A DICTIONARY

OF

ENGLISH AND WELSH SURNAMES

WITH SPECIAL AMERICAN INSTANCES

BY THE LATE

CHARLES WAREING BARDSLEY, M.A.

WORCESTER COLLEGE, OXFORD

LATE VICAR OF ULVERSTON, LANCS., AND HONORARY CANON OF CARLISLE CATHEDRAL

AUTHOR OF 'ENGLISH SURNAMES, THEIR SOURCES AND SIGNIFICATIONS'

'CURIOSITIES OF PURITAN NOMENCLATURE,' ETC.

REVISED FOR THE PRESS BY HIS WIDOW

VOLUME II
Surnames J - Z

CLEARFIELD

Originally published: London, 1901

Reprinted by Genealogical Publishing Co., Inc.
Baltimore, Maryland
1967, 1968, 1980, 1996
Library of Congress Catalogue Card Number 67-25404

Reprinted, one volume in two, for Clearfield Company
by Genealogical Publishing Company
Baltimore, Maryland
2010

ISBN, Volume II: 978-0-8063-5484-2
Set ISBN: 978-0-8063-0022-1

Made in the United States of America

A DICTIONARY
OF
ENGLISH AND WELSH
SURNAMES

Volume II
Surnames J - Z

J

Jack, Jackes, Jacks, Jacke.— Bapt. 'the son of John,' from nick. Jack; v. Jakes. It seems probable that for a short period after Jack was becoming the nick. for John, robbing James of the distinction, Jakes with an *s* answered for Jacques or Jacobus, and Jake or Jack without an *s* for John.

John le Warner, *or* Jacke le Warner, co. Norf., 1273. A. i. 441–2.
John de Bondec', *or* Jakke de Bondec, co. Bucks, ibid. ii. 344.
Jacobus Amadur, *or* Jakes Amadur, co. Linc., ibid. i. 357, 353, 385, 396.
1753. Married—William Jack and Eliz. Davison : St. Geo. Chap. Mayfair, p. 252.
1788. — John Tobias and Eliz. Jacks : St. Geo. Han. Sq. ii. 2.
London, 9, 2, 3, 0 ; New York, 7, 1, 2, 1.

Jackaman.—A variant of Jackman, q.v. ; cf. Jackaway.

MBD (co. Suffolk), 1.

Jackaway, Jackways, Jakeway.—Bapt. 'the son of Jacques,' variants of the French Jacques. First it would become Jackway, then Jackaway ; cf. Greenaway for Greenway, or Hathaway for Hathway.

1613. Married—Fawke Marrow and Isabell Jackway : St. Jas. Clerkenwell, p. 39.
1614. — Robert Jaquey and Margery Paine : ibid. p. 40.
These instances are conclusive.
Philadelphia, 6, 0, 0 ; MBD. (co. Soms.), 0, 1, 1.

Jackett, Jacquette. — Bapt. 'the son of Jack,' from dim. Jacket; cf. O.F. Jaquette, a girl's name. The dictionary 'jacket' has probably a similar origin, being the dim. of O.F. *jaque*, a jack or coat of mail, which Ducange assigns to the Jacquerie, or revolt of the peasantry nicknamed Jacques Bonhomme, A.D. 1358 ; v. Skeat.

John Jaket, C. R., 1 Hen. V.
1411. Roger Jaket : Cal. of Wills in Court of Husting (2).
1680. Married—Thomas Stringfeild and Deboray Jacket : St. Jas. Clerkenwell, iii. 180.
1753. — John Nash and Ann Jackett : St. Geo. Chap. Mayfair, p. 263.

1788. — William Jackett and Susannah Norman : St. Geo. Han. Sq. ii. 16.
1808. — Thomas Jacquet and Mary Hanell : ibid. p. 392.
— — Robert Jaquet and Sarah Springford : ibid. p. 381.
Philadelphia, 0, 2 ; MDB. (co. Cornwall), 1, 0.

Jackling, Jacklings, Jacklin.—Bapt. 'the son of Jacqueline,' a. name probably introduced from Flanders. It lingered as a font-name till the Reformation : ' 1598, March 15. Buried Jacolyn Backley, widow' (St. Dionis Backchurch, London). The final *g* is excrescent as in Jennings. And the final *s* in Jacklings is the patronymic as in Williams or Jennings.

Jakoline le Blonde, temp. Hen. III : E. & F.; co. Cumb., p. 102.
Johannes Jakolini, co. Camb., 1273. A.
Jakelina Vanne, C. R., 2 Edw. II.
Thomas de (sic) Jaclyn, 1379 : P. T. Yorks. p. 112.
Petrus Jaclyn, 1379 : ibid. p. 218.
1749. Married—James Walker and Mary Jackling : St. Geo. Han. Sq. i. 42.
1794. — John Pearce and Mary Jacklin : ibid. ii. 117.
London, 1, 1, 0 ; MDB. (co. Camb.), 0, 0, 1 ; (co. Lincoln), 0, 0, 13.

Jackman.—Occup. 'the man of Jack,' i.e. the servant of Jack ; cf. Addyman, Peterman, Matthewman. I find no evidence that Jackman was a man who wore a *jack*, as suggested by Mr. Lower ; cf. Jakeman. The following are entered together :

Johannes de Clyfford, 1379 : P. T. Yorks. p. 153.
Robertus Jakman, 1379 : ibid.
Johannes Dycson, 1379 : ibid.
Thomas Jak-son, 1379 : ibid.
Johannes Jak-man, 1379 : ibid.
Cf. Elias Joneman, 1379 : ibid. p. 149.
Johannes Joneman, 1379 : ibid. p. 181.
Willelmus Joneman, 1379 : ibid. p. 209.
Thomas Jonman, 1379 : ibid. p. 213.
Cf. also, Willelmus Jakknave (i.e. Jack's knave, the servant of Jack), 1379 : ibid. p. 267.
Robertus Jakman, 1379 : ibid.
1545. William Jackman and Ann Woodford : Marriage Lic. (Faculty Office), p. 5.
1564. Edward Jackman and Anne Style : Marriage Lic. (London), i. 27.
London, 9 ; Oxford, 4 ; Boston (U.S.), 4.

Jackson.—Bapt. 'the son of John,' from the popular nick. Jake or Jack, q.v. Instances are unneeded, but I furnish a few.

Robert fil. Jake, co. Camb., 1273. A.
Henricus fil. Jake, co. Camb., ibid.
Johannes Jakson, 1379 : P. T. Yorks. p. 301.
Willelmus Jacson, 1379 : ibid. p. 8.
Robertus Jackeson, 1379 : ibid. p. 23.
Willelmus Jakeson, 1379 : ibid. p. 32.
1547. Bapt.—John, s. Thomas Jacson : Kensington Ch. p. 2.
1582. Married—Steven Roodes and Marget Jakson : ibid. p. 62.
London, 260 ; New York, 344.

Jacob, Jacoby, Jacobson, Jacobs.—Bapt. 'the son of Jacob.' Although the personal names prefixed to these surnames in the London Directory generally denote a Jewish origin, it is not so in all cases. There are Jacobs and Jacobsons of purely English descent. The same remark applies to Jacob and possibly to Jacoby. The last was well established as a personal name in the 13th century.

Thomas Jacoby, co. Camb., 1273. A.
William Jacob, co. Camb., ibid.
William fil. Jacobi, co. Kent, ibid.
Jacobus de Broxton, 1379 : P. T. Yorks. p. 112.
Alicia fil. dicti Jacoby, 1379 : ibid. p. 6.
Johannes fil. Jacoby, 1379 : ibid. p. 7.
Jacobus fil. Ricardi, 1379 : ibid.
1598. Edward Woorall and Mary Jacobson : Marriage Lic. (London), i. 248.
1780. Married—Bryan Sergeant and Avis Jacobs : St. Geo. Han. Sq. ii. 34.
London, 19, 6, 14, 82 ; Philadelphia, 20, 85, 3, 142.

Jacomb.—? Local, ' of Jacomb.' I cannot find the spot. Probably a West-country name, where the suffix is, and was, so common ; v. Combe.

1676. Bapt. — Thomas, s. William Jacomb : St. Mary Aldermary, p. 103.
1677. Thomas Jacomb, D.D., and Amy Forth, *widow* : Marriage Alleg. (Canterbury), p. 265.
1724. Married—Henry Jacomb and Frances Hinde : St. Michael, Cornhill, p. 63.
London, 5.

Jacox.—Bapt. ; v. Jeacock.

Jadis.—Bapt. 'the son of Jadis.' The history of this personal name is quite unknown to me. I do not find it mentioned in any work on the subject.

Jadis de Hangerhale, co. Camb., 1273. A.
Richard fil. Jadis, co. Camb., ibid.
Richard Jado, co. Camb., ibid.
William Jado, co. Camb., ibid.
1785. Married—Charles Skyrme and Isabella Jane Jadis: St. Geo. Han. Sq. i. 381. Philadelphia, 1.

Jaffray.—Bapt. 'the son of Geoffrey,' a popular pronunciation.

1653. Married — Robert Jeffery and Mary Moxham : Reg. Broad Chalke, co. Wilts, p. 71.
1659. Bapt.—Mary, d. Robert Jaffery : ibid. p. 68.
1753. Married — Taylor Ansell and Sophia Jaffray : St. Geo. Chap. Mayfair, p. 258.
London, 2 ; Philadelphia, 1.

Jaggard.—Bapt. 'the son of Jaggard'; cf. the French Jacquard.

William Jagard, co. Camb., 1273. A.
1609. John Jaggard and Anne Chapman : Marriage Lic. (London), ii. 314.
1621. Richard Jaggard, co. Middlesex : Reg. Univ. Oxf. vol. ii. pt. ii. p. 391.
1702. John Jaggard, curate of St. Nicholas, Lynn : FF. viii. 504.
1729. Married—John Tobias Jaccard and Christian Moody : St. Geo. Han. Sq. i. 6.
1781. — Samuel Jaggard and Eliz. Abell : ibid. p. 328.
London, 1 ; MDB. (co. Suffolk), 1 ; (co. Warwick), 2 ; Philadelphia, 7.

Jagger, Jaggar.—Occup. 'the jagger,' one who works draught-horses for hire (Halliwell). Only found in Yorkshire. Probably from the personal name Jack (O.E. Jagg), and related to Jockey, i.e. one who rides horses for hire ; v. Jack. Cf. 'Jagge the jogelour,' Piers Plowman's Vision, Pass. Sext. 3935.

Thomas Jager, 1379 : P. T. Yorks. p. 93.
Johannes Jagher, 1379 : ibid. p. 185.
1625. Married—Anthony Callis and Susan Jagger : St. Jas. Clerkenwell, iii. 55.
1652. — James Jaggar and Phillis Richardson : St. Dionis Backchurch, p. 29.
1660. Richard Pibus and Eliz. Jagger, widow, Marriage Alleg. (Canterbury), p. 51.
1803. Married—Thomas Jagger and Isabella Appleton : St. Geo. Han. Sq. ii. 294.
West Rid. Court Dir., 1, 1 ; Flockton (West Rid. Yorks), 4, 0 ; Fixby (West Rid. Yorks), 1, 0 ; Philadelphia, 9, 0.

Jaggs.—Bapt. ' the son of Jack,' from the lazy pronunciation Jagg. ' Jagge the jogelour,' Piers Plowman. v. Jagger and Jiggens. Jaggs is the genitive form ; cf. Jones, Williams, Tompkins, &c.

MDB. (co. Essex), 1 ; New York, 1.

Jago.—Bapt. ' the son of James,' from the Spanish Iago, which must have crossed over into Cornwall at some early period. The surname is fairly well established in that county ; cf. Bastian for Sebastian, a fontal name familiar to the same shire.

Thomas Jagoe, 1583 : Reg. St. Columb Major, p. 141.
Oliver Jagoe, 1617 : ibid. p. 208.
1608. Married—John Jago and Margaret Griffin : Kensington Ch. p. 65.
1754.— Thomas Jago and Margaret Deane: St. Geo. Chap. Mayfair, p. 273.
1809. — Thomas William Jago and Jane Bridges : St. Geo. Han. Sq. ii. 406.
London, 2 ; Philadelphia, 1.

Jaine ; v. Jane.

Jakeman, Jakerman. — Occup. 'jakesman,' i.e. the servant of Jake, i.e. Jack ; v. Jackman. Jackerman is a corruption. The first stage would be Jake-a-man, as in Green-a-way and Hath-a-way ; cf. Jackaman.

1692. Charles Jakeman and Sarah Waldoe : Marriage Alleg. (Canterbury), p. 222.
1714. Bapt.—Margaret, d. Nicholas Jakeman : St. John the Baptist, Wallbrook, p. 178.
1790. Married — John Jakeman and Catherine Baker : St. Geo. Han. Sq. ii. 50.
London, 2, 0 ; Tadcaster, 1, 0 ; Tadcaster East, 1, 0 ; MDB. (co. Worc.), 4, 1 ; Philadelphia, 2, 0.

Jakes, Jaques. — Bapt. 'the son of John,' from the nick. Jack or Jake, but when found as a Christian name Jakes stood for Jaques = James. It is curious to notice that Jakes has been avoided for some generations, Jacks or Jacques being the popular forms. The local *jakes* (a house of office) has caused the objection.

Agnes Jakkes, 1273. A.
Jake Heriet, ibid.
Robert fil. Jake, ibid.
Richard Jakes, co. Soms., 1 Edw. III : Kirby's Quest, p. 198.
Ricardus Jakes, 1379 : P. T. Yorks. p. 61.

Robertus Jakes, 1379 : ibid. p. 103.
Robertus Jak', 1379 : ibid. p. 104.
Johanna Jacke-wyf, 1379 : ibid. p. 111.
Johannes Jake, 1379 : ibid.
1618. Married — William Carter and Abigall Jaques : St. Dionis Backchurch, p. 19.
1636. Bapt.—John, s. Thomas Jakes : St. Peter, Cornhill, i. 87.
London, 0, 17 ; MDB. (co. Lincoln), 1, 7 ; Philadelphia, 0, 1.

Jakeway ; v. Jackaway.

Jakins. — Bapt. ' the son of John,' either a corruption of Jankin, or more directly from Jack-kin.

Jakynus atte Boclond, C. R., 32 Edw. I.
1803. Married—William Jakins and Bidey Coffee : St. Geo. Han. Sq. ii. 279.
London, 2 ; MDB. (co. Camb.), 1.

Jalland.—Bapt. ; v. Jolland.

Jamaison, Jamason.—Bapt. Variants of Jamieson ; v. James.
New York, 1, 1.

Jamaway.—A corruption of Janaway, q.v.
MDB. (co. Warwick), 1.

Jamblin.—Bapt. ' the son of Gamelin ' ; v. Gambling, of which it is a variant ; cf. Joslin and Goslin.
MDB. (co. Cambridge), 1.

James, Jameson, Jamieson, Jamison, Jamson.—Bapt. 'the son of James.' The purely English Jamison and its variants are almost entirely confined to North England, and indeed the great majority are of Lowland Scottish descent. On the other hand, James as a surname is as often South English as North, which accounts for the multitude of its modern representatives. It is particularly strong in the West country.

James or Jacobus Audithleg', co. Salop, 1273. A.
Walter James, co. Soms., 1 Edw. III : Kirby's Quest, p. 122.
Jacobus Maldeson, 1379 : P. T. Yorks. p. 216.
Willelmus Jamesson, (sic) 1379 : ibid.
Johannes Jamesman (i.e. the servant of James), 1379 : ibid. p. 146.
Alicia James, doghter, 1379 : ibid. p. 225.
Henricus Jamsman, 1379 : ibid. p. 272.
Johannes James, 1379 : ibid. p. 300.
1566-7. Robert Mowlde and Alice James : Marriage Lic. (London), i. 35.
1769. Married—William Jamison and Mary Smith : St. Geo. Han. Sq. i. 186.
— — Thomas Jameson, of Alnwick, and Ann Wilson : ibid. p. 193.

London, 187, 25, 5, 2, 2; MDB. (co. Soma.) (James), 45; Philadelphia, 180, 17, 12, 68, 0.

Janaway, Janeway, Jannaway, Gannaway, Janway, January, Jennaway.—Local, 'of Genoa'; cf. Lombard. The Genoese traded much with England, both in silks and spices.

'The Janneys comyne in sondre wyses, Into this londe wyth dyverse merchaundysses': Libel on English Policy.

January is a curious imitative corruption.

Benedict de Janua. E.
William de Janua, co. Kent, 1273. A.
1670. Buried—Jeremiah Jenowaye: St. Michael, Cornhill, p. 257.
1715. Bapt.—Sarah, d. Richard Jannaway: St. Jas. Clerkenwell, ii. 84.
1717. — Thomas, son of Thomas Janeway: St. Antholin (London), p. 130.

Another curious imitative corruption is found in a London register.

1787. Married—John Nibbs and Sarah Johnaway: St. Geo. Han. Sq. i. 308.
London, 1, 3, 1, 5, 1, 1, 0; MDB. (co. Berks) (Jennaway), 1; Philadelphia (Janeway), 2.

Jane, Jayne, Janes, Janson, Jannings, Jankin, Jaine, Jaynes, Jans, Janse.—Bapt. 'the son of Jan,' i.e. John. Hence also Jannings for Jennings, or Jankin for Jenkin. In the North there was a strong tendency towards Jan. Johnson is entered as Janson from 1545 to 1700 in the church registers at Ulverston; cf. Tamplin for Tomlin.

Janne le Lordig, co. Oxf., 1273. A.
Walter Jankin, co. Hunts, ibid.
Robert Janes, co. Soms., 1 Edw. III: Kirby's Quest, p. 117.
William Janes, co. Soms., 1 Edw. III: ibid. p. 190.
William, son of John Jane, 1548: Reg. St. Columb Major, p. 5.
John, son of William Jane, 1605: ibid. p. 22.
1539. Bapt.—Gabella, d. Robert Jans: St. Peter, Cornhill, i. 1.
1540. — Emme, d. Robert Jance: ibid. p. 2.
1555. — John Janes: ibid. p. 7.
1606. Bapt.—a servant of William Jansonne, vintner: ibid. p. 162.
Thomas Jan, Janne, or Jane, bishop of Norwich, 1499: FF. iii. 543.
1438. Roger Janneson, vicar of Shernbourne, co. Norf.: ibid. x. 361.
1471. John Jannys, of Norwich: ibid. v. 350.

Later on this became Janes:

1716. Elizabeth Janes, spinster, co. Norf.: FF. viii. 339.
1805. Married—John Jaynes and Mary Cutts: St. Geo. Han. Sq. ii. 330.
London, 3, 0, 10, 5, 1, 0, 0, 0, 0; MDB. (co. Gloucester), 2, 2, 0, 0, 0, 0, 0, 1, 0, 0; Boston (U.S.) (Jans), 1; (Janse), 4; Philadelphia, 2, 9, 5, 5, 0, 0, 0, 1, 0, 0.

Janet, Jannett.—Bapt. 'the son of Jan,' from dim. Jan-et or Janot; cf. Emmett or Emmott, the dim. of Emm, i.e. Emma. Probably at first masculine as well as feminine.

Henry Janot, co. Soms., 1 Edw. III: Kirby's Quest, p. 250.
1781. Married—James Peter Janet and Mary Liddle: St. Geo. Han. Sq. i. 320.
London, 1, 0; Boston (U.S.), 0, 1.

Janion, Jenions, Jannance. —Bapt. 'the son of Janion' (i.e. John), a Welsh variant of English Jenin; v. Jennings.

John Janion, of Lower Bebington, 1587:Wills at Chester (1545-1620), p. 109.
Thomas Janion, of Great Saughall, 1591: ibid.
Ellen Janion, of Chester, 1611: ibid.
John Jennyon, of Christleton, 1687: ibid. (1681-1700), p. 141.
Robert Janyon, of Liverpool, shipwright, 1698: ibid.
Liverpool, 2, 1, 0; Manchester, 1, 0, 1; London, 1, 0, 0.

Janney.—Bapt. 'the son of John'; v. Jenney, Jannings, Jane.
'At Macclesfield, the Monday next after the feast of the Exaltation of the Holy Cross, 9 Hen. IV (1408) before Richard de Manley, escheator, by the oaths of Robert de Huyde, Nicholas de Davenport, . . . John Janny, William Wilot, &c.: Hist. East Cheshire, ii. 157.
1566. Married—Randelle Jannye and Alice Wilkeson: Prestbury Ch. (co. Ches.), p. 19.
1570. Bapt.—Edward Jannye: ibid.p.29.
1758. Married—John Janney and Mary Hart: St. Geo. Han. Sq. i. 82.
1778. — William Gelson and Sarah Janney: ibid. p. 202.
MDB. (co. Lincoln), 7; Philadelphia, 25.

Jannings, Janning.—Bapt. 'the son of John,' a variant of Jennings (q.v.), from the O.F. Jenin, the dim. of Jean; v. Jane.
1346. Nicholas Janing, rector of Sparham, co. Norf.: FF. viii. 260.
London, 1, 0; MDB. (co. Suffolk), 3, 0.

Jans(e, Janson; v. Jane.

Jaques.—Bapt.; v. Jakes.

Jardine, Jarden.—Local, 'at the garden,' from residence thereby. An old Scottish form; v. Garden or Gardyne.

1725. Thomas Jardin and Eliz. Washington: Marriage Lic. (Faculty Office), p. 250.
1750. Married—Andrew Gray and Jane Jardine: St. Geo. Han. Sq. i. 86.
London, 2, 0; MDB. (co. Suffolk), 2, 0; (co. Surrey), 0, 1; Manchester, 3, 0; Boston (U.S.), 2, 0; Philadelphia, 6, 24.

Jarman, Jarmain, Jermyn, Jermin, Jerman.—Bapt. 'the son of German,' q.v.; cf. Jeffrey and Geoffrey, Joscelyn and Goslin, Jarratt and Garrard.

John Germyn, 20 Edw. I. R.
Jerman Bradbone, 1634: Visitation of London (1633-5), i. 97.
John Jermin, 1647: St. Jas. Clerkenwell, i. 168.
Margarett Jerman, 1670: ibid. p. 244.
1623. Margaret Jarman, of Upholland: Wills at Chester (1621-50), p. 123.
1665. Peter Arrowsmith and Rose Jermyn: Marriage Alleg. (Canterbury), p. 106.
1673. Joseph Day and Hannah Jerman: ibid. p. 216.
1750. Married—Harvey Combe and Christian Jarman: St. Peter, Cornhill, ii. 86.
London, 5, 1, 4, 1, 0; Philadelphia, 5, 0, 0, 1, 5.

Jarratt, Jarred, Jarrett, Jarritt, Jarrad, Jerrette.—Bapt. 'the son of Gerard'; v. Garrard. This form does not seem older than the Reformation.

Jarret Blithman, Newcastle, 1539: PPP. ii. 174-94.
Jarrard Gore, temp. Eliz. Z.
Jarat Nycholson, co. York. W. 9.
Elizabeth, d. of Jarrett Dashwood, gent, and Anna-Maria his wife, Jan. 18, 1741, aged 7 weeks, St. Gregory, Norwich: FF. iv. 279.
1688. Buried—William, son of Thomas Jarrad: St. John the Baptist on Wallbrook, p. 189.
1728. Bapt.—John, son of John Jerratt: ibid. p. 158.
1778. Married — Jarrett Juson and Hannah Hickman: St. Geo. Han. Sq. i. 293.
London, 1, 2, 7, 1, 0, 0; MDB. (co. Lincoln) (Jarrad), 1; Philadelphia (Jarrett), 16; New York (Jerrette), 1.

Jarrold.—Bapt. 'the son of Gerald' (q.v.); a variant.

MDB. (co. Suffolk), 3.

Jarrom; v. Jerome.

Jarvis, Jervis, Jervois.— Bapt. 'the son of Gervase.' The initial *g* ruled supreme at first, but *j* in the end almost entirely monopolized the position. Gervas (q.v.), however, still exists.

John fil. Gervacil, co. Camb., 1273. A.
William fil. Gervasii, co. Hunts, ibid.
Stephen Gerveis, co. Camb., ibid.
Henry Gerveys, co. Norf., ibid.
Geruasius, et uxor, 1379: P. T. Yorks. p. 152.
Johannes Jerwas, 1379: ibid. p. 110.
1560. Bapt.—Eliz. d. Edmond Jervice: St. Michael, Cornhill, p. 79.
1662. Richard Chandler and Winifred Jervoise: Marriage Alleg. (Canterbury), p. 77.
1729. Bapt. — Jervoice, son of John Finch: St. Peter, Cornhill, ii. 36.
London, 67, 6, 0; Crockford, 6, 6, 1; Philadelphia, 34, 1, 0; New York, 45, 3, 1.

Jasper. — Bapt. 'the son of Jasper'; Fr. Gaspard. Very rare in England as a surname. I have not found any early instances, but it was at one time common as a Christian name.

Jasper Cranwell, 1545: Reg. St. Dionis Backchurch, p. 73.
1647. Bapt. — Jesper, son of Jesper Loward: St. Jas. Clerkenwell, i. 169.
1672. — Mary, d. John Jessper: ibid. p. 254.
1689. Buried—Margarett Jesper: St. Mary Aldermary, p. 200.
London, 1; MDB. (co. Cornwall), 4; Boston (U.S.), 4.

Jauncey.— Local, a variant of Chauncey, q.v.; cf. Chubb for Jubb.

1784. Married — Robert Digby and Eleanor Jauncey: St. Geo. Han. Sq. i. 363.
1795. — John Scott and Ann Jancey: ibid. ii. 127.
1808. — George Green and Eliz. Jancey: ibid. p. 381.
London, 1; MDB. (co. Hereford), 2; co. Worc.), 3; New York, 1.

Javens, Javan.— Bapt. 'the son of Javin'; v. Jevon. Javens is a genitive form; cf. Williams, Jones, &c.

Adam Javin, co. Camb., 1273. A.
1703. Buried—Sarah Rutter, a lodger at Mr. Javin's: St. Mary Aldermary, p. 208.
MDB. (co. Lincoln), 4, 0; London, 1, 1.

Jay, Jaye.— (1) Nick. 'the jay,' a chatterer, a gaily-dressed person. (2) Local, ' of Jay,' a township in the parish of Leintwardine, co. Hereford.

John le Jay, 1313. M.
Thomas le Jay, Fines R., 20 Edw. II.

William le Jay, co. Soms., 1 Edw. III: Kirby's Quest, p. 102.
Richard Jay, C. R., 32 Hen. VI.
Thomas Jaye, 1511: Reg. Univ. Oxf.i. 77.
1630. Married — Thomas Smith and Eliz. Jaye: Kensington Ch. p. 70.
1722. Bapt.—Thomas, s. William Jay: St. Jas. Clerkenwell, ii. 33.
London, 19, 3; MDB. (co. Hereford), 7, 0; Philadelphia, 1, 0; Boston (U.S.), 1, 0.

Jayne(s; v. Jane.

Jaycocks, -cox; v. Jeacock.

`Jeacock, Jeacocke. Jacox, Jecock, Jaycocks, Jaycox.— Bapt. 'the son of John,' from the nick. Jack and suffix -*cock*. Jack-cock was soon abbreviated to Jacock, and this became corrupted into Jeacock. The patronymic Jacocks, of course, became Jacox; cf. Wilcock and Wilcox, and v. Cocks. Jancock is found early:

1397. Richard Jancock: Cal. of Wills in Court of Husting (2).
1669. Married—Edward Endell and Margarett Jeccockes: St. Jas. Clerkenwell, iii. 158.
1700. — Caleb Jacock and Eliz. Thornhill: ibid. p. 222.
1712. — James Sharplers and Eliz. Jeacock: ibid. p. 235.
London, 1, 3, 0, 0, 0; Crockford, 0, 0, 1, 0, 0; Manchester, 9, 0, 0, 1, 0, 0; New York, 0, 0, 0, 0, 1, 2.

Jeakins, Jeakes.— Bapt. 'the son of John,' from the nick. Jack, and dim. Jack-kin. In the same way we derive Jeacock (q.v.) from Jack-cock; cf. Wilcock and Wilkin. Just as Dawkins became corrupted to Dawkes, and Perkins to Perkes, and Wilkins to Wilkes, so Jeakins became corrupted to Jeakes.

1772. Married—John Jakins and Mary Pettis: St. Geo. Han. Sq. i. 223.
1806. — Robert Jeakins and Eliz. Winsall: ibid. ii. 352.
London, 3, 1.

Jealous.—! ——. Probably nothing to do with the quality *jealous*, but an imitative corruption of some baptismal name.

1603. Bapt.—George, s. William Jellis: St. Jas. Clerkenwell, i. 41.
1783. Married—Henry Gillies and Mary Downing: St. Geo. Han. Sq. i. 344.
MDB. (co. Camb.), 2; (co. Lincoln), 4.

Jean(s, Jeanes; v. Jeens.

Jeavons.—Bapt. ; v. Jevon.

Jebb, Jebson.—Bapt. 'the son of Geoffrey,' from nick. Gepp or

Jepp; v. Jephson – Jepps and Jepson. A lazy pronunciation; cf. Slagg and Slack, &c.

1642. Buried—Sarath Jebson, Mr. Pecke his servant: St. Mary Aldermary, p. 172.
1719. Married—Edward Thompson and Eliz. Jebb: St. Michael, Cornhill, p. 60.
1735. — Rev. John Jebb and Ann Gansel: St. Geo. Han. Sq. i. 15.
London, 2, 0; MDB. (North Rid. Yorks), 0, 1; Philadelphia, 3, 0.

Jeckell, -kills, -kyl(1; v. Jekyll.

Jecks.—Bapt. 'the son of John'; v. Jex.

Jee.—Local, a variant of Gee, q.v.

1563. Buried—Johane, d. Thomas Jee: St. Jas. Clerkenwell, iv. 3.
1797. Married—William Jee and Eleanor Farrell: St. Geo. Han. Sq. ii. 163.
1803. — John Jee and Margaret Brunt: ibid. p. 292.
London, 3; MDB. (co. Leicester), 2; New York, 1.

Jeens, Jeans, Jean, Jeanes, Jeynes, Jeynson, Jeannes.— Bapt. 'the son of John.' To the influence of the O.F. dim. Jenin we owe our English Jennings (q.v.). To the influence of Jean we owe the variants of Jones here given ; v. Jane and Jones.

Alan fil. Jene, co. Linc., 1273. A.
1595. Married—John Johnson and Jone Geynson: Prestbury Ch. (co. Ches.), p. 126.
1663. Thomas Lovell and Mary Jeenes: Marriage Alleg. (Canterbury), p. 90.
1667. Thomas Jeynson, vicar of Prestbury, co. Ches.: Wills at Chester (1660-80), p. 152.
1801. Married—Robert Jeanes and Eliz. Jones: St. Geo. Han. Sq. ii. 233.
— — John Jeans and Martha Chater: ibid. p. 235.
London, 1, 4, 1, 2, 1, 0, 0; Philadelphia, 0, 0, 0, 9, 0, 0, 1; New York (Jeens), 2.

Jeeves, Jeves.—Bapt. 'the son of Geoffrey,' from nick. Jeff, patronymic Jeffs. The Yorkshire Poll Tax contains endless references to Jeff, or Geff, or Gep ; v. Gipp and Jeffs and Jephson. No wonder therefore that corrupted forms have come down to us ; v. Geeves, where the Yorkshire instances will be found clearly explained.

Thomas Jeve, co. Soms., 1 Edw. III: Kirby's Quest, p. 264.
1570. William Jeffes, of Gray's Inn: Marriage Lic. (Westminster), p. 3.

1578. James Jeve and Catherin Cowarne: Marriage Lic. (London), i. 80.
1671. John Jeffs and Eliz. Elliston: Marriage Alleg. (Canterbury), p. 197.
London, 2, 2; Sheffield, 3, 0; West Rid. Court Dir., 4, 0.

Jeff; v. Jeffs.

Jeffcock, Jeffcoat, Jephcott, Jeffcott. — Bapt. 'the son of Jeffrey' or 'Geoffrey,' q.v., from the nick. Jeff, with suffix -*cock*; v. Cock. With the corrupted Jephcott, cf. Glasscock for Glascott, a kind of reverse parallel.

Reginald Geffecok, C. R., 1 Hen. V.
John Jeffcocke, temp. Eliz. Z.
1616. Married—Thomas Merrett and Agnes Jefcott : St. Mary Aldermary, p.13.
1713. — John Hall and Mary Jephcott: St. Dionis Backchurch (London), p. 56.
London, 0, 2, 2, 0; MDB. (West Rid. Yorks), 2, 0, 0, 0; Philadelphia, 0, 0, 0, 1; New York (Jeffcott), 4.

Jefferson, Jeffreson.—Bapt. 'the son of Geoffrey,' q.v.; cf. Jarratt, Gerald, &c.

1545. Buried—Agnes Giffersonne: St. Antholin (London), p. 5.
1747. — Sarah Jefferson : St. Mary Aldermary, p. 227.
London, 8, 1; Philadelphia, 22, 0.

Jeffery, Jefferay, Jefferey, Jefferies, Jefferis, Jefferiss, Jefferys, Jeffree, Jeffrey, Jeffreys, Jeffries, Jeffryes, Jeffrie, Jeffry.—Bapt. 'the son of Geoffrey,' q.v. The various forms cited and the numbers of their representatives furnish some sort of idea of the enormous popularity of this now old-fashioned font-name in the 13th and 14th centuries. To give more than one or two modern references would be superfluous.

Rogerus Jeffray, 1379: P. T. Yorks. p. 198.
1613-4. Married—Thomas Cook and Alice Gowen, alias Jefferey : St. Dionis Backchurch (London), p. 18.
1635. Buried—Captayne William Jefferyes: St. Jas. Clerkenwell, iv. 217.
1636. — John, s. William Jefferie: ibid. p. 220.
— — Roberte Jefferies: ibid.
1664. — Richard Jeoffries: ibid. p. 355.
London, 32, 1, 1, 6, 2, 4, 14, 1, 8, 7, 14, 7, 0, 0; Philadelphia, 1, 0, 0, 5, 17, 0, 5, 0, 12, 3, 56, 0, 1, 1.

Jeffkins, Jeffkyns. — Bapt. 'the son of Geoffrey,' from the nick. Jeff, and dim. Jeff-kin; cf. Watkin, Wilkin, &c. Jeffkins is

the genitive form, as in Watkins, Wilkins, &c.

1792. Married—Thomas Jeffkins and Mary Wilson : St. Geo. Han. Sq. ii. 76.
1804. — William Neighbour and Eliz. Jefkins: ibid. p. 305.
London, 1, 0; MDB. (co. Surrey), 1, 1.

Jefford, Jeffords.—Bapt. 'the son of Giffard,' q.v.; cf. Gervase and Jarvis, Gannaway and Jannaway.

1639. Andrew Jefford and Mary Steevens: Marriage Lic. (Westminster), p. 38.
1720. Buried—John Jafford: St. Mary Aldermary, p. 216.
1755. Married—John Jefford and Sarah Gatfield : St. Geo. Han. Sq. i. 59.
London, 2, 0; Philadelphia, 2, 3.

Jeffreson; v. Jefferson.

Jeffrey(s, -ries; v. Jeffery.

Jeffs, Jeffes, Jeff.—Bapt. 'the son of Geoffrey,' q.v. The old nick. was Gef or Geff, but J is almost invariably the initial of the surname formed from it ; v. Jeeves.

Alan.fil. Gef, co. Linc., 1273. A.
Alicia Gef-doghter, 1379: P. T. Yorks. p. 124.
Alicia Gefray-wyf, 1379 : ibid.
1527. Thomas Jeffes and Margery Evered: Marriage Lic. (London), i. 6.
1635. Thomas Hollbacke and Eliz. Jeffes: Marriage Lic. (Westminster), p. 35.
London, 5, 0, 0; MDB. (co. Suffolk), 1, 3, 0; (North Rid. Yorks), 0, 0, 1; Boston (U.S.), 1, 0, 0.

Jeggins, Jeggs; v. Jiggens.

Jekyll, Jeckell, Jeckyll, Jeckyl, Jeckills, Jickles, Jeckel.—Bapt. 'the son of Jukel' or 'Gikel.' Although the personal name soon died out, the surname formed from it struggled into existence and still lives. Jeckills is the genitive form (as in Williams, Jones, &c.), and of this Jickles is a manifest variant.

Jukel Alderman, sheriff of London, 1194: WWW. p. 187.
'Gikel de Smithetun gave to Saint Cuthbert one carucate,' temp. 1200: DDD. iii. 288.
Johannes Jukel, co. Bucks, 1273. A.
Richard Gikell, co. Linc., 1273.
Nicholas Gikel, *carnifex*, 3 Edw. III : Freemen of York, i. 25.
Johannes Jekyll, temp. 1400 : Hist. Dunelmensis (Surt. Soc.), cccviii.
1670. John Catesby and Eliz. Jekyll (co. Essex): Marriage Alleg. (Canterbury), p. 178.
1739. Married—Robert Jeckell and Mary Rogers: St. Geo. Han. Sq. i. 23.

London, 1, 1, 1, 0, 0, 0, 0; MDB. (co. Camb.)(Jeckyl), 1; (co. Lincoln)(Jeckills), 1; (Jickles), 1; New York (Jeckel), 1.

Jelbart.—' The son of Gilbert, q.v. ; a Cornish variant.

1782. Married—Laurence Collins and Mary Jelbeart: St. Geo. Han. Sq. i. 340. MDB. (co. Cornwall), 4.

Jellet, Gellett. — Bapt. ' the son of Julian,' popularly Gillian, whence dim. Juliet, popularly Geliet, whence *jilt*, a wanton, a flirt ; v. Julian.

Robertus Gelietson, 1379: P. T. Yorks. p. 286.
Adam Gelietson, 1379 : ibid.
Robertus Geliot, 1379 : ibid.
1618. Bapt.—Anne, d. Andrew Jellit : St. Jas. Clerkenwell, i. 81.
1668. Thomas Powell and Dorothy Jellett : Marriage Alleg. (Canterbury), p. 239.
1833. Married—George Gillett and Mary Ann Goodwin : Canterbury Cathedral, p. 104.
Crockford, 3, 0; London, 0, 1; Philadelphia, 5, 0.

Jelley, Jelly.—(1) Bapt. A corruption of Jenney, q.v. In the same way Jennison became Jellison, q.v. (2) Bapt. 'the son of Juliana,' from the nick. Jill ('Jack and Jill') turned into the pet Jilly or Jelly; cf. Jelyan for Gillian :

1570. Married—Myles Jelyan and Agnes Smythe: St. Jas. Clerkenwell, i. 4.

Or Jelson for Gilson or Jilson :

1661. Married—Benedict Jelson and Ann Merrill: St. Jas. Clerkenwell, p. 108.

Hence the shorter form Jill became Jell, Jelley, or Jelly.

1562.—John Gellye (co. Herts) and Katherine Fallys: Marriage Lic. (London), i. 24.
1610. Married—William Jelley and Iland Crosse: St. Jas. Clerkenwell, iii. 36.
1748. — John Jelley and Joyce Whitehead: St. Geo. Han. Sq. i. 41.
1784. — John Jelly and Rachel McDuggull: ibid. p. 360.
London, 8, 0; Manchester, 0, 1; Boston (U.S.), 2, 3.

Jellicoe, Jellico, Jellicorse.—
? Nick. The old nickname Gentilcors naturally arises to one's mind. This would popularly become Jellicour or Jellicorse. In the United States this name has assumed the form of Jericho, q.v. It will be seen that Jellicorse still exists, and

Jellicour existed so late as the 17th century.

William Gentilcorps, 1301. M.
Richard Gentylcors, London. X.
James Jelicoe, of Whitchurch, co. Salop, *yeoman*, 1648: Wills at Chester (1621–50), p. 123.
Mark Jellicour, of Handbridge, 1678 : ibid. (1660–80), p. 151.
John Jolycoe, of Great Barrow, *blacksmith*, 1667: ibid. p. 155.
1644. Bapt.—William, s. William Jellico: St. Jas. Clerkenwell, i. 159.

It is almost certain that Handsomebody is a translation of Gentilcors. 'Thy fayre body so gentyl' (Robert of Gloucester, p. 205), i.e. graceful, noble, *genteel*.

Crockford, 2, 0, 1 ; Liverpool, 0, 1, 0 ; Manchester, 0, 0, 1 ; London, 1, 0, 0.

Jellison, Jellerson. — (1) Bapt. ; v. Jennison ; cf. *bannister* for *baluster*. Although now only found, I believe, in America, it was an English corruption, finding its way, no doubt, with the Pilgrim Fathers. (a) Bapt. A variant of Jillson, q.v.

1592. Richard Gelyson and Mary Hope: Marriage Lic. (London), i. 203.
1593. Bapt.—Luce, d. William Jellyson, or Gennysson : St. Jas. Clerkenwell, i. 27.
1621. — Henry, s. Robart Jellison: ibid. p. 92.
1663. Married—John Gillison and Susanna Parker: St. Mary Aldermary, p. 30.
1665. Bapt.—Thomas, s. John Jellison and Susanna, his wife: ibid. p. 101.

This conclusively proves that Jellison is sometimes 'the son of Gill,' the nick. of Juliana, whence we get Gillson and Jillson, q.v., Jellison being a variant.

Boston (U.S.), 9, 2.

Jemison ; v. Jimpson.

Jemmett.—Bapt. 'the son of James,' from nick. Jem and dim. Jemm-et; cf. Emmett (little Emma), Hewett (little Hugh), &c. Although the derivation is certain I have not discovered an early instance.

1657. Married—William Banes, *carman*, and Marye Jemmett: St. Michael, Cornhill, p. 32.
1661. Samuel Jemmatt (co. Berks) and Avelin Bateman : Marriage Alleg. (Canterbury), p. 66.
1712. Married—Thomas Bishop and Mary Jemmett: St. Mary Aldermary, p. 41.
London, 2 ; MDB. (co. Kent), 2.

Jenckes; v. Jinks or Jinkins.
Boston (U.S.), 1.

Jenifer. — Bapt. 'the son of Guinevere,' one of Arthur's wives. Still in use in Cornwall as Jenifer or Jennifer (v. Yonge, ii. 132) ; v. Genever, which is the more correct form. Also v. Juniper.

Jenefer, d. of Thomas Bosowarne, 1554: Reg. St. Columb Major, p. 7.
Jenniphret Norton, *widdow*, 1623 : ibid. p. 210.
1623. John Foster, Stepney, and Jenefer Foster, of St. Mary Woolnoth : Marriage Lic. (London), ii. 126.
'Comes Captain Jenifer to me, a great servant of my Lord Sandwiches,' 1666–7: Pepys' Diary, Chandos edit., p.371.
Jennifer, d. of John Stephens, 1770 : Reg. St. Columb Major, p. 285.
1661. Married—Walter Jeniver and Jane Wright: St. Jas. Clerkenwell, iii. 107.
Boston (U.S.), 1.

Jenions.—Bapt. ; v. Janion.

Jenkin, Jenking, Jenkins, Jenkinson, Jenkyns. — Bapt. 'the son of John,' from dim. Jenkin ; cf. Wilkin, Watkin, Tompkin, Simpkin, &c. The *g* in Jenking is excrescent, as in Jennings. The tendency at first was to Jonkin, but the influence of the N. French Jenin was too strong ; v. Jennings.

Adam Janekyn, co. Soms., 1 Edw. III : Kirby's Quest, p. 183.
Johannes Wayte, et Agnes uxor ejus, 1379 : P. T. Yorks. p. 59.
Johannes serviens ejus, 1379 : ibid.
Robertus Jonkinson, 1379 : ibid.

The last three entries occur together.

Alicia Jonkyn, 1379 : P. T. Yorks. p. 104.
Johanna Jonkyn-wyf, 1379: ibid. p. 123.
Johannes Jonkynson, 1379 : ibid.
Jenkin Vaughan, prebendary of St. David's, 1621: Hist. and Ant. St. David's, p. 361.
1602. Ralph Jenkinson, alias Johnson, of Longton: Wills at Chester (1545–1620), p. 109.
London, 4, 1, 74, 15, 1 ; Philadelphia, 0, 0, 140, 13, 0.

Jenks ; v. Jinks or Jinkins.
London, 2 ; Boston (U.S.), 29.

Jennaway ; v. Janaway.

Jenner.—Occup. 'the engineer,' a military officer who worked the catapult, &c. As *engine* became shortened to *gin* or *ginne*, so Engi-

ner became Ginner ; v. my English Surnames, 5th edit. p. 229.

Waldinus Ingeniator, co. Linc.: Domesday.
Richard le Engynur, C. R., 18 Edw. I.
Hugh le Ginnur, co. Oxf., 1273. A.
William le Engynur, co. Suff., ibid.
Richard le Enginur. B.
Ernulf le Enginnur. E.
William le Genour, 1306. M.
1598. Robert Pascall and Gresagon Jeynor: Marriage Lic. (London), i. 254.
1608. Bapt.—John, the son of Henrye Jenoure, *marchant*: St. Peter, Cornhill, i. 58.
1781. Married—Samuel Jenner and Catherine Roberts : St. Geo. Han. Sq. i. 323.
London, 13 ; Philadelphia, 11.

Jennett, Jennette, Jinnett.—Bapt. 'the son of John' or ' Joan,' from dim. Jennet. It is as likely to be masculine as feminine ; v. Janet.

1589. William Cookes and Ann, d. Humphrey Jennetts : Marriage Lic. (London), i. 183.
1615. Bapt.—Robert, s. James Jennettes: St. Peter, Cornhill, i. 63.
1762. Married—Richard Jennet and Mary Colclough : St. Geo. Han. Sq. i. 113.
London, 1, 1, 0 ; Philadelphia, 1, 0, 1.

Jenney.—(1) Bapt. 'the son of John.' For instances, v. Jennison. (a) Local, 'de Gyney,' or ' Gisnei,' or 'Gisney,' no doubt from Guisnes, near Calais.

Roger de Gisnei, or Gisney, 9 Ric. I, co. Norf. : FF. x. 452.
1250. Ingelram de Gisnei, or Gyney, co. Norf. : ibid. iv. 454.
James Gyney, co. Norf., 1395 : ibid. ix. 308.

Later on, and after the prefix was dropped, the orthography was changed to Jenney.

John Jenney, of Intwood, sheriff of Norwich, 1486: FF. iii. 191.
Roger Jeney, co. Norf., 20 Edw. III : ibid. xi. 75.
Suckling Jenny, co. Norf., 1691 : ibid. viii. 237.
1565. Married—William Dowdall and Joane Jenny: St. Jas. Clerkenwell, iii. 3.
London, 1 ; Boston (U.S.), 13.

Jenningham ; v. Jerningham.

Jennings, Jenyns, Jennens.—Bapt. 'the son of John '; O.F. Jehan; O.E. Jan; dim. Jan-in ; cf. Col-in, Rob-in, &c. Jan or Jehan left us Jan-et and Janson. Jan-in (through influence of later Jean) became Jenin, with excrescent *g* Jenning, and with patronymic *s* Jennings.

'Item, to Janyn Marcazin, mynstrelle, 66s. 8d.': Privy Purse Exp., Elizabeth of York, p. 100.

Janyn le Breton, co. Lanc., 1332: Lay Subsidy (Rylands), p. 120.

Janyn de Gynes, 1379: P. T. Yorks. p. 240.

Janyn serviens Johannes warde, 1379: ibid.

Jenyn de Fraunce, 1379: ibid. p. 139.

Jane, d. of Stephen Jenyn, 1548: Reg. St. Columb Major, p. 5.

John Genens, or Jenens, citizen of Oxford, 1573: Reg. Univ. Oxf. vol. ii. pt. i. pp. 302-3.

Francis Jenance, or Jennens, or Jenens: ibid. pp. 303-4.

Thomas Jennyns, co. Norf., 13 Eliz.: FF. viii. 432.

1571. Buried—Jeames Jennynges: St. Peter, Cornhill, i. 121.

1610. Ralph Jenyngs, of Chester: Wills at Chester (1545-1620), p. 109.

London, 91, 0, 0; MDB. (co. Camb.), 4, 2, 0; Philadelphia, 90, 0, 3.

Jennison, Jenney, Jenny.— Bapt. 'the son of John,' from O.F. Jean, dim. Jenin; v. Jennings. The feminine Jenny was probably not in use at this time. It is almost certain that it was a masculine form at first and a modification of Jenin, just as Colly was of Colin.

Alan fil. Jene, co. Linc., 1273. A.

John Jenysyn. F.

Joan Geneson, co. York. W. 11.

Willelmus Gyneson, 1379: P. T. Yorks. p. 77.

Ricardus Gene, 1379: ibid. p. 78.

Thomas Genne, 1379: ibid. p. 82.

Agnes Gine, 1379: ibid. p. 86.

Agar Genyson, 1546: St. Dionis Backchurch (London), p. 2.

Robert Jennison, *merchant*, 1668. Tomb, St. Nicholas, Newcastle-on-Tyne: Brand's Hist. of Newcastle, i. 281.

1666. John Jenney and Mary Reading: Marriage Alleg. (Canterbury), p. 128.

Manchester, 2, 0, 0; Boston (U.S.), 9, 13, 1; Philadelphia, 2, 0, 2.

Jentle. — Nick. 'the gentle'; v. Gentle.

1555. Bapt.—Mathew Jentyll: St. Peter, Cornhill, i. 7.

1577. Buried — Raphe Jentle: St. Michael, Cornhill, p. 195.

1591-2. Edmund Jentill and Johanna Hussey: Marriage Lic. (London), i. 195.

London, 1; New York, 1.

Jephcott.—Bapt. ; v. Jeffcock, a corruption.

Jephson, Jepps, Jepson.— Bapt. 'the son of Geoffrey,' from nick. Geff or Gepp ; v. Gipp for

several instances. South Lancashire is a well-known habitat of Jepson.

Thomas Gepson, 1379: P. T. Yorks. p. 123.

Jeppe de Hesilden, 1379: ibid. p. 271.

Johannes Jepson, 1379: ibid. p. 86.

Nicholas Jepson, of Mostyn, 1595: Wills at Chester (1545-1620), p. 109.

Robert Jepson, of Oldfield, Manchester, 1614: ibid.

1603. Bapt.—William, s. Robert Jeppes: St. Jas. Clerkenwell, i. 41.

London, 3, 3, 6; Manchester, 0, 0, 8; Boston (U.S.), 0, 0, 12.

Jeremy. — Bapt. 'the son of Jeremy,' i.e. Jeremiah ; M.E. Jeremy.

Jeremy de Caxton, co. Norf., 1239: FF. iii. 46.

1638. Married—Gilbert Jeremi and Eliz. Raulinges: St. Michael, Cornhill, p. 28.

London, 3 ; Philadelphia, 1.

Jericho.—An imitative corruption of Jellicoe, q.v.

Philadelphia, 2.

Jerman, Jermin ; v. Jarman.

Jermy, Jermey. — Bapt. 'the son of Jermin.' At first sight this name would seem to be Jeremy, q.v., but Blomefield in his History of Norfolk, to which county the Jermys belong, says positively that Jermin is the true parent ; v. Jarman. This is likely to be true, as Jermyn has been for centuries a Norfolk patronymic.

Sir John Germyn, or Jermy, *knight*, temp. 1300, co. Norf.: FF. v. 386.

Robert Jermye, of Norwich, 1533: ibid. i. 382.

Thomas Jarmy, co. Norf., 1652: ibid. v. 387.

In opposition to the above cf.

Jeremye Gooch, 1617, co. Norf.: FF. iv. 248.

Jermey Gooch, 1652, co. Norf.: ibid. p. 321.

Perhaps the explanation is that surnames were then beginning to be fashionable as fontal names, and Jermey being thus used was miswritten or confused with Jeremy.

'1658. Married—Thomas Knowles and Eliz. Jermy: St. Jas. Clerkenwell, iii. 101.

1666. Francis Jermy and Ann Wilsford: Marriage Lic. (Faculty Office), p. 92.

MDB. (co. Norfolk), 4, 0; London, 0, 1.

Jermyn ; v. Jarman.

Jerningham,   Jernegan, Jenningham. — Bapt. 'the son of Gernegan.' The second *n* is excrescent ; cf. Pottinger and Messinger for Potager and Messager. In some documents bearing the seal of Queen Elizabeth (1572), concerning the town of Yarmouth, Sir Henry Jerningham, knight, is set down as 'Sir Henry Jernegam' not less than three times ; v. FF. xi. 288-91. Blomefield says, 'That Jernegan was anciently a Christian name is very true, as numerous records prove. In 1195, there was a fine levied of lands in Edricheston, in Warwickshire, between Reginald de Claverdon and Gernagan his brother, and about this time it was a common name in France, as we find from Lobineau, in his History of Britain (i. 105), where Jernegon de Pontchasteau and some others of the name are mentioned' (FF. ii. 411).

Jernegan Fitz-Hugh, 1180, co. Norf.: FF. ii. 411.

Walter Gernegan, co. Suff., 1273. A.

William Gernegon, co. Norf., ibid.

1675. Francis Jernegan (co. Norf.) and Anna Blount : Marriage Alleg. (Canterbury), p. 243.

1767. Married—William Jerningham and Frances Dillon: St. Geo. Han. Sq. i. 166.

MDB. (co. Devon), 0, 0, 1 ; Boston (U.S.), 0, 5, 0.

Jerome, Jerram, Jerrems, Jarrom. — Bapt. 'the son of Jerome.' I do not find any early English instances. It must have been a rare name in this country. Miss Yonge writes, 'The spear raven, Gerramn, is the old English Jerram that has become lost in Jerome' (Hist. Christian Names, ii. 328'). I cannot discover any trace of an old English name Jerram as distinct from Jerome. Jerrems is the genitive form, as in Jones, Williams, &c.

1614. John Watson and Eliz. Jerome: Marriage Lic. (Westminster), p. 21.

1729. Married—Joseph Jerram and Ann Elgar: St. Geo. Chap. Mayfair, p. 286.

1748. — Stephen Jerom and Mary Callard : ibid. p. 124.

1770. — John Fisher and Eliz. Jerrom : St. Geo. Han. Sq. i. 196.

1779. Married — Joseph Jerome and Eliz. Elsmore: St. Geo. Han. Sq. i. 303. London, 2, 1, 0, 0; MDB. (co. Lincoln), 0, 1, 1, 0; (co. Leicester) (Jarrom), 2.

Jervis,-vois.—Bapt.; v. Jarvis.

Jessmaker.—Occup. 'a maker of *jesses*,' the straps of silk or leather by which the hawk was held.

Robert le Jesemaker, co. Linc., 1273. A.

Jesson. — Bapt. 'the son of Geoffrey,' from nick. Geff, whence Geffson, which gradually assumed the form of Gesson, then Jesson; cf. Joslin and Goslin.

Willelmus Gesson, 1379: P. T. Yorks. p. 18.
1628. Married—Henry Jesson and Amy Munden: St. Michael, Cornhill, p. 25.
1661. John Jesson and Anne Artson: Marriage Lic. (Canterbury), p. 59.
1790. Married—Thomas Jesson and Ann Green: St. Geo. Han. Sq. ii. 41.
London, 3; Philadelphia, 3; MDB. (co. Leicester), 2.

Jessop, Jessup, Jessopp, Jessupp. — Bapt. 'the son of Joseph'; O.E. Josep. Any doubt on the subject is settled by the sub-joined references from the York Poll Tax:

Willelmus Josop, 1379: P. T. Yorks. p. 170.
Johannes Jesop, 1379: ibid.
Richard fil. Josep, co. Camb., 1273. A.
Adam Josep, c. 1300. M.
Josep le Taverner. J.

No doubt the pronunciation was influenced by the Lombardic merchants and Italian Jews. Jessop is simply Giuseppe Anglicized. 'Isaac of York' could have told us something about it.

1612. William Newsam and Eliz. Jesopp: Marriage Alleg. (Canterbury), p. 20.
1663. William Jesup (co. Linc.) and Eliz. Woolby: ibid. p. 90.
1746. Married—Thomas Jessapp and Ann Hill: St. Geo. Chap. Mayfair, p. 80.
London, 9, 10, 0, 0; MDB. (co. Essex), 1, 0, 1, 1; West Rid. Court Dir., 12, 0, 0, 0; Crockford, 0, 0, 2, 0; Philadelphia, 0, 6, 0, 0; Boston (U.S.), 4, 1, 0, 0.

Jester. — Occup. 'the jester,' the professional fool or jester in attendance on the king or baron; v. Fool.

1665. Married—Thomas Straford and Sarah Jester: St. Jas. Clerkenwell, i. 121.
1666. Bapt.—Eliz., d. Christopher Jester: ibid. p. 230.

1802. Married—George Groom and Lydia Jester: St. Geo. Han. Sq. ii. 257.
Coventry, 1; Philadelphia, 16.

Jeune.—Nick. 'le jeune,' i.e. the young; v. Young and Jung.

Agnes le Jevene, co. Oxf., 1273. A.
William le Jeuene, London, ibid.
Bartholomew le Jevene, co. Bedf., ibid.
Bartholomew le Jouene, C. R., 36 Hen. III.
London, 2.

Jeves.—Bapt.; v. Jeeves.
London, 2.

Jevon, Jevons, Jeavons.—Bapt. (Welsh) 'the son of Jevan' or 'Yevan' or 'Evan'; v. Evans. Jevan appears in the list of early *arch*bishops of St. David's; v. Crockford (1891), p. xxxvii.

Heine fil. Yevan, co. Salop, 1273. A.
John ap Howell ap Jevan: Visit. of Gloucestershire (Harl. Soc.), p. 179.
Howell ap Yevan. H.
Jevan ap Rees. G.
Jevan ap Adam, 1327. M.
Javin Coke, 1384: Hist. and Ant. St. David's, p. 369.
1594. Hopkin ap Jevan, co. Glamorgan: Reg. Univ. Oxf. vol. ii. pt. ii. p. 207.
1600. Jevan, or Evan Thomas, co. Glamorgan: ibid. p. 243.
1658. Buried—Ann, wife of Thomas Jevon: St. Thomas the Apostle (London), p. 132.
Liverpool, 0, 4, 0; Dalton-in-Furness, 0, 0, 1; Lanc. Court Dir., 0, 1, 2; MDB. (co. Stafford), 4, 1, 3; New York (Jevons), 1.

Jew.—Nick. 'the Jew,' a common entry in mediaeval registers; v. Jewson.

John le Gyw, C. R., 28 Hen. III.
Thomas le Jeu, co. Notts, 1273. A.
Moses le Jeu, co. Northampt., 20 Edw. I. R.
Mirabilla Judaeus. C.
1557. Richard Jewe: Cal. of Wills in Court of Husting (2).

The editor seems doubtful of the name in the following entry:

1582. Buried—Thomas Renoldes, servant to Mr. Jew (?): St. Antholin (London), p. 29.

Jewell, Jewelson.—Bapt. 'the son of Joel'; O.E. Juel and Jewel. v. Joel; cf. Job and Jubb, Jordan and Jurden, &c.

Warin fil. Juelis, co. Devon, Hen. III-Edw. I. K.
Juel de Stanhuse, co. Devon, ibid.
Juel de Buketon, co. Devon, ibid.
Jordan fil. Juel, 25 Edw. I: BBB. p. 543.
Jordan fil. Jowell, 25 Edw. I: ibid.

William Juel, co. Soms., 1 Edw. III: Kirby's Quest, p. 202.
John Juell, C. R., 18 Ric. II.
John Jowell, sheriff of Norwich, 1486: FF. iii. 191.
Robert Jewelson, of Skipton, Yorks, 1741: Dawson's Hist. of Skipton, p. 363.

A curious mixture of the old form and the new is found in the following entries:

1615. Buried—Elizabeth, d. Joell Jewell: St. Columb Major, p. 207.
1639. — Senobie, widow of Joell Juell: ibid. p. 216.
London, 20, 0; Philadelphia, 10, 0.

Jewett, Jewitt.—Bapt. 'the son of Juliana,' from the dim. Juliet, popularly, in North England, Juet; v. Jowett.

William Juet, co. Hunts, 1273. A.
1629. Bapt.—Gabriel, s. John Jeuett: St. Jas. Clerkenwell, i. 111.
1778. Married—James Jewett and Eliz. Clarke: St. Geo. Han. Sq. i. 292.
London, 1, 1; MDB. (West Rid. Yorks), 0, 3; Philadelphia, 7, 2.

Jewison.—Bapt. A corruption of Jewelson, a Yorkshire surname, where Jewell was the form for Joel; v. Jewelson (s.v. Jewell).

West Rid. Court Dir., 3; MDB. (East Rid. Yorks), 2.

Jewkes; v. Jukes.

Jewsbury.—(1) Local, 'at the jewsbury,' i.e. the district or part of a town set apart for the residence of Jews; v. Jury. The surname is North English, and not found in the London Directory. The York Pageant (1417) was arranged to play at certain points of the city, amongst others 'at the end of Jubir-gate' (query Jewbury-gate): York Mystery Plays, p. xxxiii, ed. Toulmin Smith. (2) Local, 'of Dewsbury,' a town in W. Rid. Yorks. Probably a corruption, as suggested by Mr. Lower. This view is strengthened by the fact that the surname seems confined to Lancashire and Yorkshire.

MDB. (West Rid. Yorks), 1; Manchester, 3.

Jewson, Juson.—Nick. 'the Jew's son' (?). Nevertheless, the instance below seems to refute this statement since Peter would not be used as a personal name by a strict Jew. With the variant

Juson, cf. Jury for Jewry; v. Jewison for a second and different origin.

Peter fil. Gewe, co. Linc., 1273. A.
1600. Thomas Fewson, or Jewson, co. Bucks: Reg. Univ. Oxf. vol. ii. pt. ii. p. 240.
1745. Married — Samuel Cobley and Eliz. Jewson: St. Geo. Chap. Mayfair, p. 55.
1778. — Jarrett Juson and Hannah Hickman: St. Geo. Han. Sq. i. 293.
London, 3, 1.

Jex, Jecks. — Bapt. 'the son of Jacques'; v. Jakes.

Agnes Jakkes, co. Hunts, 1273. A.
1384. Jeffery Jeckkes, rector of St. Peter, Norwich: FF. iv. 330.
1475. George Jekkes, rector of South Pickenham, co. Norf.: ibid. vi. 74.
The Vicarage of Corpesty, co. Norf., was sold by Heydon (temp. Elizabeth) to Thomas Jecks and John Shakle, and by them to the Bacons, and in 1611 William Bacon separated,' &c.: ibid.

Thomas Jecks is again referred to:

1589. Thomas Jex presented to rectory of Irmingland, co. Norf.: FF. vi. 322.

Cf. Cox for Cocks, Dix for Dicks, Dixon for Dickson.

1783. Married — William Raker and Ann Jex: St. Geo. Han. Sq. i. 350.
London, 3, 1; New York, 3, 3.

Jeynes, Jeynson; v. Jeens.

Jibb. — (1) Bapt.; v. Jebb. (2) Bapt. 'the son of Gilbert,' from the nick. Gib; v. Gibb, and cf. Goslin and Joslin.

MDB. (co. Lincoln), 1.

Jickles; v. Jekyll.

Jiffard. — Bapt. 'the son of Giffard,' q.v.

Johannes Juffard, 1379: P. T. Yorks. p. 37.
Johanna Juffard, 1379: ibid. p. 54.

Jiggens, Jeggins, Jeggs, Jegen. — Bapt. 'the son of Jegg,' whence the dim. Jeggon. Jiggens or Jeggins is the genitive, as in Jennings, Jones, Williams, &c. There can be little doubt that the original name was Jackson (i.e. little Jack), which became Jaggin or Jeggin. Jack is found as Jagg in early rolls, and is so styled by the author of Piers Plowman. The surname Jeggins seems to have arisen in co. Essex, where Jeggins, Jeggs, and Jaggs are still to be met with.

In 1590 John Jeggon, son of Robert Jeggon, of Coggeshall, co. Essex, was appointed Warden of Bennet College (now Corpus Christi), Cambridge. He was a strict disciplinarian. He fined the undergraduates for some offence and with the mulct whitened the college hall. — On one of the screens a young fellow wrote: —
'Doctor John Jeggon, of Bennet College, Master,
Broke the Scholars' heads, and gave the Hall plaister.'
The Doctor, seeing it as he passed by, subscribed extempore:
'Knew I but the wag, that writ this in a bravery,
I'd commend him for his wit, but whip him for his knavery': FF. iii. 562.
Claricia Jagun, co. Norf., 1273. A.
1613. John Jeggon, Bishop of Norwich: FF. vi. 443.
1621. Robert Jegon, of Norwich: ibid.
'Mr. William Jeg gave a small piece of land in this parish' (East Dereham): ibid. x. 218.
1667. Thomas Walker and Arabella Jiggons: Marriage Alleg. (Canterbury), p. 132.
1673. Thomas Bland and Anne Jegon, widow: ibid. p. 220.
London, 1, 0, 0, 0; London Court Dir., 0, 1, 0, 0: MDB. (co. Essex), 0, 2, 1, 0; Philadelphia (Jegen), 1.

Jigger. — Occup. 'the jigger,' a player on the gige or gigue, a musical instrument; hence jig, a dance. Italian giga, a fiddle; cf. Crowder or Crowther, and Fiddler. This surname lasted till the 16th century. I suspect it is now extinct.

John le Gigur, co. Oxf., 1273. A.
Walter le Gigur, co. Oxf., ibid.
Alexander le Gigur. T.
Bigelot le Gigur. DD.
John Gygour, co. Soms., 1 Edw. III: Kirby's Quest, p. 227.
1544. Buried — Anne Giger: St. Peter, Cornhill, i. 107.

Jillings. — Local; v. Gilling(s.

Jillson. — Bapt. 'the son of Juliana,' from the nick. Jill, which is the usual English form, although Jill was more common than Gill; v. Gillson and Jellison.

1603. Buried — Richard Smyth, servant to Richard Jellson: St. Jas. Clerkenwell, iv. 84.
1626. — William, s. Benedict Jilson: ibid. p. 187.
1661. — William, s. William Jelson: ibid. p. 339.
Philadelphia, 2.

Jimpson, Jimison, Jemison. — Bapt. 'the son of James,' from the nick. Jim. The p is in-

trusive, as in Simpson and Thompson.

William Gimmison, co. York. W. 20.
1808. Married — John Handley and Eliz. Jimerson: St. Geo. Han. Sq. ii. 389.
Manchester, 1, 0, 0; Philadelphia, 0, 3, 3.

Jinkins, Jinks. — Bapt. 'the son of John,' from dim. Jenkin, whence Jinkin, the patronymic of which was Jinkins. This passed through the usual stages of modifications into Jinks, and was turned into Ginx in the story of 'Ginx's Baby,' which created a certain sensation a few years ago; cf. Dawks, Wilks, Perks, Tonks, &c., from Dawkins, Wilkins, Perkins, Tonkins, &c.; cf. Jinckson for Jenkinson in the following:

1577-8. James Nicolls and Johanna Jinckson: Marriage Lic. (Westminster), p. 6.
1603. Buried — Mr. Bernard Jynkes, parson of this parishe: St. Dionis Backchurch (London), p. 207.
1606. Married — Robert Lymbarr and Amye Jenckes: ibid. p. 15.
1658-9. — Robert Jenkes and Grace Halsey: ibid. p. 34.
1666. Francis Jenkes and Sarah Wallwin: Marriage Alleg. (Canterbury), p. 116.
1670. Bapt. — Francis, son of Francis Jinckes: St. Michael, Cornhill, p. 146.
London, 1, 2.

Joachim. — Bapt. 'the son of Joachim.' Modern immigration has helped to preserve the surname.

Richard Joachim, co. Camb., 1273. A.
Nicholas Jochim, co. Camb., ibid.
London, 2; Philadelphia, 1; New York, 3.

Job, Jobson, Jobe. — Bapt. 'the son of Job'; v. Jupp, Chubb, Jobling, &c. Job was a favourite personal name in the hereditary surname period, and in consequence has left many descendants. No doubt the Mystery Plays had much to do with its popularity.

William Jobba, co. Oxf., 1273. A.
Elyas Jobbe, co. Suff., ibid.
John fil. Job, co. Camb., ibid.
Nicholas Jobbe, vicar of Swerdeston, co. Norf., 1318: FF. v. 52.
1567. Married — Thomas Jackson and Eliz. Jobson: St. Dionis Backchurch (London), p. 6.
1589. Bapt. — Katherine, d. Michael Jobson: St. Jas. Clerkenwell, i. 22.
1672. Thomas Clithero and Jane Job: Marriage Alleg. (Canterbury), p. 206.
London, 6, 6, 0; Philadelphia, 1, 2, 1.

Jobbins.—Bapt. 'the son of Job,' from the dim. Jobbin ; cf. Col-in, Rob-in, &c. The final *s* is the genitive form, as in Jennings, Williams, &c.

1623. Married—John Jobbins and Susan Wetherley : St. Jas. Clerkenwell, iii. 53.
1704. Bapt.—Elizabeth, d. Isaac Jobbins : St. Michael, Cornhill, p. 161.
London, 3 ; MDB. (co. Wilts), 1 ; Philadelphia, 3.

Jobling. — Bapt. 'the son of Job,' from dim. Jobelin ; cf. Hewling ; v. Joplin and Jopling. Jobelin seems to suggest the origin of Jobelin, a stupid man. ' Jobelin, a sot, a fool ' (Cole's Eng. Dict., 1684). 'Joblin, a stupid boy. Somerset' (Halliwell). 'As patient as Job' is even now not used complimentarily. Job's patience has even seemed to imply want of energy, and the term would easily become a nickname for lethargy, but was not easily distinguished from sheer stupidity ; v. Joppe, Joppus, and Joppa, Prompt. Parv., where Joppe may be Job. Jobling may therefore belong to the nickname class without affecting the origin given above.

1738. Bapt.—Jane, d. Henry Jobling : St. Jas. Clerkenwell, ii. 241.
1788. Married—Charles Turner and Susanna Joblin : St. Geo. Han. Sq. ii. 14.
1809. — Isaac Watts and Margaret Jobling : ibid. p. 415.
Crockford, 3 ; Manchester, 1 ; Boston (U.S.), 2.

Jobson ; v. Job.

Joce, Jose. — Bapt. 'the son of Goce' ; v. Joyce. A well-known West-country surname, but formerly generally familiar as a personal name.

Geoffrey Jose, co. Hunts, 1273. A.
Nicholas Jose, co. Hunts, ibid.
Philip Joce, co. Norf., temp. Edw. II : FF. vii. 288.
William Jose, co. Soms., 1 Edw. III : Kirby's Quest, p. 199.
John Joce, co. Soms., 1 Edw. III : ibid.
Joceo de Bayouse, co. Soms., 1 Edw. III : ibid. p. 95.
John Joce, co. Norf., 50 Edw. III : FF. vii. 289.
Thomas Jose, 1379 : P. T. Yorks. p. 266.
1752. Married—Thomas Joce and Sarah Massa : St. Geo. Chap. Mayfair, p. 214.
MDB. (co. Devon), 6, 0 ; (co. Cornwall), 0, 14 ; New York, 0, 2.

Joel, Joell.—Bapt. 'the son of Joel' or 'Johel,' a fairly favourite name in the 13th and 14th centuries ; v. Jewell.

Joel de Stok, C. R., 47 Hen. III.
Joelus de Bosco, Hen. III–Edw. I. K.
William Joel, co. Hunts, 1273. A.
Joel le Warrener. H.
Johel Thenkersman, C. R., 1 Edw. II.
Joel de Bukyngton, C. R., 15 Ric. II.
1723. Married—John Joel and Eliz. Hippeth : St. Mary Aldermary, p. 46.
1789. — William Gibb and Mary Joel : St. Geo. Han. Sq. ii. 31.
London, 7, 0 ; West Rid. Court Dir., 8, 1 ; Sheffield, 2, 0 ; New York, 6, 0.

John.—Bapt. 'the son of John,' a Welsh surname. John was never an English surname. Johnson monopolized the honours.

Edward ap-John, archdeacon of Caermarthen, 1509 : Hist. and Ant. St. David's, p. 360.
Robert ap-Edward John, of Bangor, 1599 : Wills at Chester (1545–1620), p. 109.
William ap-Thomas John, of Pulford, 1606 : ibid.
Edward ap-John, of Hanmer, *laborer*, 1584 : ibid.
1666. Married—Robert Ralt and Charity John : St. Jas. Clerkenwell, iii. 120.
1751. — Thomas John and Joanna Russell : St. Geo. Chap. Mayfair, p. 204.
London, 2 ; Liverpool, 3 ; MDB. (co. Pembroke), 25 ; New York, 23.

Johns, Johnson, Johnes.—Bapt. 'the son of John,' originally pronounced and spelt Jone ; v. Jones. It will be well to give a fairly large number of instances.

Robert Johns, co. Soms., 1 Edw. III : Kirby's Quest, p. 126.
Johannes Webster, 1379 : P. T. Yorks. p. 187.
Willelmus Joneson, 1379 : ibid.
Willelmus Johnson, 1379 : ibid. p. 221.
Robertus Johanson, 1379 : ibid. p. 36.
Juliana Jonesson, *webster*, 1379 : ibid. p. 161.
Ricardus Joneson, 1379 : ibid. p. 2.
Robertus Jonson, 1379 : ibid. 187.
Lewis Johns, prebendary of St. David's, 1486 : Hist. and Ant. St. David's, p. 361.

The following represents one of the earliest Puritan Christian names :

1583. Bapt.—Evangeliste, s. Evangeliste Johnson : St. Michael, Cornhill, p. 92.
1600. Lewis Johnes, co. Monmouth : Reg. Univ. Oxf. vol. ii. pt. ii. p. 244.
— William Johnes, co. Montgomery : ibid. p. 245.
London 21, 343, 1 ; New York, 16, 680, 4.

Joice.—Bapt. ; v. Joyce.

MDB. (co. Essex), 1 ; Boston (U.S.), 1 ; New York, 2.

Joiner, Joyner.—Occup. 'the joiner,' rare. Probably *joiner* as an occupative term came into use somewhat later than *carpenter*. The surname seems barely to have maintained an existence, while Carpenter and Wright are represented by thousands.

'Carpenters, coupers, and joyners.'
       Cocke Lorelle's Bote.
Hugh le Joignour. G.
Alan le Jovgnour. N.
Richard Joynere, 1564 : Reg. Univ. Oxf. i. 254.
1566. Stephen Wyseman and Mary Joyner : Marriage Lic. (London), i. 34.
1743. Married—Thomas Joiner and Mary Walters : St. Dionis Backchurch, p. 68.
1767. — Francis Willince and Ann Joyner : St. Geo. Han. Sq. i. 162.
London, 1, 8 ; Boston (U.S.), 4, 0.

Jolin, Joline.—Bapt. 'the son of Jolin' or 'Jollan' ; v. Jolland.

Jolin de Dunholme, co. Hunts. 1273. A.
Henry fil. Jolani, co. Linc., ibid.
1649. Married—Samuel Jollins and Anne Mosely : St. Jas. Clerkenwell, iii. 84.
1738. Buried—E. Jollins : St. Thomas the Apostle (London), p. 154.
London, 1, 0 ; Philadelphia, 0, 4.

Joll ; see Jull.

Jolland, Golland, Galland, Jollands, Jollans, Jalland.—Bapt. 'the son of Jollan,' possibly, as stated by Camden, a corruption of Julian. The *d* in Jolland is excrescent ; cf. *riband*, Simmond, and Hammond, for *ribbon*, Simon, and Hamon. The font-name is almost entirely found in co. Lincoln, where also the surname seems to have originated. It is interesting to notice that Lincolnshire is still the chief habitat of all the various forms. With the initial G, cf. Gill and Jill, Garrett and Jarratt, Gosling and Joscelyn. The final *s* in Jollands and Jollans is the patronymic, as in Williams, Jennings, &c.

Jollan de Hamby, co. Linc., Hen. III Edw. I. K.
Jollanus de Heyling, co. Linc., ibid.
Jodlanus de Nevill, co. Linc., ibid.
Jollan de Hemby, co. Linc., ibid.
Gilbert fil. Jolani, co. Linc., 1273. A.
William fil. Jollani, co. Linc., ibid.

Robert Jollayn, co. Linc., 1273. A.
Ricardus Joland, 1379: P. T. Yorks.
p. 8.
Katerina Golland, 1479, York: W. 11,
p. 106.
1536-7. Richard Joland and Agnes In-
kersall: Marriage Lic. (London), i. 9.
1698. Married—William Joland and
Anne Gurney: St. Dionis Backchurch,
p. 47.
London, 1, 1, 2, 0, 0, 1; MDB. (co.
Lincoln), 1, 4, 2, 1, 1, 0; (East Rid.
Yorks) (Jalland), 2; Philadelphia (Galland), 2.

Jolliff, Jolliffe, Joliffe. —
Nick. 'the jolif,' i.e. the festive,
sportive; O.F. *jolif*, the earlier
form of jolly; cf. *bailiff* and *bailey*..
'Forth he goth, jolif and amorous.'
          Chaucer, C. T. 3355.
John Jolyf, co. Hunts, 1273. A.
Henry Jolyffe, c. 1300. M.
Robertus Jolyf, 1379: P. T. Yorks.
p. 208.
Alicia Jolyff, 1379: ibid. p. 270.
John Jolyf, C. R., 1 Hen. IV. pt. i.
1670. William Hawkins and Edith
Joliffe (of Dorchester): Marriage Alleg.
(Canterbury), p. 179.
Liverpool, 0, 1, 0; MDB. (co. Kent),
0, 1, 1; (co. Worcester), 0, 0, 1; New
York (Joliffe), 1.

Jolly, Jolley, Joly, Jollie.—
Nick. 'the jolly,' merry, gay, festive;
v. Jolliff. Prof. Skeat connects
it with Yule; Icel. *jol.* The following entries referring to the
same individual are interesting:
Johannes Yoly, 1379: P. T. Yorks.
p. 265.
Agnes, serviens Joly Johan, 1379: ibid.
p. 226.

Hence the double forms Little
and Little-john in our directories.
In the latter case the font-name
becomes permanently incorporated
with the nickname. Jolly-john
might as easily have been perpetu-
ated. Note, however, Y and J in
the instance given; v. Joy for
similar instance.
William Golye, 1273. A.
Henricus Joly, 1379: P. T. Yorks.
p. 142.
Ricardus Jolyman, 1379: ibid. p. 119.
Willelmus Jolyman, 1379: ibid. p. 16.
Johannes Jolyman, 1379: ibid. p. 32.

With these instances, cf. Merriman and Merry.

1715. Buried—Theodorius Joley, servant to Mr. Philips, the barber: St.
Michael, Cornhill, p. 283.
London, 12, 1, 0, 0; Philadelphia, 12,
8, 5, 3.

Jollypace. — Nick. With the
merry step, lively gait; M.E.
pas; cf. Golightly, Lightfoot.
Henry Jolypas, C. R., 17 Ric. II.
'And forth we riden a litel more than
pas.'   Chaucer, C. T. 825.

Jonas. — Bapt. 'the son of
Jonas.' Generally of Jewish de-
scent, but in early use as an
English font-name.
Jonas de Powis, Pipe Roll, 11 Hen. II.
1548-9. Richard Jonas (? Jones) and
Joanna Smyth: Marriage Lic. (Faculty
Office), p. 14.
1736. Bapt.—Ann, d. William Jonas:
St. Jas. Clerkenwell, ii. 226.
London, 13; Philadelphia, 7.

Jones, Joneson.—Bapt. 'the
son of John (?), or 'Johan,' or
'Jone,' as at first written and pronounced, both masculine and feminine. In the 13th and 14th centuries Johan stood for both Johannes and Johanna. This being
awkward, the masculine took the
form of John (Jon), the feminine
of Joan (Jone). But it is quite
clear from evidence that for a time
the sound Jone represented both.
In the Poll Tax, 1379, co. Yorks
(p. 43), we find for instance :
Johan Chapman et Lesot sa femme.
Johan servant de dit Johan.
Henri de Nortburne et Johan sa femme.
Robert Geslyng et Johan sa femme.
Johan Quenyld.
Matilda Jones, co. Hunts, 1273. A.
Walter fil. Jone, co. Hunts, ibid.
Ralph Jones-man, C. R., 30 Edw. I.
Walter Jones, co. Soms., 1 Edw. III:
Kirby's Quest, p. 231.
Ricardus Jone-son, 1379: P. T. Yorks.
p. 104.
Alicia Jone-doghter, 1379: ibid.
Johanna Jone-wyf, 1379: ibid. p. 23.
Jane Joneson, of Audlem, *widow*, 1594:
Wills at Chester (L. and C. R. S.), p. 111.
Jane Joneson, of Marton, *widow*, 1605:
ibid.

Joneson has become absorbed
by Johnson. Indeed, Joynson is
the only variant that remains.
London, about 650, 0; Philadelphia,
1262, 0.

Jonet, Jonetson.—Bapt. 'the
son of John' (?) ; M.E. Jone, dim.
Jonet. Probably for a time Jonet
was masculine as well as feminine.
But Janet (q.v.) won the day.
Johannes Jonetson, 1379: P. T. Yorks.
p. 18.
Willelmus Jonet, 1379: ibid. p. 88.

Johannes Jonet, 1379: ibid. p. 91.
William Jonetson, C. R., 9 Ric. II.

Jonson. — Bapt. 'the son of
John,' for Johnson, but quite as
early a form; cf. Jones. I often
wonder how 'Poems by Benjamin
Johnson' would read. But 'rare
Ben's' name is several times spelt
Johnson by his friends.
Magota Jon-wyf, 1379: P. T. Yorks.
p. 86.
Margareta Jon-dowtter, 1379: ibid.
p. 88.
Thomas Jon-son-Dycon-son, 1379: ibid.
p. 240.
1527. Rawlyns and Johanna Jonson:
Marriage Lic. (London), i. 6.
1556. Christning of Ellen Jonsonne: St.
Peter, Cornhill, i. 7.
Christopher Jonson, or Johnson, 1557:
Reg. Univ. Oxf. i. 234.
London, 1 ; New York, 6.

Joplin, Jopling.—Bapt. 'the
son of Job,' from dim. Joblin ; v.
Jobling. In Jopling the final *g*
is excrescent, as in Jennings; cf.
Hamlin and Hamling from Hamo,
and Tomlin or Tomling from Tom
(Thomas). The change from *b* to
p is common ; cf. Hoblin and Hop-
lin, Hobson and Hopson, Hobbs
and Hopps, Robson and Ropson,
all from Robert. Also cf. Jopson
for Jobson.
1742. Married—John Hague and Hannah Joplin: St. Geo. Chap. Mayfair,
p. 28.
1763. — John Taylor and Eliz. Jopling :
St. Geo. Han. Sq. i. 120.
1804. — Robert Haines and Sarah
Joplin: ibid. ii. 313.
MDB. (co. Camb.), 1, 0 ; Lancashire
Court Dir., 1, 1; Manchester, 0, 1;
Liverpool, 1, 0.

Jopson. — Bapt. 'the son of
Job'; v. Job, Jupp, and Joplin.
Jopson was an early sharpened
form of Jobson.
Johannes Jopson, 1379: P. T. Yorks.
p. 289.
1579. Thomas Jopson, co. York: Reg.
Univ. Oxf. vol. ii. pt. ii. p. 89.
1597-8. Francis Jopson, or Jobson, co.
Westm. : ibid. p. 226.
Liverpool, 2.

**Jordan, Jordanson, Jordi-
son, Jordeson, Jorden, Jor-
don.**—Bapt. 'the son of Jordan.'
This great personal name, that has
made such a strong impression
on English and West European
nomenclature, received its impetus,

like Ellis (Elias), John, and Baptist, from the Crusades. Flasks of Jordan water, we know, were brought home to be used for fontal purposes. John the Baptist was the second Elias, and the baptizer of Jesus Christ. Naturally Jordan was added to the list, and became popular throughout Western Europe. Only a trained student of nomenclature can know what a favourite it became in England. Every register has its muster of instances. Judd was the nick. (whence Judd, Judde, and Judson, q.v.), and Judkin the dim. after the prevailing fashion that gave us Watkin, or Wilkin, or Simpkin, or Tompkin (whence Judkins toned down to Juckins, Juggins, Juckes, and Jukes, q.v.). Dean Stanley says, 'The name of the river has in Italy and Spain, by a natural association, been turned into a common Christian name for children at the hour of baptism, which served to connect them with it' (Sinai and Palestine, p. 333). The late dean did not seem aware that the practice was equally common in England.

Roger fil. Jurdan, co. Camb., 1273. A.
Robert fil. Jordan, co. Oxf., ibid.
Jordan atte Mull, temp. 1300. M.
Matilda relicta Jordani, 1379: P. T. Yorks. p. 210.
Jordanus Thorneton, 1379: ibid. p. 211.
Thomas Jordanson: Three Lancashire Documents (Cheth. Soc.), p. 51.

Jordy or Jurdy is early found as the nick. of Jordan:

Bartholomew Jurde, co. Camb., 1273. A.
Henry Jurde, co. Hunts, ibid.
Jurdi (without surname), co. Suff., ibid.
James Jurdeson. GG.
1763. Married—Francis Nelson and Rachel Jurdison: St. Geo. Han. Sq. i. 118.
London, 65, 0, 2, 1, 0, 0; Philadelphia, 183, 0, 0, 0, 8, 5.

Jose; v. Joce.

Joseph, Josephs.—Bapt. 'the son of Joseph'; v. Jessop. Many of the modern directory Josephs are of Jewish extraction, but there are also a fair number of Josephs who have a purely English descent.

Galian' relict Joseph, co. Oxf., 1273. A.
Thomas Joseph, co. Soms., 1 Edw. III: Kirby's Quest, p. 89.
Edith Josep, co. Soms., 1 Edw. III: ibid. p. 95.
1577. John Joseph, co. Kent: Reg. Univ. Oxf. vol. ii. pt. ii. p. 74.
1754. Married—Anthony Joseph and Mary Thomas: St. Geo. Chap. Mayfair, p. 276.
1799.—John Gough and Jane Josephs: St. Geo. Han. Sq. ii. 198.
1803.—William Burrell and Amelia Joseph: ibid. p. 278.
London, 39, 5; New York, 56, 11.

Joslin, Joselin, Josolyne, Josselin, Josslyn, Joscelyne, Josling, Joslyn, Josline. — Bapt. 'the son of Josse' or 'Goce,' dim. Josselin or Gocelin; v. Joyce. The g in Josling is excrescent; cf. Jennings, Rawling, Hewling, &c.

Thomas Jocelyn, co. Essex, 1273. A.
Jocelinus de Braggrowe, co. Devon, ibid.
Stephen Jocelin, co. Warw., Hen. III-Edw. I. K.
1548. John Heron and Jane Joslyn: Marriage Lic. (Faculty Office), p. 13.
1590. Thomas Josselyn and Dorothy Scott (excommunication removed): Marriage Lic. (London), i. 188.
— John Joslinge and Joanna Humfrye: ibid. p. 191.
1672. Robert Sawyer and Mary Joscelyn: Marriage Alleg. (Canterbury), p. 80.
London, 4, 1, 1, 1, 1, 0, 0, 0, 0; Crockford (Joscelyne and Josling), 2, 1; Philadelphia, (Joslin) 8, (Joslyn) 1, (Josline) 1.

Joule, Joul, Jowle, Joules.— Bapt. 'the son of Joel.' This was popularly styled Jowel. In course of time this became a monosyllable, and is now commonly found in Derbyshire as Joule or Jowle. The patronymic or genitive form is Joules; cf. Jones, Williams, Simpkins, &c. For instances of Jowel, v. Jewell.

1643. Married—Robert Jole and Eliz. Dennis: St. Antholin (London), p. 76.
1650.—Augustine Jowles and Dorothy Ridley: St. Jas. Clerkenwell, iii. 85.
1662. Henry Jowles and Rebecca Alleyn: Marriage Alleg. (Canterbury), p. 75.
1762. Married—George Joules and Margaret Potter: St. Geo. Han. Sq. i. 113.
1767.—John Stent and Sophia Joules: ibid. p. 164.
MDB. (co. Derby), 4, 2, 1, 0; Philadelphia, 2, 0, 0, 0.

Jourdan, Jourden. — Bapt. 'the son of Jordan,' q.v.

William Jurdan, co. Oxf., 1273. A.
Magot Jurdan, vidua, 1379: P. T. Yorks. p. 42.
Isabella Jurdan, 1379: ibid. p. 99.
1573. Thomas Jourden and Marcia Burstowe: Marriage Lic. (London), i. 57.
1585-6. Thomas Shereman and Secile Jourden: ibid. p. 144.
London, 2, 0; Boston (U.S.), 0, 1.

Jowett, Jowitt.—Bapt. 'the son of Juliet.' A New England corruption. There can be, I suspect, no controversy on the origin of these names. Julian or Gillian early took to itself a dim. Juliet or Gilot. The more correct Juliet would, of necessity, almost become Juwet in Yorkshire and the north of England generally: v. Jewett. Of course this modification was not wholly northern.

Robert Jouet, co. Soms., 1 Edw. III: Kirby's Quest, p. 207.
Johannes Juwett, 1379: P. T. Yorks. p. 249.
Robertus Jowet, 1379: ibid. p. 105.
Adam Jowete, 1379: ibid. p. 185.
Johannes Jowete, 1379: ibid.
Willelmus Jowet, 1379: ibid. p. 195.
1539. Married—Richard Juet and Katherine Averell: St. Peter, Cornhill, i. 221.
London, 1, 1; West Rid. Court Dir., 23, 5; New York, 0, 2; Philadelphia, 2, 0.

Joy.—Nick. for one of joyous disposition. Perhaps baptismal; cf. Joyce. The dim. Joyet is found in the case of Richard Joyet, co. Camb. (1273. A.) Joy is a common entry in early registers.

Elena Joye, co. Hunts, 1273. A.
Simon Joye, co. Camb., ibid.
John Joye, co. Oxf., ibid.
Martin Joye, co. Soms., 1 Edw. III: Kirby's Quest, p. 206.
Robertus Yoy, 1379: P. T. Yorks. p. 289.
Robertus Yoy, junior, 1379: ibid.
Willelmus Joye, 1379: ibid. p. 3.

With Yoy, cf. Yoly for Jolly.

1472. Godfrey Joye, alderman of Norwich, died: FF. iv. 213.
1593. Henry Joye and Eliz. Fisher: Marriage Lic. (London), i. 208.
London, 11; Philadelphia, 14.

Joyce, Joycey, Joysey, Jowsey.—Bapt. 'the son of Josse' or 'Goce.' Cognate in origin with joy and joyous; Latin gaudere. Rendered popular by St. Josse the hermit, who refused the sovereignty of Brittany (v. Yonge, i.

396). Nearly forgotten as it is, this name was parent of the dim. Jocelyn, and thus secured immortality through its offspring. From the first there was in England a choice of initials, G or J. If G, then the name was pronounced hard as in *gospel*, if J, soft as in *gentile*. Thus it is that we have Gosling and Joscelyn in our directories, while both are the same name. The early entries of Josse or Goce are numerous, the diminutives at first being rare. Such are some of the registrations :

Goce Fitz-peter, sheriff of London, 1211 : WWW. pp. 187-90.
Goce le Pesur, sheriff, 1218 : ibid.
Goce le Juvene, sheriff, 1220 : ibid.
Josse Sephurd, 1273. A.
Alexander Joce, ibid.
John fil. Jocey, ibid.
Reginald fil. Jocei, ibid.
Nicholas Jose, ibid.
Manasseh fil. Jossy, ibid.
Goceus Gothel, Hen. III-Edw. I. K.
Robert fil. Jocei, 20 Edw. I. R.
1618. William Hercules and Jane Jowsey : Marriage Lic. (Westminster), p. 24.

The name became distinctly popular, and many diminutives arose, Josselin and Gocelin being the chief. For instances, v. Goslin and Joslin. Gosset and Goslett (q.v.) added themselves to the list. The parent form Josse became Jocey, as already seen, and through French influence (cf. *rejoice* and *joy*) Joyce and Joycey. This last is common in Durham and the Newcastle district ; v. Newcastle Directory.

William Joysey, 1561, Tweedmouth : QQQ. p. 25.
'John Moorhead, clerk, against William Joysee in a ple of trespass,' 1614 : ibid. p. 243.

It needs only to add that Joyce became a favourite girl's name, though some of the early instances may be masculine.

Joyce Faukes. H.
Joyce Tibetot, ibid.
Joice Frankline, co. York. W. 9.
1563. Buried—Joyce, wife of Thomas Armstrong : St. Dionis Backchurch (London), p. 187.

I find that the name Joyce occurs once as a nickname, equivalent to joyous :

Richard le Joyce. J.
London, 30, 1, 4, 0 ; Sunderland (Jowsey), 1 ; Philadelphia, 76, 0, 10, 0.

Joyner.—Occup. ; v. Joiner.

Joynson, Joynes.—Bapt. 'the son of John' ; v. Johns. This form has existed in Cheshire for several centuries. It was a compromise between Johnson and Joneson ; v. Jones. The latter is found in Cheshire at an early period :

'William le Crouther, William le Baron, Robert de Bookynton, Henry Jonesson of Werford,' &c. : Hist. East Ches. i. 424.
Robert Joynson, of Eaton, co. Ches., 1582 : Wills at Chester (1545-1620), p. 111.
John Joynson, of Eaton, co. Ches., 1613: ibid.
1619. Arthur Joynson, of Waverton : Hist. East Ches. ii. 146.

Of course Welsh influence had much to do with these Cheshire variants of Johnson.

Sheffield, 0, 2 ; Manchester, 6, 0 ; London, 0, 2 ; MDB. (co. Chester), 6, 0 ; Philadelphia, 0, 2.

Jubb, Jupp, Juppe.—Bapt. 'the son of Job.' Jubb was, generally speaking, the North-English, Jupp or Joppe the South-English form. This probably explains *jubbe*, a drinking vessel, i.e. a Job's comforter.

'With bred and chese, and good ale in a jubbe.' Chaucer, C. T. 3628.

Jack and Jug (Joan) were both similarly employed ; *jug* still exists. v. Jupp.

Elyas Jubbe, co. Suff., 1273. A.
Warin Jubbe, co. York, ibid.
Johannes Jubbe, 1379 : P. T. Yorks. p. 104.
Ricardus Jubbe, 1379 : ibid.
Ales Jubbe, temp. 1495, co. York : Visitation of Yorkshire (Harl. Soc.), p. 57.
1502-3. Martin Jubb and Ursula Smith : Marriage Lic. (London), i. 205.
1864. Married—Gartland and Selina Fanny Jubb : Canterbury Cathedral, p. 108.
West Rid. Court Dir., 13, 0, 0 ; London, 0, 13, 0 ; Boston (U.S.) (Jubb), 1 ; New York (Juppe), 1.

Juckins, Jukinson. — (1) Bapt. 'the son of Jordan,' from the nick. Judd, and dim. Judkin. The patronymic Judkins was modified into Juckins ; v. Jukes and Juggins.

I have only seen one instance of Jukinson.

1641. Married—Ralfe Jukinson and An Lane : Canterbury Cathedral.

(2) Bapt. Possibly a Flemish name, from a nick. Jo (Joseph ?), and dim. Jokin.

William Jokin, co. Suff., 1273. A.
John Jowkin, 1379 : P. T. Yorks. p. 295.

In spite of these two entries I cannot but think that the extremely popular font-name Jordan with its nick. Judd is the parent. Judkins was bound to become Juckins and Jukinson or Juckinson.

Judd, Judde, Jude.—Bapt. 'the son of Jordan,' from nick. Jud, but possibly an early form of Jude. The former is much more probable as Jordan (q.v.) was one of the favourite names of the surname era. Jurdi occurs as a single name (A. ii. 198), also Jurdy (A. ii. 148), which are obviously nicks. of Jordan. Henry Jurde and Bartholomew Jurde occur in the same register. These would readily become popularized into Juddy. In the account of Wat Tyler's insurrection Gower says :

'*Hudde* ferit, quem *Judde* terit, dum Tibbe juvatur.'

Henry Judde, co. Camb., 1273. A.
Aaron Judde, co. Linc., ibid.
Alicia Jude-doghter, 1379 : P. T. Yorks. p. 172.
Johannes Juddeman (i. e. the servant of Judde), 1379 : ibid. p. 93.
Johannes Judd', 1379 : ibid. p. 165.
John Jude, 1585 : Reg. St. Columb Major, p. 142.
John Judde, 1593 : ibid. p. 143.
1774. Married—John Jude and Betty Harman : St. Geo. Han. Sq. i. 243.
London, 31, 0, 4 ; New York, 24, 0, 1.

Judge.—? Offic. 'the judge' ; cf. Justice. So far I have come across no early instances, and suspect it is generally Judds corrupted (i.e. the son of Jordan) ; v. Judd and Judkins. In this case Judge would be imitative.

1575. William Judges and Agnes Okendale : Marriage Lic. (London), i. 66.
1616. Richard Judge, co. Montgom. : Reg. Univ. Oxf. vol. ii. pt. ii. p. 348.
1675. Matthew Wright and Mary Judge : Marriage Alleg. (Canterbury), p. 245.
1746. Married—Simon Norcut and

Sarah Judge: St. Geo. Chap. Mayfair, p. 80.
London, 13; New York, 32.

Judkins, Judkin.

—Bapt. 'the son of Jordan,' from nick. Jud, dim. Judkin ; v. Jukes, which is a modification.

1648. Buried—Thomas Judkins, servant to Mr. Thomas Lucis : St. Dionis Backchurch, p. 39.
1668. James Taylor and Grace Judkin : Marriage Lic. (Faculty Office), p. 103.
1677. Married — Edward James and Jane Judkin : St. Dionis Backchurch, p. 226.
1778. — George Gundrey and Eliz. Mary Judkins : St. Geo. Han. Sq. i. 291.
London, 5, o ; MDB. (co. Warwick), o, 1 ; Boston (U.S.), 15, o.

Judson.

— Bapt. 'the son of Jordan,' from nick. Jud ; v. Judd.

Ricardus Jodson, 1379 : P. T. Yorks. p. 71.
Willelmus Judson, 1379 : ibid. p. 203.
Thomas Judson, 1379 : ibid. p. 90.
Johannes Jodson, 1379 : ibid. p. 108.
Agnes Jod-doghter, 1379 : ibid. p. 263.
William Juddeson, Pardons Roll, 15 Ric. II.
1574. Buried—Briget, d. John Judson : St. Peter, Cornhill, i. 123.
1594. Bapt.—Dority, d. Robert Judson : St. Antholin (London), p. 37.
London, 2 ; Philadelphia, 25.

Juggins, Juggings.

— Bapt. 'the son of Jordan,' from the nick. Judd, whence the dim. Jud-kin, whence Judkins. This became modified to Juckins, and this to Juggins. The g in Juggings is excrescent, as in Jennings, Collinge, &c. ; cf. Slack and Slagg. The surname is somewhat rare. v. Judkins.

1650. Married—Thomas Juggins and Alice Wentworth : St. Jas. Clerkenwell, iii. 85.
1651. Buried—John, s. John Juggin : ibid. iv. 286.
1793. Married — Edmund Hall and Mary Juggins : St. Geo. Han. Sq. ii. 89.

An amusing leading article on the case of Mrs. Juggings occurs in the Daily Telegraph, Nov. 5, 1889.

London, 1, o ; Oxford, 4, o ; Boston (U.S.), 1, o.

Jugler.

—Occup. 'the juggler.'

Robert Jugler, C. R., 21 Ric. II. pt. i.
Richard Juggolir : Kirby's Quest, p. 273.
Henricus Juglore, 1379 : P. T. Yorks. p. 284.

Jugson ; v. Juxon.

Jukes, Jewks, Juckes, Jewkes.

— Bapt. 'the son of Jordan,' from nick. Judd, and dim. Jud-kin. With a patronymic s (as in Williams) this became Judkins, by-and-by corrupted into Judkiss, Juckiss, and finally Jukes, &c. ; cf. Hawkins, Hawkiss, Hawkes from Henry, or Perkins, Perkiss, Perkes from Peter; v. Dawkins. Also v. Juckins, Judkins.

1570-1. Thomas Jeux and Ellen Johnson : Marriage Lic. (London), i. 48.
1588. George Jucks, co. Salop, Reg. Univ. Oxf. vol. ii. pt. ii. p. 164.
1594. Simon Juckes, London : ibid. p. 205.
1615. Francis Juckes, co. Salop : ibid. p. 337.
1621. Bapt.—James, s. Thomas Jucks : St. Jas. Clerkenwell, i. 90.
1630. Richard Jucks and Eliz. Taunton : Marriage Lic. (Westminster), p. 38.
1768. Married—Joel Jukes and Mary Garlick : St. Geo. Han. Sq. i. 175.
London, 5, o, o, o; Liverpool, o, o, 1, o; Boston (U.S.), 1, o, o, 1.

Julian, Julien, Julyan, Julyans.

—Bapt. 'the son of Juliana,' from the martyr of that name, beheaded at Nicomedia under Galerius (Yonge, i. 320). Popular at an early period, both in the Low Countries and in Normandy. It attained such favour in England that Jack and Jill took the place of Godric and Godgivu as representatives of the sexes. The ordinary form was Julyan and Gillian, in which latter shape it reached the 16th century.

1573. Married—John Carrington and Gillyan Lovelake : St. Dionis Backchurch, p. 7.
1586. Bapt.—Gillian, d. Thomas Jones, grocer : St. Peter, Cornhill, i. 30.

Earlier instances are easily obtainable :

' Jelyan Joly at signe of the Bokeler.'
Cocke Lorelle's Bote.

Gillian Coc, co. Camb., 1273. A.
Robert Gilion, co. Camb., ibid.
Hugh fil. Juliane, co. Oxf., ibid.
Peter fil. Juliane, co. Hunts, ibid.
Roger Juliane, co. Camb., ibid.
Geoffrey Julyan, C. R., 17 Edw. III. pt. i.
Alanus Alscy, et Juliana uxor ejus, 1329 : P. T. Yorks. p. 7.
1574. William Bragdon and Bennet Julyans : Marriage Lic. (London), i. 61.
1591. Bapt.—Robert, s. Miles Julyon : St. Jas. Clerkenwell, i. 25.

1774. Married—James Julian and Eliz. Yandley : St. Geo. Han. Sq. i. 243.
1793. — Jean Jullien and Edith Hunt : ibid. ii. 101.

The nick. of Julian, as will have been understood above, was Jill or Gill.

'I am careful to see thee carelesse, Jylle.
I am woful to see thee wytlesse, Wyll.'
Heywood's Epigrams.
'Sir, for Jak nor for Gille
Wille I turne my face.'
Towneley Mysteries, Noah.
Richard fil. Gille, co. Camb., 1273. A.
Gille Hull, co. Camb., ibid.

This nick. gave birth to Gill and Gillson, q.v. The dim. was Juliet, a name later on to be made familiar for ever. This was ordinarily corrupted to or modified into Juet, Jewett, or Jowett, q.v.

Juetta fil. William. T.
Roger fil. Jowette. ibid.
William fil. Juet, co. Camb., 1273. A.
Jowet Barton, co. York. W. 11.

Hence our various Jewitts, Jewetts, and Jowitts, also our Jewitsons, Jowetsons, Jewisons, and Jewsons.

Christopher Jewitson. Z.

Besides Juliet there was the corresponding form Gillot or Gillet. In one of the old Metrical Sermons it is said :

' Robin will Gilot
Leden to the nale,
And sitten there togedres,
And tellen their tale.'
Gillot Carel. (BB.)

But our Gilletts and Gillotts must as a rule be referred to William ; v. Gillott. From Juliet or Gilot we got ' jilt.' Constant association with Jack made it a cant term for an inconstant girl :

'All shall be well, Jack shall have Gill :
Nay, nay, Gill is wedded to Will.'

Shakespeare has a similar slighting allusion, flirt-gill (Romeo, ii. 4) ; flirt-gillian (Beaumont and Fletcher, The Chances, iii. 1). ' A jillet brak his heart at last' : Burns, On a Scotch Bard. Another instance of the disrepute of Julian lies in the local ' Julian Bowers ' or ' Gelyan Bowers,' a name for the old-fashioned mazes or labyrinths formed by hedges. To find Jillian seated laughing in the centre was the gallant's difficulty. Correspondents in N. and Q. (1855, pp. 65, 132, 193) ascribed them to the Roman period and the Emperor Julian or Julus, son of Aeneas, and quote Virgil, Aen. v. 1. A Julian Bower is noticed in Stukeley's Itinerarium Curiosum, p. 91. Several of the above observations will be found elsewhere, but I thought it better, with a fontal name that has made such a deep impression on our nomenclature, to give a somewhat complete statement.

London, 5, 2, 1, o ; New York, 8, 5, o, o.

Jull, Joll.—Bapt. 'the son of Julian' (q.v.), from the nick. Jill, or more correctly Jull. A Cornish name.

John Jolle, 1549: Reg. St. Columb Major, p. 5.
Richard Julle, 1575: ibid. p. 9.
John Joulle, 1579: ibid. p. 140.
Joane Jule, 1585: ibid. p. 142.
1704. Married—Robert Jull and Sarah Stone : Canterbury Cathedral, p. 67.
1802.—William Warner and Harriot Jull: St. Geo. Han. Sq. ii. 250.
London, 4, o ; Boston (U.S?), o, 1.

Jump.—Local, 'of Jump,' probably the hamlet of Jump in the parish of Wombwell, co. Yorks.

William Jump, of Hesketh, 1612 : Wills at Chester (1545-1620), p. 112.
Robert Jump, of North Meols, 1614 : ibid.
1569. Married—John Willyams and Margery Jumpe: St. Jas. Clerkenwell, iii. 4.
1688-9. Thomas Jump and Eliz. Martendale: Marriage Alleg. (Canterbury), p. 93.
London, 1 ; Liverpool, 5 ; Crockford, 2 ; Philadelphia, 5.

Jung, Junge, June.—Nick. 'the young'; Fr. 'le Jeune.' With an excrescent g ; cf. Jennings.

Matilda Jun, co. Camb., 1273. A.
Johannes le Junge, co. Camb., ibid.
Robert le Jevene, co. Wilts, ibid.
Simon le Jevene, co. Oxf., ibid.
London, 4, o, o ; New York, 44, 5, 3.

Junior. — Nick. 'the junior,' the younger of two men bearing the same name ; cf. Senior. It was a very common thing for two or three brothers to bear the name of John. This necessitated some mark of distinction ; v. my Curiosities of Puritan Nomenclature, p. 4.

Robert Junior, co. Linc., 1273. A.
'John le Senior, *priest*, and John le Junior': FF. v. 384.

These were brothers.

1752. Married—Lewis Brunet and Jeane Junier : St. Geo. Chap. Mayfair, p. 213.
London, 1 ; Philadelphia, 8.

Juniper, Junifer.—Bapt. 'the son of Gwenever' or 'Guinevere'; v. Jenifer. Another name of King Arthur's court. Lancelot was her lover. In Cornwall it has been a font-name for hundreds of years in the several forms of Junipher, Jenifer, and Jennefair. It was still common in the 17th and 18th centuries.

1691. Bapt.—Junipher, d. of Edward Rickard : St. Colomb Major, co. Cornwall.
1692. — Junipher, d. of Robert Dunkin : ibid.
1700. — Jenifer, d. of Richard Janes: ibid.
1701. — Jenifer, d. of Matthew Battrell : ibid.

The surname has been made familiar by Mr. Juniper of the Sussex county cricket eleven. It is in the London Directory. (v. Miss Yonge, Christian Names, ii. 132, for the story of Gwenever.)

1753. Married—John Juniper and Eliz. Keckerman : St. Geo. Chap. Mayfair, p. 239.
London, 1, o ; MDB. (co. Worcester), o, 1 ; (co. Norf.), 3, o ; Boston (U.S.), 1, o.

Jupiter.—Bapt. No doubt an imitative corruption of Juniper, q.v.

1798. Married—William Jupiter and Catherine Davis: St. Geo. Han. Sq. ii. 187.
Jane Jupiter, *tailoress*, 1 Shawmut Terrace : Boston (U.S.).

Jupp, Juppe.—Bapt. 'the son of Job'; M.E. Joppe. The story of Job told in the religious plays would make the name very popular; v. Jopson and Joplin ; v. also Jubb and Chubb. With Jupp, cf. Ropps for Robbs, or Hopps for Hobbs.

Joppe (without surname), co. Bedf., 1273. A.
Thomas Jop, co. Oxf., ibid.
John Joppe, co. Hunts, ibid.
Henry Joppe, co. Wilts, ibid.
John Joppe, co. Soms., 1 Edw. III : Kirby's Quest, p. 257.
1618. Bapt. — Elizabeth, d. Thomas Juppe : St. Dionis Backchurch, p. 97.
1676-7. William Hampton and Judith

Evans, alleged by Benjamin Jupp : Marriage Alleg. (Canterbury), p. 185.
London, 13, o ; New York, o, 1.

Jurden, Jurdon.—Bapt. 'the son of Jordan,' q.v.

Jurdana de Cantok, co. Soms., 1 Edw. III : Kirby's Quest, p. 261.
William Jurdan, co. Soms., 1 Edw. III : ibid.
1582-3. Married—William Shearland and Katherine Jurdenne : St. Dionis Backchurch, p. 10.
1669. — Humfrey Jurden and Allice Andrew : St. Jas. Clerkenwell, iii. 166.
1670. — John Jurden and Mary Hurbin : ibid. 170.
Boston (U.S.), 1, o ; Philadelphia, o, 1

Jury.—Local, 'of the Jewry,' that part of a town which was set apart for the Jewish population; v. Jewsbury.

'Ther was in Asie, in a gret citee, Amonges Cristen folk a Jewerie.' Chaucer, C. T. (beginning of Prioress' Tale).
'And I am juge of all Jury' (i. e. Judea): York Mystery Plays, p. 130, l. 127.

Cf. Jewry in London.

John Jewrie : Pat. Roll, 19 Eliz. pt. xii.
1670. Married—John Jury and Allice Tealor : St. Jas. Clerkenwell, iii. 171.
1804. — William Bennett and Mary Jury : St. Geo. Han. Sq. ii. 306.
London, 3 ; Boston (U.S.), 3.

Juson ; v. Jewson.

Just. — Nick. 'the just,' the righteous, the fair-dealing ; cf. Righteous. I have not found any early instances, and to-day the name is rare.

1764. Married—Adam Just and Margaret Burkit : St. Geo. Han. Sq. i. 134.
London, 1 ; Manchester, 1 ; Grange-over-Sands (N. Lanc.), 2 ; Philadelphia, 1 ; Boston (U.S.), 1.

Justan ; v. Justin.

Justice, Justis. — Offic. 'the justice,' a judge. A feminine form occurs twice in the Hundred Rolls.

'Joseph was justice Egipte to loke.'
Piers P. 4825-6.

Eva la Justice, co. Norf., 1273. A.
John le Justice, co. Oxf., ibid.
Henry Justis, co. Bucks, ibid.
Robert le Justise. E.
Johanna Justys, 1379 : P. T. Yorks. p.60.
Robertus Justys, *wryght*, 1379 : ibid.
Johannes Justis, 1379 : ibid.
1571. John Justice, London : Reg. Univ. Oxf. vol. ii. pt. ii. p. 51.
1636. William Justice and Mary Hooker : Marriage Lic. (London), i. 226.
London, 3, o ; MDB. (co. Salop), 4, o ; Boston (U.S.), 6, 1.

Justicer.—Offic. 'the justice,' augmented into Justicer.

'Come, sit thou here, most learned justicer': K. Lear, Act iii. sc. vi.
'A perfect patterne of an upright justicer': Holinshed, Hist. of Scotland, p. 63, quoted by Halliwell.
Michael Justicer, C.R., 5 Hen. IV. pt. ii.

Justin, Justyne, Justan, Juston.—Bapt. 'the son of Justin.' In spite of St. Justina and Justin Martyr, Justin was little used in England, but it was popular in Wales. 'Yestin was one of the many old Roman names that lingered on long among the Welsh' (Yonge, i. 398).

Jestyn ap Owen, ap Holl: Visit. Glouc. (Harl. Soc.) p. 113.
Justian Hill: ibid. p. 30.
Jenetta fil. Nevan, ap-Lyon ap-Jestin: ibid. p. 98.
London, 0, 1, 0, 0; Liverpool, 0, 0, 1, 0; Oxford, 1, 0, 0, 0; Philadelphia, 2, 2, 0, 1.

Jutson, Jutsum.—Bapt. 'the son of Jordan,' from nick. Jud, whence the patronymic Judson, sharpened to Jutson. The change from the final *n* to *m* in Jutsum is not uncommon; cf. Ransom for Ranson, Milsum for Milson, and v. Sanson and Sansom.

1777. Married—Richard Jutson and Eliz. Young: Canterbury Cathedral, p.97.
London, 1, 3.

Juxon, Jugson.—Bapt. 'the son of Jordan,' from nick. Jud. A corruption of Judson; cf. Jutson; also cf. Coxon for Cockson.

1583-4. Thomas Juxon and Eliz. Ireland: Marriage Lic. (London), i. 126.
1614. Buried—A stillborn of Albion Jugsonn: St. Antholin (London), p. 50.

With the above entry, cf. Juggins for Judkins.

1545. John Jugson: Cal. of Wills in Court of Husting (2).
1619. Married—Arthur Juxon and Anne Saunders: St. Thomas the Apostle (London), p. 18.
1665.—William Juxon and Eliz. Tymson: St. Michael, Cornhill, p. 39.

K

Kable.—Bapt.; v. Cabbell and Kibble.

London, 1; Philadelphia, 1.

Kain, Kane, Kayne.—(1) Bapt.; v. Cain. (2) Local, 'of Caen' in Normandy.

Roger de Kana, co. Linc., 1273. A.
John Kane, co. Bedf., ibid.
William de Kan, co. Essex, Hen. III–Edw. I. K.
Lucia Cayne, 1379: P. T. Yorks. p. 242.
'Nicholas Bever from a gimnasium at Kane in Normandy, sup. for B.D. June 15, 1506': Reg. Univ. Oxf. i. 46.
1618. Bapt. — Benjamin, s. Robert Kaine: St. Michael, Cornhill, p. 213.
1751. Married — Charles Kain and Judith Jones: St. Geo. Chap. Mayfair, p. 195.
1752. — Francis Kane and Ann Wilcocks: ibid. p. 217.
London, 6, 2, 0; MDB. (co. Lanc.), 0, 1, 1; Philadelphia, 32, 325, 1.

Kaines, Kains.—Local, 'of Kaynes' or 'Keynes.' I cannot identify the place, probably Norman.

Robert de Kaynes, co. Northampton, 1273. A.
Robert de Kaynes, or Keynes, co. Wilts, 20 Edw. I. R.
Hawysia (Avice) de Kaynes, co. Northampton, ibid.
Roger de Kaynes, co. Devon, ibid.
1572. Humphrey Keynes, St. Alban Hall: Reg. Univ. Oxf. vol. ii. pt. ii. p. 40.
— James Keynes, St. Alban Hall: ibid.

1749. Married — John Boaz and Ann Kaines: St. Geo. Chap. Mayfair, p. 132.
1770. — Robert Lamb and Mary Kaines: St. Geo. Han. Sq. i. 200.
Philadelphia, 0, 1.

Kaiser, Kazer, Keyser, Kezar, Kezor, Keyzor.—Nick. 'the emperor'; v. Cayzer and Caesar; cf. Lemprière. Some of the American instances, especially those in New York, are of German extraction, and merely modern importations.

Robert le Keser, co. Kent, Edw. I–Edw. III. R.
Lambert Keser, co. Kent, ibid.
1663. Thomas Keysar and Rachael Ward: Marriage Alleg. (Canterbury), p. 99.
1670. John Keyser and Alice Pike: ibid. p. 40.
1672. George Kezar and Eliz. Oldom: ibid. p. 78.
1739. Married—Adam Keiser and Mary Milborn: St. Geo. Chap. Mayfair, p. 13.
London, 3, 0, 3, 0, 0, 1; Boston (U.S.), 5, 1, 7, 4, 3, 0; New York (Keyser), 37.

Karl, Karle; v. Carle.

Karslake, Kearslake, Kerslake.—Local, 'of Karslake.'

1586. John Kerslake, or Kersleck, co. Cornwall: Reg. Univ. Oxf. vol. ii. pt. ii. p. 156.
1677-8. John Kerslake and Mary Larcomb: Marriage Alleg. (Canterbury), p. 213.

London, 5, 0, 6; Warwick, 0, 1, 0; Philadelphia, 0, 0, 2.

Kay, Kaye.—(1) Local, 'at the quay,' from residence thereby.

'Et de 5s. de firma unius tenementi jacen' in le *Kaysyd* (i.e. Kay-side) in tenura Johannis Blakeston,' 30 Hen. VIII: Brand's Hist. of Newcastle-on-Tyne, i. 408.
John del Kai, sheriff of London, 1201: WWW. p. 187.
Jordan Kay, 1273. A.
Robertus Cay, 1379: P. T. Yorks. p. 242.
Alanus Kay, 1379: ibid. p. 47.
Johanna Caa, 1379: ibid. p. 112.
Willelmus Ka, 1379: ibid. p. 58.
Thomas Key, or Cay, master of University College, Oxford, died 1572: Oxford Hist. Soc. viii. 183.
1557-8. Robert Kaye and Lucy Barbur: Marriage Lic. (London), i. 18.
1674. Bapt.—Mary, d. Arthur Key: Canterbury Cathedral, p. 15.
1700. Married—Thomas Kay and Eliz. Cotton: St. Dionis Backchurch, p. 49.

A clergyman named Kaye once said in my hearing that his surname might be spelt with one, two, three, or four letters, as it pleased the scribe, viz. K, Ka, Kay, Kaye.

London, 26, 5; New York, 13, 2.

Kayne.—Bapt.; v. Kain.

Keal, Keel, Keele, Keale.—
Local, 'of Keal.' East and West
Keal are parishes in co. Lincoln.
Robert de Kele, co. Linc., 1273. A.
William de Kele, co. Linc., ibid.
1570. Sebastian Keele, co. Bucks:
Reg. Univ. Oxf. vol. ii. pt. ii. p. 87.
1598. Robert Keale, co. Essex, and
Eliz. Smythe : Marriage Lic. (London),
i. 253.
1602-3. William Austen and Katherine
Keale, *widow* : ibid. i. 274.
1604. Bapt.—Henrie, s. Thomas Keele :
St. Jas. Clerkenwell, i. 45.
1618. — Jeffrey, s. William Keale :
ibid. i. 82.
London, 0, 1, 3, 0 ; MDB. (co. Lincoln),
6, 1. 0, 0 ; New York, 3, 0, 1, 1.

Kean, Keen, Keene, Keane,
Kene.—(1) Nick. 'the keen,' the
sharp, the quick, the eager. (2)
Local, ' of St. Keyne,' a parish in
co. Cornwall, near Liskeard, from
St. Kayne, or Keyne, a saint of
the 5th century. The nick. is
undoubtedly the chief parent; cf.
Quick, Snell, Sharp, &c.
Hugh le Kene, co. Oxf., 1273. A.
Reginald le Kene, co. Bucks, ibid.
William le Kene, co. Bucks, ibid.
Simon de Kyne, co. York, Edw. I-
Edw. III. R.
Thomas Kene, co. Soms., 1 Edw. III:
Kirby's Quest, p. 109.
Gilbertus Kene, 1379: P. T. Yorks. p. 17.
Willelmus Kene, *wryght*, 1379 : ibid.
p. 19.
Robertus Kene, 1379 : ibid. p. 25.
1587. William Kine, co. Dorset (=
Keyne): Reg. Univ. Oxf. vol. ii. pt. ii.
p. 159.
1598. Married—Richarde Fludde and
Hester Keane: St. Michael, Cornhill,
p. 16.
1617. — John Keene and Katherine
Andrews : ibid. p. 21.
1681. Buried — Thomas Keyne : ibid.
p. 265.
London, 21, 35, 20, 0, 0 ; New York,
13, 4, 6, 21, 2.

Kearsey.—Local, ' of Kersey,'
q.v. ; cf. Karsley for Kearsley,
Kearshaw for Kershaw.
Richard de Karsy, co. Worc., Hen.
III-Edw. I. K.
London, 3 ; MDB. (co. Wilts), 1.

Kearshaw; v. Kershaw. A
North-Yorkshire variant.
Middlesborough, 1.

Kearslake ; v. Karslake.

Kearsley, Keasley.—Local,
' of Kearsley,' a township in the
parish of Dean, co. Lanc.

Richard Kersley, of Westhoughton,
1604 : Wills at Chester, i. 114.
Roger Kersley, of Westhoughton, 1620 :
ibid.
1610. John Kersly, Glouc. Hall : Reg.
Univ. Oxf. i. 402.
1618-9. John Karsley and Elmina
Barton : Marriage Lic. (London), ii. 70.
1673. Philip Burton and Eliz. Kearsly :
Marriage Alleg. (Westminster), p. 221.
London, 2, 2 ; Manchester, 6, 0.

Kearton.—Local, ' of Kirton,'
a North-Yorkshire variant ; v.
Kirton. In the same district Kearshaw is found for Kershaw.
MDB. (North Rid. Yorks), 5.

Keasbey, Kisbee, Kisby,
Kisbey.—Local, ' of Keisby,' a
hamlet in the parish of Lavington,
co. Linc.
(Dominus) de Kiseby, co. Linc.,1273. A.
1574-5. Robert Kisbie, co. Berks : Reg.
Univ. Oxf. vol. ii. pt. ii. p. 61.
1581. Paul Kysbie, co. Berks: ibid.
p. 111.
MDB. (co. Linc.), Kisby, 1 ; (co. Hunts),
0, 1, 3, 0 ; (co. Lancaster), Kisbey, 2 ;
Philadelphia (Keasby), 3 ; London (Kisbee), 1.

Keast.— ? ——. A Cornish
name.
MDB. (co. Cornwall), 4 ; London, 3.

Keat, Keate, Keates; Keats.
—Bapt. ' the son of Kett,' but
whether Kett represents a nick. of
Catherine, or, like Kit, of Christopher, I cannot say. The forms
are found all over England, con-
firming a baptismal derivation. The
variants given in the Oxford
Registers are : Keete, Keighte,
Keit, Ket, Keyt, Kight, Kighte,
Kite, Kitte, and Kyte. Several
of these are variants of Kite, q.v.
Keats or Keates is the genitive, as
in Williams, Jones, &c.
William Ket, co. Norf., 1273. A.
1575. Jerome Kighte, co. Oxf. : Reg.
Univ. Oxf. vol. ii. pt. ii. p. 68.
1581. Thomas Keate, or Keighte : ibid.
p. 113.
1589. Edward Keat, co. Berks : ibid.
p. 175.
1780. Married — Jeremiah James and
Ann Keate : St. Geo. Han. Sq. ii. 34.
1791. — James Watts and Hannah
Keates : ibid. p. 53.
1795. — Richard Keats and Mary
Widdison : ibid. p. 125.
1803. Joseph Hyde and Frances Keet :
ibid. p. 293.
London, 2, 1, 7, 3 ; Philadelphia
(Keates), 2.

Keatch, Keech, Keach,
Ketch, Keitch, Kedge.—Nick.
' Kedge,' brisk, active. It occurs
as *Kygge* or *Kydge*=jocundus, in
Prompt. Parv. p. 274. Hence we
need not be surprised to find the
home of the surname to be in
co. Norfolk and the neighbouring
shires. ' *Kedge*, brisk, budge, hale,
lively. Suff.': Ray and Moor (v.
Wray's note on Kygge in Prompt.
Parv.).
Peter Kech, co. Norf., 1273. A.
Emma Kech, co. Camb., ibid.
Adam Kyg, co. Bucks, ibid.
John Keche, co. Soms., 1 Edw. III :
Kirby's Quest, p. 100.
1430. John Keche, rector of Erping-
ham, co. Norf. : FF. vi. 411.

On a brass plate in the ancient
church of St. Helen's, Norwich,
could be read :
' Hic jacet corpus Dni. Edmundi
Keche, presbyteri ': FF. iv. 379.
1620. Henry Keitch and Magdalen
Chambers : Marriage Lic. (London),
ii. 95.
1621. Married — Andrew Stucke and
Edey Kege : St. Mary Aldermary, p. 14.
1673. John Keech and Mary Rutland :
Marriage Alleg. (Canterbury), p. 226.
London, 0, 1, 0, 0, 0, 2 ; Crockford
(Keitch), 1 ; Boston (U.S.) (Keach), 7 ;
Philadelphia (Keech), 6.

Keatley.—Local. Either a variant of Kettley or Keighley, q.v.
1752. Married—William Keetly and
Eliz. Sayers : St. Geo. Chap. Mayfair,
p. 215.
Birmingham, 1 ; New York, 1 ; Boston
(U.S.), 1.

Keable, Kebbel, Keble, &c.
—Bapt. ; v. Kibble.

Keddington.—Local, (1) ' of
Keddington,' a parish in co. Lincoln,
near Louth; (2) ' of Kedington,'
a parish in co. Suffolk, on the
border of Essex.
John de Kediton, co. Essex, 1273. A.
Godfrey de Kediton, co. Camb., ibid.
1582. Henry Keddington, rector of
Bergh-Apton, co. Norf. : FF. x. 100.
MDB. (co. Suffolk), 2.

Kedge, Keech ; v. Keatch.

Keedwell, Kidwell.— ? Bapt.
' the son of Kedwell ' ; seemingly
a Welsh personal name, possibly
an abbreviation of Cadwallador, or
Cadwallon (v. Yonge, ii. 94). There

is a parish of Kidwelly in the dioc. of St. David's.

1589. Roger Kidwall: St. Mary Aldermary, p. 8.
1508. Bapt.—Kedwallader, son of Kedwell Rogers: ibid. p. 65.
1747. Married—John Saxon and Catherine Kidwell: St. Geo. Han. Sq. i. 39.
London, 1, 1; MDB. (co. Glouc.), 4, 0; (co. Somerset), 2, 0; (co. Monmouth), 1, 1; Philadelphia, 0, 2.

Keefe, Keeff, Keeffe.—?Local.
1797. Married—William Hearn and Margaret Keefe: St. Geo. Han. Sq. ii. 175.
1800. — Michael Shine and Margaret Keif: ibid. p. 210.
1806. — John Keeffe and Sarah Shaw: ibid. p. 344.
London, 3, 1, 1; Philadelphia, 30, 0, 2.

Keel, Keele; v. Keal.

Keeler, Keelar.—Occup. 'the keeler,' a bargeman, one who navigated a keel. Brockett has quotations in 1378 and 1440 (p. 244). The surname is found on the East coast, just where one would expect it.
1750. Married — Thomas Keeler and Jane Plaw: St. Geo. Chap. Mayfair, p. 183.
1799. — Alexander Keeler and Jean Duncan: St. Geo. Han. Sq. ii. 208.
West Rid. Court Dir., 1, 0; Sheffield, 1, 0; London, 3, 0; MDB. (co. Kent), 6, 1; Philadelphia, 26, 0.

Keeley, Kealey, Keely.—Local, 'of Keighley,' q.v. The variants of this name are many. From the epitaphs in the churchyard of Keighley it is clear that the place was often pronounced Keeley in the last century.
1563. Buried—Martha Keely: St. Peter, Cornhill, i. 116.
1689. Bapt. —Anne, d. of William Kealy: St. Jas. Clerkenwell, i. 332.
1747. Married — Thomas Brislet and Ann Keeley: St. Geo. Chap. Mayfair, p. 87.
1793. — Martin Kealey and Hester Curren: St. Geo. Han. Sq. ii. 92.
1794. — Charles Bullock and Ann Keely: ibid. p. 123.
London, 4, 1, 0; Philadelphia, 22, 1, 53.

Keeling, Keelinge, Keiling, Keelin.—(1) Nick. 'the keeling,' i.e. a special small cod; Icel. *keila*, a kind of small cod. On visiting the North-east coast in the summer of 1886, I failed to find the word in use, yet both word and name were there for centuries.
'Item, 189 Kelinges and codlinges,

&c., £16 13s. 7d.' 1350, Account of Holy Island Monastery: QQQ. p. 99.
John Kelynge, master of Greatham Hospital, 1463: DDD. (Durham), iii. 136.
Henry Keling, rector of Houghton-le-Spring, 1482: ibid. i. 156.

(2) Local, 'of Keelin.' I suspect the Staffordshire, Cheshire, and Lancashire Keelings are of local origin. But I cannot find the spot. The final *g* is in this case an excrescence, as in Jennings, Hewlings, &c.
' In 56 Hen. III (1272), Henry de Lascy granted for his service all that land which William of Keelin and William his son formerly held, and which reverted to the grantor by the felony of William de Keelin': Baines' Lanc. (Croston's edit.), ii. 404.
Walter de Kelin, co. Hunts, 1273. A. Osbert Kelyng, co. Hunts, ibid.
1526. William Kelyng and Anne Lacy: Marriage Lic. (London), i. 5.
1582. Daniel Keeling, co. Oxf.: Reg. Univ. Oxf. vol. ii. pt. ii. p. 119.
1645. Nathaniel Waterhouse and Eliz. Kelinge: Marriage Lic. (London), ii. 276.
1661. Edward Keling and Alice Cave: ibid. p. 284.
London, 12, 0, 0, 0; MDB. (co. Stafford), 11, 1, 1, 0; Philadelphia, 1, 0, 0, 1.

Keen, Keene; v. Kean.

Keenlyside, Kinleyside.—Local, probably 'of Kinneyside,' a township in the parish of St. Bees, co. Cumberland. A purely North-English surname.
Sunderland, 2, 0; MDB. (co. Durham), 1, 1.

Keep.—Local, 'at the keep,' the donjon or stronghold of a castle.
William atte Kep, C. R., 18 Edw. I.
Roger Kep, co. Soms., 1 Edw. III: Kirby's Quest, p. 163.
Richard atte Kippe, co. Soms., 1 Edw. III: ibid. p. 168.
1617. Henry Keepe, co. Berks: Reg. Univ. Oxf. vol. ii. pt. ii. p. 365.
1643. Buried—Mr. Cristever Keape, a stranger: St. Michael, Cornhill.
1661. Bapt. — Peter, s. Peter Keepe: St. Jas. Clerkenwell, p. 210.
1743. Married — Thomas Nelson and Joanna Keep: St. Geo. Han. Sq. i. 30.
London, 8; New York, 12.

Keeper.—Offic. 'the keeper,' a woodward, also the keeper of any stronghold; v. Keep. 'The keeper of the prison' (Acts xvi. 27).
'John Keeper, or Woodward, of Buckholt-wood: Rudde's Gloucestershire, pp. 140-1.

William Kepere, co. Hunts, 1273. A.
John Keeper, temp. Eliz. Z.
1567. John Keper: Reg. Univ. Oxf. i. 268.
1568. John Keeper, or Keper, or Kepar, Hart Hall: ibid. vol. ii. pt. ii. p. 39.
Johannes Kauper, 1379: P. T. Yorks. p. 87.

Keetley.—Local. A variant of Kettley or Keighley, q.v.
Birmingham, 1.

Keeton; v. Ketton.

Keevil.—Local, 'of Keevil,' a parish in co. Wilts, four miles from Trowbridge.
1620. Bapt.—Jaîne, d. Henry Kevill: St. Jas. Clerkenwell, i. 87.
London, 2; New York, 1.

Keighley, Keeley, Kealey, Keithley, Keightley, Keightly.—Local, 'of Keighley,' a well-known town in the W. Rid. Yorks. Many of these variants are to be seen in the epitaphs of the parish churchyard of Keighley. For other variants, v. Kightley.
Henry Kighele, co. Lanc., Edw. I-Edw. III. K.
Johannes de Kyghelay, 1379: P. T. Yorks. p. 199.
William de Kigheley, 1397: Preston Guild Rolls, p. 6.
1576. John Kighlye, co. Linc.: Reg. Univ. Oxf. vol. ii. pt. ii. p. 72.
1583. Philip Kyghley, co. Kyglaye, co. Worc.: ibid. p. 127.
1612. Robert Keigley, of the Whitelee, in Goosnargh: Wills at Chester, i. 112.
1662. Joseph Dey and Margaret Keighley: Marriage Alleg. (Canterbury), p. 69.
1676. Holmer Lunne and Elizabeth Keightly: ibid. p. 260.
London, 6, 4, 1, 0, 0, 0; West Rid. Court Dir., 10, 0, 0, 2, 0, 0; Kendal (Keightley), 1.

Keitch; v. Keatch.

Keith.—Local, 'of Keith,' an estate in the parish of Humble, co. Haddington. Mr. Lower adds that several parishes and places in Scotland bear this name.
1582. Robert Keathe, co. York: Reg. Univ. Oxf. vol. ii. pt. ii. p. 119.
1675. John Keith and Ann Sweeting: Marriage Alleg. (Canterbury), p. 147.
London, 13; Philadelphia, 24.

Keithley; v. Keighley.

Kekewick, Kekewich, Kékwick.—Local, 'of Kekewick,' co. Chester. Spelt Kekewicke and

Kekewike in the Accounts of Norton Abbey (v. Lanc. and Ches. Records, i. 103–4). The name passed into Cornwall several centuries ago.

Peter Kykewhych, 1518 : Reg. Univ. Oxf. i. 105.
1574–5. Gregory Keckwiche, co. Cornwall : Reg. Univ. Oxf. vol. ii. pt. ii. p. 81.
John Keakwich, of Aughton, *yeoman*, 1650 : Wills at Chester (1621–50), p. 127.
John Keyquick, Liverpool, 1677 : ibid. (1660–80), p. 72.
Robert Darwell, of Keckquick, co. Chester, *husbandman* : ibid. (1660–80), p. 159.
1622. Peter Rawson and Ellen Kewquitt : Marriage Lic. (London), ii. 110.
Cumberland Court Dir., 0, 0, 1 ; London, 0, 1, 0 ; MDB. (co. Cornwall), 1, 0, 0.

Kelby.—Local ; v. Kilbey.

Kelcey.—Local ; v. Kelsey.

Keld, Kell.—Local, 'at the keld,' from residence thereby. 'Keld, a well (Craven dialect), smooth reaches of water in a rough stream' (Halliwell). A common term in Yorks., Westm., and Cumb. for a well or spring. Icel. Kelda, *palus* (Brockett). The *d* seems to have been entirely disconnected from the name in Yorkshire.

Willelmus atte Keld, 1379 : P. T. Yorks. p. 242.
Johannes atte Keld, 1379 : ibid. p. 3.
Dionisius del Kell', 1379 : ibid. p. 22.
Rogerus Kell, 1379 : ibid. p. 123.
Thomas atte Keld, 1379 : ibid. p. 255.
William del Keld, 1396 : FFF. p. 566.
Cf. Johannes de Kelfeld (i.e. the wellfield), 1379 : P. T. Yorks. p. 16.
1730. Married—Lancelot Kell and Jane Wilsby : St. Dionis Backchurch, p. 67.
London, 0, 5 ; West Rid. Court Dir., 0, 5 ; Philadelphia, 0, 2.

Kelham, Kellam.—Local, 'of Kelham,' a parish in co. Notts, two miles from Newark.

Walter de Kelome, co. Notts, 1273. A.
Peter de Kelum, co. Notts, Hen. III-Edw. I. K.
1696. Married — Christopher Kelham and Grace Bennett : St. Michael, Cornhill, p. 48.
1700. — John Kelham and Sarah West : ibid. p. 50.
1763. — Joseph Kelham and Sarah Flower : St. Geo. Han. Sq. i. 125.
London, 1, 0 ; MDB. (co. Northampton), 0, 1 ; (co. Notts), 2, 0 ; New York, 0, 2.

Kelk.—Local, 'of Kelke.' 'The estate of Kelke, co. Linc., was owned by a family so designated from it. There are also two townships in Yorkshire called Kelk' (Lower, Patr. Brit. p. 176). Great and Little Kelk, the townships referred to, are about five miles from Great Driffield, E. Rid. Yorks.

Walter Kelke, co. Norf., 1273. A.
1656. Thomas Kelke and Anne Milton (publication) : St. Michael, Cornhill, p. 36.
1731. Married—John Kelke and Alice Tompson : St. Geo. Han. Sq. i. 8.
1754. — John Tomlinson and Eliz. Kelk : St. Geo. Chap. Mayfair, p. 268.
London, 3 ; Crockford, 2 ; Sheffield, 2 ; New York, 1.

Kell.—Local ; v. Keld.

Kellaway, Kelleway.—Local, 'of Kellaways,' a parish in co. Wilts, near Chippenham. It seems to have been known in earlier times as Kellaway, not Kellaways. With Kelloway, cf. Solloway in the same district.

Elyas de Kaylewey, co. Wilts, Hen. III-Edw. I. K.
1592. Richard Keyllwaye, co. Soms. : Reg. Univ. Oxf. vol. ii. pt. ii. p. 191.
1598. Francis Kellway, co. Devon : ibid. p. 228.
1599. Bapt.—Henrie, s. Henrie Kellway : St. Jas. Clerkenwell, i. 35.
1604. Ralph Kellway, co. Soms. : Reg. Univ. Oxf. vol. ii. pt. ii. p. 274.
1612. Thomas Kelloway of Bettefield, parish of Hanmer : Wills at Chester (1545–1620), p. 112.
1639. John Starkey and Susan Kellaway : Marriage Lic. (London), ii. 244.
— Thomas Pate and Winifred Kellaway : ibid. p. 246.
1754. Married—William Kelloway and Ann Arnold : Reg. Stourton, Wilts, p. 57.
London, 5, 0 ; MDB. (co. Hants), 1, 5 ; Sheffield, 0, 1 ; Boston (U.S.), 0, 1.

Keller.—(1) Local, 'of Keller.' I cannot find the spot. Perhaps from the Low Countries. (2) Occup. 'the keller,' probably a kilner. 'A furnace or kell': Cleaveland, p. 40. 'A kiln, as lime kell. South' (Halliwell).

Elias de Keller, London, 20 Edw. I. R.
John Keller, 1379 : P. T. Yorks. p. 235.
Symon le Keller, de London, 16 Edw. II : Freemen of York, i. 20.
1686. Godfrey Keller and Eliz. Savery : Marriage Alleg. (Canterbury), p. 236.
1716. Married — Richard Keller and Sarah Neal : St. Jas. Clerkenwell, iii. 239.
London, 4 ; Boston (U.S.), 1.

Kellett, Kellet.—Local, 'of Kellett,' a village near Carnforth, North Lanc. This surname still holds its place in Furness and the district round the village.

Orme de Kellet (de Lonesdale), co. Lanc., 20 Edw. I. R.
Johannes Kelett, 1379 : P. T. Yorks. p. 253.
1557. Married — Edward Kellet and Anne Fell : St. Mary, Ulverston, p. 20.
1575. George Turner and Isabel Kellett : Marriage Lic. (London), i. 66.
1562. Ewan Kellett, *mylner* : Preston Guild Rolls, p. 29.
1589. John Kellatt, of Cartmell : Lancashire Wills at Richmond (1457–1680), p. 172.
1604. Hugh Kellett, of the High, Cartmell : ibid.
London, 1, 0 ; Manchester, 6, 0 ; Lanc. Court Dir., 8, 2 ; Philadelphia, 3, 1.

Kellington.—Local, 'of Kellington,' a parish in W. Rid. Yorks.
1681–2. Job Kellington and Rachael Wyld : Marriage Alleg (Canterbury), p. 87.
1714. Bapt.—John and William Kellington : St. Jas. Clerkenwell, ii. 79.
1736. Buried—Joseph Kellington : St. Michael, Cornhill, p. 293.
Hull, 2.

Kellow, Kellough.—Local, 'of Kelloe,' a parish in co. Durham, six miles from Durham.
Patrick de Kellawe, co. York, Edw. I-Edw. III. R.
William de Kellawe, co. Linc., ibid.
1612–3. John Kellowe, *poulter*, and Mary Presson : Marriage Lic. (London), ii. 18.
1616. Bapt.—Susan, d. John Kellowe : St. Jas. Clerkenwell, i. 75.
1640. Samuel Kello and Mary Emelie : Marriage Lic. (London), ii. 254.
1789. Married—Job Dowsing and Jane Kellow : St. Geo. Han. Sq. ii. 17.
London, 3, 0 ; Boston (U.S.), 0, 2.

Kelsall, Kelsey, Kilshall, Kilshaw, Kelsell, Kelsow.—Local, 'of Kelsall,' a township in the parish of Tarvin, co. Chester. For a second derivation of Kelsey, v. Kelsey. The Lancashire Kelseys, however, must be referred to Kelsall in Cheshire.
Reginald de Keleshalle, co. Camb., 1273. A.
Roger de Keleshelle, co. Camb., ibid.
Johannes Kelesall, 1379 : P. T. Yorks. p. 75.
1561. Buried—John Kelsow (Kelsall) : Reg. Prestbury, co. Ches., p. 5.
— Married—James Kelsow and Blaunch Broke : ibid. p. 4.
1570. Bapt.—Elizabeth Kelsall : ibid. p. 30.

The name is also spelt Kilshaw in the same register.

Manchester, 7, 5, 0, 0, 0, 0; Lanc. Court Dir., 10, 2, 1, 1, 0, 0; Philadelphia, 1, 10, 0, 0, 2, 0; New York (Kelsey), 16; (Kelsow), 1.

Kelsey, Kelcey.—Local, 'of Kelsey,' two parishes, North and South Kelsey, in co. Lincoln.

Brice de Keleseye, co. Linc., 1273. A.
Peter de Keleseve, co. Linc., ibid.
1550. Bapt.—Elizabeth Kelsaye: St. Michael, Cornhill, p. 76.
1552. Married—William Keltredge and Agnes Kelsaye: ibid. p. 6.
1574. — William Kelsea and Isabell Imme: St. Dionis Backchurch, p. 7.
1795. — Thomas Kelsey and Maria Thomas: St. Geo. Han. Sq. ii. 123.
MDB. (co. Kent), 7, 6; (co. Lincoln), 32, 0; London, 21, 0; Boston (U.S.), 15, 0.

Kelston, Kelson.—Local, 'of Kelston,' a parish in co. Somerset, four miles from Bath. Many local surnames ending in -ston become -son.

1687-8. John Kelson and Eliz. Clark: Marriage Alleg. (Canterbury), p. 52.
London, 0, 3; MDB. (co. Somerset), 1,3.

Kemball, Kemble. — Local, 'of Kemble,' a village and parish near Cirencester, co. Wilts. Not to be confounded with Kimbell, although that must have been occasionally done.

1657. Married—John Kemball and Jane Jones: St. Jas. Clerkenwell, iii. 99.
1680. John Kembell and Grace Grey: Marriage Alleg. (Canterbury), p. 45.
1736. Married—James Kemble and Judith Davies: St. Geo. Han. Sq. i. 18.
1742. — George Kemble and Eliz. Pool: St. Geo. Chap. Mayfair, p. 23.
London, 1, 4; Crockford, 0, 3; MDB. (co. Suffolk), 4, 0; Philadelphia, 0, 32.

Kember, Kimber.—(1)Occup. 'the comber,' a wool-comber; cf. Kembester, now Kempster, a female wool-comber. (2) Local, 'of Kimber.' South Kimber in co. Cornwall. The first is the more probable origin; v. Kemper.

1617. John Neave and Thomasine Kember: Marriage Lic. (London), ii. 56.
1770. Married—Thomas Kimber and Alice Hastings: St. Geo. Han. Sq. ii. 301.
— — George Mansfield and Eliz. Kember: ibid. p. 304.
London, 1, 10; Devon Dir. (Farmers' List), 0, 1; New York, 0, 6.

Kemble.—Local; v. Kemball.

Kemme, Kemm, Kem. — Local, 'at the keme.' 'Kemb,' a stronghold. North England' (Halliwell).

Katherine dil. Keme, co. Suff., 1273. A.
Adam Keme, co. Camb., ibid.
Antec' de Kembe, co. Linc., ibid.
Agnes Kemme, 1379: P. T. Yorks. p. 105.
Thomas Keme, 1379: ibid. p. 114.
1602. Married—John Kemme and Sara Potter: St. Dionis Backchurch, p. 14.
1626-7. Edmund Beane and Hannah Keme: Marriage Lic. (London), ii. 184.
London (1887), 2, 0, 0; Crockford, 2, 0, 0; MDB. (co. Wilts), 3, 0, 0; Philadelphia, 0, 1, 1.

Kemmish, Kimmis, Kemish, Kimmish.—Local, 'of Kemeys,' two parishes in co. Monmouth. 'The Baronets, created 1642, extinct 1735, claimed to be of the noble house of Camois. . . . The family were early settlers in Wales, where as lords of Camaes and St. Dogmaels in Pembrokeshire they exercised authority little short of regal' (Lower, quoting Burke's Ext. Barts.).

Arthur Kemys (co. Somerset), Queen's Coll., 1586: Reg. Univ. Oxf. vol. ii. pt. ii. p. 151.
William Kemys of the Began: Visit. Glouc., 1623, p. 98.
Jevan ap Moris Kemys: ibid.
1553-4. Christopher Nappe and Eliz. Kemyes: Marriage Lic. (London), i. 14.
1570. Married—Richard Foster and Ellyn Kemyshe: St. Dionis Backchurch, p. 6.
1608. — Henrie Callis and Fraunces Kemish: St. Michael, Cornhill, p. 19.
1637. Walter Kemis and Anne Pascall: Marriage Lic. (London), i. 230.
MDB. (co. Wilts), 0, 0, 1, 0; (co. Hants), 0, 0, 4, 1.

Kemp, Kempe, Kempson.—Offic. or occup. 'the kemp,' a knight, a soldier, a champion.

'Then it is time for mee to speake,
Of Kern Knightes and Kempes greate.'
Guy and Colbrand.
' Here is Kempis full Kene to the Kyng for to care ': York Mystery Plays, p. 291, l. 521.

Alan Kempe, co. Suff., 1273. A.
William Kemp, co. Oxf., ibid.
Ricardus Kempe, 1379: P.T.Yorks.p. 28.
Johannes Kempe, 1379: ibid. p. 47.
1775. Married—John Dixon and Ann Kempe: St. Geo. Han. Sq. i. 254.
London, 51, 1, 3; Philadelphia, 26, 1, 0.

Kemper.—Occup. 'the kember,' a wool-comber; v. Kempster, with its feminine terminative as in

spinster,' Brewster, &c. This seems to be an American variant; v. Kember.

Philadelphia, 10.

Kemplay.—Local, 'of Kempley,' a parish in co. Gloucester.

1800. Married—Robert Carlisle and Ursula Kempley: St. Geo. Han. Sq. ii. 224.
Beverley (E. R. Yorks), 2; London, 1.

Kempson, Kempston. — (1) Nick. 'the kemp's son'; v. Kemp; cf. Wrightson, Smithson, Hindson, &c. (2) Local, 'of Kempston,' parishes in cos. Bedford and Norfolk. The suffix -ston frequently became son; cf. Kelson for Kelston.

Richard Kemson, 1379: P. T. Yorks. p. 291.
1661-2. Nicholas Kempsone and Hester Busby: Marriage Alleg. (Canterbury), i. 21.
1683-4. Nicholas Kempston and Eliz. Best: ibid. ii. 156.
1729. Married—William Lyley and Mary Kempson: St. Geo. Chap. Mayfair, p. 308.
London, 3, 0; Birmingham, 3, 0; Boston (U.S.), 0, 1.

Kempster, Kemster.—Occup. 'the kembster,' a wool-comber. 'Kempstare, pectrix': Prompt. Parv. Originally a feminine occupation; cf. spinster. Johanna la Kempster (X). Margery la Kembestere (Close Roll, 18 Edw. I). A prayer to the Commons in 1464, respecting the importations of foreign goods, mentions 'the makers of wollen cloth within this Reame (Realm) as Wevers, Fullers, Dyers, Kempsters, Carders, and Spinners ' (Rot. Parl. Edw. IV). Cf. 'unkempt locks.'

' Hir brighte heer was kempt, untressed all.' Chaucer, C. T. 2289 (Skeat's ed.).
Peter Cambestre, co. Camb., 1273. A.
Agnes Kembester, 1379: P.T. Yorks. p. 219.
Johanna Saper, kemster, 1379: P. T. Howdenshire, p. 12.
Robertus Kembster, 1379: ibid. p. 8.
1684. William Watts and Eliz. Kempster: Marriage Alleg. (Canterbury), p. 165.
1747. Married—Richard Kempstar and Susanna Chips: St. Geo. Chap. Mayfair, p. 99.
1791. — Joseph Wright and Eliz. Kempster: St. Geo. Han. Sq. ii. 68.

1806. Married—Isaac Olive and Mary Kempester: St. Geo. Han. Sq. ii. 355. London, 5, 0; MDB. (co. Salop), 6, 0; Birmingham, 2, 0; New York, 1, 0; Boston (U.S.), 1, 0.

Kempthorne, Kimpthorne. —Local, 'of Kempthorne.' This family name was derived from Kempthorne, an estate in the parish of Beer-Ferris, co. Devon; v. C. S. Gilbert's Cornwall (quoted by Lower).

1585. Bapt.—John, s. George Kempthorne: St. Jas. Clerkenwell, i. 17.
1602-3. Richard Kempthorne, co. Cornw.: Reg. Univ. Oxf. vol. ii. pt. ii. p. 263.
Crockford, 4, 0; MDB. (co. Cornwall), 1, 1.

Kempton.—Local, 'of Kimpton' (q.v.), probably a variant.

1599. Bapt. — Robarte, s. William Kempton: St. Antholin (London), p. 39.
1707. Married — James Calcott and Mary Kempton: St. Peter, Cornhill, ii. 67.
1720. Bapt.—Eliz., d: William Kempton: St. Dionis Backchurch, p. 290.
1749. Married—John Kempton and Mary Turner: St. Geo. Chap. Mayfair, p. 149.
London, 9: Philadelphia, 10.

Kench; v. Kinch.

Kendal, Kendall, Kendell, Kendle, Kendel. — Local, 'of Kendal,' co. Westm. The manufacture of 'Kendal green' made this town early famous, and of necessity caused the surname to be common. The result is that it is familiar to every directory in the English-speaking world. The river *Kent*, I need not say, still flows through the *dale*. The surname is frequently met with in all the adjacent villages and towns of the Furness district of North Lancashire.

Johannes de Kendall, 1379: P. T. Yorks. p. 268.
Thomas de Kendale, 1379: ibid. p. 99.
Edmundus de Kendall, 1379: ibid. p. 200.
Johannes de Kendall, *webster*, 1379: ibid. p. 206.
John Kendall, of Aldyngham, 1571: Lancashire Wills at Richmond (1457-1680), p. 173.
Roger Kendoll, of Ulverston, 1582: ibid.
Elizabeth Kendall, of Clitheroe, *widow*, 1593: Wills at Chester (1545-1620), p. 113.
London, 0, 32, 1, 1, 0; Manchester, 6, 4, 0, 0, 0; New York, 0, 31, 0, 0, 1.

Kenderdine.—(?)

MDB. (co. Stafford), 4; New York, 13.

Kendrew.— ? Bapt. A corruption of Kendrick, q.v.

1744. Married—Samuel Barratt and Susanna Kendra: St. Geo. Chap. Mayfair, p. 41.
1747. — Thomas Evans and Mary Kendrey: ibid. p. 86.
1785. — Robert Kendrew and Harriot Garbutt: St. Geo. Han. Sq. i. 369.
London, 1; Liverpool, 1.

Kendrick, Kenrick, Kenrack, Kenwright, Kenwrick. —Bapt. 'the son of Kenwrec.' Domesday Kenricus and Kenric. It is the still earlier Cynric, one of which name defeated the Welsh at Salisbury (Freeman, N.C. i. 319). With Kenwright (which seems to imply an occupation; cf. Cartwright, Arkwright), cf. Allwright for Aldrich.

Nicolas Kenewrek, co. Soms., 1 Edw. III: Kirby's Quest, p. 90.
Kenwrec fil. Maddoc, 7 Hen. II: Pipe Roll, iv. 39.
Ennian fil. Kenewrec, 7 Hen. II: ibid.
Hugo fil. Kenewrec, 7 Hen. II: ibid.
David ab-Kenewrek, Wardrobe Roll, 14-15 Edw. I-III. 3/23.
Davyd Kenrycke, 1565: Reg. St. Dionis Backchurch (London), p. 79.
Richard Kendrick, of Rape, 1593: Wills at Chester (1545-1620), p. 113.
Kendrick Eyton, of Eyton, 1602: ibid. p. 61.
Kenrick Evans, of Chester, alderman, 1613: ibid. p. 62.
1601. David Kendrighe and Eliz. Overton: Marriage Lic. (London), i. 264.
1666. Bapt.—John, son of Rise Kendricke: St. Jas. Clerkenwell, i. 229.
Lanc. Court Dir., 3, 3, 1, 2, 0; Liverpool, 4, 3, 0, 0, 0; London, 12, 2, 0, 0, 0; MDB. (co. Worcester), 9, 0, 0, 0, 1; Philadelphia (Kendrick), 27.

Keningale.—Local, 'of Kenninghall,' a parish in co. Norfolk, three miles from East Harling.

1451. John de Kenninghale, Norwich: FF. iv. 420.
Dr. John Kenninghall, Norwich, temp. Hen. V: ibid. p. 349.
London, 2.

Keniston, Kenniston, Kennison, Kennerson.—Variants of Kynaston, q.v. The American forms of Kennison and Kennerson seem to suggest a baptismal derivation. But such is not the case. There are dozens of parallel instances in this dictionary. The

suffix -*ston* or -*stone* is frequently corrupted to -*son*. The instances below show how the ball of corruption was set rolling; cf. Kelson for Kelston.

1592. Buried — Francis Kennystone: St. Michael, Cornhill, p. 203.
1598. — William Kennyston, *upholder*, ibid. p. 209.
1641. Marmaduke Dollman and Margaret Kennaston: Marriage Lic. (London), ii. 258.
London, 2, 0, 0, 0; Boston (U.S.), 3, 8, 7, 1.

Kenn. — (1) Nick. 'le ken,' from N.F. *ken*; O.F. *chien*, a dog, whence *kennel*, a place for dogs; v. Kennet. Both (1) and (2) represent another instance of a name that seems to be nearly defunct.

Walter le Ken, co. Oxf., 1273. A. Eborard le Ken, co. Camb., ibid.
Thomas le Chene, co. Norf., ibid.
Geoffrey le Ken. B.
Reginald le Chien, C. R., 24 Edw. I.

(2) Local, 'of Kenn,' a parish in co. Somerset, ten miles from Axbridge.

John de Ken, co. Soms., 1 Edw. III: Kirby's Quest, p. 113.
Walter de Ken, co. Soms., 1 Edw. III: ibid.
1670-1. John Kenn and Mary Bland: Marriage Alleg. (Canterbury), p. 50.
1753. Married — Richard Kenn● and Rachael Jackson: St. Geo. Chap. Mayfair, p. 266.
New York, 1.

Kennard; v. Kenward.

Kennell, Kennel.—Local, 'of Kenell.' I cannot find the spot, but evidently it is in the West country.

John de Kenell, co. Hereford, Hen. III-Edw. I.
1601. Richard Keynell, co. Dorset: Reg. Univ. Oxf. vol. ii. pt. ii. p. 247.
1607. Buried—Eliz., d. Thomas Kennell: St. Jas. Clerkenwell, iv. 98.
1774. Married — John Kennell and Martha Church: St. Geo. Han. Sq. i. 240.
London, 2, 0; Philadelphia, 0, 2; New York, 4, 7.

Kennerley.—Local, 'of Kennerleigh,' a parish in co. Devon, five miles from Crediton.

1661. Married—John Kennaley and Margaret Hill: St. Jas. Clerkenwell, iii. 106.
1746. — Henvill Anderson and Ann Kennerly: St. Geo. Chap. Mayfair, p. 65.
1798. — John Stevenson and Mary Kennerley: St. Geo. Han. Sq. ii. 189.
Birmingham, 2.

Kennet, Kennett.—(1) Nick. ' le kenet.' N.F. *kenet* ; M.E. *kenet*, a little dog, a dim. of *ken* (v. Kenn). ' Kenet, hownde, *caniculus*' : Prompt. Parv. ' Kenettys, teroures, butchers houndes, dunghyll dogges': Dame Julyan Berner's Doctryne, quoted by Way. ' A kenit ; *caniculus*' : Cath. Ang. (2) Local, ' of Kennett,' a parish in co. Camb., five miles from Newmarket. Also East and West Kennett, parishes in co. Wilts.

Peter de Kenet, co. Norf., 1237: FF. i. 349.
Nicholas de Kenet, co. Kent, Hen. III-Edw. I. K.
Thomas de Kenete, co. Berks, ibid.
Peter de Kenet, co. Wilts, 1273. A.
William de Kenet, co. Camb., ibid.
1586. William Kennett and Barbara Eglesfield : Marriage Lic. (London), i. 152.
1596. Richard Clark and Susan Kennett (co. Essex) : ibid. p. 229.
1789. Married—Peircy Kennett and Catherine Carty : St. Geo. Han. Sq. ii. 29.

It is manifest that (2) is the chief parent.

London, 3, 16 ; Philadelphia, 0, 4.

Kennicott.—Local, ' of Kencott,' a parish in co. Oxford, five miles from Burford. With the intrusive *i* in Kennicott, cf. the *a* in Ottaway, Greenaway, and Hathaway.

MDB. (co. Durham), 2.

Kenninton, Kennington.—Local, ' of Kennington,' (1) a parish in co. Kent, two miles from Ashford ; (2) a district in the parish of Lambeth, London ; (3) a parish in co. Berks, two miles from Oxford.

Ivo de Kenington, co. Suff., 1273. A.
Thomas de Kenington, co. Suff., ibid.
Walter de Keninton, co. Oxf., ibid.
1795. Married—Richard Woodington and Ann Kenington : St. Geo. Han. Sq. ii. 127.
· 1802. — John Kenington and Frances Jenkins : ibid. p. 257.
London, 1, 0 ; MDB. (co. Lincoln), 0, 6 ; New York, 0, 1 ; Boston (U.S.), 0 3.

Kennison, Kenniston, &c. ; v. Keniston.

Kenrack, -rick; v. Kendrick.

Kensall, Kensal, Kensel, Kensil, Kensill. — Local, ' of Kensal,' now familiarly known as Kensal Green, co. Middlesex.

John de Keneshal, or Keneshale, co. Norf., 1273. A.
1591. William Kensall : Reg. Univ. Oxf. i. 338.
1624. John Kensall : ibid. p. 339.
London (Kensall), 1 ; Philadelphia, 0, 1, 4, 21, 5.

Kensington.—Local, ' of Kensington,' a parish in co. Middlesex. This surname seems to have crossed the Atlantic and made its home there.

Reginald de Kensington, co. Norf., 1273. A.
(Persona) de Kensinton, co. Middlesex, 20 Edw. I. R.
1791. Married—James Kensington and Hannah Bues : St. Geo. Han. Sq. ii. 66. Philadelphia, 9.

Kent.—Local, ' of Kent' ; cf. Derbyshire, Cornish, Cheshire, &c., and v. Kentish. The Kentish people seem to have possessed strong migratory tendencies, de Kent being a common entry in early registers. Hence the numbers in modern directories.

Robert de Kent, co. Norf., 1273. A.
Gilbert de Kent, co. Linc., ibid.
Richard de Kent, co. Hereford, Hen. III-Edw. I. K.
Benedict de Kent, co. Bedf., 20 Edw. I. R.
Johannes de Kent, *smyth*, 1379 : P. T. Yorks. p. 17.
Johannes Kent et Ibbota uxor ejus, 1379 : ibid. p. 44.
Thomas de Kent, 1379 : ibid. p. 160.
1607. John Kent, co. Wilts : Reg. Univ. Oxf. vol. ii. pt. ii. p. 295.
1623. Richard Kent and Awdrie Twyneowe : Marriage Lic. (London), ii. 121.
London, 64 ; West Rid. Court Dir., 5 ; Boston (U.S.), 56.

Kentish.—Local, ' the Kentish,' a man of Kent ; cf. Devonish, Cornish, or Cornwallis.

Ricardus Kenteys (co. Kent), Hen. III-Edw. I. K.
William de (le ?) Kenteys, ibid.
Richard le Kenteys, co. Hants, 1273. A.
Robert le Kenteys, co. Camb., ibid.
William le Kenteys. E.
1582. Thomas Fuller and Alice Kentishe (of St. Albans, Herts) : Marriage Lic. (London), i. 108.
1777. Married — Ross Kentish and Maria Read : St. Geo. Han. Sq. i. 277.
London, 6 ; New York, 1.

Kenward, Kennard.—Bapt. ' the son of Kenward,' a Domesday personal name.

' Keneward, a freeman of King Edward, held Duntesborne,' Domesday : v. Atkyns' Hist. Glouc. p. 213.

Ralph Keneward, co. Kent, 1273. A.
Ricardus filius Kenardi, Fines Roll, 10 Edw. I.
1751. Married—David Kennard and Jesse Cummins : St. Geo. Chap. Mayfair, p. 192.
1809. — Richard Kennard and Frances Hamlin : St. Geo. Han. Sq. ii. 408.
1858. Bapt.—Mary Jane, d. Geo. Kenward : Canterbury Cath. p. 50.
London, 2, 15 ; Philadelphia, 0, 21 ; Boston (U.S.), 1, 19.

Kenworthy.—Local, ' of Kenworthy,' a manor in East Cheshire ; cf. Langworthy for Langworth or Longworth ; v. Worth.

Roger de Kenworthey, co. Ches., 1276: East Ches. p. 130.
William de Kenworthey, co. Ches., 1389 : ibid. p. 196.
Robert de Tatton, of Kenworthey, 1370 : ibid. i. 307.
James Kenworthy, of Saddleworth, 1588 : Wills at Chester (1545-1620), p. 113.
Richard Kenworthy, of Saddleworth, 1616 : ibid.
Manchester, 7 ; West Rid. Court Dir., 8 ; Philadelphia, 8.

Kenwrick; v. Kendrick.

Kenwright.—Bapt. ' the son of Kenwrec' ; v. Kendrick. Woolright and Allwright are similarly corrupted from Woolrich and Aldrich.

Manchester, 1 ; Liverpool, 1 ; MDB. (co. Lanc.), 1.

Kenyon, Kenion, Kennion.—Local, ' of Kenyon,' a township in the parish of Winwick, co. Lanc.

Jordan de Kenyon, 25 Edw. I : Baines' Lanc. ii. 211.
Adam Kenyon, de Kenyon, 1358 : ibid.
1562. Jacobus Kenyon, *shoemaker* : Preston Guild Rolls, p. 30.
Katherine Kenion, of Altham, *widow*, 1594 : Wills at Chester (1545-1620), p. 113.
Elizabeth Kenyon, of Warrington, 1596 : ibid.
William Kenion, of Manchester, 1608 : Lancashire Inquisitions, p. 115.
Manchester, 25, 0, 0 ; London, 6, 0, 0 ; New York, 7, 0, 0 ; West Rid. (Yorks) Court Dir., 7, 2, 1.

Kerbey, Kerby ; v. Kirkby.

Kerchiefwasher. — Occup. ' a washer of kerchiefs' ; M.E. *covenchef*, a cloth used for a head covering. As a favourite decoration of the ladies of the period it would require a special ' stiffener.' Although it could not live it is a surname of some antiquarian interest as descriptive of the times.

Isabella Kierchiefwassher, 1379 : P. T. Yorks. p. 237.

Kerford, Kerfoot, Kerfut.—
Local, ' of Kerford.' I cannot identify the spot, and have only one early instance. Kerfoot is, of course, a corruption. Lancashire and Yorkshire are manifestly the district within which the place must be found.

Ricardus de Kerfforth, 1379 : P. T. Yorks. p. 79.
1572. Buried—Margarette Kyrfote, of Bollington : Reg. Prestbury, co. Ches., p. 39.
1583. John Kirfoote, or Kyerfoote, co. Ches.: Reg. Univ. Oxf. vol. ii. pt. ii. p. 131.
John Kerford, 1661, Wrexham : Exchequer Depositions (co. Lanc.), p. 35.
Thomas Kirfoote, 1664, Lancaster : ibid. p. 41.
1688. Nathan Kerfoot and Bridgett Gaton : Marriage Alleg. (Canterbury), p. 88.
1741. Married—Samuel Kerfoot and Eliz. Jones : St. Geo. Chap. Mayfair, p. 15.
Manchester, 1, 2, 0 ; Boston (U.S.), 0, 0, 1.

Kernel, Kernell.—Local, ' at the kernel,' i.e. battlement. One more instance of a surname, seeming to have died out in England, being found on American soil.

'The maydene, whitt as lely-floure,
Laye in a kirnelle of a towre.'
MS. Lincoln A. i. 17, f. 107 (Halliwell).
Robert del Kernell, co. Hunts, 1273. A.
Robert de la Kirnele, co. Hunts, 20 Edw. I. R.
New York, 0, 1 ; Philadelphia, 0, 2.

Kerr, Ker.—Local, ' at the kerr,' a low-lying meadow, from residence thereby ; v. Carr.

John del Ker, co. Notts, Edw. I–Edw. III. R.
John del Kar, co. Lanc., ibid.
Henricus del Kerre, *webester*, 1379 : P. T. Yorks. p. 26.
Johannes del Kerre, 1379 : ibid. p. 9.
Roger del Kerre, 1379 : ibid. p. 35.
Petrus in the Kare, 1379 : ibid. p. 42.
Willelmus atte Karr, 1379 : ibid. p. 44.
Johannes del Karr, 1379 : ibid. p. 67.
John in the Kerr, C. R., 21 Ric. II. pt. i.
London, 27, 1 ; Philadelphia, 55, 3.

Kerrey, Kerry, Kery.—Local, ' of Kerrey,' a parish in co. Montgomery.

1616. Richard Kerie, co. Salop : Reg. Univ. Oxf. vol. ii. pt. ii. p. 254.
1620-1. William Kery, or Kerry, co. Salop : ibid. p. 385.

1590. Buried—Fayth Kerye : Kensington Parish Ch. p. 93.
1594. Ould father Kerrey buryed his daughter, Eliz. Kerry : ibid. p. 94.
— Ould father Kerye buryed an other of his daughters : ibid.
1599. Married—Henry Egleton and Agnes Kerry : ibid. p. 64.
London, 1, 0, 0 ; Oxford, 0, 3, 0 ; Boston (U.S.), 0, 1, 1.

Kerridge, Kerrich.— Local, ' of Kerridge,' an elevated locality in the parish of Prestbury, co. Cheshire. Alfred Gatley, the sculptor, was born at Kerridge in 1816. Lower, under Courage, has ' Currage, a manor in the parish of Cheveley, co. Bucks.' The latter place seems to be the chief parent of the name.

Thomas Kerridge, London, 1631 : FF. i. 166.
Mary Carreige, 1631 : Reg. St. Dionis Backchurch (London), p. 102.
Susanna Carriage, d. of Thomas Kerridge, 1632 : ibid. p. 103.
Hester Kerridge, 1633 : ibid.
John Kerrich, rector of Banham, co. Norf., 1735 : ibid. i. 353.
Samuel Kerrish, vicar of Dersingham, co. Norf., 1761 : ibid. viii. 400.
1753. Married—Daniel Kerridge and Rebecca Brightman : St. Geo. Chap. Mayfair, p. 252.
London, 6, 0 ; MDB. (Norfolk), 4, 2 ; (Suffolk), 5, 1 ; Manchester, 2, 0.

Kerrison.—Local, ' of Kerdeston,' a parish in co. Norfolk, near Reepham. There is no escape, so far as I can see, from this conclusion. Otherwise, one of the earliest and commonest of Norfolk names has left no descendant. On the other hand, where else has the great Norfolk name of Kerrison sprung ? It is not a baptismal surname. Finally, Kerdeston would readily become Keriston, and then Kerrison. Personally I have not a doubt about this derivation ; cf. Kelson for Kelston.

Roger de Kerdeston, co. Norf., 1273. A.
William de Kerdeston, co. Norf., 20 Hen. III : FF. x. 112.
Leonard Kerdeston, co. Norf., 9 Ric. II : ibid. p. 114.
Thomas Kerdeston, co. Norf., 1446 : ibid.

The histories of Norfolk teem with these entries. If the reader will repeat Kerdeston six times over to himself he will see how easily the corruption would arise.

Robert Karrison, of Milton Green, co. Chester, 1620 : Wills at Chester, i. 212.
Hugh Kerrison, of Dodleston, 1640 : ibid. ii. 129.
1802. Married—James Kerrison and Eliz. Pearce : St. Geo. Han. Sq. ii. 272.
London, 3 ; MDB. (co. Norfolk), 11 ; Boston (U.S.), 1 ; New York, 1.

Kerry ; v. Kerrey.

Kersey.—Local, ' of Kersey,' a parish in co. Suffolk, near Hadleigh.

Selvestre de Kereseye, co. Suff.,1273. A.
Robert de Kersy, co. Soms., 1 Edw. III : Kirby's Quest, p. 185.
1715. Married — John Kersey and Rebecca Taylor : St. Jas. Clerkenwell, iii. 239.
1745. Buried — Juliana Kersey, Mr. Hare's mother : St. Michael, Cornhill, p. 297.
1786. Married—Thomas Kersey and Nancy Larkin : St. Geo. Han. Sq. i. 393.
MDB. (co. Suffolk), 11 ; London, 6 ; Philadelphia, 2.

Kershaw, Kershow.—Local, ' of Kirkshaw,' in the parish of Rochdale, co. Lanc. For the loss of *k*, cf. Kirby for Kirkby. 'Lands in Kirkshaw, Little Wardle . . . and Spotland' (Lanc. and Cheshire Records, pt. ii. p. 330). The surname that has sprung therefrom has ramified in an extraordinary manner, and is known in all English-speaking countries.

Matthew de Kyrkshagh, co. Lanc., 1281 : Baines' Hist. Lancashire(Croston's edit.), pt. xxxi. p. 69.
Geoffrey del Kyrkeshagh, of Rochdale parish, 1390 : ibid.
John de Kyrkshagh, or Kershaw, of Townhouses, in Rochdale, 1424 : ibid.
Edward Kershaw, of Upper Townhouse, 1572 : Wills at Chester (1545-1620), p. 114.
Edward Kershaw, of Townhouse, 1617 : ibid.

From this period the surname is invariably found as Kershaw. The meaning, of course, is the shaw or wood by the church. I find two instances of the earlier form in the first two following entries.

Agnes Kirkeschagh, 1379 : P. T. Yorks. p. 189.
1630. Bapt.—Thomas Kirkshawe : Reg. Prestbury, co. Ches., p. 273.
1752. Married—Charles Kershaw and Eliz. Sooby : St. Geo. Chap. Mayfair, p. 228.
Rochdale, 27, 0 ; Manchester, 40, 0 ; West Rid. Court Dir., 32, 0 ; London, 14, 0 ; Philadelphia, 51, 5.

Kerslake; v. Karslake.

Kerswell, Kerswill.—Local, 'of Kerswell.' There are two parishes of this name, both in co. Devon, viz. Abbots Kerswell and Kings Kerswell; v. Carswell.

William de Kareswalle, co. Salop, 1273. A.
1598. William Kerswell and Joane Warde: Marriage Lic. (London), i. 252.
1621. John Kerswell: Reg Univ. Oxf. vol. ii. pt. ii. p. 401.
1682-3. Thomas Stone and Sarah Karswell: Marriage Alleg. (Canterbury), p. 120.
London, 1, 2; New York, 1, 1.

Kerton; v. Kirton.

Kerwin.—Local; v. Curwen. Originally Culwen, a lordship in Galloway, Scotland.

1571. Married — Androe Kerwyn and Margaret Swarhande: St. Michael, Cornhill, p. 10.
1621-2.—Richard Dowdswell and Barbara Keruin: St. Dionis Backchurch, p. 20.
1679. — Henry Kerwin and Ann Barlow: St. Mary Aldermary, p. 32.
London, 1; Philadelphia, 6.

Kestell, Kestle, Kessell, Kessel.—Local, 'of Kestell,' in the parish of Egloshayle, co. Cornwall. A family of this name was settled there from the time of King John till about the year 1737 (C. S. Gilbert's Cornwall).

1602-3. Walter Kestell, co. Cornwall: Reg. Univ. Oxf. vol. ii. pt. ii. p. 263.
1619. John Kestell, or Kestle, co. Cornwall: ibid. p. 376.
1700. Married — James Kessall and Hannah Maud: St. Dionis Backchurch, p. 49.
Devon Court Dir., 1, 0, 0, 0; London, 0, 0, 0, 1; MDB. (co. Cornwall), 0, 4, 2, 0; Cornwall Dir. (Farmers' List), 0, 2, 1, 1; New York (Kessel), 3; Boston (U.S.), 0, 1, 0, 1.

Kesterton.—Local, 'of Kesterton.' I have not found the spot.

Birmingham, 5; London, 1.

Kesteven.—Local, 'of Kesteven.' Lower says, 'A division of co. Lincoln.' I doubt not this is true, as nearly all the early local references belong to that county.

(Coronator) de Kestevene, co. Linc., 1273. A.
(Coronator) de Ketstevene, co. Linc, ibid.

Alexander de Kestevene, co. Northumb., 1273. A.
Johannes de Kesteven, 1379: P. T. Yorks. p. 63.
Hugo Kesteven, 1379: ibid. p. 91.
Adam de Ketsteven, 6 Edw. III: Freemen of York, i. 26.
London, 2; West Rid. Court Dir., 1; MDB. (co. Notts), 1.

Keswick, Kissick.—Local, 'of Keswick,' the town so called at the head of Derwentwater; also a parish in co. Norfolk, and a township in W. Rid. Yorks. With Kissick, cf. Physick for Fishwick.

Ralf Kesewic, co. Norf., 1378: FF.iv.180.
Johannes de Kesswyk, 1379: P. T. Yorks. p. 100.
Johannes de Keswyk, 1379: ibid. p. 208.
Philadelphia, 0, 9.

Ketch; v. Keatch.

Ketelbern.—Bapt. 'the son of Ketelbern'; cf. Osborn, and v. Kettle. Alongside the first of my instances we find Ketelbert de Kelesholt; probably a relative. As usual, these names of Norse derivation are found on the East coast.

Ketelbron de Keles, co. Linc., Hen. III–Edw. I. K.
Roger Ketilbern, co. Suff., 1273. A.
1641. Buried — Marye Kettlbourne: St. Jas. Clerkenwell, iv. 247.

Kettering, Ketring.—Local, 'of Kettering,' a market-town and parish in co. Northampton.

Robert de Keteringe,co.Camb.,1273. A.
Richard Ketering, co. Northampt., 20 Edw. I. R.
1382. Roger Ketering, rector of Burnham Ulp, co. Norf.: FF. vii. 32.

It is interesting to notice how frequently a surname that seems to have died out in England is found across the Atlantic.

Philadelphia, 3, 1.

Ketteringham, Kitteringham.—Local, 'of Ketteringham,' a parish in co. Norfolk.

Agnes de Keteringham, co. Norf., 1273. A.
Thomas de Keteringham, co. Norf., 1342: FF. v. 97.
William de Keteringham, co. Norf., 40 Edw. III: ibid. vi. 40.
Birmingham, 1, 0; MDB. (co. Norfolk), 6, 2.

Kettle, Kettell, Kettelle.—Bapt. 'the son of Kettle.' Ketel, Ketil, Cytel, or Chetel, the sacrificial cauldron of northern mytho-

logy. A large number of surnames are founded on Kettle and its compounds; v. Chettle, Oskettle, Arkettle, Grimkettle, Steinkettle, Wulfkettle; also their abbreviations, such as Kell and Chell, Oskell, Arkell, Thurkle, &c.

Ketil, son of Tostig: Freeman, Norm. Conq. iii. 375.
The father of William of Lancaster, baron of Kendel, was Gilbert, the son of Ketel, the son of Eldred, the son of Ivo de Taillebois (of Domesday): West's Ant. of Furness, p. 28.
'Alan, son of Ketell, gave one-half of Kinemund.' Revenues of the Priory of Conishead: ibid. 'p. 193.
Emma fil. Ketel, co. Camb., 1273. A.
Kettle le Mercer, co. Camb., ibid.
Reyner Ketel, co. Norf., ibid.
Robert fil. Ketell. J.
Willelmus Ketyll, 1379: P. T. Yorks. p. 128.
Thomas Ketill, 1379: ibid. p. 153.
1582-3. Edmund Kettle, or Kettell, co. Worc., Reg. Univ. Oxf. vol. ii. pt. ii. p. 125.
1583. Christopher Kettell, co. Hertf.: ibid. p. 131.
1612. Robert Vincent and Alice Kettle: Marriage Lic. (London), ii. 12.
1700. Bapt. — Deborah, d. Henry Kettle: St. Jas. Clerkenwell, i. 387.

For variants, v. Chettle.

London, 13, 0, 0; Boston (U.S.), 2, 6, 5.

Kettleborrow, Kettleborough.—Local, 'of Kettleburgh,' a parish in co. Suffolk, near Framlingham. For derivation, v. Kettle and Burrough.

William de Ketelbergh', co. York, 1273. A.
John de Ketelbergh', co. Norf, ibid.
1317. Steven de Ketelburgh, rector of Fincham, co. Norf.: FF. vii. 361.
1347. John de Kettlebury, rector of West Walton, co. Norf.: ibid. ix. 141.
1630. Married — Daniel Callis and Hellin Kettleboorow: St. Antholin (London), p. 64.
1682-3. Joseph Tullie and Ann Kettleborough: Marriage Alleg. (Canterbury), p. 124.
MDB. (co. Leicester), 1, 0; (co. Lincoln), 0, 2.

Kettleby.—Local, 'of Kettleby,' a hamlet in the parish of Wrawby, co. Lincoln; the by or dwelling of Kettle, the first settler.

1589. John Kettlebie, co. Worc.: Reg. Univ. Oxf. vol. ii. pt. ii. p. 169.
1604. Thomas Ketilby, co. Worc.: ibid. p. 271.
1652. George Kettleby and Eliz. Kinaston: St. Antholin (London), p. 81.

1688. Arthur Lowe and Susanna Kettleby : Marriage Alleg. (Canterbury), p. 90.
1693. Ralph Ketelbey and Mary Freeman : ibid. p. 266.
1704. Harrington Kettilby and Margaret Beverly : Marriage Lic. (London), ii. 332.

Kettlewell.—Local, 'of Kettlewell' (i.e. the well of Kettle (q.v.), the first settler), a market-town and parish in W. Rid. Yorks, fifteen miles from Skipton.

Stephen de Ketelwelle, co. York : Edw. I-Edw. III. R.
John Ketelwel, 1379 : P. T. Yorks p. 238.
Alessander Katelwell, co. York. W. 11.
1583. Richard Kettlewell and Fortune Rydall : Marriage Lic. (London), i. 125.
1676. William Beresford and Ann Kettlewell : Marriage Lic. (Westminster), p. 259.
London, 4 ; West Rid. Court Dir., 11 ; Boston (U.S.), 1 ; New York, 1.

Kettlewood.—Local, 'of Kettlewood' (i.e. the wood of Kettle (q.v.), the original proprietor), some small spot in E. Rid. Yorks. One member of the family of Kettlewood seems to have reached London more than three centuries ago.

1551-2. Married — Thomas Francke and Elyn Ketellwoode : St. Dionis Backchurch, p. 3.
1586. John Kettlewood, of London, grocer, and Eliz. Penny : Marriage Lic. (London), i. 156.
MDB. (East Rid. Yorks), 3.

Kettley, Kitley.—Local, 'of Ketley,' a chapelry in the parish of Wellington, co. Salop.

1561. Married—Richard Wilch'm and Eliz. Kitly : St. Thomas the Apostle (London), p. 3.
1573. Henry Roe and Susanna Keteley : Marriage Lic. (London), i. 58.

Possibly the above is a variant of Keighley, q.v.

1742. Bapt. — William, s. Ambrose Kitely : St. Jas. Clerkenwell, ii. 261.
1781. Married—George Thornton and Amey Ketly : St. Geo. Han. Sq. i. 321.
London, 1, 1.

Ketton, Keeton, Kitton.—Local, 'of Ketton,' (1) a township in the parish of Lamplugh, co. Cumberland ; (2) a parish in co. Rutland, near Stamford.

Johannes de Keton, 1379 : P. T. Yorks. p. 63.
Henry de Ketton, 1379 : ibid. p. 237.

1506. Thomas Keton, rector of Langale and Kirksted, co. Norf. : FF. x. 165.
1805. Married — Thomas Keeton and Ann Fuller : St. Geo. Han. Sq. ii. 331.
Lanc. Court Dir., 2, 0, 0 ; MDB. (co. Norfolk), 2, 0, 1 ; London, 0, 1, 0.

Kevan, Kevin.—Bapt. 'the son of Kevin' (Yonge, ii. 108), evidently a Welsh name.

Kavan ap Howell, 20 Edw. I. R.
London, 2, 0 ; Philadelphia, 0, 3.

Kew.—(1) Occup. 'the cook.'

Nicholas le Keu, co. Notts, 1273. A.
Walter le Keu, co. Oxf., ibid.

The same individual is thus described :

William le Keu, 1301. M.
William Cocus, 1302. M.
William le Keu, or Cocus, 1306. M.

(2) Local, 'of Kew,' the well-known parish in the dioc. of Rochester.

1688. Thomas Palfrey and Mary Kew : Marriage Alleg. (Canterbury), p. 79.
1809. Married—John Kew and Flora Sharman : St. Geo. Han. Sq. ii. 416.
London, 4.

Kewell, Kevell.—Local, 'of Kewell,' seemingly some small spot in co. Somerset with the local suffix -well.

John Kewel, co. Oxf., 1273. A.

This name seems sometimes to have been registered Kevell.

William de Kiwell, co. Soms., 1 Edw III : Kirby's Quest, p. 159.
1598. George Rewitt, co. Warwick : Reg. Univ. Oxf. vol. ii. pt. ii. p. 227.

In a footnote the editor says that this last name is indistinct. It might be Rewill, or Revell, or Kevel.

1620. Bapt. — Janie, d. Henry Kevill : St. Jas. Clerkenwell, i. 87.
1751. Married — William Garrett and Eliz. Kevell : St. Geo. Chap. Mayfair, p. 193.
London, 2, 0 ; Philadelphia, 0, 1.

Kewley, Cully.—Local, 'of Quilli,' near Falaise, Normandy.

Hughe de Cuilly, 1313. M.
Hugo de Cully, 1314. M.
Roger de Cuilly, 1315. M.
Roger de Kuly, 1318. M.
Roger de Kuylly, 1322. M.

The Isle of Man Kewleys are said to be a mere variant of Kelly, the great Manx patronymic. It is a question I am not able to decide.

1777. Married — William Kewley and Joyce Verty : St. Geo. Han. Sq. i. 274.
Crockford, 9, 0 ; London, 0, 2 ; Philadelphia, 0, 8.

Keymer, Keymar.—Local, 'of Keymer,' a parish in the dioc. of Chichester, co. Sussex.

1601. Richard Kemer, co. Kent : Reg. Univ. Oxf. vol. ii. pt. ii. p. 247.
Richard Kemeyre, 1604 : St. Dionis Backchurch, London, p. 15.
1713. Married — Samuel Keymer and Sarah Beer : St. Mary Aldermary, p. 42.
1793. Married — Francis Keymer and Anne Gilman : St. Geo. Han. Sq. ii. 93.
London, 4, 0 ; New York, 1, 1.

Keyser, Keyzor, Kezar, Kezor.—Nick. ; v. Kaiser.

Keyworth.—Local, 'of Keyworth,' a parish in co. Notts, seven miles from Nottingham.

1590. Buried—Tobie Keworth, servant to Mr. John Hodgkins : St. Mary Aldermary, p. 145.
1786. Married—George Cheshire and Catherine Keyworth : St. Geo. Han. Sq. i. 3'6.
MDB. (co. Notts), 10 ; London, 4 ; New York, 2.

Kibble, Keable, Kebbel, Kebbell, Kebble, Keeble, Keble, Kibel.—Bapt. 'the son of Kibble,' i.e. Cubold. A strong confirmation of the view that Kibbel was an old personal name is the existence of such local names as Kibblethwaite, Kibbleworth, Kibblestone, Cobbledick, q.v. The absence of prefixes in the instances below is additional evidence. I doubt not it is the Domesday Cubold, and therefore a mere variant of Cobbold, q.v.

Michael Kibbel, co. Hunts, 1273. A.
William Kibbel, co. Camb., ibid.
Thomas Kibel, co. Linc., ibid.
Reginald Kibel, co. Linc., ibid.
Stephen Cubbel, co. Oxf., ibid.
1525. George Kebyll and Katharine Terell : Marriage Lic. (London), i. 5.
1686. Bapt. — John, s. John Keeble : St. Jas. Clerkenwell, i. 320.
1607. Thomas Keble, co. Suff., and Mary Tirrell : Marriage Lic. (Westminster), p. 15.

The variants of this surname have simply run riot in our registers, especially in modern times. I append a few from one record :

1804. Married — Thomas Keable and Millicent Shepherd : St. Geo. Han. Sq. ii. 303.

1806. Married—John Kibble and Ann Mary Lockley: St. Geo. Han. Sq. ii. 346.
— — Henry Strong and Eliz. Kebble: ibid. p. 341.
1807. — Richard Keeble and Mary Whiting: ibid. p. 366.
1809. — John Kebbell and Sarah Parsons: ibid. p. 414.
London, 5, 3, 3, 1, 3, 10, 0, 0; Crockford (Keble), 3; New York (Kibel), 2; Boston (U.S.), Kibble, 5.

Kibblewhite.—Local, ‘of Kibblethwaite’; cf. Applewhite for Applethwaite. The prefix represents the personal name of the settler. The meaning is, ‘the thwaite (clearing) of Kibble’; v. Kibble and Thwaite. I cannot find the spot.

1575. Michael Kiblewhite, of London: Reg.Univ. Oxf. vol. ii. pt. ii. p. 68.
1560. Bapt. — Michael, s. John Keblewhite: St.MaryAldermary (London),p.53.
1597. Married — Roger Gwine and Joane Kebelwhite: ibid. p. 6.
1678. Bapt. — Eliz., d. Edward Kiblwhite: Marriage Alleg. (Canterbury), p. 16.
1684. — Ann, d. Edward Kiblewhite: ibid. p. 18.
1805. Married—Abraham Boxall and Sarah Kibblewhite: St. Geo. Han. Sq. ii. 322.
London, 2.

Kibby, Kibbee, Kibbe.—Local, ‘of Kirkby,’ a variant of Kirby; v. Kirkby. With Kibbee, cf. Applebee for Appleby.

Birmingham, 7, 0, 0; Boston (U.S.), 0, 1, 0; Philadelphia, 5, 0, 2.

Kidd.—Nick. ‘the kid,’ a man of a frisky disposition; cf. Doe, Roe, Buck, Roebuck, &c.

Reginald Kyd, co. Oxf., 1273. A.
Ricardus Kyd, 1379: P. T. Yorks. p. 226.
Thomas Kydde, 1379: ibid. p. 222.
Willelmus Kydde, 1379: ibid. p. 209.
1611. Anthony Kydde and Julian Percy: Marriage Lic. (London), ii. 4.
1631-2. Archibald Kyd and Sara Butler: ibid. p. 204.
1799. Married — William Kidd and Christian Willson: St. Geo. Han. Sq. ii. 202.
London, 20; Philadelphia, 33.

Kidder.—Occup. ‘the kidder,’ i.e. a huckster. ‘Kiddier, a huckster. East’ (Halliwell). An Act of Edward VI speaks of ‘the buying of anye corne, fyshe, butter, or cheese by any such Badger, Lader, Kyddier, or Carrier as shal be assigned and allowed to that office’

(5 and 6 Edw. VI, c. 14). A confirmation of this Act by Elizabeth alters Kyddier to Kydder. The name is frequently found in the Poll Tax, 1379, W. Rid. Yorks, several instances being given below.

William le Kydere, 25 Edw. I: BBB. p. 542.
Johannes Kyder, 1379: P. T. Yorks. p. 18.
Johannes Kydder, 1379: ibid. p. 58.
Johannes Kydder, 1379: ibid. p. 155.
Richard Kydder, temp. Eliz. Z.
1580. John Kydder and Christian Morgan: Marriage Lic. (London), i. 96.
1635-6. Buried — Richard, s. Richard Kidder: St. Jas. Clerkenwell, iv. 219.
1790. Married — John Kidder and Phoebe Ross: St. Geo. Han. Sq. ii. 40.
London, 1; Philadelphia, 1; Boston (U.S.), 34.

Kiddle, Kiddall, Kidall, Kiddell.—(1) Local, ‘of Kiddal,’ a hamlet in the parish of Barwick-in-Elmet, seven miles from Leeds. (2) ? Bapt. ‘the son of Kedwall’; v. Keedwell. If this be correct it would explain the large number of Kiddles in cos. Gloucester and Somerset, as Kidwell would readily become Kiddle.

Thomas de Kidale, 1379: P. T. Yorks. p. 227.
Beatrix de Kydhall, 1379: ibid. p. 224.
Walterus de Kydhall, 1379: ibid.
1606. John Sedgewicke and Petronella Kiddall: Marriage Lic. (Westminster), p. 15.
1718. Married — Thomas Kiddle and Mary Maidman: Reg. Stourton, co. Wilts.
1802. — Jonathan Lock and Susanna Kiddell: St. Geo. Han. Sq. ii. 264.
London, 3, 0, 0, 1; MDB. (co. Somerset), 18, 0, 0, 0; (co. Norfolk), 5, 0, 2, 0; New York, 1, 0, 0, 0.

Kidgell.—? Bapt. ‘the son of Kiggel.’ It is curious to find the surname still lingering in co. Somerset.

Matilda Kiggel, co. Hunts, 1273. A.
Robert Kiggel, co. Soms., 1 Edw. III: Kirby’s Quest, p. 178.
MDB. (co. Soms.), 1.

Kidman. — (1) Occup. ‘the kidman,’ a man who looked after young goats; cf. Cowman, Gooseman, Bullman, &c. (2) Bapt. ‘the son of Kideman’; probably a variant of Cadman, q.v. This must be accepted as the chief parent.

Alan Kydeman, co. Norf., 1273. A.
Walter Kademan ,co. Soms., ibid.

Guy Kidman, C. R., 4 Edw. IV.
Alfric, son of Kideman, co. Norf.: FF. vii. 145.
1735. Charles Kidman, rector of Banham, co. Norf.: ibid. i. 353.
1743. Buried — Bathsheba, wife of the Rev. Brewer Kidman: St. Michael, Cornhill, p. 296.
1744. Married — John Parkinson and Sarah Kidman: St. Geo. Han. Sq. i. 33.
London, 3; MDB. (co. Hunts), 5.

Kidner.—Local, ‘of Kitenare,’ some estate or manor in co. Somerset that I am unable to identify. The modification of the name into Kidner is a natural one.

William de Kitenare, co. Soms., 1 Edw. III: Kirby’s Quest, p. 192.
William Kytenor,co. Soms., ibid. p. 142.

The surname is well represented in the county in the 19th century. A member of the family seems to have travelled into Yorkshire at an early period:

Adam Kitener, 1379: P. T. Yorks. p. 165.
London, 2; MDB. (co. Somerset), 8; Boston (U.S.), 1.

Kidney.—Local. An imitative corruption of Gidney, q.v. A good example of the principle laid down in this dictionary; cf. Kilby and Gilbey.

1593. Buried—John Kidney, or Kydney: St. Jas. Clerkenwell, iv. 52.
1665. Married — Thomas Kidney and Mary Vellis: ibid. iii. 118.

Private Kidney (co. Lanc.) scored high in the first stage of the Queen’s Prize at Wimbledon, July 10, 1888 (v. Daily Papers).

London, 1; Philadelphia, 6.

Kidson.—Bapt.; v. Kitson.

Kidwell; v. Keedwell.

Kifford, Kefford. — ? Local, ‘ of Guildford’; possibly an old pronunciation. But perhaps a sharpened form of Giffard, q.v.; v. Kidney.

George Guldeford, or Gilford, or Kifforde, 1556: Reg. Univ. Oxf. i. 232.
1623-4. John Kifford and Alice Butcher: Marriage Lic. (London), ii. 134.
1744. Married —Thomas Kefford and Mary Bunyan: St. Geo. Chap. Mayfair, p. 35.
London, 1, 3.

Kift.—Nick. ‘the kift,’ i.e. the ungainly, the awkward. ‘Kift,

G g

awkward, clumsy. West' (Halliwell).

John Kyft, co. Soms., 1 Edw. III: Kirby's Quest, p. 80.

We find similar nicknames, such as Snell (q.v.) and Crees, in the same register; v. Crease.

1616. Edward Kyfte, co. Glouc.: Reg. Univ. Oxf. vol. ii. pt. ii. p. 352.
1674. Joseph Smart and Mary Herbert, alleged by Richard Kiff: Marriage Alleg. (Canterbury), p. 124.
1675. Henry Hinton and Eliz. Corbett, alleged by Richard Kift: ibid. p. 152.
1703. Married — Joseph Lester and Eliz. Kift: St.Dionis Backchurch, p. 51.
MDB. (co. Soms.), 1; Philadelphia, 3.

Kightley, Kightly.—Local, 'of Keighley,' q.v. The variants of this old surname are many.

1574. George Kyghtelye and Grisill Crayforde: Marriage Lic. (London), i. 63.
1808. Married—Samuel Kightley and Mary Costelow: St. Geo. Han. Sq. ii. 389.
London, 1, 1.

Kilbey, Kilby, Killby, Kilbee, Kelby.—Local, (1) 'of Kilby,' a parish in co. Leicester; (2) 'of Kelby,' a parish in co. Lincoln. The latter seems to be the chief parent. Probably Gilbey, Gillbee, Gilby, &c., are in many cases but variants.

Richard de Kelby, co. Linc., 1273. A.
William de Kelby, co. Linc., ibid.
Roger de Kelleby, co. Linc., ibid.
William de Kyleby, co. Leic.: Hen. III-Edw. I. K.
1351. William de Keleby, rector of Kelling, co. Norf.: FF. ix. 406.
Roger de Kileby, co. Norf.: ibid. viii. 465.
1712. Died—Anchor Kilby, sub-sacrist, co. Norwich: ibid. iv. 24.
1797. Married — Richard Kilbey and Eliz. Coffee: St. Geo. Han. Sq. ii. 172.
London, 4, 5, 3, 0, 0; Philadelphia, 0, 0, 0, 0, 3; New York (Kilby), 2; Oxford (Kilbee), 2.

Kilbrick.—Local, 'of Kelbrook,' a chapelry in the parish of Thornton, W.R. Yorks, near Colne.

1704. John Kelbreck, of Hambleton: Lancashire Wills at Richmond (1681-1748), p. 155.
MDB. (co. Lanc.), 1.

Kilburn, Kilbourn, Kilborn, Kilbourne, Kilborne.—Local, 'of Kilburn,' (1) a hamlet, partly in the parish of Hampstead, co. Middlesex; (2) a parish in N. Rid. Yorks, seven miles from

Thirsk; (3) a township in the parish of Horsley, co. Derby.

Ralph de Kylburn, co. Derby, 1273. A.
1587. Married—Richard Kylborne and Alice Sackfelde: St. Michael, Cornhill, p. 14.
1626. — Isaac Kilbourne and Mary Fayrefax: St. Jas. Clerkenwell, iii. 56.
1746. — William Killbourn and Ann Killbourn: St. Geo. Chap. Mayfair, p. 75.
1807. — John Kilbourn and Mary Ann Jennings: St. Geo. Han. Sq. ii. 370.
London, 2, 1, 0, 0, 0; MDB. (co. Warwick), 0, 0, 1, 0, 0; New York, 3, 0, 0, 5, 1; Philadelphia, 7, 0, 0, 0, 0.

Kilford. — Local, 'of Guildford' (?). This is highly probable; cf. Kisby and Gisby, Kilbey and Gilbey, &c.

1556. George Kilforde: Reg. Univ. Oxf. vol. ii. pt. ii. p. xiv.

The following seems to be a curious variant:

1550. William Cocks and Margaret Kyllyfedd: Marriage Lic. (London), p. 13.
London, 1.

Kilham, Killam.—Local, 'of Kilham,' a parish in E. Rid. Yorks, near Great Driffield; also a township in the parish of Kirk-Newton, co. Northumberland.

John de Kyllum, co. York, Hen. III-Edw. I. K.
1709. Married — Richard Marsh and Jane Kilham: Canterbury Cath. p. 69.
1845. — Marmaduke Kelham and Julia Ann Christie: ibid. p. 106.
MDB. (co. Sussex), 1, 0; (West Rid. Yorks), 1, 0; London, 0, 1; Philadelphia, 0, 2.

Killbull, Killbullock, Killhare, Killhog.—Nicknames for a pig-sticker or slaughter-man. Prof. Skeat says kill was originally to strike, to deaden with a blow. Thus Killbull and Killbullock meet the case exactly; M.E. culle, kill.

Reginald Cullebel (-bol?), co. Oxf., 1273. A.
Henry Cullebulloc, co. Bedf., ibid.
William Cullehar', co. Oxf., ibid.
William Cullehog', co. Oxf., ibid.

Killer.—(1) Occup. 'the kilner,' q.v.; a variant; cf. Keller (2). But v. Killbull. Perhaps it means a slaughterer or pig-sticker. (2) Local, 'of Keller'; v. Keller (1).

MDB. (co. Derby), 3; New York, 1.

Killhare, -hog; v. Killbull.

Killick; v. Killwick.

Killigrew.—Local, 'of Killigrew.' Mr. Lower says, 'In charters, Cheligrovus, a manor in the parish of St. Erme, co. Cornwall, where this celebrated family resided from an early date down to the reign of Richard II': Patr. Brit. p. 179.

1590. Robert Killegrew, co. Hants: Reg. Univ. Oxf. vol. ii. pt. ii. p. 181.
1615. Henry Killygrew, co. Cornwall: ibid. p. 336.
1722. Married—Charles Killigrew and Eliz. Vaughan: St. Antholin (London), p. 136.
1743. Bapt. — Thomas, s. Thomas Killigrew: St. Michael, Cornhill, p. 173. Boston (U.S.), 4.

Killingback, Killingbeck.—Local, 'of Killingbeck.' I do not know the spot.

Mr. Killeingbeck, curate of St. Nicholas Chapel, Lynn, co. Norfolk, 1682: FF. viii. 504.
1688. Richard Baines and Francis Killingbeck: Marriage Alleg. (Canterbury), p. 54.
1722. Bapt. — Thomas, s. William Killingbeck: St. Jas. Clerkenwell, ii. 134. London, 2, 0; Philadelphia, 0, 1.

Killingsworth, Killingworth, Chillingworth, Chillingsworth.—Local, 'of Killingworth,' a township in the parish of Long Benton, co. Northumberland. Possibly another spot so called may have existed in co. Norfolk. Of course Shillingsworth is an imitative corruption of Chillingsworth. With Chillingworth, cf. Church and Kirk.

Adam de Kellyngworthe, co. Norf., 1273. A.
1388. Thomas de Killingworth, vicar of Windham, co. Norf.: FF. ii. 508.
1561. Richard Killingworth, co. Norf.: ibid. p. 214.
1576. John Kyllingworthe and Alice Smithe, widow: Marriage Lic. (London), i. 71.
1616. John Killingworth, of London: Reg. Univ. Oxf. vol. ii. pt. ii. p. 353.
1713. Married — John Shillingsworth and Isabella Boyce: St. Jas. Clerkenwell, iii. 235.
London, 1, 0, 3, 0; MDB. (co. Norfolk), 0, 1, 0, 0; Philadelphia, 0, 0, 0, 0.

Killmaster; v. Kilminster.

Killwick, Killick, Killik.—Local, 'of Kildwick.' a parish in W. Rid. Yorks. With Killick, an inevitable variant, cf. Physic for Fishwick.

1601. Buried — John Kylleck : St. Dionis Backchurch, p. 205.

1662. John Killicke and Isabel Covell : Marriage Alleg. (Canterbury), p. 57.

1745. Married—William Killick and Diana Bateman : St. Geo. Chap. Mayfair, p. 45.

1789. — George Samples and Amy Killick : St. Geo. Han. Sq. ii. 25.

London, 2, 7, 1.

Kilminster,.   Killmaster, Killmister.—Local, 'of Kilminster,' near Wick, Scotland (Lower). The suffix -minster generally corrupts to -master or -mister ; cf. Buckmaster and Kittermaster.

1753. Married — William Kilmaster, alias Bradley, and Betty Povey : St. Geo. Chap. Mayfair, p. 247.

1760. — John Bankes and Ann Killmister : St. Geo. Han. Sq. i. 91.

1793. — Joseph Beeson and Eliz. Killmaster : ibid. ii. 102.

London, 1, 0, 0 ; MDB. (co. Oxf.), 0, 1, 0 ; (co. Glouc.), 2, 0, 2 ; (co. Stafford), 0, 0, 1.

Kilner.—Occup. ' the kilner,' a limeburner, one who superintended a kiln. Kilner has been for many centuries a Furness (North Lanc.) surname, but it seems to have nearly died out. I could furnish scores of entries from the Ulverston register. The name survived in the town till some thirty years ago.

1545. Bapt.—Elizabeth Kilner : St. Mary Ulverston, p. 1.

1546. Buried — Esabell Kilner : ibid. p. 3.

1560. Bapt.—Anthonie Kilner : ibid. p. 37.

1587. Thomas Kilner, of Aldingham : Lancashire Wills at Richmond, i. 174.

1598. John Lendall and Margaret Kilner : Marriage Lic. (London), i. 248.

1626. James Killner, of Ulverston : Lancashire Wills at Richmond, i. 174.

1732. Married—Nathaniel Killner and Sarah Bishop : St. Geo. Han. Sq. i. 10. London, 4 ; Manchester, 1 ; Boston (U.S.), 2.

Kilpack, Kilpeck.—Local, 'of Kilpeck,' a parish in co. Hereford.

Hugh de Kilpec, co. Salop, Hen. III-Edw. I. K.

1583. Married — John Kilbecke and Cecily Masterson : St. Jas. Clerkenwell, iii. 10.

London, 1, 0 ; Crockford, 1, 1 ; Oxford, 1, 0.

Kilpin.—Local, 'of Kilpin,' a township in the parish of Howden, E. Rid. Yorks.

1594. Richard Kilpin : Reg. Univ. Oxf. vol. ii. pt. ii. p. 204.

1603. Robert Kilpin, co. Bucks : ibid. p. 267.

1690. Bapt.—Sarah, d. William Killpin : St. Jas. Clerkenwell, i. 338.

1720. Married—Benjamin Kilpin and Susanna Butler : St. Mary Aldermary, p. 45.

London, 3.

Kilsby.—Local, ' of Kilsby,' a parish in co. Northampton, six miles from Daventry.

1678-9. William Killsbe and Ann Whiting : Marriage Alleg. (Canterbury), p. 223.

1732. Married — John Killsbey and Sarah Dyer : St. Jas. Clerkenwell, iii. 260.

1744. — Edward Kilsby and Ann Meridith : St. Geo. Chap. Mayfair, p. 34. London, 4.

Kilshaw.—Local ; v. Culshaw. A corruption of Culcheth. For a second derivation, v. Kelsall.

1570. Married — Wylliam Kylshaye and Sarah Sturlay : St. Dionis Backchurch, p. 6.

1617. William Kilshaw, of Burscough : Wills at Chester, i. 115.

1619. John Kilshaw, of Burscough : ibid.

1622. John Kilshawe : Preston Guild Rolls, p. 67.

1688. Buried — Margaret, d. Edw. Kilshaw : Reg. Leyland, co. Lanc., p. 247. MDB. (co. Chester), 1.

Kilvington.—Local, 'of Kilvington,' (1) a parish in co. Notts, seven miles from Newark ; (2) a parish in N. Rid. Yorks, near Thirsk.

1733. Buried—Eliz. Kilvington : St. Mary Aldermary, p. 222.

1736. — Thomas Kilvington : ibid. p. 223.

1763. Married—Joseph Shout and Eliz. Kilvington : St. Geo. Han. Sq. i. 120. Hull, 1 ; MDB. (North Rid. Yorks), 5 ; Manchester, 1.

Kimball, Kimble, Kimbel.—Local, 'of Kimble'; v. Kimball. Familiar American forms.

1654-5. Married — Henry Finch and Margrett Kimball : St. Dionis Backchurch, p. 30.

1729. — William Kimbal and Joanna Pickett : St. Geo. Chap. Mayfair, p. 298.

1751. — Albin Hadon and Eliz. Kimble : ibid. p. 199.

1754. — Timothy Honnor and Mary Kimbell : ibid. p. 269. Philadelphia, 24, 14, 3.

Kimbell. Kimble.—Local, 'of Kimble.' Great and Little Kimble are parishes in co. Bucks, near

Wendover, and should be carefully distinguished from Kemble (v. Kemball), although at times, no doubt, they have become confused. For other variants, v. Kimball.

Richard de Kinebelle, co. Bucks, 1273. A.

John de Kinebelle, co. Oxf., ibid.

Nicholas Kymbell, co. Norf., 3 Hen. IV : FF. ix. 430.

1718. Married—John Phillibrown and Mary Kimbell : St. Michael, Cornhill, p. 60.

1775. — John Kimbell and Eliz. Plumb : St. Geo. Han. Sq. i. 250.

MDB. (co. Warwick), 4, 0 ; London, 0, 1.

Kimber ; v. Kember.

Kimberley,   Kimberly.—Local, ' of Kimberley,' a parish in co. Norfolk.

Eustace de Kimberle, co. Norf., 1308 : FF. iv. 442.

Hugh de Kymberly, burgess of Great Yarmouth, 17 Edw. III : ibid. viii. 30.

1571. Robert Kymberlie and Rose Ive : Marriage Lic. (London), i. 50.

1611. Bapt.—John, s. William Kemberley : St. Jas. Clerkenwell, i. 63.

Birmingham, 10, 0 ; London, 5, 0 ; MDB. (co. Warwick), 2, 0 ; New York, 0, 3.

Kime, Kyme. — Local, ' of Kyme.' South Kyme is a parish in co. Lincoln, eight miles from Tattershall ; North Kyme is a township in the same parish.

Philip de Kyme, co. Linc., 1273. A.

Rosa de Kyme, co. Linc., ibid.

William de Kyma, co. Linc., ibid.

Lucia de Kyme, co. York, 20 Edw. I. R.

Symon de Kyme, co. Linc., Hen. III-Edw. I. K.

1638. Robert Lloyd and Eliz. Kyme : Marriage Lic. (London), ii. 237.

1641. Nightingale Kyme and Eliz. Pigeon : ibid. p. 259. MDB. (co. Lincoln), 7, 1.

Kimmis(h ; v. Kemmish.

Kimpthorne ; v. Kempthorne.

Kimpton.—Local, 'of Kimpton,' (1) a parish in co. Hertford ; (2) a parish in co. Hants, five miles from Andover.

Thomas de Kymynton, co. Soms., 1 Edw. III : Kirby's Quest, p. 80.

1674. John Kimpton and Sarah Pense : Marriage Alleg. (Westminster), p. 228.

1682. Thomas Kimpton and Eliz. —— : Marriage Alleg. (Canterbury), p. 93. London, 19 ; New York, 2.

Kinch, Kinnish, Kench.—Bapt. A Manx surname, corresponding to the Irish McGuiness and Gaelic McGinnis. The Manx forms are McInesh, 1511; Kynnishe, 1601; Kinnish, 1626; Kennish, 1732 (v. Manx Note Book, ii. 65).

Donold Kynyshe, 1601: The Manx Note Book, i. 61.
1685. Richard Kinch and Martha Sheppard: Marriage Alleg. (Canterbury), p. 207.
1731. Bapt.—Ann, d. Nathaniel Kinch: St. John Baptist on Wallbrook, p. 183.
Liverpool, o, 2, o; Manchester, 2, o, o; Birmingham, o, o, 1; New York, 3, o, o; Oxford, 1, o, 1.

Kindell.—Local, ' of Kendall.' One of several variants.

London, 2; Boston (U.S.), 1.

Kinder, Kynder, Kender.—Local, ' of Kinder,' a hamlet in the parish of Glossop, co. Derby, near Chapel-en-le-Frith.

Philota de Kender, co. Derby, 1273. A.
1576. Married—John Kynder and Ales Holme: Reg. Prestbury (co. Ches.), p. 53.
1581. John Kinder, or Kynder, co. Linc.: Reg. Univ. Oxf. vol. ii. pt. ii. p. 102.
1752. Married — John Kinder and Martha Attersoll: St. Geo. Chap. Mayfair, p. 219.
1793. — William Kinder and Catherine Butcher: St. Geo. Han. Sq. ii. 94.
1800. — William Kinder and Mary Stokes: ibid. p. 219.
London, 2, o, o; MDB. (co. Derby), 3, o, o; (co. Lanc.), 1, 1, o; Birmingham, 3, o, 1; Boston (U.S.), 3, o, 1.

Kindersley.—(1) Local, ' of Kinnersley,' q.v. The d is intrusive; cf. riband for ribbon, or Simmonds for Simmons. (2) Local, ' of Kingsley.' There is evidence in favour of this view. Kingsley became Kinsley, as we know. This with the intrusive d would become Kindsley. The intrusive r also presents no difficulty; cf. Patterson for Patteson, &c.

1597. Thomas Kindesley, or Kingsley, London: Reg. Univ. Oxf. vol. ii. pt. ii. p. 220.
— William Kindesley, London: ibid.
1618. Thomas Kyndesley, of Warrington: Wills at Chester, i. 116.

As this name occurs in the vicinity of Kingsley it helps to support the above suggestion (v. Kinsley for further confirmation).

1613. Married—Robert Kindersly and Mary Anston: St. Antholin (London), p. 40.
MDB. (co. Dorset), 1.

Kindon; v. Kingdon.

King.—Offic. 'the king.' There are four columns of Kings in the London Directory. An explanation is manifestly needed. Our Kings are of no royal descent; nor yet is the title always a mere nickname, like Caesar, Kaiser, Emperor (q.v.), from the royal bearing or appearance of the original nominee. The entries are in this direct and plain fashion:—Hamond le King. A. Robert le Kynge. G. Saher le King. H. The Hundred Rolls (1273) also furnish a William Littleking. There is also a Roger Wyteking. K. Stature and dress will account for these. The fact is the progenitors of our Kings acted in that capacity in the numerous festival and mock ceremonials of mediaeval times. At Epiphany-tide the Magi ('Kings of the East') were represented in every village.

'Thy mummeries, thy twelfe-tide kings
And queens, thy Christmas revellings.'
Herrick.

Besides the king and queen enthroned on May-day (who would maintain their regal title through the year, at least), there was the familiar 'King of Misrule,' whom every great nobleman possessed. In the manor of Ashton-under-Lyne (1422) we find 'Hobbe the King,' and a festival to be held there is under the supervision of 'Margaret, widow of Hobbe the King, Hobbe Adamson, Jenkin of the Wood,' &c. (v. Three Lancashire Documents, Cheth. Soc.). One more quotation will suffice:

'We, Adam Backhous and Harry Nycol, hath made account for the Kenggam (King-game) that same tyme don William Kempe, Kenge, and Joan Whytebrede, Quen, and all costs deducted, £4 5s. od.': Churchwarden's Accounts, Kingston-upon-Thames (Lysons).

'Queen' also existed as a surname, q.v. That King should be so largely represented now simply proves that every town and village had its festival, and that the 'King' was proud of his title; so were his

children. Thus it became hereditary; v. Kingsman and Kingson.

John le Kyng, co. Norf., 1273. A.
Walter le Kyng, co. Camb., ibid.
Willelmus Kyng', 1379: P. T. Yorks. p. 35.
1611-2. William Kinge and Elliner White: Marriage Lic. (London), ii. 9.
London, 355; Philadelphia, 360.

Kingaby.—Local, ' of Kingerby,' a parish in co. Lincoln, five miles from Market Rasen.

1794. Married — James Kingaby and Ann Andrews: St. Geo. Han. Sq. ii. 106. London, 2.

Kingcombe, Kingcome, Kingscomb.—Local, *of Kingcombe,' a tithing in the parish of Toller Porcorum, near Beaminster, co. Dorset.

1789. Married — John Nicholas and Bridget Kingcome: St. Geo. Han. Sq. ii. 19.
Bristol, 1, 3, o; London, 1, o, o; MDB. (co. Devon), o, 2, 1.

Kingdon, Kingdom, Kindon.—Local, ' of Kingdon,' or more probably ' Kingsdon,' a parish in co. Somerset, near Somerton. Kingdom is an imitative corruption; cf. Hansom for Hanson, or Ransom for Ranson. With Kjndon, cf. Kinsley for Kingsley, or Kinsman for Kingsman. No doubt, as intimated in the index to the two registers, the two following entries concern the same couple:

1709. Married — Henry Kindon and Eliz. Plucknet: St. Antholin (London), p. 122.
1710. Bapt.—Eliz., d. Henry and Eliz. Kingdom: St. John Baptist on Wallbrook, p. 176.

Thus Kindon and Kingdom are variants of Kingdon.

1752. Married — Bryan Connor and Mary Kingdon: St. Geo. Chap. Mayfair, p. 217.
Bristol, 3, 2, o; London, 6, o, 1; Tenby, o, 1, o; MDB. (co. Devon), 20, 2, o; Philadelphia, 1, o, 2; Boston (U.S.), 3, o, o.

Kingett, Kinggett. — Nick. 'the kinget' or 'kinglet,' a dim. of King. In the same way we have the two dims. of Hew (Hugh), viz. Hewett and Hewlett, v. King.

Johannes Kinglot, 1379: P. T. Yorks. p. 156.
London, 2, 2.

Kingham.—Local, 'of King-ham,' a parish in co. Oxford, four miles from Chipping Norton.

1721. Buried — Mary Kinghom : St. Thomas the Apostle (London), p. 149.
1749. Married — Edward Ralph and Mary Kingham : St. Geo. Chap. Mayfair, p. 146.
1774. — Edward Wench and Mary Kingham : St. Geo. Han. Sq. i. 239. London, 3 ; MDB. (co. Oxford), 1.

Kinglake.—Local, 'of King-lake.' I cannot find the spot. Assuredly a West-country name.

1608. William Kinglacke, co. Soms. : Reg. Univ. Oxf. vol. ii. pt. ii. p. 302. MDB. (co. Somerset), 12.

Kingman ; v. Kingsman.

Kingsbury.—Local,'of Kings-bury,' (1) a parish in co. Middle-sex ; (2) a parish in co. Warwick ; (3) a parish in co. Somerset.

Adam de Kinggesbire,co.Linc.,1273. A. Philip de Kingesbire, co. Dorset, Hen. III–Edw. I. K.
1603. Married — John Stacye and Katheryn Kyngssberie : Reg. Stourton, co. Wilts, p. 50.
1791. — John Gibbs and Mary Kings-bury : St. Geo. Han. Sq. ii. 61. London, 8 ; Birmingham, 1 ; Philadel-phia, 4.

Kingscomb ; v. Kingcombe.

Kingscote,   Kingscott.— Local, 'of Kingscote,' a parish in co. Gloucester, eight miles from Stroud.

William Kingescott, of Kingescott, co. Glouc. : Visitation of Gloucester (1623), p. 99.
Troyolus Kingescott, co. Glouc., 1623 : ibid. p. 100.
1603. Bapt.—John, s. John Kingscot : Reg. Cowley, co. Glouc.
1722. Married — Nicholas Kingscote and Margaret Merrett : Reg. Stone, co. Glouc.
London, 1, 0 ; MDB. (co. Gloucester), 1, 1.

Kingsey.—Local, 'of Kingsey,' a parish in co. Bucks, two miles from Thame. The suffix is -hay, as in Fotheringhay ; v. Hay.

John de Kyngeshaye, co. Suff., 1273. A. William de Kyngeshaye, co. Suff., ibid.
1710. Married — Peter Kingsey and Ann Amler : St.Antholin (London), p. 123.
1764. Married — Evan Kingsey and Mary Platts : St. Geo. Han. Sq. i. 136.

Kingsford.—Local, 'of Kings-ford,' a hamlet in the parish of Wolverley, near Kidderminster, co. Worcester. Other spots would naturally bear this title.

Avicia de Kyngesford, co. Worc., Hen. III–Edw. I. K.
Henry de Kyngesford, co. Devon, 1273. A.
John de Kingsford, co. Norf., 1372 : FF. vii. 51.
1746. Married — William Lott and Eliz. Kingsford : Canterbury Cath. p. 88.
1751. — John Kingsford and Eliz. Rose : ibid. p. 92.
London, 9 ; New York, 3.

Kingsland.—Local, 'of Kings-land': (1) a parish in co. Hereford, four miles from Leominster ; (2) a chapelry in the parish of Islington, co. Middlesex. Other spots would naturally bear this name.

Mathew de Kyngeslond, co. Kent, 1273. A.
1596. Bapt.—Robert, s. James Kings-land : St. Jas. Clerkenwell, p. 31.
1708. Married — John Kingsland and Jane Minge : Canterbury Cath. p. 68.
1711. — Thomas Kingsland and Eliz. Worham : ibid. p. 70.
MDB. (co. Kent), 6 ; New York, 26.

Kingsley.—Local, ' of Kings-ley.' (1) A township in the parish of Frodsham,co. Cheshire. Although Kingsley is somewhat scarce to-day in Cheshire and South Lan-cashire, it must not be forgotten that its variants Kinsley and Kindersley (q.v.) are familiar there. (2) A parish in co. Southampton, near Alton. (3) A parish in co. Stafford, near Cheadle.

Adam de Kyngeslegh : East Cheshire, ii. 161.
William Rutter, of Kyngesleye, 7 Hen. VIII : ibid. p. 86 n.
1588. Edmund Kingsley, of Wigan : Wills at Chester, i. 115.
1620. John Kingsley, of Haigh : ibid.
1803. Married — John Kingsley and Peggy Barber : St. Geo. Han. Sq. ii. 289. London, 2 ; Manchester, 1 ; Philadel-phia, 10.

Kingsman, Kinsman, King-man. — (1) Official, 'the king's man,' i.e. servant, a royal servitor. Probably also one who looked after royal property, a steward, a wood-ward, &c. (2) Occup. 'the king's man,' or assistant in the many festivities in which the king was personated ; v. King.

William Kingman, co. Soms., 1 Edw. III : Kirby's Quest, p. 130.

Thomas Kyngesman, Close Roll, 19 Ric. II.
Richard Kyngesman, 1273. A.
Ralph Kyngesman, 1311. M.
Alanus Kyngesman, 1379 : P. T. Yorks. p. 134.
1611. Robert Kingman, co. Soms. : Reg. Univ. Oxf. vol. ii. pt. ii. p. 325.

There is no trace of Kinsman being what it seems to imply ; cf. Kinsley for Kingsley. It is an imitative corruption of Kingsman, the said corruption being as old as the reign of Elizabeth.

John Kynnesman. ZZ.
Leonard Kinsman. Z.

Since writing the above I find

Simon Kynnesman, C. R., 9 Hen. VI.

Nevertheless this earlier date does not militate against the view I hold. For conclusive evidence, v. Kinsman. An analogous instance is met with in Kinsley (q.v.), a corruption of Kingsley through an intermediate form Kindsley. Thus, too, we find Kindsman as a similar intermediate step.

1639. Bapt.—Owen, s. Richard Kins-man : St. Jas. Clerkenwell, p. 143.
1656. — Mary, d. Reuben Kindsman : St. Dionis Backchurch, p. 114.
1659. Married—William Hopkins and Sarah Kindsman : ibid. p. 34.

But the earlier forms of entry are after this fashion :

1533. Jeffrey Kingsman, rector of Sutton, co. Norf.: FF. ix. 348.
1573. Myles Kyngesman and Johanna Walker : Marriage Lic. (London), p. 58.

We may take it that the cor-ruptions began at the beginning of the reign of Henry VI, when, the original meaning being for-gotten, the possessors of the name took up the *significative* form of Kinsman.

London, 0, 2, 0 ; New York, 1, 0, 0 ; Boston (U.S.), 0, 13, 39.

Kingsmill. — Local, 'at the king's mill,' a mill held of the king by the miller. One of these was in co. Hants.

Hugo de la Kingesmille, co. Southamp-ton, 1273. A.
Peter de Kingesmill, co. Wilts, ibid.
1574. Richard Kyngsmyll and Eliz. Stonehouse : Marriage Lic. (London), i. 61.
1582. Francis Kingsmell, co. South-ampton : Reg. Univ. Oxf. vol. ii. pt. ii. p. 123.

1585. John Kingsmill, co. Norf.: FF. vii. 188.
1610. Robert Spatman and Amy Kingesmeale: Marriage Lic. (London), p. 325.
1684. Col. Heneage Finch and Anne Kingsmell: Reg. Univ. Oxf. vol. ii. pt. ii. p. 305.
London, 2; Crockford, 3; Philadelphia, 1.

Kingsnorth.—Local, 'of Kingsnorth,' a parish in co. Kent, three miles from Ashford.
1732. Married—Charles Coombs and Margaret Kingsnorth: St. Geo. Han. Sq. i. 9.
1762. — Thomas Kingsnorth and Mary Howard: ibid. p. 112.
London, 1; MDB. (co. Kent), 6.

Kingson, Kinson.—Nick. 'the king's son,' i.e. the son of the man who acted as king in the local festivals (v. King). It is impossible to entirely separate Kingson and Kingston: many of the latter, no doubt, started life as Kingson.
Reginald Kyngesone, co. Hunts, 1273. A.
Simon Kyngeson, 1307. M.

The first three of the following entries occur together:
Johannes Kyng, hosteler, 1379: P. T. Yorks. p. 270.
Johannes Kyngson, 1379: ibid.
Thomas Kyngson, 1379: ibid.
Thomas Kyngson, 1379: ibid. p. 177.
Cf. Johanna Kyng', doghter, 1379: ibid. p. 175.

This is sufficient evidence of the derivation given above.
1585-6. Richard Kingson, laborer, and Margaret Wood: Marriage Lic. (London), i. 146.
1753. Married — James Millson and Ann Kingson: St. Geo. Chap. Mayfair, p. 239.
MDB. (co. Devon), 0, 1; Birmingham, 0, 1.

Kingston, Kingstone.—Local, (1) 'of Kingston,' parishes in cos. Cambridge, Devon, Somerset (2), Southampton, Sussex (2), Berks, Wilts, E. Rid. Yorks, &c.; (2) 'of Kingstone,' parishes in cos. Kent, Stafford, and Hereford.
Peter de Kyngeston, London, 1273. A.
Robert de Kingeston, co. Glouc., ibid.
Cristina de Kyngeston, co. Camb., ibid.
Lenote de Kyngeston, co. Sussex, ibid.
William de Kyngeston, co. Wilts, ibid.
Amicia de Kyngeston, co. Oxf., ibid.
John de Kyngeston, co. Soms., 1 Edw. III: Kirby's Quest, p. 85.

1578-9. Edward Kingeston and Barbara Piellowe: Marriage Lic. (London), p. 85.
1618. Edmund Kingstone, co. Glouc.: Reg. Univ. Oxf. vol. ii. pt. ii. p. 368.
1788. Married—Thomas Kingston and Ann Johnson: St. Geo. Han. Sq. ii. 14.
1806. — John Robertson and Jane Kingstone: ibid. p. 345.
London, 11, 1; MDB. (co. Somerset), 0, 2; Philadelphia, 20, 0.

Kingswell, Kingwell, Kingwill.—Local, 'at the king's well,' from residence thereby. The surname evidently hails from Hampshire, whence also Kingsmill comes. Indeed the two names are confounded in one instance.
1581. Ferdinando Kingswell, Hants: Reg. Univ. Oxf. vol. ii. pt. ii. p. 105.

A footnote to this entry records that in Matriculation he was returned as Ferdinando Kingsmell (v. Kingsmill).
1597. Buried—Harrye Kyngewell: St. Michael, Cornhill, p. 208.
1602. Edward Kingswelle, Hants: Reg. Univ. Oxf. vol. ii. pt. ii. p. 256.
1604. Richard Kingeswell, or Kinswell, Hants: ibid. p. 277.
1607. Richard Kingswell, Hants: ibid. p. 298.
London, 1, 4, 1; MDB. (co. Devon), 0, 3, 2.

Kington, Kinton.—Local, 'of Kington.' parishes in cos. Hunts, Warwick, Wilts, Worcester, and Dorset. With the variant Kinton, cf. Kinsley for Kingsley, or Kinsman for Kingsman.
Stephen de Kington, co. Norf., 1273. A.
Robert de Kington, co. Oxf., ibid.
1586. John Kynton and Margery Pemerton: Marriage Lic. (London), i. 153.
1752. Married — Weackham Kington and Sarah Armistmie (sic) Stead: St. Geo. Chap. Mayfair, p. 231.
London, 2, 0.

Kingwell, Kingwill.—Local; v. Kingswell.

Kinleyside; v. Keenlyside.

Kinmond, Kinman, Kynman.—Bapt. 'the son of Kinmond.' All personal names with suffix -mond corrupt to -man; cf. Osman, Wyman, Wayman, Tesseyman, &c.
1620. Married — Edward Kennyman and Mary Quince: St. Dionis Backchurch (London), p. 20.
1623-4. William Kynman and Joane Fowler: Marriage Lic. (London), ii. 134.

1711. Bapt. — Elizabeth, d. Francis Kinman: St. Jas. Clerkenwell, ii. 63.
1753. Married—Hill Burton and Eliz. Kinnimond: St. Peter, Cornhill, ii. 86.
London, 0, 1, 0; MDB. (co. Lincoln), 0, 0, 3; Sunderland, 1, 0, 0.

Kinnard.—Bapt.; v. Kenward. An American variant.
Philadelphia, 6.

Kinnersley, Kinnersly, Kinseley, Kynnersley.—Local, 'of Kinnersley,' a parish in co. Salop, five miles from Wellington; also a parish in co. Hereford, four miles from Weobley. v. Kindersley, and cf. Kinsley.
Hugh de Kinardeslegh, co. Hereford, Hen. III–Edw. I. K.
Richard de Kinardesle, co. Hereford, ibid.

Thus the name means the field of Kenward, the original settler or proprietor; v. Kenward.
1576. Nicholas Kinnersley, co. Linc.: Reg. Univ. Oxf. vol. ii. pt. ii. p. 72.
1581. Buried—Dorothye Kynnerseleye: Reg. Prestbury, co. Ches., p. 72.
1597. Married—Henry Kinnerslie and Margery Butler: St. Mary Aldermary, p. 9.
1676. Thomas Kinnersley and Mary London: Marriage Lic. (Canterbury), p. 259.
MDB. (co. Stafford), 2, 2, 0, 0; (co. Worcester), 0, 0, 0, 1; London, 0, 0, 1, 0; Birmingham, 0, 0, 0, 1; New York (Kinnersley), 1.

Kinnish; v. Kinch.

Kinsey.—Local, (1) 'of Kilnsea,' a parish in E. Rid. Yorks; (2) 'of Kilnsay,' a hamlet in the parish of Burnsall, W. Rid. Yorks; (3) 'of Kingsley'(?). I cannot help coming to the conclusion that Kinsey in cos. Ches. and Lanc. is a variant of Kingsley. The g was lost in Kinsley, q.v., and the l in Kinsey. I doubt not that in the South of England most of our Kinseys are modifications of Kingsey (q.v.); cf. Kinsman for Kingsman, or Kinsley for Kingsley.
1471. William Kynnesay, vicar of Hitcham, co. Norf.: FF. x. 311.
1586. William Chinseie, or Kinssee, co. Ches.: Reg. Univ. Oxf. vol. ii. pt. ii. p. 154.
1592. Married — Thomas Joneson and Eliz. Kynseye: Reg. Prestbury, co. Ches., p. 114.
1602. John Kynsey, co. Ches.: Reg. Univ. Oxf. vol. ii. pt. ii. p. 258.

1608. Married — John Kinsey and Dorithie Byrtles: Reg. Prestbury, co. Ches., p. 179.
1729. — Charles Kinsey and Kerthrine Rever: St. Antholin (London), p. 143. London, 8; Philadelphia, 21; MDB. (co. Ches.), 4.

Kinsley, Kinsly, Kinseley, Kinzley.—Local. ' of Kingsley,' q.v. This name is found in the Cheshire and Lancashire neighbourhood of Kingsley. No doubt a variant. In the Index to the Wills at Chester (v. infra) the two names are treated as the same. A parallel case is met with in Kinsman for Kingsman, q.v. We even find the intermediate form of Kindsman. Under the one heading Kingsley, the Index to the Reg. Univ. Oxf. gives the following variants: Kindesley, Kingesley, Kinsley, and Kyngysley. The d in the instances below is therefore merely intrusive. v. Kindersley.

Adam Kindsley, of Charnock Richard, 1627: Wills at Chester (1621-50), p. 130.
John Kindsley, of Duxbury, *husbandman*, 1639: ibid.
Robert Kindsley, of the City of London, 1699: ibid. (1681-1700), p. 148.
1662. Thomas Kindsley: Preston Guild Rolls, p. 157.
1800. Married—William Carroll and Mary Kinsley: St. Geo. Han. Sq. ii. 230. Liverpool, 3, 0, 0, 0; Manchester, 1, 0, 0, 0; MDB. (co. Chester), 0, 1, 0, 0; Philadelphia, 31, 0, 0, 3; London, 0, 0, 1, 0.

Kinsman.—Occup. ; v. Kingsman. All the evidence is in favour of this derivation. For a parallel case, v. Kinsley for Kingsley. For further evidence, v. Kingsman.

1588-9. George Kinesman, co. Northampton: Reg. Univ. Oxf. vol. ii. pt. ii. p. 168.
The two following entries settle the question:
1674. Bapt.—Deborah, d. Herold and Deborah Kingsman: St. Michael, Cornhill, p. 148.
1676. — Eliz., d. Herold and Deborah Kinsman. — ibid. p. 149.
Boston (U.S.), 14 ; Philadelphia, 2.

Kinson ; v. Kingson.

Kinton ; v. Kington.

Kipling, Kepling, Kippling. —Local, ' of Kiplin,' a township in the parish of Catterick, N. Rid. Yorks. The final *g* is excrescent,' as in Jennings, &c.

1756. Married—Samuel Platt and Eliz. Kippling : St. Geo. Han. Sq. i. 60. London, 4, 0, 0 ; MDB. (N.Rid. Yorks), 6, 0, 0 ; Stockton-on-Tees, 0, 1, 0 ; New York, 3, 0, 0 ; Philadelphia (Kippling), 1.

Kippax.—Local, ' of Kippax,' a village eight miles east of Leeds.

Adam Kypas, 1379 : P. T. Yorks. p. 95.
Johannes de Kypax, 1379 : ibid. p. 205.
Johanna Kepas, 1379 : ibid. p. 18.
Johannes de Kepax, 1379 : ibid. p. 82.

With the forms Kypax and Kypas, cf. Lomax and Lomas in the neighbouring county of Lancaster.

1749. Married—Paul Bowns and Mary Kippax: St. Geo. Chap. Mayfair, p. 157.
1751. Buried—John, s. Thomas Kippax : St. Michael, Cornhill, p. 299.
1754. Bapt.—Mary, d. Thomas Kippax : ibid. p. 176.
Lanc. Court Dir. (1887), 8.

Kipping, Kippen. — ? Bapt. ' the son of Kiping ' (?). The surname occurs frequently, but always without prefix, in the Hundred Rolls. Still, it may be local ; cf. Browning and Harding, both personal names.

Ralph Kiping, co. Norf., 1273. A.
Henry Kipping, co. Camb., ibid.
Adam Kyping, co. Oxf., ibid.
Alexander Kippinge, co. Hertford, 20 Edw. I. R.
Robert Kipping, co. Soms., 1 Edw I. R.
1591-2. Herman Kyppinge, or Kyppyn, and Faith Etheridge: Marriage Lic. (London), i. 196.
1795. Married — James Kipping and Dinah Offin : St. Geo. Han. Sq. ii. 129. London, 6, 1.

Kipps, Kipp.—? Bapt. Probably a corruption of Gipp, q.v. ; cf. Gilbey and Kilbey.

1752. Married—John Foord and Jane Kipps: St. Geo. Chap. Mayfair, p. 207.
1805. — Thomas Kipps and Jemima Irwin : St. Geo. Han. Sq. ii. 321. London, 4, 0 ; Philadelphia, o, 6.

Kirby ; v. Kirkby.

Kirk, Kirke.—Local, ' at the kirk,' from residence beside the church ; v. Church.

William atte Kirke, C. R., 19 Ric. II.
Robert atte Kirke. J.

Robertus del Kirke, 1379 : P. T. Yorks. p. 183.
Johannes de Kirke, 1379 : ibid. p. 57.

A curious intermediate form between Kirk and Church is found in the Hundred Rolls.

John de la Chirke, co. Linc., 1273. A.
1547. Married — Guylberte Johnson and Jawbyn Kyrke: St. Michael, Cornhill, p. 5.
1742. — Alex. Kirk and Eliz. Hunter : St. Geo. Chap. Mayfair, p. 30.
London, 19, 2 ; Philadelphia, 174, 2.

Kirkaldy, Kirkaldie, Kirkcaldie.—Local, ' of Kirkcaldy,' a royal burgh and parish in co. Fife. A modern importation into England.

London, 5, 2, 1.

Kirkbank. — Local, ' at the kirk bank,' from residence on the side of the slope on which the church was built ; cf. Kirkup and Chappelow.

MDB. (co. Kent), 2 ; London, 3.

Kirkbride, Kirkbright. Local, ' of Kirkbride,' a parish in co. Cumb., about six miles from Wigton.

Richard de Kirkebride co. Cumb., 20 Edw. I. R.
1742. Married — George Holride and Katherine Kirkbride : St. Geo. Chap. Mayfair, p. 18.
Philadelphia, 11, 0 ; MDB. (co. Westm.), 2, 0 ; Lofthouse (co. Yorks), 0, 4 ; West Riding Court Dir., 1, 0.

Kirkby, Kirby, Kerbey, Kerby. — Local, ' of Kirkby.' Parishes and hamlets too numerous for particular mention, chiefly in the North of England and in the counties along the East coast. Just as Kirkby became Kirby, so Kirkton became Kirton, q.v.

Adam de Kyrkeby, co. York, 1273. A.
Alex. de Kyrkeby, co. Linc., ibid.
Thomas de Kirkeby, co. Norf., ibid.
John de Kyrkeby, co. Westm., 20 Edw. I. R.
Roger de Kyrkeby, co. Hunts, ibid.
Alan de Kirkeby, co. Linc., ibid.
Johannes de Kirkeby, 1379 : P. T. Yorks. p. 50.
1594. John Kerbie and Eliz. Bendowe : Marriage Lic. (London), i. 216.
1806. Married—George Kerbey and Ann Woodford : St. Geo. Han. Sq. ii. 339. London, 4, 36, 2, 6 ; Philadelphia, 0, 46, 1, 1.

Kirker; v. Churcher.
Boston (U.S.), 5.

Kirkham. — Local, 'of Kirkham,' a parish in co. Lanc. This parish is one of the largest in the county, comprising about 130 square miles, or 41,736 statute acres. Naturally such an area gave birth to a local surname, and although no great family of Kirkham can be recorded, the name made its way among the less important classes. To-day it is a familiar cognomen throughout the country, America, and the Colonies.

Walter de Kirkham, co. Northumb., Edw. I-Edw. III. R.
Adam de Kirkham, 1379: P. T. Yorks. p. 30.
Agnes de Kyrkham, 1379: ibid. p. 300.
Johannes Kvrkam, 1376: ibid. p. 79.
1575. John Kirkham, co. Surrey: Reg. Univ. Oxf. vol. ii. pt. ii. p. 65.
1582. William Kirkeham and Eliz. Smith, widow: Marriage Lic. (London), p. 111.
1597-8. Robert Kyrkham, or Kirkham, co. Middlesex: Reg. Univ. Oxf. vol. ii. pt. ii. p. 225.
London, 5; Manchester, 14; New York, 7.

Kirkland, Kirtland, Kartland, Keartland. — Local, ' of Kirkland,'(1) a parish in co. Cumberland; (2) a township in the parish of Torpenhow, co. Cumb.; (3) a township in the parish of Garstang, co. Lanc.; (4) a township in the parish of Kendal, co. Westm. Kirtland is a manifest corruption.

(Homines) de Kyrkelaund, co. Cumb., 20 Edw. I. R.
Hugh de Churchlond, co. Soms., Edw. III: Kirby's Quest, p. 163.
1585. Henry Woode and Johanna Kirkelande (co. Derby): Marriage Lic. (London), i. 142.
1586. David Jones and Anne Kyrtland, widow of Henry Kirtland: ibid. i. 150.
1790. Married — Andrew Milne and Catherine Kirkland: St. Geo. Han. Sq. ii. 45.
1797. — James Kirkland and Eliz. Brown: ibid. p. 160.
London, 5, 2, 1, 1; Philadelphia, 5, 0, 2, 0.

Kirkley, Kirley, Kirly. — Local, 'of Kirkley,' (1) a township in the parish of Ponteland, co. Northumberland; (2) a parish in co. Suffolk, near Lowestoft. With the variants Kirley and Kirly, cf. Kirby for Kirkby.

1232. Richard de Kirkely, vicar of Buxton, co. Norf.: FF. vi. 441.
William de Kirkely, prior of Norwich: ibid. iv. 444.
Abraham de Kirkele, co. Suff., 1273. A.
Thomas de Kirkele, co. Suff., ibid.
1639. Robert Kirkley and Mary Penny: Marriage Lic. (Westminster), p. 39.
1686-7. Charles Kirly and Eliz. Hunter: Marriage Alleg. (Canterbury), p. 272.
1745. Married — Thomas Kirkly and Sarah Page: St. Geo. Chap. Mayfair, p. 54.
Manchester, 4, 0, 0; London, 0, 1, 3; Boston (U.S.), 1, 0, 0.

Kirkman. — Offic. ' the kirkman,' the keeper or guardian of the church; v. Churchman.

Roger le Kyrkeman, co. Linc., 1273. A.
Symon Kirkeman, co. Suff., ibid.
Alan Kyrkeman, co. Norf., ibid.
Gilbertus Kyrkman, 1379: P. T. Yorks. p. 26.
Johannes Kyrkman, 1379: ibid.
Ricardus Kirkeman, 1379: ibid. p. 64.
1597. Charles Kyrckman, co. Linc.: Reg. Univ. Oxf. vol. ii. pt. ii. p. 224.
1609. William Kynder and Anne Kirkeman: Marriage Lic. (London), i. 316.
London, 10; Philadelphia, 5.

Kirkness. — Local, ' of Kirkness,' a headland in_ Shetland. The following entry is thoroughly Scotch:

1753. Married — John Isbister and Jennet Kirkness: St. Geo. Chap. Mayfair, p. 256.
London, 1.

Kirkpatrick. — Local, 'of Kirkpatrick,' parishes in cos. Dumfries and Kirkcudbright; the church dedicated to St. Patrick. Cf. Marychurch, Kirkbride, &c.

1687-8. Thomas Kirkpatrick and Mary Turner: Marriage Lic. (London), ii. 309.
1747. Married — David Cockburn and Agnes Kirkpatrick: St. Geo. Chap. Mayfair, p. 90.
1803. — Guthrie Kirkpatrick and Mary Green: St. Geo. Han. Sq. ii. 294.
London, 2; MDB. (East Rid. Yorks), 3; Philadelphia, 80.

Kirkshaw; v. Kershaw.
Worcestershire Court Dir., 1.

Kirkup. — Local, 'at the kirk hope,' i.e. the hope on which the church stands; v. Kirk and Hope; cf. Greenup (s. v. Greenhalgh), Trollope, &c.

1754. Married — George Morwick and Sarah Kirkup: St. Geo. Han. Sq. i. 54.
1786. — William Davis and Mary Kirkup: ibid. i. 386.

London, 1; MDB. (co. Durham), 3; Newcastle, 2; New York, 1; Boston (U.S.), 1.

Kirkus, Churchouse. — Local. ' of the kirkus,' i.e. kirk-house or parsonage, but afterwards applied to the inn by the church gate, where at weddings, christenings, or funerals 'refreshments' might be had. There is a 'kirkus' by the church at Ulpha, beyond Broughton-in-Furness. Kirkus as a surname of course dates from the earlier meaning, and may be set beside Parsonage, Monkhouse, Vickridge, &c.

John Kyrkhuse and Richert Kyrkus occur as men capable and fit to bear arms in Newcastle-upon-Tyne, 1539: PPP. ii.181.
1552. Married — Humfrey Kyrkys and Beatrixe Thomson: St. Dionis Backchurch, p. 3.
'To John Milburn of Kirkehous for tith,' 1617: VVV. p. 99.
Henry Kirkhouse was Master of Trinity House, Newcastle-on-Tyne, for the year 1662: Brand's Newcastle, ii. 337.
Manchester, 1, 1; Hull, 5, 0.

Kirkwood. — Local, ' at the kirk wood,' from residence in the wood beside the church.

1699-1700. Married — John Kirkwood and Bridget Heath: St. Dionis Backchurch, p. 48.
1751. — William Kirkwood and Mary Lotan: St. Geo. Chap. Mayfair, p. 198.
1775. — Thomas Kirkwood and Catherine Wright: St. Geo. Han. Sq. i. 258.
London, 1; Philadelphia, 7.

Kirland. — Local, 'of Kirkland,' q.v. Just as Kirkby has become Kirby, so Kirkland has become Kirland.
Philadelphia, 3.

Kirley, Kirly; v. Kirkley.

Kirshaw. — Local. A variant of Kershaw, q.v.

1716. Bapt. — Catherine, d. Edmund Kirshaw: St. Mary Aldermary, p. 121.
1754. Married — Kirshaw and Mary Bellamy: St. Geo. Chap. Mayfair, p. 270.
MDB. (co. Warwick), 2.

Kirsopp, Kirsop. — Local. A Northumberland local name with the suffix -hope (v. Hope); cf. Blenkinsopp in the same county; v. Kirkup, of which it may be a variant, the more probably as both belong to the same district.

1791. Married — John Lee and Sarah Kirsop: St. Geo. Han. Sq. ii. 60.
Liverpool, 2, 0; Newcastle, 0, 3.

Kirtland.—Local, 'of Kirkland,' q.v.

New York, 4.

Kirtley.—Local, 'of Kirkley,' a township in the parish of Ponteland, ten miles from Newcastle, co. Northumberland. A corruption; cf. Kirtland for Kirkland.

Sunderland, 3; Newcastle, 1.

Kirton, Kerton.—Local, 'of Kirton,' (1) a parish in co. Lincoln, near Boston; (2) a parish in co. Suffolk, nine miles from Ipswich; (3) also Kirton-in-Lindsey, co. Lincoln, eighteen miles from Lincoln. All three seem to be modifications of Kirkton; cf. Kirby for Kirkby.

Alicia de Kirketon, co. Norf., Edw. I-Edw. III. R.
Alex. de Kirketon, co. Linc., ibid.
Simon de Kirketon, co. Linc., ibid.
Sir John de Kirton, co. Norf., 33 Edw. III : FF. ix. 107.
Robert Kyrton, co. Norf., 13 Edw. IV: ibid. xi. 208.
1576. Henry Kyrton and Eliz. Canler: Marriage Lic. (London), i. 72.
1591-2. William Kirton, co. Northampton : Reg. Univ. Oxf. vol. ii. pt. ii. p. 188.
1622. Bapt.—Amy, d. William Kertone, dwelling in the backe lann : St. Mary Aldermary, p. 77.
London, 4, 3 ; MDB. (co. Lincoln), 5, 1 ; New York, 1, o.

Kisbee, Kisbey, Kisby. — Local ; v. Keasbey.

Kislingbury. — Local, ' of Kislingbury,' a parish in co. Northampton.

1651. Bapt. — Sarah, d. Edward Kislingberry : St. Thomas the Apostle (London), p. 60.
1653. Buried—Ann, d. Edward Kislingbery : ibid. p. 129.
MDB. (co. Berks), 1.

Kiss.— ? ——. Probably some early personal name ; of kin to the German Kisch, instances of which are in the London Dir.

1455. Thomas Kysse, bailiff of Yarmouth : FF. xi. 325.
1573. Married—Lawrence Kyshe and Bridgett Phillipson : St. Jas. Clerkenwell, iii. 5.
1765. — William Woodward and Sarah Kish : St. Geo. Han. Sq. i. 146.
London, 1 ; New York, 1.

Kisser.—Occup. 'the kisser,' a maker of cuishes, thigh-armour.

F. *cuisse*, the thigh ; O.F. *cuissaux*. 'Cuisses, armour for the thighs': Cotgrave.

'And no son of a great lord, that is to say, of an earl or baron, shall have other armour than mufflers and cuishes'—('ne seit arme fors de mustilers e de quisers ') : Stat. of Realm, i. 231.
Walter de Bedefont, *kissere*, London. X.
Richard le Kissere, ibid.
1760. Married — Edward Kishere and Sibell Clipsham: St. Geo. Chap. Mayfair, p. 169.
1738. Married—Benjamin Kishere and Rachel Benefold : St. Geo. Han. Sq. i. 21.
1754. — William Burton and Mary Kisher: St. Geo. Han. Sq. i. 55.
London, 1.

Kissick ; v. Keswick.

Kitcat, Kitcatt. — ? Local. Probably an imitative corruption of some local name ending in *-cott* ; cf. Westcott, Kingscott, Caldecott.

London, 1, o; MDB. (co. Dorset), o, 1 ; (co. Glouc.), 1, o.

Kitchen, Kitchin, Kitching. —Local, 'at the kitchen,' equivalent to Kitchingman, q.v. The *g* in Kitching is, of course, excrescent, as in Jennings and a hundred other surnames.

Henry atte Kychene, temp. 1300. M.
Richard del Kechin. H.
Nicholas de la Kechyn : Patent Roll, 17 Ric. II. pt. ii.
Johannes del Kechyn, 1379: P. T. Yorks. p. 21.
Johannes del Kychyn, 1379: ibid. p. 142.
Thomas del Kichyn, 1379: ibid. p. 188.
1578. James Kytchen, of London: Reg. Univ. Oxf. vol. ii. pt. ii. p. 81.
1616. Abel Kitchen, of Bristol: ibid. p. 356.
London (1874), 9, 6, 8; West Rid. Court Dir., 4, 2, 5; Philadelphia, 27, 2, o; New York, 10, o, 10.

Kitchener, Kitchiner. — Occup. 'the kitchener,' equivalent to Kitchingman (q.v.), and v. Kitchen.

'John Silvester, *kychynner*,' a member of the dissolved Abbey of Hayles, co. Glouc.: Rudder's Hist. Glouc. p. 487.
Adam Kitener (?), 1379: P. T. Yorks. p. 165.
1569. Married—Edward Kychener and Mary Pyers : Marriage Lic. (London), p. 43.
1618. Thomas Kechener, co. Devon: Reg. Univ. Oxf. vol. ii. pt. ii. p. 371.
1716. Married—John Kitchener and Eliz. Hare: St. Jas. Clerkenwell, ii. 239.
London (1874), 2, 3.

Kitchingman, Kitchingham, Kitchenman. — Occup. 'the kitchen-man,' a scullion, a cook. The corrupted Kitchingham is more common in the reverse case ; cf. Deadman and Swetman for Debenham and Swetenham.

Willelmus Kychynman, 1379: P. T. Yorks. p. 203.
Johannes Kychynman, 1379: ibid.
Beatrix Kychynman, 1379: ibid. p. 204.
Hugo Kychynman, 1379 : ibid. p. 206.

Four Kychynmans occur also on p. 209, resident in the village of 'Colyngham.' The surname is common in Yorkshire records.

1661. Willoughby West and Ester Kitchingman: Marriage Lic. (Canterbury), p. 61.
1666. Thomas Kitchinman and Anne Browne: ibid. p. 123.
London (1874), 2, 1, o ; West Rid. Court Dir., 3, o, o ; Leeds (Kitchenman), 1 ; Philadelphia, o, o, 21.

Kite. — Nick. 'the kite,' a sobriquet for one of wild, voracious habits ; cf. Hawk, Falcon, Sparrowhawk.

Hugo Kyte, 1379 : P. T. Yorks. p. 213.
John Kyte, rector of Wolferton, co. Norf., 1507: FF. ix. 196.
1739. Married — Edward Kite and Phebe Jefferys : St. Antholin (London), p. 150.
1783. — John Kite and Jane Lever : St. Geo. Han. Sq. i. 345.
1790. — Henry Kyte and Jane Sullivan : ibid. ii. 42.
London, 9 ; Philadelphia, 33.

Kitewild.—Nick. 'wild as a kite' (?) ; v. Kite.

Jordanus Kitewilde, co. Bucks, 1273. A.

Kitley ; v. Kettley.

Kitson, Kidson.—(1) Bapt. 'the son of Christopher,' from nick. Kit, patr. Kitson. (2) Bapt. 'the son of Katherine,' from nick. Kit. This nick. lasted in the North till the 16th century. I had several in my own registers at Ulverston. We still use the pet Kitty.

Johannes Lund et Kit uxor ejus, 1379 : P. T. Yorks. p. 175.
Thomas Ketson, 1379 : ibid. p. 170.
Johannes Kytson, 1379 : ibid. p. 211.
Alicia Kytson, 1379 : P. T. Howdenshire, p. 7.
1579. John Kytson, co. Salop: Reg. Univ. Oxf. vol. ii. pt. ii. p. 98.
1581. Robert Kitson, co. York: ibid.p.98.
1585. Richard Kitson, or Kidson, co. York : Reg. Univ. Oxf. vol. ii. pt. ii. p. 148.

1590. John Kitson, co. Glouc.: Reg. Univ. Oxf. vol. ii. pt. ii. p. 178.
1746. Married — Richard Wynn and Mary Kitson: St.Geo.Chap.Mayfair, p. 70.
1752. — Thomas Kidson and Mary Bell: ibid. p. 208.
London, 7, 2; West Rid. Court Dir., 7, 1; Lanc. Court Dir. (Kidson), 4; Leeds, 2, 2; New York, 5, 1.

Kitt, Kitts.—Bapt. 'the son of Christopher,' from the nick. Kit; v. Kitson.

Nicholas Kitte, co. Northampton, 1273. A.
William Kitte, co. Camb., ibid.
Osbert Kyt, co. Soms., 1 Edw. III: Kirby's Quest, p. 155.
1621. Buried — Jone Kitts: St. Jas. Clerkenwell, iv. 154.
1667-8. Henry Kitt and Mary Long: Marriage Alleg. (Canterbury), p. 233.
1669. Married — Thomas Rolley and Jane Kitte: St. Jas. Clerkenwell, iii. 169.
Plymouth, 3, 1; Boston (U.S.), 0, 4.

Kitten.—Nick. 'the kitten'; cf. Catt.

William Kytene, co. Oxf., 1273. A.
But cf.
Johanna de Ketyne, 1379: P. T. Yorks. p. 167.
Nevertheless this *de* may be a misreading of the text, and ought to be *le*.
Philadelphia, 3.

Kitteringham; v. Kettering-ham.

Kittermaster. — Local, 'of Kidderminster'; cf. Buckmaster and Killmaster. Lower, quoting Burke's Landed Gentry, shows that the Kittermasters of Meriden, co. Warwick, spelt their name Kydermister in 1543, Kydermaster in 1568, and Kittermaster in 1649 (Patr. Brit. p. 181).

Richard Kidderminster, abbot of Winchcombe, 1498: Dict. Nat. Biog. (Colet), xi. 323.
1594. John Keedomister, or Keedermister, co. Bucks: Reg. Univ. Oxf. vol. ii. pt. ii. p. 201.
1597. Robert Kederminster, or Kidermister, co. Bucks: ibid. p. 219.
1663. William Kittermaster and Margaret Harland: Marriage Lic. (Faculty Office), p. 74.
1693. Jonathan Seyton and Hester Kittermaster (co. Warw.): Marriage Alleg. (Canterbury), p. 257.
F. J. Kittermaster, of Shrewsbury School, has taken an open Scholarship at King's Coll., Cambridge': Manchester Courier, Dec. 31, 1887.
Crockford, 1; MDB. (co. Warwick), 2.

Kittle. — Bapt. 'the son of Kettle' (q.v.).
'Robert Ketyll, or Kyttell, sup. for B.A., April, 1513': Reg. Univ. Oxf. i. 86.
1608. Buried—an abortive, the sonne of Francis Scotte, the sonne-in-law to Edward Kittle, dwellinge in Cornhill: St. Peter, Cornhill, i. 163.
1676. Richard Small and — Kittle: Marriage Alleg. (Canterbury), p. 180.
London, 1; New York, 10.

Kitto, Kittoe, Kittow.— ? Local. A Cornish surname.
John Kittowe and Elizabeth Bland, 1543: Marriage Lic. (Faculty Office), p. 1.
Tamson (i.e. Thomasine) Kyttowe, 1581: Reg. St. Columb Major, p. 141.
John, son of Joane Kettoe, 1604: ibid. p. 201.
James Kettowe, or Kittowe (co. Somerset), Queen's Coll., 1608: Reg. Univ. Oxf. vol. ii. pt. ii. p. 301.
London, 3, 1, 0; Cornwall Dir. (Farmers), 3, 0, 11; MDB. (co. Cornwall), 2, 0, 8.

Kitton; v. Ketton and Kitten, of either of which it may be a modification.

Kitts; v. Kitt.

Knabwell. — Local, 'at the knap-well,' i.e. the well at the hilltop; v. Knap.
Robert de Cnapwell, 1273. A.
John de Cnabwelle, ibid.

Knaggs.—Local, 'at the knaggs' or 'knagg,' from residence thereby. A Yorkshire surname, as might be expected. 'Knag, the rugged top of a hill. North' (Halliwell). 'Knaggs, pointed rocks, or rugged tops of hills' (Brockett).
1620-1. Thomas Reekes and Joane Knagges: Marriage Lic. (London), ii. 96.
1637. Buried — Prina, d. William Knagge: St. Jas. Clerkenwell, iv. 231.
1665. — Alice Knagg: ibid. iv. 365.
London, 3; Hull, 3; MDB. (N. Rid. Yorks), 6; New York, 1.

Knapman.—Local, 'the knap-man,' the man on the knap or hilltop, from residence thereon (v. Knap); cf. Bridgman, &c. A well-known Devonshire surname.
James Knapman. Z.
William Knapman. ZZ.
1601. James Knapman, co. Devon: Reg. Univ. Oxf. vol. ii. pt. ii. p. 246.
1607-8. John Knapman, co. Devon, Exeter Coll.: ibid. p. 300.

1648. Married—Richard Hill and Eliz. Knapman: St. Michael, Cornhill, p. 30.
1799. — William Knapman and Susanna Davis: St. Geo. Han. Sq. ii. 211.
London, 3; Plymouth, 4; MDB. (co. Devon), 14.

Knapp.—Local, 'at the knap,' a summit, a hilltop, from residence thereon. 'Some high knap or tuft of a mountaine': Holland, trans. of Pliny, bk. xi. c. 10 (v. Skeat on Knop). 'Knap, a hillocke, or knap of a hill': Cotgrave. Cf. *knop* (Exod. xxv. 31), the earlier form of *knob*, a round protuberance. So *knab* or *nab* for *knap*. 'Nab, the summit of an eminence. North' (Halliwell). v. Knabwell.
John Cnape, co. Camb., 1273. A.
John Knapp, co. Bucks, ibid.
Capella de la Cnappe. DD.
Margaret atte Cnappe, co. Soms., 1 Edw. III: Kirby's Quest, p. 206.
Johannes Knape, 1379: P. T. Yorks. p. 15.
Johannes Knaype, 1379: ibid. p. 200.
1553-4. Christopher Nappe and Eliz. Kemyes: Marriage Lic. (London), i. 14.
1681. Bapt.—Robert, s. Robert Knapp: St. Jas. Clerkenwell, i. 296.
London, 9; Philadelphia, 52.

Knapper.—Local, 'the knapper,' i.e. the man on the hilltop; cf. Bridger, and v. Knapp.
William Knapper. G.
1710. Married—Isaac Beckett and Ann Knaper: St. Jas. Clerkenwell, iii. 232.
1730. — John Gray and Jane Knopper: St. Geo. Chap. Mayfair, p. 319.
New York, 1; Philadelphia, 1.

Knapton, Napton. — Local, ' of Knapton,' i.e. the town on the knap, (1) a township in the parish of Acomb, W. Rid. Yorks; (2) a township in the parish of Wintringham, E. Rid. Yorks; (3) a parish in co. Norfolk, three miles from North Walsham; v. Knapp and Town.
Estrilda de Knapeton, co. Norf., 1273. A.
Thomas de Cnapeton, co. Suff., ibid.
Adam de Knapeton, of Norwich, 1292: ibid. iv. 386.
William Knapton, co. York. W. 16.
Elisabet de Knapton, 1379: P. T. Yorks. p. 212.
Thomas Knapton, 1379: ibid. p. 125.
Clement de Knapton, co. Norf., 1386: FF. iv. 122.
1586. Albinus Knapton, co. Wilts: Reg. Univ. Oxf. vol. ii. pt. ii. p. 157.
1759. Married—John Nickelson and Mary Knapton: St. Geo. Han. Sq. i. 85.

1790. Married—Bartholomew Napton and Susanna Hine: Reg. Univ. Oxf. vol. ii. pt. ii. p. 47.
London, o, 1 ; Boston (U.S.), 6, o.

Knatchbull.—I cannot classify this singular surname. Mr. Lower says (quoting Shirley's Noble and Gentle Men), 'The first recorded ancestor of the family is John Knatchbull, who had lands in the parish of Lymne, co. Kent, in the reign of Edward III, and there some of the name remained down to the time of Charles I. The main branch were at Mersham-Hatch, in the same county, by purchase temp. Henry VI, and there the present baronet yet resides' (Patr. Brit. p. 181).
1592. Buried — Thomas, s. Richard Nashbull, of Madehatche, co. Kent: St. Michael, Cornhill, p. 204.
1613. Married — George Knatchbull and Jone Gilbarde: Canterbury Cath. p. 55.
1667. Richard Sheafe and Mary Knatchbull, of Cranbrook, co. Kent: Marriage Lic. (Faculty Office), p. 98.
1734. Married — Edward Hearst, of New Sarum, and Alicia Knatchbull, of Mersham, co. Kent: St. Geo. Han. Sq. i.13.
London, 1 ; MDB. (co. Kent), 4.

Knave.—Occup. 'the knave,' i.e. a servant, a lad ; v. Good-knave.
Adam le Cnave, co. Soms., 1 Edw. III: Kirby's Quest, p. 259.

Kneebone.—?Local. A Cornish name.
Jane, d. of Grace Kneebone, 1585: Reg. St. Columb Major, p. 13.
Anthony Kneebone, of Gwenapp, 1753: ibid. p. 112.
1681. Married—William Holmes and Mary Kneebone: St. Jas. Clerkenwell, iii. 190.
1692. Amor Steffe and Susan Kneebone : Marriage Alleg. (Canterbury), p. 232.
1796. Married—William Pummis and Margery Kneebone: St. Geo. Han. Sq. ii. 148.
London, 2 ; MDB. (co. Cornwall), 2 ; Cornwall Dir. (Farmers' List), 6.

Kneedler.—Occup. ;v. Needler.
Philadelphia, 21.

Kneeshaw.—Local, 'of Kneesall,' a parish in co. Notts, four miles from Ollerton. As is common in such names, the suffix has -aw instead of -all; cf. Shallcross and Shawcross, Lindall and Lindow,

Preesall and Presow, Picthall and Picthaw.
(Ballivus) de Kneshale, co. Notts, 1273. A.
Richard de Knewshale, rector of Beetley, co. Norf., 1341: FF. ix. 467.
Ricardus Knesall, 1379: P. T. Yorks. p. 210.
Lanc. Court Dir. (1887), 1 ; Liverpool, 2 ; Philadelphia, 1.

Knell, Knill.—Local, ' of Knill,' a parish in co. Hereford, three miles from Kingston.
Henry de Knell, co. Bedf., Hen. III-Edw. I. K.
Gille de Knille, co. Camb., 1273. A.
Robert de Knille, co. Camb., ibid.
John atte Knyle, co. Soms.: Kirby's Quest, p. 184.
1571-2. John Knell and Margaret Barrell: Marriage Lic. (London), i. 51.
1600. John Knell, co. Kent : Reg. Univ. Oxf. vol. ii. pt. ii. p. 240.
1656. Married—James Knell and Eliz. Berry : Canterbury Cath. p. 58.
London, 4, 6 ; Crockford, 1, o; MDB. (co. Hereford), o, 5 ; New York, 6, o.

Kneller.—Occup. 'the kneller,' a bellringer ; v. Knowler (1). The surname is English in spite of Sir Godfrey Kneller. Mr. Lower says it was formerly common in East Sussex (Patr. Brit. p. 181). But I cannot for one moment accept the local derivation he suggests.
London, 1 ; Philadelphia, 3.

Kneresboro. — Local, ' of Knaresborough,' a market-town in the W. Rid. Yorks. The surname seems almost extinct.
Stephen de Knaresburg', co. York, 1273. A.
Thomas de Knaresburg', co. York, ibid.
1583. Thomas Knaresboroughe and Margarett Wytter: Marriage Lic. (London), i. 121.
Philadelphia, 1.

Knevitt, Knyvett. — Local, ' de Knyvet.' I cannot find the place.
Mathew de Knyvet, co. Notts, 1273. A.
Geoffrey Knyfet, co. Camb., ibid.
Thomas Knyvet, co. Essex, ibid.
John de Knevet, co. Norf., temp. 1430: FF. i. 378.
1523. William Knevett, of the Household of our Lord the King, and Katherine Grey : Marriage Lic. (London), p. 3.
Nathaniel Knevet, co. Norf., 1633 : FF. xi. 167.
1571. Henry Knevet, London : Reg. Univ. Oxf. vol. ii. pt. ii. p. 51.

1789. Married—Thomas Knevit and Easter Hart: St. Geo. Han. Sq. ii. 19.
London, 1, 1.

Knewstub, Knewstubb.—Local, ' of Knewstubb,' a spot in or near the parish of Ravenstonedale, co. Westm. The suffix is -stubb; v. Stubbs.
Thomas Knewstupp, his wife, and 2 children : Hist. and Traditions of Mallerstang Forest, co. Westm., W. Nicholls, p. 95.
John Knewstupp and his mother : ibid. p. 97.
John Knewstupp and 2 children : ibid.
1696. Buried—Ann Knewstub: St. Michael, Cornhill, p. 275.
1698. — Mary Knewstub : ibid. p. 276.
1734. William Knewstub : Hist. and Traditions of Ravenstonedale, co.Westm., W. Nicholls, p. 116.
— Anthony Knewstub : ibid. p. 117.
London, 1, 1.

Knibb, Knibbs.—Bapt. ' the son of Isabel,' from the nick. Ibb. This became popularly Nib or Nibb, whence the patronymic Nibbs (q.v.). Knibb and Knibbs are variants of Nibbs ; cf. Nobbs.
1604-5. William Knebb and Susan Awsten: Marriage Lic. (London), i. 294.
1734. Married — Isaac Knibbs (co. Northampton), and Eliz. Hawkins : St. Antholin (London), p. 146.
1705. — John Colbeck and Susanna Knibb : St. Geo. Han. Sq. ii. 139.
1803. — Henry Knibs and Sarah Rook : ibid. p. 292.
London, 3, 1 ; Manchester, 1, 1 ; Birmingham, 3, 1 ; Boston (U.S.), o, 1.

Knifesmith, Neasmith, Nasmith.—Occup. 'the knifesmith,' a maker of knives ; cf. Cutler. It has been stated as beyond need of evidence that Nasmith and Neasmith are corrupted forms of Nailsmith, a maker of nails. The instances furnished below seem to point strongly in favour of knifesmith. For the other theory I have found no evidence.
1594. Married — Roberte Knysmithe and Eliz. Weekes : St. Michael, Cornhill, p. 15.
1595. Bapt. — Eliz., d. Robert Knysmythe: ibid. p. 99.
The earlier and complete form is found in the Valor Ecclesiasticus, viz. Henry Knyfesmythe (F.). I forgot to note date and page (v. Index). But it will be seen at once by any candid observer that, failing evidence to the contrary,

Neasmith and Nasmith are corruptions of the old Knifesmith. Besides, Nailer (v. Naylar) was the accepted occupative term for a maker of nails.

London, 0, 1, 1.

Knifton, Knyfton. — Local, 'of Kniveton,' a parish in co. Derby, near Ashbourn.

John de Knyveton, co. Derby, 20 Edw. I. R.
1605. Gilbert Knyveton : Reg. Univ. Oxf. i. 237.
1630. Married—Thomas Knifton and Katherine Swetna : Reg. Prestbury, co. Ches., p. 274.
Charles Knifton, of Raby, 1685 : Wills at Chester (1681-1700), p. 149.
1788. Married — William Bowerman and Eliz. Knifton : St. Geo. Han. Sq. ii. 4.
London, 1, 0 ; MDB. (co. Somerset), 0, 1.

Knight.—Official, 'the knight,' a man-at-arms, a military follower; A.S. *cniht*, a servant.

John le Cnihth, co. Suff., 1273. A.
Gilbert le Knyt, co. Camb., ibid.
Roger le Knith, co. Oxf., ibid.
Ellis le Knyght, co. Wilts, ibid.

Other forms in the same registers are Knicht, Knyght, Knict, Kneyt, Knigt, Kniht, Knyth, and Knit.

Roger le Knyt, C. R., 3 Edw. I.
Johannes Knyght', 1379 : P. T. Yorks. p. 21.
Willelmus Knighte, 1379 : ibid. p. 27.
Thomas Knycht, 1379 : ibid. p. 28.
Willelmus Knygth, 1379 : ibid. p. 76.
1599. Married—Thomas Burves and Jone Knight : St. Antholin (London), p. 40.

A curious Puritan Christian name is seen in the following :

1638. Bapt.—John, s. of Know-God Knight : St. Jas. Clerkenwell, p. 140.

I fear his enemies would pronounce it No-Good !

London, 151 ; Philadelphia, 152.

Knightley, Knightly.—Local, ' of Knightley,' a township in the parish of · Grosall, co. Stafford. The variant Knightly is imitative.

Robert de Knyghstelee, co. Staff., Edw. I-Edw. III. R.
Robert de Knyghistele, co. Staff., ibid.
1574. Edward Knightlie, co. Northampton : Reg. Univ. Oxf. vol. ii. pt.ii.p.58.
1597-8. Seymour Knightley, co. Northampton : ibid. p. 225.
1698. Thomas Knightley (co. Northampton), and Sarah Mitford : Marriage Lic. (London), ii. 324.

1808. Married—James Knightley and Eliz. Bennett : St. Geo. Han. Sq. ii. 391.
London, 2, 2 ; New York, 1, 0.

Knighton.—Local, ' of Knighton.' (1) West Knighton, a parish in co. Dorset, four miles from Dorchester ; (2) a chapelry in the parish of Lindridge, co. Worcester ; (3) a chapelry in the parish of St. Margaret, Leicester.

Thomas de Knyghton, 1379 : P. T. Yorks. p. 147.
1544. John Alen and Margaret Knyghton : Marriage Lic. (Faculty Office), p. 3.
1583-4. George Knighton and Susan White : Marriage Lic. (London), i. 127.
1688. John Knighton and Eliz. de Champner : Marriage Alleg. (Canterbury), p. 89.
London (1884), 4 ; New York, 3.

Knightson.—Nick. ' the son of the knight' ; cf. Wrightson, Taylorson, Smithson, or Hindson.

Alicia fil. Ricardi Knyghtson, 1379 : P. T. Yorks. p. 217.
1721. Married—William Fareley and Eliz. Knightson : St. Jas. Clerkenwell, iii. 245.

Knill.—Local ; v. Knell.

Knipe.—Local, ' at the knap ' (v. Knapp) ; a variant. This North-English surname existed for several centuries in Cartmel parish, North Lancashire. Though it died out there it made its way into the surrounding district. It must be considered a Furness surname.

1597. Elizabeth Knype, of Warton : Lancashire Wills at Richmond (1457-1680), p. 178.
— William Knype, of Cartmel : Stockdale's Annals of Cartmel, p. 34.
1601. Bapt.—Marie, d. Isaac Knypp : St. Mary, Ulverston, p. 91.
1612. Jenkin Knype, of Hawkshead : Lancashire Wills at Richmond (1457-1680), p. 178.
1661. William Knipe, of Grysdale : ibid.
Agnes Knipe, of Town-end, *widow,* 1698 : Wills at Chester (1681-1700), p. 149.
London, 3 ; Liverpool, 1 ; New York, 8.

Knock.—(1) Local, 'atten-oak,' from residence beside some specially prominent oak-tree. The surname at first was Noke or Nock (v. Noakes). Then by imitation it became Knock. (2) Local, ' at the knock,' a hill, a knoll ; Celtic and Gaelic, *cnoc,* ' collis ' (Lower).

Tenentes de la Knocke, co. Kent, 1273. A.
1717. Married — Robert Knock and Sarah Keete : Canterbury Cath. p. 73.
1788. — Robert Pattle and Charlotte Knocke : St. Geo. Han. Sq. ii. 7.
1797. — William Taylor and Caroline Knocke : ibid. p. 171.
London, 3 ; Boston (U.S.), 2.

Knocker.—?Local. Like Knowler (2), one who dwelt on a knoll, Knocker may mean one who dwelt on a knock (v. Knock). I cannot suggest any other derivation. But in favour of it is the fact that both Knock and Knocker are Kentish names. This will seem fairly strong evidence to some.

1685. Bapt. — Friswith, d. George Knocker ; St. Antholin (London), p. 102.
1693. Buried — Richard, s. George Knocker : St. John Baptist on Wallbrook, p. 191.
1726. Married—Jacob Thompson and Eliz. Knocker : St. Michael, Cornhill, p. 63.
MDB. (co. Kent), 4 ; New York, 1.

Knoll, Knollys, Knowles, Knolles.—Local, ' at the knoll,' from residence thereon ; M.E. *knol,* a hill, a summit. The final *s* in Knowles, Knollys, &c., may be patronymic, as in Brooks, Styles. Holmes, &c., corresponding to Jones, Williams, &c., in surnames of the baptismal class.

Roger de la Cnolle, co. Devon, 1273. A.
John Cnolle, co. Dorset, ibid.
Robert de la Cnolle, co. Sussex, ibid.
John atte Knolle. B.
Cecilia de Knolle, 1379 : P. T. Yorks. p. 123.
Johannes Knoll', 1379 : ibid. p. 160.
Thomas de Knoll', 1379 : ibid. p. 276.
Robert de Knollys, 1397 : Preston Guild Rolls, p. 6.
1583. Bapt. — Eliz., d. William Knowiles : St. Jas. Clerkenwell, i. 15.
1598-9. Married—Robert Knowels and Mary Wryght : St. Dionis Backchurch, p. 14.
London, 1, 1, 40, 0 ; Philadelphia, 11, 0, 81, 1.

Knoller, Knollman ; v. Knowler.

Philadelphia, 1, 1.

Knollys.—Local ; v. Knoll.

Knope, Knopp, Knop. — Local, ' at the knop,' from residence thereon ; v. Knapp and Knipe.

1771. Married—John Greenfield and Betty Knopp : St. Geo. Han. Sq. i. 212.
London, 1, 0, 0 ; Philadelphia, 0, 4, 3.

Knott, Knotts.—(1) Local, 'at the knot,' the summit of a rocky hill, from residence thereon; cf. Knapp, Knaggs, and Knoll, all of similar origin. (2) Bapt. 'the son of Cnut' (Canute). (3) Nick.; v. Nott.

Richard Knotte, London, 1273. A.
Peter Cnotte, co. Salop, ibid.
Robertus Knotte, 1379: P. T. Yorks. p. 46.
Ricardus Notte, 1379: ibid. p. 70.
Isabella Notte, 1379: ibid. p. 71.
Thomas Knot, 1379: ibid. p. 224.
1662. Married—James Rokeby and Judith Knott: St. Dionis Backchurch, p. 37.
London, 20, 3; Philadelphia, 21, 0.

Knowell, Knoell.—Bapt. 'the son of Nowell'; v. Nowell and Knowlson.

1655. Married — John Knouell and Abigal Straley: St. Dionis Backchurch, p. 31.
MDB. (co. Somerset), 1, 0; Philadelphia, 0, 4.

Knowlden; v. Knowlton.

Knowler, Knowlman.—(1) Occup. 'the knowler' or 'knowlman,' a bellringer, a chimer; v. Ringer, Bellringer. (2) Local, 'one who dwelt on a knoll'; v. Knoll and Knocker.

'Carillonneur, a chymer, or knowler of bels': Cotgrave's Dict. 1611.
'Where bells have knolled to church': As You Like It, ii. 7. 114.
1616. Buried—Wilmore Knowleman, servant to Mr. Norman Paynter: St. Peter, Cornhill, i. 172.
— John Knowler, co. Kent: Reg. Univ. Oxf. vol. ii. pt. ii. p. 348.
1618. Richard Knoller, co. Kent: ibid. p. 375.
1691. Married—George Knowler and Bridget Foucke: St. Dionis Backchurch, p. 42.
1743. Bapt.—Ann, d. John Knowler, recorder of this city: Canterbury Cath. p. 28.
1770. Married—Henry, Lord Digby and Mary Knowler: St. Geo. Han. Sq. i. 202.
1805. — William Knowler and Hannah Butcher: ibid. ii. 317.
London, 3, 2; MDB. (co. Devon), 0, 3; New York, 0, 1.

Knowles, Knowlys.—Local; v. Knoll.

Walter atte Cnolle, co. Soms., 1 Edw. III: Kirby's Quest, p. 232.
Roger de Knolle, co. Soms., 1 Edw. III: ibid. p. 245.
New York, 27, 0.

Knowlman; v. Knowler.

Knowlson.—(1) Bapt. 'the son of Olive' or 'Oliver,' from the nick. Noll, patronymic Nollson; cf. Towler for Toller, or Toulson for Tolson, or Coulson for Colson. (2) Bapt. 'the son of Nowell' or Noel'; v. Noel.

Alexander Nouelson, Pardons Roll, 6 Ric. II.

Of these two derivations the last must be accepted as the more probable, as possessing evidence. But it must not be forgotten that the first is in strict accordance with rule; cf. Nibbs, Nobbs, Nabbs, Nopps, &c. In either case the initial K is imitative of the local Knowles, q.v.

1757. Married—Richard Nowlson and Margaret Wilcocks: St. Geo. Han. Sq. i. 71.
York, 4; London, 1; MDB. (N. Rid Yorks), 5.

Knowlton, Knowlden.—Local, 'of Knowlton,' a parish in co. Kent. There seems to be little doubt that Knowlden is a lazily pronounced variant. Knowlton has flourished for some time in the United States. Various small spots would naturally bear the name; v. Knowles and Town.

Richard de Knolton, co. Soms., 1 Edw. III: Kirby's Quest, p. 253.

The two following Kentish entries are strongly conclusive of the view that Knowlden is a variant of Knowlton:

1658. Married—Thomas Godfrey and Anne Knowlden: Canterbury Cath. p. 59.
1665. — John Smyth and Mary Knolden: ibid. p. 60.
1776. — William Knowlton and Mary Howse: St. Geo. Han. Sq. i. 261.
1799. — Francis Knowlton and Sarah Widley: ibid. ii. 196.
London, 0, 4; Worcester (U.S.), 20, 0; New York, 19, 0.

Knowsley.—Local, 'of Khowsley,' a township in the parish of Huyton, co. Lanc., three miles from Prescot.

1570. Bapt. — William, s. Robert Knowesley: St. Jas. Clerkenwell, i. 6.
1585. Thomas Steere and Isabell Knowsley, d. William Knowsley, late of Denbigh, in Wales: Marriage Lic. (London), i. 142.

1586-7. Henry Knowsley, or Knousley, co. Denbigh: Reg. Univ. Oxf. vol. ii. pt. ii. p. 157.
James Knowsley, of the city of Chester, 1689: Wills at Chester (1681-1700), p. 150.
Plymouth, 2; Exeter, 1.

Knox. — Local, 'of Knocks,' from residence on the lands of Knocks or Knox, co. Renfrew. The Knoxes were of that ilk at an early period, and sometimes wrote themselves of Ranfurly, whence the family of Knox, earls of Ranfurly in Ireland. The great Reformer was of this family (Lower's Patr. Brit. p. 182).

London, 18; Boston (U.S.), 44.

Knyfton; v. Knifton.

Knyvett; v. Knevitt.

Kohn.—Offic. 'the cohen' or priest (Hebrew). A German immigrant.

London, 3; Philadelphia, 45.

Kortright.— ?

Worcestershire Court Dir., 1; New York, 1.

Kramer, Kramar, Kreamer, Kreemer, Kremer.—Occup.; v. Creamer.

London, 1, 0, 0, 0, 0; Philadelphia, 98, 9, 16, 1, 9.

Kripps, Krips; v. Cripps. These are American variants.

Philadelphia, 3, 8.

Kyffin.— ? Bapt. 'the son of Kyffin' (?), seemingly a Welsh personal name, perhaps a variant of Griffin.

1586. Lewis Kyffin, co. Denbigh: Reg. Univ. Oxf. vol. ii. pt. ii. p. 153.
1590. John Kyffin, co. Salop: ibid. p. 178.
1620. Cadwalader Kyffin, Hart-Hall: ibid. i. 293.
1622. Bapt.—Annis, d. Robart Kiffen: St. Jas. Clerkenwell, i. 93.
1639. William Marsh and Anne Kiffin: Marriage Lic. (London), ii. 243.
London, 1; MDB. (co. Denbigh), 5; (co. Carnarvon), 4; Philadelphia, 1; Liverpool, 1.

Kyme; v. Kime.

Kynaston, Kynston, Keniston.—Local 'of Kynaston.' I

cannot find the spot; but it is a Shropshire surname.

Richard de Kynestan, co. Notts, Hen. III-Edw. I. K.

1610. Buried—Anne Byrtles, of Byrtles. A footnote says, 'daughter of Roger Kynaston, of Lightwick, co. Salop': Reg. Prestbury, co. Ches., p. 187.

1510. Bapt. — Thomas, s. Thomas Kynaston : St. Peter, Cornhill, i. 22.
1583. — William, s. Thomas Kynaston : ibid. p. 26.
Charles Kynston, *tripe dresser*, 94, Hill Street, Birmingham : Birmingham Directory (1872).
MDB. (co. Surrey), 2, 0, 0 ; (co. Salop), 7, 0, 0 ; London, 4, 0, 2.

Kynder ; v. Kinder.

Kynman ; v. Kinmond.

Kynnersley ; v. Kinnersley.

Kyte.—Nick. ; v. Kite.

Oxford, 1 ; Boston (U.S.), 3.

L

Labern, Laborn.—Local ; v. Layburn.

Labourer. — Occup. 'the labourer'; cf. Workman, Tasker, &c. I do not think this surname now exists, but it reached the 16th century. v. Labrey.

Avicia Laborer, 1379 : P. T. Yorks. p. 219.
Isabel Laborer, c. 1560. ZZ.
Robert Laborer, ibid.
1618. William Laborer, London : Reg. Univ. Oxf. vol. ii. pt. ii. p. 369.

Labrey, Labbree, Labrie.— Occup. 'the labourer,' q.v. I suspect this is the true origin of this curious surname. Indeed, the following three entries seem conclusive on the point :

Thomas Laborer, Over Burrow, 1599 : Lancashire Wills at Richmond (1457-1680), p. 179.
John Labray, of Burton in Kendall, 1645 : ibid.
Thomas Labrey, of Burton, 1665 : ibid.

The following, too, shows the half-stage :

William Laboura, of Brows in Midleton, 1710 : ibid. (1681-1748), p. 161.

Thus the several stages would be : Laborer, Labberer, Labbere, Labrey, or Labbree ; v. Labourer, for earlier instances.

Manchester, 2, 0, 0 ; Philadelphia, 0, 3, 0 ; New York, 3, 0, 1.

Lach, Lache.—Local, 'at the lache,' from residence beside a lache or lake. No doubt Lache as a surname is lost in Leach, and has materially helped to swell the large list in the Lancashire and Cheshire directories. In proof of this, v. Blackleach, i.e. 'the black lache or lake.'

Henry del Lach, Preston, 1397 : Preston Guild Rolls, p. 6.
Richard Lach, *husbandman*, Preston, 1642 : ibid. p. 100.
Thomas Lache, of Great Harwood, *woollen-weaver*, 1590 : Wills at Chester (1545-1620), p. 116.
Edward Lache, of Facit, co. Lanc., 1603 : ibid.
George Lach, of Bretton, co. Flint, 1620 : ibid. (1621-50), p. 132.
New York, 3, 0 ; Philadelphia, 2, 0.

Lack.—Local, 'at the lake,' from residence thereby ; a variant ; cf. the French Du Lac, and v. Lach and Lake.

William Lack, co. Soms., 1 Edw. III : Kirby's Quest, p. 223.
William Lack, jun., co. Soms., 1 Edw. III : ibid.
1682. Samuel Holleway and Ann Lacke : Marriage Alleg. (Canterbury), p. 113.
1800. Married—John Lack and Frances Moss Parry : St. Geo. Han. Sq. ii. 220.
1807. — Thomas Lack and Eliz. Yeatman : ibid. p. 376.
London, 13 ; Philadelphia, 2 ; New York, 4.

Lackey, Lackie. — ? ——. Mr. Lower says, 'A personal attendant, a footman.' I do not think there is any connexion, but I cannot suggest another derivation.

1750. Married—John Lackie and Rebecca Baxter : St. Geo. Chap. Mayfair, p. 180.
London, 1, 0 ; Philadelphia, 20, 1.

Lacklove.—Nick. 'lack love,' a cold, phlegmatic man, the opposite of 'full love.'

Simon Lakelove, co. Bedf., 1273. A.

Lacy, Lacey, Lassey, Lassy. —Local, 'de Laci,' from some place of that name in Normandy. Ilbert de Laci (Domesday). The surname has spread widely, and has representatives in every grade of

society. The variants Lassey and Lassy are met by early forms of a similar character.

Gilbert de Lascy, co. Salop, 1273. A.
Walter de Laci, co. Salop. ibid.
Robertus Lascy, 1379 : P. T. Yorks. p. 121.
Isabella Lassy, 1379 : ibid.
1571. Peter Lacye and Hester Shawe : Marriage Lic. (London), i. 48.
1761. Married—Thomas Lasey and Mary Vipoint : St. Geo. Han. Sq. i. 107.
London, 16, 17, 0, 0 ; MDB. (West Rid. Yorks), 7, 0, 4, 0 ; Philadelphia, 19, 34, 0, 1.

Ladbrook, Ladbrooke. — Local, 'of Ladbroke,' a parish on the road from Oxford to Coventry, co. Warwick.

Juliana de Lathebroc, co. Oxf., 1273. A.
Henry de Lodbroc, co. Warw., ibid.
1618. Robert Ladbrooke, co. Warw. Reg. Univ. Oxf. vol. ii. pt. ii. p. 368.
1627. Married—Cristofer Martyn and Margret Lagbrooke (sic) : St. Jas. Clerkenwell, iii. 58.
1662. Buried—Thomas Ladbroke, servant to Mr. Savage Barrell, *hosier* : St. Dionis Backchurch, p. 234.
London, 3, 0 ; MDB. (co. Warwick), 0, 1.

Ladbury. — Local, 'of Lathbury,' q.v.

Ladd.—Offic. 'the lad,' i.e. the servant, the young servitor, the page.

Roger Ladde, co. Hunts, 1273. A.
Thomas Ladde, co. Camb., ibid.
John le Ladde, 1322. M.
John le Ladde, C. R., 8 Edw. III.
1587. William Callaway and Joane Lad, *widow* : Marriage Lic. (London), i. 101.
1688. Bapt.—James, son of John Ladd : St. Jas. Clerkenwell, i. 329.
London, 5 ; New York, 15.

Laddington.—Local. A variant of Loddington or Luddington, q.v.
MDB. (co. Northampton), 1.

Lade.—Local, 'at the lade' or 'lathe,' equivalent to Barnes; v. Barne (1). 'Lathe, a barn. North England' (Halliwell). 'Berne, or lathe' (Prompt. Parv.). 'Grangia, lathe, or grange' (Ortus). 'Lathe, *apotheca, horreum*' (Cath. Ang.); v. Leathes.

'Why ne had thou put the capel in the lathe?' Chaucer, The Reeve's Tale.
John de la Lade, co. Lanc., 1273. A.
Richard de la Lade, C. R., 28 Edw. I.
Edmund de la Layde, C. R., 17 Edw. I.
Thomas atte Lathe, C. R., 16 Ric. II.
Hugh de la Lade, Fines Roll, 11 Edw. I.
1729. Buried—Thomas Lade: Canterbury Cathedral, p. 138.
London, 1.

Ladychapman. — Occup. A curious compound; v. Chapman.

William Ladychapman, C. R., 25 Edw. III.

Ladyman.—Occup. 'the lady's man,' i.e. the servant of the lady, i.e. the baron's or squire's wife; cf. Matthewman, Addyman, Priestman, Vickerman. The origin is easily settled by a comparison of the first batch of entries, all but one being recorded in close juxtaposition.

Ricardus Ledyman, 1379: P. T. Yorks. p. 233.
Johanna ye Laydimayden, 1379: ibid. p. 33.
Johannes Serve-ledy, 1379: ibid. p. 231.
Willelmus Masterman, 1379: ibid.
Willelmus Halle-man, 1379: ibid. p. 232.
Alan Ladyman, temp. Edw. II: GGG. p. 286.
1581. John Ladyman and Margarett Collsell: Marriage Lic. (London), i. 102.
1700. Bapt.—Dianah, d. Charles Ladyman: St. Jas. Clerkenwell, i. 389.
1787. Married—Thomas Ladyman and Ann Ludlow: St. Geo. Han. Sq. i. 403. Liverpool, 2.

Laidler, Laddler. — Local. Variants of the Scotch Laidlaw.

1752. Married—James Sams and Jane Ladler: St. Geo. Chap. Mayfair, p. 218.
MDB. (co. Northumberland), 3, 0; (co. Cumberland), 0, 1; New York, 1, 0.

Laird.—Occup. or offic. 'the lord'; v. Lord. A Scotch form; cf. Layard.

1781. Married—John Laird and Eliz. Monk: St. Geo. Han. Sq. i. 318.
1782. — John Laierd and Catherine Jones: ibid. p. 331.
London, 3; New York, 17.

Lait, Layt, Laight.—Local, 'at the lathe' or 'barn' (v. Lade); cf. Leathes.

Thomas atte Lathe, C. R., 16 Ric. II.
Sibota at Layte, 1379: P. T. Yorks. p. 161.
1746. Married—John Russell and Ann Laight: St. Geo. Chap. Mayfair, p. 73.
London, 2, 1, 0; New York, 0, 0, 3.

Laithwaite; v. Lewthwaite.

Lake.—Local, 'at the lake,' from residence thereby; v. Lach and Lack.

William atte Lake, co. Oxf., 1273. A.
William de la Lake, co. Salop, ibid.
William de la Lake, Fines Roll, 11 Edw. I.
Philip atte Lake, co. Soms., 1 Edw. III: Kirby's Quest, p. 257.
William of the Lake, Pardons Roll, 6 Ric. II.
Arthur Lake, co. Southampt., 1588: Reg. Univ. Oxf. vol. ii. pt. ii. p. 165.
1620. Bapt.—Anne, d. Francis Lake: St. Jas. Clerkenwell, i. 87.
London, 33; New York, 23.

Lakeman. — (1) Local, 'of Lakenham,' a parish in co. Norfolk. This corruption is one of many of a similar character; cf. Buckman for Buckenham, Putman for Putnam (Puttenham), Swetman for Swetnam (Swetenham), Deadman for Debnam (Debenham), &c. Lower's suggestion that it means the lake man, the man who lived by the lake, is not supported by any proof. (2) ? Bapt. 'the son of Lacman,' an old personal name. Lacman assisted Duke Richard of Normandy against Odo of Chartres (Freeman, Norm. Conq. i. 456). Lacman was king of Man, 1075–1093 (ibid. ii. 632). A Scandinavian name corresponding to Engl. Lawman. But I can find no corroborative evidence in the rolls of the 12th, 13th, and 14th centuries.

Reginald de Lakeham, co. Norf., 1273. A.
Geoffrey de Lakenham, co. Herts, 20 Edw. I. R.
Simon de Lakenham, vicar of Tibenham, co. Norf., 1394: FF. v. 278.
William Lakenham, rector of South Rungton, co. Norf., 1511: ibid. vii. 402.

For another probable variant of Lakenham, v. Larkman.

London, 3; New York, 1; Boston (U.S.), 11.

Lamacraft.—Local, 'of Lambcroft,' a hamlet in the parish of Kelsterne, co. Lincoln. For suffix -craft instead of -croft, v. Craft and Crafter. There is one drawback to this derivation. Devonshire seems to be the home of the name. Probably there is or was a Lambcroft in that country. The second a is intrusive; cf. Ottaway and Greenaway for Ottway and Greenway.

1647. Bapt.—Mary, d. Michael Lamcroft: St. Jas. Clerkenwell, i. 167.
1648. — Christopher, s. Michael Lamecraft: ibid. p. 169.
London, 1; MDB. (co. Devon), 1; Upton Pyne (Devon), 2; Exeter, 1.

Lamb, Lambe.—(1) Nick. 'the lamb'; cf. Bull, Bullock, Fox. Affixed to one of a mild, inoffensive character.

William le Lambe, co. Camb., 1273. A.
Richard le Lam', co. Northampt., ibid.
Ingrida Lomb, co. Hunts, ibid.

(2) Bapt. 'the son of Lambert,' from Lamb the nick., whence such diminutives as Lamb-in and Lamb-kin (q.v.) were found.

1558. William Justyce and Jane Lambe: Marriage Lic. (London), i. 19.
1665. Buried—Ann Lam, servant to Mr. Clark: St. Dionis Backchurch, p. 236.
London, 57, 4; New York, 60, 0; Philadelphia, 76, 1.

Lambard, Lambarde.—Bapt. 'the son of Lambert,' q.v. It might be thought that this was a corrupted form of Lombard (q.v.), a native of Lombardy, but the evidence is entirely in favour of the personal name Lambert; cf. Hibbard for Hibbert. For a Saxon origin, v. Lambert (1), and cf. Coward for Cowherd.

Hugo Lambard, co. York, 1273. A.

Lambert Godfrey, a local justice, thus describes himself:

'Lambarde Godfrey, 1654, Maidstone, co. Kent': Burn's History of Parish Registers, p. 168.
1581. Anthony Lambarte, *silk weaver*, and Awdrie Stone: Marriage Lic. (London), p. 102.
1596. William Lambard, co. Bucks: Reg. Univ. Oxf. vol. ii. pt. ii. p. 216.
1764. Married—William Lambart and Ann Batty: St. Geo. Han. Sq. i. 138.

1784. Married—John Hallward and Mary Lambard: St. Geo. Han. Sq. i. 364. London, 1, 0; MDB. (co. Kent), 1, 2; New York, 1, 0.

Lambelet. — Bapt. 'the son of Lambert,' from the nick. Lamb (q.v.), and dim. Lambelot; cf. Hewlett and Ablett for Hughelot and Abelot.

1772. Married—John Lambelet and Sarah Starbuck: St. Geo. Han. Sq. i. 223.
New York, 1.

Lambert. — (1) Occup. 'the lamb-herd'; cf. Calvert, Coward, Stoddart, Swinnart, and Shepherd; v. Hind. Most unquestionably many of our Lamberts represent the occupation of lamb-herd. The Yorkshire Calverts all stand for the old occupative calveherd.

Johannes le Lambehirde, 1310: Whitaker's Craven, p. 462.
John Lambherde, C. R., 5 Edw. IV.
Johannes Lamberd, 1379: P. T. Yorks. p. 272.
Thomas Lambhyrd, 1379: ibid.

The two last named are set down together.

Willelmus Lamhird, 1379: P. T. Yorks. p. 183.
Barbara Lamheard, 1596: St. Dionis Backchurch (London), p. 89.

(2) Bapt. 'the son of Lambert.'

Lambert Suet, C. R., 36 Hen. III.
Adam fil. Lamberti, co. Linc., 1273. A.
Roger Lambert, co. Norf., ibid.
Stephen Lambert, co. Oxf., ibid.
William Lambryt, co. Hunts, ibid.
London, 77; New York, 66.

Lambertson, Lamberson.— Bapt. 'the son of Lambert.' I am not certain whether or not this surname still exists in England.

John Lambertson, son of Nicholas Lambertson, 1603, co.: Exchequer Depositions, L. & C. R. S. p. 11.

The above lived at Warton, Lancaster. A century later we find the name, slightly abbreviated, in a neighbouring parish:

Thomas Lamberson, of Bolton-le-Sands, 1715: Lancashire Wills at Richmond (1681–1748), p. 162.
John Lambertson, of Warton, 1647: Lancashire Wills at Richmond (1457–1680), p. 180.
Agnes Lambertson, of Bolton-le-Sands, 1661: ibid.
George Lamberson, of Warton, 1637: ibid.

1559. Buried—Richard Lamerson: St. Peter, Cornhill, i. 114.
New York, 1, 4.

Lambeth, Lamberth, Lambirth.—Local, 'of Lambeth,' a parish in co. Surrey.

Richard de Lambeth, citizen of London, 5 Edw. III: FF. x. 10.
1786. Married—Thomas Lamberth and Esther Hagar: St. Geo. Han. Sq. i. 394.
1789. — William Ward and Abigail Lambeth: ibid. ii. 18.
1796. — William Gray and Mary Lambeth: ibid. p. 158.
London, 2, 2, 0; Boston (U.S.), 0, 0, 3.

Lambin, Lampin, Lamin, Laming, Lammin, Lamming, Lamping. — Bapt. 'the son of Lambert,' from the nick. Lamb and dim. Lamb-in; cf. viol-in, Rob-in, Col-in. The g in Laming, &c., is excrescent (cf. Jennings), and the p for b in Lampin is a common exchange; cf. Lampson and Lampett.

Lambyn Clay played before the King at Westminster, at the great festival in 1306 (Popular Music of the Olden Time, Chappell, i. 29). The Flemish Lambert had a great influence on English nomenclature for a time, nearly as great, in fact, as Baldwin.

John Lambyn, co. Camb., 1273. A.
Henry Lambin, London, 20 Edw. I. R.
Edmund Lambin, London, ibid.
William Lambyn, 1379: P. T. Yorks. p. 48.

Later the b has been dropped, and Laming or Lamming are the usual forms, especially in co. Lincoln, where Lambert (owing to Flemish immigration) was exceedingly common in the surname period. As an interesting proof of this, v. Lammiman.

1683. Married—Roger Laming and Rachel Ball: St. Michael, Cornhill, p. 43.
London, 1, 0, 0, 6, 1, 1, 1; MDB. (Lincoln), 0, 0, 0, 8, 3, 6, 0; Boston (U.S.) (Laming), 3.

Lambkin, Lampkin, Lambking, Lamkin.—Bapt. 'the son of Lambert,' from the nick. Lamb and dim. Lamb-kin. A Flemish introduction, no doubt; cf. Wilkin, Simpkin, &c. The g in Lambking is an excrescence, as in Jennings.

Lambekin de Lamburne, London, 1273. A.

Lambekin de Carsell, London, ibid.
Lamkynus de Braban, 1379: P. T. Yorks. p. 250.
Lambekyn fil. Eli. C.
Lamkyn Loker. O.
Lambekin Taborer: Wardrobe Account, 48 Edw. III–1 Ric. II. 41/10.
1608–9. William Money and Christian Lamkin: Marriage Lic. (London), i. 311.
1643. Married—Henry Palmer and Eleanor Lamkin: St. Dionis Backchurch, p. 24.
Philadelphia, 0, 0, 1, 0; Boston (U.S.), 0, 0, 0, 4.

Lambole, Lamboll, Lamble. —Local, 'of Lampole.' I do not know where the locality is. Of course the suffix is -pole = pool.

John Lampole, co. Norf., 1366: FF. vii. 242.

The final d in the following name is an excrescence:

1610. John Lambold, co. Berks: Reg. Univ. Oxf. vol. ii. pt. ii. p. 317.
1797. Married—Richard Lamble and Mary Weston: St. Geo. Han. Sq. ii. 163.
1807. — James Bush and Rebecca Lamble: ibid. p. 369.
London, 1, 1, 1.

Lamborn, Lambourn, Lambourne.—Local, 'of Lambourn,' (1) a parish in co. Berks, near Hungerford; (2) a parish in co. Essex, near Romford (for suffix, v. Burn).

William de Lamburne, co. Suff., 1273. A.
Alicia de Lamburne, co. Oxf., ibid.
Lambekin de Lamburne, London, ibid.
John de Lamborne, co. Soms., 1 Edw. III: Kirby's Quest, p. 85.
1525–6. John Lamburn and Alice —— (blank): Marriage Lic. (London), i. 5.
1583. William Vincent and Anne Lamborne (co. Bucks): ibid. p. 125.
1663. Henry Goddard and Margaret Lamburne: Marriage Alleg. (Canterbury), p. 87.
London, 1, 1, 0; MDB. (co. Bucks), 0, 2, 1; (co. Oxford), 2, 0, 1; Philadelphia, 2, 0, 0.

Lambshead, Lamzead. — ? Local. 'A Scottish local surname' (Lower). This may be so, but all my directory examples are from cos. Devon and Cornwall; cf. Sheepshead. Lamzead is a curious variant.

Agnes Lambesheved, co. Hunts, 1273. A.
Ilsington (co. Devon), 4, 0; MDB. (co. Devon), 4, 1.

Lambson, Lampson, Lamson.—Bapt. 'the son of Lambert,' from Lamb, the popular nick. of Lambert; v. Lambertson.

Godwin Lambesune, co. Berks, Hen. III-Edw. I. K.
Johannes Lambeson, 1379: P. T. Yorks. p. 253.
Ricardus Lambeson, 1379: ibid.
Thomas Lamson, C. R., 4 Edw. IV.
William Lampson, temp. Eliz. ZZ.
Edward Lamson. FF.
1626. Married—Clement Lamson and Francis Spinke: St. Michael, Cornhill, p. 24.
1689. Buried—Thomas Lambson, *mariner*: St. Dionis Backchurch, p. 256.
1770. Married—George Lamson and Catherine Lovett: St. Geo. Han. Sq. i. 202.
London, 2, 1, 1; Boston (U.S.), 0, 1, 32.

Lambton, Lampton.—Local, 'of Lambton,' a township in the parish of Chester-le-Street, co. Durham.

1461. William Lambton, master of Balliol College: Reg. Univ. Oxf. i. 26.
1663. Ralph Marshall and Isabell Lambton: Marriage Lic. (Faculty Office), p. 75.
1732. Married—Edward Lambton and Harriet Santlow: St. Jas. Clerkenwell, iii. 260.
MDB. (North Rid. Yorks), 1, 0; (co. Durham), 0, 1.

Lamerton.—Local, 'of Lamerton,' a parish in co. Devon, three miles from Tavistock.
MDB. (co. Cornwall), 2; London, 1.

Lamin, Laming; v. Lambin.

Lamkin; v. Lambkin.

Lammas.—Local, 'of Lammas,' a parish in dioc. of Norwich. Not from the season or festival of Lammas, as is the case with Christmas, Nowell, Pentecost, and Whitsunday, q.v. The first three instances probably concern the same individual.

Richard de Lammesse, London, 1273. A.
Richard Lammasse, co. Camb., ibid.
Richard de Lamnesse, co. Camb., ibid.
Richard de Lammesse, prior of Austin Friars, Norwich, 1367: FF. iv. 91.
Thomas Lammas, co. Norf.: FF.
Daniel Lammas, 1620: St. Mary Aldermary, p. 14.
1642. Married—John Lamas and Sara Donaldson: St. Jas. Clerkenwell, i. 75.
London, 2; Oxford, 3; MDB. (Norfolk), 1.

Lammiman, Lamminam, Lamyman. — Occup. 'the man of Lammin,' i.e. Lambert's servant.

All these forms are peculiar to co. Lincoln, where Lammin, Lamin, and Lamming are also common; cf. Matthewman, Addyman, Ladyman, &c. This class of surname is largely represented in our directories. Lambert, swelled by Flemish immigration, was a very familiar fontal name in the Eastern Counties; v. Lambin.

1542. Buried—Maye Lamymam (sic): St. Peter, Cornhill, i. 106.
MDB. (Lincoln), 3, 1, 8.

Lammin(g; v. Lambin.

Lampard, Lampert. — (1) Bapt. 'the son of Lambert,' q.v. (2) Local, 'of Lamport,' q.v.

1620. Richard Crolley and Eliz. Lampert: Marriage Lic. (London), p. 94.
1683. John Lampard and Ann Cockquerell: Marriage Alleg. (Canterbury), p. 146.
1745. Bapt.—John, s. Thomas Lampard: Reg. Stourton, co. Wilts, p. 30.
1770.— Edward, s. Thomas Lampard: ibid. p. 37.
London, 4, 1; Boston (U.S.), 5, 0.

Lampet, Lampitt. — Local, ' de Lampet.' I cannot find the spot. Probably it lies in Normandy.

1356. William de Lampet: FF. v. 328.
1444. Ralph Lampet, bailiff of Yarmouth: ibid. xi. 325.
'To Julian Lampit, recluse at Carhoe, 10s.,' Will of Sir Thomas Erpingham, 1427: ibid. iv. 39.
1621. William Lampit, co. Worc.: Reg. Univ. Oxf. vol. ii. pt. ii. p. 400.
The Vicar of Ulverston, William Lampett, was one of the dispossessed ministers in 1662. Probably the last entry refers to the same individual.
Leamington, 1, 0; MDB. (co. Essex), 1, 0; (co. Worc.), 0, 3.

Lampin(g.—Bapt.; v. Lambin.

Lampkin; v. Lambkin.

Lamplough, Lamplugh. — Local, ' of Lamplugh,' a parish in co. Cumberland.

Robert de Lamplugh, temp. Hen. II: E. and F. (co. Cumb.), p. 29.
Adam de Lamplugh, temp. John: ibid.
Johannes de Lamplogh, co. Cumb., 1319. M.
George Lamplugh, or Lampleughe, co. Cumb., 1588: Reg. Univ. Oxf. vol. ii. pt. ii. p. 164.
1655-6. Married—Thomas Lamplugh and Katherine Meuerell: St. Dionis Backchurch, p. 31.

London, 4, 1; MDB. (East Rid. Yorks), 10, 8; Philadelphia, 0, 3.

Lamport, Lampert.—Local, (1) 'of Lamport,' a parish in dioc. of Peterborough; (2) 'of Landport,' a parish in dioc. of Winchester. Lower adds, 'An estate now called Landport at Lewes, Sussex, had owners called Lamport, temp. Edward III.' One instance below agrees with this statement.

Richard de Lamport, co. Wilts, 1273. A.
Walter Lamport, co. Sussex, ibid.
1789. Married—Joseph Hughes and Eliz. Lamport: St. Geo. Han. Sq. ii. 33.
London, 1, 1; MDB. (co. Surrey), 2, 0; New York, 2, 4.

Lamprey, Lampray.—Local, 'of Lamprey,' evidently a Devonshire name. No more a fish-name than is Salmon, or Chubb, or Spratt, or Herring. The same individual is thus referred to:

William de Lanteprey, co. Devon, 1273. A.
William Lampreye, co. Devon, ibid.
Simon de Lampree, co. Devon, Hen. III-Edw. I. K.
Devon Court Dir., 1, 0; MDB. (co. Warwick), 0, 1; Boston (U.S.), 11, 0.

Lampson, Lamson.—Bapt.; v. Lambson.

Lamyman; v. Lammiman.

Lancashire. — Local, 'from Lancashire'; cf. Wiltshire, Derbyshire, &c. Oddly enough we often find these county names well represented in the very shires which the bearers had left to seek their fortunes. The explanation is, these wanderers did not go far, probably over the border only, into the next county, and their sons or grandsons were likely to return, bearing the surname that had been given to them in the place of their brief sojourn.

1604. Robert Lancashire, of Syddall: Wills at Chester (1545-1620), p. 117.
1625. James Lancashire, of Blakeley: ibid. (1621-50), p. 132.
1693. Bapt.—Ellen, d. Robert Lankishire: St. Antholin (London), p. 108.
London, 1; Manchester, 9.

Lancaster, Lankester. — Local, 'of Lancaster,' the well-known county town of Lancashire.

Willelmus de Lancastre, 1379: P. T. Yorks. p. 99.

H h

1454. Robert Lankester, B.C.L.: Reg. Univ. Oxf. i. 22.

1568–9. Walter Lancaster and Magdalen Shinghleton, *widow*: Marriage Lic. (London), i. 41.

Four varieties of spelling occur in the following three entries relating to one and the same family. The clerk started well, but fell off:

1598. Married—Christofer Lancaster and Mary Cripps: St. Antholin(London), p. 39.

1600. Bapt.—Robart, s. Cristifer Lanckister: ibid. p. 40.

1602.—Ane Lankkester, d. Crestofer Lankester: ibid. p. 41.

London, 21, 5; New York, 8, 0.

Lance. — Bapt. 'the son of Lancelot,' from nick. Lance (v. Yonge, ii. 120), not from Lawrence. The nick. form is found for centuries on the Anglo-Scottish border, where Lancelot was one of the favourite font-names. The same individual is described under both guises in the two following entries:

Lancelot Hodshon, 1663: KKK. iv. 299.

Lance Hodgshon, 1663: ibid.

Mabil Lance, co. Oxf., 1273. A.

Johanna Lance, co. Oxf., ibid.

Lance Car, 1516: QQQ. p. ix.

Lance Newton, 1663: KKK. iv. 286.

1692. Bapt.—Mary, d. Richard Lance: St. Jas. Clerkenwell, p. 345.

London, 8; New York, 1; Philadelphia, 17.

Lancelin.—Bapt. 'the son of Ancell'; O.F. L'ancell; dims. Lancel-in and Lancel-ot. v. Ancell and Aslin.

'Ivo, the Chaplain and his homagers, and the homage of Master Anseline, and Hubert de Shimpling,' 1266 : FF. i. 208.

Lancelyn de Pira, co. Essex, 1273. A.

John Lancelin, co. Oxf., ibid.

William Lancelyn, co. Hunts, ibid.

Henry Launcelyn, co. Linc., ibid.

Roger Lanseleyene, Fines Roll, 12 Edw. I.

Aunselen de Gise, *miles*, 7 Edw. II : v. Pedigree of Gyse, Visitation of Gloucestershire, 1623, p. 72.

Beauma, uxor. Aunselin, 7 Edw. II: ibid.

'The oath of John Launcelyn was taken at Chester concerning the property of Margaret de Arderne, Sept. 29, 1423': East Cheshire, i. 323.

Jane Lancellen, of Neston, *widow*, 1605: Wills at Chester (1545–1620), p. 117.

Lancelot, Launcelotte. — Bapt. 'the son of Lancelot.' Very common in Cumberland and N. England generally for many centuries. The nick. was Lance, q.v. For further information, v. Lancelin.

Acelot Bryon, co. Camb., 1273. A.

Acelota Palmer, co. Hunts, ibid.

Lanslot Colynson, 1509: Reg. Univ. Oxf. i. 65.

Lancilot Colynson, co. York, 1513. W. 11.

Lancelot Hethe, 1548: St. Dionis Backchurch, p. 74.

Lancelot Hutton, 1640: VVV. p. 502.

Lancelot Crow, 1612: ibid. p. 491.

1568. Bapt. — William, s. Fryseley Launcelott: St. Michael, Cornhill, p. 84.

John Lancelott, of Neston, 1618: Wills at Chester (1545–1620) p. 117.

Hugh Lancelott, of Little Neston, *husbandman* : ibid. (1660–80), p. 162,

London, 2, 0; MDB. (co. Chester), 0, 1.

Lanchester.—Local, 'of Lanchester,' a parish in co. Durham.

Roger de Lancastre, co. Northumb., 1273. A.

1750. Married—James Pickernell and Eliz. Lanchester: St. Geo. Chap. Mayfair, p. 182.

1790. — James Lancester and Mary Dorrington: St. Geo. Han. Sq. ii. 35.

MDB. (co. Suff.), 2; London, 2.

Land.—Local, 'at the land,' from residence beside the *launde* or land, the open wood ; v. Landman, and Lund or Lowndes. The modern word is *lawn*.

William de la Lande, co. Oxf., 1273. A.

Jacob de la Lande, co. Warwick, 20 Edw. I. R.

Richard de la Lande. B.

William atte Land, c. 1300. M.

1579. Married — Richard Land and Eliz. Fuller: St. Jas. Clerkenwell, iii. 8.

1651. — Hugh Joanes and Susan Land: St. Peter, Cornhill, i. 258.

1741. Buried—James Land : Reg. Stourton, co. Wilts, p. 78.

London, 9; New York, 2; Philadelphia, 31.

Lander, Landor. — Occup. 'the lavender'; early contracted to Launder, q.v., and later on to Lander or (as in the poet's case) Landor.

1592. Buried—Thomas Lander : St. Antholin (London), p. 35.

1688. Bapt.—Ann, d. Edward Lander: St. Jas. Clerkenwell, p. 131.

1710. — Mary, d. Ephraim Lander : St. Michael, Cornhill, p. 166.

London, 7, 0 ; MDB. (co. Stafford), 6, 5; New York, 19, 0.

Landless. — Local. In the Modern Domesday Book for co. Lancaster occurs 'Ralph Landless,

Blackpool, 25 acres, 2 roods, 2 perches.' This has a very contradictory look, but no doubt the surname is of local origin, the suffix being -*lees* ; v. Lees.

MDB. (co. Lancaster), 1; Manchester, 1; Philadelphia, 3.

Landman.—Occup. 'the landman,' one who looked after the *launde* or open wood, especially the beasts of chase that found covert around ; v. Land, Lund, &c.

Richard le Landman, c. 1300. M.

1609. Richard Landeman and Martha Darby : Marriage Lic. (London), i. 316.

1623. John Landman, living in Virginia : Hotten's Lists of Emigrants, p. 172.

New York, 6; Philadelphia, 1.

Landor.—Occup. ; v. Lander.

Landry.—Local ; v. Laundry.

Lane. — Local, 'at the lane,' from residence therein ; v. Lone. Naturally this surname is well represented in our directories all over the country.

William atte Lane, C. R., 48 Hen. III.

Robert de la Lane, co. Devon, 1273. A.

Cecil in the Lane, co. Oxf., ibid.

Emma a la Lane, co. Oxf., ibid.

Jurdan atte Lane, co. Soms, 1 Edw. III : Kirby's Quest, p. 257.

1575. John Lane and Johanna Noxe : Marriage Lic. (London), i. 66.

1580. William Lane, co. Berks: Reg. Univ. Oxf. vol. ii. pt. ii. p. 94.

London, 81; New York, 150.

Laner, Lanyer.—Occup. 'the laner,' a wool-merchant, a woolcomber. Fr. *lainier*, a wool-stapler, a wool-sorter. With Lanyer, cf. Sawyer or Bowyer.

Bartholomew le Laner, co. Hunts, 1273. A.

Symon le Laner, co. Hunts, ibid.

William Lannator, co. Wilts, ibid.

Ivo le Laner, C. R., 19 Edw. I.

Richard Lanour, co. Soms., 1 Edw. III : Kirby's Quest, p. 131.

Walter de (? le) Laner, 2 Edw. III : Freemen of York, i. 24.

John le Laner. T.

1567. Evan Forges and Joanna Lanyer : Marriage Lic. (London), i. 36.

1645. Buried—Æmilia Laneire : St. Jas. Clerkenwell, iv. 263.

Lang, Lange.—Nick. 'the lang,' i.e. the long, the tall. Hence such nicks. as Langbachelor, and such local surnames as Langabeer, Langdale, Langford, Langham, Langley, Langmead, Langridge, Langston, or Langton, q.v.; cf. Strang for Strong.

Hamo le Lang, c. 1300. M.
John le Lange. L.
Richard le Lange, co. Soms., 1 Edw.
III : Kirby's Quest, p. 266.
Ricardus Lang, 1379: P. T. Yorks.
p. 36.
1639. Buried—'Ellis Lange, brought
home from Tyborne' (!): St. Jas. Clerkenwell, iv. 238.
1665. — Sarah Lang : ibid. p. 367.
London, 19, 7 ; New York, 162, 63.

Langabeer.—Local, 'of Langabeer.' 'In this neighbourhood
(Lidford, co. Devon) we find Langabeer, Beardon, Beer Alston, Beer
Ferrers' (Taylor's Words and
Places, p. 179). The meaning of
this place-word is the long byre,
the long dwelling, or farm ; cf.
Scotch *byre*, a stall, Icelandic *boer*,
a farmstead. The *a* is intrusive for
the sake of euphony ; cf. Greenaway, Ottaway, or Hathaway.
London, 1.

Langbachelor. — Nick. 'the
long bachelor.' The instance below is amusing, with its intrusive
a ; cf. Greenaway for Greenway ;
v. Bacheller.
William le Langabacheler, co. Soms.,
1 Edw. III : Kirby's Quest, p. 180.

Langcake. — ! Nick. ; cf.
Blanchpain, Whitbread, Cakebread, &c. Seemingly a N. England
name.
1750. Married—Thomas Langcake and
Mary Wilkinson : St. Geo. Chap. Mayfair,
p. 169.
1784. — James Wyer and Sarah Langcake, of Greenwich : St. Geo. Han. Sq.
i. 364.
London, 1 ; MDB. (co. Cumb.), 4 ;
New York, 1 ; Boston (U.S.), 1.

Langdale, Langdell.—Local,
'of Langdale,' a parish in co. Westmoreland.
Robert de Langedale, co. Westmoreland, 20 Edw. I. R.
Alban Langdale, 1554 : Reg. Univ.
Oxf. i. 224.
1673. Married—Edward Langdale and
Eliz. Landoys : St. Michael, Cornhill,
p. 40.
London, 4, 1 ; Philadelphia, 1, 1.

Langdon. — Local, 'of Langdon.' Parishes in cos. Kent and
Essex. The Kent Langdon is
divided into East and West Langdon.
Bartholomew de Langedon, co. Essex,
1273. A.

Cecil de Langedon, co. Kent, ibid.
William de Langedone, co. Essex, ibid.
John de Langedone, co. Soms., 1 Edw.
III : Kirby's Quest, p. 177.
1587. Robert Langdon and Alice
Garshe, *widow*: Marriage Lic. (Lon-
don), i. 161.
1791. Married — George Stillors and
Ann Langdon : St. Geo. Han. Sq. ii. 60.
London, 9 ; New York, 16.

Langfit.—Local, 'of Langford.'
A corruption.
William de Langfit, co. Northumb., 20
Edw. I. R.
1586. William Dickenson, *damasker*,
and Eliz. Langfitt, relict of Peter Langfitt, *cordwainer*: Marriage Lic. (London),
i. 152.

Langford.—Local, 'of Lang-
ford' (i.e. the long ford). Eight
parishes are so called in various
counties.
Nigel de Langeford, co. Derby, 1273. A.
John de Langeford, co. Essex, ibid.
Beatrice de Langeford, co. Oxf., ibid.
John de Langefford, co. Wilts, ibid.
1309. Thomas de Langeford, vicar of
Swaffham, co. Norf.: FF. vi. 224.
Ralph de Langeford, co. Soms., 1 Edw.
III : Kirby's Quest, p. 85.
John Langforde, co. Oxf., 1581 : Reg.
Univ. Oxf. vol. ii. pt. ii. p. 110.
1609. William Langford and Margaret
Deux: Marriage Lic. (London), i. 316.
1718. Married—John Langford and
Susanna Barton: St. Dionis Backchurch,
p. 59.
London, 16 ; Boston (U.S.), 8.

Langham, Lanham.—Local,
'of Langham.' Parishes in diocs.
Ely, Peterborough, St. Albans, and
Norwich.
William de Langham, co. Suff., 1273. A.
Henry de Longeham, co. Linc., ibid.
Dionis de Langham, co. Norf., ibid.
1575-6. Henry Langham and Jane
Northroffe, *widow*, Marriage Lic. (London), p. 68.
1621. Edward Langham, co. Northampt.:
Reg. Univ. Oxf. vol. ii. pt. ii. p. 389.
1647-8. Married— Thomas Langham
and Sarah Turgis : St. Dionis Backchurch, p. 25.
London, 7, 3 ; Oxford, 3, 1 ; New York,
3, 0.

Langhorn. — ? Local. At first
sight this might seem to be a nick.
for a huntsman, &c., from the
length of the horn he carried ; cf.
Shakespear, Wagstaff, &c. Probably, however, it is local, from
some piece of land so called from
its shape. Then the surname would
originally be 'at the lang horn,'
from residence thereby ; cf. Harts-

horn, which is local. Also v.
Horn.
1581. William Langhorne, co. Cumb. :
Reg. Univ. Oxf. vol. ii. pt. ii. p. 102.
1648. Christopher Conyers and Eliz.
Langhorne, of Putney : Marriage Lic.
(Faculty Office), p. 40.
1795. Married—Samuel Langhorn and
Mary Jones: St. Geo. Han. Sq. ii. 129.
London, 3 ; Philadelphia, 1 ; New
York, 1.

Langland.—Local, 'of Lang-
land.' I cannot find the spot.
Hugh de Langelonde, co. Soms., 1
Edw. III : Kirby's Quest, p. 249.
London, 1.

Langley.—Local, 'of Langley.'
Parishes in diocs. Canterbury,
Norwich, Worcester, and Bath and
Wells.
Thomas de Langeleye, co. Oxf., 1273. A.
Peter de Langlege, co. Wilts, ibid.
Ralph de Langleye, co. Kent, ibid.
Geoffrey Langleg, C. R., 8 Edw. I.
Richard de Langela, co. Soms., 1 Edw.
III : Kirby's Quest, p. 259.
1538-9. Married—Petter Skreven and
Alys Langlee : St. Dionis Backchurch,
p. 1.
1581. William Price and Dorothy
Langley, *widow*: Marriage Lic. (London),
i. 102.
— Thomas Langley, co. Salop : Reg.
Univ. Oxf. vol. vii. pt. ii. p. 100.
London, 28 ; Boston (U.S.), 32.

Langman.—Nick. 'the long
man' ; v. Shortman ; cf. Long-
fellow, Long, and Longman.
William Langman, co. Soms., 1 Edw.
III : Kirby's Quest, p. 82.
William Langeman, C. R., 7 Ric. II.
1729. Married—Gamaliel Maud and
Alice Langman : St. Jas. Clerkenwell,
iii. 256.
London, 3 ; MDB. (co. Devon), 1 ;
New York, 1 ; Philadelphia, 3.

**Langmead, Langmaid,
Longmate.** — Local, 'of Lang-
mead,' i.e. the long meadow.
Langmaid shows the usual later
tendency towards an imitative cor-
ruption. Seemingly a Devonshire
surname, judging by the directories.
And yet it is clear that there was
another Langmead in the Eastern
counties. Longmate is a palpable
corruption. Cf. Broadmeadow.
Geoffrey de Longo Prato, co. Camb.,
1273. A.
John de Longo Prato, co. Camb., ibid.
Richard Langemede, co. Soms., 1
Edw. III : Kirby's Quest, p. 240.
Hugh Langemede, co. Soms., 1 Edw.
III : ibid. p. 241.

1802. Married—James Longmate and Eliz. Callender: St. Geo. Han. Sq. ii. 270.
1808. — James Langmead and Maria Brien: ibid. p. 392.
London, 4, 0, 0; Devon Court Dir., 4, 1, 0; MDB. (co. Lincoln), 0, 0, 2; Boston (U.S.), 0, 4, 0.

Langridge, Langrish, Langrick.—Local, (1) 'of Langridge,' a parish in co. Somerset, near Bath; (2) 'of Langrish,' a tithing in the parish of Petersfield, co. Hants. These separate surnames are now inextricably mixed. With Langrick, cf. Longrigg; v. Longridge.
Stephen de Langerigg', co. Kent, 1273. A.
Robert de Langerich, co. Herts, 20 Edw. I. R.
Walter de Langereche, co. Kent, Hen. III-Edw. I. K.
William Langerugg, co. Soms., 1 Edw. III: Kirby's Quest, p. 272.
1519. Richard Langrysh, or Langrige: Reg. Univ. Oxf. i. 112.
1585. Roger Langrishe, co. Hants: ibid. vol. ii. pt. ii. p. 144.
— Robert Langrishe, co. Hants: ibid. vol. ii. pt. ii. p. 145.
1765. Married—Thomas Langrish and Sarah Cole: St. Geo. Han. Sq. i. 147.
1775. — Joseph Porter and Jane Langridge: ibid. p. 257.
London, 9, 1, 0; MDB. (East Rid. Yorks), 0, 0, 1; New York, 2, 0, 0.

Langstaff; v. Longstaff.

Langston, Langstone, Lankston.—Local, 'of Langstone,' a parish in co. Monmouth, near Newport.
1564. Thomas Langstone and Eliz. Baughe, *widow*: Marriage Lic. (London), i. 29.
1745. Bapt.—Daniel, s. Benjamin Langstone: St. Jas. Clerkenwell, ii. 276.
London, 5, 0, 1; MDB. (co. Hereford), 2, 1, 0.

Langstroth, Langstrath, Langstreth, Longstreeth, Longstreth.—Local, 'of the lang strother,' i.e. the long marsh; v. Strother, a North-English and Border name. The last syllable seems to have been dropped in modern times.
Richard Langstrothyr, sup. for B.C.L., 1448: Reg. Univ. Oxf. i. 1.
William Langstrother, 1450: ibid.
John Langstreth, of Forsbancke, parish of Tatham, 1676: Lancashire Wills at Richmond (1457-1680), p. 180.
'Private Langstroth, of the Canadian team, was a winner of £15 in the shooting for the Queen's Prize at Wimbledon, July 19, 1887': Standard, July 20, 1887.

London (Longstreeth), 2; MDB. (co. Lancaster), 1, 0, 1, 0, 0; Philadelphia (Longstreth), 27; New York, 5, 1, 1, 0, 0.

Langton.—Local, 'of Langton.' There are at least eight parishes in England so termed, two in co. York, three in co. Lincoln.
Geoffrey de Langeton, co. Linc., 1273. A.
William de Langeton, co. Linc., ibid.
Robertus de Langeton, 1379: P. T. Yorks. p. 222.
1576. John Lancton, co. Linc.: Reg. Univ. Oxf. vol. ii. pt. ii. p. 71.
Ellen Langton, of Caton, 1595: Lancashire Wills at Richmond (1457-1680), p. 180.
John Langton, of Preston, 1680: ibid.
1598. Thomas Langton and Mary Stockmeade: Marriage Lic. (London), i. 251.
London, 23; Manchester, 5; MDB. (co. Lincoln), 7; New York, 5.

Langtree, Langtry. — (1) Local, 'of Langtree,' a parish in co. Devon, eight miles from Bideford, in the Hundred of Shebbear. It is spelt Langtrewe in the Hundred Rolls (i. 78) of 1273.
Agnes Langtree, 1538: Reg. Broad Chalke, co. Wilts, p. 6.
Thomas Lantree, 1548: ibid. p. 7.

(2) Local, 'of Langtree,' a township in the parish of Standish, four miles from Wigan, co. Lanc.
Richard Langtree, of Langtree, 1596: Wills at Chester (1545-1620), p. 117.
Edward Langtree, of Langtree, 1624: ibid. (1621-1650), p. 133.
Manchester, 1, 0; Crockford, 0, 2; Boston (U.S.), 0, 5; New York, 1, 0.

Langworth, Langworthy.—Local, 'of Langworth'; v. Worth; cf. Kenworthy, Whitworth, &c. Probably the name may be referred to Upper Langwith, a parish in co. Derby; cf. Askwith for Askworth.
William de Langwathe, co. Linc., 1273. A.
John Langworthe, co. Worc., 1576: Reg. Univ. Oxf. vol. ii. pt. ii. p. 71.
1524. Thomas Barthelett and Agnes Langwyth: Marriage Lic. (London), i. 4.
1762. Married—Arthur Langworth and Sarah Buckoke: St. Geo. Han. Sq. i. 116.
1803. — Peter Flinn and Sarah Langworthy: ibid. ii. 286.
London, 2, 3; MDB. (co. Devon), 0, 10; Boston (U.S.), 0, 2; New York, 0, 3.

Lanham; v. Langham.

Lankasheer.—Local, 'of Lancashire,' a variant; v. Lancashire.
1808. Married—John Lankshear and Margaret Pearson: St. Geo. Han. Sq. ii. 381.
MDB. (co. Somerset), 1.

Lankester.—Local, 'of Lancaster,' q.v.

Lansdell, Lansdale.—Local, 'of Lonsdale,' q.v. The instances below conclusively prove that Lansdell and Lansdale are mere variants of Lonsdale, and originated in North Lancashire.
William Landysdale, or Londysdall, 1511: Reg. Univ. Oxon. i. 75.
Richard Lonsdale, of Booths, 1595: Wills at Chester (1545-1620), pp. 117-118.
Thomas Lonsdale, of Simonstone, 1591: ibid.
Richard Lansdale, of the Booths, 1588: ibid.
Robert Lansdale, of Simonstone, 1598: ibid.
1571. Alexander Rigbye and Margaret Landesdale: Marriage Lic. (London), i. 48.
1577-8. Thomas Golde and Margaret Lansdall: ibid. p. 79.
1665. Buried—John, s. of John Lansdall, *barber*: St. Dionis Backchurch, p. 236.
London, 3, 1; Philadelphia, 0, 4.

Lansdown, Lansdowne. — Local, 'of Lansdowne,' a level tract of country in the neighbourhood of Bath. A battle was fought here in 1643 between Charles I and the Parliamentary forces.
Jacob de Launtesdoune, co. Soms., 1 Edw. III: Kirby's Quest. p. 86.
1753. Married—John Lansdown and Betty Phillot: St. Geo. Chap. Mayfair, p. 235.
1795. — John Lansdown and Catherine Shury: St. Geo. Han. Sq. ii. 140.
London, 2, 1.

Lanyer.—Occup. 'the lanyer'; v. Laner.

Lapage.—Occup. 'a law-page'; v. Lappage.

Lapish.—Offic. 'a law-page'; v. Lappage.

Lappage, Lapage, Lapish, Lapidge.—Offic. 'the law-page.' Probably an apparitor or summoner, a servant of the law. Not 'le Page,' the evidence being contrary. Lapish and Lapidge are somewhat curious variants.
Johannes Lawpage, 1379: P. T. Yorks. p. 289.
Agnes Lawpage, co. York. W. 2.
Christopher Lawpage. FF.
1778. Married—Samuel Lapidge and Sarah Lowe: St. Geo. Han. Sq. i. 290.
1787. — Peter Reynolds and Susannah Lappage: ibid. p. 399.

London (Lappage), 1; West Rid. Court Dir., 1, 2, 2, 0; Thorne, near Doncaster (Lapidge), 1; New York (Lapage), 1.

Lappin, Lapping, Lappine. —Bapt. 'the son of Lapin.' Probably, however, a contraction of Lampin or Lambin, q.v., the pet name of Lambert. The *g* in Lapping is an excrescence, as in Jennings.

Lapinus Roger, M.P. for Canterbury, C. R., 8 Edw. III.
Thomas Lapyn, C. R., 18 Ric. II.
Makinus Lappyng. XX. 1.
1749. Married—James Merchant and Susanna Lapine: St. Geo. Chap. Mayfair, p. 143.
London, 1, 1, 0; New York, 5, 0, 2.

Lapworth.—Local, 'of Lapworth,' a parish in co. Warwick, near Henley-in-Arden.

1562. Michael Lappworthe: Reg. Univ. Oxf. i. 248.
1588-9. Edward Lapworth, co. Warwick: ibid. vol. ii. pt. ii. p. 168.
1744. Married—Francis Lapworth and Eliz. Loder: St. Jas. Clerkenwell, i. 275.
London, 4; MDB. (co. Warwick), 1; Philadelphia, 1; Boston (U.S.), 1.

Larder.—Local, 'of the larder,' an official who superintended the larder or place for the reception of lard. O.F. *lardier*, 'a tub to keep bacon in' (Cotgrave). 'Lardery, a larder; v. Ord. and Reg. p. 21: *lardarium*, a lardyr-hows. Nominale MS.' (Halliwell). v. Lardner.

William del Larder, C. R., 37 Hen. III.
John Larder: Privy Seal Bills, Nov. 1-16, 1559, 1 Eliz.
1616. John Larder, co. Dorset: Reg. Univ. Oxf. vol. ii. pt. ii. p. 357.
London, 1; MDB. (co. Lincoln), 7.

Lardner, Lardiner, Lardnar. —Offic. and occup. 'the lardiner,' a bacon-salter, a steward of the larder. Lard, the melted fat of swine; 'larde of flesche' (Prompt. Parv.). Lardiner, the officer who superintended, as well indoors as out of doors, the supply of pigstock.

'David le Lardiner holds one serjeantry, and he is keeper of the gaol of the Forest, and Seizer of the Cattle which are taken for the King's debts': Hist. and Ant. of the City of York, vol. iii. (York, 1785.)
'The fleshours' sale serve the burgessis all the time . . . in preparing of their flesh, and in laying in of their lardner.'—The Lawes and Constitutions of Burghs in the Regiam Majestatim, p. 243, Edin-

burgh, 1774: quoted by Brand, Pop. Ant. i. 220, edit. 1841.
Ywon the Lardaner, co. Glouc., 1289: Household Exp. Ric. de Swinfield, Camd. Soc. p. 168.
Thomas le Lardiner, c. 1300. M.
Philip le Lardiner. B.
Hugh le Lardiner. L.
1693-4. John Lardner and Hannah Moore: Marriage Lic. (Faculty Office), p. 210.
1701. Bapt.—Edward, s. John Lardner, *apothecary*: St. Dionis Backchurch, p. 140.
London, 3, 0, 0; New York, 1, 0, 0; Philadelphia, 4, 0, 1.

Large.—Nick. 'the large,' the big, the bulky; cf. Small, Bigg, Little, Fatt, Lean, &c.

Robert le Large, co. Oxf., 1273. A.
William le Large, co. Essex, ibid.
Andrew le Large, C. R., 6 Edw. I.
Thomas le Large, co. Soms., 1 Edw. III: Kirby's Quest, p. 209.
1595. Thomas Large, co. Sussex: Reg. Univ. Oxf. vol. ii. pt. ii. p. 210.
1630. Bapt.—Ane, d. Thomas Large: St. Jas. Clerkenwell, i. 116.
1647-8. Dudley Avery and Jane Large: Marriage Lic. (Faculty Office), p. 38.
1787. Married—John Large and Mary Rawlings: St. Geo. Han. Sq. i. 403.
London, 10; New York, 2.

Larimer; v. Lorimer.

Lark, Larke.—Nick. 'the lark,' one who sang 'like a lark'; cf. Nightingale. Bird-names were very popular, as our directories prove; v. Finch, Spinks, Jay, Goldfinch, &c. Lark is a contraction of O.E. *laverock* (v. Laverack).

Hamo Larke, co. Norf., 1273. A.
William le Lerk, C. R., 7 Edw. I.
1545. Buried—Cecyly Lavoroke: St. Dionis Backchurch, p. 181.
Nicholas Larke, co. Linc., 1584: Reg. Univ. Oxf. vol. ii. pt. ii. p. 140.
1670. Bapt.—Ane, d. Robert Larke: St. Jas. Clerkenwell, i. 285.
London, 6, 2; New York, 0, 1; Philadelphia, 4, 1.

Larkin, Larking.—Bapt. 'the son of Lawrance,' pronounced Larance, whence the nick. Larry, dim. Lar-kin; cf. Wil-kin. The *g* is, of course, excrescent. Although I have not much direct evidence, there can be no doubt about the origin.

Larance Kyllum: Visit. Yorks, 1563, p. 178.
Larance Hamerton: ibid. p. 153.
Larance Hamerkine, 1623: St. Mary Aldermary, p. 15.

1546. Thomas Larkyng and Clare Sanders: Marriage Lic. (Faculty Office), p. 8.
1620. Bapt.—Joane, d. Thomas Larkings: St. Jas. Clerkenwell, i. 87.
1684. Buried—Eliz. Larkin, servant to Mr. James Bayly: St. Dionis Backchurch, p. 251.
London, 10, 5; Philadelphia, 40, 0.

Larkman.—Local, 'of Lakenham,' a parish in co. Norfolk. The local surname became unquestionably Lakeman, q.v. As Larkman is a Norfolk and Suffolk surname, we may suppose that it is the result of a local pronunciation with long *ā*; Lahkman would soon become Larkman. I doubt not this is the true derivation; cf. Swetman for Swetenham, or Deadman for Debenham.

William Lacknam, 1524: Reg. Univ. Oxf. i. 135.
London, 4; MDB. (co. Norfolk), 3; (co. Suffolk), 1.

Larnder; v. Launder.

Larrett, Larritt.—Bapt. 'the son of Lora,' or 'Laura,' or 'Laurencia'; dim. Lorett or Laurett. 'It was the Provençal Lora de Sades, so long beloved of Petrarch, who made this one of the favourite romantic and poetical names, above all, in France, where it is Laure, Lauretta, Loulon' (Yonge, i. 368). But possibly Larrett or Larrit is a dim. of Larry, the nick. of Laurence. Still the origin would be the same.

Laurencia, comitissa de Leycestre, Hen. III–Edw. I. K. p. 236.
Loretta, com'de Leycestre, ibid. p. 166.
Lauretta de Wyum, ibid. p. 328.
Lora de Scaccario, 1273. A.
Lora de Herthill, 1379: P. T. Yorks. p. 14-15.
Lora Mawer, 1379: ibid.
Lora de Grenelef, 1379: ibid.
Lora Soker, 1379: ibid.
1577. Edward Larratt and Katherine Wheelor: Marriage Lic. (London), i. 75.
London, 1, 2.

Lasbury. — Local, 'of Lasborough,' a parish in co. Gloucester, near Tetbury.
London, 1.

Lascelles, Lassells, Lascell, Lassell, Lasselle, Lasell, Laselle.—Local, 'de Lascelles.' Mr. Lower says 'la Lacelle is a place in the arrondissement of Alençon in Normandy' (Patr. Brit. p. 187).

William de Lassell, co. Linc., Hen. III-Edw. I. K.

Alan de Lascelle, co. Northampt., 1273. A.

William de Lasceles, co. York, ibid.

Roger de Lascelles, co. York, ibid.

1574. Francis Lassells, co. Richmond: Reg. Univ. Oxf. vol. ii. pt. ii. p. 57.

1665. Cuthbert Wytham and Lucy Lassell: Marriage Alleg. (Canterbury), p. 142.

London, 5, 0, 0, 0, 0, 0, 0; Crockford, 5, 0, 0; 0, 0, 0, 0; New York, 1, 0, 3, 0, 0, 3, 1; Boston (U.S.), 0, 0, 0, 4, 2, 0, 0.

Lasham, Lassham, Lassam.—Local, 'of Lasham,' a parish in co. Southampton.

Richard de Lasham, co. Suff., 1273. A.

A single register will suffice to give instances of the variants.

1800. Married—Thomas List and Sarah Lasham: St. Geo. Han. Sq. ii. 215.

1808. — Michael Lassam and Eliz. White: ibid. p. 394.

1809. — Henry Lassham and Eliz. Hill: ibid. p. 412.

London, 1, 1, 2.

Lassey.—Local; v. Lacy.

Latchford, Letchford. — Local, 'of Latchford,' a chapelry in the parish of Grappenhall, co. Chester. Also a hamlet in the parish of Great Haseley, co. Oxford. It is quite possible that Latchford and Letchford represent two different places; v. Letchford.

1609. Nicholas Latchford, of Pinnington: Wills at Chester (1545-1620), p. 118.

1666. Married—Edward Blacford and Margett Litchford: St. Jas. Clerkenwell, iii. 130.

1679. John Lachford, of Macclesfield: Wills at Chester (1660-80), p. 161.

1788. Married — George Cobb and Frances Letchford: St. Geo. Han. Sq. ii. 9.

1806. — George Tweedle and Ann Latchford: ibid. p. 358.

London, 4, 3; Manchester, 0, 1; Philadelphia, 0, 4.

Latham, Leatham, Lathom, Laytham, Leethem, Leatheam, Leetham, Lethem.—Local, 'of Lathom,' a chapelry in the parish of Ormskirk, co. Lanc. The surname has ramified very strongly and spread far and wide, probably from lade or lathe, a barn. A distinguished family took their name from this place. In Yorkshire this

surname took the form of Leatham and Leathom, unless it had a separate local origin. But the meaning is the same (v. Leathes), as leath is found to be a Yorkshire form of lade or lathe mentioned above; literally, therefore, 'the barn-house.'

Henry de Latham, co. Soms., 1 Edw. III: Kirby's Quest, p. 169.

Johannes de Lethom, 1379: P. T. Yorks. p. 241.

Thomas de Lathom, co. Lanc., 1382: Baines' Lancashire, ii. 414.

1605-6. Edward Lathom, co. Lanc.: Reg. Univ. Oxf. vol. ii. pt. ii. p. 288.

1616. John Lathom, or Latham, co. Lanc.: ibid. p. 353.

London, 21, 0, 0, 0, 0, 0, 0, 0; Manchester, 9, 0, 0, 1, 0, 0, 0, 0; West Rid. Court Dir., 3, 8, 0, 0, 1, 0, 0, 0; Hull, 1, 0, 0, 0, 0, 0, 3, 1; New York, 21, 0, 0, 0, 0, 2, 0, 0; Philadelphia, 13, 1, 0, 0, 0, 3, 0, 1.

Lathbury, Ladbury.—Local, 'of Lathbury,' a parish in co. Bucks, near Newport Pagnell. Ladbury may be for Ledbury; but the prefix seems to be lade or lathe, a barn; v. Lade.

(Domina) de Lathbiry, co. Bucks, 1273. A.

John de Lathebyr, co. Bucks, ibid.

1578. Francis Lathburye, co. Derby: Reg. Univ. Oxf. vol. ii. pt. ii. p. 80.

1579. Ralph Barton and Rose Lathburie: Marriage Lic. (London), i. 92.

1609. Bapt.—Marie, d. Isak Lathburie: St. Michael, Cornhill, p. 108.

1745. Married—Edward Ladbury and Frances Dale: Canterbury Cathedral, p. 88.

London, 3, 3; Philadelphia, 4, 0.

Lathom; v. Lathom.

Lathrop, Lathrope.—Local, 'of Lowthorp,' q.v.

Latimer, Lattimer, Lattimore. — Occup. 'the latimer,' an interpreter; lit. a speaker of Latin. O.F. Latinier. 'Latonere, or he that usythe Latyn speche' (Prompt. Parv. p. 289); v. Way's note. 'Sir John Maundevile, speaking of the routes to the Holy Land, says of the one by way of Babylon, "And alle weys fynden men Latyneres to go with hem in the contrees ... in to tyme that men conne the langage"': Voiage, p. 71. An old poem says:

'Lyare was mi latymer,
Sloth and sleep mi bedyner.'
　　Wright's Lyric Poetry, p. 49.

Hugo Latinarius, 1086: Domesday.

William le Latiner. G.

Warin le Latymer. B.

Nicholas le Latimer. M.

Alan le Latimer, co. Suff., 1273. A.

Symon le Latiner, co. Suff., ibid.

William Latymere, 1513: Reg. Univ. Oxf. i. 89.

1586. John Hollowaie and Johanna Latimer: Marriage Lic. (London), i. 151.

For a second derivation, v. Latoner.

London, 5, 1, 0; Crockford, 1, 0, 0; MDB. (co. Warwick), 0, 0, 1; Philadelphia, 19, 3, 4.

Latoner, Latner. — Occup. 'the latoner,' one who worked in laton or latten, probably a mixture of lead with brass or copper. M.E. laton.

'He had a crois of laton, ful of stones.'
　　Chaucer, C. T. 701.

As a surname inextricably mixed with Latiner or Latimer, an interpreter. Thus Latimer has two distinct origins; v. Latimer.

Thomas le Latoner, temp. 1300. M.

Nicholas Musket, latoner, 3 Edw. II : Freemen of York, i. 12.

Richard le Latonere. V. 9.

Robertus Latoner, 1379: P. T. Yorks. p. 39.

Richard Latoner, bailiff of Yarmouth, 1341: FF. xi. 323.

1579. Edward Latner, co. Glouc.: Reg. Univ. Oxf. vol. ii. pt. ii. p. 89.

1583. Oswold Greated and Dorcas Moncke, widow, relict of John Moncke, latten-founder: Marriage Lic. (London), i. 125.

New York, 0, 2.

La Touche. — Local, 'de la Touche.' David Digues de la Touche, a Huguenot, settled in Ireland after the revocation of the Edict of Nantes. He was a scion of the noble house of Blesois, who held considerable lands between Blois and Orleans (Lower, quoting Burke's Landed Gentry).

Crockford, 4; Oxford, 1.

Launcelotte. — Bapt. ; v. Lancelot.

Laund.—Local, 'at the laund'; v. Land and Lund.

Gernes de la Launde, co. Warw.: Hen. III-Edw. I. K.

John de la Launde, co. Linc.: ibid.

Robert de la Laund, co. Essex, 1273. A.

Nicholas atte-Launde, co. Norf., 1401: FF. v. 6.

1585-6. Richard Westemyll and Dorothy Launde : Marriage Lic. (London), i. 148.

Launder, Lavender, Larnder.—Occup. 'the lavender,' a washerwoman or a washerman. '*Buandière*, launderer': Hollyband's Dictionarie, 1593. 'Lauender, wassher, or lawndere, *lotrix*': Prompt. Parv. Mr. Way in a note quotes Caxton (Boke for Travellers), 'Beatrice the lauendre shall come hethir after diner, so gyve her the lynnen clothis.'

'Envy is lavender of the Court alway.'
Legend of Good Women.

Beatrice Ap Rice, laundress to Princess Mary (daughter of Henry VIII), is always set down as 'Mistress Launder':

'Item, paid for 2lb. of starche for Mts. Launder, viiid.': Privy Purse Expenses, Princess Mary, p. 160.
1530. 'Item, paied to the lawnder that wasshith the children of the kinges pryvat chambre, 48s. 4d.': ibid. Henry VIII. p. 75.
Alice la Lavander, co. Bedf., 1273. A.
Cecilia la Lavender, co. Camb., ibid.
Peter le Lavender, co. Camb., ibid.
1538. William Launder: Reg. Univ. Oxf. i. 192.
Isabel la Lavendre. E.
1752. Married—Richard Morris and Ann Lavender: St. Geo. Han. Sq. i. 47.
London, 1, 4, 1; Boston (U.S.), 1, 5, 0.

Laundry, Landry. — Local, 'of the laundry'; v. Launder, the officer who superintended the washing department; cf. Wardrop (at the wardrobe) and Wardroper (the wardrober). Practically the local form is the same as the official. This surname has crossed the Atlantic and flourishes in the States, although all but extinct in England.

Alice atte.Lauendre, C. R., 3 Edw. I.
Robert de la Lavendrye, Fines Roll, 11 Edw. I.

The first two following names occur together :

William le Lavender, co. Soms., 1 Edw. III: Kirby's Quest, p. 205.
Roger atte Louendrye, co. Soms., 1 Edw. III: ibid.
1773. Married—John Bidwell and Jane Landry: St. Geo. Han. Sq. i. 233.
Boston (U.S.), 7, 19.

Laundy. — Local, 'of the laundry'; v. Landry. A corruption.

1790. Married—Edward Moggridge and Sarah Laundy: St. Geo. Han. Sq. ii. 43.
London, 3.

Laurence. — Bapt. ; v. Lawrance.

Laurie. — Bapt. 'the son of Lawrence'; v. Lowrie.

Lavender; v. Launder.

Laverack, Laverick, Lavrick, Loverock. — Nick. 'the laverock' or 'lavrock,' i.e. the lark, probably because the bearer was a good blithe singer, or of bright and cheery habits; cf. Nightingale, Finch, Goldfinch, &c. ; v. Lark.

Richard Laverock, co. Notts, 1273. A.
Willelmus Lauerok, 1379: P. T. Yorks. p. 277.
1750. Married—Grey Elliott and Mary Laverik : St. Geo. Han. Sq. i. 80.
1764. — John Laverick and Ann Weston : ibid. p. 133.
Hull, 4, 1, 1, 0; Stourbridge (co. Worc.), 0, 0, 0, 1.

Lavington.—Local, 'of Lavington,' a parish in co. Lincoln, four miles from Folkingham ; also two parishes (East and West Lavington) in co. Wilts.

Hugh de Lavinton, co. Linc.: Hen. III-Edw. I. K.
Ralph de Lavinton, co. Linc. : ibid.
Reginald de Lavinton, co. Wilts, 1273. A.
William de Lavinton, co. Wilts, ibid.
Hugh de Lavington, rector of Bircham Magna, co. Norf., 1310: FF. x. 293.
Robert de Levyngton, co. Soms., 1 Edw. III: Kirby's Quest, p. 272.
1669. Married—Edward Top and Anne Lavinton: St. Jas. Clerkenwell, iii. 167.
London, 4.

Law, Lawe, Lawes. — (1) Local, 'at the low,' i.e. hill ; v. Low. The seeming plural form Lawes represents the common tendency to tack on an s in monosyllabic local surnames; cf. Styles, Oakes, Brooks, Sykes, Dykes, &c. Probably the patronymic s, as in Williams, Jones, &c.; v. Brook. (2) Bapt. 'the son of Lawrence,' from the nick. Law. For instances, v. Lawson. The final s in Lawes will here represent the patronymic, as in Jones, Williams, Jennings, &c.

William de la Lawe, co. Northumb., 1273. A.

Ralph de la Law, or Lowe, co. Salop: ibid.
Robertus del Lawe, 1379 : P. T. Yorks. p. 210.
Johannes de la Law, 1379: ibid. p. 140.
1527-8. John Brewer and Agnes Lawes: Marriage Lic. (London), i. 6.
1591. John Lawe, *yeoman*, and Eliz. Manfeilde: ibid. p. 191.
London, 36, 0, 7; West Rid. Court Dir., 21, 1, 0; New York, 30, 1, 2.

Lawday.—? Bapt. 'the son of Loveday' (?), q.v. A corruption. London, 1.

Lawford.—Local, 'of Lawford,' parishes in cos. Essex and Warwick.

1682. Married—Edward Golding and Mary Lawford: St. Michael, Cornhill, p. 43.
1710. Buried—Anne Lauford: Reg. Stourton, co. Wilts, p. 74.
London, 12; Boston (U.S.), 3.

Lawless.—Nick. 'the lawless,' uncontrolled, unrestrained ; M.E. *laweles*, lawless.

Hugo Laghlese, 1314. M.
John Laweles, C. R., 19 Ric. II.
John Laweles, C. R., 1 Hen. IV. pt. i.
1619. Francis Godingham and Alice Lawlesse : Marriage Lic. (London), i. 79.
1746. Married—William Coolley and Ann Lawless: St. Geo. Chap. Mayfair, p. 74.
London, 3 ; Philadelphia, 16.

Lawley.—Local, 'of Lawley.' I cannot find the spot.

1595-6. George Lawley, co. Salop: Reg. Univ. Oxf. vol. ii. pt. ii. p. 213.
1652. Bapt.—John, s. William and Sibbell Lawly : St. Jas. Clerkenwell, i. 179.
1698. Robert Palmer and Hester Lawley : Marriage Lic. (Faculty Office), p. 229.
MDB. (co. Salop), 3; London, 7; Philadelphia, 6.

Lawman.—Offic. 'the lawman,' i.e. the lawyer, 'the man of law,' as Chaucer would say.

Ranulf Lawman, co. Hunts, 1273. A.
Peter Laweman, co. Camb., ibid.
Thomas Laweman, co. Oxf., ibid.
Willelmus Lawghman, 1379: P. T. Yorks. p. 273.
1607. Married — Edward Lawman, *girdler*, and Fraunces Keuall : St. Michael, Cornhill, p. 18.
London, 3.

Lawrance, Lawrence, Laurance, Laurence, Lawrenson.—Bapt. 'the son of Laurence.' This saint 'of universal popularity' has made a deep impression upon our nomenclature; v. Law (2), Lawson, Lowrie, Laurie, Larkin, Larrett, &c.

Gilbert Laueronce, co. Camb., 1273. A.
John fil. Laurence, co. Linc., ibid.
Simon fil. Laurencii, London, 20 Edw.
I. R.
Nicholas Lawranson, of Poynton, co.
Ches., 1584: Wills at Chester (1545-1620), p. 119.
James Lawranson, of Maghull, 1613:
ibid.
Josiah Lawrenson, of Frodsham: ibid.
(1681-1700), p. 152.

Memorials to members of one and the same family represent the name as follows :

Mary, wife of John Laurence, 1736:
FF. iv. 133.
Ester, wife of John Lawrence, 1796:
ibid.
Mary, d. of John and Ester Laurance,
1727: ibid.
London, 13, 126, 1, 12, 0; Liverpool,
0, 15, 0, 1, 8; New York, 5, 37, 0, 10, 0.

Lawrey, Lawrie, Lawry.—Bapt. 'the son of Lawrence'; v. Lowrie.

Lawson.—Bapt. 'the son of Laurence' or 'Lawrence,' from the nick. Law; v. Law (2).

Willelmus Lauson, 1379: P. T. Yorks.
p. 146.
Law Robynson, 1379: ibid. p. 255.
Henricus Laweson, 1379: ibid. p. 135.
Agnes Law-wyf, 1379: ibid. p. 291.
1554. James Castelys and Eliz. Lawson: Marriage Lic. (London), i. 15.
1576. William Lauson, co. Lanc.: Reg.
Univ. Oxf. vol. ii. pt. ii. p. 72.
1664. Bapt.—Jone, d. Randall Lawson:
St. Jas. Clerkenwell, i. 222.
London, 46; West Rid. Court Dir.,
16; New York, 66.

Lawton.—Local, 'of Lawton,' a parish in co. Ches., now Church-Lawton, but simply Lawton in earlier records; v. Earwaker's East Cheshire, ii. 207, 239. In South England probably sometimes confused with Laughton.

1575. Thomas Lawton, co. Ches.: Reg.
Univ. Oxf. vol. ii. pt. ii. p. 67.
Mr. Lawton, parson of Lawton, 1620:
Lanc. and Ches. Rec. Soc., p. 51.
Thomas Lawton, 1634: Earwaker's
East Ches. ii. 211.
Thomas Lawton, of Lawton, 1595:
Wills at Chester (1545-1620), p. 119.
John Lawton, of Church Lawton, co.
Ches., 1607: ibid.
Randle Lawton, of Chester, 1604: ibid.
1587. Christopher Walker, bricklayer,
and Anne Lawton: Marriage Lic. (London), i. 160.

Manchester, 29; London, 11; New
York, 23.

Lawyer.—Occup.'the lawyer';
v. Lawman, and cf. Sawyer and Bowyer.

New York, 3; Philadelphia, 3.

Lax, Laxe.— ? Local, 'at the lake,' from residence thereby. The chief home of this surname is co. Somerset, where we find Lack (i.e. Lake) at an early period. A.S. lac (Skeat); Fr. lac, a lake. Hence a surname Lack, and with the final s (cf. Holmes, Styles, Brooks, Sykes, &c.) Lacks. This by and by would become Lax; cf. Dix Rix, Wix, Wilcoxon, for Dicks, Ricks, Wicks, Wilcockson. This seems to me a simple solution.

1729. Married—Joseph Lax, of Whitby,
co. York, and Anne Dodd: St. Geo.
Chap. Mayfair, p. 295.
MDB. (co. Soms.), 8, 0 ; Philadelphia,
1, 0; New York, 6, 1.

Laxton.—Local, ' of Laxton.'
(1) Laxton or Lexington, a parish in co. Notts; (2) Laxton, a parish in co. Northampton.

Henry de Laxington, co. Linc., 1273. A.
Robert de Laxinton, co. Linc., ibid.
Simon de Laxton, co. Norf., 1361: FF.
v. 33.
1542. Married—Thomas Eswell and
Annes Laxtonne: St. Peter, Cornhill,
i. 221.
1578-9. Morgan Laxton and Margaret
Smithe, widow: Marriage Lic. (London),
i. 84.
1680. Martin Laxton and Eliz. Jones:
Marriage Lic. (Faculty Office), p. 153.
1799. Married—William Robert Laxton and Phoebe Parker: St. Geo. Han.
Sq. ii. 209.
London, 8.

Lay.—Local, 'at the lay,' from residence thereby; v. Lee.

John de la Lay, co. Linc., 1273. A.
John du Lay, co. Hunts, ibid.
John du Lay, co. Bedf., 20 Edw. I. R.
1615. Married—Olyver Laye and Eliz.
Wildicott: St. Jas. Clerkenwell, iii. 41.
1770. — Benjamin Lay and Winifred
Robinson: St. Geo. Han. Sq. i. 197.
London, 5; Oxford, 5; New York, 11.

Layard.— ? Occup. or ? offic. ; probably 'the lord.' A variant of Scottish Laird, q.v.

1743. Daniel Peter Layard and Susanna
Henrietta Boysragon: Marriage Lic.
(London), ii. 345.
Crockford, 2.

Layburn, Layborn, Laybourn, Laborn, Labern.—Local, (1) 'of Leyburn,' a parish in the N. Rid. Yorks; (2) 'of Leybourn,' a parish in co. Kent.

William de Leybourne, co. Kent,
1273. A.
Roger de Leyburne, co. Hunts, ibid.
Henry de Leyburne, co. Kent, 20 Edw.
I. R.
Thomas de Layburn, 1379: P. T. Yorks.
p. 209.
1618. Married—William Myllarde and
Thomyzin Labourne: St. Michael, Cornhill, p. 21.
1781.—Matthew Gilpatrick and Margt.
Laybourn: St. Geo. Han. Sq. i. 320.
London, 0, 3, 1, 1, 2; New York, 2, 0,
1, 0, 0.

Laycock.—Local, 'of Laycock,' now a suburb of the town of Keighley, W. Rid. Yorks, one of the five manors into which that town was divided.

Johanna Lakkoc, 1379: P. T. Yorks.
p. 197.
Johannes de Laccok, 1379: ibid. p. 263.
Thomas de Lacokke, 1379: ibid.
1640. Married—John Painter and Dorothy Laycock: St. Peter, Cornhill, i. 253.
— — William Bartlemew and Ann
Laycock: St. Antholin, London, p. 64.
London, 3; West Rid. Court Dir., 24;
Philadelphia, 12.

Layer.—Occup. 'the layer,' i.e. a stone layer (Latinized into cubatores), one who sets the stones in building, a waller. ' Layere, or werkare wythe stone and mortere, cementarius' : Prompt. Parv. p. 294, and v. Way's note thereon. Probably the term was familiar to co. Norfolk, as the above quotation suggests, for Layer has been a Norfolk surname for many centuries. In the contract for building Fotheringay Church, 1425, the chief mason undertakes neither to 'set mo nor fewer freemasons, rogh setters, ne leyers' upon the work but as appointed (Dugdale, Mon. iii. 164).

George Layer, of Bury, co. Suff., 1429:
FF. vi. 354.
William Layer, sheriff of Norwich,
1526; mayor, 1537: ibid.
'Here resteth the body of Mary, daughter of Christopher Layer, citizen and alderman of Norwich, who deceased the 9th of October, 1602': ibid. p. 357.
Mary Layer, 1710, Boughton, Norfolk:
ibid.
1661. Francis Layre, of Hanningham,

co. Norf., and Eliz. Bowle: Marriage Alleg. (Canterbury), p. 64.
New York, 3 ; Philadelphia, 21.

Layland, Leyland, Leeland, Leland.—Local, 'at the lay land.' Two parishes in co. Lanc. bear the name of Layland or Leyland. A valuable note by Way in the Prompt. Parv. (p. 285) on the word ' *lay*, londe not telyd,' explains the meaning. Amongst other authorities he quotes ' laylande ; *terre nouvellement labourée* ' (Palsgrave); ' a leylande, *frisca terra* ' (Cath. Ang.) ; ' *selio*, a lee lande ' (Ortus). Thus Layland means fallow or unploughed land. For the connexion of *lay* with *lea* and *lee*, v. Lee.

Johannes Leyland, 1379: P. T. Yorks. p. 161.
Ellis Leyland, of Nether Wyersdale, 1679 : Lancashire Wills at Richmond (1457-1680), p. 182.
Thomas Lealand, of Nether Wyersdaile, 1670 : ibid.
1688. Bapt.—William, son of Richard Layland : St. Jas. Clerkenwell, i. 329.
London, 6, 1, 0, 0; West Rid. Court Dir., 1, 2, 0, 0 ; MDB. (co. Warwick), 0, 0, 1, 0; New York, 0, 0, 0, 17.

Layman. — ? ——. Mr. Lower thinks this is a personal name, and the same as Layamon, who transcribed the Roman de Brut. I would suggest that it is only a variation of Lawman, q.v.—or perhaps of Leman, q.v.
' Here lyeth the body of Habbakuk Layman, surgeon, who departed this life the 5th day of April, an Dom. 1699,' Kenninghall, co. Norf.: FF. i. 223.
London, 2 ; Philadelphia, 7 ; New York, 4.

Laytham ; v. Latham.

Layton.—Local, ' of Layton.' East and West Layton, two townships in N. Rid. Yorks ; also a township in the parish of Bispham, co. Lanc. Doubtless many small spots are so called ; cf. Leighton.

Richard de Layton, co. Cumb., 20 Edw. I. R.
1581. Thomas Laitone, co. York: Reg. Univ. Oxf. vol. ii. pt. ii. p. 96.
1626. Thomas Heylen and Anne Layton, *widow*: Marriage Lic. (London), ii. 167.
— Bapt. — Ann, d. William Layton : St. Jas. Clerkenwell, i. 103.
1057. — Mary, d. Richard Laighton : ibid. p. 198.
London, 18 ; Philadelphia, 20.

Lazenby, Lazonby.—Local, ' of Lazonby,' a village in co. Cumberland. But the Yorkshire Lazenbys hail from Lazenby, a manor in the parish of Kirk Leatham, co. York.

Ricardus Lasynbi, 1379: P. T. Yorks. p. 285.
Willelmus de Lethom, 1379: ibid.
William Laysynby, C. R., Ric. II. pt. ii.
1632. Bapt.—Benjamine, s. Richard Lazonby: St. Antholin (London), p. 66.
1696. Buried—Robert Lasinby, rector of St. Antholin : ibid. p. 110.
1701. Bapt.—Mary, d. William Lasingby, *haberdasher of hats* : St. Dionis Backchurch, p. 140.
London, 2, 0 ; West Rid. Court Dir., 2, 0 ; Manchester, 0, 2 ; Boston (U.S.), 1, 0 ; Philadelphia, 2, 0.

Lea, Leah.—Local, 'at the lea'; v. Lee. Leah is unquestionably a variant. It is not Jewish, but purely English. The intermediate stage was Leay.

William de la Lea, co. Oxf., 1273. A. John atte Lea, 1301. M.
Richard Lea, of the Lea, co. Ches., 1563 : Wills at Chester (1545-1620), p. 119.
Robert Lea, of Sutton, 1588: ibid.
1682. Bapt.—Henry, s. William Leay : St. Jas. Clerkenwell, i. 300.
1799. Married—John Leah and Eliz. Barker : St. Geo. Han. Sq. ii. 197.
London, 29, 3 ; Manchester, 11, 4 ; MDB. (co. Chester), 16, 1 ; New York, 4, 0.

Leach, Leech, Leachman.—(1) Occup. ' the leech,' a physician ; M.E. *leche*. ' Leche, *medicus*' : Prompt. Parv.
' The divel made a reve for to preche, Or of a souter a shipman, or a leche.'
Chaucer, C. T. 3902.
' Harpemakers, leches, and upholsters, Porters, fesycyens, and corsers.'
Cocke Lorelle's Bote.
With Leachman, cf. *merchantman*, Priestman, &c.

Edmund le Leche, co. Oxf., 1273. A.
William le Leche, co. Oxf., ibid.
Robert le Leche, 1307. M.
John le Leche. X.
Robertus Leche, *taverner*, 1379 : P. T. Yorks. p. 161.

(2) Local, ' at the lache,' i.e. the lake. In co. Lancaster Leach has absorbed Lache (q.v.), which explains the commonness of that surname in that shire.

London, 47, 11, 1 ; Oxford, 8, 6, 0 ; New York, 33, 15, 0.

Leacroft.—Local, ' of Leacroft,' a township in the parish of Cannock, co. Stafford.

1576. Bapt.—Robert, s. Robert Lecroft : *armorer* : St. Peter, Cornhill, i. 18.
1593. Buried—Margery, *ignoti cognominis*, Mr. Lecrafte's mayd, of the plague: ibid. p. 141.
1607. Bapt.—Richard Leycraft, s. Sampson Leycrafte : ibid. p. 57.
1614. Married—Daniel Barker and Mary Leacrofte : ibid. p. 248.
Crockford, 1.

Leadbeater, Leadbetter, Leadbitter, Lidbetter, Liberty(?).—Occup. ' the lead-beater'; cf. Goldbeater. It is probable that Liberty is a corruption, the intermediate form being Libiter. The following entry strongly confirms this view :

1669. Married—John Bayley and Saray Libiter : St. Jas. Clerkenwell, i. 156.
Gonnilda le Ledbetere, co. Bucks, 1273. A.
Ricardus Ledebatter, 1379 : P. T. Yorks. p. 193.
Robertus Ledebeter, 1379: ibid. p. 20.
1561-2. John Leadbeater and Christiana Andrewes : Marriage Lic. (London), i. 23.
1788. — John Winkfield and Margaret Leadbitter : St. Geo. Han. Sq. ii. 1.
1792. — William Leadbetter and Eliz. Miller : ibid. p. 72.
London, 3, 2, 1, 0, 1 ; Manchester, 2, 2, 0, 0, 0 ; Crockford, 0, 0, 1, 0, 1 ; New York, 2, 2, 0, 0, 0 ; Boston (U.S.) (Liberty), 1.

Leader.—Occup. ' the leader,' a carrier, a carter. Farmers still *lead* hay in the North, as for instance in my old parish (Ulverston). ' Lede wythe a carte, *caruco* ' : Prompt. Parv. Mr. Way quotes from the *Liber Niger Regis*, Edw. IV, an ordinance commanding that no seller of wheat for the use of the King's house ' be compelled to lede or carye his wheete ' more than ten miles at his own cost. Waterleaders for water-carriers was the old familiar term for the occupation ; v. Waterleader ; cf. Loder or Loader, q.v.

1519. Richard Ledar, rector of Fouldon, co. Norf. : FF. vi. 34.
1601. Bapt.—Alexander, s. Henrie Leeder : St. Jas. Clerkenwell, i. 38.
1654. Thomas Leader, co. Norf. : FF. vi. 35.
1688. George Leader and Mary Newnam : Marriage Alleg. (Canterbury), p. 91.

1771. Married—James Leader and Jane Gardner : St. Geo. Han. Sq. i. 205. London, 6 ; Philadelphia, 1.

Leadley.—Local ; v. Leathley.

Leadman.—Occup., probably a water-leader ; v. Leader and Loadman. A.S. *ladman*, a carrier.

1618. Married—Thomas Leadman, of St. Gyles, Creplegate, and Marie Smythe : St. Michael, Cornhill, p. 21.
1633. William Ledman and Ellen Burrowes : Marriage Lic. (London), p. 212. Philadelphia, 2.

Leaf, Leefe, Lief, Leafe.—Nick. ' the lief,' i.e. dear ; v. Leif-child. The dim. *lief-kin*, a term of endearment, occurs in Palsgrave's Acolastus, 1540 ; v. *leefekyn*, Halliwell's Dict.

Pagan Lef, co. Norf., 1273. A.
Alice le Lef, co. Camb., ibid.
Lone the Lef, co. Hunts, ibid.
Nicholas Leve, co. Soms., 1 Edw. III : Kirby's Quest, p. 123.
Lucia le Lyf, co. Soms., 1 Edw. III : ibid. p. 140.
1677. Married—Richard Owen and Susanna Leefe : St. Michael, Cornhill, p. 41.
1754. — James Leaf and Eliz. Clarke : St. Geo. Chap. Mayfair, 277.
London, 4, 2, 0, 0 ; MDB. (North Rid. Yorks), 0, 1, 2, 1.

Leah.—Local ; v. Lea, of which it is a manifest variant.

Leak, Leake, Leek. — Local, ' of Leek,' a parish in dioc. of Lichfield ; also ' of Leake,' parishes in diocs. of York, Lincoln, and Southwell.

John de Lek, co. Linc., 1273. A.
Roger de Leke, co. Linc., ibid.
Teobald de Lek, co. Linc., ibid.
John de Leek, co. Notts, 20 Edw. I. R.
1595. Thomas Leeke, co. Northampt. : Reg. Univ. Oxf. vol. ii. pt. ii. p. 211.
— Bapt.—John, s. Arthur Leake, *merchant-tailor* : St. Peter, Cornhill, i. 42.
London, 1, 10, 1 ; New York, 3, 4, 2.

Leaman ; v. Leman.

Lean.—Nick. ' the lean,' a spare man ; cf. Large, Small, Bigg, Little, Lyte, &c. Thus Lean is the opposite of Fatt, q.v.

Walter Lene, co. York, 1273. A.
Roland le Lene, co. Bucks, ibid.
Henry le Lene, co. Soms., 1 Edw. III : Kirby's Quest, p. 278.
1605. Matilda Leene, of Chester, *widow* : Wills at Chester, i. 120.
1797. Married—Thomas Joyner and Eliz. Lane, or Leane : St. Geo. Han. Sq. ii. 171.

1800. Married—Guy Waterman and Henrietta Lean : ibid. p. 218.
MDB. (co. Soms.), 4 ; Boston (U.S.), 2.

Lear, Leer.—Local, ' de Leyre,' probably Lire, in the arrondissement of Evreux in Normandy.

William de Leyre, Leic., 1273. A.
William de Leyre, London, 20 Edw. I. R.
1602. Buried—Thomas, s. of Christofer Leere : St. Mary Aldermary, p. 150.
1647. Married — Vincent Lear and Anne Carter : St. Thomas the Apostle, London, p. 18.
1722. Bapt.—Mary, d. James Leeer : St. Jas. Clerkenwell, ii. 134.
London, 3, 3 ; Crockford, 3, 0 ; New York, 4, 0 ; Philadelphia, 13, 1.

Learoyd.—Local, ' of the learoyd,' from *lee, lea, legh*, or *leigh*, a meadow, and *royd*, a ridding ; v. Royd.

Alicia Legh-rode, 1379 : P. T. Yorks. (Sowerby), p. 195.
Richard Leyrod, of Manchester, *clerk* : Wills at Chester (1621–50), p. 139.
West Rid. Court Dir., 12 ; Boston (U.S.), 3.

Leason. — Bapt. ' the son of Lettice ' ; v. Leeson.

Leatham.—Local ; v. Latham.

Leather, Leathers. — Bapt. ' the son of Leather.' Although I have scarcely any instances, there can be no doubt of the origin of names prefixed with Leather. Leather was a personal name. ' One *Lethar* was a bishop in the days of Æthelbert. Cod. D.pl. 981 '(Lower, Patr. Brit. p. 190). Hence such localities as Letheringham and Letheringsett, and such local surnames as Leatherdale, Leatherby, Leatherhead, or Leatherbarrow. Leatherwine occurs as a single name (without surname), co. Camb. 1273. A. (vol. ii. p. 493). With this cf. Bald-win, Un-win, &c. ; v. Liverpool.

1582. Buried—Alyce Lether, daughter of William, of the plague : St. Michael, Cornhill, p. 197.
1623. Peter Leather and Sarah Bainam : Marriage Lic. (London), ii. 127.
1633. Married—Nathaniel Carter and Ann Leather : St. Antholin (London), p. 67.
1663. Samuel Pine and Sarah Leather: Marriage Alleg. (Canterbury), p. 87.
London, 5, 1 ; New York, 1, 0 ; Oxford, 1, 0.

Leatherbarrow, Leatherberry, Leatherbury, Letherbury.—Local, ' of Leatherbarrow' ; v. Leather and Barrow. One Leatherbarrow is a hill by Windermere Lake.

1581. Nicholas Letherborow, co. Warw. : Reg. Univ. Oxf. vol. ii. pt. ii. p. 107.
1582. Anthony Leatherbarrow, of Aughton : Wills at Chester, i. 120.
1600. Married—Edward Leatherborow, of Coventry, and Cibell Pywell : St. Peter, Cornhill, i. 241.
1618. Cicely Leatherbarrow, of Wigan : Wills at Chester, i. 120.
1661-2. John Booth and Mary Letherbarrow : Marriage Alleg. (Canterbury), p. 23.
London, 1, 0, 0, 0 ; Philadelphia, 0, 3, 14, 3.

Leatherby, Letherby, Leatherbee. — Local, ' of Letherby.' I do not know where the place is ; v. Leather.

London, 1, 1, 0 ; Boston (U.S.), 0, 0, 12.

Leatherdale. — Local, ' of Leatherdale,' a parish in dioc. Ripon, co. York. v. Leather.

London, 2.

Leatherhead. — Local, ' of Leatherhead ' or ' Letherhead,' a parish in dioc. of Winchester, co. Surrey. Lower says, ' formerly Lederede.' v. Leather.

John de Leddred, co. Soms., 1273. A.
Richard Leddred, co. Soms., ibid.
John de Ledrede, co. Wilts, 20 Edw. I. R.
1733. Married—Thomas Leatherhead and Eliz. Upshot : St. Geo. Han. Sq. i. 12.

Leatherhose.—Nickname for one who wore or sold buskins ; cf. Shorthose.

John Letherhose, co. Oxf., 1273. A.
Richard Letherhose, co. Glouc., 20 Edw. I. R.

Leatherman, Letherman.—Occup. ' the leatherman,' a dealer in leather. Possibly the man or servant of Leather ; v. Leather and Matthewman.

Adam Letherman, C. R., 12 Edw. III. pt. iii.
Philadelphia, 6, 1.

Leathes, Leathe, Leath. —Local, ' of the lathes,' i.e. the barns, the grange ; v. Lade. The surname has arisen in several localities.

' Lathes is a hamlet next unto Warnpool, and was so called of a grange or farm which the Lord of Whitrigg had there. Of that place the family of the Lathes took their name . . . until Adam Leathes, now owner of the demesne thereof, sold the tenements and residue of the hamlet to the inhabitants. . . It was given by Robert, the son of Robert de Dunbretton, to his kinsman Henry, whose posterity were thereupon called *de le Leaths* ': E. and F., co. Cumb., p. 76.

Appended is a quotation :

' Robertus filius Roberti dedit Leathes Henrico fratri suo, Hen. III ' : Gilpin.

Thomas atte Lathe, rector of Stokesby, co. Norf., 1356 : FF. xi. 251.

Johannes del Lethe, 1379 : P. T. Yorks. p. 50.

A family of Leathes sprung up in co. Norfolk, and is still represented.

' The manor house was lately called the Lathes, it stands a little distance from Pokethorp Street.' Pokethorp Manor, Norwich : FF. iv. 428.

Again, we read of the same manor :

' John Corbet (4 Edw. VI), had a lease of the Cellerie's, or St. Leonard's meadow, containing six acres, lying between the river and street, the *Lathes* close, and fold-course, and liberty of shak . . . in the manor house and yard, and all thereon built, called the Lathe-yard ' : ibid. iv. 429.

The origin of the Norfolk Leathes is thus distinctly apparent.

Stanley Leaths, rector of Matlask, Norfolk, 1741 : ibid. viii. 137.

' Thomas Atte-lathe married first Alice, daughter and heir of Sir William Wisham, and Margaret his wife, and in her right presented as lord to the church of Elingham Parva, in Norfolk, in 1468 ' : ibid. vii. 449.

Gilbert del Lathes, 25 Edw. I : Freemen of York, i. 6.

London, 1, 0, 2 ; Crockford, 2, 0, 0 ; York, 0, 1, 0 ; MDB. (Norfolk), 3, 0, 0 ; New York, 0, 0, 1 ; Boston (U.S.), 0, 1, 0.

Leathley, Leadley. — Local, ' of Leathley,' a parish in the W. Rid. Yorks, i.e. ' the meadow by the barn '; v. Lade and Leathes.

1579-80. Henry Leathelye and Fortune Hallywell : Marriage Lic. (London), p. 94.

London, 1, 0 ; Leeds, 3, 1 ; MDB. (North Rid. Yorks), 0, 6; Philadelphia, 0, 1.

Leavenbread.—Nick. Probably Isabel was so familiarly entitled because she baked this sort of bread ; cf. Blanchpain, Whitbread, Cakebread, &c.

Isabella Leuanbrede, 1379 : P. T. Yorks. p. 199.

Leaver, Lever. — Local, ' of Lever,' q.v. Although the variant Leaver is not now very common in South Lanc., it formerly was frequently found in that district.

1621. Robert Leaver, of Darcey Lever : Wills at Chester, ii. 135.

1635. James Leaver, of Darcey Lever : ibid.

1647. Roger Leaver, of Bolton : ibid.

Here the true spelling of the locality is preserved, while the surname originated by that same locality has changed its orthography.

London, 15, 8 ; Manchester, 2, 14 ; New York, 0, 2.

Leaversuch.—Local ; v. Liversage, of which it is a variant.

MDB. (co. Essex), 1.

Leche.—Occup. ; v. Leach.

1552. John Leche, of Carden, co. Ches.: Wills at Chester, i. 120.

1605. James Leche, of Lower Place, in Castleton : ibid. Liverpool, 1.

Lechmere. — Local, ' of Lechmore,' probably some moor in the vicinity of Lechlade, a parish twenty-eight miles from Gloucester. The surname seems to have arisen in that district.

1587-8. Richard Lechmore, or Lichmoore, co. Heref. : Reg. Univ. Oxf. vol. ii. pt. ii. p. 162.

1599. Edmund Leachmore, or Lechemoore, or Lechmoor, co. Heref. : ibid. p. 233.

1679. Sandys Lechmere and Joan Holmes : Marriage Lic. (Faculty Office), p. 148.

1677. Thomas Lechmere and Jane Blagrave : Marriage Alleg. (Canterbury), p. 273.

MDB. (co. Hereford), 1 ; Crockford, 1.

Leck. — Local, ' of Leck,' a township in the parish of Tunstall, near Lancaster.

Johannes de Lek, 1379 : P. T. Yorks. p. 199.

Willelmus de Lek, 1379 : ibid.

1575. Barnabas Hills and Catherine Lecke : Marriage Lic. (London), i. 67.

1587-8. Anthony Lecke, co. Herts, and Mary Knagge : ibid. p. 167.

Ulverston, 1 ; New York, 2 ; Philadelphia, 1.

Ledgar(d, Ledger ; v. Legard.

Ledsham, Ledson. — Local, ' of Ledsham,' a parish in W. Rid. Yorks, six miles from Pontefract.

Ledson is a corrupted form ; v. Lettsom and Lett.

1540. Buried—Thomas Ledsam : St. Dionis Backchurch (London), p. 178.

1582. Thomas Ledsum, co. Ches.: Reg. Univ. Oxf. vol. ii. pt. ii. p. 123.

1606. Buried—Jane, d. Cuthbert Ledsome : St. Jas. Clerkenwell, iv. 95.

— George Ledsham, of Inner Temple, London : Wills at Chester, i. 120.

1809. Married—Charles Hope and Sarah Ledson : St. Geo. Han. Sq. ii. 401.

Melling, near Liverpool, 0, 3 ; MDB. (co. Ches.), 1, 0.

Lee.—Local, ' at the lea,' from *ley*, *legh*, *lea*, or *lay*, a meadow, a grassy plain. The local names with which this word is incorporated as affix or suffix are innumerable ; cf. Leighton, Chudleigh, Eckersley, Leyburn, &c. Of itself, also, it represents countless spots styled Lee, Lees, Leigh, Lea, Leece (a village in Furness), &c. The local surnames built upon it are equally numerous, comprising (without adducing compound forms) Lee, Lees, Leese, Leece, Legg, Legge, Legh, Leigh, Ley, Lay, and Lea, all of which see under their respective heads.

Henry de la Lee, co. Camb., 1273. A Richard de la Lee, co. Wilts, ibid.

John de la Lee. J.

Roger de la Lee. B.

Johannes del Lee, 1379 : P. T. Yorks. p. 155.

1550-1. John Lee and Agnes Masset : Marriage Lic. (London), i. 13.

1565. Bapt.—Anne, d. Henry Lee : St. Jas. Clerkenwell, p. 3.

London, 191 ; New York, 258.

Leece.—(1) Local, ' at the lees,' v. Lees ; cf. Ellice for Ellis, or Avice for Avis. (2) Local, ' of Leece,' a hamlet near Ulverston, in the Furness district of North Lancashire. The derivation is the same as (1). Leece is still found as a surname in Ulverston and the neighbourhood. It is commonly met with in the Ulverston Church registers.

1546. Buried—Eliz. Leece : St. Mary, Ulverston, p. 5.

1561. Bapt.—Brian Liese : ibid. p. 38.

1593. Jenet Leece, of Coulton, Furness : Lancashire Wills at Richmond (1457-1680), p. 183.

1597. William Leice, of Bardsey, Furness : ibid.

Ulverston, 1.

Leech.—Occup. ; v. Leach.

Leedham, Leedam, Leedom.—Local, ' of Lathom '; v. Latham. One familiar form of Lathom is Leatham or Leetham, and of this Leedham, Leedam, and the American Leedom are variants. It is astonishing how many variants of Lathom are to be found scattered over the world.

Hull, 1, 0, 0; MDB. (co. Stafford), 5, 0, 0; Philadelphia, 0, 0, 28; Boston (U.S.), 1, 0, 0.

Leeds.—Local, ' of Leeds,' the well-known town in the W. Rid. of Yorks.

1565. Buried—Elizabethe Leedes, alias Grove: St. Michael, Cornhill, p. 188.
1575. Edward Leedes, co. Sussex: Reg. Univ. Oxf. vol. ii. pt. ii. p. 65.
1609. Thomas Leedes, co. Sussex: ibid. p. 305.
1647-8. Charles Leeds of Biddenden, Kent, and Sarah Taylor: Marriage Lic. (Faculty Office), p. 38.
Crockford, 1; New York, 17.

Leek.—Local; v. Leak.

Leeland.—Local; v. Layland.

Leeman, Leemon; v. Leman.

Leeming. — (1) Local, ' of Leeming,' a village near Bedale, co. York. (2) Personal, ' the son of Leming ' (v. Halliwell, and Prompt. Parv. pp. 295-6). In the Towneley Mysteries Leming is a horse's name, from its bright, flashing colour.

' Say, Malle and Stott, wille ye not go? Lemynge, Morelle, White-horne, io.'

The editor (Preface, p. xii) says that Leming as a cow's name occurs in the will of a West Riding yeoman. That Leming was a personal name and became a surname seems indubitable.

Stephen Leming, co. Oxf., 1273. A.
William Leming, co. Oxf., ibid.
Stephen de Leminge, co. Kent, ibid.
Johannes Lemyng, 1379: P. T. Yorks. p. 5.
Isolda Lemyng, 1379: ibid.
Willelmus Lemyng, *sutor*, 1379: ibid. p. 277.
1545. Buried—Urseley (Ursula) Lemynge: St. Dionis Backchurch, p. 180.
1645. William Leming (Essex) and Ellen Rolt: Marriage Lic. (London), ii. 276.
London, 2; West Rid. Court Dir., 7; Philadelphia, 3.

Leeper, Leaper.—Nick. ' the leper,' a variant; v. Lepper. The

fact that Leper or Lepper is now nearly extinct shows a tendency to throw it off as objectionable. Hence, probably, the deceptive-looking Leeper.

1567. Thomas Leper, of Over Kellet: Lancashire Wills at Richmond (1457-1680), p. 182.
1598-9. John Leaper and Florence Dawson: Marriage Lic. (London), i. 259.
1611. Robert Leaper, of Over Kellet: Lancashire Wills at Richmond (1457-1680), p. 182.
1746. Married—William Leapper and Ann Manning: St. Geo. Chap. Mayfair, p. 72.
London, 2, 0; New York, 1, 0; Philadelphia, 5, 0; Oxford, 0, 1.

Leer.—Local; v. Lear.

Lees, Leese, Leighs.—Local, ' at the lees ' (v. Lee), from residence thereby. Also ' of Lees,' a hamlet in the parish of Ashton-under-Lyne. This has originated a large number of the South Lancashire Lees.

Roger de Lees, co. Norf., 1273. A.
John de Lees, co. Norf., ibid.
Avelina de Leys. J.
William de Leghes, ibid.
1577. William Sulham and Anne Lease, *widow*: Marriage Lic. (London), i. 76.
1582. Robert Leese, of Ashton-under-Lyne: Wills at Chester, i. 121.
1593. Edward Leese, of Ashton-under-Lyne: ibid.
1687. Bapt.—Richard, son of Richard Leighs: St. Jas. Clerkenwell, i. 323.
London, 12, 4, 0; Manchester, 47, 1, 0; MDB. (co. Stafford), 18, 10, 0; New York, 13, 0, 0.

Leeson, Leason.—(1) Bapt. A corruption of Levison, v. Lewis. I am told that the Levison-Gowers call themselves the Lesson-Gowers. (2) Bapt. ' the son of Lece,' i.e. Lettice. Lecia and Lece seem to have been popular forms.

Lecia de Eltesle, co. Camb., 1273. A.
Robert fil. Lece, co. Camb., ibid.
Lecia Arnet, co. Camb., ibid.
Johannes Lesson, 1379: P. T. Yorks. p. 79.
Gryfyn Leyson, 1524: Reg. Univ. Oxf. i. 135.
1625. Joseph Willmor and Sarah Leason: Marriage Lic. (London), ii. 154.
1666. Francis Bromley and Frances Leeson: Marriage Alleg. (Canterbury), p. 197.
London, 5, 3; Liverpool, 2, 0; New York, 2, 1.

Leete.—Bapt. ' the son of Let-tice,' from the nick. Lete; v. Lett.

We find a dim. Letelin also existing at the hereditary surname period.

Walter Letelin, co. Norf., 1273. A.

Cf. Hewelin, i.e. little Hew (v. Hewling).

Letia (without surname), co. Camb., 1273. A.
Nicholas fil. Lete, co. Bedf., ibid.
Roger Lete, co. Oxf., ibid.
Walter Lete, co. Suff., ibid.
1745. Married—Thomas Leett and Rebecca Wittaker: St. Geo. Chap. Mayfair, p. 54.
1778. — Edward Griffiss and Mary Leet: St. Geo. Han. Sq. i. 284.
London, 9; New York, 3.

Leetham, -them; v. Latham.

Leftwich. — Local, ' of Leftwich,' a township in the parish of Davenham, co. Chester.

Johannes Lethewyche, 1379: P. T. Yorks. p. 54.
1602. John Leftwich, of Leftwich, co. Ches.: Wills at Chester, i. 121.
1641. William Leftwich, of Northwich, *gentleman*: ibid. ii. 136.
1647. Ellen Leftwich, of Weaverham, *widow*: ibid.
1751. Married—James Pritchard and Mary Leftwich: St. Geo. Chap. Mayfair, p. 196.
London, 8.

Legard, Ledgard, Ledger, Ledgar, Ledgerson.—Bapt. ' the son of Leger.' I find no evidence in favour of Lower's statement that the origin is ' le garde,' the guard or keeper. The final *d* is a common excrescence. St. Leger was a canonized priest of Chalons, the French form being Leguire (Yonge, ii. 430). With the intrusive *d* in Ledger, cf. Rodger for Roger.

Leggard de Aula, co. Camb., 1273. A.
Lyger de la Frache, co. Oxf., ibid.
Adam Leger', co. Camb., ibid.
Andrew fil. Legg', co. Camb., ibid.
Thomas Leggard, co. Norf., ibid.
Johannes Leggard, *hostiler*, Bradforth (Bradford), 1379: P. T. Yorks. p. 190.
Willelmus Lyggard, 1379: ibid.
1584. John Legerde and Alice Alsopp, *widow*: Marriage Lic. (London), i. 132.
1595-6. Christopher Roffie and Catharine Leger, *widow*: ibid. p. 227.
1746. Bapt.—Eliz., d. John Ledgerson: St. Jas. Clerkenwell, ii. 281.
London, 0, 1, 7, 1, 0; West Rid. Court Dir., 0, 5, 1, 0, 0; MDB. (co. Stafford) (Ledgerson), 1; Leeds (Ledgard), 1; Sheffield (Ledger), 5; Philadelphia (Ledger), 8.

Legerton.—Local, 'of Legerton.'

Hugh de Legerton, co. Notts, 1273. A. London, 1.

Legg, Legge.—(1) Local, 'at the leigh' or 'legh' (v. Lee); cf. Whitelegge and Whiteley.

John de Leg, co. Oxf., 1273. A.
Pagan de la Leg, co. Wilts, Hen. III–Edw. I. K.
Avice de Leg, co. Salop, ibid.

(2) Bapt. 'the son of Legg,' a personal name of the history of which I know nothing. Perhaps a nick. of Legard, q.v.

Andrew fil. Legge, co. Camb., 1273. A.
Nicholas Legge, co. Hunts, ibid.
Roger Legge, co. Soms., ibid.
John Legge, co. Soms., 1 Edw. III: Kirby's Quest, p. 260.
William Legge, co. Hunts, 1581: Reg. Univ. Oxf. vol. i. pt. ii. p. 100.
1630. Bapt.—Robert, s. John Legge: Reg. Stourton (co. Wilts), p. 7.
1770. Married—William Legg and Ann Cawdron: St. Geo. Han. Sq. i. 200.
London, 19, 4; New York, 1, 1; Philadelphia, 6, 1.

Leggatt, Leggett, Leggitt, Leggott, Leggate, Leggat.—(1) Local, 'at the lidgate' (q.v.), an inevitable corruption; 'atte Lidgate' or 'Lidyate' was one of our commonest entries, and must have left many representatives. (2) Offic. 'the legate,' an ambassador, a commissioner; M.E. *legate*, *legat*; O.F. *legat*.

Geoffrey le Legat, co. Devon, 1273. A.
Robert Legat, co. Camb., ibid.
Thomas Legat, co. Norf., ibid.
Ricardus Leget, 1379: P. T. Yorks. p. 268.
1585. Married—Richard Colfe and Elsabeth Legget: St. Dionis Backchurch, p. 10.
1770. — Henry Legitt and Catherine Eagan: St. Geo. Han. Sq. i. 198.
London, 0, 8, 16, 1, 2, 0; MDB. (co. Lincoln), 0, 1, 2, 21, 1, 0; New York, 3, 36, 0, 0, 0, 6.

Legh, Leigh.—Local, 'at the legh'; v. Lee. The reason why Leigh has so much larger a representation in the Manchester Directory than that of London lies in the fact that Leigh, a parish in South Lanc., early gave rise to a family name that has very strongly ramified. Of course the origin of the name is the same. The *i* in Leigh was inserted in more recent times.

Pagan a la Legh, co. Wilts, 1273. A.
Richard de la Legh, co. Oxf., ibid.
Johel de Legh, co. Devon, ibid.
Avelina de la Legh, co. Surrey, 20 Edw. I. R.

An old Cheshire family still preserve the old form Legh.

1580. Thomas Legh, of Atherton: Wills at Chester, i. 121.
1617. Jane Leigh, of High Leigh, *widow*: ibid.
1636. William Legh, of Bolton, *linen-draper*: ibid. ii. 137.
London, 0, 17; Manchester, 0, 44; New York, 0, 6.

Leicester; v. Lester.

Leifchild, Liefchild.—Nick. 'lief child,' i.e. dear child (v. Leaf); *lief*, dear, still exists in 'I had as lief'; cf. Darling.

William Lefchild, C. R., 3 Edw. I.
William Levechilde, C. R., 13 Hen. IV.
Cf. Cecilia Levebarne, 1379: P. T. Yorks. p. 141.
1696. Bapt.—Henry, s. Henry Liftchild: St. Jas. Clerkenwell, p. 367.
1763. Married—John Church and Martha Leafchild: St. Geo. Han. Sq. i. 120.
London, 1, 1.

Leigh.—Local; v. Legh.

Leighton.—Local, 'of Leighton,' parishes in cos. Hunts, Salop, and Bedford. Also two townships in co. Ches., in the parishes of Nantwich and Neston; v. Layton, Lee, and Legh.

Henry de Leyton, co. Bucks, 1273. A.
Roger de Leyton, co. Hunts, ibid.
Clement de Leyton, co. Hunts, ibid.
Adam de Leytun, co. Salop, Hen. III–Edw. I. K.
1601. Robert Leighton, co. Salop: Reg. Univ. Oxf. vol. ii. pt. ii. p. 253.
1750. Married—Thomas Leighton and Mary Ann Tash: St. Geo. Chap. Mayfair, p. 182.
London, 15; Philadelphia, 10.

Leishman, Lishman.—Nick. 'leish' or 'lish,' nimble, strong, active, stout, alert, lithe. A North-English term.

'Wha's like my Johnny,
Sae leish, sae blithe, sae bonny?'
The New Keel Row (v. Brockett).

Cf. Blythman, Merriman, Strongman.

1783. Married—Joseph Lishman, *husbandman*, and Betty Macartney, *widow*: St. Mary, Ulverston, p. 427.

1785. Married—Robert Lishman and Jane Park: ibid. p. 429.
1806. — Stephen Hagan and Frances Leisman: St. Geo. Han. Sq. ii. 349.
1809. — Henry Hawkins and Mary Lisseman: ibid. p. 410.
London, 2, 0; West Rid. Court Dir., 0, 1; New York, 2, 0.

Leitch, Leitche.—Local and occup.; v. Leach. This is probably a Scottish variant.

London, 2, 0; Liverpool, 4, 1; New York, 6, 0.

Leland; v. Layland.

Leman, Lemmon, Lemon, Leeman, Leemon, Leaman, Limon.—Bapt. 'the son of Leman,' a corruption of Liefman. No doubt in some instances employed as a nickname, meaning dear one, sweetheart; cf. Leifchild.

'And hail that madyn, my lemman.'
Towneley Mysteries.

But its use as seen below compels us to place it mainly in the category of fontal names. The forms in the London Directory show little change. It was a familiar joke some few years ago to say that there were two Lemons in the House of Commons and only one Peel.

Leman Bru, co. Norf., 1273. A.
Alan fil. Leman, co. Camb., ibid.
Eldred Leman, co. Suff., ibid.
Thomas Leiman, co. Oxf., ibid.
William Lemon, of Preston, 1642: Wills at Chester (1621–50), p. 138.
1672. James Wynstanley and Eliz. Leman: Marriage Alleg. (Canterbury), p. 83.
1746. Married—William Lemon and Mary Newman: St. Geo. Chap. Mayfair, p. 66.

The following has an excrescent *d*, as in Simmonds or Hammond:

1752. Married—John Lemond and Dorcas Massey: St. Geo. Chap. Mayfair, p. 214.
1790. — John Newton and Lucy Lemmon: St. Geo. Han. Sq. ii. 45.
London, 4, 4, 15, 2, 0, 0; MDB. (co. Lincoln) (Limon), 3; (East Rid. Yorks) (Leaman), 1; Plymouth (Leaman), 2; New York, 7, 2, 5, 2, 1, 0.

Lemprière.—Nick. 'the emperor'; cf. King, Caesar, &c.

'In the Chartuleries of the Abbaye de la Trinité, at Caen, this patronymic goes through the various gradations of Imperator, L'Empereur, Lemprere, Lempreur, to Lempriere': Lower, Patr. Brit. p. 192.

1580-1. Hugh Lamprier, of Jersey: Reg. Univ. Oxf. vol. ii. pt. ii. p. 96.
1610. Philip Lempriere, of Jersey: ibid. p. 314.
1735. Married—James Lemprier and Sarah Atkinson: St. Mary Aldermary (London), p. 47.
London, 1; MDB. (co. Surrey), 1; New York, 1.

Lenecock.—Bapt. 'the son of Leonard,' from the nick. Lenny and the suffix -cock (v. Cock, and cf. Wilcock, Simcock, &c.); v. Leney.
Robertus Lenecok, 1379: P. T. Yorks. p. 102.
Ricardus Lenecok, 1379: ibid.
Margareta Lenecok, 1379: ibid.

Leney, Lenney, Lenny.—Bapt. 'the son of Leonard,' from the nick. Lenny.
Lenne Textor, co. Camb., 1273. A.
Osbert fil. Lene, co. Suff., ibid.
William Leny, co. Worc., ibid.
1786. Married — George White and Eliz. Lenny: St. Geo. Han. Sq. i. 382.
London, 2, 2, 2; Philadelphia, 0, 4, 8.

Lennard; v. Leonard.

Lent. — ? Bapt. 'the son of Lent' (?), from the ecclesiastical season; cf. Nowell, Midwinter, Christmas, Pentecost, Pask, &c.
William Lent, co. Oxf., 1273. A.
1675. Bapt.—John Hengoe, s. Hengoe Lentt: St. Thomas the Apostle, p. 67.

The two following entries may bear on the season:
Willelmus Lenten, 1379: P. T. Yorks. p. 30.
Johannes Lentyn, 1379: ibid. p. 257.
London, 2; New York, 29.

Lenthall, Lentell.—Local, 'of Leinthall': (1) Earls Leinthall, a chapelry in the parish of Aymestrey, co. Hereford; (2) Leinthall-Starkes, a parish in co. Hereford.
1377. Roger de Leynthale, rector of Mundham, co. Norf.: FF. x. 171.
1575. William Lentall, co. Hereford: Reg. Univ. Oxf. vol. ii. pt. ii. p. 65.
1611. Robert Leynthall, co. Oxf.: ibid. p. 324.
1669. Bapt.—William, s. William Lentall: St. Jas. Clerkenwell, i. 238.
1799. Married—Maurice Lenthall and Mary Hastings: St. Geo. Han. Sq. ii. 206.
London, 1, 1; Boston (U.S.), 0, 1.

Lenton.—Local, 'of Lenton,' a parish in co. Notts, near Nottingham.
Clemence de Lentone, co. Hunts, 1273. A.

Simon de Lenton, co. Derby, 20 Edw. I. R.
1579. William Buckley and Eliz. Lenton: Marriage Lic. (London), i. 92.
1613. Bapt.—William, s. John Lenton: St. Jas. Clerkenwell, i. 67.
London, 2; Philadelphia, 1.

Leo.—Bapt. 'the son of Leo.' Seemingly in the hereditary surname period a Jewish personal name.
Leo le Horsmongere, co. Camb., 1273. A.
Jacobus fil. Leonis, co. Linc., ibid.
Judeus Leo, co. Linc. ibid.
London, 3; New York, 5.

Leonard, Leonards, Lennard, Lenard.—Bapt. 'the son of Leonard.' For history of the name, v. Miss Yonge's Christian Names, i. 180. St. Leonard was a popular saint both in England and in France.
William Leonard, co. Hunts, 1273. A.
1546. James Leonard and Alice Barber: Marriage Lic. (Faculty Office), p. 8.
1606. Sampson Lennard, co. Norf.: FF. vi. 302.
1650. John Lennard and Jane Binding, widow: Marriage Lic. (Faculty Office), p. 45.
1791. Married—George Leonard and Eleanor Martin: St. Geo. Han. Sq. ii. 65.
London, 14, 1, 4, 1; Philadelphia, 134, 1, 6, 0.

Leopard, Lepard, Leppard, Lippard.—Nick. 'the leopard'; cf. Bull, Fox, &c.
John Lyppard, co. Norf., 1273. A.
Reginald Leopard, C. R., 28 Edw. I.
John Lepard. H.
1738. Married—Thomas Rogers and Eliz. Leopard (co. Surrey): St. Antholin (London), p. 149.
1790. — Richard Leopard and Sarah Wheeler: St. Geo. Han. Sq. ii. 38.
1794. — James Evans and Ann Lippard: ibid. ii. 117.
London, 0, 5, 2, 2; MDB. (co. Sussex), 1, 0, 6, 0; Middlesborough (Leopard), 2; New York (Leopard), 1.

Lepper.—Nick. 'the leper.' It has been said that leprosy was brought into Europe by the Crusaders. There were several spitals or hospitals for lepers in England. In the Assisa de Foresta, assigned by Manwood to 6 Edw. I, it is enacted that if any beast of chase be found wounded or dead, 'caro mittatur ad domum leprosi, si qua prope fuerit.' 'Lepyr, or lepre, man or woman or beeste, leprosus.

Lepyr, or lepre, sekenesse, lepra': Prompt. Parv., and see Way's note thereon.

Geoffrey le Lepere, co. Oxf., 1273. A.
Walter le Lepere, co. Bucks, ibid.
Robert Leper, co. Linc., ibid.
William le Lepar, C. R., 13 Edw. I.
Cf. Magister et Fratres Hospital' Sti. Jacobi Leprosi, London: A. i. 420.
Alicia Lepar, 1379: P. T. Yorks. p. 154.
1558. Buried—Thomas Leper, bowyer: St. Mary Aldermary, p. 133.
1576. John Hunte and Joyce Leper, widow: Marriage Lic. (London), i. 72.
West Rid. Court Dir., 1; New York, 2; Philadelphia, 6.

Leppington.—Local, 'of Leppington,' a chapelry in the parish of Scrayingham, E. Rid. Yorks.
1634. Bapt.—Marie, d. Roberte Lepington: St. Jas. Clerkenwell, i. 130.
1680-1. Lemuell Leppington and Sarah Allen: Marriage Alleg. (Canterbury), p. 50.
MDB. (West Rid. Yorks), 1.

Lermit. — Occup. 'l'hermite,' the hermit; cf. Armitage.
Dennis Lermitt, or Lermyt, of Norwich, 1621: FF. iii. 365.
Crockford, 1.

Lescombe.—Local, 'of Lescomb.' One of the many place-names ending in -comb, so frequently to be met with in the West country (v. Combe).
Thomas de Lescomb, co. Soms., 1 Edw. III: Kirby's Quest, p. 138.
London, 1.

Lesingham.—Local, 'of Lessingham,' a parish in co. Norfolk, near Stalham.
1674. Thomas Lessingham and Sarah Francklin: Marriage Alleg. (Canterbury), p. 113.
1676. Henry Lesingham and Dinah Penny: ibid. p. 174.
1713. Married—Samuel Lesingham and Mary Miller: St. Mary Aldermary, p. 42.
London, 1.

Lester, Leicester, Leycester.—Local, 'of Leicester,' the well-known capital of the county of that name.
Ongar de Leycestre, co. Devon, 1273. A.
Sandre de Leycestre, London, ibid.
Robert de Lestre, co. Camb., ibid.
Henry de Laycestre, specer (i.e. spicer), 6 Edw. II: Freemen of York, i. 15.
1578. Ralph Lester, co. Ches.: Reg. Univ. Oxf. vol. ii. pt. ii. p. 80.

1604-5. Thomas Leycester, or Lester, co. Essex: ibid. p. 270.
London, 24, 1, 1; Crockford, 10, 3, 0; MDB. (co. Chester), 0, 0, 2; New York, 31, 1, 0.

L'Estrange. — Nickname, 'le Estrange,' the stranger; v. Strange, the recognized English form.
Alex. le Estraunge, co. Norf., 1273. A.
Roger le Estraunge, co. Linc., ibid.
Roger Extraneus, co. Bedf., ibid.
Roger le Extrange, co. Bedf., ibid.
1546-7. Nicholas Lestrange and Catharine Men: Marriage Lic. (Faculty Office), p. 9.
1661. Alex. Scott and Ann Lestrange: ibid. p. 55.
Crockford, 2; New York, 6.

Lesturgeon, Lestourgeon.— Nick. 'the sturgeon,' q.v. Evidently a French importation.
1746. Married—Peter Lesturgeon and Mary Hide: St. Geo. Chap. Mayfair, p. 69.
1768. — Aaron Lestourgeon and Caroline Douxsaint: St. Geo. Han. Sq. i. 178.
1772. — Isaac Lesturgeon and Ann Wragg: ibid. p. 225.

Letchford.—Local, 'of Lechford,' possibly Leckford, a parish in co. Southampton. But v. Latchford.
Alex. de Lecheford, co. Oxf., 1273. A.
Philip de Lecheford, co. Oxf., ibid.
Walter de Lecheford, co. Oxf., ibid.
1592. Married—William Marten and Isabel Lechforde: St. Mary Aldermary, p. 8.
1616. Arthur Knight and Eliz. Lechford: Marriage Lic. (London), ii. 45.
Oxford, 1; Philadelphia, 4.

Letchworth. — Local, 'of Letchworth,' a parish in co. Hertford, near Hitchin.
Urban de Lecheworth, co. Essex, Hen. III-Edw. I. K.
1579. Giles Holden and Ellen Lechworthe: Marriage Lic. (London), i. 89.
London, 1; Philadelphia, 3.

Lethbridge.—Local, 'of Lethbridge.' Like Mr. Lower (Patr. Brit. p. 193), I cannot find the spot. It is evidently a Devonshire surname, and no doubt the locality is or was in that county.
1615. Anthony Lethbridge, co. Devon, *gentleman*: Reg. Univ. Oxf. vol. ii. pt. ii. p. 339.
1803. Married—Thomas Buckler Lethbridge and Ann Goddard: St. Geo. Han. Sq. ii. 280.
London, 4; Plymouth, 9; MDB. (co. Devon), 11; New York, 3; Boston (U.S.), 3.

Letherby; v. Leatherby.

Letheridge.—Bapt. ; v. Leveridge, of which this is an American variant. Cf. Leverton for Letherton.
Boston (U.S.), 1.

Leton ; v. Letton.

Lett, Letts, Lettson, Lettsom, Letson.—Bapt. 'the son of Lettice' (Latin, *laetitia*, gladness). As a girl's name Lettice was very popular in its day. It is now rare. It suffered at the Reformation, and still more so in the Puritan era, not being a Bible name, and implying hilarity. Lett was the nick., Letts and Lettson being the patronymics. Lettsom is occasionally a corrupted form of Lettson (cf. Ransom for Ranson, or Hansom for Hanson), but in general it is local (v. Lettsom). It is said that a well-known doctor of the last century used to sign his prescriptions 'I. Lettsom,' whence the following:
  'When any patient calls in haste,
  I physics, bleeds, and sweats 'em ;
  If after that they choose to die,
  Why, what care I?
            I Lettsom.'
Nicholas fil. Lete, co. Bedf., 1273. A.
John fil. Lettice, co. Camb., ibid.
Warin fil. Letice, co. Suff., ibid.
Lettice Kygelpeny, C. R., 28 Edw. I.
John Lettesone, c. 1300. M.
Johannes Leteson, 1379: P. T. Yorks. p. 211.
Willelmus Letis, 1379: ibid. p. 130.
Alicia Letis, 1379: ibid.
1683. Bapt.—Ann, d. Ralph Lett: St. Jas. Clerkenwell, i. 301.
1782. Married—Richard Hammonds and Ann Lettes: St. Geo. Han. Sq. i. 332.
London, 2, 8, 0, 0, 0; New York, 2, 1, 0, 0, 8.

Lettice.—Bapt. 'the son of Lettice'; v. Lett for further information and earlier instances.
John Lettice. PP.
1568. George Bell and Judith Lettice: Marriage Lic. (London), i. 30.
1647. Buried—William, s. George Lettice: St. Jas. Clerkenwell, iv. 274.

Letton, Letten, Leton.— Local, 'of Letton,' a parish in co. Norfolk, one mile from Shipdham.
Simon de Leton, or Letton, co. Norf., 1273. A.
1337. William de Letton, rector of Buckenham Parva, co. Norf.: FF. ii. 269.
'John, son of Richard de Letton, for 4 marks and a gold ring, gave lands in Heringeshae,' &c. : ibid. x. 48.

1808. Married—William Little and Mary Letten: St. Geo. Han. Sq. ii. 390.
London, 1, 1, 0; New York, 0, 0, 1.

Lettsom. — Local, 'of Ledsham.' Although Lettsom is undoubtedly baptismal in some cases (v. Lett), it is as unquestionably local in others. Ledsham is a parish six miles north from Pontefract. Lettsom is a sharpened form.
Robertus de Ledesam, 1379: P. T. Yorks. p. 154.
Johannes de Ledsam, 1379: ibid. p. 145.
1570. Henry Ledsham: Reg. Univ. Oxf. i. 277.
1602-3. Hugh Rymell and Anne Ledsam, *widow*: Marriage Lic. (London), p. 276.
1603. Thomas Ledsham and Eliz. Danvers: ibid. p. 279.
1775. Married—Joseph Webb and Eliz. Letsome: St. Geo. Han. Sq. i. 249.

Lever. — Local, 'of Lever.' Great Lever is a township in the parish of Middleton, co. Lanc. Little Lever is a chapelry in the parish of Bolton, co. Lanc.
Alexander Lever, of Burnley, 1560: Wills at Chester (1545-1620), p. 122.
Richard Lever, of Little Lever, 1588: ibid.
Margaret Lever, of Lever, 1603: ibid.
Mary Lever, of Bolton-in-le-Moors, *widow*, 1668: ibid. (1660-80), p. 168.
1587. James Tanner and Cicely Leaver (co. Essex): Marriage Lic.(London), i.161.
Robertus Leyver, 1602: Preston Guild Rolls, p. 65.
Manchester, 14; London, 8; New York, 2.

Leverett.— ? Nickname, 'the leveret (?),' a young hare; v. Hare.
William Leverit, co. Oxf., 1273. A.
Agnes Leverit, co. Oxf., ibid.
1577-8. William Leverett and Juda Cole: Marriage Lic. (London), p. 78.
1601. Bapt.—Anthonie, son of Godfrey Leveritt: St. Jas. Clerkenwell, i. 30.
1625. Married—Thomas Leueritt and Ann Nicholls: ibid. iii. 55.
1702. — Roger Leveret and Hanah Speak: ibid. p. 225.
London, 1; Manchester, 2; Oxford, 3; New York, 2.

Leveridge, Leverick, Leverich.—Bapt. 'the son of Leofric'; cf. Aldridge for Aldrich. Many surnames ending in -*ridge* seem to be of local origin ; yet they merely represent the -*rich* or -*rick*, that is, the suffix of so many early personal names. Coleridge is local, Leveridge is personal.
Mariota Leverich, co. Hunts, 1273. A.

Henry Leverige, co. Camb., 1273. A.
Robert Leverikke, co. Linc., ibid.
Roger Lefrich, co. Salop, ibid.
Richard Leverich, co. Soms., 1 Edw.
III : Kirby's Quest, p. 153.
1587. John Leveridge, co. Northampt. :
Reg. Univ. Oxf. vol. ii. pt. ii. p. 161.
1613. Bapt.—Charles, s. John Lyve-
ridge : St. Jas. Clerkenwell, i. 67.
1733. Buried—Joshua Leverick : St.
Dionis Backchurch, p. 302.
1778. Married—William Levridge and
Eliz. Turner : St. Geo. Han. Sq. i. 294.
London, 2, 0, 0 ; New York, 6, 0, 11.

Leversha.—Local, 'of Levi-
shagh,' a manor in the parish of
Buxton, co. Norfolk.
Halfred de Leveshagh, co. Norf.,
c. 1200 : FF. vi. 445.
Henry de Leveshagh, co. Norf., c. 1260 :
ibid.
William de Leveshaye, co. Norf., 20
Edw. I. R.
London, 1.

Leverton.—Local, 'of Lever-
ton,' parishes in cos. Notts and
Lincoln. Also found as Letherton,
proving its origin, viz. 'the town of
Lether,' its first settler ; cf. Liver-
pool for Litherpool ; v. Litherland.
William de Letherton, co. Linc.,
1273. A.
William de Levertone, co. Linc., ibid.
Henry de Leverton, co. Linc., ibid.
Thomas de Leverton, co. Linc., 20
Edw. I. R.
1572. Bapt.—Jane, d. John Leverton :
St. Mary Aldermary, London, p. 57.
1578. Walter Hunt and Eliz. Leverton :
Marriage Lic. (London), i. 82.
London, 6 ; MDB. (co. Lincoln), 4 ;
Philadelphia, 1.

**Levett, Levet, Levette, Le-
vitt.**—(?) Local, 'of Livet.' Mr.
Lower says, 'From one of the places
in Normandy called Livet. The
Itin. de la Normandie mentions no
less than eight of these' (Patr.
Brit. p. 194). This derivation
seems probable.
William Levett, co. Linc., 1273. A.
Eustacius de Livet, co. York, Hen. III-
Edw. I. K.
1537. John Shelley and Johanna Levet :
Marriage Lic. (London), i. 9.
John Leavett, or Levet, co. Sussex,
1590 : Reg. Univ. Oxf. vol. ii. pt. ii. p. 176.
Thomas Levite, or Levet, co. York,
1610 : ibid. p. 318.
1694. Richard Levett and Ann Sweet-
apple : Marriage Lic. (London), ii. 316.
London, 8, 1, 1, 0 ; New York, 3, 1, 0, 1.

Levin (son ; v. Lewin.

Levison.—Bapt. 'the son of
Lewis,' q.v. Also v. Leeson.

Roger Leveson, co. Oxf., 1273. A.
William Leveson, co. Oxf., ibid.
The Levisons in the New York
Directory are mostly of Jewish
parentage, 'the son of Levi,' as
is shown by the personal names
appended.
London, 1 ; New York, 14.

Lew, Lewe.—Local, 'at the
lew,' i.e. lee, a sheltered place
(v. *lee*, Skeat, who says the word
lee is Scandinavian) ; cf. Lewthwaite, a local Cumberland surname, i.e. sheltered meadow.
Professor Skeat adds, 'The true
English word is *lew*,' and quotes
its provincial use from Halliwell.
Alicia ate Lewe, co. Hunts, 1273. A.
John ate Lewe, co. Salop, ibid.
1614. Married—Robert Lew and Prudence Greene : St. Jas. Clerkenwell, iii. 41.
1749.— Mark Demontherand and Sarah
Lew : St. Geo. Chap. Mayfair, p. 137.
New York, 0, 1 ; Boston (U.S.), 3, 0.

Lewd.—Nick. 'the lewd,' i.e.
the ignorant, untaught, one of the
laity, a layman. 'Lered and lewed,'
i.e. clergy and laity (v. Piers Plow-
man, Bk. iv. 11).
William le Lewed, c. 1300. M.
Robert le Lewed, ibid.
Robert le Lewede, C.R., 5 Edw. III. pt. i.
Roger Lude, co. Soms., 1 Edw. III :
Kirby's Quest, p. 184.
Nicholas Lude, co. Soms., 1 Edw. III :
ibid.

Lewes.—Local, 'of Lewes,' a
market-town in co. Sussex. The
surname is almost entirely lost in
Lewis (q.v.), that name also being
found in the form of Lewes.
John de Lewes, co. Oxf., 1273. A.
1555. Thomas Lewes and Alice Poole :
Marriage Lic. (London), i. 16.
1577. Thomas Lewes, co. Monmouth :
Reg. Univ. Oxf. vol. ii. pt. ii. p. 75.
— Lewes Hewes, co. Glamorgan : ibid.
1580. William Lewes, London : ibid. p. 92.
Crockford, 1.

**Lewin, Levin, Levine, Le-
vene, Levinson, Levenson,
Lewinson.**—Bapt. 'the son of
Leofwin,' from the popular form
Lewin or Levin. Of one Leofwine,
a Warwickshire thegn, Professor
Freeman quotes, 'Leuuinus emit
ab Alwino fratre suo,' and again,
'Hanc terram dixit Leuuinus se
tenere de Vlstano Episcopo' (Hist.
Norm. Conq. v. 785).

Leofwin, son of Hugh, temp. Ric. I :
Freeman, Norm. Conq. v. 894.
Leofwin, son of Godwin, temp. Ric. I :
ibid. iii. 361.
This Leofwin was in command
at Stamford Bridge.
Robert Lefwyne, co. Oxf., 1273. A.
Cecilia Leffeyne, co. Hunts, ibid.
Nicholas Leffeyne, co. Hunts, ibid.
William Lewine, co. Norf., ibid.
Henry Lewyn, co. Northumb., ibid.
The above references very clearly
mark the stages by which Lewin
was reached.
Lewin Scani, co. Bedf., 20 Edw. I. R.
Henry Lewyn, burgess of Newcastle-
on-Tyne, 1292 : Brand's Hist. of New-
castle, i. 41.
1626. Bapt.—Barbary, d. Levin Wel-
den : St. Michael, Cornhill, p. 118.
1674. Buried—A child of Charles and
Levine Hornsby : St. Thomas the Apostle
(London), p. 140.
London, 18, 1, 1, 2, 1, 0, 0 ; New York,
16, 20, 10, 2, 7, 7, 5.

Lewington, Lewinton. —
Local, 'of Levington,' a parish in
co. Suffolk, five miles from Ipswich ;
cf. Lewin and Levin in the preceding article.
1662-3. John Hill and Sarah Lewington : Marriage Alleg. (Canterbury),
p. 84.
1749. Married—John Lewington and
Mary Crowhurst : St. Geo. Chap. Mayfair, p. 147.
1765.— Samuel Lewington and Jemima
Paice : St. Geo. Han. Sq. i. 139.
London, 3, 2.

Lewis, Lewison, Levison.—
Bapt. 'the son of Louis' or 'Lewis'
(for the history of this personal
name read an interesting account
in Yonge, ii. 387-9). Miss Yonge
thinks Lewis is used by the Welsh
as an Anglicanism of Llewelyn.
This view is confirmed by the following entry :
Llewelyn ap-Madoc, alias Lewis Rede,
archdeacon of Brecon, 1437 : Hist. and
Ant. St. David's, p. 360.
John Levesone, co. Soms., 1 Edw. III :
Kirby's Quest, p. 110.
Lewis ap-Owen, archdeacon of Car-
digan, 1487 : Hist. and Ant. St. David's,
p. 361.
Lewis ap-Rhys, prebendary of St.
David's, 1502 : ibid. p. 361.
William Lewson, archdeacon of Caer-
marthen, 1554 : ibid. p. 360.
1521. William Lewys and Alice Mason :
Marriage Lic. (London), i. 2.
1586. Humphrey Smith and Ursula
Lewson, alias Levison : ibid. p. 150.
London, 220, 1, 1 ; New York, 344, 2, 14.

Lewknor, Luckner.—Local, ' of Lewknor,' a parish in co. Oxf. I am informed that this surname still exists in Sussex.

Geoffrey de Lewekenore, co. Oxf., 1273. A.
Alina de Leuekenore, co. Bucks, ibid.
Roger de Leukenore, co. Sussex, 20 Edw. I. R.
1568. Mathew Machell and Mary Lewckenare: Marriage Lic. (London), i. 39.
1625. Edward Lewkner and Sarah Richardson: ibid. ii. 151.
Boston (U.S.), 0, 1.

Lewtas.—Local. I cannot find the spot. It is essentially a Lancashire name.

George Lewtus, of Out Rawcliffe, 1675: Lancashire Wills at Richmond (1457-1680), p. 183.
Manchester, 2; Lancaster, 1; MDB. (co. Lancaster), 4.

Lewthwaite, Laithwaite.— Local, ' of Lewthwaite,' some spot in co. Cumberland, or Furness, North Lancashire, with the familiar suffix -thwaite (v. Thwaite); probably a corruption of Leathwaite (v. Lea); cf.

1670. William Bisbrowne, of Leathwayte, Furness: Lancashire Wills at Richmond (1457-1680), p. 34.
Cf. Lucraft for Leacraft; v. Leacroft.
1546. Buried—George Lewteth (Lewthwaite): St. Mary, Ulverston, p. 3.
1553. Married—John Greene and Agnes Lewteth: ibid. p. 21.
1670. — George Fell and Helenar Leauthet: ibid. p. 151.
1650. James Lewthwaite, of Bardsey, parish of Urswick: Lancashire Wills at Richmond (1457-1680), p. 183.
1697. John Lewthwaite, of Lancaster: ibid. (1681-1748), p. 166.
1750. Married—Joseph Speck and Eliz. Leathwait: St. Michael, Cornhill, p. 72.
1792. — John Lewthwaite and Mary Tweedie: St. Geo. Han. Sq. ii. 84.
London, 2, 0; MDB. (co. Cumberland), 5, 0; Manchester, 1, 1.

Lewty. — ? Local. I cannot find any definite information about this North Lancashire surname.

Leonard Lewtie, of Much Plumpton, 1608: Lancashire Wills at Richmond (1457-1680), p. 183.
Edmund Lewtie, of Lea, 1673: ibid.
John Lewtye, of Plumpton Magna, 1676: ibid. p. 184.
London, 1; MDB. (co. Lancaster), 1; Preston, 2.

Ley.—Local, ' at the lea' or ' legh' (q.v.), from residence thereby.

William de Ley, co. Hunts, 1273. A.
John de Leya, co. Oxf., ibid.
Philip de la Ley, co. Northumb., 20 Edw. I. R.
1546. Thomas Dodsworth and Eliz. Ley, widow: Marriage Lic. (Faculty Office), p. 8.
1593. Married—Robart Leymine and Katharine Ley: St. Dionis Backchurch, p. 12.
1699. Bapt.—Mary, d. Robert Ley: St. Jas. Clerkenwell, i. 382.
London, 8; New York, 10.

Leycester.—Local, ' of Leicester'; v. Lester. Leycester is the oldest form.

Leyland.—Local; v. Layland.

Leyson, Lewson, Leyshon. —Bapt. ' the son of Lewis,' a Welsh surname. The h in Leyshon is intrusive, as in Dodgshon or Hodgshon; v. Lewis.

1453. Lewis Leyson: Reg. Univ. Oxf. i. 20.
1454. Robert Lewson: ibid. p. 24.
1524. Gryffyth Leyson: ibid. p. 135.
Ystrad Rhondda (South Wales), 0, 0, 1; Llantrissant, 0, 0, 1.

Liard.—Nick.; v. Lyard.

Libbe, Libby, Libbie, Libbey, Libbis.—Bapt. ' the son of Isabel,' from the nicks. Ibb and Libb, popularly Libby or Libbie. The variants of this surname are very well represented in the United States. The present nursery name is still Libby; for Elizabeth and Isabel are the same name, and are interchangeable in mediaeval records.

William Lybbe, chaplain, 1506: Reg. Univ. Oxf. i. 45.
John Libb, co. Oxf.: ibid. vol. ii. pt. ii. p. 149.
London, 0, 2, 0, 0, 2; Boston (U.S.), 1, 86, 4, 26, 0.

Liberty.— (?) Occup. Probably a corruption of Leadbeater, q.v. But Mr. Lower thinks it must be considered local. Then it would be ' of the liberty,' from residence in some early franchised district so called. There is a village called Liberty in co. Fife.

1669. Married—John Bayley and Saray Libiter: St. Jas. Clerkenwell, iii. 156.

This looks like a halfway house between Leadbeater, q.v., or Lidbetter, and Liberty.

London, 1; Crockford, 1; Boston (U.S.), 1; Worcester (U.S.), 5.

Libtrot; v. Liptrott.

Licence; v. Lysons, an imitative variant.

Lickbarrow; v. Litchbarrow.

Lickfold, Lickfeld.—Local, ' of Lickfold,' a place near Petworth, co. Sussex (Lower).

MDB. (co. Sussex), 2, 0; London, 4, 0; Philadelphia, 0, 3.

Lickorish; v. Liquorish.

Lidbetter.—Occup.; v. Leadbeater.

Crockford, 1.

Liddell, Liddle, Liddall, Liddel.—Local, ' of the Liddel,' a river in Roxburghshire. The surname settled in Newcastle at an early period; v. Lower, Patr. Brit. p. 194.

1586. George Gardener and Mary Lyddall: Marriage Lic. (London), i. 154.
1680. Bapt.—Mary, d. William Lydall: St. Dionis Backchurch, p. 154.
1752. Married—William Goodchild and Mary Liddell: St. Geo. Chap. Mayfair, p. 220.
1775. — John Claxton and Mary Liddle, St. Geo. Han. Sq. i. 258.
MDB. (co. Cumberland), 5, 1, 0, 0; (co. Northumberland), 5, 0, 0, 1; London, 6, 6, 1, 0; New York, 5, 2, 0, 0.

Liddington, Lidington. — Local, ' of Liddington': (1) a parish in co. Rutland, near Uppingham; (2) a parish in co. Wilts, near Swindon.

Robert de Liddinton, co. Oxf., Hen. III-Edw. I. K.
(Tenentes) Lidinton, co. Rutland, 1273. A.
Fulco de Lydinton, co. Oxf., ibid.
Thomas de Ledintone, co. Soms., 1 Edw. III: Kirby's Quest, p. 203.
1603. Bapt.—Eliz., d. Thomas Liddington, armorer: St. Peter, Cornhill, i. 53.
1795. Married—Thomas Bullivant and Susannah Liddington: St. Geo. Han. Sq. ii. 134.
MDB. (co. Northampton), 1, 2.

Liddon.—Local, ' of Lydden,' a parish in co. Kent, near Dover. Probably this is the true parent; but there may have been a spot bearing this name in the West country.

John de Lyddone, co. Soms., 1 Edw. III: Kirby's Quest, p. 177.

Adam de Lyddone, co. Soma., 1 Edw. III : Kirby's Quest, p. 177.
1543-4. John White and Johanna Lydden, of Whittsam, co. Kent : Marriage Lic. (Faculty Office), p. 2.
1800. Married—William Lyddon and Bessey Goldsmith : St. Geo. Han. Sq. ii. 224.

London, 3 ; New York, 1.

Lidgate, Lidgett, Liggett, Ligate, Ligget, Lydiate, Liddiatt.—Local, ' at the lidgate,' from residence thereby, a common local term in old records. Lidgate, a gateway, an entrance, perhaps a covered way (v. Skeat on *lid*). As a child I played on a spot called Lidgate, near Waterhead, Oldham. ' John Dodds dwellynge at Lodgayte at the signe of the spayd ' : *Liber Bursarii Eccles. Dunelmensis*, Surt. Soc. Bishop Hotham in 1320 gave for alms ' tenementum vocatum Lythgates ' : *Hist. Elien. Ang. Sacra.* p. 643.

Robert atte Lidgate, C. R., 14 Edw. I.
Walter atte Lideyate. H.
Matilda atte Lydeyate, 1379 : P. T. Yorks. p. 119.
Robertus atte Lytheyate, 1379 : ibid. p. 122.
Johannes Robert-man atte Lythgat, 1379 : ibid. p. 123.

For the suffix *-yate*, v. Yate.

1591. Thomas Lidiot, co. Oxf.: Reg. Univ. Oxf. vol. ii. pt. ii. p. 187.
1602. John Death and Mary Lidiatt : Marriage Lic. (London), i. 269.
1627.. Married—Edward Underwood and Dorothy Lidyate : St. Jas. Clerkenwell, iii. 58.

Ludgate is found as well as Lidgate ; cf. Ludgater in next article.

1784. Married—Thomas Harper and Rebecca Ludgate : St.Geo. Han.Sq. i. 365.

Hence the local Ludgate, London.

Manchester (Liggett), 1 ; London (Lidgett), 1 ; Liverpool (Lidgate), 1 ; MDB. (co. Chester) (Lydiate), 1 ; (co. Salop) (Ligget), 1 ; (co. Derby) (Ligate), 1 ; (co. Glouc.) (Liddiatt), 2 ; New York (Lidgate), 1.

Lidgater, Ludgater.—Local, ' the lidgater,' one who resided at a lidgate (q.v.). This surname incidentally proves the former familiarity of the local term *lidgate* ; v. Bridger.

1738. Married—William Ludgater and Ann Langstaff : St. Geo. Han. Sq. i. 21. Crockford, 0, 2.

Lidington ; v. Liddington.

Lidlington.—Local, ' of Lidlington,' a parish in co. Bedf., near Ampthill.

London, 1.

Lidster.—Occup. ' the litster,' a dyer. The later and almost universal form was Lister, q.v. Lidster is naturally found in Yorkshire, the great home of the litsters, both as regards occupation and name.

Hull, 2 ; Sheffield, 3 ; West Rid. Court Dir., 1 ; MDB. (co. Lincoln), 1.

Lidstone.—Local, ' of Lidstone,' a hamlet in the parish of Church Enstone, co. Oxf.

London, 7 ; Philadelphia, 2.

Lief ; v. Leaf.

Liefchild ; v. Leifchild.

Liefqueen. — Nick. ' dear quean.' M.E. *lef*, dear ; and M.E. *quene*, a woman, a quean, a strumpet. But probably here simply ' dear woman,' a title of endearment like Bellamy ; cf. Leifchild.

Edith Lefquene, 1273. A.
Johannes Lefquen, ibid.

Ligget(t ; v. Lidgate.

Light.—Nick. ' the little,' a variant of Lyte ; cf. Lightman, a later variant of Lyteman (i.e. Littleman) ; v. Lyte. It is quite possible that Light might refer to the light tread of the original bearer of the sobriquet, but I find no evidence.

1586. William Bellamye and Hester Lighte : Marriage Lic. (London), i. 150.
1626. Married—Thomas Broughe and Ann Light : St. Michael, Cornhill, p. 24.
London, 7 ; MDB. (Hants), 8.

Lightbody.—Nick. for one of light weight, nimble and agile.

London, 1 ; New York, 4.

Lightbourn, Lightbourne, Lightbound, Lightbown, Lightbowne.—Local, ' of Lightbourn.' Probably there are several spots so called in co. Lancashire. A suburb of my old parish (Ulverston, North Lancashire) is called Lightburne, the beck or burn flowing alongside (v. Burn). With the corrupted Lightbound, cf. Simmonds for Simmons, or *riband* for *ribbon*. The *d*, of course, is an excrescence. That Lightbown and

Lightbowne are variants of Lightbourn is proved below, although proof is not needed. There is no representative of any of the forms in my London Directory (1870). It is well confined to co. Lancashire.

Roger Lightborn, of Caton, 1593 : Lancashire Wills at Richmond (1457-1680), p. 184.
Robert Lightbourne, of Eccles, 1598 : Wills at Chester (1545-1620), p. 123.
William Lightbourne, of Bolton-le-Moors, 1614 : ibid.

In the next generation the name is written Lightbowne :

James Lightbowne, of Manchester, 1621 : Wills at Chester (1621-50), p. 139.
Alexander Lightbowne, of Eccles, 1638 : ibid.

In Ulverston, Lightburn is a name over a shop in close proximity to the suburb Lightburne.

1781. Bapt.—Ann, d. George Lightburn : St. Mary, Ulverston, p. 498.
MDB. (co. Lancaster), 1, 1, 1, 0, 0 ; Manchester, 0, 1, 0, 1, 2 ; Liverpool (Lightbound), 4 ; New York (Lightbourn), 1.

Lightfoot.—Nick. ' light foot,' from the light springy tread of the bearer ; cf. Golightly and Pettifer ; also Lithefoot, below.

William Lightfot, co. Camb., 1273. A.
Henry Lithfot, co. Oxf., ibid.
Robert Lightfot, 1301. M.
Willelmus Lightfote, 1379 : P. T. Yorks. p. 239.
1571. Randall Smythe and Mary Lightfoot, *widow*: Marriage Lic. (London), i. 49.
London, 8 ; Crockford, 8 ; New York, 1.

Lightoller, Lightowler, Lightowlers.—Local, ' of Lightowlers,' an estate in the parish of Stockport.

John Lightowlers, of Withnell, co. Lanc., 1606-7 : Lancashire Inquisitions, pt. i. p. 74.
Robert Lightowler, of Wyndybank, 1620 : Wills at Chester, i. 123.
James Chadwick, of Lightowlers, parish of Stockport. 1621 : ibid. ii. 45.
Edmund Lightowler, of Castleton, 1623 : ibid. p. 139.
1624. Bapt.—John, s. Thomas Lightollors : St. Jas. Clerkenwell, i. 98.
1631. Married—Thomas Godfrey and Ann Lightellers : ibid. iii. 62.
Chorley (co. Lanc.), 1, 0, 0 ; North Bierley (Yorks), 0, 3, 5 ; New York, 0, 3, 0.

Liley, Lilie ; v. Lilly.

Lill.—Local, ' of Lille,' i.e. the French town of that name.

Robert de Lill, co. Oxf., Hen. III-Edw. I. K.
William de Lille, co. Oxf., 1273. A.
Robert de Lille, co. Oxf., ibid.
1734. Married—William Lill and Eliz. Randal: St. Geo. Han. Sq. i. 13.
London, 4; MDB. (co. Lincoln), 10; Boston (U.S.), 2.

Lillicrap, Lillicrapp, Lilly-crap, Lillycrop.—Local. This curious surname is found in cos. Devon and Cornwall. I cannot suggest a derivation, but no doubt it is the name of some locality.
Plymouth, 6, 0, 0, 0; London, 0, 1, 0, 0; MDB. (co. Cornwall), 0, 0, 2, 1.

Lillingston.—Local, ' of Lillingstone,' two parishes, one in co. Bucks, the other in co. Oxf.
1689. Marmaduke Constable and Eliz. Lillingstone: Marriage Alleg. (Canterbury), p. 123.
Oxford, 1.

Lillington.—Local, ' of Lillington': (1) a parish in co. Dorset, near Sherborne; (2) a parish in co. Warwick, near Leamington.
1616. John Lillington: Reg. Univ. Oxf. i. 360.
1691. Nathaniel Huthnance and Susanna Lillington: Marriage Alleg. (Canterbury), p. 196.
1800. Married—Thomas Barnett and Susanna Lillington: St. Geo. Han. Sq. ii. 214.

Lilly, Lilley, Lillie, Liley, Lillee, Lilie.—(1) Bapt. ' the son of Lily.' The dim. Lilion (now Lilian) must have been in early use, as it is found as a surname in the Hundred Rolls; cf. Marion for Mary, now Marian.
Geoffrey Lilion, co. Bedf., 1273. A.

(2) Local, ' of Lilley,' a parish in co. Hertf., four miles from Luton. (3) Local, ' of Lilly,' a hamlet in the parish of Catmore, co. Berks. My two first instances occur in the neighbourhood.
Nicholas Lilie, co. Oxf., 1273. A.
William Lilie, co. Oxf., ibid.
Beatrix Lyly, 1379: P. T. Yorks. p. 214.
Robert Lyllye, 1546: Reg. Univ. Oxf. i. 213.
1564. Gilbert Lyllye and Joanna Matthewe, widow: Marriage Lic. (London), i. 30.
1571. John Lyllie, co. Kent: Reg. Univ. Oxf. vol. ii. pt. ii. p. 51.
1605. Bapt.—William, s. Raphe Lylly: St. Jas. Clerkenwell, i. 45.

London, 8, 16, 5, 2, 0, 0; MDB. (co. Lincoln), 1, 8, 0, 0, 1, 0; New York, 14, 7, 5, 0, 0, 2.

Lillyman, Lilleyman, Lilleman, Lilliman.—Occup. ' the servant of Lilly,' q.v. One more instance of a fairly large class of surnames compounded of -man (i.e. servant) as suffix to the baptismal name of the master. The most conspicuous instances are Matthewman, Addyman, and Perryman, q.v. Although not entirely confined to that county, Yorkshire must be looked upon as the home of this batch of surnames.
Ricardus Lilyman, 1379: P. T. Yorks. p. 72.
Johannes Lelman, 1379: ibid. p. 75.
Thomas Lelyman, 1379: ibid. p. 63.
1752. Married—James Lillyman and Ann Pugh: St. Geo. Chap. Mayfair, p. 232.
Sheffield, 1, 1, 0, 0; Swinton (near Rotherham), 0, 0, 1, 0; MDB. (co. Lincoln), 0, 0, 0, 1; Boston (U.S.) (Lillyman), 2.

Lillywhite.—Nick. ' the lily-white,' one whose complexion was white as a lily. One of endless surnames of a similar class; v. White, Reid, Black, Russell, Burnell, &c.
1664. Married—Thomas Lilliwhite and Rebecca Benbrigg: St. Jas. Clerkenwell, iii. 116.
1723. William Washington and Sarah Lillywhite, widow: Marriage Lic. (Faculty Office), p. 250.
1788. Married—Emery Mussett and Mary Lillywhite: St. Geo. Han. Sq. ii. 12.
1796. — Charles Hensley and Lucy Lillewhite: ibid. p. 157.
London, 4.

Lilter.—Occup. ' the lilter,' a player on an instrument, a singer.
Roger le Lilter, co. Hunts, 1273. A.

Lilwall.—Local, ' of Lilwall,' a township in the parish of Kington, co. Hunts.
1783. Married—John Wolf and Eliz. Lilfwell: St. Geo. Han. Sq. i. 342.
London, 1.

Limbert, Limbird. — Bapt. ' the son of Lambert ' (?). This corruption is found in co. Norfolk three centuries ago. This county being adjacent to the Low Countries we naturally expect to see Lambert and its corruptions familiar there.

Stephen Lymbert, died Oct. 10, 1589, Norwich: FF. iv. 61.
1785. Married—John Limbird and Ann Elborn: St. Geo. Han. Sq. i. 375.
London, 1, 2; New York, 5, 0.

Limbrey.—Local, ' of Limbury, a hamlet in the parish of Luton, co. Bedf.
1605. John Lymberie, co. Soms.: Reg. Univ. Oxf. vol. ii. pt. ii. p. 284.
1666. William Limbery and Sarah Swanley: Marriage Alleg. (Canterbury), p. 188.
1686. James Field and Eliz. Limbrey: ibid. p. 230.
London, 1.

Limbrick, Limrick. — (1) Local, ' of Lambrigg ' (?), a township in the parish of Kendal, co. Westm. The suffix -brigg (bridge) often becomes brick; cf. Philbrick and Maybrick. (2) Local ' of Limerick ' (?), with an intrusive b after m, as is so common. The surname would first become Limrick, then Lim-b-rick. I have an impression that if there are any low-lying hills about Limber in co. Linc. the origin is Limberigg, i.e. Limberidge, one who lived on the ridge thereby; cf. Coleridge, &c.
1564-5. James Limbericke: Reg. Univ. Oxf. vol. ii. pt. ii. p. 24.
— Thomas Limbericke: ibid.
1667. Married—Thomas Wall and Mary Lemericke: St. Jas. Clerkenwell, iii. 137.
1748. — Thomas Limberick and Eliz. Chamberlain: St. Geo. Chap. Mayfair, p. 114.
London, 1, 0; Liverpool, 0, 1; New York, 0, 1; Boston (U.S.), 0, 1.

Limburg, Limberg.—Local, ' of Limburg.' But more probably ' of Limber,' a parish and a hamlet (Magna and Parva) in co. Linc. Mr. Lower writes these as Limbergh.
Johannes de Lymbergh', 1379: P. T. Yorks. p. 113.
Robertus de Lymburgh', 1379: ibid.
London, 1, 0; New York, 1, 0; Boston (U.S.), 0, 1.

Limeburner. — Occup. ' the limeburner.' It is never safe to say a surname is extinct. Limeburner was in existence at the latter end of last century; cf. Limewright. Since writing the above I find the surname has crossed the Atlantic, and is in a fairly flourishing condition.
John le Lymberner, Rot. Fines, 7 Edw. I.

Robert le Lymbrennere, C. R., 13 Edw. II.
1760. Married—Benjamin Limeburner and Sarah Wilkshire: St. Geo. Han. Sq. i. 94.
Philadelphia, 4.

Limehirst.—Local, 'at the limehurst,' from residence beside a wood of lime-trees; v. Hirst.
Johannes del Lymehirst, 1379: P. T. Yorks. p. 35.

Limes.—Local, 'at the limes,' more correctly 'lines,' i.e. the linden-trees, from residence beside some particular lime-tree or trees; v. Limehirst.
Hugo del Lymbe, 1379: P. T. Yorks. p. 179.
1708. Married—John Limb and Mary West: St. Antholin (London), p. 121.
London, 1.

Limewright. — Occup. 'the limewright,' a limeburner. M.E. *lym*, lime.
Hugh de Limwryte, co. Bucks, 1273. A.

Limiter.—Offic. 'the limiter,' i.e. a friar licensed to beg within certain prescribed limits; cf. Fryer, Monk, &c.
1581. George Limiter, or Lymiter, co. Kent: Reg. Univ. Oxf. vol. ii. pt. ii. p. 103.
Mary, d. of George Limiter of Canterbury: Visitation of Glouc., 1623, p. 166.
Turning, however, to the Canterbury register, I find:
1712. Buried—Peter Lemastre: Reg. Canterbury Cathedral, p. 314.
which the register of affidavits spells Lematre. So it may be but a French name Anglicized. There are six Lemaitres in the London Dir.

Limmer.—(1) Local, 'of Limber' (?). Limber Magna is a parish, and Limber Parva a hamlet, in co. Lincoln, near Caistor. Limmer is probably a variant, but v. Limner. (2) Occup. 'the limer,' a limeburner; v. Limewright and Limeburner. Limer would naturally settle down into Limmer.
Thomas de Limer, bailiff of Norwich, 1245: FF. iii. 58.
William de Lymar, co. Northampt., 1273. A.
John de Limer, co. Hunts, ibid.
Agnes Limer, co. Hunts, ibid.
Adam Lymer, co. Camb., ibid.
1620-1. Robert Limber and Jane Roberts: Marriage Lic. (London), ii. 96.

1627. Married—Thomas Limer and Bridget Wilkinsone: St. Mary Aldermary, p. 16.
1776. — Stephen Limmer and Eliz. Deewes: St. Geo. Han. Sq. i. 263.
There can be little doubt that both (1) and (2) share the parentage of Limmer.
London, 2; New York, 3.

Limner, Limmer, Lomer, Lommer.—Occup. 'the limner,' an illuminator of books, missals, &c. (v. Limmer for a different origin.)
'Parchemente makers, skynners and plowers,
Barbers, boke-bynders, and lyminers.'
Cocke Lorelle's Bote.
Nicholas Cotes, *lummer*, 1421, York. W. 11.
'*Lymnyd*, as bookys, *elucidatus*; lymnore, *elucidator, miniographus*': Prompt. Parv. It is natural to find Oxford and Cambridge represented in the Hundred Rolls, as seen below. In the *Mun. Acad. Oxon.*, p. 550, we find a quarrel settled between 'John Conaley, lymner,' and John Godsend, 'stationarius.' It is arranged that the former shall occupy himself 'liminando bene et fideliter suos libros.'
Thomas Liminor, co. Camb., 1273. A.
Ralph Illuminator, co. Oxf., ibid.
John de Gippeswyk, *lomenoure*, 14 Edw. III: Freemen of York, i. 34.
Henry Lumynour, C. R., 15 Ric. II.
Thomas Lumpner, 1470, York. W. 11.
Godfrey le Lomynour. T.
Limner lingered on till the 18th century, and perhaps is not yet defunct.
'John Limner, of Chevington, and Eliz. Sibbes, of this town, were married August 22nd, 1700': Sibbes' Works, i. cxlii.
1767. Married—Donald McDonald and Sarah Lomer: St. Geo. Han. Sq. i. 167.
1787. — William Collin and Prudence Limmer: ibid. p. 407.
There need be no hesitation in accepting these as modern forms of this old and interesting occupative name. It is found, as already seen, as Lummer (with the *n* dropped) in Yorkshire in the 15th century. The following is unmistakable:
1562. Buried—William, son of Harry Lomner: St. Dionis Backchurch, p. 78.
1374. Henry Lumnor, or Liminour, or Lomynour, or Lumnour, or Luminour: FF. iv. 185, iv. 180, iii. 113, ii. 398, v. 56.

London, 0, 2, 2, 0; MDB. (co. Suffolk), 0, 2, 0, 0; Boston (U.S.), 0, 1, 0, 1.

Limon; v. Leman.

Limrick; v. Limbrick.

Linacre, Linaker, Lineker, Linneker.—Local, 'of Linacre,' a township in the parish of Walton-on-the-hill, co. Lancaster. One of many local terms with *-acre* as suffix; cf. Stirzaker, Whittaker.
Peter de Linacre, co. Camb., 1273. A.
Mabilia de Linacre, co. Camb., ibid.
1573. Robert Pepper and Agnes Lynecar: Marriage Lic. (London), i. 58.
Thomas Linaker, of Chester, 1602: Wills at Chester (1545-1620), p. 124.
Robert Linaker, of Great Meols, 1613: ibid.
John Lynacre, of Stourton, parish of Bebbington, 1614: ibid. p. 128.
Elizabeth Lynacre, of Linacre, *widow*, 1616: ibid. p. 110.
1809. Married—Michael Edward Jacob and Catherine Liniker: St. Geo. Han. Sq. ii. 411.
Liverpool, 4, 2, 0, 0; MDB. (co. Ches.), 0, 1, 0, 0; (West Rid. Yorks), 0, 0, 1, 0; Sheffield (Linneker), 1.

Lincey; v. Lindsey.

Linck, Lincke; v. Link.

Lincoln.—Local, 'of Lincoln,' the cathedral city of the shire of that name. The surname has ramified strongly in the United States.
Robert de Linccolne, co. Notts, 1273. A.
Richard de Linccolne, co. Hunts, ibid.
Hugh de Lyncoln, *piscator*, 3 Edw. II: Freemen of York, i. 12.
Daniel de Lyncoln, 1324. M.
Adam de Lincoln, 1379: P. T. Yorks. p. 296.
William Lincoln, 1537: Reg. Univ. Oxf. i. 189.
1753. Sibella Lincon, carried to be buried at Epping, Essex: St. Dionis Backchurch, p. 319.
London, 15; Boston (U.S.), 149.

Lind, Lynde, Lynd.—Local, 'at the lind,' i.e. the linden-tree, modernly, the lime-tree. *Lind* is the true subs., and *linden*, like woollen or golden, is the adj. (Skeat). Lind is the root of many local names, such as Lyndhurst, Lindley, Lindale, and Lindow, q.v.
Henry de la Lynde. B.
Robert ate Lynde, temp. 1300. M.
Thomas de la Lynde, co. Soms., 1 Edw. III: Kirby's Quest, p. 197.
1596. Humphrey Linde, of London: Reg. Univ. Oxf. vol. ii. pt. ii. p. 218.

1800. Married—Peter Snowdon and Harriot Linde: St. Geo. Han. Sq. ii. 222. London, 3, 1, 0; New York, 0, 8, 1.

Lindale, Lindall, Lindell, Lyndall.—Local, 'of Lindall'; v. Lindow.

London, 0, 0, 0, 1; Philadelphia, 1, 0, 2, 9.

Lindley, Linley.—Local, 'of Lindley,' a parish in the outskirts of Huddersfield, co. Yorks. Smaller spots will, no doubt, be so called; v. Lind.

Robert de Linleye, co. Bedf., 1273. A. Augustin Lynleye, co. Soms., 1 Edw. III: Kirby's Quest, p. 94.
1594. Arthur Lindley, co. York: Reg. Univ. Oxf. vol. ii. pt. ii. p. 207.
1670. John Lindeley and Anne Wilson: Marriage Lic. (Faculty Office), p. 116.
London, 5, 5; West Rid. Court Dir., 4, 11; New York, 4, 1.

Lindow, Lindo.—Local, ' of Lindall,' in Furness, North Lancashire, a hamlet two miles from Ulverston. This became Lindaw, and then Lindow. Thus in the same district Presow (as a surname) represents the older Preesall, and Picthaw stands for Picthall. Lindow has crossed the Duddon into Cumberland.

1546. Bapt.—Elesabeth Lindoe: Reg. Ulverston Ch., p. 2.
—— Kataran Lindoe: ibid.
George Lindo, or Lyndoe, of Urswick, 1592: Lancashire Wills at Richmond, p. 184.
Margaret Lindowe, of Ulverston, 1598: ibid.
James Lindall, of Ulverston, Furness, 1661: ibid.
Elizabeth Lindaw, of Aradfoot, Ulverston, 1662: ibid.
London, 1, 4; MDB. (co. Cumberland), 2, 0; Ulverston, 1, 0; New York. 0, 5.

Lindraper.—Occup. 'the linendraper.' Linen, like woollen, is an adjective; the subs. is lin. God made 'ffor to cover us and clethe us also lyne, and wolle, and lethire' (Mirror of St. Edmund, E.E.T.S., p. 21). Cocke Lorelle's Bote includes 'lyne-webbers' and 'lyne-drapers'; v. Liner.

Ino le Lyngedraper, C. R., 52 Hen. III. William le Lyndraper. G.
Wymund le Lyngedraper, co. Oxf., 1273. A.
Elias le Lyndraper, temp. 1300. M.
William le Lynged(r)aper, 7 Edw. II: Freemen of York, i. 15.

Lindsey, Lindsay, Linsey, Linzee, Lincey. — Local, 'of Lindsey.' Lindsey, a parish in co. Suffolk; no doubt it means the ' linden-isle.' Probably other spots are so called. A division of co. Lincoln is still called the 'Parts of Lindsey.' The instances below are widely separated, and point to more than one spot so called.

Walter de Lyndesay, 56 Hen. III: Nicolson and Burn's Hist. Westm. and Cumb., i. 35.
Thomas de Lyndesey, co. Derby, 1273. A.
Henry de Lindeseye, co. Kent, ibid.
Robert de Lindesay, co. Notts. ibid.
William de Lyndeseye, co. Northampt., 20 Edw. I. R.
William de Lyndesaie, 11 Edw. I: Nicolson and Burn's Hist. Westm. and Cumb., i. 35.
Willelmus de Lyndesay, 1379: P. T. Yorks. p. 273.
Jacobus de Lyndesay, 1379: ibid. p. 164.
1546. Ralph Brooke and Eliz. Lynseye: Marriage Lic. (London), i. 9.
1793. Married—William Ball and Margaret Lindsey: St. Geo. Han. Sq. ii. 99.
London, 14, 17, 2, 0, 0; MDB. (co. Berks), 0, 0, 0, 1, 0; Crockford (Lincey), 1; Philadelphia, 19, 124, 2, 0, 0.

Line, Lyne.—Local, 'at the lane' (?), from residence therein. Probably one of the many dialectic forms of the word lane.

Thomas in ye Lyen, 1379: P. T. Yorks. pp. 140-1.
Willelmus in ye Lyne, 1379: ibid.
Johannes del Lyen, 1379: ibid.
1582. Buried—William Lyne, sonne of John Lyne; he dyed of ye plague, yers 29: St. Peter, Cornhill, i. 129.
1606. Richard Lyne, co. Hants: Reg. Univ. Oxf. vol. ii. pt. ii. p. 289.
London, 11, 4; New York, 0, 1: Boston (U.S.), 2, 0.

Lineaweaver. — Occup. ; v. Linwebb.

Lineaker.—Local; v. Linacre.

Liner, Lyner.—Occup. 'the liner,' a flax-dresser; v. Lindraper.

Richard de Wymondham, lyner. 9 Edw. III: Freemen of York, i. 29.
1668. Married—Thomas Lynear and Saray Browne: St. Jas. Clerkenwell, iii. 160.

With Lynear, cf. Bowyer, lawyer, &c., the e being for euphony as the y in Bowyer.

Philadelphia, 1, 0; New York, 0, 1.

Linford, Linforth. —Local, 'of Linford,' two parishes (Great and Little Linford) in co. Bucks. The suffix -forth = ford (v. Forth).

Roger de Lynford, co. Bucks, 1273. A.
1591. William Osborne and Parnell Lyndeforde: Marriage Lic. (London), i. 194.
1670. Bapt.—John, s. John Linford: Kensington Ch. p. 53.
London, 4, 2; New York, 1, 0.

Ling, Linge.—(1) Local, 'at the ling,' one who resided on the heath or ling; cf. Heath, Gorst, Furse. 'Lynge of the hethe (lynge, or hethe)' : Prompt. Parv. Mr. Way in a note easily proves that ling was a common term for heath. He adds, 'Skinner gives ling as the common appellation of heath in Lincolnshire.' (2) Local, ' of Ling,' a parish in co. Somerset, six miles from Bridgewater. Both Ling and Linge are familiar surnames in the county. Probably the origin is the same.

Henry atte Lyng, co. Norf., 52 Hen. III: FF. x. 117.
John de Ling, co. Norf.. 1273. A.
Roger de Lyng, bailiff of Norwich, 1370: FF. iii. 100.
1570. Married—James Bland, draper, and Ellen Ling, widow: St. Mary Aldermary, p. 6.
Henry and John Linge were resident in Virginia, in 1623: Hotten's Lists of Emigrants, p. 72.
1661. Buried—Ann Ling: St. Antholin (London), p. 88.
London, 13, 0; MDB. (Norfolk), 6, 0; (Somerset), 13, 1; Boston (U.S.), 5, 0.

Lingard, Linguard.—Occup. 'the ling-ward' (?) or 'ling-guard' (?). I can only suggest this solution. The great Catholic historian was of Lincolnshire parentage. Canon Tierney, after stating this fact, says, 'The family name, with the accent on the first syllable, is still common in the district. (Claxby), which, within the memory of persons yet alive, was a wild expanse covered with furze and ling' (Lingard's Hist. of Eng. i. 2, edit. 1854). Lancashire and Cheshire have been familiar with the surname for at least five centuries; cf. Woodward, and v. Ling.

Robert Lyngard, de Preston, co. Lanc., 1415: Preston Guild Rolls, p. 10.

1566. Married—Lawrence (blank) and Dorythye Lyngarde, *widow*: St. Michael, Cornhill, p. 9.
Thomas Lingard, of Eccles, *butcher*, 1569: Wills at Chester (1545-1620), p. 124.
John Lingard, of Middlewich, 1595: ibid.
Laurence Lingart, of Fullwood: Lancashire Wills at Richmond (1457-1748), p. 185.
London, 4, 0; Manchester, 8, 0; MDB. (co. Lincoln), 3, 1; Philadelphia, 3, 0.

Lingen, Lingain.—Local, ' of Lingen,' a parish in co. Hereford; v. Lingham.

John de Lyngayne, co. Salop, 1273. A.
1586-7. John Lingen, of Gloucester Hall: Reg. Univ. Oxf. vol. ii. pt. ii. p. 157.
1698. Married—John Lingen and Sarah Muddiclip: St. Michael, Cornhill, p. 49.
MDB. (co. Hereford), 1, 0; (co. Worc.), 1, 0; Boston (U.S.), 0, 1.

Linger.—Local, ' of Lingure.' Probably of Norman extraction. It is interesting to note that the early Oxfordshire Lingures are still to be met with in the neighbouring county of Buckingham.

Robert de Linguire, co. Berks, Hen. III-Edw. I. K.
Henry de Lingure, co. Oxf., ibid.
Alice de Lyngure, co. Oxf., 1273. A.
1609. Buried—Jane, d Nicholas Lingar: St. Jas. Clerkenwell, iv. 106.
1628. — Joyce Linger: ibid. p. 193.
1632. — Ursula Linger: Canterbury Cath. p. 117.
MDB. (co. Bucks), 2; New York, 1; Philadelphia, 1.

Lingham.—Local, ' of Lingen,' a parish in co. Hereford. Mr. Lower says, ' Lingham, a known corruption of Langham.' I think this must be a mistake. The evidence is distinctly in favour of the derivation given above; v. Lingen.

Leonard Lyngham, or Lyngam, 1541: Reg. Univ. Oxf. i. 200.
Richard Lingam, or Lingen, from Stoke Edyth in co. Hereford, 1542: ibid. pp. 204, 313.
1650. Married—Edmund Lingham and Margarett Jackson: St. Dionis Backchurch, p. 27.
London, 1; Crockford, 3; MDB. (co. Worc.), 1; New York, 2.

Lingwood.—Local, ' of Lingwood,' a parish in co. Norfolk.

John de Lyngwood, of Norwich, 1294: FF. iv. 386.
William de Lingwood, co. Norf., 9 Edw. II: ibid. vii. 237.

1568. Buried—Rowlande, s. John Lyngwood: St. Michael, Cornhill, p. 189.
Thomas Lyngwoode, rector of Ovington, co. Norf., 1601: FF. ii. 296.
London, 1; MDB. (co. Essex), 1; (co. Suffolk), 3.

Link, Linke, Linck, Lincke.—Local, ' atte ling,' a variant; v. Ling. Way in his note to *lynge* in the Prompt. Parv. (p. 305) quotes, ' In Wiltshire nere Shaftesbery is an heth that growth ful of that (Junipere femel) and of lynk, and the lynk is heyere than that,' &c. Nevertheless, this surname may be a variant of Lynch, q.v.

1594. William Lincke (or Linke), co. Oxf.: Reg. Univ. Oxf. vol. ii. pt. ii. p. 202.
1781. Married—Charles Howse and Mary Link: St. Geo. Han. Sq. i. 325.
London, 3, 0, 0, 0; New York, 23, 4, 6, 3.

Linklater, Linkletter. — Local. A Shetland name; cf. Findlater.

London, 2, 0; Boston (U.S.), 0, 3.

Linneker; v. Linacre.

Linley.—Local; v. Lindley.

Linnell.—Bapt. ' the son of Lionel,' which is proved below to have become popularly Lynell or Linel.

Leonel de Anvers. H.
Lunell Wodeward, co. Essex, 1273. A.
Reginald Linel, co. Linc., ibid.
1513. Richard Lyonell: Reg. Univ. Oxf. i. 87.
1577. Richard Lynell and Margery Awsten, of Kensington: Marriage Lic. (London), i. 76.
1579. John Barnefeilde and Margery Lyonell, *widow*, of Kensington: ibid.
Probably Margery is the same person in both instances. This is very strong evidence in favour of my view.
1612. Married—Henry Lynnell and Margaret Rothley: St. Dionis Backchurch, p. 18.
1620. — Robert Spriggins and Ann Linnell: St. Jas. Clerkenwell, iii. 48.
London, 1; MDB. (co. Northampton), 13; Boston (U.S.), 23.

Linnett, Linnet.—Bapt. ' the son of Linot,' which, no doubt, is the dim. of some familiar girl's name. Now we turn Caroline into the nick. Lina, which would become Linot with the dim. suffix. But Caroline was unknown in the sur-

name epoch. Probably it was for Elenot, a dim. of Elen or Ellen. It must be remembered that Eleanora was a most popular girl's name at the period, and must have had its nicks. and dims.

Lenote de Kyngeston, co. Soms., 1273. A.
Linota atte Feld, ibid.
Linota the Widow, ibid.
Lyna de Stoford, co. Soms., 1 Edw. III: Kirby's Quest, p. 145.
Beatrix Linot, 1379: P. T. Yorks. p. 41.
Willelmus Lynot, 1379: ibid. p. 43.
1550-1. Thomas Bond and Ellen Lynnett: Marriage Lic. (London), i. 13.
1753. Married—Jasper Linnet and Ann Redman: St. Geo. Chap. Mayfair, p. 240.
London, 2, 0; MDB. (co. Northampton), 1, 0; Boston (U.S.), 1, 1.

Linsey.—Local; v. Lindsey.

Linstead.—Local, ' of Linstead, a parish in co. Kent. Also two parishes (Magna and Parva Linstead) in co. Suffolk.

Richard de Lindested, co. Kent, 1273. A.
John de Linstede, parson of Cawston, 1370: FF. v. 381.
Thomas de Linstead, of Norwich, 1676: ibid. iv. 311.
1804. Married—John Widdison and Eliza Linstead: St. Geo. Han. Sq. ii. 315.
London, 2; Oxford, 1.

Linthwaite.—Local, ' of Linthwaite,' a chapelry in the parish of Almondbury, W. Rid. Yorkshire, four miles from Huddersfield.

Roger de Lingthweyt, co. Norf.,1273. A.
The above entry may represent some other spot.
Willelmus de Lyntthewayt, 1379: P.T. Yorks. p. 181.
1606. Edmund Linthwaite, of Saddleworth: Wills at Chester (1545-1620), p. 124.
1619. Buried—Alice, wife of James Lynthweight, *merchant-talor*: St. Peter, Cornhill, i. 175.
1675. James Linthwitt, of Knare: Wills at Chester (1660-80), p. 169.
London, 1; Crockford, 1.

Linton, Lynton.—Local, ' of Linton,' parishes in cos. Cambridge, Devon, Hereford, Kent, and York (W. Rid.). Also townships in cos. Derby, Hereford, York (W. and N. Rid.).

William de Lynton, co. Worc., Hen. III-Edw. I. K.
Richard de Linton, London, 1273. A.
Robert de Lynton, co. Camb., ibid.

Hugh de Linton, co. York, 20 Edw. I. R.

Laurencius de Lynton (of Linton), 1379: P. T. Yorks. p. 269.

1545-6. Robert Lynton and Katherine Johnson: Marriage Lic. (Faculty Office), p. 6.

1686. Bapt.—William, s. Thomas Linton: St. Jas. Clerkenwell, i. 317.

1719. Married—John James and Margaret Linton: St. Dionis Backchurch, p. 59.

London. 7, 0; Manchester, 1, 1; Philadelphia, 31, 0.

Lintott.—Local, 'de Lintot,' 'a place in the department of Seine Inferieure, Normandy, another in the arrondissement of Havre. The family were in Shropshire in the 12th century' (Lower's Patr. Brit. p. 196).

Ralph de Lintot, co. Essex, 1273. A.

1722. Married—Joshua Lyntott and Mary Habersham: St. Jas. Clerkenwell, i. 247.

1789.—Thomas Bonnett and Eliz. Lintott: St. Geo. Han. Sq. ii. 32.

London, 7; Philadelphia, 4.

Linwebb, Lineaweaver.—Occup. 'a linen webster.'

Alina la Lynwebbe, C. R., 6 Edw. II.

Linen is literally the adjective of *lin*, as woollen is of *wool*; cf. *lin-seed*. 'Lyne-webbers,' Cocke Lorelle's Bote: v. Lindraper. The surname persists in the United States as Lineaweaver.

Philadelphia, 0, 3.

Lippard.—Nick.; v. Leopard.

Lippett, Lippiatt.—Local; v. Lipyeatt.

Lippincott, Lippencott.—Local, 'of Luffincott,' a parish in co. Devon, seven miles from Holsworthy. Mr. Lower says, 'The baronets (extinct 1829) traced their family into Devonshire in the 16th century, and there is little doubt that the name was originally Luffincott, from a parish in that county so called' (Patr. Brit. p. 196.) The surname is now very rare in England, but it has ramified in the most extraordinary fashion in the United States. I see no reason to doubt Mr. Lower's derivation. Everything points to a Devonshire habitat.

John Lippencott, co. Cornwall, 1585: Reg. Univ. Oxf. vol. ii. pt. ii. p. 143.

Arthur Lippincot, co. Devon, 1594: ibid. p. 205.

1777. Married—Eli Lippencott and Sarah Richards: St. Geo. Han. Sq. i. 279.

MDB. (co. Gloucester), 1, 1; New York (Lippencott), 2; Philadelphia, 120, 0.

Lipscomb, Lipscombe, Lipscoumb.—Local, 'of Lipscomb.' I cannot find the spot. Possibly a variant of Liscombe, a hamlet in the parish of Soulbury, co. Bucks.

1673. William Lipscomb and Frances Gundey: Marriage Alleg. (Canterbury), p. 97.

1788. Married—William Lipscomb and Frances Longhurst: St. Geo. Han. Sq. ii. 4.

1792. — Samuel Sutcham and Susan Lipscombe: ibid. p. 70.

London, 2, 4, 1; Philadelphia, 1, 0, 0.

Liptrott, Liptrot, Libtrot.—? Local, 'of Liptrott' (?). I cannot find the spot. It is a well-established Lancashire surname. Mr. Lower, quoting Ferguson, says, 'It corresponds with a German name Liebetrut' (Patr. Brit. p. 196). In this case it would probably be a personal name.

Richard Liptrot, of Lowton, 1601: Wills at Chester (1545-1620), p. 124.

Jane Liptrott, of Haulgh, parish of Bolton, 1617: ibid.

John Liptrott, of Lawton, co. Lanc., *yeoman*, 1647: ibid. (1621-50), p. 140.

Alexander Liptrott, of Chorley, *yeoman*, 1649: ibid.

1612. Bapt.—Ann, d. William Liptrod: St. Jas. Clerkenwell, i. 64.

1749. Married—Ralph Dell and Alice Liptrot: St. Geo. Chap. Mayfair, p. 139. Bolton (co. Lanc.), 2, 0, 0; Manchester, 0, 1, 1; London, 0, 1, 0.

Lipyeatt, Lippett, Lippiatt.—Local, 'at the loop-gate,' from residence thereby. Either the gate (or yate) at the bend of the road, or the gate through a hole in the wall; cf. loop-hole (v. *loop*, Skeat). This compound local term occurs frequently in West-country records. It gave birth to a hamlet Lypeat, in the parish of Kilmersdon, co. Soms.

Robert de Luppegate, co. Wilts, 1273. A. John atte Lupeyate, co. Soms., 1 Edw. III: Kirby's Quest, p. 204.

Thomas atte Lupeyate, co. Soms., 1 Edw. III: ibid. p. 94.

Editha atte Lupeyate, co. Soms., 1 Edw. III: ibid. p. 97.

1450. Philip Lepegate, or Lypgate: Reg. Univ. Oxf. i. 10.

1460. Mr. Philip Lepeyate, rector of Salle, co. Norf.: FF. viii. 274.

1619. William Lipyeatt, co. Wilts: Reg. Univ. Oxf. vol. ii. pt. ii. p. 374.

1648. Bapt.—William, s. William Lippiat: St. Jas. Clerkenwell, i. 169.

1686-7. Thomas Hatchett and Eliz. Lippyatt (co. Wilts): Marriage Lic. (Faculty Office), p. 183.

1734. Married—William Lipyeat and Mary Jefferys: St. Antholin (London), p. 146.

The following entry mentions a Lypiat in co. Glouc.:

1749. Married—Charles Cox, of Lypiat, co. Glouc., and Eliz. Westley, of Kemble, co. Wilts: St. Geo. Han. Sq. i. 41.

London, 0, 1, 0; MDB. (co. Devon), 1, 0, 0; (co. Somerset), 0, 0, 2.

Liquorish, Lickorish, Lickrish.—Nick. ' the liquorish,' also lickerish, one dainty, or nice in his palate; one inclined to be greedy or gluttonous.

'To fulfil all thy lickerous talent.' Chaucer, C. T. 12473.

'A proud peevish flirt, a liquorish, prodigal quean': Burton's Anat. Melanc. (Introduction, p. 64).

1637. Bapt.—Ann, d. John Licorishe: St. Jas. Clerkenwell, i. 136.

1652. — William, s. John Licorish: ibid. p. 180.

1654. Buried—Eliz., d. John Licoris: ibid. iv. 301.

London, 2, 0, 0; MDB. (co. Northampton), 1, 0, 0; London Court Dir., 0, 1, 1.

Liscomb, Liscombe, Liscom.—Local, 'of Liscombe,' a hamlet in the parish of Soulbury, co. Bucks. In some instances, no doubt, a variant of Luscombe, q.v. (v. also Lipscomb).

1623. William Michell and Jane Liscombe: Marriage Lic. (London), ii. 128.

New York, 5, 1, 0; Boston (U.S.), 1, 0, 4.

Lishman.—Nick.; v. Leishman.

Lisle, Lyle.—Local, 'at the isle,' from residence thereon. In Crockford 'de Lisle.'

Robert del Ile, 1 Edw. III: KKK. iv. 83.

Richard del Isle, 1323: ibid. v. 303.

John Lisle, 1338: PPP. p. 102.

Robertus del Ile, 1379: P. T. Yorks. p. 156.

1744. Married—Nicholas Lyle and Eliz. Davenport: St. Geo. Chap. Mayfair, p. 40.

1747. — Davie Lisle and Jane Harrison: ibid. p. 95.

London, 1, 3; Crockford, 2, 2; New York, 1, 7.

Lister, Litster, Lyster. — Occup. 'the litster,' a dyer. Both trade-name and surname, founded on the trade-name, existed in Yorkshire for centuries. To-day it is one of the largest represented surnames in the shire. 'Lystare, clothe dyynge (or lytaster of clothe dyynge, s. lytstar, P.), *tinctor*': Prompt. Parv. '*Tinctor*, a lyster': Ortus. 'A littester, *tinctor, tinctrix*': Cath. Ang. A chantry in the church of All Saints, York, was erected in the 15th century by 'Adam del Bank, littester' (Hist. and Ant. of York, ii. 269). Not found in the Hundred Rolls, 1273.

Hugh le Litster, co. Notts, 20 Edw.I. R.
Andrew le Litster, 1301. M.
Joane Lyttestere, C. R., 20 Ric. II. pt. i.
Cristiana Lyttester, *lyster*, 1379: P. T. Yorks. p. 249.
Robert le Lyster, 1397: Preston Guild Rolls, p. 1.
Nycholas le Lystere. G.

Lower says the Norfolk rebellion in 1381 was called Lister's rebellion, because headed by John Lister, or Littester, a dyer of Norwich (Patr. Brit. p. 196); v. also Way's note to *lystare* in Prompt. Parv., p. 307.

1547. Married—Thomas Lyster and Mary Pugborne: St. Dionis Backchurch, p. 2.
London, 20, 0, 0; West Rid. Court Dir., 41, 0, 0; MDB. (co. Cumb.), 0, 3, 0; Oxford (Lyster), 1.

Liston, Listone, Lyston. — Local, 'of Liston,' a parish in co. Essex, near Sudbury.

Godfrey de Liston, co. Essex, Hen. III-Edw. I. K.
Thomas de Liston, co. Essex, 1273. A.
Geoffrey de Lyston, co. Camb., ibid.
Johannes de Liston, co. Essex, 31 Edw. I: BBB. p. 641.
1668. Married—Arthur Martin and Mary Lisston: St.Jas.Clerkenwell, iii. 153.
New York, 2, 0, 1; Philadelphia, 1, 1, 0.

Litchbarrow, Lickbarrow. —Local, (1) 'of Litchborough,' a parish in co. Northampton, near Towcester; (2) 'at the Lichbarrow' (i.e. the mound of the dead); cf. Litchfield, lich-gate, and lich-wake (Chaucer). A.S. *lic*, a corpse.

Thomas de Lichesbarue, Hen. III-Edw. I: K. p. 36.
In connexion with this entry

the place *Lichesbar* occurs in the Hundred of Falewesle, co. Northampton.

William Lechebarowe, C. R., 42 Edw. III.
Thomas Lychebarowe, C.R., 6 Hen. IV.
John Lychbarow, 1451: Reg. Univ. Oxf. i. 15.
1601.William Lickbarrowe, co.Westm.: ibid. vol. ii. pt. ii. p. 253.
1647. Thomas Lickbarrow: Lancashire Wills at Richmond, i. 184.
1686. Eliz. Lickbarrow, of Inskipp: ibid. ii. 167.
1709. Jane Lickbarrow, of Langdale: ibid.
1795. Buried—John Lickbarrow, of Ulverston: Reg. St. Mary, Ulverston, North Lanc. p. 618.

Litchfield. —Local, 'of Lichfield,' a city in co. Stafford.

1450. Richard Lychfeld: Reg. Univ. Oxf. i. 10.
1594. Thomas Fowler and Anne Lichefeild, *widow*: Marriage Lic. (London), i. 219.
1663. Married—Henry Cookman and Eliz. Litchfeild: St. Jas. Clerkenwell, p. 112.
London, 9; Boston (U.S.), 61.

Litherland. —Local, 'of Litherland,' a township in the parish of Sefton, near Liverpool. Liverpool itself was originally Litherpool.

Richard Litherpol, Hen. III-Edw. I. K.
William de Litherland, co. Lanc., ibid.
Thus Liverpool and Litherland are derived from the name of the original settler, viz. Lither or Leter; cf. Leverton for Letherton.

William Litherland, of Whiston, 1582: Wills at Chester, (1545-1620). p. 124.
James Litherland, of West Derby (Liverpool), 1609: ibid.
1513. Robert Lytherlond, or Lederland: Reg. Univ. Oxf. i. 87.
1572. Titus Wystocke and Susanna Letherland, co. Essex: Marriage Lic. (London), i. 53.
1646. Buried—Eliz. Leatherland, *a servant*: St. Dionis Backchurch, p. 225.
Liverpool, 5; Manchester, 4.

Lithgoe, Lithgow; v. Lythgoe.

Litster. —Occup.; v. Lister.

Little, Littell, Lytle, Litel, Lytell, Lyttle. —Nick. 'the little'; cf. Bigg, Small, and Long. Sometimes affixed as a sobriquet on the least of two bearing the same name.

Johannes de Bland, et uxor, 1379: P. T. Yorks. p. 289.
Johannes de Bland, littill, 1379: ibid.
Johannes Tailliour, parws (i. e. parvus), 1379: ibid. p. 278.
Johannes Tailliour, de Hyle, 1379: ibid.
William le Letle, co. Oxf., 1273. A.
Wiscard Litil, co. Hunts, ibid.
John le Litle, co. Berks, ibid.
Julian Litel, co. Camb., ibid.
1544-5. Simon Bedell and Margaret Litell, *widow*: Marriage Lic. (Faculty Office), p. 4.
1619. Bapt.—John, s. Davye Little: St. Jas. Clerkenwell, p. 85.
London, 45, 3, 0, 0, 0, 0; Liverpool, 23, 0, 2, 0, 0, 0; New York, 86, 19, 0, 1, 1, 1.

Littleboy, Littleboys. —Possibly a nickname, 'little boy'; synonymous with Littlepage and Smallpage (q.v.), but more probably local, -*boy* or -*boys* representing the common suffix -*bois*, a wood; cf. Mortiboy or Worboise. In this case it is doubtless the French Lillebois Anglicized and made imitative.

1603. John Wood and Sarah Littleboy, widow of John Littleboy, of Rochester: Marriage Lic. (London), i. 285.
William Littleboys, of Over Peover, *gent*, 1625: Wills at Chester (1621-50), p. 140.
1687. Bapt.—Hanna, d. Henry Littleboye: St. Jas. Clerkenwell, i. 323.
1688. Married—Joshua Taylor and Grace Litleby: St. Peter, Cornhill, ii. 58.
London, 1, 1; Philadelphia, 2, 0.

Littlebury. —Local, 'of Littlebury,' a parish in co. Essex, near Saffron Walden.

Martin de Littlebury, temp. Hen. III: FF. ix. 168.
Laurence de Lytlebory, co. Camb., 1273. A.
John de Lytlebury, co Hunts, ibid.
1605-6. Philip Littlebury, co. Linc.: Reg. Univ. Oxf. vol. ii. pt. ii. p. 287.
1693-4. John Littlebury and Susanna Dodsworth: MarriageAlleg.(Canterbury), p. 284.
London, 1.

Littlechild. —Nick. 'the little child'; cf. Fairchild, Leifchild, Child, &c.
London, 1.

Littlecot. —Local, 'of Littlecot,' a chapelry in the parish of Chilton Foliatt, co. Wilts; also 'of Littlecote,' a hamlet in the parish of Stewkley, co. Bucks.

Adam de Litlecote, co. Wilts, Hen. III-Edw. I. K.
Symon de Lutlecote, co. Wilts, 1273. A..

Philip de Luttelcot, co. Wilts, 1273. A.
Robert de Luttlecot, co. Bucks, ibid.
1550. John Cowper and Alice Litlecote:
Marriage Lic. (London), i. 12.

Littledale.—Local, 'of Littledale,' a hamlet in the parish of
Lancaster, co. Lanc.

1605. John Littledale, of Ronray (?):
Wills at Chester, i. 124.
London, 1; Liverpool, 3; MDB. (co.
Ches.), 3.

Littlefair. — ? Nick. 'little
fellow'; cf. Playfair, little play-
mate, from the North Country *fere*,
a companion, a mate.

Farewell, my doughter Kateryne, late
the *fere* to Prynce Artour, late my chyld
so dere': Halliwell.
Thomas Lytlefayr, or Litlefere, co.
Durham, 1585: Reg. Univ. Oxf. vol. ii.
pt. ii. p. 142.
MDB. (co. Durham), 1; (North Rid.
Yorks), 9.

Littlefield.—Local, 'of Littlefield,' one of the hundreds of Kent
(Lower). Of course many small
enclosures would be called the
'little field.'

1610. Thomas Littlefeild, or Lyttlefeld,
co. Hants: Reg. Univ. Oxf. vol. ii. pt. ii.
p. 317.
1684. Thomas Littlefeild and Sarah
Allen: Marriage Alleg. (Canterbury),
p. 183.
1751. Married—John Littlefield and
Mary Tempest: St. Geo. Chap. Mayfair,
p. 197.
London, 3; Boston (U.S.), 114.

Littlehale. — Local, 'at the
little hale,' i.e. at the little hall
(v. Hale), from residence therein
or thereby. The final *s* in Littlehales is too common in local surnames to need explanation; cf.
Williams, Styles, &c.

1557. Bapt.—Thomas Lyttellhaylle, son
of George Lyttyllhayle: St. Dionis Backchurch, p. 77.
1558-9. Married—George Lytilhale and
Eliz. Wryght: ibid. p. 4.
1618. Richard Wilkinson and Joane
Littleale: Marriage Lic. (London), ii. 64.
1679-80. Edward Pawlett and Hannah
Littlehayles: Marriage Lic. (Faculty
Office), p. 149.
1778. Married—John Cole and Martha
Littlehales: St. Geo. Han. Sq. i. 289.
Boston (U.S.), 4.

Littlehick.—Nickname, 'little
Richard,' from the nick. Hick,
q.v.; cf. Littlejohn.

Richard Litelhikke, C. R., 9 Ric. II.

Littlejohn, Littlejohns. —
Nick. 'little John,' equivalent to
John Little. A mere reversal of
order between baptismal name and
surname; cf. Fr. Petit-jean.

Richard fil. Parvi-Johannis, co. Camb.,
1273. A.
Parvus Johannes, 1379: P. T. Yorks.
p. 224.
Pety Jon et uxor, 1379: ibid. p. 283.
'Y met hem bot at Wentbreg, seyde
Lytyll John': Robin Hood, i. 83.
Nicholas Peti John, C. R., 35 Hen. VI.
1607-8. Hugh Littlejohn, co. Devon,
St. Mary Hall: Reg. Univ. Oxf. vol. ii.
pt. ii. p. 300.
1766. Married—Robert Littlejohns and
Eliz. Whiting: St. Geo. Han. Sq. i. 158.
London, 8, 1; MDB. (co. Devon), 0, 3;
New York, 4, 0; Boston (U.S.), 5, 0.

Littlemore.—Local, 'of Littlemore,' a liberty in the parish of
St. Mary the Virgin, partly in
Bullingdon, partly in Oxford, two
miles and a half from Oxford. Probably many spots would be similarly
entitled. There is one in Cheshire.

(Priorissa) de Lytlemore, co. Oxf.,
1273. A.
1609. George Littlemore, of Chester:
Wills at Chester, i. 124.
1650. Thomas Littlemore, of Littlemore, co. Ches., *gent*: ibid. ii. 140.
1748. Married—Samuel Littlemoore
and Ann Cantrell: St. Geo. Chap. Mayfair, p. 105.
London, 2; MDB. (co. Ches.), 3.

Littlepage.—Nick. 'the little
page,' a young or small servitor;
v. Smallpage.

Lawrence Litilpage, C. R., 1 Hen. V.
1681. Nicholas Awnsham and Ann
Littlepage: Marriage Alleg.(Canterbury),
p. 82.
1703. Robert Littlepage, co. Oxf., and
Martha Smith: Marriage Lic. (Faculty
Office), p. 245.
1762. Married—Joseph Littlepage and
Phillis Burrell: St. Geo. Han. Sq. i. 109.

Littleproud.—Nick. 'the little
proud.' Although this surname
lasted at least four centuries and
made a gallant effort to survive, it
is, I fear, extinct; cf. Smallpride.

Matilda Lytillprowd, 1379: P. T. Yorks.
p. 133.
Robertus Lyttylproud, 1379: ibid. p. 95.
Reginald Littleprowe, Mayor of Norwich, 1532: FF. iii. 219.

Of the appointment to the seventh
prebend in Norwich Cathedral we
read:

'1536. Stephen Prewet, presented by
Elizabeth Littleproud by grant from the
Bishop': FF. iv. 173.
'1619. Mr. John Littleproud, a young
man, lately in priest's orders, for the
help of his living, being but a grammar
scholar, was buried Nov. 1' (at Attle-
burgh): ibid. i. 535.
1701. Married—Robert Littleproud and
Frances Avery: St. Jas. Clerkenwell,
iii. 223.

Littler.—Local, 'of Littleover,'
a village in co. Derby. The name
crept over the border into Cheshire,
and remained firmly fixed there;
cf. the pronunciation Peevor for
Peover, a parish in co. Chester.

John de Littelore, 1401: East Ches.
ii. 9.
Richard Lytler, 1582: ibid. p. 382.
Ralph Litlor, 1602: ibid. p. 241.
1588. Married—Geffray Mottershed and
Jone Lytler: Reg. Prestbury, Ches., p. 97.
Thomas Littler, of Eddisbury, 1576:
Wills at Chester (1545-1620), p. 124.
John Littler, of Chester, *alderman*,
1619: ibid.
1623-4. Buried—Robert Littleler, ser-
vant of Gilbert Allam: St. Dionis Back-
church, p. 216.
1660. Married—Richard Littler and
Ann Knight: St. Jas. Clerkenwell, iii. 105.
1796. Married—Edmund Littler and
Eliz. Henman: St. Geo. Han. Sq. ii. 150.
London, 1; Manchester, 3; MDB. (co.
Chester), 5; Philadelphia, 2.

Littleswain.—Nick. 'the little
swain'; v. Swain.

Philip Litsweyn, co. Oxf., 1273. A.

Littleton.—Local, 'of Littleton,' parishes and townships in
cos. Chester, Dorset, Middlesex,
Somerset, Hants, Wilts, Worcester,
and Gloucester.

Michael de Lutelton, co. Wilts, 1273. A.
Henry de Luteleton, co. Soms., 1 Edw.
III: Kirby's Quest, p. 85.
Francis Littleton, co. Staff., 1575: Reg.
Univ. Oxf. vol. ii. pt. ii. p. 65.
John Littleton, co. Worc., 1576: ibid.
p. 71.
1590. John Littleton and Mereall Brom-
ley: Marriage Lic. (London), i. 189.
1751. Married—Joseph Littleton and
Sarah Bury: St. Geo. Chap. Mayfair,
p. 194.
London, 1; Boston (U.S.), 1.

Littlewood.—Local, 'of Little-
wood,' a well-established West
Riding surname, in which division
of the county of York it first arose.
The precise spot was seemingly
in the neighbourhood of Holmfirth.

Johannes de Litylwode, 1379: P. T.
Yorks. p. 174.

Willelmus de Litilwode, 1379: P. T. Yorks.

1576-7. German Fryer and Alice Little-wood: Marriage Lic. (London), i. 74.

1664. Bapt.—Ann, d. Robert Little-wood: St. Jas. Clerkenwell, i. 222.

1754. Married—Joseph Littlewood and Joyce Sharp: St. Geo. Chap. Mayfair, p. 275.

London, 8; West Rid. Court Dir., 10; Sheffield, 8; Philadelphia, 13.

Littleworth, Littlewort. — Local, 'of Littleworth,' i.e. at the little worth or farm. This surname has been corrupted into Little-work and Littlewort. Littleworth is an ecclesiastical district in the union of Faringdon, co. Berks.

1591. Edmund Littleworke, co. Berks, *pleb.*: Reg. Univ. Oxf. vol. ii. pt. ii. p. 187.

1665. William Litleworck and Sarah Edwards: Marriage Alleg. (Canterbury), p. 142.

London, 1, 1.

Litton. — Local, 'of Litton, parishes in cos. Somerset and Dorset; also townships in cos. Hereford and York (W. Rid.), and also a hamlet in the parish of Tideswell, co. Derby.

Hugh de Litton,co.Northampt.,1273.A.

Symon de Litton, co. Suff., ibid.

Alicia de Lytton, 1379: P. T. Yorks. p. 273.

1583. William Litton and Eliz. Myles, *widow*: Marriage Lic. (London), i. 125.

1607. Married—Edward Litton and Eliz. Friarson: St. Michael, Cornhill, p.18. London, 2.

Lively, Liveley. — Local (?). Mr. Lower says, 'From natural disposition.' This may be so. More probably we must look for a local origin with the common suffix -*ley*, as in Morley or Ripley.

1543. Buried—Robarte Lyvely: St. Dionis Backchurch, p. 179.

1549. Married—Robarte Kynge and Alys Lyveley: ibid. p. 2.

London, 1, 0; Philadelphia, 0, 2; New York, 2, 0.

Livens; v. Living.

Livermore.—Local, 'of Liver-mere,' two parishes, Great and Little Livermere, in co. Suffolk, about six miles from Bury St. Edmunds. From Suffolk the surname wandered into Essex, where it is still familiar as Livermore; cf. Whitmore for Whittemere.

1239. Agnes Livermere, co. Norf.: FF. vi. 150.

William de Lyvremere co.Suff.,1273. A.

1349. William de Lyvermere, rector of Croxton, co. Norf., FF. ii. 154.

1668. Married—Richard Renoles and Eliz. Livermore: St. Jas. Clerkenwell, iii. 151.

1675-6. John Livermore, co. Essex, and Eliz. Peirson: Marriage Alleg. (Canterbury), p. 251.

London, 7; MDB. (co. Essex), 7; Boston (U.S.), 26.

Liverpool.—Local, 'of Liver-pool,' a city in co. Lancaster. I fear the surname is extinct in England. For the derivation of the name, v. Litherland. Probably the same Lither who owned the 'land' owned the 'pool' also.

Richard de Liverpol, co. Lanc., 20 Edw. I. R.

Richard Litherpol,co. Lanc., Hen. III-Edw. I. K.

John de Lyverpole, 19 Edw. II: Baines' Lancashire, ii. 295.

Adam de Liverpool, temp. Edw. III: ibid. p. 296.

Edward Liverpool, of Stoke, *black-smith*, 1633: Wills at Chester (1621-50), p. 140.

Boston (U.S.), 1.

Liversage, Liversedge, Liversidge, Liverseege. — Local, 'of Liversedge,' a township in the parish of Birstall, nine miles from Leeds. But there seems to have been a place of this name also in the West country.

Ralph Leversedge, co. Soms., 1583-4: Reg. Univ. Oxf. vol. ii. pt ii. p. 133.

Thomas Leversage, co. Ches., 1607: ibid. p. 297.

Roger Liversage, of Woolston, 1582: Wills at Chester (1545-1620), p. 124.

William Liversage, of Wheelock, 1613: ibid.

1573. Bapt.—John Jeffreys, alias Lever-sedg: Reg. Stourton, co. Wilts, p. 1.

1690. Married—John Trimboy and Eliz. Leversage: ibid. p. 53.

London, 0, 0, 1, 0; Liverpool, 1, 2, 1, 0; MDB. (West Rid. Yorks), 0, 4, 3, 0; Manchester, 0, 0, 0, 1.

Livesey, Livesley, Live-zey, Livezley, Livzley, Livzey. —Local, 'of Livesey,' a township in the parish of Blackburn, co. Lanc. Livesley is a corruption. By a curious freak the American variants in all cases turn s into z. The surname has established itself strongly in the United States.

'Livesey gave name to a family, the owners of Livesey Hall, ... who became extinct early in this century, and of whom

James Levesey in 2 Edw. VI held Levesey as a manor': Baines' Lanc. ii. 80.

1578. William Sherlocke and Ellen Livesey, *widow*: Marriage Lic.(London), p. 83.

George Livesey, of Blackburn, 1592: Wills at Chester (1545-1620), p. 125.

James Livesey, of Livesey, 1619: ibid.

Roger Livesey, of Darwen (nr. Black-burn), 1620: ibid.

London, 2, 0, 0, 0, 0, 0; Manchester, 14, 3, 0, 0, 0; Philadelphia, 0, 0, 30, 2, 1, 2; New York (Livesey), 4.

Living, Liveing, Livens, Levinson, Livings.—Bapt. ' the son of Liven,' probably like Lewin (q.v.), a variant of Leofwin, the intermediate form being Liffin. Mr. Lower says, 'An Anglo-Saxon personal name. There was a Liv-ing, archbishop of Canterbury, and another Living, bishop of Wor-cester' (Patr. Brit. p. 197). The final g is excrescent.

William fil. Lyfyne, co. Bedf., 1273. A.

Richard Lyfyne, co. Oxf., ibid.

Richard Livesone, co. Camb., ibid.

Adam Livene, co. Camb., ibid.

Roger Livene, co. Camb., ibid.

1579-80. Jeffry Lyvinge and Eliz. Pattenson: Marriage Lic. (London), i. 94.

1591. Timothy Levinge, co. Warw.: Reg. Univ. Oxf. vol. ii. pt. ii. p. 183.

1593. Bapt. — Leven d. Lambrighte Vandelo, a stranger (elsewhere described as a Dutchman): St. Michael, Cornhill, p. 205.

1715. Married—John Living and Eliz. Millett: ibid. p. 58.

1791. — William Fitch and Mary Livens: St. Geo. Han. Sq. ii. 63.

1806. — Joseph Sparrow and Ann Living: ibid. p. 338.

London, 2, 2, 3, 1, 0; New York (Livings), 1; Boston (U.S.) (Living), 2.

Livingstone, Livingston.—Local, 'of Livingstone,' a parish in co. Linlithgow.

1789. Married—Alex. Cowie and Sarah Livingston: St. Geo. Han. Sq. ii. 29.

London, 1, 5; Boston (U.S.), 4, 25.

Llewellin, Llewellyn, Llew-ellen, Llewallen. — Bapt. 'the son of Llewellyn' (Welsh). The double l in Welsh has always been a stumbling-block to the English; cf. Floyd for Lloyd. An instance of the difficulty occurs in the Wills at Chester (1545-1620), Lanc. and Ches. Rec. Soc:

Richard Thwellin, of Holt, 1618: p. 192.

1715. Married—Richard Luellyn and Eliz. Bromwich: St. Peter, Cornhill, ii. 71.

1776. Married — William Gaunt and Mary Lewelling : St. Geo. Han. Sq. i. 268. London, 1, 7, 0, 0 ; Philadelphia, 2, 1, 13, 3 ; Boston (U.S.) (Lewellyn), 2.

Lloyd. — Bapt. 'the son of Lloyd,' a Welsh personal name ; v. Floyd and Bloyd. This surname is known over the whole English-speaking world.

1577. Jenkin Lloyde, co. Montgomery : Reg. Univ. Oxf. vol. ii. pt. ii. p. 74.
1579. Francis Lloyde, co. Carnarvon : ibid. p. 90.
1585. Griffith Lloid, co. Radnor : ibid. p. 143.
1559. Richard Lloyd, of Chester : Wills at Chester, i. 125.
1610. Robert Lloyd, of Chester : ibid. London, 144 ; Philadelphia, 118.

Load. — Local, 'at the lode,' from residence thereby. 'Lode, a leaning wall. Glouc.' (Halliwell). It is interesting to notice that the name is early found in the neighbouring county of Somerset.

Robert atte Lode, co. Soms., 1 Edw. III : Kirby's Quest, p. 106.
1753. Married — William Load, co. Worc., and Eliz. Read : St. Geo. Chap. Mayfair, p. 261.
1769. — Thomas Load and Sarah Squibb : St. Geo. Han. Sq. i. 184. London, 1.

Loader, Loder, Lodder. — Occup. 'the loader,' i.e. a carrier. M.E. lode, a burthen ; 'loders, carriers' (Halliwell) ; v. Leader.

Emma la Lodere, co. Oxf., 1273. A.
Agnes Lodere, co. Oxf., ibid.
Robert Loder, 1537 : Reg. Univ. Oxf., i. 188.
1559-60. William Loder and Agnes Mychell : Marriage Lic. (London), i. 20.
1781. Married — Thomas Loader and Margaret Atkins : St. Geo. Han. Sq. i. 323.
London, 14, 4, 2 ; New York, 2, 7, 0.

Loadman, Loadsman. — Occup. 'the loadman,' a carrier ; v. Loader, Leadman, or Leader. 'Lodysmane, vector, lator, vehicularius' : Prompt. Parv. p. 310. Mr. Way adds as a note, 'The lodesman seems to be here the carrier ; Anglo-Saxon ladman, ductor.'

1792. Married — Richard Loadman and Eliz. Kane : St. Geo. Han. Sq. ii. 86.
1801. — Thomas Anstead and Henrietta Loadsman : ibid. p. 240.
John Loadman, farmer, Crate house, Crakehall : North Rid. Yorks Dir., 1872. East Rid. Yorks Dir. (Farmers' List), 5.

Loadstar. — Nick. 'the lode-star' or 'load-star,' i.e. pole-star. The star that leads.

'And after was she made the lodesterre.'
Chaucer, The Knight's Tale.
James Lodsterre, co. Kent, 1273. A.

Lobb, Lob. — Nick. 'the lobb,' a loutish country bumpkin, a clownish rustic. 'A blunt countrie lob' (Stanihurst, p. 17). In Somersetshire the last person in a race is called the lob (Halliwell) ; cf. lobcock, a lubber. 'Baligaut, an unwelde lubber, great lob cocke' (Cotgrave) ; cf. the Somersetshire Crease and Kift ; cf. looby.

Adam Lobbe, co. Norf., 1273. A.
Richard Lobbe, co. Soms., 1 Edw. III : Kirby's Quest, p. 150.
1752. Married — Peter Lobb and Catherine Stranger : St. Geo. Chap. Mayfair, p. 223.
1799. — Thomas Guymerl and Eliza Lobb : St. Geo. Han. Sq. ii. 210.
London, 5, 0 ; New York, 1, 2 ; Philadelphia, 10, 0.

Lobley. — Local, 'of Lobley.' I cannot find the spot. Evidently Lancashire is its habitat.

1580. William Lobley and Margaret Allen : Marriage Lic. (London), i. 07.
Roger Lobley, of Worston, 1621 : Wills at Chester (1621-50), p. 141.
Adam Lobley, of Woodall, co. York, 1665 : ibid. (1660-80), p. 171.
London, 1 ; Liverpool, 2 ; MDB. (co. Lancaster), 3 ; New York, 2 ; Philadelphia, 5.

Lock, Locke. — Local, 'at the lock,' from residence thereby. A hatch or wicket. The English surname is not to be confounded with Gaelic loch, a lake ; v. Prompt. Parv. ; M.E. loke, a door-fastener.

Robert atte Waterlok, C. R., 45 Hen. III.
Geoffrey Loc, or Lock, co. Suff., 1273. A.
William Lock, co. Oxf., ibid.
Richard atte Loke, Fines Roll, 18 Edw. II.
John Loke, co. Soms., 1 Edw. III : Kirby's Quest, p. 261.
1577. Zachary Locke, London : Reg. Univ. Oxf. vol. ii. pt. ii. p. 76.
London, 42, 11 ; Philadelphia, 10, 12.

Locker. — Occup. 'the locker' or 'locksmith' ; v. Lockyear.

1605. Henry Locker and Eliz. Herd : Marriage Lic. (London), i. 295.
1608. Thurstan Locker, of Manchester : Wills at Chester, i. 125.
London, 2 ; Philadelphia, 10.

Locket, Lockett. — ? Bapt. Not a corruption of Lockhart, as suggested by Lower. It is found as simple Loket in the 13th century. It seems to be the dim. of some personal name ; cf. Emmett for Emma.

Eudo Loket, co. Norf., 1273. A.
Johannes Loket, 1379 : P. T. Yorks. p. 172.
1574-5. William Locket, co. Soms. : Reg. Univ. Oxf. vol. ii. pt. ii. p. 62.
1601. Giles Lockett, co. Dorset : ibid. p. 252.
London, 3, 3 ; Manchester, 0, 7 ; New York, 0, 2.

Lockington. — Local, 'of Lockington,' (1) a parish in co. Leicester, seven miles from Loughborough ; (2) a parish in E. Rid. Yorks, six miles from Beverley.

Ralph de Loketon, co. York, Hen. III-Edw. I. K.
Geoffrey de Lukinton, co. Wilts, ibid.
Robert de Lokinton, co. York, 1273. A.
William de Lokinton, co. York, ibid.
Roger de Lokynton, co. Soms., 20 Edw. I. R.
1648. Bapt. — John, s. Richard Lockington : St. Jas. Clerkenwell, i. 169.
1678. Thomas Ladd and Amy Lockington : Marriage Alleg. (Canterbury), p. 288.
1721. Buried — Stephen Lockington : St. Antholin (London), p. 134.
London, 5 ; Philadelphia, 1.

Lockley. — Local, 'of Lockerley' (?), a parish in co. Southampton, six miles from Romsey.

1549. Married — John Lockly and Ellen Oliver : St. Peter, Cornhill, i. 222.
1580. Roger Lockley and Alice Berrye, widow, Marriage Lic. (London), i. 96.
1793. Married — John James Ashley and Charlotte Sophia Lockley : St. Geo. Han. Sq. ii. 103.
London, 4.

Locksley. — Local, 'of Locksley' ; v. Loxley.
Oxford, 1.

Locksmith. — Occup. 'the locksmith.' 'Loksmythe, serefaber' (Prompt. Parv.). Locksmith, I fear, is obsolete ; but v. Lockyear, which has a vigorous existence.

Robert Locsmyth, co. Hunts, 1273. A.
William Loksmyth, c. 1300. M.
Roger Locksmyth, vicar of Wighton, co. Norf., 1384 : FF. ix. 208.
William Loksmyth, C. R., 6 Hen. VI.
1605. William Locksmith, co. Glouc. : Reg. Univ. Oxf. vol. ii. pt. ii. p. 287.
— Married — William Locksmith and Katharine Markham : St. Michael, Cornhill, p. 18.

1620. Anthony Locksmith, co. Surrey, and Susan Rogers: Marriage Lic. (London), ii. 93.

Lockton.—Local, 'of Lockton,' a chapelry in the parish of Middleton, N. Rid. Yorks.

Hugh de Loketon, co. York, Hen. III-Edw. I. K.
Ralph de Loketon, co. York, ibid.
1648. John Lockton, co. Linc., and Mary Fairfax: Marriage Lic. (Faculty Office), p. 40.
1729. Married—Richard Hawkins and Ann Lockton: St. Geo. Han. Sq. i. 6. London, 1.

Lockwood.—Local, 'of Lockwood,' a village in the ancient parish of Almondbury, W. Rid. Yorks. This local surname has ramified strongly and spread widely.

Willelmus de Lokewod, 1379: P. T. Yorks. p. 177.
Thomas de Lockewod, 1379: ibid. p. 178.
1575. Married—Roberte Clayton and Elizabethe Lockwood: St. Michael, Cornhill, p. 11.
1621-2. John Lockwood and Joane Padnowl: Marriage Lic. (London), ii. 108.
1626. John Watkyns and Margaret Lokewood: ibid. p. 169.
London, 24; West Rid. Court Dir., 31; New York, 110.

Lockyear, Lockyer, Locker.—Occup. 'the lockyer,' the locksmith; M.E. *loke*, a lock. More correctly lock-er, but *y* has intruded, as in *sawyer, lawyer, bowyer* for saw-er, law-er, bow-er.

Henry le Lockier, London, 1273. A.
Nicholas le Lokyere, co. Soms., 1 Edw. III: Kirby's Quest, p. 211.
Lucas le Lokier, co. Soms., 1 Edw. III: ibid. p. 273.
Robert Harward, *loker*, 1443: Mun. Acad. Oxon. p. 535.
1604. William Lokier, co. Soms.: Reg. Univ. Oxf. vol. ii. pt. ii. p. 276.
1608. Married—Abraham Bateman and Ursula Lockyer: St. Michael, Cornhill, p. 19.
1735.—James Sanger and Joan Lockier: Reg. Stourton, co. Wilts, p. 55.

It is interesting to notice that while Lockyer has predominated over Locksmith in our personal nomenclature, yet locksmith has nearly ousted lockyer as an occupative term.

London, 1, 15, 2; New York, 0, 4, 0; Philadelphia, 0, 10, 3.

Lodder, Loder; v. Loader.

Lodge.—Local, 'at the lodge,' a small cottage, a place to rest in.

M.E. *logge*. 'Logge, or lytylle house': Prompt. Parv. p. 311.

Roger de la Logge, C. R., 32 Edw. I.
William atte Logg, co. Soms, 1 Edw. III: Kirby's Quest, p. 195.
Johannes del Loge, 1379: P. T. Yorks. p. 283.
Thomas Lodge, or Loge, 1520: Reg. Univ. Oxf. i. 113.
1575. Bapt.—Jane, d. Robert Lodge: St. Jas. Clerkenwell, i. 9.
1577. Miles Lodge, co. York: Reg. Univ. Oxf. vol. ii. pt. ii. p. 78.
London, 19; New York, 4.

Loe.—Local, 'at the low,' from residence thereon; v. Low; cf. Hoe, sometimes a variant of How.

1598. Humphrey Lowe, or Loe, co. Ches.: Reg. Univ. Oxf. vol. ii. pt. ii. p. 229.
1621. William Loe, co. Warw.: ibid. p. 390.
1657. Buried—Emery Loe: St. Jas. Clerkenwell, iv. 315.
1788. Married—Francis Loe and Charlotte Goodman: St. Geo. Han. Sq. ii. 11. London, 2.

Loft, Lofts.—Local, 'at the loft,' an attic, a garret, a room in the roof; cf. Lodge. The final *s* in Lofts is common to all monosyllabic local names (cf. Holmes, Lowndes, Brooks), and in fact is the genitive, as in Williams, Tompkins, Jones, &c. v. Loftus.

Alenus atte Loft, co. Hunts, 1273. A.
Angnes ad le Loft, co. Hunts, ibid.
Walter ad le Loft, co. Hunts, ibid.
1669. Married—William Loft and Mary Morgan: St. Jas. Clerkenwell, iii. 171.
1738. — Stephen Hasser and Anne Loft: St. Dionis Backchurch, p. 66.
1753. — Stephen Loftes and Mary Cox: St. Geo. Chap, Mayfair, p. 247.
London, 2, 7; Crockford, 2, 0; New York, 1, 1.

Loftus, Lofthouse. — Local, 'at the loft-house,' a house with an attic or cock-loft above it. This is a Yorkshire surname and several places are so termed. The chief are Lofthouse, a village three miles north of Wakefield, and Lofthouse, a village in the parish of Kirkby Malzeard.

Robert de Lofthus, C. R., 28 Edw. I.
Richard Lofthouse, co. York. W. 16.
John Loftous, co. York, ibid.
Robertus Lofthouse, 1379: P. T. Yorks. p. 193.
John de Lofthouse, C. R., 17 Ric. II.
1593-4. William Loftous, co. York: Reg. Univ. Oxf. vol. ii. pt. ii. p. 200.
1667. Arthur Bostock and Catherine

Loftus: Marriage Alleg. (Westminster), p. 135.
London, 4, 0; Sheffield, 0, 2; Leeds, 6, 2; New York, 17, 0; Philadelphia, 34, 4.

Logsdon; v. Longsdon. An unmistakable variant.

Lomas, Lomax.—Local, 'of Lomax,' a small spot in the parish of Bury, co. Lanc. I do not know whether it can still be identified, but it has given birth to a family name that has ramified itself in a wonderful manner.

Christopher Lomax, of Bury, 1590: Wills at Chester (1545-1620), p. 125.
Jeffery Lomax, of Heap, 1590: ibid.
Laurence Smethurst, of Lomax, parish of Bury, 1624: ibid. (1621-50), p. 201.
Edmund Smethurst, of Lomax, parish of Bury, *yeoman*, 1638: ibid.
Oliver Lumas, 1602: Preston Guild Rolls, p. 63.
Oliver Lumax, 1622: ibid. p. 70.
Richard Lumas-jur', 1602: ibid. p. 63.
Richard Lumax-jur', 1622: ibid. p. 70.

The double instances given above prove, if proof were needed, that Lomax and Lomas are one and the same name.

Manchester, 31, 18; London, 7, 10; New York, 3, 4.

Lomb; v. Lumb.

Lombard, Lumbard.—Nick. 'the Lombard,' one who came from Lombardy. One or two of the names recorded below are evidently Jewish.

Jacob le Lumberd. E.
Jacobina la Lumbard, London. X.
Denteyt Lumbardus, London, 1273. A.
Richard Lomberd, co. Kent, ibid.
John Lumbard, co. Oxf., ibid.
Michael le Lumbard, C. R., 12 Edw. I.
Marcus le Lumbard, C.R., 20 Edw. I.
Nicholas Lombard, or Lumbarde,1567: Reg. Univ. Oxf. i. 267.
1657. Married—Hugh Lumbard and Jane Tayler: St. Jas. Clerkenwell, iii. 99.

Lombard Street, London, took its name from being the district in which the Italian merchants resided. It will be seen that several of the instances above hail from the metropolis.

London, 1, 0; New York, 7, 2.

Lombardy.—Local, 'of Lombardy'; v. Lombard.

New York, 1.

Lomer.—Occup.; v. Limner.

Lond; v. Lund.

Londesborough; v. Lowndesbrough.

London.—Local, ' of London '; v. Londonish.

Jordan de London, co. Berks, Hen. III-Edw. I. K.
Haginus de London, co. Northumb., 1273. A.
Gilbert de Londonia, co. Salop, ibid.
William de London, co. Wilts, 20 Edw. I. R.
Osbert de Londone, co. Soms., 1 Edw. III : Kirby's Quest, p. 261.
1570. John Harker and Susan London: Marriage Lic. (Faculty Office), p. 15.
1730. Married—Edward London and Eliz. Phillips : St. Dionis Backchurch, p. 64.
London, 21 ; New York, 18,

Londoner, Londner.—Nick. ' the Londoner,' one who hailed from London.

William Londoner, alias Tinsley, 1564 : Visitation of Yorkshire, p. 324.
'Sir Henry Tinsloo (Tinsley), *knight*, whose Aunceters were called Londoner, alias Gresbroke,' 1564 : ibid. p. 325.
New York, 1, 2.

Londonish.—Local, ' of London '; cf. Spanish, Kentish, Cornish, Devenish, Norris, &c. ' Londonoys' (Chaucer), a Londoner, one, as we now say, born within sound of Bow Bells, a cockney.

Ralph le Lundreys. T.
Richard Londoneys, co. Camb., 1273. A.
William Londeneys, co. Hunts, ibid.
William Londonissh, temp. 1300. M.

Lone.—Local, ' at the lone,' i.e. lane; v. Lane (M.E. *lane* and *lone*), from residence thereby.

Ralph de la Lone, co. Norf., 1273. A.
Beatrix Lone, co. Hunts, ibid.
1590. Edward Lone (co. Essex) and Margaret Hepcott : Marriage Lic. (London), i. 186.
1719. Bapt.—Ann, d. William Lone : St. Michael, Cornhill, p. 166.
London, 1.

Long.—Nick. ' the long,' from the stature of the original bearer; cf. Longfellow and Longman; cf. also Short, &c.

Henry le Longe, co. Bucks, 1273. A.
John le Longe, co. Hunts, ibid.
Walter le Longe, co. Salop, ibid.
Johanna Long', 1379 : P. T. Yorks. p. 130.
1536-7. Thomas Bolton and Mary Long: Marriage Lic. (London), i. 9.
London, 75 ; New York, 124.

Longacre, Longaker.—Local, ' at the long-acre,' from residence at a field so called ; cf. Fouracre.

Philadelphia, 13, 18.

Longbotham, Longbottam, Longbottom. — Local, ' at the long bottom,' i.e. the long hollow; v. Bottom, and cf. Ramsbotham, Higginbottom, and especially Broadbotham.

Thomas Langbotehom, 1379 : P. T. Yorks. p. 187.
Ricardus Longbotehom, 1379 : ibid.
1557. Thomas Longbottom, rector of Ashwell Thorp, co. Norf.: FF. v. 163.
1603-4. Richard Longbothom, co. York : Reg. Univ. Oxf. vol. ii. pt. ii. p. 270.
1612. John Longbothome and Margery Hutchins : Marriage Lic. (London), ii. 18.
1685. Bapt.—Anne, d. Samuel Longbotham : St. Jas. Clerkenwell, i. 314.
1705. Married—John Langbotham and Margaret Newman : St. Mary Aldermary, p. 38.
London, 1, 0, 0 ; Manchester, 4, 0, 0 ; Philadelphia, 0, 0, 6.

Longcroft. — Local. ' of the long croft,' i.e. the long field or enclosure (v. Croft), from residence thereby.

Stephen de la Lungecrofte, co. Wilts, 1273. A.
1646. Married—John Burlace and Sarah Longcraft : St. Dionis Backchurch, p. 25.
London, 1.

Longden.—Local, ' of Longdon' or ' Longden,' parishes in the diocs. of Hereford, Lichfield, and Worcester.

Robert de Longedon, co. Salop, 1273. A.
Roger de Longedon, co. Salop, ibid.
1577. William Longdon, co. Soms.: Reg. Univ. Oxf. vol. ii. pt. ii. p. 75.
1599-1600. George Longden, co. Derby : ibid. p. 239.
London, 5.

Longfellow.—Nick. ' the long fellow '; cf. Goodfellow, Bonfellow, Stringfellow, &c. This surname is only found in records and registers of co. York. The American poet was the descendant of a Yorkshire family.

Peter Langfellay, co. York. W. 11.
Elizabeth Longfellow, co. York. W. 16.
Margery Langfellow, 1491, co. York. W. 11.
Henry Emmott, alias Longfellow, 1590 (Reg. Skipton Ch.): Dawson's Hist. of Skipton, p. 207.

1645. Bapt. — William, s. of William Longfellow: Reg. Skipton Ch.
New York, 1 ; Boston (U.S.), 18.

Longhurst.—Local, ' of Longhurst' (v. Hurst), a township in the parish of Bothal, near Morpeth, co. Northumb. But other and smaller localities would probably bear this name.

John de Langehirst, co. Hertf., 1273. A.
Walter de Langhurst, co. Sussex, 20 Edw. I. R.
1690. John Underhill and Elliner Longhurst : Marriage Alleg. (Canterbury), p. 145.
1791. Married—John Longhurst and Sarah Killick : St. Geo. Han. Sq. ii. 53.
London, 13 ; New York, 1.

Longley.—Local, ' of Longley,' a hamlet in the parish of Ecclesfield, near Sheffield (cf. Langley), from *long*, long, and *ley* or *lee*, a meadow ; v. Lee.

Thomas de Longlegh, 1379 : P. T. Yorks. p. 169.
Willelmus Longlegh, 1379 : ibid.
1565. Married—Robart Longly and Ellen Watkinson: St. Antholin (London), p. 17.
1697. — Benjamin Longly and Ruth Tadhunter : Canterbury Cath. p. 65.
1761. — John Longlee and Sarah Saunders: St. Geo. Han. Sq. i. 107.
London, 13 ; West Rid. Court Dir., 11 ; Sheffield, 2 ; Philadelphia, 19.

Longman. — Nick. ' the long man '; cf. Longfellow, Long, Lang, Short, &c.

1547-8. Richard Longman and Agnes Ebbes : Marriage Lic. (London), i. 11.
1758. Married—Lambert Howard and Eliz. Longman: St. Geo. Han. Sq. i. 82.
1788. — James Longman and Anne Sawer : ibid. ii. 3.
London, 14 ; New York, 6.

Longmate.—Local ; v. Langmead.

1802. Married—James Longmate and Eliz. Callender: St. Geo. Han. Sq. ii. 270.

Longmire.—Local, ' of Longmire,' a well-known Westmoreland surname, whence *-mire* is a common suffix to local place-names ; cf. Blamire.

1632. Thomas Longmyre, of Claughton: Lancashire Wills at Richmond, i. 186.
1698. Dorothy Longmire, alias Jackson, of Torver: ibid. ii. 168.
1738. Buried—John, s. William Longmire: St. Mary, Ulverston, p. 261.
MDB. (co. Cumberland), 1 ; (co. Westmoreland), 10 ; New York, 4.

Longridge, Longrigg. — Local, ' of Langrigg,' a township in the parish of Bromfield, co. Cumberland. The surname derived from this place is now generally spelt Longridge (v. Langridge) and Longrigg.

Margaret Langrige, of the parish of Burton, 1598 : Lancashire Wills at Richmond (1457-1680), p. 180.
1805. Married—John Gooch and Ann Longridge : St. Geo. Han. Sq. ii. 339.
London, 1, 0 ; MDB. (co. Cumberland), 0, 7 ; New York, 0, 1 ; Philadelphia, 1, 0.

Longsdon, Logsdon.—Local, ' of Longstone ' ; v. Longson. There can be no doubt that Logsdon is Longsdon with the *n* elided. It is equally evident that both Longsdon and Logsdon are not variants of Longden, which would give a senseless signification to the name. We may safely presume that Longstone became Longsdon, and then Logsdon. It is pleasant to have a view of this kind corroborated after making the statement. Since writing the above I find Longsdon to be a familiar Derbyshire surname, and not unknown in the immediate neighbourhood of Longstone.

1617. Bapt.—Anne, d. John Logsdon : St. Jas. Clerkenwell, i. 78.
London, 2, 2 ; MDB. (co. Derby), 2, 0.

Longson. — Local, ' of Longstone.' Great Longstone is a chapelry three miles from Bakewell, co. Derby. Little Longstone is a hamlet almost equidistant from the same town. Many names ending in -*son* are local, the *t* in the suffix -*stone* being elided. It is just possible that Longson is an abbreviation of Lawrenson (the son of Lawrence), a surname peculiar to Lancashire. To many this will seem the more probable derivation. To one or the other Longson must be referred. Nevertheless the fact that Longson is a Derbyshire name is strong evidence in favour of my first view.

Ulverston, 2 ; Manchester, 2 ; MDB. (co. Derby), 1.

Longstaff, Longstaffe, Langstaff. — Nick. The sobriquet of some sergeant, bailiff, catchpoll, or other officer of the law. Nicknames from the weapon or badge of office were very common ; cf. Shakespear, Wagstaff, and *tipstaff*.

William Longstaf, co. Norf., 1273. A. William Longstaff, co. Norf., 20 Edw. III : FF. ii. 264.
1660. Married—John Longstaffe and Eliz. Blowe : St. Jas. Clerkenwell, i. 105.
1748. — William Pricklowe and Barbara Longstaff : St. Geo. Han. Sq. i. 40.
London, 3, 1, 1 ; MDB. (North Rid. Yorks), 7, 0, 0 ; New York, 1, 0, 0.

Longstreeth. — Local ; v. Langstroth.

Longtoft.—Local, ' of Langtoft,' a parish in co. Lincoln, near Market Deeping.

Godfrey de Langetot, 24 Hen. III : FF. viii. 199.
Ralph de Langetot, co. Wilts, Hen. III–Edw. I. K.
John de Langetoft, co. Hunts, 1273. A. Richard Langetot, co. Oxf., ibid.
MDB. (North Rid. Yorks), 1.

Longton.—Local, ' of Longton,' a chapelry in the parish of Penwortham, co. Lanc., five miles from Preston ; cf. Langton.

Evan Longton, of Ormskirk, 1597 : Wills at Chester (1545-1620), p. 126.
William Longton, 1602 : Preston Guild Rolls, p. 53.
Jacob Longton, *glover*, 1642 : ibid. p. 101.
Katherin Longton, of Wyersdale, *widow*, 1617 : Lancashire Wills at Richmond (1457-1680), p. 186.
Liverpool, 5 ; Preston, 1.

Longworth, Longworthy.—Local, ' of Longworth,' a township in the parish of Bolton, co. Lancaster. With Longworthy, cf. Langworthy or Kenworthy, the suffix -*worth* (v. Worth) frequently becoming *worthy*.

1572. Peter Sturer and Isabel Longeworthe : Marriage Lic. (London), i. 53.
Ralph Longworth, of Edgworth, near Bolton, *tailor*, 1587 : Wills at Chester (1545-1620), p. 126.
George Longworth, of Bolton, 1596 : ibid.
Alice Longworth, of Longworth, 1612 : ibid.
1621. John Longworth, co. Northampt.: Reg. Univ. Oxf. vol. ii. pt. ii. p. 391.
London, 1, 1 ; Manchester, 14, 1 ; New York, 3, 0.

Lonsbrough ; v. Lowndesbrough.

Lonsdale, Londsdale. — Local, ' of Lonesdale,' the vale of the Lune ; cf. Tyndale, Tweedale, Dunderdale ; v. Lansdell and Lancaster.

Thomas de Londesdale, 1379 : P. T. Yorks. p. 268.
Willelmus de Londesdale, 1379 : ibid.
John Lonsdale, of Pendle, 1592 : Wills at Chester (1545-1620), p. 126.
William Lonsdall, of Newton, 1674 : Lancashire Wills at Richmond, i. 186.
1757. Married—Christopher Lonsdale and Eliz. Reeve : St. Geo. Han. Sq. i. 69.
London, 10, 0 ; Manchester, 4, 0 ; MDB. (co. Kent), 1, 1 ; New York, 4, 0.

Look, Looke.—Bapt. ' the son of Luke ' ; v. Luke. This variant is found in co. Somerset.

1747. Married—John Look and Ann Whitcombe : St. Geo. Chap. Mayfair, p. 95.
MDB. (co. Somerset), 6, 0 ; New York, 2, 2 ; Boston (U.S.), 7, 0.

Looker, Luker.—Occup. ' the looker,' i.e. watcher, a herdsman. ' *Looker*, a shepherd or herdsman. South ' (Halliwell). ' Looker. In the south of England a herdsman, especially in marshy districts ; a man who superintends cattle and drives them to higher ground in case of sudden floods ' (Lower, Patr. Brit. p. 199).

1582. William Lookar, co. Hants : Reg. Univ. Oxf. vol. ii. pt. ii. p. 123.
1649. Robert Looker, of Chester : Wills at Chester, ii. 142.
1686. Married—Francis Looker and Katherine Stronte : St. Michael, Cornhill, p. 45.
1795. — Thomas Looker and Sarah Nocks : St. Geo. Han. Sq. ii. 129.
London, 5, 6 ; MDB. (co. Surrey), 2, 2 ; Boston (U.S.), 1, 5.

Loose.—(1) Local, ' of Loose,' a parish in co. Kent, near Maidstone. (2) Bapt. ' the son of Lewis.' An imitative variant.

Edward Lewse, co. Glamorgan, 1577 : Reg. Univ. Oxf. vol. ii. pt. ii. p. 75.
London, 2 ; Philadelphia, 8.

Loosemore.—Local ; v. Luxmoore.

Loraine, Lorraine. — Local, ' of Lorraine ' ; v. Loring.

1680. Married—Samson Lorane and Rose Dutton : St. Jas. Clerkenwell, iii. 189.
1692. William Loraine and Ann Smith : Marriage Alleg. (Canterbury), p. 216.
Crockford, 1, 0 ; Philadelphia, 3, 1.

Lord.—Offic. 'the lord,' the master, the head of the household; v. Master and Masterman.

Robert le Loverd, co. Oxf., 1273. A.
William le Loverd, co. Notts, ibid.
Roger le Lord, co. Camb., ibid.
Walter le Lord, co. Hunts, ibid.
Richard le Lord, fil. Margarete le Lord, C. R., 9 Ric. II.
1642. Bapt.—Judith, d. Richard and Avis Lord: St. Jas. Clerkenwell, i. 150.
1647. — Jesper, son of Jesper Loward: ibid. p. 169.
London, 23; Manchester, 30; New York, 68.

Lorey; v. Lowrie.

Loriman; v. Lurryman.

Lorimer, Lorymer, Larimer, Lorrimer. — Occup. 'the lorimer,' a maker of horses' bits, &c.; '*laremar*, that maketh byttes, *esperonnier*' (Palsgrave); O.F. *lorimier*, later *lormier* (Skeat). It will be seen, however, that Lormar occurs in the 13th century, also Lorimar, the more correct form.

Gervase Lorimarius, or Sadler, bailiff of Norwich, 1239: FF. iii. 58.
Adam le Lorimer, co. Salop, 1273. A.
Richard le Lorimer, co. Essex, ibid.
Thomas Lormar, co. Essex, ibid.
William Lorinar, co. Oxf., ibid.
Alan le Lorymer. T.
Thomas le Lorymer, 1313. M.
Thomas Loremar, 1379: P. T. Yorks. p. 99.
1503. 'Item, to Symond Warde of London, *lorymere*, for v DD bittes, lxxs.': Privy Purse Exp., Elizabeth of York, p. 97.
1643. Married—Richard Lorrimore and Ann Smyth: St. Mary Aldermary, p. 19.
1779. — James Lorimer and Jean Howden: St. Geo. Han. Sq. i. 296.
London, 2, 2, 0, 0; Boston (U.S.), 4, 0, 1, 2.

Loring, Lorin. — Local, 'of Lorraine,' formerly a French province.

Peter de Loring, co. Bedf., 1273. A.
John le Loreng, co. Oxf., ibid.
Alice Loring, co. Soms., 1 Edw. III: Kirby's Quest, p. 131.
Emma Loring, co. Soms., 1 Edw. III: ibid.
Sir Roger Lorynge, 1566: Visitation of Bedfordshire, p. 13.
1636. Married—William Loringe and Margret Turnore: St. Mary Aldermary, p. 18.
Crockford, 1, 0; London, 0, 1; New York, 6, 0.

Lorriman.—Occup. 'Lorry's man,' i.e. the servant of Lawrence;

cf. Matthewman, Sandeman, Addiman, &c., and v. Lowrie.

West Rid. Court Dir., 2.

Lory.—Bapt. 'the son of Lawrence'; v. Lowrie.

Lott.—Bapt. 'the son of Lott.' All my instances are from the South-Eastern counties. Probably an immigrant from the Low Countries. As Abraham was common, it seems natural that Lot should be the same. The story, as an attractive one, would be familiar to the peasantry. The leading personages of the Old Testament as well as the New were utilized at the font.

Richard fil. Lote, co. Camb., 1273. A.
Robert Lote, co. Camb., ibid.
Walter Lotte, co. Camb., ibid.
William Lot, co. Suff., ibid.
John Lotte, co. Norf., ibid.
1608. Jeoffrey Farrant and Mary Lott: Marriage Lic. (Westminster), p. 16.
1626. Henry Lott and Joane Hill: Marriage Lic. (London), ii. 180.
London, 6; MDB. (Suffolk), 7; New York, 6.

Loudan, -don; v. Lowden.

Lound, Lounds; v. Lund.

Louth.—Local, 'of Louth,' a well-known town in co. Lincoln.

Robert de Luda, co. York, Hen. III–Edw. I. K.
John de Luda, co. Linc. 1273. A.
Richard de Luda, co. Linc., ibid.
Eva Louth, co. Soms., 1 Edw. III: Kirby's Quest, p. 97.
1616. Buried—William Lowth: St. Jas. Clerkenwell, iv. 137.
1674. Henry Champante and Sarah Lowth: Marriage Lic. (Westminster), p. 231.
East Rid. Court Dir., 1; MDB. (co. Lincoln), 1; Philadelphia, 4.

Love.—(1) Bapt. 'the son of Love.' That this was a fontal name the dims. Love-cock and Love-kin (q.v.) amply prove.

Love del Hok, co. Oxf., 1273. A.
1610. Bapt.—Love Hewlett: Reg. Burgh, Norfolk.
1631-2. Buried—Love Ballard: Reg. Berwick, Sussex.
1662. Bapt.—Love Appletree: Reg. Banbury.

There is no reason to suppose that this name was introduced by the Puritan party. That it was favoured by them there can be no doubt.

(2) Nick. 'the love,' the dear one, or, as suggested by Mr. Lower, some English modification of the French 'le loup,' the wolf.

Alan le Love, co. Camb., 1273. A.
Walter Love, co. Camb., ibid.
1581. Nathaniel Love, co. Wilts: Reg. Univ. Oxf. vol. ii. pt. ii. p. 112.
London, 25; Philadelphia, 76.

Loveband; v. Lovibond.

MDB. (co. Devon), 4.

Lovecock.—Bapt. 'the son of Love' (q.v.), with suffix -*cock* (v. Cock); cf. Wilcock, Adcock, Badcock.

Roger Lovecock. B.
Matthew Lovecok, co. Oxf., 1273. A.
Henry Lovecok, co. Essex, ibid.
John Lovecok, co. Soms., 1 Edw. III: Kirby's Quest, p. 90.
Lovecok de Murifield, co. Soms., 1 Edw. III: ibid. p. 174.
Lovecok le Carter, co. Soms., 1 Edw. III: ibid.

The gen. Lovecocks also occurs; cf. Wilcocks.

Robert Lovecoks, co. Soms., 1 Edw. III: ibid. p. 91.

Loveday.—Bapt. 'the son of Loveday.' Of the same class as Christmas, Pentecost, Nowell, &c. The font-name lingered on as Lowdy in Cornwall, the last refuge of many old English favourites, till the 18th century, and is not yet extinct. 'John Lovdesman' (John, the servant of Loveday) occurs in the Hundred Rolls, 1273, in co. Norfolk (i. 439). The word occurs in Piers Plowman:

'I kan holde love-dayes
And here a reve's rekenyns.'

Halliwell says: 'A day appointed for settlement of differences by arbitration.'

'But helle is fulle of suche discorde,
That ther may be no loveday.'
Gower MS. Soc. Ant. 134, f. 37.

Walter Loveday, co. Camb., 1273. A.
Richard Loveday, co. Hunts, ibid.
Ralph Loveday, 1313. M.
Hugo Lofdey, 1379: P. T. Yorks. p. 8.
Lovdie, d. Thomas Jenkin, 1578: Reg. St. Columb Major, p. 11.
Lowdye Trelogan, 1601: ibid. p. 20.
Lowdy, d. William Trekeene, 1622: ibid. p. 210.
Loveday, wife of Thomas Vivian, 1768: ibid. p. 284.

The Devon County Directory has ' Mrs. Loveday Budd, miller,' resident in the parish of Dolton.

London, 7; New York, 1.

Lovejoy. — Nick. A pretty sobriquet ; cf. Makeblithe. Just the surname to be handed down. No fear of any male member of the family trying to get rid of it.

1578. William Randeson and Johanna Lovejoye, *widow*: Marriage Lic. (London), i. 83.
1669. Buried—Robert Lovejoy, a carpenter, killed by a fall of a piece of timber: St. Michael, Cornhill, p. 257.
1685. Bapt.—Eliz., d. John Lovejoy: St. Jas. Clerkenwell, i. 314.
1689. — John, s. John Lovjoy: St. Antholin (London), p. 105.
1756. Married—Samuel Lovejoy and Sarah Wagger: St. Geo. Han. Sq. i. 66.
London, 6; New York, 14.

Lovekin, Luffkin, Lufkin, Lufkins.—Bapt. 'the son of Love' (q.v.), from the dim. Lovekin. This has now almost universally settled down into Lufkin; cf. Watkin for Walter, or Tompkin for Thomas. From Shropshire Lovekin came northwards into Cheshire, and as Lufkin is now in the Manchester Directory.

Lovekin Dawes, co. Oxf., 1273. A.
Robert Luvekyn, co. Oxf., ibid.
Lovekyn Piscator, co. Salop, ibid.
Lovekyn Stukepenne, co. Kent, ibid.
Richard Lovekyn, 1313. M.
Margery Lovekyn, co. Soms., 1 Edw. III : Kirby's Quest, p. 111.
1546. John Osborne and Philipa Lufkyne, *widow*, of the King's Household : Marriage Lic. (Faculty Office), p. 7.
Mathew Lovekin, of Wiston, 1647 : Wills at Chester (1621–50), p. 142.
Randle Lovekin, of Wibunbury, 1691 : ibid. (1681–1700), p. 162.
'Maistres Lovekyn to give in almes, 10s.,' 1542–3 : Privy Purse Expenses, Princess Mary, p. 99.
'Maistres Luffkyn to give in almes, 10s.', 1543 : ibid. p. 114.

This conclusively proves Luffkin or Lufkin and Lovekin to be one and the same name.

London, 0, 0, 1, 1 ; Manchester (Lufkin), 1 ; MDB. (co. Salop), 1, 0, 0, 0 ; (co. Essex), 0, 0, 4, 0 ; Philadelphia, 2, 0, 1, 0.

Lovelace, Loveless. — Nick. ' the loveless ' (?).

Albricus Loveles, co. Suff., 1273. A.
Sarra Loveles, co. Hunts, ibid.

1587. Robert Lovelisse, co. Berks: Reg. Univ. Oxf. vol. ii. pt. ii. p. 160.
1734. Married—Thomas Grinaway and Sarah Loveless: St. Geo. Han. Sq. i. 13.
1754. — Joseph Lovelace and Eliz. Owen : ibid. p. 51.
London, 3, 3 ; Philadelphia, 1, 3.

Lovelady.—Local(?). A curious name, but doubtless a mutilation of some local surname ; cf. Toplady.

Ann Lovelady, of Sephton, 1679 : Wills at Chester (1660–80), p. 172.
MDB. (co. Lancaster), 1 ; Liverpool, 7.

Lovell.—(1) Bapt. ' the son of Lovel,' probably a dim. of Love, q.v.

Lovel le Clerc, co. Essex, 1273. A.
Lovel (without surname), co. Suff., ibid.

(2) Nick. ' the lovel,' i.e. the little wolf. ' It is a derivative of the Lat. *lupus*, wolf, thus : Lupus, Loup, Lupellus, Louvel, Lovel' : Lower's Patr. Brit. p. 200. Lovel was, like Talbot, a dog's name. ' William Collingborne, executed in 1484, wrote as follows of the favourites of Edward III (Catesby, Ratcliffe, and Lovel) :

"The Ratte, the Catte, and Lovell, our dogge,
Rule all England under the Hogge.""

(Lower, ibid. p. 200). It is curious to notice that Wolf was used both as fontal name and nickname at the same period ; v. Wolff, and also Lowell.

Baldewin Lovel, co. Devon, Hen. III-Edw. I. K.
Caterina Lovel, co. Oxf., 1273. A.
1576. John Lovel, co. Soms. : Reg. Univ. Oxf. vol. ii. pt. ii. p. 71.
1762. Married—William Lovell and Eliz. Dalton : St. Geo. Han. Sq. i. 110.
London, 27 ; Philadelphia, 10.

Lovelock. — Nick. ' with the lovelock,' i.e. pendant curls, &c. ; cf. Silverlock, Blacklock, &c. ; v. Lovelocker. The early *lovelock* was as familiar as the later *chignon*. A prominent lovelock would give the wearer the sobriquet.

' Why should thy sweete love-locke hang dangling downe,
Kissing thy girdle-stud with falling pride?'
The Affectionate Shepheard, 1594.
John Lovelok. J.

1611-2. Thomas Ricards and Joane Lovelacke : Marriage Lic. (London), p. 10.
1625-6. George Windor and Anne Lovelock : ibid. p. 160.
1770. Married—John Smith and Mary Lovelock : St. Geo. Han. Sq. i. 198.
London, 5; MDB. (co. Berks), 4 ; New York, 1.

Lovelocker.—Occup. Seemingly a lovelocker, one who made up lovelocks, perhaps with false hair, analogous to the later perukemaker ; v. Lovelock.

Walter le Loveloker, Oxford, 1273. A.

Did he cater for the 'Varsity dandies of the period ?

Lovelot. — Bapt. From Love (q.v.), and dim. Love-elot ; cf. Hewlett, &c. The following reference distinctly proves the popularity of Love as a font-name. Lovelock (q.v.) is additional evidence.

Lovelota Gemmete, co. Soms., 1 Edw. III : Kirby's Quest, p. 220.
Adam Lovelot, co. Soms., 1 Edw. III : ibid. p. 234.

Lovely, Lovelee.—Nick. ' the lovely.'

William Louelyk, C. R., 35 Edw. I.
1772. Married—John Tamberlin and Ann Lovely : St. Geo. Han. Sq. i. 224.
Crockford, 2, 0 ; MDB. (co. Lincoln), 0, 1 ; New York, 4, 0 ; Philadelphia, 2, 0.

Lover.—Nick. ' the lover ' ; cf. Paramor, Phillimore, &c.

William le Lovere, co. Norf., 1273. A.

I believe it has been generally thought that ' lovyer' was a modern vulgarism ; seemingly it is not so.

John le Lovyere, co. Soms., 1 Edw. III : Kirby's Quest, p. 179.
Walter le Loveyere, co. Soms., 1 Edw. III : ibid.
1762. Married—William Lover and Margaret Hornsby : St. Geo. Han. Sq. i. 114.
New York, 2.

Loveredge, Loveridge. — Bapt. ' the son of Loverich'; cf. Aldridge for Aldrich.

William Loverich, co. Oxf., 1273. A.
Robert Loverik, co. Linc., ibid.
1666. Henry Clarke and Grace Loveridge : Marriage Lic. (Westminster), p. 115.
1805. Married—Aaron Loveridge and Mary Gattfield : St. Geo. Han. Sq. ii. 319.
London, 1, 4 ; Philadelphia, 0, 2.

Loverock; v. Laverack.

Lovett, Lovitt.—? Bapt. 'the son of Love' (q.v.), from the dim. Lov-et; cf. Emmott, &c. As Love became Lovell (q.v.), so also it became Lovet. 'Little wolf' seems to be the meaning; v. Love.

Thomas Lovet, co. Northampt., 1273. A.
Henry Lovet, co. Devon, ibid.
Willelmus Louott, 1379: P. T. Yorks. p. 240.
1583. William Lovett, co. Staff.; Reg. Univ. Oxf. vol. ii. pt. ii. p. 131.
1668. Bapt.—Mary, d. William Louett: St. Michael, Cornhill, p. 146.
1800. Married—Charles Wheeler and Eliz. Lovitt: St. Geo. Han. Sq. ii. 229.
London, 7, 1; New York, 10, 2.

Lovibond, Loveband. — Nick. (?). Probably a sobriquet of a playfully satirical character affixed to one who was a slave or bond to love; v. Bond. But it may have been a personal name, for Love-bond would make a pretty child's name; cf. Love, Lovekin, Lovecock, Loveday. Also cf. Love-lot (Kirby's Quest, p. 234).

Nicholas Loveband, co. Norf., 20 Edw. I. R.
Thomas Lovehybonde, co. Soms., 1 Edw. III: Kirby's Quest, p. 231.
William Lovybonde, co. Soms., 1 Edw. III: ibid. p. 250.
160⁸. Edward Lovibond, Isle of Wight: Reg. Univ. Oxf. vol. ii. pt. ii. p. 301.
1698. Henry Lovibond and Anne Collins: Marriage Lic. (Faculty Office), p. 230.
1702. Thomas Thorpe and Anne Lovibond: ibid. p. 244.
1784. Married—John Edmonds and Theodosia Jane Loverbond: St. Geo. Han. Sq. i. 360.
London, 2, 1; New York, 2, 0.

Loving.—Local, 'of Lovaine,' a well-known city in the Netherlands. The final g is, of course, excrescent, as in Jennings and a host of names, the corruption being imitative. The instances below fully prove my statement.

Godfrey de Luvayn, co. Bedf., Hen. III-Edw. I. K.
Mathew Lovein, co. Glouc., ibid.
Muriel de Lovayn, co. Suff., 1273. A.
Mathew de Lovayne, co. Suff., ibid.
John Loveyn, co. Norf., 1365: FF. v. 186.
Ellen Loveyn, co. Norf., 1365: ibid.
1608. William Lovinge, of Newport, Isle of Wight: Marriage Lic. (London), i. 305.

1623. Bapt.—Mary, d. Stephen Loven: St. Jas. Clerkenwell, i. 96.
1703. Married—Thomas Loveing and Eliz. Rothwell: St. Dionis Backchurch, p. 51.
London, 1; Philadelphia, 1.

Low, Lowe.—Local, 'at the low,' i.e. the hill; A.S. hlaw or hlœw, a hill; v. Law (1).

Ralph de la Lowe, co. Salop, 1273. A.
Hugh de la Lowe, co. Heref., ibid.
Crist. atte Lowe, co. Soms., 1 Edw. III⁴ Kirby's Quest, p. 256.

The following occur in the list of mayors of Macclesfield:

Thomas del Lowe, 1430: East Ches. ii. 164.
Thomas Lowe, 1448: ibid.
George Lowe, 1607: ibid. p. 465.
London, 33, 46; New York, 41, 45.

Lowcock.—Bapt. 'the son of Lawrence,' from the nick. Law or Low (v. Lowson), and suffix -cock; cf. Wilcock, and v. Cock.

Alicia Lowcok', 1379: P. T. Yorks. p. 205.
Willelmus Loucok', 1379: p. 134.
1767. Married—Thomas Park and Deborah Lowcock: St. Geo. Han. Sq. i. 169.
Manchester, 2; Sheffield, 1.

Lowden, Loudan, Louden, Loudon.— Local. Probably 'of Loudson,' a parish in co. Ayr. The surname has crossed the border and is well known in co. Cumb.

1716. William Lowden, of Kirkham: Lancashire Wills at Richmond, ii. 169.
1753. Married—Thomas Dalby and Sarah Lowden: St. Geo. Chap. Mayfair, p. 265.
London, 6, 1, 0, 0; MDB. (co. Cumb.), 1, 0, 0, 0; Boston (U.S.), 8, 0, 1, 12.

Lowder; v. Lowther.

Lowell.—Nick. and bapt. There is not the shadow of a doubt that Lowell is a variant of Lovell. For a conclusive proof a Cambridgeshire Lovel is found with his name spelt both ways in the Hundred Rolls.

Fulco Lovel, co. Camb., 1273. A.
Fulco Lowel, co. Camb., ibid.
1531. Thomas Lovel, or Lowell, or Louwell: Reg. Univ. Oxf. i. 164.
1655. Married—Peter Hentton and Jenne Louell: St. Mary Aldermary, p. 24.
1745. — Charles Tarr and Elioner Lowell: St. Geo. Chap. Mayfair, p. 55.
London, 1; New York, 4.

Lowman. — (1) Occup. 'the servant of Low,' i.e. Lawrence; v. Lowson. This class of occupa-

tive names is somewhat large; v. Matthewman, Addyman, &c. (2) Local, 'the low-man,' one who lived on the low (v. Low); cf. Denman, Berryman, &c.

1587. Francis Lowman, co. Devon: Reg. Univ. Oxf. vol. ii. pt. ii. p. 159.
1664-5. John Huett and Faith Lowman (co. Hants): Marriage Lic. (Faculty Office), p. 86.
1673. Married—John Lowman and Frances Knowles: St. Peter, Cornhill, ii. 55.
1688. Buried—Frances Loman, in the North Isle: ibid. p. 101
London, 3; New York, 1; Boston (U.S.), 1.

Lowndes, Lownds; v. Lund.

Lowndesbrough, Lowndsbrough, Lowndsborough, Lonsbrough, Londesborough, Lownsbury, Lounsberry, Lounsbery, Lounsbury. — Local, 'of Londesborough,' a parish in E. Rid. Yorks, two miles and a half from Market Weighton.

MDB. (North Rid. Yorks), 1, 0, 0, 0, 0, 0, 0, 0, 0; Hull, 0, 1, 0, 0, 0, 0, 0, 0, 0; New Malton, 0, 0, 1, 0, 0, 0, 0, 0, 0; Fridaythorpe, York, 0, 0, 0, 0, 1, 0, 0, 0; Scarborough, 0, 0, 0, 0, 0, 1, 0, 0, 0; Philadelphia, 0, 0, 0, 0, 0, 0, 6, 2, 1, 2.

Lowrie, Lowry, Laurie, Lawry, Lawrey, Lawrie, Lory, Lorey.—Bapt. 'the son of Lawrence.' In the Lowlands and on the Borders, popularly Lowrie or Laurie, whence the many North-English and Scottish variations of this name. The English sobriquet of the fox was Reynard, q.v. In Scotland Lawrence stood sponsor to the animal.

'Whilk slee Tod Lowrie hads without his mow.'
Ramsay's Poems, ii. 143.
'He said; and round the courtiers all and each
Applauded Lawrie for his winsome speech.'   ibid. p. 500.

Hence 'Lowrie-like,' having the crafty look of a fox. The full name Lawrence was also applied to the fox, proving that Lowry and Lawry are the true offspring of the name.

'Lawrence the actis and the proceis wrait.'
Bannatyne Poems, p. 112, st. 4.

All my quotations are from Jamieson.

K k

1677. Buried—Mary Lowery: St. Dionis Backchurch, p. 243.
1742. Married—Edward Lowry and Sarah Gilbert: St. Geo. Chap. Mayfair, p. 20.
1784. — Hugh Laurie and Frances Storie: St. Geo. Han. Sq. i. 362.
London, 1, 8, 8, 1, 1, 10, 0, 0; MDB. (co. Cornwall), Lory, 7; New York, 4, 18, 2, 0, 0, 4, 2, 8.

Lowson.—Bapt. 'the son of Lawrence,' from the nick. Law or Low; cf. Lowrie for Laurie, and v. Lawson. Lawson is a familiar Cumberland surname.

1616. Henry Lowson, co. Cumb.: Reg. Univ. Oxf. vol. ii. pt. ii. p. 351.
1753. Married—John Baxter and Ann Lowson: St. Geo. Chap. Mayfair, p. 256.
London, 2; Boston (U.S.), 1.

Lowther, Lowder. — Local, 'of Lowther,' a parish in co. Cumb. In the Household Books of Lord William Howard of Naworth Castle (Surt. Soc.) the name is spelt variously as Lowther, Louther, Lowder, and Louder.

Robertus de Louther, 1310, co. Westm. M.
Hugo de Louthre, 1319, co. Cumb., ibid.
Ann Lowder, 1622, co. Cumb.: VVV. p. 495.

Sir John Lowther, of Whitehaven, had two daughters baptized in London at the church of St. Martin's-in-the-Fields. They are thus entered:

1664. Bapt.—Catherine, d. of Sir John Lowder, *knight*: Transactions Cumb. and Westm. Ant. and Arch. Soc. pt. ii. vol. ix. p. 341.
1667. — Jane, d. of Sir John Lowther: ibid.
1606(?). Rowland Lowder, of Staveley, in Cartmell: Lancashire Wills at Richmond, i. 186.
1670. Rowland Lowther, of Stayley, in Cartmell: ibid.
1796. Married—Anthony Jackson, *husbandman*, and Betty Lowther: St. Mary, Ulverston, p. 442.
London, 4, 1; Crockford, 2, 1; MDB. (co. Cumb.), 13, 0; New York, 8, 0; Philadelphia, 5, 8.

Lowthian, Lothian, Lowthin, Lowthing. — Local, ' of Lothian,' a Scottish surname that has crept across the Border. Lothian is a district on the south side of the Forth, including the

counties of Haddington, Edinburgh, and Linlithgow.

Ranulph de Louthiane, co. Northumb., 1273. A.
1791. Married—Robert Lowthian and Mary Bodimeade: St. Geo. Han. Sq. ii. 69.
Manchester, 2, 0, 1, 1; MDB. (co. Cumb.), 8, 0, 0, 0; Boston (U.S.), 0, 2, 0, 0; New York, 1, 2, 0, 0.

Lowthorpe, Lathrop, Lathrope, Lowthrop.—Local, ' of Lowthorp,' a parish in the E. Rid. Yorks, near Great Driffield. My first entry clearly proves that the American Lathrop is but a variant; cf. Winthrop for Winthorp, and v. Thrupp.

1602. John Lowthroppe, or Lawthrop, co. York: Reg. Univ. Oxf. vol. ii. pt. ii. p. 259.
1608. Bapt.—John, s. Robert Leythorpe: St. Jas. Clerkenwell, i. 55.
1610. — Robert, s. Robert Laytharopp: ibid. p. 59.
1740. Married—Robert Lathropp and Ann Tomkins: St. Geo. Han. Sq. i. 25.

These four entries supply, as will be seen, a complete chain of evidence.

London, 1, 0, 0, 0; Hull, 2, 0, 0, 0; East Rid. Court Dir., 0, 0, 0, 1; Philadelphia, 0, 6, 1, 0.

Loxham.—Local, ' of Loxham.' I have not found the spot. A Lancashire surname.

William Loxham, of Longton, *butcher*, 1622: Preston Guild Rolls, p. 89.
Robert Loxum, of Preston, 1675: Lancashire Wills at Richmond (1457-1680), p. 186.
Thomas Loxam, of Preston, 1677: ibid.
Eliz. Loxham, of Preston, 1733: ibid. (1681-1748), p. 169.
Edward Loxham, of Kirkham, 1737: ibid.
Preston, 2; Barrow-in-Furness, 1.

Loxley.—Local, ' of Loxley,' a liberty in the parish of Uttoxeter, co. Stafford; also a parish in co. Warwick, near Stratford.

Richard de Lokesley, *taillour*, 14 Edw. III: Freemen of York, i. 34.
Thomas de Lokeslay, 1379: P. T. Yorks. p. 35.
1740. Bapt.—Edward, s. Abraham Loxley: St. Geo. Chap. Mayfair, p. 1.
1767. Married—William Davis and Grace Loxley: St. Geo. Han. Sq. i. 167.
London, 1; MDB. (co. Glouc.), 3; Oxford, 2; Philadelphia, 1.

Luard.—? ——. ' At the Revocation of the Edict of Nantes, 1685, Robert Abraham Luard came from Caen in Normandy and settled in London, *a quo* the Luards of Lincolnshire and Essex': Lower's Patr. Brit. p. 201.

1754. Married—Peter Robert Luard and Jane Burryan: St. Geo. Chap. Mayfair, p. 273.
London, 1; MDB. (co. Essex), 5; (co. Lincoln), 2.

Lubbock.—Local, ' of Lübeck,' on the Trave, near Hamburg.

Robert de Lubyck, co. Linc., 1273. A.
Bernard de Lubic, co. York, ibid.
Hildebrand de Lubek. J.
Hellbrand de Lubeck, co. Norf., 14 Edw. I: FF. ix. 363.
1686. Bapt.—Anne, d. Herman Lewbeck: St. Jas. Clerkenwell, i. 319.
Richard Lubbock, sheriff of Norwich, 1714: FF. iii. 436.
William Lubbock, rector of Lammas, co. Norf., 1738: ibid. vi. 294.
London, 4; MDB. (co. Lincoln), 1.

Lucas. — Bapt. 'the son of Luke.' A single glance at the London Directory will suffice to show that Lucas, not Luke, was the early English form.

' And al that Marc hath y-maad,
Mathew, Johan, and Lucas.'
    Piers Plowman, 3498-9.

Lucas Cacherellus, co. Norf., 1273. A.
Lucas Bercator, co. Camb., ibid.
John Lucas, co. Soms., 1 Edw. III: Kirby's Quest, p. 261.
Willelmus Lucas, 1379: P. T. Howdenshire, p. 23.
Thomas fil. Lucas, co. York. W. 15.
1561. Richard Lucas and Alice Pumfrett: Marriage Lic. (London), i. 22.
London, 83; New York, 27.

Luccock, Lucock, Lowcock.—(1) Bapt.'the son of Luke'; with suffix -*cock*, Lukecock, popularly Luccock; v. Cock. (2) Bapt. 'the son of Lawrence,' a variant of Lowcock, q.v.

Robert Lukok, *bocher*, 13 Edw. III: Freemen of York, i. 33.
1681. Married—William Luccocke and Eliz. Wright: St. Jas. Clerkenwell, iii. 194.
1752. — John Moris and Sarah Luckock: St. Geo. Chap. Mayfair, p. 232.
1794. — John Lucock and Ann Dawson: St. Geo. Han. Sq. ii. 109.
London, 1, 3, 3.

Luck, Lucke, Luckie, Luckey.—(1) Bapt. 'the son of

Luke,' popularly Luck and Luckie on the Scottish border.

1624. Married—Sir Samuell Lucke and Eliz. Freeman: St. Michael, Cornhill, p. 24.
1627. Bapt.—Samvell, s. Sir Samvell Luke: ibid. p. 119.
'Lucke Moffett, for one howse, 4d.,' 1631: QQQ. p. 155.

Hence diminutives Luckett and Luckin, q.v.

(2) Local, ' of Luke,' probably Liege in the Netherlands, with which province and city we were closely related by commercial ties. Andrew Borde says in his Boke of Knowledge, ' The lond of Lewke is a pleasant countre, the chiefe towne is the cytie of Lewke. The speche is base Doche' (quoted by Lower).

Theobald de Luke, co. York, 1273. A.
Reynen de Luke, co. York, ibid.
William Lucke, co. Camb., ibid.
John de Luke, 1317. M.
1733. Married—Richard Luckie and Jane Warden: St. Geo. Han. Sq. i. 12.
1756. — Thomas Luck and Jane Featherston: ibid. p. 63.
London, 12, 0, 3, 0; New York, 3, 3, 1, 7.

Luckett.—Bapt. ' the son of Luke,' from dim. Luke-et, popularly Lucket (v. Luck); cf. Emmott from Emma, or Collett from Cole (Nicholas).

Matilda Luket, co. York, 1418: W. 11, p. 20.
Walter Luket, co. York, 1418: ibid.
1629. Buried—Richard, s. Richard Luckett: St. Jas. Clerkenwell, iv. 196.
1802. Married—George Luckett and Rosanna Taylor: St. Geo. Han. Sq. ii. 264.
London, 2; Oxford, 2.

Luckin, Lucking, Lukeing, Lukyn, Luckings, Lucken, Luken, Lukens. — Bapt. ' the son of Luke,' from dim. Luke-in; with excrescent g Lukeing, and with patronymic s Lukeings, popularly Luckin, Lucking, and Luckings; v. Luck.

Jane Luckin. FF.
1548. Martin Pugson and Joanna Luckynes: Marriage Lic. (Faculty Office), p. 13.
1587. John Luckyn and Anne Sampford: Marriage Lic. (London), i. 162.
1591. Walter Lukyn, co. Essex: Reg. Univ. Oxf. vol. ii. pt. ii. p. 186.

1609. Buried—Martha Lukin, servant to the Lady Denney: St. Antholin (London), p. 47.
London, 2, 3, 1, 2, 1, 0, 0, 0; New York, 0, 2, 0, 0, 0, 1, 1, 1.

Luckman, Lukeman. — Occup. ' the man of Luke,' i.e. servant. In the North popularly Luck, q.v. This is a surname of a distinct class; v. Matthewman, Ladyman, or Addyman, and cf. Lowman.

1683. Married—John Lucman and Suzanna Bennett: St. Jas. Clerkenwell, iii. 199.
London, 1, 1; Philadelphia, 3, 0.

Luckner; v. Lewknor.

Lucombe. — Local, ' of Luccombe,' a parish in co. Somerset; also written Luckham.

Geoffrey de Luccombe, co. Soms., 1 Edw. III: Kirby's Quest, p. 246.
1752. Married—Richard Shepperd and Eliz. Luckham: St. Geo. Chap. Mayfair, p. 221.
1756. — Thomas Marchant and Sarah Luckham: St. Geo. Han. Sq. i. 87.
London, 3.

Lucraft, Luckcraft, Luckraft, Loucraft.—Local, ' of Leacroft,' a township in the parish of Cannock, co. Stafford. The suffix -croft is frequently found as -craft; v. Craft. A novel published several years ago by Messrs. Besant and Rice, entitled The Case of Mr. Lucraft, has helped to give prominence to this surname. There can be little doubt that all the above forms are variants of Leycraft or Leacroft. Of course smaller spots than Leacroft in Staffordshire may have originated the surname, as the term leacroft would be a common place-word; v. Lea and Croft.

Francis Leycrofte, or Leighcrofte, London, 1584: Reg. Univ. Oxf. vol. ii. pt. ii. p. 134.
1601. Buried—Sara, d. Samson Lecraft, armorer: St. Peter, Cornhill, i. 151.
1607. Bapt.—Richard, s. Sampson Leycrafte, brasier: ibid. p. 57.
1608. Buried — Samson Leycrofte, brasier: ibid. p. 163.
London, 2, 0, 0, 0; MDB. (co. Devon), 0, 1, 3, 0; Plymouth, 0, 0, 1, 0; Boston (U.S.), 0, 0, 0, 1.

Lucy, Lucey.—(1) Local, ' de Luci.' Luci is a parish in the

arrondissement of Neufchâtel, in Normandy. The Lucys of our modern directories represent two totally different derivations, and are inextricably mixed; v. (2).

Godfrey de Lucey, 34 Hen. II: FF. x. 332.
Reginald de Lucy, co. Essex, Hen. III-Edw. I. K.
Gilbert de Lucie, co. Linc., 1273. A.
John de Luce, co. Norf., ibid.
Richard de Lucy, co. Essex, ibid.
Fulco de Lucy, co. Staff., 20 Edw. I. R.
Ancelina de Lucy. J.

(2) Bapt. ' the son of Lucy.'
Richard fil. Lucia. J.
Roger fil. Lucie, co. Norf., 1273. A.
Alice fil. Luce, co. Hertf., ibid.
Richard fil. Lucie, co. Hunts, 20 Edw. I. R.
Elena fil. Luce, co. York, ibid.
Charles Lucey, 1513: Reg. Univ. Oxf. i. 87.
1612. Bapt.—Ann, d. Robert Lucey: St. Antholin (London), p. 48.
London, 4, 3; Philadelphia, 10, 0.

Luddington.—Local, ' of Luddington,' (1) a parish in cos. Northampton and Hunts, six miles from Oundle; (2) a hamlet in the parish of Old Stratford, co. Warwick.

Henry de Ludinton, co. Soms., Hen. III-Edw. I. K.
William de Ludinton, co. Warwick, ibid.
Hamund de Lodingtone, co. Hunts, 1273. A.
Edelina de Lodinton, co. Northampt., ibid.
Walter de Lodyngton, co. Hunts, ibid.
1606. Bapt.—Eliz., d. Vallintonne Luddingtonne: St. Peter, Cornhill, i. 56.
1661-2. Stephen Lodington and Eliz. Neesham: Marriage Alleg. (Canterbury), p. 67.
1670. Married—James Tridway and Saray Ludington: St. Jas. Clerkenwell, iii. 172.
MDB. (co. Lincoln), 1; Philadelphia, 3.

Ludford.—Local, ' of Ludford,' a parish near Ludlow, partly in co. Hereford, partly in co. Salop. Also two parishes (Magna and Parva Ludford) in co. Lincoln.

John Lodeford, co. Soms., 1 Edw. III: Kirby's Quest, p. 215.
1450. John Lydford, or Ledford, or Ludford: Marriage Lic. (Faculty Office), p. 10.
1548. William Askeryck and Eliz. Ludford: Marriage Lic. (Faculty Office), p. 13.

1669. William Ludford and Vertue Roker: Marriage Alleg. (Canterbury), p. 23.
London, 3.

Ludgate.—Local, 'at the ludgate'; v. Lidgate and Lidgater.

London, 1; Boston (U.S.), 6.

Ludgater.—Local, 'the ludgater,' i.e. one who lived by the ludgate; v. Lidgate and Lidgater.

Crockford, 2; MDB. (co. Kent), 2.

Ludlam.—Local, 'of Ludlam,' seemingly some place in co. Derby. I have not found the locality.

1575. Robert Lodlam, co. Derby: Reg. Univ. Oxf. vol. ii. pt. ii. p. 68.
1707. Buried—James Ludlam: St. Michael, Cornhill, p. 279.
London, 3; MDB. (co. Derby), 4; Philadelphia, 4.

Ludlow.—Local, 'of Ludlow,' a market-town and parish in co. Salop. In the Hundred Rolls (1273) the name of the place is variously Ludelawe, Ludelawie, Ludelawye, Ludelowe.

Nicholas de Ludelawe, co. Glouc., 1273. A.
John de Ludloe, co. Glouc., 15 Edw. I: Atkyns' Hist. Glouc. p. 161.
1591. Henry Ludlowe, co. Wilts: Reg. Univ. Oxf. vol. ii. pt. ii. p. 185.
1610. Roger Ludlowe, co. Wilts: ibid. p. 311.
1695. Married—William Bracey and Mary Ludlow: St. Michael, Cornhill, p. 48.
1746. — William Ludlow and Eliz. Halbert: St. Geo. Han. Sq. i. 37.
London, 8; MDB. (co. Warwick), 3; New York, 19.

Luff.—Bapt. 'the son of Love,' whence Lovekin, q.v. Lufkin and Lufkins are corruptions of Lovekin; so no doubt Luff of Love.

William Luffe, co. Bucks, 1273. A.

Cf. the immediate entry above with

Walter Lufesone, co. Oxf., 1273. A.

which is manifestly 'the son of Love.'

1679. John Steward and Mary Luffe: Marriage Lic. (Faculty Office), p. 147.
1741. Bapt.—Mary, d. George Luff: St. Peter, Cornhill, i. 41.
London, 14; Philadelphia, 6.

Lufkin, Lufkins.—Bapt.; v. Lovekin.

Lugg.—? Local, 'at the lug' (?), from residence thereby. Lug, a

measure of land, anciently 20 ft. 'Lug, a pole in measure' (Kennett). Forty-nine square yards of coppice wood make a *lug* (Halliwell); cf. Hyde. 'Lugger, a strip of land, Glouc.' (ibid.)

Thomas Lugge, co. Kent, 1273. A.
Josep Lugge, co. Kent, ibid.
Richard Lug', co. Hunts, ibid.
1620. Toby Lugge, St. Mary Hall: Reg. Univ. Oxf. i. 405.
1638. Robert Lugge, St. John's College: ibid. p. 148.
1716. Married—Henry Harris and Rachael Lugg: St. Jas. Clerkenwell, iii. 239.
London, 8.

Luggar, Lugar.—? ——. A curious surname which I dare not attempt to classify. It is found in Norfolk three centuries ago, and probably came from the Low Countries. From Norfolk it crossed into Essex as Lugar. But v. Lugg.

1558. Philip Lewgar, co. Norf.: FF. viii. 120.
1573. Thomas Lewger, vicar of Windham, co. Norf.: ibid. ii. 508.
1800. Married—Marshall Lugar and Mary Mapes: St. Geo. Han. Sq. ii. 400.
London, 1, 0; MDB. (co. Essex), 0, 1; Philadelphia, 0, 10.

Luke, Lukes, Luks. — (1) Bapt. 'the son of Luke.' Lucas was the more popular form. Yet the diminutives seem formed from Luke; v. Luckett, Luckin, and Luccock. (2) Local, 'of Luke,' i.e. Liege. For further proof, v. Luck (2).

Lucas de Luk, London, 1273. A.
Lucas de Lukes, London, ibid.
Katerina Luke, co. Norf., ibid.
1669. Nicholas Luke and Martha Tibby: Marriage Alleg. (Canterbury), p. 22.
London, 9, 2, 1; New York, 6, 0, 0.

Lukeing, Luken (s; v. Luckin.

Luker; v. Looker.

Lumb, Lomb.—Local, 'at the lum,' from residence thereby, a North-English surname. '*Lum*, a woody valley, a deep pool. North England' (Halliwell). The final *b* is excrescent. There can be little doubt about the truth of this derivation, although I have no proofs; cf. Lumby and Lumley, North-English place-names.

1752. Married—Beaumont Bellamy and Eliz. Lum: St. Geo. Chap. Mayfair, p. 261.

1753. Married—Edward Clark and Mary Lumb: ibid. p. 262.
MDB. (co. Cumberland), 6, 0; West Rid. Court Dir., 13, 0; London, 2, 0; New York, 1, 3.

Lumbard; v. Lombard.

Lumby.—Local, 'of Lumby,' a township in the parish of Sherburn, W. Rid. Yorks; v. Lumb.

Robertus de Lumby, 1379: P. T. Yorks. p. 192.
1693-4. Zephaniah Lumby and Martha Wilson: Marriage Alleg. (Canterbury), p. 285.
London, 3; West Rid. Court Dir., 1; Sheffield, 2.

Lumley, Lumly.—Local, 'of Lumley,' a township in the parish of Chester-le-Street, co. Durham; v. Lumb.

Roger de Lumeleye, co. Leic., 1273. A.
Robert de Lumley, 1431: DDD. i. 74.
1620. Married—George Lumbly and Jone Tatnam: St. Antholin (London), p. 55.
1671. Bapt.—Richard, s. Francis Lumley: St. Jas. Clerkenwell, i. 252.
1703. Married—Stephen Anderson and Anne Lumley: St. Michael, Cornhill, p. 52.
London, 17, 0; New York, 2, 1; Boston (U.S.), 0, 1.

Lummis.—Local, a variant of Lomas, q.v.

1702. Bapt.—Eliz., d. Edward Lumis: St. Jas. Clerkenwell, ii. 18.
1796. Married—William Lummis and Margery Kneebone: St. Geo. Han. Sq. ii. 148.
Manchester, 1; East Rid. Court Dir., 1; New York, 2.

Lumpkin.—Bapt. 'the son of Lambert,' from the nick. Lamb and dim. Lambkin. No doubt a variant of Lambkin or Lampkin, q.v.

Philadelphia, 5.

Lumsden.—Local, 'of Lumsden,' an ancient manor in the parish of Coldingham, co. Berwick.

1616-7. John Lumisden, *Scotus*: Reg. Univ. Oxf. vol. ii. pt. ii. p. 358.
London, 6; Boston (U.S.), 1.

Lund, Lound, Lounds, Lowndes, Lownds, Lowne, Lond.—Local, 'at the laund' or 'lund,' i.e. lawn, which is a modern form, an open space in a wood, a glade. 'Lawnde of a wode, *saltus*': Prompt. Parv.

'At the hartes in these hye laundes.'
         Morte Arthur.

A property in my late parish (Ulverston) has been from time immemorial called 'The Lund.' A high piece of greensward, it once overlooked the forest of Furness. The final s in Lowndes, &c., is probably the patronymic, as in Williams, Jennings, &c.; cf. Knowles, Styles, Brooks, Holmes, &c.

Richard de la Lund, co. Norf., 1273. A.
Henry del Lund, co. Linc., ibid.
Robert de la Laund, co. Essex, ibid.
Thomas de Lound, co. Linc., ibid.
William de la Londe, co. Devon, ibid.
John de la Lound, co. Bedf., 20 Edw. I. R.
Alice du Lund, C. R., 32 Edw. I.
Beatrice atte Lound, co. Norf., temp. Edw. III: FF.
Johannes del Lound, 1379: P. T. Yorks. p. 24.

Lund is the commonest form of entry in early rolls.

1625-6. Thomas Madlocke and Catherine Lownes: Marriage Lic. (London), ii. 162.
1628. Thomas Lowndes and Eliz. Spenser: ibid. p. 193.
London, 10, 1, 1, 4, 2, 2, 1; Philadelphia, 9, 0, 0, 1, 0, 1, 0.

Lung. — Nick. 'the lung,' i.e. Long, q.v. A common variant in the Hundred Rolls; cf. Lang.

Geoffrey le Lung, co. Norf., 1273. A.
Thomas le Lung, co. Glouc., ibid.
Walter le Lung, Fines Roll, 12 Edw. I.
John le Lung, de Doncaster, 4 Edw. II: Freemen of York, i. 13.
London, 1; Boston (U.S.), 1.

Lungley. — Local, 'of Lungley,' a form of Langley or Longley, q.v.; cf. Lung for Long or Lang.

Robert de Lungeleye, co. Essex, 1273. A.
Ralph de Lingeley, co. Suff., ibid.
London, 3; Oxford, 1.

Lunn.—(1) Bapt. 'the son of Lune.' But while there seems every reason to suppose that some of our Lunns are thus derived, there can be no doubt that (2) is the chief parent.

Lone le Lef, co. Hunts, 1273. A.
Reginald fil. Lune, co. Linc., ibid.
William Luneson, co. Oxf., ibid.
Bartelom' Lune, co. Suff., ibid.
Robert Lune, co. Camb., ibid.
Cf. Lunell Wodeward, co. Essex, ibid.

(2) Local, 'of the lund,' q.v. In this case the final d has been dropped.

1722. Bapt.—Richard, s. Richard and Anne Lund: St. Peter, Cornhill, i. 33.
1728. — Caroline, d. Richard and Anne Lunn: ibid. p. 35.
1581. Henry Lunde, or Lunne, co. Cumb.: Reg. Univ. Oxf. vol. ii. pt. ii. p. 109.
London, 10; Philadelphia, 8.

Lunt.—Local, 'of Lunt,' a township in the parish of Sephton, near Liverpool. Probably in some cases a sharpened form of Lund, q.v.

1568. Gilbert Lunt, of Litherland: Wills at Chester (1545-1620), p. 128.
1592. Humphrey Lunt, of Maghull: ibid.
1669. Richard Lunt, of the Lunt, co. Lancaster: ibid. (1660-80), p. 174.
1678. Robert Lunt, of Lunt: ibid.
1802. Married—John Lunt and Eliz. Bishop: St. Geo. Han. Sq. ii. 257.
Liverpool, 14; London, 2; Boston (U.S.), 37.

Lupson.—Bapt. 'the son of Love,' q.v. Loveson would readily corrupt to Lupson, and no other interpretation seems possible.

Walter Lufesone, co. Oxf., 1273. A.
Roger fil. Love, co. York, ibid.
London, 2.

Lupton.—Local, 'of Lupton,' a township in the parish of Kirkby Lonsdale, co. Westmoreland. The surname crossed the border into Yorkshire at an early period, and is much more familiar in the West Riding than in its native county.

Thomas de Lupton, 1379: P. T. Yorks. p. 289.
Thomas Lupton, of Dalton, 1596: Lancashire Wills at Richmond (1457-1680), p. 187.
John Lupton, of Tatham, 1640: ibid.
1685. John Lupton and Alice Hall: Marriage Lic. (Faculty Office), p. 177.
— Bapt.—Thomas, s. Thomas Lupton: St. Jas. Clerkenwell, i. 314.
London, 11; West Rid. Court Dir., 19; Philadelphia, 9.

Lurryman, Loriman, Lorriman.—Occup. 'the servant of Lorry' or 'Lowry,' i.e. Lawrence; cf. Matthewman, Addyman, &c. Naturally we find this surname in Yorkshire, where so many of this class abound; v. Lowrie.

James Lurryman, 1662: Preston Guild Rolls, p. 133.
Thomas Lurryman, 1662: ibid.
Richard Lorriman, of Cansfield, 1687: Lancashire Wills at Richmond (1681-1748), p. 169.

West Rid. Court Dir., 0, 0, 2; Lofthouse-cum-Carlton (West Rid. Yorks), 0, 1, 0.

Lusby.—Local, 'of Lusby,' a parish in co. Lincoln, near Spilsby.

1750. Married—Samuel Lusby and Grace Fitch: St. Geo. Chap. Mayfair, p. 178.
London, 3; MDB. (co. Lincoln), 1; Philadelphia, 1.

Luscious.—Nick. 'the luscious.' Professor Skeat says (v. luscious), 'It evidently arose (I think) from attaching the suffix -ous to the M.E. lusty, pleasant, delicious.' My instance below suggests rather that the suffix was -wise (way, mode); cf. righteous from M.E. rightwis. The two corruptions go hand in hand. My instance is 300 years earlier than those usually found in dictionaries, &c.

Thomas Lustwys, co. Oxf., 1273. A.

Luscombe, Luscomb.—Local. 'of Loscoombe,' (1) a locality in the parish of Illogan, co. Cornwall; (2) 'of Loscombe,' a hamlet in the parish of Netherbury, co. Dorset; (3) 'of Luscombe,' an estate near Dawlish, co. Devon, which belonged to the family, and was their residence temp. Henry V; and probably much earlier, as the name of Hugh de Luscombe occurs in that county, 9 Edw. I' (Lower, Patr. Brit. p. 203). No doubt the last is the true home of nine-tenths of the Luscombes or Luscombs of our directories.

1587. Henry Luscombe, co. Devon: Reg. Univ. Oxf. vol. ii. pt. ii. p. 160.
1798. Married—Robert Luscombe and Mary Ford: St. Geo. Han. Sq. ii. 179.
MDB. (co. Devon), 15, 0; London, 3, 0; Boston (U.S.), 6, 6.

Lush.— ? ——. I cannot offer any solution.

1671. Robert Lush (co. Berks) and Precilla Garrard: Marriage Lic. (Faculty Office), p. 120.
Richard Lush, 1722: Reg. Broad Chalke, co. Wilts, p. 54.
Dorothy Lush, 1722: ibid.
1751. Married—George Pawson and Rachael Lush: St. Geo. Chap. Mayfair, p. 192.
London, 5; Philadelphia, 10.

Lusher, Luscher.— ? ——. I cannot suggest a solution.

1546. George Bewmond and Eliz. Lusher: Marriage Lic. (Faculty Office), p. 9.
1600. Richard Lusher, co. Surrey: Reg. Univ. Oxf. vol. ii. pt. ii. p. 241.
London, 3, 1; Philadelphia, 1, 0.

Lushington.—Local, 'of Lushington.' I cannot find the place. Manifestly of Kentish extraction.

1606-7. Thomas Lushington, co. Kent: Reg. Univ. Oxf. vol. ii. pt. ii. p. 293.
1687. George Walker and Ann Lushington, co. Kent: Marriage Alleg. (Canterbury), p. 288.
1747. Married—Nathaniel Belsey and Ellen Lushington: Canterbury Cath. p. 89.
London, 3; MDB. (co. Kent), 5.

Lusty.—Nick. 'the lusty,' full of spirit, merry, jovial; cf. Merry, Gay, &c.

1746. Married—John Lusty and Eliz. Towne: St. Geo. Chap. Mayfair, p. 67.
1784. — William Lusty and Eliz. Brumhead: St. Geo. Han. Sq. i. 356.
London, 5; Bristol, 3.

Luter.—Occup. 'the luter,' a player on the lute. In some cases this surname may be but a variant of Luther, q.v.

German le Lutrere. T.
John de Leuter, London, 20 Edw. I. R.
1537-8. 'Item, given to Philip the Luter, 11s. 4d.': Privy Purse Expenses, Princess Mary, p. 60.
1542-3. 'Haunce the Luter, 2s. 6d.': ibid. p. 104.
1578. Buried — Christopher Lewter, clothworker: St. Michael, Cornhill, p. 195.
1584. Bapt.—Anne, d. John Luter: ibid. p. 93.
New York, 2.

Luther.—(1) Local; v. Lowther. (2) Bapt. 'the son of Lothar.' This German name never became popularized in England, except as Lothario. The French form was Lothaire. Martin Luther has made the cognomen immortal.

Luther Buchard, C. R., 3 Edw. I.
1593. Bapt.—Salomon, s. Arthur Luther, or Luter: St. Jas. Clerkenwell, i. 27.
1596. — Mary, d. Arthur Luther, or Lewter: ibid. p. 30.
1649. Thomas Luther (co. Essex) and Anne Jackson: Marriage Lic. (Faculty Office), p. 42.
Philadelphia, 9.

Lutley.—Local, 'of Luttley,' a hamlet in the parish of Hales Owen, co. Worc.

Philip de Lotteleg, co. Staff., Hen. III–Edw. I. K.
Thomas de Luttelegh, co. Staff., 20 Edw. I. R.
Crockford, 1.

Luttrell.—Local. A Norman surname found in England soon after the Conquest. Lower says, 'The name is probably derived from a diminutive form of the French loutre, an otter.' We may more safely conjecture that it is of local origin.

Geoffrey de Lutterell, 7 John: FF. vii. 152.
Robert Lutrel, co. Notts, Hen. III–Edw. I. K.
Margeria Luterel, co. Soms., 1273. A.
Andreas Loterel. L.
Robert Lutterell, or Lotterel, 1532: Reg. Univ. Oxf. i. 171.
Thomas Luterel, co. Soms., 1579: ibid. vol. ii. pt. ii. p. 88.
Thomas Lutterell, or Luttrell, co. Soms.: ibid. p. 223.
London, 1; MDB. (co. Somerset), 8; New York, 2.

Lutwyche, Lutwidge. — Local, 'of Lutwich,' an estate in the parish of Munslow, nine miles from Ludlow, co. Salop.

Henry de Lotwich, co. Salop, 1273. A.
William de Lotwich, co. Salop, ibid.
Thomas Lutwich, de Lutwich, co. Salop: Visitation of Shropshire (1623), ii. 346.
Richard Lutwiche, de Lutwiche Hall, in Mu'slowe in co. Salop: ibid.
1575. Thomas Luttwyche and Johanna Warde: Marriage Lic. (London), i. 67.
1588-9. Edward Lutwyche, co. Salop: Reg. Univ. Oxf. vol. ii. pt. ii. p. 168.
London, 1, 0; MDB. (co. Kent), 0, 1; (co. Salop), 1, 0.

Luxmoore, Luxmore, Luzmore, Loosemore, Losemore.—Local, 'of Luxmoor' or 'Luxmore.' A Devonshire surname. I cannot find the locality.

1661. Benjamin Donne and Anne Loosemore: Marriage Lic. (Faculty Office), p. 52.
London, 1, 1, 1, 2, 0; Devon Court Dir., 4, 3, 0, 2, 0; MDB. (co. Devon), 4, 6, 0, 7, 1.

Luxton.—Local, 'of Luxton.' I cannot find the spot, but if it is referred to in my first instance, then the surname hails from Lewston, an extra-parochial liberty in the hundred of Sherborne, co. Dorset.

Henry de Lewistone, co. Hants, 20 Edw. I. R.

1594. Bernard Luxton, co. Devon: Reg. Univ. Oxf. vol. ii. pt. ii. p. 202.
London, 3; MDB. (co. Devon), 24; New York, 2.

Lyall, Lyel, Lyell. — Bapt. 'the son of Lionel,' from the nick. Lyell. A great Scottish border name. Endless instances proving its past popularity might be adduced. Sir Charles Lyell, the geologist, was a Forfarshire man.

Lyell Robson, 1541: TTT. p. xlix.
Gowde Lyall, 1541: ibid.
Lyell Charltoun, 1541: ibid.
Liell Gray, 1542: QQQ. p. xx.
Lyell Fenwick, 1561: ibid. p. xxxii.
Lyonel Robson, 1663: KKK. vol. iv. p. 202.
Lyonell Lister, 1663: ibid. p. 203.
David Lyonell, 1670: QQQ. p. 160.
1752. Married—Thomas Hyett and Eliz. Lyell: St. Geo. Chap. Mayfair, p. 226.
1760. — David Lyall and Mary Geed: St. Geo. Han. Sq. i. 97.
London, 6, 1, 4; New York, 6, 0, 4.

Lyard, Liard. — Nick. 'the lyard,' one with iron-grey or dapple grey hair. Burns uses liart for locks of iron-grey; and Aubrey in his Lives describes Butler, author of Hudibras, as having 'a head of sorrell haire.'

Henry Lyard, co. Oxf., 1273. A.
William Liard, c. 1300. M.
Walter Lyhert. H.
1577. Married—William Burton, stationer, and Anne Lyard: St. Peter, Cornhill, i. 231.
New York, 0, 2.

Lycett.— ?

1736. Caesar, s. William and Mary Lycett, lodgers: St. Peter, Cornhill, ii. 39.
London, 2; MDB. (co. Stafford), 5; New York, 3.

Lyde, Lyd.—Local, 'of Lyde,' a township in the parish of Pipe, co. Hereford.

1589. Allan Lyde, co. Devon: Reg. Univ. Oxf. vol. ii. pt. ii. p. 170.
1591. Bapt.—Sarai, d. John Lyde: St. Jas. Clerkenwell, i. 24.
1679. — Mary, d. Richard Lyde: ibid. p. 288.
London, 1, 0; MDB. (co. Hereford), 0, 1; Philadelphia, 3, 0.

Lydiate.—Local, 'of Lydiate,' a township in the parish of Halsall, co. Lancaster, near Ormskirk; v. Lidgate.

1555. Richard Lydiate, of Chester: Wills at Chester (1545-1620), p. 128.

1623. Richard Lydiate, of Weston: Wills at Chester (1621-50), p. 144.
1631. Thomas Lydiate, of Lydiate: ibid.
MDB. (co. Chester), 1.

Lye. — (1) Local, 'of Lye,' a chapelry in the parish of Swinford, co. Worc. (2) Upper Lye, a township in the parish of Aymestrey, co. Hereford. Evidently this is the chief parent.

Jacobus de Lye, co. Wilts, Hen. III-Edw. I. K.
Philippus de Lye, co. Wilts, ibid.
Ela de Lye, co. Wilts, 1273. A.
Hugh Lie, or Lye, co. Soms., 1575: Reg. Univ. Oxf. vol. ii. pt. ii. p. 66.

(3) Local, 'at the lye,' i.e. Lee, q.v.

Herebert de la Lye, co. Southampt., Hen. III-Edw. I. K.
Elyas de la Lye, co. Southampt., ibid.
William de la Lye, co. Notts, 1273. A.
1583-4. Robert Lye, *yeoman*, and Anne Williams: Marriage Lic. (London), i. 129.
1590. Barnaby Ligh, or Lyghe, co. Hants: Reg. Univ. Oxf. vol. ii. pt. ii. p. 180.
London, 4; New York, 1.

Lyel(l ; v. Lyall.

Lyford.—Local, ' of Lyford,' a chapelry in the parish of West Hannay, near Wantage, co. Berks; v. Lye and Ford.

John de Lyford, co. Oxf., 1273. A.
1615. William Lyford, co. Berks: Reg. Univ. Oxf. vol. ii. pt. ii. p. 336.
1661-2. John Morton and Mary Lyford: Marriage Alleg. (Canterbury), p. 19.
1742. Married—Henry Granger and Betty Lyford: St. Peter, Cornhill, ii. 84.
London, 1.

Lyle.—Local ; v. Lisle.

Lynch.—Local, ' at the linch,' from residence thereby. ' A.S. *hlinc*, a hill, but especially a balk or boundary, a sense still preserved in modern provincial English *linch* ' (Skeat, *y. link*). ' *Linch*, a balk of land (Kent). Any bank or boundary for the division of land ' (Halliwell). A large portion of the New York Lynches must be ascribed to an Irish parentage, as such prefixes as Michael, Patrick, and Terence abound (v. New York Directory).

Emma de Linches. J.
William de la Lynche, C.R., 55 Hen. III.
Roger Ate-lynch, Fines Roll, 12 Edw. I.
Simon de Lynche, co. Norf., 20 Edw. I. R.

John Uppelynch (i.e. John up the Lynch), co. Soms., 1 Edw. III : Kirby's Quest, p. 270.
1780. Married—William Lynch and Martha Richa: St. Geo. Han. Sq. i. 313.
London, 13 ; New York, 477.

Lyndall ; v. Lindale.

Lynd(e ; v. Lind.

Lyne ; v. Line.

Lyner ; v. Liner.

Lynn. — Local, ' of Lynn.' There are several parishes of Lynn in co. Norfolk. In Devon there is Lynmouth.

Cecilia de Lynn, co. Devon, Hen. III-Edw. I. K.
Reginald de Lyn, co. Devon, 1273. A.
John de Lynne, bailiff of Norwich, 1396 : FF. iii. 116.
1546. John Dyneley and Margery Lyn: Marriage Lic. (Faculty Office), p. 8.
1680. Mathew Key and Eliz. Lynn: Marriage Alleg. (Canterbury), p. 26.
London, 18 ; New York, 17.

Lynton.—Local ; v. Linton.

Lyon, Lyons.—(1) Bapt. ' of Leone.' Many Jews in modern times have taken the name of Lyon (the Lion of the tribe of Judah). This seems to have been an early custom, judging by my first reference. The London Directory will prove by its personal names how Jewish the surname is.

Lyoyne (alias Leoyn) Duningh, co. Camb., Hen. III-Edw. I. K.
Judaeus Leo, co. Linc., 1273. A.
Jacob fil. Leonis, co. Linc., ibid.
John Leon, co. Oxf., ibid.
Lyon Raithbye, C. R., 1-2 Philip and Mary, pt. viii.

(2) Local, ' of Lyons.'

Roger de Leonibus fil. Jeffrey de Lions, co. Norf., temp. Hen. III : FF. ix. 374.
John de Leonibus, co. Southampt., Hen. III-Edw. I. K.
Peter de Leonibus, co. Northampt., ibid.
Roger de Lyons, co. Wilts, 1273. A.
Richard de Lyons, co. Northampton, Edw. I. R.
John de Lyouns, co. Northampt., ibid.
Edmond de Lyons, co. Soms., 1 Edw. III : Kirby's Quest, p. 93.
London, 36, 29 ; New York, 118, 218.

Lysons, Licence. — ? Local. This name was 'spelt in the 16th century Lysans, Leyson, and Lison. Probably derived from Lison, a place in the department of Calvados, in Normandy' (Lower, Patr. Brit. p. 204). Of course Licence is an imitative variant.

1677-8.' Fergus Farrell and Ann Licence: Marriage Alleg.(Canterbury), p.275.
1739. Bapt.—Layer, d. Zebulon Licence : St. Jas. Clerkenwell, ii. 244.
London, 1, 1 ; MDB. (co. Glouc.), 1, 0.

Lyster ; v. Lister.

Lyte, Lyteman.—Nick. ' the lyte,' i.e. the little ; A.S. *lyt*, little.

Agnes le Lit, co. Soms., 1 Edw. III : Kirby's Quest, p. 201.
Richard Liteman, co. Bedf., 1273. A.
William le Lyt, 1313. M.
John Lytman, temp. 1570. Z.

The following, no doubt, is an imitative variant :

1582. Humphrey Lighteman and Agnes Woode : Marriage Lic. (London), i. 108.
1729. Married—George Lyte and Eliz. Read : St. Geo. Chap. Mayfair, p. 303.
Crockford, 1, 0.

Lyth, Lythe.—Nick.' the lithe,' soft, tender, mild, hence pliant, flexible, supple.

' To maken lithe that erst was hard ': Chaucer, House of Fame, l. 118.

' *Lithe*, calm, quiet' (Kennett).

Gonnilda le Lyth, co. Bucks, 1273. A.
Cf. Henry Lithfot, co. Oxf., ibid.
1540. Buried—John Lythe: St. Dionis Backchurch, p. 178.
London, 1, 0 ; Manchester, 2, 0 ; Beverley, 0, 1.

Lytham.—Local, 'of Lytham,'a parish in the union of Fylde, co. Lanc.

Prior de Lythom. K.
John Lythom, 1602 : Preston Guild Rolls, p. 62.
Liverpool, 1.

Lythgoe, Lithgoe, Lithgow, Lythgow.—Local, ' of Lythgoe.' I cannot find the spot. This is a South Lancashire surname; but it has a Scotch look. Lower says, ' A contraction of Linlithgow, a well-known Scotch town': Patr. Brit. p. 196. He furnishes no proof. Eight persons named Lithgow appear in the County Directory of Scotland, 1882.

Robert Lythgoe, of Abram, *husbandman*, 1578: Wills at Chester (1545-1620), p. 129.
Mathew Lythgoe, of Bedford, parish of Leigh, *yeoman*, 1633: ibid. (1621-50), p.145.
Robert Lythgoe, of Abram, parish of Wigan, *husbandman*, 1647: ibid.
1721-2. Bapt.—Joseph, s. Joseph Lythgoe: St. Dionis Backchurch, p. 157.
London, 1, 0, 1, 0 ; Manchester, 4, 1, 0, 1 ; Philadelphia, 0, 0, 9, 0.

Lyttle ; v. Little.

M

Maas, Maass.—?——. An importation from the Low Countries, probably. The published and unpublished 'Household Expenses' of kings, queens, and wealthy nobles invariably show that the minstrels in attendance were foreigners.

Hanekin Almond, varlet of the Countess of Surrey: Household Book of Queen Isabella, 1358, Cot. MS. Galba, E. xiv.
Janin Maas, varlet of the Countess of Surrey: ibid.

The first of these two was evidently a German by descent.

1795. Married — John Sudlow and Hannah Gertrude Maass: St. Geo. Han. Sq. ii. 131.
London, 3, 0; Boston (U.S.), 3, 2; New York, 28, 11.

Mabb, Mabbs, Mobbs. — Bapt. 'the son of Mabel,' from nick. Mab (v. Mapp). Oddly enough, the modern form is generally Mobbs; cf. Maggs and Mogg.

Alicia Mab, 1379: P. T. Yorks. p. 154.
Agnes Mabbe, 1379: ibid. p. 209.
1616. Married — Frauncis Mydleton and Katherain Mabb, of Woodford, co. Essex: St. Michael, Cornhill, p. 21.
1626. — Daniell Mabbes and Hannah Crakell: ibid. p. 24.
1800. — John Mobbs and Susanna Ambler: St. Geo. Han. Sq. ii. 231.
London, 0, 0, 7; Liverpool, 0, 1, 0.

Mabbett, Mabbitt, Mabbott. —Bapt. 'the son of Mabel' from nick. Mab, and dim. Mabb-ot or Mabb-et (v. Mappin); cf. Elliot, Tillotson, Emmott, &c.

Mabota Ryder, 1379: P. T. Yorks. p. 214.
Willelmus Mabotson, 1379: ibid. p. 280.
Willelmus Mabetson, 1379: ibid.
Richard Mabot, or Mabatt, 1509: Reg. Univ. Oxf. i. 65.
1646. Bapt. — William, s. William Mabbett, *pewterer*: St. Peter, Cornhill, ii. 91.
1648. Buried — William, s. William Mabbutt: ibid. p. 204.
1769. Married — Joseph Howel and Mary Mabbutt: St. Geo. Han. Sq. i. 191.
1807. Married — Joseph Bland and Martha Mabbatt: ibid. ii. 364.
London, 1, 1, 1; Philadelphia, 2, 0, 0.

Mabley, Maberley, Maberly. — Bapt. 'the son of Mabel,' familiarly Mabley. I can only furnish a few instances out of many. Not as a rule to be confounded with Moberley (q.v.), but confusion would easily arise. It is quite possible that Maberley is the same as the local Moberley, but I doubt it.

Andrew fil. Mabilie, co. Hunts, 1273. A.
Philip fil. Mabilie, co. Camb., ibid.
Nicholas Mabely, co. Oxf., ibid.
John Mably, co. Camb., ibid.
1603. Buried — Arthur Maberly: St. Antholin (London), p. 42.
1665. — John, s. Luke Mably: St. Michael, Cornhill, p. 254.
1692. — Thomas Mabley, St. John the Baptist, on Wallbrook, p. 190.
London, 1, 1, 2.

Mabon. — Bapt. 'the son of Mabel,' from the nick. Mab, and dim. Mab-on; cf. Marion from Mary, Guyon from Guy, &c.

Emanuelle Mabon, Patent Roll, 1 Eliz. pt. x.
1582. Richard Morecocke and Eliz. Mabone: Marriage Lic. (London), i. 110.
1806. Married — Andrew Mabon and Sarah Wright: St. Geo. Han. Sq. ii. 358.
London, 1.

Mabson. — Bapt. 'the son of Mab' (Mabel); cf. Mabotson (s.v. Mabbett). It will be seen that Mabel, with its nick. Mab, was popular in the hereditary surname period.

John Mabson, Patent Roll, 8 Ric. II. pt. ii.
Michael Mabson, York, 1494. W. 11.
1672. Bapt. — Steeven, s. William Mabson: St. Jas. Clerkenwell, i. 257.
Sheffield Dir., 4.

Mace.—Bapt. 'the son of Mace.' Lower says, 'Originally Macé, a French nurse-name of Matthew.' As with all other fontal names, this was turned into a feminine, as in the following instances :

Massia Billesby, C. R., 24 Hen. VI.
Macius le Teynturer, co. Devon, 1273. A.
Duce fil. Masse, co. Hunts, ibid.
Adam Mace, co. Oxf., ibid.
William Mace, co. Bucks, ibid.

The following, no doubt, refer to the same individual :

Macius de Besile, co. Oxf., 1273.
Macias de Betille, co. Oxf., ibid.
Matheus Besyl, co. Oxf., ibid.
1663. Philip Mace and Ann Right : Marriage Alleg. (Canterbury), p. 115.
1733. Bapt. — Stanfield, s. Thomas Mace: St. Jas. Clerkenwell, ii. 208.
London, 18 ; Philadelphia, 5.

Macey, Macy.—(1) Bapt. 'the son of Macy'; v. Mace. A fem. form is found.

Alan Macy, co. Suff., 1273. A.
Henry Macy, co. Suff., ibid.
Walter Masci, co. Hunts, ibid.
1391. Massia Newport : Cal. of Wills in the Court of Husting (2).

(2) Local, 'of Macei,' near Avranche, in Normandy (Lower).

Robert de Meysy, co. Wilts, 1273. A.
William de Macy, co. Wilts, ibid.
1581. Bapt.—Grace, d. Jeames Macey: St. Michael, Cornhill, p. 92.
1621. — Laurence, s. John Macye : St. Jas. Clerkenwell, i. 90.
London, 9, 0 ; New York, 0, 39.

Machell.—Nick. ; originally 'le Machel' or Manchell, 'bad whelp,' Latinized as Malus-Catulus. A certain Roger Malus-Catulus was Vice-Chancellor of England ; but I have lost my reference to this. The following occur in records of the Machells of Crackenthorpe :

Halthe le Machel, temp. Hen. I : Transactions of Cumb. and West. Ant. Arch. Soc. viii. 418-9.
Humfrey le Machel, temp. Henry II : ibid.
William Malus Catulus, 1179 : ibid.
William Manchel, 1206 : ibid.
1606. Buried—Eliz. Machell : St. Jas. Clerkenwell, iv. 95.
1619. John Machell, co. Surrey : Reg. Univ. Oxf. vol. ii. pt. ii. p. 377.
1798. William Machell and Eliz. Allen : St. Geo. Han. Sq. ii. 180.
London, 2.

Machen, Machin, Machan, Machon. — Bapt. 'the son of Matthew'; a familiar Yorkshire surname found in every district. The O.F. nick. of Matthew was Mace or Mache, and this, with the dim. -on or -in, became Machon and Machin. It is commonly found in the Poll Tax (1379). I only furnish a few instances. It has left an indelible mark upon Yorkshire nomenclature.

Thomas Mathen, 1379: P. T. Yorks. p. 186.
Eva Machon, 1379: ibid.
Ricardus Machon, 1379: ibid. p. 194.
Beatrice Machon, 1379: ibid.
Johannes Machon, 1379: ibid. p. 198.
Willelmus Mathon, 1379: ibid.

The first two entries lie in the same hamlet, so also the last three. Therefore Mathon may be looked upon as a more English form eventually settling down to Mattin, as in Mattinson; v. Mace, Masson (2), Mattin, and Maton.

1558. Married — John Rypleye and Margarett Machyn: St. Michael, Cornhill, p. 7.
1662. — Edward Machin and Cassandra Trendall: Marriage Alleg. (Canterbury), p. 58.
London, 1, 12, 0, 0; West Rid. Court Dir., 5, 2, 1, 0; Sheffield, 3, 6, 2, 2; New York, 1, 2, 0, 1; Philadelphia, 0, 0, 0, 2.

Mackareth, Mackreth, Mackereth.—Local, ' of Mackareth,' a distinctly English Lake-district surname. It is still found in the neighbourhood of Windermere. I cannot discover the spot. Probably the suffix is -heath.

1591. George Macreth of Hauxhead: Lancashire Wills at Richmond, i. 188.
1670. Brian Mackereth, of Skelwith, Hawkeshead: ibid.
Thomas Macareth, of Natland, 1602: Hist. West. and Cumb. i. 96.
Edward Maccareth of Natland, 1602: ibid.
1622. Robert Willis and Eliz. Mackreth: Marriage Lic. (Westminster), p. 28.
1664. Buried—Johanna, wife of Roberd Mackereth: St. Jas. Clerkenwell, iv. 358.
1760. Married — Edward Mackereth and Jane Brockbank: Reg. St. Mary, Ulverston, p. 403.
Ulverston, 0, 0, 1; London, 0, 2, 0.

Mackarness. — Local, ' of Maukerkeys,' seemingly some spot on the East Coast; cf. Holderness. There is no connexion with the Mac's or Mc's of Ireland or Scotland, as in Macdonald or McGrath.

William de Maukurneys, co. Linc., 1273. A.
Henry Maukurneys, 18 Edw. II: Freemen of York, i. 22.
Cecilia Maugurnays, 1379: P. T. Yorks. p. 273.
Robertus Magornays, 1379: ibid. p. 266.

1626. Bapt. — Thomas, s. Richard Makernes: St. Thomas the Apostle, London, p. 47.
1649. Buried — Ann, wife of William Mackernes: St. Jas. Clerkenwell, iv. 282.
John Mackerness, 1745: Reg. Canterbury Cath. p. 87.
Crockford, 3.

Mackerell, Mackrell, Mackrill, Mackrille, Macrell. — Nick. ' the mackerel.' M.E. and O.F. *makeral*, a fish known by that name; cf. Keeling, a Yorkshire surname, on whose coast the particular cod of that name was caught. The earlier instances below are from the Lincoln coast, although by 1273 one had reached Cambridge.

Hugh Makarel, co. Linc., Hen. III-Edw. I. K.
Walter Makarel, co. Linc., ibid.
William Makarell, co. Linc., 1273. A.
Richard Makarel, co. Camb., ibid.
Richard Makerell, Pat. Roll, 9 Edw. IV.
Richard Mackerell, 1513: Reg. Univ. Oxf. i. 86.
1546. Buried — Jone Makarell: St. Dionis Backchurch, p. 181.
1593. — One Mackerell, out of the feildes: St. Jas. Clerkenwell, iv. 52.
London, 1, 3, 2, 0, 0: Philadelphia, 3, 0, 0, 0, 0; New York (Macrell), 3; Boston (U.S.) (Mackrille), 1.

Mackeson.—Bapt. ' the son of Margaret,' from the nick. Magg or Maggy. The son of Magg or Maggy became Maggeson; this, when sharpened, became Mackeson. In the same way Moggson became Mockson and Moxon, q.v. There is no difficulty about the derivation. The solution is very simple.

John Makkesone, Disley, co. Ches., 1333: East Ches. ii. 85.
Agnes Makkesone, Disley, co. Ches., 1333: ibid.
1765. Married — Henry Mackeson, of Deal, and Eliz. Hooper: Canterbury Cath. p. 96.
London, 3.

Macklin, Mackling.—? Bapt. Seemingly ' the son of Maculin.'

Maculin Cosin, canon of the ' free chaple of Berkynge,' temp. Ric. III: Hist. Allhallows, Barking, p. 140.
1797. Married—John Maclin and Eliz. Bonn: St. Geo. Han. Sq. ii. 175.
1808. — John Maklin and Mary Dunster: St. Geo. Han. Sq. ii. 392.
London, 6, 1; Philadelphia, 5, 0.

Mackman; v. Makeman.

Mackness.—Local; v. Mackarness. London, 6.

Mackrell, Mackrill; v. Mackerell.

Mackreth; v. Mackareth.

Mackworth.—Local, ' of Mackworth,' a parish in co. Derby.

Robert de Makeworth, co. Derby, 1273. A.
1695. Married — Edmund Taylor and Ann Mackworth: St. Peter, Cornhill, ii. 61.
1761. — Herbert Mackworth and Eliz. Trefusis: St. Geo. Han. Sq. i. 103.

Macy; v. Macey.

Mad.—Nick. ' the mad.'
Jordan le Madde, co. Lanc., 20 Edw. I. R.

Maddick, Maddicks, Maddock, Maddocks, Maddox, Maddux. — Bapt. ' the son of Madoc.' An early Welsh personal name. For history, v. Yonge, ii. 29. With Maddox for Maddocks, cf. Rix, Dixon, Simcox, &c.

Kenwrec fil. Maddoc: Pipe Roll, 7 Hen. II.
Madoc de Sotton, co. Salop, Hen. III-Edw. I. K.
Tudor ab Madoc, co. Salop, 1273. A.
Walter fil. Madoc, co. Salop, ibid.
Madoc le Estrange, co. Salop, ibid.
Madoc fil. Griffin. J.
1573. Buried — Judith Madox: Reg. Stourton, co. Wilts, p. 1.
1593. Robert Madox, co. Oxf.: Reg. Univ. Oxf. vol. ii. pt. ii. p. 198.
1602. George Maddockes, co. Glouc.: ibid. p. 262.
1604. John Madocke, co. Glouc.: ibid. p. 271.
London, 4, 1, 3, 1, 6, 0; Philadelphia, 0, 0, 9, 0, 6, 1; Boston (U.S.), 0, 0, 4, 1, 6, 0.

Maddison, Madison.—Bapt. ' the son of Maud,' i.e. Matilda, either from a pet form Maddy, or a mere corruption of Maudson (v. Maud).

1558. Bapt.—Annes Maddesonne: St. Peter, Cornhill, i. 8.
Henry Maddeson, of Melling, 1670: Lancashire Wills at Richmond, p. 189.
Anne Maddesson of Whittington,1680: ibid.
' Here rest in Christian hope the bodies of Lionel Maddison, son of Rowland Maddison,' &c., 1624: Epitaph, St. Nicholas, Newcastle-on-Tyne (Brand's Hist. of Newcastle, i. 291).
1704. Bapt.—David, s. John Maddison: St. Thomas the Apostle (London), p. 69.
London, 3, 0; Philadelphia, 0, 17; Boston (U.S.), 0, 7.

Maddock(s, -dox; v. Maddick,

Maden.—Local, 'of Maden,' a small locality in the parish of Rochdale, co. Lanc., whence all the Madens have sprung.

Charles Holt, of Maden, in Spotland, 1595 : Wills at Chester (1545-1620), p. 99.
John Maden, of Hopwood, *yeoman*, 1637 : ibid. (1621-50), p. 145.
Manchester, 3 ; New York, 2.

Mader, Maderer, Maderman, Madder. — Occup. ' the maderer,' a collector and seller of madder ; cf. Garlicker, Garlickmonger, &c. Just as Pepperer is now found as Pepper, so Maderer has been reduced to Mader and Madder.

Jacob le Madur, co. Linc., 1273. A.
John Maderman, temp. 1300. M.
Laurence Maderer. H.
Thomas Maderer. XX. 1.
1748. Married — James Madder and Christian Black : St. Geo. Chap. Mayfair, p. 120.
London, 1, 0, 0, 1 ; Philadelphia, 2, 0, 0, 0.

Madge. — Bapt. 'the son of Margaret'; v. Maggs.

Madgett, Matchet, Matchett.—(1) Bapt. 'the son of Margaret,' from nick. Madge, and dim. Madg-et ; cf. Maggot, a dim. of the harder nick. Magg. (2) Bapt. ' the son of Mache,' from Mache, the O.F. nick. for Matthew, and dim. Machet ; cf. Emmett (v. Emmott),Collett, &c. The evidence seems to confirm this view; v. Machen.

Willelmus Machet, 1379 : P. T. Yorks. p. 10.
1670. Married — Franses Pickerin and Mary Matchett : St. Jas. Clerkenwell, iii. 174.
1736. — Richard Saunders and Mary Matchitt : St. Geo. Han. Sq. i. 16.
London, 1, 0, 0 ; Doncaster, 0, 1, 0 ; Sheffield, 1, 0, 0 ; Boston (U.S.), 0, 0, 1 ; New York, 0, 0, 3.

Madin ; v. Maiden.

Madison ; v. Maddison.

Madswain.—Nick. 'the foolish swain'; cf. Goodswain, Littleswain.

Alan Madsweyn, co. Essex, 1273. A.

Mager ; v. Major.

Maggot, Maggotson.—Bapt. 'the son of Margaret,' from O.F. Margot, sharpened and abbreviated in England to Magot. This form was especially liked in northern

counties. In the 14th century it was enormously popular in Yorkshire. The mag-pie was equally familiar as the magot-pie. Shakespear says :

' Augurs, and understood relations, have,
By magot-pies, and choughs, and rooks
brought forth
The secret'st man of blood.'
Macbeth, Act iii. sc. 4.

With this, cf. Magota Pye, 1379, P. T. Yorks. p. 45, an evident connexion of ideas. v. Madgett.

Maggot Fin, co. Hunts, 1273. A.
Richard Maggote, co. Camb., ibid.
Robert Maggot, co. Camb., ibid.
Thomas Magotson, 1379 : P. T. Yorks. p. 18.
Cecilia fil. Magote, 1379 : ibid. p. 190.
Magota Malet, 1379 : ibid. p. 59.
Johannes fil. Magote, 1379 : ibid. p. 121.
Magota Merchalk, 1379 : ibid. p. 45.
Johannes Magotson, 1379 : ibid.
1644. Bapt.—Joan, d. Joseph Maggot, St. Jas. Clerkenwell, i. 159.
1591. Married — John Magett and Janne Richarsone : St. Dionis Backchurch, p. 12.

Maggs, Magson, Madge.— Bapt. ' the son of Margaret,' from the nick. Magg. The mag-pie still preserves the memory of this homely name.

Magge Flie, co. Camb., 1273. A.
John Magge, co. Hunts, ibid.
Ralph fil. Henry Mag, co. Camb., ibid.
Isabella Mag-doghter, 1379 : P. T. Yorks. p. 143.
Ricardus Magge, 1379 : ibid. p. 58.
Robertus Magson, 1379 : ibid. p. 280.
Rogerus Magson, 1379 : ibid. p. 138.

The next two occur together :

Johannes Megson, 1379 : P. T. Yorks. p. 131.
Robertus Magson, 1379 : ibid.
1751. Married — Eli Maggs and Jane Mason : St. Geo. Han. Sq. i. 45.
1760. — Richard Boyden and Mary Magson : ibid. p. 92.
London, 12, 0, 1 ; West Rid. Court Dir., 0, 1, 0 ; Manchester, 0, 1, 0 ; Leeds, 0, 0, 1 ; New York, 0, 0, 3 ; Philadelphia, 0, 1, 1.

Magill. — Local, ' of Maghull,' a manor in the parish of Halsall, co. Lanc.

William de Maghull, c. John : Baines' Lanc. ii. 424.
Richard Maghull, 21 Edw. I : ibid. p. 425.
Matthew Maghull, 27 Hen. VIII : ibid.
Richard Maghall, of Maghall, 1606 : Lancashire Inquisitions, i. 66.
1646. Ellen Maghull, of Aintree, *widow* : Wills at Chester, ii. 145.
Liverpool, 2 ; Philadelphia, 32.

Magnus. — Bapt. 'the son of Magnus.' A North-British name. In Shetland, Magnus as a fontname is tenth in order of frequency, and eleventh as a surname in the form of Manson (Magnus-son). There are also seventeen Magnus-sons ; v. Scotsman, Oct. 16, 1886.

1780. Married—William Magnus and Alice Sherman : St. Geo. Han. Sq. i. 310.
London, 9 ; Boston (U.S.), 1 ; New York, 19.

Magson ; v. Maggs.

Mahenild.—Bapt. 'the son of Maginhild' (Yonge, ii. 415).

Mahenyld Brycth, co. Norf., 1273. A.
Alan Mahenyld, co. Norf., ibid.
Alan Maghenyld, co. Norf., ibid.

I do not see any of this name in modern registers.

Maiden, Madin.—Nick. 'the maiden.' Perhaps the bearer was somewhat effeminate ; cf. Milksop. But probably a servant, a female attendant ; v. Mann and Servant. This is practically settled by such an entry as :

Alicia Martynmayden, 1379 : P. T. Yorks. p. 157.
Matilda Marschalmaydyn, 1379 : ibid. p. 111.

An instance of Mayden as a surname from the same register will be found below.

Robert le Mayden : Fines Roll, 12 Edw. I.
Adam le Maiden, co. Camb., 1273. A.
Johanna Mayden, 1379 : P. T. Yorks. p. 105.
1730. Married — Thomas Hyett and Jane Maiden : St. Geo. Chap. Mayfair, p. 311.
1753. — George Madin and Ann Harris : St. Mary Aldermary, p. 52.
London, 1, 0 ; Sheffield, 0, 1 ; West Rid. Court Dir., 0, 1 ; Manchester, 2, 0 ; Philadelphia, 2, 0.

Maidment, Maidman.—Bapt. 'the son of Maymond' ; v. Mayman. For corruption into *-ment*, cf. Rayment (Raymond) and Garment (Garmund) ; for *-man*, cf. Wyman (Wymond) and Osman (Osmund).

1744. Married — John Maidman and Eliz. Anderson : St. Geo. Chap. Mayfair, p. 38.
1749. — John Maidman and Ann Walker : St. Geo. Han. Sq. i. 43.
1802. — Moses Lavell and Ann Maidment : ibid. ii. 270.
London, 5, 1.

Maidstone.—Local, ' of Maidstone,' now as a surname more generally Mayston, q.v.

1690. Bapt. — Robert, s. Robert Maidstone: St. Antholin (London), p. 107.
1702. Buried — Charles, s. John Madston: ibid. p. 115.

Maidwell.—Local, 'of Maidwell,' a village in co. Northampton, ten miles from Northampton. Probably distinct from Meadwell, q.v.; cf. Maidenwell, a parish in co. Lincoln, five miles from Louth.

John Maydenwell. Pat. Roll, 43 Edw. III.
1547. Bapt. — Annes Madewell: St. Peter, Cornhill, i. 3.
1687. Married — James Maydwell and Annabella Coningsbey: St. Mary Aldermary (London), p. 33.
London, 1.

Maile; v. Male.

Mailmaker, Maler.—Occup. 'the mail-maker.' A manufacturer of bags or wallets. M.E. *male*, a bag, whence mail-coach, &c.

John de Redinges, *maler*, 4 Edw. III: Freemen of York, i. 26.
Henry Malemaker. RR. 2.

Main, Maine.—(1) Bapt. ' the son of Main'; v. Mayne (1).

Ralph fil. Main, co. Northumb., 1166: KKK. v. 9.
Walter fil. Main, co. Northumb., 1168. KKK. vi. 11.

(2) Local, 'of Maine'; v. Mayne (2).

1798. Married — Thomas Main and Jane Dawson : St. Geo. Han. Sq. ii. 190.
1805. — William Dodson and Ann Maine : ibid. p. 331.
London, 14, 4; Boston (U.S.), 6, 4.

Mainprice, Mainprise, Mainprize, Mimpriss.—Offic. or nick. 'the mainprize,' i.e. (1) one who is security for another, or (2) one who has found sureties for his appearance on the proper day : a prisoner at large. ' Mainprize, one who is bail-pledge, or security for another person': Bailey's Dict., 1742 (v. Outlaw). Mimpriss was an inevitable modification or corruption. In another form it occurs as early as 1440, 'Maynprysed, menprisyd (maymprysyd or memprisyd), *manucaptus, fidejussus*': Prompt. Parv. An entry below exactly corresponds to one of these forms.

1625. Buried — Roberte, s. Thomas Memprisse : St. Peter, Cornhill, i. 186.
1659. Married — Isaack Mempris and Mary Allen : St. Jas. Clerkenwell, iii. 103.
1663. — William Morgan and Elizabeth Mempris : St. Dionis Backchurch, p. 37.
London, 1, 0, 0, 1 ; Wirksworth, co. Derby, 0, 1, 0, 0 ; Derby, 0, 0, 3, 0.

Mainwaring, Mannering.—Local, from ' the manor of Warin.' This family, so long established in co. Cheshire, claim to have come with the Conqueror in the person of Ranulph de Meinilwarin, and is distinctly Norman, as its earlier forms, Menilwarin and Mesnilwarin, prove. The second half of the name is Warin or Guarin, a once common font-name, introduced by the Normans into England; v. Warren (2) and Wareing. It is said that this name can be found spelt in no less than 131 different ways.

Robert de Meynwareing, co. Derby, 1273. A.
Thomas de Meynnegaryn, co. Norf., ibid.
1663. Bapt. — Ann, d. Allen Manwaring : St. Jas. Clerkenwell, i. 218.
1669. Bapt. — Elisebeth, d. Doctor Manerring : ibid. p. 242.
London, 2, 2 ; Boston (U.S.), 2, 0; Philadelphia, 1, 0.

Mair, Maire. — Offic. ' the mayor,' the magistrate of the town. M.E. *maire*. v. Meyer.

' Saloman the sage
A sermon he made
For to amenden maires.'
Piers P. 1541-3.

Ricardus Mayre, 1379: P. T. Yorks. p. 111.
Willelmus Mayre, 1379: ibid.
1574-5. Richard Maior, co. Bucks: Reg. Univ. Oxf. vol. ii. pt. ii. p. 61.
1677. Thomas Mayor and Martha Puckerin : Marriage Alleg. (Canterbury), p. 207.
London, 2, 2 ; Philadelphia, 13, 3.

Major, Mager. — Bapt. ' the son of Malger ' or ' Mauger.' The modern form is imitative. The font-name was fairly popular in the 13th century. Mauger is found as a single personal name in the Hundred Rolls (ii. 609, and again ii. 797). For other instances, v. Mauger.

Hugh fil. Magri, co. Devon, 1273. A.
Thomas fil. Magri, co. Linc., ibid.
Walter Mauger, co. Camb., ibid.

Richard Malgor, co. Bucks, ibid.
Mauger de la Neuland, C. R., 31 Hen. VI.

I find no evidence to prove that Major as a surname is the Latin *major*, i.e. mayor, a town magistrate (v. Mair). The present military *major* is modern from a surname point of view.

1561. Bapt.—Robert, s. John Maygor : St. Mary Aldermary. p. 54.
1577. — Alice, d. William Mager: St. Peter, Cornhill, i. 19.
1742. Married — Robert Major and Eliz. Davis: St. Geo. Chap. Mayfair, p. 17.
London, 13, 2 ; Philadelphia, 22, 15.

Makebliss.—Nick.

Julian Makeblise, co. Oxf., 1273. A.

Makeblithe.—Nick. A pretty nickname ; cf. Makepeace and Makejoy. This surname does not seem to have descended to modern times, although found in three different parts of the country. Makepeace has fared better.

William Makeblithe, co. Oxf., 1273. A.
Radulphus Makblyth', *textor*, 1379: P. T. Yorks. p. 290.
Robert Maykblythe, co. York, 1511: W. 11, p. 174.
1597. William Makblythe, co. Warw.: Reg. Univ. Oxf. vol. ii. pt. ii. p. 224.

Makehate.—Nick. This seems to be the opposite of Makepeace, Makejoy, &c.

Alicia Makehayt, co. Bucks, 1273. A.
William Makehayt, co. Oxf., ibid.
John Makeheyt, co. Oxf., ibid.

Makejoy.—Nick. As pretty as Makepeace and Makeblithe. 'Make-joy,' Prompt. Parv. ; ' joyñ or make-joy, *gaudeo, exulto*' (ibid.).

Maud Makejoy, c. 1300. M.

Makeman, Mackman. — ? Bapt. ' the son of Maymond ' (?), i.e. Magin-mond. Probably the *k* and *ck* represent the original *g* sound. As a Lincolnshire form this is the more likely. Other forms of the surname are Mayman, Maidman, and Maidment, q.v.

MDB. (Lincoln), 1, 2 ; New York, 0, 1.

Makepeace.—Nick. A pretty and gracious sobriquet, always to be remembered as the second name of Thackeray. It occurs early in Yorkshire, and has always maintained its existence, though it must be included among the rarer surnames ; cf. Makebliss and Makejoy.

'Joan Makepeace was the name given to the daughter of Edward II, when the long war with the Bruces was partly pacified by her marriage' : Yonge, i. 112.
Thomas Makpays, 1379 : P. T. Yorks. p. 296.
Richard Makepeace, co. York. W. 20.
1601. Laurence Makepeace, co. Northampton : Reg. Univ. Oxf. vol. ii. pt. ii. p. 247.
1706. Bapt. — Sarah, d. of Margaret Makepeace : St. Thomas the Apostle (London), p. 70.
1712. John Makepeace, rector of Quedgley, co. Glouc.: Rudder's Hist. Glouc. p. 613.
1752. — Ann, d. Jonathan Makepeace: St. Mary Aldermary (London), p. 132.
1786. Married—John McKee and Eliz. Makepeace, of Waltham Cross, Herts: St. Geo. Han. Sq. i. 393.
London, 1.

Makin, Makinson, Makein, Making, Makings, Makins.— Bapt. 'the son of Matthew' (Fr. Maheu), from nick. May (v. May, Maycock, &c.), and dim. May-kin ; cf. Wil-kin, Wat-kin. The g in Making and Makings is excrescent, and the e in Makein intrusive. The nick. May is distinguished from the nick. Mat as being the offspring of Maheu, and not Matthew.

Henry Maykin, co. Camb., 1273. A.
Mathew de Sutheworth, *dictus*, Maykyn, C. R., 20 Edw. III. pt. i.
Maykyn de Sythwrt (sic), 1379 : P. T. Yorks. p. 271.
Johannes Maykeson (i.e. Maykinson): ibid. p. 216.
Makin Lappyng, Pat. Roll, 1 Hen. VII. pt. i.
Maykina Parmunter. H.

This last is a feminine form.

1565. Married — Richard Makin and Alice Langden : St. Thomas the Apostle, p. 4.
1613. Married — Henry Jenkinson and Isabel Makinson : St. Jas. Clerkenwell, p. 39.
1753. — John Makings and Mary Scott : St. Geo. Chap. Mayfair, p. 248.

The Manchester Dir. contains fifteen Makins and nine Makinsons.

London, 3, 1, 2, 1, 1, 2 ; West Rid. Court Dir., 4, 0, 0, 1, 0, 1 ; New York, 5, 0, 0, 0, 0, 0 ; Philadelphia, 1, 5, 1, 0, 0, 1.

Malbon, Mallabone, Mallebone, Mallabund.—? Local, ' of Malbanc'(?). As Malbon undoubtedly arose in Cheshire, it probably represents the old de Malbancs of that county. Ellen de Malbanc was second wife of Sir Robert de Stokeport, who was living in 1268 (East Cheshire, i. 337-8). Otherwise I cannot explain it. The corruptions into Mallabone, Mallabund, &c., are not singular ; cf. Allibone for Alban. The d in Mallabund is excrescent, as in Simmonds, or the provincialism *gownd* for *gown*. The corruptions seem to have increased as the name extended into the further counties of Stafford and Warwick. A family named Malbon resided near Mottram, co. Cheshire, for many generations.

William Malbon, co. Ches., 1479 : East Cheshire, ii. 294 n.
Robert Malbon, co. Ches., 1479 : ibid.
William Malbon, of Great Budworth, *yeoman*, 1582 : Wills at Chester (1545-1620), p. 129.
1586. Bapt.—Thomas Malbon, of Mottram, co. Ches.: Reg. Prestbury Ch., p. 88.
1634. — George, s. Joseph Malbone : ibid. p. 292.
1651. Married — Henry Gouldsmith and Hanna Malbone : St. Jas. Clerkenwell, iii. 86.
1625. Buried—Robert Mallibone : St. Thomas the Apostle (London), p. 115.
London, 1, 0, 0, 0 ; MDB. (co. Warwick), 0, 1, 1, 1 ; (co. Stafford), 2, 0, 0, 0 ; Boston (U.S.), 1, 0, 0, 0.

Malcolm.—Bapt. 'the son of Malcolm.' 'The great St. Columba, who established the centre of his civilizing and christianizing efforts at Iona, had many a grateful disciple, as Gillecolumb, or Maelcolum ' (Yonge, ii. 116) ; cf. Gilpatrick and Gilmichael.

Melcolinus de Inghou, co. Northumb., Hen. III-Edw. I. K.
Maucolumb' Com', co. Hunts, 1273. A.
London, 8 ; New York, 14 ; Boston (U.S.), 16.

Malcovenant. — Nick. ; cf. Manclarke, Malregard. Probably n for l in the instance below.

Robertus Mancowennant, co. Linc., 1273. A.

Male, Maile.—?——. I can offer no satisfactory suggestion as to the derivation of this name.

Roger de la Male. [I have lost my reference to this.]
1607. John Mayle, London : Reg. Univ. Oxf. vol. ii. pt. ii. p. 296.
1616. Robert Mayle, London : ibid. p. 357.
1714. Married — George Male and Sarah Longworth : St. Peter, Cornhill, ii. 70.
1735. Bapt.—Sarah, d. Thomas Maile : St. Jas. Clerkenwell, ii. 221.
London, 3, 3 ; New York, 1, 0.

Malham, Maleham, Mallam, Malam.—Local, ' of Malham,' a township in the parish of Kirkby-in-Malham-Dale, W. Rid. Yorks.

John de Malghom, 1379 : P. T. Yorks. p. 269.
Stephen de Malgham, *draper*, 1379 : ibid. p. 265.
Thomas de Malgham, *cissor*, 1379 : ibid. p. 267.
Willelmus de Malghom, 1379 : ibid. p. 269.

The above instances occur in the immediate neighbourhood of Malham ; cf. also

Adam de Mallom, 1379 : P. T. Yorks. p. 254.
Thomas de Mallum, 1379 : ibid. p. 245.
1774. Married — William Barrett and Eliz. Mallam : St. Geo. Han. Sq. i. 243.
London, 2, 0, 4, 0 ; West Rid. Court Dir., 0, 2, 0, 0 ; Sheffield, 0, 4, 0, 0 ; Halifax (Malam), 1 ; Oxford (Mallam), 9 ; New York (Mallam), 1, 0.

Malin.—Bapt. 'the son of Malin'; v. Mallinson.

Malkin, Malkinson. — Bapt. 'the son of Matilda,' from dim. Malkin. ' Malkyne or Mawt, propyr name (Molt, K., Mawde, W.), Matildis (Matilda)' : Prompt. Parv. In the face of this clear statement it seems strange that Malkin should have been universally treated as the dim. of Mary. 'It was formerly a common diminutive of Mary' (Halliwell). I suspect Malkin represented Mary in the North of England, and Matilda in Norfolk and South-East England generally. At any rate, Maid Marian was also known as Malkin, and Marian, or more correctly Marion, is an unquestionable diminutive of Mary. Malkin is found early :

'Nor those prude yongemen
    That loveth Malekyn.'
A Litul soth Sermun, E.E.T.S.

'And Malkin, with hire distaf in hire hond.' Chaucer, C. T. 15391.

Hence a kitchen wench. 'The kitchen malkin pins Her richest lockram': Coriolanus, ii. 1. Burton is still more unkind. 'A filthy knave, a deformed quean, a crooked carcass, a *maukin*, a witch': Anat. of Melancholy, part iii. sect. 2, mem. 2, subsect. 3. Hence, too, *malkin*, a baker's clout to clean ovens with, or a scarecrow (v. Halliwell), on the same principle by which implements taking Jack's place took Jack's name; cf. *boot-jack*, or *jack*, a turnspit.

Thomas Malkynson, *webster*, 1379: P. T. Yorks. p. 287.
Johannes Malkynson, 1379: ibid. p. 12.
William Malkynson, 1379: ibid. p. 248.
Matilda Dikwyuemalkynson, *vidua*, i.e. Matilda, the wife of Dick, the son of Malkyn, *widow*: ibid. p. 42.
Willelmus Malkynson, ibid. p. 173.

Malkinson exists in Yorkshire, but it is rare; Malkin later on, as the name of a drab, having, like Parnall and Nan, lost caste. Nevertheless some of our Makinsons are doubtless thus originated; v. Makin.

1694. Bapt. — Joseph, s. Joshua Malkin: St. Jas. Clerkenwell, i. 358.
West Rid. Court Dir., 2, 0; Sheffield, 2, 0; MDB. (co. Linc.), 0, 2.

Mallabone, -bund; v. Malbon.

Mallalieu, Mallalue.—Nick. A corruption of Melladew; v. Merridew.

London, 2, 1; Manchester, 3, 0; Boston (U.S.), 3, 0.

Mallam; v. Malham.

Mallard.—Nick. 'the mallard,' i.e. the wild drake; cf. Wildgoose. 'Malarde, bryde, *anas*': Prompt. Parv. Probably absorbed in the course of generations by Mallet, q.v.

1580. John Malard, co. Hereford: Reg. Univ. Oxf. vol. ii. pt. ii. p. 94.
1638. Married — Ralph Beech and Marye Mallard: St. Jas. Clerkenwell, iii. 70.
1742. — Francis Mallard and Ann Hinderson: St. Geo. Chap. Mayfair, p. 17.
New York, 5; Boston (U.S.), 8.

Malledew.—Nick.; v. Merridew.

Liverpool, 1.

Malleson, Mallison.—Bapt. 'the son of Mallin,' from Mary; v. Mallinson, of which it is a modification; cf. Patteson for Pattinson. Sometimes more directly from Mally, the earlier form of Molly. It is still Mally in Furness, and Moll is still Mall.

Ricardus fil. Roberti Malleson, 1379: P. T. Yorks. p. 219.
1560. Bapt. — Fraunces Mallisonne: St. Peter, Cornhill, i. 9.
1777. Married — James Mallison and Mary Dickens: St. Geo. Han. Sq. i. 280.
London, 1, 1.

Mallet, Mallett.—Bapt. 'the son of Malet.'

Malet fil. Henry. C.
Baldwin Malet, co. Soms., 1273. A.
Sarra Malet, co. Camb., ibid.
Harvey Malet, co. Bucks, ibid.
Alan Malet, co. Derby, Hen. III–Edw. I. K.
Malet Molendinarius (Malet the Miller), Jersey: 20 Edw. I. R.
Magota Malet, 1379: P. T. Yorks. p. 59.
Johannes Malet, 1379: ibid. p. 167.
1586. Gawen Mallett, co. Soms.: Reg. Univ. Oxf. vol. ii. pt. ii. p. 151.
1619. Married — Anthony Mallet and Margaret Meredeth: St. Jas. Clerkenwell, iii. 47.
London, 3, 17; New York, 0, 1; Boston (U.S.), 2, 0.

Mallinson, Malin. — Bapt. 'the son of Mallin,' from Mary, nick. Mall, dim. Mall-in or Mal-in; cf. Rob-in, Col-in, Perr-in, Gibb-in. Molly is always Mally in the Ulverston parish registers to the close of last century; cf.

'Mall, or Maria Frears, of Ulverstone,' 1624: Lancashire Wills, Archdeaconry of Richmond, p. 116.
Malyna de Acstede, co. Kent, Hen. III–Edw. I. K.
Peter Maghlaynsone, C. R., 5 Edw. III. pt. i.
Malyn de Went, 1379: P. T. Yorks. p. 100.
Robertus Malyn, 1379: ibid. p. 163.
Johannes Malynson, 1379: ibid. p. 92.
Richard Malynson, 1379: ibid. p. 146.
Beatrix Malyn, doghter, 1379: ibid. p. 287.
Malin Gogun, co. Oxf., 1273. A.
Malin' ad Ecclesiam, co. Camb., ibid.

1655. Buried — Thomas Malin: St. Thomas the Apostle, p. 130.
London, 1, 4; Leeds, 5, 0; West Rid. Court Dir., 24, 0; Philadelphia, 4, 22; Boston (U.S.), 0, 2.

Mallory, Mallorie. — Local, 'de Malore' or 'Mallore' (three syllables). Evidently some Norman local surname.

Anketil de Malore, cos. Berks, Oxf., and York: Hen. III–Edw. I. K.
Robert Malhore, or Mallore, or Mallori, or Mallory, or Mallure, co. Northampton: ibid.
Anketil Malore, co. Salop, 1273. A.
Crispiane Malure, co. Leic., ibid.
Bertram Malore, co. Bedf., 20 Edw. I. R.
Johannes Malore, 1379: P. T. Yorks. p. 225.
Alicia fil. Johannes Maulore, 1379: ibid.
Peter Malure, co. Heref., ibid.
1578. Married—William Cotton, *gent*, and Elizabeth Mallare: St. Dionis Backchurch (London), p. 8.
1664. — Foulke Malober and Frances Mallory: St. Michael, Cornhill, p. 38.
1726. Bapt.—Mary, d. Stephen Malary: St. Jas. Clerkenwell, p. 165.
Crockford, 2, 0; West Rid. Court Dir., 0, 3; New York, 34, 0.

Malpas, Malpass.—Local, 'of Malpas,' a parish in the union of Wrexham, co. Ches.

William de Malpas, co. Ches., temp. 1230: East Ches. i. 264.
David del Malpas, co. Ches., 1391: ibid. p. 172 *n*.
1556. Married—Rycharde Wheler and Jone Mallipez: St. Michael, Cornhill, p. 7.
1737. — John Bendford and Mary Malpass: Canterbury Cath. p. 82.
1746. — Anthony Malpas and Jane Roberts: St. Michael, Cornhill, p. 71.
London, 2, 1; Philadelphia, 1, 6.

Malregard.—Nick. 'evil eye.' The English verbs *regard* and *reward* are doublets. F. *regarder*, to eye, to look.

William Malregard. T.
Geoffrey Malreward. J.
Walter Maureward, co. Linc., 1273. A.
Robert Maureward, co. Wilts, Hen. III–Edw. I. K.
Thomas Malreward, co. Wilts, 20 Edw. I. R.

Maltby.—Local, 'of Maltby,' parishes in the diocs. of York and Lincoln.

William de Malteby, co. Linc., 1273. A.
Walter de Malteby, co. Norf., ibid.
Robert de Malteby, co. Norf., 20 Edw. I. R.
Willelmus de Maltby, 1379: P. T. Yorks. p. 50.

Isabella de Maltby, 1379 : P. T. Yorks. p. 53.
1706. Married — William Maltby and Mary Westly : St. Mary Aldermary (London), p. 38.
London, 9 ; MDB. (Lincoln), 12 ; Philadelphia, 3 ; Boston (U.S.), 3.

Malter.—Occup. ' the malter ' ; v. Maltmaker and Maltster.

Thomas Malter, C. R., 35 Hen. VI.
1677. Married — William Bell and Marvell Malter : St. Jas. Clerkenwell, iii. 184.
1795. — Antoine Rousseau and Marie Ann Malter : St. Geo. Han. Sq. ii. 126.

Malthouse, Malthus.—Local, ' at the malt-house,' found early as Malthus ; cf. Loftus and Kirkus for Lofthouse and Kirkhouse.

Thomas de Malthous, 1379 : P.T.Yorks. p. 238.
Beatrix Malthus, co. York. W. 16.
1570. William Malthus, co. York : Reg. Univ. Oxf. vol. ii. pt. ii. p. 80.
1615. Married — John Thomson and Ann Malthus, of Reading : St. Mary Aldermary (London), p. 13.
London, 2, 0 ; New York, 0, 1.

Maltmaker. — Occup. ' the maltmaker.' I suspect this surname did not last more than two or three generations.

Hugh le Maltmakere,co.Bucks,1273. A.
Rosa Carttwryth : *maltemaker*, 1379 : P. T. Yorks. p. 27.

Maltman.—Occup. ' the maltman,' a maltster, a dealer in malt. As a surname, scarce.

Liverpool, 1 ; Philadelphia, 1.

Malton.—Local, ' of Malton,' two parishes (New and Old) in N. Rid. Yorks. The surname does not seem to have made much impression upon our registers.

John de Malton, *mason*, 4 Edw. II : Freemen of York, i. 4.
Thomas de Malton, 1379 : P. T. Yorks. p. 159.
1603. William Malton and Alice Cooke : Marriage Lic. (London), i. 280.
London, 1 ; MDB. (East Rid. Yorks), 2.

Maltster.—Occup. ' the maltster.' The feminine terminative is common to these domestic employments ; cf. Brewster, Baxter, Sempster or Simister, Kempster. ' Malstere or maltestere, *brasiatrix, brasiator* ' : Prompt. Parv. When men more frequently took their part in some of these avocations the feminine term was still retained. There is no Maltster in the Hundred

Rolls (1273), but Maltmaker occurs. v. Malter.

Johannes de Pillay, 1379 : P. T. Yorks. p. 87.
Dionicia ancilla ejus, *malster*, 1379 : ibid.
Thomas Malster, 1379 : ibid. p. 140.
Johannes Malster, 1379 : ibid. p. 156.
Robertus Malster, 1379 : ibid. p. 153.
John Malster. B.
Aleyn le Maltestere. H.

I dare not say that Maltster, as a surname, is extinct, but I believe such to be the case.

Manby.—Local, ' of Manby,' a parish in co. Lincoln.' With the variant Manbee, infra, cf. Applebee for Appleby.

Robert de Manby, co. Linc., 1273. A.
Ricardus Maunby, 1379 : P. T. Yorks. p. 245.
1581. Francis Manby, co. Linc. : Reg. Univ. Oxf. vol. ii. pt. ii. p. 113.
1583. William Manbee, co. Linc. : ibid. p. 127.
1788. Married — Joseph Manby and Hannah Littlewood : St. Geo. Han. Sq. ii. 8.
1804. — Thomas Pope and Maria Manbey : ibid. v. 299.
London, 5 ; West Rid. Court Dir., 3 ; MDB. (co. Linc.), 1.

Mancell, Mansel, Mansell, Maunsell.—(1) ? Local. An inhabitant of Le Mans, the capital of Maine, a native of Maine—so says Lower. I suggested in English Surnames that it might be an abbreviation of Manciple, q.v. Probably Lower is right.

Thomas le Mansell, co. Bucks, 1273. A.
Sampson le Maunsel, co. Bedf., ibid.
John le Maunsel, 1313. M.
Robert le Mansel. J.
Johannes Mauncell, 1379 : P. T. Yorks. p. 285.
Alicia Maunsell, 1379 : ibid. p. 134.

(2) Bapt. ' the son of Mansel,' possibly a form of Marcel.

Frater Maunsel, co. Norf., 1273. A.
Maunsel (without surname), co. Hunts, ibid.
Thomas Maunsel, co. Camb., ibid.

Hence the dim. Mancel-ot or Maunsel-ot.

Henricus Maunselot, rector of Gateshead, 1322 : Brand's Hist. Newcastle, i. 501.
Hugh Mancelot, co. Linc., 1273. A.
London, 2, 1, 13, 0 ; Oxford (Maunsell), 1 ; New York, 0, 0, 0, 7.

Manchester.—Local, ' of Manchester.' We do not often find

many representatives of our large cities. The tendency was to come to them, not to leave them. Hence many little spots are the fruitful parents of surnames.

John de Manchestre, 18 Edw. II : Freemen of York, i. 22.
John Manchester, C. R., 5 Hen. VI.
Richard Manchester, of Ratcliffe, 1671 : Wills at Chester (1660-80), p. 177.
Sarah Manchester, of Manchester, 1676 : ibid.
1787. Married—David Allen and Mary Manchester : St. Geo. Han. Sq. i. 407.
1726. — Laurence Bath and Abigail Manchester : St. Jas. Clerkenwell, iii. 252.
London, 2 ; Liverpool, 2 ; New York, 13 ; Boston (U.S.), 11.

Manciple.—Offic. ' the manciple,' a caterer for a college, convent, &c.

' A gentil manciple was ther of a temple, Of which achatours mighten take ensemple.'	Chaucer, C. T. 571.

The name is still officially used in several Oxford colleges. v. Mancell.

William Mannsipple : Pardon Roll, 6 Ric. II.
Thomas Mancipill, 1441 : Munim. Acad. Oxon. p. 525.

Manclarke.—Nick. Malclerk, the opposite of Beauclerk or Bonclerk, both of which existed side by side with it. Manclarke is not a modern corruption, only an early change from *l* to *n* ; v. Malcovenant, and cf. *bannister* for *baluster*.

Walter Manclerc, co. Oxf., 1273. A.
Walter Malclerk. PP.
Godfrey Mauclerk. PP.
Colman Manclarke, mayor of Yarmouth, 1770 : FF. xi. 312.
' Aug. 28, 1888. Married—Amedée F. Mieville to Rose Manclark, of Rochester ': Times, Aug. 31, 1888.
Crockford, 1 ; MDB. (Norfolk), 1.

Mander ; v. Maunder.

Manderson.—Bapt. ' the son of Magnus.' A corruption of Magnusson. This surname comes from Shetland, where Manderson and Magnusson run side by side ; v. Magnus. There need be no hesitation in accepting this solution. The corruption is of a most ordinary character.

1804. Married — William Manderson and Ann Maria Marsh : St. Geo. Han. Sq. ii. 310.
London, 1 ; Philadelphia, 17.

Mandeville, Manvell, Manville. — Local, 'of Mandeville.' I quote from Lower : 'Goisfrid de Mandeville was a Domesday chieftenant in many counties. His descendants were the famous Earls of Essex, extinct in the 13th cent. From a younger branch probably sprang the famous traveller, Sir John M., in the 14th cent. In charters "de Magna Villa" and "de Mandaville." Magneville is near Valognes, in Normandy; and there are two places called Mandeville, one near Louviers, and another in the arrondissement of Bayeux.' Manvell is a manifest variant.

Nigel de Manderville, co. Berks, 1273. A.
Ernald de Maundeville, co. Suff., ibid.
Walter de Maundeville, co. Kent, 20 Edw. I. R.
John de Maundeville, 33 Edw. I. BBB. p. 696.
Ricardus Maunfill, 1379 : P. T. Yorks. p. 171.
1667. Married — Geo. Mandevell and Eliz. Clinch : St. Jas. Clerkenwell, iii. 138.
1751. — Peter Nott and Eliz. Mandeville : St. Geo. Chap. Mayfair, p. 201.
1757. Bapt. — Eliz. Maria, d. Robert Mandeville : St. Peter, Cornhill, ii. 47.
1766. Married—Richard Manvell and Ann Richbell : St. Geo. Han. Sq. i. 160.
London, 2, 3, 0 ; New York, 9, 0, 1.

Mandley.—Local ; v. Manley.

Mandrell.—? Bapt. ' the son of Maundrell ' (?).

Thomas Maundrell, et Elena uxor ejus, 1379 : P. T. Yorks. p. 129.
1605. Henry Mandrell, co. Wilts : Reg. Univ. Oxf. vol. ii. pt. ii. p. 284.
1614. Emme Maundrell, wife of Henry Mandrell (sic) : Marriage Lic. (London), ii. 30.
1663. John Bartlet and Grace Pitts, married by Mr. Mandrill, per licence : St. Peter, Cornhill, i. 263.
1696. Married—John Jacob and Mary Mandrill : St. Jas. Clerkenwell, iii. 217.
London, 2.

Manfred.—Bapt. ' the son of Manfred '; O. Ger. Maginfred (Yonge, ii. 415).

Bernardus Manifred, 1290-1325, Compotus of Bolton Abbey : Whitaker's Craven, p. 455.
Hugo Madefray, C. R., 11 Edw. III. pt. i.
London, 1.

Manger.—Bapt. ' the son of Mangar.' A common entry in the Hundred Rolls.

Manger, father of Thomas Manger, co. Oxf., 1273. A.
Manger (without surname), co. Oxf., ibid.
Richard Manger, co. Camb., ibid.
John Manger, co. Wilts, ibid.
Johannes Maungerson, 1379 : P. T. Yorks. p. 218.
1753. Buried — Thomas Manger : St. John the Baptist on Wallbrook, p. 215.
London, 4 ; New York, 1 ; Philadelphia, 4.

Manggolfe.—Bapt. ' the son of Meginulf,' mighty wolf ; v. Yonge, ii. 415, Meïnolf.

Willelmus Manggolfe, et Beatrix uxor ejus, 1379 : P. T. Yorks. p. 110.

Manifold.—Local, 'of the Manifold,' probably from residence by the river of that name in co. Derby.

Robert Manifold, 1595 : Wills at Chester (1545-1620), p. 130.
Thomas Manifold, of Great Aldersey, 1618 : ibid.
Manchester, 1 ; Liverpool, 4 ; Philadelphia, 3 ; New York, 1.

Manikin.—Bapt. ' the son of Main,' dim. Manekin ; v. Main.

Manekyn le Heaumer. H.
Stephen Manekin, co. Kent, Hen. III-Edw. I. K.
Robert Manekin, co. Suff., 1273. A.
Simon Monekin, co. Oxf., ibid.

In course of time the surname would probably be discontinued, when confused with *manikin*, a dwarf. Nevertheless, I find two instances across the Atlantic.

New York, 2.

Manley, Mandley, Manly, Mandly.—Local, 'of Manley,' a township in the parish of Frodsham, co. Chester. The South-English variant Manly is imitative. The *d* in Mandley is intrusive.

1577. Thomas Manley, co. Ches. : Reg. Univ. Oxf. vol. ii. pt. ii. p. 74.
Nicholas Manley, of Poulton, 1595 : Wills at Chester (1545-1620), p. 130.
Ann Manley, of Chester, *widow*, 1618 : ibid.
Thomas Manley, of Manley, *husbandman*, 1665 : ibid. (1660-80), p. 177.
1621. Married—Thomas Mandley and Mary Lambert : St. Jas. Clerkenwell, iii. 50.
1629. Bapt.—Eliz., d. Tobitha Manly, *widow* : St. Michael, Cornhill, p. 120.
Manchester, 5, 1, 0, 0 ; London, 19, 0, 1, 0 ; MDB. (co. Ches.), 3, 0, 0, 0 ; New York, 18, 0, 0, 1.

Mann, Man.—(1) Occup. ' the man,' i.e. the servant, in early use.

Henry le Man, co. Camb., 1273. A.
Bartholomew le Man, co. Suff., ibid.
Michael le Man, co. Oxf., ibid.
Henry le Man, co. Soms., 1 Edw. III : Kirby's Quest, p. 108.
Richard le Man. E.

(2) Local, 'from Maine,' the French province. A common Yorkshire surname.

Patricius de Man, 1379 : P. T. Yorks. p. 151.
Johannes de Man, 1397 : ibid. p. 28.
Cecilia Manne, 1379 : ibid. p. 29.
Johannes de Manne, 1379 : ibid. p. 60.

For many other and conclusive instances, v. Mayne (2).

1586. Buried—Phillippe Colston, servant of Richard Man : St. Thomas the Apostle (London), p. 97.
1720. Bapt.—Anne, d. Daniel Mann : St. Jas. Clerkenwell, ii. 121.
London, 51, 0 ; Sheffield, 6, 0 ; Leeds, 14, 0 ; New York, 76, 7.

Mannering.—Local. Norman ; v. Mainwaring.

Manning, Mannin. — Personal, ' the son of Manning,' an early personal name. Mr. Ferguson derives it from the Old Norse *manningi*, a valiant man. The name is preserved in such local terms as Manningford, Manningham, Mannington, and Manningtree, all parishes set down in Crockford. It occurs in Domesday as Mannig (co. Suffolk).

Henry Maninge, co. Camb., 1273. A.
Nicholas Mannyng, co. Kent, ibid.
Richard Mannyng, co. Hertf., 20 Edw. I. R.
Johannes Mannyng, 1379 : P. T. Yorks. p. 238.
Nora Mannyng, 1379 : ibid.
1757. Married—Thomas Renshaw and Jane Mannin : St. Geo. Han. Sq. i. 70.
London, 48, 0 ; New York, 120, 1.

Mansel(1 ; v. Mancell.

Manser.—Bapt. ' the son of Manser.'

Manser Arsik, co. Oxf., 1273. A.
Mancer de Pentelun, co. Bedf., ibid.
Fr. (frere?) Manserus, co. Norf., ibid.
Manser de Morton, co. Hunts, 20 Edw. I. R.
Leo fil. Manser, temp. Edw. III : Kal. and Inv. (Palgrave), i. 79.
1670. William Saunders and Eliz. Manser : Marriage Alleg. (Canterbury), p. 44.
1791. Married — Edward Manser and Christiana Davis : St. Geo. Han. Sq. ii. 62.
London, 3 ; Philadelphia, 4.

Mansergh, Mansurgh.— Local, 'of Mansergh,' a manor in the parish of Kirkby Lonsdale.

Thomas de Mansergh, 12 Edw. II : Nicolson's Hist. Westm. and Cumb., i. 252.
John de Mansergh, 7 Ric. II : ibid.
Thomas Manser, or Mansergh, of Burton, 1580 : Lancashire Wills at Richmond, p. 189.
George Mansergh, 1573 : ibid.
Elizabeth Manzer, of Barwicke, 1608 : ibid.
London, 1, 0 ; Manchester, 2, 0 ; Liverpool, 1, 1 ; Lancaster, 1, 0.

Mansfield, Mansfeld.— Local, 'of Mansfield,' a parish in co. Notts.

Robertus Mannsfeld', *carpenter*, 1379 : P. T. Yorks. p. 147.
1577. Richard Mannsfeilde and Susanna Selbie : Marriage Lic. (London), i. 76.
1581. Francis Mansfield, co. Derby : Reg. Univ. Oxf. vol. ii. pt. ii. p. 105.
1606. Thomas Mansfeild, co. Leic. : ibid. p. 289.
1745. Bapt.—Sarah, d. George Mansfield : St. Peter, Cornhill, ii. 43.
London, 39, 1 ; New York, 38, 0.

Manson.—(1) Bapt. 'the son of Magnus,' q.v. Manson is a common surname in Shetland. ' Manson is the contracted form of Magnusson': Scotsman, Oct. 16, 1886. (2) Bapt. 'the son of Main.' For instances, v. Main. So far as Manson is an English surname, this is the true derivation.

1592. Thomas Manson and Edith Connaway : Marriage Lic. (London), i. 201.
1794. Married—Daniel Manson and Ann Seewell : St. Geo. Han. Sq. ii. 111.
London, 1 ; Philadelphia, 10.

Mantell, Mantle, Mantel.— ? Nick. ' Turstinus Mantel occurs in the Domesday of co. Bucks as a tenant-in-chief. Probably a sobriquet from the French *mantelé*, cloak-wearer' (Lower). This is quite possible, for we have several familiar surnames still existing taken from the dress of the bearers; v. Chaperon. The variant Mantle is purely imitative.

Robert Mantel, co. Bucks, 1273. A.
Roger Mauntel, co. Essex, ibid.
John Mauntel, co. Oxf., ibid.
1596. Tristram Mantell and Helen Duplex : Marriage Lic. (London), i. 230.
1755. Buried—Eliz. Basset Mantle : St. Peter, Cornhill, ii. 142.
London, 3, 5, 0 ; MDB. (co. Oxf.), 1, 0, 0 ; New York, 1, 2, 7.

Manton.—Local, 'of Manton. Parishes in the diocs. of Lincoln and Peterborough.

William Manton, co. Camb., 1273. A.
Robert de Mantone, co. Notts, 20 Edw. I. R.
Willelmus de Manton, *smyth*, 1379 : P. T. Yorks. p. 58.
1603. Married — James Manton and Amey Thorlbey : St. Jas. Clerkenwell, iii. 27.
1667. Richard Cutts and Dorothy Manton : Marriage Lic. (London), p. 100.
London, 7 ; New York, 8.

Manuel, Manwell, Manuell. —Bapt. ' the son of Emanuel,' nick. Manuel, corrupted to Manwell ; cf. Samwell for Samuel. A rare English surname, through lateness of its introduction into England.

Edward, son of Manuel Roger, 1542 : Reg. St. Columb Major, Cornwall, p. 2.
Humphrey, son of Emanuell Roger, 1545 : ibid. p. 3.
Manuell, son of John Tucker, 1602 : ibid. p. 21.
John, son of Emanuel Harvey, 1610 : ibid. p. 24.
1609. Buried — John Manuell : ibid. p. 204.
1778. Married—William Fielder and Sarah Manwell : St. Geo. Han. Sq. i. 287.
1806. — Anthony Manuel and Cecilia Salt : ibid. ii. 359.
London, 2, 2, 0 ; New York, 4, 2, 1.

Manvell, -ville; v. Mandeville.

Mapledoore.—Local, ' at the mapledore,' i.e. the maple-tree ; cf. Appledore, and the local names, Mapledur-well and Maple-durham, where (in the latter instance) the hyphen seems to be in the wrong place.

1629. Married—Francis Ball and Eliz. Mapledoore : St. Dionis Backchurch, p. 23.

Maples, Maiples, Marples, Mapples.—Local, 'at the maples,' from residence beside the maple-trees. Evidently some spot in W. Rid. Yorks ; cf. Mapplewell, a village near Barnsley. The modern Yorkshire form seems to be Marples.

Robert de Mapeles, co. York, 1273. A.
Willelmus de Mapples, 1379 : P. T. Yorks. p. 27.
Johannes de Mapples, 1379 : ibid.
1617. Bapt.—Thomasin, d. John Maples : St. Jas. Clerkenwell, i. 79.
London, 11, 0, 0, 0 ; West Riding Court Dir., 0, 1, 10, 0 ; MDB. (West Rid. Yorks), Mapples, 1 ; Philadelphia, 4, 0, 0, 0.

Maplesden. Mapelsden.— Local, 'of Maplesden,' a locality to be found somewhere in co. Kent.

William de Mapplesden, co. Kent, 1273. A.
Stephen de Mapplisden, co. Kent, ibid.
1600. Gervase Maplesden, co. Kent : Reg. Univ. Oxf. vol. ii. pt. ii. p. 245.
1660. Walter Croxton and Mary Maplisden : Marriage Alleg. (Canterbury), p. 53.
1666. John Maplesden and Jane Cobham : ibid. p. 131.
1667. George Mapplesdon and Katharine Horsmonden : ibid. p. 137.
1687. Benjamin Fissenden and Eliz. Maplesden, of Maidstone : ibid. p. 51.
London, 1, 3 ; MDB. (co. Kent), 4, 0 ; New York, 0, 1.

Mapleson.—Bapt. ' the son of Mabel.' The *b* is sharpened into *p*, as in Mapps, Mappin, or Maplet, all from the same name. But while it seems so natural and easy of solution, it must not be forgotten that Mapleson may be a modification of Mapleston, and thus have a local origin ; cf. Kelson for Kelston, where the *t* is similarly elided.

London, 3 ; Liverpool, 1 ; New York, 1.

Mapleston, Maplestone. — Local, 'of Mapleston,' probably for Mapleton.

1575. John Mapleston and Barsaba Newton : Marriage Lic. (London), i. 67.
1791. Married — Thomas Maplestone and Eliz. Davenport : St. Geo. Han. Sq. ii. 54.
London, 1, 2 ; Philadelphia, 1, 0.

Maplet.—Bapt. ' the son of Mabel,' from dim. Mabelot, sharpened to Mapelot, whence the shorter Maplet.

1619. Henry Maplet, or Mapelett, co. Cumb. : Reg. Univ. Oxf. vol. ii. pt. ii. p. 378.

Maplethorpe. — Local, ' of Maplethorpe,' some small spot in co. Lincoln that I cannot find.

MDB. (co. Linc.), 5.

Mapp, Mapps, Mapson.— Bapt. ' the son of Mabel ' (cf. Mapleson), from nick. Mab (sharpened to Map), whence dim. Mabbin (sharpened to Mappin). A Yorkshire surname, where Mabel was particularly popular ; v. Mabb and Mabson. Thus Nob, from Oliver, became Nopps and Nopson.

1585. John Mapes and Ann Cater: Marriage Lic. (London), i. 130.
1647. Married—Thomas Mapsonne to Elizabeth Border: St. Mary Aldermary (London), p. 20.
1722. Bapt.—Ann, d. Richard Mapp: St. Jas. Clerkenwell, ii. 137.
1737. — Mary, d. John Mapson: ibid. ii. 231.
London, 3, 0, 1; Philadelphia, 0, 1, 0.

Mappin.—Bapt. 'the son of Mabel,' from nick. Mab and dim Mab-in, sharpened to Mappin; v. Mapp.

Hugh Mapping, C. R., 3 Edw. I.
Maude Mabyn, wyfe of Roger Mabyn, 1603: St. Columb Major (Cornwall), p. 201.
1729. Married—Joseph Mapping and Mary Long: St. Geo. Chap. Mayfair, p. 294.
London, 2; Sheffield, 12; New York, 1.

Mapplebeck, Maplebeck.—Local, 'of the maple-beck,' the beck or stream where the maples grew; cf. Ellerbeck for the elder-beck. Yorkshire seems to have been a great place for maple-trees; cf. the local Mapplewell, and v. Marples.

Ricardus de Mapelbek', et Beatrix uxor ejus, webester, 1379: P. T. Yorks. p. 25.
Adam de Mappelbek', 1379: ibid. p. 129.
Doncaster, 1, 0; MDB. (West Rid. Yorks), 2, 1.

Mapples.—Local; v. Maples.

Mappleton, Mapleton.—Local, 'of Mappleton,' two parishes, one in co. Derby, the other in E. Rid. Yorks.

Robert de Mapelton, co. Derby, 1273. A.
Thomas de Mapelton, co. Derby, ibid.
1693. William Mappleton and Agnes Lowe: Marriage Alleg. (Canterbury), p. 268.
1804. Married — John Mapleton and Ann Evans: St. Geo. Han. Sq. ii. 281.
MDB. (co. Somerset), 0, 1; (co. Hants), 0, 1.

Marbiler, Marbrer.—Occup. 'the marbler' or 'marbrer,' a worker in marble, a sculptor, a marble-mason.

'Masones, malemakers, and merbelers.'
            Cocke Lorelle's Bote.

From O.F. marbre, altered in England to marbel, marbil, and marble.

Geoffrey le Merberer. B.
John le Merbrer, London. X.
Walter le Marbiler, London. X.
Agnes Mabler, 1379: P. T. Yorks. p. 141.
Johannes Marlebare (sic), 1379: ibid.
Hugh Marbeler was Sheriff of London in 1424.

Marbury, Marberough.—Local, 'of Marbury,' a parish in co. Chester, three miles from Whitchurch.

1545. John Marbery and Alice Marbery: Marriage Lic. (Faculty Office), p. 5.
1610. William Marburie, co. Ches.: Reg. Univ. Oxf. vol. ii. pt. ii. p. 375.
1627. Bapt.—Rebecca, d. Lewes Marbury: St. Thomas the Apostle, p. 48.
London, 0, 1; New York, 2, 0.

March.—(1) Local, 'of March,' a market-town and chapelry in the parish of Doddington, co. Cambridge. As with several other local surnames, the early entries have le instead of de as prefix; cf. Le Bruce for De Bruce.

Henry le March, co. Camb., 1273. A.
William le March, co. Camb., ibid.
Philip le March, co. Oxf., ibid.
Willelmus de Marche, 1379: P. T. Yorks. p. 237.
Johannes de Marche, 1379: ibid. p. 246.

(2) Local, 'at the march,' i.e. the border, limit, or boundary-line of a district.

Johannes de la Marche, 1379: P. T. Yorks. p. 261.
Ricardus del Marche, 1379: ibid. p. 245.
Agnes del Marche, 1379: ibid. p. 171.
1584. Edward Marche, co. Kent: Reg. Univ. Oxf. vol. ii. pt. ii. p. 138.
London, 16; West Rid. Court Dir., 3; New York, 14.

Marcham.—Local, 'of Marcham,' a parish near Abingdon, co. Berks; v. Markham and Marsham.

Robert de Marcham, co. Notts, 1273. A.
Peter de Marcham, 1379: P. T. Yorks. p. 13.
1742. Married — John Marcham and Mary Towell: St. Geo. Chap. Mayfair, p. 19.
London, 1; Oxford, 1.

Marchant, Marchand.—Occup. 'the merchant'; M.E. marchant. 'Marchaunte, mercator': Prompt. Parv.

Thomas le Marchaunt, co. Hunts, 1273. A.
John le Marcaunt, co. Hunts, ibid.
Samson le Marchant, co. Suff., ibid.
William Marchand, co. Hunts, ibid.
Adam Mercator, co. Oxf., ibid.
Willelmus Castleforth, merchand, 1379: P. T. Yorks. p. 159.
Isabella Marchaunt, 1379: ibid. p. 110.
1615. John Picknett and Mary Markant: Marriage Lic. (London), ii. 35.
London, 29, 2; New York, 2, 2; Philadelphia, 8, 1.

Marchington. — Local, 'of Markington,' a village near Ripley and Ripon, co. York.

Johannes de Merkyngton, 1379: P. T. Yorks. p. 259.
Alicia de Merkyngton, 1379: ibid.
West Riding Court Dir., 2; Sheffield, 1; Boston (U.S.), 2.

Marcroft.—Local, 'of Marcroft,' probably a variant of Moorcroft, q.v. The instances below from the Chester Wills settle the origin of the Lancashire Marcrofts beyond dispute. Evidently it was some small farmstead between Rochdale and Middleton.

Thomas Hardman, of Marcroft, parish of Rochdale, 1594: Wills at Chester (1545-1620), p. 82.
Thomas Marcroft, of Kersley, parish of Dean, 1607: ibid. p. 130.
Robert Marcroft, of Middleton, 1613: ibid. p. 131.
Liverpool, 2.

Marcus.—Bapt. 'the son of Mark'; cf. Lucas for Luke. 'Marke, propyr name, Marcus': Prompt. Parv.

John Marcus, co. Essex, 1273. A.
1568. Married—John Wright and Alice Marcus: St. Jas. Clerkenwell, iii. 4.
1752. Bapt.—Lewis, s. Lewis Marcus: ibid. ii. 301.
London, 5; Philadelphia, 14.

Margaret, Margretts.—Bapt. 'the son of Margaret.'

Henry fil. Margaret', co. Camb., 1273. A.
William fil. Margaret'. co. Oxf., ibid.
Hugh Margarete, co. Bucks, ibid.
Johannes Margaret, 1379: P. T. Yorks. p. 190.
1615. Married — Robert Jennison and Elizabeth Margrettes: St. Jas. Clerkenwell, iii. 42.
1642. Bapt.—Ann, d. Robert Margerets, fishmonger: St. Peter, Cornhill, i. 89.
1666. Buried — Elizabeth Margritts: St. Antholin (London), p. 92.

Margerison, Margesson, Marginson, Marjason, Marjerrison, Margisson, Margeson.—Bapt. 'the son of Margaret,' from the popular pet form Margery. Careless pronunciation has in course of time brought about the corrupted forms; v. Margery.

Robert Marjorison, 1379: P. T. Yorks. p. 243.
Richard Marjorison, 1379: ibid.
Roger Margeryson, 1379: ibid. p. 104.
1619. Griffin Margison and Anstis Hall: Marriage Lic. (Westminster), p. 28.

1716. Bapt.—Elenor, d. Richard Margeson : St. Peter, Cornhill, ii. 30.

The Blackburn Directory (co. Lanc.) has Margerison (3), Margerson (1), and Margeson (2).

London, 1, 0, 1, 1, 0, 0, 0 ; Crockford, 0, 1, 0, 0, 0, 0, 0 ; Manchester, 2, 0, 0, 0, 0, 0, 0 ; Sheffield, 2, 0, 0, 0, 2, 0, 0 ; West Rid. Court Dir., 4, 0, 0, 0, 1, 0, 0 ; MDB. (co. Linc.), 0, 0, 0, 0, 1, 1, 0 ; Philadelphia, 5, 0, 0, 0, 0, 0 ; Boston (U.S.), 0, 2, 0, 0, 0, 0, 10.

Margery, Margie, Margries.—Bapt.'the son of Margaret,' from the popular pet form Margery or Marjory. 'Margery, propyr name, *Margeria*': Prompt. Parv.

John Margerie, co. Suff., 1273. A.
Margeria (without surname), co. Oxf., ibid.
Margerie le Bercher. T.
Johannes Marjory, 1379 : P. T. Yorks. p. 197.
Marjoria Love, 1379 : p. 199.
Agnes Marjory-mayden, 1379 : ibid. p. 237.
Marjoria Norris, 1379 : ibid. p. 11.
London, 0, 4, 1.

Margetts, Margetson, Margot.—Bapt. 'the son of Margaret,' from the popular abbreviated Margot or Marget ; v. Maggot.

Margota Servant, co. York. W. 2.
Robert Margets, temp. Eliz. Z.
Francis Margetson, co. Norf. FF.
Joyce Margetson. PP.
1656. Bapt.—John, s. James Margetson, Dr. in Divinity : St. Jas. Clerkenwell, i.196.
1709. Married—Philip Margot and Anne Dauborne : Canterbury Cath. p. 69.
London, 5, 5, 2 ; Boston (U.S.), 0, 0, 8.

Margrie.—Bapt. 'the son of Margaret,' popularly Margery, q.v.

Maries ; v. Marison.

Marigold, Marygold.—?Nick. This surname seems to have had Staffordshire for its home.

John Marigold, minister of Cartmel, 1643 : Baines' Lanc. (Croston), p. 309.

Possibly the same clergyman is referred to in the following :

1643. 'Item, for charges and expenses uppon divers Ministers (to witt), Mr. Fornace, Mr. Mariegould . . . which bestowed their paines in preaching with us when wee had no constant minister ' : Northenden Church, East Cheshire, i. 293.

This is confirmed by the fact that a John Marigold occurs as 'pastor of Waverton,' in Cheshire, in 1648. He seems to have died in 1662.

1662. John Margold, of Waverton, *clerk* : Wills at Chester (1660-80), p. 177.

London, 1, 0 ; MDB. (Worcester), 1, 0 ; (Stafford), 1, 0 ; Oxford, 0, 1 ; Philadelphia, 1, 0.

Mariner, Marner, Marriner. —Occup. 'the mariner,' a sailor, a shipman ; Fr. *marinier*. Marner is a natural abbreviation.

Jacobus le Mariner, co.'Camb., 1273. A.
Roger le Mariner, co. Hunts, ibid.
Henry le Mariner. H.
John Maryner, co. Soms., 1 Edw. III : Kirby's Quest, p. 267.
1689. Bapt.—Elinor, d. James Mariner: St. Dionis Backchurch (London), p. 129.
1795. Married—John Waller and Mary Marner : St. Geo. Han. Sq. ii. 123.
London, 2, 5, 1 ; West Rid. Court Dir., 0, 0, 5 ; Philadelphia, 20, 0, 2.

Marion, Maryon, Marrian. —Bapt. 'the son of Mary,' from the dim. Mari-on, 'little Mary'; cf. Gibbon from Gib, Alison from Alice, Diccon from Dick. Marion or Marian is now a separate name from Mary, as is Eliza from Elizabeth. The doublet Mary Ann helps to perpetuate the modern idea that Marian is a compound of Mary and Ann. It is ludicrous to read that ' Marian, more frequently written Marion, is not formed from Mary and Ann, as some French writers have supposed, but more probably from Mariamne, the wife of Herod, &c.': A Lytell Geste of Robin Hode, i. 342. This is 'out of the frying-pan into the fire.' Maid Marian was as often styled ' Malkin, the May Lady,' Malkin being the English dim. of Mary. Jamieson has unfortunately permitted the 'Mariamne' view a place in his dictionary.

Marion Lambert, 1379 : P. T. Yorks. p. 41.
Mariona fil. Henry, 1379 : ibid. p. 262.
Johannes Marion, 1379 : ibid. p. 104.
Johannes Marionson, 1379 : ibid. p. 111.
Robertus Marion, 1379 : ibid. p. 214.
1391. Gilbert Marion : Cal. of Wills in the Court of Husting (2).
1638. Married—Thomas Allamby and Averine Marrian : St. Jas. Clerkenwell, p. 69.
1688. Bapt. — Thomas, s. Thomas Maryan : St. Mary Aldermary (London), p. 109.
London, 2, 5, 1 ; West Rid. Court Dir., 0, 0, 2 ; Philadelphia, 16, 0, 0.

Marison, Maris, Maries.— Bapt. 'the son of Mary.' Mariot the dim. was almost universal,

Mary being rare ; v. Marriott. Maris might seem to be one of the many early forms of Marsh (q.v.), but it seems more natural to place it here. However, v. Marriss.

Hugh fil. Mary, co. Linc., 1273. A.
William fil. Marie, co. Linc., ibid.
Henry fil. Marie, co. Devon, 20 Edw. I. R.
1621. Jasper Maries, co. Worc. : Reg. Univ. Oxf. vol. ii. pt. ii. p. 393.
1806. Married—Isaac Fitch and Maria Maris : St. Geo. Han. Sq. ii. 349.
London, 1, 4, 2 ; Boston (U.S.), 2, 0, 0 ; Philadelphia, 0, 18, 0.

Mark, Marks, Marx.—Bapt. 'the son of Mark'; v. Marcus. ' Marke, propyr name ': Prompt. Parv. In many cases Marks (and Marx) is a variant of March, q.v. Mark was a rare personal name in the 13th and 14th centuries. With Marx, cf. Dix, Rix, Cox, Wilcox, &c.

William Marke, co. Southampton, 1273. A.
Thomas Mark, co. Oxf., ibid.
Johannes Markson, 1379 : P. T. Yorks. p. 278.
1575. John Marks, co. Devon : Reg. Univ. Oxf. vol. ii. pt. ii. p. 64.
1593-4. George Marks, co. Cornwall : ibid. p. 200.
1749. Married—John Marks and Sarah Powell : St. Geo. Chap. Mayfair, p. 149.
London, 3, 49, 3 ; Philadelphia, 2, 83, 15.

Markby.—Local, ' of Markby,' a parish in the union of Spilsby, co. Lincoln.

Prior de Markeby, co. Linc., 1273. A.
1744. Married—Thomas Markby and Mary Skhellington : St. Geo. Chap. Mayfair, p. 36.
1805. — John Martin and Eliz. Markby : St. Geo. Han. Sq. ii. 334.
London, 2.

Markendale.—Local. A variant or corruption of Martindale (q.v.), a hamlet in the parish of Barton, co. Westmoreland ; v. Martindale.

1726. Married—James Markendle and Mary Thomas : St. Antholin (London), p. 141.
Manchester, 3.

Marketman. — Occup. ' the market-man.'

Nicholas Marketman. TT.
'Articles exhibited against Clement Marketman, executor of Clement Stupeney ': State Papers, July 25, 1623.

'Mr. William Markettman was appointed by the Committee of Plundered Ministers in 1650 to the rectory of Elstree': Clutterbuck's Hist. of Herts, i. 161.

Markham.—Local, 'of Markham,' a parish near Tuxford, co. Notts.

Johannes Marcam, Ibbota uxor ejus, 1379: P. T. Yorks. p. 44.
Nicholaus Marcam, Isabella uxor ejus, 1379: ibid.
Henricus de Markham, 1379: ibid. p. 154.
1573. Married—Christopher Markeham and Margerye Turke: St. Michael, Cornhill, p. 10.
1585. Henry Marcham or Markham: Reg. Univ. Oxf. vol. ii. pt. ii. p. 144.
Sheffield, 5; London, 10; MDB. (co. Linc.), 4; New York, 13.

Marking, Markin.—Bapt. 'the son of Mark,' from the dim. Mark-kin; cf. Wil-kin, Tomp-kin, Jeff-kin, &c. The final g is excrescent, as in Jennings, &c. The name has always been rare, whether as personal name or surname; but it has survived five centuries of neglect.

Johannes Markyn, 1379: P. T. Yorks. p. 78.
1626. Bapt.—Milles, s. Milles Markine: St. Mary Aldermary (London), p. 79.
1659. Bapt.—Alise, d. Ann Markin: Kensington Church, p. 44.
London, 1, 0; New York, 0, 2.

Markland.—Local, 'of Markland.' Mr. Lower, quoting Jamieson, says, 'In Scotland a division of land.' If it be a North-British surname it migrated to South Lancashire a few centuries ago.

Matthew Markland, of Wigan, 1561: Wills at Chester (1545-1620), p. 131.
John Markland, of Pemberton, 1611: ibid.
Gerard Markland, temp. 1662: East Cheshire, ii. 11 n.
1644. Married — Michael Markeland and Mary Perry: St. Dionis Backchurch (London), p. 24.
Manchester, 5; Philadelphia, 7.

Marland.—Local, 'of Marland,' an estate in the township of Castleton and parish of Rochdale.

'Marland, or Mereland (from its water), in this township (Castleton), is of high antiquity. Alan de Merland, Adam de Merland, and Andrew de Merland were living in the 13th century. . . . A branch of the family of Marland continued to reside and hold lands at Marland from the earliest period until the latter part of the 17th century — James Marland, of

Marland, gentleman, being buried within Trinity Chapel, in Rochdale Church, in 1675': Baines' Lanc. i. 505.

The name is not extinct in South Lancashire.

James Marland, of Rochdale, 1584: Wills at Chester (1545-1620), p. 131.
Alice Marland, of Bradley, 1589: ibid.
John Marland, of Hartshead, Ashton-under-Lyne, 1610: ibid.
1699. Married—James Mareland and Sarah Sanson: St. Peter, Cornhill, ii. 62.
Manchester, 2; Philadelphia, 2.

Marlborough. — Local, 'of Marlborough,' a well-known town in co. Wilts.

John de Marleberge, co. Oxf., 1273. A.
Thomas de Marleberge, co. Soms., 1 Edw. III: Kirby's Quest, p. 176.
1595. Bapt.—William, s. Mr. Marlborowe: St. Jas. Clerkenwell, i. 30.
1604. — Anne, d. Robert Marlboroe: ibid. i. 44.
1775. Married—Francis Marlborough and Eliz. Hall: St. Geo. Han. Sq. i. 259. London, 3.

Marler.—Occup. 'the marler,' one who marled fields or who worked in a marl-pit; M.E. marle, a rich earth used for manure.

'Til he was in a marle-pit yfalle.' Chaucer, C. T. 3460.
Alice le Marlere, co. Oxf., 1273. A.
Alan le Marler, C. R., 3 Edw. II.
Willelmus Marlar, 1379: P. T. Yorks. p. 79.
Johannes Merler, 1379: ibid. p. 7.
Stephen le Marlar, co. Soms., 1 Edw. III: Kirby's Quest, p. 106.
1566. Married — John Wattes and Johane Marler: St. Jas. Clerkenwell, iii. 3.
1790. — Robert Marler and Sarah Clinch: St. Geo. Han. Sq. ii. 45. London, 3; New York, 1.

Marley.—Local, 'of Marley,' now Marley Hill, in the parish of Whickham, near Gateshead. A family of this name were early settled there.

'In 1380 Gilbert de Merley held the vill of Merley,' i.e. Marley: DDD. ii. 256.
Adam de Merley, 1201: ibid.
William de Merley, 1339: ibid.
Roger de Merlay, co. York, 1273. A.
Margareta de Marlay, 1379: P. T. Yorks. p. 272.
Thomas de Marlay, 1379: ibid. p. 153.

Marley is a well-established surname in co. Durham.

1746. Bapt.—Mary, d. Joseph Marley: St. Jas. Clerkenwell, ii. 278.
London, 3; MDB. (co. Durham), 4; Philadelphia, 35.

Marmaduke.—Bapt. 'the son of Marmaduke'; somewhat rare in the surname period. Nevertheless it was popular in Yorkshire, and made the pet nicks. Doket and Doke (now Duckett and Duke) favourites long enough for them to become surnames and attain immortality in our directories. Whether the full name ever reached surnominal honours so as to live into modern times I cannot say. I have not met with it.

Marmaduc' de Twenge, co. York, 1273. A.
John Marmaduc, co. Northumberland. 20 Edw. I. R.
John fil. Marmeduc, 1315: DDD. p. 19.
Marmedoke (without surname), 1379: P. T. Yorks. p. 269.
1569. Bapt.—Margaret, d. Marmaduke Servant: St. Jas. Clerkenwell, i. 5.
1619. Marmaduke Greathead and Katherine Dorrell: Marriage Lic. (London), p. 81.

Marner.—Occup. 'a mariner, sailor'; v. Mariner.

Marples. — Local, 'at the maples,' i.e. the maple-trees. This familiar Yorkshire surname has no connexion with Marple, the parish in East Cheshire. At some period an r seems to have intruded itself into Maples or Mapples, q.v.

Thomas de Mapples, 1379: P. T. Yorks. p. 6.
Johannes de Mapples, 1379: ibid. p. 27.
Willelmus de Mapples, 1379: ibid.

The two latter dwelt in Rotherham.

Sheffield, 19; West Rid. Court Dir., 10; London, 0; New York, 2.

Marquis, Marquiss.—? Bapt. Probably a continental form of Marcus. Marquis, strange to say, is a common modern baptismal name in co. York, but it refers to the title of nobility, and is the outcome of eccentric fashion; v. Duke. Earls, Dukes, Marquises, and Squires abound in some parts of the West Riding.

Markisa Galle, C. R., 11 Edw. II.
'Item, to Marques Loryden, mynstrelle, 66s. 8d': Privy Purse Exp., Elizabeth of York, p. 100.
1797. Married—Archibald Marquisand Helen Scott: St. Geo. Han. Sq. ii. 162.
London, 1, 0; MDB. (co. Devon), 0, 3; Philadelphia, 9, 0; New York, 6, 0.

Marr.—Local, 'of Marr,' a small parish four miles from Doncaster. The Scotch Marrs are from the district of Marr, in Aberdeenshire.

Johannes de Merre, 1379 : P. T. Yorks. p. 52.
Henricus de Marre, 1379 : ibid. p. 61.
1748. Married—Joseph Meadows and Faith Marr : St. Geo. Chap. Mayfair, p. 111.
Sheffield, 1 ; London, 8 ; New York, 21.

Marrable.—Bapt. 'the son of Mirabell' (not in Yonge). Notice that in one instance the entry is *de* Mirabell, suggesting a local origin. Most of the other instances, however, are distinctly fontal.

Lucia Mirabile, co. Oxf., 1273. A.
Roger Mirabel, co. Devon, ibid.
William Mirabel, co. Essex, ibid.
Roger de Mirabell, co. Devon, Hen. III-Edw. I. K.
Mirabella Wal, co. York. W. 2.
Belina fil. Mirabilis. DD.
Mirabilla Judaeus, temp. 1300. M.
1604. James Gentleman, *tailor*, and Joane Marable : Marriage Lic. (London), i. 286.
London, 1 ; Crockford, 2.

Marriage.—? Local. The spelling is evidently imitative, and the suffix should probably be -*ridge*, as in Coleridge, Ridgway, Brownrigg, &c.

1616. Thomas Egerton and Alice Marriage (co. Warwick) : Marriage Lic. (London), ii. 41.
1626. Samuel Marredge (co. Middlesex) and Margaret Legge : ibid. ii. 180.
1709. Married—Stephen Marridge and Susanna Browning : St. Jas. Clerkenwell, iii. 231.
London, 3.

Marrian.—Bapt. 'the son of Mary,' from dim. Mary-on ; v. Marion.

Marrin.—Bapt. 'the son of Mary,' from the dim. Mari-on, corrupted to Marrin.

Walter Maryne, co. Soms., 1 Edw. III : Kirby's Quest, p. 249.
Thomas Marynson, 1379 : P. T. Yorks. p. 262.
Elizabeth, d. of James and Marrin Nettle, 1681 : Reg. St. Columb Major, p. 236.
1689. Peter Maligne and Mary Marrin : Marriage Alleg. (Canterbury), p. 126.
London, 1 ; New York, 13.

Marriott, Marryatt, Marratt, Marritt.—Bapt. 'the son of Mary,' from the dim. Mari-ot ; cf.

Philipot (fem.), Emmot (Emma), Tillot (Matilda). Another French dim., Marion, came about a century later ; v. Marion.

Nicholas Maryot, co. Suff., 1273. A.
John fil. Mariot, co. Hunts, ibid.
Mariota in le Lane, co. Camb., ibid.
Walter fil. Mariot, co. Wilts, ibid.
Ricardus Mariot, 1379 : P. T. Yorks. p. 44.
Thomas Haliday et Mariot uxor ejus, 1397 : ibid. p. 79.
Johannes Redebarne et Mariota uxor ejus, 1379 : ibid. p. 80.
1436. ' Received 10*s*. of Robert Atkynson, of Fenham, for the merchet of Mariot his daughter' : QQQ. p. 118.

In Cornwall, where diminutive forms lingered on later than in other counties, Mariot is found in the last century.

1677. Richard Marryott and Catherine Bradbourne : Marriage Alleg. (Canterbury), p. 267.
1725. Buried—Mariot Nettle, *widow* : Reg. St. Columb Major, p. 261.
London, 21, 1, 1, 1 ; New York, 4, 0, 1, 0.

Marris, Maris.—Local, 'at the marsh' (q.v.), from residence thereby. We naturally find this surname in the Fen country. Fr. *marais*, a marsh. But v. also Marison.

John de Mareys, co. Camb., 1273. A.
William du Mareys, co. Suff., ibid.
1745. Married—Henry Lane and Eliz. Marriss : St. Geo. Chap. Mayfair, p. 58.
1786. Married—William Marriss and Jane Ticklepenny : St. Geo. Han. Sq. i. 386.
MDB. (co. Linc.), 13, 0 ; (co. Camb.), 1, 2 ; London, 1, 0 ; Philadelphia, 3, 18.

Marryatt ; v. Marriott.

Marsden, Marsdin.—Local, 'of Marsden.' Parishes in the diocs. of Ripon, Durham, and Manchester. Lit. the marsh-valley, the dale in the swamp. A familiar surname in cos. Lanc. and York.

Robert de Marcheden, co. York, 1273. A.
Nicholaus Mercheden, 1379 : P. T. Yorks. p. 208.
Johanna de Mersseden, 1379 : ibid. p. 184.
1600. Richard Marsden, of the Castle, in Clitheroe : Wills at Chester, i. 131.
1677. William Gibbins and Catherine Marsden : Marriage Alleg. (Canterbury), p. 203.
London, 14, 0 ; West Rid. Court Dir., 38, 5 ; Manchester, 43, 0 ; Philadelphia, 42, 0.

Marsh.—Local, ' at the marsh' (from residence thereby), i.e.

swamp, bog. Low Latin, *mariscus* ; M.E. *mersche*.

Isabel ate Mershe, co. Oxf., 1273. A.
John in le Merse, co. Oxf., ibid.
Ricardus de Marisco, co. Suff., ibid.
Brian de Marisco, co. Wilts, ibid.
Katerina del Mersch, *huswyfs*, *webster*, 1379 : P. T. Yorks. p. 66.
1567. Married—Peter Foxe and Eliz. Marshe St. Michael, Cornhill, i. 9.
1567-8. William Woods and Isabel Marsh : Marriage Lic. (London), i. 38.
London, 70 ; New York, 98.

Marshall, Marshal.—Occup. 'the marshal,' i.e. farrier. Like the smith, the marshal was a necessity in every centre of population. Hence it is found in all counties.

William le Marechal, co. Camb., 1273. A.
Gunnilda le Marescall, co. Soms., ibid.
Robert Marescallus, co. Oxf., ibid.
' Ego Matilda, quae fuit uxor Willelmi Benetson, marschall, compos mentis,' &c., 1392 : Testamenta Ebor. pt. i. p. 180, Surt. Soc.
Thomas de Tiveryngton, *mareschal*, 28 Edw. I : Freemen of York, i. 8.
Willelmus de Scheplay, *marchall*, 1379 : P. T. Yorks. p. 171.
Johannes Mareschall, 1379 : ibid. p. 181.
1572. Christopher Marshall and Eliz. Byrde : Marriage Lic. (London), i. 54.

In the course of time, as marshal began to be associated solely with the military title, we find a kind of compromise in

Jacobus Laurence, *horsmarshall*, 7 Hen. VII : Freemen of York, i. 216.
Richard Henryson, *horsmarshall*, 7 Hen. VII : ibid.
London, 157, 1 ; New York, 116, 2 ; Philadelphia, 230, 0.

Marsham.—Local, 'of Marsham,' a parish in co. Norfolk, near Aylsham ; v. Marcham.

1610. John Marsham, co. Middlesex : Reg. Univ. Oxf. vol. ii. pt. ii. p. 378.
1754. Bapt.—Eliz., d. William Marsham : St. Antholin (London), p. 166.
London, 2.

Marshfield.—Local, 'of Marshfield,' a parish in co. Monmouth, five miles from Newport.

Peter de Marsfelde, co. Soms., 1 Edw. III : Kirby's Quest, p. 271.
London, 1 ; MDB. (co. Soms.), 1.

Marshman.—Local, 'the marshman,' from residence beside the marsh.

Richard Merischman, co. Soms., 1 Edw. III : Kirby's Quest, p. 188.

1711. Married—John Evile and Mary Marshman: Reg. Stourton, co. Wilts, p. 54.
1766. — William Marshman and Ann Anderson: St. Geo. Han. Sq. i. 157.
London, 1; MDB. (co. Soms.), 1; (co. Wilts), 1; New York, 1; Philadelphia, 3.

Marsland. — Local, 'at the marsh land,' from residence thereby. I cannot find any particular spot bearing this name, but it seems to be North English. ◄

Ricardus Mersland, 1379: P. T. Yorks. p. 180.
Thomas Marsland, of Chester, 1609: Wills at Chester (1545-1620), p. 132.
John Marsland, of Stockport, 1603: ibid.
1742. Married — Joshua Kelly and Patience Marsland: St. Michael, Cornhill, p. 69.
West Rid. Court Dir., 3; London, 5; Manchester, 10; New York, 5.

Marson.—(1) Local, 'of Marston,' q.v. No doubt occasionally it is the case that Marson is a lazy abbreviation of Marston; cf. Kelson for Kelston. (2) Nick. 'the son of the mayor'; cf. Wrightson, Taylorson, Clerkson, &c. In any case, *not* 'the son of Mary.'

David fil. Meyr, co. Linc., 1273. A.
Robert Mayerson, of Wray, parish of Melling, 1589: Lancashire Wills at Richmond, i. 193.
1601. John Marson, co. Worc.: Reg. Univ. Oxf. vol. ii. pt. ii. p. 253.
1636. Married — Francis Parker and Ann Marson: St. Peter, Cornhill, i. 255.
1660. Bapt. — Eliz., d. George Marsoone: St. Jas. Clerkenwell, ii. 206.
London, 4; Boston (U.S.), 6.

Marston.—Local, 'of Marston.' There are at least twenty-five parishes of this name in England, including parishes in the diocs. of York, Lincoln, Hereford, and Oxford, of which instances are furnished below. The meaning is, 'the town on the marsh' (v. Town); M.E. *mersche*; A.S. *mersc*, a marsh.

Petronilla de Merston, co. Oxf., 1273. A.
Rither de Merston, co. Bedf., ibid.
Gilbert de Merston, co. Linc., Hen. III-Edw. I. K.
William de Merston, co. Heref., ibid.
Margeria de Merston, 1379: P. T. Yorks. p. 147.
Johannes de Merston, 1379: ibid. p. 257.
1591. John Marston, co. Warw.: Reg. Univ. Oxf. vol. ii. pt. ii. p. 187.
1690. Francis Marston and Eliz. Goold: Marriage Alleg. (Canterbury), p. 166.
London, 9; New York, 20; Boston (U.S.), 73.

Martel, Martell, Myrtle (?). —Bapt. 'the son of Martin,' otherwise ' Martel '; cf. Martle-mas for Martin-mas, common in North England. The dim. Martinet became Martnet and Martlet, hence the bird, the *martin*, which takes its name from the saint, is also known as the *martlet*. 'Martnet, byrd, *turdus*': Prompt. Parv. 'Martynet, a byrde, *martinet*': Palsg.

Johannes fil. Mertel, co. Norf., 1273. A.
Robert Martel, co. Norf., ibid.
Walter Martel, co. Norf., ibid.
William Martell, 20 Edw. I. R.
Ricardus Martyll, 1379: P. T. Yorks. p. 100.
1574-5. John Martill, Ireland: Reg. Univ. Oxf. vol. ii. pt. ii. p. 59.
1684-5. Henry Kelsey and Sarah Martel: Marriage Alleg. (Canterbury), p. 189.
London, 1, 2, 0; Manchester, 0, 0, 1; Philadelphia, 6, 0, 1; Boston (U.S.), 0, 13, 0.

Marten, Martens.—Bapt. 'the son of Martin,' q.v. Strictly speaking the Dutch form, but sometimes merely an English variation.

1541. Buried — Thomas Marten, a *priest*: St. Peter, Cornhill, i. 105.
London, 6, 2; Philadelphia, 4, 1.

Marter.—Nick.; v. Martyr.

Martin, Martins, Martinson.—Bapt. 'the son of Martin'; v. Martel. This once popular font-name, coming as it did in the hereditary surname period, has swelled our 19th century directories enormously.

Martin de Littlebyr, C. R., 42 Hen. III.
William fil. Martin, co. Camb., 1273. A.
Mariota fil. Martini, co. Hunts, ibid.
Martin le Cordwaner, C. R., 9 Edw. II.
Johannes Martynson, 1379: P. T. Howdenshire, p. 32.

It is interesting to notice that Martinson still lives, although it does not now appear in the London Directory.

1797. Married — Thomas Martinson and Sarah Burrows: St. Geo. Han. Sq. ii. 169.
London, 243, 4, 0; MDB. (Lincoln), 34, 0, 2; (West Rid. Yorks), 8, 0, 1; New York, 600, 13, 0.

Martindale, Markendale, Martindell.—Local, 'of Martindale,' in co. Cumb. Markindale was an early corruption, as the reference below fully proves; v. Markendale.

1475. Katerina Martyngdale, co. York: W. 11, p. 98.
1476. John Markyngdale, co. York: ibid. p. 99.
Robert Martinndall, of the Grainge, in Cartmell, 1581: Lancashire Wills at Richmond, i. 191.
John Martyndall, 1590: ibid.
London, 3, 0, 0; Manchester, 2, 3, 0; Philadelphia, 10, 0, 5.

Martinet.—Bapt. 'the son of Martin,' from dim. Martin-et; v. Martel for further observations. Probably a somewhat modern importation from France.

1644. André Martinet and Mary Rosanpré: Marriage Alleg. (Canterbury), i. 289.
1670-1. John Taunay and Lucrece Martinett: ibid. ii. 50.
1775. Married—Claudy Martinet and Esther Thurston: St. Geo. Han. Sq. i. 253.
1782. — George Clarke and Priscilla Martinet: ibid. p. 338.
1845. Buried—Louis Martinet: Canterbury Cath. p. 158.
New York, 2.

Martland.—Local, 'of Markland,' a Lancashire variant of that county surname (v. Markland); cf. Martindale and Markendale.

Blackburn, 2; Manchester, 2.

Marton.—Local, 'of Marton.' Parishes in cos. Linc., Warwick, W. Rid. Yorks, and N. Rid. Yorks, besides several townships and chapelries in various counties. It is probable that Marton, as a surname, has gradually become lost in Martin, q.v.

Symon de Marton, 1379: P. T. Yorks. p. 268.
1799. Married — Geo. Rich. Marton and Ann Pocklington: St. Geo. Han. Sq. ii. 200.
MDB. (West Rid. Yorks), 1; (North Rid. Yorks), 1; Philadelphia, 2.

Martyn.—Bapt. 'the son of Martin,' q.v.

Henry Martyn, co. Hunts, 1273. A.
John Martyn, co. Norf., ibid.
Elena Martyn, 1379: P. T. Yorks. p. 236.
1580. Married—Timothie Goose and Susan Martyn: St. Jas. Clerkenwell, iii. 8.
London, 5; Philadelphia, 2; Boston (U.S.), 3.

Martyr, Marter.—(1) Nick. 'the martyr,' one who had obtained that sobriquet by suffering of some sort for his faith's sake. M.E. *martir*; A.S. *martyr*. (2) Nick. 'the martre,' the marten, a weasel. F. *martre*, a martin, Cotg.; so spelt by Caxton in Reynard the Fox (Skeat). This is the more likely origin, nicknames from animals being so common.

William le Martre. J.
John le Martre. G.
1554. Married — Thomas Graye and Eliz. Martyr, co. Surrey : St. Dionis Backchurch (London), p. 3.
1603. — John Martir and Katherin Bromely : St. Peter, Cornhill, i. 243.
1644. Bapt. — Samuel, s. George Martin : St. Antholin (London), p. 77.
1726. Married — Robert Marter and Margaret Tomkins : St. Geo. Han. Sq. i. 2.
London, 2, 2 ; Philadelphia, 0, 14.

Marvell, Marvill.—Nick. 'the marvel.' M.E. *mervaile* ; Fr. *merveille*, the wonder. Probably the name of some youthful prodigy in learning or physical prowess ; cf. Marvellous. Andrew Marvell, born at Hull in 1620, made the name familiar, and it is in Yorkshire we find the surname still existing.

Warin Merveyl, co. Camb., 1273. A.
Richard Merveyle, co. Camb., ibid.
1702. Bapt. — William, s. William Marvel : St. Jas. Clerkenwell, ii. 8.
1724. Married—Richard Marvel and Elizabeth Walford : St. Mary Aldermary (London), p. 46.
Leeds, 3, 0 ; Philadelphia, 2, 8.

Marvellous.—Nick. 'the marvellous,' the wonderful. M.E. *mervaile*, a wonder.

Robert le Mervyllous, 'clericus de Kesteven,' co. Linc., 1273. A.

Marvin, Mervin, Mirfin, Mervyn, Murfin.—Bapt. 'the son of Merfin' or 'Mervyn' (Yonge, ii. 154-6). The Brittany form of this famous name was Merlin. Miss Yonge says Mervyn is still in use in Wales as a font-name. The story of 'Mervyn Clytheroe' has made the name familiar to modern ears ; cf. Dolphin, Turpin, or Halpin, the suffix in all three cases being *-fin*. The Yorkshire form of the surname to-day is Murfin or Mirfin, practically the same as Mirfyn in the 14th century.

Mervin (without surname), rector of Chester-le-Street, 1085: DDD. ii. 144.
Matilda Marwyn, co. Hunts, 1273. A.
Willelmus Mirfyne, *smyght*, 1379 : P. T. Yorks. p. 69.
Johannes Myrfyn, 1379 : ibid. p. 16.
Thomas Mirfyn, 1379 : ibid. p. 50.
Edmund Marvyn, or Marwyn, 1537: Reg. Univ. Oxf. i. 189.
1564. Married—Danyell Ashpoole and Agnes Morfyn: St. Jas. Clerkenwell, iii. 2.
1635. James Marvyn and Eliz. Phillpott : Marriage Lic. (London), ii. 223.
1692. Bapt. — John, s. John Mirfin, *butcher* : St. Peter, Cornhill, ii. 16.
1699. Mervin Perry, vicar of Dyrham, co. Glouc. : Atkyns' Hist. Glouc. p. 216.
1710. Bapt.—Ann, d: Daniel Murfin : St. Peter, Cornhill, ii. 28.
London, 5, 0, 1, 0, 1 ; West Rid. Court Dir. (Murfin), 3 ; Sheffield (Mervine), 24 ; (Mirfin), 2 ; Philadelphia, 4, 1, 0, 0, 0.

Marwood.—Local, 'of Marwood,' a parish in co. Devon, four miles from Barnstaple. Also, a township in the parish of Gainford, co. Durham.

William Marwod, *pulter*, 6 Edw. II : Freemen of York, i. 14.
1538. William Marwode, or Merwodde : Reg. Univ. Oxf. i. 190.
1604. Thomas Marwoode, co. Devon: ibid. vol. ii. pt. ii. p. 278.
1674. Richard Covere and Jane Marrwood : Marriage Alleg. (Canterbury), p. 236.
1687. George Marwood and Constance Spencer : ibid. p. 296.
MDB. (co. Dorset), 1 ; (North Rid. Yorks), 2.

Marx.—Bapt. ; v. Mark.

Marychurch. — Local, ' of Marychurch,' a parish in co. Devon, two miles from Torbay (St. Marychurch). A family sprung from this place seem to have settled some centuries ago in co. Pembroke, where they attained to a position of importance.

1520. Anne, daughter and heiress of Rudd (or Read), of Rock Castle, Esq., married John St. Marichurch.
1684. Bapt.—Morrish, s. Jenkin Marychurch : Reg. Haverfordwest Parish Ch.
1686. — Elizabeth, d. William Marychurch : ibid.

The above references have been supplied to me by Mr. Marychurch, of Oxford.

1613. Thomas Marichurch : Reg. Univ. Oxf. vol. ii. pt. ii. p. 330.
Oxford, 1 ; MDB. (West Rid. Yorks), 1 ; (co. Pemb.), 1.

Marygold ; v. Marigold.

Maryon ; v. Marion.

Mascall, Maskall, Maskell, Maskill.—Occup. ' the marshal ' (q.v.). No doubt, as suggested by Mr. Lower, a corruption of Marscal. ' I believe that the Mascalls of Kent and Sussex were originally Marshalls. There is armorial evidence of this, and in a document of the 16th century I find the name written Marscal, which is about midway between Mareschal and Mascall' : Patr. Brit. p. 218. There is no need to go back to Mareschal, as Marscal existed so early as the 13th century, and one of my instances belongs to co. Sussex.

Gilbert le Marscale, co. Sussex, 1273. A.
Thomas le Marsscal, co. Camb., ibid.
Peter Marscallus, co. Oxf., ibid.

The transition from Marscal to Mascall was inevitable.

1360. Simon Maschal, rector of St. Buttolph the Abbot, Norwich : FF. v. 442.
1550. Bapt.—Sara Mascall: St. Peter, Cornhill, i. 5.
1551. Buried — Joane Mascoll : ibid. p. 110.
1565. Married—Harrye Maskolle and Alyce Walker : St. Michael, Cornhill, p. 9.
London, 2, 3, 4, 0 ; Leeds (Maskill), 2 ; New York, 0, 1, 1, 1 ; Boston (U.S.), 1, 0, 4, 0.

Mash, Mashman.—These are mere provincialisms of Marsh and Marshman, q.v.

1625. Richard Mash and Lucretia Johnson : Marriage Lic. (London), ii. 156.
1692. Bapt.—John, s. John Mash : St. Jas. Clerkenwell, ii. 345.
1758. Married — Perfect Mash and Familiar Ford : St. Geo. Han. Sq. i. 77.
1764. — William Mash and Susanna Wright : ibid. p. 137.
London, 7, 1 ; New York, 2, 1.

Masham, Massam.—Local, ' of Masham,' a market-town and parish in N. Rid. Yorks.

Robert de Masseham, *faber*, 8 Edw. III : Freemen of York, i. 28.
1606-7. William Masham, London : Reg. Univ. Oxf. vol. ii. pt. ii. p. 293.
1660. Buried—John Masham : Kensington Ch. p. 130.
1685. Sir Francis Masham and Mrs. Damaris Cudworth : Marriage Alleg. (Canterbury), p. 205.
London, 2, 1 ; Philadelphia, 0, 3.

Mashmaker. — Occup. One who steeped malt, or perhaps a maker of mash-vats. In any case, connected with the brewing trade. This curious name is found in the Saint Edmund's Gild, Bishop's Lynn, the ordinances of which are signed by 'Johannes Mashemaker' (English Gilds, p. 96) ; v. *maschel* and *maschyn* in Prompt Parv.

Mashrudder. — Nick. for one who steeped malt. 'Maschel, or rothyr, or maschscherel, *remulus*': Prompt. Parv. Mr. Way adds in a note, 'This term evidently implies the implement used for mashing or mixing the malt, to which, from resemblance in form, the name *rudder* is also given.' In Withal's little Dictionary, enlarged by W. Clerk, among the instruments of the brewhouse is given 'a rudder, or instrument to stir the meash-fatte with, *motaculum*.'

1517. Robert Masherudder, co. York : W. ii, p. 186.
1536. Laurence Maschrodder, co. York : ibid. p. 226.
1584. Peter Mashrether, of Chigwell, Essex, *yeoman*, and Judith Bacon : Marriage Lic. (London), i. 130.

Maskall, -kell ; v. Mascall.

Maskelyne. — Bapt. 'the son of Masculin.'
Henry Maskelyn, co. Wilts, Hen. III-Edw. I. K.
Masculin de la More, co. Worc., 2 Hen. IV : v. Pedigree of Bishop, Visitation of London, 1633-5, vol. i. p. 74.
1655. Buried — Mrs. Sarah Masklin : St. Michael, Cornhill, p. 247.
London, 2.

Maskill ; v. Mascall.

Maslen, Maslin. — Bapt. 'the son of Mazelin,' probably for Marcelin, a dim. of Marcel ; v. Masson (2).
Mazelin de Rissebi, co. Suff., 1273. A.
John Mazelyn, co. Oxf., ibid.
1629. Bapt. — Rachell, d. John Maslin : St. Michael, Cornhill, p. 120.
1772. Married — Thomas More and Esther Maslin : St. Geo. Han. Sq. p. 219.
1780. — William Maslem and Ann Allaway : ibid. p. 311.
London, 6, 5 ; Philadelphia, o, 1.

Mason. — (1) Occup. 'a stonemason, a woodmason.' M.E. *mason* ; O.F. *maçon, masson* (Skeat).
Gotte le Mazoun, co. Hunts, 1273. A.
Nicholas le Macun, co. Bucks, ibid.

Adam le Mazon, 1307. M.
Willelmus Mason, *mason*, 1379 : P. T. Yorks. p. 282.
(2) Bapt. 'the son of Matthew.' O.F. Mayheu, shortened into Maye ; v. May (2) and Mayson (1).
Roger fil. Maye, co. Salop, 1273. A.
1579. Bapt. — Eliz., d. John Mason : Kensington Ch. p. 8.
London, 137 ; Boston (U.S.), 187.

Massam ; v. Masham.

Masser. — Occup. 'the mercer,' a Lanc. provincialism for mercer (Halliwell). In the registers of the Parish Church, Ulverston, N. Lanc., I have frequently seen in entries of the 17th and 18th centuries a man described as a 'marcer.'
1727. Bapt. — Susanna, d. Thomas Masser : St. Jas. Clerkenwell, ii. 169.
1744. Married — John Bowdery and Ann Massar : St. Geo. Han. Sq. i. 32.
West Rid. Court Dir., 2 ; Philadelphia, 1.

Massey, Massie. — Local, 'of Mascy.' A Norman surname that came over with William. Hamon Massie acquired Dunham, in co. Ches., and the patronymic spread rapidly. Mr. Lower points out several places in Normandy whence the name may have come, ' viz. Macé-sur-Orne, Macei in the arrondissement of Avranches, Marcei in that of Argentan, and Marcei, on the Broise, near the town of Avranches.
Robert de Mascy, of Tatton, co. Ches., 1353 : Hist. of East Ches. ii. 157 *n*.
Ameria de Mascy, 1353 : ibid.
1583. James Massye, co. Lanc. : Reg. Univ. Oxf. vol. ii. pt. ii. p. 131.
1588. Gerard Massye, co. Ches. : ibid. p. 167.
1592. John Massie, of Shocklach, *husbandman* : Wills at Chester, i. 132.
1609. Alice Massey, of Manchester : ibid. p. 133.
London, 20, 1 ; Oxford, o, 1.

Massingberd, Massingbird. —?——. I can discover nothing satisfactory with regard to this name. I suspect it came at some fairly early period from the Low Countries. As Massingham (q.v.), however, is a parish in co. Norf., it may be that Massingberd was originally some spot called Massingbergh in co. Linc. Indeed Massingberg is in MDB. (co.

Lincoln), only I fear it is a misprint.
1581. Thomas Massingberd, co. Linc. : Reg. Univ. Oxf. vol. ii. pt. ii. p. 114.
1681. Married—William Ash and Eliz. Massinbird, of Northampt. : St. Peter, Cornhill, ii. 55.
1701. Buried — Daniel, son of John Masingbard, *gent.* : FF. iv. 501.
1774. — Charles Burrell Massingberd and Ann Blackall : St. Geo. Han. Sq. i. 248.
Crockford, 1, o ; MDB. (co. Linc.), o, 1.

Massinger. — Offic. ; for Messenger, q.v.

Massingham. — Local, 'of Massingham,' two parishes in co. Norfolk.
Walter de Massingham, co. Camb., 1273. A.
Adam de Messingham, co. Linc., ibid.
John de Messingham, London, ibid.
Thomas de Messyngham, 1379 : P. T. Yorks. p. 49.
1799. Married — Henry Ford and Harriot Massingham : St. Geo. Han. Sq. ii. 207.
London, 2 ; Oxford, 1.

Masson. — (1) Occup. 'the mason.' O.F. *maçon* or *masson* ; v. Mason.
Osbert le Masson, co. Oxf., 1273. A.
Richard le Massun, co. Salop, ibid.
John le Mascon, co. Southampt., ibid.
Ricardus de Brodesworth, *masson*, 1379 : P. T. Yorks. p. 73.
(2) Bapt. 'the son of Masse,' a nick. of Marcel. Massilia is found likewise for Marcilia (A. ii. 580).
Duce fil. Masse, co. Hunts, 1273. A.
1685. Peter Masson and Mary le Febvre : Marriage Alleg. (Canterbury), p. 282.
London, 3 ; Philadelphia, 7.

Master. — Offic. 'the master,' a superior, a teacher, ' Maystyr, *magister, petagogus, didascolus*': Prompt. Parv. v. Masters.
Angnes le Maistre, co. Camb., 1273. A.
Thomas Magister, co. Camb., ibid.
Hamund le Mester, co. Hunts, ibid.
Roger le Mestre, co. Hunts, ibid.
John Hume le Mestre, C. R., 2 Edw. I.
John Maistre, C. R., 17 Ric. II.
Thomas le Mayster, C. R., 1 Hen. IV. pt. i.
Johannes Mastere, 1379 : P. T. Yorks. p. 14.
1562. Buried—Anne, d. Thomas Master, *embroderer* : St. Mary Aldermary (London), p. 134.
1746. Married — Edward Raby and Mary Master : St. Jas. Clerkenwell, iii. 276.
Crockford, 6 ; Philadelphia, 5.

Masterman.—(1) Official, 'the master,' a superior, modern 'gaffer,' American 'boss,' with augmentative *man* as in merchantman. (2) Occup. 'the master's man,' a servant'; cf. Vickerman, Matthewman, &c. This is the more probable derivation; v. Ladyman for convincing proof.

Richard Maysterman, co. Camb., Pardons Roll, 6 Ric. II.
Johannes Maysterman, 1379: P. T. Yorks. p. 224.
Willelmus Mausterman, 1379: ibid. p. 231.
1748. Married — Robert Eastee and Sarah Masterman: St. Jas. Clerkenwell, iii. 280.
1782. — William Springal and Ann Masterman: St. Geo. Han. Sq. i. 335.
London, 6; Ripon, 2; New York, 1.

Masters, Masterson.—Nick. 'the master's son' (v. Master); cf. Taylorson, Clerkson, Smithson, Millerson. Considering the large number of early and later entries relating to this surname, it is curious that Masterson should be so rarely met with in the present generation in England. It flourishes, I find, in New York. But nomenclature is full of surprises of this kind.

Hugh fil. Magistri, co. Devon, 1273. A.
Thomas fil. Magistri, co. Linc., ibid.
Henry fil. Robert Magistri, co. Camb., ibid.
John Maisterson, 17 Edw. II: Freemen of York, i. 21.
Roger le Maistressone. G.
Dorothy Masterson, temp. Eliz. Z.
Robert Maystreson. XX. 1.
John Maysterson, C. R., 3 Hen. VI.
1583. Married — John Kilbecke and Cecily Masterson: St. Jas. Clerkenwell, iii. 10.
1616. William Pym and Eliz. Masters: Marriage Lic. (London), ii. 43.
Thomas Maisterson, of Wich Malbank, co. Chester: Wills at Chester (1660-80), p. 177.
London, 29, 1; New York, 8, 66.

Matchet; v. Madgett.

Mather.—Of this surname, so well known in co. Lanc., there seem to be two origins, one occupative, the other baptismal. But there is distinctly more evidence on behalf of the first. (1) Occup. 'the mather,' i.e. the mower; cf. Mawer, q.v., probably a general term for a husbandman. We still use *math* or *after-math* in poetry. Mr. J.

Paul Rylands, F.S.A., supplies me with my first two and most important references.
'16 August, 5 Hen. V. (1417). Writ to the Sheriff of Lancashire, commanding him to attach . . . Mathew le Madour, of Culcheth, husbandman; Ric. le Madour, of Culcheth, husbandman': Risley Charters, in the possession of Mr. Ireland Blackburne, of Hale.
Johannes Madyr, 1379: P. T. Yorks. p. 202.
Thomas Madour, 1379: ibid. p. 204.
1582. Roger Mather, of Leigh, co. Lanc.: Wills at Chester, i. 134.
1616. Ellis Mather, of Liverpool: ibid. p. 133.

(2) Bapt. 'the son of Madur.' I have only one clear reference, and it concerns co. Hunts. The genitive of this would be Mathers; cf. Williams, Jones.

Emma fil. Madur, co. Hunts, 1273. A.
1635. Married — Roland Mather and Eliz. Gibson: St. Peter, Cornhill, i. 255.
London, 12, 2; Liverpool, 6, 0; New York, 19, 6.

Matheson, Mathison, Mathieson.—Bapt. 'the son of Mathew,' from the popular form Mathie. For further instances, v. Matthey.

John fil. Mathie, co. Wilts, 1273. A.
Henry fil. Mathie, co. Oxf., ibid.
Herbert fil. Mathew, co. Devon, ibid.
1601. Robert Mathison, co. York: Reg. Univ. Oxf. vol. ii. pt. ii. p. 251.
1802. Married—Gilbert Mathison and Catherine Farquhar: St. Geo. Han. Sq. ii. 257.
London, 3, 2, 3; Boston (U.S.), 7, 4, 4.

Mathew, Mathews, Mathewson, Matthew, Matthews, Matthewson, Mathewes.—Bapt. 'the son of Mathew.' Found in French and English forms in large quantities in the early registers. The nicks. and dims. also are numerous, as the pages of this dictionary will show. The two chief nicks. were Mat (English) and May (French). Mathew or Mayheu was exceedingly popular with our forefathers. As Miss Yonge reminds us, some form or other of
'Matthew, Mark, Luke, and John
Bless the bed I sleep upon'
has existed for centuries.
Matheu Robert, 1379: P. T. Yorks. p. 174.

Willelmus Matheu, 1379: ibid.
Agnes Mathewe, 1379: ibid. p. 47.
Ricardus fil. Mathei, 1379: ibid. p. 184.
1559. Married — Robert Mathewson and Joane Goringe: St. Thomas the Apostle (London), p. 3.
London, 8, 39, 4, 5, 143, 1, 1.

Mathias.—Bapt. 'the son of Mathias'; v. Mathew.

1807. Married—George Mathias and Mary Dennison: St. Geo. Han. Sq. ii. 373.
London, 6; New York, 6.

Matkin.—Bapt. 'the son of Mathew,' from nick. Mat, and dim. Mat-kin; cf. Watkin, Wilkin, &c.

Richard Matkyn, temp. Eliz. ZZ.
Jeremiah Matkyn, ibid.
1584. Richard Price and Martha Matkyns: Marriage Lic. (London), i. 132.
1614. Francis Matkin, New Coll. Oxf.: Reg. Univ. Oxf. vol. ii. pt. iii. p. 333.
1618. John Matking, co. Linc.: ibid. vol. ii. pt. ii. p. 370.
West Rid. Court Dir., 1; London, 3.

Matley.—Local, 'of Matley,' a township in the parish of Mottram, co. Ches.

William de Mattelegh, 1316: East Ches. ii. 157.
Hugh de Mattelegh, 1316: ibid.
Richard de Mattlegh, 1300: ibid. ii. 155.
1633. James Matley, of Rixton, *husbandman*: Wills at Chester, ii. 151.
1635. Alice Matley, of Bostock, co. Ches.: ibid.
1794. Married—Matthew Matley and Martha Bothamly: St. Geo. Han. Sq. ii. 111.
Manchester, 3; New-York, 1.

Maton.—Bapt. 'the son of Matthew,' from nick. Mat, dim. Mat-on. Alison is still the dim. of Alice in Scotland. For further instances, v. Mattin and Mattinson.

William Matun, co. Norf., 1273. A.
Robertus Maton, 1379: P. T. Yorks. p. 137.
Willelmus Mathon, 1379: ibid. p. 198.
1581. Edward Maton, co. Wilts: Reg. Univ. Oxf. vol. ii. pt. ii. p. 115.
1588. William Maton, co. Wilts: ibid. p. 167.
1683. John Maton and Mary Thompson: Marriage Alleg. (Canterbury), p. 135.
London, 3.

Matterson.—Bapt. 'the son of Matthew,' v. Mathew. A Yorkshire form of Matthewson or Mattinson; cf. Dickenson, Catterson, and

Patterson for Dickinson, Cattinson, and Pattinson :

London, 2 ; York, 6.

Matthew, &c.; v. Mathew.

Matthewman.—Occup. 'the servant or labourer of Matthew'; cf. Perryman and Addyman. This is one of the most familiar representatives of this class of surname. Its origin as here deduced admits of no doubt. Perhaps the following instance will best exemplify the circumstances under which such a surname arose :

Matheus de Lofthous, *firmarius*, 1379 : P. T. Yorks. p. 241.
Willelmus Mathewman, 1379 : ibid.
Magota Mathewoman, 1379 : ibid.

Here are Mathew himself, the farmer, William his hind, and Magot his kitchen wench. The two servants took their surname from the position they occupied to their master.

Cf. Willelmus Thomasman, 1379 : P. T. Yorks. p. 210.
Ricardus Watman, 1379 : ibid.
Thomas Robertman, 1379 : ibid. p. 293.
Hugo Mathewman, 1379 : ibid. p. 248.

The master's name almost immediately precedes in each case. Matthewman is still one of the leading indigenous surnames of Yorkshire.

1762. Married — Thomas Mathewman and Ann Colgate : St. Geo. Han. Sq. i. 111.
London, 3 ; West Rid. Court Dir., 10.

Matthey, Matthes. — Bapt. 'the son of Matthew,' popularly Matthey. The final *s* in Matthes is genitive, as in Matthews, Williams, Jones, &c.

Mathy del Jarty, co. Devon, 1273. A.
Hugh fil. Mathey, co. Oxf., ibid.
William Mathy, co. Wilts, ibid.
Henry Matthe, co. Camb., ibid.
Agnes uxor Mathie, 1379 : P. T. Yorks. p. 27.
1771. Married — Henry Matthey and Ann Aston : St. Geo. Han. Sq. i. 205.
1786. — Charles Mathis and Mary Dean : ibid. p. 385.
London, 3, 5 ; Boston (U.S.), 0, 1.

Mattin, Mattinson, Mattison.—Bapt. 'the son of Matthew,' from nick. Matt, dim. Matt-in or Maton (q.v.); cf. Colin, Robin, Alison, &c.

The first three following belonged to one village :

Robertus Maton, 1379 : P. T. Yorks. p. 137.
Adam Mathin, 1379 : ibid.
Johannes Mathin, 1379 : ibid.
Johannes Mathon, 1379 : ibid. p. 183.
Willelmus Mathon, 1379 : ibid. p. 198.
Thomas Mateson, 1379 : ibid. p. 195.
1672. Bapt. .— Thomas, s. Thomas Mattison : St. Jas. Clerkenwell, p. 275.
1783. Married — John Crawford and Isabella Mattison : St. Geo. Han. Sq. p. 343.
London, 0, 2, 1 ; Philadelphia, 0, 0, 6.

Mattock, Mattocks, Mattick, Mattox.—Bapt. 'the son of Madoc' ; v. Maddock, Maddox, and Maddick, of which these are sharpened forms.

1687. Oliver Mattox and Alice Westwood : Marriage Alleg. (Canterbury), p. 33.
1750. Married—George Mattocks and Eliz. Restell : St. Geo. Chap. Mayfair, p. 166.
1753. — Francis Stewart and Mary Mattax : ibid. p. 249.
1802. — Robert Teasdale and Sarah Mattock : St. Geo. Han. Sq. ii. 263.
London, 2, 5, 1, 0 ; Bristol, 0, 0, 1, 0 ; Philadelphia, 1, 0, 0, 2.

Matts, Mattson, Matson.—Bapt. 'the son of Matthew,' from the nick. Mat; v. Mattin.

Adam Matte, co. Wilts, 1273. A.
Thomas Mateson, 1379 : P. T. Yorks. p. 195.
Marmaduke Matteson, co. York. W. 16.
Anne Mattson, co. York, ibid.
Roger Matson, of Cocken, Furness, 1605 : Lancashire Wills at Richmond, p. 193.
Robert Mattson, of Cockon, Furness, 1673 : ibid.
1729. Married—John Matts and Sarah Pickett : St. Antholin (London), p. 143.
London, 3, 0, 2 ; Sheffield, 0, 1, 0 ; New York, 0, 1, 4 ; Boston (U.S.), 0, 6, 4.

Maud, Maude, Mawd, Maudson, Mawson.—Bapt. 'the son of Matilda,' of which a popular form was Maud. Fr. Mathilde, Mahaud (Yonge, ii. 415).

Maud Gladewyse, Close Roll, 7 Edw. II.
Geoffrey Maude, co. Hunts, 1273. A.
Robertus Maweson, 1379 : P. T. Yorks. p. 219.
Johannes Mawde, 1379 : ibid. p. 184.
Willelmus Mawde, 1379 : ibid. p. 198.
1646. Bapt. — Elizabeth, d. James Maude : St. Michael, Cornhill, p. 134.

1682. Married—Thomas Mawson and Elizabeth Holden : ibid. p. 43.
London, 3, 7, 0, 1, 4 ; Leeds, 4, 5, 0, 1, 7 ; Philadelphia, 1, 3, 0, 0, 17.

Maudling.—Bapt. 'the son of Magdalene.' M.E. Maudelein or Magdelaine. The final *g* is, of course, excrescent, as in Jennings, &c.

'His barge ycleped was the Magdelaine.'
　　　　　　Chaucer, C. T. 412.
'And also Marie Maudeleyne.'
　　　　　　Piers P. 10203.

Hence such phrases as 'maudlin sentiment.'

Simon Maudeleyn, co. Oxf., 1273. A.
Maudlin Hoby. V. 2.
Robert Maudelyn. O.
1562. Bapt. — Mawdelyn, d. John Champyon : St. Jas. Clerkenwell, i. 2.
1608. Married—William Marrett and Maudlyn Tatome : ibid. p. 34.
1669. Bapt.—John, s. Thomas Maudlin : ibid. ii. 239.
1674. — Mary, d. Richard and Avis Maudlin : ibid. p. 267.
1696. Married — John Lokwex and Maudlin Lernoult : St. Michael, Cornhill, p. 49.
London, 1.

Maudsley, Mawdsley, Maudslay, Mawdesley.—Local, 'of Mawdesley,' a village parish in the old mother parish of Croston, co. Lanc., eight miles from Chorley. The place originated a surname at an early period.

Adam de Moudesley, 35 Hen. III : Baines' Lanc. ii. 118.
William Mawdsley, of Mawdsley, 1584 : Wills at Chester (1545-1620), p. 134.
Robert Mawdsley, of Mawdsley, 1617 : ibid.
1605. Thomas Mawdisley, Bras. Coll. : Reg. Univ. Oxf. vol. ii. pt. ii. p. 283.
1671. Thomas Mawdesley and Ann Cary : Marriage Lic. (Faculty Office), p. 118.
Manchester, 2, 2, 0, 1 ; London, 3, 1, 0, 0.

Maudson.—Bapt. 'the son of Maud' ; v. Maud and Mawson.

Sheffield, 1.

Mauger, Maugerson.—Bapt. 'the son of Malger' or 'Mauger.' Malger, Archbishop of Rouen, opposed William's marriage (Freeman, Norm. Conq. iii. 94); v. Major. As a personal name Mauger lasted till the 18th century in the Vavasour family (v. Vavasseur).

Malger le Clerk, co. Bucks, 1273. A.
Thomas fil. Mauger, co. Norf., ibid.
Mauger (without surname), co. Oxf., ibid.
Mauger (without surname), co. Hunts, ibid.
Walter Mauger, co. Oxf., ibid.
Mauger fil. Elie, c. 1300. M.
Mauger le Vavasour. J.
Hugh Maugason. H.
William Maugerson. FF.
Margre Warner, 1379: P. T. Yorks. p. 38.
Robert Maugere, *smyth*, 1379: ibid. p. 70.
Morker Baynbrigg, 1379: ibid. p. 259.
1569. Bapt. — Margery, d. James Mawger, or Maugere: St. Jas. Clerkenwell, i. 5.
London, 1, 0; Philadelphia, 14, 0.

Maul, Maule, Maull, Mawle.
—Local, 'of Maule,' 'from the lordship of Maule, near Paris,' says Lower, and adds, 'According to Douglas's Peerage of Scotland, Guarin de Maule, a younger son of Arnold, lord of Maule, accompanied William to the Conquest of England. Robert de Maule, his son, accompanied David I into Scotland, and obtained from him a grant of lands in Lothian.'

Xᵽia de Maulea, co. Essex, 1273. A.
Cristiana de Maule, co. Hertf., 20 Edw. I. R.
1587. Married — Thomas Maull and Anne Atkinsonne: St. Peter, Cornhill, i. 236.
1602. George Maull, co. Essex, and Suzanna Herdde: Marriage Lic. (London), i. 273.
1619. Thomas Maule, co. Salop: Reg. Univ. Oxf. vol. ii. pt. ii. p. 376.
1782. Married — Henry Maule and Hannah Rawson: St. Geo. Han. Sq. i. 339.
London, 1, 4, 1, 0; MDB.(co.Northampt.) (Mawle), 5; Philadelphia, 12, 18, 42, 0.

Maunder, Mander.—Occup. (?) 'the maunder,' a maker of baskets called *maunds.* Lower says, 'Maunder, a beggar; O.E. *maund,* to beg.' I strongly suspect my own interpretation to be the true one, although I have no early instances. 'Mawnd, skype, *spor-tula*': Prompt. Parv. Mr. Way, commenting on this word, adds, 'Caxton says, in the Book for Travellers, "Ghyselin the mande maker (*corbillier*) hath sold his vannes, his mandes (*corbilles*) or corffes."' This is strong evidence. In Ulverston registers to this day

a maker of *swills* (i.e. baskets) is set down as a *swiller,* not a swill-maker.

1566. Richard Maunder, co. Herts, and Margery Graves: Marriage Lic. (London), i. 34.
1583. Robert Maunder, co. Devon: Reg. Univ. Oxf. vol. ii. pt. ii. p. 129.
1683. Buried—Sarah, wife of Michaill Maunder: St. Mary Aldermary, p. 195.

Of course Maunder and Mander are the same:

1664. Buried—Elisha, s. George and Barbara Mander: St. Antholin (London), p. 91.
1665. — Barbery Maunder: ibid. p. 92.

We may take for granted that Barbara and Barbery refer to the same woman.

London, 11, 9; MDB. (co. Devon), 9, 0; New York, 0, 4; Boston (U.S.), 1, 0.

Maunsell; v. Mancell.

Maurice.—Bapt. 'the son of Maurice'; v. Morris.

William fil. Maurici, co. Hunts, 1273. A.
Richard fil. Maurycii, co. Camb., ibid.
Peter fil. Maurice, co. Linc., ibid.
1678. Robert Maurice and Frances King: Marriage Alleg. (Canterbury), p. 290.
1754. Married — Thomas Reeve and Margaret Maurice: St. Geo. Chap. Mayfair, p. 276.
London, 7; New York, 13.

Maw, Mawe.—Local, 'at the maw,' i.e. *mow,* a stack of hay or corn; cf. Mawer for Mower. We still sing of the 'barley-mow.' This surname is very strongly represented in co. Lincoln.

Alice de la Mawe, co. Suff., 1273. A.
William de la Mawe, co. Suff., ibid.
Sibill de la Mawe, co. Suff., ibid.
William de la Mawe, bailiff of Yarmouth, 1275: FF. xi. 322.
William atte Mawe, bailiff of Yarmouth, 1354: ibid. p. 323.
Willelmus Mawe, 1379: P. T. Yorks. p. 217.
1663. Bapt.—Margarett, d. John Mawe: St. Jas. Clerkenwell, i. 217.
1674. Thomas Mawe and Mary Monke: Marriage Alleg. (Canterbury), p. 227.
London, 5, 1; MDB. (Suffolk), 1, 0; (Lincoln), 33, 0; Boston (U.S.), 1, 0.

Mawby, Mawbey.—Local, 'of Mautby,' a village and parish in co. Norfolk. The *t* has been omitted in modern spelling. In some instances Mawby will represent Maltby, q.v.

Walter de Mauteby, co. Norf., 1273. A.
Robert de Mauteby, co. Norf., ibid.

Simon de Maudeby, 10 Ric. I, co. Norf.: FF. xi. 226.
Robert de Mauteby, 4 Hen. III, co. Norf.: ibid.
1755. Married—Jeffray Edwards and Mary Mawby: St. Geo. Han. Sq. i. 55.
MDB. (Norfolk), 2, 0; (Lincoln), 5, 0; London, 2, 1; New York, 0, 5; Philadelphia, 2, 0.

Mawditt.—Local, 'de Mauduit,' a Domesday surname. At first sight this appears to be a dim. of Maud. This is not the case. It is well represented as a local surname in the Hundred Rolls (A.) and in many guises. Only one entry in the London Directory (a confectioner) preserves its memory, 'sic transit gloria mundi.' William Mauduith was chamberlain to William the Conqueror

William de Maudut, co. Salop, 1273. A.
Flaundrina Mauduyt, co. Bedf., ibid.
John Maudeyt, co. Bucks, ibid.
Gilbert Maudit, co. Essex, ibid.
Johanna Mawduyt, 1379: P. T. Yorks. p. 241.
Robertus Maudyt, 1379: ibid. p. 60.
1616. John Everard and Elizabeth Mauditt: Marriage Lic. (London), ii. 46.
1635. William Bathurst and Eliz. Mawdett: ibid. p. 225.
Jasper Mauditt, 1687: Lanc. and Ches. Rec. Soc. xi. 77.
1752. Buried—Elizabeth Mauduit: St. Dionis Backchurch (London), p. 318.
London, 1.

Mawdsley; v. Maudsley.

Mawer.—Occup. 'the mower'; v. *mow* (Skeat). This formerly common surname seems to have become lost in Moore, which was a very natural result. It is found in its original form but rarely.

Rogerus Hamerton, *mawer,* 1379: P. T. Howdenshire, p. 14.
Henricus Mawer, 1379: P. T. Yorks. p. 127.
Johannes Rayner, *mawer,* 1379: ibid. p. 31.
Robertus Mawer, 1379: ibid. p. 32.
Robert Dymond, *mawer,* 1379: ibid. p. 91.
1623. John Mawer, *haberdasher,* and Sarah Woollet: Marriage Lic. (Westminster), p. 29.
1676. Maurice Jarvis and Eliz. Mawer: Marriage Alleg. (Canterbury), p. 256.
London, 4; Oxford, 2.

Mawle; v. Maul.

Mawley.—Local, 'de Mauley.' Mr. Lower says that Peter de Mauley, a squire of King John, who was employed to murder Prince Arthur, was a native of Poitou. He received much land from the king in the West of England.

Peter de Maulley, co. Somerset, 1273. A.
Peter de Maulay, co. Sussex, Hen. III-Edw. I. K.
1717. Bapt.—Joyce, d. Thomas Mauley: St. Jas. Clerkenwell, ii. 101.
1787. Married—Thomas Oakley and Barbara Mawley: St. Geo. Han. Sq. i. 398.
London, 3; Philadelphia, 3.

Mawson, Mawsom.—Bapt. 'the son of Matilda' (v. Maud for instances). In Mawsom *m* takes the place of *n*, as in Ransom and Hansom for Ranson and Hanson; cf. also Sansom.

1692. Bapt. — Thomas, s. Samuel Mauson : St. Jas. Clerkenwell, p. 348.
Leeds, 7, 0; West Rid. Court Dir., 14, 1; Philadelphia, 17, 0.

Mawtus.—Local, 'of the malt-house.' This, of course, became Malthus (q.v.) and then Mawtus; cf. provincial *sawt* for salt.

Miniskip, near Ripon, 1.

Maxey, Maxcy, Maxcey.—Local, 'of Maxey,' a parish in co. Northampton. A member of this family seems to have settled early in London, whence occasional registrations in the City churches. I furnish a few instances out of many :

1575. Married—John Slatur and Eliz. Maxse : St. Antholin (London), p. 24.
1658. Bapt.—John, s. Ralph Maxee : St. Jas. Clerkenwell, i. 201.
1710. Bapt. — Charles, s. Arabella Maxey (London), p. 279.
London, 1, 0, 0; New York, 3, 4, 1.

Maxfield.—Local, 'of Maccles-field,' a town in co. Cheshire. In the Index to Earwaker's East Cheshire the author has 'Max-field ; see Macclesfield.'

1539. Bapt.—William, s. John Max-feild : St. Antholin (London), p. 1.
1608. Buried—John Maxfeild, *brasier*, dwellinge in Cornhill : Reg. St. Peter, Cornhill, i. 163.
London, 2; West Rid. Court Dir., 3; Manchester, 2; New York, 4; Boston (U.S.), 6.

May.—(1) Nick. 'the may,' a young lad or girl.

'Thou glory of womanhed, thou faire may.'
     Chaucer, C. T. 5271.
Richard le Mey, co. Hunts, 1273. A.
Bateman le May, co. Bedf., ibid.
Cristin le May, co. Camb., ibid.
Emma le May, co. Oxf., ibid.

(2) Bapt. 'the son of Matthew.' Just as the English form Matthew took the nick. Mat, so the French form Maheu took the nick. May. This was augmented into May-cock and May-kin ; v. Maycock and Makin.

Roger fil. Maye, co. Salop, 1273. A.
John fil. Maye, co. Linc., ibid.
Willelmus May, 1379: P. T. Yorks. p. 145.
May de Hindley, 1379: ibid. p. 278.
May Downe, 1370: ibid. p. 130.
London, 88; New York, 135.

Mayall, Mayhall, Mayell.—? Bapt. 'the son of Michael' (?) ; v. Miell.

1616. Bapt.—Ann, d. James Mayall: Kensington Ch. p. 18.
London, 1, 0, 5; Manchester, 5, 0, 0; Oldham, 7, 0, 0; Leeds, 0, 1, 0; New York, 0, 0, 1; Boston (U.S.), 8, 0, 0.

Maycock.—Bapt. 'the son of Matthew,' from the nick. May (v. May, 2), and with suffix May-cock ; cf. Wil-cock, Dan-cock, Jeff-cock, &c. In some parts of Lancashire and Yorkshire the form was Mycock and Mocock ; v. Mycock.

Hugh Maykoc, co. Bedf., 1273. A.
John Maykoc, co. Bedf., ibid.
Alicia Makok, 1379: P. T. Howden-shire, p. 15.
1578. William Macock, co. Warw.: Reg. Univ. Oxf. vol. ii. pt. ii. p. 82.
John Macocke, 1643 : Reg. St. Dionis Backchurch (London), p. 107.
1680. Thomas Maycocke and Joane Payne : Marriage Alleg. (Canterbury), p. 38.
London, 4; Oxford, 3; New York, 1.

Mayer.—Offic. 'the mayor'; v. Meyer.

London, 19; New York, 258; Boston (U.S.), 18.

Mayes.— Bapt. 'the son of Matthew,' from the nick. May; v. May and Mays.

Mayger.—Bapt.; v. Major.

1568. Buried — Arthure, son of John Mayger, *clothworker* : St. Mary Alder-mary, p. 137.
1570. — John, son of William Maygor : ibid. p. 138.
— — Thomas, son of John Maygor, *clothworker* : ibid.
London, 2; Philadelphia, 1.

Mayhew, Mayow, Mayo, Mayhow, Mayho.—Bapt. 'the son of Matthew,' from O.F.Mayheu. It was impossible to keep this surname from corrupted forms. There is probably no connexion with co. Mayo, Ireland, in any single instance.

Adam fil. Maheu, co. Camb., 1273. A.
Robert Maheu, co. Oxf., ibid.
Mayeu de Basingbourne, c. 1300. M.
Johannes Mahewe, 1379: P. T. Yorks. p. 125.
1537. Nicholas Mayowe, or Mayo, or Mayhewe: Reg. Univ. Oxf. i. 188.
1572. Elizabeth, d. of Nowell Mayhew : Reg. St. Columb Major, p. 8.
1580. James, s. of Nowell Mathew : ibid. p. 11.
1641. Married—John Mayhoe and Eliz. Beverley : Kensington Ch. p. 71.
London, 25, 0, 13, 0, 1; New York, 18, 0, 8, 0, 0.

Maykin.—Bapt. 'the son of Matthew'; v. Makin.

Leeds, 1.

Maylin.—Bapt. 'the son of Malin' (v. Mallinson). A variant.

1741. Married — Joseph Maylin and Sarah Leavesley: St. Antholin (London), p. 151.
London, 2; Philadelphia, 1.

Mayman.—Bapt. 'the son of Maymond.' From a forgotten name 'Maymond,' i.e. Magin or Main, *mighty*, and Mund or Mond, *protection*. For other forms, v. Maidment and Maidman ; for corruption into *-man*, cf. Wyman for Wymond, or Osman for Osmond. Mr. Lower has unfortunately permitted himself to write, 'Mayman, probably the superintendent of the sports of May-day': Patr. Brit. p. 221.

Maimon, prior of Castleacre, co. Norf., temp. 1200 : FF. viii. 375.
Lucia Meymund, co. Oxf., 1273. A.
Richard Meymund, co. Oxf., ibid.
Alice Maymund, co. Hunts, ibid.
Johannes Maymund, 1379: P. T. Yorks. p. 262.
Johannes Maymond, 1379: ibid. p. 266.
Willelmus Maymund, 1379: ibid. p. 257.

Two centuries later it is found in the last-named county as Mayman.

1541. Antony Mayman, co. York : W. 11, p. 228.
1616. Thomas Bond and Margaret Mayman, widow of John Mayman, *girdler* : Marriage Lic. (London), ii. 43.

Naturally this surname was imitated into Mammon.

1651. Married—John Billing and Margaret Mammon: St. Jas. Clerkenwell, i. 86.
London, 2; Dewsbury, 1; Philadelphia, 1.

Maynard.—Bapt. 'the son of Maynard' (Yonge, ii. 415).

Maynard de Abyngdon, vicar of Dersingham, co. Norf.: FF. viii. 399.
Maynard de Capella, co. Bucks, 1273. A.
Hugh Maynard, co. Oxf., ibid.
Robert Maignard, co. Wilts, ibid.
Henricus Manerd, 1379: P. T. Yorks. p. 119.
Johannes Manerd, 1379: ibid. p. 120.
1609. Married—Mathewe Staples and Alice Maynard: St. Thomas the Apostle (London), p. 11.
1647. — James White and Cathrine Mainard: St. Jas. Clerkenwell, iii. 81.
London, 23; Philadelphia, 9; Boston (U.S.), 76.

Mayne, Main, Maine, Mann, Manns, Manson.—(1) Bapt. 'the son of Mayne' (Yonge, ii. 415).

Radulphus fil. Main, Pipe Roll, 5 Hen. II.
Walterus fil. Main, ibid.
Matilda Meyn, co. Oxf., 1273. A.
1719. Bapt.—Mary, d. Thomas Manson: St. Jas. Clerkenwell, ii. 112.

(2) Local, 'from Maine,' the French province; v. Mann (2).

Walter de Man, co. Camb., 1273. A.
Joel de Meyn, co. Devon, ibid.
Roger de Magen, co. Hereford, Hen. III–Edw. I. K.
Cristiana de Manne, co. Hertf., 20 Edw. I. R.
Peter de Manne, co. Suff., Hen. III–Edw. I. K.
Johannes de Manne, 1379: P. T. Yorks. p. 212.
Johannes de Man, 1379: ibid. p. 233.

For another interpretation of Mann, v. Mann (1).

London, 5, 13, 4, 51, 1, 1; New York (Manne), 1; Philadelphia, 10, 10, 2, 0, 0, 0.

Mayo(w ; v. Mayhew.

Mayor.—Offic. 'the mayor'; v. Meyer.

Maypowder.—Local, 'of Maypowder,' a parish in co. Dorset.

John Maupudre, co. Soms., 1273. A.
Robert Maupudre, co. Camb., ibid.

Mays, Mayes, Mayse.—Bapt. 'the son of May'; v. May (2). This solution requires no proof. As William became, through its nick. Will, patronymically Wills and Wilson, so Matthew, through its nick. May, became patronymic-

ally Mays, or Mayes, or Mayse. The only difference is that Will is still a nick. of William, while May as a nick. of Matthew (through the O.F. Mayheu) is forgotten. v. Mayhew.

1542. Bapt. — Thomas, s. Richard Mays: St. Antholin (London), p. 3.
1619-20. Richard Mays and Ellen Richmond: Marriage Lic. (London), p. 83.
1655. Buried—Elizabeth Mayes: St. Antholin (London), p. 84.
1682. Married — John Clearke and Anne Mayes: St. Jas. Clerkenwell, p. 196.
London, 4, 11, 2; Philadelphia, 13, 1, 0.

Mayson.—(1) Bapt. 'the son of May'; v. May (2).

Cf. Willelmus Mayson, Wigglesworth, 1379: P. T. Yorks. p. 278.
Maye de Hindley, 1379: ibid.
Johannes Mayson, 1379: ibid. p. 204.
William Mayesone, C. R., 7 Edw. II.

(2) Occup. ; for Mason (1), q.v.

Adam de Mortan, mayson, 1371 : P. T. Yorks. p. 37.
1745. Married — Henry Mayson and Mary Joynes: St. Geo. Chap. Mayfair, p. 53.

Mayston, Maidstone.—Local, 'of Maidstone.' There can be no doubt that Mayston is a modern variant of Maidstone, a surname taken from the important town of that name in co. Kent. It is not likely that such a once familiar surname should leave but one representative in the London Directory. Besides, the corruption is a perfectly natural one, and found where we should expect to meet with it, viz. in London and the neighbourhood; v. Maidstone.

1666-7. John Tibbs and Margaret Maidstone: Marriage Lic. (Canterbury), ii. 96.
1696. Buried—Robert, s. Robert Maidston: St. Antholin (London), p. 111.
1733. Bapt.—Charlotte, d. Nathaniel Maidstone: St. Jas. Clerkenwell, ii. 211.
1745. Married—William Mayston and Easter Donfall: St. Geo. Chap. Mayfair, p. 55.
London, 4, 1.

Mazerer, Mazeliner.—Occup. 'the mazerer' or 'mazeliner,' a manufacturer of mazers or maslins, a bowl or cup maker; so called because made of maple, which is a knotted wood. 'Masar of woode, masière, hanap': Palsgrave. 'Mazer, a broad standing-cup': New World

of Words. Maslin was a dim., a cup of smaller size.

'They fet him first the swete win,
And mede eke in a maselin.'
Chaucer, C. T. 13781.

These bowls are frequently mentioned in early wills and inventories. In my old parish of Ulverston an ancestor of Chancellor Fell bequeathed (1542) 'A masser unto the saide Leonarde after the wedowheade or death of Ann, my wife' (v. my Chronicles of the Town and Church of Ulverston, p. 65). For general information, v. Way's note, Prompt. Parv. p. 328, and Skeat on mazer.

Adam le Mazerer, co. Northampt., 1273. A.
John le Mazerere. N.
William le Mazerer, London. X.
John le Mazelyner, c. 1300. M.
William le Mazeliner, London, 20 Edw. I. R.

Meacham, Mecham.—Local; v. Measham.

Meacock.—Bapt. 'the son of Matthew'; v. Maycock. Meacock is to Maycock as Meakin is to Makin.

1585. John Mecocke, co. Oxf.: Reg. Univ. Oxf. vol. ii. pt. ii. p. 144.
1670. Married—William Mecocke and Mary Fisher: St. Jas. Clerkenwell, iii. 174.
1788. — John Meacock and Amelia King: St. Geo. Han. Sq. ii. 12.
London, 5; New York, 1.

Mead, Meade, Meed, Meads.—Local, 'at the mead,' from residence thereby; M.E. mede, a meadow; v. Meadows and Medd.

William at Mede, 1278. M.
Nicholas atte Mede, co. Soms., 1 Edw. III: Kirby's Quest, p. 236.
Henry del Myde, co. Lanc., 20 Edw. I. R.
Alan atte Mede, C. R., 14 Edw. III. pt. ii.
Willelmus del Mede, 1379: P. T. Yorks. p. 214.
1552. Bapt.—Andrew Meade: St. Jas. Clerkenwell, i. 1.
1672. John Mede and Jane Wardour: Marriage Alleg. (Canterbury), p. 201.
London, 42, 2, 1, 2; Philadelphia, 46, 28, 0, 1.

Meadley.—Local; v. Medley.

Meadowcroft, Meddowcroft.—Local, 'of Meadowcroft'; v. Metcalf. The Lancashire Meadowcrofts appear to have originated at Meadowcroft, a small estate in the parish of Middleton, near Manchester.

Ricardus de Meducroft, 1379: P. T. Yorks. p. 54.
Willelmus Miducroft, 1379: ibid. p. 67.
Isabella Birch, of Meadowcroft, Middleton, 1615: Wills at Chester (1545-1620), p. 19.

The surname is found in the immediate neighbourhood in the 16th and 17th centuries.

Richard Meadowcroft, of Smethurst, 1581: Wills at Chester (1545-1620), p. 134.
Francis Meadowcroft, of Ratcliffe, 1616: ibid.

The above solution is amply proved by the following entries:

Nicholas de Meducroft, co. Lanc., 20 Edw. I. R.
Roger de Middelton, co. Lanc., ibid.
Adam de Rodees, co. Lanc., ibid.

Rhodes is close by Middleton. The three surnames occur together. The place is again referred to:

'John, son and heir of John de Radclif, of Chaderton, deceased, was born at Medecroft, on Monday before the Purification of the Virgin, 16 Ric. II': Baines' Hist. of Lancashire (Croston's edit.), iii. 97.

Manchester, 9, 1; London, 1, 0; Rochdale, 4, 0; New York, 1, 0; Philadelphia, 10, 0.

Meadows, Meadow.—Local, 'at the meadow' or 'meadows.' The final s is probably not plural, but that so common in local names of a distinctive and specific character; cf. Brooks, Styles, Bridges, Dykes, Sykes, &c. Possibly a patronymic s, as in Williams, Jones, Collins, &c.

John atte Medowe, rector of Metton, co. Norf., 1429: FF. viii. 140.
William att the Meadow, rector of East Beckham, co. Norf.: ibid. p. 87.
1689. Bapt. — William, s. Ralph Meadowes: St. John Baptist on Wallbrook, p. 170.
1719. Married — Philip Lynall and Barbara Medowe: St. Dionis Backchurch, p. 59.
London, 25, 0; Philadelphia, 3, 0.

Meadwell, Medwell.—Local, 'of Meadwell,' which I do not find. But v. Maidwell, of which it may be a variant.

Agnes de Meydewell, co. Oxf., Hen. III–Edw. I. K.
Alanus de Meydewelle, co. Bucks, ibid.
1629. Married — John Hutchens and Margeritt Medwell: St. Michael, Cornhill, p. 26.

1694. Thomas Templer and Eliz. Medwell, co. Northampt.: Marriage Lic. (Faculty Office), p. 212.
London, 1, 0; New York, 0, 1.

Meagre, Meager (?), Meagreman.—Nick. 'the meagre,' i.e. the lean, the poor. A sufficiently common sobriquet in the 13th and 14th centuries to ensure its becoming an hereditary surname; cf. Fatt.

Robert le Megre, C. R., 48 Hen. III.
Robert le Megre, co. Leic., Hen. III–Edw. I. K.
William le Megre, co. Oxf., 1273. A.
Hugh le Megre, c. 1300. M.
John le Meaugre. O.
Basilia le Megre. T.
Martin Megreman, C. R., 35 Hen. VI.
1420. John Megre: Cal. of Wills in Court of Husting (2).
1796. Married—Thomas Meager and Amy Hooker: St. Geo. Han. Sq. ii. 143.
London, 0, 3, 0; New York, 0, 1, 0.

Meagresauce.—Nick. One who gave scanty allowance (?). *Meagre*, thin, scanty; *sauce*, salted condiments. v. Meagre.

Peter Meagresause, co. Linc. R.

Meakin, Meakins.—Bapt. 'the son of Matthew'; v. Makin and Makins, of which these are but variations.

1729. Married—John Meakins, *Indian weaver*, and Rebecca Jones: St. Geo. Chap. Mayfair, p. 294.
1804. — Samuel Meakin and Mary Ann Kendal: St. Geo. Han. Sq. ii. 298.
London, 4, 1; Boston (U.S.), 0, 2.

Mealman, Mealmonger.—Occup. 'the meal-monger,' a dealer in meal; cf. Cornmonger.

William Meleman: Fines Roll, 8 Ric. II.
John le Melmongere. M.
1499. Geoffrey Meleman: Cal. of Wills in Court of Husting (2).

Meals.—Local, 'at the meols' (i.e. the sands or sand-banks), from residence thereby. On the Cumberland and Lancashire shores are several Meols—Eskmeols and Northmeols being instances. The word is styled Meales (temp. Jas. I; Lanc. and Ches. Records, pt. ii. p. 484) and Meeles (ibid. pt. i. p. 127).

Margery de Meoles, co. Soms., 1 Edw. III: Kirby's Quest, p. 207.
John de Meoles, co. Soms., 1 Edw. III: ibid. p. 208.
1605. Katherine Meoles, of Wallasey: Wills at Chester, i. 135.

1628. William Meoles, of Wallasey, *gent.*: ibid. ii. 152.
1636. John Meoles, of Newton, near Chester, *gent.*: ibid.
Liverpool, 2.

Mearbeck, Marbeck.—Local, 'of Mearbeck,' a hamlet in the parish of Settle, W. Rid. Yorks.

Willelmus de Merebeke, 1379: P. T. Yorks. p. 284.
Robertus Merebek, 1379: ibid. p. 287.
Petronilla Merbeke, 1379: ibid. p. 236.
1581. Married — William Grosse and Barbery Marbeck: St. Antholin (London), p. 28.
West Rid. Court Dir., 2, 0.

Mears, Meares.—Local, 'at the mere,' from residence by a pool, with s as customary suffix in local surnames of one syllable; cf. Holmes, Brooks, Briggs, Styles, Sykes, Milnes. Perhaps it represents the patronymic, as in Williams, Jones, Wilkins, &c. Then Mears = Mear's son.

Stephen atte Mere, co. Soms., 1 Edw. III: Kirby's Quest, p. 91.
Gregory de la Mere, co. Wilts, 1273. A.
William ad le Mere, co. Camb., ibid.
Robert atte Meere, C. R., 4 Hen. VI.
Henricus del Mere, 1379: P. T. Yorks. p. 210.
Alex. Atte-mere, rector of Ashwell Thorp, co. Norf., 1337: FF. v. 162.
Henry Meare, of Hough, 1673: Wills at Chester (1660-80), p. 183.
William Meare, of Pott Shrigley, 1673: ibid.
London, 18, 1; Philadelphia, 6, 2.

Measham, Meacham, Mecham.—Local, 'of Measham,' a parish in co. Derby.

London, 0, 0, 5; MDB. (co. Derby), 2, 0, 0; Manchester, 2, 0, 0.

Meatyard. — ? Nick. Until proved local this must be set down in the nickname class. Possibly from the straight back of the original possessor, or his occupation as a draper. The 'meteyard' was the old measuring-stick. 'Ye shall do no unrighteousness in judgement, in meteyard, in weight, or in measure': Lev. xix. 35. A.S. *metgeard*, a measuring rod; M.E. *meten*, to measure; hence to mete out, to distribute impartially. Yard (M.E. *yerde*), a stick, a rod. 'Nothing take ye in the weye, neither yerde, ne scrippe, neither breed, ne money' (Wyclif, Luke ix. 3); v. Skeat, s.v. *mete*; cf. Shakespear, Wagstaff, &c.

1618. Married—John Meatyarde and Anne King : Reg. Broad Chalke, co. Wilts, p. 4.
London, 2.

Medcalf, -calfe, Medcraft.— ? Local; v. Metcalf.

Medd, Meed.—Local, 'at the mead,' i.e. meadow (v. Mead), from residence thereby.

Richard atte Med, co. Oxf., 1273. A.
Philip atte Medde, 1278. M.
Thomas atte Mede : Lay Roll, co. Soms., 1327.
1684. Joseph Mede and Eliz. Dede: Marriage Alleg. (Canterbury), p. 173.
1791. Married—Alexander Macintosh and Eliz. Meed : St. Geo. Han. Sq. ii. 66.
London, 0, 1 ; Crockford, 3, 0 ; Philadelphia, 1, 0.

Medland.—Local, 'of Medland' or 'at the medland,' from residence beside some particular meadow-land ; v. Medd.

Walter de Medeland, co. Camb., 1273. A.
1768. Married—John Turner and Eliz. Medlond : St. Geo. Han. Sq. i. 172.
London, 3 ; Philadelphia, 1.

Medler, Medlar.—(1) ? Nick. An obtrusive person, a busybody.

Nicholas de Medler, co. Salop, 1273. A.

(2) Local, ' of Medlar,' a township in the parish of Kirkham, co. Lanc.

Richard de Medler, co. Salop, Hen. III–Edw. I. K.

Query : as both these instances (1) and (2) occur in co. Salop, is not instance (1) a misprint or misreading for *de* Medler ? Probably such is the case.

1640. John Hicks and Anne Medler (or Needler ?) : Marriage Lic. (London), ii. 250.
London, 1, 0 ; Philadelphia, 0, 4.

Medley, Meadley. — Local, (1) 'at the mid-ley,' from residence by the middle field ; (2) 'at the mead-ley,' from residence by the meadow pasture.

Simon atte Middele, co. Soms., 1 Edw. I : Kirby's Quest, p. 258.
1578. John Medley : Reg. Univ. Oxf. i. 364.
1792. Married — George Medley and Eliz. Constance : St. Geo. Han. Sq. ii. 84.
London, 1, 1 ; Philadelphia, 2, 0.

Medlicott, Medlycott.— Local, 'of Middle-cote'; cf. Middle-

ditch, &c., and v. Coates and Cotes. I have not discovered this locality, which I doubt not lies in co. Devon, or some adjacent shire.

Richard de Middelcote, co. Dev., 1273. A.
Katherine Medlecoate, married, 1593 : Reg. St. Mary Aldermary (London), p. 9.
1586. Bapt. — Mary, d. Christopher Medlicott : St. Thomas the Apostle (London), p. 11.
London, 4, 1 ; MDB. (co. Soms.), 0, 2.

Medpleck.—Local, 'at the meadow pleck.' ' *Pleck*, a plot of ground, a small enclosure, a field. Co. Warw.' (Halliwell). ' *Plecks*, a term in hay-making applied to the square beds of dried grass. Co. Chester' (ibid.). v. also *plack* and *plek* in Halliwell.

Jordanus atte Medpleck, co. Oxf., 1273. A.

Medwin.—Bapt. 'the son of Medwin.' One of the many personal names with suffix -win ; cf. Godwin, Unwin, Baldwin, and Goldwin. 'In the unreformed calendar the feast of St. Medwyn stands for Jan. 1' (Lower). 'St. Mawdwen (or Modwin) was one of St. Patrick's Irish nuns; another later Modwin, also Irish, came to England in 840, and educated Edith, daughter of King Ethelwolf, and founded an abbey at Polsworth' (Yonge, ii. 135).

Modewine, wife of Clement Cotton, C. R., 3 Edw. IV.
1787. Married—John Morris and Patty Medwin: St. Geo. Han. Sq. i. 399.
London, 4.

Mee, Mees, Meeson, Meese. —? Bapt. 'the son of Matthew' (?). This surname is quite beyond me. I can only suggest that as May, Makin, and Maycock (q.v.) represented Matthew, and as Makin and Maycock are generally found as Meakin and Mcacock, so Mee may be also a variant of May. There is no doubt that Matthew, through the O.F. Mayheu, which was popularized in England, had many nick. forms, some of which are now obsolete. The favourite was May, and this would have variants. All this is corroborated by the existence of Mees and Meeson, corresponding to Mayes and Mayson. Circum-

stantial evidence, therefore, is entirely in favour of the above suggested solution.

1608. Robert Meese, co. Oxf. : Reg. Univ. Oxf. vol. ii. pt. ii. p. 302.
William Mee, of March Croft, co. Lancaster, 1613 : Wills at Chester (1545–1620), p. 135.
Hugh Mee, 1615: ibid.
1642. Henry Meese, of Brockhurst, in Pennington: St. Jas. Clerkenwell, ii. 152.
1691. Bapt.—Mary, d. Thomas Meeson : ibid. p. 339.
London, 6, 1, 2, 0 ; Manchester, 8, 0, 1, 0 ; Philadelphia, 2, 1, 0, 0 ; New York, 5, 0, 0, 2.

Meed.—Local ; v. Mead, Medd.

Meek.—Nick. 'the meek '; cf. Humble. 'Meke and mylde' : Prompt. Parv.

Alicia Meke, *laborer*, 1379 : P. T. Yorks. p. 223.
1692. Married—John Martin and Jane Meek : St. Antholin (London), p. 107.
1697. Anthony Meek and Eliz. Cook : Marriage Lic. (London), ii. 322.
London, 16 ; Manchester, 3 ; New York, 9.

Meggett, Meggott. — Bapt. 'the son of Margaret,' from nick. Meg, and dim. Megg-ot or Megg-et ; v. Maggot.

Robertus Meggot-son, 1379 : P. T. Yorks. p. 119.
1677. Married—George Meggott and Mary Crosse : St. Jas. Clerkenwell, i. 185.
1705. Robert Meggott and Patience Holt : Marriage Lic. (London), ii. 334.
London, 1, 0 ; Boston (U.S.), 1, 0.

Meggs, Meggeson, Megson, Meggy.—Bapt. 'the son of Margaret,' from nick. Megg, popularly Meggy ; v. Moxon.

John fil. Megge, co. Oxf., 1273. A.
Robert Megge, co. Bedf., ibid.
John Megge, co. Berks, ibid.
Adam Meggessone, c. 1300. M.
Johannes Mekson, 1379 : P. T. Yorks. p. 216.
Robertus Megson, 1379 : ibid. p. 157.
Johannes Megson, 1379 : ibid.
1578. William Megges and Alice Banckes : Marriage Lic. (London), i. 79.
1735. Married—John Megson and Ann Harrison : St. Jas. Clerkenwell, iii. 263.
London, 4, 1, 1, 2 ; Philadelphia (Meggs), 1 ; New York (Megson), 1.

Megucer.—Occup. 'a leather dresser'; Fr. *mégissier*, a tawer of leather; v. Whittawer or Whittier. According to Strype, the London 'Company of Megusers' dealt in the skins of dead horses, and flayed them. He mentions 'Walter le Whitawyer' in the same account (London, ii. 232).

John le Megucer : Munimenta Gild-hallae Londoniensis.
Richard le Megucer : ibid.
1272. Norman le Meggecer : Cal. of Wills in Court of Husting.

Meiklejohn, Meiklejon. — Nick.' big John'; one of the Scottish Border names. M.E. *mikel*. Cf. Littlejohn.

Cf. 'To Mickle Willie, £2 0s. 0d., April 23, 1607': Nicolson and Burn, Hist. Westm. and Cumb., vol. i. p. cxx.
'Mekill Henry Nikson,' 1516 : TTT. p. 207.
'Mekle Johne Burne in Branxhelm,' 1495 : ibid. p. 188.
London, 1, 0 ; Boston (U.S.), 0, 1.

Melhuish, Melluish, Mellish, Meluish.—Local, 'of Melhuish,' a place in co. Devon.

'Chagkford, xii¹; Churiton, vi¹; Eghbeare, xii¹; Melehewis, xii¹; Foleford, vi¹': Hundred Rolls, 1273, i. 84.
William de Melehywis, co. Devon, Hen. III–Edw. I. K.
John de Melewis, co. Devon, ibid.
Elinora de Melhywys, co. Devon, 1273. A.
1674. Married—Robert Mellish and Anne Smith : St. Michael, Cornhill, p. 40.

Driving through Dalton-in-Furness in Oct. 1887, I saw 'Mellish' over a small shop in the Market-place. I wondered how it had got there. The mystery was easily explained. The town is largely peopled with Cornishmen, who work at the iron-ore mines.

London, 8, 1, 8, 1 ; MDB. (co. Devon), 15, 0, 0, 0 ; Boston (U.S.), (Mellish), 5.

Melladew ; v. Merridew.

Melling.—Local, 'of Melling': (1) an extensive parish in North Lancashire, six miles from Kirkby-Lónsdale ; (2) a chapelry in the parish of Halsall, six miles from Ormskirk. This has manifestly been the chief source.

Robertus Mellyng', 1379 : P. T. Yorks. p. 113.
Richard Mellinge, 1602 : Guild Rolls, Preston, p. 62.
Alexander Mellinge, fil. ejus, 1602 : ibid.
Reginald Melling, of Liverpool, 1572 : Wills at Chester (1545-1620), p. 135.
John Melling, of Chorley, 1614 : ibid.
John Melling, of Skelmersdale, parish of Ormskirk : ibid.

John Melling, of the parish of Mellinge, 1583 : Lancashire Wills at Richmond, p. 194.
Robert Melling, of Hallett, parish of Melling, 1622 : ibid.
Manchester, 3 ; Liverpool, 8 ; Preston, 10 ; Philadelphia, 7 ; Boston (U.S.), 2.

Mellody, Mellodey, Melody, Melledy.—(1) ? Nick. The same as Mellodew. All the forms are confined to cos. Lanc. and York, where 'Merydewe' existed in the 14th century ; v. Merridew.

'Margaret Mellodey took Bishop's prize for religious knowledge': Manchester Courier, June 7, 1886.

(2) ? Nick. for a singer or minstrel; M.E. *melodie*, an air, a tune.

Richard Melodie, co. Oxf., 1273. A.
1550. Married—William Spencer and Margaret Mellody : St. Peter, Cornhill, i. 222.
Liverpool, 1, 0, 0, 0 ; Blackburn, 1, 0, 0, 0 ; New York, 0, 0, 1, 0 ; Boston (U.S.), 0, 0, 3, 5.

Mellor, Meller.—(1) Local, 'of Mellor,' a chapelry in the parish of Glossop, near Manchester. (2) Local, 'of Mellor,' a township in the parish of Blackburn, co. Lanc. (3) Occup. 'the miller,' q.v.

Hugo Bell, *meller*, 1379 : P. T. Yorks. p. 75.
Willelmus de Meller, 1379 : ibid. p. 177.
1588. Edward Mellor, of Oldham : Wills at Chester, i. 135.
1603. Eliz. Mellor, of Mottram : ibid.
1677. Charles Wynne and Eliz. Meller : Marriage Alleg. (Canterbury), p. 192.
London, 6, 3 ; Manchester, 40, 2 ; New York, 3, 7.

Melton.—Local, 'of Melton,' parishes in cos. Suffolk, Norfolk, W. Rid. Yorks, Leicester, and Lincoln.

John de Melton, co. Norf., 1273. A.
Nicholas de Melton, co. York, ibid.
Adam de Meltone, co. Suff., ibid.
Ricardus de Melton, *souter*, 1379 : P. T. Yorks. p. 301.
Henricus de Melton, 1379 : ibid. p. 74.
1593. Married—Geo. Melton and Ann Cannings : St. Antholin (London), p. 36.
1596. Buried — Alice, wife of Steven Melton : St. Jas. Clerkenwell, iv. 58.
London, 2 ; MDB. (co. Suff.), 1 ; Philadelphia, 2.

Memory.—Local. A variant of Mummery (q.v.), which is a variant of Mowbray. There can be no question as to the correctness of this solution; it is simply imitative.

1589. Christopher Membrey, or Membrye, of Corpus : Reg. Univ. Oxf. ii. 93.

1730. Bapt.—Eliz., d. Samuel and Rachael Memory : St. Jas. Clerkenwell, ii. 192.
1756. Married — John Membery and Jane Bottomley : St. Geo. Han. Sq. i. 63.
1759. — Samuel Memory and Mary Taylor : ibid. p. 87.
1784. — John Brittain and Margery Memorey : ibid. p. 356.
New York, 1.

Mendfault.—Nick. A complimentary sobriquet that does not seem to have descended to many generations ; M.E. *faute*, a fault.

1416. Walter Mendfaute, co. York : W. 11, p. 19.

Mercer, Mercier. — Occup. 'the mercer,' a dealer in clothes ; Fr. *mercier*, a draper.

Jordan de Mercer, co. Linc., 1273. A.
Adelard le Mercer, co. Oxf., ibid.
Ketel le Mercer, co. Camb., ibid.
Johannes Payge, *mercer*, 1379 : P. T. Yorks. p. 79.
Thomas Mercer, 1379 : ibid. p. 170.
1694. Bapt.—Success, son of Thomas Mercer : St. Michael, Cornhill, p. 157.
London, 19, 3 ; New York, 18, 2.

Merchant.—Occup. 'the merchant'; v. Marchant. From the rarity of this form it is clear that while as a dictionary word and in a commercial sense *merchant* has gained the superiority, as a surname Marchant has never lost its original hold ; cf. Clark, the surname, and *clerk*, the occupative term.

Beneyt Mercator, co. Camb., 1273. A.
1563. Buried—Roger Merchant : St. Thomas the Apostle (London), p. 86.
1697. Samuel Howard and Eliz. Merchant : Marriage Lic. (London), p. 322.
London, 2 ; New York, 9 ; Boston (U.S.), 9.

Meredith, Meredyth.—Bapt. 'the son of Meredith' (Welsh) ; v. Merridew.

Meredydd, son of Bleddyn : Freeman's Norman Conquest, iv. 675.
Meredydd, son of Gruffydd : ibid. p. 183.
Meredydd, son of Owen : ibid. p. 503.
Meredith ap Eynon, 1322 (co. Glamorgan). M.
Meredith Walshman, 1431 : Toulmin-Smith, Old Birmingham, 1864, p. 80.
1575. Richard Meredith, co. Radnor : Reg. Univ. Oxf. vol. ii. pt. ii. p. 68.

I remember seeing a curious pun in an epitaph in Marshfield Church, recorded by Rudder in his Hist. Gloucestershire. The monument is to the memory of A. Meredeth. A rhyming epitaph ends thus:

'Judge, then, what he did lose who lost but breath,
Lived to die well, and dyed *A Meredeth*.'

London, 27, 0; MDB. (co. Ches.), 5, 1; New York, 10, 0; Philadelphia, 54, 0.

Merrall, Merrell, Merrill.—Bapt. 'the son of Muriel.' From an early period there was a disposition to pronounce this name Meriel or Merrell.

Muriel Manekyn, co. Norf., 1273. A.
Matilda Miriel, co. Camb., ibid.
Henry fil. Mirield, co. Linc., ibid.
Robert fil. Muriel, co. Hunts, ibid.
Thomas fil. Muriel, co. Salop, ibid.
Richard Miriel, co. Norf., ibid.
1550. Married—Jeames Meriall and Margaret Shingleton: St. Antholin (London), p. 8.
1593. Buried—Nicholas Meriall: St. Peter, Cornhill, i. 143.
Meryell, d. of Sir John Burton: Visit. Yorks. 1563, p. 116.
Meryell, d. of Sir Hugh Hastings: ibid. p. 113.
'Merriall Saltonstall, aged 22, and her daughter Merriall, aged nine months, embarked in the Suzan for New England in the year 1635': Hotten's Lists of Emigrants, p. 59.
London, 1, 6, 2; New York, 1, 1, 51.

Merrick, Meyrick.— Bapt. 'the son of Merick.' Probably a variant of Almerick; v. Amery. Miss Yonge connects Meyrick, Merrik, and Merich with Almeric (Hist. Christian Names, ii. 259, and v. Glossary).

Henry Meriche, 1379: P. T. Yorks. p. 237.
Johannes Miricheson, 1379: ibid. p. 241.
Meurik de Hope, Hen. III-Edw. I: K. p. 45.
1550. Bapt.—William Mericke: St. Peter, Cornhill, i. 5.
1563. Buried—Anthonye Meryck: St. Michael, Cornhill, p. 185.
1582. Maurice Merricke, or Mayrick, or Maericke, New Coll.: Reg. Univ. Oxf. vol. ii. pt. ii. p. 118.
1610. Richard Merrick and Martha Tither, alias Walker: Marriage Lic. (Westminster), p. 18.
London, 8, 3; New York, 12, 0.

Merridew, Melladew, Mellodew, Merriday.—? Bapt. 'the son of Meredith.' An early English corruption, also a well-recognized Irish form of the same. The corruptions of this North-English surname, besides those recorded above, are Malledew, Mallalieu, Mellody,

and Mellodey, q.v. The following entries concerning the same individual are interesting as bearing on the point:

1596. Bapt.—Sybell, d. John Meredithe: St. Michael, Cornhill, p. 100.
1598. — Phillipe, s. John Meredaye: ibid. p. 101.
1599. — John, s. John Meredaye: ibid.
Thomas Merydewe, 1379: P. T. Yorks. p. 58.
Johannes Meridewe, 1379: ibid. p. 57.

The two entries following are very decisive:

1680. Bapt.—George, s. George and Eliner Merideth: St. Jas. Clerkenwell, i. 291.
1682. — Mary, d. George and Eliner Meriday: ibid. p. 301.
1711. — John, son of John Merryday: ibid. ii. 60.
London, 1, 1, 0, 0; Oldham, 0, 0, 6, 0; Philadelphia (Mellodew), 1.

Merrifield, Merrefield, Merryfield.—(1) Local, 'of Merevale,' a parish near Atherstone, co. Leicester. A corruption; cf. Tubberfield for Tubberville; v. Merrifill, infra. (2) Local, 'of Merryfield' probably for Maryfield. Mr. Lower (Patr. Brit. p. 223) says, 'The site of Salisbury Cathedral is so called in mediaeval documents, being a corruption of St. Mary's Field.' Other spots might easily be so called.

John de Merefeld, co. Soms., 1273. A.
Lovecok de Murifield, co. Soms., 1 Edw. III: Kirby's Quest, p. 174.
1582. Married—Richard Merefeild and Sislie Skeles: St. Mary Aldermary (London), p. 7.
1584. — Edward Merefeeld and Annes Foden: St. Peter, Cornhill, i. 234.
1756. — William Merryfield and Maria Harpley: St. Geo. Han. Sq. p. 65.
1781. Nicholas Merrifill (co. Worc.) and Mary Wright: ibid. p. 325.
London, 2, 0, 0; Crockford, 0, 1, 0; New York, 4, 1, 0; Boston (U.S.), 13, 0, 0; Philadelphia (Merryfield), 1.

Merriman, Merryman. — Nick. 'the merry man,' one of a joyous, festive disposition. In proof of the familiarity of this sobriquet I may remind the reader of the dog's name in the Taming of the Shrew:

'Huntsman, I charge thee, tender well my hounds:
Trash Merriman, the poor cur is emboss'd.'　　Induction, Scene 1.

For an opposite characteristic, v. Muddeman.

Adam Myryman, 1379: P. T. Yorks. p. 211.
William Merryman. F.
John Meryman, co. York. W. 15.
Gerard Merriman, co. York. W. 16.
1684. Married—John Merryman and Hester Poole: St. Michael, Cornhill, p. 44.
1778. — Thomas Jesson and Mary Merryman: St. Geo. Han. Sq. i. 285.
London, 12, 1; New York, 0, 1; Philadelphia, 1, 2; Boston (U.S.), 4, 0.

Merriott; v. Meryett.

Merritt, Merrett.—Local, 'of Merriott,' a parish in co. Somerset. As Merrett it still lives in that shire; v. Meryett for early instances.

1753. Married—Robert Merritt and Jane Backhouse: St. Geo. Chap. Mayfair, p. 245.
1808. — Silas Merritt and Sarah Mansell: St. Geo. Han. Sq. ii. 382.
London, 9, 6; MDB. (co. Soms.), 0, 1.

Merry.—Nick. 'the merry'; v. Merriman. M.E. *merie*, *mirie*, and *murie* (Skeat).

John le Mirie, co. Oxf., 1273. A.
Geoffrey le Mirie, co. Kent, ibid.
John Merie, co. Norf., ibid.
William Merrye. Z.
1625. Bapt. — Sammuell, s. Audrian Merry: St. Antholin (London), p. 59.
1663. Thomas Clarke and Eliz. Merry: Marriage Alleg. (Canterbury), p. 97.
London, 12; New York, 8; Boston (U.S.), 9.

Merrycock. — Nick. 'merry fellow.' Cock, a pert, lively young lad; v. Cock.

Richard Merricocke, rector of Flordon, co. Norf., 1555: FF. v. 73.

Merryman.—Nick. 'the merry man'; v. Merriman.

Merrymouth.—Nick. 'a ready laugher,' one given to merriment.

John Merrymouth. V.
Richard Merymouth. X.

Merryweather, Meryweather, Merewether, Mereweather.—Nick. 'merry weather'; a happy, genial, sunshiny fellow; a colloquial expression. Nothing to do with a wether sheep. Cf. Fairweather, used in exactly a similar sense, and still existing as a surname. 'Fayre, mery wedur or tyme (fayir as wedyr, K.), *amenus*': Prompt. Parv. 'Myry weder, or softe weder, *malacia*' (ibid.). Merry is here used in the sense of pleasant. Way adds a quotation from Vegecius, attributed to Trevisa, Roy. MS. 18 A. xii, where it is observed that wise warriors in olden times used to 'occupie theire foot menne in dedes of armes in the felde in mery wedire,' i.e. fair weather (v. Way's edit. Prompt. Parv.). As a surname it occurs, among some other fictitious characters, in one of the Coventry Mysteries, where mention is made of

'Bontyng the Brewster, and Sybyly Slynge,
Megge Mery-wedyr, and Sabine Sprynge.'
Andrew Muriweder, co. Oxf., 1273. A.
Thomas Murweder, co. Camb., ibid.
Henry Muriweder. O.
1617. Married — Thomas Church and Francis Merryweather : St. Peter, Cornhill, i. 250.
1667. John Ferris and Jane Merrywether (co. Wilts) : Marriage Alleg. (Canterbury), p. 134.
London, 8, 1, 2, 0 ; Crockford, 1, 0, 4, 1 ; Philadelphia (Merryweather), 1.

Merton.—Local, 'of Merton,' parishes in cos. Oxford, Devon, Norfolk, and Surrey. This surname is a proof how names rise and fall. There is but one solitary representative in the London Directory. It was familiar in its day, and one Oxford college will for ever preserve it from obscurity. The first two instances probably refer to Marton in the W. Rid. Yorks :

Alicia de Merton, 1379 : P. T. Yorks. p. 256.
Thomas de Merton, 1379 : ibid.
John de Merton, co. Oxf., 1273. A.
William de Merton, co. Wilts, ibid.
Walter de Merton, co. Norf., ibid.
Richard de Merton, co. Hertf., 20 Edw. I. R.
1759. Bapt.—Ann Theodosia, d. Luke Merton : St. Peter, Cornhill, ii. 48.
London, 1.

Mervin, Mervyn ; v. Marvin.

Meryett, Merriott.—Local, 'of Merriott,' a parish in co. Somerset, in the union of Chard ; v. Merritt.

John de Meriet, co. Linc., 1273. A.
Simon de Meriet, co. Soms., ibid.
Hugo de Meriet, co. Soms., Hen. III-Edw. I. K.

John de Meryet, co. Soms., 1 Edw. III : Kirby's Quest, p. 93.
George de Meriet, co. Soms., 1 Edw. III : ibid.
1799. Married — James Merriett and Mary Crick : St. Geo. Han. Sq. ii. 205.
1802. — Richard Meryett and Jane Dew : ibid. p. 267.
London, 1, 0 ; MDB. (co. Somerset), 0, 3.

Messenger, Massinger, Messinger.—Occup. 'the messenger'; M.E. *messager*; cf. *passenger* for *passager*, Pottinger for Potager, Clavinger for Claviger, &c.

'Item, to Owen Whitstones, messagier, xls. ' : 1503 (Privy Purse Exp. Eliz. of York. p. 100).
'Of April that is messager to May.'
Chaucer, C. T. 4427.
Reginald le Messager, co. Norf., 1273. A.
Jacob le Messager, co. Soms., ibid.
Thomas le Messager, co. Camb., ibid.
Ricardus le Messager, 12 Edw. II : Freemen of York, i. 18.
Richard le Messager, co. Soms., 1 Edw. III : Kirby's Quest, p. 205.
William Messanger, 1379 : P. T. Yorks. p. 293.
Richard Messanger, C. R., 20 Hen. VI.
1636-7. Thomas Messenger and Jane Underwood : Marriage Lic. (London), p. 229.
1693. Bapt.—William, s. Eliz. Messinger : St. Jas. Clerkenwell, p. 351.
London, 13, 1, 0 ; Boston (U.S.), 22, 1, 13.

Messer.—Occup. 'the messer.' An old and very common entry for a mower (v. Mawer), harvester, or reaper.

John le Messer, co. Camb., 1273. A.
Adam le Messor, co. Oxf., ibid.
Milo le Messer, co. Bedf., ibid.
William le Messor, co. Suff., ibid.
1658. Married—Robert Boskitt and Mary Messer : St. Jas. Clerkenwell, iii. 100.
1771. — Thomas Messer and Elizabeth Denn : St. Geo. Han. Sq. i. 215.
London, 10 ; Oxford, 3 ; Philadelphia, 6.

Metcalf, Metcalfe, Medcalf, Medcalfe, Medcraft, Meadowcroft.—? Local. I feel assured the name is local, and that it is a modification of Medcroft or Medcraft (v. Craft and Croft, and cf. Calcraft and Calcroft), of which an instance still remains in the London Dir. Mead and meadow as double forms still exist. M.E. *mede*, a grassfield, so called because mowed (Skeat). Metcalf and Turnbull were great Yorkshire names. I have seen them side by side in

Yorkshire records of 500 years ago. Horace Smith still keeps them in company :
'Mr. Metcalf ran off on meeting a cow, With pale Mr. Turnbull behind him.'
Willelmus Miducroft, 1379 : P. T. Yorks. p. 67.
Ricardus de Meducroft, 1379 : ibid. p. 54.
Nicholas de Meducroft, C. R., 7 Edw. III. pt. ii.
Nicholas de Meducroft, co. Lanc. 20 Edw. I. R.
Miles Metkalff : Patent Roll, 1 Hen. VII.
James Medcalfe, 1570 : Reg. Univ. Oxf. i. 279.
Mark Meadcalfe, 1568 : ibid. p. 271.
It is a remarkable fact that I cannot find Metcalf in the Yorks. P. T. of 1379. But the Meducrofts are there. Probably the corruption had not yet taken place ; cf. Duncalf and Duncuft, i.e. Duncroft (?), also Crostkalf infra.
Agnes de Crostkalf (i. e. Crosscroft ?), 1379 : P. T. Yorks. p. 127.
London, 5, 22, 14, 1, 1, 1 ; New York, 13, 7, 0, 0, 2, 0, 1.

Meth, Methe.—Nick. 'the methe,' i. e. courteous. '*Methe*, courteous' (Halliwell). 'Thou was methe and mee' (ibid.).
'Alle that meyné mylde and meth Went hem into Nazareth.'
Cursor Mundi, Halliwell.
Henry Methe, co. Suff., 1273. A.
John Methe, co. Salop, ibid.
1616. Bapt.—Anne, d. Thomas Mythe : St. Jas. Clerkenwell, i. 76.
New York, 2, 1.

Methley.—Local, 'of Methley,' a village situate between Leeds and Pontefract.
Ricardus de Methelay, *souter*, 1379 : P. T. Yorks. p. 80.
Emma de Methlay, 1379 : ibid. p. 94.
Johannes de Methlay, *tayllour*, 1379 : ibid. p. 95.
West Rid. Court Dir., 1 ; Sheffield, 1 ; London, 1.

Methven, Methuen, Methwin.—Local, 'of Methven,' a parish in co. Perth.
1618. Anthony Methwin, *cler.*, co. Soms. : Reg. Univ. Oxf. vol. ii. pt. ii. p. 368.
1677. Paul Methwen and Deborah Hough : Marriage Lic. (London), ii. 301.
London, 3, 0, 0 ; Boston (U.S.), 2, 1, 0.

Meuse ; v. Mewze.

Mew.—Nick. 'the mew,' a sea-mew, a gull ; v. Seafowl.
John le Mew, C. R., 20 Edw. I.

William le Mewe, co. Soms., 1 Edw. III : Kirby's Quest, p. 192.
Johannes Mewe, et Agnes uxor ejus, 1379 : P. T. Yorks. p. 118.
1625. Buried—Ellen Mew : Kensington Ch. p. 107.
1687-8. John Blanch and Hannah Mew : Marriage Alleg. (Canterbury), p. 42.
London, 4 ; Boston (U.S.), 1.

Mewett.—(1) Bapt. 'the son of Matthew,' from nick. Mew (i.e. Mahew), dim. Mewot. (2) ? Nick. ; perhaps a dim. of Mew ('the mew'), q.v.
Richard Mewot, co. Hunts, 1273. A.
1804. Married—Geo. Mewitt and Mary Sturt : St. Geo. Han. Sq. ii. 314.
London, 1.

Mewse, Meuse.—? Local, ' of Meux ' (?), a township in the parish of Waghen, E. Rid. Yorks. The evidence below seems to confirm this view:
William de Mewse, 1379 : P. T. Yorks. p. 146.
John de Mewhes, 1379 : ibid. p. 147.
These individuals are found on the borders of the East Riding.
1685. Charles Hances and Ann Meux : Marriage Alleg. (Canterbury), p. 222.
1692. Rannulph Mewsse and Ann Lee : ibid. p. 226.
London, 0, 1 ; Philadelphia, 1, 0 ; New York, 5, 0.

Meyer, Mayer, Mayor.—Offic. 'the mayor'; M.E. maire, a mayor. Generally these names in the London Directory are of modern German importation. Germ. meier, a bailiff, steward, farmer, mayor ; cf. Fr. Lemaire ; Dutch Meyer. v. Mair.
David le Meir, co. Linc., 1273. A.
William Mair, co. Camb., ibid.
Willelmus Meyre, 1379 : P. T. Yorks. p. 37.
Matilda Mayre, laborer, 1379 : ibid. p. 219.
1586. Christopher Maier, co. Durh. : Reg. Univ. Oxf. vol. ii. pt. ii. p. 150.
London, 29, 19, 6 ; Sheffield, 1, 0, 4 ; New York, 560, 124, 0.

Meyler.—Bapt. 'the son of Meyler.' Found in the Welsh Principality and on the English border.
Meyler, canon of St. David's, 1202 : Hist. and Ant. St. David's, p. 364.
Nicholas ap-Meyler, canon of St. David's, 1222 : ibid.
Meyler de Stretton, co. Salop, 1273. A.
Henry Meyler, co. Salop, ibid.
Walter Meyler, co. Salop, ibid.
Robert fil. Meilir, co. Salop, ibid.

1764. Married—Richard Henessy and Margaret Meyler : St. Geo. Han. Sq. i. 131.
MDB. (co. Pembroke), 5 ; South Wales Court Dir., 3 ; Narberth, S.W., 2 ; New York, 1.

Meyrick ; v. Merrick.

Miall.—Bapt. 'the son of Michael'; v. Miell.
1798. Married—Thomas Young and Hannah Miall : St. Geo. Han. Sq. ii. 182.
London, 4.

Michael, Michaels, Michaelson.—Bapt. 'the son of Michael,' more commonly Mitchell, q.v.
Hugh fil. Micahel, co. Linc., 1273. A.
Roger Michel, co. Norf., ibid.
Michael de Audewarp, 1379 : P. T. Yorks. p. 73.
Sometimes, perhaps, a foundling name :
1657. Bapt. — Peregrinus Michael, a foundling in this parish : St. Michael, Cornhill, p. 141.
London, 5, 3, 2 ; New York (Michaelson), 7 ; Boston (U.S.), 4, 0, 1 ; Philadelphia, 37, 22, 0.

Michell.—Bapt. 'the son of Michael,' q.v. A variant, like Mitchell, q.v.
Robert Michel, co. Oxf., 1273. A.
Walter Michel, co. Camb., ibid.
Johannes Michell, 1379 : P. T. Yorks. p. 253.
Johannes Michol', 1379 : ibid. p. 43.
1578. Married—William Smyth and Margery Michell : St. Jas. Clerkenwell, i. 7.
1645. Bapt.—Eliz., d. William Michill : Kensington Ch. p. 35.
London, 15 ; New York, 1.

Michelthwaite, Mickelthwaite, Micklethwait, Micklethwaite.—Local, ' of Micklethwaite,' part of the township of Bingley, co. York; also 'of Micklethwaite,' a village in the same parish.
Adam de Mekkelhawayth, 1379 : P. T. Yorks. p. 84.
Magota Mekkelwayth, 1379 : ibid.
Johanna de Mickilwayte, 1379 : p. 80.
William de Mickilwayte, 1379 : ibid.
1615. Paul Muclethwait : Reg. Univ. Oxf. i. 359.
1690. Joseph Micklethwait and Frances Johnson : Marriage Alleg. (Canterbury), p. 162.
1691. Nathaniel Micklethwaite and Sarah Sutton : ibid. p. 191.
West Rid. Court Dir., 1, 1, 3, 5.

Micklewright. — Nick. 'the mickle wright,' i.e. the big wright.

Evidently a North-English or Border surname ; cf. Meiklejohn.
1619. George Durye, fletcher, and Sibell Michaelwright : Marriage Lic. (London), p. 78.
1692. Married—Timothy Michelwright and Mary Brittaine : St. Jas. Clerkenwell, iii. 212.
Manchester, 1.

Midday ; v. Midnight.

Middle.—(1) Local, ' of Middle, a parish in co. Salop, eight miles from Shrewsbury.
Richard le (de ?) Midel, co. Oxf., 1273. A.
(2) Local, 'at the middle,' i.e. the middle house, field, farm, &c.
Robert atte Midle, co. Soms., 1 Edw. III : Kirby's Quest, p. 80.
Henry atte Middel, co. Soms., 1 Edw. III : ibid. p. 108.
London, 2.

Middleditch.—Local, 'at the middle dike,' from residence thereby.
1590. Bapt. — Roberte, s. Richard Myddleditche : St. Michael, Cornhill, p. 96.
1646. Elizabeth Middleditch : St. Mary Aldermary (London), p. 20.
1808. Married—William Middleditch and Ann Mills : St. Geo. Han. Sq. ii. 394.
London, 1 ; New York, 2.

Middlehurst.—Local, 'at the middle hurst,' i.e. wood, from residence thereby ; cf. Midwood. Both belong to the North.
1610. Alice Middlehurst, of Grappenhall : Wills at Chester, i. 135-6.
1615. John Middlehurst, of Latchford : ibid.
Liverpool, 2 ; Manchester, 1.

Middlemass, Middlemiss, Middlemist, Middlemost.—(1) Bapt. or nick. 'Michaelmas'; cf. Candlemas, Pentecost, Whitsunday, Christmas, Nowell, Saturday, &c., from the day or season whereon or wherein the child was born. The evidence in favour of this origin is sufficiently strong, although I suggest another interpretation infra. For one thing we find one undoubted instance :
1547. Shorman Myglemas : Churchwarden's Accounts, Ludlow (Camd. Soc., v. Index).
Michaelmas was commonly so pronounced. In the Treatise of Fishing with an Angle, in the St.

Alban's Book, the following are given as baits for roach in July, 'the not worme, and mathewes, and maggotes tyll Myghelmas': Sign. i. ii (v. Prompt. Parv. p. 331, *n.*). For further proof v. Mighill. From Migglemas to Middlemas would be an easy transition. The final *t* in Middlemast and Middlemost would thus be excrescent.

(2) Nick. or local, 'the middlemost,' i.e. the middle one in the family, or the middle house in a row of cottages, 'at the middlemost.' We find this somewhat uncouth superlative in Ezek. xlii. 5, 'the middlemost of the building.' Still earlier, c. 1450, we find it in some curious nursery lines upon the fingers (v. *fingers*, Halliwell), wherein the little finger is styled 'litylman,' and the longest 'longman.' 'Longman hat the mydilmast, for longest fynger hit is.'

1694. Married—Moses Pearepoint and Mary Midlemass: St. Jas. Clerkenwell, iii. 214.
1709. — Searles Middlemas and Elizabeth Court: Canterbury Cathedral, p. 69.
London, 3, 2, 3, 0 ; West Riding Court Dir., 0, 2, 0, 3 ; New York, 1, 1, 0, 0.

Middleton.—Local, 'of Middleton,' i.e. the middle town, or farmstead; v. Town. There are several dozen places, larger or smaller, scattered up and down England of this name.
Richard de Midelton, co. Bucks, 1273. A.
Thomas de Middilton, co. Linc., ibid.
Gilbert de Middelton, co. York, ibid.
Johannes de Midillton, 1379 : P. T. Yorks. p. 286.
Thomas de Midilton, 1379 : ibid.
Ricardus de Midilton, 1379 : ibid. p. 263.
1580. Christopher Middelton, co. Ches. : Reg. Univ. Oxf. vol. ii. pt. ii. p. 94.
London, 34 ; New York, 27.

Midgall.—Local, 'of Midghall,' some small spot near Preston, co. Lanc., which I have not as yet been able to identify.
Edward Midghall, of Goosnargh, 1662 : Lancashire Wills at Richmond, i. 195.
Anne Midgehall, of Blackehale, *widow*, 1612 : ibid.
Preston, 1.

Midgley, Midgely.—Local, 'of Midgley,' a village five miles from Halifax, W. Rid. Yorks. This sur-

name has ramified strongly in the surrounding district. Under heading of 'Migelay' (i.e. township) occurs :
Ricardus de Migeslay, 1379 : P. T. Yorks. p. 188.
Johannes Migeslay, 1379 : ibid.
1595. Richard Midgley, of Dinkerley : Wills at Chester, i. 136.
1788. Married—Thomas Midgley and Sarah Price: St. Geo. Han. Sq. ii. 10.
London, 1, 0 ; West Rid. Court Dir., 20, 0 ; New York, 1, 0 ; Worcester (U.S.), 14, 3.

Midnight.—Nick. It is curious to note that both Midday and Midnight were early surnames.
Elena Mydnyght, 1379 : P. T. Yorks. p. 200.
Adam Midday, bailiff of Norwich, 1335 : FF. iii. 98.
Roger Midday, bailiff of Norwich, 1348 : ibid. p. 99.
Boston (U.S.), 1.

Midwinter.—Bapt. 'the son of Midwinter.' Christmas and Noel were in common use as names for children born at this season. Midwinter was a synonym. 'The sheriffs, by the custom of the city, do ride to several parts thereof every year, betwixt Michaelmas and Midwinter, that is Yoole' (Hist. and Ant. York, ii. 54). Robert of Gloucester says that the Conqueror purposed 'to midwinter at Gloucester, to Witesontid at Westminster, to Ester at Wincester.' Cf. Yool and Youle.
Gounilda Midewynter, co. Oxf., 1273. A.
John Midewynter, co. Soms., 1 Edw. III : Kirby's Quest, p. 220.
William Mydwynter, C. R., 14 Hen. IV.
John Mydwinter. H.
1688. Bapt. — Mary, d. Thomas Midwinter : St. Jas. Clerkenwell, ii. 329.
This surname occurs constantly in Kirby's Quest (co. Soms.), quoted above.
London, 3.

Midwood, Middlewood.—Local, 'at the middle wood,' from residence thereby ; cf. Middlehurst.
Johannes de Middelwode, 1379 : P. T. Yorks. p. 55.
Willelmus Midrewode, 1379 : ibid. p. 161.
Manchester, 3, 1 ; Philadelphia, 2, 0.

Miell, Mihell, Myhill.—Bapt. 'the son of Michael.' Mihell was a common form of this popular

name, even when the proper orthography was preserved.
'At Michael's term had many a trial,
Worse than the Dragon and St. Michael.'
Hudibras, pt. iii. canto 2.
1626. Married—Thomas Yearly, of Sant Mihills in Cornhill : Reg. St. Dionis Backchurch (London), p. 22.
A castaway called, no doubt, after the patron saint of the parish, is thus entered in the baptisms of St. Michael, Cornhill :
1585. Joane Myhell, a foundling : St. Antholin (London), p. 93.
1549. Bapt. — Richard, s. Mihill Cristen : ibid. p. 7.
— Married — Mihill Assherst and Christian Bowen : ibid.
1770. — James Kay and Priscilla Miell : St. Geo. Han. Sq. i. 301.
There are many corruptions of this surname, as for instance, Miall, Mayall, Mayell, q.v.
London, 3, 3, 1.

Mighill.—Bapt. 'the son of Michael,' popularly called Mighel, often softened to Miell, q.v. 'Mighell = Michael' : Palsgrave. Mihill is very common in old writers.
'The sothfastenes and nothing hele,
That thou herdest of seynt Myghele.'
Cursor Mundi, Halliwell.
1598. Married—Mighell Axendall and Marye Wall : St. Mary Aldermary (London), p. 9.
1626. Francis Bevis and Margaret Mighell : Marriage Lic. (London), i. 173.
1789. Married — Philip Mighell and Sarah Bolton : St. Geo. Han. Sq. ii. 21.
For further proof, v. Middlemass.
Worcester (U.S.), 1.

Milbank, Millbank.—Local, 'of the mill-bank,' one who resided on the slope of the mill ; v. Mill and Miller. Perhaps in some cases the 'meol-bank,' i.e. the sandbank (?) ; v. Meals, and cf. the first entry following :
1621. Married — John Barker and Isabell Mealebanke : St. Jas. Clerkenwell, i. 49.
1685. John Milbanke and Margaret Lane : Marriage Alleg. (Canterbury), p. 209.
1804. Married — John Gardner and Eliz. Milbank : St. Geo. Han. Sq. ii. 304.
London, 3, 1 ; New York, 5, 2.

Milburn, Milborn, Milbourn, Milbourne.—Local, ' of Milburn,' a chapelry in the parish of Kirkby Thore, co. Westm. ; also two townships in co. Northumberland, in the parish of Ponteland. It is evidently to the latter we owe the surname with its variants.

Margaret de Milleburn, co. Northumb., Hen. III–Edw. I. K.
1594. Robert Milborne: Reg. Univ. Oxf., i. 354.
1662. Thomas Milburne and Winifred Francis: Marriage Alleg. (Canterbury), p. 54.
1679. Edward Milbourne and Mary Kemp: ibid. p. 8.
1683. Alex. Milbourn and Eliz. Watson: ibid. p. 142.
London, 3, 1, 3, 4; MDB. (co. Northumberland), 7, 0, 0, 0; New York, 2, 0, 0, 0; Philadelphia, 7, 0, 0, 2.

Mildmay.—Nick. 'the mild-maiden'; M.E. *may*, maid; v. Sadmay and May. Mild-maiden was from the earliest times a title given to the Blessed Virgin.

1546. Walter Myldmay and Mary Walsyngham: Marriage Lic. (London), i. 7.
1548. Edward Mylmaye and Joanna Awparte, ibid. p. 13.
1616. Thomas Mildmay and Anne Savile: ibid. ii. 49.
1744. Carew Hervey Mildmay (co. Somerset) and Edith Phillips: St. Geo. Han. Sq. i. 32.
Crockford, 4.

Mildred.—Bapt. 'the son of Mildred,' a fairly popular fontal name in the 13th and 14th centuries.

Melred Forest', 1170: KKK. vi. 16.
Maldred de Glentendon, 1187: ibid. vi. 41.
Robert fil. Meldredi, 1196: ibid. vi. 56.
Robert fil. Mildred, 37 Hen. III. BBB. p. 54.
William Mildrede, C. R., 4 Hen. VI.
1611. Married—John Lowdell and Isabell Mildred: St. Dionis Backchurch, p. 17.
1686. Bapt.—Anne, d. John Mildred: St. Jas. Clerkenwell, ii. 316.
London, 2.

Miles, Myles.—Bapt. 'the son of Miles'; v. Mills (2). This is still a popular personal name in North England.

William fil. Milon', co. Bedf., 1273. A.
Milo le Messer, co. Bedf., ibid.
Peter Myles, co. Kent, ibid.
Wychard Miles, co. Linc., ibid.
1584. Alex. Miles, co. Northampton: Reg. Univ. Oxf. vol. ii. pt. ii. p. 135.
1694-5. Lewis Myles, co. Pembr.: ibid. p. 281.
London, 76, 1; New York, 59, 6.

Milestone.—Local, 'of Milston,' a parish two miles from Amesbury, co. Wilts. 'Milestone, from resi-

dence near one': Lower. History, I believe, has not recorded that milestones were in use in the 13th century.

Richard de Mildestane, co. Wilts, 1273. A.
London, 2.

Milford.—Local, 'of Milford,' parishes in diocs. Winchester, York, and Southwell; also Milford Haven, in dioc. St. David's, Wales; also Long Melford, in dioc. Ely. In all cases probably the mill-ford, the mill by the ford; cf. Mulford.

John de Milforde, co. York, 20 Edw. I. R.
William de Melford, co. Camb., ibid.
Ralph de Milford, co. York, 1273. A.
Adam de Milford, co. Suff., ibid.
Hugh de Meleford, co. Suff., ibid.
Johannes de Milforth, 1379: P. T. Yorks. p. 215.
Adam de Milforth, 1379: ibid.
1618. George Milforde, co. Wilts: Reg. Univ. Oxf. vol. ii. pt. ii. p. 367.
London, 8; New York, 3.

Milkandbread.—Nick.; cf. Milksop.

William Milkanbred, 11 Edw. I.
Walter, s. William Milk-and-bred, ibid.

Unfortunately, G. H. D., who communicated these and other curiosities in nomenclature to N. and Q. (Jan. 24, 1857), did not furnish his authorities.

Milker.—Occup. 'the milker,' a milkman.

Thomas le Milkar, co. Salop, 1273. A.
William Milkar, co. Oxf., ibid.
William le Milker, co. Soms., 1 Edw. III: Kirby's Quest, p. 183.
Henry Mylker, 1379: P. T. Yorks. p. 79.
1273. William le Melker: Cal. of Wills in Court of Husting.

Milksop, Milsop, Mellsop.—Nick. 'the milksop,' a soft, effeminate kind of fellow.

'To wed a milksop, or a coward ape.' Chaucer, C. T. 13916.

Oddly enough this sobriquet continued as a surname till the middle of the last century, and as Milsop probably still lives.

Roger Melkesopp, co. Bucks, 1273. A.
Robert Mulksop, co. Oxf., ibid.
John Milesop, co. Oxf., ibid.
William Milksop, c. 1300. M.
William Milksop. J.
Hugh Milkesop. RR. 1.

Exactly three centuries after the instances in A. we find the name in the same district:

1572. James Edwards, of Reading, and Dionise Milkesopp, *spinster*, of St. Albans, Herts: Marriage Lic. (London), i. 53.

Later we find representatives in the metropolis:

1620. Buried—John, s. Thomas Milksopp: St. Thomas the Apostle (London), p. 111.
1621. Bapt. — Thomas, s. Thomas Melksopp: ibid. p. 45.

In the last century the family had contrived to get rid of the *k*.

1736. Bapt.—Mary, d. Robert Milsop: St. Jas. Clerkenwell, p. 225.

This curious and interesting surname still thrives in the United States as Mellsop.

Worcester (U.S.), 0, 0, 2.

Mill—Local, 'at the mill,' from residence thereby (v. Miln, Milnes, and Mills, 1).

Roger atte Mille, co. Oxf., 1273. A.
John del Mill, c. 1900. M.
Hugh Atte-myll, rector of Gillingham, co. Norf., 1349: FF. viii. 12.
William Atte-Mylle, rector of Mundford, co. Norf., 1412: ibid. ii. 247.
1612. William Mill and Eliz. Greene: Marriage Lic. (London), ii. 16.
1633. Pointz Mill and Eliz. Wright: ibid. p. 213.

Mill is now an extremely scarce surname, Mills having become the accepted form. This final *s* is common in monosyllabic local surnames; cf. Holmes, Sykes, Brooks, Lowndes, Knowles, &c.

London, 1; Philadelphia, 4.

Millage, Milledge. — Local, 'of Milwich,' a parish in co. Stafford (Lower).

1666. Matthias Melledge and Mary Ryal: Marriage Alleg. (Cant.), p. 122.
1690. Bapt. — William, s. William Millage: St. Jas. Clerkenwell, ii. 336.
London, 1, 1.

Millard.—Offic.; v. Millward.

Millbank; v. Milbank.

Millen.—Local, 'de Millen,' probably of Dutch origin. The bearer settled in London in the 16th century.

1583. Buried—Alexsander de Millen, *stranger*: St. Dionis Backchurch, p. 198.
1584.—William, s. Alexander Millen: ibid.
London, 5; New York, 13; Philadelphia, 6.

Miller.—Occup. 'the miller,' one who grinds corn, a 'milner' (q.v.), a surname found in the records of every county in England.

John le Mellere, c. 1300. M.
Adam le Molendinator, co. Oxf., 1273. A.
Achard Molendinarius, co. Hunts, ibid.
Wymund Molendinarius, co. Soms., 20 Edw. I. R.

Molendinarius is a very frequent entry in the Hundred Rolls (A.), but, oddly enough, no instance is given in English.

1572. George Miller, co. Warwick: Reg. Univ. Oxf. vol. ii. pt. ii. p. 54.
London, 198; New York, 1,100.

Millerson.—Nick. 'the miller's son'; cf. Taylorson, Smithson, Wrightson, Hindson, and Herdson, but this class of names is distinctly small. Possibly Milson and Millson are so originated. The surname was still in existence in the last century.

William fil. Molendinarii, co. Camb., 1273. A.
Henry fil. Molendinarii, co. Hunts, ibid.
Gilbert Millerson, co. York. W. 3.
Thomas Milnerson, 1379: P. T. Yorks. p. 279.
Ricardus Milnerson, 1379: ibid. p. 56.
John Milnerson, of Ulverston, 1589: Lancashire Wills at Richmond, i. 196.
William Milnerson, of Sowtergate, in Ulverston, 1605: ibid.

The variants in the Ulverston parish church registers are Milnerson, Millerson, Milerson, and Mellerson. All the entries relate to one family. One of the latest references is:

1727. Married — Thomas Millerson and Dorothy Gibson: Reg. Ulverston, p. 373.

Millett, Millet, Millot. — Bapt. 'the son of Mille,' (1) i.e. Miles, from dim. Mill-ot, or Mil-ot, or (2) perhaps from Mille, the nick. of Millicent, a popular girl's name in the 13th and 14th centuries, especially in Yorkshire. This again would become as dim. Mill-ot, or Mil-ot, just as in the same county Margaret gave us Magot and Magotson, and Matilda Tillot and Tillotson, the one from the nick. Magg, the other from the nick. Till. On the whole it is probable that Millicent is the parent.

Richard fil. Milot. MM.
Roger Millot, co. Notts, 1273. A.

John Milot, co. Hunts, 1273. A.
Willelmus Melot, 1379: P. T. Yorks. p. 23.
Johannes Millot, 1379: ibid.
Rogerus Millotson, 1379: ibid. p. 19.
Matilda Millot, 1379: ibid.

The last two instances are together.

Thomas Mylett, co. York. W. 9.

Members of the same family are found thus entered:

John Mylote, co. Durham, temp. 1380. QQQ. ii. 153.
William Melot, co. Durham, 1433: ibid.
Robert Millot, co. Durham, 1512: ibid.
1696. Married — William Millett and Beatre Vodell: St. Michael, Cornhill, p. 49.
London, 3, 0, 0; New York, 4, 6, 3.

Millhouse.—Local, 'at the mill-house,' the cottage where the miller lived, close beside the mill, or the body of the mill itself. 'Myllehowse, *molendina, molendinum*': Prompt. Parv.

John de Molendino, co. Oxf., 1273. A.
William de Molendino, co. Oxf., ibid.
1624. John Milnhouse, James Citty, Virginia: Hotten's Lists of Emigrants, p. 219.
London, 3; Philadelphia, 5.

Millicent, Millisent.—Bapt. 'the son of Millicent' (Yonge, ii. 257-8).

Joan fil. Milicente, co. Bucks, 1273. A.
Peter Milisent, co. Salop, ibid.
Millesenta Cruche, co. Norf., ibid.
William Millecent, C. R., 29 Edw. III.
Mylisant Wyfe, 1379: P. T.Yorks. p. 88.
John Myllicent, bailiff of Yarmouth, 1549: FF. xi. 327.
'The story of Sir John Millicent that would have had a patent from King James for every man to have had leave to have given him a shilling': Pepys' Diary, Aug. 8, 1662.
1583. Married — Richard Davis and Millysent Leather: St. Jas. Clerkenwell, p. 9.
1717. Bapt.—Mary, d. John Millissent: St. Jas. Clerkenwell, iii. 99.
London, 1, 1.

Millichamp, Millichap. — Local, 'of Millichamp,' seemingly a Norman name, like Beauchamp. Millichap is one more instance of the tendency of a surname to corrupt when it passes the border of the county of its original settlement.

1620. William Millichap, or Millechappe, or Millichamp, co. Salop: Reg. Univ. Oxf. vol. ii. pt. ii. p. 383.

1774. Married — Richard King and Mary Milchup: St. Geo. Han. Sq. i. 244.
1795. — Henry Draper and Ann Millichamp: ibid. ii. 126.
MDB. (co. Salop), 3, 0; (co. Hereford), 0, 1.

Millikin, Milliken. — Bapt. 'the son of Milligan.' Looking at the large contingent of persons bearing this name in the States, it is safe to conclude that it is simply a sharpened form of the Irish Milligan. The only evidence of a personal name with the suffix *-kin* (as in Jenkin) is furnished below. But it is an isolated instance, and probably came from the Low Countries:

John Mulkyn, co. Suff., 1273. A.

The following entry, however, practically settles the question, being the halfway house between Milligan and Millikin:

1798. Married — John Chandler and Susanna Millican: St. Geo. Han. Sq. ii. 189.
London, 2, 1; New York, 2, 18; Philadelphia, 4, 20.

Millington.—Local, 'of Millington.' There is a parish in co. York of this name. Millington has been an East Cheshire surname for centuries. This name arose from Millington, an estate near Bowdon, co. Ches. It has always kept itself in view in South Lanc. and on the Cheshire border.

Hugh de Mulynton, 1400: East Ches., ii. 59.
Roger de Mulynton, 1401: ibid. p. 9.
'John Millington, of Millington, near Bowdon,' c. 1530: ibid. p. 256.
1606. Married — Robert Milligeton and Ann Wodd: Reg. Prestbury Ch., Ches., p. 172.
1608. James Millington, of Knutsford: Wills at Chester, i. 136.
1615. Margerie Millington, of Chelford, widow: ibid.
Manchester, 3; London, 7; New York, 2; Philadelphia, 4.

Millman; v. Milman.

Millmaster. — Offic. 'the manager of a mill'; v. Millward.
'Mr. Andrew Milmaster, of the Old Jewry, died Aug. 23, 1630': Smith's Obituary.

Mills.—(1) Local, 'at the mill,' from residence thereby. There is a column of Mills in the London Directory. A large number of these are local in origin. The final *s* (probably genitive) is common to all monosyllabic local surnames; cf. Brooks, Briggs, Styles, Dykes, Holmes, &c. For instances, v. Mill and Miln.

(2) Bapt. 'the son of Miles,' a once popular font-name, or 'the son of Millicent,' from the nick. Mille, or Milly; v. Milson.

Margery Mylys, co. Camb., 1273. A.
1645. Bapt. — Ann, d. Anthony Mills : St. Jas. Clerkenwell, i. 161.

The name is so universal that modern instances are needless.

West Rid. Court Dir., 16; London, 144; New York, 14.

Millward, Milward, Millard.—Official, 'the mill-ward,' the keeper of the mill ; M.E. *melle, mulle*, and *mulne*. As with *miller* even now, so *mill* then meant always a place for grinding corn ; cf. Milman, Millmaster, and Windmilward, q.v. Millard is a modified form.

'Manumissio Thomae Haale, alias dicti Mylleward de Hextone,' 1480 : XX. 2, p. 210.
Richard Muleward, C. R., 12 Ric. II.
Walter le Meleward. N.
Robert le Muleward, co. Hunts, 1273. A.
William le Milward. G.
1662. John Milward (co. Derby), and Mary Corderoy : Marriage Alleg. (Canterbury), p. 80.
1677. Henry Plumtree and Joyce Millward : ibid. p. 272.
1696. Married — Richard Millard and Mary Rhymes : St. Dionis Backchurch (London), p. 45.
London, 4, 7, 29; New York, 1, 0, 15; Philadelphia, 9, 0, 20.

Milman, Millman.—Occup. 'a millward' ; v. Millward.

William Meleman, Close Roll, 13 Ric. II. pt. i.
1563. Buried — Harry Milman : St. Antholin (London), p. 15.
1564. Married — Nicholas Bridgman and Als (Alice) Milman : ibid. p. 17.
1791. Married — Thomas Andrews and Sarah Milman : St. Geo. Han. Sq. ii. 56.
London, 2, 1; New York, 1, 1; Philadelphia, 0, 9.

Miln, Milne, Milnes, Milns.—Local, 'at the mill' ; A.S. *myln*, a mill ; Latin *molina* ; v. Milner. The final *s* is common in these local surnames; cf. Brooks, Holmes, Styles, Knowles, &c.

Thomas atte Milne. B.
Petrus atte Milne, 1379 : P. T. Yorks. p. 41.
Johannes de Milne, 1379 : ibid. p. 287.
Thomas atte Milne, 1379 : ibid. p. 254.
Robertus del Milne. 1379 : ibid. p. 169.
1766. Married — William Nicol and Eliz. Milne : St. Geo. Han. Sq. i. 150.
1785. — Robert Shore Milnes and Charlotte Frances Bentinck : ibid. i. 380.
London, 1, 23, 4, 1; West Rid. Court Dir., 0, 3, 18, 1; New York, 1, 12, 0, 0; Boston (U.S.), 1, 2, 2, 0.

Milner.—Occup. 'the milner,' the more correct form of miller, which has slipped the *n*; A.S. *myln*, a mill; Latin *molina*. Mulliner (London Directory) is probably a reminiscence of 'mulnere,' although it may be a corruption of Molineux.

Robert le Melner, co. Derby, 1273. A.
Alan le Milner. G.
William le Melner, c. 1300. M.
Emmot Mylner, co. Yorks. W. 9.
'William Bannester, *miluer*, 1397': Preston Guild Rolls, p. 1.
Robertus Mylner, 1379 : P. T. Yorks. p. 131.
Henricus Tele, *milner*, 1379 : ibid p. 265.
London, 16; New York, 4; Philadelphia, 15.

Milnes ; v. Miln.

Milsom.—Bapt. (1) 'the son of Miles'; (2) 'the son of Millicent' (v. Milson, 3). The change from Milson to Milsom finds many parallels; cf. Ransom for Ranson, or Hansom for Hanson.

1763. Married — William Milsom and Sarah Staples : St. Geo. Han. Sq. i. 119.
1773. — John Saunders and Eliz. Millsum : ibid. p. 231.

The more correct form is found in the same register :

1777. Married — John Millson and Hanna Hyatt : ibid. p. 278.
London, 4; New York, 1.

Milson, Millson.—(1) Local, 'of Milson,' a parish in co. Salop, near Cleobury-Mortimer. (2) Bapt. 'the son of Miles,' a popular font-name in the surname period. (3) Bapt. 'the son of Millicent' (q.v.), early modified into Milson, or from the nick. Milly, whence Millison. Of these three (1) has had little influence. The real contest lies between (2) and (3), and doubtless both have contributed their due share.

Reginald fil. Militis, co. Hunts, 1273. A.
Robert fil. Militis, co. Hunts, ibid.

Amongst the inhabitants of Leeds were :

Thomas Milsson, 1379 : P. T. Yorks. pp. 214-5.
Elisota Milesson, *mayden*, 1379 : ibid.
1601. Henry Myleson, of Sutton : Wills at Chester, i. 140.
1606. William Myleson : ibid.

Of distinct connexion with Millicent, we have the following :

Iveta Milsent, co. Camb., 1273. A.
1577. Bapt.—Mylson, d. Henrie Gwynnowe : Reg. St. Columb Major, p. 10.
1584. — Mylson, child to young Cocker : ibid. p. 12.
1601. — Mellison, d. David Fyne : ibid. p. 20.

Further proof of Millicent's relationship to this name is seen from several registers :

Ann Millison, co. York. W. 16.
1689-90. Gabriell Millison, of Greenwich, and Ruth Day : Marriage Alleg. (Canterbury), p. 137.
1701. Married — Thomas Millison and Sarah Bills : Canterbury Cathedral, p. 66.
London, 1, 1; Philadelphia, 3, 0; Boston (U.S.), 0, 1.

Milsted.—(1) Local, 'of Milstead,' a parish in co. Kent. (2) Local, 'of Minstead,' a parish in dioc. Winchester. The change from *n* to *l* is too common in the dictionary and directory to need illustration.

Richard de Minsted, co. Bucks, 1273. A.
1763. Married—Francis Milstead and Ann Holmes : St. Geo. Han. Sq. i. 116.
London, 3; New York, 1; Philadelphia, 1.

Milthorp, Milthorpe.—Local, (1) 'of Milnethorp,' a hamlet in the parish of Sandal Magna, near Wakefield, W. Rid. Yorks; cf. Mill and Miln; (2) a market-town in the parish of Heversham, co. Westm. The former seems to have been parent of the name.

Geoffrey de Milnethorp, co. Linc., 1273. A.
Robertus de Milnethorp, 1379 : P. T. Yorks. p. 83.
Joanna Milnethorp, 1379 : ibid.
West Rid. Court Dir., 1, 1.

Milton.—Local, 'of Milton.' About thirty parishes of this name occur in Crockford, representing England alone. Smaller spots bearing the same name must be common. The 'mill-town' would naturally be a frequent local sobriquet. Cf. Milford.

Alan de Miltone, co. Hunts, 1273. A.
Hugh de Miltone, co. Oxf., ibid.
Gregorius de Multon, co. Camb., ibid.
Agnes de Multon, co. Norf., ibid.
Thomas de Multon, 1379 : P. T. Yorks. p. 294.
Isabella de Melton, 1379 : ibid. p. 301.

It is unnecessary to furnish modern instances.

London, 15 ; New York, 5.

Milverton.—Local, ' of Milverton,' two parishes, one in co. Somerset, the other in co. Warw.

1751. Married—Thomas Bird and Eliz. Pitt Milverton : St. Geo. Han. Sq. i. 53.
MDB. (co. Dorset), 1.

Miner, Minor.—Occup. ' the miner,' an excavator. 'And thereupon anon he bad His minours for to go and mine' : Gower, C. A. ii. 198 (Skeat).

Benedict le Mineur, C. R., 33 Hen. III.
1275. John le Minour : Cal. of Wills in Court of Husting.
Richard le Minour : co. Soms., 1 Edw. III : Kirby's Quest, p. 205.
1690. Bapt. — Easter, d. Nathaniel Minor : St. Jas. Clerkenwell, i. 334.
1760. Married — James Mineur and Eliz. Barrow : St. Geo. Han. Sq. ii. 91.
Boston (U.S.), 30, 8.

Minett, Minnitt, Minet, Minnot.—? Bapt. Lower says, ' French Protestant refugees after the Rev. of the Edict of Nantes.' But the surname existed earlier.

John Mynot, cos. Warw. and Notts, 1273. A.
Nicholaus Mynyot, 1379 : P. T. Yorks. p. 91.
1579. —— Minet, co. Glouc. : Reg. Univ. Oxf. vol. ii. pt. ii. p. 87.
1749. Married—Benjamin Minnitt and Mary Veale : St. Geo. Han. Sq. i. 42.
1770. — Martin Manney and Margaret Minnett : ibid. p. 197.
London, 3, 1, 0, 0 ; New York, 1, 0, 1, 1.

Minister, Minster. — Local, ' at the minster,' i.e. monastery ; cf. Westminster. Not a minister, an attendant, as stated by Lower. Minister is imitative.

Thomas de Mynistre, Close Roll, 45 Hen. III.
Haldanus Minister, co. Norf., 1273. A.
1768. Married — Thomas Minster, co. Oxf., and Ellen Prichard : St. Geo. Han. Sq. i. 171.

London, 2, 0 ; MDB. (co. Norfolk), 1, 0 ; (co. Warwick), 0, 1 ; Philadelphia, 5, 10.

Minn, Minns.—Bapt. 'the son of Min.' There is some evidence in favour of an old personal name Min, which was probably a nick. Minnie is still used as a girl's pet name for Emmeline. The existence of Minson strongly favours this view. Further it must be remembered that Emmeline was a very popular girl-name in the hereditary surname period, and must have had a nick.

1541. Buried—John Myn, servant to Mr. Gammadge : St. Antholin (London), p. 3.
1595. Married — William Mynne and Anne Phenney : St. Jas. Clerkenwell, p. 19.
1748. — Joseph Gant, or Grant, and Ann Mins : ibid. p. 279.
1793. — Robert Minson and Ann Dakins : St. Geo. Han. Sq. ii. 98.
London, 2, 5 ; New York, 2, 0 ; Boston (U.S.), 0, 3.

Minshall, Minshull.—Local, ' of Minshull,' now Church Minshull, a parish five miles from Nantwich, co. Chester. Minshall is a South-English variant, and seems to have arisen in the 18th century.

William Mynshull, co. Ches., 1359 : East Cheshire, ii. 160.
Thomas Minshull, of Eaton, Tarporley, 1580 : Wills at Chester (1545-1620), p. 137.
Ralph Minshull, of Minshull, 1602 : ibid. p. 137.
1746. Married — Richard Davies and Eliz. Minshull : St. Geo. Han. Sq. i. 37.
1765. — Nathan Minshall and Esther Clench : ibid. i. 144.
London, 2, 3 ; Manchester, 0, 6 ; New York, 1, 2.

Minskip.—Local, ' of Minskep,' a township in the parish of Aldborough, W. Rid. Yorks.

Sheffield 1.

Minster ; v. Minister.

Minstrel.—Occup. or offic. ' the minstrel.'

William le Menestral, Close Roll, 30 Edw. I.

Minter.—Occup. ' the minter,' a mint-master ; v. Monier, Moneymaker, Moneyman. The reason why these surnames are found scattered over the country lies in the fact that the greater lords, and more considerable cities, had power to issue coin.

Henry le Munetar, co. Salop, 1273. A.
Geoffrey Monetare, co. Salop, ibid.
William Monetaris, co. Salop, ibid.
Ralph le Myneter. N.
Theobald Monetarius, cos. Notts and Derby, Hen. III-Edw. I. K.
1723. Bapt. — Mary, d. Claudius Minter : St. Jas. Clerkenwell, ii. 140.
1781. Married—John Davis and Mary Minter : St. Geo. Han. Sq. i. 323.
London, 9 ; Boston (U.S.), 1.

Mintern, Minterne, Minturn.—Local, ' of Mintern,' two parishes (Magna and Parva) in co. Dorset. In the form of Minturn the name is fairly thriving in the U.S.

1575. John Mintorne, co. Dorset : Reg. Univ. Oxf. vol. ii. pt. ii. p. 66.
1610. Robert Minterne, co. Dorset, ibid. p. 314.
1672. Thomas Rosse and Mary Minterne, co. Soms.: Marriage Lic. (Faculty Office), p. 123.
1750. Married — John Mintern and Rebeckah Roden : St. Geo. Chap. Mayfair, p. 180.
1752. — Thomas Mintren and Sarah Watson : ibid. p. 212.
London, 1, 0, 0 ; MDB. (co. Dorset), 2, 2, 0 ; New York, 0, 0, 10.

Minting.—Local, ' of Minting,' a parish in co. Linc., about six miles from Horncastle.

(Prior) de Mintinge, co. Linc. 1273. A.
London, 1.

Minton.—Local, ' of Mindtown,' a parish five miles from Bishop's Castle, co. Salop. Probably also some smaller spot in co. Northumberland. But this family name has sprung from Shropshire.

Jordan de Minton, co. Northumberland, 1169. KKK. vi. 14.
Peter de Mineton, cos. Salop and Staff., Hen. III-Edw. I. K.
1744. Married — Samuel Minton and Ann Grimsley : St. Geo. Chap. Mayfair, p. 42.
1796. — Francis Minton and Lucy Coleman : St. Geo. Han. Sq. ii. 150.
London, 10 ; MDB. (co. Salop), 8 ; New York, 16.

Mintsmith.—? Occup. 'a maker of coin,' a minter ; v. Minter.

John le Mynsmith, c. 1300. M.

Mirfield.—Local, ' of Mirfield,' a parish near Dewsbury, W. Rid. Yorks.

Thomas de Mirfield, et Alicia uxor ejus, 1379 : P. T. Yorks. p. 80.
Johannes de Mirfeld, et Agnes uxor ejus, 1379 : ibid. p. 179.

Willelmus de Mirfeld, *chivaler,* of Mirfeld', 1379 : ibid. p. 180.
West Rid. Court Dir., 2.

Mirfin.—Bapt. ; v. Marvin.

Mirrorer.—Occup. 'the mirrorer,' a maker of looking-glasses. The manufacture seems to have been confined to London, where, as the centre of fashion, we should naturally expect to see it.

Crispian le Mirorer, London, 1273. A.
John le Mirorer. H.
Richard le Mirourer, London. X.

Misselbrook.—Local, 'of Misselbrook.' I cannot find the spot.

1575. Edward Miselbroke, New Coll. : Reg. Univ. Oxf. iii. 76.

Also found spelt as Missilbrooke, Mistilbrooke, Misselbroke, and Mislebrough.

1751. Married — Stephen Misslebrook and Mary Gough : St. Geo. Chap. Mayfair, p. 191.
London, 1.

Missenden.—Local, 'of Missenden.' Great and Little Missenden are parishes in co. Bucks ; also Missenden, a hamlet in the parish of Hitchin, co. Hertford.

Roger de Messindene, co. Bucks, 1273. A.
Hugo de Messenden, co. Northampt., Hen. III–Edw. I. K.
Roger de Messingeden, co. Middlesex, ibid.
1727. Married — William Smith and Sarah Musseldine : St. Jas. Clerkenwell, iii. 254.
1783. Married—George Missildine and Eliz. Adams : St. Geo. Han. Sq. i. 348.
London, 1.

Misson, Mizen, Mizon, Musson.—Local, 'of Misson,' a parish near Bawtry, co. Notts ; v. also Musson.

Hugo Mussun, co. Notts, Hen. III–Edw. I. K.
1697. Married — Jerimiah Myson and Susanna Darlow : St. Antholin (London), p. 111.
1753. Bapt.—George, s. Thomas Misen : St. Geo. Chap. Mayfair, p. 11.
1770. Married — Thomas Argill and Mary Misson : St. Geo. Han. Sq. i. 194.
1780. — George Musson and Ann Matthews : St. Geo. Chap. Mayfair, p. 320.
MDB. (co. Notts), (Musson), 3 ; New York (Musson), 2 ; London, 1, 4, 2, 6 ; Philadelphia, 1, 0, 0, 7.

Mister.—Nick. 'the master' ; v. Master. It seems to be merely spelt as 'master' is colloquially pronounced. Possibly, however, an abbreviation of Minister, q.v.

London, 2 ; New York, 1.

Mitcham.—Local, 'of Mitcham,' a parish in co. Surrey, nine miles from London.

Peter de Micham, London, 1273. A.
1754. Married — Daniel Thorp and Sarah Mitcham : St. Geo. Chap. Mayfair, p. 281.
1763. — Thomas Mitcham and Sarah Mash : St. Geo. Han. Sq. i. 126.
London, 3.

Mitchelboy.—Occup. 'Mitchell's boy,' i.e. his young servant ; cf. Matthewman, Addyman, &c. One of a large class.

William Michelboy, co. Suff., Edw. I. R.

Mitchell, Mitchelson.—Bapt. 'the son of Michael,' popularly Mitchell; cf. *dike* and *ditch, kirk* and *church,* &c.

Hugh fil. Micahel, co. Linc., 1273. A.
Roger Michel, co. Norf., ibid.
Mikael de Brackele, London, ibid.
Johannes Michelson, 1379 : P. T. Yorks. p. 15.
Thomas Michilson, 1379 : ibid. p. 19.
Adam Michelson, 1379 : ibid. p. 190.
1563. Bapt.—John, s. Thomas Michell : St. Jas. Clerkenwell, i. 2.
1754. Married — William Mitchel and Eliz. Herring : St. Geo. Han. Sq. i. 53.
London, 168, 4 ; New York, 258, 0 ; Philadelphia, 450, 0.

Mitchinson, Mitcheson.—Bapt. Corruptions of Mitchelson, q.v. Mitchinson is well-known in co. Cumb. The change from *l* to *n* is not uncommon ; cf. *banister* for *baluster.* With the abbreviated Mitcheson cf. Patteson for Pattinson.

1749. Married—Edward L'Epine and Ann Mitchinson : St. Geo. Chap. Mayfair, p. 151.
London, 3, 2 ; MDB. (co. Cumberland), 11, 0 ; Philadelphia, 0, 6.

Mitford.—Local (1) 'of Mitford,' a parish in the union of Morpeth, co. Northumberland. William Mitford, the historian, often resided at Newton Park in the parish, and his ancestors were early lords of Mitford ; (2) 'of Mutford,' a parish in co. Suffolk, three miles from Beccles. Probably the two streams have mingled.

Adam de Mitford, co. Suff., 1273. A.
Peter de Mitford, co. Northumb., ibid.
Robert de Mitford, bailiff of Newcastle-on-Tyne, 1275 : PPP. ii. 12.
Hugh de Mutford, co. Suff., Hen. III–Edw. I. K..
John de Mutteford, co. Kent, 20 Edw. I. R.
1685–6. Lionel Mitford and Katherine Clinton : Marriage Lic. (Cant.), p. 179.
1761. Married—Booth Brathwaite and Ann Mitford : St. Geo. Han. Sq. i. 101.
Crockford, 2.

Mitton.—Local, 'of Mitton,' a parish in the union of Clitheroe, W. Rid. Yorks, but partly in co. Lanc.

John de Miton, 17 Edw. II : Freemen of York, i. 22.
Adam de Mytton, 1379 : P. T. Yorks. p. 268.
Johannes de Mytton, *sutor,* ibid. p. 266.
Robert Mitton, of Great Marsden, *clothier,* 1558 : Wills at Chester (1545-1620), p. 137.
William Mitton, of Burnley, 1570 : ibid.
Henry Mitton, of Colne, 1597 : ibid.
West Rid. Court Dir., 8 ; London, 3 ; Manchester, 6 ; Colne, 1 ; New York, 1 ; Philadelphia, 12.

Mizen, -zon ; v. Misson.

Mobbs ; v. Mabb.

Moberley, Moberly.—Local, 'of Mobberly,' a parish in co. Chester, two miles from Nether Knutsford.

Patrick Moberlegh, c. 1220 : East Cheshire, ii. 550.
William de Modburlegh, 1308 : ibid. p. 85.
1565. Bapt. — Margery Mobberleye : Reg. Prestbury, co. Ches., p. 15.
1568. — John Moberleye : ibid. p. 24.
1585. Edward Mobberley, of Norley, *yeoman* : Wills at Chester (1545-1620), p. 137.
1756. Married—Richard Moberly and Jane Adams : St. Geo. Han. Sq. i. 62.
Crockford, 1, 6 ; London, 0, 4 ; Boston (U.S.), 0, 1.

Mocker.—Nick. 'the mocker,' one who derided, a scoffer.

William le Mokare, Fines Roll, 11 Edw. I.
Philadelphia, 2.

Mockridge ; v. Moggridge.

Moffat, Moffatt.—Local, 'of Moffatt,' a parish partly in Lanarkshire, and partly in Dumfriesshire.

1778. Married—John Curtis and Eliz. Moffatt : St. Geo. Han. Sq. i. 291.
1787. — Mathew Swan and Margaret Moffett : ibid. p. 406.
London, 2, 10 ; New York, 11, 7.

Mogford, Mugford.—Local, 'of Mogford' or 'Mockford.' I cannot identify the spot. For similar changes in the spelling of the first syllable v. Moggridge.

1777. Married — Francis Resin and Eliz. Mugford : St. Geo. Han. Sq. i. 282.

— — John Mockford and Margaret Musgrove: ibid.

London, 5, 1 ; New York, 0, 1 ; Boston (U.S.), 0, 2.

Mogg, Mogge, Moggs.—Bapt. 'the son of Margaret,' from the nick. Mogg or Moggy ; v. Moxon. Margaret ran riot among the vowels with Mag, Meg, and Mog for nicks.

William Mogge, co. Soms., 1 Edw. III : Kirby's Quest, p. 269.

Peter Mog, co. Soms., 1 Edw. III: ibid.

1729. Married — Daniel Moggs and Grace Baker: St.Geo.Chap.Mayfair,p.295.

1798. — Robert Mogg and Mary Ann James : St. Geo. Han. Sq. ii. 186.

London, 3,¹2, 0.

Moggridge, Mockridge, Muggeridge, Mogridge.— Local, ' of Moggridge.' I cannot discover the spot ; manifestly the suffix is -ridge. The curious tricks that can be played with the spelling of surnames is well exemplified by Lower, who states that he once saw Mugridge over a small shop in co. Sussex, while in the window 'Muggerages ginber-beer' was announced for sale.

1586. George Mogerege, co. Wilts, Balliol College: Reg. Univ. Oxf. vol. ii. pt. ii. p. 150.

1590. Married — Tristram Blaby and Joane Morgradge : St. Mary Aldermary (London), p. 8.

1760. — James Clarke and Ann Mugrige: St. Geo. Han. Sq. i. 97.

1773. Thomas Pring and Mary Mugridge : ibid. i. 227.

London, 10, 3, 10, 0 ; MDB. (co. Soms.), 1, 0, 0, 1 ; Philadelphia (Mogridge), 3.

Mohun.—Local, 'de Mohun' ; v. Moon, its modern representative.

Crockford, 1 ; Philadelphia, 1.

Mold.—Bapt. ; v. Mould.

Mole.—Local, ' of Mole.'

Willelmus Praepositus de Mole, co. Glouc., temp. Hen. III–Edw. I. K.

Nicholas de Mol, ibid.

London, 4 ; Oxford, 5 ; Philadelphia, 2.

Molehunt.—Occup. ' the molehunt,' one who hunted down moles for the farmers, receiving a stated price ; v. Hunt = Hunter.

William Molehunte, co. Suff., 1273. A.

Molesworth.—Local, ' of Molesworth,' a parish in co. Hunts.

John de Molesworthe, co. Hunts, 1273. A.

Richard de Molesworth, co. Hunts, ibid.

Nicholas de Mulsewrthe, co. Hunts, ibid.

1624. Bapt. — Winkfeilde, s. William Molsworthe: St. Michael. Cornhill, p. 117.

1762. Married—John Molesworth and Barbara St.Aubyn: St.Geo.Han. Sq. i. 112.

London, 2 ; Crockford, 8 ; New York, 2.

Molineaux, Molineux, Mollineux, Molyneux, Mollyneux, Mullineaux, Mullineux.—Local, ' de Molineaux.' Probably, like the noble family who trace from William the Conqueror, from Molineaux-sur-Seine, near Rouen. This name has ramified very strongly in co. Lanc., and is found in all classes of society, from the highest to the lowest. Six centuries have brought their troubles upon younger branches of the family.

Adam de Mulyneus, alias Molyneus, co. Lanc., Hen. III–Edw. I. K.

Richard de Molyneaus, co. Northumb., 20 Edw. I. R.

1578. John Molynex, co. Lanc. : Reg. Univ. Oxf. vol. ii. pt. ii. p. 79.

1608. James Mollineux, co. Lanc. : ibid. p. 300.

1583-4. John Hollande and Mary Mollenax : Marriage Lic. (London), i. 129.

1592. Thomas Molineux, of Garstang, co. Lanc. : Wills at Chester, i. 137.

1607. William Molineux, of Ormskirk: ibid.

1603. Buried — James Mullinax : St. Michael, Cornhill, p. 212.

1634. Bapt.—Henry, s. John Mollinox : St. Jas. Clerkenwell, i. 126.

London, 1, 1, 1, 6, 0, 0, 1 ; MDB. (co. Lanc.), 0, 0, 0, 0, 1, 1, 1 ; Manchester (Molyneux), 18 ; New York, 0, 2, 0, 1, 0, 1, 0 ; Philadelphia, 6, 0, 0, 0, 0, 16, 0.

Moll, Mollison, Mollinson, Molleson.—Bapt. 'the son of Mary,' from the nick. Mall, and dim. Mall-in; v. Malleson and Mallinson. Later on Mall and Mally became Moll and Molly ; cf. Magg and Mogg, the nicks. of Margaret.

Margaret Molleson, 1379: P. T. Yorks. p. 89.

1550. Bapt. —— the son of Fraunces Molsonne: St. Peter, Cornhill, i. 5.

1741. Married — Francis Mollison and Eliz. Fletcher : St. Geo. Chap. Mayfair, p. 15.

1789. — John Molisone and Miriam Seal: St. Geo. Han. Sq. ii. 28.

Manchester, 1, 1, 1, 0 ; New York, 21, 0, 0, 5.

Molland.—Local, ' of Molland,' a parish in co. Devon.

Simon de Molland, co. Devon. K.

London, 2 ; MDB. (co. Devon), 1.

Mollett, Mollet.—Bapt. ' the son of Mary,' from the nick. Moll, and dim. Moll-et or Moll-ot ; cf. Emmott, Tillot, Bartlett, &c.

Alicia Molot, 1379 : P. T. Yorks. p. 89.

1685-6. James Mollet and Mary Langdon : Marriage Alleg. (Cant.), p. 222.

1766. Married — Amos Mollett and Eliz. Sauberre : St. Geo. Han. Sq. i. 157.

London, 2, 0 ; Manchester, 1, 0 ; New York, 2, 1.

Mollison ; v. Moll.

Molyneux ; v. Molineaux.

Mompesson.—Local, ' de Mont Pinson,' a castle on the river Scie, in Normandy (Lower).

Philip de Mumpinzun, co. York, 1273. A.

Adam le Mūpincū, co. Norf., ibid.

Oliver de Mounpynson, vicar of Attleborough, co. Norf., 1320 : FF. i. 524.

John Mompesson, rector of Hasingham, co. Norf., 1717 : FF. vii. 234.

1603-4. Edward Momperson and Jane Gardner : Marriage Alleg. (Canterbury), p. 285.

1703. Charles Mompesson and Eliz. Longueville : Marriage Lic. (Faculty Office), p. 246.

Monday, Munday, Mundey, Mundy.—(1) Personal or baptismal, ' the son of Monday ' ; cf. Saturday, Friday.

Simon Moneday, co. Hunts, 1273. A.

Simon Mundi, co. Camb., ibid.

Henry Mundi, co. Camb., ibid.

Edmund Moneday, co. Soms., 1 Edw. III : Kirby's Quest, p. 245.

(2) Local, ' of Mondaye.' A correspondent writes : ' Mondaye, a hill in the parish of Juaye, about six miles from Bayeaux, is still extant, likewise the abbey. . . . The hill was originally called Mont d'Aë : in the *langue d'oïl* Aë signifies water.' It is highly probable that Monday is in some cases local, but I have not any early instances to bring forward in evidence.

1584. Married — Thomas Gibbyns and Agnes Munday : St. Jas. Clerkenwell, i. 11.

1657. — Richard Chase and Bridgett Monday : St. Michael, Cornhill, p. 37.

London, 3, 15, 1, 13 ; New York, 5, 5, 0, 6.

Money, Monney.—(1) Local, ' de Monye.' Probably ' Monnay, a place in Normandy, in the department of Orne ' (Lower).

John de Mony, co. Soms., 1273. A.

William de Monye, co. Glo., 20 Edw. I. R.

William de Money, co. Oxf., Hen. III–Edw. I. K.

(2) Official, 'the monk,' one of the endless forms of 'le Moyne' or 'le Moigne'; v. Munn.

Robert le Monhe, co. Norf., 1273. A.
William le Mone, co. Kent, ibid.
Robert Monay, co. Oxf., ibid.
Henry le Monie, co. Glouc., 20 Edw. I. R.
John le Monie, co. Glouc., ibid.
1785. Married — Joseph Money and Eliz. Withey: St. Geo. Han. Sq. i. 380.
London, 5, 0; Oxford, 7, 0; New York, 1, 0; Boston (U.S.), 3, 3.

Moneymaker, Moneyman.
Occup. 'a maker of coin'; v. Monier.

John Monemaker, co. York. W. 2.
¹ In the 38th of Henry VIII, Robert Moneyman conveyed two messuages, 40 acres of land,' &c.: Randworth, co. Norf., FF. xi. 113.

Moneypeny. — Local. One thing is very certain, this surname has nothing to do with *money* generally, nor a *penny* specifically. Although now a recognized Scotch surname, it is early found on English soil. Lower says, 'that it is local is proved by the prefix *de* with which it is found in early records.' Unfortunately my instances are without any prefix.

John Manipenyn, co. Bedf., 1273. A.
Herbert Manipeni, co. Hunts, ibid.
Henry Muddepenyng, C. R., 14 Edw. III. pt. ii.
John Manypany, C. R., 45 Edw. III.
Thomas Monipeni, co. York. W. 2.
Alex. Moneypenny. FF.
Crockford, 2; New York, 2.

Monier.—Occup. 'the money-er,' a maker of coin, a mint-master; v. Minter. The name still exists, but it is hard to find modern instances.

Henry le Moneur, co. Salop, 1273. A.
Haco le Muner, co. Suff., ibid.
Henry le Moneur, C. R., 3 Edw. II.
Walter le Monner, London, 20 Edw. I. R.
John le Monnier. N.
Hamo le Monner. T.
Gilbert le Muner. G.
Philadelphia, 2.

Monk, Monke, Munk. — Official, 'the monk,' a recluse. A.S. *munec.*

William le Monek, 1273. A.
Peter le Monek, temp. 1300. M.
John le Monck. G.
Johannes Mounke et Agnes uxor ejus, 1379: P. T. Yorks. p. 23.
Willelmus Mounke et Alicia uxor ejus, 1379: ibid.

Agnes Moncke, 1379: ibid. p. 38.
Johannes Moncke, 1379: ibid.
1638. Married—William Worslye and Agnes Monke: St. Jas. Clerkenwell, iii. 70.
London, 28, 0, 1; New York, 7, 0, 3.

Monkey.—Local, 'of the monk-haw,' i. e. the monk's enclosure; cf. Hay and Haw in Hayward or Haward, q.v.

John del Monkhagh, 1379: P. T. Yorks. p. 147.

More than a century afterwards the tendency to imitation appears:

'Johannes Monkey, nuper de Laystoff in Com. Suffochire,' 2 Hen. VIII: HHH. p. 124.

I do not find the name in modern directories.

Monkhouse.—Local, 'at the monk-house,' i.e. the house where the monk or monks resided; cf. Chanonhouse (i. e. Canon-house). With such forms as Munkus, &c., cf. Loftus for Lofthouse, or Malthus for Malthouse.

Rogerus del Munkhous, 1379: P. T. Yorks. p. 234.
Thomas Munkas, of Chorlton, Manchester, 1660: Wills at Chester (1660–80), p. 193.
1602. Married—Thomas Fulwode and Ales Munckus: St. Antholin (London), p. 41.
1762. Married — Peter Mounkhouse and Mary Booth: St. Geo. Han. Sq. i. 113.
London, 1; York, 3; Crockford, 4; MDB. (co. Cumberland), 13; Philadelphia, 7.

Monkman, Monckman, Monkmon.—Occup. 'the monk's man,' i. e. servant of the monk; v. Priestman. Almost all these names ending in man (=servant) belong to the county of York; v. Matthewman.

John Monkeman, co. York, 1273. A.
Henry Munkeman, co. York, ibid.
William Munkeman, co. York. W. 15.
Robertus Monckeman, 1379: P. T. Yorks. p. 118.
Johannes Munkman, *barker*, 1379: ibid. p. 98.

The surname still clings to York-shire. An action was tried at York to recover damages, in which one of this name appears, hailing from Malton (Manchester Evening News, March 12, 1886).

York, 2, 0, 0; Bradford, 0, 2, 1.

Monkton, Monckton.—Local, 'of Monkton,' i.e. the monk's stead or farm. Parishes in various diocs. are so called, viz. Ripon (2), York (1), Salisbury (2), Exeter (1), Canterbury (1), Bath and Wells (2), &c.

William de Moneketon, co. Wilts, 1273. A.
Peter de Munkton, *sutor*, 5 Edw. II: Freemen of York, i. 14.
Henricus de Monketon, 1379: P. T. Yorks. p. 299.
Johannes de Monkton, 1359: ibid. p. 212.
William de Muncketon, 1379: ibid. p. 47.
1774. Married — Charles Monckton and Betsey Edwards: St. Geo. Han. Sq. i. 246.
London, 3, 4; Crockford, 0, 1.

Montagu, Montague.—Local, 'of Montagu,' in Normandy. The Latinized form was 'de Monte Acuto,' whence the occasional Montacute. The 'Prior Montis Acuti' is mentioned in the Hundred Rolls (ii. 125). The parish of Montacute, co. Somerset, took its name from the family. 'Drogo de Monte-Acuto, the great Domesday tenant, came over in the retinue of Robert Earl of Mortain, the Conqueror's half-brother': Collins, quoted by Lower.

William de Monte Acuto, co. Southampton, 1273. A.
William de Montagu, co. Bucks, ibid.
Symon de Monte Acuto, co. Devon, ibid.
1526. John Muntagew and Catherine Slene: Marriage Lic. (London), i. 5.
1628. Bapt. — Edward, s. Thomas Mountague: St. Jas. Clerkenwell, i. 109.
London, 2, 11; New York, 0, 19.

Montford; v. Mountford.

Montgomery, Montgomerie, Montgomray.—Local, 'of Montgomerie,' near Lisieux, in Normandy. Of this great family, which gave name to the shire and town of Montgomery in Wales, Lower says, 'One of them, Roger de Montgomery, a kinsman of the Conqueror, accompanied him, and led the centre of his army at Hastings' (Patr. Brit. p. 228). It is more natural to refer back the surname to the Norman estate than to the county to which the family gave their name.

Fulco de Mongomery, co. Devon, 1273. A.
Lucia de Mongomery, co. Notts, ibid.

Gregory de Montgomery, co. Salop, 1273. A.
1430. John Dalton and Eliz. Mungumbery : Marriage Lic. (London), i. 7.
1745. Married — Hugh Fergusson and Margaret Montgomery : St. Geo. Han. Sq. i. 34.
1758. — George Montgomerie and Eliz. Lloyd : ibid. p. 77.
London, 11, 3, 1 ; New York, 90, 0, 0.

Monument, Mornement.—
‡ Local. Lower says, ' from residence at or near a monument.' I do not think this view satisfactory, and question its local application in the surname epoch. Perhaps it represents an early form (corrupted later on) of Monmouth. In this case the corruption would be, as usual, imitative.

John de Monemuta, co. Glouc., 1273. A.
1767. Married — Samuel Monument and Eliz. Holmes : St. Geo. Han. Sq. i. 182.
London, 0, 1.

Moody, Moodey, Moodie, Mudie.—
Nick. ' the moody,' i.e. the brave, the bold, the resolute. A common sobriquet in the Hundred Rolls. Mudie is a Scottish form. Moody also frequently hails from over the Border.

' Aslaked was his mood,' i. e. anger.
     Chaucer, C. T. 1762.
' Mody, Mwdy, adj., proud, brave. Moodie, Mudie, gallant, courageous' (Jamieson).

Adam Mody, co. Oxf., 1273. A.
Roger Mody, co. Salop, ibid.
Simon Modi, co. Camb., ibid.
Johannes Mody, husband, 1379 : P. T. Howdenshire, p. 15.
Thomas Mody and Sibota uxor ejus, 1379 : P. T. Yorks. p. 5.
Thomas Mody and Agnes uxor ejus : 1379 : ibid. p. 101.
1544. Married—Henry Mody and Anne Laurence : Marriage Lic. (Canterbury), p. 3.
1605. — Henry Modye and Deborah Dunche : St. Mary Aldermary, p. 11.
1621. Thomas Moody and Margaret Scrivenor : Marriage Lic. (London), p. 108.
London, 22, 1, 1, 7 ; West Rid. Court Dir., 12, 0, 0, 0 ; New York, 34, 1, 1, 0.

Moon, Moone, Munn.—
Local, ' de Mohun' ; cf. Boon, and in some cases Bunn for ' de Bohun.' Lower says, ' Moon, a corruption of Mohun. The Itin. de la Normandie, speaking of the place from whence the Mohuns derived their name (Moyon), says, ' Masseville appelle ce bourg Moon.' (a) Offic. ' the monk' ; v. Munn.

John de Mohun, co. Somerset, 1273. A.
Reginald de Mohun, co. Devon, Hen. III–Edw. I. K.
William de Mohun, co. Wilts, ibid.
1651. Married — Thomas Haynes and Dorothy Moone : St. Jas. Clerkenwell, iii. 87.
1661. — William Mohun and Mary Morgan : Marriage Lic. (Canterbury), p. 55.
1762. — William Moon and Mary Stuart : St. Geo. Han. Sq. i. 116.
London, 26, 1, 7 ; New York, 9, 0, 19.

Moor, Moore, More.—
Local, ' at the moor' (A.S. mór, a heath), from residence thereby ; v. Moorhouse.

John atte Mor, co. Norf., 1273. A.
Adam atte More, co. Oxf., ibid.
Fulco de la More, co. Hunts, ibid.
Pontius de la More, co. York, ibid.
Agatha atte More, co. Soms, 1327 : Tax Roll.
Alicia del More, 1379 : P. T. Yorks. p. 219.
Johannes atte More, 1379 : ibid. p. 31.
1578. Married—Henrie More and Alice Simpson : St. Mary Aldermary (London), p. 6.
London, 2,243, 6 ; New York, 3,602, 21.

Moorcock, Morcock.—
Bapt. ' the son of Maurice,' from the nick. Mor (v. Morin), with the suffix -cock (v. Cock) as in Wilcock, &c. It may possibly be a nickname = Moorcock, the red grouse, but the first definition is more natural and according to rule. The fact that Mor-kin also existed (cf. Jenkin, Wilkin, &c.) is additional evidence. On the other hand, Moorhen (q.v.) also existed as a nickname. It is hard, after all, to say which is the true definition.—Since writing the above I have lighted on an entry in Kirby's Quest which settles the matter :

Morecok Chepman, co. Soms., 1 Edw. III : Kirby's Quest, p. 264.
Nicholas Morcok, co. Soms., 1 Edw. III : ibid. p. 155.
Morekin de Vautham, London, 1273. A.
Morekin le Wolmongere, London, ibid.
Henricus Morekok, 1379 : P. T. Yorks. p. 94.
Joan Morecocke, 1661 : St. Peter, Cornhill, i. 103.
1625. Nicholas Morecocke and Anne Eate : Marriage Lic. (London), i. 163.
1773. Married — William Price and Sarah Moorcock : St. Geo. Han. Sq. i. 233.

Moorcraft, Moorcroft, Morecroft.—
Local, ' at the moor-croft,' i.e. from residence at the enclosure, or croft, on the moor (v. Croft and Craft). With the variant Moorcraft, cf. Meadowcraft. Some small spot on the borders of Cheshire has given birth to a surname which still thrives in south Lancashire. But v. Marcroft.

Brian Morecroft, priest, 1524 : East Ches. ii. 92.
Bryan Morecroft, of Ormskirk, 1589 : Wills at Chester (1545-1620), p. 138.
Henry Morecroft, of Swanscough, co. Ches., 1567 : ibid.
1594. Ferdinando Moorecroft, co. Lanc. : Reg. Univ. Oxf. vol. ii. pt. ii. p. 207.
1635. Bapt.—Phillip, d. Richard Moorcraft : St. Antholin (London), p. 69.
Liverpool, 0, 3, 3 ; London, 1, 1, 0.

Moorhen.—
Nick. ' the moorhen,' seemingly the feminine of Moorcock, q.v. It maintained its existence till the 17th century.

Magota Morehen, 1379 : P. T. Yorks. p. 54.
1627. Buried—Widdow Moorehen, one of the pencioners : St. Peter, Cornhill, i. 189.
1752. Married—William Morehen and Mary Woolly : St. Geo. Chap. Mayfair, p. 207.

I suspect this name is either extinct or lost in Morin.

Moorhouse, Morehouse.—
Local, ' at the moor-house,' the cottage situate on the moor, a local name common to many places. I had a Moorhouse in my parish (Ulverston), a farmstead still far separated from other abodes. It gave rise to a family of Moorhouses resident in the immediate district for centuries. Some of the many Yorkshire Moorhouses, or Morehouses, are doubtless sprung from Moorhouse, now increased to a hamlet in the parish of Hooton Pagnell, near Doncaster. Naturally we find this name predominant in the North.

Geoffrey atte Morhouse, co. Soms., 1 Edw. III : Kirby's Quest, p. 232.
Adam de Merehowse (sic), 1379 : P. T. Yorks. p. 274.
Johannes de Morehowse, 1379 : ibid. p. 275.
Thomas Morehowse, 1379 : ibid.
Elias de Morehous, 1379 : ibid. p. 245.

1558–9. Oliver Morehouse and Katherine Sprickeman: Marriage Lic. (Westminster), p. 1.
1621. John Morehouse, co. Cumb.: Reg. Univ. Oxf. vol. ii. pt. ii. p. 398.
London, 3, 0; West Rid. Court Dir., 14, 3; Manchester, 15, 0; New York, 1, 6; Philadelphia, 12, 2.

Moorman.—Local, 'the moorman,' one who dwelt on the moor; cf. Bridgeman, Houseman, &c.

Johannes Morman, 1379: P. T. Yorks. p. 173.
Adam Morman (sic), co. Soms., 1 Edw. III: Kirby's Quest, p. 177.
1752. Married—James Moorman and Jane Grey: St. Geo. Chap. Mayfair, p. 227.
1787. Married—James Moorman and Sarah Glover: St. Geo. Han. Sq. i. 403.
London, 1; Manchester, 1; Philadelphia, 1.

Moorsom, Morson. — Bapt. 'the son of Morris.' From Morrison to Morson was a natural transition; cf. Morse for Morris. The m in Moorsom presents no difficulty, as the final -son was often corrupted to -som; cf. Ransom, Hansom, Sansom. Nevertheless Mr. Lower's suggestion that it is for Moorsham, a township in the parish of Skelton, N. Rid. Yorks, must not be overlooked. I see the Modern Domesday Book has one instance in the North Riding. This confirms Mr. Lower's view.

1693. Richard Morson and Mary Nutt: Marriage Alleg. (Canterbury), p. 264.
1778. Married — William Morson and Catherine Coffering: St. Geo. Han. Sq. i. 291.
1784. — Richard Toms and Catherine Morsom: ibid. p. 364.
London, 3, 1; Leeds, 1, 0; MDB. (North Rid. Yorks), 1, 0; New York, 0, 3.

Moorward.—Offic. 'the moorward,' the guardian or keeper of a moor. Probably lost in the local Moorwood, q.v.

German le Morward, co. Southampton, 1273. A.
Henry le Morward. B.

Moorwood, Morewood. — Local, 'of Moorwood.' Seemingly a spot in co. Lincoln.

Ralph de Morwode, or Morewude, co. Linc., 1273. A.
Alicia de Morewod', 1379: P.T. Yorks. p. 40.

1740. Married — Andrew Moorwood and Eliz. Sherman; St. Jas. Clerkenwell, iii. 270.
London, 1, 4; New York, 0, 6.

Morby, Morbey, Murby.— Local, 'of Moorby,' a parish in co. Lincoln, near Horncastle.

Elena de Moreby, 1379: P. T. Yorks. p. 154.
1675. Joseph Moreby and Mary Wood: Marriage Alleg. (Canterbury), p. 153.
London, 3, 1; Philadelphia, 1, 0, 0.

Mordan, Morden, Murden.—Local, (1) 'of Mordon,' a township in the parish of Sedgefield, co. Durham; (2) also 'of Morden,' a parish in co. Dorset, six miles from Wareham; (3) also 'of Morden,' a parish in co. Surrey, one mile from Mitcham; (4) also 'of Morden,' two parishes in co. Cambridge.

John de Mordon, co. Camb., 1273. A.
John de Mordene, co. Camb., ibid.
Ralph de Mordone, co. Camb., ibid.
Symon de Mordone, co. Camb., ibid.
Gilbert de Mordon, Lond., 20 Edw. I. R.
Robert de Moredone, co. Devon, Hen. III–Edw. I. K.
Peter de Mordon, co. Wilts, ibid.
1619. George Morden and Martha Harris: Marriage Lic. (Westminster), p. 26.
1763. Married—James Morden and Priscilla Holdman: St. Geo. Han. Sq. i. 125.
1769. — George Mackmolt and Mary Mordin: ibid. p. 190.
London, 2, 1, 1; MDB. (Cambridge), 0, 3, 0; New York, 0, 1, 0.

Mordaunt, Mordan.—Nick. 'the biter.' The legend has ever been that this is the origin of this Norman name. Mr. Lower quotes that 'Osbert le Mordaunt possessed Radwell, co. Bedford, by gift of his brother, who had received it from the Conqueror for services rendered' (Patr. Brit. p. 229).

Robert le Mordaunt, co. Bedf., 1273. A.
William le Mordaunt, co. Bedf., ibid.
1575. Edmund Mordant, co. Bedf.: Reg. Univ. Oxf. vol. ii. pt. ii. p. 64.
1739. George Dixon and Mary Mordaunt: St. Geo. Han. Sq. i. 92.
London, 2, 2; New York, 2, 0.

More.—Local; v. Moor.

Morecroft; v. Moorcroft.

Morehouse; v. Moorhouse.

Morel, Morell, Morrall, Morrell, Morrill. — (1) Nick. 'the morel,' dark-complexioned.

A once common name for a horse. 'Morel, horse, *morellus*': Prompt. Parv. Mr. Way in a note quotes, 'Morel: noir, tanné, tirant sur le brun': Roquefort. In the Towneley Mysteries, p. 9, 'Morelle' occurs as one of the steeds yoked to Cain's plough; cf. *morel*, a species of dark cherry.

Herveus Morel, co. Norf., 1273. A.
Nicholas Morel, co. Norf., ibid.
Thomas Morel, co. Hunts, ibid.
Ralph Morell. J.

(2) Bapt. 'the son of Morel,' i. e. dark-complexioned. White, Black, and Brown (q.v.) were all employed as baptismal names.

Moral de Hulfton, 1171: KKK. vi. 19.
Morel (without surname), co. Camb., 1273. A.
The heirs of Morell, co. Camb., ibid.
1666. Stephen Brewer and Anne Morrell: Marriage Alleg. (Canterbury), p. 115.
London, 5, 3, 4, 19, 2; New York, 1, 2, 0, 26, 9.

Moreton.—Local, 'of Moreton,' i.e. the enclosure on the moor; cf. Morton. Of course there are wellnigh endless places styled by this name, some of which have originated surnames. Moreton, a township in the union of Congleton, co. Ches., seems to be the parent of the Lancashire and Cheshire Moretons.

Eustace de Moreton, co. Worc., Hen. III–Edw. I. K.
William de Moreton, co. Soms., ibid.
John Moreton, of Moreton, 1598: Wills at Chester (1545–1620), p. 138.
Brian Moreton, of Congleton, 1614: ibid.
1613. Married—James Battey and Eliz. Moreton, or Mooreton: St. Jas. Clerkenwell, p. 39.
London, 6; Manchester, 2; Liverpool, 6; New York, 1; MDB. (Cheshire), 10; Boston (U.S.), 1.

Morewood; v. Moorwood.

Morey.—Local, 'at the moorhey,' from residence by the enclosure on the moor (v. Hey or Hay). This suffix -hay or -hey frequently slips the h and becomes -ey.

William Morehay, C. R., 14 Ric. II.
1738. Bapt.—Mary, d. John Moorey: St. Mary Aldermary (London), p. 128.
1747. Married—William Coleman and Mary Morey: St. Geo. Chap. Mayfair, p. 101.

1775. Married — Thomas Eades and Barbara Jane Morey: St. Geo. Han. Sq. i. 255.
London, 8; New York, 12.

Morgan, Morgans. — Bapt. ' the son of Morgan' (Welsh). Latterly in the place of Ap-Morgan, the true Welsh patronymic, an English form Morgans has arisen; cf. Williams for Ap-William.

Walter Morgan, co. Oxf., 1273. A.
'Item, geven to David ap Morgan, xxs': 1537: Privy Purse Exp., Princess Mary, p. 45.
Morgan Gough, C. R., 20 Hen. VI.
1616. Bapt.—John, s. Morgan Davies: St. Jas. Clerkenwell, i. 76.
Thomas Morgan, of Chester, 1602: Wills at Chester (1545-1620), p. 137.
London, 200, 0; MDB. (co. Glamorgan), 64, 3; New York, 250, 0.

Morin, Moring, Morrin. — Bapt. ' the son of Maurice,' from nick. More, and dim. Mor-in; cf. Col-in, Rob-in. The name is a common one (always without prefix) in the Hundred Rolls, and the origin need not be doubted. There was evidently a nick. Mor or More, and the usual dims. Morin, Morcock, and Morkin were formed from it; v. Moorcock. The *g* in Moring is excrescent, as in Jennings.

Isabella fil. Morini, co. Camb., 1273. A.
Geoffrey Morin, co. Camb., ibid.
Ralph Moryn, co. Bedf., ibid.
Simon Morin, co. Oxf., ibid.
Flandrina Moryn, co. Northampton, ibid.
William Moryn, co. Soms., 1 Edw. III: Kirby's Quest, p. 228.

Since writing the above, I have found entries that absolutely settle the question. The same individual is thus referred to:
Morinus de la Bare, co. Devon, 1273. A.
Morinus de Bare, co. Devon, ibid.
Moritius de Bare, co. Devon, ibid.
1668-9. Thomas Morin and Susanna Barnardiston: Marriage Alleg. (Canterbury), p. 161.
1756. Married — Nicholas Perrin and Ann Morin: St. Geo. Han. Sq. i. 65.
London, 1, 3, 1; New York, 2, 1, 1.

Morley. — Local, ' of Morley.' Parishes in cos. Derby and Norfolk (2); also an ecclesiastical district in the parish of Batley, W. Rid. Yorks, besides many small localities. ' The pasture on the moor' would naturally be styled by this name.

Johannes de Morelay, 1379: P. T. Yorks. p. 56.
Adam de Morlay, 1319: ibid.
Margeria de Morlay, 1379: ibid. p. 142.
1569. Married—Richarde Morley and Avis Tucke: St. Mary Aldermary, p. 5.
London, 41; MDB. (West Rid. Yorks), 11; New York, 4; Boston (U.S.), 18.

Morling. — Bapt. ' the son of Maurice,' dim. Mor-ling; cf. Hewling, Hickling, and v. Morin.

Hugh Morlyng, co. Camb., 1273. A.
1626. William Parsonn and Anne Morlinge: Marriage Lic.(London), i. 165.
1745. Married—John Morling and Mary Musgrave: St. Dionis Backchurch, p. 69.
London, 3.

Morpeth. — Local, ' of Morpeth,' co. Northumberland.

Roger de Morpath, co. York, 1273. A.
William de Morpathe, co. York, ibid.
London, 2.

Morrall, Morrell, Morrill; v. Morel.

Morrin. — Bapt. ; v. Morin.

Morris, Morrish, Morriss, Morrison. — (1) Bapt. ' the son of Maurice,' commonly spelt Morris; v. Maurice.

Mauricius fil. Mauricii, co. Northampton, 20 Edw. I. R.
Thomas Moriz', co. Bedf., ibid.
Ricardus Morrisson, 1379: P. T. Yorks. p. 185.
William Moreson, 1379: ibid. p. 265.
Elena Morys, 1379: ibid. p. 56.
Johannes Morys, 1379: ibid.
Morice ap-Owen. XX.
Jevan ap Moris Kemys: Visit. Glouc. 1623, p. 98.

(2) Nick. ' the Moreys,' i.e. the Moorish, the Moor; cf. Norris.

Robert le Moreys, co. Soms., 1273. A.
William de (sic) Morreys, co. Suff., ibid.
1575. Married — Robert Wolfe and Johane Morrys: St. Jas. Clerkenwell, p. 6.
1602. — Israell Garrett and Alice Morrice: ibid. i. 26.
London, 174, 6, 4, 41; New York, 344, 1, 0, 8.

Morrow, Marrow. — Local, ' of the moor-row,' i.e. the cottages on the moor. Row is a common suffix to early local surnames. A.S. *raw*, a row (Skeat); cf. Towndrow. Lower says that Morrow is a corruption of Mac Murrough. This may be true in certain cases, but there is undoubtedly an English surname Morrow also which has

to be explained. Neither must it be forgotten that there is a hamlet Morrowe in the parish of Wisbeach, co. Cumb.

Willelmus de Morerawe, 1379: P. T. Yorks. p. 241.
Johannes Marowe, 1370: ibid. p. 22.
William Marrow, of Leighton Wood, 1591: Wills at Chester (1545-1620), p. 131.
1567. Married—Umphrey Marrowe and Ellyn Todd: St. Michael, Cornhill, p. 9.
London, 4, 0; Halifax, 1, 0; Liverpool, 4, 2; New York, 46, 1.

Morse, Morss. — Bapt. ' the son of Morris' (q.v.), modified into Morse.

1555. Silvester Steweley and Mary Mors: Marriage Lic. (London), i. 17.
1610. John Morse and Dorothy Burnap: ibid. p. 319.
1684. Buried—Mary, d. Eward Morss: St. Mary Aldermary, p. 196.
London, 18, 2; New York, 55, 3.

Morson. — Bapt. ; v. Moorsom.

Mortan, Morten. — Local; v. Mortyn. Not to be confounded with Morton.

Mortiboy, Martiboy. — Local. This name has been placed in the roll of fame by Sir W. Besant and the late Mr. Rice in their story Readymoney Mortiboy. It is no fancy name, as the London Dir. proves. Manifestly its last syllable is Fr. *bois* (v. Boys or Boyce), a wood, as in Talboys. This is confirmed by the entry :

1700. Bapt.—Jane, d. John Morteboyes: St. Jas. Clerkenwell, i. 389.
1702. — Rebecca, d. John Morteboys: ibid. ii. 8.

As I have found no earlier reference, I presume it is of fairly modern French extraction. I wonder where Sir W. Besant or Mr. Rice met it? Many of Charles Dickens' characters will be met with in this dictionary.
London, 2, 0; MDB. (co. Staff.), 0, 1.

Mortimer, Mortimore. — Local, ' de Mortimer,' Latinized in old rolls into de Mortuo Mari, i.e. Dead Sea. Lower says it was for this reason that the surname was supposed to have sprung from Crusading times. ' The castle and barony of Mortemer lie in the arrondissement of Neufchâtel in Normandy': Patr. Brit. p. 230.

Ralph de Mortimer, co. Linc., 1273. A.
Hugh de Mortuomari, co. Heref., ibid.
Lucia de Mortuomari, co. Heref., ibid.
Sir Robert de Mortimer, co. Norf., 1381: FF. i. 485.
Willelmus Mortimere, 1379: P.T.Yorks. p. 184.
1581. William Mortimer, co. Wilts: Reg. Univ. Oxf. vol. ii. pt. ii. p. 109.
1601. James Mortimer, co. Cardigan: ibid. p. 252.
London, 19, 10; New York, 39, 3.

Mortlock.—Local, 'of Mortlake,' a parish in co. Surrey. There can be no doubt about this derivation.

Walter Mortlake, co. Camb., 1273. A.
1565. John Mortlake and Dorothy Chesell: Marriage Lic. (London), i. 31.
1581. John Moreclacke and Eliz Woode: ibid. p. 105.
1744. Married—Geo. Brisac and Mary Mortlock: St. Geo. Chap. Mayfair, p. 41.
1746. — Richard Gale, of Mortlock, co. Surrey, and Grace Hughes: ibid. p. 65.
London, 13; Philadelphia, 1.

Morton.—Local, 'of Morton,' i.e. the moor-ton, the farm or enclosure on the moor. This naturally has given birth to many place-names, and as a consequence surnames. There are places, large and small hamlets and parishes, styled Morton in cos. Derby, Lincoln (3), Nottingham, York (4), Worcester, Warwick, Durham (2), Hereford, Norfolk, Northampton, &c.

Robert de Morton, co. Notts, 1273. A.
Egidius de Morton, co. Northampton, ibid.
Richard de Morton, co. Oxf., ibid.
Felicia de Morton, co. Linc., ibid.
Alicia de Morton, co. York, Hen. III–Edw. I. K.
Michael de Morton, co. Salop, ibid.
Rogerus de Morton, 1379: P.T.Yorks. p. 197.
Johannes de Morton, 1379: ibid.
Manser de Morton, co. Hunts, 20 Edw. I. R.
1504. John Morton, co. Leic.: Reg. Univ. Oxf. vol. ii pt. ii. p. 206.
London, 48; New York, 76.

Mortyn, Morten, Mortan.—Local, 'of Morteyn.' I cannot find the place. No doubt the surname is now generally absorbed by Morton. But it must be regarded as totally distinct in origin.

William de Morteyn, co. Notts, 1273. A.
Eustace de Morteyn, co. Notts, ibid.
Hugh de Morteyn, co. Bedf., Hen. III–Edw. I. K.
John de Mortayne, co. Salop, 20 Edw. I. R.
Roger de Morteyn, co. Cornwall, ibid.
Custance de Morteyne, co. Hunts, ibid.
1663-4. William Brom and Isabel Morten: Marriage Alleg. (Canterbury), p. 124.
London, 3, 4, 1.

Moseley, Mosley, Mosely.—Local, 'of Mossley,' till recently a hamlet, but now a rising town in the parish of Saddleworth, W. Rid. Yorks. Probably other small localities would bear the name.

Willelmus de Moslay, 1379: P. T. Yorks. p. 81.
Ricardus de Moslay, smyth, 1379: ibid. p. 82.
Thomas de Mosseley, 1379: ibid. p. 168.
1588. John Moseley, co. Middlesex: Reg. Univ. Oxf. vol. ii. pt. ii. p. 167.
1591. Ralph Mosley, of Great Sankey, husbandman: Wills at Chester, i. 139.
1617. Rowland Mosley, of the Hough, Manchester: ibid.
West Rid. Court Dir., 5, 4, 1; New York, 7, 3, 1.

Moser, Mosser.—Local, 'of Mosser,' a chapelry in the parish of Brigham, co. Cumberland. It seems almost certain that this is the parent, as the surname is familiar to that and the neighbouring counties.

1590. John Moser: Lancashire Wills at Richmond, i. 198.

The surname has ramified strongly in the United States.

London, 3, 0; MDB. (co. Westm.), 2, 0; New York, 39, 3.

Mosley; v. Moseley.

Moss.—(1) Local, 'at the moss,' from residence thereby. The name is too general to necessitate extracts from modern registers.

Henry Mosse, co. Linc., 1273. A.
Henry del Mosse, C. R., 6 Edw. III.
Robertus de Mos, 1379: P. T. Yorks. p. 247.
Johannes del Mosse, 1379: ibid. p. 295.

(2) Bapt. 'the son of Moses,' from nick. Moyse or Mosse (for instances, v. Moyse). It is curious to find that the modern practice, whereby Jews settling in England change their surname Moses into Moss, is supported by the fact that

six centuries ago Moss was the English nick. of Moses.

London, 78; West Riding Court Dir., 14; New York, 46.

Mossman.—(1) Bapt. 'the servant of Moss,' i.e. Moses (v. Moss, 2); cf. Matthewman, Wilman, Bartleman, &c. It is curious to notice that Mossman, as a modern surname, is commonest in Yorkshire, the county that has given us the largest number of surnames of this particular class. Moses was a popular font-name in the 13th and 14th centuries. (2) Local, 'the mossman,' one who lived on or close by a moss. I am obliged to suggest this, but doubt not (1) is the correct interpretation.

1687. James Mosman and Rebecca Hampton: Marriage Alleg. (Canterbury), p. 276.
1748. Married — James Mosman and Damask Rose: St. Geo. Chap. Mayfair, p. 106.
London, 3; West Rid. Court Dir., 5; New York, 1; Boston (U.S.), 2.

Mote, Moth; v. Mott.

Mothersole, Mothersill. — Local, 'of Mothersoul.' For the suffix, v. Sale. I cannot find any hall or hamlet bearing this name.

Ralph Modersoule, C. R., 6 Edw. II.
1602. Buried — Thomas Mothersowle: St. Dionis Backchurch (London), p. 206.
1635. Bapt.—Agnes, d. William Mothersoale: Reg. Deopham. co. Norfolk.
1793. Married — John Mothersall and Esther Williams: St. Geo. Han. Sq. ii. 105.
Manchester, 0, 4; Crockford, 1, 0; MDB. (co. Suffolk), 2, 0.

Motley.—Local, 'of Motley.' I cannot find the place. It must undoubtedly be sought for in co. Linc.

Thomas de Motlawe, 1379: P. T. Yorks. p. 174.
1570. Robert Dodds and Barbara Mottley: Marriage Lic. (London), i. 46.
1660. Buried—John, s. Edward Motley: St. Jas. Clerkenwell, iv. 337.
London, 1; MDB. (co. Linc.), 13; New York, 4.

Mott, Motte, Mote, Moth.—(1) Local, 'at the moat.' M.E. mote, O.F. mote, a dike, an embankment; the same as modern Fr. motte, a mound; cf. also mothe, a little earthen fortresse, Cotg.

(v. Skeat, s. v. *moat*, for full history of the word). All the above forms are found, without prefix, in the Hundred Rolls (1273); cf. French 'Delamotte.'

Saundrina de la Mote: Wardrobe Account, 21–23 Edw. III. 38/2.

(2) Bapt. 'the son of Motte.' Undeniably some of our Motts, &c., are of fontal origin. Whether this Mott was a nick. of some familiar personal name or not I cannot at present say. I give instances of both (1) and (2) together, as I cannot separate them.

Motte (without surname), co. Bucks, 1273. A.
William Moth, co. Norf., ibid.
Basilia Motte, cb. Camb., ibid.
Richard Mote, co. Oxf., ibid.
Elena Mott, 1379 : P. T. Yorks. p. 208.
Hugo Mott, 1379 : ibid. p. 209.

Since writing the above it has occurred to me that Motte was but one more attempt at Matilda. 'Malkyne, or Mawt, propyr name, *Matilda*': Prompt. Parv. v. Moulson.

1786. Married—John Pain and Mary Moth : St. Geo. Han. Sq. i. 393.
London, 14, 1, 5, 4; New York, 86, 0, 1, 2.

Mottershead, Mottershadd.—Local, 'of Mottershead,' a spot in the township of Mottram St. Andrew, in the parish of Prestbury, co. Ches.

'A family of the name of Mottershead held lands in this township from an early period. . . . An ancient deed without date, and probably of the 12th or 13th century, says that "Edward, son of Gamyl, lord of Mottram, gave to William, his son and heir, all that land in Mottersheved, in the vill of Mottram, . . . which John de Chellegh then held, from which place he was called William de Mottershead, and his descendants Mottershead of Mottram "': East Ches. ii. 355.

Richard de Mottershead, of Mottram, 1337 : ibid.
John de Mottershead, of Mottram, 1415 : ibid.
1565. Bapt.—Anne Mottershed : Reg. Prestbury, p. 15.
— Buried—Agnes Mottershedde : ibid. p. 17.
1612. Jeffry Mottershead, of Mottram Andrew : Wills at Chester, i. 140.
Manchester, 6, 1; Liverpool, 1, 0; Philadelphia, 2, 0.

Mottram, Motteram.—Local, 'of Mottram,' a parish in East Ches. Motteram occurs in the London Directory. The tendency

to variation increases as the name wanders further from its native home; cf. Barnum for Barnham.

John de Mottrum, 1310: East Ches. ii. 348.
Adam de Mottrum, 1376 : ibid.
1564. Bapt.—Elizabeth Mottram : Reg. Prestbury (East Ches.), p. 13.
1565. — Agnes Mottram : ibid. p. 16.
Hugh Mottram, of Mottram, 1595 : Wills at Chester (1545–1620), p. 140.
Mary Mottram, of Mottram Andrew, 1605: ibid.
London, 3, 1 ; Manchester, 14, 0 ; Philadelphia, 2, 0.

Mould, Moul, Moule, Mold.—Bapt. 'the son of Matilda.' For further information, v. Moulson. The final *d* has been dropped in Moul; cf. Mowl.

1566–7. Robert Mowlde and Alice James : Marriage Lic. (London), i. 35.
1568. William Molde and Susanna Totnam : ibid. p. 39.
1584–5. John Moule, or Moulde, co. Worc. : Reg. Univ. Oxf. vol. ii. pt. ii. p. 140.
1686. William Mould and Alice Hester : Marriage Lic. (Faculty Office), p. 180.
Leeds, 3, 0, 0, 0; West Rid. Court Dir., 1, 0, 0, 0; London, 6, 2, 4, 2 ; Oxford, 0, 0, 0, 3 ; Philadelphia, 2, 0, 0, 0.

Mouldsworth. — Local, ' of Mouldsworth,' a township in the parish of Tarvin, nine miles from Chester ; v. Molesworth, by which this name seems to have been absorbed.

Hamnet Booth, of Mouldsworth, *husbandman*, 1590: Wills at Chester (1545–1620), p. 23.
Humphrey Mouldsworth, of Warmingham, 1587 : ibid. p. 140.
1584. Anthony Mowlsworthe and Cicely Hurlande : Marriage Lic. (London), i. 131.

Moule ; v. Mould.

Moulson.—Bapt. 'the son of Matilda.' Fr. Mathilde, O.E. Molde or Maude (v. Yonge, ii. 415–6). Prof. Freeman says, 'In the mouths of Englishmen pronouncing French names, it (Matilda) became Mahtild, Mahault, Molde, Maud, and so forth' (Norman Conquest, ii. 291). Yorkshire has preserved a memory of this in Moulson (the *d* being dropped).

Walter Moldesone, co. Soms., 1 Edw. III : Kirby's Quest, p. 240.
Ricardus Maldson, 1379 : P. T. Yorks. p. 185.
Thomas Maltson, 1379 : ibid. p. 76.
Roger Moldson, 1379 : ibid. p. 22.
Alicia Moldson, 1379 : ibid. p. 116.

Henricus Moldson, *webster*, 1379 : ibid. p. 136.
Mauld Beeston, 31 Edw. I : Visitation of Cheshire, 1580, p. 84.
1550. Bapt.—Fraunces Molsonne : St. Peter, Cornhill, i. 5.
1565. Married—Rycharde Molson and Agnes Glazier : St. Michael, Cornhill, p. 9.
West Rid. Court Dir., 6 ; Sheffield, 7 ; New York, 1.

Moult. — Bapt. 'the son of Matilda'; v. Moulson, Mould, and Mowl.

1628. Laurence Moult, of Congleton : Wills at Chester, ii. 159.
1636. Margaret Moult, of Congleton, *widow* : ibid.
MDB. (co. Ches.), 4 ; Philadelphia, 2.

Moulton.—Local, 'of Moulton,' a village and parish in co. Chester ; also parishes in cos. Suffolk, Northampton, Norfolk, and Lincoln. Many of these seem to be represented.

Agnes de Multon, co. Norf., 1273. A.
Thomas de Multon, co. Linc., ibid.
Adam de Multon, co. Camb., ibid.
Alex. de Multon, co. Oxf., ibid.
John de Moltone, co. Soms., 1 Edw. III : Kirby's Quest, p. 188.
1591. Thomas Moulton, co. Wilts : Reg. Univ. Oxf. vol. ii. pt. ii. p. 186.
Randle Lowndes, of Moulton, 1617 : Wills at Chester (1545–1620), p. 128.
John Moulton, of Middlewich, 1616 : ibid. p. 140.
London, 6 ; Manchester, 2 ; MDB. (co. Suff.), 4 ; New York, 15.

Moultrie, Moutrie.—Local, 'of Moultrie.' As stated by Mr. Lower, 'A small river in Fifeshire, now called the Motray.'

1566–7. John Fell and Joanna Mowtrye : Marriage Lic. (London), i. 35.
1754. Married—James Moultrie and Cecilia Stanton : St. Geo. Chap. Mayfair, p. 279.
1784. — James Neubigging and Margaret Mutrie : St. Geo. Han. Sq. i. 366.
London, 2, 2.

Mounsey, Mouncey.—Local, ' de la Monceau,' i.e. at the hillock or mound (cf. Munt). O.F. Moncel or Muncel ; later Monceau. More specifically perhaps from some Norman town or hamlet of the name of Monceau or Monceaux.

Robert de Muncella, co. Wilts, 1273. A.
Robert de Munceaux, co. Norf., ibid.
Ingelram de Munceaus, co. York, ibid.
Gilbert de Munceaus, co. Linc., 20 Edw. I. R.
Ralph de Muncy, co. Suff., ibid.
1568. Married — James Munsey and Jone Hollylande : St. Michael, Cornhill, p. 10.

1724. Bapt.—Robert, s. John Mounsey: St. Michael, Cornhill, p. 71.
1747. Married—Anthony Monsey and Sarah Hines: ibid. p. 168.
London, 4, 1; Manchester, 4, 2; MDB. (co. Cumberland), 13, 0; New York, 0, 1; Boston (U.S.), 0, 3.

Mount.—Local, 'at the mount,' i.e. the rising ground, M.E. *munt*. v. Munt for further early instances.
Alan atte Mount, C. R., 12 Edw. III. pt. ii.
1569. Thomas Mounte and Mary Kyrkebye: Marriage Lic. (London), i. 44.
1626. Robert Mount and Joane Stanley: ibid. ii. 170.
London, 7; New York, 30.

Mountain, Mountan.—Local, 'at the mountain.' Not very common in England, as we have but few mountains to boast of. But Hill and Hills have made up for any deficiency, even if they sound more modest; cf. Fr. 'de la Montaigne.' No doubt in some cases this has been Anglicized to Mountain. Mr. Lower (Patr. Brit. p. 231) furnishes an instance of 'de Montaigne' settling as Mountain in co. Norfolk after the Edict of Nantes.
Hugh de Muntein, co. Salop, 1273. A.
William de Muntein, co. Oxf., ibid.
Hugh supra Montem, co. Oxf., ibid.
Matilda supra Montem, co. Oxf., ibid.
1618. John Dentithe, *goldweaver*, and Eliz. Mountaine: Marriage Lic.(London), ii. 62.
1767. Married—John Cooper and Eliz. Mountain: St. Geo. Han. Sq. i. 163.
London, 4, 0; New York, 4, 2; Philadelphia, 12, 0.

Mountainacre.—Local, 'at the mountain acre,' i.e. the arable land on the hillside. This somewhat curious and lengthy surname existed for a time.
1598. Bapt. — Susan, d. Richard Mountaynacre: St. Jas. Clerkenwell, i. 33.
1600. — William, s. Richard Mountaynaker: ibid. p. 36.
1601. — Margaret, d. Richard Mountaynaker: ibid. p. 39.

Mountford, Montford, Mountfort.—(1) Local, 'de Montfort.' Lower, in his Patr. Brit. (p. 228), says that there are two places in Normandy called Montfort, one situated near Argentan, the other near Pont-Audemer. The latter is a fortified town. (2) Local, 'of Montford,' a parish five miles from Shrewsbury, co. Salop.

Simon de Monteforte, co. Notts, 1273. A.
Petronilla de Monteforti, co. Wilts, ibid.
Henry de Monteforti, co. Soms., ibid.
Henry Mounfort, co. Soms., 1 Edw. III: Kirby's Quest, p. 84.
Reginald de Monte Forti, co. Soms., 1 Edw. III: ibid. p. 85.
1586. John Mountford, co. Warw.: Reg. Univ. Oxf. vol. ii. pt. ii. p. 155.
1602. Buried — John Mounford: St. Antholin, p. 41.
1621. Married—Frederic Steward and Abigall Mondeford, of Mondeford, in Norfolk: St. Michael, Cornhill, p. 23.
London, 9, 1, 0; New York, 1, 1, 1; MDB. (co. Salop), 0, 2, 0.

Mountjoy.—Local, 'of Muntjoy.' Lower writes, 'Fr. Mont-joie, which Cotgrave defines as "a barrow, a little hill, or heap of stones, layed in or neare a highway for the better discerning thereof, or in remembrance of some notable act performed, or accident befallen in that place."' . . . According to Sir John Maundeville, an eminence near Jerusalem was formerly so called, because it "gevethe joy to pylgrymes hertes because that there men seen first Jerusalem"': Patr. Brit. p. 231.
Ralph de Munjay, alias de Munjoie, alias de Munjau, cos. Derby and Notts, 1273. A.
Ralph de Muntjoye, co. Derby, 20 Edw. I. R.
Serl de Muntjoye, co. Derby, ibid.
Mention is made of the
Canonici et Fres de Monte Jovis, co. Essex, 1273. A.
1586. Edward Wilberfosse and Ann Monioye, alias Mountioye (co. Essex): Marriage Lic. (London), i. 152.
1610. John Montjoy and Ann Blackwood: ibid. p. 325.
1690. Married — Edmund Mountjoy and Mary Mannaton: St. Jas. Clerkenwell, iii. 221.
London, 1; New York, 1; Philadelphia, 4.

Mountney, Montanye. — Local, 'de Mounteny.' I cannot find the spot, but it looks thoroughly Norman.
Robert de Mounteny, co. Camb., A. 1273.
Alexander de Munteny, co. Essex, ibid.
Johannes Mountenay, *armiger*, 1379: P. T. Yorks. p. 31.
Johan Mountenay, Edden sa femme, *fleshewer*, 1379: ibid. p. 43.
1586. Roger Mowntney and Frances Chetham: Marriage Lic. (London), i. 153.
1676. Married—Richard Mounteney and Mary Irons: St. Michael, Cornhill, p. 41.

1745. Edward Mountency (Garlick Hith, London) and Catherine Capen: St. Antholin (London), p. 153.
New York, 0, 4; Philadelphia, 4, 2.

Mouse, Muss, Musse.—Nick. 'the mouse'; M.E. *mous*; cf. Ratt.
Roger Mus, co. Essex, 1273. A.
Isabel Mus, co. Camb., ibid.
John le Mous, burgess, returned for Wilton, 1302. M.
Hugh le Mus. E.
Richard Mowse, c. 1550. Z.
Richard Mouse, C. R., 1 Mary, pt. ix.
1661. Jacob Bodenduch and Susan Mouse: Marriage Alleg. (Canterbury), p. 14.
1720. Married—William Harrison and Mary Mouse: St. Jas. Clerkenwell, p. 244.
1768. — Michael Mows and Mary Walter: St. Geo. Han. Sq. i. 178.
New York, 0, 1, 2; Boston (U.S.), 1, 0, 0.

Mouth.—Local.
Fulk de Mouthe, C. R., 14 Hen. VI.
New York, 1.

Moutrie; v. Moultrie.

Mowbray, Mumbray. — Local, 'of Mowbray,' or 'Monbrai,' an ancient barony in Normandy. Robert de Mowbray was Earl of Northumberland, but his estates passed to his cousin Nigel de Albini, whose son Roger, at the command of Henry I, assumed the name of Mowbray, and affixed it to one of his fiefs, now Melton Mowbray. v. Lower, Patr. Brit. p. 231.
Nigel de Mumbray, temp. Hen. III—Edw. I. K.
Nigel de Moubray, ibid.
Roger de Munbray, co. Bedf., 1273. A.
London, 5, 0; Manchester, 1, 1.

Mowe.—Local, 'at the mow' (v. Maw); cf. Mower and Mawer.
Oliver de la Mowe, Fines Roll, 14 Edw. II.
New York, 1.

Mower.—Occup. 'the mower.' one who cuts grass, commonly found in the North of England as Mawer, q.v.
Roger le Mower, Pardons Roll, 6 Ric. II.
Thomas Mower, C. R., 31 Hen. VI.
1551. Buried — Cristabell Mowre: St. Jas. Clerkenwell, iv. 1.
1659. Married —Daniell Mower and Sarah Powle: St. Dionis Backchurch, p. 34.
London, 1; New York, 3; Philadelphia, 24.

Mowl, Mowll.—Bapt. 'the son of Matilda.' For further information v. Moulson. Mowl is Mould with the final *d* dropped. An instance is furnished under Mould, q.v.

1615. Thomas Moule, co. Worc.: Reg. Univ. Oxf. vol. ii. pt. ii. p. 338.
1646. Buried — Joane, wife of Richard Moule: St. Peter, Cornhill, i. 202.
London, 4, 1.

Moxon.—Bapt. 'the son of Margaret,' from the nick. Mogg or Moggy, sharpened to Mock; cf. Jagge for Jack (Piers Plow.), also Slagg for Slack, and Higg for Hick. Thus Mogson became Mockson and, of course, Moxon; cf. Coxon for Cockson, Dixon for Dickson, &c. Moxon is a Yorkshire surname, and it is there we find the early instances.

Johannes Mokesson, 1379: P.T. Yorks. p. 186.
Robertus Mokeson, 1379: ibid. p. 81.
Johannes Mokeson, 1379: ibid. p. 35.
Roger Mokson, 1379: ibid. p. 236.
1655. John Mokesone and Jane Wardsworth: Reg. Silkstone Church, co. Yorks.
1764. Martha, d. John Mokeson, died Nov. 14, 1764: Monument, Silkstone, co. Yorks.

But Moxon is found in the 16th century:

1592. Married — Antony Moxon and Annes Allenson: St. Peter, Cornhill, i. 239.

Moxon is now, I believe, the universal form.

London, 13; Leeds, 4; West Riding Court Dir., 11; New York, 1; Boston (U.S.), 6.

Moyer.—Occup. 'the mower,' a corruption of Mawer, q.v.

1776. Married—John Charles England and Mary Mower or Moyer: St. Geo. Han. Sq. i. 260.
London, 1; Philadelphia, 98.

Moyse, Moyce, Moyes.—Bapt. 'the son of Moses.' M.E. Moyses (q.v.), whence the nick. Moyse or Mosse (v. Moss); cf. O.F. Moise, i.e. Moses. This probably suggested the English forms.

Mosse fil. Jacob the Jew, co. Oxf., 1273. A.
Hasting Moyse, co. Suff., ibid.
William Movse, co. Essex, ibid.
Mosseus Judeus, co. Northampton, 20 Edw. I. R.
1604. Married — John Lambert and Katherine Moyes: St. Mary Aldermary (London), p. 1.
1643. — Edmund Moys and Clement Pincknye: St. Jas. Clerkenwell, iii. 76.

1797. Married — William Cowley and Ann Moyce: St. Geo. Han. Sq. ii. 160.
London, 1, 1, 3; Boston (U.S.), 0, 0, 3.

Moyses.—Bapt. 'the son of Moses,' always so spelt in the older records. Moyses in our directories represents an English as distinct from a Jewish descent, and stands to Moses as Salmon does to Solomon; v. Moyse.

'Yond is Moyses, I dar warand.'
York Mystery Plays, p. 81.
'Save that he, Moises, and King Salomon.' Chaucer, The Squire's Tale.
Moyses le Batur, co. Hunts, 1273. A.
Moyses Capellanus, 10 Hen. II: Pipe Roll, p. 43.
Alicia Moyses, 1379: P.T. Yorks. p. 299.
1573. Bapt.—Moyses, s. William Wood: St. Jas. Clerkenwell, i. 7.
1590. — Moyses, s. Robert Stuard: St. Peter, Cornhill, i. 36.
1592. Eliz. Moysses, or Moses, of Yealand Conyers: Lancashire Wills at Richmond, p. 198.
1629. Bapt. — Marye, d. of Robert Moyses: St. Mary Aldermary, p. 81.
April 24, 1761, Hugh Moises, A.M., morning lecturer on the death of R. Swinburne, All Saints, Newcastle-upon-Tyne: Brand's Newcastle, i. 390.
New York, 1.

Muckleston; v. Mugleston.

Muddeman, Muddiman, Muddyman.—Nick. 'the moody man,' probably with the earlier sense of being quick to anger, brave, courageous; v. Moody, and cf. Merry and Merriman.

'O mony were the moodie men
Lay gasping on the green.'
Ballad of Captain Carre (Jamieson).
London, 1, 2, 1; West Rid. Court Dir., 2, 0, 0; Sheffield, 1, 0, 0.

Mudie.—Nick.; v. Moody.

Muff.—Nick. 'the mauf' or 'maugh,' i.e. the brother-in-law, a curious surname found in the W. Rid. Yorks alongside its compound Watmuff, i.e. Walter's brother-in-law; cf. the Lancashire Hickmough, Richard's brother-in-law. In compounds it is found as *maghe, moghe, mough*, and *mouth*; v. Watmough.
West Rid. Court Dir., 5; Sheffield, 2; Philadelphia, 3.

Muffit.—Local, 'of Moffatt,' a town on the borders of Lanarkshire and Dumfriesshire. Muffitt

or Muffet seems to have been an old corruption.

1569. Married — John Buxton and Joane Muffet: St. Thomas the Apostle (London), p. 4.
1598. — John Hake and Brigett Muffet: ibid. p. 9.
1651. — Thomas Wallis and Susanna Muffett: St. Dionis Backchurch (London), p. 27.
1663. — William Moffett and Mary Borne: ibid. p. 37.
Only one letter differs in these last two entries.
London, 1.

Mugford.—Local; v. Mogford.

Muggeridge.—Local; v. Moggridge.

Muggleton.—Local, 'of Muckleston' (?). Probably a variant; v. Mugleston.

1618. Thomas Powell and Judith Muggleton: Marriage Lic. (London), ii. 67.
1637. Bapt. — Mary, d. Lodowicke Mugelltone: St. Mary Aldermary, p. 85.
London, 2.

Mugleston, Mugliston, Muckleston. — Local, (1) 'of Muckleston,' a hamlet in the parish of Shawbury, co. Salop; (2) 'of Muckleston,' a parish in the union of Market Drayton, co. Salop. The ancient form still remains, but is now generally modified into Mugliston.

1592. Edward Mucleston, co. Salop: Reg. Univ. Oxf. vol. ii. pt. ii. p. 191.
1601. Richard Mucleston, or Muckellstone, co. Salop: ibid. p. 247.
1675. John Goldwell and Ann Muggleston: Marriage Lic. (Westminster), p. 46.
1677. William Mugglestone and Eliz. Bookham: Marriage Alleg. (Canterbury), p. 209.
London, 1, 2, 0; MDB. (co. Derby), 0, 2, 0; (co. Salop), 0, 0, 1.

Mulcaster, Muncaster.—Local, 'of Mulcaster,' now Muncaster, a parish in co. Cumb.; cf. *baluster* and *banister*.

Robert de Molecastre, co. Cumb., 1279. M.
Walter de Mulecastre, co. Cumb., 1287. M.
1560. Married—Rycharde Monckestre and Katherine Ashleye: St. Michael, Cornhill, p. 8.
1662. Henry Hesketh and Sarah Mulcaster: Marriage Alleg. (Canterbury), p. 71.
Crockford, 1, 0; Ulverston, 0, 1; Philadelphia, 0, 2.

N n

Mule.—Nick. 'the mule'; A.S. *mul*, a sobriquet for an obstinate man.

Roger le Mul, co. Wilts, 1273. A.

Mulford.—Local, 'of Mulford.' Possibly, but not probably, the place now known as Mudford, a parish three miles from Yeovil, co. Soms. The earliest references are found in that district. Cf. Milford.

Gilbert de Mullford, co. Wilts, Hen. III-Edw. I. K.
Edmund de Muleford, co. Wilts, 1273. A.
Richard de Muleford, co. Wilts. ibid.
1655. Buried—Eliz., wife of William Mulford: St. Jas. Clerkenwell, iv. 305.
1675. Thomas Grice and Judith Mulford: Marriage Alleg. (Canterbury), p. 146.
London, 1 ; New York, 30.

Mullin, Mullen.—Local; v. Mullins (1 and 2).

1722. Buried—(blank) Mullin: St. Thomas the Apostle (London), p. 149.
New York, 44, 119.

Mulliner.—(1) Occup. 'a milner'; M.E. *mulnere*; v. Milner. (2) Local, a corruption of Molineaux, q.v., and cf. Mullins and Molines.

Sancheus Moliner, co. Linc., 1273. A.
1564. Thomas Mulliner, Corp. Christi Coll.: Reg. Univ. Oxf. vol. ii. pt. ii. p. 15.
1715. Buried—Charles Molineer: St. Antholin (London), p. 128.
London, 2 ; Philadelphia, 1.

Mullineux.—Local; v. Molineaux.

Mullins, Mullings.—(1) Local. An English dress of the French 'de Molines.' The *g* in Mullings is an excrescence; cf. Jennings for Jennins.

William de Molyns, co. Glouc., 1273. A.
1587-8. Barentyne Molens, co. Berks: Reg. Univ. Oxf. vol. ii. pt. ii. p. 162.
(2) Local, 'at the miln,' i.e. mill. M.E. *miln* and *mulne*. The final *s* is common to these local surnames; cf. Meadows, Brooks, Sykes, Mills, &c. Perhaps it is the patronymic *s*, as in Williams, Jones, &c.

Laurence atte Mulene, 1278. M.
Gilbert atte Mullane, co. Soms., 1 Edw. III: Kirby's Quest, p. 154.
1670. Francis Shepherd and Abigaell Mullins: Marriage Alleg. (Canterbury), p. 41.

1787. Married—John Mullens and Jane Rebecca Trevor: Canterbury Cath. p. 98.
London, 15, 3 ; New York, 38, 0.

Mullock, Mulock, Mulloch, Mullocks.—? Bapt. 'the son of Mulloc' (?). This seems to be the only natural conclusion. This view is confirmed by the fact of the existence of the genitive Mullocks, i.e. Mullock's son; cf. Williams, Jenkins, &c.

Reginald Mulloc, or Mulluc, co. Camb., 1273. A.
Thomas Mulloc, co. Camb., ibid.
Johannes Mullok, 1379 : P. T. Howdenshire, p. 29.
1750. Married—John Bassil and Eliz. Mullocks: St. Geo. Chap. Mayfair, p. 179.
Crockford, 0, 1, 0, 0; New York, 0, 0, 1, 0; Philadelphia, 0, 5, 0, 0.

Mumbray.—Local; v. Mowbray.

Mumby, Munby.—Local, ' of Mumby,' a parish in the union of Spilsby, co. Lincoln. Mumby is found as early as the 13th century; v. infra.

Alicia de Mumby, co. Linc., 1273. A.
Cf. Hereð de Munby, co. Linc., ibid.
Alan de Mumby, co. Linc., Hen. III-Edw. I. K.
Beatrice de Mumby, co. Linc., ibid.
1669. Married—Robert Hodskines and Eliz. Mumbee: St. Jas. Clerkenwell, iii. 161.
1690. Bapt. —Eliz., d. Barthollomew Mumbey: ibid. ii. 337.
London, 3, 1 ; New York, 1, 0.

Mumford, Munford.—Local, 'of Mundford,' a parish in co. Norwich, found as early as the 13th century; in the variant form Mumford was inevitable; cf. Munby for Mumby.

Adam de Mundeford, co. Norf., 1273. A.
Richard de Mundefode, co. Camb., ibid.
John de Mundeford, co. Northampton, 20 Edw. I. R.
Lora de Mumford, co. Herts, ibid.
Osbert Mundeford, C. R., 21 Hen. VI.
The following is interesting evidence :

1720. Bapt.—Anne, d. John and Mary Munford: St. Jas. Clerkenwell, ii. 184.
1733. — John, s. John and Mary Mumford : ibid. p. 208.
London, 19, 2 ; New York, 7, 1.

Mummery, Momerie.—Local, ' of Munbray ' or 'Mumbray,' variants of Mowbray, the earliest forms of which include Mumbray,

Mombray, and Munbray ; v. Mowbray.

Walter Mombray, Mayor of Bristol, 1221 : YYY. p. 669.
Roger de Moubray, 1283. M.
Roger de Mounbray, 1297. M.

The above two entries refer to the same person.

Roger de Mumbral, co. Kent, 1273. A.
Pagan de Mumbray, co. Oxf., ibid.
Roger de Munbray, alias Mumbray, co. Bedf., ibid.
Roger de Mumbray, co. York, 20 Edw. I. R.

All these Rogers, no doubt, refer to the same individual, one of the Mowbrays. Of the etymology of Mummery, therefore, there can be no question.

1660. Buried — Elizabeth Mummery : Canterbury Cath. p. 121.
London, 8, 0; Crockford, 1, 1.

Munby ; v. Mumby.

Muncaster.—Local; v. Mulcaster.

Muncey, Muncy ; v. Mounsey.

1568. Married — James Munsey and Jone Hollylande: St. Michael, Cornhill, p. 10.
London, 5, 2 ; MDB. (co. Herts), 2, 0.

Munday, Mundy ; v. Monday.

Munden.—Local, 'of Munden,' two parishes in co. Hertford, Great and Little Munden.

Henry de Mundene, co. Wilts, 1273. A.
Henry de Munden, co. Linc., Hen. III-Edw. I. K.
1565. John Munden, New Coll.: Reg. Univ. Oxf. vol. ii. pt. ii. p. 15.
1669. John Munden and Eliz. Usher : Marriage Alleg. (Canterbury), p. 15.
London, 2 ; Philadelphia, 3.

Munford ; v. Mumford.

Munk.—Offic. 'the monk'; v. Monk. This variant has always been rare as a surname. A.S. *munec*.

Beatrix le Munk, co. Hunts, 1273. A.
Peter le Munk, co. Norf. FF.
1682. Married—Robert Harrison and Mary Munke: St. Jas. Clerkenwell, iii. 196.
London, 1 ; New York, 3 ; Philadelphia, 2.

Munn.—Offic. ' the monk,' one of the many variants of 'le Moigne'; v. Money (2). Probably Moon (q.v.) in some instances is a similar variant.

Robert le Moun, co. York, 1273. A.
Walter le Moun, co. Essex, ibid.
Thomas le Mun, co. Norf., ibid.

Ralph Mun, co. Camb., 1273. A.
John le Moune, co. Kent, 20 Edw.
I. R.
1665. Married — Gabriell Seuens and
Ann Munn: St. Jas. Clerkenwell, iii. 119.
1782. — William Spencer and Mary
Munn: St. Geo. Han. Sq. i. 337.
London, 6; New York, 19.

Munt.—Local, 'at the mount.'
M.E. *munt*; A.S. *munt* (Skeat).
My first instance settles the matter
beyond dispute.
William atte Munte, co. Kent, 20 Edw.
I. R.
Walter Munte, co. Dorset, 1273. A.
Cf. Roger de Munt Feront, co. Suff.,
ibid.
1677-8. William Ediall and Eliz. Munt:
Marriage Alleg. (Canterbury), p. 276.
1692-3. Bapt.—Mary, d. John Munt,
tailor: St. Dionis Backchurch (London),
p. 132.
London, 5; Oxford, 2; New York, 1.

Murby.—Local; v. Morby.

Murch.—Local, (1) 'at the
march,' from residence thereby,
i.e. the boundary line; v. March.
(2) 'At the marsh,' from residence
thereby, i.e. the swamp; v. Marsh.
This variant seems to be of West-
country parentage.
Robert in the Merche, co. Soms., 1
Edw. III: Kirby's Quest, p. 99.
1772. Married — William Murch and
Esther Mitchell: St. Geo. Han. Sq. i. 225.
London, 4; MDB. (co. Soms.), 4.

Murcott, Murcutt.—Local, (1)
'of Murcot,' a hamlet in the parish
of Charlton - upon - Ortmoor, co.
Oxford; (2) 'of Morcott,' a parish
in co. Rutland; (3) 'of Murcott,'
a hamlet in the parishes of Long
Buckby and Watford, co. Northampton. But such a local name
as the Moorcot, i.e. the cottage on
the moor, no doubt arose in several
places; cf. Moorhouse.
William de Morcote, co. Oxf., 1273. A.
Robert Morcote, co. Oxf., ibid.
Laurence de Morcok (sic), co. Bucks,
Hen. III-Edw. I. K.
Alan de Morkote, co. Leic., ibid.
Martin de Morkot, cos. Norf. and Suff.,
ibid.
Thomas de Morcote, co. Northampton,
20 Edw. I. R.
1671. James Prescott and Ann Staper,
with consent of her mother, now wife of
Job Murcott: Marriage Lic. (Faculty
Office), p. 120.
London, 3, 4.

Murden.—Local; v. Mordan.
Stephen de Murdon, co. Norf., 1273. A.

Murdoch, Murdock.—Bapt.
'the son of Murdoch,' Celtic (Yonge,
ii. 158).
Murdac, dean of Appleby, 32 Hen. II:
Nicolson and Burn, Hist. Westm. and
Cumb., i. 428.
Murdac de Gunton, cos. Warw. and
Leic., Hen. III-Edw. I. K.
1680. Job Nutt and Sarah Murdock:
Marriage Alleg. (Canterbury), p. 34.
London, 11, 0; New York, 15, 20.

Murfin.—Bapt. 'the son of
Mervin'; v. Marvin.

Murgatroyd, Murgitroyde.
—Local, 'of Mergret's royd,' i.e.
Margaret's clearing; v. Royd. So
we read of Tom-rode, Wilimotrode, Smyth-rode (Whitaker's
Craven, p. 199). The instance
quoted below sets all doubt at
rest as to the origin. This surname has ramified strongly in
Yorkshire, the county of its birth.
Gilbert and Sullivan have immortalized the name, if it needed
immortalizing; but it was a strong
flight of fancy to place it so far
from its true home.
Johannes Mergretrode, 1379: P. T.
Yorks. p. 187.
1726. Bapt. — Benjamin, s. William
Murgytroyd: St. Dionis Backchurch,
p. 160.
1739. Married — Joseph Foster and
Eliz. Murgatroyd: St. Geo. Han. Sq.
i. 23.
West Rid. Court Dir.,16,0; New York,
4, 0; Philadelphia, 7, 6.

Muriel, Murrell, Murrells.
—Bapt. 'the son of Muriel'; v.
Merrall.
London, 0, 16, 2; Crockford, 3, 3, 0;
New York, 0, 6, 0.

Murthwaite.—Local, 'of Murthwaite,' a small hamlet in Ravenstonedale, co. Westm.
William Myrthwaite,1541: W. Nicholls,
Hist. and Traditions of Ravenstonedale,
co. Westm., p. 114.
Rowland Myrthwaite, 1541: ibid.
Lancelot Myrthwaite, 1541: ibid.
1678. William Ivatt and Mary Murthwaite: Marriage Alleg. (Canterbury),
p. 283.
1802. Bapt. — Thomas, s. John Murthwaite, *waller*: Parish Ch., Ulverston,
p. 542.
Liverpool, 2; Ulverston, 3; MDB. (co.
Cumb.), 1.

Muschamp.—Local, 'of Muschamp.' The exact locality I do

not know, probably somewhere in
North France. A family of this
name were early settled in North-
umberland.
Robert de Muscans, 1195: KKK. vi. 54.
Also, de Muschans, 1198, and de
Muschauns, 1228: ibid. pp. 63, 151.
Matilda de Muscamp, co. Northumb.,
Hen. III-Edw. I. K.
Thomas de Muscham, cos. Notts and
Derby, ibid.
Ada Muschamp, cos. Notts and Derby,
ibid.
Robert de Mustchamp, co. Northumb.,
ibid.
1587-8. Aymondesham Muschampe, co.
Middlesex: Reg. Univ. Oxf. vol. ii. pt. ii.
p. 162.
1655. Married—John Roy and Dorothy
Muschampe: St. Jas. Clerkenwell, iii. 94.
London, 2.

Musgrave, Musgrove.—Local, 'of Musgrave,' a parish near
Brough, co.Westm. It is probable,
however, that some spot in the
West of England has given birth
to a similar surname.
Roger de Mussegrave, 1277. M.
1581. John Mosgrove, co. Devon: Reg.
Univ. Oxf. vol. ii. pt. ii. p. 113.
1603. Henry Musgrove, co. Soms.:
ibid. p. 264.
1708. Married—Thomas Tompkins and
Mary Musgrave: St. Antholin (London),
p. 121.
London, 7, 6; New York, 6, 5.

Mushet, Mussett, Mushett.
—Nick. 'the musket,' a sparrow-
hawk; v. Muskett. O.F. *mouschet*
(v. Skeat on *musket*).
John Muschat, co. Oxf., 1273. A.
William Muschet: Close Roll, 17 Edw.
III. pt. ii.
1692. Married—Thomas Musset and
Ellen Rice: St. Jas. Clerkenwell, iii. 211.
1788. — Emery Mussett and Mary
Lillywhite: St. Geo. Han. Sq. ii. 12.
London, 1, 1, 0; Philadelphia, 1, 0, 2.

Muskett, Muskette. — Nick.
'the musket,' a sparrow-hawk,
afterwards a hand-gun, when the
names of birds of prey were given
to firearms; v. Mushet; cf. Spark,
Hawk.
Robert Musket, co. Camb., 1273. A.
Nicholas Musket, *latoner*, 3 Edw. II:
Freemen of York, i. 12.

That Muskett and Mushet are
the same may be seen by two
entries concerning one individual:
William Muschet, co. Camb., 1273. A.
William Musket, co. Camb., ibid.

John Musket, co. Soms., 1 Edw. III : Kirby's Quest, p. 224.
1604. Edward Myles and Agnes Muskett: Marriage Lic. (London), i. 292.
1745. Married—Septimus Musket and Mary Maynard: St. Geo. Chap. Mayfair, p. 53.
London, 3, 0 ; Philadelphia, 0, 1.

Mussard.—Nick. 'the musard,' the dreamy, meditative man (?). The name seems to have survived.
Malcolm le Musard, c. 1300. M. London, 1.

Muss (e ; v. Mouse.

Musset ; v. Mushet.

Musson.—Local, ' of Muston,' parishes in cos. York and Leicester. I can scarcely hesitate to accept this solution. The corruption was, it seems to me, inevitable. But v. Misson.
Andrew de Muston, co. Leic., Hen. III–Edw. I. K.
John de Muston, co. Linc., 1273. A.
1702. Married — Hugh Musson and Phillis Lowe: St. Dionis Backchurch, p. 51.
1766. — John Muston and Mary Merry-wether : St. Geo. Han. Sq. i. 159.
London, 6 ; New York, 2 ; Philadelphia, 7.

Mustard.—Nick. (1) for one of a sharp, keen, biting tongue, or (2) for a seller of mustard ; v. next article. Cf. Pepper and the remarks appended.
Jordan Mustard, co. Hunts, 1273. A.
John Mustard, co. Camb., ibid.
Margaret Mustard, co. Norf., ibid.
London, 3.

Mustarder. — Occup. ' the mustarder,' a maker of and dealer in mustard, an important manufacture in a day of pungent sauces ; cf. Pepper, Garlickmonger, &c.
' Wo was his coke, but if his sauce were Poinant and sharpe.'
Chaucer, C. T. 352–3.
Richard le Mustarder, co. Northampt., 1273. A.
Robert le Mustarder. H.
Thomas le Mustarder, London. X.
David le Mustarder, 1305. M.
William Mustarder, rector of Baldeswell, Norfolk, 1467 : FF. viii. 186.

Mustardman, Mustardmaker.—Occup. 'makers or dealers in mustard ' ; v. Mustarder. These surnames were too cumbrous to last, and probably were abbreviated to Mustard for convenience sake ; cf. Pepper and Pepperman.
Peter le Mustardman, co. Norf., 1273. A.
Robertus Musterdman, 1379 : P. T. Yorks. p. 41.
Johannes Mustardman, 1379 : ibid. p. 99.
Alicia Musterdmaker, 1379 : ibid. p. 97.
John Alan, *musterdemaker*, 1479, co. York : W. 11, p. 105.
Alicia Mustardmaker de Ripon, 1397 : W. 2, pt. i. p. 222.

Muttlebury.—Local, ' of Muttlebury.' This name seems to hail from co. Somerset.
Robert de Motelbury, co. Soms., 1 Edw. III : Kirby's Quest, p. 174.
Mr. Muttlebury rowed for Cambridge in the inter-University race, 1891.

Mutton. — (1) Nick. O.F. *moton*, a sheep, whence our mutton, the carcass, the flesh of a sheep. (2) Local, ' of Mutton.' I do not see any locality bearing this name, but I find the following entry :
' Robert de Mutone,' co. Soms., 1 Edw. III : Kirby's Quest, p. 280.
Perhaps *de* is a misprint for *le*.
Philip le Mutton. B.
Willelmus Moton, 1379 : P. T. Yorks. p. 27.
1729. Married—Richard Brackston and Margaret Mutton : St. Geo. Chap. Mayfair, p. 292.
London, 1.

Mycock.—Bapt. ' the son of Matthew ' ; v. Maycock. The variant Mocock, afterwards Mycock, seems to have been popular in East Lancashire and over the border into W. Rid. Yorks. It still remains in Manchester and district.
Mokock de la Lowe : De Lacy Inquisition, 1311.
Mokock del Moreclough : ibid.
Dik, son of Mocock : ibid.

Johannes Mocok', 1379 : P. T. Yorks. p. 180.
Dionisia Mocok', 1379 : ibid. p. 8.
Sheffield, 2 ; Manchester, 6.

Myers, Mires.—Local, ' at the mire,' swampy, low-lying land, a bog, found in such compounds as Hollowmire, Longmire, Blamire. The final s is common to short local surnames; cf. Holmes, Greaves, Brooks, Styles. A large number of the Myers in the London Directory are of German-Jewish descent, and have no connexion with the North-English Myers. M.E. *mire* and *myre*.
'And lette his shepe acombred in the mire.' Chaucer, C. T., Prologue.
David in the Mire, C. R., 24 Edw. I.
Henricus del Myre, 1379 : P. T. Yorks. p. 169.
Johannes del Mire, 1379 : ibid. p. 182.
Willelmus del Mire, 1379 : ibid. p. 275.
Richard del Myre, 1379 : ibid. p. 268.
1609. Thomas Awsten and Katherine Myers : Marriage Lic. (London), p. 314.
Roger Mires, 1642 : Preston Guild Rolls, p. 101.
William Mires, 1642 : ibid.
Richard Myres, of Preston, 1670 : Lancashire Wills at Richmond, p. 190.
Hugh Myres, of Docker, 1540 : ibid.
Thomas Myers, of Preston, 1671 : ibid.
West Rid. Court Dir., 14, 2 ; London, 48, 0 ; New York, 152, 0.

Myerscough. — Local, ' of Myerscough,' a township in the old parish of Lancaster. For the various early spellings, Mireschoghe, Merscowe, Myreskoo, Mirescoghe, Myrescoghe, and Myerscoe, v. Baines' Lanc. ii. 540.
'The heir of Henry de Fetherby, and William de Whytyngham, John de Staunford, and the heir of Richard de Mirscowe hold the mediety of the manor of Claghton ': Knights' Fees, 23 Edw. III, Baines' Lanc. ii. 693.
London, 1 ; Manchester, 4.

Myhill.—Bapt. ; v. Miell.

Myles.—Bapt. ; v. Miles.

Myrtle.—Bapt. ; v. Martel.

N

Nabb, Nabbs, Nabs. — (1) Bapt. 'the son of Abel,' from the nick. Nabb, gen. Nabbs; cf. Nibbs from Isabella or Noll for Oliver. In the Alchemist (1610) Abel the tobacco-man is familiarly Nab.

'Six o' thy legs more will not do it, Nab.' Act. ii. sc. 1.

(2) Local, 'at the nab,' from residence on a spot so called. Here *nab* is a variant of *knap*, the crown of a hill; v. Knapp. The Lancashire surname Nabb or Nabbs is undoubtedly of local origin.

1572. Thomas Nabb, of Tottington: Wills at Chester, i. 140.
1576. Jane Nabb, of Bury: ibid.
1596. Ann Nabbs, of Bury: ibid.
1604. John Slater, of the Nabb in Billington: ibid. p. 176.
Manchester, 1, 0, 0; Bury, 1, 2, 0; Philadelphia, 2, 0, 1.

Nagle, Nagele, Nagel. — ? Local. A corruption of Nangle (?); v. Burke's Landed Gentry. This surname seems to have made enormous strides in the United States. One cannot help thinking that there must be some second parentage. But v. Neagle.

1749. Married—James Nagle and Mary Rowson: St. Geo. Chap. Mayfair, p. 131.
1796. — James Nagle and Margaret Hughes: St. Geo. Han. Sq. ii. 155.
London, 3, 0, 0; Philadelphia, 72, 14, 27.

Nail(e; v. Nale.

Nailer, Nailor. — Occup. 'the nailer'; v. Naylar.

London, 1, 2; New York, 0, 1; Philadelphia, 0, 1.

Nairn, Nairne, Nern. — Local, 'of Nairn,' co. Nairn. A Scottish surname. Nern, as a variant, seems to be confined to the United States.

Peter Nerne, 1601: Cal. State Papers (Scotland), p. 804.
1752. Bapt.—Eliz., d. Edward Nairne: St. Michael, Cornhill, p. 175.
1806. Married — George Nairn and Mary Busby: St. Geo. Han. Sq. ii. 250.

London, 2, 3, 0; Philadelphia, 4, 0, 0; New York, 1, 1, 1; Boston (U.S.), Nern, 1.

Naish. — Local, 'atten ash'; v. Nash. Naish is simply a variant of Nash; cf. Aysh for Ash. All these forms belong to the West country, especially Devonshire and Somersetshire. In the Reg. Univ. Oxf. the name is spelt indifferently Nash, Naish, and Nasshe; v. Index.

1524. John Hurdman and Anne Naysshe: Marriage Lic. (London), i. 3.
1799. Married—Samuel Whatley and Ann Naish: St. Geo. Han. Sq. ii. 210.
1804. — Henry Naish and Jane Stiell: ibid. p. 299.
MDB. (co. Somerset), 13.

Nakerer. — Occup. 'the nakerer,' a player on the naker or kettledrum.

'Pipes, trompes, nakeres, and clariounes.' Chaucer, C. T. 2513.
Lambekyn Taborer, *minstrel*: Wardrobe Account, 48 Edw. III-1 Ric. II. 41/10.
Janyn Nakerer, *minstrel*: ibid.
Nicholas Trumpour, *minstrel*: ibid.

This surname has not survived.

Nalder, Nelder. — Local, 'atten alder,' i.e. at the alder-tree; A.S. *alr*, an alder-tree; the *d* is excrescent. The initial N is the last letter of the prefix *atten* (= at the); cf. Noakes and Nangle.

Robertus de Alre, co. Devon, 1273. A.
Alice Attenalre. J.
John Nelder. H.
1749. Married—Stephen Nalder and Sarah Pearson: St. Geo. Chap. Mayfair, p. 143.
1784. — Daniel Nelder and Mary Spundley: St. Geo. Han. Sq. i. 363.
London, 5, 0; Plymouth, 0, 2; Tiverton, 0, 1; Philadelphia, 1, 0.

Nale, Nail, Naile. — Local, 'atten ale,' i.e. at the ale-house, the final *n* of *atten* becoming the prefix of the name proper.

'And maken him gret festes at the nale.' Chaucer, C. T. 6931.

Cf. Nelmes, Noakes, &c. Nail was a natural modern variant.

1562. Married—John Nale and Sisley Barlow: St. Antholin (London), p. 14.
1584. John Naile, of Liverpool: Wills at Chester, i. 141.
1791. Married — William Naile and Sarah Wild: St. Geo. Han. Sq. ii. 66.
1798. — Robert Nale and Maria Jervaise: ibid. p. 183.
London, 0, 1, 0; Philadelphia, 0, 2, 1.

Nall. — Local, 'atten hall,' i.e. at the hall, from residence there as owner or servant. The final *n* in *atten* has become the prefix of the name proper.

1665-6. Bapt.—William, s. William Nall, servant to Sir Edmond Turner: St. Dionis Backchurch (London), p. 118.
1681. William Nall and Jane Biber: Marriage Alleg. (Canterbury), p. 60.
Manchester, 7; Liverpool, 4.

Nance. — Local, 'of Nance.' 'An estate in the parish of Illogan, co. Cornwall, which was, not many generations ago, in the possession of the family' (Lower). For the meaning of this local term, v. Nanfan, and cf. Nancy in Lorraine, Nantes in Brittany, and Trenance in Cornwall.

Crockford, 1; Cornwall Dir. (List of Farmers), 5.

Nanfan. — Local, 'of Nanfan.' 'A Cornish family of some distinction, which produced, among other worthies, John Nanfan, the first patron of Cardinal Wolsey, who had been his chaplain. The name is evidently local, probably from Nanfan in the parish of Cury' (Lower). Cf. such other Cornish names as Nancarrow, Nankivell, Nanjulian, Nankervis, Pennant, &c. The root is Celtic, *nant*, a valley; cf. Nantwich (co. Chester) and Nantglyn (co. Denbigh).

John Nanfane, C. R., 26 Hen. VI.
1660. Married—Bridgis Nanfan and Katherine Hastings: St. Dionis Backchurch (London), p. 37.

Nangle. — Local, 'atten angle,' i.e. at the angle, the bend or corner; v. Angle. In this case, as in Nale and Nall, the initial is borrowed from the prefix. The name is Latinized into 'de angulo,' or 'in angulo,' in the Hundred Rolls; cf. Nash, Nelmes, &c.

John de Angulo, co. Norf., 1273. A.
Symon in Angulo, co. Linc., ibid.
1571. Peter Nangle (Dublin): Reg. Univ. Oxf. vol. ii. pt. ii. p. 49.
London, 2; Worcester, 1; Boston (U.S.), 4.

Nanson.—Bapt. 'the son of Ann,' from nick. Nan; cf. Noll, Nabb, Nibb. Nan later on became Nanny and Nancy. The French turned it into the diminutives Nanette and Nanon. Even Ann Boleyn was 'Nan.' James Harrison, a priest, when the proclamation was read forbidding the people to call Catherine of Arragon Queen, was accused of saying, 'Queen Catherine was Queen, and Nan Boleyn was not Queen': v. Dict. Nat. Biog. ix. 299. Nan gave us nan-pie for mag-pie, the phrase 'As nice as a nanny-hen,' i.e. very affected, and 'Miss Nancy,' an effeminate man (v. Halliwell). But Nan and Nanny fell into disrepute, like Parnall and Jill. A nanny-house was well known to the dissolute of both sexes in the 16th century. In the ballad, 'The Two Angrie Women of Abington,' Nan Lawson is a wanton; indeed, in the 17th century she generally appears in the roistering songs in anything but a virtuous light. Respectable people, still liking the name, changed it to Nancy, and in that form it still lives among the peasantry.

Robertus Nanson, 1379: P. T. Yorks. p. 123.
Benedictus Nanson, 1379: ibid. p. 232.
Nicholaus Nanson, 1379: ibid. p. 272.

Our Nansons, of course, have no connexion with Nan in her degraded days. They belong to Nan in her early youth, before she became tainted with the world.

London, 1; Carlisle, 4; MDB. (co. Cumberland), 6.

Naper, Napier, Napper, Napery.— Offic. 'the naper,' 'napier,' or 'napper,' from O.F. nape, a cloth; Fr. nappe, a table-cloth. Dim. nap-kin. 'Napet or napekyn': Prompt. Parv. 'The over nape schall double be layde': The Boke of Curtasye. Thus the naper or napier had charge of the table-linen; whence also the form 'de la naperye,' corresponding to 'de la paneterie,' 'de le eurerie,' 'de le butterye,' &c. With the intrusive i in Napier, cf. the y in Sawyer (Sawer), Bowyer (Bower), or lawyer for lawer.

John le Naper, Close Roll, 43 Hen. III.
Jordan le Nappere, co. Oxf., 1273. A.
Thomas le Nappere, co. Oxf., ibid.
John le Naper. C.
Robert Napparius. E.
Walter de la Naperye. L.
Robert le Nappere, co. Soms., 1 Edw. III: Kirby's Quest, p. 259.
1546-7. Edward Napper and Anne Peyton: Marriage Lic. (London), i. 9.
1784. Married — The Right Hon. Francis, Lord Napier, and Maria Margaret Clavering: St. Geo. Han. Sq. i. 358.
1794. — Henry Rycroft and Jane Naper: ibid. ii. 114.
London, 0, 6, 5, 0; New York, 0, 11, 0, 0.

Nappy.—(1) ? Nick. This name just barely survives in Yorkshire, where it arose. 'Nap, expert. Yorks' (Halliwell). 'Nappy, strong, as ale, &c. "Noppy as ale is, vigoreaux": Palsgrave' (Halliwell). (2) ? Nick. Perhaps connected with nap, the rough surface of cloth. A likely nickname in Yorkshire; v. nap (2) (Skeat).

Walterus Napy, laborer, 1379: P. T. Howdenshire, p. 6.
Selby (co. York), 2.

Napton, Knapton.—Local, 'of Knapton': (1) a township in the parish of Acomb, near York; (2) a parish in co. Norfolk. 'The town or farmstead on the nap'; v. Knapp.

Estrilda de Cnapetone, co. Norf., 1273. A.
William de Knapeton, co. Norf., ibid.
Johannes de Knapton, 1379: P. T. Yorks. p. 295.
Ricardus de Knapton, 1379: ibid.
1752. Married—Thomas Napton and Ann Wright: St. Geo. Chap. Mayfair, p. 213.
1790. — Bartholomew Napton and Susanna Hine: St. Geo. Han. Sq. ii. 47.
London, 1, 0; Boston (U.S.), 0, 6.

Nash.—Local, 'atten ash' (at the ash), from residence beside an ash-tree. The final n in the prefix became the initial of the name proper; v. Noakes and Nalder for similar tree instances. M.E. asch, esche. 'Esche, tre, fraxinus': Prompt. Parv. Esh is still popular for ash in Furness, North Lanc. This surname is familiar to all the English-speaking world.

Agnes ate Nasse, co. Oxf., 1273. A.
Sarra Atteneshe. B.
William atte Nasche, c. 1300. M.
Pagan atte Nash. B.
1524. John Hurdman and Anne Naysshe: Marriage Lic. (London), p. 3.
1620. Married—Fardinando Simones and Alece Nashe: St. Mary Aldermary (London), p. 16.
London, 103; New York, 80.

Nasmith, Neasmith, Nesmith.—Occup. 'the nail-smith.' So says Lower, but see my remarks upon Knifesmith.

James Nasmite, co. York. W. 9.
John Naysmith, co. York. W. 13.
James Nasmith, sheriff of Norwich, 1734: FF. iii. 449.
1745. Married—James Nasmith and Mary Barthol: St. Geo. Chap. Mayfair, p. 53.
1751. Bapt.—Ann, d. Alexander Nacsmith: St. Jas. Clerkenwell, ii. 298.
London, 1, 1, 0; Philadelphia, 0, 0, 4.

Nave.—(1) Nick. 'the neve'; v. Neave. A variant. (2) Occup. 'the knave,' a lad, a servant. The older meaning of knave is not disreputable. The Yorkshire Poll Tax (1379) has many instances to prove its purely occupative character; cf. Napton for Knapton.

Johannes Jakkesknave, 1379: P. T. Yorks. p. 268.
Nicholas Gaytknave, 1379: ibid. p. 271.
Thomas Wyllknave, 1379: ibid. p. 269.
London, 1; New York, 1.

Naylar, Nayler, Naylor.—Occup. 'the nailer,' a maker of nails. In the North of England, where the occupation is early found, the surname has taken the almost universal form of Naylor, following on the lines of Taylor.

John le Naylere, co. Northumb., 20 Edw. I. R.
Stephen le Naylere, London. X.
Johannes Nayler, 1379: P. T. Yorks. p. 17.
Willelmus Nayler, 1379: ibid. p. 272.
Johannes Strenger, nayler, 1379: ibid. p. 172.
Thomas Pope, nayler, 1379: ibid. p. 17.

1565. Married—Robert Nayler and Margaret Larke: St. Jas. Clerkenwell, iii. 2.

1603. Bapt. — William, s. Wylfrecan Naylor: ibid. iv. 75.

1744. Married—John Hicks and Sarah Naylor: St. Geo. Han. Sq. i. 41.

But Nayler was the general form till the middle of the last century.

London, 1, 7, 25; West Rid. Court Dir., 0, 0, 37; Philadelphia, 0, 0, 32.

Nead, Neads, Need, Needes, Needs.—Bapt. 'the son of Eade' or 'Eede' (v. Edes, Eades, and Ede); nick. Nead, Need; gen. Needs, or Neads, or Needes; cf. Neddy, Nibbs, Nopps, Nabbs, &c. Although I have no actual proof, I am confident that this is the derivation of the surname. Ede or Eade was one of the most popular fontnames in the hereditary surname period. My first two instances are strongly confirmatory of this view:

1678. Bapt.—Mary, d. Richard Nede: St. Jas. Clerkenwell, i. 281.

1681. Married—William Smith and Barbara Nedes: ibid. iii. 189.

1729. — Charles Smith and Rachael Needs: St. Geo. Chap. Mayfair, p. 301.

1747. Bapt. — Susannah, d. William Need: St. Jas. Clerkenwell, ii. 283.

1780. Married — William Need and Mary Long: St. Geo. Han. Sq. i. 311.

London, 0, 0, 1, 4, 1; Philadelphia, 1, 3, 0, 0, 2.

Neagle.—? Local, 'atten eagle,' i.e. at the eagle, a sign-name with initial N borrowed from the prefix (v. Roebuck for other instances of sign-names); cf. Nelmes, Nash, Nangle, &c.

1673-4. John Falkon and Susanna Neagell: Marriage Alleg. (Canterbury), p. 109.

1679. Martin Neagle, in the Rebecca, for Virginia: Hotten's Lists of Emigrants, p. 39.

1762. Married—George Holland and Eliz. Neagle: St. Geo. Han. Sq. i. 110.

London, 2; Philadelphia, 3.

Neal, Neale, &c.; v. Neil.

Neame, Neames.—Nick. 'the uncle' (O.E. *neme*), gen. Neames; cf. Neaves, Watmough, Bairnfather, Cousin, &c. Names of relationship will be found scattered in considerable numbers over this dictionary. v. also Uncle.

'In evyll tyme thou dedyst hym wronge, He ys my neme.'   Halliwell.

'And angels did him gret honoure, Lo! childe, he seid, this is thy neme.' Ibid.

1584. Thomas Neame, co. Kent: Reg. Univ. Oxf. vol. ii. pt. ii. p. 135.

1587. William Neames and Margaret Burton: Marriage Lic. (London), i. 159.

1594-5. Buried—William Neame, *gent.*, in the Chauncell: St. Jas. Clerkenwell, iv. 55.

1893. Died—Richard Beale Neame, at Hastings: Daily Telegraph, Dec. 26. London, 5, 0.

Neap, Neep. — Nick. 'the grandson' or 'nephew'; cf. Cousin, &c.; v. Neave.

Henry le Nep, co. Bucks, 1273. A. Peter le Nep, co. Bucks, ibid. Emma Nep, co. Hunts, ibid.

Close beside the reference to Emma is set Adam Nepos, where the Latin form is used.

1752. Married—Thomas Mathews and Ann Neap: St. Geo. Chap. Mayfair, p. 207.

1753. — Simon Reddish and Ely Neep: ibid. p. 235.

London, 1, 2.

Neasmith. — Occup.; v. Nasmith.

London, 1.

Neat, Neate.—Nick. (1) 'the neat,' trim, tidy; Fr. *net*, clean, pure. (2) The 'neat' (Icel. *naut*), an ox, a cow (v. Neatherd); cf. Bull and Bullock.

John Net et Avice uxor ejus, co. Camb., 1273. A.

Robert le Neyt, co. Wilts, 20 Edw. I. R.

Henricus Naute, 1379: P. T. Yorks. p. 200.

Johannes Naute, 1379: ibid.

1592. Matthew Neate and Ursula Taylor: Marriage Lic. (London), i. 202.

1770. Married—John Bambridge and Sarah Neate: St. Geo. Han. Sq. ii. 158.

London, 2, 9; Boston (U.S.), 3, 0.

Neathard, Nothard, Nutter (?).—Occup. 'the neat-herd,' a tender of cattle; cf. Coward, Oxnard, Shepherd, Calvert, the suffix of all of which is -*herd*. M.E. *neet*, Icel. *naut*, cattle. Every variety of form is found in Yorkshire records. I will simply quote the Poll Tax.

Johannes Nawtehird, 1379: P. T. Yorks. p. 158.

Willelmus Nouthird, 1379: ibid. p. 14. Johannes Nedhard, 1379: ibid. p. 114. Johannes Nawtard, 1379: ibid. p. 164. Willelmus Netherd, 1379: ibid. p. 86. Cecilia Neawterd, 1379: ibid. p. 160. Adam Netehird, 1379: ibid. p. 301.

I cannot find any modern representatives of these forms, saving one Nothard in the London Directory. I doubt not the present dress is Nutter through an intermediate stage Nuttard or Nutterd. Then the final *d* was dropped, and thus as Nutter this interesting surname still maintains a respectable appearance in our larger directories.

London, 0, 1, 17; Boston (U.S.), 0, 0, 31.

Neave, Neaf, Neaves, Neeve, Neeves, Neef. — Nick. 'the nephew'; O.F. *le nevé*. 'Nevé, sonys sone, *nepos*.' 'Neve, broderys sone, *neptis*': Prompt. Parv. Neve also acquired a secondary meaning, of waster or self-indulgent man, exactly as *nepos* did in Latin. 'Neve, neverthryfte or wastour, *nepos*': Prompt. Parv.

Rayner le Neve, co. Norf., 1273. A. Walter le Neve, co. Norf., ibid. John Neven, co. Essex, ibid. Hugh Nepos, co. Linc., ibid. Robert Bernardsnef, co. Linc.: Pardons Roll, 6 Ric. II.

This means Robert, the nephew of Bernard. The final *s* in Neaves and Neeves is the genitive; cf. Williams, Jones, &c.

1662. Married—Richard Neave and Avery Mason: Reg. St. Antholin (London), p. 89.

1655. Buried—William Neeves: St. Jas. Clerkenwell, iv. 107.

1807. Married—Edward Neaves and Amy Fenton: St. Geo. Han. Sq. ii. 365.

London, 8, 0, 1, 1, 2, 0; Philadelphia, 0, 0, 1, 0, 0, 6.

Neaverson; v. Nevin.

Need, Needs; v. Nead.

Needham. — Local, (1) 'of Needham,' a parish in co. Norfolk; (2) a market-town in co. Suffolk; (3) of Needham, an estate in co. Derby, from which place Earl Kilmorey's family took their name (Lower). The surname is familiar both in cos. Lanc. and Derby, especially the first, and in that portion which is adjacent to the Derbyshire border.

Thomas de Nedham, co. Norf., 1227: FF. vii. 372.

Albric de Nedham, co. Camb., 1273. A. John de Nedham, co. Derby, ibid.

1578. Thomas Needham, co. Staff.: Reg. Univ. Oxf. vol. ii. pt. ii. p. 83.

1587. John Nedham, co. Leic.: Reg. Univ. Oxf. vol. ii. pt. ii. p. 160.
1596. Bapt.—Ann, d. Henry Needam: St. Peter, Cornhill, i. 44.
1631. James Needham, of Ringstones, co. Ches.: Wills at Chester, ii. 160.
1644. Grace Needham, of Ringstones, co. Ches.: ibid.
London, 13; Manchester, 26; MDB. (co. Derby), 12; Philadelphia, 15.

Needler, Needlemaker. — Occup. 'the needler,' a maker of needles; M.E. *nedeler* and *nedler*.
'Hikke, the hakeney-man, And Hugh the nedlere.'
    Piers Plowman, 3111-2.
'Pavyers, bellemakers, and brasiers, Pynners, nedelers, and glasyers.'
    Cocke Lorelle's Bote.
Reginald le Nedlere, co. Hunts, 1273. A.
Lucas le Nedlere, co. Camb., ibid.
Ricardus Godwynn, *nedeler*, 25 Edw. I: Freemen of York (Surt. Soc.), i. 6.
Richard le Nedlere, 1313. M.
John Nedlemakyere, ibid.
1563. Simon Nedler and Margaret Harryson: Marriage Lic. (London), i. 27.
1616. Married—Ralph Needler and Agnes Rawlins: St. Jas. Clerkenwell, iii. 43.
1661. Buried—Frauncis Baker, *gent.*, from Mr. Needler's house: ibid. iv. 343.
1667. Bapt. — William, s. William Needler: ibid. i. 230.
There must be present instances, but oddly enough I cannot find any. There is, however, an American variant Kneedler (q.v.).

Neep; v. Neap.

Neeve(s; v. Neave.

Negus. — ? Local. Doubtless from some local name ending in *-house*; cf. Kirkus, Loftus, Bacchus, &c. The beverage so named took its title from Colonel Francis Negus, who 'mixed' it in Queen Anne's reign; v. Life of Dryden (Malone), p. 414. Notes and Queries, Second Series, v. 224, records several Neguses in the neighbourhood of Norwich; v. Skeat.
1598. William Negose, of London: Reg. Univ. Oxf. vol. ii. pt. ii. p. 229.
1636. Buried—Thomas Neegoose: St. Jas. Clerkenwell, iv. 219.
1671. Bapt.—Mary, d. John Negus: ibid. i. 252.
1685. William Negus: St. Mary Aldermary (London), p. 107
1697. Bapt.—John, s. of Peter Nyhouse: St. Jas. Clerkenwell, i. 372.
1707. — Ursula, d. of John Negus, a barber on College Hill: St. Thomas the Apostle (London), p. 71.
London, 4; Philadelphia, 3; New York, 7.

Neighbour, Nabor. — Nick. 'the neighbour.' This surname has a pleasant ring in it, and nothing could be more natural than its creation.
John Neyghbour, C. R., 33 Hen. VI.
1585. Buried—Adam Neighbore: St. Dionis Backchurch (London), p. 199.
1599. — Samuell Neyghbor: ibid. p. 205.
1694. John Frith and Sarah Neighbours: Marriage Alleg. (Canterbury), ii. 288.
1772. Married—Charles August Cramer and Eliz. Neighbour: St. Geo. Han. Sq. p. 220.
1779. — Moses Nabour and Mary Rose: ibid. p. 297.
London, 4, 0; New York, 0, 2; Boston (U.S.), 0, 1.

Neil, Neild, Neill, Neal, Neale, Neall, Nell, Neilson, Neison, Nelson, Niell, Nielson.—Bapt. 'the son of Neil.' For a full history of this personal name, common to all Northern Europe, v. Yonge, ii. 60-62. It is found in every possible guise in English rolls, and although Nell and Nelson must in many cases spring from Ellen or Eleanor, there can be no doubt that in general they are descendants of Neil. For instance, we find in Settle the following householders:
Nell de Hege, Elias Neleson, and Robert Nellson, 1379: P. T. Yorks. p. 273.
Probably all these were closely related. The excrescent *d* in Neild seems peculiar to the North of England. There is no Neild in the London, while ten appear in the Manchester, Directory.
Roger fil. Nigelli, co. Linc., 1273. A.
Alan fil. Nigelli, co. Norf., ibid.
Robert fil. Nele, co. Linc., ibid.
Thomes Nel, co. Essex, ibid.
John fil. Nel, co. Camb., ibid.
Henry le fiz Neel, C. R., 31 Edw. I.
Thomas Fitz-neel, 1301. M.
Ricardus Nelleson, 1379: P. T. Yorks. p. 78.
Dionisius Nelle, 1379: ibid. p. 79.
Alicia, servant of Nele, 1379: ibid. p. 288.
London, 7, 0, 7, 32, 26, 2, 4, 6, 1, 50, 1, 0; Philadelphia, 17, 12, 50, 36, 3, 16, 15, 26, 0, 150, 0, 1.

Nelder.—Local; v. Nalder.

Nelmes, Nelms.—Local, 'atten elms,' i.e. at the elms. For ex-

planation of the initial N, v. Nash or Noakes. The name is Latinized into De Ulmo in the Hundred Rolls.
Osbert atte Elme, co. Oxf., 1273. A.
William ad Ulmum, co. Oxf., ibid.
Richard de Ulmo, co. Oxf., ibid.
1604-5. Married—Christopher Foster and Cassandra Nelme: St. Dionis Backchurch (London), p. 15.
1639. Buried — Marye, d. Jesper Nellmes: St. Mary Aldermary (London), p. 170.
1714. Married—Charles Byne and Eliz. Nelms: St. Dionis Backchurch (London), p. 57.
1803. — Thomas Degory and Eleanor Nelms: St. Geo. Han. Sq. ii. 274.
London, 1, 1; Oxford, 0, 2; Philadelphia, 0, 13.

Nelson.—(1) Bapt. 'the son of Eleanor,' from nick. Nell. (2) Bapt. 'the son of Neil.' There can be no doubt that both Eleanor and Neil are parents of Nelson; v. Neil. There are many instances in the Hundred Rolls.
Nel Fawkes, co. Camb., 1273. A.
John fil. Nel, co. Camb., ibid.
Adam Nel, co. Oxf., ibid.
William Neleson. H.
Thomas Nelson, or Ne:lson, co. York. W. 11.
Thomas Nellson, 1379: P. T. Howdenshire, p. 29.
1554. Buried—Mother Nelson: Reg. Kensington Parish, p. 83.
1687. Henry Nelson (co. Herts) and Sarah Raby (co. Camb.): Marriage Alleg. (Canterbury), ii. 20.
1740. Buried—James Nelson, in the Vault: St. Peter, Cornhill, ii. 137.
Although we now spell the nick. Nell, as in 'Little Nell,' nevertheless Nel has been the prevailing form through all the last six centuries.
London, 50; Philadelphia, 150.

Nend, Nind.—Local, 'atten end,' i.e. at the end, one who resided at the end of a row of cottages, or the end of the lane, or wood, or town; v. Ind and Townsend. Nend or Nind is formed by taking as its initial the final *n* of the prefix *atten*; v. Noakes or Nash.
John atte Nende. B.
Christopher Nend, co. York, 1443. W.11.
1795. Married — William Nind and Sarah Preston: St. Geo. Han. Sq. ii. 129.
London, 0, 11; Philadelphia, 0, 2.

Nesbit, Nesbitt, Nisbet, Nisbett, Nesbett.—Local, 'of

Nesbit.' There are several townships so called in cos. Durham and Northumberland, not to speak of Nesbit in co. Berwick. Nearly all originated a surname.

William de Nesebit, C. R., 18 Edw. I.
Thomas de Nesbyt, temp. 1380: Hist. Dunelmensis (Surt. Soc.), xlii.
1716. Married—Thomas Garbrand and Anne Nisbett: St. Antholin (London), p. 129.
1789. — Colebrooke Nesbitt and Eliza Sneyd: St. Geo. Han. Sq. ii. 32.
London, 1, 3, 3, 3, 0; Newcastle, 5, 0, 3, 0, 0; New York, 7, 26, 3, 1, 2; Philadelphia, 4, 11, 5, 0, 0.

Nesmith; v. Nasmith.

Ness, Nesse.—Local, 'at the ness,' i.e. at the promontory or headland; cf. Holderness, Sheerness, Harkness, &c.

William del Ness, of Ness, co. Norf., 10 Ric. I: FF. xi. p. 200.
Roger atte Nesse, co. Kent, 1273. A.
Alicia del Nesse, 1379: P. T. Yorks. p. 141.
Johannes del Nesse, 1379: ibid.
Simon de Ness, of Ness, co. Norf., 20 Edw. III: FF. xi. 200.
1807. Married—John Alex. Paul MacGregor and James Ness: St. Geo. Han. Sq. ii. 366.
London, 3, 0; New York, 5, 1; Philadelphia, 2, 0.

Netherclift.—Local, ' at the nether cliff,' i.e. at the lower cliff. The final t is an excrescence.

1605. Bapt.—Samuell, s. John Nethercleve: Reg. Kensington Parish, p. 15.
1742. Married—John Netherclift and Jane Barnet: St. Geo. Chap. Mayfair, p. 17.
London, 2.

Nethercote, Nethercott, Nethicott.—Local, ' of Nethercote,' a village in co. Northampton. The American Nethicott is a manifest modification of the name. The original meaning was ' the nether cot ' or cottage.

1574. Buried — Eliz. Nethercott: St. Jas. Clerkenwell, iv. 16.
1655. Married — Edward Nethercoate and Eliz. Twichell: St. Michael, Cornhill, p. 35.
1747. — Charles Osborn Nethercott and Maria Constantia Rodney: St. Geo. Chap. Mayfair, p. 87.
Crockford, 0, 2, 0; MDB. (co. Northants), 2, 0, 0; New York, 0, 2, 1.

Nethermill.—Local, ' at the nether mill,' the lower as distinct from the upper mill.

Richard Nedyrmyl, 1533: Reg. Univ. Oxf. i. 174.
1546. John Nethermyll and Winifred Dod: Marriage Lic. (Faculty Office), p. 7.

Nethersole.—Local, 'at the nether sale,' from residence therein (v. Sale); = ' nether hall '; cf. Netherwood.

1399. Edmund Nethersole: Cal. of Wills in Court of Husting (2).
1618. William Nethersole, co. Kent: Reg. Univ. Oxf. pt. ii. p. 368.
1717. Married—Jacob Sharpe and Eliz. Nethersole: Reg. Canterbury Cath. p. 73.
1748. — Abraham Portal and Eliz. Nethersole: St.Geo. Chap. Mayfair, p. 111.
London, 1; MDB. (co. Kent), 4.

Netherway.—Local, ' at the nether way,' i.e. the lower road; cf. Nethergate in the Hundred Rolls.

Gundewyn de Nethergate, co. Suff., 1273. A.
Wacelin de Nethergate, co. Suff., ibid.
1642. Buried — Charles Nethwaye, a poor servant: St. Jas. Clerkenwell, iv. 255.
1651. Bapt.—John, s. John Netherway: ibid. ii. 178.
1682. Jonathan Netheway and Mary Clarke: Marriage Alleg. (Canterbury), p. 118.
1796. Married—John Kelly and Susannah Netherway: St. Geo. Han. Sq. ii. 145. London, 1.

Netherwood.—Local, ' at the nether wood,' i.e. the lower wood.

Thomas de Netherwode, co. Essex, 1273. A.
Adam Nethyrwode, 1379: P. T. Yorks. p. 261.
John de Netherwode, 1379: ibid. p. 264.
1708. Married—Joseph Netherwood and Jane Sharp: St. Michael, Cornhill, p. 54.
1751. — Thomas Walker and Eliz. Netherwood: St. Geo. Chap. Mayfair, p. 205.
1781. — Joseph Woolley and Ann Netherwood: St. Geo. Han. Sq. i. 323.
London, 1; Sheffield, 1; MDB. (West Rid. Yorks), 3; Philadelphia, 1.

Netmaker.—Occup. ' the matmaker '; not a maker of nets. Originally ' nat maker,' i.e. a maker of mats; Fr. natte. ' Natte or matte, matta, storium ': Prompt. Parv. ' A natte maker, storiator ': Cath. Ang. ' Nat maker, natier ': Palsg. ' In the curious poem entitled "The Pilgrimage to Jerusalem," . . . one of the characters introduced is the " natte makere," who holds long

discourse with the Pilgrim ' (v. Way's note on natte, Prompt. Parv. p. 351). In spite of all this the surname may mean the net-maker.

Isabella Nettemaker, 1379: P. T. Yorks. p. 26.
1603. Married—Lawrence Netmaker and Elizabeth Rice: St. Mary Aldermary (London), p. 10.
1621. Buried—Robert Netmaker, an old man: St. Antholin (London), p. 56.
1625. — Ann Netmaker: ibid. p. 59.
1683. Married — Sackvill Nettmaker and Ann Harford: Marriage Alleg. (Canterbury), p. 148.

I have many more instances. It seems strange that I should not be able to light upon any in the directories of to-day.

Netter.—?Occup. 'the netter,' a maker of nets (?). Perhaps one who netted fish.

Johannes Netter, 1379: P. T. Yorks. p. 209.
London, 1; Philadelphia, 3; New York, 5.

Nettlefield, Nettelfield. — Local, ' of the nettle-field,' from residence thereby. I fail to identify the locality, but it would be a common local term.

1662-3. James Round and Eliz. Bishopp: alleged by Ric. Netlefield: Marriage Alleg. (Canterbury), p. 65.
1666. William Wood and Susanne Nettlefeild, of Rigate: ibid. p. 187.
London, 1, 2; New York, 1, 0.

Nettlefold. — Local, ' at the nettle-fold,' from residence thereby. I cannot find the spot.

1633. Married — George Nelson and Ann Nettlefold: St. Antholin (London), p. 67.
1635. George Nettelfold sailed in the Globe to Virginia: Hotten's Lists of Emigrants, p. 119.
1752. Married—John Poynton and Eliz. Nettlefold: St. Geo. Chap. Mayfair, p. 228.
1790. — John Nettlefold and Eliz. Humphry: St. Geo. Han. Sq. ii. 49.
' Nettlefold. On the 23rd inst. at Hallfield, Edgbaston, Birmingham, Hugh, son of the late Edward John Nettlefold ': Daily Telegraph, Dec. 27, 1893. London, 3.

Nettleship.—Local, ' of Nettleshope' (?). There can be little doubt as to the accuracy of this definition. The suffix (v. Hope) is common to place-names in North England, and in some instances has become -ship, as applied to surnames which owe their parentage to them. I have seen Blenkinsopp spelt Blenkinship; cf. Winship. Nettleship is a Yorkshire name, and seems to have arisen in the neighbourhood of Tickhell, on the borders of Notts.

1583. William Netelshippe, co. Notts, St. Alban Hall: Reg. Univ. Oxf. vol. ii. pt. ii. p. 126.
1688. Edward Nettleshipp and Susanna Nynn: Marriage Alleg. (Canterbury), p. 88.
1752. Married — Lacey Roberts and Mary Nettleship: St. Geo. Chap. Mayfair, p. 222.
1778. — James Brittain and Sarah Nettelship: St. Geo. Han. Sq. i. 291.
London, 4; Sheffield, 2; MDB. (co. Notts), 5; New York, 1.

Nettleton.—Local, 'of Nettleton,' parishes in cos. Lincoln (one mile from Caistor) and Wilts (eight miles from Chippenham).

1616. Buried—Ann Nettleton, servant to Eliz. Osborne: St. Jas. Clerkenwell, iv. 135.
1617. Robert Nettleton, gent, co. York: Reg. Univ. Oxf. vol. ii. pt. ii. p. 364.
1665. Bapt.—Ann, d. Thomas Nettleton: Kensington Parish, p. 40.
1665-6. Anthony Tye and Mary Nettleton: Marriage Alleg. (Canterbury), p. 160.
London, 4; MDB. (West Rid. Yorks), 4; New York, 2; Philadelphia, 2.

Nevett, Nevitt.—Local, 'de Knyvet.' I cannot identify the spot, but the corruption to Nevett and Nevitt is perfectly clear, although it did not commonly occur till the 17th century.

Mathew de Knyvet, co. Notts, 1273. A.
Geoffrey Knifet, co. Camb., ibid.
Alex. de Knyvet, co. Oxf., ibid.
Thomas de Knyvet, co. Essex, ibid.
1583. Married — Henry Knevit and Frances Elsin: St. Antholin (London), p. 30.
1634. Bapt.—Ann, d. Edward Nevit: ibid. p. 68.
1635. — Mary, d. Edward Nevet: ibid. p. 70.
1782. Married—John Nevitt and Mary Lovett: St. Geo. Han. Sq. i. 338.
London, 2, 0; Crockford, 0, 1.

Nevin, Nevins, Nevinson, Nevison, Niven, Nivens, Nivison, Neaverson.—Bapt. 'the son of Niven,' or Nevin. I find no clue in the 13th and 14th century records. 'This series points to an early but forgotten personal name' (Lower's Patr. Brit. p. 236).

But for the existence of Nevin and Nevens I should at once assume that Nevinson and Nevison were Neve-son (v. Neave), i.e. Nephewson, the intrusive n in the former being extremely common in such forms. Neaverson presents no difficulty. Nevinson was bound to become Neverson, and of this Neaverson is but a variant; cf. Pattinson and Patterson, or Cattinson and Catterson. The two following entries seem oddly enough to concern the same couple:

1635. Married — Robert Sharpe and Jane Nevisonn: St. Antholin (London), p. 69.
1637. — Robert Sharpe and Jone Nevinson: ibid. p. 70.

The following reference probably dates about the first year of Henry VI:

Jenetta fil. Nevans, ap Lyon, ap Jestin: Visitation of Gloucestershire, 1623, p. 98.
1602. Richard Nevinson, co. Kent: Reg. Univ. Oxf. vol. ii. pt. ii. p. 258.

My next entry denotes the change mentioned above as a natural one:

1728. Buried — John Neverson: St. Thomas the Apostle (London), p. 15.

Nevison as a variant was inevitable:

1757. Married—John Park and Susanna Nevison.

The same changes are rung upon the Yorkshire Pattinsons, Pattersons, and Pattisons from the once familiar North-English Patrick.

London, 1, 2, 0, 0, 2, 0, 0, 0; Crockford, 2, 2, 1, 0, 2, 0, 0, 0; MDB. (co. Cumb.), (Nevison), 1; (co. Northampton) (Neaverson), 1; New York, 18, 34, 0, 1, 1, 1, 4, 0.

New.—Nick. 'the new,' i.e. the new-comer, the stranger just settled in the district or village; v. Newman and Newcome.

Richard le Newe, co. Camb., 1273. A.
Robert le Newe, co. Wilts, ibid.
Simon le Neue, co. Bedf., ibid.
Richard le Nywe, co. Soms., 1 Edw. III: Kirby's Quest, p. 232.
1617. Bapt.—Thomas, s. William Newe: St. Jas. Clerkenwell, i. 77.
1683. Thomas New and Bersheba Roe: Marriage Alleg. (Canterbury),p.130.
— Charles Booth and Sarah Newe, of Oxford: ibid. p. 141.
1718. Married—Charles Fox and Elizabeth New: St. Mary Aldermary (London), p. 44.
London, 14; Philadelphia, 16.

Newall, Newell, Newhall.—Local, 'of Newhall,' townships in cos. Chester, York, &c.; cf. Sewall and Sewell. The surname means 'at the new hall,' probably as distinct from the old hall. No doubt co. Chester has supplied most of our Newalls and Newells.

Thomas atte Nywehalle, co. Soms., 1 Edw. III: Kirby's Quest, p. 196.
John de Newhalle, co. Camb., Pardons Roll, 6 Ric. II.
Hugo de Neuhalle, souter, 1379: P. T. Yorks. p. 18.
1630. Richard Newall, of Chester: Wills at Chester, i. 161.
1686. George Hunter and Honor Newell, co. Herts: Marriage Alleg. (Canterbury), p. 252.
1755. Married—Matthew Newall and Mary Moore: St. Geo. Han. Sq. i. 57.
1764. — John Newell and Sarah Caudery: ibid. p. 139.
London, 3, 19, 0; MDB. (co. Ches.), 4, 0, 0; Philadelphia, 3, 32, 11.

Newbart, Newbert.—Local, 'of Newbold,' q.v. These variants seem to be peculiar to co. Notts.

MDB. (co. Notts), 2, 2.

Newberry, -bery; v. Newbury.

Newbiggin, Newbeggin, Newbegin.—Local, 'of Newbeggin.' Two parishes, one in the dioc. of Carlisle and one in the dioc. of Newcastle, and many little farmsteads, &c., go by this name; = new building; cf. Lowland Scotch and North English big, to build; v. Halliwell. There is also a township called Newbiggin in the parish of Middleton-in-Teesdale, co. Durham; also a township in the parish of Shotley, co. Northumberland; also a township in N. Rid. Yorks.

Robert de Newbigging, 7 Edw. II: Nicolson and Burn, Hist. Westm. and Cumb., i. 365.
1745. Married—Peter Newbigging and Catherine Dowling: St. Geo. Chap. Mayfair, p. 155.
Philadelphia, 1, 1,0; Boston (U.S.),0,0,8.

Newbold, Newball, Newbolt, Newbould, Newboult.—Local, 'of Newbold,' i.e. the new dwelling. A.S. bold, a house, a dwelling (v. build, Skeat'. Naturally many places bear this name. There are parishes in cos. Warwick, Worcester, and Leicester, also hamlets in cos. Leicester, Derby.

Northants, and Warwick. New-bald represents Newbald, a parish in the E. Rid. of Yorks, near Market Weighton ; cf. Newbiggin.

John de Neubald, co. Salop, 1273. A.
Richard de Newebald, co. Oxf., ibid.
Robertus de Newbald, 1379: P. T. Howdenshire, p. 11.
Willelmus Newbald, 1379: P. T. Yorks. p. 149.
1654. Bapt.—Joseph, s. John Newball: St. Jas. Clerkenwell, p. 186.
1693-4. William Glenister (co. Bucks) and Eliz. Newboult (co. Bucks): Marriage Alleg. (Canterbury), i. 284.
1726. Married — George Ernest Eller and Mary Newbolt: St. Geo. Han. Sq. p. 2.
MDB. (co. Notts), 1, 0, 0, 1, 2 ; West Rid. Court Dir., 2, 1, 2, 7, 3 ; London, 7, 0, 1, 0, 0 ; Philadelphia, 26, 0, 0, 0, 0.

Newbond, Newbon, New-bound.—Occup. ' the new bond ' (v. Bond), i.e. the new householder, the newly-settled peasant who held under the tenure of bondage.

Roger le Neubonde, co. Bucks, 1273. A.
Henry Neubonde, co. Bucks, ibid.
Richard le Newebonde, co. Hunts, ibid.
William le Newebonde, co. Hunts, ibid.
Johannes Neubond', 1379: P. T. Yorks. p. 294.
1808. Married—John Newbound and Ann Burford: St. Geo. Han. Sq. ii. 383.
London, 0, 4, 0 ; West Rid. Court Dir., 0, 0, 1.

Newbury, Newberry, New-bery.—Local, ' of Newbury,' a town in co. Berks. Also ' of Newborough,' a parish in co. North-ants, five miles from Peterborough. Also a township in parish of Cox-wold, N. Rid. Yorks. All these places no doubt contributed their share to swell the number of Newburys, Newberrys, and New-berys in our directories. For similar changes rung on the suffix, v. Oxberry.

Henry de Neubury, co. Bucks, 1273. A.
John de Newbury, co. Soms., 1 Edw. III : Kirby's Quest, p. 161.
1680. Bapt. — Anthony, s. Anthony Newbery: St. Jas. Clerkenwell, i. 380.
1688. Jeremiah Newbrough and Eliz. Conniers: Marriage Alleg. (Canterbury), p. 62.
1691. Thomas Newborough and Martha Atkins : ibid. p. 198.
1693. David Newbery and Ann Dale: ibid. p. 268.
— Thomas James and Susanna New-bary : ibid. p. 254.

The following variants are found in the Reg. Univ. Oxf. (Index):

Neuburgh, Newberough, New-brough, Neuberrye, Newberey, Newbrye, Nubery, and Newberie.
London, 3, 3, 18 ; Philadelphia, 0, 13, 1.

Newby.—Local, ' of Newby,' a township in the union of Ripon, Yorks ; also a township in the parish of Clapham, near Settle, Yorks; also a hamlet in the parish of Harewood, near Leeds, Yorks. Also other small places.

Nicholas de Neuby, co. York, 1273. A.
Robert de Neuby, co. York, ibid.
William de Neuby, co. Cumb., 20 Edw. I. R.
Galfridus de Nuby, 1379: P. T. Yorks. p. 258.
Radulphus de Neuby, 1379 : ibid. p. 253.
London, 9 ; New York, 4.

Newcome, Newcomen, Newcomb, Newcombe.—Nick. ' the new-comen,' a newly-settled stranger; cf. Newman (q.v.). The b in Newcomb is excrescent. New-comen is the invariable form in early rolls. M.E. cumen, comen, to come, pp. cumen, comen, come (Skeat).

' But the fflemynges among these things dere
Incomen loven beste bacon and beer.'
Old Political Song.

' Newcomes, strangers newly arrived ; v. Hollinshed, Conq. Ireland, p. 55 ' (Halliwell).

Gilbert le Neucum, co. Linc., 1273. A.
Gilbert le Neucomen, co. Linc., ibid.
Robert Neucomen, co. Linc., ibid.
Robert le Newcomen, C. R., 9 Edw. I.
Ricardus Newcomen, 1379: P. T. Yorks. p. 264.
1660. Robert Maddison and Eliz. Newcomen: Marriage Alleg. (Canterbury), p. 53.
London, 0, 1, 5, 5; Philadelphia, 2, 0, 24, 3.

Newdick.—Local, ' at the new dike,' i.e. from residence by or near the new trench, mound, or dike; cf. Cobbledick, and v. Dyke.

1676. Henry Newdick and Mary Nicholls : Marriage Alleg. (Canterbury), p. 169.
1743. Bapt.—Joseph Baden, s. Henry Newdick : St. Michael, Cornhill, p. 173.
1744. — Henry, s. Henry Newdick : ibid. p. 174.
London, 2.

Newell, Newhall; v. Newall.

Newham.—Local, ' of New-ham.' There is a township of this

name in co. Northumberland. But doubtless, like Newton, it is com-mon to many counties.

John de Neuham, co. Essex, 1273. A.
Ambrose de Neuham, co. Camb., ibid.
Walter de Neuham, co. Camb., ibid.
1680. John Wyne and Eliz. Newham: Marriage Alleg. (Canterbury), p. 49.
1684. Buried—Ralph Newham, haber-dasher: St. Mary Aldermary, p. 195.
1772. Married—George Newham and Anne Quinlan : St. Geo. Han. Sq. i. 125.
London, 6.

Newhouse.—Local, ' at the new house,' from residence at a house so called. Many small spots go by this name up and down the country; cf. Newton, Newby, New-biggin, and Newham, which are strictly parallel cases, only in most cases of older origin. The family of Newhouse, however, are evi-dently sprung from co. York.

Johannes Newehowse, 1379: P. T. Yorks. p. 287.
Alicia Newhouse, 1379: ibid. p. 284.
Ricardus de Newhese, 1379: ibid. p. 282.
1686-7. William Waller and Eliz. New-house: Marriage Alleg. (Canterbury), p. 260.
1771. Married—James Newhouse and Isabel Thwaites : St. Geo. Han. Sq. p. 207.
Crockford, 1; MDB. (West Rid. Yorks), 5 ; New York, 8 ; Philadelphia, 14.

Newington.—Local, ' of New-ington,' parishes and places in cos. Kent, Oxford, Surrey, Middle-sex, &c.

Ralph de Newentone, co. Hunts, 1273. A.
Richard de Newentone, co. Sussex, ibid.
Peter de Newentone, co. Bucks, ibid.
1622. Bapt.—Amy, d. William Newing-ton : St. Jas. Clerkenwell, i. 94.
1681. Charles Bidell and Mary New-ington : Marriage Alleg. (Canterbury), p. 60.
London, 1.

Newland, Newlands.—(1) Local, ' of Newland,' parishes in co. Worc. and Glouc. ; also town-ships in the parish of Ulverston, co. Lanc., and of Drax, W. Rid. Yorks. (2) ' Of Newlands,' a township in the parish of Bywell St. Peter, co. Northumberland ; also a chapelry in the parish of Crosthwaite, co. Cumb. But from my first instances it is manifest that the chief parent-age must be allowed to land reclaimed from the great fen district.

Roger de la Neuelonde, co. Camb., 1273. A.
Richard le (de ?) Neulond, co. Camb., ibid.
Thomas de la Neulaund, co. Essex, ibid.
G. de Neuland, co. Linc., ibid.
William atte Niwelond, co. Soms., 1 Edw. III : Kirby's Quest, p. 227.
1573. John Newlande and Grace Sampson : Marriage Lic. (London), i. 58.
1670. Married—William Newland and Mary Spratt : St. Jas. Clerkenwell, iii. 169.
1748. — Peter Newland and Joyce Atkinson : St. Geo. Chap. Mayfair, p. 104.
London, 10, o ; Liverpool, o, 1 ; Philadelphia, 6, o ; Boston (U.S.), 1, 1.

Newling, Newlin.—Local, ' of Newlyn,' a parish in co. Cornwall, eight miles from Truro. With the natural adoption of an excrescent g, cf. Jennings, Collins, Collings, &c.

1614. Robert Newlin or Newling : Reg. Univ. Oxf. vol. ii. pt. ii. p. 335.
1687. Thomas Jolly and Catharine Newling : Marriage Alleg. (Canterbury), p. 280.
1707. Buried — Hannah, d. Susannah Newling : St. Antholin (London), p. 120.
1779. Married—William Matthews and Eliz. Newlyn : St Geo. Han. Sq. p. 302.
1782. — William Fordham and Sarah Newling : ibid. p. 341.
London, 11, o ; Philadelphia, o, 30 ; Boston (U.S.), 2, 1.

Newman.—Nick. ' the new man,' the newly-settled stranger ; v. New and Newcome. A.S. niwe. This is a common entry in the Hundred Rolls.

Robert Niweman, co. Camb., 1273. A.
Herbert le Niweman, co. Oxf., ibid.
Mathew le Neuman, co. Hunts, ibid.
John le Neuman, co. Bedf., ibid.
London, 116 ; New York, 146 ; Philadelphia, 65.

Newmarch, Newmark.—Local, ' of Newmarch.' The opposite of Newland (q.v.), for this seems to be land lost instead of reclaimed from the marshes ; v. Marsh. I suspect Newmark is German.

Adam de Neumarche, co. Linc., 1273. A.
1591. Buried — John, s. John Newmarch : St. Jas. Clerkenwell, iv. 44.
1785. Married — Matthias Newmarch and Mary Rouse : St. Geo. Han. Sq. ii 372.

London, 1, 1 ; New York, o, 7 ; Boston (U.S.), 1, o.

Newnham, Newnam.—Local, ' of Newnham,' parishes in cos. Glouc., Herts, Kent, Northants, Southants, Warwick, and Oxford. I have a fairly early English instance of the American way of spelling the name.

Ralph de Neunenham, co. Camb., 1273. A.
1576. Buried—William Newnam : St. Jas. Clerkenwell, iv. 18.
1743. Married — Thomas Newnham and Ann Smith : St. Geo. Han. Sq. i. 30.
1750. — Thomas Newenham and Susanna Wandesford : St. Geo. Chap. Mayfair, p. 170.
1806. — Patrick Newnham and Ann Trattell : St. Geo. Han. Sq. ii. 354.
London, 3, o ; Philadelphia, o, 10.

Newport.—Local, ' of Newport,' a large hamlet in co. Devon, a parish in co. Essex, and the well-known seaport town in Monmouthshire. It would seem as if the Essex town was the chief parent.

William de Neuport, co. Bucks, 1273. A.
Gernega de Neuport, co. Linc., ibid.
Maurice de Neuport, co. Linc., ibid.
1574. Francis Newporte, co. Salop : Reg. Univ. Oxf. vol. ii. pt. ii. p. 60.
1589. Charles Newporte, co. Northants : ibid. p. 173.
1604. Richard Newport, co. Salop : ibid. p. 276.
1654-5. Buried — John, s. Samuell Newport : St. Jas. Clerkenwell, iv. 303.
1744. Married—John Fuller and Hannah Newport : St. Geo. Chap. Mayfair, p. 36.
London, 6 ; Oxford, 7 ; Philadelphia, 6.

Newsam, Newsom, Newsome, Newsman, Newsum, Newsholme.—Local, (1)' of Newsome,' a village near Huddersfield ; (2) ' of Newsholm,' a township in the parish of Gisburne, near Clitheroe, W. Rid. Yorks. Newsman is a curious modern corruption. It occurs in the Sheffield Directory. Alongside it is found the more correct Newsome. It is needless to say that Newsham, q.v., is inextricably mixed up with the above.

Willelmus de Newsom (dwelling at Newsholm), 1379 : P. T. Yorks. p. 272.
Alicia de Neusom, 1379 : ibid. p. 137.
Willelmus de Newsome, 1379 : ibid. p. 66.

Walter de Newsom, 4 Edw. III : Freemen of York, i. 26.
1618. Thomas Newsam, co. Warw. : Reg. Univ. Oxf. vol. ii. pt. ii. p. 371.
1694-5. John Newsum and Dorothy Summers : Marriage Lic. (Faculty Office), p. 214.
1744. Married—Richard Sare Newsome and Eliz. Greame : St. Jas. Clerkenwell, iii. 274.
London, 2, 2, 1, o, o, o ; West Rid. Court Dir., 3, o, 4, o, 4, 2 ; Manchester, o, 1, o, o, o, o ; Philadelphia, o, o, 4, o, 1, o.

Newsham.—Local, ' of Newsham.' Townships in the parishes of Wressel, E. Rid. Yorks ; Kirby Wisk, N. Rid. Yorks ; Kirby Ravensworth, N. Rid. Yorks ; Kirkham, co. Lanc.; and Eaglescliffe, co. Durham. Many of the surnames which owe their parentage to these places are mixed up with Newsam, q.v. In the Index to the Register of St. George, Mayfair, the compiler has placed these names under one heading, as ' Newsham or Newsome.' In reality they ought to have been separated.

1615. Robert Newsham, of Whalley : Wills at Chester, i. 142.
1752. Married—Henry Newsham and Frances Bromley : St. Geo. Chap. Mayfair, p. 214.
1805. — John Nicholls and Elen Newsham : St. Geo. Han. Sq. ii. 337.
Manchester, 3 ; Liverpool, 1 ; Philadelphia, 13.

Newsom(e ; v. Newsam.

Newson. — Local, ' of Newsome' ; v. Newsam. This is the obvious origin ; v. Ransom for Ranson, or Sansom for Samson. It is a very natural corruption. The following entry is of considerable assistance :

1641. Married — Peter Newsan and Bridgett Jeffes : St. Jas. Clerkenwell, iii. 73.

This denotes the first change from Newsam to Newsan. Newson was then inevitable.

1682. Married—John Jones and Eliz. Newson : St. Jas. Clerkenwell, iii. 198.
1720. Buried—Dorothy Newson, from Mr. Lockyer's, *poulterer* : St. Dionis Backchurch (London), p. 290.
1745. Married — Samuel Hankinson and Margaret Newsom : St. Geo. Han. Sq. p. 35.
1777. — William Newson and Rachel Shaw : ibid. p. 273.
London, 11 ; Liverpool, 1 ; Philadelphia, 4.

Newstead.—Local, 'of New-stead,' co. Notts, where the famous abbey was founded. But there are also places in cos. Lincoln and Northumberland that bear this name. With Newstead, 'the new holding' (v. Stead), cf. Newham, Newhouse, Newton, &c.

1616. Christopher Newsteade, co. Linc.: Reg. Univ. Oxf. vol. ii. pt. ii. p. 356.
1753. Married—Thomas Newstead and Jane Graham : St. Geo. Chap. Mayfair, p. 243.
1758. — William Newstead and Ann Coleman : St. Geo. Han. Sq. i. 78.
London, 6 ; Leeds, 1 ; New York, 2.

Newton.—Local, 'of Newton.' Naturally found in every county in England ; cf. Oldham, Newham, Newstead, &c. It would be easy to furnish instances from every early register of names.

Gunnora de Neutone, co. Suff., 1273. A.
Ralph de Neutone, co. Hunts, ibid.
Alan de Neuton, co. Linc., ibid.
Willelmus de Neweton, 1379: P. T. Yorks. p. 32.
Johannes de Neuton, 1379 : ibid. p. 98.
1579. John Newton, co. Salop : Reg. Univ. Oxf. vol. ii. pt. ii. p. 86.
1683. Bapt.—Thomas, s. Thomas Newton : St. Peter, Cornhill, ii. 10.
London, 94 ; Philadelphia, 63.

Nibbs.—Bapt. 'the son of Isabel,' from nick. Ibb (v. Ibb and Ibbett). This Ibb became familiarly Nibb, just as Oliver became Noll ; cf. Nobbs. Isabel had a great many nicks., the name being very popular in its day, which happened to be the hereditary surname period. v. Knibb.

John Nybbe, co. Soms., 1 Edw. III : Kirby's Quest, p. 257.
1677. Bapt. — Margarett Nibb, d. Thomas Nib : St. Jas. Clerkenwell, i. 276.
1746. Married — William Nibbs and Mary Betts : St. Geo. Chap. Mayfair, p. 75.
1787. — John Nibbs and Sarah John-away : St. Geo. Han. Sq. i. 398.
London, 2.

Niblett.—Bapt. 'the son of Isabel,' from nick. Nib (v. Nibbs), and dim. Nib-elot ; cf. Hewlett for Hew-elot, i.e. little Hugh or Hew ; also Noblett for Nobelot, from Nob (=Hob=Robert) ; v. Nobbs.

1687. Married — Phillip Niblett and Anne Biddulfe : St. Jas. Clerkenwell, p. 204.

1740. Married — William Niblet and Mary Lambert : St. Geo. Han. Sq. i. 24.
1742. — Henry Niblett and Susanna Todd : St. Geo. Chap. Mayfair, p. 19.
1781. — James Marsh and Eliz. Niblett : St. Geo. Han. Sq. p. 319.
London, 2.

Niche.—Local, 'at the niche,' i.e. nook, the recess. This seems an early instance and worth re-cording.

Simon atte Nych, co. Soms., 1 Edw. III : Kirby's Quest, p. 105.

Nicholas.—Bapt. 'the son of Nicholas.' This once popular font-name is the parent of a very large family ; v. Cole, Collin, Nicklin, Nix, Nixon, &c. A large list of variants is given under Nicholes.

Nicholas le Hunte, co. York, 1273. A. John fil. Nicholai, co. Salop, ibid.
1585. Humphrey Nicholas, co. Camar-then : Reg. Univ. Oxf. vol. ii. pt. ii. p. 143.
1703. Bapt.—Eliz., d. John Nickless : St. Jas. Clerkenwell, ii. 12.
1730. — Robert, s. Thomas Nicholas : ibid. p. 189.
London, 16 ; Philadelphia, 34.

Nicholes, Nicholl, Nicholls, Nichols, Nicholson, Nickalls, Nickels, Nickolds, Nickoll, Nickolls, Nickols, Nicol, Nicole, Nicoll, Nicolle, Ni-cols, Nicolson, Nickoles.—Bapt. 'the son of Nicholas,' from Nichol or Nicol, the nick. ; v. Nicholas. Nichol always held a fair place in popular favour, as our directories of to-day amply prove. But Collin (q.v.) was probably the greater favourite.

William fil. Nicoll, co. Salop, 1273. A. John Nicole, co. Oxf., ibid.
Stephen Nicol, co. Oxf., ibid.
Alicia Nicholmayden and Robertus Nichol-man (i.e. the servant of Nichol), 1379 : P. T. Yorks. pp. 158, 154.
Nichol Gurdelere, C. R., 21 Edw. III. pt. ii.
John Niccolson, temp. Eliz. ZZ.
1562. Bapt.— Joane Nicholsonne : St. Peter, Cornhill, i. 10.
1575. Thomas Nicolls, co. Middlesex : Reg. Univ. Oxf. vol. ii. pt. ii. p. 62.
Nycall Spyght, 1601 : Nicolson and Burn, Hist. Westm. and Cumb., i. 96.
1687. James Nickleson and Ann Good-man : Marriage Alleg. (Canterbury), p. 25.
1707. Married—Robert Nicholls and Eliz. Moye : St. Antholin (London), p. 120.

London, 5, 10, 65, 55, 67, 1, 3, 1, 2, 1, 3, 7, 2, 12, 1, 1, 1, 1, 0 ; Philadelphia, 44, 2, 24, 122, 88, 0, 8, 0, 0, 0, 0, 3, 0, 0, 3, 2, 0, 1.

Nicholetts, Nicholet.—Bapt. 'the son of Nicholas,' from dim. Nichol-et ; cf. Collett. There is no doubt that Collett was the favourite. Nicholet made little headway. Nicklet is an obvious modification, and has managed to cross the Atlantic.

1603. Gabriel Nicholetts, co. Hereford, *pleb.* : Reg. Univ. Oxf. vol. ii. pt. ii. p. 267.
1659. Buried—Jane Nicholett, *spinster*, in the chancel : St. Jas. Clerkenwell, iv. 330.
1661. — Samuell Nicholetts : ibid. p. 340.
1743. Married—Caleb Nicholetts and Sarah Darby : St. Antholin (London), p. 152.
New York, o, 1.

Nicholl(s, &c. ; v. Nicholes.

Nickerson.—Bapt. 'the son of Nicholas,' a corruption of Nichol-son (v. Nicholes) ; cf. Patterson, Catterson. The following entry shows the preliminary step towards the corruption :

1759. Married — John Nickelson and Mary Knapton : St. Geo. Han. Sq. i. 85.
London, 3 ; Philadelphia, 13.

Nickinson, Nickisson. — Bapt. 'the son of Nicholas.' Nickinson is probably a corruption of Nicklinson (v. next article) and Nickisson an extension of Nickson (v. Nix).

London, 2, 1.

Nicklin, Nickling, Nicklin-son.—Bapt. 'the son of Nicholas,' from nick. Nicol, dim. Nicolin. Thomas Nycklyn (also written Nyclys, i.e. Nicholls) was Mayor of Coventry in 1575 (Coventry Mysteries, p. 129). The g in Nickling is excrescent, as in Jennings and hundreds of other cases. With the dim. Nicol-in, cf. *violin*, a little viol.

1733. Married — Thomas Nicklin and Sarah Tomlinson : St. Jas. Clerkenwell, p. 261.
1746. — William Nicklin and Esther Pugh : St. Geo. Chap. Mayfair, p. 62.
1771. — John Nicklin and Eliz. Doubt-fire : St. Geo. Han. Sq. i. 205.
London, o, o, 1 ; Manchester, 1, 1, o ; Derby, o, o, 5 ; Shrewsbury, 1, o, o ; New York, o, 2, o.

Nickoll(s, &c. ; v. Nicholes.

Nicks, Nickson.—Bapt. 'the son of Nicholas,' from the nick. form Nick ; v. Nix and Nixon.

1621. Edward Nickson, co. Ches.: Reg. Univ. Oxf. vol. ii. pt. ii. p. 396.
1652. Buried—Mary, d. Richard Nicks : St. Jas. Clerkenwell, iv. 292.
1741. Bapt.—Margaret, d. Henry Nickson : St. Geo. Chap. Mayfair, p. 3.
London, 2, 0 ; Manchester, 0, 5 ; New York, 0, 3.

Nidson.—Bapt. 'the son of Idonia,' from the nick. Idd, changed into Nidd (v. Iddison); cf. Nell, Ned, Noll, Numph, Nabb, Nibb, &c.
William Niddson, C. R., 4 Hen. IV. pt. i.

Niell(son ; v. Neil.

Niger-oculus.—Nick. 'black eye.'
Robertus Niger-Oculus 'pro felonia suspensus.' L.
1752. Thomas Blackeyes and Elizabeth Bridge, by Lic.: Canterbury Cath. p. 92.

Nightingale, Nightingall.—Nick. 'the nightingale,' probably given on account of the sweet voice of the nominee. Jenny Lind was called the Swedish Nightingale. A.S. *nihtegale.*
Ralph Niktègale, co. Norf., 1273. A.
Robert Nitingal, co. Norf., ibid.
Ricardus Nyetgale, 1379 : P. T. Howdenshire, p. 24.
Thomas Nightegale, co. Glouc., 20 Edw. I. R.
1572. James Nightingale, co. Yorks : Reg. Univ. Oxf. vol. ii pt. ii. p. 55.
1575. Married — Ralphe Nightingale and Eliz. Kiddar: St. Jas. Clerkenwell, iii. 6.
1787. — William Nuttall and Eliz. Nightinggall : St. Geo. Han. Sq. p. 404.
London, 14, 1 ; MDB. (co. Surrey), 4, 1 ; Boston (U.S.), 8, 0.

Nihill.—Bapt. 'the son of Nigel,' or Niel, or Neil, q.v. Possibly the *h* is a memory of the *g* in Nigel.
1565. Buried—John Nihell : St. Peter, Cornhill, i 118.
1796. Married — Matthew Nihill and Mary Foard : St. Geo. Han. Sq. ii. 152.
Crockford, 2 ; Philadelphia, 2.

Nind.—Local, 'atten end '; v. Ind and Nend.

Ninepence. — Nick. 'Ninepence'; cf. Twelvepence, Fourpence, and Fivepence. Possibly the sobriquet of some banker or moneylender. Of Thomas à Becket we read : 'He was sent to the hall of

Richer of L'Aigle, his father's friend, to learn courtly behaviour, and to the office of the wealthy Osbert Eightpenny to be taught business': Hist. England, by F. York Powell (Rivington, 1885), p. 92. We still hear lawyers called 'old six-and-eightpenny.'
John Ninepennys, ordained priest, 1334: Hist. of Newcastle and Gateshead, i. 88.
Sir Adam Ninepennvs, chaplain of the chantry in All Saints' Church, Newcastle, 1335 : ibid. p. 95.
John Ninepence, co. York. W. 9.
I need scarcely say the surname is extinct, but it is clear that it lasted for several generations.

Nisbet, Nisbett; v. Nesbit.

Niven(s.—Bapt. ; v. Nevin.

Nix, Nixon.—Bapt. 'the son of Nicholas,' nick. Nick, with patronymic s Nicks, whence Nix. Nixon, of course, is Nickson ; cf. Dixon, Jaxon, Baxter.
Henry Nix, co. Oxf., 1273. A.
William Nix, co. Oxf., ibid.
Margareta Nikeson, 1379 : P. T. Yorks. p. 10.
William Nicson, 1379 : ibid. p. 117.
1527. Thomas Nyxson and Johanna Scochyn : Marriage Lic. (London), i. 6.
1586. Married—Benedict Nix, *bacheler,* and Eliz. Cathron, *a mayden* : St. Peter, Cornhill, i. 235.
1635. Buried—Susan, d. Thomas Nixon : St. Jas. Clerkenwell, iv. 217.
London, 8, 28 ; Oxford, 5, 1 ; Philadelphia, 0, 82.

Noad ; v. Nodes.

Noakes. Noke, Nokes, Nock. Noack, Nocke.—Local, 'atten oak,' from residence beside the oak-tree. M.E. *oke.* As with Nalder and Nash, the final *n* in the prefix *atten* (= at the) becomes the initial of the name proper (v. Oak). Nokes and Noakes merely represent a cluster of oak-trees.
Philip attenoke, C. R., 3 Edw. I.
William atte Noke, London. X.
Richard Attenok. B.
Richard atte Noke. P.
Robertus Nok, 1379 : P. T. Yorks. p. 74.
1504. Bapt.—Anne, d. Robert Nocke : St. Jas. Clerkenwell, p. 29.
In the Reg. Univ. Oxf. (Index) this name is spelt indifferently Knokes, Nokes, and Nooke.

1637. Married—Nicholas Firman and Ann Nokes : St. Jas. Clerkenwell, iii. 69.
1649. — Richard Hope and Susan Noke: ibid. p. 83.
1664. — Richard Wood and Mary Noakes : ibid. p. 115.
1749. — George Nock and Eliz. Long: St. Geo. Chap. Mayfair, p. 146.
London, 15, 2, 4, 5, 0, 0 ; Philadelphia, 0, 0, 1, 7, 1, 1.

Nobbs, Nopps, Nobbe. — Bapt. 'the son of Robert,' from nick. Hob, familiarly Nob. Names beginning with vowels or the aspirate *h* were commonly nicked with prefix N ; cf. Nab (Abel), Nib (Isabel), Numph (Humphry), Noll (Oliver); v. Curiosities of Puritan Nomenclature, pp. 89,90. As regards the change from Nobbs to Nopps, cf. Ropps for Robbs, Hopps for Hobbs, Hopkins for Hobkins, &c. To 'hob and nob,' to pledge a health by touching glasses. To 'hob-nob,' to associate closely. Perhaps the explanation lies in the fact that both were recognized nicks. of the same name, Robert.
Geoffrey Nobbe, co. Norf., 1273. A.
Philip Noppe, co. Hunts, ibid.
Richard Noppe, co. Hunts, ibid.
1590. Buried—John Nobbes : St. Jas. Clerkenwell, iv. 42.
1617. John Nobes, co. Berks : Reg. Univ. Oxf. vol. ii. pt. ii. p. 363.
London, 12, 0, 0 ; Ulverston, 0, 1, 0 ; New York, 0, 0, 1.

Noble. — Nick. 'the noble,' excellent, illustrious. This complimentary sobriquet was not allowed to die out by the fortunate possessors, and they have bred a large progeny.
Amice le Noble, co. Hunts, 1273. A.
Hugh le Noble, co. Bedf., ibid.
Thomas le Noble, co. Oxf., ibid.
Robertus Nobill', 1379 : P. T. Yorks. p. 102.
1607. Michael Noble, co. Staff.: Reg. Univ. Oxf. vol. ii. pt. ii. p. 295.
1670. Bapt. — Catherine, d. Mark Noble: Kensington Parish Reg. p. 52.
London, 31 ; Philadelphia, 76.

Noblet, Noblett, Noblit.—Bapt. 'the son of Robert,' from nick. Hob, changed to Nob (v. Nobbs), and dim. Nob-elot. In the same way Hob took the diminutive -*elot* and became Hobelot. Nob would similarly become Nobelot ; cf. Niblett and Hewlett.

Constancia Hobelot, co. Camb., 1273. A.
Agnes Nobelot, co. Oxf., ibid.
Roger Nobelot, co. Hunts, ibid.
William Noblet, co. Salop, ibid.
Alicia Nobelot, co. Soms., 1 Edw. III:
Kirby's Quest, p. 216.
1578. Buried—Peter Noblott, a Dutch-
man: St. Michael, Cornhill, p. 195.
1750. Married—Nicholas Tayler and
Alice Noblet: St. Jas. Clerkenwell,
p. 282.
John Noblet, 1 Geo. I: List of Papists,
Baines' Lanc. ii. 698.
London, 0, 1, 0; Crockford, 1, 1, 0; New
York, 0, 1, 0; Philadelphia (Noblit), 12.

Nobody.—?——. This curious
surname occurs in the 17th century;
cf. Peabody, Truebody, &c.

1618. Bapt.—John and Joseph, sons of
Valentine Nobodye: St. Jas. Clerkenwell,
p. 82.

There is no evidence of these
being foundlings, although the date
of the baptism is February 4, which
is somewhat near St. Valentine's
day.

Nock(e.—Local, 'at the oak';
v. Noakes.

Nodder.—Nick. 'the sleepy.'
There seems to be no escape from
the conclusion that this well-known
Yorkshire patronymic was a nickname for one of sleepy or apathetic
habits: one who nodded. I have
tried to find an occupative origin,
but have hitherto failed.

Hugh le Nodder, of Pontefract, 1295. M.
Thomas Nodder', 1379 : P. T. Yorks.
p. 262.
1668. Edward Nodder, of Wood Plumpton: Lancashire Wills at Richmond,
i. 204.
1669. Dorothy Nodder, of Wood
Plumpton : ibid.
Sheffield, 7; West Rid. Court Dir., 4;
London, 1.

Nodes, Nodson, Noad. —
Bapt. 'the son of Ode' or Oddy
(v. Oddy), nick. Node or Noddy
(cf. Nibbs, Nobbs, Nabbs, &c.),
genitive Nodes (cf. Jones, Williams,
&c.).

Willelmus Node, 1379 : P. T. Yorks.
p. 102.
Agnes Node, 1379: ibid.
Elias Ode, 1379: ibid.
Alicia Ode, 1379: ibid.

All dwelling in Villata de Camp-
sale.

Thomas Noddessone, C. R., 12 Edw.
III. pt. i.

William Nodes, of Stevenedge, co.
Herts, 1533 : Visit. Bedfordshire, 1634,
p. 127.
1626. Married — George Nodes and
Eliz. Cooley: St. Jas. Clerkenwell, iii. 56.
1766. — John Whitnell and Eliz.
Noads: St. Geo. Han. Sq. i. 156.
1784. — John Taylor and Sarah Nodes:
ibid. p. 356.
London, 8, 0, 0; Philadelphia, 0, 0, 3.

Noel.—Bapt. 'the son of Noel,'
i.e. Christmas Day, Dies Natalis,
reduced in French to Noël. Still
given occasionally to children born
on this great feast; cf. Christmas,
Tiffany, Pascal, Pentecost, Midwinter, &c. A famous old carol
still preserves the word, and Halliwell quotes:

'Therfore let us alle syng nowelle,
Nowelle! Nowelle! Nowelle! Nowelle!
And Cryst save mery Ynglond.'

v. Nowell.

Ralph Noel, co. Hunts, 1273. A.
Noel de Aubianis, co. Suff., ibid.
Noel atte Wynde, co. Soms., 1 Edw.
III : Kirby's Quest, p. 177.
Richard Noel, 1313. M.
1667. Peter Trovell and Hannah Noell:
Marriage Alleg. (Canterbury), p. 222.
1706. Noell, son of Noell Whiting:
Reg. St. Dionis Backchurch (London).
1768. Married — Rev. Rowney Noel
and Maria Boothby Skrymsher: St. Geo.
Han. Sq. i. 178.
London, 12 ; Philadelphia, 6.

Noelson, Knowlson.—Bapt.
'the son of Noel' (q.v.). Alexander
Nouelson, co. Northumberland,
Pardons Roll, 6 Ric. II. The
surname evidently had a precarious existence. It might seem
that Nolson was 'the son of Noll'
(i. e. Oliver), but I do not find
traces of that nick. further back
than the 17th century.

1617. John Nalson, co. York : Reg.
Univ. Oxf. vol. ii. pt. ii. p. 363.
1660. Married — George Nolson and
Dorothy Rye : St. Jas. Clerkenwell,
iii. 103.
1752. — Abraham Gordon and Ann
Nolson: St. Geo. Chap. Mayfair, p. 221.
London, 0, 1.

Noke, Nokes; v. Noakes.

Noon, Noone.—? Occup. 'the
nun' (?) ; v. Nunn.

1575. Andrew Noone, co. Northants:
Reg. Univ. Oxf. vol. ii. pt. ii. p. 67.
1635. Buried—George Noone, householder : St. Jas. Clerkenwell, iv. 216.
1664. — Charles, s. Daniell Noone:
ibid. p. 358.

Died at Stoneygate, Leicester, Lucy,
widow of the late C. Noon : Daily Telegraph, July 17th, 1893.
London, 2, 1 ; Philadelphia, 13, 0.

Nopps.—Bapt. ; v. Nobbs.

**Norbury, Norbery, Nor-
bery.**—Local, 'of Norbury,' a
township in the parish of Stockport,
co. Ches. This surname has ramified somewhat strongly, but is still
best represented in the surrounding
district, as at Manchester, for instance.

Thomas de Norburie, c. 1190: East
Cheshire, i. 456.
Robert de Northbury, c. 1260: ibid.
ii. 102 n.
Lyulph de Norbury, c. 1260: ibid.
John Narbery or Northbury, 1515 :
Reg. Univ. Oxf. p. 94.
1523. Henry Humfrey and Eliz. Nor-
borowe: Marriage Lic. (London), i. 3.
1573. Buried — Roberte Norburye :
Reg. Prestbury, co. Ches., p. 43.
1616. Thomas Norbury, co. Oxon :
Reg. Univ. Oxf. vol. ii. pt. ii. p. 350.
1617. Buried—Peares Norburie : Reg.
Prestbury, co. Ches., p. 216.
1671. Married — John Norberye and
Eliz. Ferres: St. Jas. Clerkenwell, iii. 175.
London, 3, 0, 0 ; Manchester, 15, 0, 0;
Philadelphia, 6, 1, 1.

Norcross. — Local, 'at the
North Cross,' from residence
thereby. Although not common
in England, this surname has
ramified strongly in America.
There can be little doubt that
the spot lies somewhere upon
the borders of Lanc., Westm., and
Yorks.

1636. Agnes Norcrosse, of Alston,
widow: Lancashire Wills at Richmond,
i. 204.
1662. George Norcross, of Hothersale :
ibid.
1670. Eliz. Norcross, of Rawclift : ibid.
1724. Married—Jonathan Norcross and
Eliz. Odell: St. Jas. Clerkenwell, iii. 250.
1729. — James Norcross (of Trowbridge, co. Wilts) and Martha Poulton :
St. Geo. Chap. Mayfair, p. 296.
Manchester, 1 ; Liverpool, 1 ; MDB.
(co. Ches.), 1 ; Boston (U.S.), 36 ; Philadelphia, 9.

Norcutt.—Local ; v. Northcot.

Norden, Nordon.—Local, 'of
Norden,' i.e. at the north dean
(v. Dean), from residence therein.
I do not know the locality.

1580. John Norden and Margaret
Lewes : Marriage Lic. (Westminster),
p. 7.

1591. Bapt.—Martha, d. John Norden:
St. Peter, Cornhill, i. 37.
1647. John Norden and Eliz. Skinner:
Marriage Lic. (Faculty Office), p. 34.
1687. George Westhrop and Amy
Norden: Marriage Alleg. (Canterbury),
p. 36.
London, 3, 4; Philadelphia, 5, 0.

Norfolk.—Local, ' of Norfolk.';
v. Suffolk; cf. Lancashire, Cornish,
Kent, &c. County names were
very popular.

Roger de Norfolk, London, 1273. A.
Willelmus de Northfolk, *souter*, 1379:
P. T. Yorks. p. 97.
1543. William Northfolke or Norfolke:
Reg. Univ. Oxf. vol. ii. pt. i. p. 285.
1666. Thomas Drake and Margaret
Norfolk: Marriage Alleg. (Canterbury),
p. 120.
1795. Married—Richard Norfolk and
Ann Platt: St. Geo. Han. Sq. ii. 131.
London, 3; MDB. (West Rid. Yorks),
4; Boston (U.S.), 2.

Norgate.—Local, 'at the north
gate' or road. The persons below
(P. T. Yorks) lived in Pontefract,
and among other burghers is one
Diota de Bougate (p. 100).

Ralph de Northgate, co. Norf., 1273. A.
Lodewysus de Northegate, 1379: P. T.
Yorks. p. 98.
Johanna de Northgate, 1379: ibid.
1615. Married — Henry Forrest and
Jane Northgate: St. Jas. Clerkenwell,
iii. 42.
1631. — John Norgate and Rebecka
Bonnivall: ibid. p. 62.
London, 4; Oxford, 1.

Norgrave, Norgrove. —
Local, ' of Norgrave,' i.e. at the
North Grave (a wood); v. Grave
or Grove.

1632. Buried — Eliz., d. Thomas Norgrove: St. Jas. Clerkenwell, iv. 205.
1633. Bapt.—Thomas, s. Thomas Norgrave: St. Mary Aldermary (London),
p. 83.
1731. — Sarah, d. William Norgrove:
St. Jas. Clerkenwell, ii. 195.
MDB. (co. Hereford), 0, 1; Oxford,
0, 4; Philadelphia, 3, 0.

Norie.—Local, 'at the north-ey';
v. Northey, and cf. Norton for
Northton, or Norham for Northam.
The first two following instances
occur together:

John atte Northeye, co. Soms., 1 Edw.
III: Kirby's Quest, p. 258.
William Norye, co. Soms., 1 Edw. III:
ibid.
1806. Married — John Gilbert and
Martha Norrie: St. Geo. Han. Sq. ii. 340.
London, 1.

Norman, Normand. — (1)
Local, ' the Norman,' i.e. north
man. O.F. Normand, Dan. Normand. The English surname may
imply either a Norman from Normandy or from Norway.

William Northman, co. Sussex, 1273. A.
Robert Northman, co. Oxf., ibid.
Alex. le Normaunt, co. Linc., ibid.
Mathew le Norman, co. Oxf., ibid.
Lucas Normannus, co. Devon, ibid.

(2) Bapt. ' the son of Norman.'
The root is the same. From a
national the term became a personal
name (cf. German). As such it
became a component of many local
names, such as Normanby, Normanton, Normanvill, Normancote,
Normansell, &c., perpetuating the
name of the original settler.

Alicia fil. Normanni, co. Camb.,
1273. A.
Robert fil. Normanni, co. Notts, ibid.
Philip Norman, co. Camb., ibid.
Norman de Arcy, co. Linc., ibid.
Norman de Redeman, 34 Hen. II :
Hist. West. and Cumb. i. 202.
Robertus Normand, 21 Ric. II : Fur-
ness Coucher Book, i. 40.
1583. Bapt. — Geoffraie, s. Anthonie
Normand: St. Mary Aldermary (Lon-
don), p. 61.
1585. — Anne, d. Anthonie Norman :
ibid.
London, 65, 1; New York, 24, 2.

Normanby.—Local, ' of Normanby,' parishes in cos. Lincoln
(2) and York. The meaning is
the *by* or habitation of Norman
(q.v.).

Jacobus de Normanby, co. Linc.,
1273. A.
Ralph de Normanby, co. Linc., ibid.
Alan de Normaneby, co. Linc., Hen.
III–Edw. I. K.

Normancote.—Local, ' of Normancote,' i.e. the cote or cottage
of Norman; cf. Normanton, &c.; v.
Norman.

Thomas de Normonekot, co. Salop,
1273. A.

Normansell.—Local, ' of Normansell.' There has long been
a family of Normansell settled in
East Cheshire. The name went
out to Virginia, and is in the list of
dead at ' James Cittie' :

1623. Edward Normansell: Hotten's
Lists of Emigrants, p. 192.

1501. Robert Normansell, of Bollington:
East Cheshire, ii. 333.
1562. Married — James Clercke and
Agnes Normansell: Reg. Prestbury, co.
Ches., p. 7.
1567. — Hugh Normansell and Sycely
Dale : ibid. p. 22.
1763. — Thomas Normansell and Ann
Povey: St. Geo. Han. Sq. p. 117.
London, 1.

**Normanton, Norminton,
Normington.**—Local, ' of Normanton,' parishes in cos. Lincoln,
York, Nottingham, Rutland, Derby,
and Leicester. The meaning, like
that of Normanby, is obvious, viz.
the town of Norman, q.v.

Henry de Normaneton, co. York,
1273. A.
Richard de Normanton, co. Notts, ibid.
Ralph de Normanton, co. Linc., Hen.
III–Edw. I. K.
Hugh de Normanton, co. Notts, 20
Edw. I. R.
Magota de Normanton, 1379: P. T.
Yorks. p. 97.
Laurencius de Normanton, 1379 : ibid.
p. 281.
1748. Married — William Norminton
and Anne Bull: St. Geo. Han. Sq. i. 40.
London, 0, 1, 1; West Rid. Court Dir.,
2, 0, 3; Philadelphia, 0, 0, 2 ; New York,
0, 1, 0.

Normanville. — Local, ' of
Normanville,' a name exactly
corresponding to English Normanby and Normanton. Lower
says, 'The Itineraire de la Normandie
shows two places so called, one
near Yvetot, and the other in the
arrondissement of Evreux' (Patr.
Brit. p. 239).

Galiena de Northmanville, co. Kent,
1273. A.
Thomas de Normanville, co. Linc., ibid.
Ralph de Northmanvyle, co. Kent, ibid.
Richard de Normanvill, co. Notts,
Hen. III–Edw. I. K.
Ralph Normauille, *armiger*, 1379 :
P. T. Yorks p. 62.
1607. Buried — William Normavell,
lodger at the spred egle: St. Peter,
Cornhill, i. 162.

Normin(g)ton; v. Normanton.

Norrington.—Local, ' of Northampton' (?). There can be little
doubt that this is the true etymology. The early forms of the
surname were Norhampton, Norhamton, and Norhanton, and this
would soon become Norrington.
There is no Northampton in our

directories, and yet the surname was common in the 13th century. Therefore we must look for it in some corrupted form. Norrington meets every difficulty.

John de Northampton, London, 1273. A.
Michael de Northampton, co. Linc., ibid.
William de Norhamton, co. Linc., ibid.
(Prior) de Norhanton, co. Linc., ibid.
Geoffrey de Norhantone, co. Salop, ibid.

From Norhanton to Norrington is but an easy single step.

1601-2. Nathanael Norringtonne : Reg. Univ. Oxf. vol. ii. pt. ii. p. 300.
1686. ' John Broadhurst and Jane Norrington : Marriage Alleg. (Canterbury), p. 240.
1699. Bapt. — Thomas Northampton, a foundling in Wood's Close : St. Jas. Clerkenwell, p. 381.
London, 4 ; MDB. (co. Devon), 1.

Norris, Norrish, Norriss.—
(1) Local, ' the Noreis,' the northern, the man from the North : sometimes meaning a Norwegian, but generally the ' north countree.' (2) Offic. 'the nurse.' M.E. *norice.* v. Nurse.

Thomas le Noreis, 1273. A.
Robert le Norys. B.
Walter le Noreis 1313. M.
1579. Edward Norries, co. Lanc. : Reg. Univ. Oxf. vol. ii. pt. ii. p. 87.
1766 Married—John Norriss and Mary McClary : St. Geo. Han. Sq. i. 158.
London, 65, 2, 2 ; Philadelphia, 98, o, o.

Norse.—Local, ' the Noreis,' the Norseman (v. Norris) ; cf. Morse for Morris.

1562. Buried — William Norse, *embroderer* : St. Mary Aldermary, p. 134.
New York, 1.

Norsworthy.—Local ; v. Nosworthy.

North.—Local, ' of the North,' a settler from the northern direction ; cf. South, East, and West ; v. Northern.

John de North, London, 1273. A.
Robert North, co. Oxf., ibid.
Willelmus del North, 1379 : P.T.Yorks. p. 195.
Johannes del North, 1379 : ibid. p. 116.
Margareta del North, 1379 : ibid. p. 170.
1558. James Northe, of Mellinge : Lancashire Wills at Richmond, i. 204.
1706. Married—Elias Philpin and Joan North : St. Antholin (London), p. 119.
London, 40 ; New York, 17.

Northam.—Local, ' of Northam,' a parish in co. Devon, near Bideford.

1806. Married — John Northam and Susan Greenwood : St. Geo. Han. Sq. ii. 348.
MDB. (co. Devon), 4 ; London, 1 ; New York, 3.

Northcot, Northcote, Northcott, Norcutt, Norcott. — (1) Local, ' of Northcote,' a hamlet and estate in the parish of East Downe, co. Devon ; (2) ' of Northcott,' a liberty in the parish of Stone, co. Staff. Originally 'at the north cot ' or dwelling ; cf. Westcott. Other small spots would bear this name. With the corrupted Norcutt, cf. Norbury or Norfolk.

Amyas de Northcote, co. Linc., 1273. A.
Amicia de Northcotes, co. Linc., ibid.
William de Northcote, co. Soms., 1 Edw. III : Kirby's Quest, p. 192.
1656. Buried — Dorothy Northcott, *spinster* : St. Thomas the Apostle (London), p. 131.
1674. John Norcott (co. Bucks) and Grace Rockoll : Marriage Alleg. (Canterbury), p. 234.
1681. William Northcote, of Exeter, and Alice Northcote, of the same : ibid. p. 67.
1752. Married — Thomas Norcut and Sarah Appleby : St. Geo. Chap. Mayfair, p. 209.
London, 1, 5, 1, 1, o ; Philadelphia, o, o, o, 2.

Northeast.—Local, ' from the north-east' (?) ; v. North. If this is not the real origin of the name, then its modern representatives are imitative.

Ralph Northest, co. Norf., 1273. A.
1593. Bapt. — Walter Northest : Reg. Stourton, Wilts, p. 3.
1658. — Jeramiah Northest : Reg. Broad Chalke, co. Wilts, p. 68.
London, 2 ; MDB. (co. Wilts), 1.

Northern, Northen.—Nick. ' the northern,' one who has come from the north country ; cf. Southern and Western ; v. North.

Thomas le Northeryn, co. Linc.,1273. A.
Geoffrey le Northern, co. Norf., ibid.
Thomas le Northern. M.
Richard le Northerne, co. Soms., 1 Edw. III : Kirby's Quest, p. 171.
William Northern, C. R., 33 Hen. VI.
1666. Thomas Browne and Ann Northerne : Marriage Alleg. (Canterbury), i. 191.
1686. James Hall and Winifred Northern : ibid. ii. 230.
London, 1, 2.

Northey. — (1) Local, ' of Northey,' i.e. of the north islet. ' An extinct chapelry and "deserted village " near Pevensey, co. Sussex. It was anciently a member of the Cinque Ports ' (Lower). Other spots in rivers would be similarly called ; v. Norie. (2) Local, ' at the north hey,' i.e. the north edge or enclosure.

William de Northye, co. Sussex,1273. A.
William de Northie, co. Kent, ibid.
John atte Northeye, co. Soms., 1 Edw. III : Kirby's Quest, p. 258.
Roger de la Northawe de Ledes, co. York : Close Roll, 17 Hen. VI.
1529. William Northy and Johanna South : Marriage Lic. (London), i. 7.
1764. Married—Henry Rowe and Jane Northy : St. Geo. Han. Sq. i. 132.

There can be little doubt that North-hey (v. Hey) is the chief parent.

London, 2 ; Boston (U.S.), 1.

Northley.—Local,'of the north ley ' or ' leigh,' i.e. the north meadow.

1602. Robert Northleighe, or Northley, co. Devon : Reg. Univ. Oxf. vol. ii. pt. ii. p. 257.
1618. Buried—Robart Nortly, servaunt to Mr. Vowell, in ye East yeard : St. Peter, Cornhill, i. 174.
1662. Married—John Nortley, *comber of wooll*, and Ann Wheeler : St. Jas. Clerkenwell, iii. 110.
1676. Francis Alanson and Dorothy Northleigh : Marriage Alleg. (Canterbury), p. 252.
MDB. (co. Cornwall), 1.

Northover.—Local, ' of Northover,' a parish in the dioc. Bath and Wells, co. Somerset, close by Ilchester.

(Prior) de Northover, 1273. A. ii. 861.
(Homines) de Nordovere, or Northowere, 20 Edw. I : R. p. 774.
1607. James Northover, co. Soms. : Reg. Univ. Oxf. vol. ii. pt. ii. p. 294.
1664. Bapt.—George, s. William Northover : St. Jas. Clerkenwell, i. 221.
1669. — Andrew, s. Charles Northover : ibid. p. 240.
1787. Married—Robert Smith and Eliz. Northover : St. Geo. Han. Sq. i. 396.
London, 1 ; MDB. (co. Soms.), 2 ; Philadelphia, 1.

Northrup, Northorp, Northrop, Northup.—Local, ' of Northope,' a parish in co. Linc. (No doubt originally North-thorp.) The American Northup is found in

England as Northop at an early period ; v. Thorp.

Stephen de Northorp, co. Linc., 1273. A.
John de Northorp. H.
Willelmus Northop', 1379: P. T. Yorks. p. 197.
1682. Henry Tyler and Ellen Northupp: Marriage Alleg. (Canterbury), ii. 106.
1744. Married—Thomas Wheeler and Mrs. Northorp: St. Geo. Chap. Mayfair, p. 45.
1773. — John Northorp and Betty Kitchen : St. Geo. Han. Sq. i. 229.
London, 2, 0, 0, 0 ; West Rid. Court Dir., 0, 1, 1, 0 ; Boston (U.S.), 0, 0, 1, 5 ; Philadelphia, 0, 0, 3, 1.

Northway.—Local, 'of Northway,' a township in the parish of Aschurch, near Tewkesbury, co. Glouc.

London. 1 ; MDB. (co. Devon), 2 ; Boston (U.S.), 1.

Northwood ; v. Norwood.

Norton.—Local, ' of Norton,' i.e. the north town as distinct from the west town (v. Weston) or the south town (v. Sutton). The places so called are too many to mention. They may be found in almost every county in England. The Hundred Rolls (1273) teem with them.

R. de Northton, co. Norf., 1273. A.
Ralph de Norton, co. York, ibid.
Baldwin de Norton, co. Northants, ibid.
Johannes de Norton, 1379: P. T. Yorks. p. 120.
Magota de Norton, 1379 : ibid. p. 110.
Howisia de Norton, 1379 : ibid. p. 111.

The last three entries concern Norton in the parish of Campsall, near Doncaster. Another hamlet in the same parish is Sutton.

1578. Adam Norton, co. Staff. : Reg. Univ. Oxf. vol. ii. pt. ii p. 83.
London, 58 ; West Rid. Court Dir., 6 ; New York, 112.

Norway.—Local, ' from Norway'; cf. France, Espin, Portingale, &c. ; v. Norris.

Ricardus de Norway, 1379: P. T. Yorks. p. 253.
Richard de Noreweye, co. Soms., 1 Edw. III : Kirby's Quest, p. 206.
1718. Buried — Richard Norway, a lodger: St. Mary Aldermary (London), p. 215.
London, 1.

Norwood, Northwood. — Local, 'of Norwood,' parishes in cos. Middlesex and Surrey. Smaller places so called in various counties.

Also the fuller form Northwood, parishes in cos. Salop and Hampshire. In all these cases the meaning is ' the north wood ' ; cf. Eastwood.

Mauger de Northwode, co. Bedf., 1273. A.
William de Northwode, co. Suff., ibid.
John de Northwode, co. Southampton, Hen. III-Edw. I. K.
Tillot de Northwode, 1379: P. T. Yorks. p. 284.
Johannes Norwode, 1379 : ibid. p. 171.
1592. Edmund Northwoode, co. Bucks: Reg. Univ. Oxf. vol. ii. pt. ii. p. 194.
1671. Buried — Thomas Norwood : Kensington Parish Reg. p. 142.
1789. Married—William Norwood and Eliz. Higgins : St. Geo. Han. Sq. ii. 24.
1791. — James Northwood and Penelope : ibid. p. 64.
London, 6, 1 ; Philadelphia, 7, 0.

Nosworthy, Norsworthy, Noseworthy.—Local, ' of Nosworthy.' Evidently some spot in co. Devon or Wilts. The suffix -worth (v. Worth) is commonly found as -worthy; cf. Langworthy, Kenworthy.

Walter Noswuth, co. Wilts, 1273. A.
1730. Married — Joseph Nosworthy, carpenter, and Eliz. Pomfett : St. Geo. Chap. Mayfair, p. 300.
1800. — William Norsworthy and Mary Bray : St. Geo. Han. Sq. ii. 213.
London, 2, 2, 0 ; MDB. (co. Devon), 12, 1, 0 ; New York, 1, 1, 0 ; Boston (U.S.), 0, 0, 1.

Notary.—Occup. ' the notary,' a scrivener. O.F. notaire. ' Notary, notarius ' : Prompt. Parv. This surname does not seem to have survived.

Robert Notare, co. Oxf., 1273. A.
Johannes Notare, 1379: P. T. Yorks. p. 170.
Johannes Gueys, notarius, 1379 : ibid. p. 16.

Nothard ; v. Neatherd.

Notman, Nutman, Nuttman.—(1) Occup. ' the nutman,' a dealer in nuts. M.E. note and nut, a nut. (2) Occup. ' the servant of Note' (Cnut or Canute); v. Nott (2). This is the more probable origin, belonging as it does to a special class of surnames, of which Matthewman and Addyman (q.v.) are the most familiar examples. Thus Matthewman means Matthew's man - servant,

and Noteman means Note's manservant. Nevertheless (1) and (2) are open for selection.

John Noteman, co. Camb., 1273. A.
Richard Noteman, co. Bucks, ibid.
William Nuteman, co. Linc., ibid.
London, 2, 1, 3 ; New York, 3, 0, 1.

Noton ; v. Notton.

Notson. — Bapt. ' the son of Ote,' from the nick. Note ; cf. Nobbs, Nabbs, Nodes, &c. (v. Oat).

Johanne Noteson, co. Soms., 9 Edw. II : Kirby's Quest, p. 136.
London, 3.

Nott (1).—Nick. ' nott-headed.' with the hair cropped close; cf. nott, to shear :

'I have a lamb, . . .
Of the right kind it is notted.'
Drayton.
' Thou nott-pated fool.'
1 Hen. IV, Act ii. sc. iv.

Not-wheat is smooth unbearded wheat.

Alicia le Notte, co. Camb., 1273. A.
Hugh le Notte, co. Bucks, ibid.
Robert le Notte, co. Northampt., Hen. III-Edw. I. K.
Henry le Notte, co. Leic., ibid.
Willelmus Notte, 1379 : P. T. Yorks. p. 84.
1580. James Nott, co. Glouc. : Reg. Univ. Oxf. vol. ii. pt. ii. p. 92.
1751. Married—Peter Nott and Eliz. Mandeville : St.Geo.Chap. Mayfair, p 201.
London, 11 ; New York, 7.

Nott (2), Notson, Notts, Nutt, Nutson, Nutts, Nute.— Bapt. ' the son of Cnut' (Canute), found in the 13th century as Note. The diminutive Nutkins and the patronymic Notson clearly establish the fontal origin of this little batch of surnames. There are two Cnuts in Domesday, one in co. York, the other in co. Derby ; cf. Knutsford, a village in co. Ches.

Note Attehel (at the hill), co. Camb., 1273. A.
Alice Note, co. Oxf., ibid.
John Note, co. Suff., ibid.
John Noteson, co. Soms., 1 Edw. III : Kirby's Quest, p. 136.
Johannes Nottson, 1379 : P. T. Yorks. p. 266.
Magota Nutte, 1379: ibid. p. 271.
1581. George Nutt, co. Kent : Reg. Univ. Oxf. vol. ii. pt. ii. p. 100.
London, 11, 3, 0, 6, 0, 0, 0 ; West Rid. Court Dir. (Notts), 1, 0 ; Philadelphia, 0, 5, 0, 21, 0, 0, 0 ; Brixham (Nute),1 ; Oxford (Nutt), 11.

Nottage, Nottidge.—? Nick. 'the nut-hatch.' Halliwell quotes: 'Nothagge, a byrde, *jaye*,' Palsgrave; '*Fidecula*, a nuthage,' Vocab. Rawl. MS. ; 'The nuthake with her notes newe,' The Squire of Low Degree, 55. Cf. Jay, Nightingale, Sparrow, Pidgeon, Woodcock, &c. 'Nothak, byrde, *picus*': Prompt. Parv. The meaning is nut-hack, i.e. a nut-cracker. Should this derivation be deemed unsatisfactory (although the corruption into Nottage is a natural one), a local origin must be sought for.

1788. Married — John Nottage and Mary Whitehouse: St. Geo. Han. Sq. ii. 4.
1793. — Josias Nottidge and Emily Pepys: ibid. p. 103.
London, 3, 2 ; Boston (U.S.), 6, 0.

Nottingham.—Local, 'of Nottingham.'

Hugh de Notingham, co. Bucks, 1273. A.
Ralph de Notingham, co. Oxf., ibid.
Robert de Notingham, co. Notts, ibid.
1552. Married—Fraunces Nottingham and Mary Halliwell : St. Peter, Cornhill, i. 222.
1718. Bapt.—John, s. John Nottingham : St. John Baptist on Wallbrook.
London, 2 ; Philadelphia, 1.

Notton, Noton.—Local, ' of Notton,' a village near Barnsley, W. Rid. Yorks.

Robertus de Notton, 1379 : P. T. Yorks. p. 137.
Sheffield, 0, 1 ; London, 0, 1 ; Manchester, 0, 1.

Nourse ; v. Nurse.

Nowell, Nowill.—Bapt. 'the son of Noel,' q.v. The modern Nowill is a natural variant of Nowell.

'General pardon to Nowell Harper, late of Boyleston, co. Derby, gent,' 1486, July 16 : Materials for a History of Henry VII, p. 503.
1580. Bapt. — James, son of Nowell Mathew : Reg. St. Columb Major, p. 11.
1578. John Nowell, co. Sussex, *gent.* : Reg. Univ. Oxf. vol. ii. pt. ii. p. 83.
1622. Bapt. — Adam, s. Marmaduke Nowell: St. Jas. Clerkenwell, i. 94.
Petition of Nowell Warner, 1627-8 : Cal. State Papers (Domestic).
London, 8, 2 ; New York, 1, 1.

Nugent.—Local, 'of Nogent.' Several places are so called in France. The Nugents are among those who 'came in with the Conqueror.' 'Nogent, or Nugent,

says Salverte, is the name of many towns or villages built on the banks of a river in a pleasant position, such as Nogent-sur-Seine, Nogent - sur - Marne, &c.' (Essai, ii. 284) ; v. Lower (Patr. Brit. p. 240).

Bertram de Nugun, co. Norf., 1273. A.
Nicholas de Nugun, co. Norf., ibid.
Nicholas de Nugun, co. Sussex, Hen. III-Edw. I. K.
1571. William Nugent, co. Meath : Reg. Univ. Oxf. vol. ii. pt. ii. p. 49.
1748. Married—Benjamin Sargant and Mary Nugent : St. Geo. Chap. Mayfair, p. 122.
London, 8 ; Philadelphia, 76.

Nunhouse. — Local, 'at the nun-house,' from residence there, probably as a servant ; cf. Monkhouse.

Willelmus Nunhouse, 1379 : P. T. Yorks. p. 112.

Nunn.—Occup. 'the nun'; v. Nunns. Possibly sometimes a nickname for a man of demure and devout demeanour.

Alice le Nonne, co. Northampton, 1273. A.
Robert Nonne, co. Camb., ibid.
Margaret Nunne, co. Norf. FF.
1614. Married—Thomas Jenkins and Abigaell Nunn : St. Jas. Clerkenwell, p. 40.
1746. — Edmund Nunn and Mary Park : St. Geo. Chap. Mayfair, p. 70.
London, 33 ; Boston (U.S.), 5.

Nunneley, Nunnerley. — Local, seemingly 'at the nunne ley,' i.e. the nun's meadow; v. Nunne. Nunnerley is probably a variant. I cannot find the spot.

1739. Bapt.—William, s. William Nunnerly : St. Jas. Clerkenwell, ii. 243.
1790. Married—John Lilley and Margaret Nunnerley : St. Geo. Han. Sq. ii. 38.
Manchester, 1, 0 ; Liverpool, 0, 1 ; MDB. (co. Linc.), 1, 0 ; (co. Ches.), 0, 2.

Nunnery. — Local, ' at the nunnery' (?), from residence therein ; cf. Nunhouse.

1718. Bapt.—Anne, d. Anne Nunnery : St. Jas. Clerkenwell, ii. 106.
MDB. (co. Linc.), 2 ; New York, 3.

Nunns, Nunson.—Nick. 'the son of the nun,' i.e. the child of a lapsed vowess. M.E. *nonne* and *nunne*. Lower recalls an A.S. Nun, a personal name, but this was in 710, and there is no evidence

that it survived to the 13th century. On the other hand we have proof of the origin given above.

Alice la Nonne, et Robert filius ejus co. Northampton, 1273. A.
John Nunnes, co. Notts, 20 Edw. I. R.
Hugo Nunneson, 1379 : P. T. Yorks. p. 221.
1548. Robert Nonson : Reg. Univ. Oxf. vol. ii. pt. ii. p. xv.
1742. Buried — Hannah Nonson : St. Mary Aldermary (London), p. 225.
London, 1, 0 ; New York, 2, 0.

Nurse Nourse.—Occup. 'the nurse.' M.E. *norice*. v. Norris (2).

Robertus la (sic) Norice, co. Bedf., 1273. A.
Matilda Nutrix, co. Camb., ibid.
Maria le Nøreyse, co. Camb., ibid.
Alicia le Noryce. B.
Thomas Nurse. B.
Agnes Noryce, 1379 : P. T. Yorks. p. 256.
Johanna Nurys, 1379 : ibid. p. 110.
Robertus Horbery, *tayllour*, et Johanna uxor ejus : ibid. p. 96.
Nutrix ejus : ibid.
Magota le Nuris : ibid. p. 274.
1685-6. Robert Pitt and Martha Nourse : Marriage Lic. (London), p. 178.
1792. Married — John Nurse, *cordwainer*, and Mary King : St. Geo. Chap. Mayfair, p. 303.
London, 5, 0 ; New York, 3, 6.

Nussey, Nursey.—Local, ' of Nussey.' This surname is almost peculiar to Yorkshire even in the 19th century. The first two instances below are found in the township of Appletreewick, in the parish of Burnsall, near Skipton.

Robertus de Nusse, 1379 : P. T. Yorks, p. 264.
Johannes de Nussay, 1379 : ibid.
1688-9. Samuell Nussey, *vintner*, and Eliz. Herrington : Marriage Alleg. (Canterbury), p. 94.
1787. Married — William Nursey and Eliz. Bensted : St. Geo. Han. Sq. i. 402.
London, 0, 1 ; West Rid. Court Dir., 13, 0.

Nutbeam. — Local, 'at the notebem,' i.e. the hazel-tree. A.S. *hnut-beám*. From residence beside some prominent nut-tree. A.S. *beám*, a tree.

John atte Notebem, co. Oxf., 1273. A.
John apud Notebem, co. Oxf., ibid.
Jordan Notebem, co. Oxf., ibid.
'A charge against Henry Nutbeam of illegally interfering with the police in the Southampton strike was dismissed ' : Standard, Sept. 12, 1890.

I have also seen the surname in the Devon Directory, but cannot find my reference.

Southampton, 1.

Nutbrown. — Nick. 'nutbrown.' Probably from complexion of the hair: cf. 'nutbrown maid.' v. Brownnutt.

'George Nutbrowne was sworne the same daye, *pistler*, and Nathaniel Pownell, *gospeller*': Cheque Bk. Chapel Royal, p. 12, Camd. Soc.
Hugo Nuttebroune, 1379: P. T. Yorks. p. 190.
William Notbrone, 1441, co. York. W. 11.
William Nutbrowne, c. Eliz. Z.
1550. Anthony de Sancto Oelia and Eliz. Nutbrowne: Marriage Lic. (London), p. 13.
1576. Married — Thomas Nutbrowne and Jone Wright: St. Peter, Cornhill, i.230. York, 2.

Nuthall; v. Nuttall.

Nute; v. Nott (2).

Nutkins. — Bapt. 'the son of Cnut' (Canute), found in the 13th century as Note (v. Nott and Nutt). With the diminutive appended this became Notekin, now as a surname Nutkins. It is interesting to notice that the surname is found in co. Essex in 1273, and again turns up in 1666 in the same shire. The genitive suffix in Nutkins seems of recent origin.

Adam Notekyn, co. Essex, 1273. A.
1662. John Nutkin, of Stepney, and Sarah Kempton: Marriage Alleg. (Canterbury), i. 59.
1666. John Nutkin (co. Essex), *miller*, and Esther Spowse: ibid. p. 183.
1735. Married — John Nutkins and Ann Cock: St. Geo. Chap. Mayfair, p. 251. London, 3.

Nutley. — Local, 'of Nutley,' parishes in diocs. Chichester and Winchester, also smaller places in co. Bucks, &c.

Henry de Nuttele, co. Camb., 1273. A.
John de Nottele, co. Oxf., ibid.
Agnes de Nottelye, co. Devon, Hen. III-Edw. I. K.
John de Nuttele, co. Southampton, 20 Edw. I. R.
1672. William Nutley and Catherine Fettiplace: Marriage Lic. (Westminster), p. 45.
1691-2. William Nuttley and Amy Hooper: Marriage Alleg. (Canterbury), p. 213.
London, 1; Boston (U.S.), 3; New York, 3.

Nutman. — Occup.; v. Notman.

Nutson, Nutt; v. Nott (2).

Nuttall, Nuttle, Nuthall, Nuttell. — Local, 'of Nuttall' or 'Nuthall,' a parish in co. Notts. Possibly smaller spots may have assisted in spreading the name. One certainly in Cheshire has originated the numerous Nuttalls of Lancashire and Cheshire. The variants are of a natural character, and call for no notice.

Agatha de Nuthal, co. Notts, Hen. III-Edw. I. K.
1579. John Nuthall, co. Chester: East Cheshire, ii. 178.
Thomas de Nuthill: Patent Roll, 1 Hen. IV. pt. v.
1616. Richard Nuttall, of Nuttall, *gent*: Wills at Chester, i. 144.
1744. Married — John Nuttall and Jane Ellis: St. Geo. Chap. Mayfair, p. 41.
1748. — John Nuthall and Mary Sykes: ibid. p. 102.
1775. Married — James Smithson and Mary Nuthall: St. Geo. Han. Sq. p. 253.
London, 3, 0, 0, 0; Liverpool, 10, 1, 1, 0; Philadelphia, 24, 0, 0, 1.

Nutter. — ? Occup. 'the nutter' (?), a dealer in nuts. The surmise is quite a natural one, but I have not discovered any proof, which always makes a definition of this sort unsatisfactory. v. Neatherd for another explanation.

1611. William Nutter, co. York: Reg. Univ. Oxf. vol. ii. pt. ii. p. 324.
1617. George Nutter, co. Lanc.: ibid. p. 359.

1617. John Nutter, of Pendle: Wills at Chester, i. 144.
1620. — James Nutter, of Burnley: ibid.

The name was strongly represented in Pendle and the neighbourhood of Whalley Abbey, Lanc. The above are only two out of many of these will-names. One large branch of this name seems evidently to have sprung up in this district.

1747. Married — James Nutter and Eliz. Freeman: St. Geo. Chap. Mayfair, p. 100.
London, 7; Manchester, 3; Burnley 4; Philadelphia, 8.

Nutting. — ? ——. I can suggest nothing satisfactory.

Willelmus Nutyng, 1379: P. T. Yorks. p. 209.
1660. Buried — Mary, wife of Edward Nutting: ibid. iii. 337.
1659. Married — Robert Nutting and Mary Sibley: ibid. iii. 101.
London, 4; New York, 8.

Nye. — Local, 'atten ey' (?), at the *ey*, from residence on some small islet or eyot. The suffix -*ey* is common; cf. Northey, Forty, Ely, &c. In this case the final *n* in *atten* has become the prefix of the name proper; v. Nash, Noakes, Nelmes, for similar instances. The following entry seems conclusive:

Thoma atte Nye, co. Soms., 1 Edw. III: Kirby's Quest, p. 205.

We find Rodney spelt the same way:

Lucia de Rodenye, co. Soms., 9 Edw. II: Kirby's Quest, p. 112.
1613. Married — James Nygh and Isabel Hilliard: Kensington Parish Reg. p. 66.
1670. Buried — Judith, d. Philip Nye: ibid. p. 140.
1672. — Philyp Nye, *minister*: St. Michael, Cornhill, p. 258.
1677. — Rupert Nye, *dr. of physick*: ibid. p. 262.
London, 12; New York, 5.

O

Oak, Oake, Oakes, Oaks.—
Local, 'at the oak' or 'at the
oaks,' from residence thereby.

Adam at ye Ock, co. Salop, 1273. A.
Philip del Okes, co. Salop, ibid.
Henricus atte Ok', 1379: P. T. Yorks.
p. 132.
Johannes del Okes, 1379: ibid. p. 188.
Richard atte Oke. B.
Walter atte Ok, C. R., 2 Edw. II.
Roger of the Okes, 1319. M.
Walter atte Oke, co. Soms., 1 Edw. III:
Kirby's Quest, p. 150.
1604. Bapt. — William, s. George
Oakes: St. Dionis Backchurch, p. 91.
1754. Married — Arthur Ayres and
Mary Oake: St. Geo. Chap. Mayfair, p. 273.
London, 0, 2, 12, 1 ; Philadelphia, 1, 0,
9, 2 ; New York (Oake), 1.

Oakden.—Local ; v. Ogden.

Oakenfull.—Local, 'of the
oaken field.' *Oaken* is the adjective ;
cf. Linden, Birchen or Birken, as
in Birkenhead, and v. Akenhead and
Akenside ; *-full* is a corruption of
-field when a suffix ; cf. Hatfull
for Hatfield. Probably a Norfolk
surname.

Adam de Oakefeld, co. Norf., 1273. A.
1733. Married—John Oakinful and Ann
Saddleton : Canterbury Cathedral, p. 79.
1798. — John Penny and Eliz. Oakenfull : St. Geo. Han. Sq. ii. 178.
London, 1 ; New York, 1.

Oakes ; v. Oak.

Oakey, Okey, Okie.—Local,
'at the oak-ey,' i.e. the island
covered with oak-trees ; cf. Northey, &c.

Jack' Oky, co. Norf., 1273. A.
Nicholas Oky, co. Berks, ibid.
John de Oky, co. Soms., 1 Edw. I :
Kirby's Quest, p. 203.
John Oky, co. Norf., 20 Edw. I. R.
1707. Married—John Grout and Anne
Oakey : St. Antholin (London), p. 120.
London, 4, 3, 0 ; New York, 6, 0, 5.

Oakford, Ockford.—Local,
'of Oakford,' a parish in co. Devon,
three miles and a half from Bampton.

1746. Married — James Eager and
Sarah Okeford : Canterbury Cath. p. 88.
London, 1, 0 ; Philadelphia, 12, 0.

Oakley, Oakly.—Local, 'of
Oakley.' No less than eleven

parishes bear this name in diocs.
Oxford, Norwich, Ely, Winchester, &c.

Walter de Oclee, co. Wilts, 1273. A.
Godwin de Ocle, co. Suff., ibid.
Robert de Ocle, co. Oxf., ibid.
Thomas Acle, or Ocle, sheriff of Nor-
wich, 1415 : FF. iii. 136.
Simon de Akelegh. E.
Robert de Oklegh, co. Soms., 1327 : Tax
Roll.
Agnes de Acle, co. Norf., 1362 : FF.
iv. 336.
William de Acle, prior of Hoxne, co.
Norf., c. 1380 : ibid. iii. 609.
1541. Married — William Smith and
Elisabeth Okely : St. Antholin (London),
p. 3.
1687. — Benjamin Oakeley and Grace
Hardistey : St. Michael, Cornhill, p. 45.
London, 23, 1 ; Philadelphia, 4, 0 ; New
York, 51, 0.

Oastler, Osler, Ostler.—
Occup. 'the hosteler,' a keeper of
a hostel, an inn-keeper. O.F.
hostelier.

'Be thou not wroth, or we departen here,
Though that my tale be of an hostelere.'
Chaucer, The Coke's Prologue.

Wyclif has 'ostiler' in Luke x.
35. This is very like the early forms.

Godfrey le Hoselur, 1273. A.
Reginald le Osiler. T.
Richard le Hosteler, c. 1318. M.
William le Ostiller. J.
Walter le Oyselur. T.
Richard Hosteler, bailiff of Yarmouth,
1501 : FF. xi. 326.
1694. Bapt.—Martha, d. Henry Ostler :
St. Jas. Clerkenwell, i. 357.
1668. Married — Laurence Osler and
Eliz. Buttler : ibid. p. 146.
London, 1, 4, 1 ; MDB. (co. Norfolk),
0, 7, 0.

Oat, Oates, Oats, Oatson.—
Bapt. 'the son of Odo' (v. Oddy),
otherwise Otho, Oto, Otto, Othes,
and Otes. Camden says, 'Othes,
an old name in England drawn
from Otho' : Remains, p. 73.

Hotys de Parme, co. Linc., 1273. A.
Andreas Otes, co. Norf., ibid.
Oto de Bayley, circa 1300 : Baines'
Lanc. ii. 100.
Johannes Hotes, 1379 : P. T. Yorks.
p. 187.
Robertus Otesson', 1379 : ibid.
Otes de Howorth, 1379 : ibid. p. 188.
Johannes Oteson, 1379 : ibid.

John Otes, *glover*, 1439 : Rental of
Halifax, Cotton MSS. Vespasian, F. 15,
Brit. Mus.
Oto Sagar, secular chaplain, 1522 :
Reg. Univ. Oxf. p. 124.
Otes Redish, of Redish, co. Lanc., circa
1550 : Earwaker's East Cheshire, i. 260.
Otes Holland, 1541, Pendleton, Man-
chester :- Lanc. and Ches. Rec. Soc., vol.
xii. p. 141.
Otes Redyche, 1541, Radcliffe : ibid.
p. 144.
Adam, s. Otes Jeffery, 1547 : Reg. St.
Columb Major, p. 4.
Thomas, s. Otes Dyar, 1547 : ibid.
1575. Thomas Otes, Lincoln College :
Reg. Univ. Oxf. vol. ii. pt. iv. p. 67.
1743. Married — William Oates and
Margaret Preston : St. Geo. Han. Sq.
i. 29.

Oats and Oates are the present
directory forms. The form Oats
seems to be confined to America.

1679. Bapt.—Joseph, s. George Oats,
St. Michael's, Barbadoes : Hotten's Lists
of Emigrants, p. 424.
London, 0, 5, 0, 0 ; West Rid. Court
Dir., 0, 26, 0, 0 ; Philadelphia, 19, 3, 2, 0.

Oatmonger.—Occup. 'a dealer
in oats' ; cf. Cornmonger.

Denis le Otemonger, London. X.
Thomas le Otemangere, co. Soms., 9
Edw. II : Kirby's Quest, p. 128.

Oats ; v. Oat.

Obey, Obee. — ? Local, 'of
Oby' (?). Mr. Lower says, 'An
extinct parish now joined with
Ashby, co. Norfolk.' But probably
the name is a personal one, for
besides Obe without local prefix
we find the pet form Obekin, i.e.
little Obe, and such place-names
as Obley and Obthorpe. With the
variant Obee, cf. Applebee.

Robert Obe, co. Oxf., 1273. A.
Nicholas Obekyn, co. Camb., ibid.
1788. Married — William Obey and
Mary Birkett : St. Geo. Han. Sq. ii. 9.
1795. — John Morris and Ann Obee :
ibid. p. 134.
London, 1, 1.

Oborn, Oborne.—Local, 'of
Oborne,' a parish in co. Dorset,
one mile from Sherborne.

1605. Maurice Oborne, co. Soms. :
Reg. Univ. Oxf. vol. ii. pt. ii. p. 287.

1613. William Oburn, vicar of Boulton : Lancashire Wills at Richmond, i. 205.
1803. Married — Edward Jenkins and Sarah Watts Oborne : St. Geo. Han. Sq. ii. 286.
London, 1, 7 ; Philadelphia, 1, 0 ; New York, 1, 0.

Occleston, Ockleston, Ocklestone.—Local, ' of Occlestone,' a township in the parish of Middlewich, co. Chester. The meaning seems clear, i.e. the town or farmstead of Ogle. For a similar instance v. Oglethorpe, where that surname is found as Okolstorp as early as 1273.

1603. William Occleston, of Mere : Wills at Chester, i. 144.
1691. Henry Ocklestone, Prestbury, co. Ches. : East Cheshire, ii. 522.
MDB. (co. Chester). 0, 5, 1 ; Manchester, 1, 2, 0 ; Liverpool, 0, 2, 0 ; Philadelphia, 2, 0, 0.

Ockenden.—Local, ' of Ockenden,' i.e. the *dean* where the oak-trees grew (v. Dean). ' An estate at Cuckfield, co. Sussex, to which county the name seems mainly to be limited ' (Lower).

1806. Married — John Longley and Mary Oakenden : St. Geo. Han. Sq. ii. 345.
London, 2 ; Oxford, 2 ; MDB.(co.Sus.),2.

Ockford.—Local; v. Oakford.

Ockleshaw.—Local, ' of Ockleshaw,' probably a spot near Occleston, q.v. The derivation seems to be the shaw or wood belonging to Ogle.

1651. Ralph Ocleshaw : East Cheshire, ii. 68.
Liverpool, 1.

Odam, Odem, Odium.—Local, ' of Odiham,' a parish in co. Hants, twenty-six miles from Winchester.

Roger. de Odiam, co. Norf., 1273.
Richard de Odiham, co. Norf., ibid.

The following corruption looks somewhat odious :

1580. Married — Thomas Early and Agnes Odium : St. Jas. Clerkenwell, p. 8.
London, 2, 1, 0 ; Philadelphia, 0, 0, 1.

Odcock.—Bapt. ' the son of Odo,' from the popular Ode or Oddy, with suffix -*cock* (v. Cock and Oddy). One more proof of the great favour extended to this personal name. The suffix -*cock*

was only appended to the more familiar names ; cf. Wilcock, Simcock, Jeffcock, &c.

Amicus Odecok, co. Norf., 1273. A.

Oddy, Oddie, Ody, Odey.—Bapt. ' the son of Odo ' or ' Oddo,' still popular in Germany as Otto (v. Oat), a personal name, probably of Norman importation ; v. Odling.

' For a bishop he sent at morn when it was day,
Sir Ode of Wynchestre.'
Robert of Brunne, N. and Q., 1857, p. 113.
John fil. Ode, co. Hunts, 1273. A.
Matilda Odde, co. Hunts, ibid.
Henry fil. Ode, co. York, ibid.
Odo et alii thaine' : Domesday Book.
Odo Arbalister : ibid.
Richard fil. Odonis : Pipe Roll, 6 Hen. II. p. 17.
William fil. Ode, 1379 : P. T. Yorks. p. 194.

As a personal name found late :

Ottie Sagar, of Colne, 1597 : Wills at Chester, i. 168.
Robert Oth, or Odd, 1508 : Reg. Univ. Oxf. i. 59.
1751. Married—John Oddy and Grace Holmes : St. Geo. Chap. Mayfair, p. 205.
West Rid. (Yorks) Court Dir., 12, 2, 0, 0 ; New York, 1, 2, 0, 1.

Odell.—Local, ' of Odell,' a parish in co. Bedford. Lower writes, ' The seat of an ancient barony written Wodhull, and by Norman corruption Wahull. The great Domesday Baron known as Walter Flandrensis, from his being a Fleming, held it, and his posterity was called " de Wahull " ' (Patr. Brit. p. 243). Thus the derivation is wood-hill, the hill covered with trees ; v. Hull (2).

Walter de Wahull, co. Oxf., 1273. A.
John de Warhulle, co. Bedf., ibid.
Walter de Wadhulle, co. Bedf., ibid.
1615. Married—Richard Guilyams and Ruth Odill : St. Michael, Cornhill, p. 21.
1791. Married—Pierce Odell and Mary Bunning : St. Geo. Han. Sq. ii. 64.
London, 10 ; New York, 86.

Odger, Odgers, Oger, Ogier.—Bapt. ' the son of Oger ' ; v. Auger. The London Directory (1872) seems to have no instances. With the variant Odger, cf. Rodger for Roger. Also cf. Hodge and Hodgson from Roger ; similarly Dodge and Dodson from Roger.

Oger fil. Oger, Fines Roll, Richard I. GG.
Oger de Kernik, C. R., 54 Hen. III.
Alan fil Oger, Roger fil. Oger. E.
Peter fil. Oggery, co. Oxf., Hen. III-Edw. I. K.
1637. Bapt.—Jane, d. Abraham Ottgar : St. Antholin (London), p. 71.
1792. Married — James Smith and Catharine Oger : St. Geo. Han. Sq. ii. 75.
Oxford (Odgers), 2 ; Philadelphia, 0, 8, 0, 1.

Odinel.—Bapt. ' the son of Odinel,' a double dim. of Odo (v. Oddy). This name seems to have been all but wholly confined to co. Northumberland. It became popular through a local hero, Odinel de Umfrayville, lord of Prudhoe Castle.

' Odinel de Umfranvile relevad le suen cri' : Chronique de Jordan Fantosme, circa 1180, Surtees Soc., l. 1778.
Odonel de Ford, rector of Meldon, temp. 1200 : KKK. ii. 8.
Galfridus Odenel, 1233 : KKK. vi. 163.
Odinellus de Albaniaco, temp. Hen. III : BBB. p. 61.
Geoffrey Odinel, co. York, 1273. A.
William fil. Otnil, co. Linc., ibid.
Otnel Joce, co. Oxf., ibid.
Odnell Carnaby, 1561 ; QQQ. p. xxxii.
Johannes Odinell, cos. Norf. and Suff., Hen. III-Edw. I. K.
Walter Odynel, co. Soms., 1 Edw. III : Kirby's Quest, p. 210.
Odonel Selby, of Tweedmouth, 1555 : QQQ. p. 388.

Odlin, Odling.—Bapt. ' the son of Odo,' from dim. Odelin ; v. Oddy. The excrescent *g* in Odling is common ; cf. Jennings.

Richard fil. Odeline, co. Salop, 1273. A.
Henry Odelin, co. York, ibid.
Odelina uxor Elye de Bleynnaker, C. R., 36 Hen. III.
Johannes Otheline, 1379 : P. T. Yorks. p. 235.
' Odelina, wife of Roger Male-doctus' : Parker's Early Oxford, p. 273.
1786. Married — Joseph Odling and Hannah Spencer : St. Geo. Han. Sq. i. 388.
London, 2, 1 ; Oxford, 0, 1 ; Boston (U.S.), 1, 0.

Ody.—Bapt. ; v. Oddy.

Offer, Offor, Aufrere, Orfeur.—Occup. ' le Orfevre.' O.F. Orfevre, the goldsmith. The present modification can be easily traced. Orfeur still exists in co. Norfolk.

Peter le Orfeure, co. Wilts, 1273. A.
John le Orfevre, co. Camb., ibid.
Nicholas Aurifaber, co. Camb., ibid.
William le Orfeure, co. Bucks, 20 Edw. I. R.

John Barri, *orfeuer*, 6 Edw. II: Free-
men of York, i. 14.
Richard de Dorem, *orfeuer*, 11 Edw. II:
Freemen of York, i. 17.
Roger le Orfevre, 1313. M.
Richard Orfer. F.
William Offer, 1507: Reg.Univ.Oxf.i.51.
1696. Married — Thomas Orfeur and
Ann Llewellen: St. Jas. Clerkenwell,
p. 217.
1787. William Dawson and Sophia
Aufrere, of Hoveton St. Peter, co. Norf.:
St. Geo. Han. Sq. 399.
London, 1, 3, 0, 0; MDB. (Norfolk),
0, 0, 1, 0; Yarmouth, 0, 0, 0, 2.

Offley.—Local, 'of Offley,' (1)
a parish near Hitchin, co. Herts;
(2) 'of High Offley,' a parish near
Eccleshall, co. Stafford.
1176. William de Offcleghe, East
Cheshire, ii. 379.
1621. Thomas Offley, Hart Hall, London: Reg. Univ. Oxf. vol. ii. pt. ii. p. 389.
1638. John Offley, of Hulmehouse, co.
Ches.,*gentleman*: Wills at Chester,ii.164.
1808. Married—William Offley, Esq.,
and Mary Everett: St. Geo. Han. Sq.
ii. 380.
London, 4; Boston (U.S.), 1.

Offor; v. Offer.

Offord.—Local, 'of Offord,'
a parish in the dioc. of Ely, three
miles from Huntingdon. With
regard to the instance Offorth infra,
v. Forth.
Edelina de Offord, co. Hunts, 1273. A.
John de Offord, co. Hunts, ibid.
Thomas de Offorth, co. Camb., ibid.
1797. Married — James Offord and
Eliz. Pack: St. Geo. Han. Sq. ii. 161.
London, 11; New York, 1.

Offring.—Local, 'of Offring.'
I cannot find any 19th century
instances.
Richard de Offringe, co. Wilts, 1273. A.
1735. Married—Alexander Chatto and
Mary Offring: St. Jas. Clerkenwell, p. 263.

Ofspring. — Local; v. Oxpring.

Ogan.—Bapt. 'the son of Ogan'
or 'Wogan,' q.v.; cf. Orm and
Worm, Ulf and Wolf.
William fil. Ogyn, co. Salop, 1273. A.
Michael Wogan, or Ogan, 1513: Reg.
Univ. Oxf. i. 90.
London, 1.

Ogbourn, Ogborn. — Local,
'of Oxbourn,' two parishes in co.
Wilts. No doubt compounded of
oc, oak, and *burn*, a stream, the
stream flowing by the oak-trees.
For this lazy way of pronouncing

the word cf. Slagg and Slack.
Both parishes are situated near
Marlborough.
Walter de Okeburne, co.Wilts, 1273. A.
1764. Married — Jeremiah Ogbourn
and Mary Timson: St. Geo. Han. Sq. i.
133.
1793. — Thomas Delboux and Ann
Ogbourne: ibid. ii. 97.
1808. — William Ogborn and Sarah
Green: ibid. p. 385.
London, 1, 0; Philadelphia, 0, 7.

Ogden, Oakden.—Local, 'of
Oakden,' i.e. the oak-den; v. Dean.
This family name, so familiar to
South Lancashire, sprang up in the
neighbourhood of Crompton and
parish of Rochdale.
'In the reign of Edw. I. lived Sir Bald-
win de Tyas . . . who granted to Sir
Robert de Holland, in free marriage
with Joan, his daughter, all his lands in
Butterworth, the Cleggs, Garthside,
Akeden, Holynworth, &c., in Rochdale':
Baines' Lanc. i. 505.
This surname has widely ex-
tended in America, and on the map
I see a town called Ogdenville.
John de Okedon, co. York, 1273. A.
Richard de Okeden, 6 Edw. III.
1794. Married — Richard Davis and
Mary Ogden: St. Geo. Han. Sq. ii. 106.
1806. — Robert Oakden and Ann
Hughes: ibid. p. 343.
London, 6, 0; Manchester, 50, 0;
Philadelphia, 92, 0.

Ogilby; v. Ogleby.

Ogle.—Bapt. 'the son of Ogle,'
Icel. Ogvalld (Yonge, ii. 243). A
northern name found as component
in several local names; v. Oglethorpe. A Northumberland family
of Ogle sprang from Oggil in that
county (v. Lower).
Robertus Ogill, 1379: P. T. Yorks.
p. 236.
1582. Cuthbert Ogle, co. Northumb.:
Reg. Univ. Oxf. vol. ii. pt. ii. p. 123.
1637. Married—John Barnes and Eliz.
Ogle: St. Jas. Clerkenwell, iii. 68.
1802. — Charles Ogle and Charlotte
Martha Gage: St. Geo. Han. Sq. ii. 256.
London, 8; Philadelphia, 13.

Ogleby, Ogilby, Oglesby.—
Local, 'of Ogleby.' I cannot find
the spot. Of course the meaning
is 'the *by* (or dwelling) of Ogle,'
the first settler or owner; v.
Oglethorpe and Ogle.
1617. Thomas Oglebye, of Rochdale:
Wills at Chester, i. 145.

1640. Bapt. — Robert, s. Thomas
Oglebye: St. Jas. Clerkenwell, i. 146.
London, 2, 1, 1; Philadelphia, 0, 0, 4.

Oglethorpe.—Local, 'of Ogle-
thorp.' Oglestorp and Oglestun, in
Domesday Book, are two places in
co. York, near together, and under
the same possessor. That Ogle
as a component was a personal
name is clear; also that the bearers were Scandinavians; v. Ogle.
Nicholas de Okolstorp, co. York,
1273. A.
John de Okilsthorp, 1379: P. T. Yorks.
p. 146.
William Ogylthorp, *merchand*, 1379:
P. T. Howdenshire, p. 22.
1581. Robert Ogelthroppe, co. York:
Reg. Univ. Oxf. vol. ii. pt. ii. p. 100.
— Edward Ogelthroppe, co. Oxf.,
armiger: ibid. p. 98.
1604. Bapt. — William, s. Thomas
Oglethorpe: St. Jas. Clerkenwell, i. 44.
1663. Married — Robert Oglethorpe
and Sarah Haddon: Marriage Alleg.
(Vicar-General), i. 100.
Lancaster, 1.

Ointer.—Occup. 'the ointer,'
possibly a seller of ointments.
O.F. *oindre*, to anoint.
Michael le Hointer, London, 1273. A.
Michael le Oynter, London. X.

Okell, Okill.—? Bapt. 'the son
of Ogle'(?). Everything points to
this derivation. That the great
personal name Ogle was sharpened
into Occle is evident, and other
variants would follow; v. Oglethorpe, Occleston, and Ockleshaw.
The London Directory has also
Ockeford. I find no traces of
Oakhill, which would first strike
one as the parent.
1572. Thomas Okell, of Preston: Wills
at Chester, i. 145.
1598. Hugh Okell, of Withington: ibid.
1609. Robert Okell, of Sutton: ibid.
1792. Married — William Brads and
Eliz. Okell: St. Geo. Han. Sq. ii. 72.
Manchester, 2, 0; London, 1, 0; Philadelphia, 2, 2.

Okeover.—Local, 'of Okeover,'
co. Stafford. The family is an
extremely old one.
Hugo de Okouere, co. Staff., 1316. M.
Roger de Okouere, co. Staff., 1325. M.
1583. Edward Phillipps and Eliz. Okeover: Marriage Lic. (London), i. 118.
1638. John Okeover, New College:
Reg. Univ. Oxf. i. 148.
Houghton C. Okeover, of Okeover,
1874: MDB. (co. Derby).
MDB. (co. Derby), 1.

Okey, Okie.—Local; v. Oakey.

Old, Ould, Oulds, Olds.—(1) Nick. 'the old'; cf. Young, Senior, Youngman, Younghusband, &c.

Thomas le Old, co. Soms., 1 Edw. III : Kirby's Quest, p. 189.
John le Olde, co. Glouc., 1311. M.
Henry Olde, C. R., 7 Ric. II.
John Olde, incumbent of Cubington, 1548 : Dugdale's Warwickshire, p. 203.

(2) Bapt. 'the son of Old,' whence the patronymic form Oulds.

William fil. Alde, co. Salop, 1273. A.
1750. Married — John Old and Mary Duncan : St. Geo. Chap. Mayfair, p. 159.
— — Joshua Oulds and Mary Garnett : ibid. p. 186.
London, 5, 1, 2, 0 ; New York, 12, 0, 0, 0.

Oldaker.—Local, 'at the old acre,' i. e. the old field, from residence therein or thereby ; cf. Oldfield.

1767. Married — Richard Eades and Sarah Oldaker : St. Geo. Han. Sq. i. 161.
1796. — Robert Oldaker and Ann Allen : ibid. ii. 149.
London, 2.

Oldbury.—Local, 'of Oldbury,' parishes and hamlets in cos. Salop (2), Warwick, and Gloucester (2).

Thomas de Oldebury, co. Salop, 1273. A.
1614-5. Bapt.—Mary, d. Thomas Oldbury : St. Dionis Backchurch, i. 96.

Oldershaw, Olorenshaw. Ollerenshaw, Ollernshaw.—Local, 'at the alder-shaw' (v. Shaw), more correctly the 'aller-shaw,' the *d* being intrusive. Allern is adjectival, as in Linden, Beechen, Birken, Oaken. Thus Ollernshaw is the nearest to a correct form, wanting a change in the initial vowel only. I believe the spot 'Ollerenshaw' is in the parish of Taxal, co. Derby, close by Shall-cross Hall, which has made Shaw-cross and Shallcross so familiar a surname in that district. The Rev. M. Ollerenshaw was minister of Mellor, co. Derby (adjacent), in 1810 (v. East Cheshire, ii. 132) ; cf. Ellershaw, the North-English equivalent. The following entries occur in the neighbouring church of Prestbury :

1632. Buried — George Owlrenshaw and John Owlrénshaw, twines : Reg. Prestbury, p. 285.
1633. — Ellen Oulrenshawe : ibid. p. 290.
1634. Bapt. — Anne Owlrenshawe : ibid. p. 292.
London, 4, 2, 0, 0 ; Manchester, 0, 0, 3, 1 ; Philadelphia, 1, 0, 0, 0.

Oldfield.—Local, (1) 'at the old field' ; (2) 'of Oldfield.' Naturally this is a surname that belongs to various districts. Even the earliest instances are found scattered in separate parts of the country. 'Adam' or 'William at the Old Field' would be common. There is a hamlet in the parish of Heswall, co. Cheshire, which has given birth to many of the name.

Philip de la Holdefelde, co. Salop, 1273. A.
Robert de la Aldefeld, co. Camb., ibid.
Ricardus de Oldefelde, co. Glouc., 1315. M.
Thomas de Aldefeld, 1379 : P. T. Yorks. p. 296.
Adam de Aldefeld, *wright*, 1379 : ibid.
John del Oldefeld, 1438 : East Cheshire, ii. 86.
1564. Married—John Oldefeilde and Ellen Swydells : Reg. Prestbury, co. Ches., p. 13.
Roger Oldfield, *yeoman*, Sutton, co. Ches., 1641 : Wills at Chester, ii. 165.
London, 10 ; Manchester, 10 ; Philadelphia, 13.

Oldfriend.—Nick. 'old friend' ; cf. Bellamy, Belcher, &c.

William Oldfeend, C. R., 7 Hen. IV.

Oldgroom.—Nick. 'the old groom,' the aged servant ; cf. Good-groom.

Henry Eldegrome. O.
John Eldgrom. O.

Oldham.—Local, ' of Oldham,' the large and flourishing metropolis of cotton-spinning near Manchester.

Agnes de Oldom, 1379 : P. T. Yorks. p. 104.
Robertus de Oldom, 1379 : ibid.
This spelling was preserved till the 17th century :
1633. Bapt. — Susann, d. Thomas Ouldome : St. Jas. Clerkenwell, i. 123.
1610. John Oldham, co. Notts : Reg. Univ. Oxf. vol. ii. pt. ii. p. 310.
1621. William Oldham, of Manchester : Wills at Chester, ii. 165.
1746. Married — Charles Oldham and Margaret Coho : St. Geo. Chap. Mayfair, p. 66.

London, 11 ; Manchester, 26 ; Philadelphia, 11.

Oldis, Oldys.—Bapt. 'the son of Aldus' ; v. Aldhouse and Aldis, of the latter of which it is but a variant.

1610. William Oldis, co. Dorset : Reg. Univ. Oxf. vol. ii. pt. ii. p. 320.
1751. Married—Anthony Olddiss and Eliz. Banks : St. Geo. Chap. Mayfair, p. 192.
1752. — William Biddle and Hannah Oldis : ibid. p. 218.
New York, 2, 0.

Oldman.—Nick. 'the old man'; cf. Youngman. I cannot but think that the Oldhams of co. Norfolk are a corruption of Oldman ; cf. Swetman for Swetenham, Putman for Puttenham, &c. Of course in this case the change is in the opposite direction.

Walran Oldman, co. Suff., 1273. A.
Robert Oldman, co. Norf., ibid.
Richard Oldeman, of Colchester, 1307. M.
Robert Oldman, rector of Rockland Tofts, co. Norf., 1418 : FF. i. 474.
London, 2 ; MDB. (Norfolk), 1 ; (Oldham), 1 ; New York, 1.

Oldmixon.—Local, ' of Old-mixen.' I cannot find the spot, and I think the surname is extinct. But one can never be sure about the extinction of surnames. I have been taught many a lesson in these matters.

Ralph de Holdmixon, co. Somerset, 1273. A.
Nicholas de Oldemexen, co. Southampton, 20 Edw. I. R.
Ralph de Oldemexene, co. Southampton : ibid.
Thomas Oldemexon, co. Soms., 1 Edw. I : Kirby's Quest, p. 267.
John Oldemexen, co. Soms., 1 Edw. I : ibid.
1628-9. Anthony Oldmixon and Francis Watson : Marriage Lic. (London), 195.

Oldridge.—Bapt. 'the son of Alderich' ; v. Aldridge. A local etymology seems to strike one at once, 'at the old ridge,' but the above interpretation is, so far as I can discover, the best.

? Thomas Ordrich, co. Kent, 1273. A.
1728. Bapt.—Thomas, s. Thomas Oldridge : St. Jas. Clerkenwell, ii. 174.
1735. Married — James Oldridge and Susanna Harrison : St. Dionis Backchurch, p. 66.

1807. Married—James Oldridge and Sarah Swodridge: St. Geo. Han. Sq. ii. 376.
London, 3.

Oldroyd.—Local, 'of the old royd,' from residence therein (v. Royd). Possibly Holroyd (q.v.) is the same. In the Reg. Univ. Oxf., I find Oldesworth, Holdsworth, Holsworth, and Ouldsworth, a parallel instance. Of course the signification may be 'the royd of Old,' the personal name of the original settler or owner (v. Old and Ould). One thing is certain, the surname arises in Yorkshire, probably the West Riding; v. Holroyd.

1741. Married—William Moore and Eliz. Oldroyd: St. Geo. Chap. Mayfair, p. 14.
1771. — John Lee and Rachael Oldroyd: St. Geo. Han. Sq. i. 207.
London, 1; Philadelphia, 10; MDB. (W. Rid. Yorks), 13.

Oliff, Olliff, Olliffe. — Bapt. 'the son of Olive'; v. Olive and Oliver. I have come across many forms, the most popular being Olliph, Olyffe, Olif, and Olyff.

Adam Olif, 1379: P. T. Yorks. p. 196.
1579. Bapt.—Olyffe, d. Olyff Tooker: Reg. St. Columb Major, p. 10.
1581. — Olyff, d. Degorie Stubbs: ibid. p. 11.
1757. Married—Joseph Olliff and Grace Craft: St. Geo. Han. Sq. i. 71.
London, 2, 2, 0; New York, 1, 0, 1.

Oliphant, Olivant, Ollivant, Olyphant.—Nick. 'the elephant,' no doubt a complimentary allusion to the big, burly physique of the bearer. M.E. *olivaunt*.

'Item, pro aula "Olefante," Magister Kyllynworth, 1438': Mun. Acad. Oxon., p. 522.

This hall or smaller college was so called from the sign over the door or gate. Skelton has both 'olyfant' and 'olyphante.' He describes a woman in Eleanor Rummyng as

'Necked lyke an olyfant.'

I believe this is a Scottish surname.

1729. Married — Christopher Olivent and Ann Lane: St. Geo. Chap. Mayfair, p. 294.
1749. — John Olivant and Eliz. Lester: ibid. p. 152.
1753. — George Oliphant and Mary Micheau: ibid. p. 250.

London, 3, 1, 1, 0; Philadelphia, 4, 0, 0, 0; New York (Olyphant), 3.

Olive, Ollive.—Bapt. 'the son of Olive'; v. Oliff for variants.

Thomas fil. Olive, co. Oxf., 1273. A.
Margaret fil. Olive, co. Salop, ibid.
Johanna fil. Olive, 1379: P. T. Yorks. p. 139.
1797. Married—John Hickman Olive and Alice Ann Hickes: St. Geo. Han. Sq. ii. 164.
1806. — Isaac Olive and Mary Kempester: ibid. p. 355.
London, 3, 2; New York, 4, 1.

Oliver, Ollier, Olver, Olliver.—Bapt. 'the son of Oliver.' Fr. Olivier, Breton, Olier. For 'a Rowland for an Oliver,' v. Yonge, i. 419. The paladin of Charlemagne made it popular, and gave it a knightly sound. After the Protector's days its popularity waned, and it has not yet recovered itself as a baptismal name. The Breton form Olier found friends in this country, and as a surname is fairly common.

Oliver le Quarreur, C. R., 33 Hen. III.
Oliver Crane, co. Hunts, 1273. A.
Peter fil. Oliver, co. Oxf., ibid.
Holiver Hankoc, *husband*, 1379: P. T. Yorks. p. 163.
Walter Oliver, co. Soms., 1 Edw. III: Kirby's Quest, p. 160.
Oliver le Hoge, co. Soms., 1 Edw. III: ibid. p. 200.
1582. Johana, d. Thomas Olver: Reg. St. Columb Major, Cornwall.
1750. Married—David Oliver and Sarah Cocks: St. Geo. Chap. Mayfair, p. 174.
1801. — Richard Ollier and Charlotte Hull: ibid. ii. 239.
London, 80, 2, 3, 2; New York, 66, 0, 0, 3.

Oliverson.—Bapt. 'the son of Oliver,' q.v. I believe this surname to be almost if not actually extinct. I have looked in vain in Manchester and the district for representatives.

1593. John Oliverson, of Heaton Norris: Wills at Chester, ii. 145.
1594. Hugh Oliverson, of Pendlebury: ibid.
1606. Thomas Oliverson, of Heaton Norris: ibid.

Olivet, Ollett, Olyett.—Bapt. 'the son of Olive,' dim. Oliv-et. As Olley was the usual nick., naturally a dim. Olliet or Olyett was formed from it; v. Olley (2). From my first instances it will be seen that this diminutive arose in

good time to become an aspirant for hereditary honours.

William Olivat, Liberate Roll, 17 Edw. II.
Agnes Olyot, 1379: P. T. Yorks. p. 163.
1625. Buried—Eliz. Ollett: St. Jas. Clerkenwell, iv. 179.
1783. Married—John Olyet and Ann Roberts: St. Geo. Han. Sq. i. 352.
London, 1, 1, 3; New York, 1, 0, 0.

Ollerhad.—Local, 'of Ollerhead,' from residence at the head of the alder-trees; cf. Birkett, Akenhead, Birkenhead; v. Oldershaw.

Richard Ollerhead, of Foulk Stapleford, 1629: Wills at Chester, ii. 165.
Eliz. Ollerhead, of Chester, 1644: ibid. Manchester, 1.

Oller(e)nshaw.—Local; v. Oldershaw.

Ollett; v. Olivet.

Olley.—(1) Local, 'de Oilli,' or 'Oyly,' or 'Oilgi.' Robert de Oilgi appears as a tenant-in-chief in many counties; also Wido de Oilgi in co. Oxford (Domesday). Probably one of the Oullis near Falaise (Lower). At any rate, our Olleys may say they 'came over with the Conqueror.' The surname ramified strongly, and is now represented in every grade of society. v. Doyle.

Matilda de Oyly, co. Dorset, 1273. A.
Thomas de Oylly, co. York, ibid.
Henry de Oilli, Pipe Roll, 11 Hen.II.p.71.
Roger de Oilli: ibid. p. 72.
Henry de Oyly, co. Staff., Hen. III-Edw. I. K.
John de Oyly, co. Staff., 20 Edw. I. R.
1637. Buried—Mary, d. William Oylie: St. Jas. Clerkenwell, iv. 231.

(2) Bapt. 'the son of Olive,' pet form Olly; v. Olive. This being, so far as evidence goes, of more modern origin, we must gave the local derivation the first position, although both must have contributed to the number of our present Olleys.

1554. John, s. Thomas Ollye: Reg. St. Columb Major, p. 7.
1591. Olly, d. Nicholas Vallis: ibid. p. 15.
1601. John, s. Ollye Moyses: ibid. p. 20.
1639. Thomas Olye: Reg. Univ. Oxf. i. 359.
1693. Bapt.—Eliz., d. Samuel Oley: St. Jas. Clerkenwell, i. 352.
1803. Married — Thomas Olley and Eliz. Baylis: St. Geo. Han. Sq. ii. 283.
London, 15; Philadelphia, 2.

Ollier, Olliver; v. Oliver.

Olliff('e; v. Oliff.

Ollivant; v. Oliphant.

Olney.—Local, 'of Olney.' A parish in dioc. Oxford, co. Bucks.
Walter le Olnei, co. Oxf., 1273. A.
John de Olneye, co. Oxf., ibid.
William de Olneye, co. Bucks, 1322. M.
1729. Married—John Olney and Sarah Bubrick: St. Geo. Chap. Mayfair, p. 299.
1801. — Richard Ody and Jane Olney: St. Geo. Han. Sq. ii. 237.
London, 8; Boston (U.S.), 6.

Olver; v. Oliver.

Olyett; v. Olivet.

Ombler.—Occup. 'the ambler' (q.v.), an East Riding variant of the great Yorkshire surname.
Nafferton (E. Rid. Yorks), 1; Market Weighton (E. Rid. Yorks), 1.

Onehand.—Nick. for a one-handed man. This surname does not seem to have survived.
William Onhand. B.
John Onehand. D.
Richard Onhand, C. R., 23 Hen. VI.

Onion, Onions.—Bapt. 'the son of Enion,' a favourite personal name in old Welsh records. The modern directories abound with variants, &c. (v. Benyon, Pinnion, &c.). Mr. Lower says, 'In the register of East Grinstead, Sussex, in the first half of the 17th century, the name is written indifferently Ennion and Onion.' This quite tallies with my own observations.
1661. William Davies and Ann Onyon: Marriage Lic. (London), ii. 282.
1720. Married—Abraham Taylor and Margaret Onion: St. Dionis Backchurch, p. 60.
Liverpool, 0, 1; Manchester, 0, 1; New York, 2, 1; London, 1, 0; MDB. (co. Glouc.), 0, 1.

Onley, Only. — Local, 'of Onely,' a hamlet in the parish of Barby, co. Northants, seven miles from Daventry. Although I do not see any early instances, the first of my references settles the matter.
Edward Onley, or Onelie, co. Northampt., 1583: Reg. Univ. Oxf. vol. ii. pt. ii. p. 128.

The following two quotations evidently refer to the same individual:
1655. Bapt.—Eliz., d. George Only, vintner: St. Peter, Cornhill, i. 97.

1655. Buried—George Onely, vintner, in the pit: ibid. p. 209.
1633. Buried—John Onelye, a poor child: St. Jas. Clerkenwell, iv. 210.
1686. Thomas Onely and Catharine Broderick: Reg. Vicar-General (Canterbury), p. 253.
1771. Married — Edward Only and Isabella Davies: St. Geo. Han. Sq. i. 214.
London, 1, 0; Philadelphia, 0, 1; Boston (U.S.), 3, 1.

Onslow.—Local, 'of Onslow,' a place within the Liberty of Shrewsbury, co. Salop (in Domesday Book spelt Ondeslow). A family of this name early arose here. 'The Onslows were seated at Onslow in Shropshire as far back as Ric. I, and probably earlier. The punning motto of this ancient house, 'Festina lente,' On Slow, is probably one of the happiest conceits of its kind' (Lower).
1676. Married—Richard Onslowe and Eliz. Tulse: St. Dionis Backchurch, p. 38.
1800. — Emanuel Ducemetiere and Mary Onslow: St. Geo. Han. Sq. ii. 228.
London, 3; MDB. (co. Salop), 3; Philadelphia, 1.

Onthank.—Local, v. Unthank.

Onwhyn.—Bapt. 'the son of Unwin' (q.v.). A curious variant; cf. Goodwin, Baldwin, &c.
William Onwinne, co. Oxf., 1273. A.
1809. Married—Joseph Onwhyn and Fanny Thomas: St. Geo. Han. Sq. ii. 401. London, 2.

Openshaw.—Local, 'of Openshaw,' a parish and village about four miles from Manchester. The surname is strongly represented in South Lancashire.
Samuel Openshawe. ZZ.
1575. Robert Opinshawe, co. Suff.: Reg. Univ. Oxf. vol. ii. pt. ii. p. 66.
1607. Lambert Openshaw of Aynsworth: Wills at Chester, i. 145.
1611. Buried—John, s. William Openshawe: St. Jas. Clerkenwell, iv. 118.
London, 1; Manchester, 14; New York, 1; Philadelphia, 5.

Opie, Oppey, Oppy.—?——.
Lower says, 'Seems indigenous to Cornwall. Opye occurs there in the 15th century, and Oppie at a later date.' I have only met with it in the same county.
1590. Buried — Harrie Opie: St. Columb Major, p. 193.
1749. Married—John Opie and Sarah Burrows: St. Geo. Chap. Mayfair, p. 147.
Cornwall Dir. (Farmers' Lists), 3, 1, 5; Philadelphia, 1, 0, 0.

Orable, Orbell, Orbel. — Bapt. 'the son of Orable,' a variant of Arable, i.e. Arabella. The surname still clings to the neighbourhood of co. Cambridge, where the personal name was popular six centuries ago.
Orable de Hatele, co. Camb., 1273. A.
Orabilia Martin, co. Camb., ibid.
John Orable, co. Camb., ibid.
Arable de Meyhamme, co. Kent, Hen. III-Edw. I. : K. p. 209.
Orable de Meyhamme, co. Kent: ibid. p. 211.
Orabell de Caunsfeld, co. Lanc., 1332: Lay Subsidy (Rylands), p. 96.
Alexander Orable, C. R., 23 Hen. VI.
1543. Buried—Nicholas Errable, Mr. May's servant: St. Antholin (London), p. 4.
This surname is now found in the guise of Orbell.
1750. Married—Ambrose Orbell and Ann Curtis: St. Geo. Han. Sq. i. 44.
MDB. (Suffolk), 3, 0, 0; Cavendish (Suffolk), 0, 1, 0; New York, 0, 0, 1.

Oram, Orem. — Local, 'of Oram'(?). I cannot discover the spot. There are North and South Owram, two townships in the parish of Halifax. This is the probable origin.
1605. Bapt.—Henrie, s. Peter Orom: St. Jas. Clerkenwell, i. 46.
1609. Richard Oram: Reg. Univ. Oxf. vol. ii. pt. i. p. 327.
1778. Married—John Oram and Sarah Lamb: St. Geo. Han. Sq. i. 294.
Manchester, 2, 0; MDB. (N. R. Yorks), 1, 0; London, 11, 0; Philadelphia, 19, 6.

Orbater. — Occup. 'a goldbeater'; Fr. or, gold, and batteur, a beater, from battre, to beat.
Walter le Orbater, London, 1273. A.
John de Erkendene, orebatur, 28 Edw. I : Freemen of York, i. 8.

Orbell; v. Orable.

Orby.—Local, 'of Orby,' a parish in dioc. Lincoln.
Geoffrey de Orby, co. Hunts, 1273. A.
John de Orby, co. Hunts, ibid.
Fulco de Orreby, co. Linc., Hen. III-Edw. I. K.
Robert de Orreby, co. Notts, ibid.
John de Horreby, co. Linc., 1316. M.

Orchard, Orchart.—Local, 'at the orchard.' Many local terms took an initial n, which in reality was the final letter of the prefix -atten (=at the). Thus arose Noakes, Nash, Nalder, Nangle,

&c. Orchard was no exception.
I find, for instance :

Robert atte Northcherd, co. Oxf., 20
Edw. I. R.

Which more correctly should be

Robert atten Orthcherd.

But in general the entries run
thus :

John de la Orcharde, co. Soms.,
1273. A.
Richard atte Orchard, co. Soms., 1
Edw. III : Kirby's Quest, p. 212.
John atte Orchard, C. R., 14 Edw. III.
pt. i.
William de la Orchard, co. Dorset,
1316. M.
1683. Married—Robert Orchard and
Elisebeth Goodlad : St. Jas. Clerkenwell,
iii. 201.
London, 11, 1 ; Philadelphia, 5, 0.

Orchardson.—Bapt. A curious
patronymic ; perhaps a corruption
of Richardson.

London, 1.

Ord, Orde.—Local, ' of Orde,'
a township in North Durham.

Peter de Orde, 1281 : Raine's North
Durham, p. 147.
' John Orde for lands in Orde, £6
13s. 4d.,' 1631 : ibid. p. 156.
John Owrde, 1542 : ibid. p. xx.
Thomas Ord, of Ord, 1631 : ibid. p. 156.
1585. Richard Orde, co. Northumb. :
Reg. Univ. Oxf. vol. ii. pt. ii. p. 145.
Bartram Ord, of Fenwick, 1631 : ibid.
' Mr. Lance Ord, for the tyth, £10,'
1663 : Hodgson's Northumberland, iv. 276.
1750. Married—John Buckland and
Dorothy Ord : St. Geo. Chap. Mayfair,
p. 162.
London, 3, 0 ; Crockford, 3, 5 ; New
York, 5, 0.

Ordiner.—Offic. ' the ordinary,'
a bishop or overseer. Fr. ordinaire.
I see no signs of its present existence, but one cannot speak
positively on this question. These
surnames turn up when least expected.

Walter Ordinar', co. Camb., 1273. A.
Elena Ordiner, co. Camb., ibid.
Thomas Ordiner, co. Suff., ibid.
Isabel Ordiner, co. Camb., ibid.
John de Ordeiner, 1326. M.

Ordway.— ? Bapt. (?). Seemingly a personal name ; v. Ottaway
for a similar instance. Without
doubt it belongs to the south-
eastern counties.

John Ordwy, co. Oxf., 1273. A.
Ralph Ordwey, co. Bedf., ibid.
Matilda Ordivy, co. Norf., ibid.

1613. William Ordway : Reg. Univ.
Oxf. vol. ii. pt. ii. p. 321.
1658. Married—William Billington and
Anne Ordway : St. Jas. Clerkenwell,
p. 100.
1742.—Humfrey Maynwaring Howorth
and Sarah Ordway : St. Geo. Chap.
Mayfair, p. 28.
London, 3 ; Boston (U.S.), 30.

Orem ; v. Oram.

Orfeur ; v. Offer.

Orford.—Local, ' of Orford,'
a parish in co. Suffolk. Also ' of
Orford,' in the parish of Warrington, whence the Lancashire
Orfords. Orford Hall still stands,
and was the residence of John
Blackburne, ' the Evelyn of his
day.'

(Homines) de Oreford, co. Suff., 1273. A.
Robert Holbrooke, of Orford, in the
parish of Warrington, 1594 : Wills at
Chester (1545-1620), p. 96.
John Orford, of Haydock in Maker-
field, 1616 : ibid. p. 145.
1778. Married—Mark Gibbs and Ann
Orford : St. Geo. Han. Sq. i. 232.
London, 2 ; Manchester, 2 ; Phila-
delphia, 1.

Organ. — Bapt. ' the son of
Organ,' probably a form of Ogan
or Wogan, q.v. ; cf. Orgar.

Organus Pipard, co. Oxf., Hen. III-
Edw. I. K.
Simon Organ, C. R., 37 Edw. III.
John Organ, C. R., 7 Ric. II.
1397. William Organ : Cal. of Wills in
Court of Husting (2).
Richard Orgen, 1589 : Reg. Univ. Oxf.
vol. ii. pt. ii. p. 169.
Edward Organ, vintner, 1616 : Reg.
St. Dionis Backchurch, p. 96.
1707. Bapt.—Edward, son of Maurice
Organ : St. Jas. Clerkenwell, p. 37.
London, 1 ; Oxford, 3 ; New York, 3 ;
Boston (U.S.), 2.

Organer.—Occup. ' the organ-
ist' or ' the organ-maker.' An
interesting name which existed
till the 18th century, and probably
still lives, although I have found
no instances.

Peter le Organer, co. Warw., 1318. M.
1761. Married—William Organer and
Eliz. Fuller : St. Geo. Han. Sq. i. 111.
1764. — Robert Organer and Sarah
Dickenson : ibid. p. 129.
1797. — Thomas Harington and Mary
Orgainer : ibid. ii. 166.

Orgar, Orger.—Bapt. ' the son
of Orgar.' In Domesday Orgar is
found in cos. Somerset, North-

ampton, and Essex ; cf. Orgars-
wick, a parish in co. Kent, i.e. the
dwelling of Orgar, the first settler.
v. Worger.

Geoffrey fil Orgari, co. Camb., 1273. A.
Bernard Orgar, co. Camb., ibid.
Matilda Oregar, co. Oxf., ibid.
William Oregar, co. Oxf., ibid.
Roger Orger, co. Middlesex, 20 Edw.
I. R.
1748. Married—Thomas Garner and
Susannah Orgar : St. Geo. Chap. May-
fair, p. 327.
London, 2, 1.

Oriel, Oriol.—Local, ' at the
oriel,' i.e. the gilded chamber ;
cf. Bower, and v. oriel (Skeat).

Nicholas de Oryel, co. Kent, 20 Edw.
I. R.
Poncius Oriol, Bristol, 1320. M.
1788. Married—John Biss and Jane
Oriell : St. Geo. Han. Sq. ii. 12.
1808. — George Keith and Sarah
Oriell : ibid. p. 384.
London, 2, 0 ; New York, 0, 1.

Orlebar.—Local, ' of Orling-
bury,' four miles from Wellingborough, co. Northampton, in
which neighbourhood the surname
has existed since Edw. III. This
surname does not seem to have
crossed the Atlantic.

Robert de Orlingbir', co. Northampt.,
1273. A.
Ralph de Orlingbir', co. Northampt.,
ibid.
Hugh de Orlingbere, co. Northampt.,
1316. M.
1679. Bapt.—Richard, s. Henry Orli-
ber : St. Jas. Clerkenwell, i. 285.
1687. Cooper Orlebar, of Hinwicke, co.
Bedf., and Eliz. Powney : Marriage
Alleg. (Canterbury), p. 298.
Crockford, 3 ; MDB. (co. Northampt.),
1 ; (co. Bedford), 5.

Ormandy. — Local, ' of Osmotherly,' a township in the parish
of Ulverston, co. Lanc. This surname is still almost entirely confined to the Furness district of
N. Lanc. The former name of
Osmotherly was Osmunderlaw,
and Ormandy is found in the
neighbourhood since the beginning
of the 15th century. Everything
points to prove the above origin ;
v. Osmotherly.

1552. Married—William Holme and
Agnes Ormundie : Reg. St. Mary, Ulverston, p. 18.
1553. Bapt.—Ann Ormundie : ibid. p.
129.

1597. Richard Ormandie, of Ulverston: Lancashire Wills at Richmond, i. 205.
1663. Bapt.—Alice, d. John Ormandy: Reg. St. Mary, Ulverston, p. 17.
1673. John Ormondy, of Smiddy Greene, in Ulverston: Lancashire Wills at Richmond, i. 205.
Crockford, 1; Ulverston, 7; Preston, 1.

Orme, Ormes, Ormson, Orm.—Bapt. 'the son of Orme' (Orm, Domesday); cf. the local Urmston, Ormston, Ormsby, Ormskirk, Ormerod, and the Great Orme's Head. In this last the meaning Orm, the serpent (whence *worm*), comes out, i.e. 'the serpent's head.' Miss Yonge (ii. 290) says there are twenty-two Ormes in the Landnama-bok.

Alice fil. Orme, co. Camb., 1273. A.
William Orm, co. Notts, ibid.
Orme de Neville, co. Linc., 20 Edw. I. R.
Ormus Archebrgge, co. Westm., ibid.
John fil. Orme, co. York. W. 19.
Gospatric, son of Orme, 32 Hen. II: Nicolson and Burn, Westm. and Cumb., i. 428.

Very popular in the Cumb. and North Lancashire district.

Orm fil. Bernulfi, 21 Ric. II: Furness Coucher Book, i. 188.
Robert fil. Orm, 21 Ric. II: ibid.
Orm de Orgrave, 21 Ric. II: ibid.

Hence a common surname in the North.

1593. Buried—Thomas Scott, servant to John Orme: St. Jas. Clerkenwell, iv. 52.
1609. Bapt.—Edward Ormeson: Reg. Prestbury Ch., co. Ches., p. 181.
London, 16, 1, 1, 0; Manchester, 8, 0, 0, 0; Liverpool (Ormson), 1; Philadelphia, 5, 0, 0, 1.

Ormerod, Ormrod, Omrod.—Local, 'of Ormerod,' i.e. Ormeroyd; Orme's ridding or clearing; v. Orme and Royd, and cf. Murgatroyd, i. e. Margaret's clearing. Ormerod is in the parish of Whalley, co. Lanc.

'Ormerod is a house of great antiquity, which remained in the family of that name from 1311 until 1793': Baines' Hist. of Lanc. ii. 41.
1593. John Ormerod, of Gambleside: Wills at Chester, i. 146.
1600. George Ormerod, of Crawshaw Booth: ibid.
1732. Married — Peter Ormred and Isabel Davis: St. Geo. Han. Sq. i. 10.
1784. Laurence Ormerod, of Ormerod, co. Lanc., to Martha Anne Leghe: East Ches. ii. 301.

Manchester, 7, 12, 0; London, 2, 0, 0; West Rid. Court Dir., 6, 1, 0; MDB. (West Rid. Yorks), 8, 1, 1; Philadelphia, 1, 5, 0.

Ormesher, Ormshire.—Local, 'of Ormeshaw,' the shaw, coppice, or wood of Orme, the proprietor or first settler. The corruption is a very natural one. v. Orme.

Gilbert Ormeshaw, of Scarisbrick, 1590: Wills at Chester, i. 146.
Roger Ormeshaw, of Burscough, 1620: ibid.
1718. Married—Aaron Hawkins and Mary Ormishaw: St. Michael, Cornhill, i. 59.
Manchester, 1, 0; Liverpool, 1, 0; MDB. (co. Lanc.), 0, 1.

Ormiston, Ormston.—Local, 'of Ormiston,' the town or stead of Orme, the first settler (v. Orme), a parish in co. Haddington, also a locality in co. Roxburgh. The *i* is intrusive, just as *a* is intrusive in Greenaway, q.v.

1733. Married—John Slamaker and Eleanor Ormaston: St. Geo. Han. Sq. i. 12.
London, 1, 7; MDB. (co. Northumberland), 0, 1; Philadelphia, 2, 3.

Ormond.—Bapt. 'the son of Osmond' (?), q.v.; a variant (?); cf. Ormandy for Osmunderly. But it is quite possible that Ormond in that form was a personal name as distinct from Osmond. The variant from Osmond to Ormand is not natural.

Thomas Ormu(n)de, 1379: P. T. Yorks. p. 260.
1602. William Ormond, co. Pembroke: Reg. Univ. Oxf. vol. ii. pt. ii. p. 255.
1634. John Ormond, of Huncote, co. Lanc.: Wills at Chester, ii. 166.
London, 2; MDB. (co. Lancaster), 6; Boston (U.S.), 5.

Ormsby, Ornsby, Ormsbee.—Local, 'of Ormsby,' parishes in diocs. of York, Lincoln, and Norwich. The meaning is manifestly the by or dwelling of Orme (v. Orme). It is now becoming recognized that a large proportion of our place-names are compounded with the personal name of the original settler. Ormsbee is a natural Americanism (cf. Applebee).

William de Ormesby, co. Norf., 1273. A.
Robert de Ormesby, co. Linc., ibid.

William de Ormesby, co. Camb., 20 Edw. I. R.
Thomas de Ormesby, co. Norf., 1324. M.
1685. John Ormsby and Eliz. Kingdon: Marriage Alleg. (Canterbury), p. 198.
1761. Married—Arthur Ormsby, Esq., and Eliz. Greene: St. Geo. Han. Sq. i. 102.
London, 0, 1, 0; Crockford, 7, 0, 0; Philadelphia, 14, 1, 1.

Ormshire; v. Ormesher.

Ormson; v. Orme.

Ormston; v. Ormiston.

Orne, Ornsby.—Probably corruptions of Orme and Ormsby, q.v.

1602. John Orne, of Holt: Wills at Chester, i. 146.
London, 0, 1.

Orped, Orpedman. — Nick. 'the orped,' i.e. brave, daring. 'Orpud, *audax, bellipotens*': Prompt. Parv.; v. Way's notes thereon.

'Doukes, kinges, and barouns, Orped squiers, and garsouns.'
Arthour and Merlin, p. 81 (Halliwell).
Walter le Orpede, co. Bucks, 1273. A.
Sym Orpedeman, London, ibid.
Thomas Orpedeman, London, ibid.
Stephen le Horpede, co. Kent, ibid.
Peter Orpedeman. H.
John Orpood, co. Oxf., 1589: Reg. Univ. Oxf. vol. ii. pt. ii. p. 174.

The present form is Orpwood, q.v. This surname is to be found in co. Bucks. It was there in the 13th century as 'le Orpede.'

Orpen, Orpin.—'The family of Orpen or Erpen is of remote antiquity, and is stated to be derived from Erpen, a French noble of royal descent.' Such is the statement in Burke's Landed Gentry, though the pedigree as there given does not go further back than the 16th century (v. Lower's Patr. Brit. p. 250).

1680. John Orpen and wife. List of the Inhabitants of St. Michael's, Barbadoes: Hotten's Lists of Emigrants, p. 438.
1806. Married—Charles Orpin and Sarah Watson: St. Geo. Han. Sq. ii. 339.
1861. Married—William Orpin and Esther Cooper: Reg. Canterbury Cath. p. 107.
Boston (U.S.), 2, 6.

Orpwood.—Nick. 'the orped'; v. Orped. 'Orpud (ornwode, s. sic pro orpwode?), *audax, bellipotens*': Prompt. Parv. p. 371.

1584. Christopher Orpudde, co. Oxf.: Reg. Univ. Oxf. vol. ii. pt. ii. p. 138.

1617. Paul Orpwood, co. Berks: ibid. p. 365.

1791. Married—William Benwell and Eliz. Orpwood: St. Geo. Han. Sq. p. 67. London, 2; Oxford, 1.

Orr.—Local, ' of Orr,' a parish in co. Kirkcudbright.

Egidius de Or, co. Kent, 1273. A.
Matilda Orre, 1379: P. T. Yorks. p. 16.
Johannes Ore, 1379: ibid. p. 164.
1744. Buried—Ann Orr: St. Michael, Cornhill, p. 207.
1789. Married—Samuel Dimeto and Eliz. Ore: St. Geo. Han. Sq. ii. 21.
London, 4; Philadelphia, 104.

Orred.—Local, ' of Orred.' A Cheshire surname; probably, as suggested by Lower, a place-name whose suffix was originally *-head*; cf. Birkenhead, &c.

1588. Eliz. Orred, of Manchester: Wills at Chester, i. 146.
1636. Gyles Orred, of Lower Hulton, Dean, *blacksmith*: ibid. ii. 166.
MDB. (co. Ches.), 1.

Orrell, Orrill.—Local, (1) ' of Orrell,' a township in the parish of Wigan, co. Lanc. The suffix, as will be seen below, is *-hull*, i.e. *-hill*.

' Richard de Horul in the reign of Richard I. held half a carucate in thanage': Baines' Lanc. ii. 186.
' In 32 Edw. I. Robert de Holand had a charter for free warren in Holand, Hale, Orhull, and Martlan': ibid.

(2) ' Of Orrell,' a township in the parish of Sephton, co. Lanc.

"In 13 Edw. III. Henry Blundell, of Crosby, gave to William, his son, all his property in Rainil, Orel, Downlitherland, Thornton, and Sephton': Baines' Lanc. ii. 398.

The surname passed over the border into co. Cheshire, and is well known there and in Lancashire.

1590. Peter Orrell, co. Lanc.: Reg. Univ. Oxf. vol. ii. pt. ii. p. 176.
1602. William Orrell, of Wigan: Wills at Chester, i. 146.
1610. Alexander Orrell, of Orrell, parish of Wigan: ibid.
1781. Married—Anthony Holmes and Ann Orrell: St. Geo. Han. Sq. i. 327.
Liverpool, 6, 0; Manchester, 4, 0; Philadelphia, 7, 0; Boston (U.S.), 1, 1.

Orton. — Local, ' of Orton,' parishes in diocs. Norwich, Peterborough, Ely, and Carlisle. All these places seem to have contributed their share of surnames.

Robert de Orton, co. Oxf., Hen. III-Edw. I. K.
Henry de Orton, co. Suff., 1273. A.
Walter de Orton, co. Linc., ibid.
Alan de Orreton, co. Cumb., 20 Edw. I. R.
John de Orreton, co. Cumb., 1321. M.
1592. James Ortonne, co. Ches.: Reg. Univ. Oxf. vol. ii. pt. ii. p. 194.
1774. Married—William Orton and Ann Chandler: St. Geo. Han. Sq. i. 242.
London, 6; Philadelphia, 6.

Osbaldston, Osbaldeston, Osbaldiston. — Local, ' of Osbaldeston,' a township in the parish of Blackburn, co. Lanc. The Osbaldestons of Osbaldeston had a charity in Blackburn Parish Church (Baines' Lanc. ii. 66). The meaning is ' the town (i.e. settlement) of Osbald.' The *i* and *e* in Osbaldiston and Osbaldeston are intrusive; cf. Greenaway for Greenway, where the *a* is equally intrusive.

Edward Osbaldeston, Esq., of Osbaldeston, 1590: Wills at Chester, i. 146.
Matilda Osbaldeston, of Blackburn, 1592: ibid.
Henry Osboston, 1595: Reg. St. Dionis Backchurch (London), p. 13.
John Osbaldeston, Esq., of Osbaldeston, 1605: ibid.
1786. Married—John Osbaldeston and Susanna Crook: St. Geo. Han. Sq. i. 387.
London, 1, 0, 0; Manchester, 0, 2, 1; Preston, 0, 2, 0.

Osbert.—Bapt. ' the son of Osbert.' This surname does not seem to have survived. I cannot find any modern instances. Strange that its rival Osborn should be so familiar to our directories to-day.

Robert fil. Osbert, co. Hunts, 1273. A.
Osbert le Ferrur, co. Camb., ibid.
Roger fil. Osbert, co. Suff., ibid.
Richard Osbert, co. Camb., ibid.
William fil. Osbert. C.
Osbert de Bellebeck, co. York, 20 Edw. I. R.
Osbert Houbard, co. Soms., 1 Edw. III: Kirby's Quest, p. 227.

Osborn, Osborne, Osbourn, Osbourne.—Bapt. ' the son of Osbern,' a favourite personal name in the hereditary surname period. It is scarcely ever used now at the font, but flourishes strongly as a surname.

Gerard fil. Oseberne, co. Hunts, 1273. A.
Robert Oseberne, co. Oxf., ibid.

Osborne le Haukere. H.
Osbarn Dawson, 1379: P. T. Yorks. p. 23.
'Thomas Smithson and Osberne Walynton, servauntes of Sir Edward Wydevile,' 1489: Wardrobe Accounts, Edw. IV. p. 164.

In the Register of the University of Oxford the following forms are found: Osborne, Osbern. Osberne, Osborn, Osbourne, and Osburne (v. Index). The following variants are found amongst the marriages of a single register:

1790. George Avius and Ann Osburn: St. Geo. Han. Sq. ii. 85.
— Richard Osborne and Ann Smith: ibid. p. 163.
1792. William Osbon and Mary Thackham: ibid. p. 43.
1797. Frances Phillips and Lucy Orsborn: ibid. p. 46.
1798. William Osburne and Eliz. Yates: ibid. p. 148.
London, 42, 41, 1, 2; Philadelphia, 34, 47, 5, 1.

Osborough.—Local, ' of Oxborough.' For this change of *x* for *s*, v. Oscroft. For variants of Osborough, v. Oxberry.

Philadelphia, 1.

Oscroft.—Local, ' at the oxcroft,' i.e. the enclosure for oxen. Naturally the surname would settle down into Oscroft. A parallel instance will be found in the case of Oxspring and Ofspring, q.v. Another example of the change is to be seen in the Philadelphia Directory, where Osborough takes the place of Oxborough.

Stephen de Oxercroft, co. Suff., 1273. A.
1746. Married—John Brand and Margaret Oscroft: St. Geo. Chapel, Mayfair, p. 64.

Oscroft was a familiar figure some years ago on the Notts county cricket-ground, and a young Oscroft played for the same county in the season of 1894.

MDB. (co. Notts), 1.

Osekin, Oskins.—Bapt. One of the many pet forms ending in *-kin* (cf. Wilkin). Oskin would be the familiar appellation of some Osmund, Osbern, Oswin, or Osbert. It is quite possible that Hoskins is its present representative. The aspirate presents no difficulty, and the final *s* is of course genitive, as in Tompkins or Jones; v. Hosken.

Osekin (without surname), London, 1273. A.
Robert Osekin, London, ibid.
Philadelphia, 0, 3.

Osgathorpe, Osgathorp. — Local, 'of Osgarthorpe,' i.e. the thorp of Osgod, the first settler; a parish in co. Leicester, four miles from Ashby; v. Osgerby and Osgood.

Sheffield, 2, 0; Oxford, 0, 1.

Osgerby. — Local, 'of Osgodby': (1) a township in the parish of Lavington, co. Linc.; (2) also a parish in co. Linc., four miles from Market Rasen; (3) also a township in the parish of Hemingbrough, near Selby, E. Rid. Yorks. The change of the surname to Osgerby was very natural. The origin is plain, 'the dwelling of Osgod,' from the name of the first settler or proprietor; v. Osgood.

Eva de Osgoteby, co. York, 1273. A.
Hugh de Osgoteby, co. York, ibid.
Dionise de Osgotby, co. Linc., ibid.
1598. Buried—John, s. John Osgerbye: St. Michael, Cornhill, i. 208.
— Bapt.—John, s. John Osgerby: ibid. p. 101.
1609. Married—Edward Wilson and Jane Osgrobie: ibid. p. 19.
1614. Robert Osgoodby: Reg. Univ. Oxf. vol. ii. pt. ii. p. 372.
1668. William Osgodby, of Exeter House, Strand: Marriage Alleg. (Canterbury), p. 255.
1668-9. William Osgoodby, of Exeter House, Strand: ibid. p. 260.
MDB. (East Rid. Yorks), 1.

Osgood. — Bapt. 'the son of Osgod' (v. Yonge, ii. 181); v. Osgerby.

Tofig the Proud married Gytha, the daughter of Osgod Clapa: Freeman, Norm. Conq. i. 523.
Alveva fil. Osgod, Fines Roll, 7 Ric. I-16 John.
John Osegod, co. Oxf., 1273. A.
William Osegod, co. Oxf., ibid.
Gilbert Osegot, co. Camb., ibid.
John Osgode, co. Hertf., 20 Edw. I. R.
Ricardus Osgod, 1379: P. T. Howdenshire, p. 23.
William Osgood, co. Soms., 1 Edw. III: Kirby's Quest, p. 232.
1605. Tristram Osgood, co. Cornw.: Reg. Univ. Oxf. vol. ii. pt. ii. p. 286.
1614. John Osgood: ibid. p. 334.
1789. Married—William Oakey and Sarah Osgood: St. Geo. Han. Sq. ii. 20.
London, 1; New York, 10.

Oskettle, Oskell. — Bapt. 'the son of Oskettle,' 'divine cauldron,' a compound of Kettle (q.v.). A Norman guise of the same name was Anskettle (q.v.) or Askettle. The Abbot of Croyland in 992 was Osketyl.

Oskell Somenour. AA. 3.
Osketil atte Mere, Fines Roll, 57 Hen. III.

Oskins; v. Osekin.

Osler. — Occup.; v. Oastler.

Osman; v. Osmond.

Osmar. — Bapt. 'the son of Osmar,' a personal name found in Domesday Book as Osmar and Osmer.

1790. Married — Charles Shoubridge and Ann Osmer: St. Geo. Han. Sq. ii. 35. London, 1.

Osmond, Osmund, Osman, Osment, Osmint, Osmon, Osmand, Osmun. — Bapt. 'the son of Osmond,' the Scandinavian Asmundr; cf. Wyman for Wymond, and Mayman for Maymond. This personal name gave rise to several local names; v. Osmotherly, and cf.

John de Osemundeston, co. Norf., 1273. A.
Geoffrey Osmund, co. Devon, ibid.
Nicholas Osemund, co. Suff., ibid.
Richard Osmund, co. Middlesex, 1313. M.
John Osmond, co. Hertf., 1315. M.
1603. Buried — Thomas Osmond: St. Thomas the Apostle (London), p. 104.
1649. Married—William Bannister and Margaret Osman: ibid. p. 18.
Edward, son of Edward Osman, 1658: Reg. Broad Chalke, co. Wilts, p. 68.
John, son of Edward Osmand, 1660: ibid.
Grace, d. of Edward Osmund, 1663: ibid.
1788. Married—Charles Ballard and Sarah Osmon: St. Geo. Han. Sq. ii. 18.
London, 0, 17, 6, 1, 1, 1, 0, 0; Oxford, 1, 0, 2, 0, 0, 0, 0, 0; Philadelphia, 11, 0, 1, 0, 0, 1, 1, 1; Liverpool (Osmond), 1; Boston (U.S.) (Osman), 1.

Osmotherly. — Local, 'of Osmotherly,' a parish in N. Rid. Yorks, and a township in the parish of Ulverston, North Lancashire. It is found early in the Furness district as Asmunderlaw. It is curious that while the surname has long disappeared from the North, it should be found at Cliffe, near Rochester (but v. Ormandy). The derivation is simple,

i.e. 'the law of Osmund,' a *law* meaning a rising ground; v. Low.

Ywan de Asmunderlaw, 1440: Coucher Book of Furness, ii. 351.
Walter de Osmunderlaw, c. 1300: ibid. p. 383.
1598-9. John Osmotherley, B.A., Magd. Coll.: Reg. Univ. Oxf. vol. ii. pt. ii. p. 213.
Mr. E. Osmotherly, Gravesend: National Benevolent Institution Report, 1891.
1635. William Osmotherly embarked in ship the Globe for Virginia: Hotten's Lists of Emigrants, p. 119.
MDB. (co. Kent), 1.

Osney. — Local, 'of Oseney,' near the river on the west side of Oxford, the site of a famous monastery.

Richard de Oseney, co. Oxf., 1273. A.
Walter de Oseney, co. Oxf., ibid.
1682. Thomas Smally and Eliz. Osney: Marriage Alleg. (Canterbury), p. 101.

I cannot find any later instances.

Ostcliffe. — Local, 'of Oxcliffe,' a township in the parish of Lancaster. The surname therefrom has received many modifications. For a similar change from *x* to *s*, v. Oscroft. For loss of *c* in Osliff, cf. Antliff. The surname seems to have crossed the Morecambe Sands to Furness at an early period.

1591. Brian Osklef, of Winderin Cartmell: Lancashire Wills at Richmond, i. 205.
1626. John Oscliffe, of Pennington (Ulverston): ibid.
1633. Henry Osliffe, of Pennington (Ulverston): ibid.
1638. Bapt. — Margaret, d. Raphe Osliffe: St. Jas. Clerkenwell, iv. 235.
1639. — John, s. Raph Osliff: ibid. p. 237.
1686. Buried—Bryan Oslief, of Trinkalt: Reg. of Ulverston, i. 175.
1702. Thomas Osliffe, of Warton: ibid. ii. 186.
Bradford, 1.

Ostler. — Occup. 'a keeper of an hostelry'; v. Oastler.

Ostringer, Astringer. — Offic. 'the ostricer,' a falconer. Dame Julyan Berners says, 'Ye shall understonde that they ben called Ostregeres that kepe goshawkes or tercelles' (edit. 1496, Bk. iii). I dare not hazard a guess at its origin, but the earliest form is Ostricer. This became Ostriger. 'John Woodde, one of the Os-

tregers of ower soveregyn Lord'
(30 Henry VIII; v. Notes and
Queries, 1885, p. 306). This same
individual is styled in a deed a
fortnight earlier, ' Oistrynger'
(ibid.). Shakespeare has it *astringer*. Astringer and Ostringer are
natural corruptions (cf. Pottinger
from Potager, *messenger* from *messager*, &c.). Ostringer occurs in
Blount's Gloss. p. 459 (Halliwell).

Robert Ostriciator, co. Notts, 1273. A.
Alan Ostriciare, co. Hunts, ibid.
Robert le Ostricer, co. Norf., ibid.
Alan le Ostrizur. L.
William le Ostricer. T.
Sybil la Ostricer, Close Roll, 27 Edw. I.

**Oswald, Oswell, Oswill,
Oszwald, Oszwold, Oswalt.—**
Bapt. 'the son of Oswald,' cor-
ruptly Oswell or Oswill. A very
early personal name; cf. Oswald
Kirk, a parish in co. York.

'Osewold the Reve': Chaucer, C. T.
3857.
Simon Aswald, co. Oxf., 1273. A.
John Oswald, co. Glouc, 1325. M.
Oswell Faireweather, 1540: Reg. St.
Antholin (London), p. 2.
Oswall Mosley, 1620: Reg. St. Mary
Aldermary (London), p. 14.
Ozwell Stephens, 1744: Reg. Canter-
bury Cath., p. 87.

All Manchester people are familiar with the name of Sir Oswald
Mosley.

1570. Married—William Osewell and
Marye Mills: St. Michael, Cornhill, p. 10.
1632 Bapt.—John, s. John Oswell: St.
Jas. Clerkenwell, i. 120.

I need not furnish modern instances of Oswald.

London, 4, 3, 0, 0, 0, 1; Philadelphia,
20, 1, 1, 1, 1, 0.

Oswin.—Bapt. ' the son of Oswin' (v. Yonge, ii. 185).

Oswin Ogle, co. York. W. 9.
Oswin Sharparrow, co. York. W. 3.
1671. Bapt.—Eliz., d. Robert Oswin:
St. Jas. Clerkenwell, i. 252.
1691. — James, s. James Oswine: ibid.
p. 340.
London, 5.

Otley, Ottley.—Local, ' of Otley,' parishes in co. Suffolk and
W. Rid. Yorks; v. Uttley.

Richard de Otteleye, co. Suffolk,
1273. A.
Henry Otleghe, co. Soms., 1 Edw. III:
Kirby's Quest, p. 83.

Henry Hotlay, 1379: P.T.Yorks. p. 161.
1405. John Oteleve: Cal. of Wills in
Court of Husting (2).
1789. Married—John Otley and Mary
Rivers: St. Geo. Han. Sq. ii. 29.
1808. — William Denley and Mary
Ottley: ibid. p. 382.
Sheffield, 2, 0; West Riding (Yorks)
Court Dir., 2, 2; Philadelphia, 3, 0; New
York, 0, 2.

Ottaway, Ottway, Otway.—
? Local, ' of Ottway' (!). I cannot
identify the spot. The *a* will be
intrusive, as in Greenaway for
Greenway. Probably the way or
road that belonged to Ote (v.
Oat). I have not found any
instances in the leading American
Directories.

John Otewy, co. Suff., 1326. M.
Richard Otewy, co. Suff., ibid.

The two instances above, the
earliest I can find, seem to suggest
a personal rather than a local derivation.

1790. Married — Henry Otway and
Sarah Cave: St. Geo. Han. Sq. ii. 37.
1797. — John Mann and Hannah Ottway: ibid. p. 162.
1806. — John Brown and Mary Ottaway: ibid. p. 339.
London, 3, 1, 1.

Otter.—(1) Bapt. ' the son of
Ottur' (v. Yonge, ii. 305). (2)
Nick. ' the otter.' M.E. *oter*.
The former is evidently the chief
parent of the surname, as will be
seen below. Oter was a great
Scandinavian personal name (v.
Lower, p. 251).

Edward Oter, co. Camb., 1273. A.
Robert Oter, co. Suff., ibid.
Walter Oter, co. Oxf., ibid.
Otuer de Insula, Hen. III–Edw. I. K.
p. 344.
Otverus de Insula, ibid. p. 382.
Johannes Otour, *spicer*, 1379: P. T.
Yorks. p. 125.
1766. Married — Robert Otter and
Sarah Henslow: St. Geo. Han. Sq. i. 150.
London, 3.

Ottiwell, Ottewell, Ottwell.
—Bapt. 'the son of Otewel.' Halliwell under *larder* quotes :

' Thowas Otuwel fol of mood
And faught as he were wood.'
Romance of Otuel, p. 64.

A popular favourite in its time,
but now, I fear, quite obsolete as
a font-name, but found till the beginning of the last century. An

early legendary name (v. Yonge).
As a surname it still survives the
ravages of time. Ottiwell, natural
son of Hugh Lupus, Earl of Chester,
was tutor to the children of Henry I,
who perished at sea in 1120
(Lower). Perhaps this may account for the popularity of the
baptismal name in Cheshire. Ottiwell Higgynbotham gave evidence
in 1522 as to the boundary of
Marple (Earwaker's East Cheshire,
ii. 52). .

1549. Otewell Shallcrosse: Earwaker's
East Cheshire, i. 276.
Ottiwell Worsley, temp. Henry VI:
ibid. ii. 52*n*.
Ottiwell Rowbotham : ibid. p. 276.
1564. Married—William Ottiwell and
Margret Street: St. Mary Aldermary
(London), p. 4.
1580. Bapt.—William, s. Otuell Rilance:
Reg. Wigan, Lanc.
— Married—John Otwell and Joane
Smith: St. Antholin (London), p. 28.
1587. Robert Rychardson and Magdalen Ottwell: Marriage Lic. (London),
i. 163.
1588. Ottiwell Hodgkinson, of Manchester: Wills at Chester, i. 96.
1607. Buried—Ralph Ottewell, *clothworker*: St. Thomas the Apostle (London), p. 106.
1639. Othowell Merverell: Reg. Royal
Coll. Phys.: N. & Q. 1857, p. 305.

I could give many other instances of the font-name as well
as surname, but these will suffice.

London, 0, 1, 0; Derby, 0, 6, 0; New
York, 4, 0, 0; Philadelphia, 0, 0, 3.

Ottley; v. Otley.

Ould, Oulds; v. Old.

Oulston, Ouston, Owston.—
Local, ' of Oulston,' a township in
the parish of Coxwold, N. Rid.
Yorks. Ouston and Owston were
inevitable variants of the surname,
and it will be seen that the N. and
E. Rid. of Yorks have most of
these variants.

1674. Edward, s. Masster Oulton, hee
being the Erle of Albery's butler: St.
Jas. Clerkenwell, i. 265.
New York, 1, 0, 0; MDB. (Yorks, N.
R.), 0, 4, 0; (Yorks, E. R.), 0, 0, 6.

Oulton.—Local, ' of Oulton.'
Parishes, townships, &c., in cos.
Norfolk, Suffolk, W. Rid. Yorks,
Cheshire, and Cumberland. The
family, however, seem to have
sprung, so far as North England is

concerned, from the township of Oulton, near Tarporley, co. Ches.

Thomas Olton, Mottram, co. Ches., 1455: Earwaker's East Ches. ii. 114.
Richard Olton, of Congleton, 1588: Wills at Chester, i. 145.
Blanch Oulton, of Bradley, *widow*, 1629: ibid. ii. 167.
Liverpool, 3; Manchester, 2; Boston (U.S.), 2.

Ousby.—Local, 'of Ousby,' a parish in co. Cumb., nine miles from Penrith.

1635. Buried—William Ousby or Ousbye, *householder*: St. Jas. Clerkenwell, iv. 635.
Manchester, 1.

Ouseley, Ousley.—Local, 'of Ouseley.' As Lower and others suggest, 'the meadow by the Ouse' is probably the correct derivation. I cannot find the spot. v. Houseley.

1684. Newdigate Owsley and Eliz. Jones: Marriage Alleg. (Cant.), i. 183.
1688. John Sheffield and Ann Ousley: ibid. ii. 58.
Crockford, 1, 0; Philadelphia, 0, 1.

Ouston; v. Oulston.

Outerbridge, Outbridge.—Local, 'at the outer bridge,' from residence thereby. I have not identified the spot.

1571. Married—Nicholas Outbridge and Eliz. Peccowe: St. Thomas the Apostle (London), p. 5.

I find an instance of one who died of the plague raging in London at the period :

1625. Buried — Helen Outerbridge, servant to Mr. Sanbroke, plague: St. Michael, Cornhill, p. 228.
Philadelphia, 6, 0; New York, 1, 0.

Outlaw.—Offic. 'one out of protection of the civil law'; perhaps, more spiritually, one excommunicated.

Richard Utlawe, co. Bedf., 1273. A.
John Outlagh, co. Camb., 1322. M.
Roger Outlawe, C. R., 16 Edw. III. pt. i.
William Outlawe. V. 9.
Richard Outlaw, rector of Necton, co. Norf., 1661: FF. vi. 53.

The Ulverston News of Dec. 4. 1886, announced the marriage of Florence J. Outlaw, of Birmingham.

MDB. (Norfolk), 1; Boston (U.S.), 1.

Outram, Outran, Owtram, Owttrim.—Local, 'of Outram,' probably for Outerham (cf. Outerbridge), i.e. the outer *ham* or dwelling. I cannot find the spot.

1806. Married — Joseph Outram and Ann Locke: St. Geo. Han. Sq. ii. 343.
London, 1, 1, 1, 2; Manchester, 0, 0, 2, 0; New York (Outram), 1.

Outred, Oughtred. — Bapt. 'the son of Ughtred.' Domesday Book, Uctred. One of the earliest priors of Hexham was 'Uthred erl Killer sune' (Priory of Hexham, Surt. Soc.). 'Uhtred . . . gathered an army, rescued Durham, and gained a signal victory over the Scots.' This was a famous Earl of Northumberland. Hence we find the surname in that district (v. Freeman's Norman Conquest, i. 326).

Ughtred de Preston, C. R., 12 Edw. I: Hist. West. and Cumb. i. 202.
Ketel fil. Uchtred, 34 Hen. II: ibid.
Uhtred de Witingeham, 7 Hen. II: Pipe Roll, iv. 24.
John Vtreth, 1379: P. T. Yorks. p. 144.
1642. William Oughtred, prebend of Heathfield: Walker's Sufferings of the Clergy, edited by Whitaker, p. 26.

I once saw Oughtred over a public-house by the bridge at Newcastle. I also saw in the Visitors' book at Conishead Priory, Lanc., 'W. Oughtred, Didsbury, Manchester, Sept. 4, 1886.'

Ovenden.—Local, 'of Ovenden,' a township in the parish of Halifax, W. Rid. Yorks.

Ricardus de Ovenden, 1379: P. T. Yorks. p. 189.

This instance occurs in Halifax.

1601. Married—Robert Ovenden and Katherine Stevens: St. Peter, Cornhill, i. 242.
1775. — Rice James and Mary Ovenden: St. Geo. Han. Sq. i. 258.
London, 3; Philadelphia, 1.

Over.—Local, 'of Over,' parishes in diocs. Ely and Chester. The first seems to have been the parent of the surname. I do not find any traces of an old settled family in the county of Cheshire. 'Over, A.S. *ofer*, . . . a shore': Taylor, Words and Places (ed. 1885), p. 331. '*Ofer*, the land bordering

on water, a river-bank, sea-shore, *over* in local names': Bosworth and Toller, A.S. Dict.

Richard de Overe, co. Hunts, 1273. A.
Nicholas Over, co. Oxf., ibid.
Sybil de Ouere, co. Camb., ibid.
John de Ouere, co. Camb., ibid.
Lucas de Overe, 1300. M.
1714. Bapt. — Letitia, d. Mathew Over: St. Jas. Clerkenwell, ii. 76.
1780. Married — William Over and Sarah Crissick: St. Geo. Han. Sq. i. 316.
London, 4; Philadelphia, 1.

Overall.—Local, 'of the Overhall.' The suffix is, of course, -*hall*, with the *h* dropped; cf. Blackall, &c. Overall, therefore, means the hall by the shore of the sea or near the bank of a river; v. Over.

Thomas del Ouerhalle, 1379: P. T. Yorks. p. 173.
1647. William Overall, of Bury: Wills at Chester, ii. 167.
1750. Married— John Morgan and Ann Overall: St. Geo. Chap. Mayfair, i. 180.
London, 4; Manchester, 1; New York, 1.

Overbury.—Local, 'of Overbury,' a parish in co. Worc., five miles from Tewkesbury; v. Over and Bury.

1606. Giles Overbury, co. Glouc.: Reg. Univ. Oxf. vol. ii. pt. ii. p. 292.
1610. Walter Overbury, co. Glouc.: ibid. p. 313.
1623-4. William Overbury and Gertrude Gee: Marriage Lic. (London), ii. 135.
1641. Married—William Watson and Eliz. Orwerbere: St. Michael, Cornhill, i. 29. New York, 1.

Overdo. — ? Nick. The sobriquet of a kitchener or cook (?).
'Thing that is overdon . . . it is a vice.' Chaucer, C. T. 16113.
Henry Overdo, Close Roll, 14 Edw. IV.

Such nicknames were common and popular, but few survived.

Overend.—Local, 'at the Overend'; cf. Townsend, Woodend, Fieldsend, &c. (v. Over). With Overheynd, cf. Townshend. The letter *h* seems to have crept in easily. 'At the end of the shore' seems to be the derivation. All these compounds of *Over* go to prove that the affix implied a flat river-side as well as the sea-shore.

Michael de Overende, co. Bedf., 1273. A.
William de Overende, co. Bedf., ibid.
Robertus del Overheynd, 1379: P. T. Yorks. p. 276.

1694. John Overend, of Melling, *husbandman*: Wills at Chester, iv. 337.
1805. Married—Wilson Overend and Wilhelmina Eliz. Pringle: St. Geo. Han. Sq. ii. 329.
London, 3; Liverpool, 5; Philadelphia, 3.

Overman. — Offic. 'the overman,' a gaffer (?). William le Overer occurs (Close Roll, 2 Edw. I). Overman still lives, but seems to have found its latest home in America.

1647. Thomas Overman and Eliz. Ross: Marriage Lic. (London), ii. 278.
1650. Married—George Saunders and Alice Overman: St. Dionis Backchurch, i. 27.

In the London Directory occurs 'Overman's Alm Houses, Montague Close, Borough, S.E.'; probably an old endowment. This surname seems to have gone to America and taken the whole family with it.

New York, 1; Boston (U.S.), 2; Philadelphia, 2.

Overstone.—Local, 'of Overstone,' a parish in co. Northampton, five miles from the capital town.

MDB. (co. Warwick), 2.

Overton.—Local, 'of Overton,' parishes in diocs. of Winchester, Peterborough, Manchester, York, St. Alban's, and Sarum.

Adam de Overton, co. Oxf., 1273. A.
Ode de Overton, co. Hunts, ibid.
Geoffrey de Overton, co. Salop, ibid.
John de Overton, co. Hunts, 1324. M.
Sarra de Overtone, co. Som., 1 Edw. III: Kirby's Quest, p. 261.
1624. Jane Overton, of Overton: Wills at Chester, ii. 167.
1788. Married—Francis Parish and Eliz. Overton: St. Geo. Han. Sq. ii. 7.
London, 10; Liverpool 1; New York, 17.

Overy, Ouvry. — Local, 'of Overy.' Mr. Lower says that this is an extinct parish in co. Oxf. If it be true that the Ouvrys came into England at the Revocation of the Edict of Nantes in 1685, a statement which seems to be well established, then Ouvry has a separate parentage.

Richard de Overe, co. Hunts, 1273. A.
Robert Overhe, co. Camb., ibid.
1683. Thomas Rodan and Catherine Ovrey: Marriage Alleg. (Canterbury), i. 145.

1711. Married — William Overy and Martha Scott: Reg. Canterbury Cath., p. 70.
1774. Married—William Musgrove and Mary Overy: St. Geo. Han. Sq. i. 241.
London, 5, 1; Philadelphia, 1, 0.

Owen, Owens.—Bapt. 'the son of Owen.' Owens is the genitive form; cf. Jones, Jennings, Williams, Simmonds, &c.

Hoel fil. Oeni, Pipe Roll, 7 Hen. II.
Oenus de Porchint', ibid.
Nicholas fil. Oweyn, co. Oxf., 1273. A.
Richard fil. Owen, co. Camb., ibid.
Matthew Owen, co. Wilts, 1316. M.
1742. Married—Cornelius Owen and Eliz. Rowell: St. Geo. Chap. Mayfair, p. 31.
1747. — Rowland Owens and Sarah Narboys: ibid. p. 96.
London, 76, 6; Philadelphia, 43, 56.

Owston; v. Oulston.

Owtram, -rim; v. Outram.

Ox, Oxx.—Nick. 'the ox'; cf. Bullock, Bull, Cow, &c. This surname has not made much way. Bull has done better; v. Oxnard.

Stephen Oxe, Pardons Roll, 6 Ric. II.
1745. Married—John Gedion Stone and Mary Oxx: St. Geo. Chap. Mayfair, p. 59.
New York, 0, 2; Philadelphia, 4, 0.

Oxberry, Oxborrow, Oxenbury, Oxbrow, Oxenberry.—Local, 'of Oxburgh' (or Oxborough), a parish in co. Norfolk, three miles from Stoke Ferry. All the variants are of an extremely natural character.

William de Oxeburgh, co. Norf., 1273. A.
Nicholas de Oxeburgh, co. Norf., 1316. M.
1669. Thomas Oxborow and Ellen Corker: Marriage Alleg. (Cant.), p. 17.
1796. Married—Stephen Dear and Eliz. Oxborough: St. Geo. Han. Sq. ii. 141.
London, 1, 3, 1, 0, 0; Exeter (Oxenberry), 2.

Oxenden.—Local, 'of Oxendon,' now Oxendon Magna, a parish in co. Northampton, two or three miles from Harborough.

John de Oxendon, co. Northampt., 1273. A.
Stephen de Oxindon, co. Bucks, ibid.
Adam de Oxindon, co. Northampt., Hen. III-Edw. I. K.
Ivo de Oxinden, co. Northampt., 1316. M.
1572. Henry Oxenden: Reg. Univ. Oxf. vol. ii. pt. ii, p. 38.
1661. William Dalton and Rebeccah Oxenden: Marriage Alleg. (Cant.), 18.
Crockford, 1.

Oxenford, Oxford. — Local, 'of Oxford.' Oxenford is an old form of Oxford. Thus Bristow represents Bristol as Stopford represents Stockport.

'Whilom ther was dwelling in Oxenforde A riche gnof.' Chaucer, C. T. 3186.
William de Oxenford, *pelter*, 7 Edw. II: Freemen of York, i. 15.
Johannes de Oxenford, 1379: P. T. Yorks. p. 23.
Cristiana de Oxenford, 1379: ibid.
John Oxeneford, co. Soms., 1 Edw. III: Kirby's Quest, p. 83.
1693. John Cux, or Cox, and Mary Oxenford: Marriage Alleg. (Canterbury), p. 266.
1763. Married — Thomas Oxford and Olle Woolldridge: St. Geo. Han. Sq. i. 118.
1779. — Thomas Oxford and Ann Thomas: ibid. p. 208.
London, 1, 4; Philadelphia, 1, 2.

Oxenham, Oxhenham. — Local, 'of Oxenham.' I cannot find the spot.

Richard Oxnam, 1590: Reg. St. Columb Major, co. Cornwall, p. 193.
Richard Oxenham, 1602: ibid. p. 200.
1778. Married—John Oxenham and Mary Mills: St. Geo. Han. Sq. i. 285.
London, 4, 1; Boston (U.S.), 2, 0.

Oxenhird.—Occup. 'a tender of oxen'; v. Oxnard.

Oxford; v. Oxenford.

Oxlade, Oxlid. — Local, 'of the oak-slade' (v. Slade). The modification of Ocslade into Oxlade was inevitable. Probably some spot in co. Oxon. Both cos. Berks and Bucks have instances still existing.

Michael de Ocslade, co. Oxf., 1273. A.
1621. Francis Oxladde: Reg. Univ. Oxf. i. 343.
1717. Bapt.—Ann, d. Robert Oxlade: St. Jas. Clerkenwell, p. 97.
1750. — Ann, d. Benjamin Oxlid: ibid. p. 295.
1783. Married — Thomas Frost and Mary Oxlade: St. Geo. Han. Sq. i. 349.
London, 1, 0; MDB. (co. Bucks), 1, 0; (co. Berks), 1, 0.

Oxley, Oxlee.—Local, 'of Oxley.' I cannot find the spot. A familiar Yorkshire surname, but probably known to other counties, as the 'ox-meadow' would readily become a local title.

1562. Robert Oxeley, *weaver*, and Eliz. Goodchild: Marriage Lic. (London), i. 24.
1731. Married—Daniel Oxlee and Mary Surman: St. Geo. Han. Sq. i. 8.

1780. Married — Richard Oxley and Mary Foster: St. Geo. Han. Sq. i. 314. London, 14, 2; New York, 4, o.

Oxnard, Oxner.—Occup. 'the oxen-herd,' a keeper of oxen; cf. Coward, Calvert, Shepherd, Gozzard. A North-English name, as are most of the compounds of -*herd.* Bullockherd is found in co. Somerset:

Adam Bollokhurd, 9 Edw. II: Kirby's Quest, p. 136.
Johannes Oxinhird, 1379: P. T. Yorks. p. 216.
Thomas Oxenhyrde. W. 3.
John Oxenhyrde. W. 3.
Peter Oxhird. W. 2.
Alice Hoxherd, C. R., 4 Hen. IV. pt. i.

The abbreviation to Oxnard was inevitable:

1640. Christopher Oxnard and Faith Toulson: St. Dionis Backchurch (London).
1604. Christopher Oxnerd, *laborer,* recusant in Yorkshire: Dawson's Hist. of Skipton, p. 315.
— Stephen Oxnerd, *laborer,* recusant in Yorkshire: ibid.
1729. Henry Oxenard, *coachman,* and Jane Chillingworth: St. Geo. Chap. Mayfair, p. 308.
1793. Married—Jeremiah Oxnard and Mary Blakiston: St. Geo. Han. Sq. ii. 105.

For several years I thought Oxnard was extinct. I was much pleased, therefore, on leaving Cullercoats Station, Newcastle, Aug. 29, 1886, to see the name over a shop in the immediate street to the left. Afterwards I found several instances in the Newcastle Directory.

Newcastle-on-Tyne, 2, o; Boston (U.S.), 3, o; New York, o, 1.

Oxpring, Oxspring, Ofspring.—Local, ' of Oxspring,' a village in the parish of Penistone, W. Rid. Yorks. There is good evidence that all who bear this name, wherever settled in later times, spring from this spot. Under the title ' Villata de Oxpryng ' occur the names:

Richard de Oxpring co. York, 1273. A.
Matilda de Oxpring', 1379: P. T. Yorks. p. 86.
William Oxpring, 1379: ibid.
Gervase de Ospringe: Pipe Roll, 11 Hen. II. p. 103.

Ofspring is a manifest corruption, although a manor named Offspring is mentioned (A.D. 1273; v. A. i. 226) in the Hundred of Folkestone, co. Kent.

'Thomas Ofspringe, alias Oxspringe, of Kent, whose came out of Yorkshire.'

His son Charles Ofspringe was rector of St. Antholin's, London, in 1634: Visitation of London, 1635, ii. 129.

No doubt Offspring Blackall, Bishop of Exeter (1654-1716), born in London, was a connexion, as surnames turned into fontal names were becoming fashionable at that period.

1771. Married—Offspring Webb and Mary Withington: St. Geo. Han. Sq. i. 207.
Sheffield, 1, 4, o; Philadelphia, o, 1, o.

Oxton. — Local, of ' Oxton,' parishes in diocs. Chester and Southwell, and spots elsewhere. One more instance in which the oak-trees figure in local names.

Richard de Okeston, co. Devon, 1273. A.
Alexander de Ockeston, co. Devon, ibid.
Johannes de Oxton, 1379: P. T. Yorks. p. 145.
1663. Thomas Oxton and Ann Rutlish: Marriage Alleg. (Canterbury), p. 109.
1681. Married—Netor Oxston and Eliz. Gillford: St. Jas. Clerkenwell, iii. 190. London, 1, 1.

Oyler, Ollier.—? Occup. 'the oiler' (?), i.e. an oilman. Far more likely to be a form of Oliver, q.v.

Roberte Deane, *oylman*, 1642: Reg. St. Mary Aldermary, London, p. 88. London, 2, 2.

P

Pace, Pacey.—Bapt. ' the son of Pace,' pet Pacey. The variants of this Easter name are many; v. Pash, Pask, Peace, &c. Easter-egging in North Lancashire is still Pace-egging, and in my old parish (Ulverston) the sale of pace-eggs is large as the Easter comes round; cf. Noel, Pentecost, &c.

Hugo Pacy, co. Notts, 1273. A.
William Pacy, co. Linc., ibid.
William Pace, co. Devon, Hen. III—Edw. I. K.
Alexander Pacye, 1564: Reg. Univ. Oxf. vol. ii. pt. ii. p. 29.
1583. Edward Spendlowe and Eliz. Pace: Marriage Lic. (London), i. 117.
London, 4, 2; Boston (U.S.), 5, o.

Pack, Pakes, Packe.—Bapt ' the son of Pack.' Probably it is a harder form of Patch, q.v. Pakes is the genitive form; cf. Jones, Williams, Collins, &c. (v. Paxon for further evidence).

John fil. Pake, co. Camb., 1273. A.
Alex. Pake, co. Camb., ibid.
William Pakke, co. Camb., ibid.
Agnes Pake, co. Bedf., ibid.
Edward Pake, co. Soms., 1 Edw. III: Kirby's Quest, p. 193.
1568-9. Humfrey Pakes and Martha Brittaine: Marriage Lic. (London), i. 41.
1590. Matthew Pake and Eliz. Rogers: ibid. p. 187.
1603-4. Edward Pack and Hester Blunt: p. 281.
London, 9, 1, o; Philadelphia, 4, o, 1.

Packard.—No doubt, as suggested by Mr. Lower, a corruption of Picard, q.v. This form is very strongly represented in the United States.

1770. Married — Peter Packard and Jane Coleben: St. Geo. Han. Sq. i. 198. London, 2; Boston (U.S.), 76.

Packer.—Occup. 'the packer,' a packman. In Yorkshire a wool-packer. v. Packman (1).

Walter le Packere, co. Bedf., 1273. A.
' Richard, the son of William, the son of Orme, quit-claimed the whole of his land in Prestbury, to St. Werbergh and the Abbey. . . Similar grants were made by William, the son of Robert Pigot, Robert, the son of William le Paker, and others ': East Cheshire, ii. 180 n.
Mathew le Packere. D.
Adam le Packer. M.
William le Packere. J.
Robert de Lyndesay, *pakker*, 8 Edw. II: Freemen of York, i. 16.

1583-4. Edward Packer and Eliz. Leonard: Marriage Lic. (London), i. 126.
1642. Bapt.—John, s. Andrew Packer, dwelling in Bowe Lane: St. Mary Aldermary, p. 88.
London, 21 ; Philadelphia, 28.

Packham, Peckham.—Local, 'of Peckham,' two parishes in co. Kent. The variation was a natural and easy one. For a second derivation of Packham, v. Pakenham.
1575. George Peckam, co. Bucks: Reg. Univ. Oxf. vol. ii. pt. ii. 64.
1588. Henry Peccam, co. Sussex: ibid. p. 164.
1808. Married — William Hale and Sarah Packham: St. Geo. Han. Sq. ii. 383.
London, 3, 4 ; MDB. (co. Kent), 2, 1.

Packman.—(1) Occup. 'the packman'; v. Packer. (2) Occup. a variant of Pakeman, q.v.
1580. Arthur Gynne and Mary Packeman : Marriage Lic. (London), i. 96.
1669. Married—Richard Pacman and Saray Pane : St. Jas. Clerkenwell, iii. 166.
London, 8 ; Philadelphia, 1.

Packwood.—Local, 'of Packwood,' a parish in co. Warwick, near Henley-in-Arden.
1617. Josiah Packwood, co. Warwick: Reg. Univ. Oxf. vol. ii. pt. ii. 361.
1640. Bapt. — Christofer, s. Thomas Packwood : St. Jas. Clerkenwell, i. 145.
London, 2.

Pacy.—Bapt. 'the son of Pace,' from the pet Pacey ; v. Pace.
London, 2.

Padbury.—Local, 'of Padbury,' a parish in co. Bucks, three miles from Buckingham.
Robert de Padeburi, co. Bucks, 1273. A.
Symon de Padeburi, co. Oxf., ibid.
1778. Married — Nathaniel Gardner and Eliz. Padburey : St. Geo. Hanover Sq. i. 287.
MDB. (co. Oxf.), 2 ; London, 4.

Paddey, Paddie, Paddy.—Bapt. 'the son of Patrick,' from the nick. Pat, and pet form Patty or Paddy. All these forms are purely English ; v. Paddison or Pattison, and Patey or Pate.
1560. John Borne and Margaret Paddye, of Hadley, co. Essex : Marriage Lic. (London), i. 20.
1585. John Paddie, co. Bucks : Reg. Univ. Oxf. vol. ii. pt. ii. p. 144.
1770. Married — Joseph Paddy and Eliz. Cope : St. Geo. Han. Sq. i. 203.
London, 1, 1, 1.

Paddison.—Bapt. 'the son of Patrick'; v. Pattinson, of which Paddison is a lazier form. Although Paddy is Irish, Paddison is purely of English descent. It must never be forgotten that Patrick was a most popular North-English personal name in the surname period.
1678. Bapt. — Bartholomew, s. John Paddyson : St. Jas. Clerkenwell. i. 281.
1795. Married—Samuel Paddison and Eliz. Vergette : St. Geo. Han. Sq. ii. 138.
MDB. (co. Linc.), 13 ; London, 2.

Padget, Padgett.—Official; v. Paget.

Padley.—Local, 'of Padley,' a hamlet in the parish of Hope, co. Derby. The surname has crossed the border into Nottinghamshire.
Nicholas de Paddeleye, co. Derby, 1273. A.
Henricus de Padelay, 1379: P. T. Yorks. p. 30.
London, 3 ; MDB. (co. Notts), 3.

Pagan.—Bapt. 'the son of Pagan.' A very familiar font-name in the 13th century, and earlier, leaving a large legacy to our directories in the shape of Paine, Payn, Payne, and their other forms (q.v.). Edmundus filius Pagani (Domesday). For a history of this word, v. Gibbon's Decline and Fall, ch. xxi. ad finem. For diminutives, v. Paynel and Pannett.
Paganus de Vilers, temp. 1109: Lincolnshire Survey, p. 9.
Geoffrey, s. Paganus: ibid. p. 2.
Pagan de Shenefeld : Pipe Roll, 11 Hen. II, p. 18.
Pagan de Staning : ibid. p. 92.
Pagan a la Legh, co. Wilts, 1273. A.
Pagan de la Hale, co. Kent, ibid.
Roger fil. Pagan, co. Devon, ibid.

This surname has been gradually shuffled off or changed into Paine, Payne, &c., the bearers not caring to be so entitled. Yet it is one of the most interesting names in our directories.
Crockford, 1 ; Philadelphia, 3.

Page, Paige.—Official, 'the page,' a young servitor, a personal attendant in a noble's house.
Lambert Page, co. York, 1273. A.
Philip Page, co. Essex, Hen. III—Edw. I. K.
John le Page, 1300. M.
William le Page. BB.

1584. Anthony Page and Eliz. Blounte: Marriage Lic. (London), i. 131.
London, 128, 2 ; MDB. (co. Devon), 2. 11 ; Boston (U.S.), 57, 36.

Paget, Pagett, Padget, Padgett, Padgit.—(1) Nick. 'the page,' dim. Paget. Boy pages seem to have been held in high esteem. No instance, however, occurs in the Hundred Rolls or other contemporary records so far as my observation goes. I presume it is a 14th or 15th century importation from France, and corresponds exactly to our Littlepage and Smallpage, q.v.
Johannes Paget, taylour, 1379: P. T. Yorks. p. 118.

(2) Bapt. 'the son of Pachet.' If Paget be (occasionally) a corruption of Pachet, then early instances abound in plenty; v. Patchett. Padget or Padgett would also be natural corruptions.
1779. Married — John Briggs and Mary Padget : St. Geo. Han. Sq. i. 207.
1807. — John Kellick and Eliz. Paggitt : ibid. ii. 379.
London, 11, 0, 0, 5, 0 ; West Rid. Court Dir., 2, 0, 2, 5, 0 ; New York, 0, 1, 0, 0, 1.

Pagnam.—Local, 'of Pakenham,' a parish in co. Suffolk, five miles from Bury St. Edmunds. The corruption to Pagnam is according to recognized custom ; cf. Slagg for Slack, and Debnam for Debenham. An early instance occurs below.
William de Pakenham, co. Norf., 1273. A.
Henry de Pakenham, co. Norf., 1373: FF. i. 480.
Ralph de Pagenham, co. Soms., 1 Edw. : Kirby's Quest, p. 154.
1574. Married — Robert Pagnam and Curlellaw (sic) Chicheley : St. Jas. Clerkenwell, i. 6.
1626. Oswald Tilman and Eliz. Packnam : Marriage Lic. (London), i. 179.
George Frederick Pagnam, butcher, Eccles New Road, Salford : Manchester Directory.
Manchester, 1.

Pagnel.—Bapt. ; v. Paynel.

Paice.—Bapt. 'the son of Pace'; v. Pash and Pace. One of many variants of this Easter name ; cf. Whitsunday, Christmas, Nowell, Pentecost, &c.

1616. Barnard Paise and Eliz. Surbey: Marriage Lic. (London), ii. 41.
1765. Married — Samuel Lewington and Jemima Paice: St. Geo. Han. Sq. i. 139. London, 9.

Paige ; v. Page.

Pailthorpe, Palethorp, Palethorpe.—Local, 'of Palethorpe,' a chapelry in co. Notts (Lower).

1753. Married—George Sylvester and Sarah Pailthorpe: St. Geo. Han. Sq. i. 50.
1763. — William Pailthorpe and Eliz. Woolcott: ibid. p. 127.
MDB. (co. Lincoln), 0, 0, 3; (co. Notts), 2, 0, 2; London, 1, 0, 1; Philadelphia, 0, 5, 0.

Pain, Paine, Payn, Payne. —Bapt. 'the son of Pagan,' popularly Pain and Payne. How great a favourite this font-name was in the 12th, 13th, and 14th centuries will be seen by a glance at the London and provincial directories. The softened form of pagan (a countryman) is found in Chaucer:

'The Constable, and Dame Hermegild, his wife,
Were payenes, and that country everywhere.'   Man of Lawes Tale.

Pagan or Payn was of Norman introduction. It is curious that a great leader of atheistical principles should have borne this name.

'He never knew pleasure who never knew Payn,'

has been said of several jovial bearers of the cognomen.

Payn de Santon, co. Norf., 1273. A.
Robert fil. Payn, co. Hunts, ibid.
Gilbert Payn, co. Essex, ibid.
Elis le Fitz-Payn, 1297. M.
Pain del Ash, 1301. M.
Payne le Paumer, C. R., 33 Hen. III.
Payen le Doubber. N.
Thomas Payn, co. Soms., 1 Edw. III: Kirby's Quest, p. 110.

For diminutives, v. Pannett and Paynel. Also v. Penson. It would be useless to furnish modern instances. They abound in every church register and in every city directory.

London, 31, 37, 2, 120; Philadelphia, 1, 14, 0, 50.

Painter, Paynter. — Occup. 'the painter,' one who depicted in colours. This surname has made a strong impression upon American directories.

John Peyntur, co. Camb., 1273. A.
Ric. le Paintur, C. R., 4 Edw. II.

William de Blida, *payntour*, 8 Edw. II: Freemen of York, i. 16.
Ricardus Peyntour, 1379 : P. T. Yorks. p. 161.
Richard Peyntour, rector of Congham, co. Norf., 1439 : FF. viii. 389.
1636. Married — Richard Painter and Katherine Witt: St. Jas. Clerkenwell, iii. 67.
London, 20, 2; Philadelphia, 45, 31.

Pairpoint. — Local ; v. Pierpoint, of which it is a palpable variant.

Paisley.—Local, 'of Paisley.' Found chiefly in the North of England and near the Scottish border.

MDB. (co. Cumberland), 4.

Paitson.—Bapt. 'the son of Patrick,' from the nick. Pait or Patey ; v. Patey and Pattinson. A North-English form.

Pate Stevinson, 1528 : TTT. p. xxx.
Pait Tailyeour, 1541 : ibid. p. xlix.
Pait Graham, 1544 : ibid. p. liii.
Richard Pateson, of Wray, 1611 : ibid.
Jenet Pateson, of Much Singleton, *widow*, 1623 : Lancashire Wills at Richmond, i. 211.
Ulverston, 1 ; MDB. (co. Cumberland), 1 ; (co. Westm.), 1.

Pakeman.—Occup. 'the servant of Pake' ; v. Pack; cf. Addyman, Matthewman, &c., one of a fairly large class.

John Pakeman, co. Oxf., 1273. A.
William Pakman, co. Derby, 20 Edw. I. R.
Simon Pakeman, C. R., 7 Hen. VI.
1714. Married—Jasper Roffe and Mary Pakeman : St. Jas. Clerkenwell, iii. 237. London, 1.

Pakenham, Packham, Packenham, Packingham.—Local, 'of Pakenham,' a parish in co. Suffolk, near Bury St. Edmunds. Very early corrupted to Packham. Several variants of the name seem peculiar to the United States.

John de Pakeham, co. Norf., 1273. A.
William de Pakenham, co. Norf., ibid.
William de Pakeham, or Pakenham, co. Suff. : ibid.
Thomas de Pakeham, co. Norf.: FF. x. 449.
Edmund de Pakenham, co. Norf., 1388 : ibid. i. 253.
1808. Married — William Hale and Sarah Packham : St. Geo. Han. Sq. ii. 383.
London, 0, 3, 0, 0; Crockford, 1, 0, 0, 0; New York, 2, 0, 2, 4.

Pakes.—Bapt. ; v. Pack.

Palcock.—Bapt. 'the son of Paul,' from the pet Paulcock; cf. Wilcock, Simcock, &c. ; v. Cock.

Jordan Palcock, co. Bucks, 1273. A.
Johannes Palcock, et Beatrix, uxor ejus, 1379 : P. T. Yorks. p. 52.

This surname, I believe, still exists, but I have not met with an instance.

Palethorp(e.—Local ; v. Pailthorpe.

Paley.—Local, 'of Paley,' now Paley Green, in the parish of Giggleswick, W. Rid. Yorks, consisting of two farmsteads. Mr. Lower writes, 'This was borne as a personal name by a powerful Dane, mentioned in the Saxon Chronicle as Pallig, A.D. 1101' (Patr. Brit. p. 255). My derivation is manifestly the correct one, as all the Paleys come from Yorkshire.

Robertus de Palay, of Litton, in the parish of Arncliffe, 1379 : P. T. Yorks. p. 278.
Adam de Palay, of Giggleswick, 1379 : ibid. p. 279.
John Paley, of Melling, on the Yorkshire border, 1591 : Wills at Chester, i. 147.
Richard Paley, of Clifton, 1673 : Lancashire Wills at Richmond, i. 206.

These four references conclusively show that the Paleys are sprung from the spot indicated above.

London, 2 ; West Rid. Court Dir., 7 ; Philadelphia, 1.

Palfrey.—Nick. 'the palfrey,' a saddle-horse for a lady's use. M.E. *palfrei* ; O.F. *palefrei* ; v. Palfreyman.

'And to the paleis rode ther many a route Of lordes, upon stedes and palfreis.'
     Chaucer, Knight's Tale, l. 2495.

Thomas Palfrei, co. Linc., 1273. A.
Richard Palefray, co. Salop, ibid.
Gilbert Palfrey, co. Norf., ibid.
John Palefrey, co. Norf., ibid.
1667. Thomas Palfrey and Margaret Maxham: Marriage Lic. (Faculty Office), p. 100.
1668. Married—Richard Pallfrey and Mary Halton : St. Jas. Clerkenwell, iii. 140.
London, 2 ; Philadelphia, 1.

Palfreyer.—Official, 'the palfreyer,' the keeper of 'my lady's' palfreys; v. Palfreyman.

Gile Palfreur, co. Camb., 1273. A.
Richard le Palefreyur, C. R., 3 Edw. I.
Roger le Palefrour, ibid.
Roger le Palefreyour, co. York. W. 2.
This surname seems to have become extinct.

Palfreyman, Palframan, Palfreeman.—Official, 'the palfreyman,' the keeper of 'my lady's' palfreys.

'Item, the same daye to John Stormy ... for keping of twoo palfrayes of the Quenes after the decease of Richard Payne, palfreyman, xs.' 1502, May: Privy Purse Expenses, Elizabeth of York, p. 17.
'10 hobyes and palfreys the whiche the kinges highnesse yave unto my lady, Duchesse of Bourgoinge': Privy Purse Expenses, Edw. IV, 1480, p. 153. v. Hobman.
John le Palfreyman, co. Camb.,1273. A.
Robert Palfreyman, co. Bucks, ibid.
Thomas Palfrayman, 1379: P. T. Yorks. p. 300.
1553. Bapt. — Mary Pauefreman: St. Peter, Cornhill, i. 117.
1578. Buried — Anne Palphreman: ibid. p. 211.
1576. John Paphraman, or Palframan: Reg. Univ. Oxf. vol. ii. pt. iii. p. 57.
West Rid.Court Dir., 2, 1, o; Sheffield, 5, o, o; Coneythorpe (Knaresboro'), o, o, 1; Boston (U.S.), 1, o, o; Philadelphia, 1, o, o.

Palgrave.—Local, 'of Palgrave,' a parish in co. Suffolk, one mile from Diss; also a hamlet in the parish of Sporle, co. Norfolk. This surname has no connexion with the German Pfalzgraf, a Count-Palatine, as has been several times suggested. It is local, not official.

1311. Sir Ralph de Palegrave, rector of Bodney: FF. iii. 631.
1728. Bapt. — Susanna, d. Robert Paulgrave: St. Jas. Clerkenwell, ii. 181.
London, 2; MDB. (Norfolk), 1.

Paliser, Palliser, Palser, Palister, Pallister.—Occup. 'the palliser,' or with feminine suffix 'the pallister,' a surname seemingly peculiar to Yorkshire, where it still flourishes. The Surtees Society records contain early references (unfortunately I have mislaid my notes) to such persons as 'Robert Redman, palayser.'

'Paid to James Foster, palycer, as a present for making the payle (i. e. fence) near the dwelling of the Lord Prior, near

the butgarth, 12d.': Liber Bursarii. Eccles. Dunelmensis, Surt. Soc.
The *palliser* (Fr. *palis*, a pale, a stake) was a kind of parker, one who guarded or fenced enclosures. As regards *pallister*, it may be as well to say that the Poll Tax (1379) proves that the feminine suffix *-ster* was very popular in all occupative names (v. Slaster for Slater); cf. *palisade*.
Robertus Palycer, 1379: P. T. Yorks. p. 240.
John Pallyser, co. York. W. 9.
Thomas Palysar, co. York : ibid.
William Pallyster, co. York: ibid.
John Palyster, co. York : ibid.
Robert Paylyster, co. York. W. 11.
'The Rev. Thomas Palaser, or Pallicer, born at Ellerton-upon-Swale, a Roman Catholic priest, was executed for his religion at Durham, Aug. 9, 1600': Old Yorkshire, ii. 140.
1793. Married—Alex. Paul and Sarah Pallister: St. Geo. Han. Sq. ii. 92.
1794. — Thomas Haverly and Eliz. Palser: ibid. p. 110.
Leeds, 1, 1, o, o, 1; York, 1, o, o, o, 2; Rawdon (W. Rid.), o, 2, o, o, o; New York, o, o, o, 1, 1; London (Palser), 7.

Palismaker. — Occup. 'the palis maker,' a maker of fences ; v. Paliser or Pallister.
William Palycemaker, 1379: P. T. Yorks. p. 242.

Pallet, Pallett, Pallatt.—Local, ' of Pawlett,' q.v. I doubt not these are variants. Pellatt is well established in the United States. As will be seen below, the form Palet is early found in co. Soms.
John Palet, co. Soms., 1 Edw. III: Kirby's Quest, p. 208.
Robert Palet, co. Soms., 1 Edw. III: ibid.
1797. Married — Richard Brooks and Lucy Pallet : St. Geo. Han. Sq. ii. 168.
1798. — Joseph Pallett and Mary Youngman : ibid. p. 191.
London, 1, 6, o; Philadelphia, 1, 1, 12.

Palmer.—Occup. 'the palmer,' a pilgrim to the Holy Land ; a common entry in the Hundred Rolls.
'The faded palm-branch in his hand, Showed pilgrim from the Holy Land.' Scott.
Alice le Palmere, co. Camb., 1273. A.
Ralph le Palmere, co. York, ibid.
Robert le Palmere, co. Linc., ibid.
Richard le Palmere, co. Soms., 1 Edw. III : Kirby's Quest, p. 219.

Roger le Palmere, co. Middlesex, 20 Edw. I. R.
Ricardus Palmer, *mason*, 1379: P. T. Yorks. p. 25.
1565. Henry Palmer and Agnes Hayes. *widow* : Marriage Lic. (London), i. 31.
London, 225 ; Boston (U.S.), 153.

Palphramand. — Offic. A curious corruption of Palfreyman. q.v. The York Directory has also Palfreeman and Palfreman.
York, 1.

Palser.—Occup. 'the paliser' (q. v.). Palser is now the commoner form.

Pamphilon, Pamplin, Plampin, Pampling.—Local or nick. For meaning of the name 'Papillon,' of which these are corruptions, v. Papillon. The following in Halliwell's Dict. may, however, prove that a different application of the word gave them existence. 'Pampilion, a coat of different colours, formerly worn by servants. It occurs with this explanation in Hollyband's Dictionarie, 1593. There was a kind of fur so called.' If a cant name for a servitor attired in butterfly colours, then Pamphilon and Pamplin are nicknames. But the local origin seems the more probable, for which v. Papillon.
Miriel Pampilwn, co. Hunts, 1273. A.
Godfrey Paunphilon, C. R., 33 Edw. I.
Galfridus Pamphilun, 34 Edw. I : BBB. p. 728.
1603. Married —William Mandesford and Margaret Pamplyn: Marriage Lic. (London), i. 277.
Edward Pamphilon, 1710: Reg. St. Mary Aldermary (London), p. 40.
1767. — Thomas Simmons and Esther Pamphilon : St. Geo. Han. Sq. i. 164.
London, 3, 2, 1, o ; Boston (U.S.) (Pampling), 1.

Pancefoot, Pauncefort. — Local, 'de Pauncevote,' probably of Norman extraction. 'In charters it is Latinized De Pede Planco, that is, "of the Splay Foot," but for this rendering there appears to be no authority. The first of the name on record is Bernard Pancevolt, a Domesday tenant-in-chief in Hampshire. Geoffrey de Pauncevote was steward to the household of King John': Lower. Patr. Brit. p. 255.

Isabel Pancefote, C.R., 51 Hen. III.
Lamual Pancevot, co. Hamp., Hen. Edw. I. K.
Elena Pancefot, co. Heref., ibid.
Grimbald Pancefot, co. Hertf., 1273. A.
Walter Pancevot, co. Somerset, ibid.
Richard Pauncefot, co. Glouc., 20 Edw. I. R.
John Paucefot, co. Soms., 1 Edw. III : Kirby's Quest, p. 208.
1544. Robert Barker and Margery Pawnfott : Marriage Lic. (Faculty Office), p. 3.
1676. Tracy Paunsforth and Jane Partridge : ibid. p. 136.
1681. James Bourne and Eliz. Pauncefort : ibid. p. 156.
London, 0, 1 ; Boston (U.S.), 0, 1.

Panckridge.—Bapt. 'the son of Pancras,' popularly styled Pancridge.

'Whilst Pancradge Church, arm'd with a samphier blade,
Began to reason of the businesse thus.'
Taylor's Workes, 1630, i. 120.

For meaning and history of Pancras, v. Miss Yonge's History of Christian Names, i. 211.

'Pancrace Grout sup. for B. Grammar, June, 1532, has been teaching boys thirteen years in the county, &c.': Reg. Univ. Oxf. i. 170.
1698. Married — Robert Panckridge and Margaret Dolman : St. Jas. Clerkenwell, iii. 219.
Crockford, 1 ; MDB. (co. Oxf.), 1.

Pancoast.—Local; a corruption of Pankhurst, q. v. This well-established American surname went out as Pancrust (obviously for Pankhurst). By degrees it settled down as Pancoast.

1635. Anus (Agnes) Pancrust, to New England : Hotten's Lists of Emigrants, p. 87.
1798. Married—Owen Evans and Eliz. Pancoust : St. Geo. Han. Sq. ii. 192. Philadelphia, 47.

Pangbourne, Pangborn.—Local, 'of Pangbourne,' a parish in co. Berks, six miles from Reading.

— Pangeburn (personal name not given), co. Oxf., 1273. A.
London, 1, 0 ; Philadelphia, 0, 2.

Pankhurst.—Local, 'of Penkhurst,' an estate in East Sussex (Lower). For a curious corruption, v. Pancoast.

1798. Married — Nicholas Pankhurst and Eliz. Walter : St. Geo. Han. Sq. ii. 183.
— — Owen Evans and Eliz. Pancoust : ibid. p. 192.

MDB. (co. Kent), 3 ; (co. Sussex), 1 ; London, 7.

Pannell.—Bapt. 'the son of Paynel' (q.v.)', a dim. of Payn or Pain, q.v. ; v. Pannett for a parallel instance. The same individual is thus referred to :

Fukey Panel, co. Notts, Hen. III-Edw. I. K.
Fulco Painel, co. Notts, ibid.

If any doubt existed as to the origin of Pannell, the above quotation settles it.

1584. William Poore and Alice Panell : Marriage Lic. (London), i. 33.
1658. Buried — Ann, wife of Edward Pannell : St. Peter, Cornhill, i. 211.
London, 13.

Pannett.—Bapt. 'the son of Paynot,' a dim. of Payn or Pain, q.v. ; cf. Pannell for Paynel, q.v. In the same way we get Emmett or Emmott from Emma.

Henry Paynot, co. Hunts, 1273. A.
John Paynot, co. Hunts, ibid.
Walter Paynet, co. Soms., 1 Edw. III : Kirby's Quest, p. 141.
Geoffrey Paynet, co. Soms., 1 Edw. III : ibid. p. 230.
Emma Paynot, co. York. W. 2.
John Paynett, temp. Eliz. Z.
1690-1. Francis Milles and Mary Pannot : Marriage Lic. (Faculty Office), p. 198.
London, 2.

Pannier.—Occup.'the pannier,' one who carried bread from house to house for sale, or more officially one who superintended the pantry (v. Pantry) where the bread was kept. v. next article.

Editha Panier, co. Camb., 1273. A.
Robert le Pannier, C. R., 3 Edw. I.
1680. Bapt.—Sarah, d. Daniel Panyer : St. Michael, Cornhill, p. 155.
1690. Buried — Mary Panyer : ibid. p. 272.

I do not suppose the name is extinct, but I cannot find an instance.

Panter, Panther, Pantler.—Offic. 'the panter,' the steward of the pantry, also the baker for the household, a paniter; Fr. pannetier.

Richard le Paneter. C.
Robert le Panter, co. Camb., 1273. A.
Geoffrey le Paneter. G.

The serjeant 'which is called the Chief Pantrer of the kinges mouthe'

(Liber Niger domus Edw. IV, Household Ord., p. 70, quoted by Way in Prompt. Parv.). The Prompt. Parv. has 'panthere, panitarius.' Mr. Way reminds us in a note that this form survives in the surname 'Pantler.' John Russell, in his Boke of Nurture, directs :

'The furst yere, my son, thou shalt be pantere, or buttilare,
Thou must have three knyffes kene in pantry, I say thee, evermare.'

One duty of the monastery panter was the distribution of loaves to the poor (v. Lower, Patr. Brit.). Panther is a somewhat ferocious-looking corruption ; cf. Gunther and Gunter.

1758. Married — Samuel Panter and Mary Smith : St. Geo. Han. Sq. i. 76.
1768. — Daniel Hocknell and Eliz. Panther : ibid. p. 182.
London, 4, 1, 0 ; Oxford, 4, 0, 0.

Panton, ?Pantin, ?Panting.—Local, 'of Panton,' a parish in co. Lincoln.

Hugh de Panton, co. Linc., 1273. A.
Jacop de Panton, co. Linc., ibid.
Baldwin de Panton, co. Linc., Hen. III-Edw. I. K.
William de Panton, co. Linc., ibid.
1769. Married — Peter Morgan and Emry Panton : St. Geo. Han. Sq. i. 189.
London, 2, 1, 1 ; Oxford, 0, 0, 3 ; Philadelphia, 1, 1, 0.

Pantry.—Official, 'at the pantry,' the officer of the pantry ; v. Panter, and cf. Wardrober and de la Wardrobe, Spencer and de la Spence, Kitchener and de la Kitchen.

John de la Paneterie, London, 1273. A.
Henry de la Paneterie, 1307. M.
John atte Pantery, C. R., 6 Hen. IV.
1551. William Pantrie, citizen of Oxford : Reg. Univ. Oxf. pt. i. p. 297.
John Pantrey, M.A., sup. for B.D., 1509, Provost of Queen's, but resigned in 1534 : ibid. p. 66.
1693. Bapt.—Eliz., d. William Pantry : St. Jas. Clerkenwell, i. 353.

Panyerman. — Occup. 'the panyerman,' a peddler, cheap jack.
Richard Panyerman, co. York, 1471. W. 11.

Pape.—Nick. 'the pape,' i.e. Pope. Fr. pape, Latin papa; cf. Cardinal, King, Emperor, &c. ; v. Pope.

Hugo Pape, London, 1273. A.
Ricardus Pap, co. Camb., ibid.
Nicholas Pappe, co. Camb., ibid.
Hugh le Pape. J.
William le Pape, C. R., 39 Hen. III.
pt. i.
Robertus Pape, 1379: P. T. Yorks.
p. 261.
1785. Married — David James and
Betty Pape: St. Geo. Han. Sq. i. 375.
London, 4; MDB. (co. Cumberland),
7; Philadelphia, 7.

Papillon.—Local, ' of the pa-
vilion.' Fr. *pavillon*, ' a pavillion,
tent' (Cotg.). ' So called because
spread out like the wings of a
butterfly. Latin, *papilionem*, acc.
of *papilio*, (1) a butterfly, (2) a tent'
(Skeat). The word was in early
use, and is largely used in our
Authorized Version; cf. Pamphilon
and Pamplin, which are mere
corruptions, but are placed separately, as a different use of the
term *papillon* may have brought
them into the directory.

Toraldus de Papilloyn, co. Dorset, Hen.
III–Edw. I. K.
Nicholas Papalion, co. Linc., 1273. A.
John le Pavillioner (a maker of pavi-
lions), 16 Edw. II: Freemen of York,
i. 21.
Turaldus de Papileon: Hist. Dunelm-
ensis, Surt. Soc. v.
Turald de Papeleon: ibid. vii.
1686–7. Married—Thomas Weely and
Mary Papillon: St. Dionis Backchurch,
p. 41.
1791. Married — Thomas Papillon and
Anne Pelham: St. Geo. Han. Sq. ii. 61.
Crockford, 4.

Papworth.—Local, ' of Papworth,' a parish four miles from
Huntingdon, but on the Cambridgeshire border. This surname
has ramified strongly and extended
far beyond the limits within which
it arose. ' Benjamin Papworth,
shoemaker,' occurs in the Philadelphia Directory (U.S.A.).

John de Pappeworth, co. Camb., 1273.
A.
Aylboda de Papworth, co. Camb., ibid.
Walter de Pappewrth, co. Camb., ibid.
1547. Richard Papworth and Margery
Griffinge: Marriage Lic. (London), i. 11.
1732. Bapt.—Anne, d. Ralph Papworth:
St. Michael, Cornhill, p. 171.
London, 7; MDB. (co. Camb.), 20;
(co. Hunts), 6; Philadelphia, 1.

Paradice, Paradise, Paradis.
—Local, ' of Paradise.' It was
seemingly as common to call a

pretty spot ' a perfect Paradise '
six centuries ago as to-day. The
surname was taken from residence
in some spot familiarly known as
' Paradise.'

'Item, do et lego Willielmo filio meo
unum burgag in Sadlergate, et unum
gardinum in tenurâ Ricardi Arnald juxta
Paradys emptum de Johanne Cuthbert':
Will of Matilda Bowes, 1420 (DDD. i.
278).
John de Paradyshowe, C. R., 5 Ric. II.
Anthony Paradise, C. R., 1–2 Philip and
Mary, pt. ii.
1564. Married—Rychard Paradyse to
Elyzabeth Savage: St. Dionis Back-
church.
John Paradise, 1622: Reg. Broad
Chalke, co. Wilts, p. 16.
Thomas Paradice, vicar of All Saints,
Bristol, 1693: Barrett's Bristol, p. 441.
1791. Married—George Paradice and
Eliz. Guppy: St. Geo. Han. Sq. ii. 67.
London, 1, 0, 0; Boston (U.S.), 0, 3, 0;
New York, 0, 1, 2.

**Paramor, Paramore, Parra-
more.** — Nick. ' the paramour,'
a lover in an honest sense. But
Chaucer says :

' My fourthe husbonde was a revellour,
This is to sayn, he had a paramour.'
John Paramour, co. Linc., 1273. A.
Roger Paramour, 1301. M.
1581. Robert Paramour and Katherine
Warde: Marriage Lic. (London), i. 101.
1623. Bapt. — Mathew, s. Thomas
Parramour: St. Jas. Clerkenwell, i. 96.
'1635. April 18, Whitehall. Captain
Thomas Paramour, appointed to the
Adventure': State Papers, 1635 (Do-
mestic).
1701. John Paramour and Mary
Wallbanke, by banns: Canterbury
Cathedral.
MDB. (co. Devon), 0, 5, 0; Crockford,
0, 3, 0; London, 1, 0, 0; Philadelphia, 0,
7, 2.

Parcheminer. — Occup. ' le
parcheminer,' a maker of parchment, used for testamentary, legal,
and other literary purposes. Fr.
parchemin, parchment. ' Alle bedels,
... alle stacioners, alle bokebynders,
lympners, wryters, pergemeners':
Mun. Acad. Oxon. p. 346. ' The
Parchemyners and Bukbynders
marched together in the York
Pageant': York Mystery Plays,
p. xx.

John le Parchmyner. B.
Hamo le Parchemener. L.
Cristiana le Parchemyner. G.
Geoffrey le Parcheminer. J.
Helena Parchemener, 1379: P. T. Yorks.
p. 98.

Johannes Parmyner, 1379: P. T. Yorks.
p. 48.
The surname seems to have
become extinct.

Parchmenter. — Occup.; v.
Parcheminer. William Parch-
mentar was seized for holding
independent views of the Sacra-
ments (1389); v. Nicholl's Leicestershire Index.

Parchmentmaker.—Occup.;
v. Parcheminer.
William Parchmentmaker, Close Roll,
4 Hen. V.

Pardew, Pardoe.—Nick. ' par
dieu.' This is Lower's suggestion,
and may be true. The common
use of the oath might readily
inflict on the user the epithet.
Parde and *pardy* were the later
forms of the expletive. Nevertheless a local origin for the surname
may be forthcoming; v. Purday.

John Pardieu. H.
1808. Married — James Pardoe and
Sarah Birt: St. Geo. Han. Sq. ii. 397.
London, 0, 2.

Pardon. — Nick. Probably a
sobriquet for one who had received
the royal clemency; cf. Outlaw,
Mainprice, &c. Of course it may
be local, -don being a common
suffix in place-names.

Thomas Pardoun, C. R., 17 Edw. III.
pt. i.
1671. Bapt. — William, s. William
Pardon: St. Jas. Clerkenwell, i. 252.
London, 1.

Pardoner.—Offic. and eccles.
' the pardoner,' a licensed seller
of the Pope's indulgences.
' With him ther rode a gentil pardonere.'

His wallet lay beforne him in his lappe,
Bret-ful of pardon come from Rome al
hote.'
Canterbury Tales, Prologue.
Matthew le Pardouner, Close Roll,
1 Edw. III. pt. i.
Walter le Pardoner, c. 1300. M.
Thomas Pardoner. O.
Johannes Queldryk, *pardoner*, 1379:
P. T. Yorks. p. 99.
This surname does not seem to
have lasted long.

Parfett, Parfitt.—Nick. ' the
perfect.' M.E. *parfit, parfet*; O.F.
parfit.

'He was a veray parfit gentil knight.'
              Chaucer, C. T. 72.
'The Apostle St. Peter, like a perfit workman, . . . first layeth a sure foundation': Archbishop Sandys, Works, Parker Soc., p. 386.
Robert Parfyte. B.
Robert Parfite. H.
1620. Anthony Parfitt: Reg. Univ. Oxf. i. 405.
1717. Married — William Littlebury and Mary Parfitt: St. Jas. Clerkenwell, iii. 241.
1780. — John Parfit and Esther Vickers: St. Geo. Han. Sq. ii. 313.
London, 3, 9; New York, 0, 1.

Pargeter, Pargiter.—Occup. 'the pargeter,' a plasterer, one who rough-casted walls. ' Parget, or playster for wallys, *gipsum*': Prompt. Parv. Way quotes (in a note to above), 'for lathing, pargetting, tiryng and white casting all the roves, walles, particyons, &c., for pargetments, and zelyng with mortre and here': Rokewode's Thingoe Hund. pp. 146, 148.

1533. James Pergetor, co. Norf.: FF. i. 46.
1617. Edmund Pargitur, co. Oxf.: Reg. Univ. Oxf. vol. ii. pt. ii. p. 366.
1644. Married—Thomas Pargiter and Tomsin Dickens: St. Peter, Cornhill, i. 257.
1761. — John Hooke and Mary Pargitter: St. Geo. Han. Sq. i. 106.
London, 3, 0; MDB. (co. Stafford), 2, 0.

Parham, Parram.—Local, 'of Parham,' parishes in cos. Sussex and Suffolk.

Richard de Parham, co. Camb., 1273. A.
John de Perham, co. Sussex, ibid.
Nicholas de Perham, co. Wilts, ibid.
Ralph de Parham, co. Norf. (no date): FF. vi. 170.
1594. Married — John Parham and Margaret Egerton: St. Dionis Backchurch, p. 13.
London, 0, 1; Oxford, 1, 0; Philadelphia, 7, 0.

Paris, Parriss, Parris, Pariss.—Local, 'of Paris.' A common entry in early registers. Of course Parish is inextricably mixed up with it.

Lotyn de Paris, co. Linc., 1273. A.
Robert de Paris, London, ibid.
Ralph de Paris, co. Kent, ibid.
Roger de Paris, London, 20 Edw. I. R.
Simon de Parys, London, 20 Edw. I. R.
Johannes de Parys, 1379: P. T. Yorks. p. 201.

John Parys, co. Soms., 1 Edw. III: Kirby's Quest, p. 142.
1526-7. John Paris and Elena Hevercroft: Marriage Lic. (London), i. 5.
1743. Married — Thomas Paris and Ann Sommons: St. Geo. Han. Sq. i. 29.
London, 20, 3, 1, 0; Boston (U.S.), 5, 0, 4, 1.

Parish, Parrish.—Local, ' of the parish,' from residence within its limits. M.E. *parische*. 'Parysche, *parochia*': Prompt. Parv. p. 384. No doubt at times confounded with Paris, q.v.

Willelmus de Parysch, 1379: P. T. Yorks. p. 164.
Thomas de Parysch, 1379: ibid. p. 123.
Marjoria Parysch, co. York, 1455. W. 11.
1787. Married — Samuel Parrish and Eliz. Farrant: St. Geo. Han. Sq. i. 410.
London, 12, 4; MDB. (co. Linc.), 11, 5; Boston (U.S.), 3, 1.

Park, Parke, Parkes, Parks.—Local, 'at the park,' from residence therein. It must not be forgotten that while Park may be pluralized into Parks and Parkes (cf. Bridges, Styles, Sykes, Dykes), it is just as likely that they are abbreviations of Parkins; cf. Perkins (v. Parkin).

John del Parc, co. Suff., 1273. A.
Roger atte Parke, 1301. M.
William atte Park, C. R., 29 Edw. III.
William Aparke was seized of the manor of Parke, co. Glouc.: Visitation of Glouc., p. 169 (Harl. Soc.).
1611. Bapt. — Eliz., d. Thomas Parkes: St. Jas. Clerkenwell, i. 61.
London, 12, 4, 19, 14; Philadelphia, 81, 19, 5, 37.

Parker.—Occup. ' the parker,' the guardian, keeper, or custodian of a park. Found in every early register all over the country. I furnish but a few instances; v. Park. 'Parcar, *verdier*': Palsgrave. 'Parkere, *indagator*': Prompt. Parv. This surname has almost become a rival of Smith, Wright, Green, Brown, Jones, and Robinson for numbers.

John Parcar, co. Dorset, 1273. A.
Adam le Parker, co. Norf., ibid.
Peter le Parker, co. York, ibid.
Martin le Parkar, co. Soms., 1 Edw. III: Kirby's Quest, p. 205.
Hamo le Parkere. B.
Robert le Parkere. G.
1570. Hugh Parker and Alice Bate-

man, *widow*: Marriage Lic. (London), i. 46.
London, 196; Boston (U.S.), 387.

Parkerson.—Bapt. 'the son of Peter' (v. Parkin); cf. Patterson for Pattinson, or Catterson for Cattinson. Of course, it may be 'the son of the parker' (v. Parker), and belong to a small class of which Smithson, Wrightson, Taylorson, or Hindson are prominent members. But the baptismal derivation is the more probable.

1737. Married — Richard Cook and Margaret Parkerson: St. Geo. Han. Sq. i. 19.
Philadelphia, 5.

Parkes; v. Park.

Parkhill.—Local, 'of the park hill,' i. e. from residence on the hill in the park. I do not know the spot.

Philadelphia, 9.

Parkhouse.—Local, 'at the park house,' the cottage where the parker lived. From residence therein.

Johannes del Parkhouse, 1379: P. T. Yorks. p. 127.
London, 4; New York, 4.

Parkhurst.—Local, ' at the park hurst,' i. e. the wood in the park; v. Hurst. I cannot discover the spot. Mr. Lower says, 'A place in the Isle of Wight.' Of course many places might be so styled.

1581. John Parkehurst, co. Surrey: Reg. Univ. Oxf. pt. ii. p. 95.
1619. Robert Parkhurst, co. Middlesex: ibid. p. 376.
1772. Married — Fleetwood Parkhurst and Ann Danforth: St. Geo. Han. Sq. i. 218.
London, 4; Boston (U.S.), 14.

Parkin, Parkins, Parkinson, Parkisson, Parkeson, Perkin, Perkins, Perkinson, Parkyn, Parkyns.—Bapt. 'the son of Peter,' from the pet Perkin or Parkin; cf. Wat-kin, Wil-kins, Wil-kinson, &c. There are no Perkins or Parkins in the Hundred Rolls, while the French diminutives Perrin and Perrott are common. What may be called the Flemish forms appeared in Yorkshire and the East counties about the beginning of the 14th century. With Perkins and Parkins, cf. Clerk and Clark, Derby and Darby, &c.

Johannes Perkynson, 1379 : P. T. Howdenshire, p. 5.
Johannes Parkynson, 1379: P. T. Yorks. p. 270.
John Perkyn, co. Soms., 1 Edw. III : Kirby's Quest, p. 171.
Robert Perkinson, or Parkinson, 1564 : Reg. Univ. Oxf. i. 254.

Of all the other forms it would be useless to furnish modern instances. Every register has them in abundance.

London, 12, 12, 26, 1, 0, 1, 66, 0, 2, 1 ; MDB. (co. Cornwall), Parkyn, 9; Philadelphia, 5, 1, 37, 0, 1, 0, 75, 2, 1, 0.

Parkman.—Occup. 'the park man.' The same as Parker, q.v. ; cf. Bridger and Bridgman.

1668. Married — Humfrey Parkman and Alice Hyon : St. Jas. Clerkenwell, iii. 151.
1790. — Edmund Smallman and Jane Parkeman : St. Geo. Han. Sq. ii. 37. London, 2 ; New York, 1.

Parlebien, Parlby (?).—? Nick. This name was so generally established in the 13th and 14th centuries that it ought to have left some descendants. Probably Parlby is one of them.

Peter Parlebon, co. Linc., 1273. A.
William Parleben, co. Kent, ibid.
Walter Parleben, co. Linc., 20 Edw. I : R.
John Parlebien, 1336 : PPP. i. 95.
Ricardus Parlebene, 1379 : P. T. Yorks. p. 155.
Robertus Parlebeneson et uxor, 1379 : ibid.
Richard Parlben, vicar of Hemenhale, co. Norf., 1397 : FF. v. 181.
1806. Married—John Parlby and Eliz. Harper : St. Geo. Han. Sq. ii. 347. London, 0, 2.

Parlour, Parlor.—Local, 'at the parlour,' the servant who attended the parlour, literally, 'the room for conversation,' a sitting-room ; cf. Kitchen, Pantry, Spence.

Richard ate Parlur, 1301. M.
Henry del Parlur. B.
William Parlour, co. York. W. 19.
Symon Parler, for the Barbadoes, 1635: Hotten's Lists of Emigrants, p. 73.
1619. David Parler and Anne Pullocke : Marriage Lic. (London), ii. 78.
London, 1, 0 ; MDB. (co. Hereford), 2, 1.

Parman.—Local, 'of Parnham.' Almost every local surname ending in -nham becomes -man by corruption ; cf. Swetman for Swetenham, Deadman for Debenham, &c.

1759. Married—Thomas Parnham and Eliz. Ayscough : St. Geo. Han. Sq. i. 84.
1785. William Bennett and Ann Parnum : ibid. p. 385. London, 2.

Parmelee, Parmele, Parmly, Parmalee.—Local, 'of Palmerley.' I cannot find the spot, though doubtless it exists somewhere in the south of England, nor can I discover any trace of the surname on English soil. It went out to America with the Pilgrim Fathers as Palmerley, i.e. 'the meadow that belonged to the palmer' (v. Palmer); cf. Palmerston.

John Palmerley (aged 20), for New England, 1635, in the Elizabeth and Ann barque : Hotten's Lists of Emigrants, p. 58.

His descendants may be found in most of the cities in the United States in the various disguises enumerated above.

Boston (U.S.), 16, 0, 0, 0 ; New York, 3, 2, 6, 0 ; Philadelphia, 0, 0, 0, 7.

Parmenter, Parmiter, Parminter, Parmater.—Occup. 'le parmentier,' the tailor; O.F. parmentier. 'Parmentier, a taylor' (Cotgrave, quoted by Lower).

Ralph le Parmenter, co. Camb., 1273. A.
Robert Parmintre, co. Oxf., ibid.
Walter le Parmunter, co. Salop, ibid.
John Permonter, co. Soms., 1 Edw. III: Kirby's Quest, p. 153.
Roger Permonter, co. Soms., 1 Edw. III : ibid.
John le Permonter, co. Soms., 1 Edw. III : p. 220.
Roger le Parmenter : Close Roll, 51 Hen. III.
Saher le Parmenter. H.
Hamo le Parmenter. T.
Isabella Parmeter, 1379 : P. T. Yorks. p. 264.
Johannes Parmenter, 1379 : ibid. p. 64.
1530. John Parmynter and Margaret Dunnyngton : Marriage Lic. (London), i. 7.
London, 4, 1, 0, 0 ; Devon Court Dir., 0, 0, 4, 0 ; West Rid. Court Dir., 0, 0, 0, 1 ; Boston (U.S.), 13, 0, 0, 0.

Parnall, Parnell.—Bapt. 'the son of Petronilla.' This was abbreviated to Paronel, and then to Parnel or Pernel. One of our commonest girl-names, it lost character, like Nan and Nanny, by becoming a cant term for women of ill repute. 'Parnel, a lascivious girl' (Bailey). Halliwell says, 'Pernel, the pimpernel, a flower that always shuts up its blossoms before rain.' Then he quotes, 'But these tender pernels must have one gown for the day, another for the night': Pilkington's Works, p. 56. But is not the Puritan bishop referring to Pernel in the sense ascribed above? Endless instances might be given of the name in its earlier and more honest popularity. As usual, Cornwall kept to the name long after it had been given up by the rest of the world :

1706. Bapt. — Peternell Michell : Reg. St. Columb Major, Cornwall.
1714. — Petronell Peters : ibid.

St. Petronilla was besought for fevers. Barnyby Googe says :

'The quartane ague and the rest
  Doth Pernell take away :
And John preserves his worshippers
  From prison every day.'

Petronilla de le Le, co. Oxf., 1273. A.
Pernel Clere, co. Hunts, ibid.
William Peronel, co. Camb., ibid.
Alexander Pernel, co. Camb., ibid.
Johannes Peronele, Hen. III–Edw. I. K.
Ricardus Jannel et Paronel, uxor ejus, 1379 : P. T. Yorks. p. 44.
1528-9. John Thomplynson and Parnell Saunder : Marriage Lic. (London), i. 6.
1680. Bapt. — Robert, s. Arthur and Parnell Dogood : St. Mary Aldermary, p. 105.
1686-7. — William, s. Robert Parnell: St. Dionis Backchurch, p. 128.
London, 2, 12 ; Boston (U.S.), 0, 5.

Parnham.—Local, 'of Barnham' (?). Probably a sharpened form of Barnham, in America found as Barnum ; cf. Peverley for Beverley ; v. Barnum.

1803. Married — William Hoad and Eliz. Parnum : St. Geo. Han. Sq. ii. 295.
1806. — Thomas Parnam and Ann Bearfoot : ibid. p. 358.
Boston (U.S.), 1.

Parnwell.—Bapt. 'the son of Petronilla,' from the popular Parnell (v. Parnall). This was corrupted into Parnwell ; cf. Samwell for Samuel.

Parnwell Graystocke, of Preston, 1670 : Lancashire Wills at Richmond, i. 126.

1801. Married — William Parnewell and Sarah Cockerton: St. Geo. Han. Sq. ii. 245.
London, 1.

Parr.—(1) Local, 'of Parr,' a township in the parish of Prescot, co. Lanc. 'Brian Parre died seised of the manor of Parre in 20 Henry VIII': Baines' Lanc. ii. 248. Catharine Parr, wife of Henry VIII, was sprung of the Parrs of Parr. (2) Bapt. 'the son of Peter,' from Pierre, commonly in England Parr; cf. Parratt and Parkin.

Alan de Par, co. Lanc., 46 Edw. III : Lanc. and Ches. Rec. Soc. vol. viii. p.370n.
Richard Parr, co. Lanc., 1637: ibid. vol. xi. p. 25.
1618. Alexander Parr, parish of Prescot, co. Lanc.: Wills at Chester, i. 148.
1649. Richard Parr, co. Surrey, and Eliz. Moyse: Marriage Lic. (Faculty Office), p. 42.
London, 22; Manchester, 9; Philadelphia, 17.

Parram; v. Parham.

Parramore.—Nick.; v. Paramor.

Parratt, Parrett, Parritt, Parrott, Perratt, Perrett, Perot, Perrot, Perrott, Porrett. — (1) Bapt. 'the son of Peter,' from Fr. Pierre, dim. Perrot or Parrot (little Peter). *Par* and *Per* are similarly found in Parkinson or Perkinson, Parkins or Perkins; v. Porrett. (2) Nick. 'the parrot,' i.e. the chatterer. The origin is exactly the same, the application only being different. In France *pierrot*, i.e. little Peter, is still the name for a sparrow, as Robin with us for the redbreast. The first instance below will prove how early the diminutive of Peter gave name to the tropical bird we are familiar with, and how popular the name of Peter was; cf. *mag-pie*, and v. Philipshank.

William le Perot, 1277. M.
Ralph Perot, 1277. M.
Simon Peret, 1290. M.
Perot Gruer. G.
Thomas Perret. H.
Perrot Loppes: see Index, Wars of English in France, Henry VI.
John Porrett, or Perott, or Parott, or Parrett, 1520: Reg. Univ. Oxf. i. 113.
Edward Parrett, or Perott, or Perrett, 1546: ibid. p. 212.

Parrott is the commonest form in the United States.

London, 1, 8, 1, 12, 2, 6, 9, 0, 0, 1; Oxford (Parrott), 5; Philadelphia, 1, 0, 0, 12, 0, 3, 1, 0, 16, 5.

Parrin.—Bapt. 'the son of Peter,' a variant of Perrin, q.v.; cf. Parkin and Perkin, or Parratt and Perrott, all from the same source.

Lawrence Parrin, of Manchester, *felt-maker*, 1647: Wills at Chester (1621-50), p. 169.
Adam Perrin, of Pendleton, Manchester, *yeoman*, 1666: ibid. (1660-80), p. 204.
Manchester, 1.

Parris, Parriss; v. Paris.

Parrish; v. Parish.

Parrock, Parrick. — Local, 'at the parrock,' i.e. park. 'Parrocke, a lytell parke, *parquet*' (Palsgrave). The modern form *paddock* is a corruption (v. Skeat, *paddock* 2); Halliwell, *parrick*; Prompt. Parv. *parrok*. A.S. *pearroc*, a small enclosure. The surname Parrick is a modern variant of Parrock.

Elwin de Parrok, co. Kent, 1273. A.
John de la Parocke, co. Sussex, ibid.
John de la Parroke, co. Sussex, 20 Edw. I. R.
1553. Philip Parrock, rector of Feltwell, co. Norf.: FF. i. 198.
1791. Married—William Worster and Eliz. Parrock: St. Geo. Han. Sq. ii. 59.
1805. Samuel Croft and Hannah Parrick: ibid. p. 332.
London, 3, 0; Boston (U.S.), 0, 1.

Parrott; v. Parratt.

Parry.—(1) Bapt. 'Ap-Harry' (Welsh), i.e. 'the son of Harry'; cf. Pritchard, Bowen, Price, Bethell, &c.

Stephen ap-Parry: Cal. State Papers, Hen. VIII (see Index).
John Ap-harry, 1541: Reg. Univ. Oxf. i. 202.
1569-70. Hugh Apparrye and Elizabeth Pynner: Marriage Lic. (London), i. 44.
1584. Richard Jones and Dousam Apharrye: ibid. p. 134.

(2) Bapt. 'the son of Peter,' from Fr. Pierre. This was popularly Parr (v. Parr, 2). Hence Par-kin, Par-son, Parr-att, q.v. Hence also the pet form Parry; cf. Charley, Teddie, Willy, &c.

John Pary, co. Camb., 1273. A.
Johannes Parrey, 1379: P. T. Yorks. p. 92.

For a similar double English and Welsh name, cf. Powell.

London, 36; Philadelphia, 31.

Parsley, Parslow.—Local, 'of Passelewe,' further corruptions of a once famous name; v. Pashley and Pashler.

1794. Married — Thomas Cropp and Jane Parsley: St. Geo. Han. Sq. ii. 121.
1802. — William Parsloe and Ann Raine: ibid. p. 262.
London, 4, 2; Oxford, 1, 2.

Parson. — (1) Official, 'the parson.' For further instances, v. Parsonson.

William Persona, co. Norf., 1273. A.
John Person, co. Soms., 1 Edw. III:
Kirby's Quest, p. 206.
Walter le Persone. H.
1570. Married—John Bayes and Margaret Persone: St. Jas. Clerkenwell, p. 4.

(2) Bapt. 'the son of Peter,' from Fr. Pierre, popularly in England (among other forms) Parr.

John Parson, co. Soms., 1 Edw. III:
Kirby's Quest, p. 142.
1425. John Paresson, rector of Yaxham, co. Norf.: FF. x. 283.
1581. Married — John Willson and Hellen Parson: St. Jas. Clerkenwell, iii. 9.
London, 5; Devon Court Dir., 5; Philadelphia, 7.

Parsonage. — Local, 'of the parsonage,' from residence therein as attendant on the minister; cf. Vickridge, Priestman.

John Parsonage, 1575: St. Dionis Backchurch (London), p. 194.
1789. Married — James Ackland and Phoebe Parsonage: St. Geo. Han. Sq. ii. 16.
London, 1; Manchester, 2; Sheffield, 1.

Parsonson, Parsons.—Nick. 'the parson's son'; cf. Taylorson, Hindson, Smithson, Clerkson, &c. A small but distinct class of surnames. Parsons is genitive; cf. Williams, Jones, &c.

Clemens fil. Persone, co. Norf., 1273. A.
William Parson, co. Soms., 1 Edw. III:
Kirby's Quest, p. 104.
John Personson, Pardons Roll, 6 Ric. II.
Johannes Parsonson, 1379: P. T. Yorks. p. 18.
Isabel Parsones, co. Soms., 1 Edw. III:
Kirby's Quest, p. 173.
1570. Married — Thomas Parsons and Agnes Smythe: St. Jas. Clerkenwell, iii. 4.

1775. Married — William Horrex and Ann Parsonson : St. Geo. Han. Sq. i. 258.
West Rid. Court Dir., 3, 3 ; Sheffield, 1, 1 ; Oxford, 0, 14 ; Philadelphia, 0, 52.

Part. — ? Bapt. 'the son of Peter' (?), an abbreviation of Parot ; v. Parratt. I have no actual proof, but strongly suspect this is the derivation. v. Peart.

John Part, of Hale, 1590 : Wills at Chester, i. 148.
Robert Part, of Ditton, 1610 : ibid.
1618. James Part and Anne Hayward: Marriage Lic. (London), ii. 65.
London, 4.

Partington.—Local, ' of Partington,' a parish in co. Chester. This surname is well known in South Lancashire.

Adam Partington, Barton-on-Irwell, 1541 : Subsidy Roll, Salford Hundred, L. & C. R. S., p. 140.
1616. Married—John Partington and Ellen Foster: Prestbury Church, co. Ches., p. 210.
George Partington, of Partington, yeoman, 1646 : Wills at Chester, ii. 169.
Manchester, 15 ; London, 4 ; New York, 4.

Partree ; v. Peartree, of which it is a variant.

Boston (U.S.), 1.

Partridge.—Nick. 'the partridge.' M.E. partriche, pertriche. Cf. Nightingale, Wildgoose, Sparrow, &c. Also cf. Aldridge for Aldrich.

Walter Purtrich, co. Camb., 1273. A.
Gilbert Partrich, co. Oxf., ibid.
Ancelm Partrich, c. 1300. M.
Hugh Pertrich, C. R., 3 Edw. I.
Adam Pertrich, co. Soms., 1 Edw. III : Kirby's Quest, p. 89.
Thomas le Partrich, co. Soms., 1 Edw. III : ibid. p. 91.
Robertus Pertryk, 1379 : P. T. Yorks. p. 201.
1719. Married—Wharton Partridge and Joanna Roberts: St. Michael, Cornhill, p. 671.
London, 46 ; Philadelphia, 17.

Pascall, Paskell, Pascal.—Bapt. 'the son of Pascall'; v. Pash and Pask. This font-name lingered on in Cornwall long after the Reformation.

Pascowe, son of John Langdon, 1571 : Reg. St. Columb Major, p. 7.
Philep, d. of Paskell Langdon, 1606: ibid. p. 22.
Richard, son of Paskell Langdon, 1608 : ibid. p. 24.

1585. William Pascoll and Agnes Urlyn : Marriage Lic. (London), i. 139.
1803. Married—Robert Brown and Eliz. Paskall : St. Geo. Han. Sq. ii. 288.
London, 3, 2, 0 ; Philadelphia, 0, 2, 1.

Paschall.—Bapt. 'the son of Pascall,' q.v., a variant ; cf. Pash and Pask.

John Paschall, Suffragan Bishop of Norwich, 1344 : FF. iv. 422.
1578. John Paschall (co. Essex) and Mary Bridges : Marriage Lic. (London), i. 83.
Philadelphia, 10.

Pascoe.—Bapt. 'the son of Pascall'; an English provincialism ; cf. Pentecost, Nowell, Christmas, Tiffany, &c. Pascoe still exists as a font-name in Cornwall, that last sanctuary of decayed English personal names.

Pascow, d. of Henrie Yolde, 1542 : Reg. St. Columb Major, p. 2.
John, son of Stephen Pascowe, 1549 : ibid. p. 5.
Pascowe, son of John Langdon, 1571 : ibid. p. 7.
James, son of Pauscow Anhey, 1551 : ibid. p. 6.
Paskow, son of Thomas Vivian, 1590: ibid. p. 15.
1725. Married — William Pascoe and Mary Ridge, widow : St. Jas. Clerkenwell, p. 252.
1796. — Edward Pasco and Mary Phillips : St. Geo. Han. Sq. ii. 152.
London, 6 ; MDB. (co. Cornwall), 19 ; Philadelphia, 17.

Pash, Pashson.—Bapt. 'the son of Pasche' (i. e. Easter); v. Pask. 'Also, we command that no manner of men walk in the city, nor in the suburbs by night, without torch before him, from Pasche to Michaelmas after ten of the clock, and from Michaelmas to Pasche after nine of the clock': Hist. and Ant. York, ii. 54.

Hugh fil. Pasche, co. Camb., 1273. A.
Joseph Pach, co. Camb., ibid.
Felicia relicta Pasche, co. Camb., ibid.
Robertus Pache, 1379 : P. T. Yorks. p. 62.
Thomas Pasch, 1379 : ibid. p. 114.
Antony Paschesoun, Norwich, 1571 : FF. ii. 288.
1770. Married—Edward Wild and Ann Pash : St. Geo. Han. Sq. i. 204.
London, 5, 0.

Pashler.—Local. Doubtless a variant of Passelewe (v. Pashley). It is found in the district wherein

the surname flourished for many centuries.

MDB. (co. Hunts), 5 ; (co. Suffolk), 1.

Pashley, Pasley.—Local, ' of Passelewe,' now Pashley or Pasley, a manor in the parish of Ticehurst, co. Sussex (Lower). I doubt whether this is correct. There is no trace of a Sussex parentage. I suspect it is of Norman extraction, although we need not accept Skinner's etymology : ' à Fr. passe l'eau, sc. a tranando vel transeundo aquam.' This is a meaningless guess. Possibly Lower is correct, and it may be that the name passed from Sussex to Norfolk at an early period. Nevertheless, without proof it is not satisfactory.

Robert Passelewe, co. Norf., 1273. A.
Ralph de Passelewe, co. Norf. (no date): FF. vii. 72.
1450. John Passelaw, canon of West Dereham, co. Norf. : ibid. vi. 93.
1622. Married — Robert Northam and Alice Paslew : St. Jas. Clerkenwell, iii. 51.
1809. — John Pasley and Maria Jackson: St. Geo. Han. Sq. ii. 408.
For further corruptions v. Parsley, Parslow, and Pashler.
London, 1, 1 ; MDB. (co. Norfolk), 1, 0 ; (co. Suffolk), 1, 0 ; Philadelphia, 1, 0.

Pask, Paske.—Bapt. 'the son of Pask' (i. e. Easter) ; cf. Pascall, Noel, Christmas, Pentecost, Whitsunday, &c. v. Pash. The harder Pask is found in Wyclif. 'Whanne Jhesus hadde endid all these words, he seide to his disciplis, ye weten that after tweyn days Paske schal be made': Matt. xxvi. 1.

' Witnesse in the Pask wyke
Whan he yede to Emaus.'
Piers P. 7027-8.

John Pask, co. Oxf., 1273. A.
1634. Thomas Paske, co. Norf. : FF. vi. 285.
1651. Married—Thomas strato (sic) and Paskey Prideaux : Reg. St. Peter, Cornhill, i. 258.
1702. — Samuel Boldwin and Martha Paske: St. Dionis Backchurch, p. 50.
London, 4, 1.

Paskell.—Bapt. ; v. Pascall.

Pasket. — Bapt. 'the son of Pask' (q.v.), dim. Pask-et ; cf. the softer form, Patchett. No doubt Baskett (q.v.) is an imitative corruption.

William Pasket, co. Berks, 1273. A. New York, 1.

Paskin, Paskins.—Bapt. 'the son of Pask,' dim. Pask-in (v. Pask); cf. French and Italian Pasquina or Paschina.

Paskinus Mercator. C.
London, 0, 1 ; West Rid. Court Dir., 1, 0; MDB. (co. Stafford), 0, 1.

Pasmore.—Local, 'of Pasmore.' I cannot find the spot.

Adam Passmere, co. Soms., 1 Edw. III : Kirby's Quest, p. 234.
London, 7.

Pass.—Bapt. 'the son of Pash' (q.v.). One more of the endless variants of this great Easter name.

Richard dict' Pas, co. Camb., 1273. A.
Robert Passe, co. Sussex, ibid.
Nigel Passe, co. Norf., ibid.
William Pas, 1379 : P. T. Yorks. p. 218.
Johanna Pas, 1379 : ibid.
London, 4 ; West Rid. Court Dir., 2.

Passage.—Local, ' of the passage,' from residence in an entry or narrow thoroughfare ; cf. Twitchen, Gore, Goreway, &c.

Adam de Passagio, co. Suff., 1273. A.
Agnes del Passage, co. Suff., ibid.
Walter Passage, co. Soms., 1 Edw. III :
Kirby's Quest, p. 154.

Passavant.—Offic. 'a pursuivant,' a messenger, one who attended upon the herald in royal processions or journeys. This seems to be the meaning.

Adam Passevaunt, co. Wilts, 1273. A.
Walter Passavant, C. R., 33 Hen. III.
Roger Passavant. E.
William Passavaunt. H.
West Rid. Court Dir., 3.

Passenger, Passager.—Nick. 'the passenger,' a wayfarer, a traveller, from O.F. *passager*, with intrusive *n* ; cf. Messenger.

1771. Married—William Leutten and Rebecca Passenger : St. Geo. Han. Sq. i. 208.
London, 2, 0 ; Philadelphia, 0, 1 ; MDB. (co. Kent), 1, 0.

Passey.—Local, ' de Pasey.' Probably from some spot in Normandy.

Robert de Pasey, co. Linc., 1273. A.
1635. Bapt. — Richard, s. Valentine Passie : St. Jas. Clerkenwell, i. 130.
1798. Married — William Blain and Mary Passey : St. Geo. Han. Sq. ii. 176:
London, 1 ; Oxford, 1.

Passingham.—Local, ' of Passenham,' a parish in co. Northampton.

1762. Married—Robert Passingham and Eliz. Lloyd : St. Geo. Han. Sq. i. 115.
London, 2 ; MDB. (co. Bedford), 1 ; (co. Camb.), 1.

Paston.— Local, ' of Paston.' Parishes in cos. Norfolk and Northampton ; also a township in the parish of Kirk Newton, co. Northumberland.

Eustace de Paston, co. Norf., 1273. A.
Warin de Paston, co. Norf., ibid.
Alicia de Paston, 1379 : P. T. Yorks. p. 50.
1665. Buried—John Paston, servant to John Clerke, *stationer* : St. Peter, Cornhill, i. 219.

Patch.—(1) Bapt. 'the son of Pache' (i.e. Easter), one of almost endless variants of Pasche ; v. Pask, Pash, Pass, Pace, Peace, Pease, &c. For a dim., v. Patchett.

John Pacche, co. Bucks, 1273. A.
Richard Pacche, co. Oxf., ibid.
Robertus Pache, 1379 : P. T. Yorks. p. 62.

(2) Nick. 'Patch,' an old name for the official fool, a very honourable personage in his day. Wolsey had two fools, both occasionally called Patch (v. Douce, Illustrations of Shakespeare, i. 258). It is hard to say which, (1) or (2), is meant in the following :

'Item, the same day to Pache in rewarde for bringing a present,' 1502 : Privy Purse Exp., Eliz. of York, p. 74.
'Item, delivered to Pache, for a present of poyngarnettes oranges,' 1503 : ibid. p. 93.

The following is obvious :

'And ii payer (of hosen) for patche, the kinges fole (fool),' 1530 : Privy Purse Expenses, Henry VIII, p. 86.
1610. Married — Richard Patch and Catherine Major : St. Jas. Clerkenwell, iii. 36.
1614. John Blague and Anne Patche : Marriage Lic. (London), ii. 30.
London, 3 ; Boston (U.S.), 41.

Patchell.—(1) Bapt. 'the son of Pascal,' q.v. This became Paschall and Patchell ; v. Patch and Patchett. (2) Local, 'of Pattishall,' a parish in co. Northampton (v. Pateshall). It is possible this is the true derivation. From Pateshall

to Patchell is but a single and easy step.

1738. Martha Patchell, *pensioner*, died Aug. 15 : St. Dionis Backchurch, p. 306.
Boston (U.S.), 2 ; Philadelphia, 10.

Patchett.—Bapt. 'the son of Pache' (i.e. Easter), from the dim. Pachet, one becoming popularly Patch (q.v.) and the other Patchet. There can be no doubt about this derivation (v. Pash, Pask, Pace, Peace, Pease, &c.). Patchett is still a well-known Yorkshire surname.

Gilbert Pachet, co. Suff., 1273. A.
Richard Pachet, co. Oxf., ibid.
John Pachet, co. Soms., 1 Edw. III :
Kirby's Quest, p. 125.
Henry Pachet, co. Soms., 1 Edw. III :
ibid. p. 186.
Cecilia Pachet, *souster*, 1379 : P. T.
Yorks. p. 229.
Alicia Pachot, 1379 : ibid. p. 126.
1571. Richard Pachet, rector of Litcham, co. Norf. : FF. x. 14.
1766. Married—Thomas Robinson and Ann Patchitt : St. Geo. Han. Sq. i. 154.
1790. — George Patchett and Eleanor Vaughan : ibid. ii. 39.
London, 1 ; West Rid. Court Dir. 8; Boston (U.S.), 1 ; Oxford, 1.

Patching, Patchen. — (1) Bapt. 'the son of Pachin,' from Pach (Easter), dim. Pachin or Pachon ; cf. Patch (q.v.) for Pach. The g is, of course, excrescent, as in Jennings. Rob-in and Col-in are familiar examples of this dim. in England, and Alison (little Alice) in Scotland.

Johannes Pachon, co. Oxf., 1273. A.

(2) Local, 'of Patching,' a parish in co. Sussex, five miles from Arundel. As I find the surname is well known in co. Sussex, this must claim first place.

1422. Thomas Pacchyng : Cal. of Wills in Court of Husting (2).
1783. Married—William Watson and Ann Patching : St. Geo. Han. Sq. i. 342.
1809. — Payn Patching and Sarah Whitehouse : ibid. ii. 420.
London, 1, 0 ; MDB. (co. Sussex), 4, 0 ; New York, 0, 4.

Pate, Pates.—Bapt. 'the son of Patrick,' from nick. Pate or Pait (Irish Pat). A great North-English name in its day ; v. Patey and Paitson.

Walter Patte, co. Camb., 1273. A.
Willelmus Payt, 1379 : P. T. Yorks. p. 59.

Cecilia Payt, 1379 : P. T. Yorks. p. 227.
Johannes Patte, 1379 : ibid.
1573. Henry Pate and Ann Stebber-
yncke : Marriage Lic. (London), i. 56.
1574. Robert Pates and Johanna Vynte,
widow : ibid. p. 58.
1723. Bapt.—John, s. William Pate :
St. Jas. Clerkenwell, ii. 140.
London, 1, 2 ; New York, 6, 0.

Pateman, Patman. — (1)
Occup. ' Pate-man,' i.e. the servant of Pate, i.e. Patrick ; cf.
Addyman, Matthewman, Jackman,
&c. ; a fairly large class. (2) Bapt.
' the son of Bateman ' (q.v.), a
sharpened form ; cf. Peverley for
Beverley or Parnham for Barnham.
1652. Married— Francis Patman and
Mary Graunt : St. Jas. Clerkenwell, iii. 88.
1786. — Thomas Harwood and Ann
Patman : St. Geo. Han. Sq. ii. 383.
London, 5, 4.

Paternoster. — Occup. ' the
paternostrer,' a maker of pater-
nosters, rosaries, chaplets, beads
strung together for pattering aves.
Paternoster Row may have been
the Paternosters' Row.
' And thanne was it a pece of the pater-
  noster,
  Fiat voluntas tua.'
     Piers Plowman's Vision, 9006.
1276. Robert Ornel, *paternoster* :
Riley, Memorials of London, p. xxi.
William le Paternostrer, London. X.
Robert Paternoster, co. Camb., 1273. A.
John Paternoster, co. Camb., ibid.
Stephen Paternoster, co. Norf., ibid.
Roger Paternoster, C. R., 17 Ric. II.
1789. Married — George Paternoster
and Sarah Collins : St.Geo. Han. Sq. i. 18.
London, 7.

Paterson ; v. Pattinson.

Pates ; v. Pate.

Pateshall.—Local, ' of Pattis-
hall,' a parish in co. Northampton,
four miles from Towcester ; cf.
Patchell (2).
John de Pateshulle, co. Bedf., 1273. A.
Robert de Patheshulle, co. Oxf., ibid.
1583-4. Philip Tourner and Katherine
Pattsell : Marriage Lic. (London), i. 129.
1596. William Patshall, co. Hereford :
Reg. Univ. Oxf. vol. ii. pt. ii. p. 213.
MDB. (co. Hereford), 3 ; London, 2.

Patey, Paty.—Bapt. ' the son
of Patrick,' from nick. (North England and Border) Pait, Pate, or
Patey ; v. Paitson. In the North
this nick. lasted till modern times ;
v. Pattie.

John Pati, co. Linc., 1273. A.
Hugh Paty, co. Notts, ibid.
Robert Paty, co. Soms., 1 Edw. III :
Kirby's Quest, p. 120.
' Geordie of Calfhill, Patie of the Haire-
lowe, Willie Cany, &c.,' 1587 : Nicolson
and Burn, Hist. Westm. and Cumb., vol. i.
p. xxxv.
Patie Grannie, 1587 : ibid.
' Patie's Geordie's Johnie,' 1552 : ibid.
p. lxxxii.
1581. Robert Patye or Patie : Reg.
Univ. Oxf. vol. ii. pt. iii. p. 97.
1706. Bapt.—John, s. Humphrey Paty :
St. Jas. Clerkenwell, ii. 29.
London, 6, 0 ; Boston (U.S.), 0, 1.

Patman ; v. Pateman.

Patmore,Pattemore.—Local,
' of Patmer,' a hamlet in the parish
of Albury, co. Hertford.
Philip de Patmere, co. Camb., 1273. A.
1802. Married—Edward Patmore and
Hannah Isaac : St. Geo. Han. Sq. ii. 256.
MDB. (co. Essex), 7, 0 ; (co. Herts),
3, 0 ; (co. Somerset), 0, 2.

Paton. — Bapt. ' the son of
Patrick,' from nick. Pate or Pat,
and dim. Pat-on ; v. Patten. This
was the favourite Border form, and
remains a Scottish surname to-day ;
cf. Alison for Alice, or Marion for
Mary. It must be remembered
that Patrick was one of the most
popular of North-English font-
names in the surname period.
Agnes Paton-wyf, i. e. the wife of Paton,
C. R., 18 Hen. VI.
The following is decidedly
Scottish :
1774. Married—David Paton and Jane
Blair : St. Geo. Han. Sq. i. 236.
London, 9 ; New York, 17.

Patrick, Patrickson.—Bapt.
' the son of Patrick.' A once great
North-English font-name, leaving
many descendants ; v. Pattinson,
Patterson, Pate, Paitson, Patey,
Pattie, &c. The Cumberland sur-
name of Patrickson is almost extinct,
but has a representative living in
Furness, North Lancashire.
William Patric, co. Linc., 1273. A.
Ivo Patryk, co. Essex, ibid.
Ralph Paterik, co. Hertf., 20 Edw.
I. R.
Patric de Culwen, 35 Edw. I : Westm.
and Cumb. i. 91.
Willelmus Patrik, 1379 : P. T. How-
denshire, p. 25.
Johannes Patryk, 1379 : P. T. Yorks.
p. 47.
John Paterik, 1379 : ibid. p. 141.

1566. William Patrickson, fellow of
Queen's, 1569 : Reg. Univ. Oxf. i. 251.
Queen's is, by its endowments,
the recognized Cumberland college.
1793. Married—John Patrick and Mary
Ann Mills : St. Geo. Han. Sq. ii. 103.
London, 15, 0 ; Scales (Ulverston), 0,
1 ; Philadelphia, 17, 0.

Pattemore ; v. Patmore.

Patten, Patton.—Bapt. ' the
son of Patrick,' from the nick. Pate,
and dim. Patt-in or Patt-on ; v.
Paton and Pattinson. Mr. Lower
quotes Burke's Landed Gentry to
the following effect :
' Richard Patten, son and heir of
Richard Patten, was of Patine, or Patten,
near Chelmsford, co. Essex, in 1119.
From him the Pattens of Bank Hall, co.
Lanc., claim lineal descent' : Patr. Brit.
p. 258.
I do not assert that this is true or
false. All I say is that the Scottish
and North-English Pattens have
no local derivation, but are the
sons of Patrick.
1583. Edward Patten and Dorothy
Wainforde : Marriage Lic. (London),
i. 122.
1695. Bapt.—Martha, d. Thomas Patton : St. Jas. Clerkenwell, i. 361.
London, 10, 4 ; New York, 21, 22.

Pattenden.—Local, ' of Pattenden.' I do not know where the
spot is located.
Henry Pattenden, or Battenden, B.A.,
1582-3 : Reg. Univ. Oxf. vol.ii. pt.iii.p. 112.
1790. Married — George Fowle and
Margaret Pattenden : St. Geo. Han. Sq.
iii. 39.
London, 3.

Pattenmaker, Pattener.—
Occup. ' the pattener,' i.e. a maker
of pattens. ' Pateyne, of tymbyre
or yron to walke with, *calopo-
dium*' : Prompt. Parv. ' Calopifex,
a maker of patens or styltes ' :
Ortus. ' Paten-maker, *patinier* ' :
Palsg. Mr. Way says : ' Used by
ecclesiastics when treading the
cold pavement of a church,' and
quotes church accounts of St. Mary
Hill, London, 1491, ' for ii pair of
pattens for the priests.' But he
adds that they were part of every
gentleman's costume. In 1464 the
Patynmakers of London alleged as
a grievance that the ' fletchers
alone could use aspen wood; the

lightest tymbre to make of patyns and clogges': Rot. Parl. iv. 567.

'Alys easy a gay tale-teller,
Also Peter Patynmaker.'
Cocke Lorelle's Bote.

John Rykedon, *patynmaker*, 1412 : R R. 1.
Robert Patener, et Mariona uxor ejus, co. York. W. 11.
James Patynmakere. S.
1641. John Pattener and Anne Rainer : Marriage Lic. (London), ii. 256.

Patterson ; v. Pattinson.

Pattie, Patty.—Bapt. 'the son of Patrick,' from nick. Pate, dim. Patie and Pattie ; v. Patey for instances. Chiefly found in Northumberland, as would be expected.

1795. Married — James Hannam and Martha Patty : St. Geo. Han. Sq. ii. 129.
1804. — Philip Hind and Lucy Pattey : ibid. p. 309.
London, 1, 0 ; Newcastle, 3, 0 ; New York, 0, 1.

Pattinson, Pattison, Patteson, Pattisson, Patterson, Paterson.—Bapt. 'the son of Patrick' (q.v.), from the nick. Pate and dim. Patt-in ; cf. Colin, Robin. Patterson is a corruption of Pattinson ; cf. Matterson, Dickerson, Catterson, for Mattinson, Dickinson, Catterson. Patrick was a great North-English font-name in the surname period. It would be useless furnishing many instances. Sufficient will be found under Pate, Patten, Paton, &c.

Patricius Syke, 1379: P. T. Yorks. p. 263.
Patricius Hyrd, 1379 : ibid. p. 268.
Patricius et uxor, 1379 : ibid.
Robert Pattenson, co. York. W. 15.
1598. Bapt. — Margaret, d. William Pattinson : St. Jas. Clerkenwell, i. 34.
1614. — Hector, s. Daniell Pattisonne : ibid. i. 69.
1697. Thomas Pateson, rector of Welborne, co. Norf. : FF. ii. 453.
London, 5, 15, 4, 3, 20, 20 ; New York, 0, 9, 3, 0, 151, 21.

Patton ; v. Patten.

Paul, Paulson, Pawle.—Bapt. 'the son of Paul'; v. Pawson.

Stephen Paul, co. Notts, 1273. A.
1521. John Pawle : Reg. Univ. Oxf. i. 120.
1588. John Paule and Agnes Haywarde : Marriage Lic. (London), i. 174.
1702. Bapt.—Eliz., d. Richard Paulson : St. Jas. Clerkenwell, ii. 7.
Sheffield, 0, 1, 0 ; London, 32, 1, 2 ; Boston (U.S.), Paulson, 3.

Paulden, Paulding.—Local, 'of Paulden.' I cannot find the

spot. The *g* in Paulding is excrescent, as in Jennings. Evidently a Yorkshire or, at least, North-English local surname.

Johannes de Paldeyn, 1379 : P. T. Yorks. p. 284.
1402. Richard Paldene, rector of Northenden : East Cheshire, i. 289.
1672. John Palden, of Bowdon : Wills at Chester (1660–80), p. 203.
1771. Married — William Woods and Ann Paulden : St. Gro. Han. Sq. i. 211.
1784. — William Broderick and Eliz. Paulding : ibid. p. 359.
Manchester, 2, 0 ; Boston (U.S.), 0, 6.

Paulett, Pawlett, Paulet.—Local, 'of Pawlett,' a parish in co. Somerset.

Isabel Pawlett. B.
Amys Pawlet. H.
John Paulett. H.
Agnes Poulet, co. Soms., 1 Edw. III : Kirby's Quest, p. 171.
1579. Anthony Paulet, co. Soms. : Reg. Univ. Oxf. vol. ii. pt. ii. p. 91.
1580. George Paulet, co. Soms. : ibid.
1742. Bapt. — John, s. Thomas Pawlet : St. Jas. Clerkenwell, ii. 258.
Crockford, 1, 0, 1.

Pauley, Pauly ; v. Pawley.

Paulin, Pawlin, Paullin, Pauline, Pauling, Pawling.—Bapt. 'the son of Paul,' from the dim. Paul-in ; cf. Col-in, Rob-in. The *g* in Pauling is, of course, excrescent ; cf. Jennings.

Paulinus de Bointon, co. Oxf., 1273. A.
Paulin de Basset, co. Oxf., ibid.
Augustin fil. Paulin, co. Hunts, ibid.
Roger Paulyn, co. Oxf., ibid.
Poleyn le Webbe, co. Soms., 1 Edw. III : Kirby's Quest, p. 125.
John Paulyn, co. Soms., 1 Edw. III : ibid. p. 18.
William Pawelyn, 1397 : Preston Guild Rolls, p. 1.
1581-2. Thomas Pawlyn and Eliz. Hope : Marriage Lic. (London), i. 107.
1607. William Paulinge, co. Worc. : Reg. Univ. Oxf. vol. ii. pt. ii. p. 299.
1702. Bapt.—Adam, s. William Paulin : St. Jas. Clerkenwell, ii. 9.
London, 2, 0, 0, 0, 0 ; Oxford (Pauling), 2 ; Philadelphia, 5, 0, 18, 4, 2, 3.

Paulson ; v. Paul.

Pauncefort.—Local; v. Pancefoot.

Pauper.—Nick. 'the pauper'; v. Power.

Mathew le Pauper, London, 1273. A.
William le Pauper, co. Oxf., ibid.

Pavely.—Local, 'of Pavely.' I cannot find the place.

John de Pavely, co. Norf., 1273. A.
Robert de Pavely, co. Bucks, ibid.
Geoffrey de Pavely, co. Oxf., ibid.
Reginald de Pavely, co. Wilts, 20 Edw. I. R.
Walter de Pavely, co. Soms., 1 Edw. III : Kirby's Quest, p. 84.
1572-3. John Paveley and Eliz. Spryver ; Marriage Lic. (London), i. 55.
1800. Married — Mark Scadding and Ann Pavely : St. Geo. Han. Sq. ii. 224.
London, 6.

Pavett, Pavitt.—Bapt. 'the son of Pavia' (q.v.), popularly Pavey, dim. Pav-ette.

1591. Buried—Edward, s. John Pavet, *cuntryman* : St. Peter, Cornhill, i. 139.
1763. Married — Joseph Stafford and Jane Pavet : St. Geo. Han. Sq. i. 121.
1805. — Charles Pavitt and Ann Wykes: ibid. ii. 331.
London, 2, 7 ; Philadelphia, 0, 6.

Pavia, Pavey, Pavy, Pavie.—Bapt. 'the son of Pavia,' popularly Pavey. Probably closely related to Paulina (v. Yonge, i. 351). Lat. Parva. With the diminutives Pavin and Pavett (q.v.), cf. Paulin and Paulett, strengthening the view taken above.

Pavia, widow of Robert de Grinsdale, E. and F., co. Cumb., p. 155.
'In the 12th year of King Henry III, Radulph, the son of said William de Bochardby, entered to the seignory. His sisters Alice, Pavy, and Agnes were his heirs' : ibid. p. 102.
1604. Richard Pavye, London : Reg. Univ. Oxf. pt. ii. p. 277.
1614. Buried — Martha, d. Thomas Pavie : St. Dionis Backchurch, p. 212.
1747. Married — William Pavey and Susanna Winch : St. Geo. Han. Sq. i. 38.
London, 2, 4, 2, 0 ; New York, 0, 0, 0, 2.

Pavier, Pavyer, Paver, Paviour.—Occup. 'the pavior,' more correctly paver (cf. *sawyer* and *lawyer* for *saw-er* and *law-er*), a maker of pavements.

Gerard le Pavier. E.
1621. Tristram Pavier, co. Soms. : Reg. Univ. Oxf. vol. ii. pt. ii. p. 399.
1648. Marlion Rithe and Sarah Paviour : Marriage Lic. (London), ii. 280.
1669. Married — William Paveer and Frances Tealor : St. Jas. Clerkenwell, iii. 162.
London, 1, 1, 1, 0 ; MDB. (co. Soms.), 0, 0, 0, 1 ; Oxford (Pavier), 4.

Pavin.—Bapt. 'the son of Pavia' (q.v.), popularly Pavey, dim. Pav-in. Lower says Pavin still exists, and is found in the 13th century.

Pavitt ; .v. Pavett.

Paw.—Nick. 'the peacock'; A.S. *pawe*, Lat. *pauo*. *Cock* is ex-crescent; cf. *peahen*; v. Pea, Pay, or Poe.

Alan Pawe, Close Roll, 5 Edw. II.

Pawle; v. Paul.

Pawlett; v. Paulett.

Pawley, Pauley, Pauly.—Bapt. 'the son of Paul,' from the pet form Pauley; cf. Charley, Teddie, &c. I cannot find any trace of a local origin. Paul was one of the favourite personal names in the 13th century. Thus I am driven to the above conclusion. Of course Pawley has a very local look.

Geoffrey Pauly, co. Camb., 1273. A.
William Pauly, co. Camb., ibid.
1574. Thomas Haynes and Eliz. Pawlye, *widow*: Marriage Lic. (London), i. 59.
1575. Thomas Pawlie, co. Cornwall: Reg. Univ. Oxf. pt. ii. p. 64.
London, 7, 2, o; Boston (U.S.) o, o, 1; Philadelphia, o, 6, 2.

Pawlin(g.—Bapt.; v. Paulin.

Pawson, Porson.—Bapt. 'the son of Paul,' a familiar Yorkshire surname. Dialectically, *all* frequently becomes *aw*. 'I'm going to t'haw' (i. e. to the hall). In Ulverston, Picthall (a common local surname) is only known as Pictaw.

Simon Paweson, 1379: P. T., Yorks. p. 220.
Ricardus Paweson, 1379: ibid.
Thomas Paweson, 1379: ibid.
Hugo Paueson, 1379: ibid. p. 269.
William Paweson, co. York. W. 13.
1564-5. John Pape and Marion Pawson: Marriage Lic. (London), i. 30.
West Rid. Court Dir., 6; London, 4.

Paxon, Paxson.—Bapt. 'the son of Pack' (i. e. Easter). One of very many variants of this once familiar personal name (v. Pack); cf. Dixon for Dickson. In some cases, no doubt, a corruption of Paxton, q.v.

1608. William Stanborough and Catherine Paxen: Marriage Lic. (London), i. 307.
1678. Ann Packson, Christ Church, Barbadoes: Hotten's Lists of Emigrants, p. 489.
London, 2, o; Philadelphia, 3, 48.

Paxton.—Local, 'of Paxton,' two parishes (Great and Little Paxton) near St. Neot's, co. Hunts.

Clemencia de Pacston, co. Hunts, 1273. A.

Thomas de Paxton, co. Hunts, 1273. A.
1550. John Paxton and Gertrude Mylborn: Marriage Lic. (London), i. 12.
MDB. (co. Oxf.), 2; London, 8; Philadelphia, 5.

Pay, Paye.—Nick. 'the pay,' i. e. peacock; A.S. *pawe*; v. Poe and Pea.

Elias Paye, co. Devon, 1273. A.
William Pa, *zonarius*, 14 Edw. II: Freemen of York, i. 19.
Hugo Paye, et Cecilia uxor ejus, 1379: P. T. Yorks. p. 58.
Cf. Johannes Pakok, 1379: ibid. p. 218.
1808. Married—Thomas Pay and Sarah Young: St. Geo. Han. Sq. ii. 387.
London, 3, o; New York, o, 2; Philadelphia, 2, o.

Payan. — Bapt. 'the son of Pagan' or Pain. q.v.

Worcester (U.S.), 1.

Paybody; v. Peabody.

Payn, Payne.—Bapt. 'the son of Pain,' q.v.

Paynel, Pagnel, Pennell, Pinnell, Pannell, Painell.—Bapt. 'the son of Paganel' or 'Paynel,' a dim. of Pagan or Pain, q.v. One of the chief tenants *in capite* in Domesday is a Ralph Paganel. The corruptions are many, but natural.

Katerina Paynel, co. Oxf., 1273. A.
John Painel, co. Wilts, ibid.
Hugo Paignel, Hen. III–Edw. I. K.
William Paganoll, ibid.
Fulco Painel, ibid.
Warin Pinel, ibid.
Paganel, or Pain, del Ash, 1301. M.
Robert Paynel, co. Soms., 1 Edw. III: Kirby's Quest, p. 100.
John Pennel, or Penell, sup. for B.A., 1524: Reg. Univ. Oxf. i. 136.
1619-20. John Smeeth and Anne Paynell: Marriage Lic. (London), ii. 83.
1783. Married—Thomas Weldon and Rose Pagnell: St. Geo. Han. Sq. i. 347.
London, o, o, 4, 2, 13, 1; Philadelphia (Pennell), 12.

Paynter.—Occup.; v. Painter; cf. Payne for Paine.

Payton.—Local, 'of Payton,' a township in the parish of Leintwardine, co. Hereford. But v. Peyton.

1594. Edward Payton, co. Warwick: Reg. Univ. Oxf. pt. ii. p. 206.
1606-7. Samuel Payton, co. Kent: ibid. p. 292.
1779. Married — James Payton and Sally Watmer: St. Geo. Han. Sq. i. 304.
London, 3; Philadelphia, 5.

Pea.—Nick. 'the pea,' a peacock or peahen; v. Pay and Poe.

Richard le Pe, co. Berks, 1273. A.
1640. Married — Thomas Allen and Alice Pea: St. Jas. Clerkenwell, iii. 72.
London, 1.

Peabody, Paybody.—? Nick. I find no early trace of this name. Paybody seems to have been the original form of the prefix, but what it means I cannot say; cf. Gentilcorps, Freebody, Goodbody, Baldbody, &c.

1615. Thomas Paybodie, co. Leic.: Reg. Univ. Oxf. vol. ii. pt. ii. p. 347.
— Married—Thomas Stubbs and Eliz. Pyebody: St. Jas. Clerkenwell, iii. 42.
1629. — Thomas Mason and Susan Payboddye: ibid. p. 42.
1635. Francis Peboddy sailed for New England: Hotten's Lists of Emigrants, p. 45.
London, 1, o; MDB. (co. Bucks), o, 1; Philadelphia, 10, o.

Peace, Pease.—Bapt. 'the son of Pece,' a great Yorkshire surname. No doubt Pece was one of the many variants of Pace, i.e. Easter, so given because born or baptized on that day; v. Pask, Pace, Pass, Pacey, &c. In Lancashire Easter-egging is still Pace-egging or Peace-egging.

John Pese, co. Bedf., 1273. A.
Willelmus Pece, 1379: P.T.Yorks. p.286.
Thomas Paas, 1379: ibid.
1566. John Pease and Margery Robertes: Marriage Lic. (London), i. 33.
1649. Bapt.—John, s. John Peace: St. Jas. Clerkenwell, i. 173.
London, 6, 1; Sheffield, 22, o; New York, o, 32.

Peach, Petch.—Local, 'de Peche,' probably a spot in Normandy. The same individual is thus referred to in the following three entries:

Almaric Pecche, co. Suff., 20 Edw. I. R.
Almaric Petche, co. Norf., ibid.
Almaric de Peche, co. Norf., 1 Edw. I: FF. xi. 118.
John de Pecche, co. Salop, 1273. A.
Reginald Peche, co. Hunts, ibid.
Bartholomew de Pecche, alias Bartholomew Peche, co. Berks, Hen. III–Edw. I. K.
John Petche, co. Warwick, 20 Edw. I. R.
1807. Married — Thomas Smith and Dorothy Petch: St. Geo. Han. Sq. ii. 377.
London, 7, 4; Boston (U.S.), 8, 2.

Peacock, Peacocke, Pocock, Pococke, Pycock.—Nick. 'the

peacock,' the gaudy, the proud. Probably the sobriquet would not be unacceptable to the bearer. At any rate the surname is common to-day. M.E. *pecok, pacok, pocok, pehen*, and *pohen*; v. Skeat.

Geoffrey Pokoc, co. Camb., 1273. A.
Hugh Pokok, co. Oxf., ibid.
Robert Pokoc, co. Linc., ibid.
Margaret Pakok, 2 Edw. II : Freemen of York, i. 24.
Adam Pacok, C. R., 19 Edw. II. pt. ii.
Walter Pokok, co. Soms., 1 Edw. III : Kirby's Quest, p. 107.
Roger Pokok, co. Soms., 1 Edw. III : ibid. p. 278.
John Pekok. H.
William Pecocke, sup. for B.C.L., 1510 : Reg. Univ. Oxf. i. 73.
London, 51, 1, 19, 2, 0; Leeds (Pycock), 3 ; New York (Peacock), 13.

Peak, Peake, Peek, Peeke.—Local, 'at the peak,' i.e. the hill-top ; v. Peck and Pick (2).

William del Peke, *pistor*, 17 Edw. II : Freemen of York, i. 21.
Isabella del Pek,1379: P. T. Yorks. p. 76.
Martyn del Pek, 1379 : ibid. p. 77.
1557. Anthony Peake and Margaret Vippan : Marriage Lic. (London), i. 18.
1724-5. Buried—Mary Peak : St. Dionis Backchurch, p. 294.
1806. Married—John Peek and Sophia Pike : St. Geo. Han. Sq. ii. 345.
London, 3, 26, 6, 1 ; Philadelphia,⟩ 27, 4, 1, 0.

Pearce, Pearse. — Bapt. ; a variant of Piers, q.v.

Oxford, 12, 1.

Peard, ?Peart.—? Nick. 'the pear-headed,' from the shape of the head. This solution seems strange, but it is highly probable. The surname Pearhead occurs in the Hundred Rolls, as may be seen below :

Robert Perheved, co. Notts, 1273. A.
1581. Edward Peard, co. Devon : Reg. Univ. Oxf. vol. ii. pt. ii. p. 99.
1588. John Pearte and Eliz. Eyre : Marriage Lic. (London), i. 170.
1618. Hugh Peard, of Bristol : Reg. Univ. Oxf. vol. ii. pt. ii. p. 373.
MDB. (co. Notts), 0, 1 ; (co. Devon), 4, 0.

Pearl.—Nick. or personal name; M.E. *perle*, a precious gem.

Thomas Perle, C. R., 17 Edw. III. pt. ii.
1805. Married — Matthew Pearl and Sarah Ellen Morris : St. Geo. Han. Sq. ii. 317.
London, 6; Philadelphia, 5.

Pearman, Pearmain, Pearmine, Permain.—Local, 'de

Permond,' probably a spot in Normandy or the Low Countries. As with all other names ending in *mond*, the final *d* is dropped ; cf. Osman, Wayman, &c.

John de Permond, bailiff of Norwich, 1316 : FF. iii. 79.
John Pyrmund, bailiff of Norwich, 1336: ibid. iv. 356.
1675. Married—Thomas Permount and Jone Turner : St. Jas. Clerkenwell, iii. 178.
1738. — Richard Sound and Catherine Perman : ibid. p. 266.
1800. — Thomas Pearman and Mary Hitchcox : St. Geo. Han. Sq. ii. 220.
London, 7, 5, 1, 2.

Pears, Pearse.—Bapt. 'the son of Peter' ; v. Pearson and Piers.

Robert Peres, co. Soms., 1 Edw. III : Kirby's Quest, p. 250.
Ralph Peyres, co. Soms., 1 Edw. III : ibid. p. 255.
Adam Pereys, co. Soms., 1 Edw. III : ibid. p. 276.
London, 4, 18 ; New York, 1, 6.

Pearsall, Pearsaul, Piersol, Persoll, Peirsol.—Local, ' of Pearshall ' or ' Pershall,' a township in the parish of Eccleshall, co. Stafford.

Thomas de Peshale, co. Stafford, Hen. III–Edw. I. K.
Edmund Pershall, of Over, 1676: Wills at Chester, iii. 208.
Thomas Peashall, of Checkley, co. Chester, 1634 : ibid. ii. 171.
London, 2, 0, 0, 0, 0 ; MDB. (co. Stafford), 0, 0, 0, 3, 0 ; Philadelphia, 8, 2,11, 0, 7.

Pearson, Pierson, Peirson.—Bapt. 'the son of Piers,' i.e. Peter; Fr. Pierre, O.E. Pearse or Piers. I furnish examples only of the more peculiar spellings. The settled orthography is to all intents and purposes Pearson, and every register or directory has its instances.

Walter Peressone, co. Soms., 1 Edw. III : Kirby's Quest, p. 241.
Richard Peresone, co. Soms., 1 Edw. III : ibid.
Robertus Perisson, 1379 : P. T. Yorks. p. 152.
Johannes Pereson, 1379: ibid. p. 116.
Hugo Perison, 1379 : ibid. p. 131.
1510. John Peyrson, or Pereson, or Person : Reg. Univ. Oxf. i. 73.
1554. John Peerson and Dorothy Stoderd : Marriage Lic. (London), i. 15.
1629. Bapt.—Frances, d. John Peirson : St. Dionis Backchurch, p. 105.
London, 74, 2, 6; Philadelphia, 79, 37, 8.

Peart, Pert.—? Bapt. 'the son of Perot' (?) ; v. Perrott. A modification ; cf. Part for Parot.

Agnes Pert, 1379 : P. T. Yorks. p. 64.
Henricus Pert, 1379 : ibid. p. 265.
1593. Buried—Emlyn Pearte, of plague: St. Michael, Cornhill, p. 204.
1615. Bapt. — Richard, s. Richard Pearte : St. Jas. Clerkenwell, i. 72.
London, 8, 0 ; New York, 0, 1.

Peartree.—Local, 'at the pear-tree,' from residence beside some conspicuous tree ; cf. Crabtree, Plumptre, or Rowntree.

Emma ate Peretre, co. Hunts, 1273. A.
Nicholas Peretre, co. Hunts, ibid.
Hutchin Grame, of Peretree, 1587: Nicolson and Burn, Hist. Westm. and Cumb., vol. i. p. xxxiv.
Mary Peartree, of Aston, 1671: Wills at Chester (1660–80), p. 206.
1738. Married—John Ward and Ann Peartree : St. Geo. Han. Sq. i. 21.
London, 3.

Peascod, Peasegood, Peasgood.—Nick. ' Peas-cod,' a pea-pod. ' Pescodde, *siliqua* ': Prompt. Parv. ' Pescodes ': Lydgate's London Lickpenny. Probably, like Freshfish, a nick. from the street cry of ' hot peascods.' It still remains with us as a surname; cf. Peppercorn and Barleycorn. Peasegood is a manifest corruption.

1502. 'Item, to wif of William Greneweye for bringing a present of peesecoddes to the Quene, 11s ': Privy Purse Exp., Elizabeth of York, p. 16.
1443. Godwin Pescod, of Norwich : FF. iv. 179.
1622. William Emerton and Mabell Peascodd : Marriage Lic. (London), ii. 119.
1664. Married—William Spencer and Katherine Peasgood: St. Jas. Clerkenwell, iii. 117.
1665. Nicholas Pescod, co. Norf.: FF. iv. 365.
London, 1, 0, 0 ; West Rid. Court Dir., 0, 1, 0 ; MDB. (co. Cumb.), 3, 0, 0 ; (co. Linc.\, 0, 0, 7; Philadelphia, 0, 0, 3.

Pease.—Bapt.; v. Peace.

Peasnall, Peasnell.—Local, ' of Peasenhall,' a parish in co. Suffolk.

Ralph de Pesenhal, co. Suff., 1273. A.
William de Pessenhall, bailiff of Norwich, 1259 : FF. iii. 59.
1793. Married — John Commins and Martha Peasnell : St. Geo. Han. Sq. ii. 104.
MDB. (co. Northampton), 1, 2.

Peat, Peatt, Peet, Peete.—(1) Nick. A delicate person, a pampered pet ; the older form of *pet.*

'A pretty peat': Taming of the Shrew, Act i. sc. 1.
'I overtook the wench, the pretty peat': Donne's Poems, p. 90 (Halliwell).
'As sick as a peate': Notes and Queries, 1857, p. 382.

I can suggest no other derivation; cf. Sweetlove, Sweet, Leifchild, Leaf, &c.

(2) Local, 'at the peat,' from residence thereby.

Richard de Peyt, co. Soms., 1 Edw. III: Kirby's Quest, p. 80.
1655. Married — Enock Peate and Barbery Salter: St. Peter, Cornhill, i. 260.
1664. — John Peat and Isabel Rosse: St. Jas. Clerkenwell, iii. 117.
London, 10, 0, 4, 1; New York, 2, 1, 20, 0.

Peattie, Peaty. — Bapt.; for Beattie, q.v. One more instance of change from B to P; cf. Peverley for Beverley.

1802. Thomas Peatey and Jane Young: St. Geo. Han. Sq. ii. 254.
London, 1, 0; Oxford, 1, 1.

Peberdy, Pipperday. — Doubtless variants of Peabody, q.v.

London, 2, 0; MDB. (co. Leic.), 1, 1; Philadelphia, 15, 0.

Peck. — Local, 'at the peck,' i.e. the hilltop; v. Peak. M.E. *pek*, 'the hul of the pek,' i.e. the hill of the Peak, in Derbyshire, Rob. of Glouc. p. 7 (v. *peak* in Skeat's Dict.). v. Peak and Pick (2).

John del Pek, London, 1273. A.
Henry Pek, co. Soms., 1 Edw. III: Kirby's Quest, p. 162.
Ricardus del Pecke, 1379: P. T. Yorks. p. 17.
Magota del Pecke, 1379: ibid. p. 4.
1590. Buried—An, wife of John Peck: St. Antholin (London), p. 34.
1660. Bapt. — Katherine Pecke: St. Peter, Cornhill, i. 100.
London, 17; New York, 108.

Peckham; v. Packham.

Peddell, Peddle. — Offic. 'the beadle.' German, *Pedell*. If not of German descent, the name is English by change of *b* to *p*; cf. Peverley for Beverley, or Peattie for Beattie.

1801. Married—William Coe and Eliz. Piddle: St. Geo. Han. Sq. ii. 242.
1808. — William Peedle and Sarah Bolton: ibid. p. 384.

With Piddle, cf. Biddle (v. Beadle).

London, 1, 2.

Pedder, Pedlar, Pedler. — Occup. 'the pedder,' a chap-man, a pedlar. 'Peddare, *calatharius, piscarius*' (Prompt. Parv.), i.e. one who makes baskets, or one who hawks fish, from *ped*, a pannier or basket. The market in Norwich was, or is, a ped-market, according to Way, from the fact that the wares were brought in from the country in peds, and thus exposed for sale. Hence in general a hawker or pedlar. Way has many references from the Paston Letters, Tusser, and others to the 'ped,' or wicker basket. Skeat explains *pedlar* from a diminutive *peddle*, a little ped, hence through *peddle-er* to *pedler* and *pedlar*.

Martin le Peddere, co. Norf., 1273. A.
Hugh le Pedder, c. 1300. M.
William Pedeleure, ibid.
Thomas le Pedeler. DD.
William Pedman, Pipe Roll, Ric. I.
Johannes Fox, *pedder*, 1379: P. T. Yorks. p. 13.
1616. Married — Richard Pedder and Ann Gayle: St. Jas. Clerkenwell, iii. 42.
1771. — James Evans and Mary Pedder: St. Geo. Han. Sq. i. 210.
London, 4, 1, 1; MDB. (co. Cornwall), 0, 2, 3; Boston (U.S.), 0, 2, 0.

Peek, Peeke; v. Peak.

Peel, Peal, Peall, Peale. — Local, 'at the peel,' from residence at a fortified house so termed. There can be no doubt about this derivation. '*Peel*, a square tower, a fortress' (Halliwell).

Geoffrey atte Pele, co. Soms., 1 Edw. III: Kirby's Quest, p. 169.

Many old mansions still bear the name of 'the Peel' in the North of England. Peel Castle in Furness is well known, and no doubt 'John Peel' of Cumberland hunting celebrity got his name from that spot. The name is still well known in that county. 'Within my recollection almost every old house in the dales of Rede and Tyne was what is called a *peel-house*, built for securing the inhabitants and their cattle in moss-trooping times': Archaeologia Aeliana, i. 246. The surname still keeps to the North. For other variants, v. Peil and Piel.

1541. Roger Pele, parson of Dalton-in-Furness: Lancashire Wills at Richmond i. 213.

1577. Robert Peel, of Blackburn. co. Lanc.: Wills at Chester (1545-1620), p. 149.
London, 5, 1, 1, 2; MDB. (co. Cumb.), 0, 0, 0 0; Manchester, 15, 0, 0, 1; Boston (U.S.), 2, 0, 0, 2.

Peerless, Pearless. — ? Local. I cannot find the spot. No doubt this is an imitative corruption of some local surname with suffix -*leys*, the plural of -*ley*, a meadow. Mr. Lower says: 'Unequalled, referring to character'(Patr. Brit. p. 261). I cannot accept this derivation. It is altogether unsatisfactory.

1796. Matried — William Wood and Patience Pearless: St. Geo. Han. Sq. ii. 145.
MDB. (co. Sussex), 4, 4.

Peet, Peete; v. Peat.

Pegg, Peggs. — Bapt. 'the son of Margaret,' from nick. Peg and Pog (v. Pogson). A much earlier nick. than is usually imagined.

Peter Peg, co. Oxf., 1273. A.
John Pegge, co. Oxf., ibid.
Martin Peggi, co. Oxf., ibid.
Bartholomew Peggi, co. Oxf., ibid.
Henry Pegge, co. Soms., 1 Edw. III: Kirby's Quest, p. 184.
Peter Pegge, co. Soms., 1 Edw. III: ibid. p. 262.
Johannes Pegge, 1379: P. T. Yorks. p. 14.
Magota Pegge, 1379: ibid. p. 7.
1680. Married—John Harrison and Martha Pegg: St. Jas. Clerkenwell, iii. 187.
1739. Married — John Pegg and Eliz. Traunter: St. Geo. Han. Sq. i. 22.
London, 9, 2; Philadelphia, 1, 1.

Pegram, Pegrum, Peggram, Piggrem, Pigram. — Bapt. 'the son of Peregrine.' O.F. *pelegrin*, a pilgrim. The first two instances below strongly confirm this view; in fact, all but settle it. The change from *n* to *m* is common; cf. Ransome for Ranson. v. Peregrine.

William Pegrin, co. Camb.. 1273. A.
Alicia Pegrin, co. Camb., ibid.
1604. Robert Pigrome (co. Essex) and Eliz. Butler: Marriage Lic. (London), i. 288.
1785. Married — Isaac Pegram and Martha Wyatt: St. Geo. Han. Sq. i. 325.
London, 3, 1, 1, 0, 2; MDB. (co. Essex), 0, 2, 0, 0, 0; Boston (U.S.), 1, 0, 0, 3, 0.

Peil, Peile, Peill. — Local, 'at the peel,' from residence therein; v. Peel.

1601. Edward Peele, or Peile, co. Cumb.: Reg. Univ. Oxf. pt. ii. 246.
1623. William Peile, of Netherlawton, Furness: Lancashire Wills at Richmond, i. 213.
London, 0, 1, 0; MDB. (co. Cumb.), 2, 2, 1.

Peirson; v. Pearson.

Pelham.—Local, 'of Pelham.' There are three Pelhams, parishes in co. Hertford, viz. Pelham Brent, Pelham Furneaux, and Pelham Stocking.

Geoffrey de Pelham, co. Suff., 1273. A.
Walter de Pelham, co. Camb., ibid.
Roger de Pelham, 13 Edw. II: Freemen of York, i. 19.
1791. Married—Thomas Papillon and Anne Pelham: St. Geo. Han. Sq. ii. 61.
London, 4; Boston (U.S.), 8.

Pelican.—Nick. 'the pelican'; cf. Nightingale, Sparrow, Goldspink, &c.

Robert Pellican, Close Roll, 6 Ric. II. pt. ii.

Pell, Pelle, Pells.—(1) Bapt. 'the son of Pell,' probably for Phil, i.e. Philip.

Walter fil. Pelle, co. Hunts, 1273. A.
William Pelle, co. Oxf., ibid.
1414. John Pelles, rector of Twyford, co. Norf.: FF. viii. 283.

(2) Local, 'at the pell.' 'Pell, a hole of water, generally very deep, beneath an abrupt waterfall' (Halliwell). The evidence is in favour of (1), especially as Pells exists; with the patronymic s cf. William and Williams, Simon and Simmonds, &c.

1724. Married — Robert Bates and Sarah Pells: St. Jas. Clerkenwell, iii. 240.
1757. — John Pell and Eliz. Hunt: St. Geo. Han. Sq. i. 73.
London, 1, 1, 5; MDB. (Lincoln), 7, 0, 9; (Suffolk), 0, 0, 2.

Pellegrin.—Bapt. 'the son of Peregrine' (q.v.); v. Pegram.

Philadelphia, 2.

Pelling.—Local, 'of Pilling,' a parish in co. Lanc. The variant was an early one; v. Pilling.

Wylelmus Pylyng, 1379: P. T. Yorks. p. 269.
Johannes Pellyng-man, i. e. servant, 1379: ibid.
1755. Married—John Pelling and Hannah Feild: St. Geo. Han. Sq. i. 56.
London, 4.

Pellipar.—Occup. 'a furrier,' a dealer in hairy skins, a pilch-

maker; v. Pelliter and Pilcher.
'A pylche-maker, pelliparius': Cath. Ang. 'Pelliparium, a pylchery': Ortus (v. Way's note on pylche in Prompt. Parv.).

Miles Pelliparius, co. Camb., 1273. A.
Ricardus Skynner, pelliparius, 1379: P. T. Yorks. p. 262.
Hugo Pelliperarius, co. Norf.: FF. vi. 2.
Ralph Pellipar, co. Norf.: ibid. xi. 246.

Pelliter, Pilter, Pelter.—Occup. 'the pilter,' a dealer in furs, a pilch-maker; v. Pilcher and Pellipar. Way (Prompt. Parv. p. 398) quotes Caxton's Book for Travellers: 'Wauberge the pylchemaker (pelletière) formaketh a pylche well.'

Richard de Peleter, co. Hunts, 1273. A.
John Pelletare, co. Camb., ibid.
Adam de Peleter, co. Norf., ibid.
John le Peleter. G.
Reyner le Pelter, c. 1300. M.
Johannes Pelter, merchaunt, 1379: P. T. Yorks. p. 155.
Geoffrey le Pelter, Close Roll, 50 Hen. III.
1608. Bapt. — John Pelliter, son of Matthew Pelliter: St. Michael, Cornhill.

A rare surname in the 19th century.

West Rid. Court Dir., 0, 1, 0; MDB. (co. Cumberland), 0, 0, 1.

Pells.—Bapt. 'the son of Pell,' possibly like Phil, a pet-name of Philip; v. Pell.

Pelly.—Local, 'of Pelly.' I cannot find the spot.

Elys de Peleye, co. Norf., 1273. A.
London, 4.

Pelton.—Local, 'of Pelton,' a township in the parish of Chester-le-Street, co. Durham.

1805. Married—John Pelton and Cecilia Beckett: St. Geo. Han. Sq. ii. 336.
London, 2; Philadelphia, 2.

Pemberton.—Local, 'of Pemberton,' a township in the parish of Wigan, co. Lanc.

Adam de Pemberton, c. Ric. I.
Alan de Pemberton, 3 John: Baines' Lanc. ii. 188.
Thomas Pemberton, of Whitley, 1595: Wills at Chester, i. 150.
William Pemberton, of Wigan, 1602: ibid.
1619. John Pemberton, of London, goldsmith, and Mary Lyndsey: Marriage Lic. (London), ii. 81.
Manchester, 10; London, 12; Philadelphia, 11.

Pembridge.—Local. 'of Pembridge,' a parish in co. Hereford.

John de Penbrigge, co. Glouc., 1273. A.
Reginald de Penbrugg', co. Glouc., ibid.
William de Pennebrigge, co. Glouc., 20 Edw. I. R.
1604. Anthony Pembridge or Penbridge, co. Hereford: Reg. Univ. Oxf. vol. ii. pt. ii. p. 276.
London, 1.

Pembroke.—Local, 'of Pembroke.'

1621. William Pembroocke, co. Berks: Reg. Univ. Oxf. vol. ii. pt. ii. p. 389.
1649. Buried—Katherine Pembrooke: St. Peter, Cornhill, i. 204.
1760. Married — Henry Tatchell and Jane Pembroke: St. Geo. Han. Sq. i. 183.
London, 2; Boston (U.S.), 1.

Pendegrass, Pendergast, Pendergrast, Pendergrass, Pendergest, Penderghest.—Local. Corruptions of Prendergast. These forms are largely represented in the leading cities of the United States. This is almost entirely due to Irish immigration. For history of the name, v. Prendergast.

1758. Married—James Pendergrass and Ann Williams: St. Geo. Han. Sq. i. 78.
1766. — Nicholas Pendergrass and Ann Blagrave: ibid. p. 156.
Liverpool, 2, 1, 1, 0, 0, 0; London, 0, 1, 0, 1, 0, 0; Boston (U.S.), 0, 49, 0, 1, 0, 0; Philadelphia, 1, 6, 2, 0, 1, 1,

Pender.—Offic. 'the pinder,' a keeper of a pound or penfold; v. Pinder.

Edmundus del Rodes, pendder, 1379: P. T. Yorks. p. 17.
William le Pendere. N.
1625. Buried—David Pendere, a clothworker, in Basing Lane: St. Mary Aldermary, p. 163.
Manchester, 2; Liverpool, 2; Philadelphia, 1.

Pendered, Pendred. Pendreth. — Bapt. 'Ap - Henrich' (Welsh). This has taken the forms given above; v. Pendrick, Pendry, and Penry.

Robert Pendred sailed for Barbadoes, 1635: Hotten's Lists of Emigrants, p. 52.
Lieutenant Pendred, co. Ches., 1644: Hist. East Cheshire, i. 431.
1704. Bapt.—William, s. William Pendred: St. Jas. Clerkenwell, ii. 19.
London, 1, 1, 1.

Pendergast, &c.; v. Pendegrass.

Pendlebury, Pendleberry.—Local, 'of Pendlebury,' a township in the parish of Eccles, near Manchester.

Margaret Pendlebury, of Bolton, 1584: Wills at Chester, i. 150.
James Pendlebury, of Westhoughton, 1618: ibid.
1602. Bapt. — Thomas, s. William Pendleburie: St. Jas. Clerkenwell, i. 41.
London, 2, 0; Manchester, 13, 0; Philadelphia, 9, 1.

Pendleton.—Local, 'of Pendleton,' formerly a chapelry in the parish of Eccles, near Manchester.

Thomas de Penelton, 1379: P. T. Yorks. p. 284.
William Pendleton, of Pendleton, 1588: Wills at Chester, i. 150.
Isabella Pendleton, of Pendleton, *widow*, 1592: ibid.
Hugh Pendleton, of Manchester: ibid.
London, 1; Manchester, 3; Boston (U.S.), 20.

Pendred, -dreth; v. Pendered.

Pendrick, Appenrick. — Bapt. 'the son of Henry'; Welsh Ap-Henry, abbreviated to Pendry and Pendrick (*d* is intrusive). Henry, Hendry, and Henrick were all common forms in the Principality. Philip Henry, father of Matthew Henry, the commentator, went by the name of Hendry and Henrick in his own circle of friends. He was a Welshman by birth (v. Life of Philip Henry); cf. Parry for Ap-Harry, and v. Pendry.

1788. Married — John Pendrick and Ann Shepherd: St. Geo. Han. Sq. ii. 4.

Pendry.—Bapt. 'the son of Henry' (Welsh Ap-Henry), corruptly Pendry, *d* being intrusive as in Simmonds, Hammond, &c. (v. Hendry); cf. Bevan, Pritchard, Bowen, Bethell, Price, &c. v. Penry.

1605. Robert Jennings and Joane Pendrie, of Hereford: Marriage Lic. (London), i. 298.
1677. Bapt. — Saray, d. of Thomas Pendrey: St. Jas. Clerkenwell, i. 277.
London, 2; MDB. (co. Monmouth), 1.

Penfold, Pinfold.—Local, 'at the pinfold,' a pound for strayed cattle, from residence thereby. Probably the original 'at the pinfold' was the Pinder himself; v. Pinder and Pender.

Robert del Punfold, co. Suff., 1273. A.
Philip de la Pundfold, co. Sussex, ibid.
Roger de la Pundfaude. co. Oxf., ibid.
Philip atte-punfold, C. R., 3 Edw. I.

William Punfold, co. Soms., 1 Edw. III: Kirby's Quest, p. 201.
Richard Punfolde, 1513: Reg. Univ. Oxf. i. 88.
1706. Bapt. — John, s. John Pinfold: St. Jas. Clerkenwell, ii. 29.
1769. Married — John Collings and Mary Penfold: St. Geo. Han. Sq. i. 186.
London, 14, 2; New York, 5, 0.

Penistone, Penistan, Peniston.— Local, 'of Penistone,' a market-town and parish eight miles from Barnsley, W. Rid. Yorks.

Helewise de Penneston, co. Suff., 1273. A.
1793. Married—Samuel Penistone and Ann Barker: St. Geo. Han. Sq. ii. 95.
1805. — Joseph Robinson and Mary Penniston: St. Geo. Han. Sq. p. 326.
West Rid. Court Dir., 1, 0, 3; MDB. (co. Derby), 3, 0, 0; London, 0, 1, 0; Philadelphia, 0, 0, 1.

Penketh.—Local, 'of Penketh,' a manor in the ancient parish of Prescot, co. Lanc.

1363. Jordan de Penket, 37 Edw. III: Baines' Lanc. ii. 255.
'Thomas Penketh, the famous Scottish doctor, was a monk of the Warrington monastery (1487) . . . who, writing with Dr. Shawe in support of Richard against Edward V, brought a stain upon his order in England. He is mentioned by Shakespeare:—

"Go, Lovel, with all speed to Doctor Shaw;
Go thou [*to Catesby*] to Friar Penker;
    bid them both
Meet me within this hour at Baynard's Castle ": Ric. III, Act iii. sc. 5.'
                                                    ibid. p. 224.

The surname was found at Warrington nearly 150 years after.

Mary Penketh, of Warrington, 1621: Wills at Chester, ii. 172.
John Penketh, of Warrington, 1630: ibid.
1570. Robert Penkeathe and Anne Brisowe: Marriage Lic. (London), i. 48.
London, 1; Liverpool, 1.

Penkethman, Penkeyman.—Nick. 'the man of Penketh,' i.e. Penketh's servant. Of this somewhat large class of surnames Matthewman (q.v.) is one of the most familiar instances. In this particular case Penketh is a local surname. The spot Penketh is mentioned frequently in Lancashire and Cheshire Records, pt. ii. (v. index of *places*). It is quite possible Penkethman may mean exactly what it seems to represent, 'a Penketh man,' a man from Penketh;

but this class of surname is extremely rare. v. Penketh.

Cf. Robertus Wortleyman (i. e. from Wortley), 1379: P. T. Yorks. p. 170.
1581. Hammet Penketman and Isabell Browne: Marriage Lic. (London). i. 103.
Richard Penkethman, of Warrington, *husbandman*, 1593: Wills at Chester i. 150.
Thomas Penkethman, of Warrington, 1641: ibid. ii. 172.
Peter Penkethman, 1671: St. Mary Aldermary (London), p. 102.

The Penkeths were long settled at Warrington; v. Penketh.

Manchester, 4, 0; Liverpool, 0, 1.

Penn.—(1) Local, 'at the pen, i.e. the pound, fold, from residence thereby; cf. Penfold, Penner. As every village and town had its pound, the name was naturally common. I could furnish many more instances.

William de la Penne, co. Norf., 1273. A.
John de la Penne, co. Berks, ibid.
Adam de la Penne, co. Oxf., ibid.
William atte Penne, co. Soms., 1 Edw. III: Kirby's Quest, p. 134.
Richard atte Penne, co. Soms., 1 Edw. III: ibid.
Nicholas de la Penne, temp. Hen. III: BBB. p. 190.

(2) Local, 'of Penn,' parishes in dio. s. Lichfield and Oxford.

William de Penna, co. Oxf., 1273. A.
Hugh de Penna, co. Berks, ibid.
Peter de Penna, co. Oxf., ibid.
Warin de Penne, co. Staff., 20 Edw. I. R.

Both parishes are represented in the above instances.

1667. Married—John Pen and Mary Chantree: St. Jas. Clerkenwell, iii. 130.
London, 15; Oxford, 6; Philadelphia, 39.

Pennant.—Local, 'of Pennant,' a parish in co. Montgomery. There may have been some other spot of that name.

Philip de Penant, cos. Norf. and Suff., Hen. III-Edw. I. K.
1504. Edward Pennant, otherwise Edward ap Rees, rector of Newton, co. Norf.: FF. v. 68.

This is strongly corroborative of the Welsh origin.

London Court Dir., 1.

Pennell.—(1) Bapt. 'the son of Petronilla,' which became Peternel, finally Pernel, Parnel, and Pennell; v. Parnall. (2) Bapt.

'the son of Painel' (v. Paynel). The three following are the children of one household :

Thomas, s. of Pethericke Pernell, 1580: Reg. St. Columb Major, p. 10.
John, s. of Pethericke Pennell, 1583: ibid. p. 12.
Zenobia, d. of Petherick Pennell, 1586: ibid. p. 13.
1671. Bapt. — Samuel, s. of Mathew Penell : St. Mary Aldermary, p. 102.
1707. Married — Richard Burroughes and Sarah Pennell : St. Geo. Han. Sq. ii. 164.
London, 4 ; Boston (U.S.), 6.

Penner.—Offic. ' the penner,' or pinder, one who impounded strayed cattle ; v. Pinner and Penfold.

John le Penner, co. Soms., 1 Edw. III : Kirby's Quest, p. 20.
Willelmus Penner, 1379 : P. T. Howdenshire, p. 21.

Perhaps the two following entries concern the same occupation : ·

Eborard Penier, co. Linc., 1273. A.
Thomas le Peniur, co. Norf., ibid.

Cf. *lawyer* for *law-er*, or *sawyer* for *saw-er*.

1793. Married — Thomas Palmer and Eliz. Penner : St. Geo. Han. Sq. ii. 192.
London, 1.

Penniger, Pennigar, Pinnegar, Pinniger, Pinnijer, Pinnigar.—Offic. 'the pennager,' an ensign - bearer.· In the York Mystery, *pennagers* walked between the various crafts in the procession (v. Hist. and Antiquities of City of York, ii. 119).

Thomas le Penniger. E.
William le Pennager. E.

The following is a curious corruption :

1803. Married — George Pindgar and Lucy Elmer : St. Geo. Han. Sq. ii. 277.
'Mr. Thomas Pinnegar, Calne, 1l. 1s. 0d.' : List of subscribers to the Religious Tract Society, Report, 1887, p. 458.
MDB. (co. Wilts), 0, 0, 0, 7, 1, 0 ; (co. Glouc.), 0, 0, 0, 1, 0, 1 ; New York (Pinniger), 2.

Penniman.—(1) Occup. ' the servant of Penny ' (q. v.) ; cf. Matthewman or Addyman. (2) Nick. equivalent to Pennyfather, q. v.

William Peniman, co. Camb., 1273. A.
1538. Nicholas Pennyman, *chaplain*, Norwich : FF. iv. 368.

1676. Married—John Faukingham and Catherine Pennyman : St. Michael, Cornhill, p. 41.
1706. Buried — John Pennyman : St. Dionis Backchurch, p. 275.
Boston (U.S.), 9. ·

Penny, Penney, Penson, Pensom. — Bapt. ' the son of Penny.' There can be no doubt, I think, about the derivation of this name. Pennyson is early found. With Pensom, cf. Ransom for Ranson, and Sampson for Sansom. If conclusive evidence were required for this derivation, we have it in the contemporaneous Penycock (cf. Wil-cock, Sim-cock, and v. Cock).

Hurtin Peni, co. Kent, 1273. A.
Alexander Peny, co. Camb., ibid.
Agatha Peny, co. Oxf., ibid.
Robert Peni, co. Kent, ibid.
Walter Peny, co. Soms., 1 Edw. III : Kirby's Quest, p. 128.
Johanne Peny, co. Soms., 1 Edw. III : ibid. p. 100.
John Pennesone, C. R., 17 Edw. III. pt. ii.
Johanna Penson, 1379 : P. T. Yorks. p. 162.
Mergareta Penycok, 1379 : ibid. p. 51.
Thomas Penycok, 1379: ibid.
William Penson, sup. for B.A., 1561 : Reg. Univ. Oxf. i. 246.
London, 20, 10, 1, 1 ; New York, 12, 5, 0, 0.

Pennyfather, Pennefather.—Nick. ' the penyfather,' i.e. a miser, a niggardly man. 'Sordidus, a niggard, a penyfather' : Junius, Nomenc. ' Pinse-maille, a pinchpenny, scrape - good, niggard, penny-father' : Cotg. (v. Prompt. Parv. p. 400).

' The liberall doth spend his pelfe, The pennyfather wastes himself.' Cotg. (quoted by Lower).

Richard Penifadir, co. Oxf., 1273. A.
John Penifader, co. Bucks, ibid.
Robert Penifader, co. Sussex, 20 Edw. I. R.
Roger Penyfader, London. X.
John Penyfader, C. R., 35 Edw. III.
1795. Married—Thomas Marshall and Sarah Pennyfather : St. Geo. Han. Sq. i. 132.
London, 2, 0 ; Crockford, 0, 2.

Penrith.—Local, ' of Penrith,' a well-known town in co. Cumberland ; very rare.

Beatrice de Penreth, co. Cumb., 20 Edw. I. R.

William de Penryth, co. Cumb., ibid.
Robert de Penreth, 1 Edw. II : Freemen of York, i. 11.
MDB. (co. Westm.), 1.

Penrose.—Local, ' of Penrose,' a parish in co. Monmouth.

1611. Married — Alex. Penrose and Margaret Goldinge: St. Jas. Clerkenwell, iii. 36.
1619. — Rowland Pendrye and Alice Penrose: ibid. p. 47.
London, 5 ; Philadelphia, 38.

Penruddocke. — Local, ' of Penruddock,' a hamlet in the parish of Greystoke, co. Cumb.

Simon de Penredek, co. Cumb., 20 Edw. I. R.
1672. Thomas Penruddock (co. Wilts) and Frances Hanham : Marriage Lic. (Faculty Office), p. 123.
Crockford, 1 ; MDB. (co. Somerset), 2.

Penry. — Bapt. ' the son of Henry.' The Welsh patronymic of this was Ap-Henry or Ab-Henry, compounded into Penry, equivalent to our Henrison, just as Parry (Ap-Harry) corresponds to our Harrison (v. Pendry).

Cadogann Ab-Henry, 23 Edw. I : BBB. p. 507.
Philip ap-Henry : Cal. State Papers, Hen. VIII.
1748. Bapt. — Joseph Penry, *parish clerk* : St. Jas. Clerkenwell, ii. 288.
1796. Married — William Dockwray and Winifred Eleanor Penry: St. Geo. Han. Sq. ii. 126.
London, 1 ; MDB. (co. Glamorgan), 1.

Penson, Pinson.—Bapt. ' the son of Pain' (!) ; v. Pagan and Pain. Nevertheless, v. Penny, which I believe to be the more correct derivation.

Pentecost, Pentycross. — Bapt. ' the son of Pentecost.' Originally a name given at the font to children born on the festival ; cf. Whitsuntide, Nowell, Pascal, and Christmas. The name is found very early. It is almost certain that Pentycross is a corruption.

' —filius Pentecosti,' Pipe Roll, 11 Hen. II, p. 32.
William Pentecoste, co. Oxf., 1273. A.
1278. Pentecost le Gras: Cal. of Wills in Court of Husting.
Pentecost de London. E.
Pentecost Servius. E.
Pentecost de Morton, C. R., 4 Edw. III.
John Pantecost, C. R., 45 Edw. III.

In Cornwall, the home of decayed personal names, especially those that lost caste at, and after, the Reformation, the name was used at baptism till the close of the 17th century.

1610. Bapt.—Pentecost, d. of William Tremain: St. Columb Major.
1696. Bapt. — Pentecost, d. of Mr. Ezekiel and Pentecost Hall: St. Dionis Backchurch (London).
London, 2, 0; Crockford, 0, 1.

Pentlow, Pentelow, Pentelowe.—Local, ' of Pentlow,' a parish in co. Essex, near Clare.

William de Pentelauwe, co. Essex, 1273. A.
London, 1, 0, 0; MDB. (co. Hunts), 0, 2, 1.

Pentney.—Local, 'of Pentney,' a parish in co. Norfolk, eight miles from Swaffham.

John de Penteneye, co. Norf., 3 Ric. II: FF. viii. 518.
Roger de Penteneye, co. Norf., 1290: ibid. iv. 336.
1805. Married — Joseph Wright and Ann Pentoney: St. Geo. Han. Sq. ii. 318.
London, 1.

Penyon.—Bapt.; v. Pinnion.

Pepin, Pippin, Pipping.—Bapt. 'the son of Pepin'; v. Peppiatt. This royal French name made but little impression in England, and was never properly naturalized. Among the early kings of France were Pepin l'Heristal and Pepin le Bref. The g in Pipping is an excrescence, as in Jennings. See, however, Pippin for another derivation of that name.

Richard Pepin, co. Hunts, 1273. A.
William Pepin, co. Hunts, ibid.
William Pippin, co. Bedf., ibid.
Hugh Pepin, C. R., 20 Edw. I.
1793. Married — Thomas Pippen and Mary Evans: St. Geo. Han. Sq. ii. 98.
London, 1, 0, 0; Boston (U.S.), 1, 0, 1.

Pepper. — Occup. ' the pepperer,' a spicer; cf. Salter, Mustarder, &c. Upholsterer has gained an er, Pepper has lost one; cf. Pewter for Pewterer.

Martin Peper, co. Hunts, 1273. A.
Ricard Pepir, co. Linc., ibid.
John le Peper. H.
Robertus Pepir, 1379: P. T. Yorks. p. 133.
Margareta Pepir, 1379: ibid.
1573. Robert Pepper and Agnes Lynecar: Marriage Lic. (London), i. 58.

1655. Bapt.—Mary, d. Allen Pepper: St. Michael, Cornhill, p. 140.
London, 16; West Rid. Court Dir., 9; Boston (U.S.), 18.

Pepperall, Pepperell, Pepperill; v. Peverall.

Peppercorn, Peppercorne.—Nick. Undoubtedly the sobriquet of a spicer or pepperer. The second instance below is valuable; v. Pepper, Peascod; cf. 'Old John Barleycorn.'

Geoffrey Peppercorn, co. Hunts, 1273. A.
Ricardus Pepercorne, *spysar*, 1379: P. T. Yorks. p. 95.
1430. Robert Pepirkorne, co. York. W. 11.
London, 1, 2; MDB. (co. Bedford), 4, 0; Oxford, 1, 0; Philadelphia, 1, 0.

Pepperman.—Occup. 'a dealer in pepper'; cf. Mustardman. I suspect the surname is now obsolete.

1590. Buried—A son of Andrias Pepperman: St. Dionis Backchurch, p. 200.

Peppiatt, Peppiett, Peppiette, Pippet, Pippett, Pippitt.—Bapt. ' the son of Pepin,' dim. Peppiette. The personal name Pepin, common in France, made little mark on English nomenclature, and the diminutives are probably the result of later immigration; v. Pepin.

1627. Bapt.—Eliz., d. Robert Peppit: St. Mary Aldermary, p. 80.
1678-9. Thomas Holgate and Rebecca Peppyatt: Marriage Alleg. (Canterbury), p. 294.
1794. Married — George Peppett and Eliz. Brewer: St. Geo. Han. Sq. ii. 109.
1797. — Thomas Peppet and Hannah Coldwell: ibid. p. 163.
1800. — William Peppiatt and Grace Nicholls: ibid. p. 218.
1804. — John Fisher and Mary Peppitt: ibid. p. 306.
London, 4, 1, 1, 0, 1, 0; Philadelphia, 0, 0, 0, 1, 2, 2.

Pepys.—Bapt. (?). Like Mr. Lower, I give up this surname in despair. Probably it is of easy solution, but I cannot at present come to any safe conclusion. It is a Norfolk surname.

Richard Pepis, co. Camb., 1273. A.
John Pepes, co. Camb., ibid.
John Peppes, 1602: Reg. St. Dionis Backchurch (London), p. 14.
1526-7. Richard Walker and Johanna Peppis: Marriage Lic. (London), ii. 280.

1581. Fermer Pepys, co. Norf.: FF. vii. 83.
1647-8. Robert Faukoner and Temperance Pepes: Marriage Lic. (London), i. 5.
1660. Edward Pepes, co. Norf.: FF. viii. 144.
London, 2.

Perceval, Percival, Percivall.—Bapt. 'the son of Percival.' Instances in early registers are extremely rare. Probably the following entry concerns the name:

Robert Passingbal, co. Camb., 1273. A.
Maurice Perceval, co. Soms., 1 Edw. III: Kirby's Quest, p. 248.

The varieties of spelling in church registers are amusing reading. I furnish a few instances:

Percyvallus Pensax, 1379: P. T. Yorks. p. 247.
1666. Bapt.—Persefall, son of William Persefall: St. Jas. Clerkenwell, i. 230.
Parcevill Fell, 1720: Annals of Cartmel, p. 260.
1776. Married — Thomas Warburton and Sally Parsivell: St. Geo. Han. Sq. i. 262.
1793. — Joseph Caythorp and Ann Persifull: ibid. ii. 88.
London, 2, 18, 4; Philadelphia, 0, 11, 0.

Perch.—Nick. ' the perch,' from the fish of that name. M.E. *perche*.

Nicholas le Perche, Fines Roll, 11 Edw. I.
New York, 1.

Percival; v. Perceval.

Perckings.—Bapt. ' the son of Peter'; v. Parkin. The g is excrescent, as in Jennings.

Boston (U.S.), 1.

Percy.—Local, ' of Perci,' a parish and canton near St. Lo, Normandy. William de Perci is set down as a tenant *in capite* in Domesday in many counties, notably in York and Lincoln (Lower). Percy is one of the earliest examples of a local surname becoming a font-name. In modern times, of course, the practice has become familiar, as in the case of Sidney in England, and Chauncy and Washington in the United States.

William de Percy, co. York, 1273. A.
Peter de Percy, co. York, ibid.
John de Percy, co. Sussex, ibid.
Robert de Percy, 1277. M.

William Percehay, C. R., 7 Ric. II.
Edmund Percehay: Visitation of
Yorks, 1563, p. 120.
William Percy, co. Soms., 1 Edw. III:
Kirby's Quest, p. 128.
1668. Married—John Percey and Mary
Willimes: St. Jas. Clerkenwell, iii. 151.
London, 14; Boston (U.S.), 8.

Peregrine.—Bapt. 'the son of
Peregrine'; v. Pegram.

Peregrinus Bernard, co. Northampt.,
20 Edw. I. R.
1781. Married — Owen Peregrine and
Lettice Cane: St. Geo. Han. Sq. i. 326.
London, 1.

Perfect.—Nick. 'the perfect,'
very excellent. A modern form of
O.E. *parfitt*; v. Parfett.

London, 4; MDB. (West Rid. Yorks), 3.

Perham.—Local, 'of Perham.'
A West-country name. I cannot
find the spot.

Johanna de Perham, co. Soms., 1 Edw.
III: Kirby's Quest, p. 174.
John de Perham, co. Soms., 1 Edw.
III: ibid. p. 202.
MDB. (co. Soms.), 2.

Perkin(s.—Bapt.; v. Parkin.

Perler.—Occup. 'the pearler,'
seemingly a dealer in pearls. M.E.
perle.

Thomas le Perler, London. X.
Margareta Perler, 1379: P. T. Yorks.
p. 270.
Johannes Pyrler, 1379: ibid. p. 271.
William Pirler, co. York. W. 2.

Permain; v. Pearman.

Perot; v. Parratt, Perrott.

Perowne.—Bapt. 'the son of
Peter,' from O.F. dim. Perron
(v. Perrin). The form Perowne
was introduced into England by
a French family who settled at
Norwich after the Revocation of
the Edict of Nantes. Several members of this family now occupy high
positions in the Anglican Church.

Crockford, 3.

Perrier; v. Perryer.

**Perrin, Perrins, Perring,
Perrings, Perren, Perin.**—
Bapt. 'the son of Peter,' from
O.F. Pierre, dim. Per-in or Per-on.

Perina Clanvowe, Close Roll, 20 Ric.
II. pt. i.
'The wife of Peryn.' Manor of Ashton-
under-Lyne: Cheth. Soc. p. 97.

The list in the London Directory
(of English descent, not counting
foreigners) is conclusive proof of
the popularity of this pet-form of
Peter; v. Perowne. The *g* in
Perring and Perrings, of course, is
excrescent; cf. Jennings.

William Perin, co. Linc., 1273. A.
John Perin, co. Camb., ibid.
Purand serviens Johannes de Hyperon:
1379: P. T. Yorks. p. 96.

As might be expected, Perin
lingered longest in Cornwall.

1524. John Peron and Alice Champyon:
Marriage Lic. (London), p. 10.
1546. William Perynne and Eliz.
Russell: ibid. p. 4.
1578. Married—James Nankevell and
Peren Eves: Reg. St. Columb Major,
p. 140.
1606. — Richard Jeninges and Jone Perrin: St. Mary Aldermary (London), p. 11.
London, 25, 1, 2, 1, 4, 0; Boston (U.S.),
14, 4, 0, 0, 0, 2.

Perrott, Perrot.—Bapt. 'the
son of Peter,' from nick. Pierre,
dim. Perr-ot; v. Parratt.

Ralph Perot, co. Bedf., 1273. A.
Robert Perot, co. Kent, ibid.
Perrot de Pyketon, co. York, ibid.
Adam Perottessone, 1340: KKK. vol.
vi. p. xl.
Perot Tempest, 1379: P. T. Yorks. p. 285.
1625. Richard Perrott and Anne Tilly:
Marriage Lic. (London), i. 154.
1662. Bapt.—Eliz., d. Adam Perrott:
St. Jas. Clerkenwell, i. 215.
London, 9, 0; Philadelphia, 1, 5.

Perry.—(1) Local, 'at the pery,'
i.e. the pear-tree; v. Pury.

'And thus I let him sitting in the pery,
And January and May roming ful
mery.'   Chaucer, C. T. 10091.

Walter atte-pyrie, co. Oxf., 1273. A.
Roger de la Peyre, co. Camb., ibid.
Richard de la Pirie, co. Oxf., ibid.
Richard atte Pyrye, co. Soms., 1 Edw.
III: Kirby's Quest, p. 106.
William atte Perye, C. R., 26 Edw. III.

(2) Bapt. 'the son of Perry,'
i.e. Peter, from O.F. Pierre, rendered popular in England as Perry;
v. Perryman.

John Pery, co. Oxf., 1273. A.
1619. Daniel Perry and Eliz. Pye:
Marriage Lic. (London), ii. 72.
1644. Bapt. — Thomas, s. William
Perry: St. Peter, Cornhill, i. 90.
London, 91; Philadelphia, 116.

Perryer, Perrier, Purrier.—
Local, 'at the pear-tree.' F. *poirier*,
a pear-tree; cf. Perry (1) and Pear-
tree.

Robert del Perer, London, 1273. A.
Ernulph del Perer, co. Wilts, ibid.
Roger de la Perere, co. Salop, ibid.
1592. Henry Gourney and Margaret
Perryer: Marriage Lic. (London), i. 199.
1610. Married — William Rivis and
Mary Purryor: St. Jas. Clerkenwell, iii. 36.
London, 1, 4, 3; New York, 0, 1, 1.

Perryman.—(1) Occup. 'the
servant of Perry,' i.e. Peter; v. Perry
(2); cf. Matthewman and Addy-
man. No relation with the growth
or sale of pears, or the making of
perry. The following were members
of one household:

Petrus Baylle, *taverner*, Johanna uxor
ejus, 1379: P. T. Yorks. p. 100.
Johannes Perys-man, 1379: ibid.
Robertus Perys-man, 1379: ibid.
Alicia serviens dicti Petri, 1379: ibid.
Johannes serviens Petri, 1379: ibid. p. 215.

Perys here is Piers, but the favourite form was Perry (i.e. Pierre).

William Peryman, co. Camb., 1273. A.

(2) Occup. 'a man who looked
after the pear orchard'; v. Pury.

Adam Puryman, co. Soms., 1 Edw. III:
Kirby's Quest, p. 125.
1580-1. John Perryman and Rose
Griffyn, *widow*: Marriage Lic. (London),
i. 99.
1600. Married — Richard Perryman
and Anne Stewardson: St. Jas. Clerkenwell, iii. 24.
London, 6.

Pershouse, Purshouse. —
Local, 'of the purse-house' (?),
a Staffordshire name. The suffix
is, of course, -house. Like Countinghouse (q.v.), it probably means the
office where the purser received
and paid accounts for his lord.
Thus Thomas or William 'de la
Purse-house' would easily originate
a surname.

William Persehouse, co. Staff., 1589:
Reg. Univ. Oxf. vol. ii. pt. ii. p. 169.
1806. Married—John Gray and Mary
Pearcehouse: St. Geo. Han. Sq. ii. 344.
MDB. (co. Stafford), 6, 3.

Persoll.—Local; v. Pearsall.

Pescott, Peskett. — Nick.
'Peascod,' q.v.; a natural corruption.

London, 1, 2.

Pessoner. — Occup. 'le pessoner,' i.e. the fisher. The pes-
soners and mariners went together
in the York Pageant (v. York
Mystery Plays, p. xx).

Egeas Fisher, alias Pessoner, was Mayor of Gloucester in 1241 : Rudder's Glouc. p. 113.

Ralf le Pecimer was bailiff of Norwich in 1239 : Bromefield's Norfolk, iii. 58.

A similar corruption is furnished in one of the instances below:

William le Pessoner, or Pessimer, co. Northampt., 1273. A.

Robert Pessoner, London, 20 Edw. I. R.

Richard le Pessoner, 1303. M.

Henry le Pessoner. C.

Pester.—Occup. ' le pestour,' i.e. the baker, pastry-cook.

Herman le Pestur, co. Norf., 1273. A.
Richard le Pester, co. Bedf., ibid.
John le Pestour, co. Oxf., ibid.
1371. Walter le Pestour, Pistor, or Baker, Norwich : FF. iv. 109.
Reginald le Pesthur, co. Linc., 20 Edw. I. R.
1599. Bapt. — Marie, d. Alexander Pistore : St. Antholin (London), p. 40.
1736. Married—John Hayes and Eliz. Pistar : St. Geo. Han. Sq. i. 17.
London, 1 ; Philadelphia, 6.

Petch.—Local ; v. Peach.

Peter, Peters, Peterson.—Bapt. ' the son of Peter.' This personal name has naturally been the parent of many forms and variations; cf. Parkin, Parnall, Perkin, Perkinson, Parkinson, Peterman, &c.

Henry fil. Pet', co. Camb., 1273. A.
Simon fil. Pet', co. Camb., ibid.
William Petres, co. Soms., 1 Edw. III : Kirby's Quest, p. 126.
London, 5, 37, 2.

Peterkin, Peterken.— Bapt. ' the son of Peter,' dim. Peterkin ; cf. Wat-kin, Tomp-kin, Lamb-kin.

London, o, 4 ; Manchester, 1, o ; Boston (U.S.), 1, o ; New York, 1, o.

Peterman.—Occup. ' the servant of Peter '; cf. Perryman, Matthewman, or Addyman.

1691. Married—Robert Peaterman and Eliz. Ladam : St. Michael, Cornhill, p. 46. Philadelphia, 42.

Peterson ; v. Peter.

Pether. — Bapt. ' the son of Peter '; v. Pither.

Petherick, Pethick.—Bapt. ' the son of Patrick.' The Cornish form, I presume, of Patrick, where it still exists as a font-name. There is a parish of Little Petherick in the dioc. of Truro, probably from the patron saint.

Pethroke, son of John Trevanan, 1547: Reg. St. Columb Major, p. 4.
Pethericke, son of John Snell, 1579 : ibid. p. 10.
Pethericke, son of Richard Reynolds, 1580: ibid. p. 11.
Thomas, son of Pethericke Pernell, 1580: ibid.
Thomas, son of John Pathicke, 1592: ibid. p. 16.
1789. Married — Lionel Pethick and Margaret Hanison: St. Geo. Han. Sq. ii. 25.
London, 2, 3 ; MDB. (co. Cornwall), 2, 9.

Peticurteis. — Nick. for one scant of courtesy.

Walter Peticurteis, co. Oxf., 1273. A.
William Petitkorteys, co. Oxf., ibid.

Petipas, Petitpaw. — ? Nick. ' Little-step,' one who stepped shortly ; cf. Lightfoot, Golightly, Purchase, &c.

William Petipas, co. Camb., 1273. A.
John Petypase, co. York. W. 11.
Thomas Petitpas. MM.
Boston (U.S.), 4, 1.

Petit, Petitt, Pettet, Pettit, Pettitt.—Nick. ' le petit,' the little ; cf. Little and Petty.

Roger Petyt, co. Norf., 1273. A.
Hamo le Petit, co. Suff., ibid.
Robert Petet, co. York, ibid.
William le Petit, C. R., 2 Edw. I.
Robert le Petit, co. Heref., 20 Edw. I. R.
1552-3. Richard Petytte and Philippa Turke : Marriage Lic. (London), i. 14.
1671. Married—Josiah Petit and Eliz. Petit : St. Michael, Cornhill, p. 40.
1712. Buried. — Thomas Pettit : St. Antholin (London), p. 124.
London, 4, 1, 6, 17, 7 ; Philadelphia, 2, 2, 0, 44, 0.

Pett.—Local, ' of Pett,' a parish in co. Sussex.

Carolus de Pette, co. Kent, 1273. A.
1562. Married — Nicholas Charnocke and Margery Pette : St. Jas. Clerkenwell, i. 2.
1681. Phineas Pett and Sarah Harden : Marriage Lic. (London), ii. 304.
1717. Bapt.—William, s. William Pett : St. Jas. Clerkenwell, i. 97.
London, 4.

Pettengell, Pettingell, Pettingill, Pettengill.—Local. From Portugal. ' Portingall, a Portuguese ' (Halliwell) ; v. Pettingell ; cf. Spain and Espin.

1566. Buried—John Pettingale, clothworker : Reg. St. Mary Aldermary (London).
1568. Married — Elizabeth Pettingale : ibid.
London, 1, 0, 0, 0 ; Boston (U.S.), 0, 1, 6, 1.

Petter, Petters, Petterson.—Bapt. ' the son of Peter,' an old dialectic form.

1538-9. Married—Petter Skreven and Alys Langlee : St. Dionis Backchurch (London).
Petter Newton : Visit. Glouc. p. 116.
1775. Married—Robert Elliot and Ann Petters or Peters : St. Geo. Han. Sq. i. 251.
London, 2, 1, 0 ; Philadelphia, 0, 0, 2.

Pettifer, Petifer, Pettafer, Pettafor, Pettepher, Pettifor, Pettipher, Pettyfor, Puddifer.—Nick. O.F. Pedefer, 'iron-footed'; cf. Dent-de-fer, 'iron-tooth'; also Brazdefer and Firebrace, 'iron-arm,' and M.E. Ironsides. Mr. Lower's 'petite-fere,' little wild beast, is very fanciful.

Patrick Pedefere, 7 Edw. III : Freemen of York, i. 27.
Robertus Pedefer, gentil, 1379 : P. T. Yorks. p. 277.
Bernard Pedefere. G.
Fulbert Pedefer. X.
William Pedefer. E.

By the close of the 16th century many of the modern forms had come into vogue :

William Petifer, or Petefer, or Petipher, or Petyfre, 1548 : Reg. Univ. Oxf. i. 216.
Robert Pettifer, Sheriff of Gloucester, 1603 : Rudder's Glouc. p. 116.

The most curious corruption of all is the imitative Pottiphar :

1777. Married—Moses Pottiphar and Jane Lee : St. Geo. Han. Sq. i. 283.

Pharaoh (q.v.) occurs as a surname in the same register.

1633. Married—John Pettiver and Eliz.
——: St. Jas. Clerkenwell, iii. 64.
1651. — Edward Petiver and Mary Keys : ibid. p. 86.
1668. — William Faukner and Mary Petifar : ibid. p. 147.
1703. — Samuel Pettifur and Ann Aslin : ibid. p. 226.
London, 5, 1, 1, 1, 1, 1, 1, 1, 0 ; Liverpool (Puddifer), 1.

Pettingell, Pettingle, Petingale, Pettengill. — Local, ' of Portugal,' ' a Portuguese '; v. Portingale, of which these are variants ; v. Pettengell.

1622. Bartholomew Pettingall : Reg. Univ. Oxf. vol. ii. pt. iii. p. 412.
1791. Married — Rev. S. Smith and Susanna Pettingel : St. Geo. Han. Sq. ii. 59.
1792. Married—Ward Pettingell and Ann Pettingall : ibid. p. 78.

MDB. (co. Cambridge), 2, 0, 0, 0; Great Yarmouth, 0, 1, 0, 0; New York, 0, 0, 1, 4.

Pettinger, Petinger.—Occup. A North-English form of Pottinger, q.v.

1805. Married — John Pettinger and Sarah Holmes Foster: St. Geo. Han. Sq. ii. 335.
Manchester, 4, 0; West Rid. Court Dir., 1, 1; MDB. (co. Linc.), 8, 0.

Pettit(t; v. Petit.

Petty, Pettey, Pettee.—Nick. 'the petty,' i.e. small in stature; v. Petit. The people bearing this name in the United States have selected Pettee as a preferable form; cf. Little, Littlejohn, Small, or Smallman.

Willelmus Pete, 1379: P. T. Yorks. p. 286.
Robertus Petyson, 1379: ibid. p. 287.
Richard Peteson, 1379: ibid.
Robertus Pety, 1379: ibid. p. 49.
1602. Married—Thomas Pettie and Joane Hanson: St. Jas. Clerkenwell, iii. 26.
London, 8, 0, 0; Boston (U.S.), 0, 1, 19.

Petyclerk.— ? Offc.

John Petitclerk, Close Roll, 32 Edw. I.
Richard Petyclerk, c. 1300. M.
William Peticlerk, ibid.
John Peticlerk, co. York. W. 2.

Perhaps a nickname for small stature or meagre learning (though compare Beauclerk and Manclerk, q.v.), but rather 'an under clergyman,' a vicar. The frequency of the name in separate districts is against the nickname theory. Again, it is significant that the French Petyclerk is met by the seeming English translation, 'Smallwriter' (q.v.). A large number of such translations appear in this dictionary; cf. Handsomebody, Fairchild, Fairbrother (q.v.).

Peverall, Peverell, Pepperall, Pepperell, Pepperill.— — ? 'William Peverel was a natural son of William the Conqueror, who entered England at the Conquest.' . . . 'In Domesday it is continually spelt Piperellus. Mr. Planché (Journal of Arch. Assoc. viii. 196) conjectures that it had a personal signification, and

that 'it is a corruption of Puerulus, which is almost identical with Peuerellus, as we find it written in the Anglo-Norman Pipe and Plea Rolls' (v. Lower's Patr. Brit. p. 265). This would make the meaning to be Littleboy. It does not seem satisfactory. In any case Pepperall, Pepperell, and Pepperill are variants of Peverall.

Pagan Peverel, co. Camb., 1273. A.
Richard Peverel, co. Hunts, ibid.
Sir Hugh le Peverel (sic), 1344: FF. xi. 53.
1757. Married—Benjamin Pepperel and Mary Grange: St. Geo. Han. Sq. i. 72.
1806. — George Hillem and Margaret Peverell: ibid. ii. 355.
London, 1, 1, 1, 1, 1; Philadelphia, 1, 0, 0, 0, 0.

Peverley.—Local, a corruption of Beverley.

London, 1.

Pew.—Bapt. 'the son of Hugh,' a variant of Pugh, q.v. (In the same way Hugh is found as Hew; cf. Hew or Hewson for Hugh or Hughson.) Thus we find Pewes for Pughs:

1607. Bapt. — Joan, d. John Pewes: St. Jas. Clerkenwell, i. 51.

For several instances, v. Pugh.

Hugh Pue, of Hoole, 1685: Wills at Chester (1681–1700), p. 203.
Lewis Pew, of Wigland, yeoman, 1698: ibid. p. 196.
1808. Married — Thomas Collins and Hannah Pew: St. Geo. Han. Sq. ii. 391.
London, 1; Boston (U.S.), 1.

Pewterer, Powter.— Occup. 'the pewterer,' a worker in lead and tin. 'Pewtyr, metalle': Prompt. Parv. 'Pewtrere, electuarius, vel stannarius': ibid. The Pewterers and Founders marched together in the York Pageant (York Mystery Plays, p. xx). The surname Pewterer has dropped the final er; cf. Pepper for Pepperer.

Nicholas le Peuterer, C. R., 29 Edw. III.
Henry Pewterer, temp. Eliz. ZZ.
William Peuterere. S.
1795. Married — Luke Pewter and Mary Jackson: St. Geo. Han. Sq. ii. 125.
1798. — Abraham Pewter and Mary Darby: ibid. p. 182.
London, 0, 4.

Pewtress.—Occup. 'the pewteress,' a female worker in lead and

tin (v. Pewterer); cf. Huntress and Hunter.

1753. Married—Thomas Pewtress and Eliz. Barber: St. Geo. Han. Sq. i. 49. London, 2.

Peyton.—Local, 'of Peyton,' a chapelry in the parish of Bampton, co. Devon. But v. Payton.

London, 4; Philadelphia, 7.

Pharaoh, Pharoah, Pharo. — ? Local. A manifest imitative corruption of some local or other surname; cf. Pottiphar (v. Pettifer). The tendency to imitate Scripture names seems to have amounted to a fascination. Probably the local Farrow is the true parent; cf. Physick for Fishwick. All the above corruptions have found their way across the Atlantic.

1655. Bapt. — Eliz., d. James Pharo: St. Jas. Clerkenwell, i. 192.
1702. — Eliz. Pharao: St. Jas. Piccadilly, p. 22.
1763. Married — Giles Pharaoh and Sarah Vincent: St. Geo. Han. Sq. i. 118.
1770. — William Clark and Mary Farrow: ibid. p. 197.
London, 2, 0, 0; MDB. (co. Surrey), 0, 1, 1; Oxford, 3, 1, 0; Philadelphia, 1, 2, 2.

Pheasant.—Nick. 'the pheasant'; 'fesaunt' (Chaucer). O.F. faisan. The wilder birds were popular nicknames; cf. Partridge, Hawk, Kite, Heron.

Robert Fesant, co. Oxf., 1273. A.
John ffesaunt, co. Norf., 1379: FF. x. 280.
Willelmus Faysand, 1379: P. T. Yorks. p. 150.
William Fesaunt, rector of Wood Rysing, co. Norf., 1380: FF. x. 280.
James Phesaunte, c. 1550. ZZ.
1767. Married—Morris Jones and Eliz. Pheasant: St. Geo. Han. Sq. i. 168.
London, 2; MDB. (co. Linc.), 2; Boston (U.S.), 1; Philadelphia, 1.

Phelps, Phelp, Phelips. — Bapt. 'the son of Philip,' from the nick. Philp or Phelp, whence the genitive Phelps; cf. Jones, Coles, Williams. &c. Philip is early found as Phelip, and nearly all the surnames formed from it are Westcountry.

Richard Phelip, co. Soms., 1 Edw. III: Kirby's Quest, p. 218.
Simon Phelip, co. Soms., 1 Edw. III: ibid. p. 243.
John Phelpes, temp. 1570. Z.
Charles Felpes, 1603: Reg. St. Dionis Backchurch (London), p. 14.

Margaret Felpes, 1590: Reg. Broad Chalke, co. Wilts, p. 2.
1583. Richard Phelpes, co. Somerset : Reg. Univ. Oxf. vol. ii. pt. ii. p. 129.
1611. Married — Thomas Woodcock and Philippa Phelps : St. Michael, Cornhill, p. 20.
London, 14, 0, 0 ; MDB. (co. Soms.), 26, 3, 2 ; Philadelphia, 16, 0, 0.

Phennemere ; v. Finnemore.
MDB. (co. Salop), 1.

Phethean ; v. Phythian.

Phetteplace. — An American corruption of Fettiplace, q.v. ; cf. Phillimore and Filmore.
Worcester (U.S.), 8.

Pheysey. — Local, 'de Vesci.' For proof absolute, v. Vesey.

1578. Buried—Sara Feseye, *a maiden*, plague : St. Michael, Cornhill, p. 195.
1788. Married — Edward Briscoe and Catherine Pheasey : St. Geo. Han. Sq. ii. 14.
1802. — Louis Humeau and Ann Phesay : ibid. p. 271.
—— — Thomas Phesey and Mary Evans: ibid. p. 272.
London, 1.

Philbert.—Bapt. ; v. Filbert.

Philbrick, Philbrook.—Local, 'of Felbrigg,' a parish in co. Norfolk, three miles from Cromer ; cf. Phillimore. The variants be easily proved by the evidence given below.

Matilda de Felbregge, co.Norf., 1273. A.
Roger de Felebregge, co. Norf., 20 Edw. I. R.
Robert de Fellbrigg, abbot of North Creak, co. Norf., 1412 : FF. vii. 77.
1577. Married—Harrye Felbricke and Susan Sowthwicke : St. Michael, Cornhill, p. 13.
1652. — John Langstone and Martha Filbrigg, *widow*, of Chelmsford, in Essex: ibid. p. 31.
1658. Walter Tooker and Abigail Filbricke : St. Jas. Clerkenwell, iii. 100.
1702. — William Smith and Mary Philbrook : St. Geo. Han. Sq. ii. 165.
1797. — George Philbrick and Eliz. Ballamy : ibid.
London, 3, 0 ; MDB. (co. Essex), 1, 0 ; Philadelphia, 1, 0 ; New York, 3, 3.

Philby. — Local, 'of Filby' (q.v.) ; cf. Phillimore and Philbrick.

1325. Richard de Phileby, rector of Stokesby, co. Norf. : FF. xi. 251.
1800. Married — Thomas Dennis Philbey and Jane Jones: St. Geo. Han. Sq. ii. 215.
London, 1.

Philcox.—Bapt. 'the son of Philip,' from nick. Phil, with suffix *-cock* (v. Cocks) ; cf. Philkin, and Wilcock or Wilcox.

Ricardus Filkok, 1379 : P. T. Yorks. p. 160.
1613. Bapt. — Peludia, d. Richard Filcockes : Canterbury Cathedral, p. 3.
1617. — Kathern, d. Richard Filcock : ibid. p. 4.
London, 1 ; MDB. (co. Sussex), 2.

Philibert.—Bapt. ; v. Filbert.

Philip, Philipp, Philipps.
Philips, Phillipp, Phillipps,
Phillips, Phillipson. — Bapt. 'the son of Philip.' There is little need of instances for this batch of familiar surnames. Philip ceased to be popular as a font-name after the reigns of Mary and Elizabeth for patriotic reasons. Nevertheless its earlier predominance has given it immortality in our directories.

Simon fil. Philippi, co. Kent, 1273. A.
Henry Phelipe, co. Norf., ibid.
Alicia Philippes, co. Hunts, ibid.
Ellis fil. Philip', co. Hunts, ibid.
Cecilia Philipp.1379 : P. T.Yorks. p. 83.
1617. Hugh Fisher and Eliz. Philipson : Marriage Lic. (London), ii. 54.
London, 3, 2, 4, 4, 1, 6, 287, 3.

Philipshank. — Nick. Sparrow-legged, from *shank* and Philip, the familiar name for the sparrow ; cf. Sheepshank.

Johannes Philipschank, 1379 : P. T. Yorks. p. 104.

Philkin.—Bapt. 'the son of Philip,' from the nick. Phill (v. Philson), and the dim. Philkin ; cf. Watkin from Walter, or Wilkin from William. For examples, v. Filkin, the modern form.

Robert Philkynn sailed for Barbadoes, 1635 : Hotten's Lists of Emigrants, p. 52.

Phillimore, Filmore.—Nick. of endearment, 'fin amour,' pure love (v. Douceamour and Plainamour). The change of *n* to *l* was common ; cf. Bannister for Ballister (v. Bannister), and *banister* for *baluster*. For instances, v. Finnemore. *Ph* and *f* interchange frequent civilities ; v. Fillpot for Philpot, Filbert and Philbert, Farrimond and Pharamond, &c.

1683. Married — Thomas Foster and Saray Phillmore : St. Jas. Clerkenwell, iii. 200.
1795. — William Phillimore and Eliz. Davis : St. Geo. Han. Sq. ii. 130.
London, 5, 2.

Phillipp(s ; v. Philip.

Phillis. — Bapt. 'the son of Phillis,' i.e. Felicia. The letters *f* and *ph* are commonly interchangeable in English nomenclature.

'And fecche Felice hom
Fro the wyuen pyne.'
Piers P. 2529-30.

Thomas Coline et Felisia uxor ejus, 1379 : P. T.·Yorks. p. 67.
Emma Felis, 1379 : ibid. p. 104.
Johannes Fylysson, 1379 : ibid. p. 201.
Alan Nelleson et Filisia uxor ejus : 1379 : ibid. p. 17.
1436. John Phelysson, bailiff of Yarmouth : FF. xi. 325.
1564. Michael Philles, 'plumber to Merton College' : Reg. Univ. Oxf. vol. ii. pt. i. p. 288.
1569. Bapt.—Fillys, d. Robert Grymes: St. Jas. Clerkenwell, i. 5.
1666. — Elisabeth, d. Steven and Phillis Griffith : ibid. p. 230.
1603. Phillis, wife of Ralphe White : Reg. Broad Chalke, co. Wilts, p. 42.
1677. Bapt. — Thomas, s. Thomas Dam, and Fillis, his wife : St. Thomas the Apostle (London), p. 68.
London, 1.

Phillot, Phillots.—Bapt. 'the son of Philot,' from Philip, nick. Phil, dim. Philot. Phillots represents the full patronymic ; cf. William and Williams, Philpott and Philpotts.

Philota de Kender, co. Derby, 1273. A.
MDB. (co. Dorset), 0, 1.

Philpot, Phillpott, Phillpotts, Philpots, Philpott. — Bapt. 'the son of Philip,' from the dim. Philip-ot, abbreviated to Philpot ; cf. Marri-ot or Emm-ot for Mary and Emma. The name was used for both sexes. v. Fillpot.

Thomas Phylypotte. B.
John Philpot. N.
Johannes Schikyn, Philipot uxor ejus, 1379 : P. T. Yorks. p. 75.
Nov. 1543. Item, geven to Fylpot, my lady of Suffolk's lackaye, viis. viid.' : Privy Purse Expenses, Princess Mary.
William Phellpot, co. Hereford, 1587 : Reg. Univ. Oxf. vol. ii. pt. ii. p. 159.
1583. John Phillpott and Judith Thompson : Marriage Lic. (London),i. 121.
London, 1, 1, 2, 14, 7.

Philp, Phillp, Philps.—
Bapt. 'the son of Philip,' from the

nick. or abbreviated form Philip: cf. Peart for Perrot. A North-English and Border form ; v. Phelps.

Philip Gledstanes, 1541 : TTT. p. lxxxi.
Patrik Phylp, 1547 : ibid. p. lii.
John Philpe, c. Eliz. Z.
1714. Married — John Philip and Rebecca Snelgrove : St. Jas. Clerkenwell, iii. 237.
1790. — Sparks Philp and Martha Honnor : St. Geo. Han. Sq. ii. 42.
London, 15, 2, 3.

Philpot(t ; v. Phillpot.

Philson, Phill.—Bapt. 'the son of Philip,' from the nick. Phil.

1601. Edward Phill, co. Glouc. : Reg. Univ. Oxf. vol. ii. pt. ii. p. 253.
Philadelphia, 4, 0.

Phin, Phinn, Phinney.— Bapt. ; v. Finn.

Crockford, 1, 0, 0 ; Boston (U.S.), 0, 0, 42 ; New York (Phin), 1.

Phippen, Phippin. — Bapt. 'the son of Philip,' from nick. Phip, dim. Phip-in ; cf. Colin (Nicholas), Lambin (Lambert).

George Phippen, co. Dorset, 1606–7 : Reg. Univ. Oxf. vol. ii. pt. ii. p. 293.
Elizabeth Fippin, 1628 : St. Jas. Clerkenwell, i. 110.
1792. Married — William Phippen and Catherine Merrett : St. Geo. Han. Sq. ii. 80.
1799. William Phippin and Ann Willey: ibid. p. 205.
London, 3, 0 ; Manchester, 0, 1 ; MDB. (co. Somerset), 9, 4 ; Boston (U.S.), 11, 0.

Phipps, Phipson.—Bapt. 'the son of Philip,' from the nick. Phip. 'Phip, a sparrow.' The noise made by a sparrow': Halliwell. I think this is not the true derivation. The sparrow went by the name of Philip (v. Philipshank), as the redbreast by the name of Robin. Phip was merely the nick. of Philip, and applied familiarly to the sparrow.

1583. Roger Phippes, co. Glouc. : Reg. Univ. Oxf. vol. ii. pt. ii. p. 130.
1587. John Fipp, saddler, and Catherine Easterbye : Marriage Lic. (London), i. 160.
Christopher Phipp, of Bold, yeoman, 1592 : Wills at Chester, i. 151.
1765. Married — Henry Black and Mary Phips : St. Geo. Han. Sq. i. 147.
London, 19, 2 ; Oxford, 20, 0 ; Philadelphia, 17, 0.

Phisackerley. — Local ; v. Fazackerley.

Phoenix.—? Bapt. 'the son of Felix' (!), an imitative corruption ; cf. Phillis for Felicia, and *banister* for *baluster*.

MDB. (Lincoln), 4 ; Philadelphia, 3.

Physick.—Local, 'of Fishwick.' A natural and an inevitable imitative corruption of a well-known Lancashire name ; v. Fishwick.

1617. Nicholas Phisicke : Reg. Univ. Oxf. vol. ii. pt. iii. p. 362.
1620. Bapt. — John, s. Eliz. Fishick : St. Jas. Clerkenwell, i. 87.
London, 4.

Phythian, Phethean.—Bapt. 'the son of Fithion,' i.e. Vivian. When passing through Bolton, Lanc., on Sept. 27, 1886, I saw ' John Phethean, plumber and gasfitter,' over a window in a street leading to Halliwell.

Henry Fithion, co. Kent, 1273. A.
Richard Fithion, co. Kent, ibid.
Hugh Fifiane, co. Soms., 1 Edw. III : Kirby's Quest, p. 122.
Robertus Fethethyan, 1379 : P.T.Yorks. p. 262.
Hugh Phytheon, of Tetton, 1582 : Wills at Chester, i. 65.
John Fitheon, of Overton, 1613 : ibid. p. 151.
Richardus Phytheon, of Moston, 1593 : Wills at Chester, i. 151.
'In the 6th Hen.VIII (1514–5), "William Byrtheles, son and heir of Fithian (or Vivian) Byrtheles," grants to trustees all his messuages,' &c. : East Cheshire, ii. 357.
1624. Married—Thomas Fytheone and Jane Smith : Reg. Prestbury, co. Ches., p. 246.
London, 2, 0 ; Bolton (Lanc.), 0, 1 ; Manchester, 1, 1.

Picard, Pickard, Pitcher.— Bapt. 'the son of Pichard' or ' Picard' ; cf. Richard and Ricard. The commonest form was Pichard, and of this Pitcher is doubtless an imitative corruption. Very common in Yorkshire records.

Roger fil. Pichard : Pipe Roll, 11 Hen. II, p. 41.
Alan Pichard, co. York, 1273. A.
Stephen Picard, co. Northumb., ibid.
Nicholas Pichard, co. Salop, ibid.
Roger Pichard, co. Camb., ibid.
Alan Piccard, co. Linc., 20 Edw. I. R.
Emma Picard, 1379 : P. T. Yorks. p. 207.
Ricardus Picard, 1379 : ibid.
1524. Anthony Sylver and Margaret Pykkarde : Marriage Lic. (London), p. 4.
1784. Married — Richard Pickard and Eliz. Reason : St. Geo. Han. Sq. ii. 366.
London, 4, 11, 8 ; Philadelphia, 8, 5, 5.

Pick.—(1) Nick. 'the woodpecker.' Fr. *pic*. v. Speck ; cf.

Goldfinch, Spark, Nightingale, Crow, Raven, &c.

Simon Pic, co. Suff., 1273. A.
Agnes Pick, co. Hunts, ibid.
Hugh Pick, co. Oxf., ibid.
Thomas Pik, co. Soms., 1 Edw. III : Kirby's Quest, p. 277.
Richard Pyk, co. Soms., 1 Edw. III : ibid. p. 131.

(2) Local, 'at the pike,' a peaked hill ; cf. Langdale Pikes in the Lake district. v. Peak and Pike.

Ralph del Pikke, co. Hertf., 20 Edw. I. R.
1590. Bapt.—Richard, s. Philip Pick : St. Antholin (London), p. 34.
1668. — Saray, d. Thomas Picke : St. Jas. Clerkenwell, i. 237.
1721. — Leonard, s. John Pick : ibid. p. 130.
London, 7 ; New York, 8.

Pickard ; v. Picard.

Pickavance, Pickavant, Pickvance, Pickance. — Nick. ' Prick-advance,' spur forward. We must not be tempted to refer these various forms to the pikedevant or piked beard. 'A young, pittivanted, trim-bearded fellow': Anatomy of Melancholy, Tegg's edit. p. 533. Found in the portraits of courtiers in the 16th and 17th centuries, it was not an early enough fashion to be immortalized by a patronymic. 'Tis true the following entry occurs :

1600. Married—John Gibbs and Joan Pickedevant : St. Jas. Clerkenwell, p. 24.

But the date itself would suffice to show that it was an imitation of the term for the then prevailing fashion. No doubt her real name was Pickavant. Prikeavant was, no doubt, the nickname of a harbinger, pursuivant, or herald, from *prick* ; M.E. *prike*, to put spur to horse (cf. 'kick against the pricks,' Auth. Vers.), and *avance*, forward, to the front. A herald was one who 'rode to the front.' The instances amply confirm this view :

William Prikeavant, co. Bedf., 1273. A.
1678. Buried — Simon Prickadvance : Reg. Peasmarsh, co. Sussex.

A similar surname is Sturtevant, q.v.

Edward Pickavance, of Much Woolton, *husbandman*, 1662 : Wills at Chester (1660–80), p. 209.

Manchester, o, o, 1, o; Liverpool, o, o, o, 1; Southport, o, 1, o, o; St. Helens, 3, o, o, o.

Picker, Pecker.—Occup. ' the picker.' Probably one engaged in fruit-picking or in the fields.

William le Pekkere, co. Hunts, 1273. A.
Roger le Peckere, co. Hunts, ibid.
Simon le Peckere, co. Hunts, ibid.
Paulin Peckere, co. Hunts, ibid.
1784. Married — Richard Angle and Mary Pecker: St. Geo. Han. Sq. ii. 356.
London, 1, o; Boston (U.S.), o, 4.

Pickerdite. — Local. A corrupted form of Bickerdike, q.v.; cf. Peverley for Beverley, &c.

London, 1.

Pickering.—Local, ' of Pickering,' a parish in the N. Rid. Yorks.

Hugh de Pikering, co. York, 1273. A.
William de Pikering, co. York, ibid.
Jacobus de Pikeryng, *pistor*, 1 Edw. I: Freemen of York (Surt. Soc.), i. 1.
John Pykeryng, co. Soms., 1 Edw. III: Kirby's Quest, p. 87.
Diota de Pykeryng, 1379: P. T. Yorks. p. 143.
Johannes de Pykerryng, 1379: ibid. p. 67.
1592. Anthony Pykerynge, co. Hants: Reg. Univ. Oxf. vol. ii. pt. ii. p. 192.
1705. Bapt.—Ann, d. William Pickering: St. Jas. Clerkenwell, ii. 25.
London, 22; Sheffield, 6; MDB. (North Riding Yorks), 14; Boston (U.S.), 44.

Pickernell. — Official, ' the spigurnel' (v. Spicknell), a curious corruption, but not without precedent; cf. Sturgess for Thurges, Pichfat for Spichfat, or Pilsbury for Spilsbury. Thus may an ancient and honourable name be disguised.

1769. Married — John Tillier and Ann Pickernell: St. Geo. Han. Sq. i. 183.
1781. — Richard Pink and Eliz. Pickernell: ibid. p. 328.
London, 1.

Pickersgill.—Local, ' of Pickersgill.' Some spot in the N. Rid. of Yorks which I have failed to discover.

1679. Married—Henry Boyce and Eliz. Picersgill: St. Jas. Clerkenwell, iii. 186.
MDB. (W. R. Yorks), 3; (N. R. Yorks), 5; London, 2; Philadelphia, 1.

Pickett.—Bapt. 'the son of Picot.' Mr. Lower says, 'A well-known corruption of Pigott.' This is to reverse the true order. Pigott is a corruption of Pickett, or, more correctly, Picot or Pichot. It is

strange that while the name has ramified so strongly, so little can be gleaned of its history. Camden's derivation from O.F. *picote*, the small - pox, *picote*, pock - marked, freckled, is unkind; but he gave no authority for the statement. That Picot was a personal name is clear, for Picot, a chief tenant in Hampshire, and Picot de Grentebrig', both occur in Domesday. It is curious, too, to observe that two families in Cheshire, the Pigots and Pichots, ran side by side for some generations, and Dr. Ormerod long ago surmised that both sprang from one common ancestor—Gilbert Pichot, lord of Broxton (Earwaker's East Cheshire, ii. 361). Radulphus Picot (Pipe Rolls, 6 Hen. II, pp. 53, 55). Also Picot and Picotus, as a personal name (ibid. pp. 32, 46).

Picotus de Laceles, temp. 1109: Lincolnshire Survey, p. 12.
Picot de Tani, Pipe Roll, 7 Hen. II, p. 67.
Picot de Flexbergh, co. Wilts, 1273. A.
Elis Pyket, co. Bucks, ibid.
Walter Pycot, co. Camb., ibid.
Godfrey Piket, co. Soms., 1 Edw. III: Kirby's Quest, p. 137.
London, 20; Boston (U.S.), 25.

Pickford, Pitchford.—Local, ' of Pitchford,' a parish in co. Salop. ' No doubt the same as Pitchford in Shropshire. In the Rotuli Hundredorum of the county the possessor of that estate, spelt Picheford, is styled Sir John de Picford ' (Lower).

John de Picford, or Picheford, co. Salop, 1273. A.
Ralph de Pickford, or Picheford, co. Salop, Hen. III–Edw. I. K.
John de Pycheford, 1277. M.
Galfridus de Picheford, 1296. M.
1591. Bapt. — Moyses Pickford: St. Jas. Clerkenwell, i. 25.
1599. — Theoder, s. John Pitsfort: ibid. p. 34.
London, 12, 1; Philadelphia, 3, o.

Pickin; v. Piggins.

Pickles, Pighills.—Local, ' of Pickhill,' a parish in the N. Rid. Yorks. I suspect this is the origin, and that there was an irresistible tendency to imitate the dictionary word on the part of the bearers of the surname. Several

early entries, however, point to some small locality in the West Riding.

Ricardus de Pighkeleys, 1379: P. T. Yorks. p. 182.
Stephanus de Pykedleghes, 1379: ibid. p. 183.

These persons dwelt in the village of Haworth, in which district the two names are now so familiar. In this case the word means ' the meadows on the hilltop,' the owner taking his name from residence thereon; v. Pick(a). The Directory for Wilsden, W. Rid. Yorks, contains the two following names, seemingly related :

Nathan Pickles, *beer-retailer*.
Nathan Pighills, *farmer*.

It is curious to note how little the name has wandered from its native county. Nevertheless, it has reached America.

MDB. (W. R. Yorks), 34, 4; London, 2, o; Philadelphia, 4, o.

Pickman.—Occup. ' the pikeman,' a soldier, one who carried a pike; cf. Spearman. With the form Pickman may be set *pick* and *pick-axe*.

Stephen Pykeman, London, 1273. A.
Geoffrey Pykeman, London, ibid.
Thomas Pikeman, or Pikman, London, 20 Edw. I. R.
Giles Pykeman. X.
1587. Married—George Pickman and Gillmett Johnson: St. Jas. Clerkenwell, iii. 12.
1628. Bapt.—Eliz., d. Philip Pickman: ibid. i. 109.
London, 2; Boston (U.S.), 2.

Picknell.—Local, ' of Pikenhall.' I cannot find the spot.

Thomas de Pikenhale, co. Camb., 1273. A.
1680. Married — John Pecknell and Mary Thomas: St. Dionis Backchurch, p. 39.
MDB. (co. Linc.), 1; London, 1; Boston (U.S.), 5.

Picksley, Pixley.—Local; v. Pikesley.

Pickston, Pickstone. — Corruptions of Pingston, q.v.

Pickup, Pickop.—Local, ' of Pickup.' A Lancashire surname from a township and village in the parish of Walley, now styled Yatecum-Pickup Bank. The name has ramified strongly, and can be easily traced back to the neighbourhood of Blackburn as its original home.

1584. Roger Piccop, of Over Whiteley: Wills at Chester, i. 152.
1592. James Piccop, of Nether Darwen: ibid.
1623. John Piccope, of Rawtenstall: ibid. ii. 173.
— John Piccopp, of Eccleshill: ibid.
Robert Holden, of Picope Bank, 1595: ibid. i. 97.
John Tattersall, of Piccope, 1581: ibid. p. 188.
Robert Tattersall, of Piccope, yeoman, 1587: ibid.
Manchester, 8, 1; Blackburn, 23, 3; Philadelphia, 15, 1.

Pickwell.—Local, 'of Pickwell,' a parish in co. Leicester, near Melton Mowbray.

MDB. (co. Lincoln), 7.

Pickwick.—Local, 'of Pickwick' or Bickwick, some spot in the West country; cf. Buckle and Puckle, Burser and Purser, Bickerdike and Pickerdike,&c. My earliest reference is from the county of Wilts. This is interesting. The Pall Mall Gazette (March 3, 1888) says: 'During the hearing of a case in the High Court of Justice yesterday, Mr. Dickens, a son of the famous novelist, and counsel for the defendant, said he should call as a witness a Mr. Pickwick (laughter). He added: It may interest your lordship (Baron Huddleston) to learn that this gentleman is a descendant of Mr. Moses Pickwick, who kept a coach at Bath, and I have very good reason to believe that it was from this Mr. Moses Pickwick that the name of the immortal Pickwick was taken.' Evidently the surname is a West-country one, and has existed there at least six centuries.

William de Pikewike, co. Wilts, 1273. A.
Thomas de Bykewyk, co. Soms., 1 Edw. III: Kirby's Quest, p. 103.
Ralph de Bykewyk, co. Soms., 1 Edw. III: ibid.
Walter de Bykewyk, co. Soms., 1 Edw. III: ibid.

The three last-named were all resident in Redlysch.

1647. Married — Charles Pikwik and Maria Potter: Reg. Darrington, co. York.

For this last entry I am indebted to Notes and Queries, Feb. 5, 1887, p. 112.
MDB. (co. Soms.), 1; Neath (South Wales), 1; Philadelphia, 1.

Pickworth.—Local, 'of Pickworth,' a parish in co. Lincoln, near Falkingham. The meaning is 'the farmstead on the sharppointed hill'; v. Pike and Worth.

Robert de Pickewurth, co. Linc., Hen. III–Edw. I. K.
Hugo de Pykewurth, co. Linc., ibid.
Richard de Pikeword, co. Linc., 1273. A.
William de Pikworth, co. Linc., ibid.
1739. Bapt. — Ann, d. Thomas Pickworth: St. Jas. Clerkenwell, ii. 247.
London, 5; MDB. (co. Lincoln), 6.

Picthall.—Local, 'of Pickthall,' an old house in the parish of Ulverston, Furness. The surname is well known in the district, and pronounced Picthaw.

1545. Bapt. — Esabell Picthawe: Reg. Ulverston Church, p. 1.
1547. Buried—Jenet Pickthowe: ibid. p. 5.
John Turner, of Pickthawe, 1644: Lancashire Wills at Richmond, i. 289.
James Pickthowe, of Pickthowe Ground in Dunerdale, 1610: ibid. p. 216.
Thomas Picthall, of Sandscale, parish of Dalton, 1718: ibid. ii. 197.
James Picthall, of Pickthall Ground in Dunnerdale, 1734: ibid.
MDB. (co. Cumberland), 3; Ulverston, 1; Liverpool, 1; Boston (U.S.), 2.

Picton.—Local, (1) 'of Picton,' a place close by Haverfordwest. William de Picton came to Pembrokeshire (N. and Q., 1858, p. 329), whence the Pictons in that district. Nevertheless, my instances point to Picton nearer at hand, viz. (2) 'of Picton,' a township in the parish of Plemonstall, four miles from Chester.

Hugh Picton, canon of St. David's, Hist. and Ant. St. David's, p. 364.
Thomas Picton, prebendary of St. David's, 1399: ibid. p. 361.
Jane Taylor, of Picton, 1615: Wills at Chester (1545-1620), p. 189.
John Picton, of Newton, near Chester, 1593: ibid. p. 152.
Henry Picton, of Acton Grange, 1610: ibid.
London, 1; Liverpool, 1; New York, 1.

Pidcock, Piddocke. — Bapt. 'the son of Peter,' from Peter-

cock, a corruption (v. Cocks); cf. Wilcock, Simcock, &c. Lower quotes from Burke's Landed Gentry, 'The surname is derived from the armorial bearing of the family, a pied cock!' Lower adds, 'The cock is not pied, but simply parted per fesse, Or and Argent.' This is setting the cart before the horse with a vengeance.

Gilbert Pittcok, co. Camb., 1273. A.
1738. Married — Thomas Piddock and Mary Gaudy: St. Geo. Han. Sq. i. 21.
1755. John Spencer and Ann Pidcock: ibid. p. 59.
Crockford, 5, 1; MDB. (co. Derby), 1, 2; Philadelphia, 2, 0.

Piddington.—Local, 'of Piddington,' parishes in cos. Northampton and Oxford.

Richard de Pidinton, co. Oxf., 1273. A.
William de Pidinton, co. Oxf., ibid.
Walter de Pidington, co. Oxf., ibid.
1802. Married—Peter Piddington and Anna Rapley: St. Geo. Han. Sq. ii. 269.
London, 4; MDB. (co. Hunts), 1.

Pidgeon, Pigeon, Pidgin.—Nick. 'the pidgeon'; cf. Dove, Woodcock, Pye, &c. Bird-names are among the most common of the nickname class of surnames. M.E. pygeon.

William Pigun, co. Norf., 1273. A.
Richard Pigun, co. Camb., ibid.
Walter Pygeon, C. R., 1 Hen. V.
Henricus Pygyn, 19 Edw. I: BBB. p. 431.
1757. Married—John Pidgin and Eliz. Collins: St. Geo. Han. Sq. i. 74.
London, 4, 1, 0; Boston (U.S.), 6, 3, 4.

Pidgley, Pidsley.—Local, 'of ——?' The first entry is manifestly the parent of the name.

Walter de Pideneslegh, co. Devon, 1273. A.
1761. Married — Samuel Taunton and Martha Pidgley: St. Geo. Han. Sq. i. 105.
Devon Court Dir., 2, 7; London, 0, 2.

Piebaker.—Occup. 'the piebaker,' a pastry-cook. 'Pye-baker, cereagius': Prompt. Parv. Way adds as a note, 'Cereagius, pistor qui ad modum cere deducit pastam': Cath. Ang.

'Drovers, cokes, and pulters,
Yermongers, pybakers, and waferers.'
    Cocke Lorelle's Bote.

Andrew le Pyebakere, London. X.
Hugh Pybakere, C. R., 47 Edw. III.

Piel.—Local, 'at the peel,' from residence therein; v. Peel or Peil.

New York, 2.

Pierpoint, Pierpont, Pairpoint, Pearpoint, Pierrepont.—Local, ' of Pierrepont,' from the castle of that name on the southern borders of Picardy (Lower). The name is Latinized into ' de Petro-Ponte.' Godfrey de Perpont occurs in Domesday.

Henry de Perpunt, co. Linc., 1273. A.
Hugh de Perpont, co. Notts, ibid.
John de Perpunt, co. Notts, Hen. III-Edw. I. K.
Simon de Perepont, co. Suff., 20 Edw. I. R.
Henry Perpunt, co. Linc., 20 Edw. I. R.
1575. George Perpount and Agnes Raynoldes: Marriage Lic. (London), i. 65.
London, 5, 1, 4, 1, 0; Boston (U.S.), 1, 3, 0, 0, 1.

Piers, Pierce, Pears, Pearse, Peers, Peirce, Pierse.—Bapt. 'the son of Peter,' from O.F. Pierre, O.E. Piers or Pierce. Although Peter, and with it Piers, lost much of its popularity after the Reformation, we cannot fail to see from our directories (Pearson, &c.) how extremely familiar the name was in all parts of England at the time surnames were becoming hereditary.

Richard Perys, co. Soms., 1 Edw. III: Kirby's Quest, p. 133.
Isolda Peer-doghter, co. York. W. 15.
Magota Peres-wyf, 1379 ; P. T. Yorks. p. 117.
Peres Rothwell, 1541, Tottington, Lanc.: Lanc. and Ches. Rec. Soc. vol. xii. p. 144.
Peares Armerod, temp. Eliz. ZZ.
Pearse Edgcombe, temp. Eliz. Z.
Robert Pearce, temp. Eliz. Z.
Jane, d. of Pears Marten, 1541 : Reg. St. Columb Major, p. 1.
John, s. of Peirce Penhale, 1604 : ibid. p. 22.
William Pearce, or Perce, or Peirs, or Perse, or Peirce, or Peirse, or Pearse, adm. B.A. 1601 : Reg. Univ. Oxf. vol. ii. pt. iii. p. 221.
1692. Married — George Peares and Anna Padgett : St. Michael, Cornhill, p. 47.
1738. — Thomas Pearce and Eliz. Jones: ibid. p. 68.
London, 0, 13, 4, 18, 1, 10, 14.

Piersol.—Local; v. Pearsall.

Pierson; v. Pearson.

Pigg.—Nick. 'the pig'; cf. Hogg, Wildbore, Purcell. Probably the epithet would be less offensive then than now. Two gentlemen named Pigg were about 1882 among our best county cricketers.

Goceline Pig, co. Norf., 1273. A.
Richard Pig, co. Berks, ibid.
Walter Pigge, co. Northampt., ibid.
John Pyg. H.
1626. John Pittman and Alice Pigge, *widow*: Marriage Lic. (London), ii. 179.
1787. Married — Richard Waite and Mary Pigg : St. Geo. Han. Sq. i. 399.
Manchester, 1.

Piggins, Piggin, Pickin, Picking.—Bapt. 'the son of Richard' (?). Probably popular variants of Higgins, Higgin, and Hickin, q.v. We still talk of higgledy-piggledy. The g in Picking is an excrescence, as in Jennings, &c.

1386. Roger Pickyn, rector of Billingford, co. Norf.: FF. viii. 194.
1574-5. Anthony Pickins, co. Worc.: Reg. Univ. Oxf. vol. ii. pt. ii. p. 59.
1614-5. Anthony Piggin and Sarah Ireland : Marriage Lic. (London), ii. 30.
1619. Thomas Hoggery and Joane Piggyn : ibid. p. 81.
1807. Married — Daniel Daniel and Alice Picking : St. Geo. Han. Sq. ii. 364.
London, 0, 1, 1, 1; MDB. (co. Linc.), 3, 0, 0, 0; (co. Notts), 1, 5, 2, 0.

Piggott, Pigot, Pigott.—Bapt. 'the son of Pigot' or 'Picot'; v. Pickett. The personal name Pigot without surname occurs in the Hundred Rolls; no doubt a variant of Picot.

'De dono Pigoti et Reginaldi': A. i. 336.
Astin Pigot, co. York, 1273. A.
Richard Pigot, co. Linc., ibid.
Robert Pigod, co. Salop, ibid.

The parish of Framlingham Pigot, co. Norfolk, is in Bromefield's History of Norfolk (v. 435) headed Framlingham Picot.

Thomas Pygot, or Picot, co. Norf., 1434 : FF. v. 435.

The popular form in co. Norfolk is Pickett, q.v.

1561. Richard Piggotte : Reg. Univ. Oxf. i. 245.
London, 16, 4, 4; Boston (U.S.), 1, 0, 9.

Pigherd.—Occup. 'the pigherd,' a tender of pigs; v. Swinnart, Calvert, Herd, &c.

Walter Pyghurde, co. Soms., 1 Edw. III : Kirby's Quest, p. 112.

Pighills; v. Pickles.

Pigram; v. Pegram.

Pigsflesh. — Nick. Cf. Hogsflesh.

Reyner Piggesflessh, Close Roll, 13 Edw. II.

Pike.—Local; v. Pick (2).

Walter Pik, co. Hunts, 1273. A.
Richard Pik, co. Wilts, ibid.
Baldewyn Pike, co. Soms., 1 Edw. III : Kirby's Quest, p. 114.
London, 53; Worcester (U.S.), 18.

Pikesley, Pixley, Picksley.—Local, 'of Pixley,' a parish in co. Hereford, three miles from Ledbury.

Hugo de Pikesley, co. Hereford, Hen. III-Edw. I. K.
1632. Married — Edmund Davy and Alice Pixly : St. Jas. Clerkenwell, iii. 63.
1682. — John Nero and Eliz. Pickesley: ibid. p. 198.
1764. — George Miller and Sarah Pixley : St. Geo. Han. Sq. i. 133.
London, 1, 2, 0; Manchester, 0, 0, 1; MDB. (co. Oxf.), 1, 0, 0; (co. Linc.), 0, 1, 3.

Pilbrow. — Local, 'of Pulborough,' a parish in co. Sussex ; cf. Plimpton for Plumpton.

1795. Married — George Pratt and Mary Pilbrough : St. Geo. Han. Sq. ii. 136.
1803. — Henry Pilbrough and Eliz. Swinton : ibid. p. 292.
MDB. (co. Bucks), 1; Philadelphia, 1.

Pilcher, Pilger.—Occup. 'the pilcher,' a pilch-maker. 'Pylche, *pellicium*': Prompt. Parv. Mr. Way has a long and interesting note on the word (pp. 397-8). Properly a fur gown, a garment of skin, with the hairs on. Bishop Ridley in his letter of farewell, quoting Heb. xi. 37, says, ' Some wandered to and fro in sheep's pilches, in goats' pilches.' v. Pelliter and Pellipar.

' After great heat commeth cold ;
No man cast his pilche away.'
Chaucer, Proverbs.

Hugh le Pilecher, co. Camb., 1273. A.
Nicholas Pilchere, co. Camb., ibid.
Ralph Pilkere, co. Camb., ibid.
John Pilcher. G.
1625. Buried—John Pilcher, *merchant*: St. Dionis Backchurch, p. 217.
1761. Married — John Wise and Eliz. Pilcher: St. Geo. Han. Sq. i. 103.
London, 6, 0; MDB. (co. Kent), 22, 0; New York, 2, 8.

Pile.—Local; v. Pill.

Pilgrim.—Occup. 'the pilgrim,' a wanderer, one who went long distances to visit a shrine. It is possible the name was sometimes given in baptism; v. Pegram and Peregrine. A good instance of the intermediate stage is found in the following:

Edmund Pylgrvne, rector of Sydistrond, co. Norf.: FF. viii. 170.
Henry Pelrim, co. Camb., 1273. A.
Robert Pelerin, co. Suff., ibid.
Leticia Pelrin, co. Camb., ibid.
John Pilegrim, co. Oxf., ibid.
Geoffry Pilegrim, co. Norf., ibid.
Richard Pilgrym, C. R., 2 Hen. V.
Willelmus Pylgrem, 1379: P. T. Yorks. p. 51.
1762. Married — James Ridley and Ann Green, with consent of Rev. John Pilgrim: St. Geo. Han. Sq. i. 110.
London, 8; MDB. (co. Essex), 5.

Pilkington.—Local, 'of Pilkington,' a manor in the parish of Prestwich, co. Lanc.

'Roger de Pilkington, for an oxgang of land in Pilkington, homage and service of 12d.,' 1311: Baines' Lanc. i. 483.
Roger de Pilkinton, 19 Edw. I: ibid. p. 448.
Oliver Pilkington, of Bolton, co. Lanc., 1594: Wills at Chester (1545-1620), p. 153.
Adam Pilkington, of Salford, *gentleman*, 1596: ibid.
Manchester, 13; London, 4; Philadelphia, 10.

Pill, Pile.—Local, 'at the peel' or fortified house (v. Peel), from residence therein. 'Pile, a small tower' (Halliwell).

Richard de la Pille, co. Soms., 1273. A.
Benedict de la Pille, co. Devon, ibid.
Nicholas de Pille, co. Essex, ibid.
Walter atte Pyle, co. Soms., 1 Edw. III: Kirby's Quest, p. 98.
Richard atte Pile, co. Soms., 1 Edw. III: ibid. p. 140.
William atte Pyle, co. Soms., 1 Edw. III: ibid. p. 194.
Thomas del Pille, 1379: P. T. Yorks. p. 155.
1780. Married — Benjamin Pile and Ann Meredeth: St. Geo. Han. Sq. ii. 32.
1804. George Tunks and Margaret Pill: ibid. p. 302.
London, 2, 12; Philadelphia, 0, 12.

Pillar, Piller.—Local, 'at the pillar,' from residence thereby. M.E. *piler*, a column, a support.

Walter atte-piler, C. R., 10 Edw. I.

The following instance is probably 'de le,' the *de* being omitted, as is so common in early rolls.

John le Piler, co. Soms., 1 Edw. III: Kirby's Quest, p. 219.

1666. Married — William Piller and Mary Leager: St. Jas. Clerkenwell, iii. 126.
1745. — Thomas Miles and Eliz. Piller: ibid. p. 275.
Philadelphia, 0, 1: Boston (U.S.), 0, 2.

Pilley.—Local, 'of Pilley,' a manor, now the property of Lord Wharncliffe, in the parish of Tankersley, nine miles from Sheffield, W. Rid. Yorks.

Johannes de Pillay, of Tankersley, 1379: P. T. Yorks. p. 87.
Magota de Pillay, of Tankersley, 1379: ibid.
Gilbert de Pilleghe, co. Soms., 1 Edw. III: Kirby's Quest, p. 152.

This entry probably represents a different place in the West Country.

1780. Married—John Pilley and Mary Crush: St. Geo. Han. Sq. j. 308.
London, 2; Sheffield, 1; Philadelphia, 5.

Pilling. — Local, 'of Pilling,' a township in the parish of Garstang, co. Lanc. 'The township is characterized by its fence-dykes, mentioned in the ballad of Flodden Field:

"They wth ye Standley howte forth went From Pemberton and Pillin Dikes."'
v. Baines' Lanc. ii. 537.

Rowland Pilyn, Bras. Coll. 1579: Reg. Univ. Oxf. vol. ii. pt. i. p. 391.
Hugh Pilling, of Tunstead, 1579: Wills at Chester, i. 152.
Edmund Pillinge, of Bacup, 1595: ibid.
Edmund Pilling, of Baxtenden, 1592: ibid.
1671. Married — Abraham Pillin and Jane Snosedale: St. Jas. Clerkenwell, p. 175.
London, 3; Manchester, 16; MDB. (co. Lanc.), 11; Philadelphia, 16.

Pillinger.—Offic.; v. Penniger; cf. *banister* for *baluster*, or *messenger* for *messager*.

London, 1; MDB. (co. Somerset), 1.

Pillington.—Local, 'of Billington' (q.v.), a sharpened form; cf. Pickerdite for Bickerdike, or Peverley for Beverley.

Johannes de Pyllyngton, 1579: P. T. Yorks. p. 167.
1673. Married—Samuel Pillington and Anne Wright: St. Jas. Clerkenwell, iii. 177.
London, 1.

Pilsbury, Pillsbury.—Local, 'of Spelsbury,' a village in co. Oxford; v. Spilsbury. These cor-

rupted forms are commonly found in the United States. I met with instances daily in the course of a tour through the States in May and June, 1888. But the correcter forms, Spilsbury and Spillsbury, are not unknown. The corruption into Pilsbury is a very natural one.

1792. Married — John Pilsbury and Ann Westmacott: St. Geo. Han. Sq. ii. 73.
— Richard Pilsbury and Anna Maynard: ibid. p. 76.
Philadelphia, 0, 1; Boston (U.S.), 2, 36.

Pilson.—Local, 'of Puleston.' This surname Puleston is found in the Reg. Univ. Oxon. (v. Index) as Pilston and Pillson; cf. Paxon for Paxton.

1522. Hugh Pylstone: Reg. Univ. Oxf. i. 123.
1569. William Weston and Katherine Pylson: Marriage Lic. (London), i. 42.
1580. Edward Pilson, co. Denbigh: Reg. Univ. Oxf. vol. ii. pt. ii. p. 94.
1601. John Puleston, co. Oxf.: ibid. pt. ii. p. 249.
1675. Married—Robert Pulleston and Mildred Eastland: St. Jas. Clerkenwell, p. 181.
Edward Pilson, 1679, bound for New England: Hotten's Lists of Emigrants, p. 397.

I cannot find the place Puleston. Philadelphia, 3.

Pilsworth, Pillsworth. — Local, 'of Pilsworth,' a township in the parish of Middleton, near Manchester.

1548. Roger Pyllysworthe and Ellen Polkynhorne: Marriage Lic. (Faculty Office), p. 13.
1577. William Pilsworth, London: Reg. Univ. Oxf. vol. ii. pt. ii. p. 76.
Jane Pilsworth, of the parish of Eccles (Manchester), 1603: Wills at Chester (1545-1620), p. 153.
1807. Married—Robert Pillsworth and Mary Hissey: St. Geo. Han. Sq. ii. 375.
Boston (U.S.), 1, 0; MDB. (co. Linc.), 1, 1.

Pilter.—Occup.; v. Pelliter.

Pilton.—Local, 'of Pilton,' a parish in co. Devon.

Richard de Pilton, co. Devon, 1273. A.
Adam de Pylton, co. Soms., 1 Edw. III: Kirby's Quest, p. 255.
1790. Married — William Pilton and Ann Oxley: St. Geo. Han. Sq. ii. 37.
London, 5.

Pim, Pimm, Pymm, Pym.—Bapt. 'the son of Pimme.' Considering that Eufemia is fairly common in the Hundred Rolls, that Pimme is feminine, and Phemie is still the nick., it is all but certain that we have here the solution of the name in question. Personally I have no doubt that this derivation is correct.

Eufemmia de Neville, co. Linc., 1273. A.
Katerina Eufemme, co. Norf., ibid.
Pimme, widow of Peter Seman, co. Cumb., ibid.
Bartholomew fil. Pimme, co. Hunts, ibid.
Chun Pimme, co. Camb., ibid.
Henry Pimme, co. Camb., ibid.
Roger Pym, co. Soms., 1 Edw. III: Kirby's Quest, p. 142.
Eufemia fil. Rogeri, co. Suff., 20 Edw. I. R.
Eufemmia Craker, 1379 : P. T. Yorks. p. 234.
Euphemia Forster, 1379 : ibid. p. 91.
Agnes Pyme, 1379 : ibid. p. 280.
Johannes Pymson, 1379 : ibid. p. 266.

Probably the following entries concern the same name :

1564. Bapt.—Effam Adlington : Reg. St. Peter, Cornhill, i. 11.
1620. — Frauncis, son of Alexander Brounescome and Effym, his wife : ibid. p. 68.
1635. Buried—Epham Vowell, *widow* : ibid. p. 195.
London, 6, 7, 3, 0 ; New York, 3, 0, 0, 1.

Pimlott, Pimblett, Pimblott, Pimblotte, Pimlock.—Bapt. 'the son of Pim' (q.v.), dim. Pimelot ; cf. Hewlett for Huelot (Hugh), &c. I have no proof of this statement. It is a name of Cheshire parentage. Of course the *b* in Pimblett, &c., is intrusive. In America a corrupted form, Pimlock, has sprung up ; cf. Glasscott and Glasscock.

1561. Buried—Mergret Pymlot : Reg. Prestbury, Cheshire, p. 6.
1562. Bapt.—Robert Pymlot, ibid.
Richard Pimlott, of Buglawton, 1624 : Wills at Chester (1621–50), p. 174.
Isabell Pimlott, 1648 : East Cheshire, i. 25.
Manchester, 4, 1, 0, 0, 0 ; MDB. (co. Chester), 3, 0, 1, 2, 0 ; Philadelphia, 1, 0, 0, 0, 1.

Pinchard.—Local ; v. Punchard.

Pinchback, Pinchbeck. — Local, 'of Pinchbeck,' a parish near Spalding, co. Lincoln.

Gilbert de Pincebek, co. Linc., 1273. A.
Walran de Pincebek, co. Linc., ibid.
William de Pincebek, co. Linc., ibid.

Thomas de Pincebeck, co. Linc., Hen. III–Edw. I. K.

The form Pinchback is found so early as the 16th century :

1551. Married — William Pyncheback and Jone Hamson : St. Michael, Cornhill, p. 6.

Pinchbeck is now a dictionary word, one Christopher Pinchbeck having given his name to an alloy of copper and zinc.
London, 1, 3 ; MDB. (co. Linc.), 0, 4 ; Philadelphia, 1, 0.

Pinchin (g ; v. Punshon.

Pinckard ; v. Punchard. A variant.
MDB. (co. Northampton), 3.

Pinckney ; v. Pinkney.

Pinder, Pindar, Pindard.—Offic. 'the pinder,' an impounder of strayed cattle ; v. Pinner. 'Pyndare of beestys, pynnar, *inclusor*': Prompt. Parv. 'A pynder, *inclusor*': Cath. Ang. The final *d* in Pindard is excrescent.

Hugh le Pinder, co. Linc., 1273. A.
Walter le Pinder, co. Linc., ibid.
Henry le Pynder, c. 1300. M.
John le Pindere. T.
John le Pinder. E.
1661. William Pindar and Catherine Jorden : Marriage Lic. (Faculty Office), p. 55.
1749. Married — John Pinder and Mary Butterfield : St. Geo. Han. Sq. i. 42.
London, 9, 4, 2 ; Philadelphia, 10, 0, 0.

Pine.—Local ; v. Pyne.

Pingeon ; v. Punshon.

Pinfold.—Local ; v. Penfold.

Pingston, Pinkstone, Pixton, Pickston, Pickstone.—Local, 'of Pinxton,' a parish in co. Derby. Over the border in Lancashire this surname has become popularized into Pixton, Pickston, &c.

1670. William Peckston, of Wrenbury : Wills at Chester (1660–80), p. 207.
1680. William Penkston, of Middlewich : ibid. p. 206.
1785. Married — William Dove and Mary Pinkstone : St. Geo. Han. Sq. i. 375.
London, 1, 0, 0, 0, 0 ; Manchester, 0, 0, 3, 2, 1.

Pink, Pinke.—Nick. 'the pink,'

i.e. chaffinch ; cf. Finch, Goldfinch, Chaffinch, Goldspink, and Spink.

Adam Pink, co. Norf., 1273. A.
John Pynke, co. Soms., 1 Edw. III : Kirby's Quest, p. 267.
1665. Bapt. — Eliz., d. John Pincke : St. Jas. Clerkenwell, i. 226.
London, 13, 0 ; New York, 3, 2.

Pinkerton.—Local, 'of Punchardon.' Mr. Lower says, 'We search in vain the gazetteers of England and Scotland for any locality bearing the designation of Pinkerton.' He declares that it is a corruption of Punchardon, and asserts that Punchardon is found as Pynkerton in Ragman Roll, A.D. 1296 (Patr. Brit. p. 268). I doubt not he is right. It is believed that Punchardon is the place now called Pont-Chardon, in the arrondissement of Argentan, Normandy. In Domesday the surname is found as Ponte-Cardon. We may take it therefore that the family came into England at the Conquest (v. Patr. Brit. p. 279).

Olyver de Punchardon, co. Devon, 1273. A.
Eudo de Punchardon, co. York, ibid.
Robert de Punchardun, co. Devon, Hen. III–Edw. I. K.
1752. Married — William Lake and Susanna Pinkerton : St. Geo. Han. Sq. i. 48.
London, 2 ; Philadelphia, 20.

Pinkney, Pinckney.—Local, 'de Pincheni.' It is probable that the name came into England at the Conquest. Mr. Lower says that Giles de Pincheni (temp. Henry I) endowed the monks of St. Lucien, in France, with lands at Wedon, co. Northants (Patr. Brit. p. 268).

Hamon de Pinkeney, co. Norf., temp. Hen. III : FF. vii. 195.
Henry de Pinkeni, co. Bucks, 1273. A.
Roesia de Pinkeny, co. Norf., ibid.
1751. Married—Richard Pinkney and Susanna Leisnot : St. Geo. Han. Sq. i. 46.
1756. — Roger Pinckney and Susanna Parsons : ibid. p. 64.
London, 2, 5 ; New York, 41, 11.

Pinn.—Local ; v. Pyne.

Pinnell. — ?———. I find no prefix 'de' or 'de la' to the early instances. Ralph Pinel was a tenant *in capite* in cos. Essex and Suffolk at the date of Domesday. Two centuries later, as will be seen below, the surname was still settled there. I cannot classify the name, but probably it is local in spite of the absence of local prefixes, and of Norman extraction.

John Pinel, co. Essex, 1273. A.
Henry Pinel, co. Hunts, ibid.
Roger Pinel, co. Oxf., ibid.
Mathew Pinel, co. Suff., ibid.
Warin Pinel, co. Oxf., Hen. III-Edw. I. K.
1564. Robert Brown and Eliz. Pynell: Marriage Lic. (London), i. 27.
London, 2; MDB. (co. Oxf.), 3; New York, 2.

Pinner.—(1) Offic. 'the pinner,' a pinder, an impounder of strayed cattle; v. Pinder. 'Pyndare of beestys, pynnar, *inclusor*': Prompt. Parv. Mr. Way in a note (p. 400) says, 'Amongst manorial or municipal officials the pounder of stray cattle is still in some places, as in Warwickshire, termed the pinner.' v. Penfold. (2) Occup. 'the pinner,' a pin-maker.

'Pynners, nedelers, and glasyers.'
               Cocke Lorelle's Bote.
Andrew le Pynner. G.
Walter le Pinner. X.
1569-70. Hugh Apparrye and Eliz. Pynner: Marriage Lic. (London), i. 14.
1788. Married — William Pinner and Eliz. Edwards: St. Geo. Han. Sq. ii. 8.
London, 5; New York, 15.

Pinnigar, -ger; v. Penniger.

Pinnington.—Local, 'of Pennington'; two parishes in co. Lanc. are so named.

1621. John Pinnington, of Horwich: Wills at Chester (1621-50), p. 175.
1639. Gilbert Pinnington, of Wigan: ibid.
Huyton (co. Lanc.), 2.

Pinnion, Pinyon, Penyon.—Bapt. 'Ap-Einion' (Welsh); v. Benyon, Baynham, or Bunyan.
MDB. (co. Kent), 0, 2, 1; London, 1, 1, 0.

Pinnock, Pinnick.—Local, 'of Pinnock, two parishes in cos. Cornwall and Gloucester.

William Pinnoc, co. Oxf., 1273. A.
Walter Pinnock, co. Wilts, ibid.
Roger Pynnock, co. Soms., 1 Edw. III: Kirby's Quest, p. 236.
London, 10, 1; MDB. (co. Soms.), 2, 0.

Pinson; v. Penson.

Pipe.—(1) Bapt. 'the son of Pipe.' A personal name in Domesday (Lower). (2) Local, 'of Pipe,'

a parish in co. Hereford, about three miles from Hereford.

Alicia Pipe, co. Hunts, 1273. A.
Harvey Pippe, co. Camb., ibid.
Margery Pipe, co. Soms., 1 Edw. III: Kirby's Quest, p. 130.
John Pype, co. Soms., 1 Edw. III: ibid.
London, 8.

Piper.—Occup. 'the piper,' a player on the bagpipes.
'A baggepipe cowde he blowe and sowne.
              Chaucer, C. T. 567.
Henry le Pipere, co. Oxf., 1273. A.
Adam le Piper, co. Camb., ibid.
Arnald le Pyper. P.
Robert le Pipere. M.
Peter le Pipre, Close Roll, 4 Edw. I.

Whether this was the Peter Piper who originated the alliterative nursery rhyme, 'Peter Piper picked a peck of pickled peppercorns,' I cannot say.

John le Pipere, co. Soms., 1 Edw. III: Kirby's Quest, p. 216.
Robert le Pipere, co. Soms., 1 Edw. III: ibid. p. 276.
Ema Piper, 1379: P. T. Yorks. p. 136.
1714. Married—Hugh Piper and Eliz. Matthews: St. Geo. Han. Sq. i. 14.
London, 25; Philadelphia, 34.

Pipester.—Occup. 'a female piper'; v. Piper.
Alice Pipestre, Close Roll, 30 Edw. I.

Pippett, Pippitt, &c.; v. Peppiatt.

Pippin.—(1) Bapt. 'the son of Philip.' A variant of Phippen (q.v.), and found in co. Somerset, where Phippen is a familiar name. (2) Bapt. 'the son of Pepin,' q.v. Probably a variant in some cases.

William Pippin, co. Bedf., 1273. A.
Richard Pipping, co. Soms., 1 Edw. III: Kirby's Quest, p. 217.
John Pippyng, co. Soms., 1 Edw. III: ibid. p. 243.

In the last two references the *g* is excrescent, as in Jennings, &c.
William Pippin, co. Bedf., 1273. A.
MDB. (co. Somerset), 2.

Pirie.—Local, 'at the pirie,' i.e. the pear orchard; v. Pury.

Geoffrey de la Pirie, co. Camb., 1273. A.
Robert del Pirie, co. Oxf., ibid.
William de la Pirie, co. Salop, ibid.
London, 2.

Pitcairn.—Local, 'of Pitcairn,' a village in the parish of Redgorton, co. Perth.

London, 5; Philadelphia, 1.

Pitcher.—Local. Not an occupation, but an abbreviation of Pichard'(v. Picard). Many instances will be found in this dictionary with the final *d* dropped.

Alan Pichard, co. York, 1273. A.
Walter Pichard, co. York, ibid.
John Picher, co. Soms., 1 Edw. III: Kirby's Quest, p. 182.
Gilbert Pycher, co. Soms., 1 Edw. III: ibid. p. 243.
1759. Married — John Pitcher and Catherine Shannon: St. Geo. Han. Sq. i. 85.
London, 8; Philadelphia, 5.

Pitchford.—Local; v. Pickford.

Pitchfork.—Local, 'of Pitchford'; v. Pickford. An imitative corruption. The intermediate form is represened in the following:

John de Picford, or de Picheford, or de Pichefort, co. Salop, Hen. III-Edw. I. K.
1601. Bapt.—Barnaby, s. John Pitchfort: St. Jas. Clerkenwell, i. 38.
1608-9. William Nocke and Eliz. Pitchfork (co. Salop): Marriage Lic. (London), i. 310.
MDB. (co. Lincoln), 2.

Pither, Pether.—Bapt. 'the son of Peter.' Pither must be looked upon as a variant of Pether, and that seems undoubtedly to represent Peter.

Thomas Pither, co. Glouc., 20 Edw. I. R.
John Peter, or Pether, B.A., 1526: Reg. Univ. Oxf. i. 181.
1778. Married—Thomas Pether and Arabella Fancourt: St. Geo. Han. Sq. i. 286.
1780.—John Pithor and Ann Benham: ibid. p. 310.
1783. — James Dredge and Sarah Pither: ibid. p. 351.
MDB. (co. Berks), 6, 0; London, 3, 3; New York, 0, 1.

Pithouse.—Local, 'at the pithouse,' from residence in the house by the pit.

Thomas Bennett, of Pitthouse, co. Dorset, 1623: Visitation of Dorset, 1623.

The grandfather of the above was John Bennett of Pitthouse. Oddly enough, his younger brother is styled in the same document Thomas Bennett, alias Pitt. And Bennett, alias Pite of Knockbillingsby, co. Limerick and co. Wilts, appears in Burke's General Armory, ed. 1878. (Communicated by T. Paul Rylands.)

London, 1 ; Langley (co. Bucks), 1.

Pitkethly.—Local, 'of Pit-caithly.' 'A well-known locality in the parish of Dumbarnie, co. Perth' (Lower).

London, 1 ; Boston (U.S.), 1.

Pitkin. — Bapt. 'the son of Peter,' from dim. Peterkin, corrupted to Pitkin ; v. Peterkin.

1545. John Pitkyn and Margaret Forward : Marriage Lic. (London), i. 10.
Franses Pittkin, 1668 : Reg. St. Jas. Clerkenwell, i. 235.
1760. Married—William Pittkin and Martha Roseblade : St. Geo. Han. Sq. i. 93.
1762. John Redhead and Sarah Pitkin : ibid. p. 111.
London, 6 ; Boston (U.S.), 5.

Pitman, Pittman.—Local, 'the pitman,' one who dwelt beside a deep hollow or pit ; cf. Bridgman, Styleman, &c. ; v. Pitt.

John Piteman, co. Bucks, 1273. A.
1626. John Pittman and Alice Pigge : Marriage Lic. (London), ii. 179.
1643. Buried—Andrew Pitman : St. Dionis Backchurch, p. 224.
London, 12, 18 ; Philadelphia, 6, 3.

Pitney.—Local, 'of Pitney,' a parish in co. Somerset.

London, 2 ; MDB. (co. Somerset), 1.

Pitt, Pitts.—Local, 'at the pit' or 'pitts,' from residence beside a hole, natural or artificial, or precipitous hollow, so called ; cf. coal-pit. Pitts represents several such hollows : or the final s is the patronymic, as in Williams, Jones, Wilkins, &c. ; cf. Brooks, Styles, Knowles, Holmes, &c. v. Putt.

Simon de la Pitte de Shottebrok, C. R., 36 Hen. III.
Robert in the Pyt, c. 1300. M.
Simon atte-Pitte, C. R., 26 Edw. III.
Richard Attepitte, 4 Hen. IV, co. Norf. : FF. vii. 189.
1588. Married—Richard Pit and Mary Bates : St. Antholin (London), p. 33.
1630-1. Arthur Pittes and Anne Pennington : Marriage Lic. (London), ii. 201.
1655. Bapt. s. John Pitt : St. Jas. Clerkenwell, i. 190.
London, 36, 15 ; Philadelphia, 19, 18.

Pittam, Pittom.—Local, 'of Petham,' a parish in co. Kent.

1575. John Pittam, co. Oxf. : Reg. Univ. Oxf. vol. ii. pt. ii. p. 69.
1671. Married—John Pittham and Anne Wilmote : St. Jas. Clerkenwell, iii. 175.
London, 1, 0 ; MDB. (co. Northampton), 2, 3.

Pitts.—Local ; v. Pitt.

Pittway, Pittaway.—Local, 'at the pit-way,' the way or path to the pit or hollow. Pittaway is formed like Ottaway, Greenaway, or Hathaway, from Ottway, Greenway, or Hathway.

1704. Bapt.—John, s. John Pitway, milliner : St. Dionis Backchurch, p. 143.
1757. Married— John Pittaway and Mary King : St. Geo. Han. Sq. i. 72.
London, 1, 0.

Pixley.—Local ; v. Pikesley.

Pixton ; v. Pingston.

Place, Plaice.—Local, 'at the place,' i.e. the stead, the farm, &c., any building or locality styled 'the Place' ; Fr. place. 'A place, a room, a stead . . . a faire large court' : Cotgrave. Hence place in the titles of mansions and villas. The surname arose from residence at such a spot.

William de la Place, co. Linc., 1273. A.
John atte Place, co. Soms., 1 Edw. III : Kirby's Quest, p. 258.
1592. Richard Prieste and Agnes Playce, widow : Marriage Lic. (London), i. 204.
1604-5. John Place, co. Yorks : Reg. Univ. Oxf. vol. ii. pt. ii. p. 280.
1627-8. Married—John Place and Eliz. Richardson : St. Dionis Backchurch, p. 22.
London, 5, 0 ; Philadelphia, 7, 0 ; Northumberland Court Dir., 1, 1.

Plackett.—Local. A sharpened form of Blackett, q.v.

1666. Married—William Placket and Eliz. Hutchinson : St. Jas. Clerkenwell, iii. 123.
London, 1.

Plaice.—Local ; v. Place.

Plain.—Local ; v. Plane.

Plaisted.—Local ; v. Playsted.

Plaister, Plaster.—Occup. 'the plasterer.' The usual term was Dauber, q.v.

John le Cementarius. B.
Adam le Plastier. X.
Walterus Plasterar, 1379 : P. T. Yorks. p. 132.
Joanna Plaisterer, co. York. W. 13.
William Plaisterer, co. York, ibid.

1660-1. Married—Thomas Diason and Margrett Plasterer : St. Dionis Backchurch, p. 36.
1713. Bapt.—John, s. Abraham Plastrier : St. Jas. Clerkenwell, ii. 74.
1793. Married—Samuel Plaster and Eliz. Symes : St. Geo. Han. Sq. ii. 103.
London, 1, 1 ; Oxford, 4, 0.

Plaistow, Plaistowe, Plasto, Plastow.—Local, 'at the playstow,' i.e. playground, the place set apart for games and sports ; M.E. stowe, a place (cf. Chepstow, Stowmarket, &c.). There are several parishes called Plaistow (v. Crockford), all of similar origin.

Robert atte Pleistowe, co. Oxf., 1273. A.
Nicholas de la Pleystowe, co. Oxf., ibid.
John de la Playstowe, co. Wilts, ibid.
Gunilda Attepaleystowe, C. R., 6 Edw. I.
1760. Married—John Welch and Mary Plaistow : St. Geo. Han. Sq. i. 94.
1783. — Matthew Plestowe and Charlotte Houghton : ibid. p. 352.
London, 1, 1, 1, 1.

Plampin ; v. Pamphilon.

Plane, Playne, Plain.—Local, 'at the plane-tree,' from residence thereby ; cf. Box, Maple, Ash, Oak, Birch, Birk, &c.

Gilbert Plane, co. Camb., 1273. A.
1581. William Playne and Mary Lusher : Marriage Lic. (London), i. 102.
1797. Married — William Plane and Louise Middlecott : St. Geo. Han. Sq. ii. 159.
MDB. (co. Essex), 2, 0, 0 ; (co. Gloucester), 0, 10, 0 ; (co. Norf.), 4, 0, 2 ; London, 1, 2, 0.

Plank.—Local, 'at the plank,' from residence thereby ; M.E. planke, Fr. planche. The derivation seems curious, but cf. Box, Peartree, Birch. Surnames taken from residence beside single trees were common.

William de la Plaunke, C. R., 46 Edw. III.
Matilda de la Plank, 17 Edw. I. BBB.
Jacobus de la Planche and Plaunche : 34 Edw. I. BBB.
1788. Married—Edward Plank and Susanna Willis : St. Geo. Han. Sq. ii. 13.
London, 4 ; Philadelphia, 5.

Plant, Plante.—? ——. I give this up. I can suggest no satisfactory solution.

Robert Plante, co. Camb., 1273. A.
Roger Plante, co. Camb., ibid.
1605. Married — Symon Plante and Catherine Weaver : St. Jas. Clerkenwell, iii. 30.

R r

1809. Married — John Plant and Ann Stubbs : St. Geo. Han. Sq. ii. 417.

London, 11, 2 ; Philadelphia, 10, 0.

Planterose.—?——. It seems impossible to offer any satisfactory solution of such a name as this ; cf. Pluckrose.

John Plannterose, tenet 1 mes' et 1 croft, co. Camb., 1273. A.

London, 1.

Plaskett, Plasket, Plaskitt. —Local, ' of Plaskets,' a township in the parish of Falstone, co. Northumberland (Lower).

1683. Married—Robert Plaskett and Mary Ebsworth : St. Jas. Clerkenwell, iii. 201.

1761. — Abraham Plasket and Susanna Pocock : St. Geo. Han. Sq. i. 107.

London, 2, 1, 2.

Plaster ; v. Plaister.

Plasto, Plastow.—Local ; v. Plaistow.

Plater, Platter.—Occup. ' the plater,' i.e. a maker of metal plates, flat dishes, &c. ; v. Platesmith.

Walter Playtur, co. Hunts, 1273. A.
Anne Playter. V.
1435. Edmund Playter, co. Norf. : FF. ii. 454.
1767. Married—John Lane and Martha Playter : St. Geo. Han. Sq. iii. 168.
London, 3, 0 ; New York, 0, 2.

Platesmith.—Occup. 'the plate-smith,' one who hammered metal into plates, flat dishes, &c. The surname is quite extinct.

Johannes Platesmyth, 1379 : P. T. Yorks. p. 70.
Johanna Platesmyth, 1379 : ibid. p. 80.

Platfoot.—Nick. ' splay-footed.' ' Plat-footed, splay-footed ' (Halliwell) ; cf. Barefoot, Proudfoot.

William Platfote, C. R., 1–2 Philip and Mary, pt. ii.

Platt, Platts.—Local, ' of the plat,' i.e. a small patch of ground, the same as plot ; v. Skeat, who adds that ' the spelling is probably due to M.E. plat, Fr. plat, flat,' whence our plate, a flat dish. Monosyllabic surnames often take an s at the end ; cf. Holmes, Lowndes, Bridges, Styles, &c. Hence Platts.

1349. James de Plat, rector of Trimingham, co. Norf. : FF. viii. 178.

Robertus del Platte, 1379 : P. T. Yorks. p. 190.
Johannes de Plattes : 1379 : ibid. p. 221.
1577. John Platt and Elis. Longe : Marriage Lic. (London), i. 76.
1668. Bapt.—Elis., d. John Plattes : St. Jas. Clerkenwell, i. 235.
London, 23, 3 ; West Rid. Court Dir., 5, 2 ; New York, 62, 0.

Player.—Occup. 'the player,' probably on a musical instrument, and therefore similar in origin to Piper, Tabor, Trumper, Fiddler, &c.

Arthur Player, temp. Elis. Z.
1582. John Badsey and Edith Player : Marriage Lic. (London), i. 113.
1619. John Player : Reg. Univ. Oxf. vol. ii. pt. i. p. 361.
1755. Married—Michael Player and Eliz. Reeves : St. Geo. Han. Sq. i. 58.
London, 5 ; MDB. (co. Somerset), 7 ; Philadelphia, 1.

Playfair.—Nick. 'the playfere,' a playfellow. Now almost entirely a Scotch surname : the word occurs in Jamieson's Scottish Dictionary. ' Pleyfere, collusor ' : Prompt. Parv. (1440). ' And whanne sche hadde go with hir felowis and pleiferis ' (sodalibus, Vulg.) : Judges xi. 38 (Wyclif).

1596. Thomas Playfere : Reg. Univ. Oxf. vol. ii. pt. i. p. 347.
1608. Thomas Playfere, rector of Shipdam, co. Norf. : FF. x. 247.
1796. Married—Thomas Playfair and Sarah Boyer : St. Geo. Han. Sq. ii. 157.
London, 2.

Playne ; v. Plane.

Playsted, Playstead, Plested, Plaisted.—Local, ' at the playstead,' i.e. playground, from residence thereby ; cf. Plaistow.

Alex. atte Pleystude, co. Soms., 1 Edw. III : Kirby's Quest, p. 81.
John atte Pleystude, co. Soms., 1 Edw. III : ibid. p. 110.
Philip atte Pleystede, co. Soms., 1 Edw. III : ibid. p. 158.
1581. Edward Plaisteed, co. Sussex : Reg. Univ. Oxf. vol. ii. pt. ii. p. 99.
1652. Robert Plasteed : St. Mary Aldermary (London), p. 22.
1711. Married—James Plaisted and Lettitia Tayler : St. Dionis Backchurch, p. 56.
1794. Married — Samuel Cook and Mary Playsted : St. Geo. Han. Sq. ii. 106.
London, 1, 0, 1, 0 ; MDB. (co. Glouc.), 0, 2, 0, 0 ; Philadelphia, 0, 0, 0, 2.

Pleader.—Occup. 'the pleader,' i.e. a lawyer, one who pleaded a case before a judge. Fr. plaideur, a lawyer.

' Pledoures shulde peynen hem to plede ' : P. Plowman, B. vii. 42 (quoted by Skeat).

Henry le Pleidour, co. Salop, 1273. A.
Roger Pleadour, C. R., 13 Edw. III. pt. i.
Ralph Pledour, C. R., 31 Edw. III.

Pleasant, Pleasance. — (1) Bapt. ' the son of Pleasant,' or Pleasance ; cf. Clement and Clemence, Constant and Constance.

Pleysaunt Aylmar. H.
Plesencia Fromund, C. R., 29 Hen. III.

The font-name lingered on into the last century.

1612. Married — Pleasance Beales (fem.) : Reg. Burgh, Norfolk.
1681. Bapt.—Pleasant Tarlton (fem.) : Reg. St. Dionis Backchurch (London).
1757. Married—Pleasant Dadd (fem.) : Reg. Canterbury Cath.
Robert Pleasance, rector of Boldon, 1655 : DDD. ii. 62.

(2) Local, ' of Plesence.'

Reginald de Plesence, co. Linc., 1273. A.
Peter de Plesenc', co. York, ibid.
Astin de Plesenz, co. Linc., ibid.
London, 1, 1 ; MDB. (co. Camb.), 0, 1.

Pledger.—Occup. 'the pledger,' one who gave securities (?).

1805. Married—James Stanton and Sarah Pledger : St. Geo. Han. Sq. ii. 324.
MDB. (co. Camb.), 1 ; (co. Essex), 5.

Plevin. — Bapt. ' the son of Blethyn,' a Welsh personal name. The usual patronymic is Blevin, but Plevin is not without representatives (v. Blevin and Blethyn) ; cf. Pinnion and Benyon, Pumphrey and Boumphrey, also Welsh surnames.

Alice Plethin, alias Mayo, of the city of Chester, 1670 : Wills at Chester (1660-80), p. 212.
William Plevin, of Kinnerton, 1685 : ibid. (1681-1700), p. 199.

The Manchester Courier, October 26, 1886, announces the marriage of ' George James, son of the late James Plevin, Nantwich, to Rhoda,' &c. Nantwich is near the Welsh border.

Manchester, 1.

Plews, Plues. — Bapt. Ap-Lewis (Welsh), whence Plewis, Plews, now found also as Plues. One of these latter tells me his great grandfather wrote it Plews; cf. Price, Pritchard, Ployd, &c. I lack absolute proof of the above derivation.

Griffin Lewys, or Lews, 1518 : Reg. Univ. Oxf. i. 108.
1792. Married—Thomas Plews and Charlotte Boyce: St. Geo. Han. Sq. ii. 80.
1802. — Michael Francis Plues and Mary Birley : ibid. p. 254.
London, 4, 0 ; Philadelphia, 6, 0 ; Kendal (Plues), 1.

Pleynamour.—Nick. ' full of love' (v. Fullalove); cf. Paramor, Douceamour, Phillimore.

'And geven me pleyne (full) poure and might
The kyngdom of heuene for to preche.'
York Mystery Plays, p. 160, ll. 103-4.
' Men speken of romaunces of pris,
Of Hornchild, and of Ipotis,
Of Bevis, and Sire Guy,
Of Sire Libeux, and Pleindamour,
But Sire Thopas, he bereth the flour
Of real chevalrie.'
Chaucer, C. T. 13825-30.
Andreas Pleynamur, co. Suff., 1273. A.
Cristiana Playnamur, co. Suff., ibid.
Philip Pleyndamour, C. R., 14 Edw. II.
Agnes Playnamour, 1379 : P. T. Yorks. p. 282.
Thomas Pleynamour, C. R., 4 Hen. IV. pt. i.

Plimley.—Local, ' of Plumley,' q.v., a variant ; cf. Plimpton for Plumpton.

1665. Bapt.—Ann, d. John Plimley: St. Jas. Clerkenwell, i. 226.
1796. Married—Rev. Henry Plimley and Thomasin Porter : St. Geo. Han. Sq. ii. 147.
London, 1.

Plimmer.—Occup. ' the plumber ' ; a variant of Plummer (q.v.). Cf. Plimpton for Plumpton, or Plimley for Plumley.

1780. Married—James Plimmer and Jane Talbot : St. Geo. Han. Sq. i. 313.
Manchester, 2.

Plimpton, Plympton.—Local, ' of Plympton,' a parish in co. Devon. Sometimes, however, a variant of Plumpton, q.v.

Robert de Plimpton, co. York, 20 Edw. I.
Simon de Plympton, co. Soms., 1 Edw. III : Kirby's Quest, p. 278.
London, 4, 0 ; Boston (U.S.), 16, 11.

Plimsaul, Plimsoll.—Local, ' of Plemonstall' (?), a parish about four miles from Chester. From Plimstall to Plimsoll would be an easy stage. I have no certain proof of this.

London, 1, 1 ; MDB. (co. Norf.), 1, 0 ; Sheffield, 0, 1.

Plomer; v. Plummer.

Plowden. — Local, ' of Plowden,' an estate in co. Salop. The Plowdens of Plowden Hall in that county still exist.

Roger de Ploeden, co. Salop, 1273. A.
1618. Edward Ployden, co. Salop : Reg. Univ. Oxf. vol. ii. pt. ii. p. 374.
MDB. (co. Salop), 2 ; New York, 1.

Plowman. — Occup. ' the ploughman,' a farm labourer, one engaged in ploughing.

John le Ploghman, co. Rutland, 1273. A.
John le Plouman, co. Linc., ibid.
John le Ploman, co. Soms., 1 Edw. III : Kirby's Quest, p. 232.
Luke le Ploman, co. Soms., 1 Edw. III : ibid.
Willelmus Ploghman, 1379 : P. T. Yorks. p. 256.
Alicia Plughman, 1379 : ibid. p. 96.
1602-3. Humphrey Dovey and Juliana Plowman : Marriage Lic. (London), i. 275.
London, 8 ; Philadelphia, 11.

Plowright. — Occup. ' the ploughwright,' a maker of ploughs; cf. Plowsmith.

William le Plowritte, co. Camb., 1273. A.
William le Ploughwryte, 1307. M.
Thomas Hyneson, *ploghwryght*, 1379 : P. T. Yorks. p. 292.
Catherine Ploughwright, co. York. W. 2.
1778. Married — Thomas Lloyd and Mary Plowright : St. Geo. Han. Sq. i. 290.
Manchester, 1 ; New York, 1.

Plowsmith. — Occup. ' the plowsmith,' a maker of ploughs. Plowright was the usual name, but we have proof that Plowsmith existed.

' Until a *smith*, men callen Dan Gerveis,
That in his forge smithed *plow*-harness.'
Chaucer, Milleres Tale, 3758-9.
William le Plousmith, Rot. Fin., 7 Edw. I.

Ployd. — Bapt. ' the son of Lloyd,' from the Welsh Ap-Lloyd. This is found in England generally as Bloyd (q.v.), in America as Ployd ; cf. Breese and Preece.

Philadelphia, 7.

Pluck. — I do not know the origin of this surname, and therefore simply confine myself to instances. Perhaps a French importation.

John Pluk, C. R., 3 Edw. IV.

1775. Married — Auguste François Plique and Jeanne Josephine Viulley : St. Geo. Han. Sq. i. 249.
London, 3.

Plucknett.—Local, ' of Pluke-net '; v. Plunkett, of which it is a variant.

William de Plukenet, co. Berks, 1273. A.
Alanus de Plugenet, 50 Hen. III : BBB. p. 122.
Alanus de Plukenet, 28 Edw. I : ibid. p. 587.
Eliner Plucknete, 1652 : Reg. St. Mary Aldermary (London), p. 93.
John Plucknet, 1655 : ibid. p. 94.
1735. Married — John Austin and Susanna Plucknett : St. Geo. Han. Sq. i. 15.
London, 1.

Pluckrose.—Nick. This surname is as old as the 13th century. Lower suggests that it and Pull-rose arose out of feudal custom. He finds them in Sussex in 1296, and in the same county knows property close to Ashdown Forest held of the Duchy of Lancaster by one *red rose*. The reeve of the manor comes periodically and plucks a rose from the tree (v. Patr. Brit. p. 271).

Alan Pluckerose, co. Suff., 1273. A.
Richard Pluckerose, co. Wilts, ibid.
London, 6.

Plues; v. Plews.

Plum, Plumb, Plumbe, Plume, Plumm.—Local, ' at the plum,' i.e. plum-tree (v. Plumptre); cf. Crabb and Crabtree. The *b* in Plumb and Plumbe is, of course, excrescent.

Richard Plumbe, co. Camb., 1273. A.
Symon Plumbe, co. Hunts, ibid.
Agnes Plombe, of Woodbank, *spinster*, 1590 : Wills at Chester, p. 153.
Robert Plumb, of Wavertree, 1618 : ibid.
London, 2, 6, 3, 2, 1.

Plumber; v. Plummer.

Plumbly; v. Plumley.

Plumbridge; v. Plumridge.

Plumer.—Occup. ' the plumber.' For early instances, v. Plummer.

1566. Ralph Plumer and Agnes Lendall : Marriage Lic. (London), i. 34.
1739. Married—Richard Plumer and Deborah Atkins : St. Geo. Han. Sq. i. 23.
1779. — John Plumer and Ann Finch : ibid. p. 305.
London, 1 ; New York, 9.

Plumley, Plumly, Plumbly, Plumbley.—Local, 'of Plumley,' a township in the parish of Great Budworth, co. Chester. The *b* in Plumbly is the usual excrescence. For a variant, v. Plimley. Of course many other small spots would be called Plum-ley, 'the meadow where the plum-trees grew.'

Henry Plomlegh, co. Soms., 1 Edw. III : Kirby's Quest, p. 108.
1552-3. Buried — Thomas Plumlye : St. Dionis Backchurch, p. 183.
1773. Married—George Plumley and Dorothy Avis : St. Geo. Han. Sq. i. 231.
London, o, o, 1, o; Liverpool, 1, o, o, 1; Philadelphia, 6, 9, o, o.

Plummer, Plumber, Plomer.—Occup. 'the plumber.' Cotg. 'plummer.' Fr. *plomb*, lead. 'Plumber or plomere, *plumbarius*' : Prompt. Parv. 'The Plummers and Patenmakers marched together in the York Pageant' (York Mystery Plays, p. xxii).

William le Plummer, C. R., 39 Hen. III. pt. i.
Henry le Plomere, London, 1273. A.
Andrew le Plumer, or Plummer, co Kent, ibid.
John le Plumer, co. Oxf., ibid.
Gilbert le Plomer, co. Camb., ibid.
Henry le Plummer, 25 Edw. I: Freemen of York (Surt. Soc.), i. 6.
Ricardus Plummer, 1379 : P. T. Yorks. p. 161
1631. Married—George Arnold and Eliz. Plummer : St. Jas. Clerkenwell, iii. 62.
1804. — Jarrard John Howard and Margery Plomer : St. Geo. Han. Sq. ii. 298.
MDB. (co. Kent), 4, 1, 6; London, 22, o, o; Boston (U.S.), 74, o, o; New York, 11, 2, o.

Plumpton.—Local, 'of Plumpton' : (1) a township in the parish of Kirkham, co. Lanc. ; (2) a parish in co. Sussex; (3) a parish in co. Northumberland. Also other smaller spots in various counties ; cf. Plimpton and Plympton.

William de Plumton, co. Northampton, 1273. A.
Robert de Plumpton, co. Northampton, ibid.
John Plumpton, of West Derby, co. Lanc., 1582 : Wills at Chester, i. 153.
Thomas Plumpton, of West Derby, co. Lanc., 1619 : ibid.
1576. Richard Plumpton and Johanna Husband : Marriage Lic. (London), i. 73.
London, 3.

Plumptre, Plumptree, Plumtre.—Local, (1) 'of Plumtree,' a parish in co. Nottingham, five miles from the capital ; (2) 'at the plum-tree,' from residence by some particular fruit-tree ; cf. Peartree, Crabtree, Rowntree, &c.

John Plumtre, or Plumtree, 1538 : Reg. Univ. Oxf. i. 191.
Alban Plumtree, co. Bedford, 1585 : ibid. vol. ii. pt. ii. p. 140.
1755. Married—Francis Plumptre and Dorothy Bury : St. Geo. Han. Sq. i. 56.
London, 2, o, o; MDB. (co. Notts), o, 1, 1.

Plumridge, Plumbridge, Plummeridge.—Local, 'at the plum-ridge.' I cannot discover the precise locality. Plumbridge is a manifest variant, the *b* being intrusive ; cf. Plumb for Plum.

1784. Married—James Plumridge and Susanna Clarke : St. Geo. Han. Sq. i. 357.
London, 3, 4, 2; Oxford, 9, 1, o; Boston (U.S.), 1, o, o.

Plumstead.—Local, 'of Plumstead,' a parish in co. Kent.

Simon de Plumpstede, co. Norf., 1205 : FF. v. 461.
William de Plumstede, co. Norf., Hen. III–Edw. I. K.
1764. Married—Thomas Martin and Eliz. Plumstead : St. Geo. Han. Sq. i. 127.
1771. — John Lawrence Jones and Ursula Plumstead : ibid. p. 210.
Philadelphia, 1.

Plunkett, Plunket, Plunkitt.—(1) Local, 'of Plukenet.' The same as the once great name of Plucknett (q.v.), by transference of *n* from the second to the first syllable. There are many such instances in this dictionary.

Joceus de Plukenet, co. Berks, 1273. A.
Joceus de Plunkenet, co. Berks, ibid.

(2) Nick. (?) from the complexion : *blanchet*, *blanket*, white ; whence blanket and plunket for a coarse woollen cloth (v. *plunket*, Halliwell). A statute of Richard III calls it 'plonket.' The form in Prompt. Parv. is 'plunket.' Mr. Way quotes a line from Awntyrs of Arthure :

'Hir belte was of plonkete, with birdis fulle baulde.'

Nevertheless, although some of our Plunketts may owe their name to (2), like Russell, Burnett, Blount, &c., the general derivation is undoubtedly (1).

1574-5. Edward Plunket, of Ireland : Reg. Univ. Oxf. vol. ii. pt. ii. p. 59.
1786. Married—Christopher Plunkett and Sarah Fimester : St. Geo. Han. Sq. i. 387.
London, 7, o, o; New York, 38, 5, 1.

Plympton; v. Plimpton.

Pobjay, -joy ; v. Popjay.

Pochin.—Bapt. 'the son of Pochin,' evidently the dim. of some personal name.

Adam Pochon, co. Soms., 1 Edw. III : Kirby's Quest, p. 83.
Manchester, 1.

Pocklington.—Local, 'of Pocklington,' a parish in E. Rid. Yorks. From the East Riding the surname crossed the river into co. Lincoln, where it is familiarly known to-day.

Remigius de Poclinton, co. York, 1273. A.
Adam de Poklyngton, *mercer*, 2 Edw. I : Freemen of York (Surt. Soc.), i. 1.
Ricardus Pokelyngton, 1379 : P. T. Howdenshire, p. 17.
1575. William Pocklington, co. Linc. : Reg. Univ. Oxf. vol. ii. pt. ii. p. 67.
1700. Married — Joseph Pocklington and Eliz. Roberts : St. Geo. Han. Sq. ii. 206.
London, 2 ; MDB. (co. Linc.), 10.

Pocock.—Nick. ; v. Peacock.

Podger.—A variant of Proger (q.v.), 'the son of Roger.'

1780. Married—William Baker and Ann Podger : St. Geo. Han. Sq. ii. 28.
London, 1 ; MDB. (co. Somerset), 4.

Podmore. — Local, 'of Podmore,' a township in the parish of Eccleshall, co. Stafford. The surname crossed over the border into Cheshire.

John Podmore, of Sandbach, 1626 : Wills at Chester, ii. 176.
Reginald Podmore, of Hassall, co. Ches., 1628 : ibid.
Richard Podmore, of Sandbach, c. 1650 : East Cheshire, ii. 405.
London, 4 ; MDB. (co. Staff.), 3 ; New York, 1.

Poe.—Nick. 'the peacock' ; cf. Pocock for Peacock. '*Poe*, a turkey. North England' (Halliwell). The name seems in this case to have been transferred from one fowl to another ; v. Pea and Pay.

1660. Thomas Jenner and Anne Poe (co. York): Marriage Lic. (Faculty Office), p. 48.
Leeds, 1; New York, 4.

Pogmore, Pogmoor.—Local, 'of Pogmore,' some spot in the W. Rid. Yorks.
Willelmus de Poggemore, 1379: P. T. Yorks. p. 17.
Thomas Pogemore, 1379: ibid.
Adam Pogemore, 1379: ibid.

The above lived in the township of Brampton Bierlow, in the parish of Wath-upon-Dearne, near Barnsley.
Sheffield, 0, 1; MDB. (co. Ches.), 1, 0.

Pogson, Pockson, Poxon, Pogge.—Bapt. 'the son of Margaret.' Pog was the earlier form of Peg, as Mog was of Meg. As Mogson became also Mockson (now Moxon), so Pogson became Pockson and Poxon. Why names in M should take P for their initial in the nick. form I cannot say; cf. Patty from Martha, and Polly from Mary, the intermediate form being Matty and Molly.
Margareta Pogge, 1379: P. T. Yorks. p. 141.
Adam Pogge, 1379: ibid. p. 106.
1577. Married — Robert Pogge and Agnes Camden: St. Antholin (London), p. 26.
1620. John Pogson, of Manchester, *barber*: Wills at Chester (1545-1620), p. 153.
1666. Married—Richard Scrooke and Eliz. Pog: St. Jas. Clerkenwell, p. 128.
1754. — John Pogson and Eliz. Mary Milward: St. Geo. Han. Sq. i. 52.
London, 3, 1, 0, 0; Linthwaite (Yorks), 1, 0, 0, 0; West Rid. Court Dir., 1, 0, 0, 0; MDB. (co. Derby), 0, 0, 1, 0; New York, 0, 0, 0, 1.

Poignant.—Nick. One who was sharp, biting, stinging, in retort. There is no reason why the surname should not have lived, but I fear it has disappeared.
John Poignant, C. R., 15 Ric. II.
Gilbert Poygnant. J.
1790. Married—Albanis Beaumont and Louisa Poignand: St. Geo. Han. Sq. ii. 50.

Pointdexter, Poingdestre.—Nick. An heraldic term. One of the nine chief local points of an escutcheon. 'Point-dexter parted ten (in Heraldry), an abatement due to a Braggadochio': Bailey's

Dictionary, 1742. John Poyndexter, Fellow of Exeter College, Oxford, was dispossessed of his living in 1642 (Walker's Sufferings of the Clergy). The name still exists. 'Poingdestre and Truman, Chemists, 187 Newington Butts': London Directory.
1767. Married — John Troulliet and Eliz. Poingdestre: St. Geo. Han. Sq. i. 170.
London, 0, 1.

Pointer, Poynter, Pointmaker.— Occup. 'the pointer,' a maker of points. A manufacturer of tagged lace, for fastening hose and doublet together, &c. Falstaff in the act of saying, 'Their points being broken,' is interrupted by the remark, 'Down fell their hose' (1 Henry IV). The name and occupation occur in the Privy Purse Expenses, Elizabeth of York (p. 120): 'John Poyntmaker, for pointing of XL dozen points of silk pointed with agelettes of laton.' An Act passed 1 Edw. IV mentions, among others, 'Keper of oure Armour in the Toure of London, maker of poyntes, constable of oure castell of Hadleigh, &c.': Rot. Parl. Edw. IV.
Vasse le Poynter, co. Camb., 1273. A.
John le Poyntour. B.
Robert le Poyntour. T.
William Poyntmakere. S.
Robert Ponyter (sic), co. Soms., 1 Edw. III: Kirby's Quest, p. 240.
1607. Bapt. — William, s. Andrew Poynter: St. Jas. Clerkenwell, i. 50.
1617. John Poynter, London: Reg. Univ. Oxf. vol. ii. pt. ii. p. 359.
London, 3, 4, 0; Philadelphia, 2, 9, 0.

Pointing, Pontin, Ponting, Poynton.—Local, 'of Pointon,' formerly a chapelry in the parish of Semperingham, co. Lincoln. But v. Poynton.
Emecina de Poynton, co. Linc., 1273. A.
Jordan de Poynton, co. Linc., ibid.
Thomas de Poynton, co. Linc., ibid.
1790. Married—Jonathan Poynton and Mary Wood: St. Geo. Han. Sq. ii. 36.
1795. — James Bewley and Esther Ponton: ibid. p 140.
1809. William Pointing and Eliz. Wright: ibid. p. 419.
London, 4, 1, 4, 0; Philadelphia, 0, 0, 0, 2.

Pole, Poll.— Local, 'at the pool,' from residence beside a pond

or small lake; v. Pool. In some cases the parent of this name is Poole, a seaport in co. Dorset. The etymology is the same.
Hugh de la Pole, co. Camb., 1273. A.
Peter de la Pole, co. Oxf., ibid.
Anthony de la Pole, co. Devon, Hen. III-Edw. I. K.
Griffin de la Pole, co. Salop, 20 Edw. I. R.
Richard de la Pole, co. Derby, ibid.
John atte Pole, co. Soms., 1 Edw. III: Kirby's Quest, p. 118.
Robert atte Pole, co. Soms., 1 Edw. III: ibid. p. 126.
Francis Pole, or Poole, co. Devon, 1609-10: Reg. Univ.Oxf.vol.ii.pt.ii.p.300.
David Pole, or Poole, Bishop of Peterborough, 1557: ibid. vol. i. p. 141.
1736. Married—John Marshall and Jane Pole: St. Jas. Clerkenwell, iii. 264.
London, 4, 0; Philadelphia, 12, 1.

Polecat.— ? Nick. 'the polecat' (?).
Bernard Pilechat, co. Hunts, 1273. A.

Polkin.—Bapt.'the son of Paul,' from the dim. Paulkin; cf. Watkin, Wilkin, &c.
John Polkyn, or Palkyn, sup. for B.A., 1526: Reg. Univ. Oxf. i. 142.

Polkinghorne, Polkinhorn, Puckinghorne.—Local, 'of Polkinhorne.' An estate in the parish of Guinear, co. Cornwall.

'From this place were denominated an old family of gentlemen, surnamed Polkinhorne': Gilbert's Cornwall, ii. 152 (quoted by Lower).
Robarte Pokenghorne, 1541: Reg. St. Dionis Backchurch (London), p. 71.
1808. Married—Henry Polkinghorne and Mary Hill: St. Geo. Han. Sq. ii. 394.
London, 0, 1, 0; MDB. (co. Cornwall), 5, 0, 2.

Pollard.—Nick. 'pollard,' one who had his hair cropped short, from *poll*, the head, and suffix *-ard*, Hence a pollard tree, a tree lopped at the top; cf. Ballard.
John Polhard, C. R., 56 Hen. III.
William Polard, co. Camb., 1273. A.
Stephen fil. Pollard, co. Kent, ibid.

In this last case the father is simply called by his nickname, not his personal name.
Henry Pollard, c. 1300. M.
1548. Ellis Pollard and Johanna Chapman: Marriage Lic. (London), i. 11.
1717. Bapt.—Eliz., d. Edward Pollard: St. Dionis Backchurch, p. 154.
London, 27; Philadelphia 25.

Pollett, Pollitt, Poulett, Powlett.—(1) Bapt. 'the son of Paul,' from the popular form Poll, and dim. Poll-ett. Another familiar form was Powl, whence the dim. Powl-ett. (2) Local, ' of Pawlett,' a parish in co. Somerset; v. Paulett.

Quintinus Poulet, Pat. R., 7 Hen. VII.
John Pawlet, or Poulett, or Pollett, sup. for B.A., March, 1530: Reg. Univ. Oxf. i. 159.
Robert Paulet, or Pollett, 1538: ibid. p. 190.
1661. Elias Hirons and Joane Pollett: Marriage Lic. (London), ii. 288.
1759. Married—Edmund Powlett and Frances Kelly: St. Geo. Han. Sq. i. 83.
London, 7, 1, 0, 0; Philadelphia, 1, 12, 0, 0.

Polley, Polly.—(1) Bapt., a variant of Pawley, q.v. (cf. Polson for Paulson). (2) Local, a variant of Pooley; v. Pulley. It is probable that both (1) and (2) have contributed to the existence of these surnames.

1574. Robert Polley and Grace Gooddaye: Marriage Lic. (London), i. 61.
1805. Married—William Polley and Eliz. Hodsdon: St. Geo. Han. Sq. ii. 319.
London, 4, 1; Boston (U.S.), 4, 0.

Pollinger, Bollinger.→Occup.; v. Bullinger and cf. Pullinger.

William Pallinger, c. Eliz. Z.
London, 1, 1.

Pollman; a variant of Pullman, q.v.

New York, 2.

Pollyblank, Polyblank. — Local. An undoubted local Cornwall name beginning with ' Poly,' so familiar to that county. Perhaps it is a corruption of Polyphant, a hamlet in the parish of Lewannick, near Launceston.

By Tre, Pol, and Pen
You may know Cornish men.'
London, 1, 3; Devon Court Dir., 0, 2.

Polson. — Bapt. ' the son of Paul,' from the popular form Pol; v. Powle.

1571. James Polson, New College: Reg. Univ. Oxf. vol. ii. pt. iii. p. 10.
Pol Withipol summoned to attend the Council: Proc. and Ord. Privy Council, vii. 156.
1796. Married — Thomas Polson and Hannah Solitzky: St. Geo. Han. Sq. ii. 157.
London, 2; Manchester, 1; Boston (U.S.), 5.

Pomeroy, Pomroy. — Local, ' de la pommeraye,' at the apple orchard, from residence thereby; cf. Pury, i.e. at the pear orchard.

Joan de la Pomeroy. H.
Henry de la Pomereye, or Pomeraye, co. Devon, 1273. A.
John Pomeray, co. Oxf., ibid.
Isota de la Pomerey, co. Devon, Hen. III-Edw. I. K.
Robert Pomeroy, co. Soms., 1 Edw. III: Kirby's Quest, p. 156.
1594. Andrew Pomeroy, or Pomroy, co. Devon: Reg. Univ. Oxf. vol. ii. pt. ii. p. 201.
1638-9. Pascoe Pomroy and Eliz. Wilson: Marriage Lic. (London), ii. 239.
MDB. (co. Devon), 5, 0; London, 2, 1; New York, 16, 3.

Pomfret, Pontefract, Pomfritt, Pomphrett.—Local, ' of Pontefract,' co. York. As everybody knows, Pomfret is the usual pronunciation, and has been for many centuries.

Robert Pumfret, co. Norf., 1273. A.
Thomas le Lang, de Pontefracto, 3 Edw. II: Freemen of York, i. 13.
Johannes de Poumefrgyte, 1370: P. T. Yorks. p. 108.
1579. Garrett Florence and Catherine Pomfrett: Marriage Lic. (London), i. 91.
1776. Married—William Pomfrett and Sarah Burton: St. Geo. Han. Sq. i. 265.
London, 1, 1, 0, 0; MDB. (co. Kent), 3, 0, 0, 0; Manchester, 0, 1, 1, 0; Boston (U.S.), 0, 0, 0, 1.

Pond. — Local, ' at the pond,' i.e. the pound, or enclosure for strayed cattle, from residence thereby; v. Ponder.

Geoffrey ad le Pond, co. Bedf., 1273. A.
Bartholomew de la Ponde, co. Bucks, Hen. III-Edw. I. K.
Sewal atte Ponde, c. 1300. M.
Henry Ponde, co. Soms., 1 Edw. III: Kirby's Quest, p. 223.
Roger atte Ponde, C. R., 17 Edw. III. pt. ii.
1626. ' Ellionem '. Pond and Mary Chamberlaine: Marriage Lic. (London), ii. 177.
1650. Married—Thomas Pond and Ann Hathaway: St. Jas. Clerkenwell, iii. 85.
London, 12; Philadelphia, 11.

Ponder.—Offic. ' the ponder,' the keeper of the pond or pound; v. Pond. Other forms are Pounder and Pinder.

William le Pondere, co. Camb., 1273. A.
Symon Pondere, co. Hunts, ibid.
1561. John Ponder (co. Essex) and Eliz. Wroughte: Marriage Lic. (London), i. 21.
1589. Married — Henry Ponder and Amy Fisher: St. Jas. Clerkenwell, iii. 14.
London, 9.

Ponsonby, Ponsaby.—Local, ' of Ponsonby,' a parish in co. Cumberland.

' The Ponsonbys of Hale were originally of Ponson, where they are to be traced before the reign of Edward II. At an earlier period the first of the family of whom we find any mention was called Ponson, and his son Fitz-Ponson ': Hist. of Allendale Ward, co. Cumb., by S. Jefferson, p. 56.

Thus Ponsonby means the by or dwelling of Ponson, a then familiar Norman personal name; v. Punshon.

1624-5. Simon Ponsonbey, *stationer*, and Eliz. Turner: Marriage Lic. (London), ii. 150.
1731. Married—William Punsonby and Jane Jenkinson: Reg. Parish Church, Ulverston, p. 375.
MDB. (co. Cumberland), 2, 0; Philadelphia, 0, 2.

Pontefract; v. Pomfret.

Pontifex.—Nick. ' the pontiff.' A Latinization like Faber; cf. Pope, Pape, Cardinal, Bishop.

Adam Pontif, co. Norf., 1273. A.
Richard Pontif, co. York, ibid.
London, 13.

Pook.—Nick. ' the puk,' from the complexion of the hair or dress, a colour between russet and black (v. Halliwell); cf. Russell and Black, or Borrell. But perhaps of Dutch parentage.

William le Puk, co. Soms., 1 Edw. III: Kirby's Quest, p. 102.
John Pouk, co. Soms., 1 Edw. III: ibid. p. 123.
Richard Pouk, co. Soms., 1 Edw. III: ibid. p. 195.
1667. Samuell Pooke, *weaver*: St. Peter, Cornhill, ii. 87.
1787. Married—James Albon and Ann Pook: St. Geo. Han. Sq. i. 401.
London, 6.

Pool, Poole.—Local, ' at the pool ' (v. Pole), from residence thereby.

Walter atte Pulle, C. R., 39 Hen. III.
Walter de la Pulle, co. Oxf., 1273. A.
Boniface atte Poule, co. Soms., 1 Edw. III: Kirby's Quest, p. 102.
Stephen atte Poule, co. Soms., 1 Edw. III: ibid.
Philip atte Poule, co. Soms., 1 Edw. III: p. 223.
Johanna de Pulle, 1379: P. T. Yorks. p. 118.
1595. Bapt.—John, s. William Poole: St. Jas. Clerkenwell, i. 30.
London, 19, 71; Boston (U.S.), 26, 61.

Pooley.—Local, 'the islet in the pool'; v. Pulley.

Poore, Poor.—Nick. 'the poor'; v. Power and Pauper.

William le Poure, C. R., 1 Edw. I.
1580. Married—John Poore and Eliz. Budworth: St. Dionis Backchurch, p. 9.
1797. — Richard Poor and Jane Brook: St. Geo. Han. Sq. ii. 169.
London, 7, 0; Boston (U.S.), 7, 44.

Poorfish.—Nick.; cf. Rottenherring, Hardfish.

John Pourfisshe, 1313. M.

Pope.—Nick. 'the pope'; cf. Bishop, &c. A sobriquet for one of an austere, ascetic, and ecclesiastical appearance.

Alan le Pope, co. Oxf., 1273. A.
Hugh le Pope, co. Suff., ibid.
Robert le Pope, co. Soms., 1 Edw. III:
Kirby's Quest, p. 201.
London, 39.

Popham.—Local, 'of Popham,' a parish in co. Hants, seven miles from Basingstoke.

1620. Bapt.—Eliz., d. John Popham: St. Jas. Clerkenwell, i. 89.
1621. Alex. Popham, co. Wilts: Reg. Univ. Oxf. vol. ii. pt. ii. p. 393.
1763. Married—William Leyborn Leyborn and Ann Popham: St. Geo. Han. Sq. i. 121.
London, 3; MDB. (co. Berks), 2; (co. Hants), 2; Philadelphia, 3.

Popjay, Popjoy, Pobgee, Pobjoy, Pobjay. — Nick. 'the popinjay,' the talking jay, i. e. parrot; the sobriquet of a chatterer. M.E. *popingay*, O.F. *papegay*. The *n* is excrescent, as in Pottinger, Messenger, Clavinger. Mr. Lower has found Popjay and Popjoy still existing. The curious corruption Pobgee, however, is in the London Directory. The change from *p* to *b* seems to have occurred at the close of the 18th century.

1502. 'Item, for bringing of a popyngay to the Quene to Windesore, 13s. 4d.': Privy Purse Exp., Eliz. of York, p. 30.
Robert Papyngeye, C. R., 45 Edw. III.
Richard Popingay. TT.

Of the Popinjay Inn at Norwich, Blomefield writes:

'The middle messuage belonged to the prior and convent, and the other two messuages in 1330 to Roger Papinjay, in whose family it continued till Roger Papinjay, his grandson, turned the corner house into an inn, and in allusion to his

own name made it the sign of the " popinjay, or great green parrot, from which time it hath been a publick-house to this day, it now being the Popinjay Tavern " ': FF. iv. 117.

'Richard Popynjay, surveyor of the works at Portsmouth,' July 8, 1568: Rec. Office, Cal. State Papers (Domestic), i. 311.
1759. Married — William Popjoy and Mary Maynard: St. Geo. Han. Sq. i. 84.
1770. — John Francis Popejoy and Mary Freeman: ibid. p. 200.
1784. — James Pobjoy and Margaret Harris: ibid. p. 366.

From this latter the transition to the Pobgee of the London Directory is easy.

London, 0, 0, 1, 0, 0; MDB. (co. Somerset), 0, 0, 0, 1, 0; New York, 0, 0, 0, 0, 1.

Popkin, Popkins, Popkiss.—Bapt. 'the son of Robert,' from nick. Hob, and dim. Hobkin, sharpened to Hopkin, whence Welsh Ap - Hopkin = Popkin or Popkins, corrupted into the curious-looking Popkiss of the London Directory; cf. Perkins and Perkiss, or Hotchkins and Hotchkiss. Thus English Hopkinson, Welsh Popkins.

Hopkyn ap Popkyn, temp. Eliz. Z.
John ap Hopkin, temp. Eliz. ZZ.
Thomas Hopkis, 1602: Reg. St. Mary Aldermary, p. 10.
1759. Married—Thomas Popkins and Hannah Forrister: St. Geo. Han. Sq. i. 90.
1787. — John Popkin and Mary Long: ibid. p. 403.
London, 0, 0, 1; MDB. (co. Carmarthen), 1, 1, 0.

Poplar.—Local, 'at the poplar,' from residence thereby; cf. Plumptre, Rowntree, Crabtree, Birch, Oak, Ash. M.E. *poplere*, a poplar tree.

Thomas Popeler, 1379: P. T. Yorks. p. 150.
Johannes Popeler, 1379: ibid.
Willelmus Popler, 1379: ibid. p. 226.
1667. Bapt.—Ann, d. Richard Popler: St. Jas. Clerkenwell, i. 233.
1779. Married—Ralph Popler and Sarah Letsom: St. Geo. Han. Sq. i. 302.
London, 2.

Pople; v. Popple.

Poppinger.—Nick. 'the popinjay,' i.e. the talkative man; v. Popjay.

Boston (U.S.), 2.

Popple, Pople. — Local, 'at the popple-tree,' from residence

thereby. Provincial English for a poplar-tree : ' Popple, a poplar-tree ' (Halliwell); cf. Ash, Birch, Oak, &c.; v. Poplar.

1690. Bapt. — Frances, d. William Pople : St. Jas. Clerkenwell, i. 334.
1788. Married — Joseph Spinks and Mary Popell: St. Geo. Han. Sq. ii. 7.
1794. — James Pople and Ann Holmes: ibid. p. 112.
1797. — Richard Popple and Mary Ann Potter: ibid. p. 163.
London, 1, 0; MDB. (co. Linc.), 13, 0; (co. Soms.), 0, 11; New York, 1, 0.

Poppleton.—Local, 'of Poppleton,' a parish in W. Rid. Yorks.

Willelmus de Popilton, *sutor*, 12 Edw. I: Freemen of York (Surt. Soc.), i. 4.
Johannes de Popilton, 12 Edw. I: ibid. i. 5.
Johanna de Popelton, 1379: P. T. Yorks. p. 18.
London, 2; West Rid. Court Dir., 4; MDB. (co. Linc.), 2.

Popplewell, Poppwell. — Local, 'of Popplewell,' lit. 'the well by the poplar-tree.' Provincial English, 'popple, a poplar-tree' (Halliwell); cf. Poppleton. The spot Popplewell must be sought for in the immediate neighbourhood of Heckmondwike, W. Rid. Yorks.

Thomas Popilwell, of Cleckheaton, 1379: P. T. Yorks. p. 182.
Johannes de Popiwell, of Heckmondwike, 1379: ibid. p. 185.

Curious to note, there are two Popplewells in the Heckmondwike Directory of to-day.

1563. Buried—Betteris (Beatrice) Popplewell, servant to Robert Diconson: St. Antholin (London), p. 16.
1771. Married—Richardson Warburton and Ann Popplewell: St. Geo. Han. Sq. i. 209.
London, 4, 0; West Rid. Court Dir., 6, 0; Philadelphia, 1, 1.

Porch, Portch.—Local, 'at the porch.' M.E. *porche*, a covered entrance or portico. Probably a door-keeper, or doorward; v. Dorward.

Richard atte Porche, co. Soms., 1 Edw. III: Kirby's Quest, p. 218.
Stephen atte Porche, C. R., 43 Edw. III.

This surname seems to have become corrupted into Porridge:

1601. Bapt.—Anne, d. Simon Porridge: St. Antholin (London), p. 40.

1657. Married — Robert Porch and Elizabeth Barton : St. Mary Aldermary, p. 27.

It is interesting to notice that Mr. R. B. Porch played for Somerset v. Essex, and carried out his bat for 85, July 11, 1885.

London, 1, 5 ; MDB. (co. Soms.), 5, 1 ; Boston (U.S.), 1, 0 ; Philadelphia, 0, 1.

Porcher.—Occup. 'the porker,' a swineherd, lardiner, a feeder of pork. Fr. *porc*, a hog, pork.

John Porcarius, co. Essex, 1273. A.
Emma la Porcher, co. Oxf., ibid.
John le Porker, co. Camb., ibid.
Thomas le Porker, co. Oxf., ibid.
Nicholas Porker, co. Bucks, ibid.
Roger le Porcher. B.
Gilbert le Porcher. H.
London, 3 ; New York, 2.

Porrett, Porritt.—Bapt. 'the son of Peter,' from Pierre, dim. Perrot, Parrot, Porret, &c. ; v. Parratt.

John Porrett, or Perott, or Parott : Reg. Univ. Oxf. i. 13.
Robert Porrett, or Perrott : ibid. p. 98.
1775. Married — William Porrott and Margaret Thomas : St. Geo. Han. Sq. i. 257.
1780. — Thomas Porrett and Eliz. Haley : ibid. p. 316.
London, 1, 0 ; Manchester, 0, 2.

Port.—(1) Nick. (?). Perhaps an abbreviation of de la Porte ; v. (2).

John le Port, 1273. A.
Charles le Port. BB.
Oliva le Port. BB.

(2) Local, 'of the port.' Latin *portus*, a haven, as in Portsmouth ; or Latin *porta*, a gate, as in *portal*, *porter*, *portcullis*. The same as Porter (2), q.v. ; cf. Kitchen and Kitchener, Spence and Spencer.

Hugh de la Port gave land to the Church of St. Peter, at Gloucester, 1096 : Atkyns' Hist. Glouc. p. 75.
William de la Porte, Close Roll, 39 Hen. III. pt. i.
Walter de la Porte, co. Soms., 1273. A.
Henricus del Port, co. Bucks, ibid.
Adam ad Port, co. Camb., ibid.
Robert ad Portam, co. Hunts, ibid.
1601. Bapt.—Robert, s. Robert Porte : St. Jas. Clerkenwell, i. 39.
London, 5 ; New York, 7.

Portbury.—Local, 'of Portbury,' a parish in co. Somerset.

Adam Portbury, co. Soms., 1 Edw. III : Kirby's Quest, p. 154.
London, 4.

Portch.—Local ; v. Porch, a corruption.

Porteous, Porteus.—(1) Nick. 'port-horse,' i.e. a pack-horse ; cf. *porter*, a carrier, also *portfolio* and *portmanteau*. Just the sort of name that would be affixed to some hardworking, plodding man.

John Portehors, Close Roll, 54 Hen. III.
Robert Portehors, 1273. A.
John Portehors. V. 8.
Ralph Portehors. V. 8.
Ralph Portehors, 20 Edw. I. R.

(2) Local, 'at the porter-house,' i.e. a lodge-keeper, from residence at the lodge.

Robertus de Porterhouse, 1379 : P. T. Yorks. p. 202.
1667. Married—Timothy Weaver and Ann Portris : St. Jas. Clerkenwell, iii. 132.
1788. — William Porthouse and Eliz. Tinkler : St. Geo. Han. Sq. ii. 6.
London, 2, 1.

Porter.— (1) Occup. 'the porter,' a carrier. Fr. *porteur*. 'Portowre, *portator*' : Prompt. Parv. (2) Offic. a door-keeper. Fr. *portier*. 'Portere, *janitor*' : Prompt. Parv.

Francis le Porter, C. R., 45 Hen. III.
Robert le Porter, 1273. A.
Richard le Porter, 20 Edw. I. R.
William de Hodeles, *portour*, 21-2 Edw.I : Freemen of York (Surt. Soc.), i. 5.
Albin le Portour. N.
Adam Porter, co. Soms., 1 Edw. III : Kirby's Quest, p. 118.
Richard le Porter, co. Soms., 1 Edw. III : ibid. p. 130.
1674. Buried—Mr. John Portter : St. Antholin (London), p. 95.
London, 86 ; New York, 123.

Portingale, Portigall, Portugal, Puttergill. — Local, ' of Portugal.' An immigrant from Portugal ; v. Pettingell.

1543-4. Buried — Fransys Wallar, *a portyngall* : St. Dionis Backchurch, p. 180.
John Portingale, of Youghall, 1569 : Cal. State Papers (Domestic), i. 331.
1574. Bapt.—Jone Portingale : Prestbury Church, co. Chester, p. 43.
MDB. (co. Linc.), 0, 1, 1, 1.

Portingdon. Portington. — Local, ' of Portington,' a township in the parish of Eastrington, E. Rid. Yorks. Thence it has passed over the Humber into Lincolnshire.

Robert de Portington, co. Yorks, 1273. A.

1580. Robert Portington, co. Yorks : Reg. Univ. Oxf. vol. ii. pt. ii. p. 92.
1653. Bapt. — George, s. Hugh Portington : St. Jas. Clerkenwell, i. 183.
MDB. (co. Linc.), 1, 4.

Portman. — Offic. 'the portman,' equivalent to Portreve, q.v.

John Portman, co. Soms., 1 Edw. III : Kirby's Quest, p. 274.
Thomas Portman, co. Soms., 1 Edw. III : ibid.
Oxford, 1.

Portreve. — Offic. 'the portreeve,' the chief magistrate of a town ; see a brief dissertation on the origin of the portreeve of Gravesend in Lambard's Perambulation, 1596, p. 483 (Halliwell).

Augustin le Portereve, co. Hertf., 1273. A.
Henry Porterewe, co. Kent, ibid.
William le Portereve, co. Oxf., ibid.
Philip le Portreve, co. Soms., 1 Edw. III : Kirby's Quest, p. 138.
John Protereave, co. Soms., 1 Edw. III : ibid. p. 214.

Portsmouth.—Local, 'of Portsmouth.'

MDB. (co. Berks), 1.

Portugal.—Local ; v. Portingale.

Portway.—Local, 'at the portway,' i.e. gateway ; v. Port (2). Fr. *porte*, 'a port, or gate,' Cotg. The surname has not wandered much. Found in the 13th century in co. Hunts, it is familiar in the 19th to co. Essex.

Matilda de la Portweye, co. Hunts, 1273. A.
Richard de la Portweye, co. Hunts, ibid.
'The chair was occupied by Mr. G. R. Portway' : Liberal meeting at Leeds, Yorkshire Post, April 7, 1887.
West Rid. Court Dir., 2 ; MDB. (co. Essex), 4.

Portwine.—Local, 'le Poytevin,' from Poictou, a Poictevine. An imitative corruption.

Robert Pevtewin, co. Devon, 1273. A.
Robert le Peytevin, co. Glouc., ibid.
Preciosa Potewyne, co. Camb., ibid.
Peter le Pettevin. L.
Henry le Poytevin. J.
William Peytevyn, co. York, 20 Edw. I. R.
John Peytevyn, co. Soms., 1 Edw. III : Kirby's Quest, p. 217.
William Paitefyn, co. Soms., 1 Edw. III : ibid. p. 262.
Willelmus Paytfyn, 1379 : P. T. Yorks. p. 217.
London, 1.

Posnett. — Local, ' of Postle-thwaite.' This familiar Cumberland and Furness surname is abbreviated to Poslett in colloquial intercourse. It is frequently so registered. By the common change from *l* to *n*, Poslett has become Posnett; cf. *baluster* and *banister*. v. Postle-thwaite.

Gerard Postlet, of Dalton, 1596: Lanc. Wills at Richmond, i. 218.
William Postlet, of Marton, 1597: ibid.

In the Ulverston Church Registers it is found as Postlat.

Philadelphia, 2.

Posselwhite.—Local. A cor-ruption of Postlethwaite, q.v.; cf. Applewhite for Applethwaite.

John Postelwaite, of Kirkbie, 1587: Lancashire Wills at Richmond, i. 218.
1766. Married — Richard Postlewhite and Ann Terry : St. Geo. Han. Sq. i. 154. London, 1.

Postill, Postel, Postol. — Nick. ' the Apostle '; cf. Bishop, Archbishop, &c. For lapse of initial vowel, cf. Potticary for *apothecary*. Halliwell (s.v. Postle) quotes :

' Like a postle I am,
For I preche to man.'
Armonye of Byrdes, p. 7.

' Posteles,' Piers Plowman, B. vi. 151 (Skeat). A.S. form *apostol* (ibid.).

Geoffrey Postel, London, 1273. A.
Hugh Postoyle, co. York, ibid.
William Postel, co. Sussex, Hen. III-Edw. I. K.
1560. William Yonge and Eliz. Postle : Marriage Lic. (London), i. 20.
1679. John Postle, of Lodmore Lane : Wills at Chester (1660-80), p. 214.

Probably the local Postlethwaite refers to the settlement or clearing of some early apostle or preacher, who had found his way into Cum-berland. Cf.

Richard de Postelcumbe, co. Oxf., 1273. A.
William de Postlecumbe, co. Oxf., ibid.
London, 2, 0, 0 ; Philadelphia, 0, 2, 1.

Postlethwaite. — Local, ' of Postlethwaite.' I cannot discover the spot. There can be little doubt that the surname originally arose on the Cumberland side of the Duddon, and advanced eastward into Furness. To this day it is an established Furness name; v. Postill

for probable origin. For suffix, v. Thwaites.

1546. Buried—Richard Postlethwaite : Reg. Ulverston Church, p. 3.
1547. Married—William Postlethwait and Sebell Asburner : ibid. p. 5.
1587. John Postlethwayt, co. Westm. : Reg. Univ. Oxf. vol. ii. pt. ii. p. 161.
John Posteltwhett, of Ulverston (in Furness), 1622 : Lancashire Wills, i. 218.
William Postlewhat, of Kirkbie Ierleth (in Furness), 1592 : ibid. p. 219.
MDB. (co. Cumberland), 8; (co. Lanc.), 22 ; London, 4 ; Philadelphia, 1.

Potkin. — Bapt. ' the son of Philip,' from the dim. Philip-ot, whence the abbreviation Pot, and further dim. Pot-kin; cf. Watkin, Wilkin, &c. v. Potts.

Thomas Potekin, co. Camb., 1273. A.
Alice Potekyn, co. Camb., ibid.
Geoffrey Potekine, co. Camb., ibid.
Thomas Potkin. HH.
Peter Potkyn, 1506 : Reg. Univ. Oxf. i. 46.
1581. Christopher Pottkyn and Ann Heron : Marriage Lic. (London), i. 101.

Probably this name has become lost in Popkin, q.v.

Pott.—Bapt. ' the son of Philip '; v. Potts.

Potter.—Occup. ' the potter,' a maker of pots, vessels for cooking or drinking. A common entry in 13th century registers.

Michael le Potere, London, 1273. A.
John le Pottere, London, ibid.
Ranulph le Poter, co. Essex, ibid.
Nicholas le Potter, bailiff of Yarmouth, 1303 : FF. xi. 322.
1598. Robert Bruffe and Margaret Potter : Marriage Lic. (London), i. 258.
London, 96 ; Boston (U.S.), 97.

Potterton.—Local, ' of Potter-ton,' a township in the parish of Barwick-in-Elmett, W. Rid. Yorks.

1664. Bapt. — Mathew, s. Mathew Potterton : St. Jas. Clerkenwell, i. 224.
MDB. (co. Linc.), 1 ; London, 1 ; Phila-delphia, 2.

Potticary, Pothecary. — Occup. ' the apothecary.' Origin-ally one who kept a store for non-perishable goods, such as spices, drugs, and preserves. The spicer and apothecary sold between them what the grocer now sells, minus the modern tea, coffee, &c. (v. Groser).

William Apotecarius, co. Northampton, 1273. A.

1591. Christopher Potticary, co. Wilts : Reg. Univ. Oxf. vol. ii. pt. ii. p. 186.
William Clapham, London, *potticary*, 1633 : Visitation of London, 1634, p. 164.
Josias Barnard, *pottycary*, 1645 : Reg. St. Mary Aldermary (London), p. 89.
1788. Married—James Potticary and Ann Knight : St. Geo. Han. Sq. ii. 13.
1803. — Richard Hancock and Maria Potticary : ibid. p. 291.
London, 0, 1 ; MDB. (co. Cambridge), 1, 0.

Pottin. — Bapt. ' the son of Potin,' i.e. Philip from Pot (the nick. of Philipot), dim. Pot-in (v. Pottle) ; cf. Cobbin (v. Coppin), the dim. of Cob, the nick. of Jacob.

John Potin, co. Kent, 1273. A.
Benedict Potin, co. Kent, ibid.
Simon Potin, co. Kent, ibid.

Pottinger.—Occup. ' the pota-ger,' a maker of pottage, i.e. thick soup or broth, a favourite mess in older days. The intrusive *n* is regular ; cf. Messinger and *passen-ger*, for Messager and *passager*.

' Suppe not with grete sowndynge,
Neither potage ne other thynge.'
Boke of Curtasye.

Ralph Prestbury was sworn to keep the peace towards

'Thomam Halle, *potygare*, alias *chirur-gicum*,' 1439 : Mun. Acad. Oxon. p. 523.

From his knowledge of herbs the potager gradually became looked upon as a ' medicine man,' or herbalist (v. English Surnames, 5th edit., p. 207).

Walter le Potager, 1303. M.
John le Potager, co. Soms., 1 Edw. III : Kirby's Quest, p. 272.
Simon de Wederhale, *potager*, 2 Edw. III : Freemen of York, i. 24.
Robert le Potager. G.
John Potenger. F.
1575. Simon Pottinger, co. Hants : Reg. Univ. Oxf. vol. ii. pt. ii. p. 64.
1762. Married — Benjamin Pottinger and Eliz. Dance : St. Geo. Han. Sq. i. 112.
1776. — John Bostock and Anne Potenger : ibid. p. 261.
Sheffield, 1 ; London, 4 ; Boston (U.S.), 3.

Pottiphar.—Nick. An imitative corruption of Pettifer. The half-way house was Pettipher ; v. Pet-tifer.

Gilbert Portefer, co. Soms., 1 Edw. III : Kirby's Quest, p. 106.

Pottle. — Bapt. 'the son of Potel,' i.e. Philip, from Pot (the nick. of Philipot), dim. Pot-el; v. Potts, Pottin, and Potkin. Once more in such a surname as this we see the early and widespread influence of the apostolic name of Philip.

Richard Potel, co. Bucks, 1273. A.
Nicholas Potelle, Pat. Roll, 1 Hen. VII. pt. i.
1779. Married — Thomas Pottle and Jane Simmons : St. Geo. Han. Sq. i. 297. London, 6.

Potton. — Local, 'of Potton,' a parish and market-town in co. Bedford.

Gilbert de Pottone, co. Bedf., 1273. A.
Simon de Pottone, co. Camb., ibid.
1805. Married — Timothy Potton and Eliz. Oldham : St. Geo. Han. Sq. ii. 337. London, 2.

Potts, Pott. — Bapt. 'the son of Philip,' dim. Philipot or Philpot, whence nick. Pot (v. Potkin). The frequency of Potts as a surname (see London Directory) is owing to the once great popularity of the apostolic name. The Spanish Armada and the marriage of Mary with Philip ruined the prospects of Philip at the font as much as the Gunpowder Plot ruined the name of Guy. Cf. the French importation Potelette in the London Directory, evidently a diminutive formed on the nick. Pot. The Hundred Rolls have 'John Potin, co. Kent,' another diminutive (cf. Col-in from Nicholas) which corresponds with Coppin (q.v.), a dim. of Cob, the last syllable of Jacob or Jacop.

Colin Pot, co. Linc., 1273. A.
Ricard Pot, co. Essex, ibid.
Reginald Pot, co. Hunts, ibid.
William Pote, co. Norf., ibid.
London, 22, 10.

Poucher. — Occup. 'the poucher,' a maker of pouches, pokes, or bags; v. Pouchmaker.

John Poucher, C. R., 19 Edw. II. pt. ii. MDB. (co. Lincoln), 2.

Pouchmaker. — Occup. 'the pouchmaker.' This surname, although well established, did not live. But it is represented by the shorter Poucher, q.v.

Nicholas Pouchemakere, C. R., 51 Edw. III.
William Pouchemaker. H.

Walter Pouchmaker, C. R., 24 Edw. III. pt. ii.
Nicholaus Pouchmaker, 1379 : P. T. Yorks. p. 98.
Agnes Pouchemaker, co. York. W. 2.

Poulett; v. Pollett.

Poulson. — Bapt. 'the son of Paul,' from a provincial form Poul; v. Powle.

Poulter, Poulterer. — Occup. 'the poulter,' a poulterer. O.F. *polete*, a young hen, a pullet.

'Pulter, *gallinarius*,' Prompt. Parv.

'I have no peny,
  Poletes to bugge (buy).'
          Piers Plowman.
'Drovers, cokes, and pulters.'
          Cocke Lorelle's Bote.

Osbert le Puleter, Close Roll, 52 Hen. III.
Osbert le Puleter, 1273. A.
Adam le Poleter, c. 1300. M.
Willelmus de Menthorp', *pulter*, 1379 : P. T. Howdenshire, p. 16.
Elyas Pulter, *husband*, 1379 : ibid. p. 17.
Ricardus Pulter, 1379 : P. T. Yorks. p. 242.
1621. William Poulter and Alice Belley : Marriage Lic. (London), i. 106.
1781. Married — Robert Poulter and Mary Axtell : St. Geo. Han. Sq. i. 326.
London, 10, 0 ; Philadelphia, 1, 9.

Poulton. — Local, 'of Poulton.' There are several parishes and townships of this name in cos. Lancaster and Chester ; also a parish in co. Wilts, near Cirencester. 'The homestead by the pool' would naturally cause many Poultons to arise in different districts.

Henry de Pulton, co. Soms., 1 Edw. III : Kirby's Quest, p. 104.
Walter de Pulton, co. Soms., 1 Edw. III : ibid.
1627. John Rogers and Dorothy Poulton : Marriage Lic. (London), ii. 189.
Ellen Poulton, of Dalton, 1635 : Lancashire Wills at Richmond, i. 217.
Richard Poolton, of Barton, 1670 : ibid. i. 219.
London, 14 ; Manchester, 2 ; Philadelphia, 4.

Pound. — Local, 'at the pound,' the enclosure for strayed cattle, the pin-fold; v. Pond for early instances.

William atte Pounde, co. Soms., 1 Edw. III : Kirby's Quest, p. 105.
Adam atte Pounde, co. Soms., 1 Edw. III : ibid. p. 130.
Henry del Pount de Eldreford, C. R., 47 Hen. III.
1579. Ralph Proby and Alice Pounte : Marriage Lic. (London), i. 91.

1634. Bapt. — Marie, d. Thomas Pound : St. Jas. Clerkenwell, i. 128.
London, 11 ; Philadelphia, 6.

Pounder. — Offic. 'the pounder,' the keeper of the pinfold; v. Pinder and Ponder.

1601. John Cartwright and Amy Pownder : Marriage Lic. (London), i. 266.
1803. Married — Robert Pounder and Esther Mays : St. Geo. Han. Sq. ii. 284.
London, 1 ; Boston (U.S.), 3.

Poundsend. — Local, 'at the pound's-end'; v. Pound, and cf. Townsend.

John de Poundesend. D.

Pourtrayer. — Occup. 'the pourtrayer,' a drawer, one who depicts, a painter. O.F. *portraire*, to depict.

Richard le Pertriur, co. York. W. 4.
Geoffrey le Purtreour, London. X.

Povey, Povah. — Nick. 'the povey,' i.e. owl. Almost all birds are represented in our directories; cf. Nightingale, Sparrow, Goldfinch, &c. 'Povey, an owl' (Halliwell). It is in Shropshire and on the Welsh border that the surname is so familiarly known. In Ellesmere I saw (in 1886) Povah and Povey over shops within fifty yards one of the other.

Richard Povah, of Shocklach, 1581 : Wills at Chester (1545-1620), p. 154.
David Povey, of Shocklach, 1593 : ibid.
Edward Povey, of Shocklach, 1595 : ibid. p. 155.
Randle Povah, of Shocklach, 1605 : ibid. p. 154.

It is quite manifest that Povah and Povey are the same name under two guises.

London, 8, 0 ; Crockford, 0, 4 ; MDB. (co. Glouc.), 1, 0.

Powdrell, Powderhill. — Local, 'of Powderhill' (?).

Willelmus Powdrell, 1379 : P. T. Yorks. p. 83.
1586. George Powderhill, co. Berks : Reg. Univ. Oxf. vol. ii. pt. i. p. 394.
1592. Martin Powdrill, co. Berks : ibid. p. 419.
1610. William Powdrell, co. Berks : ibid. p. 327.
1660. John Poudrell, of Great Peover, *yeoman* : Wills at Chester (1660-80), p. 214.
London, 1, 0 ; Philadelphia, 0, 1.

Powell. — (1) Bapt. Ap-hoel or Ap-howel (Welsh), 'the son of Hoel'; v. Howel.

Elizabeth Ap-Howell. B.
John Ap-Howell. D.
John Appowell. F.
1547. William Pypar and Jone Appowell : St. Dionis Backchurch (London).
John ap-Howell, prebendary of St. David's, 1554 : Hist. and Ant. St. David's, p. 461.
William ap John ap Howell : Visit. of Glouc., Harl. Soc., p. 179.

(2) Bapt. 'the son of Poul,' or Powl, or Powel, i. e. Paul (v. Powle). ' Powle, a propyr name, Paulus' : Prompt. Parv. 'Powel' (i.e. Paul), Piers Plowman.

Henry Powel, London, 1273. A.
Geoffrey Powel, co. Camb., ibid.
Mazelina Powel, co. Suff., ibid.
Hugh Poul, co. Buck, ibid.
John Powell, or Powle, sup. for B.A., June, 1532 : Reg. Univ. Oxf. i. 170.

Probably half of our Powells are of pure English descent. That all Powells are Welsh is a great fallacy.

London, 139.

Power. — Nick. ' the poor.' Although a great name, there can, it seems to me, be no doubt as to the derivation of the name. All the early entries point to one and the same source. Probably the vow of poverty would give the devotee such a sobriquet among his friends, and the title would be proudly borne ; cf. Barefoot. v. Pauper and Poore. The instances are very numerous ; only a few can be given.

John le Poer, co. York, 1273. A.
Warin le Powre, co. Norf., ibid.
William le Povre, co. Devon, ibid.
Ralph le Pouwer, co. Bucks, ibid.
John Povere, co. Camb., ibid.
Emma le Pouere, co. Oxf., ibid.
1561-2. Robert Power and Eliz. Gilbert : Marriage Lic. (London), i. 23.
1667. Bapt.—Susanna, d. Richard Pore : St. Jas. Clerkenwell, i. 230.
London, 13 ; Philadelphia, 52.

Powle, Powles, Powlson, Poulson.—Bapt. 'the son of Paul,' from a provincial form Poul. Poulson has ramified strongly in the United States. ' Powle, propyr name, Paulus' : Prompt. Parv.

' Poul, after his prechyng,
  Paniers he made.'
            Piers Plowman, 10195.
' Rob Peter, and pay Poule, thou sayst
  I do.
But thou rob'st and poul'st Peter and
  Poule too.'   Heywood.

John Poul, co. Soms., 1 Edw. III : Kirby's Quest, p. 117.
1521. John Pawle, or Powle : Reg. Univ. Oxf. i. 120.
1529. Richard Pawll, or Powle : ibid. p. 158.
1593-4. Richard Powle, *sadler*, and Ann Hockley : Marriage Lic. (London), ii. 213.
1681. Alice Poulson, of Chipping : Lancashire Wills at Richmond, ii. 200.
1797. Married — Henry Poulson and Mary Short : St. Geo. Han. Sq. ii. 171.
London, 1, 5, 0, 3 ; Manchester, 0, 0, 2, 0 ; Philadelphia, 0, 0, 0, 24.

Powlesland, Powsland, Pousland. — Local, ' of Paulsland,' land belonging to Paul (v. Powle).

London, 3, 1, 0 ; Boston (U.S.), 0, 0, 5.

Powlett ; v. Pollett.

Powley.—A variant of Pawley, q.v. ; v. Powle.

1805. Married—James Rudd and Mary Powley : St. Geo. Han. Sq. ii. 320.
London, 2.

Powling.—Bapt. 'the son of Paul,' a variant of Paulin ; v. Powle.

London, 1.

Powlson ; v. Powle.

Pownall, Pownell. — Local, ' of Pownall,' a township in the parish of Wilmslow, co. Ches.

1561. Buried—Edmund Pownall : Wilmslow Church.
1592-3. Bapt.—Uryan Pownall : ibid.
Humphrey Pownall, of Bramhall, 1604 : Wills at Chester (1545-1620), p. 155.
John Pownall, of Styal, Wilmslow, 1614 : ibid.
London, 9, 0 ; Manchester, 16, 1 ; Philadelphia, 4.

Pownceby.—Local, ' of Ponsonby,' q.v. ; a corruption. This is Mr. Lower's suggestion, and it seems satisfactory. In the United States the corrupted form is Ponsaby.

London, 4.

Poxon ; v. Pogson.

Poynter.—Occup. ; v. Pointer.

Poynton, Pointon, Poynting. Pointing.—Local, ' of Poynton,' a chapelry in the parish of Prestbury, near Stockport, co. Ches. Poynting, &c., is a corruption, the

g being an excrescence, as in Jennings. For another local origin, v. Pointing. Both have become inextricably mixed.

John de Poynton, *barber*, 12 Edw. II : Freemen of York, i. 18.
William- Poynton, parish of Bunbury, 1617 : Wills at Chester (1545-1620), p. 155.
Randal Poynton, of Congleton, 1620 : ibid.
Manchester, 4, 2, 1, 0 ; London, 0, 0, 0, 4 ; Philadelphia, 2, 0, 0, 0.

Poyntz. — Bapt. ' the son of Poynz.'

' Walter fil. Ponz, a tenant-in-chief at the time of the Norman survey, and Drogo, his brother, . . . were sons of Walter Ponz, a noble Norman. From Drogo fil. Ponz descended the family of Clifford' : Lower's Patr. Brit. p. 275.
Hugo Poynz, co. Kent, 1273. A.
Nicholas Poynz, co. Kent, ibid.
William Poynz, co. Devon, ibid.
1614. William Duncumbe, Esq., and Elizabeth Morris, daughter of Sir John Poyns, Kt. : Marriage Lic.(London), ii. 27.
Crockford, 2.

Poyser, Poysere. — Occup. ' the poiser,' i. e. the weigher, probably a maker of scales ; v. Balancer. M.E. *poisen, peisen*, to weigh ; O.F. *pois, peis*, a weight. Poyser is a common surname in Derbyshire. Hence George Eliot's use of the name in Adam Bede.

Joscens le Peisur. DD.
London, 2, 0 ; Manchester, 3, 0 ; MDB. (co. Derby), 4, 0 ; Philadelphia, 1, 1.

Prance. — ? Nick. One who pranced in his gait (?). Cf. Golightly, Lightfoot, &c.

Ricardus Praunce, 1379 : P. T. Yorks. p. 134.
Willelmus Prance, 1379 : ibid. p. 226.
1787. Married — William Prance and Mary Honnor : St. Geo. Han. Sq. i. 400.
London, 3.

Prankerd.—Bapt. ' the son of Prankard.' Perhaps a variant of Punchard, q.v.

William Praucard (sic), co. Soms., 1 Edw. III : Kirby's Quest, p. 199.

Probably a misprint for Prancard. Close by in the same roll occurs Agnes Punchard (p. 200).

MDB. (co. Soms.), 5.

Pratt.—Bapt. ' the son of Prat' (?). It seems strange that the origin of this surname should be in any doubt. No less than thirty Prats are mentioned in the Hundred Rolls (1273), proving a very early popularity. In no single case, however, is there any prefix *de*, or *de la*, or *atte*, pointing to a local derivation. I see no other conclusion than that it was a personal name. Sprat or Sprot was, we know, a familiar personal name at the same period. Mr. Lower suggests that as the surname Meadow is Latinized into 'de Prato' in early registers, Pratt is a 'contraction.' This is utterly beside the mark.

Norman Prat, co. Camb., 1273. A.
Thomas Prat, co. Glouc., ibid.
Osbert Prat, co. Hunts, ibid.
Eustace Prat, co. Camb., ibid.

So the name runs. Until proof to the contrary is advanced, I am driven to the conclusion that Prat was an old personal name.

Richard Pratt, co. Soms., 1 Edw. III: Kirby's Quest, p. 168.
1579-80. Henry Pratt, *collier*, and Avice Sharpe: Marriage Lic. (London), i. 95.
London, 70; Philadelphia, 55.

Preacher. — Official, 'the preacher,' one who was set apart to preach. Equivalent to Sermoner, q.v.

John le Precheur, co. Notts, 1273. A.
John le Prechur, C. R., 43 Hen. III.
Thomas le Prechur. T.
Jacob Preacher. W. 20.

After looking vainly for years in search of a modern instance, I concluded the surname was obsolete. I was therefore delighted to find it existing in Hampshire.

1750. Bapt.—Jane, d. William Preacher: St. Jas. Clerkenwell, ii. 297.
MDB. (co. Hants), 1.

Precious; v. Pretious.

Preece, Preese. — Bapt.; v. Price.

Preferment.—? ——. A curious surname, manifestly a corruption.

MDB. (co. Hereford), 1.

Preist; v. Prest.

Prelate.—Nick. 'the prelate'; cf. Bishop, Pontifex, Pope, Cardinal.

William Prelate, C. R., 15 Hen. VI.

Prendergast.—Local, 'of or from Prendergast,' a parish in co. Pembroke. Hence went forth Maurice de Prendergast to assist Strongbow in the Conquest of Ireland. In the many corruptions of this name the first *r* has been dropped; v. Pendegrass.

London, 2.

Prentice, Prentis, Prentiss. —Occup.'the apprentice,'familiarly 'prentice or 'prentis; cf. Potticary for *apothecary*. These forms are often found in church registers.

Thomas Prentys, London, 20 Edw. I. R.
William Prentys, co. Soms., 1 Edw. III: Kirby's Quest, p. 134.
Ricardus Prentys, 1379: P. T. Yorks. p. 237.
Johannes Prentys, 1379: ibid. p. 14.
1563. Buried—Richarde Skott, prentice to Roger Beawe: St. Mary Aldermary, p. 135.
— — William Ashforde, prentis to Roger Beawe: ibid.
1737. Bapt. — Mary Ann, d. Anthony Prentice: St. Jas. Clerkenwell, ii. 235.
London, 15, 2, 0; Philadelphia, 4, 3, 2.

Prescott.—Local, 'of Prescott,' parishes in cos. Lancaster, Oxford, and Gloucester. This surname has ramified strongly in the United States. The meaning is Priesthouse, 'the house the priest lived in.' The Lancashire town gave rise to a family that still flourishes in its local directories.

(Heredes) de Prestecote, co. Oxf., 1273. A.
Adam le Prestecote, co. Soms., 1 Edw. III : Kirby's Quest, p. 247.
1580. Bapt.—Alice, d. Thomas Prescott: St. Jas. Clerkenwell, i. 12.
Robert Prescott, of Standish, *yeoman*, 1596: Wills at Chester (1545-1620), p. 155.
Thomas Prescott, of Burscough, 1619: ibid.
Manchester, 11; London, 10; Boston (U.S.), 93.

Presow.—Local, 'of Preesall.' Hackersall and Preesall form a township in the parish of Lancaster. The surname as Presow has crossed the sands into Furness; cf. Lindow for Lindall. How early the name was so pronounced we find from the following entries:

Rogerus de Presawe, 1379: P. T. Yorks. p. 163.
'Richard de Hakenshawe holds the manor of Hackinsawe cum Prisowe, ...

by homage . . . and two cross-bows': Baines' Hist. Lancashire, ii. 541.
Alice Prisoe, *widow*, of Dalton, 1605: Lancashire Wills at Richmond, i. 221.
James Priseye, of Dalton, 1600: ibid.
Thomas Presoe, of the parish of Aldingham, 1593: ibid. p. 200.
Agnes Presoo, of Stanke, 1615: ibid.
John Presall, of Preston, 1668: ibid. p. 220.
Ulverston, 1; MDB. (co. Lanc.), 3.

Press. — Bapt. Ap-Rees, the son of Rees. A Welsh surname, a variant of Preece, &c.; cf. Pritchard, Prodger, Ployd, Price, &c.

1580. Simon Presse, co. Staff: Reg. Univ. Oxf. vol. ii. pt. ii. p. 92.
London, 6; Philadelphia, 17.

Pressland. — Local, 'at the priest-land,' the land belonging to the parson, from residence on land so styled.

William Prestlond, co. Chester, 1453: East Cheshire, ii. 89.
John Prestland, of Sounde, *gent.*, 1580: ibid. i. 252.
Margaret Priestland, of Prestland Greaves, co. Chester, *widow*, 1620: Wills at Chester, i. 156.

Of course the *t* was bound to be dropped in social intercourse, and the name is now found as Pressland.

1800. Married — John Presland and Mary Combs: St. Geo. Han. Sq. ii. 228.
London, 2.

Presson; v. Priestson.

Prest, Priest, Preist.—Offic. 'the priest.'

John le Prest, co. Hunts, 1273. A.
Roger le Prest, co. Wilts, ibid.
John le Prest, co. Soms., 1 Edw. III : Kirby's Quest, p. 167.
Adam Prest, et Magota uxor ejus, 1379: P. T. Yorks. p. 134.
1615. Richard Warne and Susan Preist: Marriage Lic. (London), ii. 37.
1799. Married—Thomas Priest and Charlotte Yerbury: St. Geo. Han. Sq. ii. 200.
London, 3, 11, 3; Philadelphia, 0, 24, 0.

Prestage.—Local. Mr. Lower says, 'A corruption of Prestwich,' which is possible. I would, however, suggest that as we have Vicar-age and Parson-age (the latter a surname), so our forefathers may have spoken of a Prest-age, 'the residence of the Priest'; v. Prest.

1791. Married — John Cox and Eliz. Prestage: St. Geo. Han. Sq. ii. 53.
1801. — Francis Woodley and Isabella Prestidge: ibid. p. 245.
London, 3; Manchester, 1.

Prester, Priester.—Official, 'the prester,' i.e. presbyter. O.F. *prestre*; M.F. *prêtre*; cf. Prester John, in Mandeville's Travels (Skeat).

Richard le Prestre, co. Norf., 1231: FF. i. 481.
Thomas le Prestre, co. Essex, 1273. A.
Gervase le Prestre, co. Soms., 1 Edw. III: Kirby's Quest, p. 206.
1591. John Jesopp and Margaret Prestar: Marriage Lic. (London), i. 195.
New York, 0, 2.

Preston.—Local, 'of Preston.' No less than twenty-four parishes, situated in every part of England, bear this name in the Index to Crockford. No wonder the surname is so familiar. I furnish a few early instances out of many.

Laurence de Preston, co. Linc., 1273. A.
Alice de Preston, co. Northampt., ibid.
Adam de Preston, co. Westm., 20 Edw. I. R.
Robert de Preston, co. Salop, ibid.
John de Prestone, of Preston, co. Soms., 1 Edw. III: Kirby's Quest, p. 212.
Johannes de Pryston, 1379: P. T. Yorks. p. 281.
Isabella de Preston, 1379: ibid. p. 285.
1562. Rowland Preston and Anne Mellowe: Marriage Lic. (London), i. 24.
London, 30; Boston (U.S.), 53.

Prestwich.—Local, 'of Prestwich,' a parish near Manchester, and now practically a suburb; v. Prestage.

Adam de Prestwich, 1325: Baines' Lanc. i. 446.
Henry de Prestwich, 1331: ibid.
'In 12 Hen. VI, Ralph de Prestwych granted the manor house (Hulme Hall, Manchester) to Henry de Byron': ibid. p. 400.
Laurence Prestwich, of Gorton, Manchester, 1587: Wills at Chester (1545-1620), p. 156.
Ellis Prestwich, of Broughton, Manchester, 1611: ibid.
Nicholas Prestwyk, co. Soms., 1 Edw. III: Kirby's Quest, p. 160.
Whitefield (a village in parish of Prestwich), 4; Manchester, 3; London, 1.

Pretious, Precious. — Bapt. 'the son of Precious' (i.e. dear). Mr. Lower writes of this Yorkshire surname, 'A correspondent sends me the following anecdote: "Walking through a town with

a friend, I noticed the name of Precious. My friend said to me, 'You knew John Priesthouse; he was the father of this Precious.' Here the vulgar had corrupted the name, probably in ridicule of Priesthouse."' Whatever truth may attach to this story communicated to Mr. Lower, it does not alter the fact that the surname Pretious or Precious is descended of a personal name Precious or Preciosa, as it was sometimes found in formal documents.

Presiosa Potewyne, co. Camb., 1273. A.
Preciosa de Kirkeby: Pat. Roll, 13 Edw. III.
Preciosa Scherwynd, *webester*, 1379: P. T. Yorks. p. 98.
Johannes Precyus, 1379: ibid. p. 241.
Richard Pretiouse, co. York, 1471: W. 11.
1730. Married — James Bickett and Mary Precious: St. Geo. Han. Sq. i. 24.
London, 1, 0; MDB. (co. Suffolk), 0, 2; (East Rid. Yorks.), 0, 5.

Prett; v. Pritt.

Prettyjohn, Prettejohn. — Nick. 'Prettyjohn.' But possibly an English corruption of the French Petit-jean. John was so very common in the 13th and 14th centuries, that such nicknames as Littlejohn, Properjohn, or Micklejohn were given in order to secure identity.

1530. 'Item, . . . paied to petit-John and his fellawe in rewarde by the Kinges commandment': Privy Purse Exp., Hen. VIII, p. 52.
London, 0, 1.

Prettyman, Pretyman. — ? Nick. 'the prettyman' (?), i.e. the comely or clever one (v. *pretty* in Skeat's Dict.). A surname of East Anglian parentage; still found in co. Suffolk. The name has flourished across the Atlantic.

1631. Peter Prettiman, co. Norf.: FF. i. 362.
1635. William Prettiman, rector of Hilburgh, co. Norf.: ibid. vi. 115.
1669. Married — Thomas Prittman and Margaret Banes: St. Jas. Clerkenwell, iii. 168.
MDB. (co. Suffolk), 3, 0; London, 0, 1; Philadelphia, 22, 0.

Prevost, Provost, Provis, Provest.—Official, 'the provost,'

i.e. the prefect, the chief magistrate, or mayor of a town. Commonly entered as Prepositus in the Hundred Rolls. O.F. *provost*, or *prevost.*

Walter le Provost, co. Wilts, 1273. A.
Henry Prepositus, co. Bucks, ibid.
Alan Prepositus, co. Norf., ibid.
Nicholas le Proust: Close Roll, 39 Hen. III. pt. i.
Geoffrey le Provost. H.
Robert fil. Provost. T.
John le Preost, co. Soms., 1 Edw. III: Kirby's Quest, p. 128.
1766. Married — Thomas Provis and Ann Robinson: St. Geo. Han. Sq. i. 160.
London, 5, 1, 1, 0; Boston, U.S. (Provest), 1; New York, 5, 7, 0, 0.

Prewett, Pruitt.—Nick. 'the proud,' the arrogant, the haughty. M.E. *prute.* The surname early assumed a disyllabic form; v. Proud for further information.

Andrew Pruet, co. Camb., 1273. A.
William Pruet, co. Camb., ibid.
Thomas Pruwet, co. Soms., 1 Edw. III: Kirby's Quest, p. 124.
Walter Prowet, co. Soms., 1 Edw. III: ibid. p. 142.
Juliana Prouet, co. Soms., 1 Edw. III: ibid. p. 264.
1680. Buried—May Pruett, nurse at Mr. Parr's: St. Dionis Backchurch, p. 247.
1717. Married — John Pruet and Mary Pruit (sic): ibid. p. 58.
London, 1, 0; Philadelphia, 1, 3.

Price, Preece, Preese.—Bapt. Welsh Ap-Rice or Ap-Rees=son of Rice (q.v.).

'Item, geven to Harry ap-Rice, xvis.', 1544: Privy Purse Exp., Princess Mary, p. 158.
Philip ap Rys. C.
Lodovicus Apprise. F.
John Apryce. F.
Lewis ap-Rhys, prebendary of St. David's, 1502: Hist. and Ant. St. David's, p. 361.
1563. Arnold Appryce and Elizabeth Andrewes: Marriage Lic. (London), i. 27.
1579. Thomas Aprees and Margaret Barker: ibid. p. 88.
London, 167,9,1; Boston (U.S.),44, 1, 0.

Prichard; v. Pritchard.

Prichett.—Bapt. A variant of Prichard or Pritchard; cf. Prickett for Prickard; v. Pritchard. The form Prichett, without the *t*, seems peculiar to the United States.
Philadelphia, 10.

Prickard.—Bapt. Ap-Rickard, a variant of Pritchard, q.v.; cf. Rickard and Richard (v. Prickett).
MDB. (co. Radnor), 3.

Prickett, Prickitt.—(1) Bapt. Ap-Richard (Welsh), i.e. the son of Richard. Just as Richard is met by the harder Rickard, so is the Welsh Prichard met by the harder Prickard (q.v.). And just as Pritchard or Prichard became corrupted into Pritchett and Pritchitt, so also did Prickard become corrupted into Prickett and Prickitt. The origin is thus simple enough.

(2) Nick. 'the pricket,' a buck in his second year; cf. Buck, Stagg, Roebuck, &c.

'Weele haunt the trembling prickets as they rome
About the fields, along the hauthorne bushes.'
    The Affectionate Shepheard, 1594.
'And I say beside that 'twas a pricket that the princess killed': Love's Labour's Lost, Act iv. Sc. 2.

Mr. Lower says, 'The crest of the family is allusive, being "a pricket—tripping, proper"': Patr. Brit. p. 277.

Richard Priket, co. Derby, 1273. A.

The above, of course, represents (2), not (1).

1793. Married—William Prickett and Hannah Weston: St. Geo. Han. Sq. ii. 91.
London, 2, 1; MDB. (co. Pembroke), 1, 0; Philadelphia, 5, 7; New York, 0, 3.

Prickhorse. — Nick. 'prickhorse,' a sobriquet for a hot rider, equivalent to Hotspur; cf. Touchprick.

Johannes Prikehors, 1379: P. T. Yorks. p. 217.

Priddy, Pridee.—Local, 'of Priddy,' a parish in co. Somerset, four miles from Wells. The surname is familiar to the district. Not to be confounded with Prideaux.

1792. Married—Abraham Priddy and Mary Pain: St. Geo. Han. Sq. ii. 73.
1805. — Thomas Flint and Ann Priddey: ibid. p. 334.
London, 2, 0; MDB. (co. Somerset), 1, 0; (co. Wilts), 3, 0; Boston (U.S.), 0, 1.

Pride, Pryde.—(1) Local, 'of Pride.' Some spot seemingly in co. Devon. (2) Nick. 'Pride,' probably the sobriquet of one who took the part of Pride in an early Mystery Play. But it may have been a nickname affixed on one of a haughty demeanour.

Roger de Prid, co. Devon, 1273. A.
W. de Prid, co. Devon, ibid.
Roger Pride, London, ibid.
John Pride, co. Derby, Hen. III–Edw. I. K.
Stephen Pride, co. Soms., 1 Edw. III: Kirby's Quest, p. 122.
Richard Pryde, co. Staff., co. Derby, 20 Edw. III. R.
1760. Married — William Pride and Ann Rogers: St. Geo. Han. Sq. i. 93.
London, 3, 0; Boston (U.S.), 7, 1.

Prideaux. — Local, 'of Prideaux.' 'The ancient family of Prideaux trace their descent from Paganus, lord of Prideaux Castle, in Luxilion, co. Cornwall, in the time of William I': Shirley's Noble and Gentle Men (quoted by Lower). There is no doubt Prideaux gave name to the family of Prideaux. They are early found in the neighbouring county of Devon.

Roger de Prydeaus, or Prydyaus, or Prudeaus, co. Devon, 1273. A.
Thomas de Prideas, co. Cornwall, 20 Edw. I. R.
Geoffrey de Pridias, co. Devon, Hen. III–Edw. I. K.
London, 6; Devon Court Dir., 10.

Pridgeon. — Nick. 'Prujean,' valiant John, a corruption of a French name; cf. Grosjean, Pettijohn, Littlejohn, Micklejohn, &c.

Philip Pridgeon, co. Linc., 1596: Reg. Univ. Oxf. vol. ii. pt. ii. p. 218.
Crockford, 1; MDB. (co. Linc.), 4.

Pridham.—Nick. A variant of Prudhomme, q.v.

Priest; v. Prest.

Priester; v. Prester.

Priestfather. — Nick. 'the father of the priest.'

Walter Prestfadre, Close Roll, 11 Edw. III. pt. ii.

Priestknave. — Occup. 'the priest's knave,' i.e. the servant of the priest.

1564. Bapt.—Elizabeth Presteknave: Reg. Prestbury, co. Ches., p. 13.
1565. Married—John Presteknave and Anne Duncalfe: ibid. p. 17.

Priestley, Priestlay, Priestly.—Local, 'of Priestley' (i.e the priest's meadow), some small estate in the near neighbourhood of Bradford, W. Rid. Yorkshire. The surname is familiar in all

English-speaking countries. But other spots would bear the same name.

Walter Prestlegh, co. Soms., 1 Edw.III: Kirby's Quest, p. 132.

The two following lived in Hipperholme, near Bradford:

Elena de Presteley, 1379: P. T. Yorks. p. 194.
Johannes de Presteley, 1379: ibid.
1561. William Priestlye and Margaret Sorrowgold: Marriage Lic. (London), i. 22.
London, 13, 0, 0; Philadelphia, 18, 0, 0; West Rid. (Yorks) Court Dir. 24, 1, 2.

Priestman. — Occup. 'the priest's man,' i.e. the servant of the priest; cf. Matthewman, Addyman, Priorman, Monkman. Nevertheless, it may be an augmentative as in Masterman, merchantman, husbandman, &c. The former is by far the most satisfactory derivation.

Roger Presteman, co. York, 1273. A.
Robert Prestman, co. York, ibid.
Robertus Prestman, 1379: P. T. Yorks. p. 200.
Isabella Prest, seruant, 1379: ibid.
1574. John Prestman: Reg. Univ. Oxf. vol. ii. pt. iii. p. 46.
1590. Christopher Wright and Alice Presteman: Marriage Lic.(London). i. 187.
London, 3; West Rid. Court Dir., 5; Philadelphia, 1.

Priestnall, Priestner.—Local, 'of Priestnall,' probably some spot in co. Chester. Priestner is a corruption of Priestnow, which is the usual pronunciation in the north of names ending in -all; cf. Preesow for Preesall, Shawcross for Shallcross, &c.

1566. Bapt.—Anne Prestenall: Reg. Prestbury, co. Chester, p. 18.
1581. Married—John Baret and Sibell Priestnowe: Cheadle Ch., East Cheshire, 231.
Richard Pristnall, of Styal, in Wilmslow Parish, 1595: Wills at Chester, i. 156.
1601. Buried — Geffrey Prestener: Reg. Prestbury, co. Chester, p. 152.
London, 1, 0; MDB. (co. Chester), 0, 2: Liverpool, 1, 0.

Priestson, Presson. — Bapt. 'the son of the priest.' One of a small class of patronymics from office and occupation; cf. Clarkson, Frearson, Taylorson.

John le Prest, et Ivo filius ejus: co. Hunts, 1273. A.
'Walter Prestfadre and Walter Prestson': Close Roll, 11 Edw. III. pt. ii.
William le Prestessone. G.

Doubtless this became Preson and Presson; cf. Pressland for Prestland.

1564. Married—John Russell and Margery Presson: St. Dionis Backchurch, p. 5.
1621. John Preson and Jane Marsh: Marriage Lic. (London), ii. 99.
Boston (U.S.), 0, 2.

Priggen. — Nick. This is a modification of Prujean. There is a Prujean Square in Old Bailey, London.

London, 2.

Primate.—Nick. 'the primate'; v. Prelate, and cf. Prince.

1611. Richard Primmitt, co. Linc.: Reg. Univ. Oxf. vol. ii. pt. ii. p. 398.
1621. Stephen Primatt, co. Linc.: ibid. p. 323.
Richard Primate, of Chester, *innkeeper*, 1618: Wills at Chester, i. 156.
1729. William Primate, rector of West Walton, co. Norf.: FF. ix. 140.

Primmer. — Official (?), 'the primer.' Probably a priest whose duty it was to conduct 'prime'; cf. Sermoner, Preacher, Chanter.

Petrus le Primur, co. Camb., 1273. A.
1795. Married—Richard Primmer and Ann Edwards: St. Geo. Han. Sq. ii. 128.
1803. — John Hubbard and Mercy Primer: ibid. p. 292.
London, 1.

Primrose.—Local, ' of Primrose,' an estate in co. Fife (Lower's Patr. Brit. p. 277). The name is in general found on Scottish soil.

Henry Prymros: Pardons Roll, 12 Ric. II.
Johannes Primerose, 1379: P. T. Yorks. p. 180.
Thomas Primerose, C. R., 3 Hen. VI. pt. ii.
1438. Robert Primerose, vicar of Easton, co. Norf.: FF. ii. 394.
1618. Duncan Primrose and Nichola Primrose: Marriage Lic. (London), ii. 59.
New York, 4.

Prince.—Nick. ' the prince'; cf. King, Bishop, Primate, Prelate, &c.

Willelmus Prynce, 1379: P. T. Yorks. p. 272.
Isolda Prynce, 1379: ibid. p. 273.
John Prince, priest in St. Michael's Church, Norwich, 1418: FF. iv. 492.
1690. Bapt.—Eliz., d. Joseph Prince: St. Mary Aldermary, p. 109.
London, 29; Philadelphia, 28.

Pring.—Nick. (?). ' Pryne, chief, first ? (A.N.). "Hym wyl he holde

most pryne"': Halliwell. The final *g* in Pring is modern and excrescent; cf. Hewling for Hewlin, or Jennings from Jenin.

William Prin, co. Berks, 1273. A.
John Prynne, or Pryn, 1506: Reg. Univ. Oxf. p. 49.
Thomas Pryn, of Swanswicke, co. Somerset, 1618: Abstract of Somersetshire Wills, p. 10.
London, 6; MDB. (Somerset), 10.

Pringle.—Local (?). A Scottish surname, of which I can gather no satisfactory account.

Alanus Prynkayle, 1379: P. T. Yorks. p. 131.
1784. Married — Robert Pringle and Jane Balneavis: St. Geo. Han. Sq. i. 362.
London, 12; New York, 11.

Prior, Pryor.—Official, 'the prior,' the head of a convent.

Hugh le Priur, co. Suff., 1273. A.
Richard le Prior, co. Suff., ibid.
Hugh Priour, co. Hunts, ibid.
John Priour, co. Som., 1 Edw. III: Kirby's Quest, p. 80.
John Priour, London, 20 Edw. I. R.
1577. Anthony Prior and Eliz. Sharsey: Marriage Lic. (London), i. 75.
1610. Bapt. — Susan, d. Edward Pryor: St. Jas. Clerkenwell, i. 58.
London, 36, 8; Philadelphia, 4, 23.

Pritchard, Prichard, Pritcher, Pritchett, Pritchitt, Prichett.—Bapt. Ap-Richard (i.e. the son of Richard), a well-known Welsh surname with several variants.

'Item, geven to William ap-Richard vs.,' 1536: Privy Purse Exp., Princess Mary, p. 4.
David Aprycharde, 1521: Reg. Univ. Oxf. i. 123.
William Prichard, or Ap-Richard, 1545: ibid. p. 215.
Thomas Prichett, London, 1616: ibid. vol. ii. pt. ii. p. 356.
London, 61, 16, 1, 7, 7, 0; Philadelphia, 13, 8, 0, 5, 0, 10.

Pritt, Prett.—Local, ' of Pret' or Preet. I cannot find the spot.

Peter Pret, co. Worc., 1273. A.
Robert de Preet, co. Lanc., 20 Edw. I. R.
William de Preet, or Pret, co. Lanc., ibid.
Richard Prett, sup. for B.A., 1543: Reg. Univ. Oxf. i. 205.
1610. Married — Edward Prett and Alice Parks: St. Dionis Backchurch, p. 17.
MDB. (co. Cumberland), 2, 0; London, 1, 1; Philadelphia, 0, 1.

Privett.—Local, ' of Privett,' a parish in co. Hants, near Petersfield.

1792. Married — Joseph Hallson and Ann Privett: St. Geo. Han. Sq. ii. 75.
London, 2; MDB. (co. Hants), 1.

Probart, Probert.—Bapt. Ap-Robert (Welsh), equivalent to English Robertson; cf. Pritchard, Price, &c.

1540. Buried — Thomas Uprobarte, prentice with Toson: St. Antholin (London), p. 2.
Lloyd ap-Robert. ZZ.
Ellice ap-Robert. Z.
'Item, given to oon Davyd ap-Robert, xvis.,' 1544: Privy Purse Exp., Princess Mary, p. 159.
1792. Married — Joseph Probert and Sarah Owen: St. Geo. Han. Sq. ii. 71.
London, 1, 3; MDB. (co. Hereford), 0, 11; (co. Radnor), 0, 2.

Probyn.—Bapt. Ap-Robin (the son of Robin = Robinson); cf. Probert = Ap-Robert. This surname crept across the borders of the Principality into Cheshire, and acquired a solid footing there.

William Ap-Robyn. H.
William Ap-Robyn. XX. 1.
William Probin, of Oldcastle, parish of Malpas, 1576: Wills at Chester (1545-1620), p. 156.
Bryan Probin, of Newton, 1578: ibid.
Hugh Probyn, of Newton, 1616: ibid.
William Probyn, archdeacon of Caermarthen, 1789: Hist. and Ant. St. David's, p. 360.
London, 3; MDB. (co. Monmouth), 3; (co. Gloucester), 5.

Proctor, Prockter, Procktor, Procter.—Offic. 'the proctor,' an attorney in a spiritual court. 'Proketowre, *procurator*': Prompt. Parv.

Thomas le Procurator, co. Linc., 1273. A.
John le Procuratour. D.
William le Procuratur, co. Linc., 20 Edw. I. R.
Willelmus Proktour, 1379: P. T. Yorks. p. 292.
1579. Edward Proctor and Effie Shewte: Marriage Lic. (London), i. 87.
1625. Bapt. — Ann, d. John Procter: St. Jas. Clerkenwell, i. 101.
London, 7, 8, 2, 14; Philadelphia, 22, 0, 0, 10.

Proffitt, Profit; v. Prophet.

Oxford, 2, 1.

Proger, Prodger. — Bapt. (Welsh) Ap-Roger = Prodger; cf. Price, Pumphrey, Powell, Pritchard, Prothero, &c. The *d* in Prodger is, of course, intrusive, as in Rodger.

John ap-Roger ap. Gilliant: Visit. Glouc. 1623, p. 104.
Roger A proger. ZZ.
1607. Charles Proger, Jesus Coll., co. Monmouth: Reg. Univ. Oxf. vol. ii. pt. ii. p. 299.
London, 1, 0.

Prophet, Proffitt, Prophett.—Nick. 'the prophet,' one who was credited with a forecasting faculty. Thus 'Prophet, Priest, and King' are all English surnames.

Ricardus Profet, 1379: P. T. Yorks. p. 283.
Willelmus Profet, 1379: ibid.
1673. Ann Prophett, of Kingsley: Wills at Chester (1660-80), p. 216.
1764. Married—William Bricknell and Winifred Profit: St. Geo. Han. Sq. i. 139.
1771. William Proffett and Susanna Richardson: ibid. p. 214.
Manchester, 3, 1, 0; London, 0, 1, 0; MDB. (co. Chester), 0, 0, 1.

Prosser, Prossor.—Bapt. Ap-Rosser (Welsh) = the son of Rosser.

Thomas ap-Rosser. H.
John Approsser. Z.
David ap-Rosser. F.
Howell ap-Rosser: Visit. London, 1634, ii. 359.
1059. Married—John Currey and Ann Prosser: St. Dionis Backchurch, p. 35.
Henry Prosser, 1694: Reg. St. Mary Aldermary (London), p. 111.
London, 9, 1; Philadelphia, 9, 0.

Prothero, Protheroe, Protho-roe, Prytherch, Prytherat, Prythuch.—Bapt. Ap-Rhydderc, Welsh. The English form would be Roderickson. Some remarks on this name will be found in Miss Yonge's History of Christian Names (ii. 370).

Evan Prhydderch, co. Carnarvon, 1617: Reg. Univ. Oxf. vol. ii. pt. ii. p. 366.

A note is appended by the editor to say that he was the son of Roderic Evans, of Llanor, co. Carnarvon. Thus after the Welsh custom he became Evan Ap-Roderic or Prhydderch; v. Rhydderch.

William Prythergh, or Protherugh, or Protherough, Jesus Coll., B.C.L., 1580-1: Reg. Univ. Oxf. vol. ii. pt. iii. p. 99.

The above entry supplies the stages by which Prothero or Protheroe was reached. The fact that the individual concerned was at Jesus College practically settles his nationality.

Walter ap-Riderch, 1384: Hist. and Ant. St. David's, p. 374.
Rhydderch, bishop of St. David's, 961: ibid. p. 357.

The following is very Welsh:

Rhys Caradoc Pytherch, *chemist*: South Wales Dir. (Llanwrtyd).
1575. Roderohe Powell, co. Merioneth: Reg. Univ. Oxf. vol. ii. pt. i. p. 390.
1784. Married—William Pearson and Eliz. Prothero: St. Geo. Han. Sq. i. 355.
1797. — Thomas Prythergch and Ann Phillips: ibid. ii. 161.
London, 3, 4, 0, 0, 0, 0; MDB. (co. Carmarthen), 2, 3, 2, 7, 1, 1.

Proud.—Nick. 'the proud,' an arrogant man. M.E. *prud, proud, prut,* or *prout,* arrogant, haughty (v. Skeat). v. Prout.

Hugh le Proude, co. Bedf., 1273. A.
Robert le Proud, co. Bedf., ibid.
John Proude, co. Bucks, ibid.
Cristina le Prute, co. Oxf., ibid.
Herbert le Prute, co. Wilts, ibid.
1740. Married — John Bannister and Mary Proud: St. Geo. Han. Sq. i. 25.
1802. — John Skinner and Eliz. Prout: ibid. ii. 270.
London, 2; Philadelphia, 5.

Proudfellow. — Nick. 'the proud fellow'; cf. Longfellow, also a Yorkshire surname, and Goodfellow.

Rogerus Proudefelawe, 1379: P. T. Howdenshire, p. 6.

Proudfoot, Proudfit.—Nick. One who walked with a haughty step.

Thomas Proudfot, co. Hunts, 1273. A.
John Protfot, co. Oxf., ibid.
Robert Prudefot, co. York, ibid.

A common entry in the Hundred Rolls—evidently a familiar and colloquial term for a haughty man.

William Proudfot. H.
Richard Prudfot: Close Roll, 27 Hen. III. pt. i.
Agnes Proudefote, 1379: P. T. Howden-shire, p. 17.
1801. Married — John Proudfoot and Eliz. Sparks: St. Geo. Han. Sq. ii. 244.

In the United States this surname is occasionally found in the corrupted form of Proudfit.

London, 4, 0; New York, 2, 2.

Proudlove.—Nick.; cf. Phillimore, Sweetlove, &c. This surname seems to have had South Lancashire and East Cheshire as its chief habitat.

Wyllyam Proudlove, Manchester, 1541: Lanc. and Ches. Rec. Soc. vol. xii. p. 139.
Georgius Prowdlove de Manchester, 1600: ibid. p. 250.
Eliz. Proudlove of Manchester, 1608: Wills at Chester (1545-1620), p. 156.
Richard Proudlove, of Sandbach, 1614: ibid.
West Rid. Court Dir., 1; MDB. (co. Chester), 4.

Proudman.—Nick. 'the proud man'; v. Proud, Proudfellow, &c. Cf. Prudhomme.

1792. Married — John Proudman and Ann Chapman: St. Geo. Han. Sq. ii. 82.
London, 2; Boston (U.S.), 3.

Prout. — Nick. 'the prout,' haughty, proud (*prut,* Ancren Riwle; *prout,* Layamon; v. Skeat; *proud*). v. Proud.

Cristina le Prute, co. Oxf., 1273. A.
Herbert le Prute, co. Wilts, ibid.
John le Prute. H.
John le Proute, co. Soms., 1 Edw. III: Kirby's Quest, p. 138.
Cristina le Prout, co. Soms., 1 Edw. III: ibid. p. 216.
1609-10. Henry Lloyd and Mary Prout: Marriage Lic. (London), i. 318.
1802. Married — John Skinner and Eliz. Prout: St. Geo. Han. Sq. ii. 270.
London, 8; Philadelphia, 3.

Provis, Provost; v. Prevost.

Prowse, Prouse, Pruce.—Local (?), 'of Pruce,' i.e. of Prussia. If this be the origin, then the prefix *le* should be *de* in the Hundred Roll instances furnished below—a common error.

'And som wol have a Pruce sheld or a targe.' Chaucer, C. T. 2124.
Richard le Prouz, co. Devon, 1273. A.
William le Prouz, co. Devon, ibid.
William Prous, co. Oxf., ibid.
1758. Married—Edward McLean and Mary Prowse: St. Geo. Han. Sq. i. 79.
London, 6, 2, 1; MDB. (Devon), 3, 2, 0.

Prudhomme, Pridham, Proudman (?), Prudame, Pruden (?).—Nick. 'Prudhomme.' An old name for a superior craftsman; 'a good and true man, a man well versed in any art or trade': Sadler. Green (Hist. Eng. People, i. 223), speaking of the conflict between the Merchant Guilds and the Crafts Guilds, says: 'It is this struggle, to use the technical terms of the time, of the 'greater folk' against the 'lesser folk,' or of the 'commune,' the general mass of the inhabitants, against the 'prud-hommes,' or 'wiser' few, which brought about ... the great civic revolution of the 13th and 14th centuries.' The surname was common at the same period.

John Prodhome, co. Devon, 1273. A.
Richard Prodham, co. Bucks, ibid.
Geoffrey Prudhomme, or Prodomme, co. Bucks, ibid.

Many other early instances might be given, but these are sufficient. Pruden doubtless is a corruption. Pridham is found as Prudham in the 13th century.

Symon Prudham, co. Norf., 1277: FF. x. 244.
1789. Married — Richard Bunn and Eliz. Prudden: St. Geo. Han. Sq. ii. 27.
London, 0, 3, 2, 0, 1; Philadelphia, 0, 1, 1, 0, 3.

Pruitt.—Nick. 'the proud'; v. Prewett.

Prust. — Offic. 'the prust.' Doubtless a form of Priest. A.S. *preóst.* v. Prest.

Thomas le Prust, co. Oxf., 1273. A.
Henry Prust, co. Oxf., ibid.
Robert Prust, co. Oxf., ibid.
1804. Married — Stephen Prust (co. Glouc.) and Sarah Summers: St. Geo. Han. Sq. ii. 304.
London, 4; MDB. (Devon), 7.

Pryor.—Offic.; v. Prior.

Prytherat,   Prytherch. — Bapt.; v. Prothero.

Puckridge.—Local, 'of Pucke-ridge,' a hamlet in the parish of Standon, co. Hertford.

1709. Bapt.—James, s. Richard Pucke-ridge: St. Jas. Clerkenwell, ii. 48.
1775. Married—Robert Anderson and Susanna Puckridge: St. Geo. Han. Sq. i. 256.
London, 7.

Puddephatt,   Puddefoot, Puddifoot.—Nick. (?). The sur-name is first found in co. Bucks. It is well known there to-day.

Walter Podefat, co. Bucks, 1273. A.
1755. Married — John Puddephatt, of Berkhamsted, co. Herts, and Mary Bed-ford: St. Geo. Han. Sq. i. 59.
1785. — John Breech and Mary Pudde-phatt: ibid. p. 376.
London, 1, 1, 1; MDB. (co. Bucks), 3, 0, 0.

Puddifer.—Nick.; v. Pettifer.

Puddle.—Local, 'at the puddle,' from residence thereby. M.E. *podel,* a muddy pond.

John Podel, co. Soms., 1 Edw. III: Kirby's Quest, p. 106.
Thomas Podel, co. Soms., 1 Edw. III: ibid.
Johanna del Podell', 1379: P. T. Yorks. p. 23.
Robertus del Podell', 1379: ibid.
1574. Bapt. — Joan Puddell: St. Jas. Clerkenwell, i. 8.
London, 1.

Pudsey.—Local, 'of Pudsey,' a parish in W. Rid. Yorks, six miles from Leeds.

Willelmus de Puddesay, 1379: P. T. Yorks. p. 268.
Johannes de Puddesay, 1379: ibid. p. 51.
Nicholas de Pudesay, of Pudesay, 1379: ibid. p. 192.
1667-8. Bapt.—Elizabeth, d. Nathaniel Pudsey: St. Jas. Clerkenwell, i. 233.
MDB. (North Riding Yorks), 1.

Pugh. — Bapt. 'Ap - Hugh' (Welsh), i.e. 'the son of Hugh,' of which an early form was Hew. The better class Welsh seemingly began to adopt the English style in the 17th century. William Ap-Hugh, of the parish of Llanegfan, co. Anglesey, gentleman, by will dated May 18, 1665, bequeathed legacies to his brother Edmund Ap-Hugh, and to his sons Hugh Hughes, and Henry Hughes. The will is printed in N. and Q., Sept. 3, 1887 (p. 186). For a variant, v. Pew.

1610. Jevan Ap-Hugh and Katherine Whitfield: Marriage Lic. (Westminster), p. 18.
1614-5. Richard Ap-Hugh, alias Hughes, and Anne Knight: ibid. p. 22.
John Apew, 1642: Peacock's Army List of Roundheads and Cavaliers, p. 29.
John Pew, 1642: ibid.
London, 23; Boston (U.S.), 6.

Puleston.—Local, 'of Puleston'; v. Pilson. Perhaps the following represents the place:

Roger de Pynelesdon, co. Salop, 1273. A.
MDB. (co. Salop), 1.

Pulford.—Local, ' of Pulford,' a parish in co. Chester, five miles from Chester.

1590. Randall Pulford, co. Denbigh: Reg. Univ. Oxf. vol. ii. pt. ii. p. 181.

Bryan Pulford, of Barton, 1593: Wills at Chester, i. 156.
Griffith Pulford, of Pulford, 1612: ibid.
MDB. (co. Chester), 1; Manchester, 2; London, 3.

Pulham.—Local, 'of Pulham,' a parish in co. Norfolk.

Nicholas de Pulham, co. Norf., 1273. A.
Richard de Pulham, vicar of Tofts, co. Norf., 1348: FF. vii. 205.
William de Pulham, co. Norf., 1372: ibid. iv. 100.
1607. Richard Chambers and Alice Pulham, *widow,* relict of Robert Pulham, of Garbledisham, co. Norf.: Marriage Lic. (London), i. 301.
London, 4; MDB. (Suffolk), 1; New York, 1.

Pullen,   Pullan,   Pullein, Pulleng,   Pulleyn,   Pullin. Pulling.—Nick. 'le Pullen.' If *pullen* was used in the singular as well as plural sense, the origin of this not uncommon surname is very obvious, and is synonymous with 'chicken,' and takes its place in the class of poultry and bird nicknames; cf. Duck, Drake, Jay, Nightingale, &c. In a note to *pullayly* (Prompt. Parv. p. 416) Mr. Way quotes the use of *pullen* for poultry by Tusser; also *pullayne* by Palsgrave. He adds, 'Gerarde observes that in Cheshire they sow buck-wheat for "their cattell, pullen, and such like."'

Nicholas le Pullen, co. Salop, 1273. A.
John Puleyn, co. Wilts, ibid.
Thomas Pulein, co. York, ibid.
Richard Puleyn, co. Dorset, ibid.
John Polayn, co. Soms., 1 Edw. III: Kirby's Quest, p. 124.
Nicholas Polayn, co. Soms., 1 Edw. III: ibid. p. 210.

The *g* in Pulleng and Pulling is, of course, excrescent, as in Jennings and a hundred other names. The forms Pullan (8), Pullein (1), Pullen (2), Pullin (1), Pullon (3), and Pullyen (1) occur in the W. Rid. Court Directory. As Paulin (or Powlin) was so common a font-name in co. York and elsewhere, it is probable that many of the above are of baptismal origin. If so, v. Paulin.

London, 33, 1, 1, 1, 1, 4, 6.

Pulley,   Pooley,   Polley, Poley.—Local, ' of Pooley,' i.e. the islet in the pool; cf. Pooley

S s

Bridge on Ulleswater. M.E. *pol* or *pole*, a pool. The forms Polhey and Polhay, however, suggest a different origin, i.e. the enclosed pool. But it is impossible to separate the two. They have become as surnames inextricably mixed.

Peter de Poleye, co. Herts, 1273. A.
William de Poleye, co. Bucks, ibid.
Ralph de Polhay, or Poley, co. Essex, ibid.
Elyas de Polhey, or Poleye, co. Essex, ibid.
George Polley, or Pooley, vicar of Attleborough, co. Norf., 1516 : FF. i. 524.
London, 5, 9, 4, 2 ; Philadelphia, 3, 5, 0, 6.

Pullin(g ; v. Pullen.

Pullinger. — Occup. A corruption of Bullinger, q.v. ; cf. Peverley for Beverley, &c. This form has ramified strongly in the United States.

1769. Married — John Twidd and Rebecca Pullinger : St. Geo. Han. Sq. ii. 186.
London, 1 ; Philadelphia, 18.

Pullman, Pulman. — Occup. 'the pool-man,' a resident by the pool ; cf. Bridgman, Stileman.

1617. Bapt. — William, s. John Pulman : St. Jas. Clerkenwell, i. 77.
1803. Married — John Gill and Sarah Poullman : St. Geo. Han. Sq. ii. 292.
1805. — John Pulman and Ann Evans : ibid. p. 323.
London, 1, 5 ; Philadelphia, 4, 0.

Pumphrey, Pumfrey. — Bapt. 'the son of Humphrey.' Welsh Ap-Humphrey ; cf. Price, Probert, Prodger, &c.

1564. John Graye and Annable Pumfrey : Marriage Lic. (London), i. 27.
1633. Whitlocke Pumfrey and Magdalen Gray : ibid. ii. 210.
London, 18 ; MDB. (co. Berks), 0, 3 ; Oxford, 0, 1.

Punch. — Nick. (?). I cannot explain this name. Halliwell has '*punch*, short, fat' ; and Little, Short, Fatt, &c., are well-known surnames. Punch may belong to this class of sobriquets.

Robert Punche, co. Oxf., 1273. A.
Philip Punche, co. Suff., ibid.
Roger Punch, temp. Hen. III. T.
John Punche, yeoman of the crown. H.
1809. Married — Benjamin Punch and Mary Norris : St. Geo. Han. Sq. ii. 408.
London, 1 ; Boston (U.S.), 9.

Punchard, Puncher, Pinchard. — Local, 'de Ponte-cardon' (Domesday). Probably from Pont-Chardon, in the arrondissement of Argentan, Normandy, as suggested by Lower. The family gave the suffix to Heanton Punchardon, co. Devon. We may fairly surmise that Punchard is a contraction, Puncher and Pinchard being corruptions of the second stage. v. Pinkerton.

Robert de Punchard, co. Southampton, Hen. III–Edw. I. K.
Richard de Punchardon, co. Southampt., ibid.

The above pair are placed together as if members of the same family.

Robert de Punchardun, co. Devon, Hen. III–Edw. I. K.
Nicholas de Punchardon, 1323 : Hodgson's Northumberland, v. 303.
1681. Married — Robert Reeves and Mary Puncher : St. Jas. Clerkenwell, iii. 192.
1785. — John Hulse and Jane Punchard : St. Geo. Han. Sq. i. 370.
London, 2, 1, 1 ; Boston (U.S.), 2, 0, 0.

Puncheon ; v. Punshon.

Punderson. — Nick. 'the son of the pounder' (v. Pounder) ; cf. Taylorson, Clerkson, Herdson.

MDB. (North Riding Yorks), 1.

Punshon, Pinchin, Pinching, Pingeon, Puncheon. — Bapt. 'the son of Puncun,' or 'Pincun,' a Norman personal name, not a corruption of Punchardon, as suggested by Lower. Representatives are found in every 13th century register.

' Ranulf, Bishop of Durham, two carucates which Pinceon Dapifer holds,' 1109 : Lincolnshire Survey, p. 13.
Oliva Pingun, co. Suff., 1273. A.
Robert Pinchun, co. Hunts, ibid.
John fil. Punzun, 1180 : RRR. p. 25.
Hugo fil. Pincun : Pipe Roll, 5 Hen. II.
William Puncyn, 1313. M.
Robertus Pynchon, 1379 : P. T. Yorks. p. 51.
Thomas Pynchon, 1379 : ibid. p. 50.
William Pownshon, 1539 : Hist. Newcastle and Gateshead, p. 11.
Henry Poynschon, 1539 : ibid. p. 174.
John Punsion, 1548 : Reg. Univ. Oxf. i. 215.
John Punchon, 1663 : Hodgson's Northumberland, iv. 252.
London, 0, 2, 1, 1, 0 ; MDB. (co. Middlesex), Puncheon, 1.

Punt. — Local, 'at the punt,' from residence beside the punt, a kind of boat ; cf. Shipp. The word was in early use.

Martin del Punt, Fines Roll, 11 Edw. I.
1579. George Punte and Margery Goslinge : Marriage Lic. (London), i. 92.
London, 1 ; Philadelphia, 1.

Punter. — Occup. 'the punter,' one who worked a punt ; v. Punt. The only other possible derivation is Punder (i.e. Pounder, q.v.), sharpened into Punter. Punder for Pounder is found below, and this might easily become Punter. Perhaps this is the true solution.

William Punter, C. R., 3 Hen. IV. pt. ii.
1557. William Puntare : Reg. Univ. Oxf. pt. ii. p. 17.
1586. Married — George Pounter and Alice Manning : St. Peter, Cornhill, i. 235.
1592. Bapt. — Golde, d. Henry Punder, St. Jas. Clerkenwell, i. 26.
1730. Married — Daniel Punter and Anne Kirby : ibid. iii. 258.
1795. — John Punter and Ann Morris : St. Geo. Han. Sq. ii. 125.
London, 2.

Purcell, Purssell, Pursell. — Nick. 'the porcel.' M.E. *pork*, O.F. *porc*, a pork, a hog ; dim. *porcell*, a young pig. 'Porcellys, young pigs' (Halliwell). Ital. *porcella*, 'a sow-pig, a porkelin' (Florio). Cf. Pigg, Grice, Hogg, Bacon ; also the dim. Porchet (O.F. *porquet* ; Eng. *porket*).

Reyner Porchet, co. Salop, 1273. A.
Edward Porcel, co. Bucks, ibid.
Roger Porcel, co. Salop, ibid.
Agnes Purcel, co. Oxf., ibid.
John Purcel, 1313. M.
1633. Bapt. — Sara, d. Joseph Purcell : St. Jas. Clerkenwell, i. 123.
1634. Anne, d. Joseph Pursell : ibid. p. 127.

This name with its variants is very familiar to the United States. It went out with the Pilgrim Fathers.

1635. William Pursell, for Virginia (aged 26) : Hotten's Lists of Emigrants, p. 136.
London, 4, 0, 0 ; Crockford, 6, 0, 0 ; MDB. (co. Bucks), 0, 2, 0 ; Boston (U.S.), 33, 1, 1.

Purchas, Purchase, Purches, Purchese. — Nick. Purchase (= eager pursuit). One of a class of names given to pursuivants, messengers, heralds, couriers, &c. (v. Swift, Lightfoot) ; cf.

Bonaventure, also a pursuivant title.

Geoffrey Purchaz, co. Devon, Hen. III–Edw. I. K.

John Purkace, co. Linc., 1273. A.

'Adam Purcas, servant of the (late) Black Prince': C. R., 14 Ric. II.

Roger Purcheiz, co. Som., 1 Edw. III: Kirby's Quest, p. 159.

'Purchace the Pursuivant': Wars of England in France, Hen. VI, (v. index).

1620. Bapt. — Henry, s. William Purchase: St. Jas. Clerkenwell, i. 88.

1763. Married—Thomas Warner and Susanna Purches: St. Geo. Han. Sq. i. 126.

London, 1, 7, 1, 5; Philadelphia, 0, 2, 0, 0.

Purchaser.—Offic. A pursuivant, courier. O.F. *purchacer*, to pursue intently.

Thomas Purchassour or Purchaceour, C. R., 15 and 29 Edw. III.

John Purchasour, Pardons Roll, 6 Ric. II.

Purday, Purdey. Purdie, Purdy, Purdue.—? Nick. Probably corruptions of Pardew, q.v. The instances suggest early corrupted forms.

Cf. Thomas Dampurday, rector of Wood Rysing, co. Norf., 1383: FF. x. 280.

Also cf. Flowerday.

John Purdeu, co. Camb., 1273. A.
William Purdeu, co. Camb., ibid.
John Purde, co. Camb., ibid.

1667. Married — William Pen and Grace Purdey: St. Jas. Clerkenwell, iii. 131.

1713. — John Penny and Eliz. Purdue: ibid. p. 236.

In the United States the surname has settled down to one form, that of Purdy.

London, 1, 1, 4, 7, 1; Philadelphia, 0, 0, 0, 16, 0.

Purdon, Purdom.—Local, 'of Purdon' or Purden. For suffix, v. Downe or Dean.

John Purden, co. Camb., 1273. A.
Adam Purdone, co. Soms., 1 Edw. III: Kirby's Quest, p. 114.
London, 1, 1.

Purefoy. — Nick. (?). O. F. *pure-foy* (?), pure faith, i.e. staunch and true. The family were seated at Misterton, co. Leic., in 1277. The motto borne by one branch is 'Pure foy est ma joie' (Lower, p. 279).

1546-7. William Fawnte and Jane Pureffey or Purfrey: Marriage Lic. (Faculty Office), p. 9.

Francis Purefei, 1569: Reg. Univ. Oxf. vol. i. p. 275.

1581. Francis Purferey (co. Essex) and Johanna Berington: Marriage Lic. (London), i. 101.

Richard Purifey, co. Bucks, 1585: Reg. Univ. Oxf. vol. ii. pt. ii. p. 139.

Arthur Purefaye, co. Norf., 1585: FF. v. 360.

Crockford, 2.

Purey; v. Pury.

Purrier.—Local, 'at the pear-tree'; v. Perryer.

Purser.—Offic. 'the purser,' a purse-bearer, one who paid the expenses, a treasurer, though possibly a purse-maker sometimes; v. Burser.

'And by hire girdel heng a purse of lether.'   Chaucer, C. T. 3251.

John le Pussar (sic), co. Soms., 1 Edw. III: Kirby's Quest, p. 139.

John Haunsy, *purser*, 11 Edw. III: Freemen of York, i. 32.

Robert le Pursere. G.

William Purser. D.

Johanna Pursar, 1379: P. T. Yorks. p. 98.

1805. Married — William Purser and Ann Bailes: St. Geo. Han. Sq. ii. 320.

London, 10; New York, 2.

Pursell; v. Purcell.

Purshouse; v. Pershouse.

Purslow,? Pursglove, Purseglove. — Local, 'of Purslow,' a hundred in the county of Salop. Mr. Lower, with some show of reason, declares that Pursglove is a corrupted form.

1587. Thomas Purslowe, co. Salop: Reg. Univ. Oxf. vol. ii. pt. ii. p. 162.

1595. Thomas Barrowe and Eliz. Purslowe: Marriage Lic. (London), i. 226.

MDB. (co. Derby), 0, 2, 0; (co. Notts), 0, 0, 1; London, 1, 0, 0.

Purton.—Local, (1) 'of Puriton,' a parish in co. Somerset, near Bridgewater; (2) 'of Purton,' a parish in co. Wilts, near Wootton Bassett.

Adam de Piriton, co. Oxf., 1273. A.
Robert de Puriton, co. Soms., ibid.
Simon de Purytone, co. Soms., 1 Edw. III: Kirby's Quest, p. 245.
Gilbert de Puritone, co. Soms., 1 Edw. III: ibid.

From these entries it seems obvious that the meaning is 'the

farmstead with the pear-orchard'; v. Pury and Town. Alongside my last two instances is 'Walter atte Purye' (p. 246).

London, 1.

Pury, Purey.—Local, 'at the perry,' i.e. the pear-tree or pear-orchard; v. Perry, and cf. Purrier for Perrier.

Ralph de la Purye, co. Somerset, 1273. A.
Nicholas de la Purie, co. Oxf., ibid.
Andrew de Purie, co. Oxf., ibid.
Lucia atte Purye, co. Soms., 1 Edw. III: Kirby's Quest, p. 86.
William atte Purye, co. Soms., 1 Edw. III: ibid.,p. 127.
Robert atte Purye, co. Soms., 1 Edw. III: ibid. p. 231.

Thus we find such entries as 'at the pury bridge':

William atte Purybrigge, co. Soms., 1 Edw. III: Kirby's Quest, p. 252.
London, 2, 0; Crockford, 0, 2.

Puryer.—Local, 'at the pear-tree'; v. Perryer.

London, 2.

Pusey, Puzey. — Local, ' of Pusey,' a parish in co. Berks. There is also Pewscy, a parish in co, Wilts, near Marlborough. The two surnames are inextricably mixed.

Henry de Pusey, co. Berks, 1273. A.
John Pusey, co. Bucks, 1579: Reg. Univ. Oxf. vol. ii. pt. ii. p. 87.

1626. Married — Robert Pewsye and Judith Atkins: St. Jas. Clerkenwell, iii. 57.

1659. — Edward Alder and Mary Pusey: St. Dionis Backchurch, p. 35.

London, 0, 12; Crockford, 1, 0; Philadelphia, 22, 2.

Putman, Putnam. — Local, ' of Puttenham,' parishes in cos. Hertford and Surrey. Putman was an inevitable corruption (cf. Deadman for Debenham, or Swetman for Swettenham); not to be connected with Pitman, I think, which, nevertheless, see.

Richard de Puteham, co. Bucks, 1273. A.

1621. Edward Putman or Putnam (v. Index): Reg. Univ Oxf. vol. ii. pt. ii. p. 403.

1774. Married — John Putnam and Catharine Hust: St. Geo. Han. Sq. i. 240.

London, 4, 4; Philadelphia, 1, 4.

Putney. — Local, 'of Putney,' a parish in co. Surrey, four miles from London.

1795. Married — Thomas Putney and Ann Shephard : St. Geo. Han. Sq. ii. 127. London, 1 ; Boston (U.S.), 7.

Putt.—Local, 'at the pit,' from residence thereby ; v. Pitt.

Nicholas de la Putte, co. Oxf., 1273. A.
John de la Putte, co. Oxf., ibid.
John atte Putte, co. Soms., 1 Edw. III : Kirby's Quest, p. 92.
William atte Putte, co. Soms., 1 Edw. III : ibid. p. 101.
Ostin atte Putte, co. Soms., 1 Edw. III : ibid. p. 185.
London, 8 ; Oxford, 4.

Puttergill.—Local ; v. Portingale.

Puttock, Puttick.—Nick. 'the puttock,' i.e. the kite ; 'metaphorically applied to a greedy, ravenous fellow' (Halliwell) ; cf. Kite, Hawk, Sparrow, Sparrowhawk.

'Some bileve that yf the kite or the puttock fle ovir the way afore them that they should fare wel that daye' : Brand, iii. 113.

Richard Puttac, co. Kent, 1273. A.
Walter Puttok, co. Hunts, ibid.
Leticia Puttoc, co. Camb., ibid.
1601. William Puttocke, co. Sussex : Reg. Univ. Oxf. vol. ii. pt. ii. p. 251.
1755. Married — Emery Puttick and Mary Elvin : St. Geo. Han. Sq. i. 59.
London, 5, 3 ; Boston (U.S.), 0, 1.

Puxon.—Local, 'of Puxton,' a parish in co. Somerset.

London, 2.

Puzey ; v. Pusey.

Pyatt.—Nick. ; v. Pyett.

Pybus.—Local, 'of the pyke-busk' (?), i.e. the bush on the pike, that is, the hill. Until absolutely conclusive evidence is shown to the contrary, I cannot doubt my conclusion. The surname is a Yorkshire one, and with the entry

below no other interpretation can be accepted.

Elena Pykebusk, 1379 : P. T. Yorks. p. 12.
Humphrey Pybus, merchant adventurer, April, 1691, St. Nicholas', Newcastle-on-Tyne : v. Brand's Hist. Newcastle, i. 290.
1787. Married—Benjamin Davies and Sarah Pybus : St. Geo. Han. Sq. i. 402.
MDB. (North Rid. Yorks), 8 ; London, 1.

Pycock ; v. Peacock.

Pye, Py.—Nick. 'the pie,' i.e. magpie ; cf. Nightingale, Lark, Finch, Goldfinch. A common entry in early registers.

Agnes relicta Pye, co. Oxf., 1273. A.
John Pye, co. Norf., ibid.
Walter Pye, co. Norf., ibid.
Willelmus Py, 1379 : P. T. Yorks. p. 202.
Robertus Pye, 1379 : ibid.
1607. Bapt.—Thomas, s. Robert Pye : St. Jas. Clerkenwell, i. 49.
1615. Otwell Pye, co. Cornwall : Reg. Univ. Oxf. vol. ii. pt. ii. p. 345.
London, 15, 0 ; New York, 9, 5.

Pyecroft.—Local, 'at the pye-croft,' the enclosure frequented by magpies ; v. Croft and Pye. From residence beside an enclosure so called.

John Pycroft, of Manchester, *linen webster*, 1590 : Wills at Chester, i. 156.
Edward Pycroft, of Manchester, 1614 : ibid.
MDB. (co. Linc.), 2.

Pyefinch.—Nick. ' a piefinch' ; cf. Goldfinch and Finch, and v. Pye.

1785. Married — William Cross and Margaret Pyefinch : St. Geo. Han. Sq. i. 372.
MDB. (co. Hereford), 1 ; Hull, 1.

Pyeshank.—Nick. ; cf. Cruikshank, Sheepshank, Philipshank, &c.

John Pyeschanke, Close Roll, 15 Edw. I.

Pyett, Pyott, Pyette, Pyatt.—Nick. ' the piot,' i.e. magpie ; a dim. of pie (v. Pye).

William Pyatt, co. Soms., 1 Edw. III : Kirby's Quest, p. 105.
1584. Richard Pyott and Margery Roberts : Marriage Lic. (London), i. 131.
1744. Married — Richard Pyott and Eliz. Grout : St. Geo. Han. Sq. i. 32.
1778. — George Pyott and Eliz. Norris : ibid. p. 292.
London, 1, 0, 0, 2 ; MDB. (co. Derby), 0, 1, 0, 0 ; New York, 0, 1, 1, 5.

Pyke.—Local, ' at the pike,' or peaked hill ; v. Pick (2).

William Pyk, Hen. III-Edw. I. K. Oxford, 3.

Pym.—Bapt. 'the son of Pimme.' v. Pim.

Pyne, Pine, Pinn.—Local, 'at the pine,' i.e. the pine-tree, from residence thereby ; cf. Lind, Crabb, Birch, Box, Oak, &c. A well-known Devonshire name, though not confined to that county. All the forms are common to Devon directories. Pinn is a hamlet in the parish of Otterton, co. Devon, probably derived from the pines that grew there.

Thomas de Pyn, co. Devon, 1271. A.
Herbert de Pyn, co. Devon, ibid.
Radulphus del Pyn, co. Devon, Hen. III-Edw. I. K.
Richard atte Pynne, co. Soms., 1 Edw. III : Kirby's Quest, p. 252.
Hercules Pine, 1563 : Reg. Univ. Oxf. p. 252.
1585-6. Tertullian Pyne and Mary Charles : Marriage Lic. (London), i. 145.
London, 11, 3, 9 ; Topsham (Devon), 0, 2, 0 ; Devon Court Dir., 6, 2, 5 ; New York, 10, 22, 0.

Pyser.—Occup. ; v. Poyser, of which it is a variant.

New York, 1.

Q

Quadling; v. Quodling.

Quaife.— ? ——? Mr. Lower, knowing cos. Kent and Sussex well, says that this name was spelt 'Coyf and Coyfe, 150 years ago, both in East Sussex and West Kent.' I suppose it is a nickname from the dress of one of the mediaeval ecclesiastical or monastical orders; v. Capron or Chapron for an exactly similar instance.

1701. Bapt.—Catherine, d. John Quoif, of ye Padocke: Canterbury Cathedral, p. 22.
1761. Married—David Coyfe (co. Middlesex) and Ann Fry: St. Geo. Han. Sq. i. 107.
1789. — William Quaife and Eliz. Whittington: ibid. ii. 24.
MDB. (co. Kent), 2.

Quail, Quaile, Quayle.— (1) Nick.; a bird, the quail.

John Quaille, C. R., 30 Edw. III.

(2) Bapt. A Manx surname. It has crossed into Lancashire, 'contracted from Mac-Phail, Paul's son. This is one of the most widely distributed names in the Island. Early forms are Mac Quayle, Quayle, 1540; Quale, 1602; Quaille, 1604; Quail, 1656.' v. The Manx Note Book, i. 134; cf. Quirk.

1793. Married—Edward Hickmott and Jane Quayle: St. Geo. Han. Sq. ii. 93.
London, 5, 0, 0; Liverpool, 0, 2, 18; Philadelphia, 6, 0, 3.

Quaint, Quant.—Nick. 'the Quaint,' that is, neat or spruce. O.F. *coint*, 'quaint, ... spruce, brisk, trim': Cotg.

'And of Achilles for his queinte spere.'
Chaucer, C. T. 10553.
Michael le Queynt. M.
John le Quent, C. R., 14 Edw. II.
Margaret le Coynte. B.
1664. Bapt. — William, s. Thomas Quaint: St. Jas. Clerkenwell, i. 222.
1692. — John, s. William Quint (sic): ibid. p. 345.
1707. Married — Dows Quant and Frances Johnson: ibid. iii. 229.
MDB. (co. Linc.), 0, 1.

Quaintance. — ? Nick. 'the acquaintance'; cf. Friend, Neighbour, &c. This is Mr. Lower's suggestion, and I see no difficulty in accepting his view. I cannot find any English instance, although he writes of it as an English surname. It has crossed the Atlantic.

Philadelphia, 1.

Quaintrell, Quantrell, Queintrell.—Nick.; v. Cantrell, of which these are variants.

Richard Queynterel, co. Camb.,1273. A.
Robertus Quintrell, 1379: P. T. Yorks. p. 86.
Johannes Quayntorell, 1379: ibid. p. 28.
1446. Gregory Queyntrill, of Norwich: FF. iv. 443.
1473. John Queyntrell, vicar of Ormsby, co. Norf.: ibid. xi. 239.
London, 2, 1, 1; Philadelphia, 0, 3, 0.

Qualter, Qualters.—Bapt. 'the son of Walter.' From Gualter, sharpened to Qualter. v. Quilliam and Quelch.

Liverpool, 1, 0; Boston (U.S.), 3, 2.

Quant; v. Quaint.

Quantock, Quantick.—Local, 'of Quantock,' probably some spot in co. Somerset; cf. East and West Quantoxhead, two parishes in that county.

MDB. (co. Somerset), 3, 0; London, 1, 0; Cardiff, 0, 1.

Quarell, Quarrell. — Local, 'at the quarel,' from residence beside a quarry. 'Quarel, a stone quarry.' 'Saxifragium, a quaryle,' Nominale MS. (Halliwell).

Ivo de Quarel, co. Camb., Hen. III-Edw. I. K.
John Quarel, C. R., 16 Edw. III. pt. i.
Johannes Qwarell, 1379: P. T. Yorks. p. 190.
1620. George Quarrell and Eliz. Webling: Marriage Lic. (London), ii. 88.
1779. Married — Edward Charlwood and Betty Quarrell: St. Geo. Han. Sq. i. 305.
London, 1, 0; MDB. (co. Worc.), 0, 7.

Quarles.—Local, 'of Quarles.' 'An extra-parochial district in the Hundred of North Greenhoe, co. Norfolk': Lower.

'Richard Quarles, *husbandmon* super de Weveton in Com. Norfolk,' 17 H. n. VII: HHH. p. 135.

The above-named was at this time settled at Beverley, co. York.

Francis Quarles, the sacred poet, was born in 1592 at Romford in Essex, a distance from Quarles not far for a surname to travel. There need be no hesitation in deciding that this is the original home of the family.

'Half a fee formerly held by Robert de Quarles, in Quarles, but now by Edmund de Baconesthorp': FF. v. 146.
1565. Bennett Quarles, New College: Reg. Univ. Oxf. vol. ii. pt. ii. p. 22.
1622. Bapt.—Jonas, s. Jonas Quarles: St. Jas. Clerkenwell, i. 93.
Philadelphia, 1.

Quarmby, Quarnby.—Local. 'of Querenby,' now Quarnby, in the parish of Huddersfield, co. York. I need not say that Quarmby is a variant of Quarnby.

Willelmus de Querenby, 1379: P. T. Yorks. p. 134.
Alexander de Quernby, 1437: East Cheshire, i. 349.
1589. Married—John Warren and Margery Quarmeby: Reg. Prestbury, co. Ches., p. 102.
MDB. (West Rid. Yorks), 9, 1; London, 1, 0.

Quarrell; v. Quarell.

Quarrier.—(1) Occup. 'the quarrier,' one who worked in a stone quarry.

Hugh le Quareur, co. Oxf., 1273. A.
Thomas le Quareur, co. Oxf., ibid.

(2) Local, 'at the quarry,' from residence thereby. M.E. *quarrere*, a quarry.

Henry de la Quarrere, co. Oxf., 1273. A.
Isabella ad Quarere, co. Camb., ibid.
William atte Quarrer, co. Soms., 1 Edw. III: Kirby's Quest, p. 158.
Richard atte Quarrer, co. Soms., 1 Edw. III: ibid. p. 226.
1635. James Quarrier embarked for Virginia: Hotten's Lists of Emigrants, p. 94.
Andrew Querrier, of Nether Alderley, 1698: Wills at Chester (1681-1700), p. 204.

Quarrington.—Local, (1) 'of Quarrington,' a township in the parish of Kelloe, near Durham ; (2) a parish in co. Lincoln, near Sleaford.

1726. Married—Joseph Patterson and Ann Quarrington : St. Geo. Han. Sq. i. 2. London, 1 ; Crockford, 1.

Quartermain, Quartermaine, Quarterman. — Nick. 'four hands.' It is possible the name is local, but I find no trace of such an origin.

Clare Quatremayns, co. Oxf., 1273. A.
William Quatremeyns, co. Oxf., ibid.
Thomas Quatermains, 1313. M.
Guy Quatreman. B.
Richard Catermayn. H.
1622. Roger Quatermaine and Emeria Nicholls : Marriage Lic. (London), ii. 116.
1711. Married—John Quatermayne and Catherine Barnes : St. Mary Aldermary, p. 40.
1798. — Richard Quarterman and Ann Reed : St. Geo. Han. Sq. ii. 192.
London, 1, 1, 9 ; Oxford, 0, 0, 6.

Quarton.—Local, 'of Wharton' (q.v.) ; cf. Quixley for Whixley, or Quickfall for Wigfall, or wick, a provincialism for quick. \

William de Querton, co. Notts, Hen. III-Edw. I. K.
Gilbert Querton, co. Westm., 20 Edw. I. R.
Francis Quarton, of Lancaster, 1707 : Lancashire Wills at Richmond, ii. 203.

Thus we find instead of Whitehead :

Henry Quytheved, 20 Edw. I. R.
William Qwythed, 1557 : Lancashire Wills at Richmond. i. 224.

Or, in place of Whiteside :

Merget Quitesyd, or Whytsyd, 1562 : Lancashire Wills at Richmond, i. 224.
MDB. (East Rid. Yorks), 3 ; (West Rid. Yorks), 1.

Quatermass. — Local, ' de Quatremars.' Some spot across the Channel that I have not identified.

Colin de Quatremars, co. York, Hen. III-Edw. I. K.
Adam de Quatremars, co. Kent, ibid.
William Quatremeys, co. Oxf., 1273. A.
Simon de Quatremarch, co. Norf.: FF. ix. 159.
1809. Married—Thomas Quartermass and Sophia Anderson : St. Geo. Han. Sq. ii. 402.
Thomas Quatermass, bootmaker, 94 Aldersgate St., E.C.: London Directory. London, 1.

Quayle ; v. Quail.

Queen.—(1) Nick. 'the Queen'; cf. King, &c. (2) Bapt. A variant in America of Quinn ; cf. McQueen for McQuinn. In the Philadelphia Directory I find seven McQueens and two McQuinns. With (2) this dictionary has nothing to do. The following references relate to (1), the nickname.

Matilda le Quen, co. Oxf., 1273. A.
Simon Quene, co. Camb., ibid.
Alicia Qwene, 1379 : P. T. Yorks. p. 272.
Richard Qwene, or Quene, 1511 : Reg. Univ. Oxf. i. 78.

The following entries are interesting :

Johannes Quencson, 1379: P. T. Yorks. p. 55.
Alicia Queneson, 1379: ibid.

This is good evidence that Queen was a nickname for one who acted as Queen of the May, &c. The sobriquet stuck and became the surname. Kingson arose in a similar way, only that survives and Queenson is gone.

Boston (U.S.), 4 ; Philadelphia, 12.

Queenborough. — (1) Local, 'of Queniborough,' a parish in co. Leicester ; (2) ' of Queenborough,' a parish in co. Kent.

Nicholas Quenbure, co. Leic., Hen. III-Edw. I. K.
Osceline de Quinbergh, co. Norf., 4 Edw. III : FF. x. 272.
MDB. (co. Leicester), 1 ; (co. Kent), 1.

Queintrell ; v. Quaintrell.

Quelch.—Local, ' the Welsh,' i.e. the Welshman. Cf. Gwyllim for William, Quilliams for Williams, and Quhitelaw for Whitelaw, and v. Whitehead. In the instances below an intermediate form Gwelch is given :

1612. Thomas Quilche and Mary Wellam : Marriage Lic. (London), i. 12.
William Quelch, 1613 : St. Mary Aldermary, p. 13.
1655. Married—Henry Quelch and Jane Collins : St. Peter, Cornhill, i. 259.
Margaret Gwelch, 1686 : St. Jas. Clerkenwell, i. 315.
Margaret Quelch, 1688 : ibid. p. 327.

These last two entries refer to the same person.

London, 3 ; Oxford, 8 ; Boston (U.S.), 1.

Quennell, Quinnell. — (1) Bapt. 'the son of Quenilda' or ' Quenild,' the Norman form of Gunnilda, already resident in England before the Conquest. Miss Yonge has an interesting account of Gunhild or Gunnilda (ii. 316), but she is mistaken in saying, 'After the Conquest Gunhild died away in England.' It was fairly popular for three centuries in both the Danish as well as the Norman dress ; v. Gunnell.

Richard fil. Qwinild. FFF.
Thomas Qwinild. W. 4.
Thomas Quenild, co. Norf., 1273. A.
Alicia Quenild, co. Bucks, ibid.
Quenilda Dewicar, co. Lanc., 1332 : Lay Subsidy, Rylands, p. 112.

There are eight Gonnilds to one Quenild in one single township in 1273 ; v. Hundred Rolls, vol. ii. pp. 354-5. It is needless to say that Quenild would be sure to become Quennell.

(2) Local. Mr. Lower suggests that Quennell is the French Quesnel, equivalent to our English Oak or Oakes. In some instances this may be quite possible. Nevertheless (1) must be considered the general parent.

1602. Robert Quennell, or Quennyl, co. Surrey: Reg. Univ. Oxf. vol. ii. pt. ii. p. 262.
1621. Peter Quennell, co. Surrey: ibid. p. 403.
London, 2, 2 ; Boston (U.S.), 3, 0.

Quentin ; v. Quintin.

Quested.—Local, ' of Quested.' I cannot find the spot. The suffix seems to be -stead, as in Playsted, Hampstead, &c.

1622. Mark Quested and Eliz. Halsall, widow : Marriage Lic. (London), ii. 110.
1692. Bapt.—John, s. Samuel Quested : St. John Baptist on Wallbrook, p. 171.
London, 1.

Quick, Quicke.—Nick. ' the quick'; v. Quickman. One of active and lively disposition.

Robert Quic, co. Camb., 1273. A.
William Quykke, C. R., 14 Hen. VI.
John Quicke, C. R., 3 Edw. IV.
1602. Bapt.—John, s. John Quicke : St. Michael, Cornhill, p. 103.
1613. Philip Quicke : Reg. Univ. Oxf. vol. ii. pt. ii. p. 330.
London, 25, 1 ; Philadelphia, 24, 0.

Quickfall.—Local. A corruption of Wigfall, q.v. ; cf. Quixley for Whixley ; v. Quarton.

1794. Married—John Quickfall and Ann Wyatt: St. Geo. Han. Sq. ii. 111. West Rid. Court Dir., 1; MDB. (co. Lincoln), 3.

Quickley, Quigley. —?——. Seemingly an Irish name. In the Boston Directory there are eight Michael and ten Patrick Quigleys. Evidently Quickley is a sharpened variant.

1793. Married—John Quickly and Su sanna Bort: St. Geo. Han. Sq. ii. 99.
Manchester, 1, 2; Boston (U.S.), 0, 96.

Quickman.—Nick. 'the quick man,' lively, energetic ; v. Quick, and cf. such double forms as Merry and Merriman, Long and Long- man, &c.

Adam Quikeman, co. Kent, 1273. A.
Thomas Quikman, 1303. M.
Denis Quicman, C. R., 17 Ric. II.

Quickman as a surname may still exist, but I cannot find any instances.

Quiddington. — Local, ' of Quiddington.' I cannot find the spot. But evidently it must first be looked for in co. Surrey.

1594-5. Married—Stockdall Queding- ton and Frances Ismangale, of Rigate in Surrey: St. Dionis Backchurch, p. 13.
1764. Married—Henry Quittenton, of Titsey, co. Surrey, and Eleanor Hinck- len: St. Geo. Han. Sq. i. 137.

A note appended by the editor says:

'Son of John Quiddington, baptized at Titsey, Nov. 26, 1743.'
London, 1.

Quigley; v. Quickley.

Quilliam.—Bapt. 'the son of William' (Welsh), a sharpened form of Gwilliam (q.v.); cf. Quelch for Welch.

Liverpool, 5.

Quilter.—Occup. ' the quilter,' a manufacturer of quilts. ' Quylte, of a bedde, *culcitra*' : Prompt. Parv.

Richard le Quilter, co. Oxf., 1273. A.
Thomas le Queylter. T.
Egidius le Quylter. J.
Robert le Quilter, Fines Roll, 12 Edw. I.
John Quylter, B. A., 1507: Reg. Univ. Oxf. i. 55.
London, 8.

Quiltmaker. — Occup. ; v. Quilter.

John Quyltemaker. H.

Quin, Quinn.—Bapt. ' the son of Quin,' an ancient Celtic personal name found commonly as McQuinn or McQueen ; v. Queen (2).

London, 6, 3; Boston (U.S.), 2, 269.

Quinby, Quimby. Quenby, Quemby.—Local, ' of Quenby,' a hamlet in the parish of Hungerton, co. Leic.

Ralph de Quenebi, co. Hunts, 1273. A.
1791. Married — William Beech and Jane Quenby : St. Geo. Han. Sq. ii. 59.
Liverpool, 2, 1, 0, 0; London (Quemby), 1; Oxford, 0, 1, 1, 0 ; Boston (U.S.), 12, 23, 0, 0.

Quince.—?——. Mr. Lower says 'the same as Quincey,' but fur- nishes no evidence. I cannot arrive at any satisfactory conclusion. The original form seems to have been Quinch.

1454. Jeffery Quinch, sheriff of Norwich: FF. iii. 165.
1620. Married — Edward Kennyman and Mary Quince: St. Dionis Back- church, p. 20.
1622. Edward Sayve and Margaret Quince: Marriage Lic. (London), ii. 116.
MDB. (co. Camb.), 2 ; (co. Hunts), 1.

Quincy, Quinsey.—Local, ' de Quency.' Probably a Norman local surname. Saier de Quency was a favourite of Henry II, and his son was created Earl of Winchester by King John.

Robert de Quency, co. Essex, 1273. A.
Hawyse de Quency, co. Bedf., ibid.
1670. Richard Cumberland and Anne Quinsey (co. Linc.): Marriage Lic. (Lon- don), ii. 297.
1730. Married—William Quincey and Mary Seager : St. Geo. Han. Sq. i. 8.
1742. Buried — William Quincy: St. Mary Aldermary, p. 226.
London Court Dir., 2, 0; Birmingham, 0, 1; Liverpool, 0, 1; Boston (U.S.), 13, 0.

Quiney.—I can furnish no his- tory of this surname, but I append instances.

1619-20. George Quiney, or Quinney, co. Warw.: Reg. Univ. Oxf. vol. ii. pt. ii. p. 382.
1788. Married—Thomas Quinney and Ann Towler : St. Geo. Han. Sq. ii. 10.
London, 4.

Quinland.—Not a variant of Queenland, but the Irish Quinlan (so familiar to the United States) with an excrescent *d*; cf. Jolland for Jollan, or Simmonds for Simmons.

Boston (U.S.), 1.

Quinn; v. Quin.

Quinnell; v. Quennell.

Quinsey; v. Quincy.

Quintin, Quentin.—(1) Bapt. ' the son of Quentin.' Quentin became a somewhat popular per- sonal name in Scotland, and has been immortalized by Walter Scott. It was still familiar in the 17th and 18th centuries, but is gradually losing ground.

Quintinus Poulet, Patent Roll, 7 Hen. VII.
Quintine Routledge, 1617: VVV. p. 440.
Quintine Foster, 1618 : ibid. p. 443.

(2) Local, ' of St. Quentin,' on the Somme, called after the mis- sionary martyred there in 287. It was he who caused the Quentin mentioned above to be a popular baptismal name. Probably the ' St.' was occasionally dropped, as seems to have been the case in several instances below.

Richard Quintine, co. Wilts, 1273. A.
John de St. Quintino, co. Wilts, ibid.
Adam Quintin, co. Hunts, ibid.
Robert Quintyn, co. Norf., ibid.
Willelmus de Qwyntyn, 1379 : P. T. Yorks. p. 128.
1647. Married—Thomas Quintin and Ann Tunstall: St. Jas. Clerkenwell, iii. 81.

It is clear that (1) rather than (2) is in general the chief parent. But both are now practically lost in Quinton, q.v.

Philadelphia, 4, 2.

Quinton.—Local, ' of Quinton.' Parishes in cos. Northampton and Gloucester.

Richard de Quenton, co. Northampt., 1273. A.
Thomas de Quenton, co. Oxford, ibid.
1665. Married—Richard Quinton and Marg. Midletich : St. Jas. Clerkenwell, iii. 121.
1713. John Quinton, rector of Thwayt, co. Norf.: FF. x. 184.
1729-30. Married—John Quinton and Eliz. Walker: St. Dionis Backchurch, p. 63.
London, 7; Philadelphia, 8.

Quirk.—Bapt. A Manx sur- name, being a contraction of Mac Cuirc, i.e. Corc's son. McQuyrke, Quyrke, 1511 ; Queerke. 1601 ; Quirk, 1641 (Manx Note Book, ii. 60). v. Quail.

1590. Married—Richard Querck and Jane Palnes: St. Antholin (London), p. 34.

1623. William Querke, living in Virginia: Hotten's Lists of Emigrants, p. 188.
Crockford, 4; Liverpool, 9; Philadelphia, 33.

Quixley.—Local, 'of Quixley,' now Whixley, a parish in the dioc. of Ripon, called Quixley in P. T. Yorks. 1379; v. Quarton. ·

Johannes de Quixley, 1379: P. T. Yorks. p. 227.
London, 2.

Quodling, Quadling, Codling.—Nick. 'Cœur-de-lion,' lion-hearted.

Robert Querdelioun, C. R., 2 Edw. III. pt. i.

Ralph Querdelyun. T.
William Querdelion, London. X.

By the middle of the 15th century the form assumed was Querdling. In 1433 John Querdling occupied a magisterial position in Norwich. Of him or an immediate descendant a rhyme is quoted:
'Whoso hath any quarrel or ple,
If he but withstand John Hankey,
John Qwerdlyng, Nic. Waleys, John
 Belagh, John Meg,
Sore shall him rewe,
For they rule all the Court with their
 lawes newe.'
 FF. iii. 145.

Later on it became Codling or Codlin (q.v.), but even to this day

in Norfolk and Suffolk Quodling or Quadling exists as a surname. No doubt Richard I made the sobriquet popular. I had the pleasure of pointing out in Notes and Queries (1888) that *codling*, an apple, is the same word as *cœur-de-lion* (sound to the core), the same intermediate stages having been gone through. 'Querdlynge, appulle, *duricenum*': Prompt. Parv.

'In July come . . . plummes in fruit, ginnitings, quadlins': Bacon, Essay 46 (Of Gardens).
1436. Simon Codlyng, rector of Bittering, co. Norf.: FF. ix. 460.
London, 1, 1, 2; MDB. (co. Norfolk), 0, 1, 0; (co. Suffolk), 0, 1, 1.

R

Raban.—(1) Bapt. 'the son of Raban,' i.e. Raven, a popular personal name in the 12th century (v. Raven). O.H.G. *hraban*, a raven (v. Skeat's Dict.). It is curious to note that the only modern instances of the surname I have seen are in Somersetshire and Gloucestershire, in which latter county we find Raban a personal name as long as eight centuries ago. This must be ranked amongst the curiosities of nomenclature.

'Raban the Englishman gave land to the Church of St. Peter, Gloucester, c. 1150': Atkyns' Hist. Glouc. p. 73.

(2) Local, 'de Raban.'

Elias de Raban, or Rabeyn, co. Linc., 1273. A.

I cannot discover the spot.

MDB. (Somerset), 1; (Gloucester), 1.

Raby.—Local, 'of Raby,' a township in the parish of Neston, co. Chester.

Thomas Penkett, of Raby, 1670: Wills at Chester (1660-80), p. 207.
Nicholas Raby, of Cuerden, 1674: ibid. p. 217.
Manchester, 4.

Rackstraw, Rexstrew. — ? Local. This surname is still familiar to Lancashire and Yorkshire. where it has flourished for

centuries. I suggested in my English Surnames, 2nd edit., p. 483, that it was a nickname for a scavenger or dust-heap searcher, quoting Piers Plowman's 'ratoner and rakyer of Cheape,' i.e. ratcatcher and scavenger of Cheapside. I have grown more careful as I have proceeded in my studies, and feel sure it is a local surname, but I cannot find the spot.

William Rakestraw, co. York. W. 11.
George Raikestray, of Ulverston, 1603: Lancashire Wills at Richmond, i. 225.
Thomas Rakestrawe, of Heysham, 1618: ibid.
1628. Bapt.—Eliz., d. Edward Rakestraw: St. Jas. Clerkenwell, i. 110.
1632. Married — Arthur Swann and Mary Rakestrawe: ibid. p. 64.

The name may be a nickname after all. I have seen Rackstraw as one of the dramatis personae in a 17th-century play, but I cannot lay my hand on it, having lost the reference. In any case the name is of North-English origin.

London, 3, 1; Sheffield, 2, 0.

Radbone.—Local; v. Rathbone.

Radborne, Radburn, Radbron.—Local, (1) 'of Radbourne,' parishes in cos. Derby and Warwick; (2) 'of Redbourne,' parishes

in cos. Herts and Lincoln. The modern pronunciation is Rad-, not Red-.

Robert de Redeborne, co. Hunts, 1273. A.
William de Redeburn, alias Redborn, co. Linc., ibid.
John de Reddeburn, co. Linc., ibid.
1797. Married—William Williams and Eliz. Redburn : St. Geo. Han. Sq. ii. 172.
1805. — Nathaniel Rogers and Sarah Redborn : ibid. p. 338.
London, 1, 3, 1.

Radcliff, Radcliffe, Radclyffe, Ratcliff, Ratcliffe. — Local, 'of Radcliffe,' a parish in co. Lanc., one of four only places in the Salford Hundred mentioned in Domesday. Radcliffe is two miles from Bury, and it is in this district the surname is especially common.

William de Radeclive, 6 Edw. I : Baines' Lanc. i. 528.
'John de Radeclif holds the tenth part of one Knight's fee in Rissheton': Knight's Fees, 23 Edw. III, ibid. ii. 694.
Willelmus de Radclif, 1379: P. T. Yorks. p. 201.
1608. Richard Radcliffe, co. Lanc., St. Mary Hall: Reg. Univ. Oxf. vol. ii. pt. ii. p. 301.
Alys Radcliffe, of Wymersley, 1554 Wills at Chester (1545-1620), p. 157.
Robert Ratcliffe, of Manchester, 1616: ibid. p. 158.
1708. Married—William English and Ann Radcliff: St. Geo. Han. Sq. ii. 189.

With this corruption, cf. Cunliffe for Cuntcliffe.

London, 1, 8, 6, 13, 10; Manchester, o, 12, o, 6, 8; MDB. (co. Lanc.), o, 23, o, o, 8; Philadelphia, 9, 25, o, 4, 1.

Radford, Radforth.—Local, 'of Radford,' 'villages and hamlets in cos. Notts, Oxford, and Warwick' (Lower). For suffix, v. Ford and Forth. Radford in co. Notts originated a surname which spread over the border into Derbyshire, and thence to Cheshire and Lancashire. In fact, it is the chief parent.

Ralph de Radeford, co. Oxf., 1273. A.
Adam de Radeford, co. Oxf., ibid.
Serlo de Radeford, co. Notts, ibid.
William de Radeford, co. Notts, ibid.
Thomas de Ratford, co. Soms., 1 Edw. III: Kirby's Quest, p. 133.
John de Raddeford, co. Soms. 1 Edw. III: ibid. p. 229.
Katherine Radforth, *widow*, 1584: Wills at Chester, i. 157.
Ralph Radford, of Chester, *tanner*, 1595: ibid.

Radford, a parish in co. Dorset, has manifestly been a parent of some of the Radfords.

London, 13, 0; Liverpool, 2, 1; Manchester, 10, 0; MDB. (co. Notts), 9, 0; (co. Derby), 19, 0; Philadelphia, 8, 0.

Radley, Redley.—Local, 'of Radley,' a parish in co. Berks.

Roger de Redlee, co. Essex, 1273. A.
Warin de Redleye, co. Essex, ibid.
Richard de Redlege, co. Essex. ibid.
1671-2. Charles Radley and Bridgett Cracroft: Marriage Lic. (London), ii. 199.
1781. Married—George Radley and Betty Cooke: St. Geo. Han. Sq. ii. 322.
London, 10, 1; Philadelphia, 3, 0.

Radmall, Radmell.—Local, 'of Rodmill,' co. Sussex, formerly written Radmell. 'It had owners of its own name, called de Rademylde, in the 14th century' (Lower, Patr. Brit. p. 283). But Redmall is a parish in co. Norwich; and Redmile, a parish in co. Leicester; and Rathmell, a parish in dioc. Ripon. Probably all have one and the same root origin as local names.

1305. William de Rademelde, vicar of West Rudham, co. Norf.: FF. vii. 161.
London, 3, 0.

Radmond, Radmon; v. Redmond, of which they are variants.

Manchester, 1, 0; Philadelphia, 1, 1.

Radnall.—Local, 'of Redenhall,' a parish in dioc. Norwich. But some spot in North England of the same name may have originated the surname in that part of the country. One of my instances lies in co. Northumberland.

Warin de Redenhale, co. Norf., Hen. III-Edw. I. K.
Thomas de Redinhale, co. Northumb., ibid.
John de Radenhale, co. Bedf., 20 Edw. I. R.
1314. Stephen de Redenhall, Rector of Holveston, co. Norf., FF. v. 488.
Ulverston, 1.

Radway.—Local, 'of Radway,' a parish in co. Warwick, and dioc. of Worcester. For further information, v. Rodway, the commoner modern form.

Geoffrey de Radeweye, co. Devon, Hen. III-Edw. I. K.
Thomas de Radeweye, co. Devon, ibid.
London, 1.

Rae.—Nick. 'the roe,' a Scottish form. North English *ra*; A.S. *ráh*; v. Ray and Roebuck.

London, 10; Philadelphia, 5.

Raeburn, Reyburn.—Local, 'of Raeburn,' a stream in the parish of Eskdalemuir, co. Dumfries.

1803. Married—Allan Raeburn and Mary Saunders: St. Geo. Han. Sq. ii. 291.
Newcastle, 1, 0; Philadelphia, 0, 4.

Raffe. — Bapt. 'the son of Ralph,' popularly Raff. 'Raaf, propyr name, Radulphus': Prompt. Parv. Cf. Ruff, Roof, Rofe, &c., for Rolf, from Rudolph.

Amice Raffe, co. Camb., 1273. A.
Thomas Rauf, co. Hunts, ibid.
Adam Rauf, co. Soms., 1 Edw. III: Kirby's Quest, p. 252.
Margerie, d. of Raff Mirkett, 1548: Reg. St. Columb Major, p. 5.
Raff Aslakeby, temp. 1550: Visitation of Yorkshire, p. 4.
Mawde, d. to Raff Grey, temp. 1550: ibid.
1668. Bapt.—Mary, d. Thomas Rafe: St. Jas. Clerkenwell, i. 237.
London, 1; Philadelphia, 7.

Raffles.—Local, 'of Raffles.' Lower says, 'A place in the parish of Mouswald, in Dumfriesshire. That parish contains five old border fortresses; the least dilapidated is that of Raffles' (Patr. Brit. p. 283).

Crockford, 1; Liverpool, 1.

Raffman.—Occup. 'a dealer in raff' (cf. *riff-raff*). So far as I can find, both surname and occupation (so termed) are peculiar to co. Norfolk. The Prompt. Parv. has 'Raaf, ware.' Raff meant refuse, shearings of cloth, wool—any rubbish in fact that was saleable. In the Guild of St. George, Norwich, 1385, occurs the name of John Raffman, also Robert Smith, raffman, and John Smith, raffman (Early Eng. Text Soc., English Gilds). Nevertheless Blomefield (FF. iii. 207), enumerating the companies in the procession of Corpus Christi Day, mentions the 'grocers and raffmen,' and explains in a note, 'i.e. raftermen, those that deal in rafts or timber pieces.' I do not think this will bear investigation.

1406. Henry Rufman, bailiff of Yarmouth: FF. xi. 324.
1506. Richard Hill, *rafeman*, gave a suit of vestments: ibid. iv. 249.

Ragg, Ragge.—Bapt. 'the son of Ragg,' a nick. of Ragner (Reyner) or Raginhold (Reynold), both very familiar personal names in the surname period. The instances adduced are from Yorkshire, where Ragg, Ragge, and Wragg (q.v.) are well-known surnames, and where Reyner (Ragner) was at the same time one of the favourite font-names. Wragg is the favourite modern Yorkshire form; cf. Wray and Ray (2).

Johannes Reyg', 1379: P. T. Yorks. p. 43.
Johannes Rage, 1379: ibid. p. 39.
Isabella Rage, 1379: ibid. p. 20.
Johanna Rage, 1379: ibid.
1743. Married—William Rhodes and Ann Ragg': St. Geo. Han. Sq. i. 30.
1747. — Richard Hunter and Ann Ragg: St. Jas. Clerkenwell, iii. 277.
London, 1, 1; West Rid. Court Dir., 4, 0; Sheffield, 4, 1; Philadelphia, 1, 0.

Raggett, Ragget.—Nick. 'the ragged,' i.e. the shaggy, the rough-haired. Lower says, 'Reigate, in Surrey, locally so pronounced.' It may be so. But a familiar entry in mediæval records is 'le Ragged,' and that seems the more natural elucidation. 'Raggyd (or torne, P.), *laciniosus, lacinosus*': Prompt. Parv. v. Ragman.

Thomas le Ragged, co. York, 1273. A.
Richard le Raggide, co. Derby, ibid.
Robert le Raggidde, co. Derby, ibid.
1705.Married—GeorgeRaggett and Ann Grimwood: St. Geo. Han. Sq. ii. 127.
London, 4, 0 ; Boston (U.S.), 0, 1.

Ragman.—Nick. 'one who went ragged.' 'Ragmann, or he that goythe wythe jaggyd clothys, *pannicius, vel pannicia*': Prompt. Parv. It is, once more, interesting to notice that Prompt. Parv. was written in Norfolk, the county whence my instance comes.

Richard Ragman, co. Norf., 1273. A.

Rain, Raine, Raines, Rains, Rayne, Raynes.—(1) Bapt. 'the son of Reine.' Fr. Reine (Queen).

Reine Bacun, co. Camb., 1273. A.
Alice Reine, co. Camb., ibid.
John Reyn, co. Linc., ibid.
Nicholas Reyn, co. Linc., ibid.

(2) Bapt. 'the son of Rayne,' seemingly a nick. of Reyner or Reynold, common in N. England, where Reyner was extremely popular.

Robert Rayne, 1379: P. T. Yorks. p. 65.
Johannes Rayne, ibid.
Richard Rayneson, ibid. p. 39.
William Rayne, ibid. p. 118.

(3) Local, 'of Rennes.'

Robert de Rennes, co. Oxf., 1273. A.
Richard de Rennes. R.
William de Rainis. E.
Ricardus de Raines, Pipe Roll, 11 Hen. II, p. 20.
London, 2, 6, 3, 7, 2, 1.

Rainbird, Raynbird.—Bapt. 'the son of Reynebaud.' A manifest corruption, and found in the district where Reynebaud or Reynebold was an early and familiar personal name (v. Rumball for instances). The corruption is, as usual, imitative. My instances are decisive.

'Witnesses, Roger, sub-prior, Rainbird, the sacrist, and William, the deacon,' temp. 12th cent., co. Norf.: FF. ii. 207.
1483. Thomas Reynberd, of Thetford, co. Norf.: ibid. ii. 62.
1540. Robert Raynbald, of Norwich: ibid. iv. 232 n.
London, 2, 1 ; MDB. (Suffolk), 0, 1 ; Norwich, 1, 0 ; Ipswich, 1, 0.

Rainbow.—Bapt. 'the son of Reynebaud' (v. Rainbird). Doubtless an imitative corruption as found in co. Norfolk, the habitat of the Rainbirds. I have no doubt in my own mind as to the truth of this derivation.

1524. Stephen Rainbow, sheriff of Norwich: FF. iii. 219.
London, 3 ; Oxford, 1 ; Philadelphia, 1.

Rainford, Rainforth.—Local, 'of Rainford,' a chapelry in the parish of Prescot, co. Lancaster. For suffix, v. Ford and Forth.

Margaret Rainforth, of Winstanley, 1612: Wills at Chester, i. 157.
Robert Rainforth, of Pemberton, 1613: ibid.
John Rainford, of Rainford, 1673: ibid. iii. 218.
William Rainford, of Weetton, 1705: Lancashire Wills at Richmond, ii. 204.
Thomas Rainforth, of Weetton, 1717: ibid.
Manchester, 2, 1 ; Liverpool, 1, 0 ; Preston, 4, 0.

Rainger, Ranger. — Occup. 'the ranger,' a forester. Lower quotes Nelson's Laws of Game, where the ranger's specific duties are described.

1615. Adam Ranger, co. Wilts: Reg. Univ. Oxf. vol. ii. pt. ii. p. 338.
1801. Married—William Rainger and Esther Hardy : St. Geo. Han. Sq. ii. 237.
London, 4, 1 ; MDB. (co. Sussex), 0, 2.

Rainscroft; v. Ravenscroft.

Raistrick.—Local; v. Rastrick.

Raively; v. Reveley. An American variant.

Raleigh, Rawley, Ralley.—Local, 'of Raleigh.' Some spot (I cannot find it) in co. Devon where the family were settled so long ago as six centuries. Sir Walter Raleigh's father lived at Fardel in that county, and he was born at Hayes on the coast. Rawley seems to have been the pronunciation (the present orthography), hence the point of the many epigrams on Sir Walter.

The following spellings occur in the Index to Reg. Univ. Oxf.: Ralegh, Raleighe, Rallegh, Raughley, Raughlie, Raughly, Raugleigh, Rauleigh, Rauly, Rawlie, Rawleigh, Rawley, Rawleygh, Rawlei, Rawlighe, Rawlye, and Raylye.

William de Raleigh, or Ralee, or Rayley, or Radley, or Rawleigh, bishop of Norwich, formerly 'treasurer of the church at Exeter,' 1239: FF. iii. 484.
Hugh de Ralegh, co. Devon, 1273. A.
Warin de Raleghe, co. Soms., ibid.
Peter de Ralegh, co. Cornwall, 20 Edw. I. R.
Wymund de Ralegh, co. Devon, Hen. III-Edw. I. K.
Simon de Raleghe, co. Soms., 1 Edw. III : Kirby's Quest, p. 167.
John de Raleghe, co. Soms., 1 Edw. III : ibid.
London, 0, 5, 0 ; Philadelphia, 5, 6, 1.

Ralf, Ralph.—Bapt. 'the son of Ralph'; v. Randolph.

John Radulphus, 1273. A.
Ralph le Gras. B.
Ralph fil Ivo. T.
London, 0, 9 ; Boston (U.S), 0, 6.

Ram, Ramm.—(1) Nick. 'the ram'; cf. Bull, Bullock, &c.

Geoffrey le Ram, co. Essex, 1273. A.
John le Ram', co. Bucks, ibid.
Nicholas le Ram, Fines Roll, 11 Edw. I.
Robert le Ram, C. R., 30 Edw. I.
Robert le Ram, co. Soms., 1 Edw. III : Kirby's Quest, p. 94.

(2) Local, 'at the Ram,' an inn-sign ; cf. Roebuck and Roe (2).

William atte Ramme, Fines Roll, 14 Edw. II.
1809. Married—Thomas Hamilton Miller and Mary Ann Ram : St. Geo. Han. Sq. ii. 405.
London, 3, 1 ; MDB. (co. Norf.), 0, 3.

Ramage, Ramadge.—Nick. 'the ramage,' i.e. the wild. 'The term was very often applied to an untaught hawk' (Halliwell); cf. Wild, Wildgoose, Hawk, &c.

'No more than is a gote ramage.'
Chaucer, R. R. 5384.

Perhaps allied to *rammish*, ram-like, strong-scented :

'For all the world they stinken as a gote;
Hir savour is so rammish.'
Chaucer, C. T. 16355.
William le Rameys, co. Soms., 1273. A.
William Ramage. B.
London, 5, 1 ; Philadelphia, 14, 0.

Rambart, Rambaut, Rambeau.—Bapt. 'the son of Rambald'; v. Rimbault.

Johannes fil. Rambaldi, co. Berks, 1273. A.
1773. Married—James Poirier and Marie Rambault : St. Geo. Han. Sq. i. 232.
London, 1, 0, 1 ; Crockford, 1, 2, 0.

Rampton.—Local, 'of Rampton,' a parish in co. Camb., dioc. Ely.

Simon de Rampton, co. Camb., 1273. A.
Eustace de Rampton, co. Camb., ibid.
1660. Married—James Rampton and
Fraunces Williams: St. Jas. Clerkenwell,
iii. 104.
1662. — John Baker and Dorothy
Rampton: ibid. p. 109.
London, 1.

Ramsbotham, Ramsbottom, Ramsbotton.—Local, 'of Ramsbottom,' a populous village in the township of Tottington-Lower-End, and in the ancient parish of Bury, co. Lanc. Nearly all the surnames with suffix -*bottom* or -*botham* hail from S.E. Lancashire or the Cheshire border ; v. Higginbotham, Shufflebotham, Sidebotham, &c.

Adam Romsbotham, Rossendale, co. Lanc., 1556 : Wills at Chester, i. 164.
Ellis Romsbotham, *husbandman*, co. Lanc., 1587: ibid.
William Romesbotham, 1602: Preston Guild Rolls, p. 63.
John Romsbottom, of Romsbottom, 1614 : Wills at Chester, i. 165.
John Ramsbothom, of Elton, parish of Bury, 1693 : ibid. iv. 205.
London, 1, 1, 0; Bury (co. Lanc.), 0, 6, 0 ; Manchester, 1, 7, 1 ; Philadelphia, 1, 4, 0.

Ramsden.—Local, 'of Ramsden,' i.e. the ram's den or dean. A.S. *ram, rom + den*, a dell, glen, or dingle. Some small spot, probably in the W. Rid. of Yorkshire, has given birth to a large contingent of Ramsdens resident in that county ; cf. the places Ramsbotham, co. Lanc., and Ramsgill, W. Rid. Yorks ; cf. also Ramsden, a parish in dioc. Oxford.

Thomas de Rammesden, co. Essex, 1273. A.
Mathæus de Romsdeyn, 1379 : P. T. Yorks. p. 174.
1562. Married—Humfraye Ramsdon and Alys Skepens : St. Dionis Backchurch, p. 2.
1607. Hugh Ramsden, co. York, 'Magd. Hall : Reg. Univ. Oxf. vol. ii. pt. ii. p. 298.
1801. Married—John Ramsden and Mary Salter : St. Geo. Han. Sq. ii. 232.
London, 10 ; West Rid. Court Dir., 40.

Ramshire ; v. Ravenshear.

Ramskill.—Local, 'of Ramsgill,' now a parish in the valley of the Nidd, not far from Pateley Bridge, W. Rid. Yorks ; v. Gaskell for a similar sharpening of pronunciation of *gill*, a ravine, dell. Cf. Ramsden.

Leeds, 1 ; Crockford, 1 ; West Rid. Court Dir., 4.

Ranacre ; v. Runacres.

Rance ; v. Rand.

Rancock.—Bapt. 'the son of Randolph,' from the nick. Ran or Rand, with suffix -*cock* (v. Cock) ; cf. Rankin, Wilcock, Simcock, &c.

Isabel Rancok, 1510. W. 11, p. 171.

Rand, Rands, Rance, Randson.—Bapt. 'the son of Randolph,' from the nick. Rand. 'Rande, or Randolf, propyr name: *Ranulphus, non Radulphus, Raaf*' : Prompt. Parv. Rand was a Yorkshire favourite, and the surnames founded on it survive there (v. Rankin). For other forms, v. Ranson.

Thomas Randson, co. York. W. 3.
Janet Rande, co. York : ibid.
Thomas Ranson, co. York. W. 20.
Adam serviens Ran Wiles, 5 Edw. II : Freemen of York, i. 14.
Alicia Randoghter, 1379 : P. T. Yorks. p. 203.
Johannes Randson, 1379 : ibid. p. 200.
Ricardus Randes, 1379 : ibid. p. 65.
Agnes Randewyf, 1379: ibid. p. 65.
Robert Randson, 1379 : ibid. p. 220.

Rance for Rands is natural ; cf. Evance for Evans.

1735. Bapt. — William, s. William and RebeccaRants: St. Jas.Clerkenwell,ii.221.
1736. — Mary, d. William and Rebecca Rance : ibid. p. 227.

Here Rands has become Rants, then Rance.

1742. Bapt.—John, s. John Rands : ibid. p. 262.
London, 7, 2, 3, 0 ; West Rid. Court Dir., 4, 0, 0, 0 ; MDB. (Norfolk), 0, 1, 0, 0 ; (Suffolk), 2, 4, 0, 0 ; Boston (U.S.), 89, 0, 1, 0.

Randall, Randell, Randle, Randal. — Bapt. 'the son of Randolph,' from the nick. Randle. For the popularity of Randle in Cheshire, v. Randolph.

Randle de Arclet, co. Ches., temp. 1290 : East Cheshire, ii. 375.
Randle Poole, co. Ches., 1600 : ibid. p. 383 *n*.
1571. Randall Smythe and Mary Lightfoot,*widow*: Marriage Lic. (London),i.49.
1637. Bapt.—Alexander, s. Cristofer Randall : St. Jas. Clerkenwell, i. 137.
1640. Bapt. -- William, s. Richard Randall : St. Michael, Cornhill, p. 130.
1652-3.Buried—Randle Newton: Wilmslow Ch., Cheshire.
1664.Bapt.—Jone, d. Randall Lawson : St. Jas. Clerkenwell, i. 222.
London,59,8,4,0 ; Philadelphia,61,1,3,1.

Randolph.—Bapt. 'the son of Randolph.' The Lond. Dir. owes many entries to this once famous name. Randle was the favourite nick. form, and for centuries held its own as a font-name in Cheshire on account of the popularity of Randle, Earl of Chester, the Crusader. On the same page of the Index to Earwaker's East Cheshire I find Rander Borowes, Randle Blackshaw, and Randle Blundeville. The directory forms are Randle, Randall, and Randell. Rand was another abbreviation, and to it we owe Rand, Rands, and Ranson. With the diminutive *kin* added we get Rankin, Ranken, and Ranking. Ralph was, however, the most generally favoured corruption of Randolph. Primary stages will be found below :

Robert fil. Ranulf, co. Linc., 1273. A.
Peter Randulf, co. Bedf., ibid.
Ranulph fil. Ranulph, co. Suff., ibid.
Engilard fil. Radulf, co. Salop, ibid.
William fil. Radufi, co. Hunts, ibid.
Richard Randolf, bailiff of Yarmouth, 1290 : FF. xi. 322.
William Randolf, co. Soms., 1 Edw. III : Kirby's Quest, p. 96.
Henricus Randolf, *osteler*, 1379 : P. T. Yorks. p. 161.
London, 3 ; Crockford, 9 ; Philadelphia, 32.

Ranford ; v. Rainford ; a corruption. In the same way Ravensford became Rainsford and Ransford, q.v.

Liverpool, 2.

Ranger.—Occup. ; v. Rainger.

Ranigar ; v. Runacres.

Ranken ; v. Rankin.

Rankill.—Bapt. 'the son of Ravenchil,' an old personal name, very early reduced to Rankil. I am confirmed in my view by the fact that all my instances belong to one locality.

Rauenchil, co. York : Domesday.
Ranchil, co. York : ibid.
Rankil, the Miller (Molendinarius),1176: RRR. p. 162.
Robertus Rankell, 1379 : P. T. Yorks. p. 43.
Robert Ravenchil, Yorks, temp. 1390 : FFF. p. 106.
Robert Ravenkil, Yorks, temp. 1390: ibid.
Stephen Ravenchil, Yorks, temp. 1390: ibid. p. 47.

Stephen Ramchel, Yorks, temp. 1390: FFF. p. 106.

Thus it is clear that the Yorkshire personal name Ravenchil or Ranchil became a surname in the guise of Rankil or Rankill. I believe Ravenhill (q.v.) is the present descendant. It is incredible that the surname should have entirely died out. Query: Is Rankin (a Yorkshire surname) sometimes a corruption of Rankil?

Rankin, Ranken, Ranking.—Bapt. 'the son of Randolph,' from nick. Ran or Rand, and dim. Rand-kin or Ran-kin. The first two instances below, however, rather point to Reyner or Reynold as the parent source. Cf. Rancock.

Gilbert Reynkyn, co. Kent, 1273. A.
Richard Reynkyn. H.
John Rankyn, co. Soms., 1 Edw. III: Kirby's Quest, p. 124.
Elena Rankyn, 1379: P. T. Yorks. p. 96.
1612. Giles Rankin, of London: Reg. Univ. Oxf. vol. ii. pt. ii. p. 328.
London, 3, 3, 1.

Ransdale.—Local, 'of Ravensdale.' There is a Ravendale, a hamlet, in the parish of Muggington, co. Derby. But probably several places of this name exist. With the corrupted Ransdale, cf. Rainscroft for Ravenscroft, or Ransley for Ravensley. v. Raven.

London, 1.

Ransford.—Local, 'of Ravensford.' I do not know where the spot is. The meaning is 'the ford which belonged to Raven'; v. Raven and Ransdale, or Rawnsley.

1670. Married—Robert Ransford and Katharin Willson: St. Jas. Clerkenwell, iii. 171.
1695-6. Dominick Melochling and Mary Ransford: Marriage Lic. (London), ii. 318.
London, 6; Philadelphia, 5.

Ransley.—Local; v. Rawnsley.

Ranson, Ransom, Ransome.—Bapt. 'the son of Randolph,' from nick. Rand, and patr. Randson. This became Ranson, and then Ransom or Ransome; cf. Hansom for Hanson (q.v.), or Sansom for Sanson (v. Sampson),

or Milsom (q.v.) for Milson. The Ransons and Ransoms run side by side in cos. Norfolk and Suffolk. For further particulars, v. Rand. Mr. Lower says, 'I should judge this name was originally Ransham, though I find no place so called' (!!). Mr. Ferguson finds the etymon in the O. Norse *ransamr*, praedabundus, piratical. 'What curious changes,' says he, 'the whirligig of time brings round! We take our money to the descendant of the old sea-robber to take care of for us—Ransom & Co., bankers, Pall Mall. Another Ransome has turned his sword into a ploughsnare, and become famed as a maker of agricultural implements at Ipswich' (!!!). All this is purely imaginary.

1601. Bapt.—Margaret, d. Anthony Rannson, or Rannsom: St. Jas. Clerkenwell, i. 38.
1788. Married—John Ransom and Jane Jones: St. Geo. Han. Sq. ii. 1.
1796. — Robert Ranson and Mary Ann Stanton: ibid. p. 156.
London, 8, 9, 9; MDB. (Norfolk), 0, 2, 3; (Suffolk), 3, 3, 4; Boston (U.S.), 1, 24, 0.

Rant.—Bapt. 'the son of Rand,' q.v., a sharpened form; cf. Brand and Brandt. As Rand is almost peculiar to Yorkshire, so is Rant to Norfolk and Suffolk.

Henry Rant, co. Norf., 1444: FF. v. 491.
1598. Buried—Robert Rant, St. Stephen's, Norwich: ibid. iv. 152.
William Rant, of Yelverton, co. Norf., died 1687: ibid. v. 492.
1635. William Rant and Jane Dingley: Marriage Lic. (London), ii. 222.
MDB. (Suffolk), 2.

Raper.—Occup. 'the roper,' a ropemaker. N. England *raper*; v. Roper.

Alan de Postoill, *raper*, 10 Edw. III: Freemen of York, i. 30.
Willelmus Raper, *raper*, 1379: P. T. Yorks. p. 222.
Johannes Raper, 1379: ibid. p. 241.
1715. Bapt.—Hellen, d. Edward Rapier (sic), St. Jas. Clerkenwell, ii. 85.
1736. Married—William Raper and Ruth Grosvenor: St. Michael, Cornhill, p. 67.
London, 6; West Rid. Court Dir., 3.

Rapkin, Rapkins.—Bapt. 'the son of Ralph,' from the nick. Rap (one of the many nicks. of a fontname that has made such a mark

on our directories), and dim. Rapkin; cf. Wilkin, Jeffkin, &c.
London, 2, 1.

Rapson.—Bapt. 'the son of Ralph,' from the nick. Rap; v. Rapkin.

John Rapson, temp. Eliz. Z.
1581. Thomas Rapshion, co. Soms.: Reg. Univ. Oxf. vol. ii. pt. ii. p. 111.
1804. Married—William Oak and Mary Rapson: St. Geo. Han. Sq. ii. 309.
London, 1; Philadelphia, 5.

Rascal.—Nick. 'the rascal,' a lean ragged deer, afterwards applied to the rabble (v. my English Surnames, 3rd edit., p. 488, for several instances); cf. Hart, Stagg, Ray, &c. As the term rascal grew more opprobrious, the surname seems to have been silently changed into Rastall, q.v.

John Raskele. H.
Robert Rascal was persecuted for his religion in 1517: Foxe.
'Received for a pewe in the lower end of the churche set to Richard Rascalle, vi²:' Ludlow Churchwarden's Accounts, Camden Soc.
Thomas Rascall, 1578: Reg. Univ. Oxf. vol. ii. pt. ii. p. 81.
Thomas Rascall, or Rastall, M.A., of Balliol Coll., 1584: ibid. vol. ii. pt. iii. p. 93.
John Raskell, Poulton-le-Fylde, 1672: Lancashire Wills at Richmond, i. 225.

Rashleigh, Rassleigh.—Local, 'of Rasleigh.' 'Rashleigh, in the parish of Wemworthy, in Devonshire, gave name to this ancient family, the elder line of which became extinct in the reign of Henry VII': Shirley's Noble and Gentle Men (quoted by Lower).

1576. John Rashlighe, co. Cornwall: Reg. Univ. Oxf. vol. ii. pt. ii. p. 71.
1592. Thomas Rashley, co. Devon: ibid. p. 191.
1643. Walter Blurton and Mary Rashleigh; Marriage Lic. (London), ii. 271.
London, 3, 0; Boston (U.S.), 0, 1.

Rastall, Restall, Restell.—?——. I can offer no suggestion as to the derivation of this name. Cf. Rascal.

Nicholas Rastel, co. Hants, Hen. III-Edw. I. K.
Roger Rastell, co. Notts, ibid.
Ralph Rastel, or Rastal, co. Hunts, 1273. A.
1574. Roger Rastall and Dionise Mayre: Marriage Lic. (London), i. 37.
1621. Roger Rastell and Joane Lewson: ibid. ii. 104.
'William Rastall, of Wisbeach, hanged

on the charge of helping in an insurrection in favour of Charles II, 1650 ': FF. iii. 400.

London, 2, 2, 4 ; Oxford, 0, 2, 0 ; Philadelphia, 1, 1, 0.

Rastrick, Raistrick.—Local, ' of Rastrick,' formerly a chapelry in W. Rid. Yorks, three miles from Huddersfield.

Katerina Rastrike, 1379 : P. T. Yorks. p. 221.

1803. Married—William Reid Rastrick and Elizabeth Emery : St. Geo. Han. Sq. ii. 287.

London, 1, 0 ; MDB. (co. Surrey), 2, 0 ; (W. Rid. Yorks), 0, 7 ; Philadelphia, 0, 1.

Rat.—Nick. ' the rat,' possibly intended as a complimentary sobriquet.

Jordan le Rat, co. Linc., Hen. III- Edw. I. K.

Robert le Rat, co. Linc., ibid.

Nicholas le Rat, co. Oxf., 1273. A.

Walter le Rat. J.

William le Rat, co. Soms., 1 Edw. III : Kirby's Quest, p. 213.

Ratcliff, Ratcliffe. — Local, ' of Radcliff,' q.v. Simply a sharpened pronunciation.

Rathbone, Rawbone, Rawbon, Rathborne, Radbone.— ? Local, ' of Ruabon ' (?). There seems little doubt that these surnames hail from co. Ches., also that Ruabon is the parent. The change to Rathbone is peculiar, but perhaps the place-name Ruabon has undergone a change. I furnish an instance of Rawbone from the Prestbury registers (co. Ches.) dated 1603. A Thomas Rathbone was living there in 1695. His name occurs in a document ; v. East Cheshire, ii. 226. This is corroborative. I see Lower says, ' Rawbone, a corruption of Rathbone.' It may be the other way about.

1547. Robert Radbone and Eliz. Smyth : Marriage Lic. (London), p. 11.

1592. Peter Rathbone, of Brereton : Wills at Chester (1545-1620), p. 158.

1605. Ann Rathbone, of Moreton, widow : ibid.

1604. Married—Thomas Rawbone and Alice Okes : Reg. Prestbury Ch. (co. Ches.), p. 163.

London, 7, 2, 1, 1, 0 ; MDB. (co. Ches.), 3, 0, 0, 0, 0 ; Liverpool, 8, 0, 0, 0, 0 ; Oxford (Radbone), 4.

Rathmell.—Local, ' of Rathmell,' a village three miles from Settle, co. York.

Willelmus de Rauthelm, 1379 : P. T. Yorks. p. 286.

Ricardus Rauthemell, 1379 : ibid.

John Rathmell, of Poulton, 1587 : Lancashire Wills at Richmond, i. 225.

Richard Rathmell, of Garstang, 1621 : ibid.

MDB. (West Rid. Yorks), 2 ; Hawkswick (Arncliffe, Yorks), 1.

Rattray.—Local, ' of Rattray,' a parish in co. Perth. Lower says, ' Derived from a barony of the same name in Perthshire. The first of the name on record is Alan de Ratheriff, who lived in the reigns of William the Lion and Alexander III. The family still reside at Craighall, in the parish of Rattray ' : Patr. Brit. p. 285.

London, 1.

Raveley.—Local, ' of Raveley,' two parishes (Great and Little Raveley) in co. Hunts.

Emma de Ravele, co. Hunts, 1273. A.

Richard de Ravele, co. Hunts, ibid.

Philadelphia, 1.

Raven. — Bapt. ' the son of Raven.' In Domesday the name existed both in Derbyshire and Cheshire ; cf. Sparrowhawk, also a personal name at the same period. In place-names like Ravenscroft, Rawnsley, &c., the probability is that the spot took its name from Raven, the proprietor, rather than from the fact that ravens abounded there.

Raven de Slinghawe, 1155 : DDD. i. 2.

Gospatric fil. Raven, 1177 : Hodgson's Northumberland, vi. 26.

William Raven, 1190 : ibid. p. 49.

Raven de Riding, 1233 : ibid. p. 163.

Henry Raven, co. Camb , 1273. A.

1618. John Raven and Leah Cotton : Marriage Lic. (London), ii. 61.

1791. Married—Robert Hoodless and Eliz. Raven : St. Geo. Han. Sq. ii. 55.

London, 11 ; Philadelphia, 1.

Ravenhill.—? ——. Mr. Lower says, ' Local, " the hill frequented by ravens." ' This is easy enough to write, and, of course, it is well-nigh impossible to contradict the statement. At the same time I cannot discover a hill so called, nor any entry with a local prefix. Yet the surname is a familiar one, there being eight in the London Dir. alone. May it not be the once great personal name of Ravenchil ? ' Rauenchil, co. Yorks ' (Domesday). In the same county we find later on :

Roger fil. Ravenkelli, 21 Ric. II : Furness Coucher Book, i. 188.

William fil. Robert Ravenchil : FFF. p. 47.

Stephen Ravenchil : ibid. p. 106.

Ravenhill is now found in the West Riding ; cf. also

Mariota Ravenild, co. Kent, 1273. A.

Robertus Ravenild, co. Kent, ibid.

a manifest font-name, which would easily corrupt to Ravenhill ; v. Rankill for many instances.

1700. Bapt.—Anna Maria, d. John Ravenell : St. Mary Aldermary, London, p. 114.

1787. Married—John Ravenhill and Mary Patrick : St. Geo. Han. Sq. i. 400.

London, 8 ; Sheffield, 1.

Ravenscroft, Rainscroft.— Local, ' of Ravenscroft,' a township in the parish of Middlewich, co. Chester.

1565. Martin Raynscrofte, Ch. Ch. : Reg. Univ. Oxf. vol. ii. pt. ii. p. 12.

1574. Richard Ravenscrofte, of Occleston : Wills at Chester, i. 158.

1618. John Ravenscroft, of Wettenhall, co. Ches. : ibid.

1757. Married—John Ravenscroft and Eliz. Colman : St. Geo. Han. Sq. i. 68.

London, 7, 0 ; MDB. (co. Chester), 5, 0 ; Boston (U.S.), 1, 0.

Ravenshear, Ramshire.—(1) Bapt. ' the son of Ravenswar,' a Domesday personal name (v. Yonge, ii. 286). I have no instances, but the origin seems unimpeachable, being one of the many compounds of Raven. (2) Local, ' of Ravenshaw' ; v. Renshaw.

1606. Robert Ravenshaw, of Bromall, yeoman : Wills at Chester, i. 158.

1617. Robert Ramshaw, of Bridgemere : ibid.

The modern general form is Renshaw, q.v. In proof we may point out that one of the Bridgemere family is thus recorded :

1613. Randle Renshaw, of Bridgemere : Wills at Chester, i. 159.

1802. Married—William Ramshaw and Eliz. Maria Hall : St. Geo. Han. Sq. ii. 251.

London, 2, 1.

Raw, Rawe.—(1) Bapt. ' the son of Ralph,' from the nick. Raw, whence such surnames as Raw-son or Raw-kins, q.v. (2) Local, ' at the Row,' i. e. the row of cottages. N.E. raw, from residence therein or thereby. Probably the latter is in general the true parent, being a North-English surname.

1574. Married—William Rawe and Dorothy Tanner: St. Jas. Clerkenwell, iii. 6.
1591.—Robert Rawe and Ann Filkes: ibid. p. 16.
Katherine Raw, of Barrow, 1613: Lancashire Wills at Richmond, i. 225.
Richard Raw, of Bispham, 1631: ibid.
William Raw, of Poulton, 1660: ibid.
London, 2, 1; Manchester, 3, 0.

Rawbon, Rawbone; v. Rathbone.

Rawcliffe; v. Rowcliffe.

Rawdon.—Local, 'of Rawdon,' a chapelry in the parish of Guiseley, W. Rid. Yorks.
John de Rawdon, 1379: P. T. Yorks. p. xv.
West Rid. Court Dir., 1.

Rawkins.—Bapt. 'the son of Ralph,' from the nick. Raw, dim. Raw-kin; with patronymic s, Rawkins. Cf. Wil-kin and Wilkins, &c., and v. Rawson.
Joane Rawkyns, temp. Eliz. Z.
Walter Rawkyns, temp. Eliz. Z.
1579. Married—Edward Rawkyns and Eliz. Robartes: St. Dionis Backchurch, p. 9.
1672. John Rawkins and Mary Thornborough: Marriage Alleg. (Canterbury), p. 201.
London, 1; Preston, 1.

Rawle, Rawles.—Bapt. 'the son of Raoul,' i.e. Ralph; Fr. Raoul. Hence Rawle and Rawles are equivalent to Rowle, Rolle, Rolls, and Rowles. v. Rawkins.
Thomas Raules, co. Soms., 1 Edw. III: Kirby's Quest, p. 188.
John Raweles, co. Soms., 1 Edw. III: ibid.
1612. Stephen Rawle and Alice Greenley: Marriage Lic. (London), ii. 14.
1726. Bapt.—Mary, d. Noah Raoul: St. Michael, Cornhill, p. 168.
London, 3, 1; Philadelphia, 10, 0.

Rawlence.—Local; v. Rylands.

Rawley.—Local; v. Raleigh.

Rawlin, Rawling, Rawlings, Rawlins, Rawlinson. — (1) Bapt. 'the son of Ralph,' i.e. Randolph, dim. Rawlin and Rollin; through French Raoul-in, the dim. of Raoul; cf.
Raoul Partrer: v. Index, Wars of English in France in reign of Henry VI.
Raoulin Reynault: ibid.
Raoulin Meriel: ibid.
Raoul de Saige: ibid.

Miss Yonge says Raoul is the French Rodolphe, not Randolph. In any case, I am sure the dim. Raoulin in England represented Randolph, i.e. Ralph.
Raulyn de la Fermerie, 1306. M.
Anabella Raulyn, 1379: P. T. Yorks. p. 139.
Raulinus Bassett. E.
Raulina de Briston. FF.
Robert Rawlyngson. ZZ.
John Rawlynson. F.

(2) Bapt. 'the son of Rowland,' pronounced Rawland and Rolland in Furness and co. Cumb., where a large family of Rawlinsons has sprung up, undoubtedly descendants of Rowland through Rawlandson.
London, 2, 5, 24, 18, 11.

Rawnsley, Ransley.—Local, 'of Ravensley,' i.e. the meadow that belonged to Raven, the original settler (v. Raven). I cannot find the spot.
Ralph de Ravenleg, co. Bedf., 1273. A.
Margareta de Rauenslawe, 1379: P. T. Yorks. p. 189.
1749. Buried—Mary Ransley, widow: St. Michael, Cornhill, p. 290.
1789. Married—Robert Ransley and Eliz. Nichols: St. Geo. Han. Sq. ii. 31.
London, 1, 4; West Rid. Court Dir., 3, 1; Philadelphia, 6, 9.

Rawson, Raws.—Bapt. 'the son of Ralph' or 'Rauf,' nick. Raw. Rawson has been a familiar Yorkshire surname for the last five hundred years.
Willelmus Raufson, 1379: P. T. Yorks. p. 134.
Johannes Rauson, 1379: ibid. p. 135.
Ricardus Raweson, 1379: ibid. p. 136.
1570. Buried—Edmonde Rawson: St. Michael, Cornhill, p. 191.
London, 8, 0; West Rid. Court Dir., 21, 0; Philadelphia, 9, 5.

Rawsthorne, Rawstorne, Rawstion, Rawstron, Rostron, Roston, Rosthern.—Local, 'of Rostherne,' a parish and village in co. Ches. A family of Rosthernes seem early to have removed into the neighbouring county of Lancashire, and settled in the district around Bury, thence distributing themselves over the county. A representative family named Rawsthorne still holds a good position

in co. Lancashire. The corrupted forms are many, the favourite being Roston. Five Rostons are still found in the Bury Directory.
Roger de Venables, parson of Roustorn, 1399: Hist. East Ches. i. 48.
James Legh, rector of the church of Rosthorn, 1484: ibid. ii. 426.
William Rawstorne, gentleman, of co. Lancaster, 1580: Wills at Chester (1545-1620), p. 165.
Agnes Rawstorne, widow, of the parish of Bury, 1594: ibid. p. 165.
Jane Rosthern, widow, of Ainsworth, 1613: ibid.
John Rawstorne, co. Ches. 1610: Reg. Univ. Oxf. vol. ii. pt. ii. p. 311.
Laurence Rowsterne (? Warrington), 1684-5: Exchequer Depositions (co. Lanc.), p. 66.
Thomas Stubbs, parish of Rawsthorne, 1638: Wills at Chester (1621-50), p. 210.

This last entry sets all doubt at rest.
MDB. (co. Lanc.), 7, 4, 2, 7, 13, 0, 0; Manchester, 0, 1, 0, 1, 8, 1, 0.

Ray.—(1) Nick. 'the roe'; cf. Stagg, Buck, Roebuck, and Scottish Rae, q.v. North English; ra; A.S. rāh. Such sobriquets were highly popular and gladly retained, being of a complimentary character.
Reginald le Raye, co. Oxf., 1273. A.
Nicholas le Ray, co. Suff., ibid.
Richard le Ray, co. Camb., ibid.
William le Ray, co. Soms., 1 Edw. III: Kirby's Quest, p. 239.
John le Ray, co. Soms., 1 Edw. III: ibid.
Etheldreda le Ray, C. R., 17 Edw. III, pt. i.

(2) Local, 'of the Wray'; v. Wray. This would inevitably be stripped of the initial w in many cases.
1790. Married—Robert Ray and Eliz. Adlington: St. Geo. Han. Sq. ii. 45.
London, 32; Philadelphia, 59.

Raybold, Reybold, Raybould.—Bapt. 'the son of Reinbold,' a corruption; v. Rimbault and Rumball.
1600. Edward Raybould: Reg. Univ. Oxf. vol. ii. pt. iii. p. 219.
London, 0, 0, 1; Philadelphia, 4, 7, 0.

Rayment, Raymond.—Bapt. 'the son of Raymond'; cf. Garment for Garmond, Osment for Osmond.
Reimond de Luka, C. R., 29 Hen. III.
Richard fil. Reimund, co. Camb., 1273. A.

Robert fil. Reimund, co. Camb.,1273. A.
Philip Remond, co. Soms., 1 Edw. III :
Kirby's Quest, p. 91.
1582. Bapt.—Margery, d. John Rayment, *poulter*: St. Mary Aldermary, p. 24.

Among Drake's companions in the Golden Hind in 1580 was Gregory Raymon (World Encompassed, pp. 168-170). In the State Papers (Domestic) Elizabeth he is set down as Gregory Raymente; v. N. and Q., Sept. 3, 1887, p. 187.
A curious Christian name is found in the following entry :

1717. Bapt.—Bargerlijah, son of Bargerlijah Raymond: St. Antholin (London), p. 129.
London, 22, 9; Philadelphia, o, 36.

Raynbird; v. Rainbird.

Rayne, Raynes; v. Rain.

Rayner, Raynor, Reyner.—Bapt. 'the son of Reyner' (v. Yonge, ii. 378). In Domesday Raynar, a common font-name in the 13th and 14th centuries, especially in Yorkshire and on the East Coast generally.

Reyner le Blake, co. Norf., 1273. A.
Reyner Custance, co. Norf., ibid.
Reyner Piggesflessh, C. R., 13 Edw. II.
Reyner, son of Reyner Fleming, temp.
Edw. II : Visitation of Yorks, 1563, p. 103.
Anabilla Rayner, 1379 : P. T. Yorks. p. 196.
Thomas Rayner, 1379 : ibid. p. 137.
1601. Edward Reyner, or Reinar, co. Yorks : Reg. Univ. Oxf. vol. ii. pt. ii. p. 248.
1740. Married—John Rayner and Priscilla Elliot : St. Jas. Clerkenwell, iii. 269.
London, 41, o, o; West Rid. Court Dir. 23, 1, o ; Philadelphia, 8, 16, o.

Rayson.—(1) Bapt.; v. Reason. (2) Local, ' of Rasen,' now three parishes, Middle, West, and Market Rasen, co. Lincoln. This will probably represent the Cambridge and York instances given under Reason, q.v. In a word, Rayson is almost certainly local, and Reason and Reeson may be the same.

Robert de Rasen, co. Linc., 1273. A.
Thomas de Rasne, co. Linc., Hen. III–Edw. I. K.
William de Rasne, co. Linc., ibid.
Robert de Rason, co. Linc., 20 Edw. I. R.
William Ryson, co. Soms., 1 Edw. III :
Kirby's Quest, p. 95.
1790. Married—Symonds Rayson and Mary Hiley: St. Geo. Han. Sq. ii. 225.

1800. Married—Edward Rayson and Mary Creick: ibid. p. 30.
London, 2 ; Philadelphia, 4.

Read, Reade, Reed, Reid.—Nick. ' the red,' a sobriquet given on account of the ruddy face or the sanguine red complexion of the hair ; cf. Black, White, Russell, Blunt, &c. M.E. *reed* or *rede*, red. Reid is a Scottish and N. English variant. Our directories teem with the name in all its forms, as is the case with all nicknames taken from the complexion of hair or face.

Godwin le Rede, co. Norf., 1273. A.
Roger le Rede, co. Hereford, ibid.
Robert le Rede, co. Surrey, Hen. III–Edw. I. K.
Martin le Rede, et Jacoba uxor ejus,
Fines Roll, 1 Edw. III.
William Red, co. Soms., 1 Edw. III :
Kirby's Quest, p. 118.
Robert le Rede, co. Soms., 1 Edw. III :
ibid. p. 202.
1568. Married—George Warde and Denys Reade: St. Michael, Cornhill, p. 9.
1592-3. Richard Read, co. Bedf. : Reg. Univ. Oxf. vol. ii. pt. ii. p. 195.
1788. Married—Edward Reed and Eliz. Mellon : St. Geo. Han. Sq. ii. 8.
— — Alex. Reid and Nancy Lewer: ibid. p. 14.
London, 95, 3, 72, 56; Philadelphia, 103, 5, 334, 59.

Reader, Reeder.—Occup. 'the reeder,' i. e. a thatcher. ' Redare of howsys, *calamator*': Prompt. Parv. Naturally we find a ' Robertus Brown, redere,' in the Guild of St. George, Norwich.

Emma le Redere, 1273. A.
Adam le Redere, ibid.
John de Redere, ibid.
William Redere, rector of Baldswell, co. Norf., 1420 : FF. viii. 186.
' In 1512 John King, *reder*, was buried in the churchyard, and gave 20s. towards building St. Vaste's new porch' : FF. iv. 105.
' The Reders, Thaxters, Rede-sellers,' Corpus Christi Guild Procession, Norwich, 1533: ibid. ii. 148.
William le Redere, London. X.
1661. Richard Eaton and Eliz. Reader: Marriage Lic. (London), ii. 285.
London, 7, 3 ; Boston (U.S.), 2, 1 ; Philadelphia, 9, 27.

Readford.—Probably for Retford. But v. Redford.

London, 2.

Reading, Redding. — Local, ' of Reading,' an important market-town in co. Berks.

1305. Henry de Reding, rector of Matlask, co. Norf.: FF. viii. 137.
1328. John de Reding, rector of Aldeburgh, co. Norf. : ibid. v. 352.
1621. Bapt.—Eliz., d. Symond Reading: St. Jas. Clerkenwell, i. 91.
1714. Henry Redding and Mary Tomlinson : St. Michael, Cornhill, p. 57.
London, 11, 7; MDB. (co. Warwick), 10, o ; Philadelphia, 16, 12.

Readwin.—Bapt. ' the son of Redwin,' one of the endless compounds of -*win*. Some surnames linger on curiously. There is but one entry in the Hundred Rolls, yet it is represented in the London Directory also by one; cf. Goldwin, Unwin, Baldwin, &c.

Simon Redwin, co. Kent, 1273. A.
1722. Peter Redwin, of Norwich : FF. iv. 470.
London, 1.

Reams.—Local, ' of Rheims.' The surname has crossed over from Norfolk to Lincoln. The spelling is much corrupted.

Hugo de Reymes, co. Norf., 1273. A.
Richer de Reymes, co. Norf., 34 Hen. III : FF. viii. 143.
William de Reymes, co. Suff., 20 Edw. I. R.
1653-4. Married—William Reymes and Dorothy Fowke: St. Dionis Backchurch, p. 30.
MDB. (co. Lincoln), 1.

Reason, Reeson, Rayson.—(1) Bapt. ' the son of——' (?). (2) Local, ' of Rasen ' (?). Several instances below suggest that the suffix is not -*son*, but the dim. -*on* or -*in*, as in Mari-on, Rob-in, &c. Possibly it is the dim. of the once popular Rose (q.v.), of which the German dim. was Roschen, the French Rosine, and the later English Rosanne. All is conjecture, but I feel nearly positive that -*son* is not the terminative. The entries in the Hundred Rolls (A.) would be John fil. Ray, not John Raysun, as below. But v. Rayson, which will explain much.

Henry Reson, co. Oxf., 1273. A.
Richard Resen, co. Oxf., ibid.
Geoffrey Resun, co. Suff., ibid.
Betricia Raysun, co. Camb., ibid.
John Raysun, co. Camb., ibid.
Albray Rayson, 1379 : P. T. Yorks. p. 41.
Willelmus Reyson, 1379 : ibid.
1792. Married—John Lennon and Susanna Reason : St. Geo. Han. Sq. ii. 84.
London, 4, 2, 2 ; Philadelphia, 5, 0, 4.

Rebbeck. — ? Bapt. 'the son of Rebecca (?); Fr. Rebecque. It has nothing to do with *rebeck*, an old name for a violin, as suggested by Lower. The dim. Ribek-on is early found. Abraham, Sarah, Jacob, and Isaac were very popular at the same time.

Gilbert Ribekon, co. Camb., 1273. A.
1804. Married—Isaac Rawlings and Sarah Rebbeck: St. Geo. Han. Sq. ii. 299.
London, 1.

Record. — (?) Local. Lower says, 'Record, a known corruption of Rickword. A Sussex family in the 18th century wrote themselves Record, alias Rickword.' This is confirmed by the registers of St. Mary Aldermary, London, where Record, Rikecord, and Rikeworth are entries that seem to belong to one and the same family.

1595. Buried—Anne, d. John Record, &c.: St. Mary Aldermary, p. 144.
1599. — A still-born childe of John Rikecord, sonne of Malliard Rikecord, stranger, in Mr. Hassald's house, &c.: ibid. p. 148.
1601. — John Rikeworth, stranger, out of Mr. Hassald's house, &c.: ibid. p. 151.
1794. Married—James Record and Jane Evans: St. Geo. Han. Sq. ii. 118.
London, 5; Boston (U.S.), 4.

Redbeard. — Nick. 'with the red beard'; v. Beard, Brownbeard, Blackbeard. M.E. *berd* and *berde*.

Richard Redberd, co. Soms., 1 Edw. III: Kirby's Quest, p. 188.
Thomas Redberd, bailiff of Yarmouth, 1407: FF. xi. 324.

A contributor to Notes and Queries, Jan. 14, 1860, quotes an old Ipswich record, in which is mentioned an 'Alexander Redberd' dwelling there in the early part of the 16th century.

Reddall, Reddell. — Local: (1) 'at the red hall' or red hill, from residence therein or thereby; cf. Blackall, &c. (2) v. Riddell.

Richard atte Redehulle, co. Soms., 1 Edw. III: Kirby's Quest, p. 108.
London, 3, 1.

Reddick; v. Ruddock.

Redding. — Local; a variant of Reading, q.v.

Reddish. — Local, 'of Reddish,' a village near Stockport, co. Ches.

Mathew de Redish, 1260: East Ches. ii. 102 n.

John Reddish, of Reddish, 1557: Wills at Chester, i. 159.
George Reddish, of Reddish, 1588: ibid.
1571. Married—John Reddiche and Dorothe Shrigleye: Reg. Prestbury Ch., co. Ches., p. 35.
1572. Buried—Jone Redyche: ibid. p. 39.
1578. Alexander Redyche, co. Lanc.: Reg. Univ. Oxf. vol. ii. pt. ii. p. 80.
1603. Married—Roger Reddiche and Ellyn Haigh: Reg. Mottram-in-Longendale, co. Ches.
London, 3; Manchester, 4; Boston (U.S.), 5.

Reddock; v. Ruddock.

Redfern, Redfearn, Redferne. — Local, 'of Redfern,' a well-known Lancashire surname. I cannot identify the spot. Probably it will be found near Rochdale. The name has spread into Lancashire and travelled to London, not to say the United States. Probably it was the name of some small estate or homestead.

James Redfearn, of Redfern, 1604: Wills at Chester, i. 159.
Edmund Redfearn, of the parish of Rochdale, 1616: ibid.
Thomas Redferne, Rochdale, 1610: Baines' Lanc. i. 489.
1661. Married—Thomas Redferne and Mary Tomkins: St. Jas. Clerkenwell, iii. 108.
London, 10, 4. 0; MDB. (co. Derby), 17, 6, 0; Manchester, 11, 0, 0; Philadelphia, 17, 4, 1.

Redford. — Local, 'of Radford,' q.v. A variant. It must be remembered, however, that East Retford in co. Notts was spelt Redeford (v. R. p. 162).

William de Redford, co. Northumb., 20 Edw. I. R.
1804. Married—Thomas Fowler and Ann Redford: St. Geo. Han. Sq. ii. 315.
London, 3; MDB. (co. Lincoln), 2; Philadelphia, 3.

Redgrave, Redgrove. — Local, 'of Redgrave,' a parish in co. Suffolk. In meaning equivalent to Redwood, q.v. (v. Grave and Grove.)

1344. Robert de Redgrave, of Norwich: FF. iv. 172.
1477. Adam de Redgrave, co. Norf.: ibid. v. 115.
1801. Married—William Redgrave and Mary Reynard: St. Geo. Han. Sq. ii. 240.
London, 6, 1; Philadelphia, 2, 0.

Redhead. — Nick. 'with the red head'; cf. Whitehead, Silverlock, Brownbeard, &c. It is quite possible the name is local, from some red-coloured headland of rock or soil. There are such spots so called in Forfarshire and Orkney. But one thing is certain, Yorkshire is the source of the family of Redheads that have drifted westwards into the Furness district of North Lancashire. No prefix is found, pointing distinctly to a nickname origin.

William Redhed, co. York, 1273. A.
John Redheved, co. Camb., ibid.
John Redeheued, C. R., 25 Edw. III.
Thomas Redhed, 1379: P. T. Yorks. p. 153.
Johannes Redhed, 1379: ibid. p. 254.
1547. Buried—Isabell Redhead: Reg. Ulverston Ch. p. 5.
Richard Redhead, of Water-end in Blawith, Furness, 1627: Lancashire Wills at Richmond, i. 227.
Marian Readhead, of Nibthwaite, Furness, 1641: ibid.
London, 3; MDB. (co. Lanc.), 3; New York, 3.

Redhouse. — Local, 'of Redhouse,' or 'at the red house,' from residence at a dwelling so called. Cf. Reddall.

William de Redhus, co. Southampton, Hen. III-Edw. I. K.
London, 2; Fulbourn (co. Camb.), 2; Boston (U.S.), 2.

Redley; v. Radley.

Redmakere. — Occup. Probably a cutter of rushes or reeds for the candlemaker or thatcher; v. Reader.

John Redmakere, C. R., 45 Edw. III.

Redman; v. Redmond.

Redmile. — Local, 'of Redmile,' a parish in co. Leicester, nine miles from Grantham.

MDB. (co. Lincoln), 3.

Redmond, Redman, Redmayne. — (1) Bapt. 'the son of Redmond' (v. Yonge, ii. 371). Of course Redmond was occasionally corrupted into Redman; cf. Wyman for Wymond, or Mayman for Maymond. (2) Local, 'of Redmain,' a township in the parish of Isell, co. Cumb.

Norman de Redman, 34 Hen. II: Hist. Westm. and Cumb. i. 202.
Matthew de Redman, temp. Edw. I: ibid. p. 89.

Thomas de Redeman, 49 Edw. III: Hist. Westm. and Cumb. i. 37.

Mathew de Redeman, co. Lanc., Hen. III-Edw. I. K.

Henry de Rydeman, co. Westm., 20 Edw. I. R.

John Redman, or Redmand, 1537: Reg. Univ. Oxf. i. 188.

There can be no doubt that (2) is the true parent of the vast majority of Redmans, Redmaynes, and Redmonds. But the two streams now flow in one common channel; cf. Simonds for Simons.

London, 4, 16, 1; MDB. (co. Lanc.), o, o, 5; Philadelphia, 41, 15, o.

Redpath, Ridpath.—Local, 'of Redpath,' a village in co. Berwick.

1801. Married—James Cooper and Jane Redpith: St. Geo. Han. Sq. ii. 239.

1805. — George Redpath and Charlotte Whisker: ibid. p. 335.

London, 2, 3.

Redshaw.—Local, 'at the redshaw,' from residence beside the shaw or wood of a red soil (v. Shaw). I cannot find the spot; cf. Redgrave and Ridley.

1575. Richard Redshawe, co. Oxf.: Reg. Univ. Oxf. vol. ii. pt. ii. p. 67.

1712. Married—Christopher Redshaw and Eleanor Kirby: St. Michael, Cornhill, p. 56.

1746. Bapt.—Ann, d. William Redshaw: St. Jas. Clerkenwell, ii. 279.

London, 1; MDB. (co. Lincoln), 4; Philadelphia, 1.

Redsmith.—Occup. 'the redsmith,' a goldsmith (?); cf. Whitesmith (tin), Blacksmith (iron), Greensmith (lead or laten), Brownsmith (copper or brass).

John Rodesmithe (?). D.

Redwood. — Local, ' of Redwood'; cf. Redshaw and Redgrave.

John de Redewode, co. Northumb.: Hen. III-Edw. I. K.

1767. Married—William Redwood and Ann Newton: St. Geo. Han. Sq. i. 171.

London, 2; Philadelphia, 2.

Ree.—Local, 'at the ree.' I do not know what Ree means. One of my entries refers manifestly to Rye, a town in Sussex. Lower says, ' La Rie, meaning a bank, is a very common name of localities in Normandy' (Patr. Brit. p. 298). It is not to be confounded with the Cumberland Reay, or Scotch Rae, q.v.

Philip ad Ree, co. Bedf., 1273. A.

Robert de Ree, co. Sussex, ibid.

Ralph de Ree, co. Salop, ibid.

John atte Ree, C. R., 3 Edw. IV.

1646. Bapt.—Robart, s. Robart Re: St. Michael, Cornhill, p. 134.

London, 1.

Reed; v. Read.

Reeder; v. Reader.

Rees, Reese, Reece.—Bapt. ' the son of Rhys' (Welsh). Other variants and derivations are Rice, Price, Preece, q.v.

Edward Reece, co. Hereford, 1601: Reg. Univ. Oxf. vol. ii. pt. ii. p. 250.

Reese Myricke (co. Glamorgan), Jesus Coll., 1607: ibid. p. 298.

Thomas ap-Reese, 1606: Wills at Chester, i. 159.

Thomas Rees, of Tybroughton, 1647: ibid. ii. 182.

Giles Reece, combmaker, of Chester: ibid. iii. 221.

London, 36, 1, 7; MDB. (co. Glamorgan), 42, o, o; Philadelphia, 59, 93, 3.

Reeson; v. Rayson, Reason.

Reeve, Reeves. — Offic. ' the reeve,' a bailiff, a steward.

' His lordes shepe, his nete, and his deirie,
His swine, his hors, his store, and his paltrie,
Were holly in this reves governing.'
Chaucer's C. T., Prologue.

Hence *borough-reeve, port-reeve,* &c.

Sampson le Reve, co. Suff., 1273. A.

John le Reve, co. Camb., ibid.

William le Reve, co. Soms., 1 Edw. III: Kirby's Quest, p. 92.

John le Reveson, co. Soms., 1 Edw. III: ibid. p. 163.

William le Reveson, co. Soms., 1 Edw. III: ibid. p. 103.

Sager le Reve. H.

1611. William Reve and Joyce Headley: Marriage Lic. (London), ii. 7.

1638-9. John Trott and Eliz. Reeve: Marriage Lic. (Westminster), p. 37.

Reeves is a genitive form (= ' the son of the reeve '), just as Williams is the genitive of William.

1686. James Petre and Eliz. Reves: Marriage Lic. (London), ii. 307.

1729. Bapt.—Ann, d. William Reeves: St. Dionis Backchurch, p. 162.

London, 40, 58; Philadelphia, 16, 112.

Reginald.—Bapt. ' the son of Reginald '; v. Reynold.

Roysia fil. Reginaldi, co. Camb.,1273. A.

Reginald le Porter. J.

Philadelphia, 1.

Register, Regester. — Offic. ' the registrar,' a recorder. M.E. *registrere*; cf. Breviter. Lower says,

' A corruption of Rochester.' This is not probable.

MDB. (co. Norfolk), 2, o; Lynn (co. Norfolk), o, 2.

Reid; v. Read.

Remblant; v. Remnant.

Remfry.—Bapt. ' the son of Reinfreid ' (Remfrid, Yonge, ii. 378). In Cornwall, where the font-name has lingered on for many centuries, this surname is not unfamiliar.

Gilbert fil. Reinfridi, alias Reymfrey, co. Notts, Hen. III-Edw. I. K.

Reynfrey de la Bruere, co. Camb., 1273. A.

Luke, son of Remfrey Carter, 1542: Reg. St. Columb Major, p. 2.

Remfrey, son of Harrie Phluyesie, 1551: ibid. p. 6.

Rempfrey, son of John Rowse, 1591: ibid. p. 15.

Elizabeth Renfrey, *widow*, 1603: ibid. p. 200.

Renfreid, son of John Moyle, 1604: ibid. p. 21.

1729. Married—Gilbert Remphrey and Eliz. Ullithorn: St. Geo. Han. Sq. i. 7.

London, 1; Crockford, 1; MDB. (Cornwall), 4.

Remington, Riminton. — Local, ' of Rimmington,' a township in the parish of Gisburn, W. Rid. Yorks. This surname crossed over the border and settled in North Lancashire several centuries ago.

Alan de Rymyngton, 8 Edw. III: Freemen of York, i. 28.

Matilda de Remyngton, 1379: P. T. Yorks. p. 264.

Robertus de Rymyngton, 1379: ibid. p. 283.

1551. Matthew Remyngton, of Melling: Lancashire Wills at Richmond, i. 228.

1599. Reginald Remington, of Melling: ibid.

1733. Married—Abraham Harris and Eliz. Rimington: St. Geo. Han. Sq. i. 11.

London, 2, 1; MDB. (co. Lanc.), 7, o; Boston (U.S.), 6, o.

Remnant, Remblant.—Bapt. ' the son of Rembrandt '; cf. the name of the artist Rembrandt. This was really his baptismal name: probably he was Rembrandt Hermanszoon (Hermanson), or Rembrandt van Rhyn of Leyden. He was buried as ' Rembrant van Rign,' Oct. 8, 1669 (v. Chambers' Encyclop. viii. 180). I suspect Remnant (an imitative corruption) is an immigrant from the Low

Countries. Remblant is an intermediate stage.

1619. Robert Remnant and Margaret Collyer: Marriage Lic. (London), ii. 78.
1620. Married—Anthonye Remnante and Catherin Drewe: St. Mary Aldermary, p. 250.
1800. Married—Edward Remnant and Eliz. Maskall: St. Geo. Han. Sq. ii. 218.
London, 3, 0; MDB. (co. Surrey), 2, 0; Bungay (co. Suffolk), 0, 2.

Renaud, Renaut, Rennard. —Bapt. ' the son of Reynold,' i.e. Reynard, not always of French extraction. The form has existed in England for six centuries; cf. Arnaud for Arnold; v. Reginald and Reynolds.

Richard fil. Renaut, co. Salop, Hen. III—Edw. I. K.
John Reynaud, co. Norf., 1273. A.
Sampson Reynaud, co. Norf., ibid.
William fil. Reynaud, co. Camb., ibid.
Robert Reynaud, co. Suff., ibid.
John Renaud, co. Soms, 1 Edw. III: Kirby's Quest, p. 92.
1769. Married—Jonathan Rennard and Mary Stephenson: St. Geo. Han. Sq. ii. 28.
1798. — David Renand and Jane Probeart: ibid. p. 190.
London, 2, 1, 0; Crockford, 3, 1, 0; West Rid. Court Dir., 0, 0, 1.

Rendall, Rendel, Rendell, Rendle.—Bapt. Probably mere changes rung upon Randle or Randal, the nick. of Randolph (v. Randall). Perhaps, however, it would be more natural to refer them to Rennell (q.v.), a popular form of Reynold. Then the d would be merely intrusive, as is common after n; cf. Simmonds, Hammond, riband, and the vulgar gownd.

Solomon Rendoll, 1678: Reg. Canterbury Cath. p. 61.
1757. Married—James Rendall and Rachel Witcomb: St. Geo. Han. Sq. i. 68.
London, 12, 3, 8, 1.

Render, Rinder.—Occup. or official, ' the renderer,' one who paid rent, one who held by an annual payment; v. redditus (i.e. rent) capitalis, redditus mobilis, redditus servicii, redditus assisus, &c. (Introduction to Pipe Roll, p. 90). v. Rinder. This surname still exists in Yorkshire, where it is found five centuries ago.

Willelmus Rendrour, 1379: P. T. Yorks. p. 155.
Johannes Rendrour, 1379: ibid. p. 155.
Matilda Rendurer, 1379: ibid. p. 200.
Johannes Rendoar, 1379: ibid. p. 293.

1667. Thomas St. George and Damaris Render: Marriage Alleg. (Canterbury), p. 139.
Harrogate, 2, 0; Leeds, 1, 0; Liverpool, 2, 0; West Rid. Court Dir., 0, 6; Philadelphia, 1, 0.

Rendfrey.—Bapt. ' the son of Reinfred '; v. Remfry. The d is intrusive.

Philadelphia, 1.

Rennard; v. Renaud.

Rennell, Rennels.—Bapt. ' the son of Reynold,' popularly Rennel; v. Reynell and Reynold. The first instance below is very conclusive:

1769. Married—Robert Rennelds and Eliz. Bond: St. Geo. Han. Sq. i. 188.

Later on the d is omitted.

1788. Married—John Rennels and Sally Fenn: St. Geo. Han. Sq. ii. 5.
1809. — John Tremayne Rodd and Jane Rennell: ibid. p. 416.
London, 1, 1; Philadelphia, 0, 2.

Rennick; v. Renwick.

Rennison, Renison. — (1) Bapt. ' the son of Reynold,' a corruption of Reynoldson. (2) Bapt. ' the son of Reyner ' (v. Rayner), a corruption of Reynerson. No doubt both (1) and (2) have contributed. But as Reyner was a great Yorkshire font-name in the 13th and 14th centuries, (2) must be looked upon as the chief parent.

Anne Rennison, co. York. W. 14.
John Reynerson, co. York. W. 10.
Thomas Rennison, co. York. W. 20.
John Rennison, of Tunstall, 1695: Lancashire Wills at Richmond, ii. 207.
1739. Married—Lancelot Rennyson and Mary Billington: St. Geo. Han. Sq. i. 23.
1753. — Richard Renneson and Mary Robinson: St. Jas. Clerkenwell, iii. 285.
Farmers' Dir. (North and East Rid. of Yorks), 5, 0; Boston (U.S.), 1, 4; Philadelphia, 1, 0.

Renshaw.—Local, ' of Ravenshaw,' some small but, I fear, lost spot in East Cheshire. The surname has ramified very strongly. The suffix is found alike as -shall or -shaw; cf. Henshall and Henshaw, Shallcross and Shawcross, in the same district. Ravenshaw means the shaw or wood belonging to Raven, an early personal name of much popularity (v. Rawnsley and Raven, and cf. Ravenscroft, a surname found in East Cheshire

also). The full form ran alongside the abbreviated for a time.

John Ravenshaw, of Walkerton, 1673: Wills at Chester (1660–80), p. 220.

The first step towards the modern form was Rainshaw (cf. Rainow, formerly Ravenowe, a township in the parish of Priestbury).

1570. Bapt.—Alice Raynshawe: Prestbury Ch. (Cheshire), p. 33.
Sir Ralphe Raynshae, vicar of Potte, 1548: East Cheshire, ii. 330.

This same Ralph was buried at Prestbury:

1561. Buried—Sir Rauffe Renshae, preste: Prestbury Ch. (Cheshire), p. 6.

Thus in two entries concerning the same individual we see the last stage practically reached.

John Rainshaw, of Sale, 1647: Wills at Chester (1621–50), p. 180.
John Renshaw, yeoman, of Mobberley, 1661: ibid. (1660–80), p. 221.
John Renshall, of Sale, 1679: ibid.
Ralph Renshall, of Mobberley, 1680: ibid.
Richard Renshaw, of Sale, 1680: ibid.
London, 10; Manchester, 28; MDB. (Cheshire), 4; Philadelphia, 14.

Renton.—Local, ' of Renton.' Lower says, ' Renton, a small town in Dumbartonshire.' Probably some of our English-seeming Rentons hail from this place, but evidently, from the large number, not all.

Mathew de Renedon, or Reneton, co. Devon, 1273. A.
Robert de Reyndon, co. Warw., ibid.
1802. Married—Robert Downham and Margaret Renton: St. Geo. Han. Sq. ii. 257.
London, 10; Boston (U.S.), 2.

Renwick, Rennick.—Local, ' of Renwick,' a parish in co. Cumb., eleven miles from Penrith. With Rennick, cf. Physic for Fishwick.

1726. Married—John Elliot and Ann Rennick: St. Geo. Han. Sq. i. 2.
London, 1, 0; MDB. (co. Northumberland), 4, 0; (co. Cumb.), 1, 0.

Repington, Rippington.—Local, ' of Repton,' a parish in co. Derby, ' otherwise written Repinton,' says Mr. Lower (Patr. Brit. p. 288). This is borne out by the Hundred Rolls:

Prior de Repindon, co. Derby, 1273. A.
Also cf.
Prior de Reppendon, or Reppedon, co. Derby, Hen. III—Edw. I. K.

Later on we find the *d* sharpened into *t* :

John Reapington, co. Warw., 1574 : Reg. Univ. Oxf. vol. ii. pt. ii. p. 57.
Humphrey Repington, co. Warw., 1590 : ibid. p. 180.
Edward Repington, or Rippington, 1598 : ibid. p. 227.

It is quite manifest that Rippington and Repington originally hail from Repton in Derbyshire.

London, o, 2 ; MDB. (co. Suffolk), 1, o; Oxford, o, 3.

Reskimer.—Local, 'of Reskymer.' Seemingly an old Cornish font-name. The instances are before the period when surnames were (saving in exceptional cases) turned into Christian names. Nevertheless Lower, quoting Gilbert's Hist. of Cornwall, says, 'The family (Reskymer) became extinct in the 17th century. They had resided for fourteen generations on their estate of Reskymer, in the parish of St. Mawgan, near Helston.' Doubtless therefore the name is local. The surname still exists in the form of Reskimer, as I have personally met with a gentleman of that name.

Reskimer, son of Henrie Sprey, 1605 : Reg. St. Columb Major.
Reskimer, son of John Pearse, 1606 : ibid.

Restall ; v. Rastall.

Reston.—(1) Local, 'of Reston,' two parishes (North and South Reston) in co. Lincoln. (2) Local, 'of Riston,' a parish in E. Rid. Yorks.

Richard de Riston, co. Notts, Hen. III- Edw. I. K.
Ralph de Riston, co. Linc., 1273. A.
Gomer de Riston, co. Norf., ibid.
1603. Bapt.—John, s. William Reston : St. Jas. Clerkenwell, i. 41.
1634. Daniel Eyres and Eliz. Reston : Marriage Lic. (London), ii. 219.
London, 1 ; Philadelphia, 2.

Reuter.—Occup. ; v. Rutter.

Reveley, Raively.—Local, 'of Reaveley,' a township in the parish of Ingram, co. Northumberland. Lower says, 'The Reveleys, who trace their pedigree to the reign of Edward II, were originally seated at the manor-house of Reveley, on the northern bank of the river Breamish, at the south-

eastern foot of Cheviot.' The surname is thus distinctly Northumbrian.

1801. Married—John Gregory and Isabel Revely : St. Geo. Han. Sq. ii. 244.
1808. — John Stevenson and Hannah Reaveley : ibid. p. 380.
MDB. (co. Northumberland), 1, o ; (North Rid. Yorks), 1, o; Philadelphia, o, 3.

Revell, Revill.—Bapt. 'the son of Revel,' a forgotten personal name. Mr. Lower says, 'Two places in Normandy bear the name of Réville, one near Bernai, the other in the arrondissement of Valognes. The surname still exists in Normandy.' The objection to this is that there is no prefix *de* in our instances, not even in the Testa de Neville, and it is found familiarly in different places widely scattered. The matter is practically settled by the occurrence of Revel as a personal name, without surname, in the Hundred Rolls. It is a common surname in present Yorkshire directories.

Richard Revel, co. Soms., Hen. III- Edw. I. K.
William Revel, co. Berks, ibid.
Revel (without surname), co. Soms., 1273. A.
Alan Revel, co. Camb., ibid.
Thomas Revel, co. Wilts, ibid.
Thomas Ryuell, 1379 : P. T. Yorks. p. 36.
Roger Ryuell, 1379 : ibid.
Adam Reuell, 1379 : ibid. p. 45.
Ricardus Ryuyll, 1379 : ibid. p. 35.
London, 7, 1 ; Sheffield, 2, 12 ; Philadelphia, 1, o.

Reveter.—Occup. 'the revetor,' a man who made rivets for armour. 'Ryvet, revet,' Palsgrave (v. Skeat).

Richard le Reveter, 7 Edw. II : Freemen of York, i. 15.
'William Revetor, a chantry priest' : v. York Plays (L. Toulmin Smith), Introduction, p. xxx.

Rew.—Local, 'at the rew,' a row, from residence therein. 'The shadyside of a street. Devon') (Halliwell) ; v. Raw and Row (2).

'And lete anon commande to hacke
    and hewe
The okes old, and lay hem on a rew.'
        Chaucer, C. T. 2868.
John atte Rewe, co. Soms., 1 Edw. III : Kirby's Quest, p. 258.
Richard atte Rewe, co. Soms., 1 Edw. III : ibid.
William in the rew, co. Soms., 1 Edw. III : ibid. p. 106.

Adam atte Rewe, co. Soms., 1 Edw. III : ibid. p. 99.
1603. John Rewe : Reg. Univ. Oxf. i. 316.
1677. Bapt.—Anne, d. John Rewe : St. Jas. Clerkenwell, i. 279.
1780. Married—Alex. Rew and Eliz. Wright : St. Geo. Han. Sq. ii. 18.
London, 6 ; MDB. (co. Devon), 3.

Rex.—(1) Nick. 'the king.' Latinized into Rex. This is quite possible ; cf. Faber for Wright ; v. King.

Adam Rex, co. Camb., 1273. A.
John Rex, co. Camb., ibid.

(2) Bapt. 'the son of Richard,' from the nick. Rick (cf. Dick and Hick), whence the genitive Ricks. (cf. Williams for William) modified to Rix (cf. Dix for Dicks), and lastly to Rex. Nine-tenths of our Rexes must be thus derived. For instances, v. Rix and Rixon. The change from Rix to Rex is modern, and, of course, imitative of the Latin.

1718. Bapt.—Rebecca, d. Ann Rex : St. Jas. Clerkenwell, ii. 104.
London, 1 ; Philadelphia, 31.

Rexstrew.—Nick. ; v. Rackstraw.

Reybold; v. Raybold.

Reyburn ; v. Raeburn.

Reynell.—Bapt. 'the son of Reynold,' popularly Reynell ; v. Rennell.

1778. Married—James Doran and Mary Reynell : St. Geo. Han. Sq. i. 292.
1803. — George Reynell and Frances Linney Hutchinson : ibid. ii. 281.
London, 4.

Reyner ; v. Rayner.

Reynold, Reynolds, Reynoldson. — Bapt. 'the son of Reynold,' i.e. Reginald. Fr. Regnauld and Renaud. One of the most popular font-names of the surname period; v. Reginald and Renaud.

John Reynold, co. Camb., 1273. A.
Roger fil. Reynald, co. Oxf., ibid.
William fil. Reynaud, co. Camb., ibid.
Rainaldus fil. Willelmi, 1379 : P. T. Yorks. p. 192.
Ricardus Raynoldson, 1379 : ibid. p. 91.
Reginald, or Reynold Reading, 1566 : Reg. Univ. Oxf. vol. ii. pt. i. p. 420.
1617. Robert Reyghnoldes and Jane Watts : Marriage Lic. (London), ii. 51.
London, 1, 122, o ; Boston (U.S.), o, 127, o.

Rhind, Rind.—Local, 'of Rhynd,' a parish in co. Perth. There is also a place called Rhind in co. Fife. The name occurs in the Chartulary of Moray early in the 13th century, and it has been variously spelt Rhynd, Rhind, Rynd, and Rind (v. Lower's Patr. Brit. p. 288).

1728. Married—John Rind and Edith Barwell: St. Michael, Cornhill, p. 64.
1789. — Robert Rhind and Mary Atkinson: St. Geo. Han. Sq. ii. 17.
London, 4, 1; Manchester, 4, 0; Boston (U.S.), 1, 0.

Rhodes, Rhoads.—(1) Local, 'of Rhodes.' Many of the Manchester Rhodes hail from Rhodes, two estates, one between Prestwich and Ringley, and the other near Middleton. Probably both local terms are equivalent to *royds* and imply an early *ridding*. (2) Local, 'at the roads,' i.e. cross-roads. Here the *h* is intrusive. This was a common Yorkshire entry, and explains the large number of Rhodes in the West Riding Dir. For instances, v. Roades.

London, 30, 2; West Rid. Court Dir., 84, 0; Manchester, 19, 0.

Rhydderch.—Bapt. 'the son of Rhydderch,' the Welsh accepted form of Roderic; v. Prothero for fuller statement.
MDB. (co. Carmarthen), 1.

Rhys.—Bapt. 'the son of Rhys' (Welsh); v. Rice, Rees, Reece, or Price for further information.
1790. Married—John Rhys and Mary Williams: St. Geo. Han. Sq. ii. 49.
MDB. (co. Glamorgan), 3.

Ribble.—(1) Nick. 'a ribald,' a low fellow. M.E. *ribaud.*
William le Ribote. J.
Philip Riband, co. York. W. 15.
(2) Bapt. 'the son of Ribald,' probably a curtailment of Rimbault, q.v.
Ralph fil. Ribaldi, Pipe Roll, 11 Hen. II, p. 9.
Folco Ribald, ibid. p. 36.
Ribald de Middleham, co. Norf., temp. 1200: FF. iii. 483.
Ribaldus (without surname), co. Norf., 1273. A.
Philadelphia, 5.

Ribchester.—Local, 'of Ribchester,' near Preston, co. Lanc.

Richard Ribchester, of Ribchester, 1662: Lanc. Wills at Richmond, i. 228.
Robert Ribchester, of Dutton, 1676: ibid. Preston, 3.

Ribston.—Local, 'of Ribston,' townships in the parishes of Hunsingore and Spofforth, in W. Rid. Yorks.
Robert de Ribstan, co. York, 1273. A.
Margareta de Ribstane, 1379: P. T. Yorks. p. 298.

Ricard, Ricards, Riccard, Ricart.—Bapt. 'the son of Ricard,' i.e. Richard (v. Rickard). Probably the earlier form. For change from *c* to *ch* see Skeat, s.v. *rich* (Etym. Dict.).
Hamo fil. Ricardi, co. Norf., 1273. A.
Alice Ricardiswyf, C. R., 8 Edw. I.
Adam Ricard, co. Soms., 1 Edw. III: Kirby's Quest, p. 92.
Walter Rykard, 1379: P. T. Yorks. p. 109.
Johannes Ricard, 1379: ibid. p. 71.
Thomas Ricards and Joane Lovelacke: Marriage Lic. (London), ii. 10.
Philadelphia, 0, 2, 2, 1.

Rice.—Bapt. 'the son of Rhys' (Welsh); v. Price, Reece, Rees, or Rhys. As with these other variants, Rice is strongly represented in the United States, and proves that the Welsh are great wanderers.
Rice, or Rise Powell, 1570: Reg. Univ. Oxf. vol. i. 276.
Thomas Rice, of Great Saughall, 1605: Wills at Chester, i. 159.
Henry Rice (co. Carmarthen), 1607, Jesus Coll.: Reg. Univ. Oxf. vol. ii. pt. ii. p. 299.
Rice Evans, of Hawarden, 1693: Exchequer Depositions (Cheshire), p. 161.
1607. Bapt.—Francis, s. Rice Winn: St. Mary Aldermary, p. 112.
London, 33; Manchester, 159.

Rich, Riches.—(1) Bapt. 'the son of Richard,' nicked occasionally into Rich, whence with patronymic *s* Riches; cf. Ricks, Rix, and Rixon. Also cf. Hitch (q.v.), another nick. of Richard.
Johannes Riche, 1379: P. T. Yorks. p. 258.
Matilda Ryche, 1379: ibid.
These paid the peasants' tax of 4*d.*
(2) Nick. Nevertheless Rich is also a nickname, denoting a man of fortune. Riches in this case has no connexion, being strictly of the baptismal class.
Reimbal le Riche. C.
Gervase le Riche. H.

Henry le Ryche, co. Oxf., 1273. A.
Hugo le Ryche, co. Oxf., ibid.
Bruman le Riche, co. Oxf., ibid.
William le Riche, co. Soms., 1 Edw. III: Kirby's Quest, p. 249.
John le Riche, co. Soms., 1 Edw. III: ibid. p. 113.
London, 17, 35.

Richard, Richards, Richardson. — Bapt. 'the son of Richard'; v. Ricard.
London, 7, 158, 188; Philadelphia, 19, 216, 240.

Richart, Richert.—Bapt. 'the son of Richard,' q.v. These American variants are closely allied to the German Reichart.
Philadelphia, 12, 4.

Richbell.—Bapt. 'the son of Richbell'; cf. Richard.
Richebelle Pirse, Fines Roll, 10 Edw. I.
John Richebele, C. R., 4 Edw. IV.
1674. Bapt. — Rebecca, d. William Richbell: St. Jas. Clerkenwell, i. 264.
1766. Married—Richard Manvell and Ann Richbell: St. Geo. Han. Sq. i. 160.
1767. — John Richbell and Eliz. Moore: ibid. p. 194.
London, 1; MDB. (co. Surrey), 1.

Richelot.—Bapt. 'the son of Richard,' from the dim. Richelot. Rikelot is the dim. of the harder form Ricard; cf. Hewlett for Hughelot, or Hamlet for Hamelot.
Richard Rikelot, co. Hunts, 1273. A.
Rikelot. CC. 1.
Robert Richelot, co. York. W. 15.
Robert Richelot. RR.

Richer. — Bapt. 'the son of Richer' (Yonge, ii. 381). To be distinguished from Richard, but absorbed by it so far as English surnames are concerned. It was very common in its day.
Cuthbert Ricerson, co. York. W. 3.
John Rycerson, co. York. W. 3.
Henry fil. Richer, co. Norf., 1273. A.
Rannlf Richer, co. Glouc., ibid.
Geoffrey fil. Richer, co. Camb., ibid.
1665-6. John Richer and Mary Gerrard: Marriage Lic. (London), ii. 294.
1668. Married—Antony Richer and Cristian Robinson: St. Jas. Clerkenwell, iii. 150.
London, 1; Boston (U.S.), 1; Philadelphia, 2.

Riches.—(1) Bapt. 'the son of Richer' (q.v.), from the genitive Richers, imitated into Riches. (2) Bapt. 'the son of Richard,' from the nick. Rich, genitive Riches, as in the case of Watts, Williams, Jones, &c. But the first derivation is the correct one in most instances. The following doubtless refer to one individual :

Henry Richers, co. Norf., 1572: FF. ii. 492.
Henry Riches, co. Norf., 1573: ibid. p. 484.
John Richers (of Walpole), co. Norf., 1707: ibid. ix. 113.
Edmund Riches, of Norwich, 1740: ibid. iv. 161.
1769. Married—Thomas Newton and Martha Riches: St. Geo. Han. Sq. i. 185.
London, 34 ; MDB. (co. Norfolk), 29 ; Philadelphia, 1.

Richey, Richie.—Bapt. ' the son of Richard ' ; v. Ritchie.

Riching, Richings. — Bapt. ' the son of Richard,' from nick. Rich, and dim. Richin ; the g is intrusive, the s in Richings, patronymic.
Oxford, 0, 5 ; Philadelphia, 1, 0.

Richman, Rickman.—Bapt. ' the son of Richman ' or Rickman ; cf. Richard and Rickard. The local Rickmansworth in the diocese of St. Alban's is thus explained. Richman le Savener, with his daughters Alvena, Mabilia, and Matilda, sold soap to the undergraduates of Cambridge in **1273** (A. ii. 382).. v. Richmond.

John fil. Rikeman, co. Hunts, 1273. A.
Richeman fil. John, co. Hunts, ibid.
Lucia Richeman, co. Camb., ibid.
William Richeman, co. Soms., 1 Edw. III : Kirby's Quest, p. 88.
John Rycheman, C. R., 15 Ric. II.
1577. Buried — Lawrence Rickman : St. Michael, Cornhill, p. 195.
1672-3. John Kirk and Anne Richman : Marriage Alleg. (Canterbury), p. 211.
London, 3, 2 ; Philadelphia, 10, 1.

Richmond.—Local, ' of Richmond,' a parish in co. York (N.Rid.). No doubt sometimes confounded with Richman, q.v.
Roald de Richemond, co. York, 20 Edw. I. R.
Geoffrey de Richemond, 26 Edw. I : Freemen of York, i. 7.
Nicholas Richemonde, co. Soms., 1 Edw. III : Kirby's Quest, p. 183.
Adam Rikemound, co. Soms., 1 Edw. III : ibid.
Nicholas Richeman, co. Soms., 1 Edw. III : ibid.
Agnes de Richemond, 1379 : P. T. Yorks. p. 250.
Johannes de Richemond, 1379 : ibid.
Thomas Rychmond, Cistercian : Reg. Univ. Oxt. i. 158.
1581. John Richman or Richmonde : ibid. vol. ii. pt. ii. p. 107.

1624. Bapt.—John, s. Robart Richmond, or Richman : St. Jas. Clerkenwell, i. 98.
London, 19 ; West Rid. Court Dir., 7 ; Philadelphia, 44.

Rick, Ricks.—Bapt. ' the son of Richard,' from the nick. Rick ; like Dick, taken from the harder form Ricard. The modern dress of Ricks in England is Rix (q.v.) ; cf. Dix for Dicks.
London, 0, 1 ; Philadelphia, 9, 7.

Rickaby ; v. Rickerby.

Rickard, Rickards.—Bapt. ' the son of Richard ' ; v. Ricard.
1602. Bapt.—Henry, s. George Rickardes : St. Jas. Clerkenwell, i. 40.
1625-6. Nathaniel Rickard and Grace Wosted : Marriage Lic. (London), ii. 163.
London, 7, 18 ; Philadelphia, 19, 19.

Rickart, Rickarts. — Bapt. ' the son of Richard ' ; v. Ricard and Rickard.
Philadelphia, 3, 2.

Rickatson, Ricketson. — Bapt. ' the son of Ricard ' (i.e. Richard), from the nick. Rick, and dim. Rick-et (cf. Emmett from Emma, nick. Emm), whence the patronymic Ricketson ; v. Ricket.
London, 1, 0 ; Boston (U.S.), 0, 9.

Rickerby, Rickaby.—Local, ' of Rickerby,' a township in the parish of Stanwix, co. Cumberland. Rickaby is a corrupted form. The original name of the place was Ricardby, i.e. the dwelling of Ricard (Richard), the proprietor.
(Homines) de Ricardeby, co. Cumb., 20 Edw. I. R.
1563. Buried—Jenet Rickobye : Reg. St. Mary Ulverston, p. 42.
1758. Married—William Baker and Catherine Rickerby : St. Geo. Han. Sq. i. 82.
1773. — George Brown and Rachel Rickerby : ibid. p. 234.
1785. — William Parkins and Rachel Rickaby : ibid. p. 369.
London, 3, 2 ; Sunderland, 0, 5 ; MDB. (co. Cumb.), 5, 0 ; Philadelphia, 1, 0.

Rickerson.—Bapt. ' the son of Richard,' a variant of Ricardson ; v. Ricard.
Philadelphia, 1.

Rickert, Rickerts. — Bapt. ' the son of Richard ' ; v. Ricard and Richart.
Philadelphia, 7, 3.

Ricket, Rickets, Rickett, Ricketts. — Bapt. ' the son of Ricard,' from the nick. Rick, and dim. Rick-et. Ricketts is the genitive ; cf. Williams, Jones, &c. v. Rickson.
1606. Married—John Scarbroughe and Hester Rickett : St. Mary Aldermary, p. 11.
1659. Bapt.—Eliz., d. Ralph Ricketts : St. Jas. Clerkenwell, i. 206.
1694. Married—Samuel Ricketts and Hannah Hughes : St. Michael, Cornhill, p. 48.
London, 2, 1, 4, 12; Philadelphia, 2, 0, 3, 21.

Rickman.—Bapt. ; v. Richman.

Rickon.—Bapt. ' the son of Richard,' from nick. Rick, dim. Rick-on ; cf. the corresponding forms Dick and Dickon or Diccon (v. Dicconson, s.v. Dickens).
Thomas fil. Ricun, co. Hunts, 1273. A.
London, 1 ; MDB. (co. Kent), 2.

Rickson.—Bapt. ' the son of Ricard,' from the nick. Rick, whence the patronymic Rick-son. The usual modern dress is Rixon, q.v.
1551. Anthony Ricson, of Bleasdale : Lanc. Wills at Richmond, i. 230.
1791. Married—Francis Rickson and Eliz. Wood : St. Geo. Han. Sq. ii. 54.
Boston (U.S.), 3.

Riddell, Riddall, Riddel, Riddal, Riddle, Ridel.—(1) Local, ' of Riddell,' in the parish of Lilliesleaf, co. Roxburgh. A clan name of great antiquity. (2) Local ; v. Reddall (1).
1761. Married—William Ridell and Mary Simpson : St. Geo. Han. Sq. i. 106.
1768. — James Riddle and Mary Humphry : ibid. p. 172.
1770. — Samuel Harper and Helen Riddell : ibid. p. 194.
London, 8, 2, 0, 0, 0, 0 ; Philadelphia, 17, 0, 1, 1, 29, 1.

Ridding.—Local ; a variant of Reading, q.v.
Crockford, 3.

Riddington. — Local, ' of Wrightington,' a township in parish of Eccleston, co. Lancaster. Wrightington first became Rightington, then Riddington ; cf. Ridlington.
Mary Wrightington, of Wrightington, 1580 : Wills at Chester, i. 219.
1713. Bapt.—John, s. John and Eliza Rightington : St. Jas. Clerkenwell, ii. 73.
1716. — Eliz., d. John and Eliz. Wrightington : ibid. p. 93.

In the next generation we find the following:

1736. Bapt.—Mary, d. John and Mary Ridington: St. Jas. Clerkenwell, ii. 229.
1738. Bapt.—Eliz., d. John and Mary Rightington: ibid. p. 241.

Thus Riddington is conclusively proved to be a corruption of Wrightington.

MDB. (co. Lincoln), 3.

Riddle; v. Reddall and Riddell.

London, 4.

Riddlesworth. — Local, ' of Riddlesworth,' a parish in co. Norfolk. This place gave birth to a local surname at a very early period; v. FF. i. 279 for an account of the family of Riddlesworth of Riddlesworth.

Gunner of Ridlesworth, co. Norf., temp. 1100: FF. i. 285.
Peter de Redelesworth, co. Norf., 1289: ibid. p. 279.
Roger de Redelesworth, co. Norf., 1335: ibid.
MDB. (co. Norf.), 1.

Ridehalgh, Riddeough, Redihalgh, Redihough. — Local, ' of the riddyhough.' The suffix -hough is generally found as -halgh in co. Lanc.; cf. Whitehalgh and Greenhalgh (pronounced halsh). Ridehalgh lay in the neighbourhood of Preston without doubt.

Robt. del Riddyough, 1397: Preston Guild Rolls, p. 1.
Edw. Riddihough, 1682: ibid. p. 174.
Edw. Riddihalgh, 1682: ibid. p. 201.
James Riddihough, of Preston, 1678: Lanc. Wills at Richmond, i. 230.
John Riddihalgh, Skipton-in-Craven, 1697: Exchequer Depositions (co. Lanc.), p. 93.
Manchester, 2, 1, 0, 0; West Rid. Court Dir., 0, 0, 1, 1.

Rideout, Ridout, Ridoutt. —? Local, ' of the redoubt' (?). Of this surname and its variants I can find no satisfactory derivation. Mr. Lower says, ' Possibly from redoubt, a military fortification. Fr. reduit; Ital. ridotto; Span. reduto. The Hundred Rolls' Ridhut will, however, hardly bend to this etymology': Patr. Brit. p. 289. v. Skeat's Dict. on redoubt.

Elyas Ridhut, co. Soms., 1273. A.
Willelmus Rydhowt, 1379: P. T. Yorks. p. 272.

1718. Bapt.—Maria, d. Giles Ridout: St. Jas. Clerkenwell, ii. 107.
1730. Married—Theophilus Ridout and Love Barnes: St. Geo. Han. Sq. i. 7.
London, 0, 2, 1; Crockford, 2, 0, 0; Leeds, 0, 1,0; Boston (U.S.), 11, 0, 0.

Rider, Ryder.—Occup. ' the rider,' i. e. trooper; v. Ritter or Rutter.

Roger le Ridere, co. Camb., 1273. A.
Stephen le Ridere, co. Hunts, ibid.
Adam le Rydere, co. Hunts, ibid.
John le Ridere, C. R., 9 Edw. II.
Nicholas le Ridere, co. Soms., 1 Edw. III: Kirby's Quest, p. 146.
John le Rider, 2 Edw. III: Freemen of York, i. 24.
Ricardus Rydere, textor, 1379: P. T. Yorks. p. 261.
1789. Married—William Minchin and Mary Rider: St. Geo. Han. Sq. ii. 24.
— — Robert Ryder and Sarah Gore: ibid. p. 28.
London, 21, 14; Leeds, 10, 1; Boston (U.S.), 3, 88.

Ridge, Rigg.—Local, ' at the ridge,' from residence on the rig or back of a hill; cf. Bridge and Brigg. In North Lancashire and Cumberland Rigg is a very familiar surname, almost as common as Fell; v. Riggs.

Thomas de la Rigge, co. Hants, 1273. A.
John de Legh del Rigge, 1437: Earwaker's East Cheshire, ii. 527.
Edward Rigge, of Hawkshead, 1586: Lanc. Wills at Richmond, i. 231.
Clement Rigg, of Hawkshead, 1590: ibid.
Robert Rig, of Hawkshead, 1611: ibid.
William Rigg, of Satterthwaite, 1611: Wills at Chester, i. 161.
1620. Thomas Ridge and Jane Waters: Marriage Lic. (London), ii. 89.
London, 13, 6; MDB. (co. Cumberland), 0, 14; Philadelphia, 13, 11.

Ridgway, Ridgeway.—Local, ' at the ridge-way,' i. e. the road over the back of the hill. A Cheshire family so called ramified strongly.

Lucia atte Rugewey, co. Soms., 1 Edw. III: Kirby's Quest, p. 105.
Johannes de Rygeway, 1379: P. T. Yorks. p. 5.
John del Ruggeway, co. Ches., 1355: East Cheshire, i. 464.
Hugh Ridgeway, co. Ches., 1577: ibid. p. 350.
1560. Buried —Katerine Ridgeway: Reg. Prestbury Ch., co. Ches., p. 2.
1572. Married—Roger Rydgewaye and Ellen Getscare: ibid. p. 38.
James Ridgway, of Offerton, 1594: Wills at Chester, i. 160.
London, 14, 0; Manchester, 10, 0; Boston (U.S.), 7, 1.

Riding, Ridding, Ryding.— Local, ' of the ridding,' from residence beside the clearing in the woods, called a ridding.

Isolda de Riddyng, 1379: P. T. Yorks. p. 244.
Willelmus de Ryddyng, 1379: ibid. p. 288.
Henry Ryding, husbandman, of Preston, 1590: Lanc. Wills at Richmond, i. 239.
William Rydeinge, of Preston, 1668: ibid.
London, 1, 0, 0; Preston, 4, 0, 3; Manchester, 3, 0, 0.

Ridler.—Occup. ' the riddler,' a maker of riddles. M.E. ridil; cf. Sivier.

Thomas le Ridelar, co. Soms., 1 Edw. III: Kirby's Quest, p. 226.
Walter le Ridelare, co. Soms., 1 Edw. III: ibid. p. 232.
John Ridler, temp. Eliz. Z.
William Rydler, ibid.
1618. Walter Ridler, co. Glouc.: Reg. Univ. Oxf. vol. ii. pt. ii. p. 368.
1792. Married—Anthony Ridler and Mary Fielder: St. Geo. Han. Sq. ii. 71.
London, 5; MDB. (co. Somerset), 5; Philadelphia, 2.

Ridley.—Local, ' of Ridley,' i. e. the red ley, or meadow, from the complexion of the soil. Many small spots would be so entitled. One Ridley is now a parish in co. Kent. Another Ridley is a township in the parish of Bunbury, co. Ches. Again, a third Ridley is a township in the parish of Haltwhistle, co. Northumberland. Cf. Redshaw.

Ricardus de Redleye, or Redlege, co. Essex, 1273. A.
Roger de Redlee, co. Essex, ibid.
Robert de Ridley, co. Lanc., 20 Edw. I. A.
John Ridley, of Chester, 1608: Wills at Chester, i. 161.
1678. Married—Jonathan Ridley and Eliz. Bowyer: St. Michael, Cornhill, p. 42.
London, 29; Philadelphia, 3.

Ridlington.—Local, ' of Ridlington': (1) a parish in co. Norfolk; (2) a parish in co. Rutland.

Adam de Wrydlington, co. Camb., 1273. A.
Ralph de Wridlingtone, co. Camb., ibid.
1383. John de Ridlington, rector of Ridlington, co. Norf.: FF. xi. 63.
1384. Roger de Ridlington, bailiff of Norwich: ibid. iii. 116.
London, 1; MDB. (co. Lincoln), 3.

Ridout(t; v. Rideout.

Ridpath; v. Redpath.

Ridsdale, Riddelsdell. — Local, 'of Redesdale,' co. Northumberland.

1782. Married—William Harwood and Mary Ridsdale: St. Geo. Han. Sq. i. 337.
1803. — James Riddelsdell and Sarah Morton : ibid. ii. 287.

London, 5, 1 ; Newcastle, 3, 0.

Rigby, Rigsby. — Local, ' of Rigsby,' a parish in co. Lincoln, near Alford ; found in early records as Rigby also.

Thomas de Ryggesby, co. Linc., Hen. III-Edw. I. K.
John de Ryggeby, or Ryggesby, co. Linc., 1273. A.
Willelmus de Rygby, 1379 : P. T. Yorks. p. 270.
Johannes de Riggeby, 1379 : ibid. p. 26.
1623. William Simon and Martha Riggesby : Marriage Lic. (London), ii. 133.
1627. John Rigby and Margery Deacon : ibid. p. 188.

London, 11, 0 ; MDB. (co. Lincoln), 0, 1 ; Boston (U.S.), 4, 0.

Rigden. — Local, ' of Rigden.' Mr. Lower, quoting Hasted, says, ' That this name originated among the *dens* of Kent is quite certain, though I cannot find the locality. The family have long been connected, by landed possessions, with various parishes in that county' : Patr. Brit. p. 290.

London, 2 ; MDB. (co. Kent), 11.

Rigg ; v. Ridge.

Riggs. — Local, ' of the ridge' (q.v.), a variant. Practically a compromise between Rigg and Ridge.

1591. Bapt.—Frauncis, s. Cuthbert Rigges : St. Jas. Clerkenwell, i. 25.
1601-2. Thomas Riggs, co. Hants : Reg. Univ. Oxf. vol. ii. pt. ii. p. 254.
1612-3. Robert Nedler and Ellen Riggs : Marriage Lic. (London), ii. 19.

London, 3 ; Philadelphia, 22.

Righteous. — Nick. ' the righteous.'

James Rightwys, Fines Roll, 14 Edw. II.
John Ryghtwyse, co. Soms., 1 Edw. III : Kirby's Quest, p. 88.
John Rightwyse. H.
John Rightwys, London. X.
John Rightwise, sheriff of Norwich, 492 : FF. iii. 191.

Rigmaiden. — Local, ' of Rigmaden,' an estate near Kendal, co. Westm. Guessing is dangerous. Lower suggests that it is a nickname, and means ' the romping

girl' (!). Trollop, also local, has been assigned to the same class and origin !

John de Rigmarden, 16 Edw. II (1322-3) : Baines' Lanc. ii. 529.
1593. Buried—Frauncis Rygmayden : St. Michael, Cornhill, p. 205.
1654. Bapt.—Jane, d. John Riggemayden : Annals of Cartmel, p. 558.
Susannah Rigmaiden, of Holker (Furness), 1689 : Lanc. Wills at Richmond, p. 210.
Thomas Rigmaiden, of Lancaster, 1735 : ibid.

Liverpool, 1.

Riley. — Local, ' of Riley,' i.e. High Riley, in the parish of Altham, co. Lanc. Probably several places bear the name. The frequency of Riley in the United States is owing to the fact that the Irish O'Reilly, or Reilly, is there generally rendered in that form.

Johannes de Rylay, 1379 : P. T. Yorks. p. 89.
Robert Riley, of Chorley, 1595 : Wills at Chester (1545-1620), p. 162.
Reynold Riley, of High Reiley, 1605 : ibid.

London, 34 ; Manchester, 46.

Rimbault. — Bapt. ' the son of Rembald ' or Reinbold (Yonge, ii. 378) ; v. Rumball.

Willielmus fil. Erembaldi, Pipe Roll, 5 Hen. II.
Reimbald le Riche. C.
John fil. Rambaldi, 1273. A.
Renebaud le Palmer, ibid.
1549. ' An yron gonne, call'd a slyng, which gonne Robert Raynbald found in the barley without St. Austen's gates ' (Norwich) : FF. iv. 232 n.
1675. Henry Townsend and Mildred Rumbould : Marriage Alleg. (Canterbury), p. 243.

London, 1.

Riminton ; v. Remington.

Rimmer, Rymer, Rimer. — Occup. ' the rhymer,' poet, versifier, singer. M.E. *rime* or *ryme*. In South-west Lancashire Rimmer has ramified very strongly ; but it was spelt Rymer in the 16th century.

Roger Rymer, of Walton, 1579 : Wills at Chester (1545-1620), p. 168.
Peter Rymer, of North Meols, 1591 : ibid.
William Rymer, of Formby, 1614 : ibid. p. 162.
John Rimmer, of Formby, 1615 : ibid.
Gilbert Rimmer, of North Meols, 1617 : ibid.

Liverpool, 31, 0, 0 ; Manchester, 1, 1, 1 ; London, 0, 6, 3 ; MDB. (co. Lanc.), 19, 1, 0.

Rind ; v. Rhind.

Rinder. — Occup. ' the rendour ' ; v. Render.

Ringbell. — Nick. ; probably the sobriquet of a bellringer ; v. Bellman.

Henry Ringebell, co. Suff., 1273. A.
Richard Ringebelle, co. Suff., ibid.
Matilda Riggebelle, co. Suff., ibid.

Ringland. — Local, ' of Ringland,' a parish in co. Norwich.

1330. William de Ringland, rector of Felthorp : FF. x. 415.

London, 1 ; Philadelphia, 5.

Ringrose. — ? ——. I have no satisfactory derivation to offer regarding this surname. It is clearly sprung from East Yorkshire.

Robert Ryngrose, 1544, York : W. 11, p. 233.
1615. John Ringrose, co. Northants : Reg. Univ. Oxf. vol. ii. pt. ii. p. 342.
1744. Married—John Thirlwall and Hannah Ringrose : St. Geo. Han. Sq. i. 33.

London, 3 ; MDB. (East Rid. Yorks), 9 ; Philadelphia, 1.

Ripley. — Local, ' of Ripley,' a parish north of the Nidd, near Ripon, co. York.

John de Riplay, 3 Edw. III : Freemen of York, i. 25.
Matilda de Riplay, 1379 : P. T. Yorks. p. 279.
1572. Bapt.—Eliz., d. Thomas Ripley : St. Jas. Clerkenwell, i. 7.
1758. Married—Richard Ripley and Sybell Morel : St. Geo. Han. Sq. i. 83.

London, 7 ; West Rid. Court Dir., 8 ; Philadelphia, 13.

Riplingham. — Local, ' of Riplingham,' a township in the parish of Rowley, E. Rid. Yorks.

1628. Sir Henry Appleton and Alice Riplingham : Marriage Lic. (London), ii. 194.

MDB. (East Rid. Yorks), 1.

Ripon, Rippon. — Local, ' of Ripon,' a cathedral city in W. Rid. Yorks.

William de Ripon, co. York, 1273. A.
William de Ripon, 1319-20 : Freemen of York, i. 19.
Johanna de Ripofi, 1379 : P. T. Yorks. p. 167.
1601. Married — James Rippen and Joane Smithe : St. Mary Aldermary, London, p. 10.
1623. Bapt.—Thomas, s. John Rippon : St. Jas. Clerkenwell, i. 98.

London, 1, 1 ; Middlesbrough (North Rid. Yorks), 0, 1.

Rippingale, Rippingall.—
Local, 'of Rippingale,' a parish in co. Lincoln, four miles from Falkingham.

John de Repinghal, co. Linc., 1273. A.
Hugh de Repinghale, co. Linc., ibid.
John de Repinghale, co. Linc., 20 Edw.
I. R.
1587. John Reppingall, *tailor*, and Eliz.
Catlyn : Marriage Lic. (London), i. 164.
1733. John Rippinghall, rector of Boynton, co. Norf. : FF. xi. 100.
MDB. (co. Norfolk), 1, 4 ; London, 1, 0.

Rippington ; v. Repington.

Risbrough, Riseborough.—
Local, 'of Risborough,' two parishes in co. Bucks.

Thomas de Riseberghe, co. Bucks, 20
Edw. I. R.
1698. Elizabeth Riseborow, of Aylesham, co. Norf. : FF. vi. 280.
1704. John Riseborough, or Risebrow,
or Riseborow, sheriff of Norwich : ibid.
iii. 436 ; iv. 222, 204.
1729. Bapt.—John, s. Timothy Riseburer (sic) : St. Jas. Clerkenwell, ii. 187.
Long Stratton (co. Norf.), 0, 1 ; Philadelphia, 4, 0.

Riseley.—Local, 'of Riseley,' a parish in co. Bedford. This is sometimes spelt Rislṛy, q.v.

Harvey de Risle, co. Bedf., 1273. A.
Geoffrey de Risle, co. Bedf., ibid.
Richard de Risele, co. Norf., 8 Ric. II :
FF. ii. 156.
1602. Nicholas Ryselye, rector of
Harpham, co. Norf. : ibid. i. 418.
1725. Bapt.—Sarah, d. James Risely :
St. Jas. Clerkenwell, i. 153.
MDB. (co. Lincoln), 1.

Rishton ; v. Rushton.

Rishworth, Rushworth.—
Local, (1) 'of Rishworth,' a township in the parish of Halifax, W. Rid.
Yorks ; (2) of Rushworth, co. Norfolk, styled in Domesday Rusceuuorda (v. FF. i. 284). M.E.
rusche, rische, a rush. v. Worth.

Domina de Ruseworthe, co. Norf.,
1273. A.
John de Russeworthe, co. Norf., ibid.
1368. William de Rusheworth, rector
of Santon, co. Norf. : FF. ii. 157.
1594. Thomas Rishworth, co. Lincoln :
Reg. Univ. Oxf. vol. ii. pt. ii. p. 204.
1702. Married—John Rose and Alice
Rushworth : St. Michael, Cornhill, p. 51.
MDB. (West Rid. Yorks), 9, 9 ; Boston
(U.S.), 0, 1.

Rising.—Local, 'of Rising,' now Woodrising, a parish in co. Norfolk, two miles from Hingham.

Roger de Rysing, co. Norf., 12 Hen. III.
Simon de Rising, co. Norf., 1273. A.
Roger de Wode Rising, co. Norf., 14
Edw. I : FF. x. 274.
1323. Eustace de Rising, rector of
Thurgartdn, co. Norf. : ibid. viii. 177.
1654. John Riseing, of Fouldon, co.
Norf. : ibid. vi. 35.

The surname has ramified strongly in Norfolk, and has wandered little. Nevertheless, it has its representatives in the United States.

London, 1 ; Yarmouth, 6 ; MDB. (co.
Norfolk), 10 ; New York, 3.

Risley.— Local, 'of Risley' :
(1) a parish in co. Bedford, near Kimbolton ; (2) a chapelry in the parish of Sawley, co. Derby ; (3) an estate in the parish of Winwick, co. Lanc., where a family of the same name dwelt for centuries. For other references to (1) v. Riseley. All three places have become the parents of surnames.

John de Risley, co. Norf., 44 Hen. III :
FF. vii. 353.
Nigel de Risleye, co. Norf., Hen. III–
Edw. I. K.
William de Riseleg, co. Derby, ibid.
Thomas de Rysshelegh, 1379 : P. T.
Yorks. p. 91.
John Risley, of Risley, co. Lanc., 1617 :
Wills at Chester (1545-1620), p. 162.
London, 2 ; MDB. (co. Oxf.), 6.

Ritch.—A variant of Rich, q.v. ;
cf. Pritchard and Prichard.

Philadelphia, 3.

Ritchie, Richey, Richie.—
Bapt. 'the son of Richard,' from the North-English and Border nick.
Richie. In the United States Richie and Richey still live. These forms seem to be extinct in England, a *t* having crept in, as in the case of Pritchard.

Richie of the Moat, 1581-7 : Nicolson and Burn, Hist. Westm. and Cumb.,
vol. i. pp. xxxiii-xxxv.
Richie Bell, 1581-7 : ibid.
Richie Maxwell, 1581-7 : ibid.
Richie Blakeburne, 1602 : ibid. p. cxiv.
1793. Married—William Ritchie and
Letitia Robertson : St. Geo. Han. Sq.
ii. 96.
London, 21, 0, 0 ; Philadelphia, 87,
3, 16.

Ritson.—Bapt. 'the son of Richard,' from the North-English nick. Rich or Ritchie, whence the

patronymic Richson, or Richison, corrupted to Ritson. This is a familiar Cumberland surname. v.
Ritchie.

1801. Married—Richard Walker and
Margaret Ritson : St. Geo. Han. Sq. ii.
240.
1806. — William Gibbs and Sarah Rittson : ibid. p. 357.
MDB. (co. Cumb.), 8 ; Philadelphia, 3.

Ritter.—Occup. ; v. Rutter.

Rively.—Local ; a variant of Reveley, q.v.

Philadelphia, 5.

River.—Local, 'at the river,' from residence on its bank. I do not find River now existing as a surname. Probably it has taken an *s* to it, like Brooks, and is lost in Rivers, q.v.

Richard de la River, co. Bedf., Hen.
III–Edw. I. K.
Andreas de la River, co. Notts, 1273. A.
Richard de la Rivere, co. Wilts, ibid.
1709. Bapt.—George River, a foundling,
by the New River : St. Jas. Clerkenwell,
ii. 47.

Rivers.—(1) Local, 'de Rivers';
probably a Norman local surname, representing a family of importance.
(2) Local, 'at the river' ; v. River.

Margaret de Rivers, co. Essex, Hen.
III–Edw. I. K.
Richard de Rivers, co. Devon, 1273. A.
Simon de Rivers, co. Suff., ibid.
Robert de Riveres, co. Worc., ibid.
1794. Married—William Rivers and
Ann Gilbert : St. Geo. Han. Sq. ii. 107.
London, 8 ; Philadelphia, 13.

Rivington.—Local, 'of Rivington,' an old chapelry in the parish of Bolton, co. Lanc. This surname is now extremely rare in the county, and has gone to the south.

John Rivington, of Wigan, co. Lanc.,
1587 : Wills at Chester (1545-1620), p. 162.
Thomas Rivington, of Chester, *gent*.
1616 : ibid.
1642. Roger Rivington, *tailor* : Preston
Guild Rolls, p. 102.
London, 5.

Rix.—(1) Bapt. 'the son of Ricard' or Rickard, i.e. Richard ;
nicked to Rick, whence Rix and Ricks ; cf. Dix for Dicks, and v.
Rickard.

1701. Married—Richard Instance and
Eliz. Rix : St. Jas. Clerkenwell, iii. 224.
1789. — Cecil Rix and Grace Bennett :
St. Geo. Han. Sq. ii. 18.

(2) Local, 'at the rix.' Rix is sometimes local. '*Rix*, a reed. Exmoor' (Halliwell). This seems to have existed since the 13th century. 'At the reeds' would seem to be meant by

John de la Rixe, co. Soms., 1273. A.
Osbert de la Rixe, co. Soms., ibid.

unless 'ricks' (i.e. small stacks) is meant.

London, 11; Philadelphia, 1.

Rixon.—Bapt. 'the son of Ricard,' from the nick. Rick, whence the patronymic Rickson, spelt Rixon (v. Rix and Rickson); cf. Dixon for Dickson.

1731. Married—Thomas Rixon and Eliz. Smith: St. Jas. Clerkenwell, iii. 259.
1805. — Joseph Cooper and Sarah Rixon: St. Geo. Han. Sq. ii. 317.
London, 8; Philadelphia, 3.

Roach.—Local, 'at the rock'; v. Roche.

Roades, Roads, Road.—(1) Local, 'at the roads,' i.e. the cross-roads, the point where the roads meet. Also simply, 'at the road,' one who lived by the road-side. It was natural for people to live at the conjunction of roads, hence the plural form. (2) Local, 'at the rode' or rodes; v. Royd.

Simon de la Rode, co. Suff., 1273. A.
William del Rode, co. Norf., ibid.
William atte Rode, co. Soms., 1 Edw.
III: Kirby's Quest, p. 98.
Robert atte Rode, co. Soms., ibid. p. 139.
Edmundus del Rodes, 1379: P. T.
Yorks. p. 17.
Agnes del Rodes, 1379: ibid. p. 207.
Alicia del Rodes, 1379: ibid. p. 201.
Henry del Rodes, 1379: ibid.

There are eighty-four Rhodes in the West Rid. Court Dir. alone, manifestly the descendants of such persons as are named above; v. Rhodes (2).

1621. Margery Rodes, of Ribchester, *widdow*: Lancashire Wills at Richmond, i. 236.
1706. Edward Roads, or Rhodes, of Thornley: ibid. ii. 211.
London, 1, 3, 0.

Roadhouse.—Local; v. Roydhouse.

Roadnight, Redknight, Rodnight.—Offic. 'the road-knight,' a riding servitor or attendant on horseback. In feudal times rod-knights were 'certain servitors who held their lands by serving their lords on horseback' (Lower, Patr. Brit.). 'Rodknightes': Spelman's Gloss. The name still exists, though not in Lond. Dir. I met the name in my own parish (Oct. 1885) at Conishead Priory Hydropathic Establishment among the list of visitors.

1586. Elizabeth Redknighte, relict of Thomas Redknighte, *wax-chandler*: Marriage Lic. (London), i. 156.
Liverpool, 1, 0, 0; Atherstone (co. Warwick), 2, 0, 0; MDB. (co. Bucks), 1, 0, 0; (co. Northants), 0, 0, 1.

Roads; v. Roades.

Roafe. — Bapt. 'the son of Ralph'; v. Rolf.

London, 1.

Roan.—(1) Local, 'of Rouen,' the capital of Normandy; a mediaeval spelling. An old poet, speaking of Richard I, says:

'Thy bowels only Carceol keeps;
Thy corse Font Everard;
But Roan hath keeping of thy heart,
O puissant Richard.'
(v. Lower's Patr. Brit. p. 290.)

(2) Local, 'at the rowan,' from residence beside a rowan-tree; cf. Roantree for Rowantree (v. Rowntree). So also we have Crabb and Crabtree, Plumb and Plumptre. Of (1) and (2) the second is probably the true derivation in most cases.

1774. Married—John Keats and Eleanor Roan: St. Geo. Han. Sq. i. 246.
London, 6, 0; Philadelphia, 7, 3.

Roanson.—Bapt. 'the son of Rowland,' an abbreviation of Row-landson; v. Rownson and Ronson.

Roantree.—Local; v. Rowntree, a manifest variant.

Rob, Robb.—Bapt. 'the son of Robert,' from the nick. Rob. The favourite nicks. were Hob and Dob. The patronymics of the three are Robson, Hobson, and Dobson.

Manchester, 0, 2; MDB. (North Rid. Yorks), 2, 1.

Robberds.— Bapt. 'the son of Robert.' A variation of Roberts, q.v.

1622. Edmund Robardes and Jane Nicholson: Marriage Lic.(London), ii. 116.
1676. William Roberds, of Blackdyke: Wills at Chester, iii. 225.
Norfolk Court Dir., 3.

Robbey, Robbie.—Bapt. 'the son of Robert,' from the pet Robbie; cf. Charlie or Charley, Teddie, &c.

MDB. (co. Cumb.), 1, 0; Liverpool, 0, 1.

Robbins; v. Robin.

Roberson.—Bapt. 'the son of Robert,' a corruption of Robertson (v. Robert).

1788. Married—William Roberson and Grace Say: St. Geo. Han. Sq. ii. 2.
1789. — Christopher Roberson and Mary Oliver: ibid. p. 22.
London, 3; Deepham (co. Norf.), 1; Swaffham (co. Norf.), 1; Philadelphia, 4.

Robert, Roberts, Robertson.—Bapt. 'the son of Robert.' The influence of this name was enormous, as our directories prove. Its chief nicks. were Hob and Dob, whence with dims. Hobkin, Hopkin, Dobinson, &c., q.v. But the most famous dim. was Robin. Hence our Robinsons, &c. (v. Robin).

Adam fil. Roberti, co. Oxf., 1273. A.
Agatha fil. Roberti, co. Oxf., ibid.
Thomas fil. Roberti, co. Soms., 1 Edw.
III: Kirby's Quest, p. 145.

It is useless giving other illustrations. It ran a fine race with Richard and Roger, one giving us the nicks. Hick and Dick, the other Hodge and Dodge, all of which see.

London, 4, 273, 96.

Robertshaw, Robishaw.—Local, 'of Robertshaw,' i.e. the wood that belonged to Robert. This is a West Riding (Yorks) surname, but I cannot find the precise spot. v. Robert and Shaw.

Laurence Robteshay, of Clayton-in-the-Moors, co. Lanc., 1610: Wills at Chester (1545-1620), p. 164.
1794. Married—William Robertshaw and Ann Mason: St. Geo. Han. Sq. ii. 122.
MDB. (West Rid. Yorks), 9, 0; Oldham, 0, 1; Boston (U.S.), 0, 1.

Robeson; v. Robison.

Robilard.—Bapt. 'the son of Robilard.'

Robelard (without surname), co. Sussex, 1273. A.

Robilard de Boteleria (i. e. the Cellar), co. Glouc., 1200: Household Exp., Ric. de Swinfield, Cam. Soc., p. 170.

Robin, Robins, Robbins, Robinson.—Bapt. 'the son of Robert,' from nick. Rob, and dim. Rob-in; cf. Col-in from Nicholas. The number of entries in the London Directory is sufficient proof of the early popularity of Robin. Birds, flowers, and weeds soon took possession of the name, the ruddock giving way to robin-redbreast so completely as to cause the earlier name to be forgotten.

'Now am I Robert, now Robin.'
Chaucer, R. R. 6337.

Dera Robins, co. Camb., 1273. A.
John Robin, co. Oxf., ibid.
Robin le Gentyle, C. R., 4 Edw. I.
Robin le Herberjer. E.
William Robyn, co. Soms., 1 Edw. III : Kirby's Quest, p. 117.
Roger Robynsoun, 1379 : P. T. Yorks. p. 220.
Roger Robyn-man (the servant of Robin), 1379 : ibid. p. 248.
Adam Robyn-man (the servant of Robin), 1379 : ibid.
1606. Bapt.—William, s. Arthur Robinsonne : St. Peter, Cornhill, i. 56.
London, 3, 28, 20, 258 } Philadelphia, 1, 15, 108, 578.

Robinet, Robinett. — Bapt. 'the son of Robert,' from nick. Rob, and double dim. Rob-in-et ; cf. Colinet from Nicholas ; cf. also 'robinet, the cock of a cistern' (Halliwell).

Robinet de Bocland, co. Glouc., 1290 : Household Exp., Ric. de Swinfield, Cam. Soc., p. 189.
Richard Robynet. H.
Robinet of the Hill. Y.
1694. Married—Robert Hallywell and Susanna Robinett, of Saffron Walden, co. Essex : St. Dionis Backchurch (London).
1804. — Henry Standford and Lucy Rabnett : St. Geo. Han. Sq. ii. 306.
1806. — Edward Humphreys Robnet and Bertie Maria Kleboe : ibid. p. 350.
London, 0, 1 ; Foulmire (co. Camb.), 0, 1 ; Liverpool, 2, 0 ; Philadelphia, 0, 2.

Robishaw ; v. Robertshaw.

Robison, Robeson. — Bapt. 'the son of Robert,' from the pet Robbie, whence the patronymic Robison.

Thomas Robyson, *faber*, 1379 : P. T. Yorks. p. 266.
1567. James Robyson, of Wray : Lancashire Wills at Richmond, i. 236.
1801. Married — Francis MacGowran

and Eliz. Robeson : St. Geo. Han. Sq. ii. 248.
London, 2, 2 ; Philadelphia, 4, 6.

Robkin, Ropkins.—Bapt. 'the son of Robert,' from the nick. Rob, and dim. Rob-kin ; cf. Wil-kin and Tom-p-kin (with intrusive *p*). I fear the surname is nearly extinct. Robin took all the honours. Ropkins is a sharpened form ; cf. Wilkin and Wilkins, &c.

Adam Robekin, co. Oxf., 1273. A.
Stephen Robekin, c. 1300. M.
1558. Thomas Robkin, co. Norf. : FF. xi. 80.
1562. Thomas Robkins : Reg. Univ. Oxf. i. 248.
1609. Buried—William Robkin, *minister*, Reg. Pulham, co. Norf. : FF. v. 391.
London, 0, 1.

Roblet. — Bapt. 'the son of Robert,' from nick. Rob, and dim. Robelot ; cf. 'roblet, a large chicken. East' (Halliwell). The instances below are from the Eastern counties, agreeing with Halliwell's statement.

Henry Robelot, co. Suff., 1273. A.
Richard Robelot, co. Hunts, ibid.
Rus Robalot, co. Camb., ibid.
William Robelot, co. Soms., 1 Edw. III : Kirby's Quest, p. 120.
John Robolot, vicar of Lillington, 1397 : Dugdale's Warwickshire, p. 204.

Roblin.—Bapt. 'the son of Robert,' from nick. Rob, and dim. Rob-elin ; cf. Hewling (with excrescent *g*) for Hew-elin.

Simon Robelyn, co. Bedf., 1273. A.
Henry Roblyn (co. Pembroke), Jesus Coll., 1607 : Reg. Univ. Oxf. vol. ii. pt. ii. p. 299.
London, 1.

Robotham ; v. Rowbotham.

Robson.—Bapt. 'the son of Robert,' from the nick. Rob or Robbie ; cf. the other nick. Hob, and Hobson. v. Robison.

Ricardus Robson, 1379 : P. T. Yorks. p. 202.
1565. Bapt.—Thomas, s. Richard Robson : St. Jas. Clerkenwell, i. 3.
1598. John Robson, co. Westm. : Reg. Univ. Oxf. vol. ii. pt. ii. p. 230.
1625. Francis Robson and Wilseam (sic) Harbert : Marriage Lic. (London), ii. 153.
London, 33 ; West Rid. Court Dir., 17 ; Philadelphia, 25.

Roche, Roach.—Local, 'at the rock' (O.F. *roche*, a rock), from residence beside some prominent rock ; v. Rock.

Alice de la Roche, co. Camb., 1273. A.
Gilbert de la Roche, co. Wilts, ibid.
William de la Roch, co. Soms., ibid.
Agnes de la Roche, co. Camb., 20 Edw. I. R.
1660. Bapt. — Seenehouse, s. John Roche : St. Jas. Clerkenwell, i. 208.
1675-6. — Eliz., d. Thomas Roach : St. Dionis Backchurch, p. 121.
London, 11, 12 ; Philadelphia, 38, 78.

Rochester.—Local, 'of Rochester,' a cathedral city in co. Kent ; v. Rossiter, probably a variant.

Avicia de Rofa, co. Kent, 1273. A.
Ralph de Roff', co. Hertf., ibid.
Salamon de Roff', co. Berks, 20 Edw. I. R.
1549. Married—Thomas Rochester and Eliz. Starkey : St. Michael, Cornhill, p. 5.
1748. — John Harrison and Hannah Rochester : St. Dionis Backchurch, p. 69.
London, 2 ; Philadelphia, 1.

Rochford, Rochfort.—Local, 'of Rochford.' Lower says, 'The Irish family settled in that country at, or soon after, the Anglo-Norman invasion. Their name was Latinized "de Rupe Forti," of the strong rock, which is doubtless its true meaning' : Patr. Brit. p. 292. This is not satisfactory. The name has sprung from two towns in England, Rochford in co. Essex, and Rochford in co. Hereford. The meaning is the *ford* on the river Roche, so far as the Essex town is concerned, the Latinization being a mere play on the name.

Guido de Rocheford, London, 1273. A.
Eustace de Rocheford, co. Essex, ibid.
Walter de Rocheford, co. Norf., 20 Edw. I. R.
Ralph de Rocheford, co. Soms., ibid.
1601. Bapt.—Michael, s. George Rochforde : St. Jas. Clerkenwell, i. 39.
1777. Married—John Cable and Sarah Rochford : St. Geo. Han. Sq. i. 276.
1788. — William Rochfort and Eliz. Sperling : ibid. ii. 6.
London, 0, 1 ; Philadelphia, 2, 2.

Rock, Rocke.—Local, 'at the rock,' from residence beside some prominent boulder ; v. Roche.

Geof. de la Roke, co. Oxf., 1273. A.
Eudo de la Roche, co. Hunts, ibid.
Jordan de la Roche, co. Devon, ibid.
Alicia atte Roch, co. Soms., 1 Edw. III : Kirby's Quest, p. 235.
1576. Bapt.—Francis, s. Robert Rocke : St. Jas. Clerkenwell, i. 9.
1711. Married—Thomas Wanless and Mary Rock : St. Michael, Cornhill, p. 56.
London, 9, 1 ; Philadelphia, 23, 0.

Rockley.—Local, ' of the rockley,' i.e. the meadow by the rocks, from residence beside such a spot. Several places seem to have been so termed.

Roisa de la Rokele, co. Oxf., Hen. III-Edw. I. K.
Robert de la Rokele, co. Bucks, ibid.
Richard de la Rokele, co. Essex, 1273. A.
William de la Rokele, co. Norf., ibid.
Johannes Roklay, 1379: P. T. Yorks. p. 165.
1700. Married—Charles Rockley and Alice Clerke: St. Dionis Backchurch, p. 49.
London, 3; Philadelphia, 1.

Rockliffe, Rockliff, Roccliffe.—Local, ' of Rockcliff,' a parish in co. Cumb., four miles from Carlisle. No doubt, in some cases, variants of the Yorkshire Rawcliffe or Rowcliffe, q.v.

MDB. (West Rid. Yorks), 1, 1, 1; Liverpool, 0, 3, 0.

Rodbard, Rodbeard.—Bapt. ' the son of Radberd,' an early personal name; v. Yonge, ii. 372.

Thomas Radbird, 1677: St. Mary Aldermary (London), p. 104.
1792. Married—John Rodbard and Sarah Price: St. Geo. Han. Sq. ii. 79.
London, 1, 0; MDB. (co. Somerset), 6, 1; Philadelphia, 3, 0.

Rodd.—Local: (1) ' at the rod,' probably at the *rod* of land, so called from its size, measuring a rod; cf. Hyde. (2) Lower says, ' Rodd, a place near Leominster, co. Hereford, formerly the residence of the family.' (3) The most probable derivation is Rudd or Rood, q.v.

Nicholas de la Rodde, co. Devon, 1273. A.
Johannes Rodde, 1379: P. T. Yorks. p. 255.
1685. William Wardour and Anna Sophia Rodd: Marriage Lic. (London), ii. 307.
1801. Married—John Rodd and Eliz. Shaw: St. Geo. Han. Sq. ii. 248.
London, 3; Philadelphia, 2.

Roddam.—Local, ' of Roddam,' a township in the parish of Ilderton, co. Northumberland.

MDB. (co. Northumberland), 4.

Roderick, Rodrick.—Bapt. ' the son of Roderick.'

London, 0, 1; Crockford, 4, 0.

Rodger, Rodgers.—Bapt. 'the son of Roger,' q.v. The *d* is, of course, intrusive.

Rodman. — Occup. Probably the *radmannus* of Domesday: one who held by some tenure similar to that of the *radcniht*; v. Roadnight.

William Rodman, co. Northampt., Hen. III-Edw. I. K.
1783. Married—Henry Marden and Sarah Rodman: St. Geo. Han. Sq. i. 353.
London, 2; Philadelphia, 10.

Rodney.—Local, ' of Rodney,' i.e. Rodney Stoke, a parish in co. Somerset, but traced back earlier to Rodney, a small moss island in the parish of Wedmore in the same county.

Richard de Rodeneye, 32 Edw. I: BBB. p. 670.
Walter de Rodeneye, co. Soms., 1 Edw. III: Kirby's Quest, p. 87.
Thomas de Rodeneye, co. Soms., 1 Edw. III: ibid. p. 228.
Ralph de Rodeneye, co. Soms., 1 Edw. III: ibid. p. 249.
'The vicar of Wedmore has been publishing some interesting notes upon the field names of that parish in the Wedmore Chronicle. In the number for March, 1887, p. 287, he states that Rodney "is the name of a little hump, or island, rising out of Mark Moor," and he traces the Rodney family back from Rodney Stoke to Mark': N. and Q., Oct. 29, 1887, p. 350.
1665. Charles Howard and Eliz. Rodney (of Pilton, co. Soms.): Marriage Alleg. (Canterbury), p. 107.
London, 1; Philadelphia, 16.

Rodnight; v. Roadnight.

Rodway, Radway. — Local, ' of Radway,' a parish in co. Warwick, four miles from Kington; cf. Rodwell (2) for Radwell.

John de Radewaye, co. Soms., 1 Edw. III: Kirby's Quest, p. 112.
Henry de Radewaye, co. Soms., 1 Edw. III: ibid.
Stephen Rodweye, or Radwaye, London, 1581: Reg. Univ. Oxf. vol. ii. pt. ii. p. 103.
1585. William Rodway and Eliz. Sawnders: St. Mary Aldermary, p. 7.
1642. Bapt.—Thomas and Francis, sons of John Rodway: Reg. Stourton, Wilts. London, 7, 1.

Rodwell.—Local, (1) ' of Rodwell,' a parish in dioc. of Rochester; (2) ' of Radwell,' a hamlet in the parish of Felmersham, co. Bedford.

Robert de Radewell, co. Bedf., 1273. A.
John de Radewell, co. Bedf., ibid.
Alan de Rodewell, co. Leic., ibid.
1598. Married—Thomas Arundell and Honora Radwell: St. Jas. Clerkenwell, i. 21.
1789. — William Rodwell and Eliz. Smirthwaite: St. Geo. Han. Sq. ii. 30.
London, 10; Oxford, 2.

Roe.—(1) Nick. 'the roe'; cf. Buck, Hart, Roebuck, &c. M.E. *ro*, the female deer.

Geoffrey le Ro, co. Hunts, 1273. A.
John le Ro, co. Norf., ibid.
Alicia le Ro, co. Hunts, ibid.
John le Ro, co. Soms., 1 Edw. III: Kirby's Quest, p. 95.
John le Roo, co. Soms., 1 Edw. III: ibid. p. 125.

This must be looked upon as the parent of nine-tenths of our Roes. The following combination of names was a happy one:

1630. Married—Robert Roe and Eliz. Hart: St. Jas. Clerkenwell, iii. 61.

(2) Local, ' at the roe,' i.e. at the sign of the Roe; cf. Roebuck (2).

John de la Roe. O.

(3) Local, 'at the row' (v. Row).

London, 18; Philadelphia, 20.

Roebuck.—(1) Nick. 'the roebuck' (v. Roe). Found in co. Yorks for many centuries.

Thomas Rabuk, co. Linc. 1273. A.
Ricardus Rabuk, 1379: P. T. Yorks. p. 293.
Robertus Rabuk, 1379: ibid. p. 294.

(2) Local, ' at the Roebuck,' a sign-name.

William atte Robuck, 1313. M.
1795. Married—Ebenezer Roebuck and Zipporah Tickell: St. Geo. Han. Sq. ii. 138.
London, 3; Sheffield, 4; Leeds, 3; West Rid. Court Dir., 10; Philadelphia, 4.

Rofe, Roff.—Bapt. ' the son of Rudolph,' through the popular form Rolf, q.v.

1570. Bapt.—Anthony, s. Thomas Roffe: St. Jas. Clerkenwell, i. 6.
1788. Married—Thomas Jennings and Amy Rofe: St. Geo. Han. Sq. ii. 8.
London, 2, 3; Philadelphia, 0, 3.

Roffey.—Local. Probably ' of Roughwray,' a township in the parish of Wrotham, co. Kent. The surname Roffey is still familiar to that and the adjacent counties.

Amfr' de la Rogheye, co. Kent, 1273. A.
1678. Aldricke Roffey and Mary Grove:
Marriage Lic. (London), ii. 282.
1775. Married—James Masdon and Ann
Roffee: St. Geo. Han. Sq. i. 256.
London, 9; MDB. (co. Surrey), 6; (co.
Sussex), 1.

Rogecock.—Bapt. 'the son of
Roger.' An attempt was made to
add *cock* to Roger (or Rodge) as
with Wilcock, Jeffcock, Mycock,
&c., but it was cumbrous and did
not lilt, so was evidently soon
dropped. But it proves the popularity of the font-name.

Stephen Rogekoc, co. Camb., 1273. A.
Ranulf Rogekoc, co. Camb., ibid.

**Roger, Rogers, Rogerson,
Rodger, Rodgers.**—Bapt. 'the
son of Roger.' In Domesday
Rogerus, co. Norf. Exceedingly
common in the 13th century all over
the country, giving us the nicks.
Hodge and Dodge, and through
them Hodgson, Hodgkins, Hodgkinson, &c., q.v. Roger vied with
Robert, John, and William for
popularity for several centuries.
In France, too, the name was a
favourite, the French proverb for
'There's a good time coming'
being 'Roger Bon Temps.'
Hodge is now an English synonym
for a peasant or agricultural
labourer. Once a knightly name,
Roger has fallen from his high
estate, and is, as Joan, ever among
the poor. Early registers teem with
the name. I furnish one or two instances for form's sake:

Adam fil. Rogeri, co. Linc., 1273. A.
Robert fil. Rogeri, co. Norf., ibid.
Eufemia fil. Rogeri. co. Suff., 20 Edw.
I. R.
Waltero Rogero, co. Soms., 1 Edw.
III: Kirby's Quest, p. 88.
Willelmus Rogerson, 1379: P. T. Yorks.
p. 135.
Rogerus Smyth, 1379: ibid.
1788. Married—John Cooper and Eliz.
Rogerson: St. Geo. Han. Sq. ii. 2.
1808. — James Rodgers and Mary
Spencer: ibid. p. 396.
London, 2, 189, 7, 2, 6; Boston (U.S.),
0, 336, 3, 0, 12.

Rokster.—Occup. 'the rokster,'
a woman who worked the distaff.
The terminative is the feminine
-ster, as in *spinster*, a synonymous
term.

'Sir, for Jack nor for Gille
Wille I turne my face,
Tille I have on this hille
Spun a space upon my rok.'
Towneley Mysteries.

'Rokke, of spynnynge': Prompt.
Parv.
Juliana Rokster, 1388. RR. 2.
Agnes Rockestre, C. R., 6 Hen. IV.

Perhaps now lost in the local
Rochester.

Roland.— Bapt.; v. Rowland.

1802. Married—Alex. Roland and Ann
Austin: St. Geo. Han. Sq. ii. 251.
London, 2; Philadelphia, 12.

Rolf, Rolfe, Rolfes, Rolph.
—Bapt. 'the son of Rudolph,' from
the nick. Rolf or Rolph. As
Ralph represented Randolph, so
Rolph or Rolf stood for Rudolph.
Lower says it is the same as Ralph,
and adds, 'The great landowner
Goisfrid de Bec, son of Rollo, and
grandson of Crispinus, baron of
Bec, is styled in Domesday "filius
Rolf"': Patr. Brit. p. 292.

Allan Rolfe, co. Camb., 1273. A.
Roger Rolf, co. Hunts, ibid.
John Rolf, co. Oxf., ibid.
1614. Robert Rolfe and Cicely Pratt:
Marriage Lic. (London), ii. 29.
1654. Married—Jasper Devenish and
Eliz. Rolph: St. Michael, Cornhill, p. 33.
1721. — Thomas Rolph and Ann Bates:
St. Mary Aldermary, p. 45.
London, 0, 24, 1, 5; Philadelphia, 2, 2,
0, 2.

Roll, Rolls, Rolles, Rowles.
—Bapt. 'the son of Ralph,' i. e.
Randolph or Radulph, from the
Norman-Fr. Raoul, the dim. of
which was Raoul-in, whence our
Rawlins and Rawlinsons, also in
some cases our Rollins and Rollin-
sons; v. Rawlin.

Raoul Partrer: v. Index, Wars of
English in France in the reign of Henry
VI.
Raoul le Saige: ibid.

Rolls, Rolles, or Rowles, are
genitive forms; cf. Williams for
William, or Jenkins for Jenkin.

1589. John Rolles, or Rowle, co. Devon:
Reg. Univ. Oxf. vol. ii. pt. ii. p. 170.
1594. Henry Rolle, or Rowles, co.
Devon: ibid. p. 202.
1611-2. Giles Rowles and Mary Stapley:
Marriage Lic. (London), ii. 10.
1647. Thomas Rolles (co. Devon) and
Florence Rolles: ibid. p. 280.

1648. Thomas Rolls and Eliz. Jenkins:
ibid. p. 281.
London, 2, 8, 1, 1; Philadelphia, 3, 1,
1, 0.

Roller.—? Occup.

Philip le Roulour, co. Soms., 1 Edw.
III: Kirby's Quest, p. 200.
London, 1.

Rolleston, Rollston, Rolston.
—Local, 'of Rolleston,' a parish in
co. Stafford. Cf. Roulston.

1609-10. William Rollstone, co. Soms.:
Reg. Univ. Oxf. vol. ii. pt. ii. p. 309.
1619-20. Thomas Rolleston, co. Devon:
ibid. p. 382.
1675. Bapt.—Frances, d. John Roules-
ton: St. Jas. Clerkenwell, i. 271.
Crockford, 4, 0, 1; Philadelphia, 1,
1, 1.

**Rollin, Rollins, Rollings,
Rollinson, Rolling.**—Bapt. 'the
son of Ralph,' from the dim. Rawlin or Rowlin, of which Rollin
was a popular variant (v. Rawlin).
The *g* in Rolling and Rollings is
an excrescence, as in Rawling or
Rawlings.

John Rolyns, co. Soms., 1 Edw. III:
Kirby's Quest, p. 125.
1701. Married—George Evelyn and
Rebecca Rollinson: Marriage Lic. (London), ii. 327.
1809. —Thomas Rollings and Harriet
Bishop: St. Geo. Han. Sq. ii. 408.
London, 1, 1, 2, 2, 0; Philadelphia, 3,
6, 1, 0, 3.

Rollinson.—Bapt. 'the son of
Rowland.' Many of the North-
English Rollinsons are thus descended. (For origin of the South-
English Rollinsons, v. preceding
article.) In the Furness district of
North Lancashire many changes
have been rung on Rowlandson,
the following being the chief, viz.
Rollandson and Rollingson. Such
entries as the following were
common:

William Rollandson, of Cartmell, 1596:
Lancashire Wills at Richmond, i. 237.
John Rollingson, of Cartmell, 1596:
ibid.
London, 2.

Rollison.—Bapt. A variant of
Rollinson, q.v.

1720. Married—Nicholas Adams and
Mary Rollison: St. Jas. Clerkenwell, i.
244.
1805. — William Simmonds and Sarah
Rollisson: St. Geo. Han. Sq. ii. 322.
Manchester, 1; Philadelphia, 3.

Rolph; v. Rolf.

Rolt.—Bapt. 'the son of Roald.' A common personal name in the 13th and 14th centuries. As to the truth of this derivation there cannot be the shadow of a doubt. Roald, which owing to its popularity was bound to leave descendants, was gradually sharpened into Roalt, and then became Rolt.

Ricardus fil. Roaldi: Pipe Roll, 11 Hen. II, p. 15.
Roaldus de Eston, cos. Oxon and Berks, Hen. III–Edw. I. K.
Rowald de Eston, cos. Oxon and Berks, ibid.
Alanus fil. Roaldi, co. Oxon, 34 Hen. III: BBB. p. 28.
Alanus fil. Rowaldi, co. Oxon, 1273. A.
1618. Walter Rolte and Frances Dixey: Marriage Lic. (London), ii. 66.
1745. Married—John Hillam and Eleanor Rolt: St. Geo. Han. Sq. i. 35.
London, 5; Philadelphia, 2.

Romain, Romaine, Roman. —Local, 'the Roman,' i.e. from Rome; cf. Janaway, Gascoigne, Portwine, Lubbock, &c.

John Romanus, co. Linc., 1273. A.
Reginald le Romayn, co. Linc., ibid.
Thomas Romeyn, London, 20 Edw. I. R.
John le Romayn. L.
Richard Romeyn, co. Soms., 1 Edw. III: Kirby's Quest, p. 96.
1789. Married—John Roman and Grace Kennell: St. Geo. Han. Sq. ii. 20.
1790. — John Goff and Ann Romaine: ibid. p. 51.
1796. — John Romain and Ann Jones: ibid. p. 156.
London, 0, 1, 0; Philadelphia, 2, 3, 7.

Romans; v. Rummans.

Rome.—Local, 'of Rome'; cf. Romaine, Janaway, &c.

Johannes de Rome, *hostiler*, 1379: P.T. Yorks. p. 148.
Ricardus de Rome, 1379: P. T. Howdenshire, p. 21.
1616. John Hudson and Isabell Rome: Marriage Lic. 45.
London, 3; Philadelphia, 1.

Romer.—Occup. 'the romer,' i.e. the pilgrim to Rome, a pilgrim.

'And religiouse romeris': Piers P. iv. 2321.
'And alle Rome renneres': ibid. 2337.

Cf. Pilgrim and Palmer.

Cristiana la Romere, co. Suff., 1273. A.
1675. Married — Crisstopher Romor and Martha Browne: St. Jas. Clerkenwell, i. 181.

1772.— Andrew Romer and Diana Shaw: St. Geo. Han. Sq. i. 222.
London, 6; Philadelphia, 3.

Romilly.—Local, 'of Romilly'; probably Romilly, a town in Savoy, near Geneva (Lower). The present Romillys are descendants of a French Protestant who settled in England at the beginning of the last century (v. Memoirs of Sir Samuel Romilly, i. 2). Romeley existed six hundred years ago, but is evidently of English origin. It either died out or became incorporated with Romeny, now Romney and Rumney.

Robert de Romeley, co. Camb., 1273. A.
Baldwin de Romeli, co. Camb., ibid.
Lucia de Romely, co. Camb., ibid.
Avice de Romelli, co. York, 20 Edw. I. R.
London, 2.

Romney; v. Rumney.

Ronald, Ronaldson.—Bapt. 'the son of Ronald.' The Scottish form of English Reynold, q.v.

London, 1, 7.

Ronson.—Bapt. 'the son of Rowland,' a North Lancashire abbreviation of Rowlandson; v. Roanson and Rownson.

Rood; v. Rudd.

Roodhouse.—Local; v. Roydhouse.

West Rid. Court Dir., 2.

Roof, Roofe, Rooff.—Bapt. 'the son of Rudolph'; v. Rolf, of which these are variants, like Rofe and Roff.

1791. Married — John Grounds and Mary Roofe: St. Geo. Han. Sq. ii. 68.
1792. — John Westley and Sarah Roof: ibid. p. 85.
London, 1, 1, 2; MDB. (co. Norfolk), 0, 5, 0.

Rook, Rooke. — Nick. 'the rook,' a nickname given probably to one with black hair or dark complexion. A.S. *hróc*, a rook; cf. Sparrowhawk, Hawk, Crow, &c.

Geoffrey le Roke, co. Oxf., 1273. A.
William le Ruk, co. Oxf., ibid.
Adam le Roc, co. Oxf., ibid.
Richard le Rouke, co. Soms., 1 Edw. III: Kirby's Quest, p. 113.
Hugh le Rook, co. Soms., 1 Edw. III: ibid. p. 147.
Richard Rook, C. R., 45 Edw. III.
1623. Richard Stacie and Frances Rooke: Marriage Lic. (London), ii. 120.

1665. Married — George Baker and Hannah Rooke: St. Jas. Clerkenwell, iii. 122.
London, 7, 13; Boston (U.S.), 0, 2.

Rooker.—Occup. 'the rocker,' i.e. the spinner; v. Rokster, and cf. Weaver and Webster.

Richard le Rockare, co. Oxf., 1273. A.
Ralph le Roker, co. Hunts, ibid.
1697. Married—Richard Rooker and Mary Slemaker: St. Jas. Clerkenwell, i. 218.
1751. — Francis Rooker and Eliz. Hatfield: ibid. p. 283.
London, 2.

Rookherd.—Occup. 'the rookherd,' a tender or keeper of rooks; cf. Gozzard, Swanherd, Coward, &c.

Henry le Rocherde, co. Oxf., 1273. A.

Rookledge.—Local; v. Routledge. A manifest corruption.

Root, Roote, Roots.—Bapt. 'the son of Root.' There is no prefix to early examples denoting a local derivation. No doubt Root was a personal name, Roots being the genitive form; cf. William and Williams, Jenkin and Jenkins.

Simon Rote, co. Hunts, 1273. A.
Peter Rote, co. Camb., ibid.
1623-4. William Roote (co. Essex) and Eliz. Dagnet: Marriage Lic. (London), ii. 136.
1745. Bapt.—Thomas, s. Robert Rootes: St. Jas. Clerkenwell, ii. 273.
1798. Married—James Root and Eliz. Camplin: St. Geo. Han. Sq. ii. 175.
London, 5, 2, 7; Philadelphia, 42, 0, 0.

Roper.—Occup. 'the roper,' a manufacturer of ropes; cf. N.E. Raper.

Peter le Roper, co. Notts, 1273. A.
Walter le Ropere, co. Camb., ibid.
Gerald Roppere, co. Suff., ibid.
John le Roper, co. Soms., 1 Edw. III: Kirby's Quest, p. 152.
1347. Thomas le Roper, rector of Eccles, co. Norf.: FF. ix. 296.
Rogerus Roper, *roper*, 1379: P. T. Yorks. p. 267.
1613. Bapt.—Richard, s. William Roper: St. Jas. Clerkenwell, i. 68.
London, 27; West Rid. Court Dir., 12; Philadelphia, 15.

Ropkins.—Bapt. 'the son of Robert,' from nick. Rob and suffix -*kin* (v. *kin*, Introd. p. 25). Ropkins is the genitive of Robkin with the *b* sharpened to *p*; cf. Hopkins for Hobkins. v. Robkin.

Rosamund; v. Roseaman.

Roscoe, Roscow.—Local (?). Mr. Lower says, 'Possibly a corruption of Roscrowe. It is certainly a Cornish name' (Patr. Brit. p. 293). I take leave to doubt this statement. I feel sure it is a Lancashire local surname, although I cannot find the spot.

Gilbert Roscoe, of Euxton (co. Lanc.), 1293 : Wills at Chester, i. 165.
James Roscoe, of Farnworth (co. Lanc.), 1594 : ibid.
John Roscow, of Leigh (co. Lanc.), 1594 : ibid.
London, 6, 0 ; Crockford, 0, 1 ; Manchester, 4, 1 ; MDB. (co. Lanc.), 2, 4 ; Philadelphia, 7, 0.

Rose.—(1) Bapt. 'the son of Rose.' Latin *rosa*, a rose. Very popular at the period surnames were becoming hereditary ; hence strongly represented in all our directories.

Thomas fil. Rose, co. Camb., 1273. A.
Richard fil. Rose, co. Notts, ibid.
Adam Costenoght et Rosa uxor ejus, 1379 : P. T. Yorks. p. 6.
Johannes Rose, 1379 : ibid. p. 9.
Rosa Held, 1379 : ibid. p. 18.

Or, again from the same period :

Johanna Rose-doghter, 1379 : P. T. Yorks. p. 33.
Isabella filia Rose, 1379 : ibid.
Rosa de Berlowe, 1379 : ibid.

(2) Local, 'of the rose,' i.e. at the rose-tree, or at the sign of the Rose.

John de la Rose, co. Oxf., 1273. A.
Robert de la Rose, co. Oxf., ibid.
Elena de la Ros, co. Oxf., ibid.
London, 86 ; Boston (U.S.), 49.

Roseaman, Rosoman, Rosemond, Rosamund.—Bapt. 'the son of Rosamund.' A common girl's name at the surname period. The suffix *-mond* or *-mund* became by corruption *-man* ; cf. Osman, Wyman, or Redman.

Rosamunda (without surname), co. Oxf., 1273. A.
Rosamond Udelin, Fines Roll, 10 Edw. I.
1469. Edith Rosamond : Cal. of Wills in Court of Husting (2).

The following occur in early Yorkshire pedigrees :

Rosamund Monford : Index, Visitation of York, 1563-4 (Harl. Soc.).
Rosamond Mallet : ibid.
Rosamond Clapham : ibid.

1665. Married—Thomas Chaplin and Rozeman Gowen : 'St. Jas. Clerkenwell, iii. 120.
1669. — James Bell and Rosaman Davis : ibid. p. 158.
1797. — Thomas Roseman and Eliz. Jupe : St. Geo. Han. Sq. ii. 167.
London, 1, 1, 0, 0 ; West Rid. Court Dir., 0, 1, 0, 0 ; Philadelphia, 0, 0, 0, 1 ; Boston (U.S.), 0, 0, 3, 0.

Rosewarne, Rosewarn. — Local, ' of Roswarne,' an estate in the parish of Camborne, co. Cornwall (Lower's Patr. Brit. p. 285).

London, 1, 0 ; Cornwall Court Dir., 1, 0 ; Philadelphia, 3, 0.

Rosewell; v. Roswell.

Roskell.—Local, 'of Rossgill.' Some small spot on the borders of North Lancashire and the West Riding that I have not discovered ; cf. Gaskell from Gasgill.

Hugh de Rasegille, co. York, 1273. A.
Walter de Rasegille, co. York, ibid.
Crystyan Rossegyll, 1563 : Visitation of Yorkshire (Harl. Soc.), p. 271.
Robert Rossegyll, 1563 : ibid.
John Roskell, of the Black poole, *yeoman*, 1628 : Lancashire Wills at Richmond, i. 237.
John Roskell, of the Greene, parish of Cartmel, 1664 : ibid.
London, 1 ; Manchester, 1.

Roskilly, Roskelly.—Local, ' of Roskilly,' an estate in St. Keverne, co. Cornwall, anciently the residence of the family (v. Lower's Patr. Brit. p. 294).

London, 3, 0 ; Cornwall Court Dir., 1, 0 ; Boston (U.S.), 0, 1.

Roskruge, Rosekroge. — Local, ' of Roscruge,' an estate in the parish of St. Anthony, co. Cornwall. It gave ' name and original,' says Hals, ' to a family of gentlemen now or lately in possession thereof' (Lower, quoting Gilbert's Cornwall).

Cornwall Court Dir., 1, 1.

Rosling, Rusling.—Bapt. 'the son of Rocelin.' This was at an early period popular in co. Lincoln as a personal name. As a result it is to that county we now look for representatives of the surname. Lower says, 'Rosling: a corruption of Roslyn, a village in co. Edinburgh.' He does not furnish a tittle of evidence. The final *g* is,

of course, an excrescence, as in Jennings.

' Three carucates which the sons of Rocelin hold,' temp. 1199 : The Lincolnshire Survey, p. 21.
Rocelinus de Bracton, co. Wilts, Hen. III-Edw. I. K.
Rocelin le Bunne, co. Wilts, 1273. A.
Roscelin de Bratton, co. Wilts, ibid.
Johanna Roscelin, co. Linc., ibid.
Thomas Roscelin, co. Norf., ibid.
Johannes Rosselyn, 1379 : P. T. Yorks. p. 178.
Emma Roscelyn, 1379 : P. T. Howdenshire, p. 1.
Robertus Roscelyn, 1379 : ibid. p. 4.
Richard Roscelyn, rector of Patesley, 1408 : FF. x. 28.
1628. Married—Samewell Randall and Frances Ruslinge : St. Mary Aldermary, p. 16.
London, 1, 0 ; MDB. (co. Lincoln), 4, 3 ; Philadelphia, 0, 5.

Rosoman; v. Roseaman.

Rossall, Rossell.—(1) Local, ' of Rossall,' near Fleetwood, co. Lanc. It was formerly a grange belonging to the abbey of Deulacres, co. Stafford. In Domesday it is styled Rushale. The following dwelt close by Rossall :

Margrett Rossall, of Bispham, *widdow*, 1578 : Lancashire Wills at Richmond, i. 237.
John Rossall, of Warbrecke, *yeoman*, 1618 : ibid.
Thomas Rossall, of Norbrecke, 1667 : ibid.
Richard Rossell, of Bispham, 1730 : ibid. ii. 216.

(2) Nick. ; v. Russell.

John Rossel, co. Soms., 1 Edw. III : Kirby's Quest, p. 86.
Preston, 1, 0 ; Manchester, 0, 1 ; Fleetwood (co. Lanc.), 1, 0 ; MDB. (co. Lanc.), 7, 0.

Rosser. — Bapt. 'the son of Rosser' (Welsh), whence Prosser (=ap-Rosser), q.v. Mr. Lower says, 'A dweller upon a heath, or upon a promontory.' This is quite untenable. He connects it with the Scottish Ross. It is a purely Welsh surname.

Rosser Morres. Z.
Robert ap-Rosser. H.
John Roser, co. Soms., 1 Edw. III : Kirby's Quest, p. 88.
William Roser, co. Soms., 1 Edw. III : ibid. p. 250.
1685. Bapt.—Anne, d. Thomas Rosser : St. Jas. Clerkenwell, i. 313.
1700. — Gload, s. Lewis Rossear : ibid. p. 386.
London, 4 ; Philadelphia, 1.

Rossiter. — (1) Local, ' of Wroxeter,' a parish in co. Salop. So says Mr. Lower, and I see no reason to doubt the statement (v. Patr. Brit. p. 294). (2) Local, ' of Rochester.' This derivation is probably in most cases the correct one. From Roucester to Rossiter would be an inevitable step.

William de Roucester, co. Norf., 33 Hen. III : FF. vii. 276.
Eustace de Roucestre, co. Essex, Hen. III–Edw. I. K.
Peter de Roucestre, co. Suff., 1273. A.
1581. John Rociter, co. Soms.: Reg. Univ. Oxf. vol. ii. pt. ii. p. 109.
1601. Married—John Pratt and Joane Rosseter : St. Jas. Clerkenwell, i. 25.
1641. — Dudleye Rositer and Sara Wilson : ibid. p. 74.
1799. — Mathew Rossiter and Frances Richmond : St. Geo. Han. Sq. ii. 198.
London, 4 ; Philadelphia, 19.

Rosthern, Roston, Rostron. —Local ; v. Rawsthorne.

Roswell, Rosewell. — ? Local, ' de Rosseville ' (?). Mr. Lower writes, ' Said to be a corruption of the French Rosseville. It is therefore local, but I know not the place. Kent, in his Grammar of Heraldry, speaks of the Rev. S. Rosewell, of London, M.A., as descended from the Rosewells of Somersetshire, Wiltshire, and Devon, who came in with the Conqueror ' : Patr. Brit. p. 295. I do not think there is any ground for this. I believe the West-country Rosewells, Ruswells, Rowsells, and Rousells are all mere variants of Russell (v. Rowsell). I cannot find any early Rossevilles in English registers.

1519. Adam Russell, or Ruswell, or Rossewell : Reg. Univ. Oxf. i. 112.
1580. Alex. Ruswell, co. Soms.: ibid. ii. 92.
1599. John Roswell, co. Soms.: ibid. p. 237.
1606-7. Henry Rosewell, co. Devon : ibid. p. 293.

Rowsell seems to be the modern Somersetshire form.

London, 3, 1.

Rotherham. —Local, ' of Rotherham,' a parish in the W. Rid. of Yorks.

Robertus de Roderham, 1379 : P. T. Yorks. p. 27.

1591-2. Edmund Rotheram, co. Bedf. : Reg. Univ. Oxf. vol. ii. pt. ii. p. 188.
1709. Buried—Sara, d. William Rotheram : St. Dionis Backchurch, p. 278.
1711. — Richard, s. William Rodderam : ibid. p. 150.
London, 3 ; MDB. (West Rid. Yorks), 2.

Rothero. —Bapt. ; v. Prothero. Shrewsbury, 1.

Rothwell. —Local, ' of Rothwell,' parishes in cos. Lincoln and Northants, and also a parish in the W. Rid. Yorks.

Robert de Rothewelle, co. Linc., 1273. A.
John de Rothewell, cotoler, 7 Edw. II : Freemen of York, i. 15.
Johanna de Rothewell, 1379 : P. T. Yorks. p. 103.
Johannes de Rothewell, 1379 : ibid. p. 183.
1598. Married—Thomas Olyver and Joane Rothewelle : St. Michael, Cornhill, p. 16.
London, 9 ; Philadelphia, 9.

Rottenherring. — Nick. ; cf. Poorfish and Goodherring. ' This name occurs in the archives of Hull in the 14th century ' : Lower, Patr. Brit. p. 295.

John Rotenherring, 5 Edw. III : Freemen of York, i. 26.

Rough. —Nick. ' the rough,' the harsh, the uncouth.

Henry le Rogh, co. Soms., 1 Edw. III : Kirby's Quest, p. 132.
London, 1 ; Oxford, 1.

Roughley. —Local, ' of Roughley,' i.e. Roughlee Booth, a township in the parish of Whalley, co. Lanc.

1592. Richard Roughley, of Windle : Wills at Chester, i. 165.
1613. Thomas Roughley, of Sutton : ibid.
1664. Richard Roughley, of Sutton, co. Lanc.: ibid. iii. 229.
Liverpool, 2.

Roughton. —Local, ' of Roughton,' two parishes, one in co. Lincoln, the other in co. Norfolk.

1378. John de Roughton, dean of the rural deanery of Ingworth, co. Norf.: FF. vi. 370.
1418. Thomas Roughton, Norwich : ibid. iii. 603.
1797. Married—William Roughton and Susanna Irvin : St. Geo. Han. Sq. ii. 159.
Manchester, 1 ; MDB. (co. Leicester), 1.

Roulston. —Local, ' of Roulston,' a parish in co. Lincoln ;

occasionally, no doubt, confounded with Rolleston, q.v.

MDB. (co. Leicester), 2.

Round, Rowand. —Local, ' at the rowan,' from residence beside a rowan-tree ; cf. Ash and Nash, Oak and Oakes, Birch, &c. The excrescent *d* is natural ; cf. Simmonds and Hammond, and also *ribbon* and *riband*. Thus we find Rowntree entered :

Christopher Roundtree, 1687 : St. Jas. Clerkenwell, i. 322.

There may be a second derivation, but I have not hit upon it, supposing it exists.

1626. Bapt. — Dorothy, d. William Round : St. Jas. Clerkenwell, i. 103.
1799. Married—Thomas Round and Mary Wallis : St. Geo. Han. Sq. ii. 201.
London, 8, o ; Crake Valley (Ulverston), o, 1 ; Philadelphia, 4, o.

Rous, Rouse, Rowse, Ruse, Russ. —Nick. ' le rous,' from the reddish complexion of hair or face ; v. Russell.

Alexander le Rous, co. Camb., 1273. A.
Juliana la Rouse, co. Oxf., ibid.
Alicia Rouze, co. Camb., ibid.
John le Rus, co. Linc., ibid.
Gilbert Russ, co. Linc., ibid.
Lucia la Russe, co. Oxf., ibid.
Robert le Rous, co. Soms., 1 Edw. III : Kirby's Quest, p. 102.
1643-4. Thomas Salter and Philippa Rous : Marriage Lic. (London), ii. 273.
1659. Buried—George Ruse : St. Peter, Cornhill, i. 212.
1666. Thomas Rowse and Mary Norwood : Marriage Lic. (Faculty Office), p. 94.
1668. Married — Nicolas Rouse and Jone Woodmus : St. Jas. Clerkenwell, iii. 140.
1767. — Samuel Russ and Mary Jones : St. Geo. Han. Sq. i. 161.
London, 2, 21, 2, 3, 7.

Rousby. —Local, ' of Roxby ' (?), a parish in co. Lincoln, nine miles from Barton-on-Humber.

Geoffrey de Rauceby, co. Linc., Hen. III–Edw. I. K.
Adam de Rouceby, co. York, 1273. A.
Iseware de Rouceby, co. Linc., ibid.
Ranulf de Rouceby, co. Linc., ibid. Crockford, 1.

Rousell ; v. Rowsell.

Routledge, Rookledge, Rucklidge. —Local, ' of Routledge.' I cannot find the spot. It has representatives in every part of the world. It is a great Border name, and whether it be Scotch or

English, it must live for ever. The suffix *-ledge* is *-lake*; v. Depledge. For other variants, v. Rutledge.

1781. Married—John Routledge and Ann Jones: St. Geo. Han. Sq. i. 327.
1789.— Robert Routledge and Phœbe Sherol: ibid. ii. 27.
London, 8, 0, 0; York, 1, 1, 1; MDB. (co. Cumberland), 15, 0, 0.

Row, Rowe, Roe.—(1) Bapt. 'the son of Rowland,' from the nick. Rowe. A once familiar personal name on the Scottish border and in North England generally.

Rowe Elwald, 1515: TTT. p. 205.
Rowe Crosier, 1586: QQQ. p. xxxvi.

(2) Local, 'of the row,' i.e. the row of cottages. M.E. *rowe*, A.S. *raw* and *rawe*; North Eng. *raw*. v. Roe (3) and Raw.

William del Rawe, 1350: DDD. vol. ii. p. 340.

The following names occur in the list of the mayors of Macclesfield:

Richard del Rowe, 1368.
Stephen del Rowe, 1426.
Roger del Rowe, 1441.
Hugh Rowe, 1477.
Roger Rowe, 1581, &c., &c., &c.
Charles Roe, 1747.

Evidently all were of the same family (v. East Cheshire, ii. 464-8).

London, 11, 44, 18.

Rowan.—Local, 'at the rowan,' from residence beside some prominent rowan-tree; v. Roan, Round, and Rowntree. A North-English and Scottish surname.

1714. Married—Edmund Roune and Anne Nash: St. Mary Aldermary, p. 42.
1805.— Charles Maclaren and Sarah Rowan: St. Geo. Han. Sq. ii. 336.
London, 2; Philadelphia, 69.

Rowand; v. Round.

Rowbotham, Rowbottom, Robotham, Robottom.—Local, 'at the roe-bottom,' from residence in the depressed ground frequented by the deer. I cannot find the spot, but the name sprung up in the same district as Shufflebotham, Winterbottom, and Ramsbottom (q.v.), somewhere in the south-east corner of Lancashire. The surname is strongly represented across the Atlantic.

1546. Married — Robert Rowe and Dorythye Robotom: St. Michael, Cornhill, p. 5.

1592. Oliver Robotham, co. Bucks: Reg. Univ. Oxf. vol. ii. pt. ii. p. 192.
1613. Thomas Rowbotham, of Winwick, co. Lanc.: Wills at Chester, i. 165.
1626. William Rowbotham and Sarah Owen: Marriage Lic. (London), ii. 169.
Sheffield, 6, 1, 0, 0; Manchester, 11, 2, 1, 0; MDB. (co. Lincoln), 3, 5, 1, 1; Philadelphia, 17, 5, 1, 0.

Rowcliffe, Rawcliffe.—Local, 'of Rawcliff,' a parish in the W. Rid. Yorks, eleven miles from Selby; also a township in the parish of Snaith, W. Rid. Yorks.

Ricardus de Rouclyff, 1379: P. T. Yorks. p. 127.
Henricus de Rouclyffe, 1379: ibid. p. 209.
John Rawcliffe, of Chipping, 1682: Lancashire Wills at Richmond, ii. 204.
George Rawcliffe, of Ribchester, 1729: ibid.
London, 8, 0; Leeds, 0, 1; Philadelphia, 0, 1.

Rowcroft; v. Rycroft.

Rowe; v. Row.

Rowell.—Local, 'of Rowell,' an extra-parochial hamlet in the union of Winchcomb, co. Glouc.

Letitia de Rowelle, co. Bedf., 1273.
1621. Bapt.—Ann, d. Thomas Rowell: St. Jas. Clerkenwell, i. 91.
London, 11; MDB. (co. Devon), 6; Oxford, 6; Boston (U.S.), 37.

Rowland, Rowlands, Rowlandson.—Bapt. 'the son of Roland.' Roland or Orlando was the nephew of the great Charles, who fell at Roncesvalles.

'Before the Duke the minstrel sprung,
And loud of Charles and Roland sung.'
                         Walter Scott.

Rouland de Flamville, Hen. III-Edw. I. K.
Robert Rouland, co. Wilts, 1273. A.
William Roulond, co Worc., ibid.
Roulandus Bloet. C.
Roulandus fil. Roulandi. T.
1683. Bapt.—Saray, d. William Rowland: St. Jas. Clerkenwell, i. 303.
1790. Married—Thomas Rowlandson and Anne Waters: St. Geo. Han. Sq. ii. 43.
1803. — Samuel Richardson and Eliz. Rowlands: ibid. p. 284.
London, 28, 11, 2; Philadelphia, 86, 1, 0.

Rowlatt, Rowlett.—Bapt. 'the son of Ralph,' from the Fr. Raoul, dim. Raoulin (whence our Rawlin and Rowling) and second dim. Raoulet, whence Rowlett and Rowlatt; cf. Emmett from Emm (Emma) or Hewlett from Hew (Hugh).

'June 25, 1679. Mr. John Rawlett appointed to Lectureship' (of St. Nicholas, Newcastle-on-Tyne). He married a daughter of a Mr. Butler. 'They had been some time in love together, but he falling sick (at her request, and that she might bear his name) married her upon his deathbed, and left her both a maid, a wife, and widow': Brand's Newcastle, i. 315.
1710. Married—Edmund Reade and Elisabeth Rowlett: St. Mary Aldermary (London), p. 39.
London, 2, 1; Philadelphia, 0, 3.

Rowles. — Bapt. Probably 'the son of Rowland,' from a nick. Rowl; v. Roll and Rowlinson.

John Roules, co. Soms., 1 Edw. III: Kirby's Quest, p. 139.
London, 1; Oxford, 8.

Rowley.—Local, 'of Rowley,' a parish in the E. Rid. Yorks; also a parish in co. Stafford. Both places have furnished surnames.

Adam de Roulay, co. York, 1273. A.
Gervase Rolegh, co. Soms., 1 Edw. III: Kirby's Quest, p. 105.
John Roley, co. Soms., 1 Edw. III: ibid. p. 106.
William Roleghe, co. Soms., 1 Edw. III: ibid. p. 205.
Johannes de Rouley, 1379: P. T. Yorks. p. 169.
1607. Richard Rowley, co. York: Reg. Univ. Oxf. vol. ii. pt. ii. p. 295.
1613. Benjamin Rowley, co. Salop: ibid. p. 332.
Ralph Rowley, of Over Peover, 1631: Wills at Chester, i. 188.
London, 27; Philadelphia, 27.

Rowling, Rowlings.—Bapt. 'the son of Ralph,' from the dim. Rawlin. Of course the *g* is an excrescence, as in Rawling or Rawlings. For further instances v. Rawlin.

1768. Married — James Soleirol and Mary Rowlings: St. Geo. Han. Sq. i. 173.
London, 3, 0; West Rid. Court Dir., 2, 0.

Rowlinson.—Bapt. 'the son of Rowland,' a corrupted form. It is found commonly in the wills of the great Rowlandson family of Furness, North Lancashire. v. Rollinson.

John Rowlinson, of Haverthwaite, 1608: Lancashire Wills at Richmond, i. 238.
Robert Rowlinson, of Knott in Ulverston, 1640: ibid.
Philadelphia, 1.

Rownson, Ronson, Roanson.—Bapt. 'the son of Rowland.' All these are abbreviated and corrupted forms of Rowlandson, and are peculiar to North Lancashire; cf. in the same district Townson for Tomlinson (pronounced Toneson).

1607. Richard Rowlandson, or Rownesonn: Lancashire Wills at Richmond, i. 237-8.
1614. Michael Rowanson, of Cartmell: ibid.
1639. John Rowanson, or Rownson, of Warton: ibid.
1715. John Rowlandson, or Rownson: ibid. ii. 216.

Many more instances might be furnished.

London, 2, 0, 0; Preston, 0, 1, 1; Preesall (co. Lanc.), 0, 1, 0; MDB. (co. Cumb.), 0, 1, 0.

Rowntree, Rountree, Roantree.—Local, 'at the rowan-tree' (the mountain ash), from residence beside such a tree. A well-known North-English surname; cf. Crabtree, Plumptre, Peartree.

William Rowentree, co. York. W. 16.
Ralph Roentree, co. York. W. 20.
1659. Bapt.—Eliz., d. John Roundtree: St. Jas. Clerkenwell, i. 204.
1683. — Mary, d. John Rantree: ibid. p. 301.
1809. Married—John Sweeting and Jean Rontree: St. Geo. Han. Sq. ii. 417.
London, 4, 0, 0; Crockford, 2, 2, 0; MDB. (North Rid. Yorks), 0, 4, 0; (East Rid. Yorks), 6, 0, 1; Philadelphia, 0, 3, 3.

Rowse.—Nick.; v. Rous, a variant.

1547. Buried—Anne Rowse: St. Peter, Cornhill, i. 108.
1618. Henry Rowse and Eliz. Matthewes: Marriage Lic. (London), ii. 65.
London, 2.

Rowsell, Rowsel, Rousell.—Nick.; variants of Russell, q.v.

London, 10, 0, 0; Crockford, 6, 0, 0; MDB. (co. Somerset), 11, 1, 3.

Rowson.—Bapt. 'the son of Ralph,' a variant of Rawson, q.v.

Reginald Rowson, of Lyme, 1611: Wills at Chester, i. 166.
Thurston Rowson, of Stockport, 1620: ibid.
London, 2; Liverpool, 5; Manchester, 1; Philadelphia, 1.

Rowton.—Local, 'of Rowton,' a chapelry in the parish of Adderbury, co. Salop.

Richard de Routon', co. Salop, 1273. A.
Ivo de Roweton, co. Salop, ibid.
London, 3; Oxford, 1.

Roxbrough, Roxburgh. — Local, 'of Roxburgh,' capital of the Scottish county of that name.

London, 1, 2; Oxford, 1, 0.

Roxby.—Local, 'of Roxby': (1) a parish in co. Lincoln; (2) a township in the parish of Pickhill, N. Rid. Yorks; (3) a chapelry in the parish of Hinderwell, N. Rid. Yorks.

1776. Married—George Creick and Mary Roxbee: St. Geo. Han. Sq. i. 260.
Crockford, 3; MDB. (East Rid. Yorks), 2.

Roy. — Nick. 'le roi,' the king; v. King and Rex.

Simon Roy, co. Camb., 1273. A.
Edonia Roy, 1379: P. T. Yorks. p. 31.
Galfridus Roye, 1379: ibid.
1614. Thomas Downton and Anne Roye: Marriage Lic. (London), ii. 27.
London, 7; Boston (U.S.), 4.

Royce, Royse.—Bapt. 'the son of Royse'; v. Yonge, i. 420, where Rohais, wife of Gilbert de Gaunt (1156), is mentioned; also Roese de Lucy, wife of Fulbert de Dover (temp. Hen. II). The name seems to have been always feminine.

Roysia Avered, 1273. A.
Henry fil. Royse, ibid.
William fil. Royse, ibid.
Radulph fil. Roysie, ibid.
Roys le Bon'e (fem.), ibid.
Roger Roys, co. Northampt., 20 Edw. I. R.

In the registers of St. Mary Aldermary the name is spelled Roise (1639), Royce (1634), Royse (1639), Roys (1636).

1720. Richard Roys and Mary Marsh: Marriage Lic. (London), ii. 341.
London, 2, 0; Doncaster, 0, 1; Philadelphia, 2, 1.

Roycraft, -croft; v. Rycroft.

Royd, Royds.—Local, 'at the rode' (so always spelt in early records), an old term implying a *ridding*, or clearing. Compounded with the Christian name of the proprietor or settler we get Murgatroyd (Mergret = Margaret) or Ormerod (Orme). Whitaker, in his Hist. and Ant. of Craven, has such spots as Tomrode and Wilimotrode (Wilmot = William): p. 199. Sometimes 'royd' is compounded with the names of the hills cleared, as in Holroyd or Acroyd; sometimes with the profession of the

resident, as Monkroyd or Smithroyd (Whitaker, p. 199); sometimes with a word descriptive of the locality, as in Huntroyd. The glossary to Hulton's Coucher Book of Whalley Abbey says: 'Roda, an assart or clearing. Rode land is used in this sense in modern German, in which the verb *roden* means to clear. The combination of the syllable *rod, rode,* or *royd* with some other term, or with the name of an original settler, has, no doubt, given to particular localities such designations as Huntroyd, Ormerod, &c.' See Notes and Queries, 1st Ser., vol. v. p. 571, for further authorities. Dr. Whitaker styles it 'a participial substantive of the provisional verb *rid*, to clear or grub up': see Hist. Whalley, 3rd edit., p. 364. v. Roades for further instances.

Johannes del Rode, 1379: P. T. Yorks. p. 154.
Adam de Roides, 1379: ibid. p. 161.
Johannes del Rodes, 1379: ibid. p. 292.
Crockford, 0, 9; Philadelphia, 0, 3.

Roydhouse, Roodhouse, Roadhouse. — Local, 'at the royd-house,' i.e. from residence in the house on the *royd,* or clearing; v. Royd, Ormerod, Murgatroyd, &c.

Henricus del Rodehouse, 1379: P. T. Yorks. p. 194.
1786. Married—Edward Cox and Eliz. Rodhouse: St. Geo. Han. Sq. i. 393.
London, 1, 0, 0; Leeds, 0, 2, 0; Rotherham, 0, 0, 1; West Rid. Court Dir., 0, 0, 1; Philadelphia, 2, 0, 0.

Roylance.—Local; v. Rylands.

Royle.—Local; v. Ryle.

Royse.—Bapt.; v. Royce.

Royston.—Local, 'of Royston': (1) a parish in W. Rid. Yorks, near Barnsley; (2) a parish partly in co. Camb. and partly in co. Hertford.

1632. Married—William Styll and Eliz. Royston: St. Jas. Clerkenwell, i. 63.
London, 4; MDB. (West Rid. Yorks), 4.

Rubbatham.—Local. A curious corruption of Rowbotham, q.v.

Southport, 1.

Rubery.—Local, 'of Rowberrow,' a parish in co. Somerset, four miles from Axbridge. The references I furnish are amply sufficient to prove my statement.

1585. Anthony Rouborow, co. Soms. : Reg. Univ. Oxf. vol. ii. pt. ii. p. 145.
1750. Married—Charles Ruberry and Eliz. Clarke: St. Geo. Han. Sq. i. 43.
1765. — Benjamin Morris and Mary Rubery : ibid. p. 150.
London, 2 ; Philadelphia, 1.

Rucklidge; v. Routledge. A manifest corruption.

Rudd, Rood.—Local, 'at the rood,' i. e. cross, from residence thereby ; cf. Cross, Crouch, Crossman, Crotchman, &c. v. Rodd.

Margaret atte Rude. J.
William de la Rude, co. Southampt., 1273. A.
Walter Rud, co. Derby, ibid.
Agnes Rudde, co. Camb., ibid.
Ralph Rudde, co. Linc., ibid.
Richard atte Reode, co. Soms., 1 Edw. III : Kirby's Quest, p. 254.
John atte Rude, C. R., 30 Edw. III.
1554. George Rudd, or Roode: Reg. Univ. Oxf. i. 224.
1620-1. Thomas Rudd and Eliz. Greene: Marriage Lic. (London), ii. 95.
1779. Married—John Rood and Susanna Sturton : St. Geo. Han. Sq. i. 297.
London, 16, 1 ; Philadelphia, 4, 1.

Ruddiman ; v. Rudman.

Ruddock, Ruddick, Reddock, Rudduck, Reddick.—Nick. 'the ruddock,' i.e. the robin redbreast ; cf. Sparrow, Nightingale, &c. Reddock is a variant.

'The tame ruddocke, and the coward kite.'
Chaucer, Assembly of Fowls, l. 349.
Edward Ruddock, co. York. W. 16.
Ralph Ruddoc, co. Herts, 1273. A.
1604. Married—William Redock and Anne Squier: St. Mary Aldermary, p. 10.
1799. — Robert Hewison and Barbara Ruddock : St. Geo. Han. Sq. ii. 209.
1803. — Thomas Reddock and Mary Blake : ibid. p. 278.
1807. — Edward Long and Amelia Rudduck : ibid. p. 369.
London, 5, 3, 1, 0, 0 ; Philadelphia, 0, 0, 0, 5, 3.

Rudge.—(1) Local, 'of Rudge,' a township in the parish of Pattingham, co. Salop. (2) Local, 'at the ridge' ; v. Rugg and Ridge. (3) Nick. 'le rouge.' Fr. *rouge*, red ; taken from the ruddy complexion ; cf. Rufus and Russell. I have no evidence for (1), and therefore must suppose (2) and (3) to be the true parents.

John le Rug, co. Oxf., 1273. A.
Mariot Ruge, co. Oxf., ibid.
Richard le Ruge, co. Essex, ibid.
Osbert le Rugge, co. Kent, ibid.
1686. Married—Thomas Rudge and Martha Hernshaw : St. Mary Aldermary, p. 33.
London, 3 ; Oxford, 3 ; Philadelphia, 3.

Rudkin, Rudkins.—(1) Bapt. 'the son of Rudolph' (?), dim. Rudkin ; cf. Watkin, Wilkin, &c. As Rudolph, saving in the form of Rolf, was not common in England, it is probable Rudkin and Rudkins are of Dutch extraction and modern immigration. I find no early instances. (2) Nick. 'the Rutterkin.' Since writing the above it has occurred to me that this is but the Dutch Rutterkin (v. Rutter). It would naturally be found on the East coast.

London, 6, 1 ; MDB. (co. Lincoln), 2, 0.

Rudman, Ruddiman.—? Nick. 'the roodman,' i.e. the man who lived by the rood or cross ; v. Rudd. An exactly analogous case is that of Cross and Crossman. The *i* in Ruddiman is euphonic ; cf. Ottaway and Greenaway for Ottway and Greenway. Perhaps both Rudman and Ruddiman represent the German Rudmann. I have no proof of the derivation I have given above.

1682. Bapt.—Ann, d. Christopher Rudman : St. Jas. Clerkenwell, i. 297.
1760. Married—James Taylor and Eliz. Ruddiman : St. Geo. Han. Sq. i. 94.
1780. — George Rudman and Mercy Brice : ibid. p. 315.
London, 1, 2.

Ruff.—Bapt. 'the son of Rudolph,' through the popular form Rolf, whence such variants as Rofe, Roff, Roof, and Ruff ; cf. Raffe for Ralph, from Randolph. The following entries will be sufficient to show that Roff and Ruff are the same :

1696. Bapt.—Susan, d. John and Eliz. Roffe : St. Jas. Clerkenwell, i. 366.
1697. — William, s. John and Eliz. Ruffe : ibid. p. 372.
1698. — Sarah, d. John and Eliz. Roffe : ibid. p. 377.
London, 5 ; Philadelphia, 16.

Rufus.—Nick. 'the red.' Latin *rufus*, red. A common entry in the Hundred Rolls ; cf. Faber for Wright.

Martin Ruffus, co. Oxf., 1273. A.
Walter Rufus, co. Oxf., ibid.
William Ruffus, co. Northumb., 20 Edw. I. R.
London, 1 ; Philadelphia, 1.

Rugg.—Local, 'at the rigg,' from residence on the rigg or rugg of the hill (v. Ridge). That Rugg is a variant of Rigg is certain. The surname Ridgway (i.e. the way over the ridge) is occasionally found as Rudgway. In the Index to Reg. Univ. Oxf. it is spelt Ridgeway, Rydgewaye and Rudgwaye.

John Rigge, or Ryge, or Rugge, 1506: Reg. Univ. Oxf. i. 45.
1700. Bapt.—William, s. William Rugg : St. Jas. Clerkenwell, i. 390.
London, 5 ; Boston (U.S.), 11.

Rumball, Rumble, Rumbles, Rumbol, Rumbold, Rumboll.—Bapt. 'the son of Reinbold' (Yonge, ii. 378) ; v. Rimbault. In Domesday there are recorded Reinbald, co. Worc., and Reinbold, co. Soms. Lower adds Rumbaldus. Cf. the local Rumboldswyke, a parish in dioc. Chichester. The surname has run riot in corrupted forms. The following is a curious proof of this statement :—

'After the Dissolution, King Henry VIII, in the year 1545, granted the impropriate rectory (of Keteringham, co. Norf.) to Robert Rumbold, alias Reynbald, and his heirs, to be held *in capite* by knight's service ; and in 1558, Anne wife of Benjamin Reynbald...had livery of it' : FF. v. 90.

To this day Rumball is a popular surname in cos. Norfolk and Suffolk. For a curious imitative corruption, v. Rainbird.

Roger Rumbold, co. Camb., 1273. A.
Adam Rumbald, co. Bucks, ibid.
Reynebaud le Paumer, co. Norf., ibid.
Rombald Cosin, co. Oxf., ibid.
1665. John Rumboll and Joane Jether : Marriage Alleg. (Canterbury), p. 111.
1688. Married — Thomas Watts and Anne Rumball : St. Mary Aldermary, London, p. 34.
1785. — Daniel Prale and Mary Rumble : St. Geo. Han. Sq. i. 370.
London, 4, 5, 1, 2, 3, 1 ; MDB. (co. Norfolk) (Rumball), 2 ; (Suffolk), 3.

Rumbelow. — Nick. 'Rumbelow,' a sobriquet for a sailor. Rumbelow was the sailor's 'Heave-ho' of later days, and the burden of all early sea-songs. In 'The Squire of Low Degree' it is said—

'Your mariners shall synge arow,
Heyhow, and rumbylow.'

Halliwell says, 'The burden of the Cornwall furry-day song is, "With halantow rumbelow."' As seen below, Rumbelow is found as a Cornish surname. 'Well, old Rumbelow, how are you?' would be the kind of way in which the sobriquet arose. The Constable of Nottingham Castle in 1369 was one Stephen Rumbilowe (v. my English Surnames, 2nd edit. p. 512).

John Rumbelow: Reg. St. Columb Major, p. 248.
Mary Rumbelow: ibid.
John Rumbelowe, or Rumblowe, B.A., 1615: Reg. Univ. Oxf. vol. ii. pt. iii. p. 339.
1803. Married—William Rumbelow and Charlotte Bush: St. Geo. Han. Sq. ii. 286.
MDB. (co. Suffolk), 4.

Rumble(s, Rumbol(l, Rumbold ; v. Rumball.

Rumfitt, Rumford.—Local, 'of Romford,' a parish in co. Essex. The corruption is a natural one ; cf. Brumfitt for Broomfield.

1796. Married—John Johnson and Mary Rumford: St. Geo. Han. Sq. ii. 114.
London, 2, 2 ; York, 1, 0 ; Philadelphia, 0, 7.

Rumley ; v. Rumney.

Rummans,   Rummens, Rumens, Rummons, Romans.—? Bapt. 'the son of Rumin' (?). Lower, quoting Ferguson, says, 'Rumun,' an Old Norse personal name.' This view seems confirmed by the fact that it is found early on the East coast.

John Rumin, co. Linc., 1273. A.

But v. Romaine, of which it may be but a vulgar corruption. Romans is found in the London Dir. side by side with Romaine. Rummen in the first of the following instances seems to be a corrupted form of Romaine :

1767. Married—William Rummen and Mary Hine : St. Geo. Han. Sq. i. 168.
1774. — John Rummins and Ann Faulkner: ibid. p. 247.
1802. — John Rumens and Marg. Catley : ibid. ii. 282.
London, 1, 2, 1, 0, 1 ; Middlesbrough, 0, 0, 0, 1, 0.

Rumminger. — Occup. 'the rummager,' a sailor who stowed away luggage in the hold of vessels. 'The master must prouide a perfect mariner called a *romager*, to raunge and bestow all merchandize in such place as is conuenient' (Hackluyt's Voyages, iii. 862) ; v. *rummage* in Skeat's Dict.

'Robert Rommongoure, alias Robert Copehed de Branketre, Rommongoure, alias Robert Copehed de Nestede, Rommongoure' : Pardons Rolls, 5-21 Ric. II, Anno 8, 1384-5.
Honorius le Rumongour. N.

For 'ing,' cf. Messinger for Messager, Pottinger for Potager, &c.

1589. Married—William Rumenger and Joane Robinson : St. Jas. Clerkenwell, i. 14.
1594. Bapt. — Elizabeth, d. William Rummenger: ibid. p. 28.

Rumney, Romney, Rumley.—(1) Local, 'of Romney,' two parishes in co. Kent. (2) Local, 'of Romilly' (q.v.), by change of *l* to *n* (cf. *baluster* and *banister*). There can be no doubt that nearly all our Romneys, Rumneys, and Rumleys are so derived. Rumney, a parish in co. Monmouth, does not seem to have given birth to any surname.

Baldwin de Rumeny, co. Worc., Hen. III-Edw. I. K.
Baldwin de Rumely, co. Worc., ibid.
Baldwin de Romeny, co. Oxf., 1273. A.
Baldwin de Romely, co. Camb., ibid.
John de Romeny, co. Oxf., ibid.
John de Romely, co. Camb., ibid.
1409. John Romley, rector of Brandeston, co. Norf.: FF. viii. 200.
1413. William Rumley, rector of Brandeston, co. Norf.: ibid.
1607. Richard Rumney, co. Cumb.: Queen's Coll. : Reg. Univ. Oxf. vol. ii. pt. ii. p. 296.
MDB. (co. Cumb.), 4, 0, 0 ; Philadelphia, 3, 1, 0 ; Boston (U.S.), 9, 1, 1.

Rump. — Bapt. 'the son of Rumpe,' probably a nick. of Humphrey, the initials R and H being interchangeable in the nicks. of personal names ; cf. Hodge for Roger, Hick for Richard, or Hob for Robert. The surname still lives in the counties where it is found six centuries ago.

Geoffrey fil. Rumphar', co. York, 1273. A.

The above looks like Humphrey in full with R for H.

Casse Rumpe, co. Cumb., 1273. A.
Robert Rumpe, of Cawston, co. Norf., 1521: FF. vi. 266.

Although this derivation is satisfactory to a certain degree, it must not be forgotten that there is a well-known German surname Rumpp. The two may have a common parent. Should that be the case, the above solution would have to be given up.

Norwich, 5 ; MDB. (co. Norfolk), 5.

Rumsey.—Local, 'of Romsey,' a parish in co. Hants, near Southampton ; cf. Rumney for Romney.

Walter de Romesy, co. Soms., 1 Edw. III : Kirby's Quest, p. 91.
John de Romesy, co. Soms., 1 Edw. III : ibid. p. 143.
John Rumsey, 1536 : Reg. Univ. Oxf. i. 186.
Walter Rumzey, 1600 : ibid. vol. ii. pt. ii. p. 241.
1670-1. John Rumsey and Eliz. Fisher : Marriage Lic. (Faculty Office), p. 116.
London, 10 ; MDB. (co. Hants), 1 ; Philadelphia, 7.

Runacres, Ranacre, Ranigar.—Local, 'of Ranacre.' I cannot find this Lancashire spot, but it is the parent of these three surnames ; cf. Greenacre or Greenacres, Whittaker, &c. The suffix is *-acre*, a field. At first the place would be styled Ravenacre, i.e. the field of Raven, the first proprietor ; v. Raven, Rawnsley, Ransford, &c.

1592. Thomas Ranicars, of Prescot : Wills at Chester, i. 158.
1623. George Ranicar, of Pinnington : ibid. ii. 180.
1641. Richard Ranikers, of Pinnington : ibid.
1665. Piers Ranakers, of Pennington : ibid. iii. 218.
1666. John Renicar, or Renicars, of Atherton : ibid. p. 221.
1672. Richard Ranikars, of Leigh : ibid. p. 218.
1807. Married—Anthony Runacres and Mary Rowley : St. Geo. Han. Sq. ii. 379.
London, 1, 0, 0 ; Manchester, 0, 1, 1.

Runciman, Runchman.—Occup. 'the runcyman,' one who dealt in *runces*, or hackney horses : cf. Palfreyman.

'Rex igitur cum persecutus esset imperatorem fugientem lucratus est *runcinum* vel jumentum sacculo retro sellam

collocato, &c.': Itinerarium of Ric. I, p. 191.
'Magistro Willelmo de Apperle, pro restauro unius runcini favi appreciati pro Roberto de Burton, valletto suo, &c., £8': Wardrobe Accounts, Edw. I, p 17.
'He rode upon a rouncie, as he couthe.'
Chaucer, C. T. 392.
1696-7. Adam Runciman and Jane Waugh: Marriage Lic. (London), ii. 320.
1797. Married—James Runcieman and Mary Burton: St. Geo. Han. Sq. ii. 170.
London, 3, 2; Boston (U.S.), 2, 0.

Runcy.—Nick. 'the runcy,' a somewhat uncomplimentary sobriquet for a porter or carrier, who was a 'beast of burden,' like a runcy or rouncy, i.e. a hackney horse; v. Runcimaon.
Thomas Runcy, co. Oxf., 1273. A.
Laurence Runci, or Runcy, or Rouncy, co. Oxf., ibid.
Roger Runcy. V. 8.

It seems to occur as a sign-name:
Ralph de la Runce, co. Notts, Hen. III-Edw. I. K.

Cf. Whitehorse, Roebuck, &c.

Rupell.—Local, 'at the rupel,' or coppice, from residence thereby. 'Ripple, a small coppice, co. Hereford' (Halliwell).
Philip atte Ruple, co. Soms., 1 Edw. III: Kirby's Quest, p. 135.

Ruse; v. Rous.

Rush.—Nick.; v. Rous. There can be little doubt that Rush is a variant of Russ, as that is unquestionably of Rous. In the Index to Reg. Univ. Oxf., Rush and Russe are placed under one heading.
1554. Anthony Rushe, B.A.: Reg. Univ. Oxf. i. 224.
1600. Married—Thomas Rushe and Eliz. Smyth: St. Ja. Clerkenwell, i. 24.
1638. Hugh Massie and Thomasine Rush: Marriage Lic. (London), ii. 235.
London, 6; Philadelphia, 69.

Rushall.—Local, 'of Rushall,' parishes in cos. Norfolk, Stafford, and Wilts.
Henry de Ryveshale, co. Norf., 1273. A.
Peter de Ryveshale, (?) co. Norf., ibid.
London, 1.

Rushbrook, Rushbrooke.—Local, 'of Rushbrooke,' a parish in co. Suffolk, three miles from Bury St. Edmunds.

William de Rushbroke, co. Norf., 1362: FF. v. 47.
Robert Rushbrooke, Norwich, 1730: ibid. iii. 452.
1789. Married—Joseph Rushbrook and Ann Deirinckx: St. Geo. Han. Sq. ii. 19.
London, 7, 1; MDB. (co. Norfolk), 2, 2; (co. Suffolk), 0, 3.

Rusher.—Occup. 'the rusher,' a thatcher, or perhaps a candle-wick maker.
Johannes Ryscher, 1379: P. T. Yorks. p. 125.
London, 1; Oxford, 1.

Rushford, Rushforth. —Local, 'of Rushford.' There is a parish so called in co. Norfolk, but I do not find the surname in the vicinity. Various fords where rushes grew may have contributed to our directories.
London, 0, 2; Oxford, 0, 1.

Rushmere, Rushmer, Rushmore.—Local, 'of Rushmere,' two parishes in co. Suffolk.
William de Rusmara, co. Linc., Hen. III-Edw. I. K.
1799. Married—Thomas Hickey and Mary Rushmore: St. Geo. Han. Sq. ii. 205.
1803. — Samuel Pearson and Sarah Rushmer: ibid. p. 277.
Yarmouth, 1, 3, 0; MDB. (co. Norfolk), 2, 1, 1.

Rushton, Rishton. — Local, 'of Rishton,' an ancient manor in the parish of Blackburn, co. Lanc. For the double prefix Rish and Rush, v. Rishworth.
'Henry, the grandson of Henry de Blackburn, took the name of Rishton, or Rushton, both orthographies being found in ancient authentic documents': Baines' Lanc. ii. 85.
1602. James Rishton, of Rishton: Wills at Chester, i. 162.
— Geoffrey Rishton, of Blackburn: ibid.
1662. Edmund Rushton, of Farnworth: ibid. iii. 225.
1668. Christopher Rishton, of Farnworth: ibid. p. 231.
London, 9, 0; Manchester, 10, 1; Philadelphia, 16, 0.

Rushworth; v. Rishworth.

Rusling; v. Rosling.

Russ; v. Rous and Russell.
1634. Buried — William Russe: St. Mary Aldermary, p. 168.
London, 7.

Russell, Russel, Rowsell, Rousell.—Nick. 'Russell,' the dim. of Rous, a sobriquet for one with hair or complexion of a reddish-brown. Just as O.F. *brun*, brown, took two dims. *burnett* and *burnell*, so *rous*, reddish brown, took two dims. *russet* and *russell*. From nicknames these became hereditary surnames, and are all in existence to-day except Russet. The fox from his colour was called Russel.
'Dan Burnel the asse.'
Chaucer, C. T. 15319.
'Dan Russel the fox.'
ibid. 15341.
Miriel Russell, co. Hunts, 1273. A.
Simon Russel, co. Camb., ibid.
Elyas Russell, London, ibid.
Johannes Russell, 1379: P. T. Yorks. p. 234.
Robertus Russell, 1379: ibid.

Endless instances might be furnished of this familiar nickname; v. Rous.
London, 154, 1, 10, 0; MDB. (co. Somerset), 13, 0, 11, 3.

Rust. — ? Bapt. 'the son of Rust' (?). Probably a Scandinavian personal name. It still flourishes in co. Norfolk, where it is found in the 13th century.
Robert Rust, co. Hunts, 1273. A.
Thomas Rust, co. Camb., ibid.
Peter Rust, co. Norf., ibid.
1492. Thomas Rust, rector of Congham, co. Norf.: FF. viii. 389.
1610. Nicholas Ruste, rector of Bixley, co. Norf.: ibid. v. 450.
1712. Married—Thomas Levett and Ann Rust: St. Dionis Backchurch, p. 56.
London, 11; Norwich, 3; Philadelphia, 11.

Ruston.—Local, 'of Ruston,' two parishes in co. Norf.
Walter de Ruston, co. Camb., 1273. A.
John de Rustone, co. Camb., ibid.

The surname passed early into the county of Cambridge and is still found there.
1666-7. Robert King and Anne Ruston: Marriage Lic. (Westminster), p. 43.
1751. Married—Benjamin Ruston and Dorothy Beech: St. Geo. Han. Sq. i. 45.
London, 5; Chatteris (co. Camb.), 6; Boston (U.S.), 4.

Rutland.—Local, 'of Rutland'; cf. Darbyshire, Cornish, Cumberland, &c.

Richard de Roteland, co. Oxf., 1273. A.
1584. William Rutland, co. Surrey:
Reg. Univ. Oxf. vol. ii. pt. ii. p. 137.
1728. Married—Barnes Rutland and
Eliz. Norman: St. Geo. Han. Sq. i. 5.
London, 9; Philadelphia, 2.

Rutlidge, Ruttledge, Ruttlidge. — Local ; v. Routledge ;
manifest variants.

1637. Bapt.—George, s. George Rutlige: St. Jas. Clerkenwell, i. 137.
1766. Married—John Burton and Mary
Rutlidge: St. Geo. Han. Sq. i. 155.
1788. — John Rutledge and Ann Richards: ibid. ii. 12.
London, 0, 1, 0; Liverpool, 0, 0, 1;
MDB. (East Rid. Yorks), 1, 0, 0.

Rutter, Ritter, Reuter.—
Occup. German *ritter*, a rider, i.e.
a trooper; ' *rutter*, a rider, a
trooper, from the German' (Halliwell); a name given to mercenary
soldiers engaged from Brabant, &c.
(v. my English Surnames, 3rd edit.,
p. 201). An old song begins :

' Rutterkyn is come into owre towne
In a cloke withoute cote or gowne,
Save a ragged hood to kover his crowne
        Like a rutter hoyda.'
                (ibid. p. 201.)
John le Rotour, co. Soms., 1 Edw. III:
Kirby's Quest, p. 87.
Thomas le Reuter. H.
Ranulph le Ruter. J.
Adam le Ruter. E.
Thomas le Roitour, C. R., 9 Edw. III.
1618. Ferriman Rutter, co. Glouc.:
Reg. Univ. Oxf. vol. ii. pt. ii. p. 372.
1627. Bapt.—Mary, d. John Rutter,
tayler: St. Peter, Cornhill, i. 77.
London, 21, 5, 2; Boston (U.S.), 2, 3, 6.

Rycroft, Roycroft, Rowcroft, Roycraft.—(1) Local, ' of
Rycroft,' a hamlet in the township
of Tong, and parish of Birstall, co.
Yorks. There are several smaller
localities bearing this name.
Margareta de Rycroft, 1379: P. T.
Yorks. p. 181.
Ricardus Rycroft, 1379: ibid.
Margaret Rycroft, of Haigh, *widow*,
1582: Wills at Chester (1545-1620),
p. 167.
George Minshull, of Rycroft, *yeoman*,
1586: ibid. p. 137.
Richard Ricroft, of Groppenhall, co.
Ches., 1638: East Cheshire, i. 179.
1779. Married—James Ryecroft and
Eliz. Diana Abbiss: St. Geo. Han. Sq.
i. 303.

London, 1, 0, 0, 1; West Rid. Court
Dir. (Rycroft), 7; MDB. (Cheshire), 2, 3,
0, 0; Manchester, 2, 1, 2, 0.

Ryder.—Occup. ; v. Rider.

Ryding; v. Riding.

Rydon.—Local, ' of Rydon.'
Alan de Rydon, co. Norf., 1273. A.
Thomas de Ridone, co. Soms., 1 Edw.
III: Kirby's Quest, p. 187.
London, 3.

Rye.—Local, (1) ' of Rye,' a
town in co. Sussex; (2) 'de la
Rie.' Mr. Lower says, 'la Rie,'
meaning a bank, is a very common
name of localities in Normandy.
There can be little doubt that this
is one, if not the chief, parent of the
surname.
Hubert de Rie, castellan of Norwich
Castle, c. 1100: FF. x. 54.
Philip de Rye, co. Linc., Hen. III-Edw.
I. K.
Robert de Rye, co. Linc., ibid.
John de Rye, co. Linc., 1273. A.
John de la Rye, co. Kent, ibid.
1791. Married—George Rye and Susanna Owen: St. Geo. Han. Sq. ii. 58.
London, 5; New York, 3.

Rygate.—Local, ' of Reigate,'
a town in co. Surrey.
John de Reygate, London, 1273. A.
Stephen de Reygate, co. Wilts, ibid.
London, 1.

Rylands, Roylance, Rylance, Rawlence, Ryland.—Local, ' of
the Rylands.' There are two places
that have originated surnames bearing this title. Mr. J. Paul Rylands,
F.S.A., says the name ' *Ryelands* is
derived from the Anglo-Saxon *rye*
or *rhee*, a water-course or stream,
and *lands*, the lands adjoining or
above the stream.' (1) Rylands,
a spot situated in the township
of Westhoughton, and parish of
Deane, co. Lanc.
Robert del Ruylondes, of West Halghton, 1 Edw. III: 'The Rylands of the
Rylands, within Westhoughton, co. Lancaster,' by J. Paul Rylands, F.S.A.
William de Rylondes, of Halghton, 6
Edw. III: ibid.
Nicholas del Rylondes, 1436: ibid.
(2) Rylands, a spot within the
parish of Wilmslow, co. Ches.

'The hamlets of Styhale, Curbichelegh,
and Northcliffe, Rylondis, Stanilondis,
and Harethorn': Earwaker's East Ches.,
i. 42.
Thomas de Ruylonds, of Wilmslow,
c. 1300: ibid. p. 138.

Roylance, although it has a
chivalrous aspect, is purely imitative. If any doubt rested on this,
it would be dispelled by the following entry concerning a farmer
who was twice sued for tithe by
his vicar :
Thomas Rylands, or Thomas Rylance,
Warmincham, co. Chester, 1686: Exchequer Depositions, pp. 148-9, L. and C.
R. S. vol. xi.

From Rylance to Roylance was
as easy as it was an inevitable
change. With Rylance cf. Sandilance for Sandilands.
Henry Sandilance, of Cotton, 1609:
Wills at Chester (1545-1620), p. 169.
London, 2, 1, 0, 1, 0; Manchester, 4,
4, 4, 0, 0; Philadelphia, 0, 1, 0, 0, 3.

Ryle, Royle.—Local, ' of Ryle.'
in the manor of Etchells, in the
parish of Northendon, co. Ches.
'Sir Nicholas de Eton ... concedes to
Sir William de Baggylegh, knt. ... one
hamlet ... in the vill of Echeles, which
is called Ruyhul ... which Richard de
Ruyhul held ... &c.' 1318: East Ches.
i. 327.

Most of the Cheshire and Lancashire Royles and Ryles are sprung
from this spot, including the late
Bishop of Liverpool. In the form
of Royle the surname has ramified
very strongly.
1574. Married — Edward Royle and
Eliz. Booth: Reg. Prestbury, co. Ches.,
p. 45.
Ellen Ryle, of Etchells, 1603: Wills at
Chester, i. 166.
Reginald Royle, of Etchells, 1609:
ibid. p. 167.
Nathaniel Royle, of Cross Acres, 1661:
Reg. Prestbury, co. Ches., iii. 231.
Ellen Ryle, of Cross Acres, 1669: ibid.
p. 232.
Manchester, 0, 50; MDB. (co. Chester),
1, 14; Philadelphia, 1, 8.

Rymer.—Occup. ; v. Rimmer.

Rynd.—Local; v. Rhind.
Oxford, 1.

S

Saar.—Bapt. 'the son of Sayer,' q.v., one of over twenty variants of this once popular personal name.

1643. Married — Edmund Saare and Anne Hukin : Canterbury Cath. p. 56.
1746. — William Greenaway and Mary Saar : St. Geo. Chap. Mayfair, p. 69.
Philadelphia, 2.

Sabbe.—Bapt. 'the son of Sabin,' from the nick. Sab and pet Sab-ey (cf. Charley, Teddie, &c.) ; v. Sabin.

Alicia uxor Sabson (i. e. Alice, the wife of the son of Sab), 1379 : P. T. Yorks. p. 110.
1583. Thomas Coles and Audrey Sabb : Marriage Lic. (London), i. 124.
1716. Married — Robert Saxby and Lydia Sabb, of Maidstone : St. Mary Aldermary, p. 43.

Mr. Lower says this surname is still existing. I have not come across it in modern directories.

Sabben, Saben; v. Sabin.

Sabey, Saby.—Bapt. 'the son of Sabine,' popularly Sabey. Sabine was a favourite font-name in the surname period; v. Sabbe and Sabin.

1641. Bapt.—James, sonne of William Saby, *blacksmith* : St. Peter, Cornhill, i. 89.
1655. Buried—Maudlin, wife of William Sabie, *blacksmith* : ibid. p. 208.
1668-9. James Sabey and Jane Lucock : Marriage Alleg. (Canterbury), p. 259.
1782. Married — John Saby and Ann Burgan : St. Geo. Han. Sq. i. 339.
London, 5, 0 ; Philadelphia, 0, 1.

Sabin, Sabine, Sabins, Sabben, Saben.—Bapt. 'the son of Sabine.' St. Sabina was martyred in Hadrian's persecution. The name was in much favour for a time in England. In one of the Coventry Mysteries occurs :

'Bontyng the Brewster, and Sybyly Slynge,
Megge Mery-wedyr, and Sabyn Sprynge.'

Also there was St. Sabinus, the martyr bishop of Assisium.

Sabyn Hubert, co. Camb., 1273. A.
Alexander Sabine, co. Essex, ibid.

Sabina Gaylard. H.
Sabinus Chambre. V. 4.
Sabyna Vesy, co. Soms., 1 Edw. III : Kirby's Quest, p. 143.
William Sabin, co. Soms., 1 Edw. III : ibid. p. 155.
Robert Sabynson, 1379 : P. T. Yorks. p. 162.
1758. Married — William Saben and Susanna Wright : St. Geo. Han. Sq. i. 78.
1791. — James Mans and Susanna Sabben : Canterbury Cath. p. 99.
Crockford, 1, 1, 0, 1, 1 ; London, 4, 7, 0, 0, 0 ; Philadelphia, 5, 1, 6, 0, 0 ; Boston (Saben), 5.

Sacheverell.— ? Local. I cannot suggest any derivation of this surname. 'Sacheverel, the iron door, or blower to the mouth of a stove' (Halliwell). This great name is represented, so far as I can see, in the 19th century by only one person, viz. : William Henry Sacheverell, clogger, Oldfield Road, Salford, Lancs.

Nicholas Saucheverel, alias Sauzcheverel, alias Saunz Cheverel, co. Camb., 1273. A.
Patricia Saucheverel, cos. Notts and Derby, Hen. III-Edw. I. K.
Patricia Sauchevel, cos. Notts and Derby, ibid.
1581. Ambrose Sacheverall, co. Leic. : Reg. Univ. Oxf. vol. ii. pt. ii. p. 109.
1590. Buried—Frances Sacheverell, a *maid*, d. of John Sacheverell : St. Peter, Cornhill, i. 138.
1776. Married — William Sacheverell and Jane Secker : St. Geo. Han. Sq. i. 260.
Manchester, 1.

Sack.—Bapt. 'the son of Sagge'; cf. Jagge for Jack, and endless instances where g becomes ck— Hick for Higg, Hickin for Higgin, &c.

Avice fil. Sage (g hard), co. Camb., 1273. A.
Alan Sage, or Sagge, co. Norf., ibid.
Thomas Sagge, co. Norf., ibid.
1798. Married—Joseph Sack and Sarah Biddle : St. Geo. Han. Sq. ii. 188.
London, 7 ; Philadelphia, 4.

Sacker.—Occup. 'the sacker,' a maker of sacks. M. E. *sak*, Chaucer, C. T. 4019. v. Secker (2).

Adam the Sakker, Fines Roll, 14 Edw. II.
Adam le Sakkere, London. X.
John Sakkere. H.

Cf. Canvaser, q.v. The occupative name *sack-weaver* existed, but did not live :

Jurdan Sakwebbe, co. Soms., 1 Edw. III : Kirby's Quest, p. 276.
1576. Married — Richard Saker and Anne Spilberrie : St. Mary Aldermary, p. 6.
1630. Buried — Eliz. Saker : St. Jas. Clerkenwell, iv. 198.
1661-2. Richard Atkinson and Mary Sacker : Marriage Lic. (London), ii. 290.
London, 3 ; Boston (U.S.), 1.

Sackerson, Sackrison.—Bapt. 'the son of Sagger,' i.e. Sagar (v. Sayer). No doubt Sackerson is the form that went out to America, as it is found in that dress in the Puritan period. The English form is Saggerson (v. Saggers).

1610. Married — Miles Crakel and Margaret Sackerson : St. Michael, Cornhill, p. 17.
1717. Bapt.—John, son of John Segerson : St. Jas. Clerkenwell, ii. 100.
1721. — William, son of John Sagesson, or Saggeson : ibid. ii. 127.
1730. — Ann, d. John Sadgerson : ibid. ii. 248.
New York, 1, 0 ; Boston (U.S.), 0, 1.

Sackville.—Local. 'A place in Normandy now called Sanqueville, about seven miles from Dieppe' (Lower) ; v. long article in Lower's Patr. Brit. p. 299. The family seem to have come in with the Conqueror, or immediately after, and were highly placed.

John de Sakewyle, co. Suff., 1273. A.
Jordan de Sakeville, co. Suff., ibid.
Gwydo de Sakevill, co. Sussex, Hen. III-Edw. I. K.
Robert de Saccavill, co. Devon, ibid.
Andrew de Sakeville, co. Norf., 20 Edw. I. R.

Like Harcourt, Sackville has not become the property of the commonalty. There is no representative in the London Directory. There is none, also, in Crockford.

Philadelphia, 1 ; New York, 1.

Sadd.—Nick. 'the sad,' i.e. the sober, the discreet, the serious. 'A sad man in whom is no pride': MS. Rawl. C. 86 (Halliwell).

Margaret Sad, co. Suff., 1273. A.
Seman Sad, co. Suff., ibid.
William Sad, co. Hunts, 20 Edw. I. R.
1429. John Sadd, prebend of Norwich: FF. iv. 173.
1600. Married — Henrie Sadd and Parnell Eaden: St. Jas. Clerkenwell, iii. 24.
1667. Thomas Cornwall and Hannah Sadd: Marriage Alleg. (Canterbury), p. 208.
London, 2.

Saddington.—Local, 'of Saddington,' a parish in co. Leicester.

Nicholas de Sadingden, co. Berks, 1273. A.
Robert de Sadyngton, *chancellor*: FF. iii. 89.
Thomas de Sadyngton, 1379: P. T. Howdenshire, p. 20.
1797. Married—Joseph Saddington and Eliz. Brown: St. Geo. Han. Sq. ii. 163.
London, 3; MDB. (co. Kent), 1; (co. Leic.), 4; New York, 1.

Saddlebow.—Nick., probably affixed to a saddler.

John Sadelbowe, co. Camb., 1273. A.
Richard Sadelbowe, co. Camb., ibid.

Saddler, Sadler, Sadtler.—Occup. 'the saddler,' a maker of saddles. An important craft in its day. v. Fewster.

John le Sadeler, co. Soms., 1 Edw. III: Kirby's Quest, p. 104.
Thomas Sadeler, 1379: P. T. Yorks. p. 47.
Willelmus Sadeler, 1379: ibid.
Nicholaus Sadiler, 1379: ibid. p. 41.
Willelmus Sadeller, 1379: ibid. p. 131.
1612. John Sadler and Jane Hogge: Marriage Lic. (London), ii. 16.
London, 1, 39, 0; Philadelphia, 3, 24, 2.

Saffery.—Bapt.; v. Savory.

Sagar, Sager.—(1) Occup. 'a sawyer.' A.S. *saga*, a saw. Yorkshire dialect *sager*, a sawyer. (2) Bapt. 'the son of Sagar' (v. Seager). This must be looked upon as the chief parent.

Richard le Saghiere, C. R., 21 Edw. III, pt. ii.
Simon Sagher, 1379: P. T. Yorks. p. 59.
Johannes Saghher, 1379: ibid. p. 16.
1621. Buried—Temperance, d. Mathew Sager: St. Jas. Clerkenwell, iv. 153.
Robert Sagar, of Billington, 1632: Wills at Chester, ii. 191.
Richard Sagar, of Padiham, 1648: ibid.
West Rid. Court Dir., 2, 2; Leeds, 3, 2; Philadelphia, 3, 16.

Sage.—Nick. 'the sage,' the wise, the sagacious. Naturally an acceptable sobriquet, and likely to be handed down.

Bernard le Sage, co. Norf., temp. Ric. I: FF. xi. 117.
Richard le Sage, co. Oxf., 1273. A.
William le Sage, C. R., 1 Edw. I.
1618–9. John Sage and Joane Vesey: Marriage Lic. (London), ii. 69.
1803. Married—James Sage and Isabella Walker: St. Geo. Han. Sq. ii. 293.
London, 12; Philadelphia, 17.

Saggers, Saggerson.—Bapt. 'the son of Sagar'; v. Seager. Sagar and Saggerson are common surnames in West Lancashire. For examples, v. Sackerson.

London, 4, 0; Prescot (co. Lanc.), 0, 5.

Saies.—Nick.; v. Sayce.

Sailer, Sailor.—Occup.; v. Saylor.

Sailes.—Local; v. Sayles.

Saint.—Nick. 'the saint,' a man of holy character, perhaps, however, given cynically for one who affected to be better than his neighbours.

John le Seynt, C. R., 39 Hen. III, pt. i.
1559. Married—Reighnold Sainct and Margarett Meridith: St. Thomas the Apostle (London), 3.
1700. —Richard Saint and Ann Bright: St. Mary Aldermary, p. 36.
1745. — John Saint and Ann Townsend: St. Geo. Han. Sq. i. 44.
London, 3; Philadelphia, 1.

Saise.—Nick.; v. Sayce.

Salamon, Salaman, Saleman, Saloman, Salomans.—Bapt. 'the son of Solomon,' found variously as Saloman, Salaman, and Saleman; v. Salman and Sloman.

Salomon Judaeus. C.
Salomon fil. Ivo. C.

The three following entries relate to the same individual:

Richard Salaman, co. Oxf., 1273. A.
Richard Saleman, co. Oxf., ibid.
Richard Saloman, co. Oxf., ibid.
Alicia Saleman, co. Camb., ibid.
Salemande Grecton, co. Camb., ibid.
Saleman pater Johannis Seliman, co. Camb., ibid.
Christian Saleman, Wardrobe Account, 1 Edw. III, 33/2.
William Saleman, co. Soms., 1 Edw. III: Kirby's Quest, p. 264.

Thomas Salman, 1379: P. T. Yorks. p. 146.
1588. Bapt.—Anne, d. Thomas Sallomon: St. Peter, Cornhill, i. 33.
London, 1, 5, 0, 5, 6; New York, 3, 0, 0, 56, 50.

Sale, Sales.—Local, 'of the sale,' i.e. the hall; cf. Fr. *salle-à-manger*, a dining-hall. Halliwell quotes:

'Sone thay sembled in sale
Bathe Kynges and Cardenale.'

Instances of the surname are found in every important 13th century roll.

Robert a la Sale, 1273. A.
Nicholas de la Sale, 20 Edw. I. R.
William de la Sale, ibid.
Robert de la Sale, bailiff of Norwich, 1327: FF. iii. 98.
Ralph de la Sale, C. R., 56 Hen. III.
John de la Sale. T.

With excrescent *s* in Sales, cf. Briggs, Brooks, Sykes, Styles, &c., a common adjunct of one-syllabled local surnames, possibly genitive.

1598. Henry Sales and Abigail Brabye: Marriage Lic. (London), i. 255.
1745. Buried—John Sale: St. John the Baptist (Wallbrook), p. 213.
London, 7, 6; Philadelphia, 4, 0; New York, 3, 1.

Sales; v. Sayles.

Salisbury, Salisberry.—(1) Local, 'of Salisbury,' a city in co. Wilts.

Robert de Salisbyr', co. Wilts, 1273. A.
1547. Married—Henry Salysberye and Jone Mathewe: St. Michael, Cornhill, p. 5.

(2) Local, 'of Salesbury.' The Lancashire Salisburys hail from Salesbury, a village-parish between Blackburn and Ribchester. The corruption is a very slight one, and simply imitative of the name of the southern cathedral city.

Ralph Salisbury, of Hindley, 1670: Wills at Chester (1660–80), p. 234.
Ann Salisbury, of Hindley, 1674: ibid.
Thomas Salisbury, of Chipping, 1669: Lancashire Wills at Richmond, p. 240.
Richard Salisbury, of Chipping, 1663: ibid.
Henry Sailsbury, of Chepin, 1626: ibid.

The last three entries place my statement of a local Lancashire origin beyond the range of controversy.

London, 13, 0; Liverpool, 5, 0; Blackburn, 4, 0; Manchester, 2, 0; West Rid. Court Dir., 0, 1; New York, 12, 0.

Salkeld.—Local, 'of Salkeld,' a parish (called Great Salkeld) in co. Cumb., three miles from Kirk-Oswald. Little Salkeld is a township in the neighbouring parish of Addingham.

1293. John de Salkild, co. Cumb., 20 Edw. I. R.
Thomas de Salkeld, co. Cumb., ibid.
1593. Thomas Salkell and Matilda Hickopp: Marriage Lic. (London), i. 207.
1610. Richard Salkeld, co. Cumb.: Reg. Univ. Oxf. vol. ii. pt. ii. p. 317.
1804. Married — James Reynolds and Mary Salkeld: St. Geo. Han. Sq. ii. 311.
London, 3; MDB. (co. Cumb.), 16; Boston (U.S.), 4.

Salman, Salmon, Salmond.—Bapt. 'the son of Solomon,' popularly in M.E. Salamon, and with excrescent *d* Salamond (cf. Simmonds and Hammond for Simmons and Hamon). These forms represent families of English descent, Solomon representing modern Jewish immigrations. Of course the London Directory has several Salamons, undoubtedly Jewish, but, speaking generally, our Salomans, Salamans, Salemans, Salmons, Salmans, Salmonds, Sammons, and Sammonds, are of English extraction, just as much as our Davies and Davidsons are (excepting when these are Welsh or Scottish).

1379. William Salman, 1379: P. T. Yorks. p. 108.
1574. Buried—Alexander Sawllmond: St. Peter, Cornhill, i. 122.
1620. John Salmon and Constance Fallwell: Marriage Lic. (London), ii. 93.
1797. Married—William Salmond and Eliz. Corns: St. Geo. Han. Sq. ii. 165.
London, 1, 48, 0; New York, 1, 22, 0; Boston, U.S. (Salmond), 1.

Salomon(s ; v. Salamon.

Salsbery, Salsbury, Salsburry.—Local; v. Salisbury.

1601. John Salsbury, or Salisbury, co. Devon: Reg. Univ. Oxf. vol. ii. pt. ii. p. 247.
— Bapt.—Marie, d. John Salsburie: St. Jas. Clerkenwell, i. 39.

The following is a still briefer form:

1670. Bapt.—Eliz., d. Robert Salsbee: St. Jas. Clerkenwell, i. 244.
1630. Married—Edward Lloyde and Ursley Sallsberye: St. Mary Aldermary, p. 17.

London, 0, 4, 0; Philadelphia, 1, 2, 0; New York, 0, 1, 1.

Salt.—Local, 'of Salt,' a township in the parish of St. Mary and St. Chad, four miles from Stafford. This is the parent of all the Salts. It is a very familiar surname in the county of Stafford.

'In the reign of Hen. III, Ivo de Saut held one Knight's fee in Saut of the Barony of Stafford': Lower's Patr. Brit. p. 302.
Ranulph de Saut, co. Camb., 1273. A.
Ivo de Saut, co. Stafford, Hen. III-Edw. I. K.
1597. Buried — Margery Sawlte: St. Jas. Clerkenwell, iv. 61.
1599. — Alyce Salte: ibid. iv. 66.
1621. Ann Salt, of Chester: Wills at Chester, ii. 191.
London, 6; MDB. (co. Stafford), 33; Philadelphia, 3.

Salter.—(1) Occup. 'the salter,' a manufacturer or dealer in salt; cf. Salthouse. The Salters' Company was early among the London Guilds.

John le Saltere, co. Camb., 1273. A.
Nygel le Salter, co. Wilts, ibid.
Ralph le Salter, C. R., 20 Edw. I.
Thomas le Saltar, co. Soms., 1 Edw. III: Kirby's Quest, p. 272.
Willelmus Salter, 1379: P. T. Yorks. p. 177.
Thomas de Wollay, *salter*, 1379: ibid. p. 92.

(2) Occup. 'the sautreour,' a player on the psaltery, or 'gay sawtrye,' as Chaucer styles it. A stringed instrument of the harp class.

William le Sautreour. X.
Janetto la Sautreour, minstrel of Queen Isabelle, Close Roll, 2 Edw. III.

This would easily get corrupted to Salter, as the form *psalterie* was in use in the 12th century.

1597. Married — William Prior and Margaret Salter: St. Mary Aldermary, p. 9.
1618. Edmund Rolfe and Dorothy Salter: Marriage Lic. (London), ii. 65.
London, 33; Philadelphia, 14.

Salters.—Local, 'of the salthouse,' a manifest corruption; v. instances in Salthouse.

Philadelphia, 2.

Salthouse, Southouse. — Local, 'of the salthouse,' the place where salt was made from sea-water

by evaporation. M.E. *salt*, Dutch *zout*. v. Southouse. In the first instance below I suspect the occupation of souter (shoemaker) is accidental. But, if not, Southouse in London Directories is an abbreviation of Souter-house, the shoemaker's house. I had a Soutergate in my late parish (Ulverston), i.e. the shoemaker's road. But this abbreviation would scarcely occur in a formal record in 1379. It is far more natural to make Southouse, the surname, a variant of Salthouse. Two small places, a Salthouse in Lytham, and a Salthouse in Furness, where salt was obtained from sea-water, have originated two families of Salthouse in North Lancashire.

Simon del Southouse, *souter*, 1379: P. T. Yorks. p. 254.
Adam de Salthus, co. Norf., 1273. A.

(This is the parish of Salthouse, co. Norfolk.)

Janet Saltehouse, of Pulton, 1562: Lancashire Wills at Richmond, p. 240.
Agnes Saltus, of Ulverston, 1596: ibid. 241.
John Salthouse, of Saltcoathouses, 1661: ibid.
William Saltus, of Banke, 1662: ibid.
Manchester, 3, 0; London, 0, 1; Blackpool (near Lytham, co. Lanc.), 3, 0; Philadelphia, 3, 0.

Saltmarsh.—Local, 'of Saltmarsh,' a township in the parish of Howden, E. Rid. Yorks.

1273. Robert Saltmerssh, C. R., 25 Edw. III.
Nicholaus de Saltmerssh', 1379: P. T. Howdenshire, co. York, p. 19.
Philippus de Saltmerssh', 1379: ibid. p. 20.
Johannes Saltemerche, 1379: P. T. Yorks. p. 151.
1618. Lawrence Saltmarsh and Margaret Jarrett: Marriage Lic. (London), ii. 65.
1650-1. Married—Jeremy Saultmarsh and Susan Thorn: St. Dionis Backchurch, p. 27.
London, 2; MDB. (co. Essex), 4; (East Rid. Yorks), 3; Boston (U.S.), 3.

Saltonstall.—Local, 'of Saltonstall.' I cannot find the spot. But it must probably be looked for in co. Essex and neighbourhood. The name of the daughter of Sir Peter Saltonstall is thus entered:

1642. Edward Chester and Anne Salt-hingston (co. Herts): Marriage Lic. (London), ii. 265.
1610. Richard Saltonstall, co. Essex: Reg. Univ. Oxf. vol. ii. pt. ii. p. 314.
1615. John Saltonstall, co. Essex: ibid. p. 343.
1805. Married—Robert Bradley and Ellen Saltonstall: St. Geo. Han. Sq. ii. 338.
Boston (U.S.), 5.

Salusbury.—Local; v. Salis-bury, a manifest variant.
1742. Bapt.—Sarah, d. John Salusbury: St. Geo. Chap. Mayfair, p. 5.
1760. Married—Gilbert Atkinson and Esther Salusbury: St. Geo. Han. Sq. i. 92.
Crockford, 6.

Sambourne.—Local, ' of Sam-bourn,' a hamlet in the parish of Coughton, co. Warwick.
Peter de Samborne, co. Soms., 1 Edw. III: Kirby's Quest, p. 254.
1577. Barnabas Samborne, co. Soms.: Reg. Univ. Oxf. vol. ii. pt. ii. p. 77.
1592. James Samborn, co. Hants: ibid. p. 193.
MDB. (co. Devon), 1.

Sambrook, Shambrook. — Local, ' of Sambrook,' a parish in the dioc. of Lichfield. If the instances below refer to this town, the terminal was originally *bridge* and not *brook*.
John de Samebrugg, co. Oxf., 1273. A.
Henry de Samebrugg, co. Oxf., ibid.
Simon de Sambrigg, co. Surrey, 20 Edw. I. R.
1645. Buried—A female, stillborn, of William and Elizabeth Shambrooke: St. Thomas the Apostle (London), p. 125.
1677-8. John English and Eliz. Sam-brooke: Marriage Alleg. (Canterbury), p. 275.
1742. Married—George Sambrooke and Hannah Purkes: St. Geo. Chap. Mayfair, p. 26.
London, 4, 1.

Sammon, Sammonds, Sam-mons, Samons, Samon.—Bapt.; v. Salman.
London, 1, 0, 0, 1, 0; Oxford (Sam-mons), 4; Philadelphia, 5, 2, 0, 1, 4.

Samms, Sams. — Bapt. 'the son of Sampson,' from nick. Sam or Samp, genitive Sams (cf. William and Williams). This name was so popular, and Samuel so rare, that we must needs give it the preference; v. Sampson.
Samme Parvus (the little), co. Linc., 1273. A.

Samme (without surname), co. Salop, ibid.
Hugelin Samp, or Sampe, co. York, ibid.
Samme (without surname), co. Linc., ibid.
Alan Samme,1379: P. T. Yorks. p. 209.
1643-4. Henry Sams and Anne Wren: Marriage Lic. (London), ii. 273.
1664. Bapt.—Dorothy, d. Aylott Sam-mes: St. Jas. Clerkenwell, i. 224.
London, o, 10; MDB. (co. Hertford), o, 3; Philadelphia, o, 1.

Samper, Semper, Sampier.—Local, ' de St. Pierre,' from some Norman chapelry of that name; cf. St. John, Semple, Sinclair, &c.
' In an Inquisition post mortem taken at Chester, 1428, Urian le (de?) Seint pierre took oath': Earwaker's East Cheshire, ii. 292.
Agnes Seynpere. B.
Robert de Seyntpere, c. 1300. M.
Brian de St. Petro, co. Salop, 1273. A.
John Seyntpere. G.
London, 1, 0, 0; Philadelphia, 0, 1, 0; New York, 0, 0, 1.

Sampford.—Local, ' of Samp-ford,' parishes in cos. Somerset, Devon, and Essex.
Roger de Samford, co. Oxf., 1273. A.
Thomas de Samford, co. Camb., ibid.
Alicia de Samford, co. Oxf., Hen III-Edw. I. K.
1574. Married — Robert Wright and Alice Samforte: St. Michael, Cornhill, p. 6.
1614-5. John Burton and Marg. Sampford: Marriage Lic.(London), ii.31.
1626. John Tapsell and Theodora Samford: ibid. p. 182.
London, 1.

Sample.—Local, ' de St. Paul'; cf. Samper, Simbarb, Sinclair, &c. The usual form is Semple, q.v.
1579. Peter Buckley and Julian Sample: Marriage Lic. (London), i. 90.
1748. Married — George Sample and Sarah Coney: St. Geo. Chap. Mayfair, p. 123.
1782. — Ephraim Sampell and Cath. Griggs: St. Geo. Han. Sq. i. 334.
New York, 4; Philadelphia, 13.

Sampson, Samson, Sansom, Sansome, Sanson, Sansum.—Bapt. ' the son of Samson.' O.E. Sampson; O.F. Sanson. With the forms Sansom, &c., cf. Ran-some for Ranson, or the dictionary word *random* for *randon*. It has been stated that Sansom stands for some local St. Anselm (cf. Semple for St. Paul, Sampier for St. Pierre). This is without foundation. As a personal name Samson was in very

early use. Mr. Freeman has three instances in Index to vol. iv (Hist. Norm.Conquest). One was Bishop of Worcester; a second, chaplain to William I; a third, messenger to Matilda. The following entries concern one individual:
Sampson Foliot, Hen. III-Edw. I. K. p. 104.
Sanson Foliot, ibid. p. 105.
Saunsum Foliot, ibid. p. 106.
Sansum le Rus, co. Camb., 1273. A.
Samson de Baterford, co. Bedf., ibid.
Sampson de Boxe, co. Wilts, ibid.
' Item, the vi. day of Aprylle, my mastyr made a couenaunt wyth Saunsam, the tylere, that he schalle perget,' &c.: Ac-counts of Sir John Howard (A.D. 1467), p. 395; v. Prompt. Parv. p. 383, ed. Way.

A well-known monastery near Rouen was built by the Archbishop of Dol, known as St. Sansone or St. Sampson. The personal name lingered long in Cornwall, where so many pre-Reformation favourites died hard.
1559. Married — John Sampson and Eliz. Clarke, *widow*: St. Michael, Corn-hill, p. 7.
1582. Bapt.—Warne, son of Sampson Morcambe: Reg. St. Columb Major, Cornwall, p. 11.
1736. Married — Abraham Sampson and Ann Lawton: St. Geo. Han. Sq. i. 16.
1756. — Thomas Younger and Ann Sansum: ibid. i. 67.
1769. — John Sansom and Eliz. Bell-ton: ibid. i. 183.
1777. — Moses Samson and Mary Best: ibid. i. 279.
London, 26, 16, 14, 1, 2, 2; Phila-delphia, 22, 4, 5, 0, 12, 0.

Sams; v. Samms.

Samuel, Samuels, Samuel-son.—Bapt. ' the son of Samuel.' Not always Jewish. There are many Samuels of English descent; v. Samwell.
Matilda Samuel, co. Soms., 1 Edw. III: Kirby's Quest, p. 139.
Geoffrey Samuel, co. Essex, 1273. A.
John Samuel, co. Hunts, ibid.
Seman fil. Samuel, co. Hunts, ibid.

All these baptismal names es-tablish the fact above stated, that Samuel and Samuels were not con-fined to Jews; v. Salman.
1626. Buried — Xpian, wife of John Samuell: St. Jas. Clerkenwell, iv. 188.
London, 30, 12, 2; New York, 25, 34, 3.

Samwell.—Bapt. ' the son of Samuel,' an early corruption.

William Samwel, co. Oxf., 1273. A.
1612. Bapt.—Alice, d. William Samwell : St. Mary Aldermary, p. 172.
1628. Married—Samewell Randall and Frances Ruslinge : ibid. p. 16.
1708. Buried—Mary Sammiwell : St. Antholin (London), p. 121.
Crockford, 1.

Sanborn.—Local, a corruption of Sambourne, q.v. ; cf. Sandbrook for Sambrook.
1799. Married—John Crick and Rebecca Sanburn : St. Geo. Han. Sq. ii. 197.
Philadelphia, 4.

Sancton.—Local, 'of Sancton,' a parish in E. Rid. Yorks.
John de Sancton, co. Linc., 1273. A. MDB. (co. Cumb.), 2.

Sanctuary. — Local, 'at the sanctuary,' from residence beside a shrine. 'Several monasteries had an ambit or surrounding space, where criminals might take refuge from immediate or impending danger, as the Sanctuary at Westminster. A person resident in a place so privileged, though no criminal, would readily acquire the name of Thomas or John at the Sanctuary' (Lower's Patr. Brit. p. 302). For a parallel instance, v. Galilee. Although I have no references at hand, there can be no doubt about this derivation.
MDB. (co. Dorset), 2 ; Crockford (1891), 1.

Sanday, Sandy.—Local, 'of Sandy,' a parish in co. Bedford.
Nicholas de Sandye, co. Hunts, 1273. A. London, 0, 2 ; Oxford, 1, 0 ; New York, 2, 2.

Sandbach, Sanbach.—Local, 'of Sandbach,' a market-town and parish in cō. Ches.
1578. Buried — Eliz. Sanbacke : St. Thomas the Apostle (London), p. 94.
1624. Mathew Sandbach, of Eaton : Wills at Chester, ii. 192.
1636. John Sandbadge, of the Nunns, parish of St. Mary's, Chester : ibid.
1749. Married—Aaron Haynes and Rebecca Sandbach : St. Geo. Chap. Mayfair, p. 143.
MDB. (co. Ches.), 9, 0 ; Manchester, 5, 1 ; Philadelphia, 1, 0.

Sandborn. — Local. A corruption of Sambourne, q.v. ; cf. Sandbrook for Sambrook.
Philadelphia, 1.

Sandbrook.—Local. A corruption of Sambrook, q.v.
1613. William Farmer and Marg. Sandbrooke (of Shrewsbury) : Marriage Lic. (London), ii. 20.
London, 2 ; Oxford, 1.

Sandell, Sandall.—Local, 'of Sandal,' a parish, now Sandal Magna, near Wakefield, co. Yorks. Also Long Sandall, a parish four miles from Doncaster.
Johannes de Sandall', 1379 : P. T. Yorks. p. 161.
Isabella de Sandale, 1379 : ibid. p. 135.
1615. Peter Letten and Anne Sandell : Marriage Lic. (London), ii. 33.
1803. Married—Thomas Sandall and Jane Chapman : St. Geo. Han. Sq. ii. 286.
London, 6, 0 ; New York, 0, 1.

Sandeman, Sanderman. — Occup. 'the servant of Sandy' or Saunder, i.e. Alexander ; cf. Addyman, Matthewman, Jackman, Ladyman, Vickerman, &c. One of a large class. Robert Sandeman, the founder of the sect styled Sandemanians, was a native of Perth. The first five of my instances occur together, settling the origin beyond dispute :
Alexander de Rokeby, marchaunt des bestes, 1379 : P. T. Yorks. p. 22.
Mergeria serviens dicti Alexandri, 1379 : ibid.
Matilda Saunder-wyf, 1379 : ibid.
Johannes Saunderman, et 'uxor ejus, 1379 : ibid.
Johannes Saundirman, senior, 1379 : ibid.
Robertus Alexsanderman, 1379 : ibid. p. 33.
Marmaduke Sandimanne, hirde, 1634. VVV. p. 322.
1682-3. John Archer and Bridgett Sandyman : Marriage Alleg. (Canterbury), p. 119.
New York, 0, 3 ; Philadelphia, 3, 0.

Sander, Sanders, Sanderson.—Bapt. 'the son of Alexander,' from nick. Sander ; v. Saunder.
London, 7, 75, 38 ; New York, 20, 60, 20.

Sandercock.—Bapt. 'the son of Alexander,' from the nick. Saunder and suffix -cock ; cf. Wilcock, Simcock, Watcock, &c., from William, Simon, and Walter (v. cock, Introd. pp. 25-6).
MDB. (co. Devon), 1.

Sandford, Sandiford, Sanford, Sandyfirth.—Local, 'of Sandford,' parishes in cos. Devon

and Oxford (2), townships in cos. Berks and Salop, and hamlets in cos. Westmoreland and Berks. For suffix, v. Ford and Forth.
Richard de Sanford, co. Oxf., 1273. A.
William de Sanforth, co. Oxf., ibid.
Ralph de Sandford, co. Oxf., ibid.
Johannes de Sandeforthe, 1379 : P. T. Yorks. p. 112.
Willelmus de Sandeforthe, 1379 : ibid.
1616. Married—John Cooke and Eliz. Sandiford : St. Jas. Clerkenwell, i. 43.
1651. — Edward Sanderford and Ann Heydon : St. Mary Aldermary, p. 22.
1684. Buried—Joseph, s. Joseph Sandford : ibid. p. 195.
1725. Bapt.—Mary, d. Samuel Sandeforth : St. John Baptist, Wallbrook, p. 181.
London, 3, 1, 7, 0 ; West Rid. Court Dir., 2, 0, 0, 0 ; Philadelphia, 2, 1, 19, 1.

Sands, Sandys, Sondes. — Local, 'at the sands,' from residence thereby. M.E. sand or sond.
Walter atte Sond, bailiff of Yarmouth, 1335 : FF. xi. 323.
Earl Sondes owns a large estate in co. Norfolk.
Johannes del Sandes, 1379 : P. T. Yorks. p. 235.
Thomas del Sandes, 16 Ric. II : E. and F., co. Cumb., p. 174.
Paulina atte Sonde, C. R., 12 Hen. IV.
Richard atte Sonde, C. R., 8 Hen. V.
1589. Henry Sandes, London : Reg. Univ. Oxf. vol. ii. pt. ii. p. 174.
1633. William Sandys and Cicily Steed : Marriage Lic. (Faculty Office), p. 31.
London, 19, 3, 0 ; Philadelphia, 46, 0, 0.

Sandy; v. Sanday.

Sanger, Sangster, Sanxter, Songster, Songer.—Occup. 'the singer' or songster. A.S. sangere, fem. sangystre.
Willametta Cantatrix. E.
Adam le Sangere. T.
Robert le Sangar, co. Soms., 1 Edw. III : Kirby's Quest, p. 112.
Thomas le Sanggere, co. Soms., 1 Edw. III : ibid. p. 244.
1640. Bapt. — Arthur, s. of Arthur Sangar : Reg. Stourton, Wilts, p. 9.
1714. Married—William Wilkins and Susanna Sangar : Reg. St. Dionis Backchurch, p. 57.
Manchester, 0, 1, 0, 0, 0 ; London, 7, 10, 0, 0, 0 ; MDB. (Wilts), 5, 0, 0, 0, 0 ; Foxton (co. Camb.), 0, 0, 1, 0, 0 ; Philadelphia, 3, 1, 0, 3, 1.

Sankey.—Local, 'of Sankey,' a township in the parish of Prescot, co. Lanc.
Gerard de Sanki, co. Lanc., Hen. III-Edw I. K.
William de Sonkey, 25 Edw. I : Baines' Lanc. ii. 211.

Roger de Sonky, 27 Edw. I: Baines' Lanc. ii. 254.
Roger Sanckey, 11 Jas. I: ibid.
Edward Sankey, of Little Sankey, 1602: Wills at Chester, i. 169.
Thomas Sankie, of Little Sankey, 1623: ibid. ii. 192.
Manchester, 4; London, 4; Boston (U.S.), 2.

Sansom, Sanson, Sansum.—Bapt.; v. Sampson.

Santer.—Nick. 'sans-terre,' i.e. Lackland. The instance below seems very conclusive. One is almost in danger of suggesting the old origin of the verb to *saunter* (v. *saunter*, Skeat). The same individual is thus referred to :
John Sansterre, co. Linc., 1273. A.
John Sansterre, co. Linc., ibid.
John Sauntere, co. Linc., ibid.
London, 2; Crockford, 1.

Santon.—Local, ' of Santon,' parishes in the diocs. of Norwich and Ely.
Payn de Santon, co. Norf., 1273. A.
Thomas de Santon, co. Linc., ibid.
1315. Harvey de Santone, patron of living of Santon, co. Norf.: FF. ii. 157.
1628. Bapt.—Margrett, d. Thomas Santon : St. Jas. Clerkenwell, i. 108.
1640. Buried—Philip Santon : ibid. iv. 246.

Santony.—Local, ' of St. Antony,' some chapelry in Normandy, no doubt; cf. Sinclair, Simbarb, St. John, &c.
Dominus St. Antonis, co. Suff., 1273. A.
1782. Married — Robert Stacey and Mary Santany : St. Geo. Han. Sq. i. 329. New York, 1.

Sanxter. — A variant of Sangster ; v. Sanger.

Sare.—Bapt. 'the son of Sayer' (q.v.). The intermediate form was Saer, then Sare. This is one more of the endless descendants of Sagar (q.v.). The truth of this derivation is absolutely certain.
William Sare, co. Glouc., 1273. A.
1605. John Sare, or Sayer, of Nantwich : Wills at Chester, i. 169.
1642. Richard Sare, of Wych Malbank, *ostler* : ibid. ii. 192.
1675. Thomas Sare, of Warrington : ibid. iii. 235.
1789. Married—Taylor Sare and Eliz. Fountain : St. Geo. Han. Sq. ii. 25.
London, 1; South Lopham (Norfolk), 1.

Sargeant, &c. ; v. Serjeant.

Sargood.— ? Bapt. 'the son of Sigurd' (?). (Yonge, ii. 306.)

1781. Married — Charles Ball and Susanna Sargood : St. Geo. Han. Sq. i. 328.
London, 4 ; Oxford, 1 ; New York, 2.

Sarjeant, &c. ; v. Serjeant.

Sarkins. — Bapt. 'the son of Sarah '; cf. Wilkins, Hopkins, &c. I find the dim. Saralin also.
William Saralyn, co. Soms., 1 Edw. III: Kirby's Quest, p. 197.
Cf. this with Hewling or Embelin, q.v.
London, 1.

Sarl, Sarle, Sarll.—Bapt. 'the son of Sarle,' i.e. Serle, q.v. It is interesting to note that the form Sarl, found as a personal name in co. Cambridge in 1273, still flourishes there as a surname.
Sarle Tinctor, co. Hunts, 1273. A.
Matilda Sarle, co. Camb., ibid.
Sometimes Sarl is registered as Sarel (cf. Serrell for Serle).
1788. Married — Edward Sarel and Mary Philcox : St. Geo. Han. Sq. ii. 15.
London, 1, 1, 1 ; Gamlingay (co. Camb.), 0, 0, 6.

Sarson.—(1) Bapt. 'the son of Sara,' i.e. Sarah, a favourite name in the 13th and 14th centuries.
Sara de Clayton, 1379 : P. T. Yorks. p. 12.
Johannes Sareson, 1379 : ibid. p. 63.
Alicia fil. Sarr', co. Hunts, 1273. A.
Laurence fil. Sarre, co. Camb., ibid.
Richard fil. Sarre, co. Bucks, ibid.
(2) Local, ' the Saracen.'
' Amonges Sarzens and Jewes ': Piers P. 6312.
Nicholas le Sarazyn, C. R., 42 Hen. III.
Peter Sarracen. C.
Henry Sarrasin. J.
William Sarrazein. C.
1742. Buried—Catherine Sarazan : St. Michael, Cornhill, p. 296.
London, 3 ; New York, 1.

Sarvant, Sarvant. — Occup. ' the servant '; v. Servant ; cf. Perkin and Parkin, Clerk and Clark, *person* and *parson.*
London, 1, 0 ; New York, 0, 1.

Sass, Sasse.—Local, ' at the sasse.' ' Sasse, a lock in a river ' (Halliwell). ' Sasse, from sass (Belgic), a sluice or lock, especially in a river that is cut with floodgates, to shut up or let out water for the better passage of boats and barges, as in Misterton Sasse ' (The Isle of Axholme, its place-names and river-names, John K. Johnstone, p. 59).
1617. John Sas and Jane Delabarr : Marriage Lic. (London), ii. 51.
London, 2, 1 ; New York, 9, 5.

Satchell.—? Bapt. 'the son of Sachel.' Lower says : ' Satchell, a small sack or bag. Probably an ancient trader's sign ' (Patr. Brit. p. 303). This is very unlikely. Probably one of the many personal names ending in -*el.*
Thomas Sachel, co. Soms., 1 Edw. III : Kirby's Quest, p. 190.
1715. Bapt.—Pritty William, s. William Satchell : St. Jas. Clerkenwell, ii. 86.
London, 6 ; Philadelphia, 4.

Satterlee, Satterley, Satterly, Saturley.—Local, ' of Satterley ' or Satterleigh, a parish in co. Devon, near South Molton.
London, 0, 0, 0, 1 ; New York, 16, 1, 4, 0.

Satterthwaite, Satterthwait. —Local, ' of Satterthwaite,' an ancient chapelry in High Furness, near Hawkshead. Small and secluded as is the spot, it has originated a surname that has spread far and wide. It seems to have reached London about the 16th century. But it is still familiar in the immediate district, as I can testify.
Robert Saterthwaite, of Coutehouse in Hawkshead, 1596 : Lancashire Wills at Richmond, i. 243.
William Satewhait, of Saterthwaite, 1604 : ibid.
George Saterwhat, of Hauxhead, 1613 : ibid. p. 244.
1642. Bapt.—Robert, s. Maylin Setterthwayte : St. Jas. Clerkenwell, i. 152.
1649. Married — John Satterthwaite, *stationer,* and Marye Peele : St. Michael, Cornhill, p. 30.
1668. Buried — Isabella, d. William Saterthwayte, of Arrad : Ulverston Parish Ch. i. 134.
London, 2, 0 ; Manchester, 2, 0 ; Ulverston, 2, 0 ; Philadelphia, 1, 5.

Saturday.—Nick. or personal ; cf. Monday, Pentecost, Whitsunday, Pask, &c.
Willelmus Ceterday, 1379 : P. T. Yorks. p. 119.

Saturley ; v. Satterlee.

Saucemaker.—Occup. ' a maker of sauces '; v. Saucer.
Joan Sausemaker, co. York. W. 11.

Saucer.—Occup. 'the saucer,' i.e. a maker of sauces, a most important avocation in the 13th, 14th, and 15th centuries, when some seasoning, like salt-pickle, for a relish was deemed a vital necessity. Hence *saucer*, a deep-rimmed plate, or shallow vessel, to hold sauce in. v. Saucemaker.

'Wo was his cook, but if his sauce were
Poinant, and sharpe, and redy all his
gere.'	Chaucer, C. T. 352.

The early registers teem with entries.

William le Sauser, co. Devon, Hen. III–Edw. I. K.
Geoffry le Sauser, co. Oxf., 1273. A.
Robert le Sauser, co. Camb., ibid.
John de Weteley, *sauser*, 25 Edw. I : Freemen of York, i. 6.
Roger le Sauser. N.
Matilda le Sausere. B.

Curiously enough, I cannot find any present representatives of the name. The latest are :

1662. Bapt.—Alexander, son of Laurance Sawcer : St. Michael, Cornhill, p. 143.
1670. Buried—Robert, son of Laurance Sawcer : ibid. p. 257.
1735. Married—Thomas Edwards and Keturah Sawcer : St. Geo. Han. Sq. i. 15.

Saucery.—Local, 'of the saucery,' practically official ; an officer of the household who had charge of the sauces ; cf. de la Pantrie, de la Spence. v. Saucer.

Robert de la Saucee, co. Northants, 1273. A.
William de la Saucery, 44 Edw. III. P.
Johannes de Sausre, 1379 : P. T. Yorks. p. 192.
Gilbert de la Saucerie, C. R., 15 Ric. II.
William Walsingham, alias William of Saucerie, C. R., 9 Hen. IV.

Saul, Saull.—(1) Bapt. 'the son of Saul' ; cf. Paul. This personal name was somewhat uncommon. (2) Local, 'at the saule' (i. e. Sale, q.v.), from residence therein as owner or servitor. O.E. *sel*, a hall ; Fr. *salle*. The surname of the famous knight commemorated by Froissart (1332–48) is variously written de la Sale, de la Saule, de Aula, or de Halle (Notes and Queries, 1st S. v. 291). No doubt both (1) and (2) have contributed to our directories.

Johannes Saule, 1379 : P.T.Yorks. p. 136.
Cecilia Saule, 1379 : ibid. p. 42.

Johannes Saule, 1379 : ibid. p. 58.
1582–3. Arnold Saule, co. Glouc.: Reg. Univ. Oxf. vol. ii. pt. ii. p. 124.
1602. Bapt.—Mary, d. Edward Saule : St. Michael, Cornhill, p. 103.
London, 8, 1 ; MDB. (co. Cumb.), 15, 1 ; New York, 18, 0.

Saulsbury, Saulsberry ; v. Salisbury, a variant.

Manchester, 1, 0 ; Philadelphia, 2, 1.

Saunder, Saunders, Saunderson.—Bapt. 'the son of Alexander,' from the nick. Saunder. In early use. v. Sander.

Alisandre, or Sandre de Leycestre, London, 1273. A.
Richard frater Sander, co. Salop, ibid.
Thomas fil. Saundre, co. Northampton, ibid.
Saunder de M're, co. Salop, ibid.
William Saundres, co. Soms., 1 Edw. III : Kirby's Quest, p. 157.
Cristiana Sawndir, 1379 : P. T. Yorks. p. 141.
Ricardus Sawndirson, 1379 : ibid.
Matilda Saunder-wyf, 1379 : ibid. p. 22.
Johannes Saundirman, 1379 : ibid.
Sawnder Manggo, 1379 : ibid. p. 109.
Johannes Saundirson (son of above), 1379 : ibid.
Saundir Saryaunte, 1379 : ibid.
London, 1, 136, 1 ; New York, 1, 41, 1.

Savage.—Nick. 'the savage' (cf. Wild). It is curious that Wild and Savage should be so popular as sobriquets, but fierceness was fascinating. The invariable forms are Salvage, Sauvage, and Savage.

Geoffrey le Sauvage, co. Leic., Hen. III–Edw. I. K.
Walter Salvage, co. Oxf., 1273. A.
Robert le Savage, co. Suff., ibid.
Beatrix Sawage, 1379 : P. T. Yorks. p. 19.
Robertus Sawfage, 1379 : ibid. p. 213.
Adelmya le Sauvage. J.
John le Savage. H.
William le Salvage. B.
1734. Married—Andrew Savage and Mary Gill : St. Geo. Han. Sq. i. 13.
London, 48 ; New York, 60.

Savill, Saville, Savile, Seville, Sevill.—Local. An old surname of the East Riding, which has penetrated into Lanc. as Saville and Seville. It looks like a surname of Norman local extraction.

Robertus Sayuill, 1379 : P. T. Yorks. p. 134.
Johannes Seyuyll', 1379 : ibid. p. 183.
Johannes Sayuyll', 1379 : ibid. p. 184.
1611. John Payne and Fridiswith Savill (co. York) : Marriage Lic. (London), ii. 1.

1616-7. Sir Thomas Mildmay and Anne Savile (parish of Wakefield, co. York) : ibid. ii. 49.
Oldham (Seville), 5, (Sevill), 1 ; London, 10, 4, 1, 0, 0 ; West Rid. Court Dir., 0, 4, 0, 0, 0 ; Philadelphia, 0, 9, 0, 4, 0.

Savoner.—Occup.'the soaper' ; v. Soper.

Nicholas le Sauoner, Close Roll, 2 Edw. I.
Agneta la Savoner. A.
Adam la Savonier. E.

Savory, Savery, Saffery, Savary. — Bapt. 'the son of Savary.' Latinized as Savaricus. The Hundred Rolls form is sometimes Saffrey, almost unaltered in the present Saffery.

Savaric de Maulcon, 1224 : Davies' Hist. of Southampton, p. 24.
Richard Saveri, co. Camb., 1273. A.
Robert Saffrei, co. Camb., ibid.
Richard Saffrey, co. Camb., ibid.
Savaricus de Fenlieze, co. Wilts, ibid.
Saufray de Som'y, co. Sussex, ibid.
Savar' de Claville, co. Bucks, ibid.
John Sauvary, co. Wilts, Hen. III–Edw. I. K.
Savericus de Bohun, 12 Edw. I. BBB. p. 345.
Saffredus de Hawkswell, 16 Edw. I, ibid. p. 388.

Savericus de Bohun is called Savary by Dugdale.

William Savery, 1605 : Reg. Broad Chalke, co. Wilts, p. 3.
1708. Bapt.—Elizabeth, d. of John and Abigail Saveory, lodging at Mr. Pitman's : St. Thomas the Apostle (London), p. 71.
1805. Bapt.—Eliz., d. James Saffery : Canterbury Cath. p. 42.
London, 8, 1, 2, 0 ; Philadelphia, 0, 6, 0, 0 ; Boston (U.S.), 8, 1, 0, 4.

Saward.—Bapt. 'the son of Siward,' one of many variants. For many instances, v. Seward (2).

Hugh Saward, co. Norf., 1273. A.
1590. Robert Boothe and Agnes Sawarde : Marriage Lic. (London), i. 187.
1736. Married—John Saward and Bridget Forsbrook : St. Geo. Han. Sq. i. 18.
1741. Bapt. — Susanna, d. William Saward : St. Antholin (London), p. 163.
London, 4 ; MDB. (co. Essex), 4 ; New York, 2.

Sawer ; v. Sawyer.

Sawkins, Sawkings.—Bapt. 'the son of Saer,' dim. Saykin, modified to Sawkin (v. Sayer). If we were sure that Saunderkin existed from Alexander, then naturally Sawkin would be the corruption. But *-kin* as a suffix was almost invariably added to a nick. monosyllable; and we have a clear case of the once great name of Saer becoming Saykin. The *g* in Sawkings is, of course, excrescent; cf. Jennings. The same individual is thus described:

Saer Bude, co. Essex, 1273. A. p. 146.
Saykinus Bude, co. Essex, ibid. p. 159.
1661. Buried—Grace Greeton, mayd servant to John Sawkins: St. Jas. Clerkenwell, iv. 338.
1720. Married—Thomas Sawkins and Sarah Wilmott: St. Dionis Backchurch, p. 60.
London, 1, 1.

Sawman.—Bapt. 'the son of Salmon,' i.e. Solomon. It is tempting to derive the name from O.F. *saumon*, English *salmon*, the fish, and make it a nickname, but this origin is improbable; v. Salmon.

William Saumon, co. Hunts, 1273. A.
Adam Sauman, co. Linc., ibid.
1551. Bapt.—Robert Sawmon: St. Jas. Clerkenwell, i. 1.
1616. — John, s. George Sawman: ibid. p. 75.
London, 1.

Sawrey.—Local, 'of Sawrey,' a hamlet on the west shore of Windermere, near Hawkshead, North Lanc. A branch of the family settled in Ulverston parish as early as the reign of Henry VI (v. West's Antiquities of Furness).

1545. Buried—John Sowraie: St. Mary Ulverston, p. 1.
1551. Bapt.—William Sowraie: ibid. p. 13.
John Saurey, of Hauxhead, 1583: Lancashire Wills at Richmond, i. 245.
William Sawrey, of Sawrey, 1593: ibid.
1619-20. Anthony Sawrey, co. Bucks: Reg. Univ. Oxf. vol. ii. pt. ii. p. 382.
MDB. (co. Cumb.), 3; Ulverston, 2.

Sawyer, Sawer.—Occup. 'the sawyer,' one who saws wood, &c.; *y* as in *law-yer* and *bow-yer* is intrusive.

Ralph le Sawiere, co. Hunts, 1273. A.
Geoffrey le Sawere, London, ibid.
Henry le Sawer, C. R., 9 Edw. I.
William Saweyer, co. Soms., 1 Edw. III: Kirby's Quest, p. 101.
Richard le Saghiere, Close Roll, 21 Edw. III. pt. ii.
Henry le Saghier. M.
Walter le Sawyere. G.
Hugo Sawer, 1379: P. T. Yorks. p. 156.
Thomas Sawer, 1379: ibid.

1767. Married—Richard Sawyer and Jane Jessatt: St. Geo. Han. Sq. i. 168.
— — Richard Meares and Frances Sawer: ibid. p. 171.
London, 30, 1; Philadelphia, 20, 0.

Saxby. — Local, 'of Saxby,' parishes in cos. Lincoln (2) and Leicester.

1577. Bapt.—Robert, son of — Sacksbye: St. Jas. Clerkenwell, i. 10.
1661. Buried—Richard Saxbee, a poore old man: ibid. iv. 343.
1808. Married—John Saxby and Mary Elkins: St. Geo. Han. Sq. ii. 394.
London, 10; MDB. (co. Kent), 5.

Saxelby, Saxelbye. — Local, 'of Saxelby,' parishes in cos. Lincoln and Leicester.

William de Saxelby, co. Linc., Hen. III—Edw. I. K.
Geoffrey de Saxelby, co. Linc., 1273. A.
1768. Married — William Evans and Eliz. Saxelby: St. Geo. Han. Sq. i. 178.
MDB. (co. Worc.), 1, 0; (East Rid. Yorks), 0, 1.

Saxon. — Local, 'of Saxton,' q.v. (2). I doubt not this is the true origin. That it means a Saxon by race and blood is chronologically absurd.

1669. Bapt.—John, s. Audery Saxson: St. Jas. Clerkenwell, i. 239.
1742. Married — Thomas Saxon and Mary Bullock: St. Geo. Chap. Mayfair, p. 24.
1791. — John Saxon and Eliz. Wilson: St. Geo. Han. Sq. ii. 54.
London, 2; Philadelphia, 2.

Saxton, Sexton, Sextone.—(1) Offic. 'the sacristan,' now sexton or verger of a church. This, without doubt, has added to the modern directories. Although my instances are few, I suspect it is the parent of many of our Saxtons and Sextons.

Hugh Sacristan, co. Kent, 1273. A.
John Sexteyn, C. R., 7 Edw. IV.

(2) Local, 'of Saxton,' a parish in the dioc. of York.

Johannes de Saxton, 1379: P. T. Yorks. p. 99.
Robertus de Saxton, 1379: ibid. p. 125.
1771. Married — Charles Saxton and Mary Bush: St. Geo. Han. Sq. i. 211.
1782. — George Sexton and Mary Liddell: ibid. p. 338.
London, 6, 14, 1; Philadelphia, 13, 30, 0.

Say.—Local, 'at the sea,' i.e. by the seaside, from residence thereby; cf. Sands, Sandys, and

Shore. The family of Say are found entered as Attsee (i. e. at the sea) and De la See in the Yorkshire Visitation, 1563; as for instance:

Sir Thomas Say, p. 168.
Johanes de Say, p. 277.
Say (otherwise Attsee, and De la See), p. 277.
John le (? de) Say, co. Soms., 1 Edw. III: Kirby's Quest, p. 243.
Henery Attsee, of Herne: Visitation of Bedfordshire, 1566, p. 167.
1619. Edward Say, co. Kent: Reg. Univ. Oxf. vol. ii. pt. ii. p. 379.
— William Say, co. Kent: ibid.
1623. Edward Say and Margaret Tooting: Marriage Lic. (London), ii. 131.
London, 6; Philadelphia, 1.

Sayce, Sayse, Saiss, Seys, Saise.—Nick. 'the foreigner,' the stranger, the Englishman. A Welsh surname; cf. Inglis, Walsh, Irish.

Anian Seys, 1309, Bishop of Bangor.
William Sys, co. Soms., 1 Edw. III: Kirby's Quest, p. 121.
Rogerus Seys, 1384: Hist. and Ant. St. David's, p. 371.
1619. Henry Sayse and Margaret Warren: Marriage Lic. (London), ii. 80.
Ilyke de Ivon Seys: Visitation Glouc. (1623), p. 98.
Joane Howell ap Evan Sais: ibid. p. 180.
'At the Chepstow police-court on Saturday, before Messrs. G. Seys and H. Lowe,' &c.: South Wales Daily News, Aug. 26, 1889.
MDB. (co. Monmouth), 1, 0, 0, 2, 0; Bristol (Saise), 3, (Sayce), 3; Tenby (Saies), 2; Pembroke (Sayse), 1; New York (Sayce), 1.

Sayer, Sayers.—Bapt. 'the son of Sayer,' also found as Sagar, Sigar, and Seger. A forgotten personal name that has left an indelible mark on our directories. From twenty to twenty-five surnames separately spelt are the offspring, and many have a large number of representatives. The name was popular so early as Domesday as Segar and Sigar, and Latinized as Sigarus. Siger de Frivile is found in the Hundred Rolls as Siger, Saer, Sayer, and Seer (ii. 152, 514, 153, 523). The following surnames (amongst others) will be found in their proper place, unquestionable descendants of Siger or Sayer, viz. Seager, Seeger, Seaker, Sugar, Sugars, Siggers, Saggers, Sagar, Sager, Secker, Sear, Sears, Searson, Seare, Seares, Seear, Syer, and Syers. Also a dim. Saykin.

John Sayer, co. Norf., 1273. A.
Saer Batayle, co. Essex, ibid.
John fil. Saeri, London, ibid.
Sayer Herberd, London, ibid.
Saher de Braban. E.
Saher Clerk. C.
Saher le King. H.
Agnes Sayer. N.
London, 24, 9; Philadelphia, 7, 12.

Sayles, Saile, Sales, Sayle. — Local, 'at the sayles,' i.e. the hurdles (cf. Paliser, also a great Yorkshire surname). 'Sales, the upright stakes of a hurdle' (Halliwell). The only instances I can find, ancient or modern, are in co. York. The name has remained there at least 500 years. But as an alternative, v. Sale.

Agnes del Sayles, 1379: P. T. Yorks. p. 66.
William Salys, 1379: ibid. p. 95.
Alanus Sayle, 1379: ibid. p. 102.
Robertus Schayle, 1379: ibid. p. 106.
Willelmus Saylles, 1379: ibid. p. 124.
Margeria del Sayle, 1379: ibid. p. 141.
John Sale, co. York, 1577: Reg. Univ. Oxf. vol. ii. pt. ii. p. 79.
West Rid. Court Dir., 2, 1, 3, 0; Sheffield, 6, 0, 1, 0; New York, 9, 3, 1, 1.

Saylor, Sailer, Sailor. — Occup. 'the sailour,' a dancer, a hopper. 'Saille, to leap (A.N.), hence sailours, leapers, dancers' (Halliwell).

'There was many a timbestere,
And sailours that I dare well swere
Couthe hir craft full perfitly.'
Chaucer, R. of R. 769-71.

Sailor is a comparatively modern term for one who sails on the sea. Mariner (q.v.) was the term in general use. Dancer and Hopper are familiar surnames. Doubtless the surname concerns the dancer. Oddly enough, I cannot find the surname on English soil. It is a common name in the United States.

John le Saillur, 1273. A.
William le Saylliur, ibid.
Nicholas le Saler, ibid.
1790. Married — John Maddocks and Frances Sayler: St. Geo. Han. Sq. ii. 45.
Philadelphia, 40, 35, 18.

Saynor. — Nick.; v. Senior.

Sayse. — Nick.; v. Sayce.

Scadlock; v. Scathlock.

Scaife. — Nick.; v. Skaife.

Scales. — Local, 'at the scales.' Norse scale, a shepherd's hut; cf. Scottish shealing (Taylor, p. 486). Hence Winterscale and Summerscales (q.v.). A hamlet in the parish of Aldingham, Furness, is called Scales. A farmstead in Ulverston parish is named Cockinskale, which gave rise to a surname corrupted to Cockinshell; cf. Portingscale, near Keswick. See, however, shale (Skeat's Dict.).

Isolda del Scales, 1379: P. T. Yorks. p. 219.
Johannes del Scales, 1379: ibid. p. 250.
Willelmus de la Scale, 1379: ibid. p. 261.
Robert Scales, of Hauxhead, 1591: Lancashire Wills at Richmond, i. 245.
George Skales, of Ulverston, 1670: ibid. p. 256.
London, 6; West Rid. Court Dir., 5; New York, 1; Boston (U.S.), 7.

Scambler. — (1) Occup. 'a scambler' (?), i.e. one who kept a stall; v. Scamell. (2) Nick. 'a scambler' (?), one who sprawled in his walk, a shambler (of which word scambler is the stronger form). Probably this is the true derivation.

Edmund Scambler, or Schambler, bishop of Peterborough, 1560: Cal. State Papers, i. 164, 374, &c.
1580. Robert Scamler, of Hornby: Lancashire Wills at Richmond, i. 245.
1588. Agnes Skamler, of Wraye: ibid. p. 256.
1793. Married — John Shambler and Hannah Coats: St. Geo. Han. Sq. ii. 96.
1794. — Joshua Thurston and Ann Scambler: ibid. p. 119.
Manchester, 1; MDB. (co. Essex), 1; (co. Lancaster), 4.

Scamell, Scammell. — Local, 'at the shamble,' i.e. the stall. M.E. schamel, a bench; A.S. scamel, a stool (v. shambles, in Skeat's Dict.). A surname for one who kept a stall or bench for meat, &c., in the street or market.

Simon de la Scamele, co. Essex, 1273. A.
Simon de la Schamele, co. Essex, ibid.
Walter Schamel, co. Dorset, ibid.
Symon del Scameles, 31 Edw. I: Freemen of York, i. 9.
Richard Skammel, co. Dorset, 1316. M.
William Scammell, 1563: Reg. Broad Chalke, Wilts, p. 1.
Mary Scammell, 1592: ibid. p. 2.

1790. Married — William Scammell and Eliz. Searle: St. Geo. Han. Sq. ii. 46.
London, 2, 4; Boston (U.S.), 1, 0; New York, 0, 5.

Scamp. — ? —. A curious name. Of course it has no connexion with the dictionary scamp. No doubt local.

Ilfracombe, 5.

Scampton. — Local, 'of Scampton,' a parish in co. Lincoln.

1705. Bapt. — Eliz., d. Francis Scampton: St. Michael, Cornhill, p. 65.
1732. Married — John Leeson and Eliz. Scampton: ibid. p. 161.
MDB. (co. Leic.), 1; Philadelphia, 3.

Scarborough, Scarbrow, Scarboro. — Local, 'of Scarborough,' co. York.

Henry de Scardeburgh, co. Linc., 20 Edw. I. R.
Johannes de Scardeburgh, 1379: P. T. Yorks. p. 265.
Nicholas de Scardburgh, 1379: ibid. p. 218.
1571. Married — Stephen Scarborough and Eliz. Eaton: St. Antholin (London), p. 21.
1606. — John Scarboroughe and Hester Rickett: St. Mary Aldermary, p. 11.
1646. Bapt. — Dennis, s. Matthew Scarbarrow: St. Dionis Backchurch, p. 108.
London, 2, 1, 0; West Rid. Court Dir., 7, 0, 0; MDB. (co. Leic.), 2, 0, 1; Philadelphia, 7, 0, 0.

Scarf(e; v. Scarth.

Scargill, Scargle. — Local, 'of Scargill,' a township in the parish of Barningham, N. Rid. Yorks. The surname has ramified strongly, and in America has assumed the guise of Scargle.

William de Scargill, co. York, 16 Edw. II: FF. x. 129.
Willelmus de Scargill, chivaler, 1379: P. T. Yorks. p. 119.
Johannes de Scargill, 1379: ibid. p. 216.
1674. Thomas Cranmer and Dorothy Scargill: Marriage Alleg. (Canterbury), p. 228.
Sheffield, 2, 0; Philadelphia, 0, 10.

Scarisbrick, Scarsbrick, Scarsbrook, Scarasbrick, Scarrisbrick. — Local, 'of Scarisbrick,' a township in the parish of Ormskirk, co. Lancashire. In London the name settled down to Scarsbrook.

1508. Thomas Scarysbrig, D.D.: Reg. Univ. Oxf. i. 56.

Edward Scarisbrick, of Scarisbrick, 1599: Wills at Chester, i. 169.
Henry Scarisbrick, of Scarisbrick, 1608: ibid.
1615. Anthony Scarsbricke, *mercer*, of London, and Jane Glascocke: Marriage Lic. (London), ii. 35.
1768. Married—Joseph Whitmore and Mary Scasbrook: St. Geo. Han. Sq. i. 177.
Liverpool, 3, 2, 0, 1, 1; MDB. (co. Ches.), 1, 0, 0, 0, 0; London, 0, 3, 0, 0, 0.

Scarlett.—Nick. 'the scarlet,' of bright red complexion in dress or person; cf. Russell, Rous, Blunt, Blundell, &c.

Henry Scarlath, alias Henry Scarlet, co. Bucks, 1273. A.
Peter Scarlet, co. Camb., ibid.
Hugh Skarlet. D.
John Scarlet, co. Soms., 1 Edw. III: Kirby's Quest, p. 83.
Robert Skerlet, 1379: P. T. Yorks. p. 46.
Thomas de Scarlett (?), 1379: ibid. p. 219.
Gregory Skarlett, 1506: Reg. Univ. Oxf. vol. ii. pt. i. 49.
1650. Married—Guy Scarlet and Ann Whitton: St. Jas. Clerkenwell, iii. 85.
London, 12; West Rid. Court Dir., 1; New York, 3.

Scarsbrick, -brook; v. Scarisbrick.

Scarth, Scarf, Scarfe, Scarff, Scarffe.—Local, 'of Scharth.' I cannot find the spot. The surname is clearly of Yorkshire parentage.

Henry Scharf, co. Linc., 1273. A.
John de Scharth, 1379: P. T. Yorks. p. 265.
1615. John Scarth, co. York: Reg. Univ. Oxf. vol. ii. pt. ii. p. 340.
1662. Married — John Milborne and Margery Scarfe: St. Jas. Clerkenwell, iii. 111.
1723. — James Wightman and Eliz. Scarfe: St. Mary Aldermary, p. 46.
London, 0, 1, 6, 2, 1; West Rid. (Yorks) Court Dir., 2, 1, 1, 0, 0; MDB. (North Rid. Yorks) Scarth, 10; Philadelphia (Scarf), 1.

Scatchard, Scatcherd, Scratcherd. — ? Occup. 'the scatch-herd'(?). I cannot find the term in the dictionaries. Yorkshire, where the surname is chiefly found, has given us a large number of this class; cf. Calvert, Shepard, Oxenhird, Coward, Geldard, Stodart, Swinnart, Coulthard, all compounds of *herd*. Of course they were not all confined to that county. Scatchard is probably of this class, Scratcherd being a manifest corruption.

1753. Married—James Finch and Esther Scatchard: St. Dionis Backchurch, p. 70.
West Rid. Court Dir., 6, 2, 1; London, 1, 0, 0; Philadelphia, 8, 0, 0.

Scathlock, Scadlock.—Bapt. 'the son of Scathlock.' Found in the district of Sherwood Forest, where we should expect to find it.

 'Readily Little John went forth,
 And Scathelock went before.'
   Robin Hood, i. 233.

Cf. Tuck, Littlejohn, and Hood.

Geoffrey Scatheloc, co. Notts, 1273. A.
York, 0, 1; London, 0, 1.

Scatliff.—Local, 'of Scaitliff,' in the parish of Rochdale, co. Lanc. Of course the suffix is *-cliff*; cf. Topliff for Topcliff, and Cunliffe for Cuncliffe.

1637. John Scatleffe and Mary Shakespeare: Marriage Lic. (London), ii. 233.
London, 1.

Scattergood.—Personal, 'the son of Schatregod.' In my book on the Sources and Signification of English Surnames I placed this in the nickname class, and said that it implied a spendthrift. There can be no doubt that it was an old personal name, one of the very many that terminate in *-god*, *-gode*, *-gaud*, or *-good*. The surname has ramified strongly in the United States; cf. Osgood, Goodwin, &c.

Wimcot Schatregod, co. Bedf., 1273. A.
Thomas Skaregoode. F.
Mathew Scatergude, co. York. W. 2.
Richard Scatergood, Patent Roll, 3 Edw. VI. pt. v.
1703. Married—Henry Edwards and Eliz. Scattergood: St. Jas. Clerkenwell, iii. 226.
London, 2; West Rid. (Yorks) Court Dir., 2; Philadelphia, 49.

Scholar, Scholer, Schollard.—Occup. 'a scholar,' one belonging to a school, a learned man.

(Magister) Scholasticus, Jersey, 20 Edw. I. R.
1619. Edward Smith and Sarah Scoller: Marriage Lic. (London), ii. 82.
1751. Married — Joseph Schollar and Grace Burgess: St. Geo. Chap. Mayfair, p. 198.
1769. — William Scholar and Mary Roberts: St. Geo. Han. Sq. i. 189.
New York, 1, 1, 0; Worcester (U.S.), 0, 0, 3.

Scholefield, Schofield, Scholfield, Schoolfield.—Local, 'at the school-field.' A Lancashire

surname, which has spread far and wide; cf. Scowcroft and Schoolcraft. Probably this *field* or *croft* was used as a playground. But I dare not pronounce definitely on this point. The plural form in Scholes (q.v.) is difficult to explain. The precise spot so termed seems to have been within the ancient parish of Rochdale, co. Lanc.

1596. Edmund Scholfield, of Middleton: Wills at Chester, i. 170.
1613. Alex. Scholfield, of Scholfield: ibid.
1623. Edmund Scholefield, of Saddleworth, ibid. ii. 193.
1665. Married — John Scofeild and Jone Hudson: St. Jas. Clerkenwell, iii. 112.
London, 2, 19, 3, 0; West Rid. Court Dir., 27, 9, 5, 0; Manchester, 2, 42, 3, 0; Philadelphia, 0, 125, 0, 0; New York (Scholfield), 2.

Scholes, Schoales.—Local, (1) 'at the school' or schools, from residence therein or thereby; cf. Scholefield, Schoolcraft, Scowcroft, &c.; v. Scholefield. Schoales is an American variant. (2) 'of Scholes,' a township in the parish of Barwick-in-Elmett, nine miles from Leeds, W. Rid. Yorks.

Johannes del Scholes, 1379: P. T. Yorks. p. 181.
Ricardus del Scholes, 1379: ibid. p. 195.
Ricardus del Scoles, 1379: ibid. p. 67.

On page 195 of the same register is found the name of Hugh Alderscholes, a manifest local surname.

Edmund Scholes, of Prestwich (Manchester), 1587: Wills at Chester, i. 170.
Francis Scholes, of Chadderton, 1596: ibid.
London, 1, 0; West Rid. Court Dir., 7, 0; Manchester, 11, 0; Philadelphia, 9, 10.

Scholey, Schooley. — Local, 'of Scoley,' some small spot in W. Rid. Yorks.

Johannes de Scolay, 1379: P. T. Yorks. p. 91.
Robertus de Scolay, 1379: ibid.
Ricardus de Scolay, 1379: ibid. p. 103.
1581-2. Richard Scholey, co. Yorks.: Reg. Univ. Oxf. vol. ii. pt. ii. p. 116.
1735. Married — Beale Scholey and Mary Carr: St. Jas. Clerkenwell, iii. 263.
1784. — John Butler and Eliz. Schoolly: St. Geo. Han. Sq. i. 361.
London, 2, 2; West Rid. Court Dir., 4, 0; Sheffield, 4, 0; Philadelphia, 11, 0.

Schoolcraft.—Local, 'at the school-croft,' from residence in the school enclosure; v. Scowcroft.

A distinguished American, Henry Rowe Schoolcraft, both ethnologist and geologist (1793–1864), bore this name ; v. Craft and Croft.

1681. John Schoolcroft and Judith Bythell: Marriage Alleg. (Canterbury), p. 80.
Worcester (U.S.), 2.

Schoolfield; v. Scholefield, an American variant.

Schoolhouse.—Local, 'at the school-house,' from residence therein. This surname lingered on for several centuries, and may still exist.—Since writing this I find it has crossed the Atlantic.

Ralph atte Skolehus, co. Norf., 1273. A.
1534. Henry Scolehouse, alderman of Norwich: FF. iii. 208.
1615. Alice Scolows, Norwich: ibid. iv. 496.
New York, 1.

Schoolmaster.—Occup. 'the schoolmaster.'

Ralph the Scolemaistre, C. R., 32 Edw. I.
Thomas Skolmayster. B.
John Scolemastre, C. R., 3 Hen. V.
New York, 1.

Scissons.—Bapt. ; v. Sisson.

London, 1.

Sclaster.—Occup. 'the slater' or 'sclater,' with feminine suffix Scla-ster ; cf. Brewster and Baxter. This form did not live, but as an occupative term *maltster* does, which is quite as uncouth in sound.

Willelmus Carter, *slaster*, 1379: P. T. Yorks. p. 61.
Robertus Clerkson, *sclaster*, 1379: ibid. p. 111.
Agnes Sclaster, 1379 : ibid. p. 3.
Hugo Sclaster, 1379 : ibid. p. 34.
Elena Slaster, 1379 : ibid. p. 23.

Sclater ; v. Slater.

Scobell, Scoble; v. Scovell.

Scoffer.—Nick. ' the scoffer.'

Matilda le Scoffar, co. Soms., 1 Edw. III : Kirby's Quest, p. 113.

Scoggins, Scoging. — Bapt. 'the son of Scogan.' Scoggins is the genitive ; cf. Williams. The final *g* in Scoging is an excrescence ; cf. Jennings. The surname still lives in cos. Norfolk and Suffolk.

Robert Scogan, co. Norf., 1357: FF. vii. 144.
Henry Scogan, co. Norf., 1407: ibid.

Robert Scoggan, co. Norf., 45 Edw. III ; ibid. x. 83.
Thomas Scoggan, co. Norf., 1420: ibid. vii. 142.
London, 3, 0 ; MDB. (co. Suffolk), 3, 1 ; Ipswich, 1, 0 ; Philadelphia, 2, 0.

Scolding, Skoulding.—? Local, ' of Shouldham ' (?). These two variants seem more or less imitative of the dictionary word *scolding*.

Rein de Sculdeham, co. Norf., temp. Hen. II : FF. vii. 514.
William de Sculdham, co. Norf., temp. Rich. I : ibid. ix. 178.

The next stage of corruption was Scoulden :

Robert Scoulden, *common-councilman*, Norwich, 1687: FF. iii. 423.

The last step was the imitative Scolding :

1654. Mr. Scolding, *ensign*, Norwich : FF. iii. 400.
London, 1, 0 ; MDB. (co. Suffolk), 1, 1.

Scorer, Scorrar.—Occup. (1) ' the scorer,' a military spy, a scourer of the country. 'The Kinge, beinge at Notyngham, and or he came there, sent the scorers al abowte the contries adjoynynge to aspie and serche yf any gaderyngs in any place were agaynst hym ': Arrival of King Edward IVth (Halliwell). (2) ' The scorer,' one who scores or counts by notches, a tally-man, one who kept accounts.

Thomas le Scorur, C. R., 4 Edw. II.
Willelmus Skorer, 1379: P. T. Yorks. p. 80.
Johannes Skorer, 1379 : ibid.
1667. John Scorror, of Disley Stanley : Wills at Chester (1660–80), p. 237.
1695. William Scorer, of Disley : ibid. (1681–1700), p. 221.
1800. Married—John Steel and Ann Scorer : St. Geo. Han. Sq. ii. 213.
London, 2, 1.

Scoresby, Sorsby, Soresby.—Local, ' of Scawsby,' a hamlet in the parish of Brodsworth, near Doncaster, co. York.

William de Schauceby, co. Northumb., Hen. III–Edw. I.
Johannes de Scausceby, 1379: P. T. Yorks. p. 46.
Ricardus de Scausceby, 1379 : ibid. p. 47.
Johannes de Scausby, 1379: ibid. p. 120.

William Scoresby, the great Arctic explorer, was son of William Scoresby, a whale-fisher, and

born at Cropton, co. York, Oct. 5, 1789.

1686. Robert Mosse and Ann Scoresby : Marriage Lic. (Faculty Office), p. 183.
West Rid. Court Dir., 0, 2, 0 ; MDB. (co. Derby), 0, 0, 3.

Scotland.—Local, ' of Scotland'; cf. Britton, Ireland, Cornwall, Burgoyne, &c.

Simon Scotland, co. Norf., temp. Hen. IV : FF. viii. 504.
1801. Married—William Spencer and Ann Scotland : St. Geo. Han. Sq. ii. 247.
Boston (U.S.), 2.

Scotney.—Local, ' of Scotney.' An estate, with castle, in East Sussex, which belonged to the family in the 13th and 14th centuries. The first of the name on record is Walter de Scotney, steward of the Earl of Gloucester, temp. Henry III, who was hanged on a charge of attempting the life of his master (Blaauw's Barons' War, p. 61, quoted by Lower).

Lambert de Scoteni, co. Linc., 1273. A.
Thomas de Scoteney, co. Linc., ibid.
Peter de Scotenye, co. Linc., ibid.
1772. Married—Stephen Scotney and Dorothy Gibson : St. Geo. Han. Sq. i. 226.
London, 2 ; MDB. (co. Camb.), 2.

Scotson.—Nick. 'the son of the Scot,' one of an extremely rare class ; cf. Taylorson, Hindson, Clerkson. It is natural to find it at first in such counties as Durham and York.

Alexander Scotteson, 1379 : P. T. Yorks. p. 206.
Gilbert Scotessun, of Durham. W. 15.
1798. Married — Abraham Bass and Margaret Scotson : St. Geo. Han. Sq. ii. 177.
Ulverston, 1 ; Manchester, 1 ; Liverpool, 4.

Scott.—Local, ' the Scot,' one who came from Scotland, q.v. This is probably the most flourishing of local surnames.

Roger le Scot, London, 1273. A.
Elias le Scot, co. Salop, ibid.
Walter Scot, co. York, ibid.
Johannes Scot, 1379 : P. T. Yorks. p. 8.
Adam Skotte, 1379 : ibid. p. 27.
1638. Robert Scott and Anne Payne : Marriage Lic. (London), ii. 37.

The double *t* in Scott is now universal.

London, 248 ; Philadelphia, 558.

Scotto.—Local; v. Skottowe.

Scotton, Scotten.—Local, ' of Scotton,' a parish in co. Lincoln. Also two townships in co. York, one in the parish of Catterick, N. Rid., the other in the parish of Farnham, W. Rid. The Lincolnshire parish seems to be the chief parent.

Robert de Scotton, co. Linc., 1273. A.
Thomas de Skotton, 13 Edw. I : Freemen of York, i. 4.
John de Scottone, co. Linc., 20 Edw. I. R.
1663. Edward Scotton and Margaret Archer: Marriage Lic. (Faculty Office), p. 71.
1750. Married — James Bracey Perry and Ann Scotton: St. Geo. Chap. Mayfair, p. 185.
London, 1, 1 ; Philadelphia, 0, 1.

Scovell, Scobell, Scoble, Scovil, Scovill, Scoville.—Local, ' of Scoville.' Lower says, ' From Escoville, now Ecoville, in the arrondissement of Caen, in Normandy.' There can be little doubt that Scobell and Scoble are variants.

Roger de Schovill, co. Norf., Hen. III-Edw. I. K.
Matilda de Scowile, co. Norf., 1273. A.
1610. Charles Skovell, co. Dorset : Reg. Univ. Oxf. vol. ii. pt. ii. p. 311.
1615. William Scoble, co. Devon : ibid. p. 339.
1663. Sir Richard Braham and Jane Scobell: Marriage Alleg. (Canterbury), p. 86.
1805. Married — Charles Andrew Scovell and Editha Slocombe : St. Geo. Han. Sq. ii. 331.
MDB. (co. Devon), 0, 2, 2, 0, 0, 0 ; London, 3, 1, 0, 0, 0, 0 ; Crockford, 0, 3, 0, 0, 0, 0 ; New York, 1, 1, 3, 1, 2, 5 ; Philadelphia, 0, 0, 0, 1, 0, 0.

Scowcroft.—Local, ' of the school-croft,' i.e. the school enclosure (v. Croft) ; cf. Scholefield. In a copy of one of the Oldham papers several years ago, dealing with local matters, I noted the following :

Adam de Scolecroft, 6 Edw. III.

I have lost all other references, but it is clear that the estate from which the name was taken lay in the ancient parish of Oldham.

Thomas Taylor, of Scolecroft, parish of Oldham, 1588: Wills at Chester (1545-1620), p. 191.
Richard Scholecroft, of Farnworth, 1589: ibid. p. 170.

Richard Scowcroft, of Haugh, co. Lanc., *husbandman*, 1689 : ibid. (1681-1700), p. 347.
Eliz. Scolecroft, of Haulgh (Bolton-le-Moors), 1690, ibid.

These last two belonged to the same family. It may be taken for granted that the change to Scowcroft became established orthographically about the year 1700. The pronunciation would be much older.

1609. Married—Stephen Scocrofte and Grace Creycall : St. Mary Aldermary, p. 11.
Manchester, 2 ; Bolton, 6 ; Philadelphia, 1.

Scraggs ; v. Scroggs.

Scratcherd. — Occup. (?) A corruption of Scatchard, q.v.

Scrimgeour, Scrymgeour, Scrimiger, Scrymigar.—Offic. ' the scrimmager '; v. Skirmisher.

1681. George Jones and Eliz. Skrymsher : Marriage Lic. (Faculty Office) p. 158.
1802. Married — William Scrimgeour and Eliz. Hawkins: St. Geo. Han. Sq. ii. 261.
New York, 3, 2, 0, 2.

Scripps.—Bapt. ' the son of Crispin,' a corruption of Cripps, q.v. Crispin took two nicks., Crisp and Crips. Both as surnames are found with an initial S in the Hundred Rolls. In one case the same individual bears both names ; cf. *crawl* and *scrawl* ; also v. Sturgess (s.v. Sturge).

Alanus Scrips, co. Camb., 1273. A.
Jacobus Scrips, co. Camb., ibid.
Geoffrey Scrisp, co. Camb., ibid.
Jacobus Scrisp, co. Camb., ibid.
London, 1.

Scripture. — Occup. ' the writer '; cf. Faber.

William Scriptor, co. Oxf., 1273. A.
1686. Bapt.—Mary, d. John Scripture : St. Jas. Clerkenwell, i. 317.
1694. — John, son of John Scripture : ibid. p. 357.
New York, 1 ; Boston (U.S.), 3.

Scriven, Screven.—(1) Occup. ' the scriven,' i.e. copyist, notary. O.F. *escrivain*, a scrivener : Cotgrave.

' But if scryveynes lie.'
Piers P. 6278.

(2) Local, ' of Scriven,' a township in the parish of Knaresborough,

W. Rid. Yorks. But (1) must be looked upon as the chief parent.

William le Scriueyn, C. R., 42 Hen. III.
Margaret Scrivein, co. Camb., 1273. A.
Henry le Escriveyn, co. Oxf., ibid.
Robert le Schrevein, co. Wilts, ibid.
William de Skrevyn, *tannator*, 3 Edw. II : Freemen of York, i. 12.
Johannes Schryuen, 1379: P. T. Yorks. p. 198.
1539. Married — Petter Skreven and Alys Langlee : Reg. St. Dionis Backchurch, p. 1.
London, 9, 0 ; West Rid. Court Dir., 1, 0 ; Philadelphia, 1, 1.

Scrivener. — Occup. ' the scrivener,' a later form of Scriven, q.v.

Johannes Scryuener, 1379: P. T. Yorks. p. 251.
Johannes Screuyner, 1379 : ibid. p. 40.
Castancia Skryvener, 1379: ibid. p. 148.
1562. Married—Thomas Browne, *skrivener*, and Wenefrid Skot : St. Mary Aldermary, p. 3.
1767. — John Scrivener and Eliz. Wargon : St. Geo. Han. Sq. i. 160.
MDB. (co. Bedf.), 2 ; Abingdon, 2 ; New York, 1.

Scroggs, Scraggs.—Local, ' of Scroggs,' a village in co. Dumfries (Lower).

1576. William Scrogges and Alice Marten : Marriage Lic. (London), i. 69.
1753. Married—William Scraggs and Mary Stevens: St. Geo. Chap. Mayfair, p. 265.
MDB. (co. Bedf.), 3, 1 ; Oxford, 3, 0.

Scrogie, Scroggie, Scroggy.—Local, ' of Scrogie,' a village in co. Perth (Lower).

1802. Married — Charles Scrogie and Eliz. Bywater : St. Geo. Han. Sq. ii. 250.
London, 0, 3, 0 ; Philadelphia, 0, 0, 2.

Scruby.—Local, ' of Scrooby,' a parish in co. Notts.

Richard de Scrobby, co. Linc., 1273. A.
1686. John Camden and Eliz. Scrooby : Marriage Alleg. (Canterbury) p. 252.
1795. Married — William Scruby and Charlotte Newling : St. Geo. Han. Sq. ii. 137.
London, 3 ; MDB. (co. Camb.), 3 ; (co. Essex), 6.

Scruton, Scrutton. — Local, ' of Scruton,' a parish in the N. Rid. Yorks.

Johanna de Scruton, 1379: P. T. Yorks. p. 254.
1749. Married—Matthew Pearson and Ann Scruton : St. Geo. Chap. Mayfair. p. 147.
1804. — William Moffatt and Hariot Scruton : St. Geo. Han. Sq. ii. 315.
London, 3, 6 ; West Rid. Court Dir., 3, 0 ; New York, 2, 0.

Scrymigar, Scrymser; v. Skirmisher.

Scudamore, Skidmore. — Local, ' of Scudamore.' I cannot trace the exact spot, but probably it will be found in the south-west of England. 'Walter de Scudamore was lord of Upton, co. Wilts, in the reign of Stephen' (Lower). Skidmore was an early variant, as the following spellings of the name of one and the same individual will show :

Walter de Scudamore, 1316. M.
Walter de Skydemor, 1319. M.
Wanter de Skidemore, 1321. M.
Petrus de Skidemore, co. Wilts, 1273. A.
Godfrey de Skidemor, co. Wilts, ibid.

The family motto is imitative, 'Scuto Amoris Divini,' but to derive on this account the name from O.F. *escu d'amour* is out of the question. The origin is manifestly local. Mottoes are made to fit names, not names mottoes. Surnames precede mottoes.

1596. Henry Scudamore and Joane Howe : Marriage Lic. (London), i. 231.
1657. Bapt.—Mary, d. Thomas Skidmore : St. Jas. Clerkenwell, i. 198.
London, 6, 7 ; New York, o, 28.

Scudder; v. Skudder.

Sculthorpe.—Local, ' of Sculthorpe,' a parish in co. Norfolk.

1325. John de Sculthorp, rector of Testerton, co. Norf. : FF. vii. 197.
1752. Buried — Mary Sculthorp : St. Michael, Cornhill, p. 300.
1798. Married—John Sculthorpe and Esther Millward : St. Geo. Han. Sq. ii. 181.
MDB. (co. Warwick), 2 ; London, 1.

Scurry, Skurray.—? Local, ' of Scurry' (?). Seemingly some spot in co. Somerset.

Seman Scury, co. Soms., 1 Edw. III : Kirby's Quest, p. 205.
John Scurye, co. Soms., 1 Edw. III : ibid. p. 206.
London, 1, 0 ; Abingdon, o, 1.

Scutt.—Nick. ' the Scot.' The temptation is strong to make Scut a variation of Schet or Sket (v. Skeate), especially as the counties referred to below comprise the district in which that name was familiar. But 'le Scut' forbids the idea.

William le Scut, co. Kent, 1273. A.
Hugh le Skut, co. Wilts, ibid.
Grimhilda Scut, co. Camb., ibid.
John Scut, co. Norf., ibid.
1807. Married — Thomas Scutt and Mary White : St. Geo. Han. Sq. ii. 366.
London, 3.

Seaber.—Bapt. ' the son of Sigborg,' modulated to Siber and Seber (v. Yonge's Christian Names, ii. 310). The surname is still familiar to co. Cambridge, where it is found six centuries ago ; cf. the local Sebergham, a parish in co. Cumb., i.e. the *ham* or home of Seberg.

John Seber, co. Camb., 1273. A.
Agnes Siber, co. Oxf., ibid.
1749. Married — Philip Pamplin and Mary Seaber : St. Geo. Chap. Mayfair, p. 153.
MDB. (co. Camb.), 5 ; London, 1 ; Boston (U.S.), 3.

Seaborn, Seaborne, Seabourne.—Bapt. ' the son of Sebern.' Icelandic Sigbjorn ; cf. Osborne. Sebern did not impress itself strongly on English nomenclature.

Alexander Sebern, co. Hunts, 1273. A.
William Seberne, co. Oxf., ibid.
Geoffrey Sebern, co. Camb., ibid.
1581. William Seiborne, co. Ches. : Reg. Univ. Oxf. vol. ii. pt. ii. p. 100.
1789. Married — Robert Seaborn and Mary Banting : St. Geo. Han. Sq. ii. 21.
1797. — William Arnett and Ann Seaborne : ibid. p. 161.
1805. — Thomas Preece and Mary Seabourn : ibid. p. 327.
London, 4, 2, 1 ; MDB. (co. Essex), 5, 1, 0 ; Philadelphia, 0, 0, 2.

Seabright, Siebert, Sebright, Seabert.—(1) Bapt. ' the son of Sigbert,' the English form of which was Seabert (Yonge, ii. 309) or Seabright (Yonge, ii. 309). (2) Local, ' of Sebright.' ' William Sebright, of Sebright, in Much Baddow, co. Essex, living in the reign of Henry II, was the ancestor of this ancient family, who removed into Worcestershire at an early period' : Lower, quoting Shirley's Noble and Gentle Men.

Sybryth fil. Roberti, co. Suff., 1273. A.
Richard Sebriht, co. Oxf., ibid.
Simon Sabright, C. R., 18 Edw. I.
1601. Edward Sebright, co. Worc. : Reg. Univ. Oxf. vol. ii. pt. ii. p. 254.
1604. Married — John Sebright and Wynnifride Whitehead : St. Dionis Backchurch, p. 15.

The above is interesting, as the spelling in the licence varies :

1604. John Seabright and Winifred Whitehead : Marriage Lic. (London), i. 289.
London, 1, 4, 0 ; New York, 0, 50, 0 ; Philadelphia (Seabert), 3.

Seabrook, Seabrooke.—Local, ' of Seabrook,' a hamlet in the parish of Ivinghoe, co. Bucks.

1613. Gilbert Seabrooke : Reg. Univ. Oxf. vol. ii. pt. ii. p. 330.
1688. John Seabrook, mayor of Thetford, co. Norf. : FF. ii. 144.
1708. Bapt. — James, s. Jonas Seabrooke : St. Jas. Clerkenwell, i. 42.
MDB. (co. Bedf.), 3, 0 ; (co. Essex), 14, 4 ; London, 10, 0 ; Philadelphia, 2, 0.

Seacombe, Secombe, Seccombe.—Local, ' of Seacombe,' a part-township in the parish of Wallasey, co. Ches. It is manifest, however, that another place in co. Devon or Cornwall is the parent of many of these names.

1630. John Seacome, of Everton : Wills at Chester, ii. 194.
1642. Ralph Seacome, of Liverpool, *alderman* : ibid.
1687. Thomas Seccombe and Eliz. Bolwell : Marriage Alleg. (Canterbury), p. 22.
London, 2, 1, 0 ; MDB. (co. Cornwall), 0, 5, 4 ; (co. Devon), 0, 0, 4.

Seafowl.—Nick. ' the sea-fowl.'

Robert Sefoul, co. Oxf., 1273. A.
Ralph Sefughel, C. R., 24 Edw. I.
Alan Sefoul, C. R., 2 Edw. II.
John Sefonghel, Fines Roll, 14 Edw. II.
John Sefoghel, co. Soms., 1 Edw. III : Kirby's Quest, p. 250.
George Sefoul, C. R., 12 Ric. II.
Thomas Sefoule, co. Norf., 1564 : FF. vii. 206.

Seager, Seeger, Seaker.— Bapt. ' the son of Sigar'; v. Sayer and Segar.

Henry fil. Sigar, co. Camb., 1273. A.
John Seger, co. Norf., ibid.
William Siger, co. Norf., ibid.
Hillarius Sigar, 25 Edw. I : BBB. p. 542.
John Seger, co. Soms., 1 Edw. III : Kirby's Quest, p. 100.
Eudo fil. Sygar. C.
Eudo fil. Seger. E.
1730. Married—William Quincey and Mary Seager : St. Geo. Han. Sq. i. 8.
London, 19, 4, 1 ; Boston (U.S.), 3, 0, 0.

Seagrave. — Local, ' of Seagrave,' a parish in the dioc. Peterborough and co. Leicester.

Gilbert de Segrave, co. Camb., 1273. A.
Nicholas de Segrave, co. Hunts, ibid.
John de Segrave, co. Kent, 20 Edw. I. R.

Stephen de Segrave, co. Kent, 20 Edw.
I. R.
1700. Buried—John Seagrave, son of
John Seagrave, haberdasher of hats:
St. Dionis Backchurch, p. 268.
1733. Bapt.—Robert, s. William Sea-
grave: St. Antholin (London), p. 160.
London, 4; Boston (U.S.), 4.

Seal, Seale, Seel, Seals.—(1)
Local, 'at the sele,' i.e. Sale, q.v.
A variant. Just as Sale is found
as Sales, so Seal has become Seals.
(2) Local, 'of Seal,' parishes in cos.
Leicester, Surrey, and Kent.

John atte Sele, C. R., 20 Edw. III,
pt. i.
1574. Richard Seale, co. Warwick:
Reg. Univ. Oxf. vol. ii. pt. ii. p. 57.
1689. Buried—Jane Seale: St. Mary
Aldermary, p. 200.
1789. Married—William Seels and Ann
Teeboe: St. Geo. Han. Sq. ii. 32.
London, 14, 6, 0, 0; Philadelphia, 22,
0, 9, 7.

Sealey, Sealy; v. Seeley.

**Seaman, Semon, Seman,
Seamons, Seamans, Seamen.**
—Bapt. 'the son of Seman,' whence
Seaman, genitive Seamans; cf.
William and Williams.

John fil. Semanni, 1160: KKK. vi. 14.
Seman de Reston, co. Suff., 1273. A.
Seman le Carpenter, co. Suff., ibid.
Seman Eche, co. Suff., ibid.
Herveus Seman, co. Camb., ibid.
Robert fil. Seman, co. Suff., ibid.
Seaman le Baylif. J.
Seaman Champayne. B.
Seman le Coliar, co. Soms., 1 Edw. III:
Kirby's Quest, p. 204.
Robertus Saymon, 1379: P. T. Yorks.
p. 206.
Semannus Joye: Pardons Roll, Ric. II.
Anno 11, 1387-8.
1795. Married — Charles Button and
Susan Seaman: St. Geo. Han. Sq. ii. 127.
London, 7, 2, 0, 1, 0, 0; MDB. (co.
Bucks), 0, 0, 0, 3, 0, 0; Philadelphia, 12,
3, 0, 1, 1, 1.

Seamer.—Local, (1) 'of Seamer,'
a parish in the N. Rid. Yorks;
(2) a variant of Seymour, q.v.
It is almost certain that (2) is the
true parent.

Thomas Semer, co. Soms., 1 Edw. III:
Kirby's Quest, p. 224.
Thomas de Semer, 25 Edw. III: Freemen of York (Surt. Soc.), i. 47.
1657. Married — Richard Seamer,
barber-chirurgion, and Martha Green-
hill: St. Michael, Cornhill, p. 37.
1744. — William Wyatt and Eliz. Sea-
mour: St. Geo. Han. Sq. i. 34.
1780. — William Seamer and Eliz.
Goode: ibid. p. 309.
London, 2.

Seanor.—Nick. 'the senior,'
a corruption of a great Yorkshire
surname; v. Senior.

West Rid. Court Dir., 2.

**Sear, Sears, Searson, Seare,
Seares, Serson.**—Bapt. 'the son
of Sayer,' q.v. All unmistakable
descendants of the great Northern
personal name that has made such
an impression on English nomenclature. Sears is the genitive of
Sear as Williams is the genitive of
William. Sears = Searson.

Walter fil. Sere, co. Notts, 1273. A.
Seer le Faber, co. Camb., ibid.
Seer de Freville, co. Camb., ibid.
Godwin Seer, co. Camb., ibid.
Thomas Seer, co. Camb., ibid.
1611. Married—William Searson and
Alice Mason: St. Mary Aldermary (Lon-
don), p. 12.
1700. — John Sears and Sarah Elliott:
St. Geo. Han. Sq. ii. 45.
1795. — Edward Martindale and Mary
Seare: ibid. p. 139.
1807. — Thomas Willshire and Eliz.
Searson: ibid. p. 369.
London, 8, 6, 1, 4, 3, 0; Crockford
(Serson), 1; Philadelphia (Sears), 23.

Seargeant. — Offic. 'the sergeant'; v. Serjeant, one of many
variants.

1754. Thomas Jackson and Katherine
Seargeant: St. Geo. Han. Sq. i. 52.
London, 1.

Searl(e, Searles; v. Serle.

Seaton.—Local, 'of Seaton,'
parishes and townships in cos.
Cumberland, Devon, Durham,
Rutland, Yorks (E. Rid.), and
Northumberland.

Richard de Seton, or Setoune, co.
Devon, 1273. A.
Elena de Seton, co. York, ibid.
John de Seton, co. Cumb., 20 Edw.
I. R.
John de Seton, co. Northumb., ibid.
Isabella de Sayton', *webester,* 1379:
P. T. Yorks. p. 221.
Johannes de Sayton', *marchant,* 1379:
ibid.
1626. Bapt.—Ann, d. Joseph Seaton:
St. Jas. Clerkenwell, i. 103.
London, 11; West Rid. Court Dir., 6;
New York, 2.

Seaward; v. Seward (2).

Sebley.—Bapt. 'the son of
Sybil'; v. Sibley.

1806. Married—Edward Taylor and
Jane Sebley: St. Geo. Han. Sq. ii. 343.
London, 2.

Seburgham. — Local, 'of Sebergham'; v. Seaber.

Henry de Seburgham, co. Cumb. R.

Secker.—(1) Bapt. 'the son of
Seger' or Segger; v. Seager;
cf. Slagg and Slack. No doubt it
is a sharpened pronunciation of
Segger. (2) Occup. 'the sacker,'
a maker of sacks; v. Sacker.

John le Sekker, 9 Edw. III: Freemen
of York, i. 29.
Icelandic *sekkr* (Skeat).
Gilbert Segger, co. Devon, 1273. A.
1754. Married—John Secker and Jane
Baxter: St. Geo. Chap. Mayfair, p. 273.
1776. — William Sacheverell and Jane
Secker: St. Geo. Han. Sq. i. 260.
London, 5; Philadelphia, 3.

Secombe; v. Seacombe.

Secular.—Offic. 'the secular,'
one unbound by monastic rules;
the opposite to religious.

'Religious folke ben full covert,
Secular folke ben more apert.'
Walter le Seculer, co. Salop, 1273. A.
Alice la Seculere, fil. and coh. Henrici
le Seculer, Close Roll, 6 Edw. I.
Alexander le Seculer. L.
Nicholas le Secular. B.

Seddon.—Local, 'of Seddon,'
some spot in south-west Lancashire,
which I cannot find. The surname
is well distributed over Lancashire,
and has found its way into distant
parts of the world.

1615. Laurence Seddon, co. Lanc.:
Reg. Univ. Oxf. vol. ii. pt. ii. p. 348.
1627. John Seddon, of Liverpool:
Wills at Chester, i. 194.
1638. Michael Seddon, of Pilkington,
yeoman: ibid.
— Margaret Seddon, of Winwick: ibid.
Manchester, 17; MDB. (co. Ches.), 4;
London, 1; Philadelphia, 8.

Sedgwick, Sidgwick.—Local,
'of Sedgwick,' a township in the
parish of Heversham, four miles
from Kendal, co. Westm. The
surname has ramified strongly.
The prefix is evidently the personal
name of the first settler in the
wick (v. Wike) and a compound of
sig; cf. Sigismund, Sigmund, Sigward, Sigwald (v. Miss Yonge, i.
cxxiii); cf. also Segar and Sayer.

Johannes de Seghswyk, 1379: P. T.
Yorks. p. 288.
Willelmus de Seglewyk, 1379: ibid.
Robertus de Seglswyk, 1379: ibid.
The above are from Dent, near
Sedgwick.

Thomas de Sigeswik, 1379 : ibid. p. 237.
Elizabeth Sigeswicke, of Botton, 1580 : Lancashire Wills at Richmond, i. 251.
George Sigeswicke, of Tatham, 1584 : Lancashire Wills at Richmond, i. 251.
Thomas Sigswicke, of Lancaster, 1624 : ibid.
London, 13, 2 ; West Rid. Court Dir., 9, 5 ; Philadelphia, 6, o.

Seear.—Bapt. 'the son of Sayer' ; v. Sear. This is quite a modern variant—one more surname that owns the famous Segar for its parent.

1805. Married — Thomas Seear and Kezia Ivory : St. Geo. Han. Sq. ii. 328.
London, 8.

Seeger ; v. Seager.

Seekins, Seekings.—Bapt. 'the son of Segin.' This personal name, in early records almost peculiar to Cambridgeshire, seems to have settled down into Seekins, the final s being patronymic as in Williams, the g in Seekings being an excrescence as in Jennings.

Richard Segin, co. Linc. 1273. A.
Alan Segin, co. Camb., ibid.
John Segyn, co. Camb., ibid.

Also spelt Segeyn. It is interesting to note that the surname is still well-nigh confined to co. Cambridge.

1757. Married—Thomas Seekins and Mary Wilkins : St. Geo. Han. Sq. i. 74.
Cambridge, 1, o ; MDB. (co. Cambridge), 1, 1 ; London, 1, o.

Seeley, Seelie, Seely, Sealey, Sealy, Seelye.—(1) Nick. 'the seely,' the simple, the innocent, the harmless ; cf. Simple. 'Seely = simple, silly' (Halliwell).

'This sely carpenter beginneth quake.'
Chaucer, C. T. 3601.

William Sely, co. Oxf., 1273. A.
Egidius Sely, co. Norf., ibid.
John Sely, co. Glouc., ibid.
Thomas Sely, London, 20 Edw. I. R.

(2) Bapt. 'the son of Cecil,' from the nick. Sill and pet Sillie ; cf. Willie, Charlie, &c. (v. Silcock). There can scarcely be the shadow of a doubt as to this being a chief parent of the surname.

Sely atte Bergh, co. Soms., 1 Edw. III : Kirby's Quest, p. 266.
Sely Percy, co. Soms., 1 Edw. III : ibid.
Sely Scury, co. Soms., 1 Edw. III : ibid. p. 205.

William Sely, co. Soms., 1 Edw. III : ibid. p. 268.
1618-9. John Symonds and Anne Seley : Marriage Lic. (London), ii. 69.
1621-2. William Stanmore and Margaret Seely : ibid. p. 109.
1760. Bapt.—William Jeffrey, son of W. Jeffrey Sealy : St. Peter, Cornhill, i. 48.
London, 9, 1, 1, 3, 7, o ; Philadelphia, 20, o, 5, 5, 2, 2.

Sefton.—Local ; v. Sephton.

Segar, Seger.—Bapt. 'the son of Sigar' ; for instances, v. Seager.

Penketh, near Warrington, 1, o ; Southport, 1, o ; Boston (U.S.), 1, 1.

Selby.—Local, 'of Selby,' a parish and market-town in E. Rid. Yorks.

William de Seleby, co. York, 1273. A.
Robert de Selby, barber, 34 Edw. I : Freemen of York, i. 11.
Johannes de Selby, 1379 : P. T. Yorks. p. 100.
Willelmus de Selby, 1379 : ibid. p. 136.
1618. Bapt. — Edward, s. George Selbye : St. Jas. Clerkenwell, i. 81.
London, 23 ; West Rid. Court Dir., 2 ; Philadelphia, 14.

Selden, Seldon.—Local, ' of Selden.' I cannot find the spot.

Ansell de Seleden, cos. Warw. and Leic., Hen. III-Edw. I. K.
1600. John Selden, co. Sussex : Reg. Univ. Oxf. vol. ii. pt. ii. p. 242.
1789. Married — Daniel Selden and Mary Gray : St. Geo. Han. Sq. ii. 32.
London, 2, 1 ; Philadelphia, 5, 1.

Self, Selfe.—(1) Local, 'of Shelf' (?), a village in the union of Halifax. The third entry is strongly confirmatory of this origin. (2) Bapt. 'the son of Seleth' (v. Selth). I suspect this is the true parent of the great majority of our Selfs, &c.

Cristiana del Schelf, 1379 : P. T. Yorks. p. 181.
Johannes de Schelf, 1379 : ibid.
Ricardus Scelue (u for v), 1379 : ibid. p. 278.
1639. Married — Randall Selfe and Alice Reaman : St. Michael, Cornhill, p. 28.
London, 9, 3 ; Boston (U.S.), 2, 2.

Selkirk.—Local, 'of Selkirk,' the county town of Selkirkshire.

London, 1 ; Philadelphia, 5.

Sellar(s ; v. Seller(s.

Selleck, Sellick.—Local, 'of Sellack,' a parish in co. Hereford, near Ross. The following entries

are quite sufficient to prove the derivation :

1603. John Sellak, co. Somerset : Reg. Univ. Oxf. vol. ii. pt. ii. p. 265.

A note appended says : 'Sellack. There was a family of Selleckes at Lydiard St. Lawrence, Somerset.'

1595. Nicholas Sellecke, or Sellick, co. Somerset : Reg. Univ. Oxf. vol. ii. pt. ii. p. 209.
1676-7. Thomas Wyne and Theophila Selleck, of Wells, co. Somerset : Marriage Alleg. (Canterbury), p. 264.
1795. Married — William Sellick and Sarah Saville : St. Geo. Han. Sq. ii. 139.
MDB. (co. Devon), 2, 1 ; (co. Somerset), o, 6 ; London, o, 2 ; Philadelphia, o, 4.

Seller, Sellar.—Occup. 'the seller,' a saddler. M.E. selle, a seat. O.F. 'selle, a stool, a seat, also a saddle' : Cotg. 'Sele, horsys harneys' : Prompt. Parv. 'Seale, horse harnesse' : Palsgrave. The 'Sellers ("sadellers", written over), Verrours, and Fuystours' (v. Fewster) went together in the York Pageant (York Mystery Plays, ed. Toulmin Smith, p. xxvi).

Bartholomew Sellarius, co. Kent, 1273. A.
Henry Sellarius, co. Warw., ibid.
Richard Sellarius, London, ibid.
Warin le Seler, temp. 1300. M.
John le Seler. O.
Hugh le Seler. O.
1615. Bapt.—George, s. Thomas Sellor : St. Jas. Clerkenwell, i. 72.
1809. Married — Joshua Hartley and Harriet Sellar : St. Geo. Han. Sq. ii. 409.
London, 3, 2 ; Philadelphia, 3, o.

Sellers, Sellars.—Local, 'of the cellar.' Practically official = the cellarer, the same as Butler or Buttery, q.v. This has become one of the most familiar of Yorkshire surnames, with an s at the end ; cf. Briggs, Styles, and Brooks. Attached no doubt to one of the monasteries or feudal houses.

Adam de Celer, co. York, 1273. A.
Roger del Celer, co. York, ibid.
Alicia del Seler, 1379 : P. T. Yorks. p. 157.
Adam del Seler', 1379 : ibid. p. 238.
Juliana del Seler, 1379 : ibid.
Agnes del Seler, 1379 : ibid. p. 296.
1617. Bapt. — Robert, s. Thomas Sellers : St. Jas. Clerkenwell, i. 79.
London, 2, 1 ; Sheffield, 4, 7 ; West Rid. Court Dir., 7, 1 ; Philadelphia, 73, o.

Sellick ; v. Selleck.

Sellinger.—Local, 'of St. Leger,' a chapelry in Normandy (?). Cf. St. John, Sinclair, Simple, &c.

Geoffrey de St. Leodegare, co. Sussex, 1273. A.
1386. Isabel de St. Legar: FF. vii. 220.
Thomas Sentlegar, Norwich, temp. Ric. III: ibid. iii. 173.
1639. Buried—The lady Thornix, wife of Mr. Anthony Sellinger: Canterbury Cath. p. 118.
Philadelphia, 1; New York, 1.

Sellman, Sellmen, Selman, Seelman, Selmond.—(1) Bapt. 'the son of Seliman,' i.e. Solomon; v. Salamon and Salman. No connexion with *sale*, a hall, as suggested by Lower. The *d* in Selmond is an excrescence; cf. Simmonds for Simmons, or Salmond for Salmon.
Cecilia fil. Selmon, co. Hunts, 1273. A.
Simon Seliman, co. Bucks, ibid.
William Seliman, co. Wilts, ibid.
Thomas Selman, co. Camb., ibid.

(2) ? Nick. 'the silly man,' i.e. the innocent, quiet man (v. Seeley, 1); or 'the servant of Silly,' a well-known personal name in the West country; cf. Matthewman, Addyman, &c.; v. Seeley(2).
Gregory Selyman, co. Soms., 1 Edw. III: Kirby's Quest, p. 79.
Walter Selyman, co. Soms., 1 Edw. III: ibid. p. 143.
1569. Bapt. — Robarte Selman, s. Robert Sellman' (sic): St. Dionis Backchurch, p. 81.
1693. — Daniel, s. Robert Sellman: St. Jas. Clerkenwell, i. 353.
London, 1, 1, 1, 1, 0; Philadelphia, 0, 0, 1, 0, 1.

Selmes.—Local, 'at the selm' (?), from residence thereby (?). ' *Selms*, gate-rails. Northumberland' (Halliwell).
John atte Selme, co. Soms., 1 Edw. III: Kirby's Quest, p. 87.
London, 2; New York, 2.

Selth, Self, Selfe.—Bapt. 'the son of Seleth.' The order of corruption was very simple, as follows: Seleth, Selth, and Self or Selfe. But for a second derivation, v. Self. Nevertheless, Seleth was so popular that it must have made its mark on our permanent nomenclature, and I doubt not Selth, Self, and Selfe are its offspring.
Selade (without surname), co. Bedf., 1273. A.
Selede (without surname), co. Camb., ibid.
Herveus fil. Selede, co. Camb., ibid.
Selithe de Wenham, co. Suff., ibid.
Robert Seled, co. Oxf., ibid.

Eustace Selede, co. Camb., 1273. A.
1775. Married—William Goodall and Mary Selfe: St. Geo. Han. Sq. i. 251.
1775. Married — John Self and Eliz. Larner: ibid. p. 253.

Selth lingered on as a surname in the district in which as a personal name it arose.
1722. William Selth, rector of Folsham, co. Norf.: FF. viii. 209.
London, 2, 9, 3; Boston (U.S.), 0, 2, 2.

Selwyn, Selwin.—Bapt. 'the son of Selwin,' one of the almost endless compounds in -*win*; cf. Sherwin, Unwin, Godwin, Baldwin, &c.
Hugo Salveyn, co. Linc., Hen. III-Edw. I. K.
Osbert Selveyn, co. Linc., ibid.
Geoffrey Selveyn, co. Linc., ibid.
Willelmus Shilwyn, 1379: P. T. Yorks. p. 163.
Agnes Saluayne, 1379: ibid. p. 52.
Nicholas Selewyne, Pat. Roll, 8 Ric. II, pt. ii.
1622. Bapt. — William, s. William Selwin: St. Jas. Clerkenwell, i. 93.
London, 1, 0; Philadelphia, 0, 1.

Seman, Semon; v. Seaman.

Semper.—Local, 'of St. Pierre,' probably a chapelry in Normandy; cf. Sinclair, Simple, Sellinger, &c.
Urian de St. Petro, co. Salop, 1273. A.
Nicholas de Seyntpiere, C. R., 19 Edw. II, pt. ii.
Thomas le (? de) Seintepier, co. Ches., 1383: East Cheshire, ii. 234.
David le (? de) Seintepier, co. Ches., 1383: ibid.
Richard Semper, alias Sentpyer, C. R., 1-2 Philip and Mary, pt. v.
1613. Buried — Owen Sempeer: St. Antholin (London), p. 50.
1628. Married — John Samues and Margret Simper: St. Mary Aldermary (London), p. 16.
Crockford, 1; Philadelphia, 1.

Semple, Sempill.—Local, 'of St. Paul,' probably some chapelry in Normandy. Not to be confounded with Simple (q.v.), although, no doubt, now inextricably mixed; cf. Sinclair, Semper, Sellinger, &c.
William de Sainpol, Hen. III-Edw. I. K.
Gunilda de St. Paul, co. Linc., 1273. A.
John de St. Paull', co. Oxf., ibid.
Emulda de St. Paul, co. Linc., ibid.
Willelmus Sayndepaule, 1379: P. T. Yorks. p. 20.
Johannes Seynpoule, 1379: ibid. p. 21.
Johanna Sayntpaule, 1379: ibid. p. 117.
1626. William Mackphell and Barbara Semple: Marriage Lic. (London), ii. 167.

London, 5, 1; West Rid. Court Dir., 1, 0; Philadelphia, 19, 0.

Sempster, Simister, Semister.—Occup. 'the sempster,' i.e. sempstress, a common entry for women. Without doubt some of the North-English Simisters (perhaps all) are thus derived. But v. Simister.
Cristiana de Belthorp', *semster*, 1379: P. T. Yorks. p. 231.
Elizabetha Semster, 1379: ibid. p. 197.
Sissot Seymster, 1379: ibid. p. 100.
Isabella Semester, 1379: ibid. p. 249.
Margareta Semester, 1379: ibid. p. 235.
Elen Semster, co. York. W. 2.
Emma Semister, co. York. W. 9.
Hellen Simster, co. York. W. 16.
Isabella Maw, *semster*, in Fosgate, York, 1433. W. 11.
Manchester, 0, 12, 0; West Rid. (Yorks) Court Dir., 0, 0, 1, 0; Philadelphia, 0, 0, 1.

Senecal. — Bapt. 'the son of Senicle.'
Senecle (without surname), co. Bucks, 1273. A.
Stephen Sinckel, co. Suff., ibid.
Senicula le Wright, Pat. Roll, 6 Edw. III.
Thomas Senycle, C. R., 18 Ric. II.
Thomas Synykill, Pat. Roll, 1 Hen. IV, pt. v.
1509. Thomas Senycle, official to the Archdeacon of Norwich: FF. iii. 660.
1775. Married — George Senegal and Sarah Womack: St. Geo. Han. Sq. i. 253.
London, 1.

Senhouse.—Local, ' of Sevenhouse ' or Senhouse, in the parish of Cross Canonby, co. Cumb. Still found in the neighbourhood of Maryport. A well-known Cumberland family.
Walter de Sevenhouse, temp. Edw. III: Hutchinson's Cumberland, ii. 268.
Thomas de Senhous, C. R., 9 Ric. II.
John Senhouse, vicar of Trimdon, 1501: DDD. i. 108.
Thomas Senowys: Visit. Yorks., 1563, p. 181.
1617. John Senhouse, co. Cumb. Reg. Univ. Oxf. vol. ii. pt. ii. p. 365.
1635. Richard Senhouse, rector of Claughton: Lancashire Wills at Richmond, i. 247.
MDB. (co. Cumb.), 3.

Senior, Senier, Seanor, Saynor, Synyer.—Nick. 'the senior,' i.e. the older of two or more persons, generally of the same personal name. This mode of expression is as early as the 13th and 14th centuries, and is very commonly found in the Yorkshire Poll Tax, 1379. The cause is simple. John was so popular that not only father and son, but two and three brothers would often bear the name. For instances, v. my Curiosities of Puritan Nomenclature, pp. 4, 5.

Johannes Holynghege, senior, 1379 : P. T. Yorks. p. 172.
Johannes Holynghege, junior, 1379 : ibid.
Johannes Bullok, senior, 1379 : ibid. p. 2.
Johannes Bullok, junior, 1379 : ibid.
Cf. Ricardus ye Elder, 1379 : ibid. p. 214 (v. Elder).

Hence such an entry as :

Willelmus Synyer, 1379 : P. T. Yorks. p. 233.

Johannes Seygnour, 1379 : ibid. p. 9.
Michael le Seigneur. E.
William le Seignour, 1302. M.
Edmund Seignyowr, co. York. W. 2.
Thomas Senior, co. York. W. 16.
'Mr. H. Synyer, of Nottingham, came first in the Two-mile Bicycle Race': Manchester Courier, Sept. 19, 1887.
West Riding Court Dir., 21, 0, 2, 0, 0; London, 10, 1, 0, 0, 0; Sheffield (Saynor), 5; Philadelphia, 14, 0, 0, 0, 0.

Sennett, Sennitt, Synnot, Sunnett, Sennott, Sinnott, Sinnett, Synett, Synnott, Synnet, Sennet. — Bapt. 'the son of Senot' or Sunot. A girl's name, but it is not mentioned in Miss Yonge's book, and I can glean no more of its history than what is recorded below. Its place as a feminine baptismal name is well marked, and that it has obtained permanent surnominal honours our directories fully prove.

Stephen Sinot, co. Suff., 1273. A.
Richard fil. Sunod, co. Hunts, ibid.
Sunod Silvestre, co. Hunts, ibid.
Sunnota fil. Jakelini, 3 Edw. I : BBB. p. 219.
Johanna fil. Sunnotoe, 3 Edw. I : ibid.
Helias stori et Senota uxor ejus, 1379 : P. T. Yorks. p. 120.
Johannes Sinhit, 1379 : ibid.
1673. John Sinnott (co. Kent) and Barbara White : Marriage Alleg. (Canterbury), p. 214.
MDB. (co. Camb.), 2, 5, 0, 0, 0, 0, 0, 0, 0, 0, 0; Manchester, 0, 0, 0, 1, 0, 0, 0, 0, 0, 0, 0; New York, 1, 0, 0, 0, 0, 20, 1, 0, 0, 1, 1; Boston (U.S.), 0, 0, 0, 0, 0, 0, 16, 17, 4, 3, 1, 0.

Senskell, Sensecal. — Offic. 'the seneschal,' a steward.

Alexander le Seneschal. B.
William le Seneschal. H.
Ivo Seneschallus. T.
1693. Married — John Henry Beckman and Sarah Senskell : St. Mary Aldermary (London), p. 35.
1793. — Richard Dearlove and Mary Senescall : St. Geo. Han. Sq. ii. 95.
1805. — Joseph Augustus Seneschal and Ann Dicker : ibid. p. 333.
MDB. (co. Oxford), 0, 1.

Sephton, Sefton. — Local, —'of Sephton,' a parish in co. Lanc., seven miles from Liverpool.

Thomas Sefton, of Skelmersdale, 1593 : Wills at Chester, i. 171.
Robert Sephton, of Mollington, 1602 : ibid.
1754. Married — Richard Etherington and Mary Sefton : St. Geo. Chap. Mayfair, p. 282.
1806. — Robert Page and Mary Sefton : St. Geo. Han. Sq. ii. 349.
London, 0, 2 ; Liverpool, 2, 4 ; Philadelphia, 1, 0.

Serf. — Occup. 'the serf' (?).

Emma le Cerf : Fines Roll, 17 Edw. II.

Sergeantston. — Local. Not to be confounded with Sergeantson.

Ricardus de Sergerstane, 1379 : P. T. Yorks. p. 58.
West Riding Court Dir., 1.

Serjeant, Sergeant, Sergent, Sargant, Sargeant, Sargeaunt, Sargent, Sarjant, Sarjeant, Sarjent, Seargeant. — Offic. 'the sergeant' or serjeant, an officer of the law, a policeman. Few surnames have undergone more varieties of spelling than this. Even in our latest dictionaries two forms are recognized. Agreeing with O.F. *sergant* and *serjant*, Serjaunt is the commonest form in early rolls.

John le Serjeant, co. Bucks, 1273. A.
Walter le Serjaunt, co. Camb., ibid.
John le Serjaunt, co. Salop, ibid.
Robert Sergant, co. Camb., ibid.
Roger le Serjaunt, co. Norf., ibid.
Nicholas le Serjaunt, co. Linc., 20 Edw. I. R.
Thomas Elys, *serjaunt*, 1379 : P. T. Yorks. p. 97.
London, 3, 3, 1, 4, 8, 1, 16, 2, 1, 1, 1; Philadelphia, 0, 8, 0, 0, 5, 0, 26, 0, 0, 0, 0.

Serjeantson, Sergeantson, Serginson, Sarginson, Sergerson, Sergeson, Sergison, Sergason. — Nick. 'the son of the serjeant,' q.v. ; cf. Taylorson, Wrightson, and Smithson. This

class of names (a very small one) seems almost peculiar to Yorkshire (v. Taylorson). There can be no doubt that that county is the home of the family.

Willelmus Sergantson, 1379 : P. T. Yorks. p. 299.
Johannes Serigantson, 1379 : ibid. p. 12.
Thomas Sergeauntson. H.
Thomas Sargandson, co. York. W. 11.
Henry Serchauntson, co. York, ibid.
Mary Sergison, co. York. W. 16.
William Surgisson embarked for Virginia, 1634 : Hotten's Lists of Emigrants, p. 36.

This early emigrant was twenty-five years old. Probably the American Sergersons, Sergesons, and Sergisons are his descendants.

Exeter (Sergason), 1 ; Manchester (Serginson), 1, (Sarginson), 1 ; Crockford (Sergeantson), 2 ; West Riding Court Dir., 1, 1, 0, 0, 0, 0, 0, 0 ; Philadelphia, 0, 0, 0, 0, 1, 11, 3, 0.

Serle, Searle, Serrell, Serlson, Searles, Serrill, Serrills, Searl. — Bapt. 'the son of Serle.' Searle is the common present surnominal form. Serle is the old baptismal form. Searles or Serrills is the genitive of Searl ; cf. William and Williams.

Serle Gotokirke, co. Camb., 1273. A.
Osbert fil. Serlonis, co. Hunts, ibid.
Richard Serle, co. Camb., ibid.
Hugh Serlson, temp. 1300. M.
Richard Serelson, temp. 1300. M.
William Serleson, co. York. W. 2.
Thomas Serlson, 1379 : P. T. Yorks. p. 213.
John Serlson, 1379 : ibid.
Serill Pynder, 1379 : ibid. p. 254.
Serell de Westwik, 1379 : ibid. p. 260.
Robert Serlys, 1512 : Reg. Univ. Oxf. i. 220.
John Seryll, or Serell, 1553 : ibid. i. 79.
1732. Married — Humphry Searls and Hester Bayley : St. Jas. Clerkenwell, i. 259.
London, 1, 40, 2, 0, 3, 0, 0, 0 ; Sheffield (Searls), 2 ; Philadelphia, 0, 11, 0, 0, 13, 8, 4, 5.

Sermoner. — Offic. 'the sermoner,' one who preached sermons. '*Sermonen*, to preach' : O.E. Homilies, i. 81, l. 14. In the North they still talk of 'listning to th' sarmon.'

'Quen He sendes his messageres,
That es at say, thir sarmonneres.'
English Metrical Homilies, p. 147, John Small, Edinb. 1862.

Richard le Sarmuner. E.
William le Sarmoner, Hen. III. T

Richard Sarmoner, co. Soms., 1 Edw.
III: Kirby's Quest, p. 118.
'I find the name John le Sarmoner
occurring in a deed dated 1316': E. H.
in N. and Q., March 12, 1887.

Serrill(s ; v. Serle.

Serson ; v. Sear.

Servant, Servent. — Occup.
'the servant.' A Yorkshire surname, found so early as the 14th
century.

Seman Serviens, co. Norf., 1273. A.
Sewall Serviens, co. Norf., ibid.
Robertus Westrin, 1379: P. T. Yorks.
p. 39.
Ricardus serviens dicti Roberti, 1379:
ibid.
Johannes Cowper, *glover*, 1379: ibid.
p. 41.
Johannes serviens ejus, 1379: ibid.
Emma Seruantman, 1379: ibid. p. 56.
Willelmus Seruantman,1379: ibid.p.63.
1699. Bapt. — Frances, d. John Ser-
vant: St. Jas. Clerkenwell, i. 383.
Leeds, 2, 1; West Rid. Court Dir., 2, 0.

Servelady. — Nick. for a lady's
maid.
Avice Serueladi, Close Roll, 1 Edw. II.
In the Yorkshire Poll Tax (1379)
there are many such entries for
the bower-maiden; v. Ladyman.

Setchell. — ? Bapt.; v. Satchell.
Oxford, 1.

Setter. — Occup. ' the setter,'
supposed to be the same as *tipper*, one
who fixed arrow-heads to the shaft.
'Sponers, torners, and hatters,
Lyne-webbers, setters, with lyne-
drapers.'
                    Cocke Lorelle's Bote.
Clement le Settere. N.
Alexander le Settere, London. X.
John de Belegame, *setter*, 18 Edw. III:
Freemen of York, i. 37.
Robertus Cetter, 1379: P. T. Yorks.
p. 261.
Walter Setter, C. R., 9 Hen. IV.
1685. Thomas Harford and Barbary
Setter: Marriage Alleg. (Canterbury),
p. 196.
London, 1.

Setterington. — Local, ' of
Settrington,' a parish in E. Rid.
Yorks.
Robert de Seterinton, co.York, 1273. A.
William de Seterington, *wayder*, 4
Edw. II: Freemen of York, i. 13.
For the occupative term *wayder*,
v. Wader.
1804. Married—John Watson and Jane
Setterington: St. Geo. Han. Sq. ii. 308.
MDB. (E. Rid. Yorks), 3.

Settle. — Local, ' of Settle,' a
parish in W. Rid. Yorks.
Alicia de Settle, 1379: P. T. Yorks.
p. 273.
Johannes de Setle, 1379: ibid. p. 272.
Johannes de Setill', 1379: ibid. p. 145.
Hugh Settle, of Cartmell, 1594: Lan-
cashire Wills at Richmond, i. 247.
James Settle, of Tatham, 1671: ibid.
1689. Richard Benson and Eliz.
Settle (co. Lincoln): Marriage Alleg.
(Canterbury), p. 195.
London, 2; West Rid. Court Dir., 3;
Philadelphia, 11.

Sevenpence. — Nick.; cf. Nine-
pence and Twelvepence.
Robert Seuenepens (*u* for *v*), Pardons
Roll, 5 Ric. II (Suffolk).

Severe, Sever, Seaver. —
Nick. ' the severe,' i.e. the grave,
the austere in manner and de-
meanour.
John le Severe, co. Hunts, 1273. A.
Henry Sever, co. Norf., 1441: FF. iii.
535.
John Seaver, co. Berks, 1616: Reg.
Univ. Oxf. vol. ii. pt. ii. p. 356.
Manchester, 0, 1, 0; Philadelphia, 0,
0, 7.

Seville ; v. Savill.

Seward (1). — Occup. ' a sow-
herd '; cf. Calvert, Coward,
Stoddard, &c. But v. Seward (2).
Alicia Sueherd, 1379: P. T. Yorks.
p. 158.

**Seward (2), Seaward,
Sewards, Suart.** — Bapt. ' the
son of Siward' (Yonge, ii. 308).
Syward Godwin. J.
Siward Oldcorn. L.
Siward, Earl of the Northumbrians,
Freeman, Norm. Conq. i. 515.
Siward, Abbot of Abingdon, ibid. ii. 67.
Cf. Sewardstone, co. Essex, and
Sewardesley, co. Northampton.
Siward de Liment', ipe Roll, 5
Hen. II.
Sygwat Kat'bode, co. Norf., 1273. A.
Syward (without surname), co. Oxf.,
ibid.
Sywardus (without surname), co. Oxf.,
ibid.
Thomas Sywat, co. Suff., ibid.
Richard Syward, co. Bucks, ibid.
Hugo Syward, 1379: P. T. Yorks.
p. 52.
Johanna Syward, 1379: ibid. p. 70.
1728. Bapt.—Ann, d. John Suertt: St.
Jas. Clerkenwell, ii. 176.
London, 7, 8, 1, 2; Philadelphia, 7, 0,
0, 0.

**Sewell, Sewill, Sewelson,
Sewall, Sewalt.** — Bapt. ' the son

of Sewal' (v. Sigwald in Miss
Yonge's History of Christian Names,
ii. 310).
Sewallus de Cleton, co. Hertf., 1273. A.
Sewale de Retcote, co. Oxf., ibid.
Robert fil. Sew', co. Northants, ibid.
Thomas Sewald, co. Oxf., ibid.
Godard Sewale, co. Camb., ibid.
Sewal atte Ponde, temp. 1300. M.
Sewall Dapifer. J.
As a personal name Sewal
lingered on into the 16th century:
Sewall Worth, of Titherington, co.
Ches., 1520: East Cheshire, ii. 290.
The modern English form is
Sewell. The United States have
preserved Sewall from oblivion.
1586. Francis Hodges and Joanna
Sewell: Marriage Lic. (Westminster),
p. 9.
1664. Robert Sewell and Jane Ryves:
Marriage Alleg. (Canterbury), p. 82.
London, 52, 2, 0, 0, 0; Manchester, 8,
0, 1, 0, 0; Philadelphia, 11, 0, 0, 2, 1;
Boston (U.S.) (Sewall), 13.

Sewer. — Offic. ' the sewer,' an
officer who brought in and took
away the dishes, one who superintended the ' courses' at table,
from O.F. *sevre*, *suir*, to follow.
A substantive ' sewes,' dishes, is
found in Chaucer, who, describing
the rich feasts of Cambuscan, King
of Tartary, says time would fail
him to tell
    ' Of their strange sewes,'
which may be from the same root.
But see Skeat, *sewer* (2), and
Wedgwood. ' Seware, at mete,
dapifer ': Prompt. Parv. ' Sewyn,
at mete,or sette mete,*ferculo,sepulo*':
ibid.
Robert le Suur, 1273. A.
Nicholas le Suur, ibid.
Henry le Suur. G.
Geoffrey le Suur, Close Roll, 50 Hen.
III.
All these references seem to
point to O.F. *sevre*, and connect
themselves naturally with such
words as *sue*, *ensue*, *pursue*, &c.
1637. Richard Sewer and Eliz. Poulter:
Marriage Lic. (Westminster), p. 37.
1675. Richard Vokins and Eliz. Sewer:
Marriage Alleg. (Canterbury), p. 145.

Sewster. — Occup. 'the sewster,'
one who sewed; cf. Simister. The
suffix is the feminine -*ster*. Cf.
Brewster, Webster, and Kempster.
1383. Robert Sewstere, vicar of Gate-
ley, co. Norf.: FF. ix. 506.

1548. Nicholas Sewester and Juliana Cave : Marriage Lic. (Canterbury), p. 14.
1802. Married — John Seuster and Martha Cull : St. Geo. Han. Sq. ii. 266.

Sexsmith ; v. Shoesmith, an American variant.

Philadelphia, 1.

Sexton ; v. Saxton.

Seymour, Seymer, Seamer. —Local, (1) 'of St. Maur,' some forgotten chapelry in Normandy. Local, (2) 'of Semer,' a parish in co. Suffolk. Bapt. (3) 'the son of Semar' (i.e. Sigmar ; v. Yonge, ii. 311). All these various names must inevitably be mixed now, the tendency being towards the aristocratic Seymour ; v. Seamer for a further derivation.

Laurence de Sancto Mauro, co. Derby, 1273. A.
Henry de Sancto Mauro, co. Oxf., ibid.
Henry de Semore, co. Hunts, ibid.
Richard de Semare, co. Bucks, ibid.
Henry de St. Maur, c. 1300. M.
Richard de Semere, vicar of Hindringham, co. Norf., 1349: FF. ix. 230.
Elizabeth Seyntmaur. B.
Adam Semar, co. Hunts, 1273. A.
Hewerad Samar, co. Camb., ibid.
William Samar, co. Hunts, ibid.
Johannes Semer, 1379 : P. T. Yorks. p. 100.
Richardus Semar, 1379 : ibid. p. 133.

These last five references evidently concern (3), the personal name. Many of our Seymours are descendants of this Scandinavian personal name, having assumed the form of Seymour in later times.

London, 39, 1, 2 ; Philadelphia, 31, 0, 0.

Seys.—Nick. ; a variant of the Welsh Sayce, q.v.

Shackel, Shackell, Shackells, Shakel, Shakell, Shackle. — Bapt. 'the son of Shakell' ; cf. the local Shackleton, i.e. the settlement of Shakell, also Shackleford and Shackerley, the latter probably standing for Shackle-ley.

Willelmus Shakelle, 1379 : P. T. Yorks. p. 160.
The Vicarage of Corpesty, co. Norf., 'was sold by Heydon to Thomas Jecks and John Shakle, and by them to the Bacons,' 1611 : FF. vi. 365.

This form still remains in Norfolk, Shackle being found in the Modern Domesday Book for that county.

1597. Married—William Shackle and Jane Durham : St. Mary Aldermary, p. 9.
1761. — Thomas Shackle and Mary Cox: St. Geo. Han. Sq. i. 101.
London, 1, 5, 1, 3, 1, 0 ; MDB. (co. Norf.) (Shackle), 1.

Shackelton, Shackleton.—Local ; v. Shackel.

London, 1, 3 ; Boston (U.S.), 0, 4.

Shacklady.—? Local, 'of Shackerley' (?) ; v. Shakerley. 'Known in Lancashire as a corruption of the ancient local surname of Shackerley' (Lower). I believe this solution to be the true one. The two surnames have run side by side for many generations. Probably Shackerley was originally Shackel-ley, i.e. the field that belonged to Shackel, the first settler (v. Shackel). This would readily corrupt into Shacklady.

1521. John Stokys and Eliz. Shaklady : Marriage Lic. (London), p. 2.
Hugh Shakerley, of Liverpool, 1623 : Wills at Chester, ii. 194.
Peter Shakerley, 1624 : ibid.
Robert Shakelady, of Wrightington, 1630 : ibid.
MDB. (co. Lanc.), 3 ; Liverpool, 1.

Shackleford, Shackelford.—Local ; v. Shackel.

Philadelphia, 0, 2.

Shacklock. — (1) Nick. 'a gaoler,' one who fetters his charge :
'And bids his man bring out the five-fold twist,
His shackles, shacklocks, hampers, gyves, and chains.'
Browne's Britannia's Pastorals, i. 129 (Halliwell).

Or perhaps, like Shakespear, Shakelance, and Shakeshaft, from his rattling the keys of incarceration. (2) Bapt. 'the son of Scathlock,' q.v., probably a variant, as found in co. Derby, on the borders of co. Notts.

Hamo Shakeloc, co. Camb., 1273. A.
Simon Shakelok, 1313. M.
1342. John Shakelok, rector of Ashby, co. Norf. : FF. x. 95.
Willelmus Schakelok, 1379 : P. T. Yorks. p. 192.
Johannes Shakelok', 1379 : ibid. p. 65.
Isolda Schakelok', 1379 : ibid. p. 222.
1568. Married—John Skott and Grace Shacklocke : St. Jas. Clerkenwell, i. 4.
London, 2 ; MDB. (co. Derby), 6.

Shadbolt, Shotbolt. —? Nick. 'Shootbolt' (?). A cross-bowman, one who shot bolts from a catapult ; cf. Drawsword, Shakespear, Wagstaff, and a hundred others, all sobriquets of employment, from the weapon or wand carried. Now found as Shadbolt.

Thomas Shotbolt, C. R., 35 Hen. VI.
John Shotbolt : Index to Clutterbuck's Hertfordshire.
Thomas Shotbolte, temp. 1570 : Cal. of Proceedings in Chancery (Elizabeth).

Shadbolt is modern, and clearly a corruption of Shotbolt.

1775. Married—William Shadbolt and Lydia Bratt : St. Geo. Han. Sq. i. 249.
London, 3, 0.

Shadd.—Personal, 'the son of Shad' ; cf. the local terms Shadwell, Shadforth, and Shadworth, i.e. the well, or ford, or worth where Shad lived. Probably the same as Chad, q.v.

Nicholas Schadd, co. Wilts, 1273. A.
1587. Married — Thomas Woolfe and Cecilia Shadd : Marriage Lic. (London), i. 164.
1693. — Thomas Shadd and Mary Henfrey : St. Jas. Clerkenwell, iii. 213.
Philadelphia, 5.

Shadforth.—Local, ' of Shadforth,' a township in the parish of Pittington, co. Durham. v. Ford and Forth.

1618-9. Thomas Shadford and Amy Rotherie : Marriage Lic. (London), ii. 70.
MDB. (co. Durham), 2.

Shadrack, Shadrake, Shadrick. — Nick. ; an imitative corruption of Sheldrake, q.v.

MDB. (co. Essex), 2, 0, 0 ; London, 0, 1, 0 ; Philadelphia, 0, 0, 1.

Shadwell.—Local, 'of Shadwell,' a parish in co. Middlesex, London, E.

William de Schadwell, 13 Edw. I : Freemen of York, i. 4.
1334. Robert de Shadwell, rector of Intwood, co. Norf. : FF. v. 42.
1620. Married—Whorwood Shadwell and Eliz. Halsey : Marriage Lic. (London), ii. 91.
1667.—John Shadwell and Alice Hickman : St. Jas. Clerkenwell, i. 130.
MDB. (co. Bucks), 1 ; London, 2 ; Boston (U.S.), 1.

Shafto.—Local, 'of Shafto,' a township in the parish of Hartburn, co. Northumberland.

John de Schafthou, co. Northumb., 1273. A.
William de Shafthou, 5 Edw. I : KKK. ii. 4.
Thomas de Shafthow, 1340 : ibid. p. 6.
William de Shafthowe, 1367 : ibid.
1794. Married — William Terry and Ann Shafto : St. Geo. Han. Sq. ii. 121.
London, 1 ; Crockford, 1.

Shakel; v. Shackel.

Shakelance. — Nick. ;   cf. Bruselance, and v. Shakespear and Shakeshaft.

Henry Shakelaunce, co. Northampt., 1273. A.

Shakerley.—Local, ' of Shack-erley,' a hamlet in the parish of Leigh, co. Lancashire, 'formerly almost exclusively the property of the Shakerleys of Somerford in Cheshire. . . . The site of the hall is marked by a moat, and continued to be the residence of the Shaker-leys till the middle of the last century' (Baines' Lanc. ii. 201). For probable derivation, v. Shackel and Shacklady.

1592. Geoffrey Shakerley, of Hulme : Wills at Chester (1545-1620), p. 172.
1596. Buried—John Shawkerley, gent : Reg. Northenden Church, East Cheshire, i. 301.
1652. Peter Shakerley, of Shakerley, co. Lanc. : ibid. ii. 505.
MDB. (Cheshire), 3.

Shakeshaft.—Nick. equivalent to Shakelance and Shakespear, q.v.

Nicholas Shakeshaft, 1542 : Preston Guild, p. 17.
Johannes Shakeshafft, 1542 : ibid. p. 22.
Henry Shakeshaft, of Warrington, 1617 : Wills at Chester, i. 172.
1744. Bapt. — Anne, d. of Hugh Shakeshaft : St. Ann, Manchester.
George Shakeshaft, 1748 : St. Peter, Cornhill, ii. 85.
1778. Married—Thomas Mort and Ann Shakeshaft : St. Geo. Han. Sq. i. 284.
Manchester, 1 ; Preston, 2 ; Boston (U.S.), 1.

Shakespear, Shakespeare.— Nick. ' a spearman.' William Shakespere (V. 1) ; cf. Simon Shakelok (M.), i.e. Shake-lock. Henry Shakelaunce, 1273 (A.), i.e. Shake-lance. Hugh Shakeshaft (Eng. Sur., 2nd edit., p. 461), i.e. Shake-shaft. It is impossible to retail all the nonsense that has been written about this name. Silly guessing has run riot on the

subject. Never a name in English nomenclature so simple or so certain in its origin. It is exactly what it looks—Shakespear ; one of a class of nicknames, nearly all of which have come down to to-day because that which was derisive in them had been soon forgotten, and they had become almost accepted as official. ' Catch-poll ' (q.v.) actually attained the honours of an authorized and official title. A serjeant who cleared the way was equally well known as ' Draw-sword ' (q.v.), a bailiff as ' Wag-staff,' a huntsman as ' Wag-horn,' a jailer as ' Shake-lock,' a pikeman or spearman as ' Shake-lance ' and ' Shake-spear,' and a well-known bird, from its customary habit, as a ' Wag-tail.' *Wag* and *shake* were the chief elements in these vigorous sobriquets ; v. names under Wag- and Shake-, and for others, not in our nomenclature, v. Halliwell.

Robertus Schaksper, *couper*, 1379 : P. T. Yorks. p. 96.
1730. Married — William Fellows and Margaret Shakespear : St. Geo. Han. Sq. i. 7.
1758. — William Guy and Rebecca Shakspar : ibid. p. 76.
MDB. (co. Warwick), 2, 3 ; Philadelphia, 0, 3.

Shallcross; v. Shawcross.

Shallis, Shalless, Shalles.— Local, ' de Schalis.' I cannot identify the spot, but probably Calais is meant. Challis, q.v., is still a Suffolk surname; cf. Shannon and Canon.

Robert de Schalis, co. Suff., 1273. A.
London, 2, 2, 0 ; Crockford, 1, 0, 0 ; Philadelphia, 0, 0, 1.

Shambrook; v. Sambrook, a variant.

Shann, Shand. — Local, ' of Shande.' Mr. Lower says, ' Philibert de Shaunde was created Earl of Bath in 1485 ': Patr. Brit. p. 310.

Johannes Schaune, *webster*, 1379 : P. T. Yorks. p. 118.
Thomas Shan, 1379 : ibid. p. 236.
1742. Married — Thomas Shand and Frances London : St. Geo. Chap. Mayfair, p. 20.
1750. — Robert Hogg and Margaret Shann : ibid. p. 175.

West Riding Court Dir., 6, 0 ; London, 0, 10 ; New York, 1,

Shannon.—Offic. ' the canon M.E. *chanon*; v. Channon.
' Monk or frere, Preest or Chanon.'
Chaucer, C. T. 16307.
The canon-house near Ulver-ston, once attached to Conishead Priory, is now a farmstead called ' Shannon - house,' but styled ' Chanon - house ' in the Church registers of last century (v. my Chronicles of Ulverston, p. 38).

1750. Married — John Shannon and Ann Smith : St. Geo. Chap. Mayfair, p. 165.
1759. — John Pitcher and Catherine Shannon : St. Geo. Han. Sq. i. 85.
London, 8 ; Philadelphia, 76.

Shaper.—Occup. ' the shaper,' a cutter-out of cloth ; v. Shapster. Sheffield, 1.

Shapster, Shepster, Ship-ster.—Occup. ' the shapster,' a female shaper or cutter-out of cloth garments.
' As a shepsteres shere.'
Piers Plowman, 8683.
'To Alice Shapster for making and washing of xxiii sherts and xxiiii stoma-chers ': Privy Purse Expenses, Eliz. of York, p. 122.

N. and Q. (1886, p. 68) has an indenture of apprenticeship dated 1552, which describes the master and mistress as ' Rogero Myners civi et cloth - worker, Lond', et Johanna uxor ejus shepstre.'

Matilda Shapistre, co. Suff., 1273. A.
Cristiana la Schippestere, C. R., 2 Edw. II.

Shard; v. Shird.

Shardlow.—Local, ' of Shard-low,' a township in the parish of Aston-upon-Trent, co. Derby.

Edmund de Scardelowe, co. Camb., 1273. A.
1684. Joseph Collins and Eliz. Shard-low : Marriage Lic. (Canterbury), p. 168.
London, 1 ; New York, 2.

Sharman.—Occup. ' a cloth-shearman'; v. Shearman.

1747. Married — John Sharman and Mary Mason : St. Geo. Chap. Mayfair, p. 80.
New York, 2.

Sharp, Sharpe.—Nick. ' the sharp,' the quick, keen, cutting. Naturally this was a sobriquet likely to be handed down as being complimentary. Several instances have lately cropped up where the child has received the baptismal name Luke, which looks as if a little humour were intended.

Alexander Scharp, co. Bucks, 1273. A.
John Scharp, co. Sussex, ibid.
William Scharpe, co. Linc., ibid.
Adam Scharpe, 1379: P. T. Yorks. p. 92.
Leticia Scharppe, 1379: ibid. p. 133.
1589. Bapt.—Anne, d. Edward Sharpe: St. Jas. Clerkenwell, i. 22.
London, 73, 48; New York, 62, 15.

Sharparrow.—Nick. 'Sharp-arrow,' a good bowman, a complimentary sobriquet.

John Sharparrow, co. York. W. 2.
William Sharparrow, co. York. W. 11.
Oswin Sharparrow, co. York. W. 3.
John Sharpearrowe, Patent Roll, 19 Eliz. pt. iii.
'Orate pro anima dom. Johannis Sharp-arrowe. quondam parsone in Eccles. Cath. Ebor., qui obiit xxv. die Oct. an. 1411': York Minster, Drake's Eboracum, i. 498.
Robertus Sharparowe, 1379: P. T. Yorks. p. 228.
Adam Sharparrow, 1379: ibid.
John Sharparrow, vicar of Shernbourn, co. Norf., 1603: FF. x. 361.

Complimentary as this Yorkshire surname was, it died out. I can find no descendants. Cf. Benbow and Sharpspear.

Sharples, Sharpless.—Local, 'of Sharples,' a township in the parish of Bolton, co. Lanc. The surname is familiar enough in South Lancashire, but does not seem to have spread far. Baines, in his History of Lancashire (i. 475), says a family of Sharples early arose there and occupied the Hall.

1602. Thomas Sharpples: Preston Guild Rolls, p. 64.
Laurence Rigby, of Sharples, 1617: Wills at Chester, i. 161.
Richard Sharples, of Sharples, 1618: p. 172.
1762. Married — Henry Penry and Mary Sharpless: St. Geo. Han. Sq. i. 108.
London, 1, 0; Manchester, 13, 1; Bolton, 6, 0.

Sharplin.—? Bapt. The suffix is clearly a diminutive; cf. Embelin, Tomlin, &c.

Alicia Sarpeline, co. Oxf., 1273. A.
1622. Buried — John Sharpling: St. Jas. Clerkenwell, iv. 157.
1801. Married — John Robinson and Eliz. Sharplin: St. Geo. Han. Sq. ii. 235.
London, 1.

Sharpspear.—Nick. 'Sharp-spear.' Cf. Sharparrow, a Yorkshire surname that lasted some centuries.

William Sharpspere, Close Roll, 6 Edw. I.

Sharrow.—Local, 'of Sharow'; v. Skirrow.

Robert de Scharhow, 28 Edw. I: Freemen of York, i. 8.
Johannes de Sharowe, 1379: P. T. Yorks. p. 300.
Ricardus Sharrowe, 1379: ibid.
London, 2.

Shavenhead. — Nick. 'the Shavenhead'; cf. Whitehead, Redhead, &c.

Robert Shevenehod, co. Camb., 1273. A.

Shaw.—Local, 'at the shaw,' from residence beside a small wood or shaw.

John atte Schaghe, co. Soms., 1 Edw. III: Kirby's Quest, p. 190.
John atte Schawe. H. (Index.)
Johannes del Schagh', 1379: P. T. Yorks. p. 25.
Radulph del Schagh', 1379: ibid. p. 104.
Alicia Shaghe, 1379: ibid. p. 131.
Robertus del Schaghe, 1379: ibid. p. 166.
1608. Bapt. — Anthonie, s. Anthonie Shawe: St. Jas. Clerkenwell, i. 55.
London, 118; New York, 172.

Shawcross, Shallcross, Shal-cross. — Local, 'of Shallcross.' Shallcross Hall lies in the parish of Taxal, Derbyshire, on the confines of Cheshire. The Shallcross's of Shallcross were considerable people in the 17th and 18th centuries. The name is still strong in the immediate district, as the Manchester Directory shows. The modern form of the surname is generally Shawcross.

James Shalcrosse, 1537: Reg. Univ. Oxf. i. 189.
1605. William Shallcross, of Stockport: Wills at Chester, i. 172.
1806. Married—Charles Fernley and Mary Shallcross: St. Geo. Han. Sq. ii. 350.
London, 2, 0, 1; Manchester, 14, 1, 0; Philadelphia, 5, 36, 0.

Shayler, Shaylor, Shailer.—Nick. One who shailed, one who walked crookedly, a cripple. 'Esgrailler, to shale or straddle with the feet or legs' (Cotgrave). 'I shayle with the feet' (Palsgrave). 'Shailer, a cripple' (Halliwell, v. shail and shale 4).

Johannes Scayler, 1379: P. T. Yorks. p. 12.
1680. Bapt. — James, s. Thomas Shayler: St. Mary Aldermary (London), p. 105.
1734. Married — Roger Evans and Anna-Maria Shaler: St. Peter, Cornhill, ii. 81.
London, 5, 0, 0; Boston (U.S.), 0, 0, 2.

Sheard.—Occup.; v. Shepard, a corruption. Cf. Shearson.

1671. Bapt. — William, s. Edward Sheard: St. Jas. Clerkenwell, i. 250.
1788. Married — Matthew Cook and Hannah Barracluf Sheard: St. Geo. Han. Sq. ii. 11.
London, 5; Oxford, 3; Philadelphia, 9.

Shearer.—Occup. 'the shearer,' i. e. a cloth shearman; v. Shear-man.

Matilda le Scherher, co. Linc., 1273. A.
Richard le Sherere, temp. 1300. M.
Reginald le Scherere, temp. 1300. M.
1809. Married — James Shearer and Margaret Ritchie: St. Geo. Han. Sq. ii. 402.
London, 3; Boston (U.S.), 3.

Shearman, Sharman, Sher-man.—Occup. 'the shearman,' a cloth-shearer, one who sheared the nap; v. Liber Albus, p. 630. The Shermen formed a company in the York Guild (York Mystery Plays, p. lxxvii and p. 337). The Shermen and Fullers appeared in the Norwich Play (Blomefield, ii. 148).

John le Sheremon, c. 1300. M.
Robert le Sherman, c. 1300. M.
William le Sherman. R.
Oliver Sherman, 1379: P. T. Yorks. p. 100.
Johannes Wykir, shereman, 1379: ibid. p. 25.
1638. Bapt.—Eliz., d. John Sherman: St. Jas. Clerkenwell, i. 139.
1792. Married — Edward Sharman and Sarah Barlow: St. Geo. Han. Sq. ii. 81.
London, 14, 24, 10; Boston (U.S.), 1, 1, 105.

Shearsmith. — Occup. 'the shearsmith,' a maker of shears.

Walter le Scheresmythe, c. 1300. M.
Thomas Schersmyth, co. York, 1440: W. 11.

1736. Bapt. — William, s. William Sharesmith : St. Jas. Clerkenwell, ii. 226.
1753. Married — Benjamin Ward and Ann Shearsmith : St. Geo. Chap. Mayfair, p. 249.
1759. Married — Samuel Shearsmith and Sarah Marshall : St. Geo. Han. Sq. i. 65.

Shearson.—Nick. A corruption of Shepherdson, q.v. A North-English corruption ; cf. Sheard for Shepherd.

Robert Shearson, of Ellel, 1675 : Lancashire Wills at Richmond, i. 249.
Edmund Sheirson, of Ellel, 1672 : ibid.
Richard Shearson, of Cockerham, 1687: ibid. ii. 226.
Margaret Shierson, of Marton, 1716 : ibid. p. 227.
Thomas Sherson, of Lancaster, 1725: ibid. p. 228.
Liverpool, 3.

Sheat, Sheate.—Bapt. 'the son of Schet' ; v. Skeate.

Walter Scheat, co. Camb., 1273. A.
1724. Bapt.—Eliz., d. John Sheat : St. Jas. Clerkenwell, ii. 149.
London, 1, 1.

Sheath.—Local, 'at the Sheath.' Possibly a bubbling spring of salt water. '*Sheath*, a fountain of salt water' (Halliwell). But more probably the name attached to some chasm in the rocks resembling the scabbard, or sheath of a knife or sword.

Humfrey de la Shethe, co. Devon, Hen. III–Edw. I. K.
1747. Married — Thomas Carpenter and Esther Sheath : St. Geo. Chap. Mayfair, p. 99.
1785. John Taylor and Sarah Sheath : St. Geo. Han. Sq. i. 372.
London, 5.

Sheather.—Occup. 'the sheather,' a maker of sword-slips ; v. Swordslipper, also a Yorkshire name. 'Schedare or schethare, *vaginarius*': Prompt. Parv. p. 444.

Henry le Schether, 31 Edw. I : Freemen of York, i. 9.
John Schether, co. Soms., 1 Edw. III : Kirby's Quest, p. 168.
Johannes de Breres, *shether*, 1379: P.T. Yorks. p. 136.
Johannes Schether, 1379 : ibid. p. 249.
Johanna Shether, 1379 : ibid. p. 59.
Thomas Schether, 1379 : ibid. p. 252.
London, 2.

Sheepdriver. — Occup. 'the sheep-driver,' a tender of sheep.

Michael le Sheepdriuere, Rot. Fin., 4 Edw. II.

Sheepshank. — Nick. 'with the sheep-shanks.' Though not complimentary, it has lived till to-day, and is respected, in one instance at least, by the whole country ; cf. Philipshank, Longshank, &c. I believe the word *leg* did not commonly exist in the popular English language at the early period of hereditary surnames. This surname sprang up in co. York. Cf. Shortshank.

Alicia Shepshank', *chapman*, 1379 : P. T. Yorks. p. 3.
Willelmus Schepschank, 1379 : ibid. p. 99.
1802. Married — John Sheepshanks, M.A., of Leeds, co. York, and Mary Anderson : St. Geo. Han. Sq. ii. 260.
West Riding Yorks Court Dir., 4 ; Harrogate, 1.

Sheepshead. — Local, 'of Sheepshed,' co. Leic.

Baldwin Shepesheued, Close Roll, 2 Hen. IV. pt. i.
John Schepishead, co. Leic. PP.
William Schepishead, co. Leic. PP.
James Hall, of Sheepshed, co. Leic. MDB.

Sheepway.—Local ; v. Shipway.

Sheffield. — Local, 'of Sheffield,' the well-known town in co. York.

Johannes de Schefeld, 1379 : P. T. Yorks. p. 74.
Johannes de Schefell', 1379 : ibid. p. 79.
Agnes Shefeld, 1564 : Lancashire Wills at Richmond, i. 249.
1601. Bapt.—Matthew, s. of Nathaniell Sheffeild : St. Michael, Cornhill, p. 103.
London, 16 ; West Rid. Court Dir., 1 ; New York, 8.

Sheldon.—Local, 'of Sheldon,' a chapelry in the parish of Bakewell, co. Derby ; also parishes in cos. Devon and Warwick. Worcestershire has for many centuries been the habitat of a family of this name.

1584-5. Francis Sheldon, co. Worc. : Reg. Univ. Oxf. vol. ii. pt. ii. p. 141.
1621. Edward Sheldon, co. Worc. : ibid. p. 401.
1737. Married — Francis Sheldon and Ann Read : St. Geo. Han. Sq. i. 19.
MDB. (co. Derby), 18 ; London, 13 ; Manchester, 6 ; New York, 42.

Sheldrake, Sheldrick, Shildrick. — Nick. 'the sheldrake,'

a kind of drake. M.E. *scheldrak* ; v. Shadrack for a modification.

Adam Sceyldrake, co. Suff., 1273. A.
John Sheldrake. D.
1662. Adam Sheldrake and Mary Pittman : Marriage Alleg. (Canterbury), p. 26.
1802. Married — William Sheldrick and Eliz. Coates: St. Geo. Han. Sq. ii. 302.
London, 2, 4, 1 ; Philadelphia, 17, 0, 0.

Shelmerdine. — Local, ' of Shermanden,' gradually corrupted to Shelmerdine. I cannot find the spot ; cf. Haseltine for Haselden. The habitat must be sought for in South Lanc. or East Ches.

1632. John Shelmerdine, of Lower Ardwick : Wills at Chester, i. 196.
1639. Ralph Shelmerdine, of Gorton : ibid.
1636. Married—Francis Shelmerdyne and Dorothy Cotterell : Reg. Prestbury Ch., East Cheshire, p. 302.
1643. 'Item, for charges and expenses uppon divers ministers (to witt), Mr. Furness, Mr. Mariegould, Mr. Worsley, Mr. Hall, Mr. Bate, Mr. Shelmerdyne,' &c. : East Cheshire, i. 293.
1647. Mary Shermantine : Cal. of Wills in Court of Husting (2).
London, 1 ; Manchester, 13 ; Philadelphia, 7.

Shelton.—Local, ' of Shelton,' a parish in co. Norfolk, near Long Stratton ; also a parish in co. Notts, six miles from Newark ; also a parish in co. Bedford, four miles from Kimbolton. Cf. Skelton.

1561. Richard Shelton and Jane Hollingworth : Marriage Lic. (London), i. 21.
1700. Bapt.—Eliz., d. Henry Shelton: St. Jas. Clerkenwell, i. 386.
MDB. (co. Camb.), 1 ; London, 12 ; Boston (U.S.), 10.

Shemeld, Shimeld.— ? Bapt. ' the son of Schwanhilde' or Svanhild, a favourite Scandinavian personal name. There can scarcely be a doubt that this is a modified form.

Adam Schemylde, 1379 : P. T. Yorks. p. 45.
Robertus Schemylde, *smyth*, 1379 : ibid.
1771. Married—Hugh Ellis and Sarah Shimeld : St. Geo. Han. Sq. i. 214.
Sheffield, 1, 3 ; West Rid. Court Dir., 1, 0 ; Philadelphia, 2, 0.

Shenston, Shenstone. — Local, ' of Shenstone,' a parish

in co. Stafford, three miles from Lichfield.

1792. Married — William Shenston and Eliz. Smith : St. Geo. Han. Sq. ii. 85. London, 1, 0 ; MDB. (co. Stafford), 0, 1.

Shenton.—Local, ' of Shenton,' a chapelry in the parish of Market Bosworth, in co. Leicester. Also some spot seemingly in co. Ches.

John Shenton, 1577, co. Ches.: Reg. Univ. Oxf. vol. ii. pt. ii. p. 76. John Shenton, of Church Coppenhull, 1607 : ibid. Thomas Shenton, of Stoke, 1611 : Wills at Chester, i. 174. 1778. Married—William Shenton and Mary Penn : St. Geo. Han. Sq. i. 286. London, 4 ; MDB. (co. Camb.), 1 ; Philadelphia, 3.

Shepard, Shephard, Shepheard, Sheppard, Shepperd, Sheppherd, Shepherd.—Occup. ' the shepherd.' With the many variants of this surname, cf. Calvert for Calve-herd, Coward for Cow-herd, Stoddard for Stot-herd, &c.

Josse le Sephurde, co. Oxf., 1273. A. Margaret le Sephirde, co. Hunts, ibid. Walter le Schepherde, co. Camb., ibid. John le Shepherde, c. 1300. M. William Shephirde, 1379 : P. T. Yorks. p. 299. Johannes Schephirde, 1379 : ibid. p. 195. James Sheppard, of Eccles, *butcher*, 1614 : Wills at Chester, i. 174. London, 7, 8, 1, 72, 8, 0, 60. Philadelphia, 7, 8, 1, 72, 8, 0, 60.

Shepherdson, Shephardson.—Nick. ' the shepherd's son'; cf. Taylorson, Wrightson, Smithson. Taylorson is peculiar to co. Yorks, as is Shepherdson. Wrightson is also familiar to that county.

John Shepherdson, 1423: DDD. ii. 370. Alice Shipperden, co. York. W. 9. William Shipperdson, co. Durham. SS. 1738. Married—William Curling and Ann Shephardson : Canterbury Cath. p. 83. 1798. — William Shepperson and Sabina Strong : St. Geo. Han. Sq. ii. 191. West Rid. Court Dir., 1, 0 ; Sheffield, 1, 0 ; Boston (U.S.), 0, 4.

Shepley, Shipley.—(1) Local, ' of Shepley,' a township in the parish of Kirk Burton, W. Rid. Yorks. (2) Local, ' of Shipley,' a parish in W. Rid. Yorks, three miles from Bradford. Both places seem to have been originally spelt Scheplay, so both Shepley and

Shipley as surnames are now inextricably mixed.

Katerine de Scheplay, 1379 : P. T. Yorks. p. 194. Joanna de Scheplay, 1379 : ibid. Adam de Scheplay, 1379 : ibid. p. 155. 1698. Bapt. — Hannah, d. Henry Shepley : St. Jas. Clerkenwell, i. 376. 1714. Buried — Samuel Shipley : St. Mary Aldermary, p. 213. London, 0, 3 ; MDB. (co. Ches.), 4, 0 ; Manchester, 3, 0 ; Boston (U.S.), 7, 17.

Sherar, Sherer, Sherrer.—Occup. ; v. Shearer.

London, 1, 1, 0 ; Boston (U.S.), 0, 0, 1.

Sherard, Sherrard, Sherratt.—Local. Probably a corruption of Sherwood, q.v. The first stage would be Sher'ood, then Sherad, then Sherratt. That this is no idle guess is proved by the fact that in the Index to the Reg. Univ. Oxf. to the name Sherwood is added, ' or Sherewood, or Sherrat.'

William Sherratt, of Moss Side, Manchester, 1588 : Wills at Chester, i. 174. John Sherratt, of Church Lawton, 1604 : ibid. 1665-6. George Sherard and Mary Deakins : Marriage Alleg. (Canterbury), p. 164. London, 0, 8, 2 ; Manchester, 0, 0, 6 ; Boston (U.S.), 0, 4, 0 ; New York, 1, 2, 0.

Sheraton, ? Sheridan.—Local, ' of Sheraton,' a village south of Castle Eden, anciently Shurveton. The name is still found in the neighbourhood of Newcastle. It is very probable that Sheridan is the modern form. The corruption was all but inevitable.

Stephen de Shurveton, 1318 : DDD. i. 54. Robert de Shirveton, 1398 : ibid. p. 54. London, 0, 4 ; Liverpool, 1, 4 ; Manchester, 0, 4 ; New York, 0, 160.

Sherborne, Sherborn, Sherburn, Sherburne.—Local, ' of Sherburne.' There are parishes and hamlets of the name of Sherborne, or Sherburne, in cos. Dorset, Warwick, Gloucester, Hants, Durham, and York.

Adam de Schirburn, *couraour*, 31 Edw. I : Freemen of York, i. 9. John de Schireburne, co. Soms., 1 Edw. III : Kirby's Quest, p. 178. William Schurebourne, co. Soms., 1 Edw. III .ibid. p. 162. William de Shirborn, co. Soms., 1 Edw. III : ibid. p. 278. Ricardus de Schyrburn, 1379 : P. T. Yorks. p. 237.

Johannes de Shirburn', of Schyrburne, 1379 : ibid. p. 147. 1585. Augustine Sherborne, co. Oxf.: Reg. Univ. Oxf. vol. ii. pt. ii. p. 143. 1598-9. Richard Sherborne, co. Lanc., ibid. p. 232. London, 2, 2, 0, 0 ; Philadelphia, 5, 0, 0, 0 ; New York, 0, 0, 1, 0 ; Boston (U.S.) (Sherburne), 30.

Shergold.—Bapt. ' the son of Shergold.' Probably a form of Sargood, q.v. Found in co. Wilts as Shergoll.

William Shergall, co. Wilts, 1552 : Reg. Broad Chalke, p. 7. Ricard Shergoll, 1603 : ibid. 1661. Buried — Percival Shergould : St. Jas. Clerkenwell, iv. 342. 1669. Bapt. — John, s. Alexander Shurgall : ibid. p. 239. 1775. Married — William Hill and Mary Shergold : St. Geo. Han. Sq. i. 256. London, 1.

Sheridan.—Local ; v. Sheraton.

Sheriff, Sherriff.—Offic. ' the Sheriff '; v. Shreeve.

Robert le Shirreve, co. Suff., 1273. A. Lena le Shireve, co. Suff., ibid. John Schiref, co. Northumberland, ibid. Thomas Shurreve, co. Soms., 1 Edw. III : Kirby's Quest, p. 122. Johannes Schyref, 1379 : P. T. Yorks. p. 91. Thomas le Shirreve. B. 1786. Married — Alex. Sherriff and Mary Chilcott : St. Geo. Han. Sq. i. 394. London, 2, 0 ; Boston (U.S.), 0, 4.

Sheringham.—Local, ' of Sheringham,' a parish in co. Norfolk, three miles from Cromer.

1793. Married — Samuel Hallaway and Mary Ann Sheringham : St. Geo. Han. Sq. ii. 105. MDB. (co. Glouc.), 1.

Sherlock.—(1) Nick. (?), 'with shorn locks.' A.S. *sceran, sciran,* to cut, to shear ; cf. Blacklock, Whitelock, Silverlock, Lovelock, &c., a large class. (2) Probably, however, Sherlock was a personal name.

Beatrice Schyrlok, co. Bedf., 1273. A. Philip Schyrlok, co. Soms., 1 Edw. II : Kirby's Quest, p. 94. Johannes Shirlok', 1379 : P. T. Yorks. p. 228. 1568-9. William Shirlocke and Aveline Stubbes : Marriage Lic. (London), i. 41. 1669. Thomas Freeman and Eliz. Shurlock : Marriage Alleg. (Canterbury), p. 11. London, 5; Manchester, 3 ; Philadelphia, 25.

Sherman.—Occup. 'the shearman,' a cloth shearman; v. Shearman.

Sherrard, -ratt; v. Sherard.

Sherrin, Sherring. — Bapt. 'the son of Sherwin,' q.v. Many of the names ending in *-win* are now *-in* or *-ing*; cf. Boddin for Baldwin, Gunning for Gundwin, Golding for Goldwin. The *g* in Sherring is therefore an excrescence, as in Jennings.

Sciring (without surname), co. Camb., 1273. A.
1629. Buried—Mary Sherryn: St. Jas. Clerkenwell, iv. 197.
London, 4, 7; MDB. (co. Somerset), 13, 4.

Sherrington. — Local, 'of Sherrington,' parishes in the diocs. of Oxford and Salisbury; cf. Cherrington, Charrington, and Carrington.

1567-8. Alex. Sherington and Edith Horne: Marriage Lic. (London), i. 38.
1642. Bapt. — John, s. William Sherrington: St. Jas. Clerkenwell, i. 152.
1662. Buried — Eliz., d. William Sherington: St. Peter, Cornhill, i. 214. London, 4.

Sherston, Sherson. — Local, 'of Sherston,' two parishes in co. Wilts.

Thomas Scherston, co. Soms., 1 Edw. III: Kirby's Quest, p. 231.
1560. Married — Thomas Sherson and Ellen Vintner: St. Peter, Cornhill, i. 225.

With this entry, cf. Kelson for Kelston, &c. These modified forms are as natural as they are common.

London, 1, 1.

Sherwell, Sherwill, Shervill. — Local, 'of Sherwill,' a parish in co. Devon, four miles from Barnstaple.

1789. Married — Ralph Shervill and Mary Clarke: St. Geo. Han. Sq. ii. 29.
MDB. (co. Devon), 3, 0, 1; London, 3, 0, 2.

Sherwin.—Bapt. 'the son of Sherwin.' One of the many personal names ending in *-win*; cf. Unwin, Baldwin, Godwin. The *d* in my instances is, no doubt, excrescent, as in Simmonds or Hammond; v. Sherrin.

John Surewyne, co. Oxf., 1273. A.
William Surewyne, co. Oxf., ibid.

Robert Serewynd, co. Camb., 1273. A.
Geoffrey Scherewynd, co. Camb., ibid
Peter Scherewynd, co. Camb., ibid.
Robert Shirwynd, C. R., 16 Ric. II.
William Sherwynd, C. R., 2 Hen. IV. pt. i.
Hugo Scherwynd, 1379: P. T. Yorks. p. 99.
Preciosa Scherwynd', *webster*, 1379: ibid. p. 98.
Thomas Schiruen, 1379: ibid. p. 192.
London, 6; New York, 2.

Sherwood.—Local, 'of Sherwood,' i.e. Sherwood Forest.

Ralph de Scirewode, co. Linc., 1273. A.
Margareta de Shyrwode, 1379: P. T. Yorks. p. 128.
Alexander de Shyrwode, 1379: ibid. p. 74.
Willelmus de Schiwode, 1379: ibid. p. 129.
1577. William Sherwood and Dionise Butler: Marriage Lic. (London), i. 75.
1610. Henry Sherwood, co. Oxf.: Reg. Univ. Oxf. vol. ii. pt. ii. p. 317.
1661. Married — John Sherwood and Judith Cooke: St. Thomas the Apostle (London), p. 21.
London, 13; West Rid. Court Dir., 2; Boston (U.S.), 9.

Sheward.—Bapt. 'the son of Seward' (q.v.), a variant. In the Index to Reg. Univ. Oxf., added to Seward is 'or Sheward, or Shewarde'; vol. ii. pt. iv. p. 376.

Henry Shewarde, co. Hereford, 1594: Reg. Univ. Oxf. vol. ii. pt. ii. p. 204.
1612. Married—Richard Sheward and Elizabeth Ashe: St. Mary Aldermary (London), p. 12.
1645. Bapt.—Jane, d. Martin Sheward: St. Thomas the Apostle (London), p. 56. London, 2.

Shields.—Local, 'of Shields,' i.e. North Shields, a seaport and market-town, co. Northumberland.

Willelmus de Scheles 1379: P. T. Yorks. p. 193.
1736. Married — William Shields and Martha Sedley: St. Geo. Han. Sq. i. 17.
1785. Thomas Pocknell and Margaret Shiells: ibid. p. 371.
London, 5; Boston (U.S.), 48.

Shilcock, Schilcock, Shillcock.—Nick. 'the shilcock'; cf. Sheldrake, and v. Skeat on *sheldrake*.

Johannes Schalkok', 1379: P. T. Yorks. p. 200.
London, 3, 0, 0; Sheffield, 0, 1, 0; MDB. (co. Leic.), 9, 0, 1; Philadelphia, 1, 0, 0.

Shildrick.—Nick.; v. Sheldrake.

Shilito, Shillito, Shillitoe, Shilleto, Shillitto.—? Local, 'of Selito' (?). This great Yorkshire name completely baffles me. Probably, like Sholto (co. Northumberland), the suffix is *-how* (v. How, 2), in which case, of course, the name is local. But I cannot identify the spot, and there is no prefix *de* to the instances. No entry is found in any of the great rolls, like the Testa de Neville, the Hundred Rolls, or the Placita quo Warranto.

Adam Selito (Houghton Grass), 1379: P. T. Yorks. p. 133.
Johannes Selito (Houghton Grass), 1379: ibid.
Jurdanus Selito (Whitwood), 1379: ibid. p. 167.
Johannes Selito (Whitwood),1379: ibid.
Cf. Ricardus Ruscheto, 1379: ibid. p. 249.
1721. Bapt.—John, s. Peter Selleto: St. Mary Aldermary (London), p. 122.
London, 0, 2, 3, 1, 0; West Rid. Court Dir., 1, 2, 0, 1, 1; Sheffield (Shillito), 4.

Shilling.—(1) Bapt. 'the son of Shilwin' or Schilling. Lower says, 'Schelin, Schelinus, a Domesday personal name.' Probably most of our Shillings descend from an old personal name Shilwin, one of the endless names with suffix *-win*; cf. Sherwin and Sherring, or Goldwin and Golding. (2) Local, 'of Schilling.' I cannot find the spot.

Henry de Scilling, co. Norf., 1273. A.
William Schilling, co. Norf., ibid.
John Schelling, co. Wilts, ibid.
Cecilia Schyllyng, 1379: P. T. Yorks. p. 140.
Willelmus Shilwyn, 1379: ibid. p. 161.
1565. Bapt.—Sara, d. Gregory Shillinge: St. Jas. Clerkenwell, i. 3.
1796. Married—John Shilling and Mary Rider: St. Geo. Han. Sq. ii. 143.
London, 4; Philadelphia, 9.

Shillingford. — Local, 'of Shillingford,' parishes in co. Berks and Devon. Probably originally Killingford; v. Killingsworth, where such variants as Chillingworth and Shillingsworth are mentioned.

1663. Charles Shillingford, alias Izard, and Mary Pryor: Marriage Alleg. (Canterbury), p. 99.
London, 7; Oxford, 1; Philadelphia, 6.

Shillingsworth. — Local; v. Killingsworth.

1753. Married—George Smedley and Elizabeth Shillingsworth.

Shillito, &c. ; v. Shilito.

Shilston, Shillson. — Local, 'of Shillingston,' a parish in co. Dorset. It is almost certain that these are variants. With Shillson, cf. Kelson for Kelston.

1689. John Chilston (or Shilston) and Ann Brady : Marriage Alleg. (Cant.), p. 111.
1801. Married—James Cormick and Sarah Shilstone : St. Geo. Han. Sq. ii. 236.
MDB. (co. Devon), 2, 1 ; London, 1, 0.

Shimeld ; v. Shemeld.

Shingler.—Occup. 'the shingler,' a tyler. Shingles were square-shaped wooden tiles for the roofs of houses. Langland speaks of Noah's ark as the 'shyngled ship.'

'Flouren cakes beth the schingles alle
Of cherche, cloister, boure, and halle.'
Halliwell.

In a statute (1563) relating to the apprenticeship of children, reference is made to the occupations of 'Tyler, Slater, Healyer, Tile-maker, Thatcher or Shingler' (5 Eliz. c. 4, 23). All these represent different modes of roofing houses, and are familiar surnames to-day. v. Hillier.

1747. Bapt.—Anne, d. Thomas Shingler : St. Mary Aldermary (London), p. 130.
1767. Married—Thomas Shinglar and Ann Selby : St. Geo. Han. Sq. i. 170.
London, 1 ; MDB. (co. Ches.), 1.

Shinn.—Local. This is clearly a variant of Chinn (v. Ching). Both hail from co. Cambridge.

1629. Buried—Mary Shinn : St. Jas. Clerkenwell, iv. 194.
1803. Married — Benjamin Hardwick Shinn and Eliz. Knight Ayres : St. Geo. Han. Sq. ii. 287.
1809. — William Shinn and Mary Nichols : ibid. p. 402.
MDB. (co. Camb.), 3 ; Philadelphia, 62.

Shipley ; v. Shepley.

Boston (U.S.), 2.

Shipman.—Occup. 'the ship-man,' a sailor, one who worked aboard a ship. 'Schypmane, nauta' : Prompt. Parv. I cannot find Sailor in our nomenclature ; Mariner and Shipman were the usual terms.

'A shipman was ther woned fer by West, ..
He knew wel alle the havens as they were,
Fro' Gotland to the Cape de Finisterre.'
Chaucer's C. T., Prologue.
Hugh le Schipman, C. R., 36 Hen. III.

William Schippeman, co. Linc., 1273. A.
Alexander Schipman. H.
Willelmus de Seyton, schypmane, 1379 : P. T. Yorks. p. 127.
Robertus Shypman, 1379 : ibid.
Richard Harman, shippeman, 1379 : ibid. p. 50.
Willelmus Shipman, 1379 : ibid. p. 30.
1602. William Shipman, of Bristol : Reg. Univ. Oxf. vol. ii. pt. ii. p. 257.
1756. Married — John Shipman and Mary Tillie : St. Geo. Han. Sq. i. 64.
London, 4 ; Sheffield, 10 ; New York, 18.

Shipp.—Local, 'at the ship,' one who was living on a ship or boat ; cf. Barge.

Ralph At Ship, Prepositor of Bristol, 1230 : YYY. p. 669.
Isolda del Shippe, 1379 : P. T. Yorks. p. 297.
1762. Married—James Hobbs and Ann Ship : St. Geo. Han. Sq. i. 115.
1789. — Robert Ship and Eliz. Jarvis : ibid. ii. 17.
London, 5 ; Boston (U.S.), 3.

Shippard, Shipperd.—Occup. 'the shepherd' ; a corruption. Nevertheless another origin is quite possible. viz. Shipward, the guardian of a ship ; cf. Millard for Millward.

John Shipward, mayor of Bristol, 1477 : Barrett's Hist. of Bristol.
George Shippherd, of Fell End, Kirby, 1666 : Lancashire Wills at Richmond, i. 250.
Cuthbert Shipperd, 1599 : ibid.
1677. Jonathan Shippard and Eliz. Beale : Marriage Alleg. (Cant.), p. 194.
London, 2, 0 ; Philadelphia, 0, 1.

Shipton.—Local, 'of Shipton,' parishes in cos. Salop, Devon, Dorset, &c. Also a chapelry in parish of Market Weighton, E. Rid. Yorks ; also a township in parish of Overton, E. Rid. Yorks.

Baldwin de Schipton, co. York, 1273. A.
Simon de Shupton, firmarius, 1379 : P. T. Yorks. p. 234.
1590-1. Edward Shipton, London : Reg. Univ. Oxf. vol. ii. pt. ii. p. 182.
1753. Married—Mark Hipworth and Anna Shipton : St. Geo. Han. Sq. i. 50.
London, 5 ; MDB. (co. Derby), 7.

Shipwash. — Local, 'at the sheepwash.' There is a spot called Sheepwash near Waterhead, Old-ham, co. Lanc. Probably many small localities would obtain this name, being favourite places for sheep-washing. Any one living beside such a running pool would readily be termed 'Robert at the sheepwash.'

1657. Bapt.—Joseph, s. Adrey Sheep-wash : St. Mary Aldermary (London), p. 96.
John Shipwash, 1725 : Reg. Canterbury Cath. p. 76.
1800. Married—Robert Shipwash and Mary Barlow : St. Geo. Han. Sq. ii. 217. London, 1.

Shipway, Sheepway. — (1) Local, 'of Shepway,' one of the lathes, or great divisions of the county of Kent (Lower). This is confirmed by the following entry :

Ballivus (the bailiff) de Shipweye, co. Kent, 1273. A.

(2) Local, 'at the sheep-way,' from residence along the track trod by the sheep ; cf. Greenway, Hathway, Otway, &c.

Richard Shippway, co. Ches., 1603 : Reg. Univ. Oxf. vol. ii. pt. i. p. 265.
1608-9. Christopher Shipway and Margaret Drake : Marriage Lic. (West-minster), p. 17.
London, 7, 0 ; MDB. (co. Glouc.), 2, 2 ; New York, 1.

Shipwright. — Occup. 'the shipwright,' a boat-builder. 'Schypwryte, naupicus' : Prompt. Parv.

Hugh le Schypwryte, co. Camb., 1273. A.
Richard Schypwryte, co. Camb., ibid.
Robert Schypwryte, co. Camb., ibid.

Perhaps made boats for the 'torpids' in the 'Varsity races of the period !

Willelmus Schypwright, 1379 : P. T. Yorks. p. 157.
Thomas Shypwryght, 1379 : ibid. p. 127.
Johannes Boteler, shippewryght, 1379 : ibid. p. 51.
1805. Married—Martin Skelt and Mary Shipwright : St. Geo. Han. Sq. ii. 324.
London, 3.

Shird, Shirt, Shard.—Local, 'of the Sherd,' a place in Disley, in the parish of Stockport. Sherds of Sherd existed at an early period, and the junior branches spread into Lancashire, Derby-shire, and beyond. As for the meaning of Sherd, cf. 'shard, an opening in a wood. Yorkshire' (Halliwell). 'Shard, a gap in a fence. Var. dial.' (ibid.) That Shirt is the modern imitative corruption of the surname is manifest.

Richard del Sherd, 1369 : v. East Cheshire, ii. 86.

William del Sherd, an archer of the Crown, 1398 : East Ches. ii. p. 87.
Hugh del Sherd, of Sherd, 1473 : ibid.
William Sherd, of Sherd, 1475 : ibid.
Jeffery Shirt, of Staley, 1593 : Wills at Chester, i. 174.
Thomas Shirt, co. Chester, *preacher*, 1618 : ibid.
Richard Sherte, co. Ches. : Reg. Univ. Oxf. vol. ii. pt. ii. p. 254.
Manchester, 1, 2, 1.

Shire, Shires.—Local, 'at the shire,' a division of territory, from residence therein; genitive Shires; cf. Brooks, Holmes, Knowles, &c. Also cf. Hallamshire.
1397. Gregory atte Shire : Cal. of Wills in Court of Husting (2).
1668. George Shyres and Sarah Rogers : Marriage Alleg. (Canterbury), p. 151,
1777. Married — William Shires and Ann Pocock : St. Geo. Han. Sq. i. 282.
London, 0, 3 ; Philadelphia, 1, 0.

Shirley.—Local, ' of Shirley,' parishes in cos. Derby, Hants, &c.
Johannes de Scherlay, 1379 : P. T. Yorks. p. 130.
Willelmus de Scherlay, 1379 : ibid. p. 120.
1573. George Shyrlye, co. Leic. : Reg. Univ. Oxf. vol ii. pt. ii. p. 56.
1579. Anthony Sherlye, co. Sussex : ibid. p. 90.
1582. John Shurley, co. Sussex : ibid. p. 361.
West Rid. Court Dir., 3 ; London, 14 ; Boston (U.S.), 5.

Shirt; v. Shird.

Shirtcliff, Shirtcliffe. — Local, 'of Shircliff.' I cannot find the spot. It is one of the many Yorkshire surnames with suffix -*cliff*; cf. Topliff, Wickliffe, &c.
Johannes de Shirclyf', 1379 : P. T. Yorks. p. 8.
Robertus de Shirclyf', 1379 : ibid.
1621. Nicholas Sheircliffe, or Sherclyff, co. York : Reg. Univ. Oxf. vol. ii. pt. ii. p. 389.
West Rid. Court Dir., 1, 6 ; Sheffield, 0, 4 ; Philadelphia, 1, 0.

Shmith.—Occup. ' the smith,' q.v. Perhaps englished out of the German Schmidt.
London, 2.

Shobbrook, Shoebrook, Shubrick, Shubrook, Shuebruk.—Local, ' of Shobrooke,' a parish in co. Devon, two miles from Crediton.
MDB. (co. Devon), 2, 1, 0, 0, 0; London, 0, 0, 1, 3, 0; Boston (Shuebruk), 1.

Shoebeggar.—Nick. 'a beggar of old shoes.' The occupation is not extinct.
Simon le Shobegg'e, co. Camb., 1273. A.

Shoebotham.—Local. Almost all our surnames in -*botham* come from East Cheshire ; v. Shufflebotham and Higginbotham ; v. also Botham.
1605. Married — Thomas Potter and Margerie Showbothom : Reg. Prestbury, co. Ches., p. 167.
Manchester, 2.

Shoemaker. — Occup. ' the shoemaker '; rare, the general trade-names were Souter and Cordwaner. Christopher Shoomaker was burnt at Newbury (1518), according to Foxe. Thomas Shomaker was an attendant upon the Princess Mary (1542); v. Privy Purse Expenses, p. 2. In the Chester Mystery the 'Corvesters and Shoemakers' marched together (Ormerod's Cheshire, p. 301).
1581. Married — Thomas Shomaker : Reg. St. Columb Major, p. 141.
Richard Shomaker. V. 3.
1591. Yeocum Shoemaker and Catharine Britten : Marriage Lic. (London), i. 225.

The name lingered on till the close of the 18th century :
1781. Buried — Mary, wife of John Showmaker : Reg. St. Ann's, Manchester.

Almost all the American Shoemakers are of German extraction.
Philadelphia, 178.

Shoesmith, Shoosmith, Shuxsmith, Sucksmith, Sixsmith, Shucksmith. — Occup. ' the shoesmith,' a maker of horseshoes, a farrier. Sixsmith may be a corruption of *sickle-smith* (v. Sucksmith) ; but it is probable, however strange it may appear, that all the above names are changes rung upon Shoesmith. Having once reached Sucksmith, the final step to Sixsmith was easy.
William le Shosmyth, C. R., 16 Edw. I.
Henry Shughsmythe, co. York. W. 2.
Margerie Shughsmythe. AA. 1.
Bryan Sukesmythe, temp. Eliz. ZZ.
1577. Bapt. — Mary, d. John Shewsmith : St. Thomas the Apostle, London, p. 27.
1576. Bryan Shusmith, of Winwick : Wills at Chester (1545-1620), p. 175.

1602. Thomas Sixsmith, of Atherton : ibid. p. 176.
1608. John Sixsmith, of Wigan : ibid.
1617. Thomas Sixesmith, or Sicksmith, co. Lanc. : Reg. Univ. Oxf. vol. ii. pt. ii. p. 359.
London, 2, 1, 0, 0, 0, 0 ; (Shoesmith), Halifax, 7 ; (Sixsmith), Manchester, 1, Liverpool, 1 ; (Sucksmith), Lightcliffe, near Halifax, 1.; Philadelphia, 0, 0, 0, 0, 8, 1.

Shooter, Shuter.—Occup.'the shooter,' one who got his living by shooting birds ; cf. Hunter, Todhunter, Fowler, &c.
Johannes Shoter,1379: P. T.Yorks.p.9 .
Willelmus Shoter, 1379 : ibid.
Johanna Schoter, 1379 : ibid. p. 41.
Johannes Schewter, 1379 : ibid. p. 165.
1784. Married — John Shuter and Ann Seller : St. Geo. Han. Sq. i. 355.
Sheffield, 1, 0 ; London, 0, 6.

Shop, Shopp.—Local, ' at the shop,' one who dwelt at a stall, or house, for sale. Cf. Shipp.
Margery atte Shoppe : Wardrobe Roll, 7 Edw. III, 35/26.
New York, 0, 3.

Shore.—Local, ' at the shore,' from residence beside the sea ; cf. Sands or Sandys.
Adam de Schore, 1379 : P. T. Yorks. p. 189.
Johannes de Schore, 1379 : ibid.
1659. Bapt.—John, s. John Shore : St. Jas. Clerkenwell, i. 204.
1768. Married — Joseph Shore and Deborah Lebarre : St. Geo. Han. Sq. i. 180.
London, 4 ; MDB. (co. Ches.), 2 ; New York, 2.

Shorland, Sherland. — Local, ' of Shorland ' (?). I cannot find the spot.
Robert de Schirlaunde, co. Kent, 20 Edw. I. R.
Richard de Scholand, co. Kent, ibid.
Richard de Scholound, co. Kent, ibid.
1607. Christopher Shorlond, co. Northants : Reg. Univ. Oxf. vol. ii. pt. ii. p. 294.
1774. Married — William Lawrence and Sarah Shorland : St. Geo. Han. Sq. i. 245.
London, 2, 0.

Short, Shortt.—Nick. ' the short,' of low stature ; cf. Long and Lang, Little, &c.
William Short, co. Suff., 1273. A.
Richard le Shorte, c. 1300. M.
Simon Schort, co. Soms., 1 Edw. III : Kirby's Quest, p. 176.
Johannes Short, 1379 : P. T. Yorks. p. 226.
Willelmus Short, 1379 : ibid. p. 115.
Willelmus Schort, 1379 : ibid.

Alice Short, of Ashton, 1672: Lancashire Wills at Richmond, i. 251. London, 36, 1; Boston (U.S.), 20, 0.

Shorter, Shotter.—Nick. 'the shorter,' to distinguish between two brothers, &c., of the same Christian name, especially in families where two or three boys were all Johns (v. my Curiosities of Puritan Nomenclature, Chatto and Windus, p. 4). Cf. Younger, Senior, Elder, &c.

John Shorter: Patent Roll, 15 Edw. IV. pt. ii.
John Shorter. H.
Anna Shawter, co. York. W. 20.
1771. Married—John Shorter and Jane Bishop: St. Geo. Han. Sq. i. 207.
London, 8, 2; Boston, 2, 0.

Shortfriend.—Nick. 'the short friend,' one who changed his intimacies frequently and soon forgot old acquaintances.

Hugo Schortfrend, co. Oxf., 1273. A.
Robertus Shortfrende, 1379: P. T. Yorks. p. 259.

Shorthose, Shorthouse.—Nick. 'with the short hose.' Still found in Derbyshire. This was the nickname of Sir Thomas Woodcock, Lord Mayor, 1405:

'Hic jacet Tom Shorthose,
Sine tomb, sine sheets, sine riches.'

William Shorthose, Close Roll, 17 Ric. II.
1585. Robert Shortus, co. Linc.: Reg. Univ. Oxf. vol. ii. pt. ii. p. 144.
John Shorthose, rector of Edlington, 1667: Hunter's South Yorks. i. 95.
1631. Married—Franses Mosse and Margery Shorthose: St. Michael, Cornhill, p. 27.
Sheffield, 1, 0; MDB. (co. Derby), 1, 1.

Shortshank. — Nick. 'short-shank,' with short legs; cf. Sheepshank, Longshank, Philipshank. Sheepshank has survived, not so the others. Yorkshire seems to have been the district of these sobriquets.

Johannes Shortshank, 1379: P. T. Yorks. p. 54.

Shott, Shot.—(1) Nick. 'the Scot'; cf. Shutt and Scutt. The two entries following are placed together:

Johannes Schote, et Matilda uxor ejus, 1379: P. T. Yorks. p. 109.
Sissot Scote, 1379: ibid.

(2) Local; v. Shutt and Shute.
West Rid. Court Dir., 1, 0; Philadelphia, 4, 1.

Shotter.—Nick.; v. Shorter, of which it is probably a variant.

1765. Married — James Shotter and Mary Anderson: St. Geo. Han. Sq. i. 157.
London, 2; New York, 1.

Shoulding; v. Shuldham.

Shoveller, Showler, Shouler. —Occup. 'the shoveler,' one who shovels with a spade; cf. Dicker. *Showl* is dialectic for shovel:

'Who'll dig his grave?
I says the owl:
With my spade and showl
I'll dig his grave.'
Cock Robin.

1609. Nicholas Shoveler and Mary Daye: Marriage Lic. (London), i. 313.
1703. Married—Daniel Shoveler and Mary Ferris: Canterbury Cath., p. 66.
1777. — Edward Crouch and Martha Shouler: St. Geo. Han. Sq. i. 274.
London, 2, 2, 0; MDB. (co. Bucks), 0, 1, 1; (Showler), Boston, 1.

Shreeve, Shreve.—Offic. 'the sheriff,' early corrupted to Shreeve; v. Sheriff. 'Schyreve, schreve, *vicecomes*': Prompt. Parv. p. 447.

'Cuthbert Conyers, shreve of the Bishopryke, 1564': Visit. Yorks. p. 71. Harl. Soc.
1580. Bapt.—Joyce, d. John Shreve: St. Jas. Clerkenwell, i. 12.
1665. William Panchast and Sarah Shreeve: Marriage Alleg. (Canterbury), p. 157.
1798. Married—John Shreve and Ann Stewart: St. Geo. Han. Sq. ii. 184.
London, 5, 0; New York, 0, 2.

Shrewsbury. — Local, ' of Shrewsbury,' the capital town of Shropshire.

Agnes de Sewesebyry, 1379: P. T. Yorks. p. 174.
1582. Henry Shrewsbury and Eliz. Turtle: Marriage Lic. (London), i. 108.
1590. Thomas Shrewesbury, co. Northants: Reg. Univ. Oxf. vol. ii. pt. ii. p. 179.
London, 2; Sheffield, 1; MDB. (co. Camb.), 3.

Shrubsole, Shrubshall. — Local, ' of Shrubsole.' I cannot find any locality of this name. The suffix will be -*sole* or -*sale*, a hall; v. Sale.

John de Sobesole, co. Kent, 1273. A.
1683. Edward Mecum and Ann Shrubsholl: Marriage Alleg. (Canterbury), p. 154.
London, 3, 1; Sheffield, 1, 0.

Shubrick, Shubrook.—Local; v. Shobbrook.

Shufflebotham, Shuffle-bottom. — Local, ' of Shippalbothom,' evidently some small spot in the ancient parish of Bury, co. Lanc., or the near neighbourhood. Like Higginbottom, Sidebotham, and several other local surnames with the suffix -*bottom* (v. Botham), Shufflebotham has East Cheshire or South-east Lancashire for its native home. The several stages of corruption after Shippobotham are Shifabottom and the imitative Shufflebotham. In the light of the subjoined entries, the assertion that the origin is Shaw-field-bottom (Lower) falls to the ground.

1582. Married — John Shippobotham and Anne Wilkynson: Reg. Prestbury (East Ches.), p. 74.
1587. Bapt.—Edwarde Shippobothom: ibid. p. 92.
1626. Married—Charles Shifabothom and Jone Horderne: ibid. p. 256.

Evidently the place is referred to in the following list of 'messuages, lands and rents' in 'Walton, Lancaster, Wigan, Haughton, Skelmersdale, ... Bury, Cheetham, Cheetwood, Tottington, Undesworth, Salford, Shuttleworth, Shippalbothan, Middleton,' &c.: (1485) Baines' Lanc. i. 516.—Since writing the above I find the following references to this family, conclusively proving my points:

James Shepobotham, of Heap, Bury, 1579: Wills at Chester (1545-1620), p. 174.
Francis Shippowbotham, Tottington, 1602: ibid.
George Shupplebotham, of the parish of Bury, 1621: ibid. (1621-50), p. 198.
James Shipplebotham, of Heap, Bury, 1642: ibid.
Richard Shufflebotham, of Betchton, 1674: ibid. (1651-80), p. 243.

The place itself also acquired the same form:

Roger Kay, of Shufflebotham, 1614: Wills at Chester (1545-1620), p. 112.
Manchester, 2, 4; London, 3, 0; MDB. (co. Ches.), 11, 0; Philadelphia, 0, 2.

Shuldham, Shuldam, Shoulding.—Local, ' of Shouldham,' a parish in dioc. Norwich. The prior of Shuldham, co. Norfolk, is several times referred to in the Hundred Rolls (1273); v. Index. Shoulding is a natural and ordinary corruption.

Thomas Shouldham, co. Norf., 1467: FF. vii. 9.
Thomas Shuldham, co. Norf., temp. 1580: ibid. i. 478.
John Shouldham, lord of Marham and Shouldham, 1551: ibid. vii. 113.
MDB. (Suffolk), 1, 0, 1; (Norfolk), 0, 1, 0.

Shute, Shutt, Shott.—(1) Local, 'of Shute,' a parish in co. Devon, two miles from Colyton.

1610. John Shute, of London: Reg. Univ. Oxf. vol. ii. pt. ii. p. 315.
1621. John Shute, co. Devon: ibid. p. 386.
1764. Married — Richard Shute and Ann Nightingale: St. Geo. Han. Sq. i. 139.

(2) Local, 'at the Shut' or Shoot, a West-country surname. '*Shut*, a narrow street. West' (Halliwell). 'Shott, a nook, an angle, a field, a plot of land; v. Carlisle's Account of Charities, p. 305' (Halliwell). Hence Aldershot, Cockshott.

Robert atte Shoete, co. Soms., 1 Edw. III: Kirby's Quest, p. 79.
Simon atte Sheote, co. Soms., 1 Edw. III: ibid. p. 83.
William atte Shote, co. Soms., 1 Edw. III: ibid. p. 98.
Walter atte Shotte, co. Soms., 1 Edw. III: ibid. p. 228.
London, 7, 1, 0; West Rid. Court Dir. (Shott), 1; Philadelphia, 10, 1, 13.

Shuter.—Occup.; v. Shooter.

Shutt, Shut.—(1) Nick. 'the Scot' (?), probably a form of that term; v. Scutt and Shott. (2) Local; v. Shute.

Alicia Schutte, 1379: P. T. Yorks. p. 244.
William Schutt, 1379: ibid. p. 245.
Henry Schutte, 1379: ibid. p. 35.
1794. Married — Thomas Shutt and Hannah Gregory: St. Geo. Han. Sq. ii. 115.
Sheffield, 2, 0; West Rid. Court Dir., 1, 0; New York, 0, 1.

Shuttleworth.—(1) Local, 'of Shuttleworth,' a township in the parish of Bury, co. Lanc. (2) Local. The Shuttleworths of Shuttleworth Hall, in the parish of Whalley, co. Lanc., were in residence there as early as 3 Edw. III (1329), when Henry de Shuttleworth died seised of it and eight oxgangs (Baines' Lanc. ii. 60).

Thomas Schytylworth, co. York, 1477. W. 11.
Richard de Shuttleworth, co. Lanc., 20 Edw. I. R.

1605. Utred Shuttleworthe, co. Lanc.: Reg. Univ. Oxf. vol. ii. pt. ii. p. 283.
1619. Richard Shuttleworth, of Bedford, co. Lanc.: Wills at Chester, i. 175.
Manchester, 3; New York, 5.

Shuxsmith; v. Sucksmith.

Shylock.—?——. This American representative of Shylock may be an imitative corruption of Sherlock (q.v.); but like Dickens, Shakespeare often took names from real life.

William Sylock, co. Soms., 1 Edw. III: Kirby's Quest, p. 244.
Philadelphia, 2.

Sibary, Sibray, Sibery, Sybry.—Bapt. 'the son of Sibry,' probably, and almost positively, a corruption of Sibley, the recognized popular form of Sybil; v. Sibley. Sybil was one of the greatest favourites in co. Yorks at the surname era, and it flourished there in every possible form. The corruption is a perfectly natural one.

Alan Sibri, co. York, 1273. A.
Stephen Sibry, co. York, ibid.
Thomas Sybry, 1379: P. T. Yorks. p. 132.
1687. John Masters and Katherine Sibrey: Marriage Alleg. (Canterbury), p. 297.
West Rid. Court Dir., 1, 4, 0, 1; London, 0, 0, 1, 0; Sheffield (Sybry), 2.

Sibbet, Sibbett, Sibbitt.—Bapt. 'the son of Sybil,' from the nick. Sib, dim. Sibbot or Sibbet; v. Sibbs. A family of Sibbitt lived for centuries at Ancroft, North Durham.

1664. Matthew Sibbitt: QQQ. p. 219.
1737. Adam Sibbitt: ibid.
1811. Isabella Sibbitt: ibid.
Sibota serviens ejus, 1379: P. T. Yorks. p. 110.
Sybota Tournour, 1379: ibid. p. 162.
Thomas Sibbotson, 1379: ibid. p. 156.
Sybil was exceedingly common. Hence are four on one page:

Sibilia Toged, 1379: P. T. Yorks. p. 74.
Sibilla de Kerre, 1379: ibid.
Sibilla de Melton, 1379: ibid.
Sibilla Schepherd, 1379: ibid.
Newcastle, 1, 0, 0; London (1886), 3, 0, 0; New York, 0, 0, 1; Philadelphia, 3, 1, 1.

Sibbs, Sibson.—Bapt. 'the son of Sybil,' from the nick. Sib; cf. Ciss and Siss, q.v.

'Neat Nancy, jolly Joan, nimble Nell, kissing Kate, tall Tib, slender Sib, will quickly lose their grace': Anatomy of Melancholy, p. 598.

'Sybby Sole, mylke wyfe of Islynton.' Cocke Lorelle's Bote.
Willelmus Sibilson, 1379: P. T. Yorks. p. 206.
Thomas Sibson, 1379: ibid. p. 40.
Agnes Sybson, *webster*, 1379: P. T. Howdenshire, p. 17.
Magota Jonwif Cybson (i. e. Magot, wife of John, the son of Sib), 1379: P. T. Yorks. p. 86.
Thomas Sibson, 1379: ibid. p. 40.
Robert Sibbs, of Counston, co. Suff., 1524: FF. i. 481.
Richard Sibson (co. Cumb.), Queen's Coll.: Reg. Univ. Oxf. vol. ii. pt. ii. p. 123.
London, 0, 2; MDB. (co. Cumb.), 0, 13; Philadelphia, 3, 9.

Sibley.—Bapt. 'the son of Sybil' (v. Sibbs), popularly Sibley. 'Sybyle, propyr name (Sibbe, K. Sybbly, P.). Sibilla': Prompt. Parv.

Geoffrey Sibilie, co. Suff., 1273. A.
Robert Sibili, co. Oxf., ibid.
Thomas Sibely, co. Camb., ibid.
Isabel Sibeli, co. Hunts, ibid.
John Sibely, co. Soms., 1 Edw. III: Kirby's Quest, p. 79.
1604. Henry Sibly, co. Soms.: Reg. Univ. Oxf. vol. ii. pt. ii. p. 273.
1732. Bapt.—Mary, d. George Sibley: St. Peter, Cornhill, ii. 37.
London, 16; New York, 7.

Sibson; v. Sibbs.

Sibthorpe. — Local, 'of Sibthorpe,' a parish in co. Notts.

William de Sibbethorp, co. Notts: Hen. III-Edw. I. K.
Theobald de Sybethorp, co. Hunts, 1273. A.
1613. Robert Fovell and Anne Sibthorpe (co. Essex): Marriage Lic. (London), ii. 23.
— Robert Sibthorp, co. Soms.: Reg. Univ. Oxf. vol. ii. pt. ii. p. 332.
London, 1.

Sickerson.—A sharpened form of Siggerson; v. Siggers, and cf. Sackerson with Saggerson, all descended from the same parent-name; v. Sayer.

New York, 1.

Sicklemore, Sickelmore, Syckelmoore.—Local, 'at the sycamore'; cf. Oak, Birch, Ash, Nash, &c. I cannot of course be positive that Sicklemore is a corruption of Sycamore, but it is highly probable.

1557-8. Richard Wade and Agnes Silkelmore: Marriage Lic. (London), i. 18.
1662-3. Edmund Sicklemore and Mary Clarke: Marriage Alleg. (Canterbury), p. 68.

Umfrid' Sicomer, 1578, incumbent of North Gosforth Chapel, Newcastle-on-Tyne: Brand's Newcastle, i. 322.
1786. Married—Johan Christian Koenig and Sally Anne Sickelmore: St. Geo. Han. Sq. i. 387.
London, 1, 2, 0; Philadelphia, 0, 0, 3.

Sickman.—Bapt. 'the son of Sigmund.' The suffix *-mund* becomes *-man*; cf. Osman, Wyman, &c. The form Sickman exists or existed both in New York and Philadelphia (Bowditch's Suffolk Surnames, pp. 388-9). It once existed in England.
Richard Sukemund, co. Wilts, 1273. A.
Ricardus Sykman, *smyth*, 1379: P. T. Yorks. p. 79.

Siddall, Siddell, Syddall.—Local, (1) 'of Siddall,' a hamlet in the parish of Halifax, co. York; (2) 'of Siddall,' some small estate in the parish of Middleton, co. Lanc.
Thomas Sydall', 1379: P. T. Yorks. p. 194.
1563. Janet Sydell, of Fullwood: Lancashire Wills at Richmond, i. 267.
John Jones, of Sidal, parish of Middleton, 1611: Wills at Chester, i. 111.
Giles Siddall, of Whitefield, in Pilkington, 1614: ibid. p. 175.
Richard Siddall, of Stockport, 1616: ibid.
1749. Married—Isaac Siddal and Ann Triggs: St. Geo. Han. Sq. i. 42.
Manchester, 9, 0, 3; West Rid. Court Dir., 5, 2, 0; Sheffield, 19, 0, 0; Philadelphia, 20, 4, 0; New York, 0, 3, 0.

Sidebotham, Sidebottom.—Local, 'of the Side-bottom,' probably the side of the hollow, or bottom, as was the term in cos. Yorks, Lanc., and Cheshire, where most of the Ramsbottoms, Higginbothams, &c., spring from; v. Botham. Like Higginbotham, Sidebotham springs from the immediate neighbourhood of Stockport.
Thomas de Sidebotham, 2 Hen. IV, 1400: Earwaker's East Cheshire, ii. 50.
Robert Sidbothom, 1445 (knights, gentlemen, and freeholders in Macclesfield Hundred): ibid. i. 17.
1576. Married—William Sydebotham and Margaret Andrewe: Reg. Prestbury, p. 53.
1581. Thomas Sidebotham, of Romiley: Wills at Chester, i. 175.
Elizabeth Sydebothome, 1675, Stockport: Exchequer Depositions (co. Lanc.), p. 140.
John Sydbotham, 1680, Manchester: ibid. p. 57.
Manchester, 11, 6; London, 1, 1; Philadelphia, 7, 7.

Sidgreaves.—Local, 'of the Sidgreaves'; v. Greaves.
Richard del Sydgreues, made member of the Guild, 1397: Preston Guild, p. 5.
'Mr. T. T. Sidgreaves has been placed on the Commission of the Peace for the Borough of Preston': Manchester Evening Mail, Sept. 17, 1887.
Five centuries of interval between the two incidents.
Manchester, 1; Preston, 1; Boston (U.S.), 1.

Sidgwick; v. Sedgwick.

Sidney, Sydney.—Local, 'de St. Denis' (?). This is the generally accepted derivation, and I doubt not it is the true one. Lower says, 'The founder of this family in England was Sir William Sydney, Chamberlain of Henry II, who came from Anjou with that monarch, and was buried at Lewes Priory in 1188': Patr. Brit. p. 337. Like Chauncy and Washington in the United States, Sidney and Percy have been turned into baptismal names in England. Sydney has also given title to one of the great cities of Australia.
Richard de Sanct' Deonise, co. Norf., 1273. A.
Robert de Sanct' Deonisio, co. Devon, ibid.
John de Sanct' Dene, co. Sussex, 20 Edw. I. R.
(Prior) de Sanct Dionisio, co. Wilts, ibid.
1627. Bapt. — Humfrie, s. Thomas Sydney: St. Jas. Clerkenwell, i. 105.
1798. Married—John Sidney and Eliz. Gumby: St. Geo. Han. Sq. ii. 182.
London, 7, 8; Philadelphia, 3, 1.

Siebert; v. Seabright.

Siggers, Sigers.—Bapt. 'the son of Seger' or Sagar; v. Sayer and Seager.
1792. Married—William Siggers and Sarah Cripps: St. Geo. Han. Sq. ii. 74.
London, 3, 0; Philadelphia, 0, 1.

Siggins.—Bapt. 'the son of Segin,' probably a later English form of Segrim, one of the many compounds of Sigg (v. Siggs); genitive Siggins; cf. William and Williams.
Richard Segrym, co. Oxf., 1273. A.
Alan Segeyn, co. Camb., ibid.
Hugh Segin, co. Oxf. ibid.
John Segyn, co. Camb., ibid.

Robert Segym, co. Camb., 1273. A.
1617. Married—William Siggins and Olive Brown: St. Jas. Clerkenwell, iii. 44.
1669. — Edmun Glover and Martha Siggines: ibid. p. 168.
London, 3; New York, 1; Philadelphia, 1.

Siggs.—Bapt. 'the son of Sigg,' found in such compounds as Sigismund, Sigfrid, Sigward, Sigwald, Sigurd, &c. The genitive of Sigg is Siggs; cf. William and Williams.
Sigge de Anemere, co. Norf., 1273. A.
1791. Married—Moses Siggs and Sarah Wood: St. Geo. Han. Sq. ii. 66.
London, 1.

Sikes.—Local; v. Sykes.

Silcock, Silcocks, Silcox.—Bapt. 'the son of Cecil,' nick. Sill (less commonly Cill), with terminative *-cock* (v. Introd. p. 25). It would appear that to preserve a distinction between the popular fem. Cecilia and masc. Cecil, the nick. of the former was Siss (v. Sisson and Sissot), and of the latter, Sil or Sill; v. Silson.
Cf. Johannes Cyllson, 1379: P. T. Yorks. p. 269.

I have not yet found a single Silas in mediaeval records. Mr. Lower's suggested origination from this Apostolic name, which I carelessly accepted in my English Surnames, is out of the question. The name was unknown. Of course Silcocks or Silcox is the genitive form; cf. William and Williams, or Wilcock and Wilcocks, or Wilcox.
Silcokkus de Altrichelun, C. R., 11 Edw. I.
Adam Silkok, 1379: P. T. Yorks. p. 20.
Johannes Silcok, 1379: ibid.
Matilda Sylkok, 1379: ibid. p. 79.
William Selecok, co. Soms., 1 Edw. III: Kirby's Quest, p. 210.
John Selcok, co. Soms., 1 Edw. III: ibid. p. 275.

In some cases very likely absorbed by Simcock or Simcox, q.v.
1785. Married—Nathan Silcock and Frances Cadney: St. Geo. Han. Sq. i. 374.
London Dir., 6, 1, 2; Philadelphia, 0, 0, 9.

Silk.—Local, 'of Silk,' a parish in co. Lincoln, now styled Silk-Willoughby.

1615. Bapt.—William, s. John Sylke:
St. Jas. Clerkenwell, i. 72.
1748. Married—Samuel Silk and Sarah
Mann: St. Geo. Chap. Mayfair, p. 121.
1769. — William Silk and Ann
Clethers: St. Geo. Han. Sq. i. 193.
London, 7; MDB. (co. Camb.), 10;
Philadelphia, 5.

Silkin.—Bapt. 'the son of
Cecil,' from the nick. Sill or Sil,
and dim. Sil-kin; v. Silcock.

John Silkyn, 1531, Tattenhall, co.
Ches.: Earwaker's East Cheshire, i. 56.

Silkman.—Occup. 'the silkman,' a dealer in silk.

Thomas Silkman, Close Roll, 51
Edw. III.
'Sylke-women, pursers, and gar-
nysshers.'   Cocke Lorelle's Bote.
New York, 3.

Silktippet.—Nick.

Roger Sylketypet: R. Pat., 4 Edw. III.
pt. ii.

Sillifant.—Bapt. 'the son of
Sullivan.' 'This Devonshire family,
originally written Sullivan, were
derived from the Sullivans of Ireland, and settled in England in the
year 1641': Patr. Brit. p. 315.

MDB. (co. Devon), 3; London, 1.

Sillito, &c.; v. Shilito.

Silson, Sills.—Bapt. 'the son
of Cecil,' from the nick. Cill or Sill
(v. Silcock); genitive Sills; cf.
William and Williams.

Johannes Cyllson, 1379: P. T. Yorks.
p. 269.
1746. Married—Samuel Sills and Eliz.
Sharp: St. Geo. Chap. Mayfair, p. 80.
1750. — Richard Sills and Mary
Stonnill: St. Geo. Han. Sq. i. 43.
London, 0, 5; Boston (U.S.), 0, 2.

Silverlock. — Nick. 'silver-
grey,' from the complexion of
a particular tress of the hair; cf.
Blacklock, Whitlock, Lovelock, &c.

Peter Siluerlok, C. R., 43 Edw. III.
Richard Selverlok, 1313. M.
James Silverlock. HH.
Alex. Silverlock. V. 5.
1622. Gilbert Seabrooke and Eliz. Sil-
verlocke: Marriage Lic. (London), ii. 117.
1634. Married — James Sylverlocke
and Ann Robinson: St. Thomas the
Apostle (London), p. 15.
1682. Hugh Nurse and Eliz. Silverlock: Marriage Alleg. (Canterbury), p. 94.
London, 4.

Silverside, Silversides. —
Local, 'of Silverside,' some small
locality in co. Lanc. which I have

not discovered. Probably near Sil-
verdale, perhaps on the slope of it.

John de Syluersyd, *sadeler*, 1397:
Preston Guild Rolls, p. 5.
1744. Married—George Silverside and
Susanna Price: St. Geo. Chap. Mayfair,
p. 36.
1800. — William Silversides and Barbara Hunt: St. Geo. Han. Sq. ii. 212.
London, 3, 1; Manchester, 0, 1.

Silverthorn, Silverthorne.—
Local, 'at the silver-thorn,' from
residence thereby; cf. Thorn and
Hawthorn.

Roger Selverthorn, co. Soms., 1 Edw.
III: Kirby's Quest, p. 159.
Richard Selverthorn, co. Soms., 1
Edw. III: ibid.
1693. Thomas Denkin and Amy Silverthorne: Marriage Alleg. (Canterbury),
p. 261.
1765. Married—Thomas Cockett and
Sarah Silverthorne: St. Geo. Han. Sq.
i. 150.
London, 1, 1; Philadelphia, 12, 0.

Silvester, Sylvester.—Bapt.
'the son of Silvester,' a fairly popular font-name in the surname era.

Robert fil. Silvestre, co. Camb., 1273. A.
Thomas Silvestre, co. Oxf., ibid.
Silvestre le Euncyse, co. Hunts, ibid.
Thomas fil. Silvestre, co. Norf., ibid.
Ganfrid fil. Silvester. C.
Silvester le Carpenter, C. R., 33
Hen. III.
Willelmus Siluestre, 1379: P. T. Yorks.
p. 141.
Robertus Siluester, 1379: ibid. p. 128.
1642. Bapt.—John, s. Walter Siluester:
St. Jas. Clerkenwell, i. 151.
London, 15, 2; Philadelphia, 0, 34;
New York, 3, 16.

**Sim, Simes, Simms, Sims,
Simpson, Simson.**—Bapt. 'the
son of Simon,' from the nick. Sim,
whence Simpson, with intrusive *p*,
as in Thompson, Hampson, &c.
Sims or Simms is the genitive of
Sim; cf. William and Williams.

Robertus Symmes, 1379: P. T. Yorks.
p. 15.
Johannes Symson', 1379: ibid. p. 288.
Thomas Symme, 1379: ibid. p. 11.
Johannes Symmeson', 1379: ibid.
Johannes Symnson, 1379: ibid. p. 136.
Christopher Sims, co. Berks, 1594:
Reg. Univ. Oxf. vol. ii. pt. ii. p. 204.
Ellen Simms, of Warrington, 1593:
Wills at Chester, i. 175.
1800. Married — Louis Baumes and
Margaret Sim: St. Geo. Han. Sq. ii. 227.
London, 5, 6, 8, 39, 149, 9; New York,
2, 2, 28, 13, 152, 4.

Simbarb. — Local, 'of St.
Barbe,' a Norman surname intro-

duced into England. Formed after
the fashion of Sinclair, &c. Even
in the Pipe Rolls (Henry II) 'de
Sancta Barbara' is sometimes
written Senbarb or Simbarb
(Introduction to Pipe Rolls, P. R.
Soc. p. 5). Barbe was the Norman
Fr. form of our Barbara (v. Babb,
Barbot, and Barbe).

Prior de Sancta Barba, co. Linc.,
1273. A.
Thomas Seymt-barbe. B.
Jordan de St. Barbe. M.
William Sembarbe. V. 3.
'Commission of rebellion to Edward
Saintbarbe (co. Somerset), Feb. 12, 1592':
Cal. State Papers (Domestic), iii. 182.
1546. William Simbarbe and Mary
Litell, of the King's Household: Marriage
Lic. (Faculty Office), p. 7.
1572. William Saintbarbe, or Simberbe:
Reg. Univ. Oxf. vol. ii. pt. iii. p. 56.

**Simcock, Simcox, Sim-
cockes, Symcox.**—Bapt. 'the
son of Simon,' from the nick. Sim,
with popular suffix -*cock* (v. Introd.
p. 25). Simcocks (varied into Simcox) is the genitive; cf. Wilcock
and Wilcox.

Robert Symcot (? Simcock), co. Camb.,
1273. A.
Vide Glasscock for change from
cock to *cott*, and vice versa.

Gregory Symekok, co. Soms., 1 Edw.
III: Kirby's Quest, p. 95.
Simon Simecok, co. Soms., 1 Edw. III:
ibid. p. 131.
James Sympcock, co. York. W. 9.
Thomas Symcoxe: Coventry Mysteries,
p. 65.
1586. Dier Simcockes, co. Soms.:
Reg. Univ. Oxf. vol. ii. pt. ii. p. 150.
1616. Thomas Simcock, of Samlesbury:
Wills at Chester, i. 175.
1669. Bapt.—Eliz., d. Robert Cim-
cockes: St. Jas. Clerkenwell, i. 241.
Crockford, 0, 3, 1, 0; London (Symcox), 1; New York (Simcox), 2; Philadelphia (Simcox), 2.

Simeon.—Bapt. 'the son of
Simeon'; kept distinct from Simon
in early records.

Ralph fil. Symeon, co. Camb., 1273. A.
Stephen Symeon, co. Oxf., ibid.
Jacobus Simeon, co. Oxf., ibid.
Roger Simeon, co. Soms., 1 Edw. III:
Kirby's Quest, p. 164.
1734. Married—Thomas Morrice and
Sarah Simeon: St. Geo. Han. Sq. i. 13.
Crockford, 3; Oxford, 2.

Simes; v. Sim.

Simister.—(1) Official (?), 'the
summaster.' I will first furnish
instances.

William Sumaster. Z.
William Summayster. B.
John Somayster. F.
William Summaster. Z.

Query (1), a summaster, i.e. chamberlain or clerk of expenses; (2) a summister, one who summarizes, abridges writings, &c. This is most probable, as the word occurs twice at least: 'Over this, if the historian be long, he is accompted a trifler; if he be short, he is taken for a summister' (Holinshed, Chron. Ireland, p. 80). 'And thus, though rudely, have I plaied the summister' (The Meane in Spending, 1598): both quoted by Halliwell. The name occurs in Mun. Acad. Oxon. (1462) as head of 'Sykyll Halle' (v. English Surnames, 5th edit., p. 206). Simister is a well-known North-English surname.

Samuel Summaster, co. Devon, 1607: Reg. Univ. Oxf. vol. ii. pt. ii. p. 297.
George Summaster, 1569: ibid. i. 274.

(2) Occup.; v. Sempster. As all the directories point to North England as the source, it is certain that some of our Simistres derive their name from the old form of Sempstress; v. instances under Sempster, which practically prove the case.

Manchester, 12; Liverpool, 2.

Simkin, Simkins, Simpkin, Simpkins, Simkinson.—Bapt. 'the son of Simon,' from the nick. Sim, dim. Sim-kin, as in Wilkin, Wilkinson, Tomkin, Tomkinson, &c. The *p* in Simpkin is, of course, intrusive, as in Simpson, Thompson, &c. For a variant of Simkins, v. Sinkins.

Simmerquin or Symchine Waller: Wars of England in France, Henry VI (v. Index).
Ralph Simpkynn: Hotten's Lists of Emigrants (v. Index).
1607. Christopher Symkinson, of Thurnham: Lancashire Wills at Richmond, i. 268.
1790. Married—Francis Simkins and Mary Edgar: St. Geo. Han. Sq. ii. 36.
1805. — James Gibson and Mary Simkin: ibid. p. 326.
London, 7, 10, 2, 3, 0; Philadelphia, 0, 8, 0, 19, 0; (Simpkin) Boston (U.S.), 1.

Simmance; v. Simmonds, of which it is a variant; cf. Evance for Evans.

1806. Married—Thomas Simmans and Sally King: St. Geo. Han. Sq. ii. 352.
MDB. (co. Essex), 1; (co. Hertford), 1.

Simmonds, &c.; v. Simon.

Simms; v. Sim.

Simnit, Simmonite, Simonett, Simnett.—Bapt. 'the son of Simon,' from the dim. Simonet.
Simonettus Mercator. E.
Symonet Villain. CC. 4.
London, 1, 0, 1, 0; Oldham Dir. (Simmonite), 1; Rotherham, 2; Derby (Simnett), 1; (Simonet) Boston (U.S.), 1.

Simon, Simmonds, Simmons, Simonds, Simons, Simonson.—Bapt. 'the son of Simon,' or Simond with excrescent *d*. 'Cym, propyr name (Cymund, H. P.), Simon': Prompt. Parv. p. 77 (cf. *gownd*, provincial for gown, *ribband* and *ribbon*, Hammond for Hamon, v. Hammon). One of the most popular font-names of the surname period (v. Sim, Simkin, Simcock). Our directories teem with examples. So do the early rolls. No connexion with Sigismund.

'He sit neither with Seint Johan,
Symond, ne Jude.'
Piers Plowman, i. 240.
'Awake, Simond, the fend is on me fall.'
Chaucer, C. T. 4283.
John Simond, co. Oxf., 1273. A.
Nicholas Simond, co. Soms., 1 Edw. III: Kirby's Quest, p. 189.
John Symondes, co. Soms., 1 Edw. III: ibid. p. 218.
'Johannes that was seruant of Symond Godewyne of Salthous': Patent Roll, 17 Ric. II. pt. ii.
Robert Symondson. W. 8.
Marquis Symondesson. H.
Alicia relicta Symonys, 1379: P. T. Yorks. p. 118.
Johanna Symond, 1379: ibid. p. 193.
Sir Simond Musgrave, 1582: Nicolson and Burn, Hist. Westm. and Cumb., vol. i. p. xxxi.
Symond Puthperker, of Muncke-Coniston, 1640: Lancashire Wills at Richmond, i. 223.
Simond Battie, of Burrow, 1623: ibid. p. 25.
London, 10, 48, 79, 8, 16, 1; Philadelphia, 152, 1, 70, 0, 70, 1.

Simpkin; v. Simkin.

Simple.—Nick. 'the simple.' A guileless, easily deceived fellow, originally more complimentary than as at present understood.
William le Simple, Close Roll, 52 Hen. III.

Jordan le Simple, co. Oxf, 1273. A.
Richard le Simple, co. Oxf., ibid.
Henry le Simple, 1307. M.

No doubt now confused with the local Semple, q.v.
1558. Buried—Margaret Simple: St. Antholin (London), p. 12.
1625. — James Simple: St. Dionis Backchurch, p. 218.
London, 1; Philadelphia, 1.

Simpson, Simson; v. Sim.

Sinclair, Sinclaire. — Local, 'of St. Clair,' some chapelry in Normandy; cf. Simbarb, St. John, &c.
John de Sancto Claro, co. Suff., 1273. A.
Robert de Sancto Claro, co. Soms.,ibid.
William de Sancto Claro, co. Kent, ibid.
Richard Seinteclere, co. Soms., 1 Edw. III: Kirby's Quest, p. 122.
William Seyncler, co. Soms., 1 Edw. III: ibid. p. 192.
1611. Bapt. — Helene, d. Nicholas Sayntcleare: St. Jas. Clerkenwell, i. 62.
1618. James Sinclar: Reg. Univ. Oxf. vol. ii. pt. ii. p. 369.
1777. Married—John Sinclaire and Ann Holborn: St. Geo. Han. Sq. i. 277.
London, 19, 0; New York, 43, 4.

Sincox.—Bapt. A corruption of Simcox, q.v.; cf. Sinkinson for Simkinson. The variants of Simcocks are placed under one heading in Index to Reg. Univ. Oxf. They include Simcox, Sincocks, and Symcockes; vol. ii. pt. iv. p. 382.
MDB. (co. Essex), 1.

Singer.—Occup. 'the singer'; v. Sanger and Sangster; cf. Dancer, Hopper, &c.
1583. John Synger and Joane Burton: St. Dionis Backchurch, p. 10.
1768. Married—John Singer and Mary Reilly: St. Geo. Han. Sq. i. 173.
London, 4; Philadelphia, 34.

Single.—Nick. 'the single,' i.e. the separate, one who lived alone.
Richard le Sengle, co. Worc., 1273. A.
London, 1; Philadelphia, 2.

Singleton.—Local, 'of Singleton,' a parish in co. Sussex, six miles from Midhurst. Also a chapelry in the parish of Kirkham, co. Lanc. Doubtless other and smaller spots are so termed.
Adam de Syngleton, 1379: P. T. Yorks. p. 276.
Thomas Singleton, of Shrigley, 1616: Wills at Chester, i. 176.
1597. Isaac Singleton, London: Reg. Univ. Oxf. vol. ii. pt. ii. p. 222.

1615. John Singleton, co. Cumb.: Reg. Univ. Oxf. vol. ii. pt. ii. p. 336.
Sheffield, 4; West Rid. Court Dir., 4; New York, 10.

Singular.—Nick. 'the singular,' the peculiar.

Robert le Senguler, C. R., 55 Hen. III.
1776. Married — Richard Parry and Ellen Singler: St. Geo. Han. Sq. i. 265.

Sinkins, Sinkinson.—Bapt. 'the son of Simon.' Sinkinson is a corruption of Simkinson; v. Simkin. Cf. Ransom for Ranson, and Milsom for Milson, an opposite tendency.

Synkyn-dogter (i. e. the daughter of Simkin), 1379 : P. T. Yorks. p. 162.
1639. Bapt.—Samuel, s. Simon Sinkinson : St. Jas. Clerkenwell, i. 144.
Cf. 1736. — Thomas, s. John Sinson : ibid. ii. 226.
1794. Married — James Evans and Susanna Sinkinson : St. Geo. Han. Sq. ii. 113.
London, 2, 0; Ulverston, o, 1; MDB. (co. Lanc.), o, 1; (co. Somerset), 4, 0; Philadelphia, 0, 4.

Sinnett, -nott; v. Sennett.

Sire, Syre.—Nick. 'the sire,' i.e. the master.

John le Sire, co. Hunts, 1273. A.
Alexander le Sire, co. Hunts, ibid.
Walter le Sire, co. Bucks, ibid.
Simon le Sire, Fines Roll, 17 Edw. II.
Cecilia Syre, 1379 : P. T. Yorks. p. 154.
Ricardus Syre, 1379 : ibid. p. 196.
1796. Married—John Syer and Catherine Green : St. Geo. Han. Sq. ii. 157.
New York, 4, 0.

Sired, Siret, Sirett, Syrett, Syratt.—Bapt. 'the son of Sigrid.' Sired (Domesday) : Yonge, ii. 310. Sigrid, mother of Cnut (Canute) and Olaf of Sweden : Freeman's Norm. Conq. i. 410.

Roger Syrad, co. Oxf., 1273. A.
John Syred, co. Hunts, ibid.
Martin Sired, co. Kent, ibid.
Sigreda de Urmeston, Close Roll, 9 Edw. III.
Sigreda de Skelton, 1346 : Accounts of the Exchequer, 19-20 Edw. III.
Cyred Tone, 1379 : P. T. Yorks. p. 240.
1722. Married — John Syrett and Susanna Hippeth : St. Mary Aldermary (London), p. 45.
1769. — John Green and Eliz. Siret : St. Geo. Han. Sq. i. 189.
London, 0, 1, 4, 5, 1.

Sirrell.—A variant of Serrill; v. Serle.

MDB. (co. Hereford), 5

Siss.—Bapt. 'the son of Cecilia,' from the nick. Ciss, Cess, and Siss. This form lasted till the 17th century, and still exists as Sissy in the nursery. Such rhymes as the following will be commonly met with in D'Urfey :

'Long have I lived a bachelor's life,
  And had no mind to marry ;
But now I would fain have a wife,
  Edith, Doll, Kate, Sis, or Mary.'

'Cesse the souteresse' (v. Sisson for quotation). Almost all the instances of names founded on Siss given below come from Yorkshire and its border. A great impetus was given to it there on account of Cicely Neville, the Rose of Raby, 'proud Ciss,' 'the Duchess of York' (v. Yonge, i. 310). The Conqueror's daughter, Cecily, Abbess of Caen, gave it favour still earlier to the country at large.

Alicia Sisse-doghter, *webster*, 1379 : P. T. Howdenshire, p. 19.

Sisselot.— Bapt. 'the son of Cecilia,' from the dim. Cecilot (cf. Hewlett from Hugh).

Alicia fil. Sisselot, 1273. A.
Bella Cesselot, co. Oxon, ibid.

Sisselson.—Bapt. 'the son of Cecil.'

Richard Sisselson. H.

Sisson, Sison, Sissons. — Bapt. 'the son of Cecilia,' from the nick. Siss or Cess ; v. Siss.

'Cesse the souteresse
  Sat on the benche.'
    Piers Plowman, l. 3105.

Johannes Sisson, 1379 : P. T. Howdenshire, p. 21.
Robertus Cisson, 1379 : ibid. p. 19.
Henricus Sisson, 1379 : P. T. Yorks. p. 226.
Thomas Cysson, 1379 : ibid. p. 269.
William Cisson, 1379 : ibid.
Henry Sysson, co. York. W. 9.

Staying at the Bull Hotel, Sedbergh (W. Rid. Yorks), in June, 1886, Sisson stared me in the face over a shop across the road. Sisson has taken a curious genitive form, Sissons; cf. William and Williams.

MDB. (co. Cumb.) Sisson, 7 ; West Rid. (Yorks) Court Dir. (Sissons), 4 ; London (Sissons), 5 ; Crockford (Sisson), 5 ; Philadelphia, 2, 4, 0.

Sissot, Sissotson, Sississon, Sisserson.—Bapt. 'the son of Cecilia,' from the nick. Cess or Siss (v. Siss), dim. Sissot or Cessot.

'Willelmus Crake and Cissot sa femme.' W.D.S.
Cissota West, co. York. W. 2.
Syssot, wife of Diccon Wilson. AA. 2.
Syssot, wife of Jak of Barsley, ibid.
John Sissotson, co. York. W. 2.
Agnes Sissotson, co. York. W. 11.
Robert Syssottysone, rector of Lecceworthe, 1478 : XX. 2, p. 187.

The nearest modern approach to the original is Sississon, found, as might be expected, in Yorkshire. Nevertheless, I am surprised that more descendants of this once common pet-name are not in existence as surnames in the 19th century. v. Sisterson.

Hull, 0, 0, 1, 0; New York (Sisserson), 2.

Sisterson.—Bapt. 'the son of Cecilia,' from the nick. Siss, dim. Sissot. Thus Sissotson became by imitation Sisterson. There can be no doubt about this origin. It is found in the very district where Sissotson arose and became familiar (v. Sissotson and Sissot). Any idea that it means a nephew, i.e. sister's son, must be discarded. The form is simply imitative; cf. Ibberson for Ibbotson from Isabella.

Corbridge-on-Tyne, 2.

Sivewright, Sievewright.—Occup. 'the sievewright,' a maker of sieves (v. Sivier). M.E. *sive*.

'And all this mullok in a sive ythrowe.'
    Chaucer, C. T. 16408.

Cf. Arkwright, Wainwright, &c.

Boston (U.S.), 1, 1.

Sivier.—Occup. 'the sievyer,' a sieve - maker ('siveyer, seve makere, *cribrarius*': Prompt. Parv.). v. Sivewright.

Ralph le Siviere, co. Camb. A.
Peter Syvyere. B.
1615. Bapt.—Sussanna, d. John Sevier : St. Jas. Clerkenwell, ii. 92.
1793. Married — John Sievier and Frances Waud : St. Geo. Han. Sq. ii. 102.
1798. — Richard Sivier and Frances Mattingley : ibid. p. 175.
London, 1.

Sixsmith; v. Shoesmith and Sucksmith.

Sizer.—Offic. 'the sizar,' probably an 'assizer,' one who jotted down the rations of bread, otherwise a poor University scholar who got his bread cheap at the buttery; v. Panter.

Willelmus Sisar, 1379: P. T. Yorks. p. 158.
1715. Buried—Samuel Siser: St. Peter, Cornhill, ii. 122.
1774. Married — Leonard Sizer and Eliz. Northorp: St. Geo. Han. Sq. i. 247.
London, 3; MDB. (co. Essex), 3; Philadelphia, 1; New York, 3.

Skaife, Scaife, Scafe, Scaif.—Nick. or personal name. 'Skafe, awkward. Lincolnshire' (Halliwell). Mr. Lower says, 'Scaif, a northern provincialism for timid or fearful.'

Henry Skayf, co. York, 1273. A.
Hugh Skave, co. Norf., ibid.
Willelmus Skayf, 1379: P. T. Yorks. p. 206.
Robertus Scayff, 1379: ibid. p. 259.
Simon Scaif', 1379: ibid. p. 232.
Alicia Scayf', 1379: ibid.
1605-6. Married — Francis Scaff, of Richmond, co. York, carrier, and Christian Fossett: St. Dionis Backchurch, p. 15.
1759. — John Channer and Eliz. Skaife: St. Geo. Han. Sq. i. 91.
London, 5, 2, 0, 0; West Rid. Court Dir., 0, 2, 1, 1; Philadelphia (Scaife), 1.

Skalls; v. Skeels.

Skeate, Skeats, Skeet.—Bapt. 'the son of Sket.' In Domesday described as Schett and Scheit, co. Norfolk. Found frequently as Sket in Norfolk and neighbouring county of Suffolk in the Hundred Rolls. Also once as a single personal name in the form of Sketh:

Sketh, co. Norf., 1273. A.
Alan Sket, co. Suff., ibid.
Nicholas Sket, co. Suff., ibid.
John Sket, co. Norf., ibid.
Warinus Sket, burgess in Parl. for Dunwich, 1311. M.
Adam Skete, 1379: P. T. Yorks. p. 157.
1616. John Skeat, co. Wilts: Reg. Univ. Oxf. vol. ii. pt. ii. p. 357.
1631. Married—Edward Skeite and Mary Lozeyer: St. Thomas the Apostle (London), p. 15.
1743. Bapt.—Mary, d. of John Skett: St. Michael, Cornhill, p. 173.

Skeats is the genitive form; cf. Williams with William.

1797. Married — Isaac Skeates and Harriet Mayriss: St. Geo. Han. Sq. ii. 160.
London, 1, 2, 5; New York, 0, 1, 0.

Skeels, Skalls, Skeeles, Skeel.—Bapt. 'the son of Schayl,' genitive Schayls, now Skalls or Skeels; cf. William and Williams. It will be seen that the surname still flourishes in the district where it is first found six centuries ago.

Dionise Schayl, co. Camb., 1273. A.
Philip Schayl, co. Hunts, ibid.
Walter Schayl, co. Oxf., ibid.
Richard Skeeles, co. Norf., 1723: FF. iv. 501.
1796. Married—Benjamin Skeel and Lucy Lambert: St. Geo. Han. Sq. ii. 152.
London, 3, 0, 1, 2; MDB. (co. Camb.), 7, 2, 0, 0; New York, 3, 0, 0, 5.

Skeffington, Skevington, Skeavington, Skivington, Skiffington.—Local, 'of Skeffington,' a parish in co. Leicester.

David de Scheftinton, co. Leic., Hen. III-Edw. I. K.
Baldewinus de Scheftinton, co. Leic., ibid.
1575-6. William Skevington, co. Staff.: Reg. Univ. Oxf. vol. ii. pt. ii. p. 70.
1611-2. Bapt.—Nicholas, s. William Skevington: St. Dionis Backchurch, p. 94.
London, 5, 0, 0, 0, 0; MDB. (co. Bedf.), 0, 1, 0, 0, 0; (co. Derby), 0, 1, 1, 1, 0; Philadelphia, 9, 0, 0, 0, 8.

Skegg, Skeggs.—? Bapt. 'the son of Skeg' (?). A Scandinavian personal name, probably (found in such local names as Skegness and Skegby). Genitive, Skeggs; cf. Williams with William.

Thomas Skegge, laborer, 1376: P. T. Howdenshire, p. 5.
Thomas Skegges, of Chelfield, Kent, 1714: Reg. St. Peter, Cornhill, ii. 70.
1715. Bapt.—John, s. James Skegg: St. Jas. Clerkenwell, ii. 86.
1790. Married — Anthony Sprigmore and Sarah Skeggs: St. Geo. Han. Sq. ii. 48.
London, 2, 5; New York, 0, 1.

Skelding.—Local, 'of Skelding,' a township in the parish of Ripon, co. Yorks.

1620. Rowland Skeldinge, of Cartmell: Lancashire Wills at Richmond, i. 256.
1678. Thomas Skelding, of Newbarnes (Dalton-in-Furness): ibid.
1640. Bapt. — Hester, d. Edmund Skeldinge: St. Jas. Clerkenwell, i. 144.
London, 3; New York, 3.

Skelton, Skeleton. — Local: (1) 'of Skelton,' a village near Ripon, co. York. Skeleton is not a happy corruption, but it is imitative, like a hundred other corrupted

spellings; cf. Deadman, Physick. (2) 'of Skelton,' a parish in co. Cumberland.

Willelmus de Skelton, 1379: P. T. Yorks. p. 242.
Thomas de Skelton, 1379: ibid.
1617. John Skelton, co. Cumb.: Reg. Univ. Oxf. vol. ii. pt. ii. p. 359.
1632-3. John Skelton and Prudence Summers: Marriage Lic. (Faculty Office), p. 26.
MDB. (co. Cumb.), 21, 0; West Rid. Court Dir., 13, 0; Newcastle, 1, 2; New York, 2, 0; Boston (U.S.), 5, 0.

Sketchley.—Local, 'of Sketchley,' a hamlet in the parish of Aston Framville, co. Leicester.

1678. John Skechley and Eliz. Crosfeild: Marriage Alleg. (Canterbury), p. 229.
1742. Married—Lewis Sketchley and Hannah Dew: St. Geo. Chap. Mayfair, p. 23.
1757. — Richard Sketchley and Susanna Stockley: St. Geo. Han. Sq. i. 74.
London, 4; MDB. (co. Leic.), 5; Philadelphia, 7.

Skidmore.—Local; v. Scudamore, of which it is a variant.

Philadelphia, 2; Oxford, 1.

Skiftling.—Nick. 'the skiftling,' one who moved from one place to another. Skift is used for shift in the Furness dialect. Dan. skifte, to remove.

Johannes Skyfftlyng, 1379: P. T. Yorks. p. 127.
Willelmus Skyftlyng, 1379: ibid. p. 128.
1566. John Skiftling, or Skiftlinge: Reg. Univ. Oxf. vol. ii. pt. ii. p. xvi.

Skillman.—? Nick. 'Skillman,' a man of reason, craft, knowledge.

Henry Skileman, co. Camb., 1273. A.
John Skyleman, co. Norf., ibid.
Richard Skyleman, co. Norf., ibid.
1802. Married — William Smith and Mary Skillmon: St. Geo. Han. Sq. ii. 267.
London, 1; New York, 5.

Skinner. — Occup. 'the skinner,' a dealer in skins.

Henry le Skyniar', co. Oxf., 1273. A.
Richard le Skynnere. B.
Robert le Skynner, 1302. M.
III: Kirby's Quest, p. 105.
Johannes Sckynner', 1379: P. T. Yorks. p. 96.
Willelmus de Parlyngton, skynnar, 1379: ibid. p. 106.
Robertus Skynner, skynner, 1379: St. Jas. Clerkenwell, i. 108.
1618. Bapt.—Richard, s. John Skinner: ibid. p. 82.
London, 65; Boston (U.S.), 76.

Skipp.—Local, 'at the skip,' from residence in or beside a ship; A.S. *scip*. v. Shipp.

1273. John Skyp: Cal. of Wills in Court of Husting.
1682. Bapt.—Thomas, s. Thomas Skip: St. Jas. Clerkenwell, i. 296.
1701. Robert Yeomans and Eliz. Skipp: Marriage Lic. (Faculty Office), p. 241.
1746. Married—Henry Skipp and Mary Parker: St. Geo. Chap. Mayfair, p. 65. London, 1.

Skipper.—Occup. 'the skipper,' a captain of a ship.

Herman le Skippere, C. R., 12 Edw. II.
1646. Married—Thomas Skipper and Ann Cornwell: St. Peter, Cornhill, i. 257.
1657. John Skipper to Elizabeth Kelke: St. Michael, Cornhill, p. 37.
James Skipper, 1738, Norwich: FF. iv. 207.
London, 6; MDB. (co. Essex), 3; Philadelphia, 1.

Skipworth.—Local, 'of Skipwith,' a parish in the E. Rid. Yorks, near Selby.

1596. Charles Skipwith, Magd. Hall: Reg. Univ. Oxf. vol. ii. pt. iii. p. 198.
1671. Bapt.—Mary, d. John Scipworth: St. Jas. Clerkenwell, i. 249.
1690. — Susanna, d. John Skipwith: ibid. p. 336.
MDB. (co. Stafford), 1.

Skirmisher, Skrimshire, Scrimshaw, Scrimgeoure, Scrymgeour, Scrimiger, Scrymser, Scrymigar. — Offic. 'the skirmisher,' a fencer. O.F. *eskirmir*, to fence. O.F. *escarmouche*, a skirmish, hence English scrimmage, and the form scrimgeour, i. e. scrimmager, one who mingled in a scrimmage.

'Qe nul teigne Escole de Eskermerye, ne de Bokeler deins la citee.'
Liber Albus.

Scrimmage was in early use, and is not in any true sense provincial. Lower quotes Crawford's Scottish Peerage as follows: 'Alexander I, by special grant, appointed a member of the Carron family, to whom he gave the name of Scrimgeour, for his valour in a sharp fight, to the office of hereditary standard-bearer.' This settles any doubt, if any doubt existed; v. Patr. Brit. p. 307.

Henry le Eskirmessur, co. York, 1273. A.

William le Shyrmisur, co. Salop, 1273. A.
Peter le Eskurmesur. E.
Abraham le Skirmisur, C. R., 34 Hen. III.
Elizebetha Skrymsher. EE.
Alexander Schirmissure. SS.
Roger le Skirmisour, London. QX.
John le Eskirmesour, co. Berks, Hen. III-Edw. I. K.
London, 0, 1, 0, 6, 0, 0, 0, 0; Crockford, 0, 4, 0, 1, 0, 0, 0, 0; Sheffield, 0, 0, 4, 0, 0, 0, 0, 0; Liverpool (Scrimiger), 1; New York, 0, 0, 0, 0, 3, 0, 6, 2.

Skirrow.—Local, 'of Sharow' (?), a village, a mile from Ripon. Possibly some spot nearer the Lancashire border of the West Riding. v. Sharrow.

Thomas de Skyrhow, 1379: P. T. Yorks. p. 290.
1570. William Skerowe, of Wray, in Melling: Lancashire Wills at Richmond, i. 256.
1611. Bapt. — Margaret, d. Henry Skerrow: St. Antholin (London), p. 48.
1620-1. Harman Curital and Frances Skerro: Marriage Lic. (London), ii. 95.
1634. Thomas Skirow, of Wray: Lancashire Wills at Richmond, i. 256.
1638. Christopher Skirroe, of Wray: ibid.
West Rid. Court Dir., 1; London, 1; Leeds (Scurrah), 2; Liverpool (Scurry), 1; Boston (U.S.) (Scurrah), 1.

Skottowe, Scotto, Scottowe.—Local, 'of Scottow,' a parish in co. Norfolk.

Jeffry de Scothowe, co. Norf., 1120: FF. vi. 341.
John de Scothowe, co. Norf., 1279: ibid.
William de Skothow, rector of Hethill, co. Norf., 1329: ibid. v. 109.
Richard Skottowe, alderman, of Norwich, 1616: ibid. iv. 292.
John Scotto, co. Norf., 1631: ibid. i. 383.
MDB. (co. Berks), 1, 0, 0; (co. Ches.), 0, 0, 1; London, 0, 1, 0.

Skoulding; v. Scolding.

Skudder, Scudder.—Occup. Probably an immigrant from Holland, equivalent to English Shooter, q.v.

1604. Married—Robert Skutter and Goodwin White: St. Mary Aldermary (London), p. 10.
1690. Bapt.—Anne, d. Robert Scudder: Canterbury Cath., p. 19.
London, 2, 1; Philadelphia, 0, 2.

Skull. —? Bapt. 'the son of Scowle' (?).

William Scowle, co. Linc., 1273. A.
1579. Ralph Skull and Margery Turnor: Marriage Lic. (London), i. 87.

1808. Married—William Adcock and Winifred Skull: St. Geo. Han. Sq. ii. 389.
London, 1; MDB. (co. Bucks), 1.

Skurray; v. Scurry.

Slack, Slagg.—Local, 'at the Slack' or Slagg, from residence thereby, a place where the road becomes less steep, a gap in the hills (slacken, to ease off). John del Slak, Pardons Roll, 6 Ric. II. With the lazier Slagg, cf. Jagg and Jack (Jagg, Piers Plowman). Probably both *slack* and *slag* refer to that point of the hilltop where the stones and earth began to dribble down the slope (hence slag, *scoria*); v. Skeate.

Johannes del Slak', 1379: P. T. Yorks. p. 180.
Thomas de Slake, 1379: ibid. p. 192.
Johannes Sclake, 1379: ibid.
1579. Thomas Lane and Eliz. Slegge: Marriage Lic. (London), i. 88.
1587. Buried—John Slake, a rogue: St. Peter, Cornhill, i. 134.
London, 9, 0; Manchester, 8, 1; MDB. (co. Cumb.), 13, 0; Philadelphia, 45, 0.

Slade.—Local, 'at the slade,' from residence thereby, a small strip of green in a woodland.

'It had been better of William a Trent
To have been abed with sorrowe,
Than to be that day in the greenwood slade
To meet with Little John's arrowe.'

In compounds *slade* is found in such local surnames as Greenslade, Moorslade, Whiteslade, Oakslade, Waldslade, and Sladen (q.v.).

Nicholas de la Slade, c. 1300. M.
Henry atte Slade, co. Soms., 1 Edw. III: Kirby's Quest, p. 178.
John atte Slade, C.R., 20 Edw. III. pt. i.
Richard atte Slade, C. R., 21 Edw. III. pt. ii.
1596. Bapt.—Mary, d. John Slade: Kensington Ch., p. 12.
1615. Ammiel Slade, co. Devon: Reg. Univ. Oxf. vol. ii. pt. ii. p. 346.
— Francis Slade, co. Berks: ibid. p. 336.
1645. Bapt.—Grace, d. George Slayd: Kensington Ch., p. 35.
London, 24; New York, 12.

Sladen.—Local, 'of Sladen,' a hamlet in the parish of Littleborough, co. Lanc. Probably other small spots are so termed (v. Slade and Dean).

Johannes Sladen, 1379: P. T. Yorks. p. 187.
Jennet Hill, of Sladen, *widow*, 1599: Wills at Chester (1545-1620), p. 93.

1767. Bapt.—Isaac, s. Isaac Sladden : Canterbury Cath., p. 33.
1806. Married—Benjamin King and Mary Sladen : St. Geo. Han. Sq. ii. 344. London, 3 ; West Rid. Court Dir., 1 ; Philadelphia, 2.

Slagg; v. Slack.

Slape.—Local, 'at the slape' (i.e. a shelving declivity), from residence thereby. A slope, a slape, or a slipe seem all to express the same meaning. In Oxfordshire the shelving bank between the base of a fortification and the moat below is a slipe. In Cumberland a farmer will say of the roads in frosty weather, 'They're terrible slape to-day,' i.e. slippery.

Matilda de Slape, co. Oxf., 1273. A.
Randulph atte Slape, co. Soms., 1 Edw. III : Kirby's Quest, p. 153.
Nicholas atte Sclape, co. Soms., 1 Edw. III : ibid. p. 240.
William atte Sclape, co. Soms., 1 Edw. III : ibid.
1604. Married—Roche Slape and Eliz. Gloover : St. Jas. Clerkenwell, iii. 29.
1610. Richard Slape, co. Soms. : Reg. Univ. Oxf. vol. ii. pt. ii. p. 316.
1696. Bapt.—Ann, d. William Slape : St. Jas. Clerkenwell, i. 368.
1749. Married—Thomas Slape and Ann Green : St. Geo. Chap. Mayfair, p. 130.

It is abundantly clear that co. Somerset was the chief habitat of the name.

London, 1 ; MDB. (co. Somerset), 1.

Slater, Sclater, Slatter.—Occup. 'the slater.' M.E. *sclat* ; v. Wyclif, Luke v. 19 (Skeat). There is no modern affectation in the forms of Sclater and Slatter. They are the unbroken use of centuries ; cf. Reader, Tyler, Thacker, Thackster, &c.

Adam le Sclattere, co. Oxf., 1273. A.
Richard le Sclattere, co. Oxf., ibid.
Walter Sclatter, co. Bucks, ibid.

Slatter is still familiar to co. Oxford.

1684. Bapt.—Eliz., d. John Sclator : St. Jas. Clerkenwell, i. 306.
1807. Married—Thomas Slatter and Esther Bael : St. Geo. Han. Sq. ii. 361.
London, 46, 1, 10 ; Oxford, 2, 0, 3 ; Philadelphia, 44, 0, 1.

Slaughter.—Local, 'of Slaughter,' two parishes in co. Glouc., viz. Upper and Lower Slaughter.

Ballivus de Sloutre, co. Glouc., 1273. A.
John de Sloghtre, C. R., 26 Edw. III.
Paris Slaughter. V. 2.

1783. Married—William Hill and Eliz. Slaughter : Canterbury Cath., p. 98.
1791. — Thomas Slaughter and Eliz. Davies : St. Geo. Han. Sq. ii. 55.
1803. — Joseph Wood and Eliz. Slafter : ibid. p. 286.
London, 6 ; Philadelphia, 18.

Slay.—Nick. 'the sly' (q.v.). Oxford, 7.

Slaymaker. — Occup. 'the slaymaker,' a maker of slays (v. Slaywright). ' "*Slay*, an instrument belonging to a weaver's loom that has teeth like a comb": Phillips. "*Slay*, a wever's tole." Palsgrave' (Skeat). The weaver's reed. A petition to Parliament in 1467 from the worsted manufacturers complains that in the county of Norfolk there are 'divers persones that make untrue ware of all manner of worstedes, not being of the assises in length or brede . . . and that the *slayes* and yern thereto belonging are untruly made and wrought' (Rot. Parl. Edw. IV).

1594. Henry Slaymaker, or Slymaker, Trin. Coll. : Reg. Univ. Oxf. vol. ii. pt. iii. p. 180.
Johannes Slaymaker, 1379 : . P. T. Yorks. p. 51.
1705. Elizabeth Slaymaker : St. Peter, Cornhill, ii. 65.
1715. Bapt.—Mary, d. John Slaymaker : St. Jas. Clerkenwell, ii. 92.
London, 2 ; Oxford, 1 ; Philadelphia, 4.

Slaywright. — Occup. 'the slaywright,' one who manufactured slays ; v. Slaymaker.

Reginald Slaywright, co. Soms., 1 Edw. III : Kirby's Quest, p. 185.
Thomas Slawryghte, co. York. W. 11.
The Prior of the Hermit Friars, Warrington, in 1520 was one Slaywright : Baines' Lanc. ii. 224.
William Slywright, C. R., 1 Mary, pt. iii.
1576. John Brockett and Margery Slewright : Marriage Lic. (London), i. 70.
1580. Thomas Sliwright, or Slywright, co. Kent : Reg. Univ. Oxf. vol. ii. pt. ii. p. 173.

I cannot find any modern representatives of this name, but it would be dangerous on that account to assert that it did not exist.

Sleddall. — Local, ' of Long Sleddale,' a chapelry in the parish of Kendal, co. Westmoreland.

Thomas Sleddall, 1586 : Lancashire Wills at Richmond, i. 256.
Richard Sleddell, of Lancaster, 1686 : ibid. ii. 234.

Maria Sleddall, of Goosenargh, 1692 : ibid.
1690. Henry Sleddall and Prudence Lucas : Marriage Alleg. (Canterbury), p. 142.
Kirkby Stephen, 1 ; Ulverston, 1.

Slee, Sleigh; v. Sly.

Sleeman.—Bapt. ; v. Slyman.

Sleep, Sleap. — (1) Local. Lower says: 'Sleep, a hamlet in the parish of St. Peter, in the liberty of St. Alban's, co. Hertford' (Patr. Brit. p. 318). The evidence below suggests another locality. (2) 'of Sleap,' a township in the parish of Wem, co. Salop. No doubt this is one of the chief parents.

Coc de Slepe, co. Salop, 1273. A.
Hugh de Slepe, co. Salop, ibid.
Richard de Slepe, co. Salop, ibid.
1574. Buried—Ursula Slepe : St. Jas. Clerkenwell, iv. 16.
1600. Married — Thomas Sleepe and Jone Lee : St. Peter, Cornhill, i. 242.
1729. — John Sleap and Parnell Buckinham : St. Geo. Chap. Mayfair, p. 288.
1749. — Charles Burney and Esther Sleep : ibid. p. 137.
London, 4, 5 ; Boston (U.S.), 2, 0.

Slemmon, Slimmon, &c. ; v. Slyman.

Slinger.—Occup. 'the slinger,' one who used the sling in warfare.

Henricus Slenger, 1379 : P. T. Yorks. p. 265.
Alicia Slynger, 1379 : ibid.
1674. Bapt. — Robert, s. Richard Slinger : St. Dionis Backchurch, p. 120.
1674-5. Buried — Eliz., d. Richard Slinger : ibid. p. 241.
Manchester, 3 ; Leeds, 1 ; West Rid. Court Dir., 3 ; New York, 2.

Slingsby.—Local, 'of Slingsby,' a parish in the N. Rid. Yorks, six miles from New Malton.

John de Slengesby, *wayder* (v. Wader), 33 Edw. I : Freemen of York, i. 10.
Henricus de Slyngesby, 1379 : P. T. Yorks. p. 245.
Ricardus de Slyngesby, 1379 : ibid.
Willelmus de Slenggesby, 1379 : P. T. Howdenshire, p. 8.
Charles Slingesbey, co. York, 1577 : Reg. Univ. Oxf. vol. ii. pt. ii. p. 78.
1787. Married—Thomas Ashley and Hannah Slingsby ; St. Geo. Han. Sq. i. 407.
London, 2 ; West Rid. Court Dir., 1.

Slipper, Sleeper.—(1) Occup. 'the slipper,' i.e. a maker of sword-slips (v. Swordslipper), an important craft in its day. (2) Nick. 'the sleeper,' a dull, heavy, sleepy sort of a fellow.

Simon le Slepar', co. Oxf., 1273. A.
Johannes Slipar, 1379: P. T. Yorks. p. 109.
London, 4, 0; New York, 2, 30; Philadelphia, 0, 9.

Slocombe, Slocum, Slocumb, Slocomb, Slocom.

—Local, ' of Slocombe,' some place in the south-west of England that I have not discovered. The suffix -comb is very common in Devonshire place-names; v. Combe.

1564. Henry Slocum, or Sloocume: Reg. Univ. Oxf. i. 255.
1596. Gilbert Slocumbe, co. Soms.: ibid. vol. ii. pt. ii. p. 216.

A curious variant is found in the following entries:

1730. Married—Thomas Slokam and Isabella Brown: St. Jas. Clerkenwell, ii. 257.
1808. — Joseph Thompson and Ann Slockham: St. Geo. Han. Sq. ii. 386.
London, 7, 0, 0, 0; MDB. (co. Devon), 2, 0, 0, 0; Boston (U.S.), 0, 18, 0, 3, 1; New York, 0, 8, 1, 0, 0; Philadelphia, 0, 13, 0, 5, 0.

Sloley, Slowley, Slowly.

—Local, ' of Sloley,' a parish in co. Norfolk.

Peter de Sloleye, co. Norf., 1273. A.
John de Sloley, of Norwich, 1420: FF. iv. 91.
1577. Robert Slowghleigh, co. Soms.: Reg. Univ. Oxf. vol. ii. pt. ii. p. 75.
MDB. (co. Devon), 5, 0, 0; London, 0, 2, 1.

Sloman, Slowman, Slomon.

—Bapt. 'the son of Solomon,' one of the many variants of this once popular font-name; v. Salman.

1571. Married—George Sloweman and Agnes Humfreye: St. Dionis Backchurch, p. 7.
1601. Robert Slowman, co. Devon: Reg. Univ. Oxf. vol. ii. pt. ii. p. 250.
1663. George Boraston and Eliz. Slowman: Marriage Alleg. (Canterbury), p. 86.
1678. Antony Sloman and Rachell Smith: ibid. p. 287.
London, 6, 0, 0; Philadelphia, 4, 0, 1.

Sloper, Slopier.

—Occup. 'the sloper,' a maker of slops. Sometimes a loose overcoat or garment, more generally large loose trousers.

' His overest sloppe is not worth a mite.'
Chaucer, Chanon Yemannes Tale.
' Item, the xxii daye paied to Cicyll for a payer of sloppes, for the Kinges Grace, vis. 8d.': Privy Purse Expenses, Henry VIII, 1532.
Agatha le Slopere, co. Hunts, 1273. A.
1610. John Sloper, co. Wilts: Reg. Univ. Oxf. vol. ii. pt. ii. p. 313.
1615. Simon Sloper, co. Wilts: ibid. p. 341.
1792. Married—William Sloper and Eliz. North: St. Geo. Han. Sq. ii. 85.

' Ally Sloper' has immortalized this name.

London, 9, 1; New York, 1, 0.

Slott.

—Local, 'at the slot,' from residence therein.

' Slot, a castle, a fort.

"Thou paydst for building of a slot
That wrought thine owne decay."
Riche's Allarme to England, 1578' (Halliwell).

Cf. slot, a bolt or bar, the fastener of a door'. 'Slot, sloot, schytyl of a dore': Prompt. Parv.

Walter de la Slot, co. Norf., 1273. A.
William de Sloth, co. Norf., ibid.
Simon de la Slode, co. Oxf., ibid.
John Slodde, co. Oxf., ibid.

In the New York Directory are Sloat, 11; Sloate, 1; and Slote, 9. Perhaps variants.

New York, 2.

Slough, Slow, Slowe.

—Local, ' of the slough,' a hollow, miry place, from residence thereby. The 'Slough of Despond' is familiar to all readers of the Pilgrim's Progress.

Stephen de la Slou, co. Bucks, 1273. A.
Matilda ad le Slow, co. Camb., ibid.
Hugh de la Slo, co. Wilts, ibid.
Adam del Slo. L.
William atte Slo', co. Soms., 1 Edw. III: Kirby's Quest, p. 110.
Nicholas atte Sloo, co. Soms., 1 Edw. III: ibid. p. 116.
1648. Married—Edward Hopkins and Mary Slow: St. Jas. Clerkenwell, iii. 83.
1806. — William Slow and Mary Brown: St. Geo. Han. Sq. ii. 340.
London, 1, 1, 0; Philadelphia, 13, 5, 1.

Slowley, Slowly; v. Sloley.

Sly, Slee, Sleigh.

— Nick. 'the sly,' the cunning. M.E. sly and sley.

Ralph Sly, co. Hunts, 1273. A.
John Sley, co. Camb., ibid.
John le Slege, co. Oxf., ibid.

John le Slegh, 8 Edw. III: Freemen of York, i. 28.
Juliana Slegh, co. Soms., 1 Edw. III: Kirby's Quest, p. 81.
1533-4. Henry Rowgholt and Matilda Slye: Marriage Lic. (London), i. 8.
1610-11. William Slee, co. Devon: Reg. Univ. Oxf. vol. ii. pt. ii. p. 321.
1658. Married—Thomas Sly and Sarah Drake: St. Thomas the Apostle (London), p. 20.
1662. Edward Nelthorpe and Mary Sleigh: Marriage Alleg. (Canterbury), p. 76.
1667. Henry Temple and Margaret Sligh: ibid. p. 136.
London, 8, 8, 5; Philadelphia, 0, 1, 4.

Slyman, Slemmon, Sleeman, Slimmon, Sleman.

—Bapt. ' the son of Seliman,' i.e. Solomon; cf. Sloman. I see no evidence in favour of 'slyman,' i. e. cunning man. The middle stage between these forms and the original Seliman was Selman or Sellman, q.v., where many instances will be found.

1588. Henry Sliman, co. Oxf.: Reg. Univ. Oxf. vol. ii. pt. ii. p. 167.
1741. Buried — Mary Slyman: St. Dionis Backchurch, p. 169.
London, 1, 1, 2, 0, 0; New York, 0, 0, 1, 2, 1.

Smale, Small.

— Nick. 'the small'; cf. Large, Bigg, Little, &c.

Robert le Small, co. Hunts, 1273. A.
Henry le Smale, co. Camb., ibid.
Richard le Smale, C. R., 9 Edw. II.
Adam le Smale, co. Soms., 1 Edw. III: Kirby's Quest, p. 117.
Willelmus Smale, 1379: P. T. Yorks. p. 220.
Thomas Smale, rector of Lerling, co. Norf., 1468: FF. i. 431.
1508. Nicholas Smale or Small: Reg. Univ. Oxf. i. 63.
1621. Bapt.—Eliz., d. John Small: St. Jas. Clerkenwell, i. 89.
1731. Married—John Smale and Ann Collett: St. Geo. Han. Sq. i. 9.
London, 12, 14; New York, 1, 44.

Smallbone, Smallbones.

— ? Nick. Seemingly a sobriquet affixed on one of small and delicate frame. But this is just a case where such a guess is tempting, and evidence of a local or other origin might at any moment upset the conclusion.

1593. Buried—William Smalbone: St. Michael, Cornhill, p. 205.
1691. Bapt.—Joseph, s. Joseph Smallbones: St. Jas. Clerkenwell, i. 341.

1740. Married—William Taylor and Mary Smallbones: St. Geo. Han. Sq. i. 25.
1787. — Frances D. Weissense and Judith Smallbone: ibid. p. 407.
London, 3, 0 ; MDB. (co. Bucks), 0, 3.

Smallcombe.—Local, ' at the small combe,' from residence thereby ; v. Smale and Combe. Of course it is a West-country surname.

John Smalecome, co. Soms., 1 Edw. III : Kirby's Quest, p. 163.
1806. Married — Thomas Smallcomb and Ann Griffiths : St. Geo. Han. Sq. ii. 340.
London, 1.

Smalley.—Local, ' of Smalley,' a chapelry in the parish of Morley, co. Derby, seven miles from Derby.

Alicia Smalhaghe, 1379 : P. T. Yorks. p. 99.
1682. James Smalley, of Liverpool: Wills at Chester, iii. 228.
1689. Edward Smalley, of Blackburn : ibid.
Sheffield, 3 ; MDB. (co. Camb.), 3 ; New York, 16.

Smallman.—Nick. ' the small man,' small of stature ; cf. Small, Bigg, Little, Longfellow, Longman, &c.

Richard Smaleman, co. Suff., 1273. A.
Alan Smalman, Pardons R., 6 Ric. II.
1590. Francis Smalman, co. Salop : Reg. Univ. Oxf. vol. ii. pt. ii. p. 181.
1605. Bapt. — William, s. William Smalman : St. Jas. Clerkenwell, i. 47.
— Married—John Smalmanne to Elizabeth Tenche : St. Peter, Cornhill, i. 244.
1790. Married — Edmund Smallman and Jane Parkeman : St. Geo. Han. Sq. ii. 37.
London, 2 ; Manchester, 3 ; Boston (U.S.), 3.

Smallpage, Smalpage. — Official, a page or servitor. The small ' tiger ' of former days ; cf. Littlepage.

' To Percivall Smallpage, for his expenses, xxs.' : Household Accounts, Princess Eliz., Camd. Soc.
' Robert Smallpage for cupboard, William Page for cellar, Thomas Drax cupbearer' : Arrangements for wedding of Roger Rockley and Elizabeth Nevill, Jan. 14, 1526 ; Whitaker's Craven, p. 380.
Thomas Smallpage, co. York. W. 2.
Ralph Smallpage. V. 3.
1535. Ralph Smalpage : Reg. Univ. Oxf. i. 184.
1564. Thomas Smallpage, manciple of Ex. Coll. : ibid. vol. ii. pt. i. p. 288.

1607. Percival Smalpage, co. Sussex : ibid. pt. ii. p. 296.
London, 0, 1 ; Manchester, 2, 0 ; Leeds, 2, 1.

Smallpiece.— ? ——. I am not able to suggest any satisfactory derivation of this surname.

Francis Smallpece, mayor of Norwich, 1622 : FF. iv. 469.
1663. Jeremy Washford and Eliz. Smallpiece : Marriage Alleg. (Canterbury), i. 120.
1675-6. Thomas Smallpeice and Ann Field : ibid. p. 160.
1676. Thomas Battin and Eliz. Smallpiece : ibid. p. 166.
MDB. (Surrey), 10.

Smallpride. — Nick. ' Small pride,' one without arrogance ; cf. Littleproud.

Richard Smalprout, co. Oxf., 1273. A.
Robert Smalprout, co. Oxf., ibid.

Smallshanks. — Nick. ' with the small shanks'; cf. Sheepshanks, Longshanks, &c.

1573. Buried—Margrett Smaleshankes : St. Michael, Cornhill, p. 192.
1803. Married — Luke Smallshankes and Isabella Forbes : St. Geo. Han. Sq. ii. 295.

Smallwood.—Local, ' of Smallwood,' a township in the parish of Astbury, co. Ches.

Robert Smallwod, C. R., 51 Hen. III.
Elizabetha Smallwode, 1379 : P. T. Yorks. p. 125.
John Turner, of Smallwood, 1675 : Wills at Chester (1660-80), p. 272.
William Smallwood, of Peover, 1674 : ibid. p. 246.
Randle Smallwood, of Lower Withington, 1673 : ibid.

Still earlier we find the entries :

James Smallwood, of Smallwood, 1617 : Wills at Chester (1545-1620), p. 176.
Randle Smallwood, of Middlewich, 1592 : ibid.
1559. Married—Thomas Pedley and Ales Smalewodde : Prestbury Ch. (Cheshire), p. 2.
Thomas Smallwood, of Chelford, 1662 : Earwaker's East Cheshire, ii. 366.
1748. Married—John Smallwood and Mary Turner : St. Geo. Han. Sq. i. 40.
Manchester, 2 ; Liverpool, 3 ; London, 3 ; MDB. (Cheshire), 2 ; Philadelphia, 9.

Smart.—Nick. ' the smart,' i.e. the brisk ; cf. Snell.

Simon Smert, co. Northumb., 1273. A.
Adam Smart, co. Oxf., ibid.
Martin Smart, co. Camb., ibid.
John Smert, co. Soms., 1 Edw. III : Kirby's Quest, p. 188.
Richard Smert, C. R., 8 Ric. II.

1651. Bapt.—John, s. John Smart : St. Jas. Clerkenwell, i. 178.
London, 54 ; New York, 25.

Smertknave. — Nick. ' the smart knave,' i.e. the brisk, active servant ; cf. Goodknave or Goodgroom.

Cristiana Smartknave, co. Oxf., 1273. A.

Smeathman.—Probably a variant of Smitheman, q.v.

MDB. (co. Bucks), 1 ; (North Rid. Yorks), 1.

Smeaton, Smeeton. — Local, ' of Smeaton,' now Kirk Smeaton, near Womersley, co. York.

Johannes Smeton, 1379 : P. T. Yorks. p. 161.
1620-1. John Mason and Rosamond Smeton : Marriage Lic. (London), ii. 95.
1756. Married — John Smeaton and Ann Jenkinson : St. Geo. Han. Sq. i. 64.
1769. — James Smeeton and Jane Sherwood : ibid. p. 192.
London, 3, 6 ; West Rid. Court Dir., 0, 4 ; Philadelphia, 0, 3.

Smedley.—Local, ' of Smythley.' I cannot identify the spot.

Willelmus de Smythlay, 1379 : P. T. Yorks. p. 4.
Magota de Smythlay, 1379 : ibid.
1693. Bapt.—Mary, d. Thomas Smedley : St. Jas. Clerkenwell, i. 351.
MDB. (co. Derby), 25 ; Sheffield, 6 ; London, 1 ; Philadelphia, 48.

Smee.— ? ——. Lower says, ' a mispronunciation of Smeeth ' (q.v.). He advances no evidence. I cannot suggest a satisfactory solution.

1573. Bapt.—Thomas, s. John Smye : St. Jas. Clerkenwell, i. 7.
1574-5. John Smy (or Sury), co. Berks : Reg. Univ. Oxf. vol. ii. pt. ii. p. 59.
London, 9 ; MDB. (co. Essex), 3 ; Philadelphia, 4.

Smeeth, Smeed.—(1) Local, ' at the smethe,' a smooth place. ' A large open level' (Halliwell) ; an open, level, smooth turf.

Johannes del Smethe, Isolda uxor ejus, 1379 : P. T. Yorks. p. 162.

(2) Local, ' of Smeeth,' a parish in co. Kent. No doubt the origin is identical with (1).

Laurence de Smethe, co. Kent, 1273. A.
1746. Married—Thomas Smeed and Mary Booker : Canterbury Cath., p. 88.
1757. — John Smethe and Rose Broughton : St. Geo. Han. Sq. i. 72.
London, 1, 3 ; MDB. (Kent), 1, 3.

Smelt. — Nick. or personal. Either (1) 'the Smelt,' which would be a nickname, or (2) 'the son of Smelt,' which would be personal or baptismal. This appears to be one of the very few names really taken from the finny tribe (v. Salman, Turbot, or Chubb). A.S. *smelt*, Danish *smelt*.

William Smelt, co. Kent, 1273. A. William Smelte, co. Norf., ibid. Richard Smelt, C. R., 19 Edw. III. pt. i. 1666. Married — Edward Hews and Jane Smelt : St. Jas. Clerkenwell, iii. 123. 1743. Bapt. — Martha, d. William Smalt : ibid. ii. 226. London, 1 ; Crockford, 3.

Smelter, Smilter. — Occup. 'the smelter,' one who smelted, or melted iron ore ; cf. Bloomer, Ashburner, and Collier.

Henricus Smelter, 1379 : P. T. Yorks. p. 265. 1762. Married — James Wigman and Hannah Smilter : St. Geo. Han. Sq. i. 116. West Rid. Court Dir., 0, 1.

Smerdon, Smerden. — Local, 'of Smarden,' a parish in co. Kent, nine miles from Cranbrook.

MDB. (co. Devon), 8, 6 ; London, 3, 0 ; New York, 0, 1.

Smethurst. — Local, 'of Smethurst,' some small spot in the neighbourhood of Rochdale or Bury, co. Lanc. I have not discovered its exact position.

Richard Meadowcroft, of Smethurst, 1581 : Wills at Chester (1545-1620), p. 134. John Smethurst, of Blakeley, 1582 : ibid. p. 177. Richard Smethurst, of Bury, 1618 : ibid. 1591-2. Richard Smethurst, co. Ches. : Reg. Univ. Oxf. vol. ii. pt. ii. p. 187. 1604. Buried—Martha Smythurst : St. Thomas the Apostle (London), p. 104. Manchester, 18 ; Philadelphia, 8.

Smilter ; v. Smelter.

Smirthwaite ; v. Smurthwaite.

Smith, Smyth, Smythe. — Occup. 'the smith.' Common to every village in England, north, south, east, and west. The *y* in Smyth is the almost invariable spelling in early rolls, so that it cannot exactly be styled a modern affectation. There are 300,000 Smiths in England ; very different from the state of Israel, when 'there was no smith found throughout all the land of Israel' (1 Sam. xiii. 19). This always seems to me the hardest verse in the Bible to read in Church without smiling ; the most difficult, with regard to proper emphasis, being Luke xxiv. 25.

Philip le Smethe, co. Hunts, 1273. A. William le Smeth, co. Oxf., ibid. William le Smyth, co. Sussex, ibid.

The following occur on one single page, representing the village of Kimberworth :

Johannes Tagge, *smyght*, 1379 : P. T. Yorks. p. 67. Willelmus Smyght, 1379 : ibid. Johannes Trogne, *smyght*, 1379 : ibid. Ricardus Sawdre, *smyght*, 1379 : ibid. Robertus Smyght, 1379 : ibid. Johannes Losseland, *smyght*, 1379 : ibid. London, 1194, 23, 3 ; Philadelphia, 2971, 84, 9.

Smitheman, Smitherman, Smithman. — Occup. 'the smithman' or smithyman, one who worked at a smithy, the smith's assistant ; cf. Priestman, Vickerman, Matthewman, Ladyman, &c.

Robert Smythyman, C. R., 2 Edw. II. Henry Smytman, C. R., 7 Ric. II. Henricus Smythman, 1379 : P. T. Yorks. p. 209. Johannes Smythman, 1379 : ibid. p. 214. Alanus Foxe, *smethyman*, 1379 : ibid. p. 219. Robertus Smytheman, 1379 : ibid. p. 279. 1624. Francis Ketelby and Mary Smitheyman : Marriage Lic. (Westminster), p. 30. 1717. Married—John Smithyman and Anne Austen : St. Michael, Cornhill, p. 59. London, 1, 0, 0 ; MDB. (co. Essex), 0, 2, 0 ; Philadelphia, 11, 1, 1.

Smithett. — Local, ' of Smurthwaite,' one of the many localities in cos. Cumberland, Westmoreland, and North Lancashire whose suffix is -*thwaite* (v. Thwaite). The first stage of corruption was Smuthwaite, the second Smethwaite. This became Smithett just as Smithwick became Smithick ; v. Smorfitt, Smithwaite, Smurthwaite. In my late parish (Ulverston) Poslet represents Postlethwaite.

1798. Married — Thomas Smuthwaite and Eliz. Maxfield : St. Geo. Han. Sq. ii. 188. 1805. Married—George Smithwaite and Mary Hancock : ibid. p. 333. London, 3.

Smithies, Smithers, Smithyes, Smither, Smythers, Smythies, Smithee. — (1) Local, 'at the smithy,' with suffix (perhaps patronymic) *s*, as in Brooks, Styles, &c. Smithers is a vulgar corruption. (2) Local, ' of Smethurst.' It seems almost certain that Smithers is more generally a corruption of Smethurst (v. Reg. Univ. Oxf. vol. ii. pt. iv. p. 384). No doubt the two are mixed.

Johannes del Smethe, 1379 : P. T. Yorks. p. 162. Margareta del Smethes, 1379 : ibid. p. 21. Johannes de Smethe, *smyth*, 1379 : ibid. p. 42. Cecilia de Smethe, 1379 : ibid. Margeria del Smythe, 1379 : ibid. Willelmus del Smithi, 1379 : ibid. p. 225. Osbert le (de ?) Smythes, co. Soms., 1 Edw. III : Kirby's Quest, p. 134. 1697. Buried — Catherine Smithyes : St. Mary Aldermary (London), p. 204. London, 3, 14, 3, 5, 1, 1, 0 ; West Rid. Court Dir., 2, 0, 0, 0, 0, 0, 0 ; MDB. (co. Norf.), Smithee, 3 ; Philadelphia, 0, 18, 0, 1, 0, 0, 0.

Smithson. — Nick. 'the smith's son' ; cf. Clarkson, Wrightson, Taylorson, Serjeantson, and Shepherdson.

Johannes Smytheson', 1379 : P. T. Yorks. p. 177. Johannes Smyth' et Alicia uxor ejus, 1379 : ibid. Johannes Smyth et uxor, 1379 : ibid. p. 214. Johannes Smythson, 1379 : ibid. Cf. Agnes Smythwyf, 1379 : ibid. p. 194. 1573. Married—Robert Watteson and Margaret Smethson : Reg. St. Dionis Backchurch, p. 7. 1579. William Smythson and Margaret Pryce : Marriage Lic. (London), i. 88. London, 7 ; York, 4 ; Philadelphia, 9.

Smithwaite. — Local, a corruption of Smurthwaite ; v. Smithett.

MDB. (West Rid. Yorks), 1.

Smithwick, Smedick. — Local, ' of Smethwick,' a township in the parish of Brereton, co. Ches., four miles from Sandbach ; also a hamlet in the parish of Harborne, co. Stafford. Of course the popular pronunciation was Smithick (cf. Physick for Fishwick). This was further corrupted to Smedick.

1311. Ralph de Smethwyk, rector of Beteley, co. Norf. : FF. ix. 467. 1621. Bapt.—Ellyn, d. Thomas Smithicke : St. Peter Cornhill, i. 70.

1663. Married—Roger Chiswicke and Jane Smethicke: St. Jas. Clerkenwell, i. 111.

1680. Thomas Smethwick, of Smethwick: Wills at Chester, i. 247.

Liverpool, 1, 0; New York, 2, 1; Boston (U.S.), 1, 0.

Smoker.—Occup. 'the smoker,' probably a maker of smocks, meaning shifts, &c.

Robert le Smoker, co. Soms., 1 Edw. III: Kirby's Quest, p. 136.

William Smoker, co. Soms., 1 Edw. III: ibid. p. 159.

John Smoker, co. Soms., 1 Edw. III: ibid.

Philadelphia, 5.

Smorfitt.—Local, a corruption of Smurthwaite; v. Smithett. It is found in a London register as Smurfoote, a kind of halfway stage in the corruption.

1661. Bapt.—Bridget, d. Robert Smurfoote: St. Jas. Clerkenwell, i. 212.

1753. Married — John Smurfit and Catherine Gainer: St. Geo. Han. Sq. p. 258.

MDB. (West Rid. Yorks), 1.

Smurthwaite, Smirthwaite. —Local, 'of Smurthwaite'; v. Smithett, Smorfitt, &c.

1733. Married—John Russell and Edith Smurthwaite: St. Geo. Han. Sq. i. 12.

1779. — Christopher Smirthwaite and Eliz. Brooksbank: ibid. p. 300.

MDB. (North Rid. Yorks), 2, 0; Manchester, 1, 0; Philadelphia, 1, 3.

Smyth(e; v. Smith.

Snaith, Sneath.—Local, 'of Snaith,' a village and parish a few miles from Goole, co. York.

Henry de Snayth, tannator, 2 Edw. I: Freemen of York, i. 1.

Ricardus de Snayth, 1379: P. T. Yorks. p. 125.

Thomas de Snayth, 1379: ibid.

Alicia de Snayth, 1379: ibid.

1751. Married—Nathaniel Snaith and Anna Maria Davis: St. Geo. Han. Sq. i. 206.

1798. — John Moulden and Catherine Sneath: ibid. ii. 189.

Liverpool, 1, 0; Philadelphia, 0, 2.

Snape. — (1) Local, 'at the snape,' from residence thereby. Most probably a piece of land with soil starved and pinched; from snape, to pine or wither. (2) Local, 'at the snape,' from residence thereby; a spring in arable ground. (3) Nick. 'the snape,' i. e. the woodcock; v. Halliwell's Dict.

Henry de la Snape, co. Sussex, 1273. A. Ralph de Snape, co. Norf., ibid.

This last entry will be connected with Snape, a parish in co. Norfolk. An estate in the parish of Scarisbrook, co. Lanc., has helped to foster the name in the co. Palatinate.

Adam del Snape, co. Lanc., 1332: Lay Subsidy Roll, co. Lanc. (Rylands), p. 6.

William Snaype, 1379: P. T. Yorks. p. 216.

1594. John Edwardson, of Snape, within Scarisbrook, husbandman: Wills at Chester, i. 60.

1600. John Lawton, of Snape: East Ches. ii. 383.

London, 4; Crockford, 3; Manchester, 7; Philadelphia, 6.

Snazle, Snazel, Snazell. — Local, (1) 'of Kneesall,' a parish in the dioc. of Lincoln; (2) 'of Knettishall,' a parish in the dioc. of Norwich. There was evidently a difficulty in pronouncing the last local term. It would readily corrupt. It is quite possible that the Lincolnshire surname Snushall is a corruption of (1); cf. Sturges for Thurgis, and v. Spurdance.

John de Gnadeshall, or Knateshall, of Knetsall, bailiff of Norwich, 1366: FF. iii. 100.

William de Knateshall, bailiff of Norwich, 1635: ibid.

William de Knateshale, or Gnatishale, burgess in Parl. for Norwich, 42 Edw. III: ibid. p. 101.

1656. Buried—Francis Snawsell: St. Jas. Clerkenwell, iv. 314.

London, 1, 1, 0; MDB. (Suffolk), 0, 1, 0; (co. Camb.), 0, 0, 1.

Snead, Sneed, Sneyd. — (1) Local, 'of Sneyd,' a township in the parish of Burslem, co. Stafford. (2) Local, 'of Snead,' a hamlet in the parish of Rock, co. Worc.

1574. William Stokes and Eliz. Snede: Marriage Lic. (London), i. 63.

1581. William Sneade, co. Stafford: Reg. Univ. Oxf. vol. ii. pt. ii. p. 100.

1590. John Sneade, co. Worc.: ibid. p. 178.

1739. Married — John Parsons and Margaret Sneed: St. Geo. Chap. Mayfair, p. 13.

1745. — Erasmus Carter and Eliz. Snead: ibid. p. 53.

London, 4, 1, 0; Philadelphia, 2, 1, 10.

Sneegum.—? Local. Probably a corruption of Snettisham, a parish in co. Norwich. I find, after writing this, that Mr. Lower is of

the same opinion (v. Patr. Brit. p. 322); cf. Barnum for Barnham.

Richard de Snetisham, co. Norf., 1273. A.

Roger de Snetesham, prebend. Norwich Cathedral, 1306: FF. iv. 173.

London, 2; MDB. (co. Essex), 1.

Snell.—Bapt. 'the son of Snel.' This name is found in the Hundred Rolls as a single personal name, a strong argument in favour of a fontal origin. If not so, it must be a nickname. 'Snell, sharp, keen, piercing. Cumberland.

"Teche hem alle to be war and snel"' (Halliwell).

As a personal name Snel is found as a compound in such local words as Snelston, Snelland, or Snelsmore.

Snel, co. Derby, 1273. A.

William Snell, co. Oxf., ibid.

Johannes Snell', 1379: P. T. Yorks. p. 116.

Willelmus Snell, 1379: ibid. p. 37.

Ricardus Snell, 1379: ibid. p. 215.

London, 31; New York, 10.

Snelling.—Bapt. 'the son of Snelling'; cf. Browning and Harding. Mr. Lower says Snelling is found in Domesday as a previous tenant (Patr. Brit. p. 322). Of course this implies a personal name.

Walter Snellyng, co. Soms., 1 Edw. III: Kirby's Quest, p. 118.

Michael Snellyng, co. Soms., 1 Edw. III: ibid. p. 119.

John Snellyng, co. Soms., 1 Edw. III: ibid. p. 132.

1582-3. Robert Snellinge and Eliz. Bull: Marriage Lic. (London), i. 114.

1790. Married—William Snelling and Sarah Jennings: St. Geo. Han. Sq. ii. 41.

London, 14; New York, 8; Philadelphia, 2; Boston (U.S.), 15.

Snelson.—Local, 'of Snelson,' a township in the parish of Rostherne, co. Ches.; in Domesday Senelestune. A family sprang up here called alike Snelson or Snelston. Both surname and local name have modernly dropped the t. Occasionally it may be 'the son of Snell'; v. Snell.

William de Snelleston, 1369: Hist. East Ches. ii. 643.

Thomas de Snelleston, 1379: ibid. p. 551.

Benedict Snelson, of Little Budworth, yeoman, 1606: Wills at Chester (1545-1620), p. 180.

1596. Richard Snellson and Katherine Mustyan: Marriage Lic. (London), i. 233.
1774. Married—David Hartley and Sarah Snellson: St. Geo. Han. Sq. i. 243.
MDB. (co. Ches.), 4; Liverpool, 1.

Sneyd; v. Snead.

Snibson.—Local, ' of Snibston,' a chapelry in the parish of Packington, co. Leic. A palpable modification; cf. Kelson for Kelston.
Liverpool, 1.

Snidall, Snidle, Snittle.— Local, 'of Snydale,' a village a mile east of Normanton, co. York.
Johanna de Snydal, 1379: P. T. Yorks. p. 159.
Johannes Snydale, 1379: ibid.
Johannes Snytall, 1379: ibid. p. 146.
Sheffield, 2, 0, 0; West Rid. Court Dir., 0, 1, 0.

Snoad.—? Bapt. 'the son of Snod.' Snod is found as a single personal name in the Hundred Rolls; cf. the local Snodgrass, where the prefix is probably the original settler's personal name.
Snod serviens Ricard Giffard, co. Suff., 1273. A.
1349. John Snod, vicar of Attlebridge, co. Norf.: FF. x. 402.
1602. Theodore Snode: Reg. Univ. Oxf. vol. ii. pt. ii. p. 259.
1657. Bapt.—Eliz., d. Charles Snode: St. Jas. Clerkenwell, i. 265.
London, 3.

Snodgrass. — Local, 'at the snodgrass,' from residence thereby. ' Snod, smooth, demure' (Halliwell). But v. Snoad for another derivation of the prefix. The surname is far more commonly found in the United States than in England.
1730. Married—Andrew Snottgrass and Ann Cressum: St. Geo. Chap. Mayfair, p. 321.
The name of Snodgrass occurs in the Cheltenham register, Aug. 1863 (N. and Q., Dec. 4, 1886).
New York, 1; Philadelphia, 23.

Snodin.—Local, 'of Snowdon'; v. Snowden. The following seems a very conclusive instance. It is clearly the half-stage of the corrupted form:
1795. Married—William Snowdin and Frances Blakes: St. Geo. Han. Sq. ii. 129.

1573. John Snodon: Reg. Univ. Oxf. vol. ii. pt. iii. p. 25.
London, 3.

Snook, Snooke, Snooks. — Local, 'of Sevenoaks' (?), a market-town and parish in co. Kent. Mr. Lower says, 'The Kentish town is usually pronounced Se'noaks.' 'The further contraction, coupled with the phonetic spelling of former days, easily passed into Snooks. Messrs. Sharp and Harrison, solicitors of Southampton, had in their possession a series of deeds in which all the modes of spelling occur, from Sevenoakes down to S'nokes, in connection with a family now known as Snooks ' (Notes and Queries, 1st S. v. p. 438, quoted by Lower). ' A Sussex family in the early part of the last century bore the name of Snooke. Sevenoke, the early orthography of the town, has also been modified into Sinnock and Cennick' (Lower).
Stephen Senevac', co. Linc., 1273. A.
Simon Senenok', co. Soms., 1 Edw. III: Kirby's Quest, p. 147.
Robert Snouk, co. Soms., 1 Edw. III: ibid. p. 218.
1617. Richard Snook, co. Dorset: Reg. Univ. Oxf. vol. ii. pt. ii. p. 366.
1642. Bapt. — Margery, d. Daniel Snoaks: Kensington Ch., p. 33.
1766. Married — Thomas Snook and Ann Autrick: St. Geo. Han. Sq. i. 266.
London, 9, 2, 2; Philadelphia, 1, 0, 0; New York, 5, 0, 0.

Snow. — Personal or, as we should now say, baptismal, 'the son of Snow'; cf. Winter, Frost, and such ecclesiastical seasons (as distinct from the natural) as Pentecost, Nowell, Pask, Whitsunday, or Midwinter. A name given originally to a child born in the time of snow. The practice is repeated to-day. A clergyman wrote to me some time ago to say he had just baptized a child by the name of Sou'-wester. This turned out to be the father's Christian name, who was born on board ship in a sou'-westerly gale.
Henry Snou, co. Bucks, 1273. A.
William Snou, co. Oxf., ibid.
Roger Snow, C. R., 14 Edw. I.
Willelmus Snawe, 1379: P. T. Yorks. p. 239.
Ricardus Snaw, 1379: ibid. p. 122.

1569. James Jobson and Saban Snowe: Marriage Lic. (London), i. 43.
London, 31; Philadelphia, 19.

Snowball.— ? Nick. I cannot suggest any satisfactory derivation. It is possible that it was a nickname for one with snow-white hair and a round head; cf. Whitehead and Snowwhite.
1546-7. William Stacye and Katherine Snowball: Marriage Lic. (Faculty Office), p. 9.
1745. Married—George Snowball and Mary Winn: St. Geo. Han. Sq. i. 34.
1746. — Richard Clingo and Jane Snowball: St. Geo. Chap. Mayfair, p. 61.
MDB. (co. Ches.), 2; (co. Durham), 6; London, 1; Manchester, 1; Philadelphia, 1; New York, 1.

Snowden, Snowdon.—Local, 'of Snowdon.' Possibly the Welsh mountain, but more probably some smaller spot in the West country. Not one in a hundred Welsh surnames is local. The parent must be sought for elsewhere.
John Snowdone, co. Soms., 1 Edw. III: Kirby's Quest, p. 93.
1558. Thomas Snowdon and Alice Heritage: Marriage Lic. (London), i. 18.
1744. Married—Patrick Hevy and Eliz. Snowden: St. Geo. Chap. Mayfair, p. 36.
London, 12, 6; Philadelphia, 22, 11.

Snowwhite. — Nick. 'with snow-white hair.' Cf. Snowball.
John Snowhite, Close Roll, 3 Hen. V.

Snushall.—Local, 'of Knesall ' (?), a parish in the dioc. of Lincoln; v. Snazle.
1580. Married—Edward Snowsell and Sisley Wilson: St. Mary Aldermary, p. 6.
MDB. (Lincoln), 4.

Soanes; v. Sones.

Soapers - lane. — Local, 'of Soapers' Lane,' a street in London where soap was manufactured.
Thomas de Sopereslane, London, 1273. A.

Soar; v. Sor.

Soden.—Local; v. Sowden.
Oxford, 4.

Sojourner. — Nick. or occup. '. the sojourner.' This surname I have only met with in North Lancashire, between Preston and the Duddon Sands. For centuries it appears in the Ulverston and Dalton registers as Suggener, and in that form a charity was left to the poor of the latter parish. In the Preston Guild Rolls occurs 'John Sojorner, butter - maker,' 1622 (p. 89). Possibly the Sojourner was, like Tasker, a worker by the day or job, a day-labourer, as we now say. If we take it in its accepted sense it will denote a new-comer, who from a passing visitor has become a settler. It is suggested in N. and Q. (Sept. 17, 1887) that the French Sigourney, or Sigournai, is of the same origin.

1547. Married—Thomas Asburner and Elisabeth Suggener : Reg. Parish Ch., Ulverston, p. 4.
1549. Buried—John Suggener : ibid. p. 10.

Sokerel.—Nick. 'the sokerel.' '*Sokerel*, a child not weaned' (Halliwell). A very likely sobriquet for a simple and silly fellow. Cf. Suckling.

Richard Sokerel, co. Soms., 1 Edw. III : Kirby's Quest, p. 155.

Sole, Soles. — Local, 'at the sole,' i.e. pond. '*Sole*, a pond. Co. Kent' (Halliwell). This solution is proved by the instances furnished below :

Peter de la Sole, co. Kent, 1273. A.
Richard atte Sole, co. Kent, ibid.
John de Soles, co. Kent, ibid.
Hamo de Soles, co. Kent, Hen. III-Edw. I. K.
1665. Married — John Knowler and Susanna Sole : Canterbury Cath. p. 60.
1690. — John Swaine and Margaret Sole : ibid. p. 64.
London, 4, 0 ; MDB. (Kent), 1, 0 ; New York, 0, 2.

Soleyndeamur.—Nick. 'seriously in love' (?).

Hugh Soleyndeamur, Close Roll, 55 Hen. III.

Cf. Finnemore, Paramor, Pleynamour, Douceamour.

Soller.—Local, 'at the soler,' an upper room, a garret, a loft. L. Lat. *solarium*. '*Solarium*, an upper room, chamber, or garret, which in some parts of England is still called a sollar' : Kennett, p. 134.

'In a soler was in that town
A childe cast another down.'
Cursor Mundi (Halliwell).

Gilbert de Solario, co. Linc., 1273. A.
Adam ad Solarium, co. Oxf., ibid.

Agnes de Solar', co. Linc., 1273. A.
Walter atte Solere, co. Soms., 1 Edw. III : Kirby's Quest, p. 123.
1607. John Soller and Mary Grammett : Marriage Lic. (Westminster), p. 16.
1711. Married — William Sollars and Eliz. Thackitt : St. Jas. Clerkenwell, iii. 234.
London, 1 ; New York, 1 ; Philadelphia, 1.

Solloway, Solway. — Local, 'at the sale-way.' This surname, so familiar to Oxford citizens, hails from co. Somerset. Its derivation is very simple. The original bearer of the name lived on the *way* that led to the *sale*, or hall (v. Sale). For change to *o*, cf. Salomon and Solomon. For the change into three syllables (for euphony), cf. Ottaway, Greenaway, Hathaway, in place of Ottway, Greenway, and Hathway.

Robert Saleway, co. Soms., 1 Edw. III : Kirby's Quest, p. 129.
John Selewey, co. Soms., 1 Edw. III : ibid. p. 133.
Richard Salweye, co. Soms., 1 Edw. III : ibid. p. 279.
1669. Married — Hercules Hale and Mary Soloway : St. Jas. Clerkenwell, iii. 158.
1752. — William Solway and Mary Mackey : St. Geo. Chap. Mayfair, p. 219.
Oxford, 2, 0 ; MDB. (co. Soms.), 0, 2 ; New York, 3, 0.

Solman, Soloman, Solomans, Solomon, Solomons. — Bapt. 'the son of Solomon.' The first *o* is very rare in early records. The spelling is almost invariably Saloman. A large proportion of the Solomons in the London Directory represents the modern Jewish invasion, as the personal names attached to them will sufficiently prove, not to mention the occupations ; v. Salman for the old English representatives of a once popular fontal name.

John Solyman, co. Wilts, 1273. A.
Walter Solyman, co. Wilts, ibid.
1705. Married—Mathew Wayne and Barbery Solman : St. Antholin (London), p. 118.
London, 1, 2, 1, 63, 13 ; New York, 0, 9, 0, 125, 7.

Solway ; v. Solloway.

Somerby.—Local, 'of Somerby,' two parishes in co. Lincoln, anciently called Somerdeby.

Robert de Somerdeby, co. Linc.,1273. A.

Hugh de Somerdeby, alias Somerteby, co. Linc., 20 Edw. I. R.
Ralph de Somertheby, co. Linc., Hen. III-Edw. I. K.
Thomas de Somerdeby, co. Linc., ibid. Boston (U.S.), 9.

Somers ; v. Summer.

Somersall, Summershall.— Local, 'of Somersall,' a parish in the co. of Derby, four miles from Uttoxeter.

1730. Married—John Springfield and Ann Somersale : Canterbury Cath. p. 78.
1737-8. John Summersol and Alice Potten : ibid. p. 82.
London, 1, 0 ; Heywood (co. Lanc.), 0, 1.

Somerset, Somersett, Summerset.— Local, 'of Somerset.' one who had left the county and received his surname as an emigrant from that particular shire ; cf. Lancashire, Wiltshire, Cornish, Kentish, &c.

William de Somersete, co. Salop, 1273. A.
Roger de Somersete, co. Soms., 1 Edw. III : Kirby's Quest, p. 204.
1591. Henry Somerset, co. Hereford : Reg. Univ. Oxf. vol. ii. pt. ii. p. 183.
1804. Married—Hugh Henry Mitchell and Harriet Isabella Somerset : St. Geo. Han. Sq. ii. 307.
MDB. (co. Derby), 2, 9, 0 ; Manchester, 2, 0, 0 ; Philadelphia, 10, 0, 0 ; New York, 0, 0, 1.

Somerton, Sommerton. — Local, 'of Somerton,' parishes in cos. Oxford, Somerset, Norfolk, and Suffolk ; v. Summer.

William de Somerton, co. Oxf., 1273. A.
Richard de Somerton, co. Norf., ibid.
Bartholomew de Somerton, co. Norf., 20 Edw. I. R.
Constancia de Somerton, co. Norf., ibid.
Robert Somerton, co. Soms., 1 Edw. III : Kirby's Quest, p. 123.
John de Somerton, co. Soms., 1 Edw. III : ibid. p. 237.
1669. Married — John Somerton and Eliz. Robertes : St. Jas. Clerkenwell, i. 158.
1766. — Thomas Hawkins and Hannah Sumerton : St. Geo. Han. Sq. i. 152.
London, 1, 0 ; Oxford, 0, 1.

Somerville, Sommerville, Somervail, Somervell, Somerwill. — Local, 'de Somerville.' Lower says, 'The progenitor of the noble family was Walter de Somerville, lord of Wicknor, &c., in Staffordshire, and of Aston Somerville, in co. Gloucester, who came into England with William the Conqueror, and left two sons, who became ancestors respectively of the English and of the Scottish Somervilles. This name has been anglicized to Somerfield': Patr. Brit. p. 323.

Jacobus de Somerwill, co. Devon, 1273. A.
Robert de Somervile, co. Staff., 20 Edw. I. R.
Roger de Somervile, co. Staff., ibid.
1639-40. Christopher Grainger and Mary Somervell: Marriage Lic. (Westminster), p. 38.
1669. Edward Sommervill and Mary Beaufoy: Marriage Alleg. (Canterbury), p. 162.
London, 4, 1, 1, 1, 2; New York, 8, 2, 0, 0, 0.

Sommer(s ; v. Summer.

Sommerlad, Sommerlat. — Bapt. 'the son of Sumalide' (Yonge, ii. 432). 1086, Summerled (Domesday). A curious instance of the survival of a probably rare personal name. Mr. Lower says Somerlad, Thane of Argyle, living in the 12th century, was founder of the Clan Macdonald (Patr. Brit. p. 323).

London, 1, 1.

Sommerton; v. Somerton.

Sommerville; v. Somerville.

Sondes ; v. Sands.

Sones, Soanes, Sounes. — ? Local, 'at the sands,' from residence thereby (v. Sands). Probably a modified form of Sondes, the early form. Sounes is unmistakably a variant.

1681. Bapt.—George, s. George and Jane Sones: St. Jas. Clerkenwell, i. 309.
1684. — Peter, s. George and Jane Sounds: ibid. p. 295.
1689. — William, s. George and Jane Soanes: ibid. p. 330.
1795. Married — John Cumberpatch and Eliz. Sones: St. Geo. Han. Sq. ii. 140.
1805. — John Souness and Ann Hamlin: ibid. p. 331.
London, 3, 4, 3 ; Oxford, 0, 7, 0 ; Boston (U.S.), 1, 0, 0.

Songer, Songster. — Occup. American variants of Sanger and Sangster, q.v.

Philadelphia, 1, 3.

Soper.—Occup. 'the soaper,' a maker of soap. M. E. *sope*, soap. Cf. Savoner.

Julian le Sopere, co. Dorset, 1273. A.
Nicholas le Sopere, co. Glouc., ibid.
John le Sopere, co. Soms., 1 Edw. III : Kirby's Quest, p. 80.
1795. Married—Joseph Soper and Eliz. Powell : St. Geo. Han. Sq. ii. 135.
London, 12 ; Philadelphia, 4 ; Boston (U.S.), 5.

Sor, Sore, Soar.—? Nick. 'the sor,' the sore, the susceptible to wounded feelings, the sensitive. But much more probably one of the endless nicknames from the complexion of the hair, from O.F. *sor*, the dim. of which was Sorel, a reddish-brown, hence a favourite name for a horse ; v. Sorrel.

Elena la Sore, co. Somerset, 1273. A.
Matheu le Sore, C. R., 26 Edw. III.
Philip le Soor, co. Soms., 1 Edw. III : Kirby's Quest, p. 170.
Roger le Sor, co. Soms., 1 Edw. III : ibid. p. 238.
John le Sor. H.
Philip le Sor. T.
1605. John Soare, Trin. Coll. Oxf. : Reg. Univ. Oxf. vol. ii. pt. iii. p. 256.
1807. Married — William Sore and Lillies Staig : St. Geo. Han. Sq. ii. 375.
London, 0, 0, 2 ; New York, 0, 0, 1.

Sorby, Sorbey. — Local, 'of Sowerby,' a parish in W. Rid. Yorks.

Johannes de Saureby, 1379 : P. T. Yorks. p. 89.
Thomas de Sawrebe, 1379 : ibid. p. 87.
Thomas de Saureby, 1379 : ibid. p. 13.
Paulinus de Saureby, 1379 : ibid. p. 80.
Thomas de Schorby, 1379 : ibid. p. 155.
1597. Thomas Sowerbye, co. Cumb., Reg. Univ. Oxf. vol. ii. pt. ii. p. 221.
1609. Francis Sowerby, co. Durham : ibid. p. 221.

The variants of these surnames in the Index to Reg. Univ. Oxf. (p. 391) are Sourbie, Sourby, Surby.

West Rid. Court Dir., 6, 0 ; Sheffield, 7, 0 ; New York, 1, 1.

Soresby.—Local ; v. Scoresby.

Sorrel, Sorrell.—Nick. 'the sorel,' a nickname of complexion, of a reddish-brown colour. O.F. *sor*, dim. sorel ; cf. Blondel, Burnell, Russell ; v. Sor.

John Sorel, co. Oxf., 1273. A.
Robert Sorel. J.
Richard Sorel, c. 1300. M.
'Sorrell Tempest, Whit Tempest, Baye Tempest,' names of three horses, 1526, belonging to Tempest family: Whitaker's Craven, p. 403.
1684. Bapt. — Timothy, s. Timothy Sorrell: St. Jas. Clerkenwell, i. 310.

1797. Married — John Sorrill and Rachel Haslewood : St. Geo. Han. Sq. ii. 160.
London, 1, 9 ; MDB. (co. Essex), 0, 6 ; Philadelphia, 1, 2.

Sorsby.—Local ; v. Scoresby.

Sotham ; v. Southam.

Sotheran ; v. Southern.

Sotherton, Southerton. — Local, 'of Sotherton,' a parish in co. Suffolk.

1581. John Sotherton or Southerton, co. Middlesex : Reg. Univ. Oxf. vol. ii. pt. ii. p. 103.
1601. Bapt. — Alexander, s. George Sotherton : St. Jas. Clerkenwell, i. 38.
1607. Nowel Sotherton, Norwich : FF. iv. 317.
London, 0, 1 ; New York, 0, 1.

Soulby. — Local, 'of Soulby,' a township in the parish of Dacre, co. Cumberland ; also a chapelry in the parish of Kirkby Stephen, co. Westmoreland.

1795. Married—John Soulby and Alice Houghton : St. Mary Ulverston, p. 440.
Liverpool, 2 ; Ulverston, 1 ; London, 1.

Sounes ; v. Sones.

Sour. — Nick. 'the sour,' i.e. sour-visaged or sour-tempered.

Gilbert le Sour, co. Camb., 1273. A.
New York, 2.

Sourbutts ; v. Sowerbutts.

Sourmilk. — Nick. 'a sour-tempered girl' ; cf. Milksop.

Alicia Sowremilke, 1379 : P. T. Yorks. p. 197.

Souster.—Occup. 'the souster,' a female shoemaker, fem. suffix -*ster* (v. Soutar) ; cf. Yorkshire Spenster (for Spenser) and Slaster (for Slater). 'Sewstare or Sowstare, *sutrix*': Prompt. Parv. Not an englished form of German Schuster, but of independent English origin.

Emma le Sowester, C. R., 35 Edw. I.
William Sewster, temp. Hen. VIII. F.
Alicia Seuster, 1379 : P. T. Yorks. p. 63.
1796. Married—Thomas Souster and Eliz. Coleman: St. Geo. Han. Sq. ii. 142.
London, 3.

Soutar, Souter, Soutter.— Occup. 'the souter,' i.e. shoemaker. Till lately in use in North England ; cf. Souter-gate in

Ulverston, North Lanc. (i. e. the shoemaker's road). 'Sowtare or cordewaner': Prompt. Parv.

'Sowters and shepherdes.'
        Piers Plowman.
'Cesse (Cecilia), the souteresse.'
                 ibid.
' Also, everych sowtere that maketh shon of newe rothes lether,' &c.: Usages of Winchester (English Gilds), p. 359.

John le Suter, co. Camb., 1273. A.
William le Sutere, co. Camb., ibid.
Johannes de Morton, *souter*, 1379 : P. T. Yorks. p. 249.
Johannes Schether, *souter*, 1379 : ibid.
Johannes Sowter, *sutor*, 1379 : ibid. p. 301.
Adam Souterson, *souter*, 1379 : ibid. p. 239.
Robert le Souter, c. 1300. M.
David le Souter, ibid.
London, 1, 6, 6 ; New York, 0, 1, 3.

South.—Local, ' of the south' ; cf. West, North, Southern, Western, &c.

William de la Sothe, co. Devon, 1273. A.
Maurice bi Suthe, co. Oxf., ibid.
Willelmus del Soth, 1379 : P. T. Yorks. p. 37.
Thomas de Sowth, 1379 : ibid. p. 269.
1664. Bapt. — Richard, s. Richard South : St. Jas. Clerkenwell, i. 223.
London, 16 ; Philadelphia, 15.

Southall, Southal. — Local, ' of Southall,' a chapelry in the parish of Hayes, co. Middlesex.

Nicholas de Suthalle, co. Norf., 1273. A.
1563. Eliz. Southall, co. Norf. : FF. v. 370.
1799. Married — John Southall and Mary Clark : St. Geo. Han. Sq. ii. 209.
London, 5, 0 ; New York, 0, 1.

Southam, Sotham.—Local, ' of Southam,' a parish and market-town in co. Warwick ; also a hamlet in the parish of Bishop's Cleeve, co. Glouc.

Thomas de Sutham, co. Oxf., 1273. A.
1388. John de Southam, rector of West Walton, co. Norf. : FF. ix. 141.
1666. Bapt. — Nicolas, s. Nicolas Southam : St. Jas. Clerkenwell, i. 229.
London, 2, 0 ; Philadelphia, 0, 1.

Southcott, Southcote. — Local, ' of Southcote.' Lower says, 'A tithing near Reading, co. Berks' (Patr. Brit. p. 324). There is also Southcoates, a township in the parish of Drypool, E. Rid. Yorks. In spite of this it is probable that the surname is of Devonshire descent, and represents some estate in that county bearing this name, *-cote* (an enclosure) being a common West-England suffix.

Richard de Suthcote, co. Wilts, 1273. A.
Walter Sowthcott, *chaplain*, 1513 : Reg. Univ. Oxf. i. 86.
1586. Richard Southcott, co. Devon : ibid. vol. ii. pt. ii. p. 155.
1595. John Southcote, co. Devon : ibid. p. 210.
London, 4, 0 ; MDB. (co. Devon), 2, 1 ; Philadelphia, 4, 0.

Southern, Sotheran, Southerne, Southren.—Local, ' the southern,' from the south. M.E. *sothern*.

'But trusteth wel, I am a sothern man.'
          Chaucer, C. T. 17342.

Naturally the surname is found in the North and not the South ; v. Western.

Willelmus Sothorn, 1379 : P. T. Yorks. p. 285.
Willelmus Sotheron, 1379 : ibid. p. 118.
Johannes Sotheron, 1379 : ibid. p. 13.
Ricardus Sothryn, 1379 : ibid. p. 25.
1586. Bapt.—Anne, d. John Sotherne : St. Dionis Backchurch, p. 86.
1587. — Mary Sotherne, d. William Southerne (sic) : ibid. p. 87.
John Southerine, 1588 : Reg. St. Dionis Backchurch (London), p. 87.
London, 4, 1, 0, 0 ; West Rid. Court Dir., 2, 0, 1, 1 ; Boston (U.S.), 3, 0, 0, 0.

Southerton ; v. Sotherton.

Southerwood, Southern-wood.—Local, ' at the southernwood,' from residence thereby ; cf. Norwood and Eastwood ; cf. also Southwood, a parish in co. Norfolk, four miles and a half from Acle.

1547. William Southerwood and Eliz. Whyskerd : Marriage Lic. (London), i. 10.
1663. John Southearnwood and Elinor Hickson : Marriage Alleg. (Canterbury), p. 110.
1803. Married—Thomas Harrison and Ann Southernwood : St. Geo. Han. Sq. ii. 274.
London, 1, 0 ; MDB. (co. Bucks), 0, 1.

Southey.—Local, 'of Southea,' a parish in the dioc. of Ely, co. Hunts.

Beatrice de Suthae, co. Norf., 1273. A.
Geoffrey de Suthae, co. Norf., ibid.
John de Southeye, co. Soms., 1 Edw. III : Kirby's Quest, p. 255.

1746. Married — Henry Southey and Dorcas Southey : St. Geo. Han. Sq. i. 36.
London, 12 ; MDB. (co. Devon), 7.

Southgate.—Local, ' of Southgate,' a parish in co. Middlesex, near London.

1349. Roger de Southgate, rector of Swainsthorp, co. Norf. : FF. v. 61.
1353. John de Southgate, rector of Barmere, co. Norf. : ibid. vii. 4.
Thomas de Southgate, 1379 ; P. T. Yorks. p. 119.
1790. Married—Christopher Southgate and Ann Mason : St. Geo. Han. Sq. ii. 47.
London, 14 ; MDB. (co. Suffolk), 4 ; Philadelphia, 1 ; Boston (U.S.), 2.

Southouse. — Local, ' of the salthouse' ; v. Salthouse. *Saut* is still a Northern provincialism for salt ; cf. Dutch *zout*, salt.

1345. John de Southouse, co. Norf. : FF. ii. 365.
Simon del Southouse, 1379 : P. T. Yorks. p. 254.
William Sauthowse, 1512 : HHH. p. 61.
1658. Martin Southouse, co. Norf. : FF. vi. 232.
1742. Married—Henry Southouse and Jane Munden : Canterbury Cath. p. 85.
London, 1 ; MDB. (co. Hants), 1.

Southrey.—Local, ' of Southery,' a parish in co. Norfolk.

Robert de Suthereye, co. Wilts, 1273. A.
Henry de Suthereye, co. Norf., ibid.
William de Suthery, co. Norf., 15 Edw. II : FF. ii. 183.
Philadelphia, 2.

Southward ; v. Southworth.

Southwell.—Local, ' of Southwell,' a market-town and parish in co. Notts.

1474. Richard de Southewell, co. Norf. : FF. viii. 57.
1592. Bapt.—Henry, s. Richard Sowthwell : St. Jas. Clerkenwell, i. 176.
1664. Married—Robert Southwell and Eliz. Dering : Kensington Ch. p. 77.
London, 8 ; Philadelphia, 8.

Southwick.—Local, 'of Southwick,' parishes in cos. Northants, Southants, and Sussex ; also a chapelry in the parish of North Bradley, co. Wilts ; also a township in the parish of Monkwearmouth, co. Durham.

William de Suthewyk, co. Hunts, 1273. A.
1617. Buried—Eliz. Southwaike : St. Jas. Clerkenwell, iv. 139.
1699. Married — Daniell Southwicke and Eliz. Taylor : St. Peter, Cornhill, ii. 62.
Philadelphia, 8.

Southwood.—Local, 'of South-wold,' a seaport and parish in co. Suffolk, in mediaeval times frequently described as Southwood. In the Hundred Rolls (1273) the following varieties of the name of the town occur: Suthwald, Suthwaud, Suthwode, Suthwold, Sutwaud (v. Index Locorum, vol. ii. p. 899).

Roger de Suthwode, London, 1273. A.
1443. Thomas Southwood, co. Norf.: FF. ii. 320.
1520. John Southwood, rector of Witchingham, co. Norf.: ibid. viii. 311.
1790. Married — Augustus Caesar Manning and Jane Southwood: St. Geo. Han. Sq. ii. 50.
London, 1.

Southworth, Southward.—Local, 'of Southworth,' a township in the parish of Winwick, co. Lanc.

1587. Thomas Southworth, of Winwick, co. Lanc.: Wills at Chester, i. 180.
1591-2. John Sothworth, co. Lanc.: Reg. Univ. Oxf. vol. ii. pt. ii. p. 189.
1599. Henry Southworth, of Witton, yeoman: Wills at Chester, i. 180.
1607. Robert Southworth of Warrington: ibid.
1615. Edmund Sowthworth, co. Yorks: Reg. Univ. Oxf. vol. ii. pt. ii. p. 337.
MDB. (co. Ches.), 1, 1; London, 2, 0; Liverpool, 2, 2; Philadelphia, 6, 0; Boston (U.S.), 18, 6.

Soutter; v. Soutar.

Sowden, Sowdon, Soudon.—Local, 'of Suddon,' i.e. the south down; cf. Sudlow, &c., a well-known West-country name.

Walter de Suddon, co. Soms., 1 Edw. III: Kirby's Quest, p. 115.
London, 2, 1, 0; Philadelphia, 12, 0, 0.

Sowerbutts, Sourbutts.—? Local. This looks very like a nickname. A brewer of bad beer would easily acquire the title. Nevertheless, it may be but a compound of butt, a mark to shoot at, and represent some long-forgotten spot. It is a Lancashire surname, and is still familiar to that county. It sprang up in the neighbourhood of Preston.

Robert Sowerbutts, 1682: Preston Guild Rolls, p. 177.
James Sowerbutts, 1682: ibid.

The earlier form is found in the following:

William Sowerbutt, of Cadate Field (Preston), 1559.
Cecilia Sorbutt, of Chepyn, 1562.

In the same record a hundred years later appears:
Arthur Sowerbutts, of Ribchester (near Preston), 1676: Lancashire Wills at Richmond, i. 260.
Preston, 3, 0; London, 3, 0; Manchester, 4, 0; Liverpool, 1, 1.

Sowerby.—Local, 'of Sowerby.' Chapelries in parishes of Thirsk and Halifax (2), townships in cos. Westmoreland and Lancaster.

Stephen de Soureby, co. York, 1273. A.
Thomas de Sawreby, 1379: P. T. Yorks. p. 87.
Johannes de Saureby, 1379: ibid. p. 89.
1597. Thomas Sowerbye, co. Camb.: Reg. Univ. Oxf. vol. ii. pt. ii. p. 221.
1609. Francis Sowerby, co. Durham: ibid. p. 307.
London, 8; MDB. (co. Durham), 4; Philadelphia, 6.

Sowter.—Occup. 'the shoemaker'; v. Soutar.

London, 3.

Spackman; v. Speakman.

Spafford.—Local; v. Spofforth.

Manchester, 1; Philadelphia, 1; New York, 3.

Spain.—Local, 'of Spain.' A very early incomer; cf. Portingale.

Michael de Ispania, co. Oxf., 1273. A.
John de Ispania, co. Hunts, ibid.
William de Spayne, co. Salop, ibid.
Henricus de Ispania, Pipe Roll, 11 Hen. II. p. 47.
Willelmus del Spayn, 1379: P. T. Yorks. p. 25.
John de Spayn, 1379: ibid.
1652. Married—John Fillpott and Mary Spaine: Canterbury Cath. p. 58.
London, 5; Philadelphia, 7.

Spalding, Spaulding.—Local, 'of Spalding,' a parish in co. Linc.

Ralph de Spaldinge, co. Hunts, 1273. A.
Ida de Spaldingge, co. Camb., ibid.
Robertus de Spaldyng, 1379: P. T. Yorks. p. 48.
Margareta de Spaldyng, 1379: ibid. p. 101.
1808. Married — William Williams, otherwise Spalding, and Maria Davis: St. Geo. Han. Sq. ii. 379.
London, 3, 0; Philadelphia, 6, 1; New York, 5, 20.

Spanald.—Local. Spanish, a Spaniard; cf. spaniel, a dog.

O. F. espqgneul, a spaniel. v. Spain.

Willelmus Spanald, Isabella uxor ejus, 1379: P. T. Yorks. p. 166.

Spaniard.—Local, from Spain, q. v.

William Spanyard, Close Roll, 6 Ric. II. pt. ii.

Sparham.—Local, ' of Sparham,' a parish in co. Norfolk, three miles from Reepham.

Geoffrey de Sparham, co. Norf., 1273. A.
William de Sparham, of Sparham, temp. Ric. I: FF. viii. 258.
1754. Married—William Sparham and Catherine Williams: St. Geo. Chap. Mayfair, p. 275.
London, 1.

Sparhawk; v. Spark, where references will be found.

1694-5. Mark Anthony and Mary Sparhauke: Marriage Lic. (Faculty Office), p. 214.
Philadelphia, 6.

Spark, Sparke, Sparks, Sparkes.—(1) Bapt. 'the son of Sparrowhawk'; found as early as Domesday in the forms Sperhauoc (co. Notts), Sparhauoc (co. Suffolk). (2) Nick. 'the sparrow-hawk.' M.E. sperhauke (Piers Plowman).

Sparheuk Sutor, co. Suff., 1273. A.
Thomas Sperheuk, co. Linc., ibid.
Nicholas Sparke, co. Norf., ibid.
Bartholomeus fil. Sparhavec, co. Norf., temp. Hen. II: FF. ix. 206.
Gilbert Sperhauk, co. Soms., 1 Edw. III: Kirby's Quest, p. 125.
John Sparhauk, rector of St. Buttolph the Abbot, Norwich, 1351: FF. iv. 442.
Magota Spark, 1379: P. T. Yorks. p. 154.
Robertus Spark, 1379: ibid. p. 14.
Olive Sparrehawke, temp. Eliz. Z.
Richard Sparhawke, rector of Fincham, 1534: FF. vii. 358.
1632-3. Married — Johan Sparrowhawke: St. Dionis Backchurch (London).
'The learned Dr. Fuller, being in company of one Mr. Sparrowhawk, unwittingly asked him, "What is the difference between an owl and a sparrowhawk?" and it is said that he received the unexpected reply, "An owl is fuller in the head, fuller in the face, and FULLER all over"': T. E. Bailey's Life of Thomas Fuller, p. 3.
1777. Married—Thomas Sparrowhawke and Susannah Hampton: St. Geo. Han. Sq. i. 279.
London, 4, 1, 26, 3; West Rid. Court Dir., 2, 1, 0, 0; Philadelphia, 1, 0, 51, 0.

Sparrow.—Nick. 'the sparrow.' A common sobriquet in

Z z

mediaeval registers. A homely, chirpy disposition would readily give rise to the surname.

John Sparuwe, co. Oxf., 1273. A.
Laurence Sparwe, co. Camb., ibid.
Hugh Sparewe, co. Camb., ibid.
Rogerus Sparowe, 1379: P. T. Yorks. p. 25.
Adam Sparowe, 1379: ibid. p. 51.
1529-30. Robert Sparrow and Eliz. Fest: Marriage Lic. (London), i. 7.
1572. Married—Francys Sparrowe and Jone Mahewe: Reg. St. Dionis Backchurch, p. 7.
London, 20; New York, 6.

Sparrowhawk, Sparhawk.
—(1) Nick.; (2) Bapt.; v. Spark.
'Charles Sparrowhawk, dealer, was charged with the unlawful possession of two ponies': Standard, Aug. 27, 1888, p. 2.
Philadelphia, 0, 6.

Sparshott.—Local, 'of Sparsholt,' parishes in cos. Berks and Hants. *-holt* (q. v.) as a suffix sometimes becomes *-hott*; cf. Aldershot. But v. Shute (2).

1744. Married — Thomas Sparshott and Jane Brathwait: St. Geo. Chap. Mayfair, p. 38.
1794. — Charles Bowden and Elizabeth Sparshatt: St. Geo. Han. Sq. ii. 120.
London, 1; Boston (U.S.), 1.

Spaulding; v. Spalding.

Spawforth.—Local; v. Spofforth.

London, 2.

Speakman, Spackman, Speckman.—Bapt. 'the son of Speakman.' There is not the slightest trace of an occupative or official origin. It must be set in the same class as Bateman and Tiddiman, all used as personal or baptismal names. It is, and has been for centuries, a familiar surname in co. Lanc.

Henry Spakeman, co. Kent, 1273. A.
Isolda Spekeman, co. Oxf., ibid.
Richard Spekeman, co. Oxf., ibid.
John Speakman, of Astley, *husband-man*, 1578: Wills at Chester (1545-1620), p. 181.
1717. Buried—John Godman, lodger at Mr. Spackman's: St. Dionis Backchurch, p. 287.
London, 2, 3, 0; Manchester, 8, 0, 0; Philadelphia, 15, 9, 2.

Spear; v. Spyer.

Speck.—Nick. 'le spec' or 'le speke,' the woodpecker; v. Speke

(2), and v. glossary to Geraldus Cambrensis, vi. 125, 'dicitur autem picus avicula lingua gallica "spec" dicta.'

William le Spek, co. Devon, 1273. A.
1642. Buried—Joane, wife of Zachary Speck: St. Peter, Cornhill, i. 199.
1750. Married—Joseph Speck and Eliz. Leathwait: St. Michael, Cornhill, p. 72.
London, 3; Philadelphia, 18.

Speckman; v. Speakman.

Speechley, Speechly.—Local, 'of Spetchley,' a parish in co. Worcester, near Worcester.

1770. Married—William Speechly and Mary Chell: St. Geo. Han. Sq. i. 209.
London, 2, 3; MDB. (co. Camb.), 1, 2.

Speed, Speedy.—? Bapt. Probably a font-name, wishing prosperity or good-speed to the child. The original meaning of speed is 'success.' If not this, it must be a nickname, significant of the quick, hasty movements of the first ancestor. If baptismal, Speedy is but a pet-form, as in the case of Charlie, Tommy, Willy, &c.

Johannes Sped, co. Suff., 1273. A.
Margaret Sped, co. Camb., ibid.
Roger Sped, co. Oxf., ibid.
1555-6. John Speede and Eliz. Cheynye: Marriage Lic. (London), i. 17.
Cicilie Speed, of Tattenhall, *widow*, 1578: Wills at Chester (1545-1620), p. 181.
London, 7, 3; Manchester, 3, 0; Philadelphia, 5, 1.

Speer; v. Spyer.

Speight, Speaight.— Nick. 'the speight' or specht, an old English name for the woodpecker.

Matilda Speght, 1379: P. T. Yorks. p. 185.
Hugo Speght, 1376: ibid.
Johanna Spite, 1379: ibid. p. 191.
John Spight, co. York. W. 16.
Richard Speight, co. York. W. 16.
1540. Buried — Richard Speite: St. Antholin (London), p. 1.
West Rid. Court Dir., 9, 0; London, 4, 2; Philadelphia, 2, 0; New York, 2, 2.

Speke, Speak, Speake.—(1) Local, 'of Speke,' a township in the parish of Childwall, co. Lanc.

Hugh Pilkington, of Speke, 1603: Wills at Chester (1545-1620), p. 153.
Ellen Speake, of Dinckley, *widow*, 1614: ibid. p. 181.
Charles Speak, of Goldshawe, 1670: ibid. (1660-80), p. 252.

(2) Nick. Lower says, 'The Spekes of Somersetshire descend from Richard le Espek, who lived in the reign of Henry II. Wemworthy and Brampton, in Devonshire, were the original seats; but temp. Hen. VI Sir John Speke married the heiress of Beauchamp, and so obtained Whitelackington, co. Somerset': Patr. Brit. p. 325. This surname has a distinct origin. It stands for 'le speke,' the woodpecker, and is a nickname of the same class as Nightingale, Lark, Sparrowhawk, &c. (v. Geraldus Cambrensis, vi. 125). For an early instance v. Speck, which is but a variant of the same name.

1701. Bapt. — Samuel, s. Richard Speake: St. Jas. Clerkenwell, ii. 1.
1725. Married—John Farrey and Mary Speake: St. Antholin (London), p. 140.
London, 1, 0, 0; Manchester, 0, 1, 0; Liverpool, 1, 0, 0; MDB. (co. Somerset), 2, 0, 0; Philadelphia, 0, 1, 1; Boston (U.S.), 0, 2, 0.

Speller, Spellar.—Occup. 'the speller.' Probably refers to the teacher, not the taught. One who spells the letters for the child to learn (v. Grammer). 'Spellare, *sillabicator*': Prompt. Parv. If the earlier sense of *spell*, a discourse, a story, originated the name, then the speller would be a professional story-teller. The surnames Speller and Spelman, q.v., are now well established.

Ralph le Speoler, co. Soms., 1 Edw. III: Kirby's Quest, p. 256.
Gerard le Speller. H.
Miles le Speller, C. R., 35 Edw. I.
Thomas Spellere, C. R., 19 Ric. II.
Thomas Speller, 1379: P. T. Yorks. p. 300.
Johannes Speller, 1379: ibid.
London, 5, 1; New York, 1, 0.

Spelman, Spellman.—Bapt. 'the son of Spileman.' I am much tempted to set the name beside Speller, but saving in one or two cases all the entries have it Spileman, without prefix *le*. I think it must go as a personal name with Bateman, Tiddiman, &c. Cf. the German Spielmann; v. Speakman.

John Speleman, co. Notts, 1273. A.
William Speleaman, co. Wilts, ibid.
Eustace Spileman, co. Oxf., ibid.

There are nine entries of Spile-man in the Hundred Rolls, repre-senting five counties.

Richard Spileman, co. Wilts, Hen. III-Edw. I. K.
Nicholas Spilman, co. Wilts, ibid.
Thomas Spyleman, C. R., 44 Hen. III. pt. i.
John Speleman, co. Soms., 1 Edw. III : Kirby's Quest, p. 133.
Roger Spileman, co. Soms., 1 Edw. III : ibid. p. 219.
London, 1, 0 ; Philadelphia, 0, 4.

Spence, Spens.—Local, 'at the spence.' The custodian of the store-room. A store-room, a store-closet, in small farms a cupboard. v. Spencer.

West Rid. Court Dir., 10, 0 ; Crockford, 5, 1 ; London, 20, 0 ; Philadelphia, 55, 0.

Spencer, Spenser.—Offic. A house-steward, one who, strictly speaking, had charge of the buttery or spence. In the Sumner's Tale the glutton is well described as :
'All vinolent as botel in the spence.'
while Mr. Halliwell quotes :
'Yet had I lever she and I
Were both together secretly
In some corner in the spence.'
In an inventory of household goods, dated 1574, I find the furniture of the hall first described, and this begins : 'A cupboard and a spence, 20s.' (Richmondshire Wills, p. 248). The office of 'la despencer' or 'la spencer' was amongst the highest in the king's household, and proportionately great among the barons. Practi-cally such a name as 'Thomas de la Spence' was as official as 'Thomas la Spencer,' but, as in similar in-stances elsewhere, I have set it down as local.

John le Spencer, co. Southampton, 1273. A.
Henry le Spenser, co. Camb., ibid.
Henry del Spens, 1292 : KKK. p. xli.
Thomas del Spens : Patent Rolls, 4 Edw. III. pt. ii.
Nicholas de la Despense, C. R., 4 Edw. III.
Thomas Spenser, 1379 : P. T. Yorks. p. 56.
Agnes Spenser, 1379 : ibid. p. 25.
West Rid. Court Dir., 25, 2 ; Crockford, 41, 0 ; London, 92, 1 ; Philadelphia, 86, 0.

Spender. — Official, 'one who spends money'; cf. Spenser or Spencer. '*Dispensier*, a spender,

also a cater, or clarke of a kitchen' (Cotgrave, quoted by Skeat).

Johannes Spender, *husband*, et Anabilla uxor ejus, 1379 : P. T. Howdenshire, p. 14.
1577-8. James Spender and Johanna Godfrey : Marriage Lic. (London), i. 79.
London, 2.

Spendlove, Spendlow, Spindelow.—Nick. or personal, 'the son of Spenlof.' No doubt of Scandinavian origin ; cf. *spend-thrift*, a 'spend-all.'

Alicia Spendelove, co. Camb., 1273. A.
William Spendelove, co. Oxf., ibid.
Thomas Spenloff, 1379 : P. T. Yorks. p. 291.
Robertus Spenlof, 1379 : ibid.
Johannes Spendlove, 1379 : ibid. p. 258.
'The heir of Robert Spendelufe holds half a bovate of land,' 23 Edw. III. Knight's Fees of Blakeburnshire : Baines' Lanc. ii. 693.

With the corrupted Spendlow, cf. Waddilove and Waddilow.

1593. Bapt.—Susan, d. William Spende-lowe : St. Jas. Clerkenwell, i. 27.
1598. — Mary, d. William Spendeloe : ibid. p. 33.
1602. — Joseph, s. William Spendlove : ibid. p. 40.
London, 2, 0, 2 ; MDB. (co. Derby), 6, 0, 0.

Spens(er ; v. Spence(r.

Spenster.—Offic. 'the spencer,' with fem. suffix -*ster* ; cf. Yorkshire Slaster for Slater, also *spinster* for *spinner.*

Thomas Spenster, 1379 : P. T. Yorks. p. 136.

Sperling, Sperlings, Spil-ling, Spillings, Spurling, Spillin.—Bapt. 'the son of Spirling,' one of the endless suffixes in -*ing* ; cf. Browning, Harding, &c. The *s* in Sperlings and Spil-lings is the genitive, as in Williams, Jones, Simmonds, &c. The only other possible origin is a nickname ; German *sperling*, a sparrow.

Geoffrey Spirling, co. Norf., 1273. A.
Henry Sperling, co. Soms., 1 Edw. III : Kirby's Quest, p. 221.
1631. Bapt. — Dennys, d. Abraham Spillinge : St. Jas. Clerkenwell, i. 118.
MDB. (Suffolk), 0, 2, 1, 1, 1, 0 ; London, 1, 0, 0, 0, 4, 0 ; Philadelphia, 2, 0, 0, 0, 1, 2.

Sperring.—Bapt. ; v. Spiring.

Spicer.—Occup. 'the spicer,' the earlier term for the modern grocer. Thus spices meant various kinds. Latin, *species.*

'Spycers speken with·hym.'
Piers P. 1332.
'Many a dyvers spyse
In bagges about thy bear.'
An old Song, written against the Mendicant Friars.
Simon le Spicere, co. Camb., 1273. A.
William le Spicere, co. Oxf., ibid.
William Speciar, co. Linc., ibid.
Sacr le Spicer. N.
Amphelisa le Spicer. O.
Richard le Spycer, co. Soms., 1 Edw. III : Kirby's Quest, p. 254.
Ricardus Chapman, *spicer*, 1379 : P. T. Yorks. p. 25.
Adam Spisar, *spicer*, 1379 : ibid. p. 27.
Giliaum Spyser, 1379 : ibid. p. 89.
London, 21 ; Philadelphia, 26.

Spichfat, Pichfatt.— ? Nick. 'Bacon-fat' (?). This derisive sobri-quet seems to have died out, but many instances occur :

William Spichefat, Close Roll, 7 Edw. II.
Benedict Spichfat, C. R., 6 Edw. III.
Robert Spichfat. X.
William Spichfat. W. 11.

These represent separate dis-tricts, north and south. 'Spyk, or set flesche (spike of fleshe), *popa*' : Prompt. Parv. 'A spycke of a bacon flycke' : Skelton, quoted by Halliwell ; cf. Hogsflesh and Pigsflesh (q.v.). Found as Pichfatt.

1684. Married — Richard Kirby and Mary Pichfatt : St. Michael, Cornhill (Harl. Soc.).
1735. — Charles Pickfatt and Jane Corr : St. Jas. Clerkenwell, iii. 263.

Spicknell, Spickernell. — Offic. 'the spigurnel,' a sealer of writs. Geoffrey Spigurnell pos-sessed this office in the reign of Henry III (Bailey's Dict. 1742).

Edmund Spigurnel, co. Notts, 1273. A.
Nicholas Spigurnel, co. Suff., ibid.
Nicholas Spikernel, co. Norf., ibid.
Henry Spigurnel, co. Kent, 20 Edw. I. R.
Matilda Sprygonell, 1379 : P. T. Yorks. p. 151.
Roger Spygurnel, co. Soms., 1 Edw. III : Kirby's Quest, p. 124.
London, 1, 0 ; MDB. (co. Hants), 0, 3.

Spier, Spiers ; v. Spyer.

Spillin, Spilling, Spillings ; v. Sperling.

Spillman.—Bapt. 'the son of Spileman'; v. Spellman.

London, 3.

Spilsbury.—Local, 'of Spels-bury,' a parish in co. Oxford, near Chipping Norton.

1621. John Spilsbury, co. Worc. ; Reg. Univ. Oxf. vol. ii. pt. ii. p. 389.

1633. Bapt.—Thomas, s. Thomas Spils-burie : St. Geo. Han. Sq. ii. 232.
1801. Married—Edgar Ashe Spilsbury and Emma Gybbon : ibid.
London, 1.

Spindelow; v. Spendlove.

Spink, Spinks.—Nick. 'the spink,' i.e. the chaffinch or gold-finch ; cf. Goldspink. A.S. *finc*, a finch ; Ger. *fink* ; Prov. Eng. *spink*. Spinks is a genitive form (cf. Williams, Styles, Brooks, &c.).

Nicholas Spinc, co. Bedf., 1273. A.
Emma Spink, co. Norf., ibid.
Johannes Spink, 1379 : P. T. Yorks. p. 100 (common in this Roll).
Hugo Spynk, 1379 : ibid. p. 208.
Willelmus Spynk, 1379 : ibid.

Pye, Cock, and Fox occur along-side these two entries.

1620. Bapt.—John, s. Edward Spinck : St. Jas. Clerkenwell, i. 89.
1788. Married — Joseph Spinks and Mary Popell : St. Geo. Hanover Sq. ii. 7.
London, 11, 9 ; West Rid. Court Dir., 5, 0 ; Sheffield, 2, 0 ; Philadelphia, 6, 0.

Spinner.—Occup. 'the spinner' ; v. Wheelspinner.

Michael le Spinner, co. Soms., 1 Edw. III : Kirby's Quest, p. 177.
Cristiana Spyner, 1379 : P. T. Yorks. p. 93.
Alicia Spynner, 1379 : ibid. p. 124.
New York, 7 ; Philadelphia, 1.

Spire ; v. Spyer.

Spirett, Spurrett.—Bapt. 'the son of Spirhard.'

Leticia Spirold, co. Saff., 1273. A.
Philip Spirhard, co. Norf., ibid.
Ricardus Spyrad, 1379 : P. T. Yorks. p. 140.
Johannes Spirard, 1379 : ibid.
Magota Spirard, 1379 : ibid. p. 151.
Willelmus Spyrad, 1379 : ibid. p. 203.
1338. Robert Spirhard, rector of Ful-modeston, co. Norf. : FF. vii. 90.
1349. Peter Spirhead, co. Norf. : ibid. v. 445.
1802. Married — Richard Dyas and Mary Spurrett : St. Geo. Han. Sq. ii. 270.
West Rid. Court Dir., 3, 0 ; London, 0, 1.

Spiring, Sperring. — Bapt. 'the son of Spiring' ; cf. Brown-ing, Harding, &c.

Reginald Spiring, co. Soms., 1 Edw. III : Kirby's Quest, p. 190.
1665-6. Roger Spering and Helen Skin-ner : Marriage Alleg. (Canterbury), p. 161.
London, 1, 2.

Spittle, Spittal, Spittall.—Local, 'at the spittle,' i.e. hospital.
Spittleman.—Offic. ' the spittle-man,' a guardian or attendant at a hospital. **Spittlehouse.**—Local, 'at the spittle-house,' from residence at the lodge of the hospital. This little batch of names is connected with the hospitals of mediaeval times ; cf. the local Spitalfields, London. 'A spittle, hospitall, or lazar-house' : Baret, 1580 (quoted by Skeat, v. *spittle*).

Gilbert de Hospitall, co. Oxf., 1273. A.
William Spitelman, co. Norf., Hen. III-Edw. I. K.
Richard atte Spitale, 1301. M.
Adam del Hospital, Fines Roll, 12 Edw. I.
Robert Spitelman, Close Roll, 39 Hen. III. pt. i.
Robert del Spitelle, C. R., 3 Hen. V.
Thomas atte Spytell, C. R., 11 Hen. VI.
Johannes del Spitilhous', 1379 : P. T. Yorks. p. 55.
Robertus de Spitell', 1379 : ibid. p. 157.

It is interesting to notice that Spittlehouse, occurring as we have just seen in Yorkshire, is still found in that county five hundred years after.

' Esau Spittlehouse, beer-retailer, Brookhouse, Laughton-en-le-Morthen' : West Rid. Yorkshire Directory.
1578. Buried—Antony Spittell : Reg. St. Dionis Backchurch, p. 195.
London, 2, 0, 0, 0, 0 ; MDB. (Yorks, West Rid.), 0, 0, 0, 0, 1 ; (co. Leic.), 0, 0, 0, 0, 1 ; Philadelphia, 0, 0, 7, 0, 0 ; New York (Spittle), 1.

Splatt.—Local, 'at the splott' or splatt, from residence thereby. '*Splat*, a row of pins as they are set upon the paper. Co. Somerset' (Halliwell). Thus *splatt* may have implied a row of cottages.

William atte Splotte, co. Soms., 1 Edw. III : Kirby's Quest, p. 216.
Hugh atte Splotte, 1379, co. Soms., 1 Edw. III : ibid. p. 246.

With the form Splot, cf. Sprott and Spratt.

London, 1 ; Philadelphia, 1.

Spofforth, Spofford.—Local, ' of Spofforth,' a parish near Knaresborough, co. Yorks. It has taken in surnames the forms of Spawforth and Spafford, q.v. (ford = forth). Thus in the P. T. Yorks. 1379, Clifford is found as Clifforth ; v. Forth.

Robert de Spofford, *seler*, 3 Edw. II : Freemen of York, i. 13.
Johannes de Spofford, 1379 : P. T. Yorks. p. 222.
Willelmus de Spoford, 1379 : ibid. p. 88.
Robertus de Spofford, 1379 : ibid. p. 301.
London, 3, 1 ; Philadelphia, 0, 1 ; Boston (U.S.), 0, 17.

Spon, Spong.—Local, ' at the spong,' from residence thereby. '*Spong*, an irregular, narrow, projecting part of a field, whether planted or in grass' : Moor (Halliwell's Dict.). 'A boggy wet place. Norfolk' (Halliwell's Dict.).

Ricardus del Spon, 1376 : P. T. Yorks. p. 193.
1741. Bapt. — George, s. George Spong : St. Geo. Chap. Mayfair, p. 3.
1749. Married — John Sponge and Martha Hatt : ibid. 143.
1802. — Thomas Spong and Jane Mary Ann Brooks : St. Geo. Han. Sq. ii. 266.
London, 1, 7.

Spooner.—Occup. 'the spooner,' a maker of spoons ; an important manufacture when no forks were used, and so many messes, stews, soups, &c., were popular ; cf. Cutler and Nasmith.

Robertus Sponer, 1379 : P. T. Yorks. p. 82.
Willelmus Sponer, 1379 : ibid. p. 127.
Henricus Spuner, 1379 : ibid. p. 266.
' 1585. Buried—John Sponer (Spooner)' —thus entered : St. Jas. Clerkenwell, iv. 33.
1625. John Spooner and Florence Fryer : Marriage Lic. (London), ii. 160.
1728. Married — Henry Spooner and Mary Taylor : St. Mary Aldermary, p. 41.
London, 24 ; Philadelphia, 8.

Spottiswood, Spottiswoode, Spottswood.—Local, 'of Spottis-woode.' 'The name is derived from the barony of Spottiswoode. The family were benefactors to the abbeys of Melrose and Kelso in early times. The ancestor ... was Robert de Spottiswood, who was born in the reign of King Alexander III, and died in that of Robert Bruce' (Lower, quoting Burke's Landed Gentry). Spottiswood is in the parish of Gordon, co. Berwick. The American form existed in England at one time.

1613. Robert Spotswood, Exeter Coll.: Reg. Univ. Oxf. i. 275.
MDB. (co. Cumb.), 2, 0, 0 ; London, 0, 2, 0 ; Philadelphia, 0, 0, 3.

Spracklin, Spratling, Sprack-len.—? Bapt. 'the son of Sparkling' ; cf. Harding, Browning, &c.

Robertus Esprakelin, co. Cornwall, Hen. III-Edw. I. K.

Geoffrey Sparkelyng, co. Soms., 1 Edw. III: Kirby's Quest, p. 230.

1645. Bapt. — Robert, s. Mr. Robert Spratling: Canterbury Cath. p. 10.

1652. — Eliz., d. Thomas Spraklin: St. Jas. Clerkenwell, i. 182.

1653. — Adam, s. Mr. Robert Sprackling: Canterbury Cath. p. 10.

London, 1, 1, 0 ; Philadelphia, 0, 0, 1.

Spradbrow, Spradbery. —

Local, ' of Sprotborough,' a parish in W. Rid. Yorks, near Doncaster, a curious corruption ; v. Spratt and Spratley for the derivation of the name ; lit. the borough of Sprot, the first settler.

Thomas Sprotburghe, co. York, 20 Edw. I. R.

Johannes de Sprotburghe, of Sprotburghe, 1379: P. T. Yorks. p. 53.

1632. Bapt., s. Edward Spradbrowe: St. Michael, Cornhill, p. 122.

1656. — Henry, s. William Sprattberry: St. Jas. Clerkenwell, i. 195.

1670. Married—Robert Spredborough and Bridget Cutberd: ibid. p. 170.

London, 0, 2 ; Liverpool, 1, 0.

Spragg, Sprague.—Nick. 'the

spragg,' the quick, the nimble ; v. Sprake.

Ralph Spragg, of Knutsford, co. Ches., 1632 : East Cheshire, ii. 343.

Thomas Spragg, of Great Budworth, 1664 : Wills at Chester (1660-1680), p. 253.

London, 0, 7 ; MDB. (co. Chester), 1, 0 ; Manchester, 2, 0 ; Philadelphia, 0, 11.

Sprake, Spragg, Sprague.—

Nick. 'the sprack,' i.e. the quick, the lively, the active ; *sprack* and *sprag* (West), Halliwell. The surname still lives in co. Somerset. With Sprake and Spragg, cf. Slack and Slagg. The dim. Spraket is also found.

William Spraket, co. Soms., 1 Edw. III: Kirby's Quest, p. 252.

William Sprak, co. Soms., 1 Edw. III: ibid. 253.

1682. Samuell Spragg and Mary Randall : Marriage Alleg. (Canterbury), ii. 116.

1690. Bapt.—Mary, d. Robert Spragg: St. Jas. Clerkenwell, i. 326.

1807. Married — Charles Spragg and Sarah Stevens : St. Geo. Han. Sq. ii. 378.

London, 2, 0, 7 ; MDB. (co. Soms.), 1, 1, 0.

Spratley.—Local, 'of Sproatley,'

a parish in E. Rid. Yorks, seven miles from Hull, lit. the field that belonged to Sprot ; v. Spratt.

1612. Edward Spratley, *cook*, and Ellen Moorton : Marriage Lic. (London), ii. 14.

1795. Married — Thomas Porter and Mary Spratley : St. Geo. Han. Sq. ii. 124.

London, 3 ; MDB. (co. Berks), 2 ; New York, 2.

Spratling ; v. Spracklin.

Spratt, Sproat, Sprott,

Sprout, Sproutt.—Bapt. 'the son of Sprot,' Domesday (co. Derby). For further instances, v. Sproat.

Henry Sprot, co. Camb., 1273. A.

Richard Sprot, co. Oxf., ibid.

Simon Sprot, co. Bedf., ibid.

John Sprot, co. Soms., 1 Edw. III : Kirby's Quest, p. 149.

Agnes Sprote, 1379 : P. T. Yorks. p. 112.

1449. John Sprott de Surlingham, co. Norf.: FF. v. 467.

1582. John Spratte and Eliz. Wheatlye : Marriage Lic. (London), i. 108.

1594. Edward Sprott or Spratt, co. Staff.: Reg. Univ. Oxf. vol. ii. pt. ii. p. 207.

MDB. (co. Soms.), Sprott, 2 ; London, 13, 4, 0, 0, 0 ; Philadelphia, 17, 0, 0, 0, 0 ; New York, 5, 1, 2, 1, 1.

Sprigg, Spriggs.—Bapt. 'the

son of Sprig,' very probably a nick. of the personal name, Sprigin (v. Spriggin). This is the more likely as Sprigg and the genitive Spriggs are found chiefly in the neighbourhood of co. Norfolk, where Spriggins and Spurgeon, &c., arose.

1607. Married — William Sprig, *blacksmith*, and Grace Percye : St. Michael, Cornhill, p. 18.

1632. Buried—Mary Spriggs : St. Jas. Clerkenwell, iv. 205.

1655. — Lidia, wife of John Sprigg : ibid. p. 306.

MDB. (co. Bucks), 1, 1, ; London, 0, 3 ; Philadelphia, 1, 4.

Spriggin, Spriggen, Spriggins, Sprigens.—Bapt. 'the son

of Sprigin,' a variant of the old Norfolk personal name, now immortalized as Spurgeon, q.v. The genitive of Spriggin is Spriggins ; cf. Williams, Jones, Tompkins, &c.

William Sprigin, co. Norf., 1273. A.

Spriginus (without surname), co. Norf., c. 12th cent.: FF. vi. 457.

Roger Spriggens, co. Norf.: ibid. vii. 350.

1559. Buried—Roger Sprigen, servant with John Hawley, draper : St. Michael, Cornhill.

1620. Married—Robert Spriggins and Ann Linnell: St. Jas. Clerkenwell, iii. 48.

1664. — Timothy Spriggin and Edith Lee : ibid. p. 115.

Spurgeon and Spurgin (q.v.) are the modern Norfolk forms of the surname.

London, 0, 0, 0, 1 ; New York, 0, 0, 1, 0.

Springall, Springhall, Springett, Springle.—Nick. or

personal. Either ' the springald,' i. e. an active, alert young man (spring), or ' the son of Springald.' The latter is the more probable.

Julian Springald, co. Oxf., 1273. A.

Walter Springaud, co. Oxf., ibid.

Alan Springold, co. Camb., ibid.

Geoffrey Spurnegold, Fines Roll, 11 Edw. I.

William Spryngold, co. Soms., 1 Edw. III: Kirby's Quest, p. 80.

Alice Spryngot, Pat. Rolls, 4 Edw. III. pt. ii.

1662. Married—Francis Springall and Rhode Padnall : St. Dionis Backchurch, p. 37.

The Manchester Evening News, Dec. 8, 1885, records the murder of an old man named Springhall at Hingham in Norfolk.

London, 2, 1, 2, 1 ; Crockford, 0, 0, 2, 0 ; New York (Springett), 1 ; Boston (U.S.), 4, 0, 0, 0.

Sproat.—Bapt. 'the son of

Sprot,' a Domesday personal name ; v. Spratt, which is a variant.

1628. William Sproate, of Hornby : Lancashire Wills at Richmond, i. 260.

1666. Henry Sprote, of Hornby, ibid.

1616. Christopher Sprote, of Tatham : ibid.

1623. Margaret Sprotte : ibid.

These last two are manifestly of one family. Their descendants are now found invariably as Sproat in co. Lanc.

1733. Christopher Sproat, of Tatham : ibid. ii. 238.

— Susan Sproat, of Tatham : ibid.

Preston, 2 ; New York, 1 ; Boston (U.S.), 2.

Sproston, Sprosson, Sproson. — Local, ' of Sproston,' a

township in the parish of Middlewich, co. Chester. With Sproston and Sprosson, cf. Snelston and Snelson in the same district.

Thomas Cranage, of Sproston, 1618 : Wills at Chester (1505-1620), p. 46.

Ralph Sproston, of Middlewich : ibid. p. 181.

Robert Sproston, of the city of Chester, alderman, 1663 : ibid. (1660-80), p. 253.

1789. Married — John Sproson and Susanna Walker : St. Geo. Han. Sq. ii. 25.

1797. — Samuel Sproston and Eliz. Kendall : ibid. p. 171.

London, 1, 1, 0 ; MDB. (co. Chester), 6, 0, 0 ; New York, 0, 0, 2.

Sprott, Sprout(t ; v. Spratt.

Spurdance, Spurdens. — ? Nick. I cannot trace the origin of this surname. Sometimes the initial s is omitted ; cf. Turges and Sturges. The surname is still found in co. Norfolk.

Richard Purdance, bailiff of Norwich, 1403 : FF. iii. 123.

Richard Spurdaunce, mayor of Norwich, 1420 : ibid. p. 136.

Richard Purdaunce, alderman of Norwich, 1424 : ibid. p. 138.

Richard, Spurdaunce, mayor of Norwich, 1433 : ibid. p. 163.

MDB. (Norfolk), 0, 1.

Spurgeon, Spurgin.—Bapt. 'the son of Sprigin.' There can be little doubt about this. It is evidently an old and long-forgotten Scandinavian personal name. Norfolk is the home. It occurs there so early as 1273. The spelling of the surname is imitative, a copy of *surgeon.* For further instances and proof, v. Spriggin.

William Sprigin, co. Norf., 1273. A.

Simon Sp'ugin, co. Camb., ibid.

Ralph Spraging, 1622 : Marriage Lic. (London), p. 28.

1566. Robert Spurgynne, vicar of Fouldon, co. Norf. : FF. vi. 35.

John Spurgeon, mayor of Yarmouth, 1712 : ibid. xi. 331.

1764. Bapt. — Daniel, s. Daniel Spurgeon : St. Peter, Cornhill, ii. 49.

London, 6, 1 ; MDB. (Norfolk), 6, 2 ; (Suffolk), 1, 1 ; New York, 1, 0 ; Boston (U.S.), 3, 0.

Spurling.—Bapt. ; v. Sperling.

Spurrett.—Bapt. ; v. Spirett.

Spurrier.—Occup. ' the spurrier,' a maker of spurs. I see no instance in the Hundred Rolls of 1273.

Robert de Gisburgh, *sporier*, 26 Edw. I : Freemen of York (Surt. Soc.), i. 7.

Nicholas Sporiare, co. Soms., 1 Edw. III : Kirby's Quest, p. 239.

Nicholas le Sporiere, C. R., 29 Edw. III.

Benedict le Sporier. J.

Nicholas le Sporiere, London. X.

1579. John Spurier, co. Somerset : Reg. Univ. Oxf. vol. ii. pt. ii. p. 88.

1798. Married—John Smith and Eliz. Spurrier : St. Geo. Han. Sq. ii. 186.

London, 3 ; Philadelphia, 1.

Spyer, Speer, Spier, Spire, Spear, Spiers. — Occup. 'the spier,' i.e. watchman ; v. Scorer. The final s in Spiers is genitive.

Robertus Spyer, 1379 : P. T. Yorks. p. 142.

Richard Spyre, 1515 : Reg. Univ. Oxf. i. 95.

1662-3. John Spier, co. Oxf., and Jane Price : Marriage Lic. (Faculty Office), p. 68.

1802. Married — Robert Spear and Maria Baker : St. Geo. Han. Sq. ii. 256.

London, 4, 6, 2, 1, 4, 1 ; Oxford, 0, 0, 0, 0, 1, 4 ; Philadelphia, 0, 20, 2, 1, 30, 0.

Squatfoot.—Nick. 'with the squat foot' ; cf. Lightfoot, Barfoot, &c.

Anabilla Squatfoot, C. R., 35 Edw. III.

Squibb. — Nick. ; a term of disdain, a poor kind of fellow ; v. Spenser's Mother Hubbard's Tale, 371 ; v. Skeat, from whom I got the reference.

John Squybbe, 1536 : Reg. Univ. Oxf. i. 187.

1693. Bapt.—Eliz., d. Thomas Squibb : St. Jas. Clerkenwell, i. 353.

London, 2 ; Philadelphia, 1.

Squiller, Skiller. — Occup. ' the squiller.' A washer of dishes, &c. 'Sqwyllare, dysche-wescheare, *lixa*' : Prompt. Parv.

John le Squylier. H.

Geoffrey le Squeller. O.

Geoffrey le Squeler : Close Roll, 52 Hen. III.

John de la Squillerye. H.

The word seems closely related to the O.F. *escuelle*, a dish, but Professor Skeat (Etym. Dict., *scullery*) says the original form was *swiller*, from *swill*, to wash, passing from *swiller* to *squiller*, and as a habitat from *squillery* to *scullery.* 'The squyler of the kechyn' is mentioned by Robert of Brunne.

'The eleven messes to the children of the kechyn, squillery, and pastrey, with porters, scowerers, and turn broches, &c.' : Ord. Henry VIII at Eltham.

We may add 'Roger de Norhamptone, squyler,' in Mr. Riley's Memorials of London. The

French *escuelle*, a dish, if not radically connected, must have influenced the changes that have passed over the word. Amongst other gifts from the City of London to the Black Prince, in 1371, were '48 esqueles and 24 salt-cellars, weighing by goldsmith's weight, 76lb. 5oz. 0dwt.'(Riley's Memorials of London, p. 350). 'Sergeant, squylloure' (Halliwell).

'Hugh Skeller, alias Dalton, was abbot of Furness, 13 Edw. III : West's Ant. of Furness, p. 84.

Squire, Squires, Squier, Squiers. — Offic. 'the esquire,' an attendant upon a knight, a shield-bearer. Squires is the genitive form ; cf. Brooks, Williams, Tompkins, &c.

John le Squier, co. Camb., 1273. A.

William Squier, co. Hunts, ibid.

Thomas le Esquier, C. R., 33 Hen. III.

Thomas Squier, 1379 : P. T. Yorks. p. 50

Agnes Squier, 1379 : ibid. p. 139.

Walter le Squier, c. 1300. M.

Squire, like Marquis, Duke, Earl, &c., has become a favourite font-name among the 'lower orders' in Yorkshire ; v. Duke for an explanation.

London, 36, 15, 0, 0 ; Philadelphia, 4, 7, 0, 0 ; New York, 13, 14, 9, 1.

Squirrel, Squirrell. — Nick. 'the squirrel,' a sobriquet referring to physical agility or prudent thrift. O.F. *escurel.*

Geoffrey le Esqurel, co. Essex, 1273. A.

Thomas Squyrelle. N. (v. Index).

Henry Squyrel, co. Soms., 1 Edw. III : Kirby's Quest, p. 217.

1279. Married — Benjamin Ruffe and Sarah Squirrell : St. Geo. Chap. Mayfair, p. 297.

London, 1, 3 ; MDB. (co. Suffolk), 0, 3 ; Philadelphia, 0, 1.

Stable, Stables.—Local, ' at the stable,' from residence thereby. Stables has the suffix s, as in Brooks, Styles, &c. (perhaps patronymic). Possibly it is really plural, implying the/ stables, as distinct from a stable.

Wido de Stabulo, co. Bucks, 1273. A.

John de Stabulo, co. Hunts, ibid.

William de la Stable, Fines Roll, 11 Edw. I.

William del Stabell, C. R., 1 Hen. V.

Radulphus del Stabill, 1379 : P. T. Yorks. p. 53.

Agnes del Stabill', 1379 : P. T. Yorks. p. 196.
Johannes del Stable, 1379 : ibid. p. 242.
1628. Bapt.—John, s. John Stables : St. Jas. Clerkenwell, i. 110.
London, 1, 3 ; West Rid. Court Dir., o, 3 ; New York, 1, o.

Stableford.—Local ; v. Stapleford.

Stabler.—Occup. ' the stabler,' a stableman, an ostler ; the keeper of an inn where horses were kept for hire.

Alan le Stabler, co. Camb., 1273. A.
William le Stabler, co. Hunts, ibid.
Thomas le Stabeler, co. Linc., ibid.
William le Stabler. R.
Anne Stabler. W. 16.
John Stabler, C. R., 20 Ric. II. pt. i.
Willelmus Stabeler, 1379 : P. T. Yorks. p. 262.
1793. Married — James Whitnell and Ann Stabler : St. Geo. Han. Sq. ii. 92.
London, 1 ; Philadelphia, 2.

Stables ; v. Stable.

Stace, Stacey, Stacy, Stacye. —Bapt. ' the son of Eustace,' from the nicks. Stace and Stacey, dim. Stacekin.

Roger Stace, co. Hunts, 1273. A.
Stacius Warewnar, co. Linc., ibid.
William Stacy, co. Devon, ibid.
Stacius 'le Boloneis. C.
Thomas Stacy, co. Soms., 1 Edw. III : Kirby's Quest, p. 148.
Stacy Hernowe, co. Soms.,1 Edw. III : ibid. p. 270.
Robertus Stasy, 1379 : P. T. Yorks. p. 44.
Ricardus Stase, 1379 : ibid.
Johannes Stase, 1379 : ibid.
Robert Stace, sup. for B.C.L., 1552 : Reg. Univ. Oxf. i. 79.

An early dim. and masculine Stacekin is met with, proving that Eustace and not Anastasia is the parent of the above; also Latinized as Stacius.

Stacekinus de Burnes, co. Kent, Hen. III–Edw. I. K.
West Rid. Court Dir., o, 15, o, 1 ; London, 3, 17, 8, o ; Sheffield, o, 19, o, 1 ; Philadelphia, o, 6, o, o.

Stafford.—Local, ' of Stafford,' the capital of co. Stafford. The surname is now far more familiar to the United States than to England.

Martin de Stafford, co. Suff., 1273. A.
Ranulf de Stafford, co. Salop, ibid.
Cf. John de Staffordsire (Staffordshire), ibid.
1562. Bapt.—Edward, sonne unto Sir Robert Stafford, knight : St. Jas. Clerkenwell, i. 2.

1576. Anthony Stafforde, co. Oxford : Reg. Univ. Oxf. vol. ii. pt. ii. p. 71.
MDB. (co. Derby), 2 ; London, 2 ; Oxford, 2 ; Philadelphia, 55.

Stagg.—Nick. ' the stag ' ; cf. Buck, Hart, Doe, &c.

Thomas Stagge, C. R., 17 Edw. III. pt. ii.
Adam Stagge, 1379 : P.T. Yorks. p. 169.
1579–80. William Stagge, co. Dorset : Reg. Univ. Oxf. vol. ii. pt. ii. p. 91.
1586. Married—William Hudson and Margaret Stagg : St. Dionis Backchurch, p. 11.
London, 13 ; Sheffield, 3 ; Philadelphia, 8.

Stailey ; v. Staley.

Stainer.—Occup. ' the stainer'; cf. Painter. Mr. Lower says, ' The London Painters and Stainers were united into one company in 1502 ' (Patr. Brit. p. 327). But v. Stanier.

John Stynour, co. Soms., 1 Edw. III : Kirby's Quest, p. 269.
1705. Buried—John Staner : St. Thomas the Apostle (London), p. 144.
1791. Married—Benjamin Stainer and Ann Davis : St. Geo. Han. Sq. ii. 67.
London, 3 ; Philadelphia, 1.

Staines, Stains, Stanes.— Local, ' of Staines,' a market-town and parish in co. Middlesex.

Richard de Stanes, co. Kent, 1273. A.
William de Staines, co. Kent, Hen. III–Edw. I. K.
1328. William de Stanes, rector of Welborne, co. Norf. : FF. ii. 453.
1677. Bapt.—John, s. Richard Stanes : St. Jas. Clerkenwell, i. 277.
London, 8, 1, 5 ; Philadelphia, 1, 2, o.

Stainforth.—Local, ' of Stainforth,' a township in the parish of Giggleswick, W. Rid. Yorks.

1749. Married — Luke Stainforth and Judith Nutt : St. Geo. Chap. Mayfair, p. 135.
West Rid. (Yorks) Court Dir., 1 ; MDB. (co. Derby), 2.

Stainsby ; v. Stanesby.

Stainton.—Local, ' of Stainton,' townships in the parishes of Stanwix (co. Cumb.), Dacre (co. Cumb.), Gainford (co. Durham), Urswick (co. Lanc.), and Downholme (W. Rid. Yorks) ; also parishes in cos. York (N. Rid. and W. Rid.), Lincoln, and Durham. v. Stanton.

Herbert de Staynton, co. Linc., 1273. A.
Robert de Staynton, co. Linc., ibid.
Thomas de Staynton, 1379 : P. T. Yorks. p. 88.

Juliana de Staynton, 1379 : ibid.
1804. Married — Robert Fernyhough and Ann Stainton : St. Geo. Han. Sq. ii. 302.
London, 6 ; West Riding Court Dir., 1 ; Ulverston, 1 ; New York, 2.

Staley, Stailey.—Local, ' of Staley,' now a parish called Staleybridge, near Ashton-under-Lyne, formerly Staveley, a common local name ; v. Staveley.

Robert de Stavelegh, or Staley, 1389 : East Ches. ii. 155.
Thomas de Staveley, 1400 : ibid. p. 167.
Ralph Staveley, or Staley : ibid. i. 79.
1608. Bapt.—John, s. Richard Staley : St. Jas. Clerkenwell, i. 52.
MDB. (co. Derby), 19, o ; Manchester, 3, o ; London, 1, o ; Philadelphia, 24, 5.

Stalker.—Occup. ' the stalker,' a huntsman, a fowler. ' Stalk, to use a stalking-horse for obtaining wild-fowl and game ' (Halliwell).

Amabil le Stalker, co. Hunts, 1273. A.
1802. Married—John Alison and Ann Stalker : St. Geo. Han. Sq. ii. 270.
1806. — John Grear and Jane Stalker : ibid. p. 340.
London, 1 ; Liverpool, 2 ; Boston (U.S.), 6.

Stallard, Stollard. — ? Bapt. Probably ' the son of Stannard' or Stonard, a once popular font-name. The change from *n* to *l* is extremely common in English nomenclature ; cf. *banister* for *baluster*, and v. Phillimore or Banister. There is no trace of a name Stallard or Stollard in the Hundred Rolls. The double variants, too, run side by side with the more correct ones ; v. Stannard. Nevertheless cf. Icelandic personal name ' Stal-hardr,' hard as steel (v. Icel. Dict. *stal*, where the name and derivation are given).

1648. Buried — Sarah, d. Thomas Stollard : St. Peter, Cornhill, i. 203.
1740. Married—Edmund Stallard and Catherine Cox : St. Dionis Backchurch, p. 67.
London, 3, 2 ; New York, 1, o.

Stallebrass, Stallibrass, Stallybrass.— ? ——. I cannot suggest any satisfactory solution.

1652. Married — Joseph Sumner and Joyce Stallowbrace, of Waltham, co. Essex : Reg. St. Peter, Cornhill, i. 259.
London, 1, 2, o ; MDB. (co. Essex), o, 3, 1.

Stallon.—Local, 'of Stalham,' a parish in co. Norfolk. The corruption took place at an early period.

Nicholas de Stalham, co. Norf., 1273. A.
Ralph Stalum, co. Norf., ibid.
Herbert Stalun, co. Norf., ibid.
1336. Jeffrey de Stalham, bailiff of Yarmouth : FF. xi. 323.
1367. William de Stallon, bailiff of Norwich : ibid. iii. 100.
1370. John de Stalham : ibid. xi. 323.
1626. Married — Anthony Griffin and Eliz. Stallonn : St. Antholin (London), 61.
1694. Christopher Stallon or Stalham, mayor of Norwich : FF. iii. 426.
MDB. (Norfolk), 2.

Stalman, Stallman.—(1) Local, ' of Stalmine,' a parish in dioc. Manchester. (2) Occup. 'the stallman.' Mr. Lower says, 'The keeper of a stall in any fair or market who paid the impost known in municipal law as stallage' (Patr. Brit. p. 327).

Adam de Stalmyn, co. Lanc., 20 Edw. I. R.
John de Stalmyn, co. Lanc., ibid.
London, 2, 0 ; Philadelphia, 0, 17.

Stalwart, Stalwartman, Stallworthy.—Nick. 'the stalwart.' M.E. *stalworth* (Pricke of Conscience, 689). For the suggested curious origin of this word, 'good at stealing,' hence brave, strong, v. Skeat. With Stallworthy, cf. the local Kenworthy and Langworthy for Kenworth and Langworth.

John le Stalewrthe, co. Oxf., 1273. A.
Henry Stalewrth, co. Camb., ibid.
Thomas Stalwrygh', 1379 : P. T. Yorks. p. 156.
John Staleworthman, C. R., 12 Ric. II.
1685. Bapt. — Mathew, s. Edward Stolwortman : St. Antholin (London), p. 102.
1794. Married — Charles Hyde and Sarah Stalworth : St. Geo. Han. Sq. ii. 108.
London, 0, 0, 1 ; MDB. (co. Bucks), 0, 0, 1.

Stamford.—Local, 'of Stamford,' a market-town in co. Lincoln. It appears that the original name of the place was Stanford (the stony ford), q.v.

Richard de Stanfordia, co. Linc., 1273. A.
Clemens de Stanford, co. Norf., ibid.

The following three references clearly attach to the same individual :

Alban de Stanford, co. Norf. : FF. x. 387.
Albon de Stamford, co. Norf. : ibid. viii. 460.
Albin de Standford, co. Norf. : ibid. p. 199.
1626. John Greene and Mary Stamford, widow of Edward Stamford (sic) : Marriage Lic. (London), i. 168.
London, 6 ; Philadelphia, 1.

Stamper.—Occup. ' the stamper,' probably a stamper of coins, a mint-man.

John Stamper, co. Camb., 1273. A.
Robert Stamper, co. York. W. 16.
1658. Married—John James and Anne Stamper : St. Thomas the Apostle (London), p. 20.
1699-1700. Robert Stamper and Ann Man : Marriage Lic. (Faculty Office), p. 235.
London, 1 ; MDB. (co. Cumb.), 9 ; Philadelphia, 1.

Stanborough, Stanbrough, Stanbury, Stanbery, Stanberry.—Local, ' of Stainbrough.' a township in the parish of Silkstone, W. Rid. Yorks. Mr. Lower says, ' A hundred in the county of Devon.' Both may have contributed, but looking at the directories it is clear that Devonshire holds the first place as parent.

Thomas de Staynburghe, 1379 : P. T. Yorks. p. 52.
1686. Married—Francis Nicholls and Jane Stanburrow : St. Dionis Backchurch, p. 41.
MDB. (co. Devon), 0, 0, 13, 0, 0 ; Plymouth, 0, 0, 9, 0, 0 ; London, 2, 1, 3, 0, 0 ; Devon Court Dir., 0, 0, 5, 0, 0 ; New York, 0, 3, 2, 1, 1 ; Philadelphia, 0, 0, 2, 0, 0.

Stanbridge.—Local, (1) ' of Stanbridge,' a chapelry in the parish of Leighton Buzzard, co. Bedford ; (2) ' of Stanbridge,' a parish in co. Dorset. This seems to be the chief parent.

Robert de Stanbrugge, co. Soms. 1 Edw. III : Kirby's Quest, p. 234.
Stephen Stenbrugge, co. Soms., 1 Edw. III : ibid. p. 243.
Walter Stenbrigge, co. Soms., 1 Edw. III : ibid.
1760. Married — Thomas Haines and Ann Stanbridge : St. Geo. Han. Sq. i. 92.
London, 3 ; MDB. (co. Bedf.), 1 ; Philadelphia, 3.

Stanbury ; v. Stanborough.

Stancliff.—Local, 'of Stancliff.' Stayncliff, a locality in co. Yorks, is mentioned in the Hundred Rolls,

1273 (vol. ii. pt. iii). No doubt the surname takes its rise from Staincliff, a hundred in the W. Rid. Yorks.

1565. Richard Stankelefe : Reg. Univ. Oxf. vol. ii. pt. ii. p. 17.
1572. James Stancleif : ibid. p. 30.
1580. Richard Stancliffe, of Atherton, *yeoman* : Wills at Chester, i. 181.
1617. Richard Stancliffe, of Atherton : ibid.
1674. Samuel Stancliffe and Eliz. Ash : Marriage Lic. (Faculty Office), p. 130.
London, 2 ; Philadelphia, 2.

Standering, Standring.—Local, ' of Stannering.' This spot in South Lancashire I have not been able to discover. It will be found in the neighbourhood of Middleton. The *d* is intrusive, as in Simmonds.

1631. John Stannering, of Hopwood : Wills at Chester, ii. 207.
1633. Eliz. Stannering, of Sidhall, parish of Middleton : ibid.
1763. Married—Samuel Standring and Sarah Storer : St. Geo. Han. Sq. i. 122.
Manchester, 0, 8 ; West Rid. Court Dir., 2, 3 ; Philadelphia, 0, 2.

Standerwick.—Local, ' o Standerwick,' a parish in co. Somerset, four miles from Frome.

1746. Married — Richard Shipley and Eliz. Standerwick : St. Geo. Chap. Mayfair, p. 77.
MDB. (co. Devon), 1 ; (co. Somerset), 2 ; New York, 1.

Standfast.—Nick. ' the firm, the steady, the resolute, the steadfast in purpose.'

Thomas Stanfast, co. Oxf., 1273. A.
John Standfast, of Lynn, co. Norf., 2 Edw. 6 : FF. vi. 507.
1765. Married — Edward Brooke and Eliz. Standfast : St. Geo. Han. Sq. i. 150.
London, 3 ; Philadelphia, 1.

Standfield ; v. Stanfield.

Standish, Standage.—Local, ' of Standish,' a parish in co. Lanc., near Wigan. With the corrupted Standage, cf. Aldridge for Aldrich.

William de Standisch, 1311 : Baines' Lanc. ii. 164.
Hugh de Standisch, 1311 : ibid.
1614. Eliz. Standish, of Standish, *widow* : Wills at Chester, i. 182.
1605. John Standish, of Wigan, *carpenter* : ibid. p. 183.
Manchester, 1, 1 ; Liverpool, 2, 0 ; Philadelphia, 6, 0.

Standring ; v. Standering.

Stanes ; v. Staines.

Stanesby, Stainsby.—Local, 'of Stainsby,' a hamlet in the parish of Ashby Puerorum, co. Lincoln; also a township in the parish of Ault Hucknall, co. Derby. Other places would be so called.

1598. John Stanesby or Stainsby, co. Wilts: Reg. Univ. Oxf. vol. ii. pt. ii. p. 227.
1663. Buried — Alice, wife of Richard Stansby: St. Jas. Clerkenwell, iv. 350.
1665. — John Stansbee: ibid. p. 365.
London, 4, 0; Philadelphia, 0, 1.

Stanfield, Standfield.—Local, 'of Stanfield.' There is a parish so called in co. Norfolk, six miles from East Dereham; but other and smaller spots would naturally bear this name, i. e. the stony field.

Geoffrey atte Stondfeld, co. Soms., 1 Edw. III: Kirby's Quest, p. 108.

The _d_ here is intrusive, as in Symonds; cf. the provincial _gownd_ for _gown_.

1587. Buried—Wenefrede Standfeild: St. Jas. Clerkenwell, iv. 36.
1683. John Stanniford and Mary Tray: Marriage Alleg. (Canterbury), p. 141.
London, 2, 1; MDB. (co. Soms.), 1, 2; Philadelphia, 2, 0.

Stanford, Staniford.—Local, 'of Stanford.' There are no less than ten parishes in the south of England of this name. The North-English form was Stanforth, and there Staniford is met by Staniforth, q.v.; v. Stamford also.

Adam de Stanford, co. Oxf., 1273.
Symon de Stanford, co. Hunts, ibid.
Florentia de Stanforde, co. Soms., 2 Edw. III: Kirby's Quest, p. 238.
1622. Thomas Stanniford, Ball. Coll.: Reg. Univ. Oxf. vol. ii. pt. iii. 408.
1630. Bapt. — George, s. Thomas Standford: St. Jas. Clerkenwell, i. 116.
London, 13, 2; Philadelphia, 11, 0.

Stanger.—Occup. 'the stanger.' Lower says it is a North-English term for a thatcher (v. Patr. Brit. p. 327). But there may be a local origin.

Jordan de Stangar, co. Soms., 1 Edw. III: Kirby's Quest, p. 179.

The following represents a still existing Cumberland baptismal name:

Gawen Stangar, Christ Ch., Oxford, 1568: Reg. Univ. Oxf. i. 259.
1784. Married—Thomas Stanger and Charlotte Jones: St. Geo. Han. Sq. i. 360.
London, 1; MDB. (co. Cumb.), 7; Philadelphia, 13.

Stanier, Stanyer, Stoner.—Occup. 'the stanyer' or stone-hewer, a hewer of stones, a quarryman. Sometimes simply 'stonier.' With the intrusive _i_ or _y_, cf. _lawyer_, Sawyer, Bowyer, &c.

Richard Stenere, 1379: P. T. Yorks. p. 18.
Richard Stonhewer. SS.
John Stonehewer. AA. 4.
Thomas Hirst, _stenyhour_, co. York, 1433. W. 11.
1689. Nathaniell Stanyar and Catherine Bryan: Marriage Alleg. (Canterbury), p. 101.
Robert Stoner, rector of Clenchwarton, co. Norf., 1736: FF. viii. 382.
London, 1, 0, 3; Philadelphia, 0, 0, 8.

Staniforth, Stainforth, Stanford, Staniford. — Local, 'of Stainforth,' a township in the parish of Giggleswick; also a township in the parish of Hatfield,' near the navigable river Don' (West Riding Dir., 1867, p. 389). This phrase reminds us of the origin of the name, viz. the stony ford, _forth_ being an early English form of _ford_; v. Forth, and cf. Sandforth and Spofforth; v. Stanford and Stamford. For suffix, v. Ford and Forth.

Henricus de Staynford, 1379: P. T. Yorks. p. 10.
Johannes de Staynford, 1379: ibid.
Thomas Stenford, 1379: ibid. p. 19.
Willelmus de Staynforth, 1379: ibid. p. 51.
1567. Vincent Pidcocke and Dorothy Stanneefoorde: Marriage Lic. (London), i. 36.
1747. Married — Richard Winkworth and Hester Staneforth: St. Geo. Chap. Mayfair, p. 86.
West Rid. Court Dir., 8, 1, 0, 0; Boston (U.S.), 0, 0, 12, 8.

Stanley.—Local, 'of Stanley.' There are at least ten ecclesiastical parishes of this name in England ('the stony meadow'). For suffix, v. Legh, Lee, or Lees.

William de Stanlegh, co. Wilts, 1273. A.
John de Stanleye, co. Oxf., ibid.
Johannes de Staynlay, 1379: P. T. Yorks. p. 252.
Robertus de Stanelay, 1379: ibid. p. 135.
Robertus de Stanelegh, 1379: ibid. p. 174.
1578-9. Edward Stanley, co. Lanc.: Reg. Univ. Oxf. vol. ii. pt. ii. p. 85.
London, 39; Philadelphia, 39.

Stannard, Stonard, Stannart.—Bapt. 'the son of Stanard' or Stanhard; v. Freeman, Norm. Conq. v. 817. A well-known Norfolk and Suffolk surname. There are two Stanards in Domesday (Stanardus, co. Essex; Stanart, co. Suffolk). Stonhard is found as a single personal name, co. Essex (Hundred Rolls, 1273, i. 154). The form Stonhard was common.

Stannard de Corton, co. Suff., 1273. A.
Stanardus Cobbe, co. Kent, ibid.
Stannard Dilker, co. Norf., ibid.
Sella Stonhard, co. Camb., ibid.
Richard Stonhard, co. Camb., ibid.
Richard Stonehard, co. Soms., 1 Edw. III: Kirby's Quest, p. 158.
John Stonard, co. Soms., 1 Edw. III: ibid. p. 179.
Richard, s. of Stannard, co. Norf.: FF. xi. 175.
William Stanard, rector of Stockton, co. Norf., 1634: ibid. viii. 44.
1607. William Stonnard, Ch. Ch., Oxf.: Reg. Univ. Oxf. i. 147.
London, II, 1, 0; MDB. (Norfolk), 5, 10, 0; (Suffolk), 9, 0, 0; Philadelphia, 1, 0, 3.

Stannus.—Local, 'of the stonehouse'; cf. Loftus for Lofthouse, or Kirkus for Kirkhouse; v. Stonehouse.

Robert de Stanehouse, co. Northumb., 1273. A.
Tuel de Stanhuse, co. Devon, Hen. III-Edw. I. K.
London, 2.

Stanton.—Local, 'of Stanton,' townships in cos. Derby, Stafford, and Northumberland; also parishes in cos. Gloucester, Suffolk, Wilts, Bucks, Derby, Somerset, Dorset, and Oxford; v. Stainton.

Alice de Stanton, co. Camb., 1273. A.
Walter de Stanton, co. Oxf., ibid.
Edmund de Stanton, co. Wilts, ibid.
1615. Francis Stanton, co. Bedf.: Reg. Univ. Oxf. vol. ii. pt. ii. p. 339.
1619. Henry Stanton or Staunton, co. Cornwall: ibid. p. 380.
1624-5. Married—Arthur Stanten and Eliz. Clapen: St. Dionis Backchurch, p. 21.
London, 23; MDB. (co. Glouc.), 10; Boston (U.S.), 49.

Stanway.—Local, 'of Stanway,' parishes in cos. Essex and Gloucester.

Hervey de Stanweye, co. Norf., 1273. A.
Hawise de Stanwey, co. Camb., ibid.
Alicia Stanwey, co. Soms., 1 Edw. III: Kirby's Quest, p. 174.

1511. William Stanwey, vicar of Besthorp, co. Norf.: FF. i. 492.
1807. Married — John Stanway and Sarah Spencer: St. Geo. Han. Sq. ii. 370. London, 3.

Stanwix.—Local, 'of Stanwix,' a parish within a mile of Carlisle, co. Cumberland.

Hugh Skot, de Staynwikes, 18 Edw. II: Freemen of York, i. 22.
MDB. (co. Cumb.), 2.

Staple, Staples, Stapler.—Local, 'at the staple,' a staple (O.F. *estaple*), a mart, a general centre of merchandise. Originally the place was the staple, not the commodity. Stapler is the occupative form, and Staples the genitive form ; cf. Styles, Brooks, Holmes, &c.

Robert de Stapel, co. Kent, 1273. A.

The above entry no doubt refers to Staple-next-Wingham, a parish in co. Kent.

Robert atte-Staple, C. R., 5 Edw. I.
Robertus Staple, *mercer*, 1379 : P. T. Yorks. p. 280.
Willelmus Staple, 1379 : ibid. p. 281.
1623. Thomas Winson and Joan Stapler : Marriage Lic. (London), ii. 124.
1666. Married — Jacob Staple and Susan Goodman : St. Jas. Clerkenwell, iii. 125.
London, 1, 22, 1 ; Philadelphia, 1, 8, 1.

Stapleford, Stableford.—Local, 'of Stapleford,' parishes in cos. Cambridge, Hertford, Leicester, Lincoln, Notts, Wilts, and Essex ; v. Staple and Ford.

Gilbert de Stapelford, co. Linc., 1273. A.
Hugh de Stapelford, co. Bedf., ibid.
Simon de Stapilford, co. Linc., Hen. III—Edw. I. K.
Robert de Stapelford, co. Linc., 20 Edw. I. R.
1572-3. William Stapleforde and Alice Wales : Marriage Lic. (London), i. 55.
1596. George Hancocke and Eliz. Stapleford : ibid. p. 232.
London, 1, 1 ; Manchester, 0, 2 ; Philadelphia, 3, 0.

Stapler ; v. Staple. But possibly for Stabler, q.v. ; and cf. Stapleford.

Stapleton.—Local, 'of Stapleton,' a village in the parish of Darrington, near Pontefract, co. York ; also parishes in cos. Cumberland, Gloucester, and Salop.

William de Stapelton, co. Oxf., 1273. A.
Nicholas de Stapelton, co. York, ibid.

Milo de Stapelton, co. York, 20 Edw. I. R.
Richard de Stapiltone, co. Soms., 1 Edw. III : Kirby's Quest, p. 144.
Margareta de Stapilton, 1379 : P. T. Yorks. p. 117.
Robertus de Stapulton, 1379 : ibid. p. 113.
Bryan de Stapilton, 1379 : ibid. p. 296.
1585-6. John Stapleton and Jane Kele : Marriage Lic. (London), i. 147.
London, 15 ; Philadelphia, 13.

Stapley.—Local, ' of Stapeley,' a township in the parish of Wybunbury, co. Chester ; also a tithing in the parish of Odiham, co. Hants.

Roger de Stapelye, co. Sussex, 1273. A.
Gilbert de Stapelyge, co. Kent, ibid.
1604. John Stapley, co. Sussex : Reg. Univ. Oxf. vol. ii. pt. ii. p. 277.
1799. Married—Richard Stapley and Jane Maitland : St. Geo. Han. Sq. ii. 194.
London, 4 ; MDB. (co. Sussex), 2.

Starbuck.—Local, ' of Starbeck,' a hamlet between Ripon and Knaresborough. Mr. Lower writes, partly quoting Mr. Ferguson, ' In O. Norse *bokki* means "vir grandis, corpore et animo." Hence *Storbocki*, from *stôr*, great, "vir imperiosus." ' This may be true, but I take it that Starbuck is simply the local Starbeck. The surname still remains in the West Riding.

Robertus Starbok', 1379 : P. T. Yorks. p. 4.
1772. Married — John Lambeld and Sarah Starbuck : St. Geo. Han. Sq. i. 223.
London, 2 ; West Riding Court Dir., 1 ; Sheffield, 1 ; New York, 2.

Starcher.—Occup. ' the starcher,' i.e. a cloth stiffener, a starcher of linen ; from *stark*, strong, stiff, weakened to starch. The occupation is referred to in Cocke Lorelle's Bote :

' Butlers, sterchers, and mustard-makers, Hardeware men, mole seekers, and ratte-takers.'

Ralph le Starkere, co. Hunts, 1273. A.

Stare.—Nick. ' the stare,' i.e. the starling (v. Starling) ; cf. Sparrow, Nightingale, &c.

Robert Stare, co. Oxf., 1273. A.
Richard le Staar, co. Soms., 1 Edw. III : Kirby's Quest, p. 259.
Ricardus Stare, 1379 : P. T. Yorks. p. 80.
1796. Married—Philip Stare and Margaret Tooley : St. Geo. Han. Sq. ii. 146.
Philadelphia, 1.

Stark, Starke, Starkman.—Nick. ' the stark,' i.e. the strong, the stiff.

' He had a pike-staff in his hand
That was both stark and strang.'
Robin Hood, i. 98.

William Starckeman or Starcman, co. Camb., 1273. A.
Geoffrey Starckman. T.
1745. Married — Francis Stark and Martha Orom : St. Geo. Chap. Mayfair, p. 52.
1757. John Starke and Honour Paterson : St. Geo. Han. Sq. i. 70.
London, 8, 1, 0 ; Philadelphia, 32, 5, 0.

Starkbone.—Nick. ' stiff,' or strong-boned.

Robertus Starkbane, 1379 : P. T. Yorks. p. 224.
Johannes Starkbayn, 1379 : ibid.

Starkey, Starkie.—Nick. ' the stark,' i.e. the strong, the stiff ; cf. Strong, &c. (v. Stark). Starkey seems undoubtedly to be a dialectic variant of Stark (cf. Teddy or Teddie for Edward). ' Starky, stiff, dry. Westmoreland ' (Halliwell).

1579. Francis Starkey, co. Derby : Reg. Univ. Oxf. vol. ii. pt. ii. p. 87.
1592. George Starkie, of Pennington : Wills at Chester, i. 182.
1609. Ellen Starkey, of Pennington: ibid.
London, 13, 2 ; Philadelphia, 16, 0.

Starling.—(1) Nick. ' the starling ' ; formed from *stare*, a bird, with dim. *ling*.

' The false lapwing, full of trecherie,
The stare, that the counsaile can bewrie.'
Chaucer, Assembly of Fowls.

(2) Nick. ' the starling,' i.e. sterling, true, from starling, a coin or true weight.

' So that ye offre nobles or starlings.'
Chaucer, C. T. 12841.

Symon Starlyng, co. Herts, 1273. A.
William Starlyng, co. Norf., ibid.
Geoffrey Starlyng, C. R., 17 Ric. II.

It is probable that (1) is the true parent of the surname.

1622. Bapt. — Christopher, s. Thomas Starling : St. Jas. Clerkenwell, i. 93.
London, 17 ; Philadelphia, 3.

Starr.—(1) Nick. ' the star ' ; M.E. *sterre*, or perhaps ' the steer,' i.e. the young ox (v. Steer). (2) Personal, ' the son of Star.' Probably Star was a personal or baptismal name as Stella is to-day.

Johannes le Ster, co. Oxf., 1273. A.
Robert le Ster, co. Sussex, ibid.

William Ster, co. Camb., 1273. A.
1416. Richard Sterre, vicar of Happesburgh, co. Norf.: FF. ix. 300.
1465. John Sterre, vicar of Quidenham, co. Norf.: ibid. i. 334.
1705. William Pynsent and Mary Starr, *widow*: Marriage Lic. (London), ii. 334.
London, 10; Philadelphia, 41.

Startup.—Local, 'of Startup,' a portion of the township of Twizle, co. Northumberland.

1592. Arthur Startupp and Margaret Lixlade: Marriage Lic. (London), i. 199.
1603. John Startuppe and Susan Tyte: ibid. p. 276.
1737. Andrew Startup rented Startup: KKK. ii. 467.
London, 1; New York, 2.

Starziker; v. Stirzaker.

Statham.—Local, 'of Statham.' I cannot find any place of this name. Possibly it stands for a parish styled Statherne, in co. Leicester. But this is pure conjecture on my part.

John de Statham, co. Camb., 1273. A.
1562. Bapt.—John, s. Thomas Statham: St. Jas. Clerkenwell, i. 2.
1689. Thomas Statham and Mary Goweth: Marriage Alleg. (Canterbury), p. 106.
Manchester, 6; MDB. (co. Derby), 8; London, 8; Philadelphia, 1.

Staunton.—Local, 'of Staunton,' parishes in cos. Worcester, Notts, Monmouth, and Hereford. v. Stanton and Stainton.

Avice de Staunton, co. Linc., 1273. A.
Nicholas de Staunton, co. Essex, ibid.
William de Staunton, co. Oxf., ibid.
Robert de Staunton, co. Derby, 20 Edw. I. R.
Harvey de Staunton, co. Camb., ibid.
John de Stauntone, co. Soms., 1 Edw. III: Kirby's Quest, p. 92.
1798. Married — William Hadnutt and Esther Staunton: St. Geo. Han. Sq. ii. 191.
London, 2; Boston (U.S.), 2.

Staveley, Stavley, Stavely.—Local, 'of Staveley.' There are parishes of this name in cos. Derby and York; a chapelry nine miles from Ulverston, co. Lanc.; and both a township and chapelry in the parish of Kendal, co. Westmoreland.

Adam de Stavell, co. Notts, 1273. A.
Adam de Staveleia, co. Cumb. K.
Adam de Staveley, co. York. R.
1560. Married — Peter Staveley and Edith Hams: Marriage Lic.(London),i.21.
1621. Miles Stavly, of Killington (Westm.): Wills at Richmond, i. 261.

1809. Bapt.— Jane, d. John Stavely: St. Mary, Ulverston, p. 569.
London, 0, 1, 0; Oxford, 1, 0, 0; Liverpool, 1, 0, 1; Philadelphia, 0, 0, 2.

St. Clair; v. Sinclair.
Philadelphia, 20.

Stead, Steade.—Local, 'at the stead,' a place, a station, a settlement; cf. homestead, market-stead (= market-place). A great Yorkshire surname. The Market-place, Manchester, was the Market-stead till the close of the last century. The Market-stead, Ulverston, is commonly so set down in the parish registers till 1790.

John Stede, co. Suff., 1273. A.
Robertus del Stede, 1379: P. T. Yorks. p. 208.
Ricardus del Stede, 1379: ibid.
Petrus del Stede, 1379: ibid.
Laurence del Stede, 1379: ibid.
1589. Bapt.— Katherine, d. John Steade: St. Jas. Clerkenwell, i. 21.
West Riding Court Dir., 31, 1; London, 9, 0; Philadelphia, 32, 0.

Steadman, Stedman, Steedman.—Occup. 'the steadman,' one who occupied a stead, a farmer; v. Stead.

Richard Stedeman, co. Camb., 1273. A.
Gilbert de Stedman, co. Oxf., ibid.
Simon le Stedman, 35 Edw. I: BBB. p. 739.
John le Stedman, 1306. M.
Johannes Stedeman, 1379: P. T. Yorks. p. 49.
Johannes Stedeman, 1379: ibid. p. 220.
1553. Married — Wyllyam Nevell and Jone Steedman: St. Michael, Cornhill, p. 6.
London, 4, 13, 3; Philadelphia, 2, 5, 0.

Stean, Steane, Steanes.—Local, 'of Steane,' a parish in co. Northants.
London, 3, 2, 0; MDB. (co. Northants.), 0, 0, 1.

Steavenson; var. of Stephenson and Stevenson (v. Stephen and Steven).

1613. Married — John Lydgold and Fayth Steavenson: Kensington Ch. p. 66. London, 2.

Stebbing, Stebbings, Stebbens, Stebbins.—(1) Local, 'of Stebbing,' a parish in co. Essex. Stebbings, &c., are genitive forms; cf. Brooks, Styles, Williams, Jones, &c.

Richard de Stebing, co. Essex, 1273. A.
Thomas Stebin, co. Camb., ibid.
1581. Bapt.—Isabel, d. George Stebyn: St. Jas. Clerkenwell, i. 12.

1615. Martin Stebbyn, Norwich: FF. iv. 354.
1807. Married—John Burton Marshall and Sarah Stebbings: St. Geo. Han. Sq. ii. 374.
London, 9, 4, 1, 0; Philadelphia, 4, 0, 0, 4.

Sted-, Steedman.—Occup.; v. Steadman.

Steel, Steele, Stell, Stelle.—Bapt. 'the son of Steel" (?). The old Danish Staal (v. Yonge, ii. 293); Icel. Stál. Lower says, 'A northern pronunciation of *stile.*' This is quite inadmissible. All early instances are without prefix. Besides, as 'atte style' became Styles, so 'atte steel' would have become Steels. It will be noticeable that all my examples are from the East Coast. The Scandinavian origin is manifest. Iron and steel are components of many of these early northern personal names; v. Stallard.

Robert Stele, co. Linc. 1273. A.
John Stel, co. Suff., ibid.
Johannes Stele, 1379: P. T. Yorks. p. 255.
Willelmus Steel, 1379: ibid. p. 250.
Willelmus Stele, 1379: ibid. p. 154.
1651. Married—John Steele, *batchler*, and Abigell Hannkok: St. Mary Aldermary, p. 22.
London, 25, 21, 0, 0; West Rid. Court Dir., 6, 6, 0, 0; Philadelphia, 115, 66, 2, 2; Manchester (Stell), 1.

Steen, Steenson; v. Stenson.

Steeple.—Local, 'of Steeple,' parishes in cos. Dorset and Essex. Of course the origin may be derived from residence beside any steeple attached to a church in the country, especially in such cases where the steeple was actually detached from the body of the church.
Morecambe, near Lancaster, 3; Philadelphia, 2.

Steer, Steere, Steers.—Nick. 'the steer,' the young ox; cf. Bull, Stott, &c. But v. Sterry, Storr, and Storey.

Willelmus Stere, 1379: P. T. Yorks. p. 106.
Johannes Stere, 1379: ibid.
1572. William Steere and Margery Pallemer: Reg. St. Dionis Backchurch, p. 7.
1580. Nicholas Steer, rector of Burnham Norton, co. Norf.: FF. vii. 18.
1697. Bapt. — Randall, s. Randall Steeres: St. Mary Aldermary, p. 112.

1748. Buried—John Steer: St. Mary Aldermary, p. 228.
Sheffield, 3, 0, 0; London, 20, 1, 3.

Steinkettle.—Bapt. 'the son of Steinketel,' i.e. 'stone cauldron.' Steinchetel is the form in Domesday, a compound of Kettle (v. Kettle and Chettle). It is found later as Stinkel; cf. Arkettle.
Richard Stinkel, co. Bedf., 1273. A.

Stelfox.—Nick.; v. Colfox.
Thomas Stelfox, of High Leigh, 1602: Wills at Chester, i. 183.
William Stilefox, of Goosnergh, 1672: Lancashire Wills at Richmond, i. 262.
London, 1; MDB. (co. Ches.), 4.

Stella.—(1) Bapt. 'the son of Stella.' (2) Local, 'of Stella,' a township in the parish of Ryton, co. Durham.
Stella de Thomholme, 1379: P. T. Yorks. p. 120.
London, 1; Philadelphia, 2.

Stemson; v. Stenson and Stimpson.

Stennett.—Bapt. 'the son of Steven' or Stephen, dim. Stevenet, modified into Stennett; v. Stephen.
1726. Bapt. — William, s. Rowland Stennet: St. Jas. Clerkenwell, ii. 163.
London, 1.

Stenning, Stennings.—Bapt. 'the son of Stening'; cf. Browning, Harding, &c. Stennings is the genitive; v. Jennings.
John Stenyng, co. Soms., 1 Edw. III: Kirby's Quest, p. 142.
1665. Richard Gardiner and Margaret Stenning: Marriage Alleg. (Canterbury), p. 104.
1750. Married — Richard Vezey and Mary Stenning: St. Geo. Chap. Mayfair, p. 159.
London, 3, 1.

Stenson, Steenson, Stemson.—(1) Bapt. 'the son of Stephen,' from the nick. Steen; v. Stimpson and Stephen. (2) Local, 'of Stenson,' a township in the parish of Barrow, co. Derby. As Stenson is a Derbyshire surname it is manifest that (2) is the more probable derivation. On the contrary it is almost certain that Steenson must be referred to (1).
Francis Steanson, co. York. W. 16.
John Steanson, co. York, ibid.
1747. Married — John Francis and Charlotte Stenson: St. Geo. Chap. Mayfair, p. 81.

1763. Married — Joseph Stenson and Ann Fareham: St. Geo. Han. Sq. i. 126.
MDB. (co. Derby), 3, 0, 0; Oxford, 0, 0, 1; Philadelphia, 5, 3, 0.

Stephen, Stephens, Stephenson, Stephan.—Bapt. 'the son of Stephen.' There is no instance of Stephen in Domesday Book. But like John and Peter, it gained popularity with great rapidity; and Stephen of Blois, of course, exercised an influence in its favour. It was enormously popular in the hereditary surname period, and, as a consequence, has endless representatives of nick. and pet forms in the directories of to-day (v. Steven, Stevens, Stevenson, Stimpson, &c.).
Gilbert fil. Stephani, co. Linc., 1273. A.
Jordan fil. Stephani, co. Essex, ibid.
Richard Stephen, co. Oxf., ibid.
Richard Stephenes, co. Soms., 1 Edw. III: Kirby's Quest, p. 101.
1585. Bapt. — Dorothy, d. William Stephens: St. Jas. Clerkenwell, i. 16.
1739. Married — James Stephen and Flora Young: St. Geo. Han. Sq. i. 22.
London, 1, 83, 35, 0; Philadelphia, 11, 81, 46, 7.

Stephings.—Bapt. 'the son of Stephen,' a corruption of Stephens, q.v. (cf. Jennings or Hewlings).
London, 1.

Stepkin.—Bapt. 'the son of Stephen,' from nick. Step, and suffix -kin; cf. Wilkin.
Lieutenant Charles Stepkin served under the Duke of Northumberland in 1640: v. Peacock's army list of Roundheads and Cavaliers, p. 78.
Theodosia Stepkin. V. 10.
1558. John Stepkyn and Alice Dades: Marriage Lic. (London), i. 18.
1628. Bapt.—Eadye, d. Roger Stepkin: St. Jas. Clerkenwell, i. 108.

Stepney, Stephany (?). — Local, 'of Stepney,' an important parish in co. Middlesex, now part of London.
1600. Robert Stepneth or Stepney, co. Herts: Reg. Univ. Oxf. vol. ii. pt. ii. p. 243.
1753. Married—William Hopkins and Eliz. Stepheny: St. Geo. Han. Sq. i. 49.
1760. — Daniel Holland and Jane Stepney: ibid. p. 95.
MDB. (co. Sussex), 2, 0; London, 0, 1; New York, 1, 4.

Steptoe, Stepto, Steptow.—Local. I cannot find the spot. The suffix is probably -how (v. How), as we find it in Shafto or

Shillito, &c. Mr. Lower says, 'Probably refers to gait.' This may be so, but the local derivation must be looked for first.
1751. Married—John Woodward and Eliz. Steptoo: St. Geo. Chap. Mayfair, p. 191.
1753. — Francis Fosset and Sarah Steptoe: ibid. p. 257.
1788. — Andrew Duncanson and Ruth Steptoe: St. Geo. Han. Sq. ii. 6.
1802. — William Steptoe and Martha Knight: ibid. p. 255.
London, 1, 3, 1; MDB. (co. Berks), 1, 0, 0; Oxford, 2, 0, 0.

Stern, Sterne. — Nick. 'the stern,' i. e. austere.
Henry Sterne, co. Camb., 1273. A.
Aubri Steryn, co. Camb., ibid.
William Sterne or Steryn, co. Camb., ibid.
1460. Henry Sterne, co. Norf.: FF. ii. 475.
1587. Bapt. — Anne, d. John Sterne: St. Jas. Clerkenwell, i. 10.
London, 4, 1; Philadelphia, 62, 4.

Sterry. — Bapt. 'the son of Sterre' (?); v. Starr.
Henricus Sterre, 1379: P. T. Yorks. p. 57.
Thomas Stere, 1379: ibid.
Henricus Sterre, 1379: ibid. p. 109.
1765. Married—Christian Sterry and Mary Frazier: St. Geo. Han. Sq. i. 147.
London, 5; Boston (U.S.), 2.

Steven, Stevens, Stevenson.—Bapt. 'the son of Stephen,' an early form; v. Stephen.
Philip Stevene, co. Soms., 1 Edw. III: Kirby's Quest, p. 240.
William Stevene, co. Soms., 1 Edw. III: ibid.
Magota Steuen-doghter (u for v), 1379: P. T. Yorks. p. 46.
Thomas Steuenson, 1379: ibid. p. 43.
Robert Steven, 1379: ibid.
1423. Laurence Stevene, rector of Wickhampton, co. Norf.: FF. xi. 136.
1600. Anthony Stephenes or Stevens, co. Wilts: Reg. Univ. Oxf. vol. ii. pt. ii. p. 242.
London, 1, 212, 54; Philadelphia, 2, 159, 251.

Steventon.—Local, 'of Steventon,' parishes in cos. Berks and Hants.
Edmund de Stewincton, co. Camb., 1273. A.
1321. Robert de Stevington, rector of Knapton, co. Norf.: FF. viii. 135.
1754. Married—James Steventon and Hannah Haynes: St. Geo. Han. Sq. i. 53.
MDB. (co. Salop), 2; London, 2.

Steverson.—Bapt. 'the son of Stephen,' a corruption of Stephenson; cf. Patterson for Pattinson, or Catterson for Cattinson.

1656. Married — Robart Warner and Katherin Steverson : St. Peter, Cornhill, i. 260.
London, 4 ; New York, 1.

Steveson.—Bapt. 'the son of Stephen,' a corruption of Stephenson ; cf. Pattison for Pattinson.

Philadelphia, 2.

Steward, Stewardson, Stewards, Stuard.—(1) Bapt. 'the son of Steuhard' or Stuard, genitive Stewards.

Stuard Cachellus, co. Norf., 1273. A.
Martin Steuhard, co. Norf., ibid.
Nicholas Staward, co. Soms., 1 Edw. III : Kirby's Quest, p. 275.
Adam Staward, co. Soms., 1 Edw. III : ibid.
Willelmus Stuard, 1379 : P. T. Yorks. p. 126.
1581. John Steward or Stuarde, co. Northampt. : Reg. Univ. Oxf. vol. ii. pt. ii. p. 101.
1710. Richard Stewardson, appointed under-usher of Grammar School attached to St. Mary's Hospital, Newcastle-on-Tyne : Brand's Newcastle, i. 95.
1800. Married — Joseph Stewardson and Eliz. Bland : St. Geo. Han. Sq. ii. 214.

(2) Offic. 'the steward.'

Adam fe Stiuuard, co. Glouc., 1273. A.
Hugh le Stiward, co. Norf., ibid.
London, 20, 1, 1, 0 ; Philadelphia, 43, 4, 0, 16.

Stewart, Stuart.—Sharpened forms of Steward and Stuard, q.v. The following entries manifestly refer to the same parents :

1723. Bapt.—John, s. Robert and Edy Steward : St. Jas. Clerkenwell, i. 144.
1725. — Jane, d. Robert and Ede Stewart : ibid. p. 152.
London, 82, 44 ; Philadelphia, 561, 89.

Stibbard.—Local, 'of Stibbard,' a parish in co. Norfolk, four miles from Fakenham.

Alice de Stiberd, co. Norf., 1273. A.
Richard de Stibarde, co. Norf., ibid.
1806. Married — Giles Stibbert and Jane Slatter : St. Geo. Han. Sq. ii. 348.
London, 2.

Sticker.—Occup. 'the sticker,' probably a pig-sticker. Wiltshire and the adjacent district are still famous for their bacon.

John le Stikkere, co. Soms., 1 Edw. III : Kirby's Quest, p. 190.
1686. Buried — Lucilla Sticher : St. Michael, Cornhill, p. 269.

The preceding entry is quoted, but it is doubtful whether or no it concerns Sticker.

New York, 1 ; Philadelphia, 4.

Stickley.—Local, 'at the Stickley,' from residence thereby ; probably some meadow of a sticky soil.

William atte Sticlegh, co. Soms., 1 Edw. III : Kirby's Quest, p. 113.
Simon Sticcle, co. Soms., 1 Edw. III : ibid. p. 194.
1606. Married — John Stickley and Rose Powell : St. Mary Aldermary, p. 11.
1752. — William Stickly and Sarah Bonus : St. Geo. Chap. Mayfair, p. 224.
London, 2 ; Oxford, 1 ; Philadelphia, 5.

Stickney.—Local, 'of Stickney,' a parish in co. Lincoln, nine miles from Boston.

1582. William Stickney and Dorothy Clenche : Marriage Lic. (London), i. 108. Philadelphia, 9.

Stiff.—Nick. 'the stiff,' rigid in feature or obstinate in temper. 'The vowel was once long' (Skeat). Hence the form of entry immediately below :

John Stife, co. Wilts, 1273. A.
Robert Stife, co. Wilts, ibid.
1682. Married — Thomas Stiffe and Margaret Pane : St. Jas. Clerkenwell, i. 196.
1702. Bapt.—William, s. Joseph Stiffe : ibid. ii. 8.
London, 9 ; Philadelphia, 1.

Stiffbow.—Nick. The opposite of Benbow, q.v.

John Stiffbowe : Patent Roll, 3 Edw. VI. pt. v.

Stiggins.—Bapt. 'the son of Stigand,' the name of the archbishop who crowned Harold ; more recently immortalized by Charles Dickens in 'Pickwick.'

Bartholomew Stegin, co. Camb., 1273. A.
Gervase fil. Stigandi, Pipe Rolls, 6 Hen. II.
1706. Married—John Carrier and Anne Stigans : St. Peter, Cornhill, ii. 66.
1747. — John Harris and Mary Stiggins : St. Geo. Han. Sq. i. 38.
Boston (U.S.), 1.

Stileman. — Local ; v. Styleman.

Stile(s.—Local ; v. Style.

Still. — Nick. 'the still,' the quiet ; cf. the opposite Snell or Quick, the active. While this

seems perfectly satisfactory, v. Style and Styleman for another parentage. But Mr. Lower says that Stille was a tenant prior to Domesday. Therefore the name may be personal.

Walter Stille, co. Oxf., 1273. A.
Robert Stille, co. Soms., 1 Edw. III : Kirby's Quest, p. 196.
1610. Nathaniel Still and Jane Whitmore : Marriage Lic. (London), i. 319.
1639. Married—John Caille and Eliz. Stille : St. Mary Aldermary, p. 18.
London, 10 ; Philadelphia, 1.

Stillingfleet.—Local, 'of Stillingfleet,' a parish in E. Rid. Yorks, seven miles from York.

Henricus de Stilyngflete, 1379 : P. T. Yorks. p. 29.
Johannes de Stilyngflete, 1379 : ibid.
Willelmus de Styllyngflete, 1379 : P. T. Howdenshire, p. 20.
1587. Married—Robert Lockson and Alice Stullingflet : St. Peter, Cornhill, i. 236.
1783. — Rev. James Stillingfleet and Eliz. Hale : St. Geo. Han. Sq. i. 346. Crockford, 1.

Stillman.—Local ; v. Styleman, a variant.

Stimpson, Stimson, Stinson. —Bapt. 'the son of Stephen' or Steven, patr. Steven-son, corrupted to Stinson or Stimson. The *p* in Stimpson is intrusive and follows *m*, as in Simpson, Thompson, or Hampson ; cf. Sinkinson for Simkinson.

Joseph Stinson, co. York. W. 11.
1624. Bapt.—Hugh, son of John Stimpson : Reg. St. Jas. Clerkenwell, i. 98.
1742. John Stimpson, Norwich : FF. iv. 448.
1793. Married—Thomas Edbrook and Mary Stempson : St. Geo. Han. Sq. ii. 90.

In a muster-roll of able-bodied men at Newcastle-on-Tyne in 1539 occur the names of

Edward Stynson : PPP. ii. 174-94.
Stewyn Sotheron : ibid.
Allen Stewenson : ibid.
John Stewynsone : ibid.
Stewne Smythe : ibid.
1705. Bapt.—Thomas, s. Thomas Stimson : St. Jas. Clerkenwell, i. 27.
London, 6, 4, 2 ; MDB. (co. Leic.), 0, 0, 3 ; Philadelphia, 0, 0, 55.

Stirk, Stirke. — Nick. 'the Stirk' (v. Stirkherd) ; cf. Bull, Stott, Steer, &c.

Juliana Sterk, co. Soms., 1 Edw. III : Kirby's Quest, p. 126.

Maurice Sterk, co. Soms., 1 Edw. III : Kirby's Quest, p. 127.
John le Sterk, co. Soms., 1 Edw. III : ibid. p. 226.
William le Sterk, co. Soms., 1 Edw. III : ibid.
Thomas Styrke, 1379 : P. T. Yorks. p. 277.
Robertus Styrke, 1379 : ibid.
1742. Bapt.—Ann, d. Robert Stirke : St. Jas. Clerkenwell, ii. 260.
1746. Married — Benjamin Stirk and Ann Gorsuch : St. Geo. Chap. Mayfair, p. 65.
London, 1, 1 ; Philadelphia, 7, 0.

Stirkherd.—Occup. 'the stirkherd,' a tender of stirks ; v. Hird and Herd. Cf. Stoddart, Calvert, Coward, Oxnard, &c.
Gilbert Stirkhirde : Pardons Roll, 6 Ric. II.
Johannes Styrkhyrd-smith, 1379 : P. T. Yorks p. 268.

Stirling.—Local, 'of Stirling,' the capital of the shire of that name in Scotland.
1770. Married—John Stirling and Ann Bunyard : St. Geo. Han. Sq. i. 195.
London, 7 ; Philadelphia, 18.

Stirrup, Stirrip.—Local, 'of Styrrup,' a township in the parishes of Blyth, Harworth, and Houghton, co. Notts.
Ingeram de Stirap, co. Notts, 1273. A.
Norman de Stirap, co. Notts, ibid.
Margery de Styrop, 44 Edw. III. P.
William de Styrapp, Close Roll, 18 Ric. II.
Willelmus Styrape, 1379 : P. T. Yorks. p. 73.
Agnes que fuit uxor Willelmi Sterappe, osteler, 1379 : ibid. p. 72.
1751. Bapt.—Mary, d. Thomas Stirrup : St. Dionis Backchurch, p. 175.
London 0, 1 ; New York, 2, 0.

Stirzaker, Starziker, Stirzacker.—Local, 'of Steresaker,' some spot not far from Preston, co. Lanc., which I have not identified. The suffix, of course, is -acre, as in Whittaker, Linaker, &c.—Since writing the above I find the spot is in Garstang parish.
Johannes de Steresaker, 1379 : P. T. Yorks. p. 262.
William Steresaker, York, 1477 : W. 11, p. 101.
1620. Thomas Styrsaker, co. Leic. (? Lanc.) : Reg. Univ. Oxf. vol. ii. pt. ii. p. 384.
John Mawdesley de Sturzaker, 1622 : Preston Guild Rolls, p. 85.

Robert Sturzaker, 1664, Garstang : Exchequer Depositions, co. Lanc., p. 38.
John Sturzaker, 1664, Garstang : ibid. p. 39.
Evan Pilkinton, of Sturzaker, in Garstang, 1668 : Lancashire Wills at Richmond, i. 216.
1738. Bapt.—James, s. George Sterzaker : St. Jas. Clerkenwell, ii. 240.
Liverpool, 4, 0, 0 ; Croston (co. Lanc.), 0, 1, 0 ; MDB. (co. Lanc.), 4, 0, 1 ; Lancaster, 3, 0, 0.

St. John.—Local, 'of St. John.' Several parishes in Normandy bear this title. It is found in England soon after the Conquest.
William de St. John, co. Bedf., 1273. A.
Robert de St. John, co. Hants, ibid.
Hugh de St. John, co. Hants, 20 Edw. I. R.
1530. Alexander Seynt John and Jane Leventhorpe : Marriage Lic. (London), i. 7.
1785. Married — Philip Hingston and Ann Saint John : St. Geo. Han. Sq. i. 376.
London, 7 ; Philadelphia, 9.

Stobbs.—Local, 'at the stobbs,' from residence thereby. A variant of Stubbs, q.v.
MDB. (co. Durham), 5 ; Philadelphia, 1.

Stock, Stocks.—Local, 'at the stock,' the stump, the trunk of a tree, post, &c., from residence thereby ; cf. Stubbs. A big, exposed tree-trunk, or clump of tree-trunks, would readily give a surname to one who lived close by. But v. Stoke.
Reginald de la Stocke, co. Oxf., 1273. A.
William de la Stocke, co. Oxf., ibid.
Jordan atte Stokk, co. Soms., 1 Edw. III : Kirby's Quest, p. 110.
William atte Stock, co. Soms., 1 Edw. III : ibid. p. 178.
Reginald atte Stocke, Close Roll, 4 Edw. III.
Johanna del Stok, 1409 : W. 11, p. 239.
1788. Married—Richard Vaughan and Mary Stocks : St. Geo. Han. Sq. ii. 2.
1790. — Thomas Stock and Eliz. Beake : ibid. p. 52.
London, 27, 4 ; Philadelphia, 28, 3.

Stockbridge.—Local, 'of Stockbridge,' a parish in co. Hants.
Cristina de Stocbrugg', co. Oxf., 1273. A.
Richard de Stokebrigg, co. Hants, 20 Edw. I. R.
Sibilla de Stokbrig', 1379 : P. T. Yorks. p. 49.
1790. Married — Robert Sharpe and Mary Stockbridge : St. Geo. Han. Sq. ii. 52.
London, 1 ; MDB. (co. Camb.), 6 ; Boston (U.S.), 8.

Stockdale.—Local, 'of Stockdale,' one of the dales in North England. I have failed to identify it. The surname is fairly familiar in the northern counties, and has crossed the Atlantic. Probably the locality will be found in Yorkshire, on the borders of Westmoreland.
Willelmus de Stokdale, 1379 : P. T. Yorks. p. 282.
Johannes de Stokdele, 1379 : ibid.
1593. Gregory Stocdalle or Stockdale, co. York : Reg. Univ. Oxf. vol. ii. pt. ii. p. 197.
1624. Francis Stockdale, of Aynsome : Lancashire Wills at Richmond, i. 263.
1695. Margaret Stockdall, of Warton : ibid. ii. 240.
1731. Married—Thomas Stockdale and Eliz. Colly : St. Geo. Han. Sq. i. 9.
1773. — Edward Stockdell and Sarah Gooch : ibid. p. 236.
London, 1 ; Lancaster, 2 ; MDB. (co. Cumb.), 5 ; Philadelphia, 7.

Stocker, Stoker.—Occup. 'the stocker,' possibly one who lived by a stub, stock, or stump. But more probably occupative. 'Stockers, persons employed to fell or grub up trees. West England' (Halliwell). With this rendering, cf. Grubber.
1260. Walter le Stockere : Cal. of Wills in Court of Husting.
Elena le Stocker, co. Bucks, 1273. A.
Cf. Alan Stayker, co. Linc., ibid.
John Stokker, C. R., 28 Hen. VI.
1740. Buried—Mary Stocker : St. Mary Aldermery (London), p. 225.
1794. Married — Alex. Stoker and Mary Maria Cook : St. Geo. Han. Sq. ii. 118.
London, 13, 5 ; Philadelphia, 24, 12.

Stockham, Stockum.—Local, 'of Stockham,' a township in the parish of Runcorn, co. Ches. Stockum is an American variant ; cf. Barnum for Barnham. As I have said of Stockwell, probably other small spots were called Stockham ; v. Stock and Ham.
William de Stockham, co. Somerset, 1273. A.
Crockford, 1, 0 ; Philadelphia, 6, 3.

Stocking, Stocken, Stockin.—Local, 'at the stocking,' i.e. the little stock, a dim. of Stock, q.v. Curiously enough, the article of dress so called is a dim. of the same word (v. *stocking*, Skeat's Dict.).

Edmund del Stocking, co. Bucks, 1273. A.
1759. Married — John Stocking (co. Norf.) and Eliz. Wright : St. Geo. Han. Sq. i. 88.
London, 1, 6, 0 ; MDB. (co. Camb.), 1, 0, 0 ; Boston (U.S.), 1, 0, 3.

Stockley, Stokley, Stokely. —Local, ' of Stockley.' Two parishes in co. Devon, and a township in the parish of Brancepeth, in co. Durham, bear this name. Other smaller spots would probably bear it ; v. Stock and Ley.

Ralph de Stockleye, co. Suffolk, 1273. A.
Pagan de Stockleye, co. Oxf., ibid.
1791. Married — Phillip Stone and Temperance Stockley : St. Geo. Han. Sq. ii. 63.
London, 2, 0, 0 ; Philadelphia, 8, 14, 3.

Stockman.—Occup. ' the stockman,' the man who lived at the stock ; v. Stock and Stoke ; cf. Stead and Steadman, Bridge and Bridgman, Style and Styleman.

Emma Stokeman, co. Oxf., 1273. A.
Johannes Stokman, 1379 : P. T. Yorks. p. 115.
1548. Buried—Mabell Stockman : St. Michael, Cornhill, p. 75.
William Stockman, Sarum, 1609 : Reg. Univ. Oxf. vol. ii. pt. ii. p. 307.
London, 6 ; Philadelphia, 15.

Stockport.—Local, ' of Stockport' ; very rare, Stopford (q.v.) being the accepted form.

MDB. (co. Lanc.), 2.

Stockton.—Local, ' of Stockton-on-Tees.' But many small spots would naturally bear this name ; v. Stock and Town.

Geoffrey de Stockton, co. Worc., 1273. A.
John de Stokton, *zonarius*, 1 Edw. II : Freemen of York, i. 11.
Johannes de Stokton, 1379 : P. T. Yorks. p. 294.
1605-6. Jonas Stockton, co. Warwick : Reg. Univ. Oxf. vol. ii. pt. ii. p. 288.
1627. Thomas Stockton, of Wiglands : Wills at Chester, ii. 209.
1650. Margaret Stockton, of Durham : ibid.
West Rid. Court Dir., 1 ; Manchester, 1 ; Philadelphia, 40.

Stockwell.—Local, ' of Stockwell,' formerly a chapelry in the parish of Lambeth, co. Surrey. Probably other and smaller spots were so called ; v. Stock and Well.

Egidius de Stokwelle, co. Oxf., 1273. A.
Alicia de Stokwell, co. Oxf., ibid.
Elias de Stokwell, 1379 : P. T. Yorks. p. 7.
1581-2. William Stockwell, co. Warwick : Reg. Univ. Oxf. vol. ii. pt. ii. p. 117.
1587. Buried—Eliz., wife of William Stockwell : St. Jas. Clerkenwell, iv. 36.
West Rid. Court Dir., 3 ; London, 3 ; Philadelphia, 7.

Stodart, Stoddard, Stoddart, Stodard.—Occup. (1) ' the studherd'; v. Studdard.

' A false stodmere,' i.e. studmare : York Mystery Plays, p. 193, l. 13.

(2) Possibly the same as Stotherd, q.v. With the sharpened forms Stodart and Stoddart, cf. Calvert for Calveherd.

1765. Married—George Stoddart and Esther Tallents : St. Geo. Han. Sq. i. 140.
1789. — Swinton Stodart and Jane Whinham : ibid. ii. 16.
1803. — John Jenkins and Mary Stoddard : ibid. p. 287.
London, 2, 1, 7, 0 ; West Rid. Court Dir., 0, 0, 2, 0 ; New York, 1, 18, 10, 1.

Stogdon, Stogden. — Local, ' of Stockton' (?). Probably a variant of Stockton, q.v. ; cf. Slagg and Slack, &c.

1753. Married — John Stogdon and Mary Britton : St. Geo. Chap. Mayfair, p. 239.
Crockford, 2, 0 ; Philadelphia, 0, 1.

Stoke, Stokes. — Local, ' of Stoke.' There are sixty-six parishes in Crockford either simply Stoke or compounded, as in such cases as Stoke Bishop, Stoke Canon, Stoke Ash, Stoke Courcy. It is to be noticed that all the entries of Stoke (with one exception) are prefixed with *de*, those of Stock with *de la* or *atte* ; ' de Stoke' implies a town or village, ' de la Stock' or ' atte Stock,' some single stump of a tree, &c., where the nominee dwelt. Etymologically, Stoke is a much older form than Stock. Monosyllabic local surnames commonly add the genitive *s*, as in Williams, Jones, &c. ; cf. Holmes, Brooks, Styles. Hence Stoke is now almost unknown.

Baldewin de Stoke, co. Suff., 1273. A.
Mariota de Stoke, co. Hunts, ibid.
Robert de Stokes, co. Oxf., ibid.
Seman de Stokes, co. Northampt., ibid.
Adam del Stoke, 1379 : P. T. Yorks. p. 270.

Walter de Stoke, co. Soms., 1 Edw. III : Kirby's Quest, p. 137.
London, 0, 49 ; Philadelphia, 0, 125.

Stokely, Stokley ; v. Stockley. The variants are American.
Philadelphia, 3, 14.

Stoker.—Occup. ; v. Stocker.

Stollard ; v. Stallard.

Stonard ; v. Stannard.

Stone, Stones.—Local, ' at the stone ' or stones (cf. Styles, Stubbs, Stocks, &c.), from residence beside some remarkable roadside stone or rock.

Warin de la Stane, co. Devon, 1273. A.
Reginald ad Ston', co. Bedf., ibid.
John de la Stone, co. Sussex, ibid.
Johannes del Stone, 1379 : P. T. Yorks. p. 53.
Robertus del Stones, 1379 : ibid. p. 180.
Elena de Stones, 1379 : ibid. p. 42.
Robert atte Stone, C. R., 31 Edw. I.
John atte Stone, co. Soms., 1 Edw. III : Kirby's Quest, p. 139.
1609. Bapt.—John, s. Francis Stone : St. Jas. Clerkenwell, i. 57.
London, 119, 3 ; West Rid. Court Dir., 4, 9 ; Philadelphia, 91, 2.

Stoneham.—Local, ' of Stoneham.' North and South Stoneham are parishes in co. Hants, near Southampton. Smaller localities bearing the name doubtless exist, and have furnished representatives.

William de Stonham, co. Camb., 1273. A.
Stephen de Stonham, co. Linc., ibid.
1603. John Stoneham : Reg. Univ. Oxf. i. 356.
1790. Married — Thomas Stoneham and Rebecca Markwick : St. Geo. Han. Sq. ii. 42.
London, 6 ; Philadelphia, 1.

Stonehewer, Stonier. — Occup. ' the stone-hewer,' a stonemason or quarryman. Similarly we find Woodhewer, Fleshhewer (q.v.), Blockhewer, and Blocker ; cf. ' hewers of wood ' (Authorized Version). My first instance is no doubt a misreading :

Thomas Stonhewaa, co. Oxf., 1273. A.
Richard Stonhewer. SS.
1605. John Stonehewer or Stonier, of Barleyford, co. Ches. : Wills at Chester, i. 184.
1638. George Stonier, of Odd Rode : ibid. ii. 209.
1702. Married—Charles Edward Pigon and Charlotte Rycroft ; witness, Richard Stonhewer : St. Geo. Han. Sq. ii. 81.

Manchester, 0, 6; MDB. (co. Ches.), 1, 0; (co. Essex), 1, 0.

Stonehill, Stonhill. — Local, 'at the stone-hall' (?), from residence therein. The evidence is, so far as I can discover, in favour of this derivation, viz. the hall or mansion built of stone, not the stony hill, which is a modern and natural corruption.

Michael de Stonehale, co. Salop, 1273. A. William de la Stonhall, co. Camb., ibid.

I cannot hesitate to say that this is the origin of the name; cf. these two entries :

1693. Buried—Richard Stonehall : St. Michael, Cornhill, p. 273.
1694. — Mary Stonell : ibid. p. 274.

The following are manifest corruptions :

1703. Married — Richard Stonell and Eliz. Spakeman : St. Jas. Clerkenwell, i. 226.
1750. — Richard Sills and Mary Stonnill : St. Geo. Han. Sq. i. 43.
1797. '— Nathaniel Stonhill and Catherine Anderton : ibid. ii. 171.
London, 0, 1; Oxford, 1, 0; Philadelphia, 2, 0.

Stonehouse, Stonhouse. — Local (1), 'at the stone-house' (v. Stannus), from residence therein; cf. Woodhouse, Moorhouse, Parkhouse, &c. Many dwellings would be so termed.

John del Stonhuse, C. R., 47 Hen. III.

(2) Local, 'of Stonehouse,' a parish in co. Gloucester.

John de Stonhus, co. Glouc., 1273. A.
1581. Walter Stonehouse or Stonhowse, co. Middlesex : Reg. Univ. Oxf. vol. ii. pt. ii. p. 111.
1618. Bapt. — Thomas, s. Cristofer Stonhowse : St. Dionis Backchurch, p. 97.
1773. Married—William Stonehouse and Rebecca Kerby : St. Geo. Han. Sq. i. 228.
London, 2, 0; Crockford, 1, 1; Boston (U.S.), 3, 0.

Stoneman.—Local, 'the stoneman,' the man who dwelt at the stone; v. Stone; cf. Bridgman, Stockman, Steadman, Styleman, &c.

1572. —— Stoneman : Reg. Univ. Oxf. vol. ii. pt. ii. p. 31.
1751. Married — John Stoneman and Hannah Clifford : St. Geo. Chap. Mayfair, p. 204.
1753. — Richard Stoneman and Mary Chipperfield : ibid. p. 236.
London, 4; Philadelphia, 2.

Stoner. — Local or occup.; v. Stanier.

Stonestreet.—Local, 'at the stone street,' i.e. the paved road, from residence therein. Mr. Lower suggests that as this name sprang up in the neighbourhood of Sussex, it may represent the old Roman road from Chichester to London, anciently called Stanistreet (Patr. Brit. p. 331).

Salomon de Stonstrete, co. Kent, 1273. A.
1616. John Coppin and Sarah Stonistreet : Marriage Lic. (London), ii. 47.
1754. Married—William Box and Mary Stonestreet : St. Geo. Han. Sq. i. 54.
MDB. (co. Sussex), 1; Worcester, (U.S.), 1.

Stoney.—Local, 'of Stoney.' Several places, Stoney Middleton (Derbyshire) and Stony Stratford (Bucks), for instance, bear this name as a prefix. But I can supply no further information.

Agnes Stany, 1379 : P. T. Yorks. p. 139.
Peter Stoney, C. R., 6 Edw. II.
1803. Married — Elijah Stoney and Sarah Weaver : St. Geo. Han. Sq. ii. 295.
London, 1; West Rid. Court Dir., 1; Philadelphia, 3.

Stonhill ; v. Stonehill.

Stonier ; v. Stonehewer.

Stonor.—Local, 'of Stonor,' an estate in co. Oxford, thus described by Leland : 'Stonor is three miles out of Henley. Ther is a fayre parke and a warren of Connes and fayre woods. . . . Sir Walter Stonor, now possessor of it, hathe augmentyd and strengthed the howse. The Stonors hath longe had it in possessyon' (v. Lower's Patr. Brit. p. 331).

Richard de Stonore, co. Oxf., 1273. A.
1545. Roger Tidder, of the household of our Lord the King, and Margery Stonar, of Dioc. Oxon, widow : Marriage Lic. (Faculty Office), p. 4.
1621-2. William Stonor, Esq., and Eliz. Lake : Marriage Lic. (London), ii. 108.
London Court Dir., 2.

Stoodley ; v. Studley.

Stopford, Stopforth.—Local, 'of Stockport.' The old name for Stockport, an important town and parish in co. Cheshire, near Manchester.

Thomas Stoppforth, 1379 : P. T. Yorks. p. 43.
Roger de Stokeport, 17 Edw. I : East Cheshire, ii. 338.

1549. Oliver Stokport, mayor of Stockport : ibid. p. 347.
1574. Married — Robert Stopforthe and Ellen Osbalston : Prestbury Ch., co. Ches., p. 45.
1594. James Stopforth, of Latham : Wills at Chester, i. 184.
1601. Married—Ralph Stockport and Margaret Collier : East Cheshire, ii. 405.
1616. William Stopford, of Melling : Wills at Chester, i. 184.
1674. William Stopford, of Macclesfield : East Cheshire, i. 457.
London, 2, 0; MDB. (co. Lanc.), 2, 2.

Stoppard.—Local, 'of Stockport,' a corruption of Stopford, an old name for Stockport; v. Stopford. There need be no hesitation in accepting this derivation.

1625. Married — Edward Mottershed and Joane Stopport : Prestbury Ch., East Ches., p. 251.
1635. — John Delves and Margaret Stoppard : ibid. p. 297.
1659. 'Mr. Stoppard, a minister in Lancashyre' : East Cheshire, i. 228.

Of this solution there cannot be the shadow of a doubt. From Stopford the popular pronunciation became Stoppard.

Manchester, 1.

Stops, Stopps, Stopp.—Local, 'at the stopps' (?), i.e. stoup or gatepost : the usual term in Ulverston, or Furness generally, for any tall stone post. Probably, however, the instance below is an early variant of Stobb or Stubb (v. Stubbs) ; cf. Hopps for Hobbs.

William del Stopp, 1379 : P. T. Yorks. p. 177.
1759. Married—John Paine and Mary Stopps : St. Geo. Han. Sq. i. 87.
London, 1, 0, 0; West Riding Court Dir., 0, 1, 0; New York, 0, 0, 2.

Storer.—Occup. and offic. 'the storer,' one who stored goods, probably an officer in the feudal household; v. Storey. But more probably a wool-storer, a warehouseman. The name is frequently met with in the Yorks. Poll Tax, 1379.

Johannes Storour, 1379 : P. T. Yorks. p. 256.
Hugo Storrour, 1379 : ibid. p. 257.
Thomas Storour, 1379 : ibid. p. 21.
Henricus Storour, 1379 : ibid.
1771. Married — Joseph Storer and Mary Kightley : St. Geo. Han. Sq. i. 216.
London, 8; West Rid. Court Dir., 1; Sheffield, 2; Philadelphia, 7.

Storey, Story, Storry, Storie, Storrie, Storrey.—Personal, 'the son of Storr' (q.v.), popularly Storry.

Thomas Storre, 1379: P. T. Yorks. p. 109.
Johannes Storre, 1379: ibid. p. 43.
Roger Storre, 1379: ibid.

Storey is still among the most familiar of Yorkshire names, but it has become, of necessity, mixed with Storer, which also is well established in that county.

Johannes Staury, 1379: P. T. Yorks. p. 40.
1554. John Williams and Agnes Storry: Marriage Lic. (London), i. 15.
1576. Bapt.—Christopher Storey: St. Jas. Clerkenwell, i. 9.
West Rid. Court Dir., 6, 5, 1, 0, 0, 0; London, 23, 11, 1, 1, 0, 0; Philadelphia, 22, 24, 3, 0, 3, 1.

Stork, Storck.—Nick. 'the stork,' the bird so called; cf. Nightingale, Hawk, Sparrow, &c.

Thomas Storck, co. Suff., 1273. A.
John Stork, C. R., 16 Hen. VI.
Simon Storke, 1535: Reg. Univ. Oxf. i. 184.
1580-1. Edward Graves and Eliz. Storke: Marriage Lic. (London), i. 100.
1784. Married — James Round and Mary Storck: St. Geo. Han. Sq. i. 355.
Sheffield, 5, 0; Philadelphia, 9, 2.

Storm, Sturm.—? Bapt. 'the son of Storm.' No doubt a personal name; cf. Frost, Winter, Snow, and, in later epoch, Christmas, Midwinter, &c.

Edmund Storm, co. Norf., 1273. A.
Hugo Storm, co. Norf., ibid.
Agnes Storme, 1379: P. T. Yorks. p. 157.
1643. Bapt.—Oliver, s. Henrye Storme: St. Jas. Clerkenwell, i. 156.
Sheffield, 1, 0; London, 0, 1; Philadelphia, 10, 14.

Storr, Storrs.—Personal, 'the son of Storr.' A.S. stor, large, big; Danish stor, large, great. Genitive Storrs; cf. Williams, Jenkins, &c.; v. Storey.

1751. Married—Holland Cooksey and Eliz. Storrs: St. Geo. Chap. Mayfair, p. 203.
1784. — John Hewett and Norris Storr: St. Geo. Han. Sq. i. 48.
London, 5, 1; West Rid. Court Dir., 2, 1; New York, 0, 11; Philadelphia, 2, 0.

Stotherd, Stodart, Stoddart, Stoddard, Stodhart, Stothard,

Stothert.—Occup. 'the stot-herd,' one who tended stots, i.e. bullocks, the bullock-herd; v. Stott. All these forms are North English, and must be distinguished from Studdard and Stuttard (q. v.), with their other corruptions, although no doubt all are now inextricably mixed; cf. Calvert, Coward, Oxnard, Shepard, &c.

Willelmus Stothyrd, 1379: P. T. Yorks. p. 278.
Willelmus Stautohird, 1379: ibid. p. 165.
1778. Married—William Stothart and Mary Heath: St. Geo. Han. Sq. i. 294.
1788. — Swinton Stodart and Jane Winhamm: ibid. ii. 16.
1802. — Benjamin Wray and Mary Stothard: ibid. p. 266.

The West Rid. Court Directory has also the form Stothert.

London, 0, 2, 7, 1, 0, 1, 0; New York, 0, 1, 10, 18, 0, 1, 0.

Stott.—Nick.; v. Stotherd. A familiar North-English surname. 'Stot, a bullock. Scandinavian' (Skeat). 'Stot, a young ox. North' (Halliwell). 'Stotte, boveau' (Palsgrave). Cf. stot-plough (Halliwell).

The live stock at Bolton Abbey (1526) included ' xx oxen, xii wedders, ix tuppes, xxvi stotts': Whitaker's Craven, p. 403.
1634. Charles Stott, of the parish of Rochdale: Wills at Chester, ii. 209.
1649. James Stott, of Heywood, parish of Bury: ibid.
1651. Bapt.—Eliz., d. Richard Stot: St. Jas. Clerkenwell, i. 178.
London, 4; West Rid. Court Dir., 18; MDB. (co. Lanc.), 30; Philadelphia, 35.

Stoughton.—Local, 'of Stoughton,' a parish in co. Sussex; also a chapelry in the parish of Thurnby, co. Leic.

Eborard de Stouton, co. Hunts, 1273. A.
1577. Thomas Whitehorne and Eliz. Stoughton: Marriage Lic. (London), i. 75.
1687. Bapt.—Mary, d. Philip Stoughton: St. Jas. Clerkenwell, i. 324.
London, 1; MDB. (co. Glouc.), 1; Philadelphia, 6.

Stout, Stoute. — Nick. 'the Stout'; cf. Bigg, Little, &c. Stout was once a familiar surname in cos. Lancaster and York. It is now somewhat rare in England, but flourishes in America.

Willelmus Stoute, 1379: P. T. Yorks. p. 300.
Johannes Stoute, 1379: ibid. p. 142.

Robert Stout, of Lowd Scales, 1692: Lancashire Wills at Richmond, ii. 241.
Jenet Stoute, of Borwick, parish of Warton, 1720: ibid.
London, 2, 0; Liverpool, 3, 0; Philadelphia, 103, 2.

Stovel, Stovell. — Local, 'of Stovile.' I do not know the place. It looks what is usually termed ' of Norman extraction.'

Agnes de Stovile, co. Camb., 1273. A.
Humfrey de Stovil, co. Bucks, ibid.
1765. Married—Robert Fortescue and Mary Stovell: St. Geo. Han. Sq. i. 141.
London, 1, 5; Philadelphia, 0, 5.

Stovin. — Local, 'of Stoven,' a parish in co. Suffolk. This surname seems to have passed through co. Lincoln into Yorkshire, and thence into North Lancashire.

1612. Edmund Stovine, of Caton: Lancashire Wills at Richmond, i. 263.
1627. William Stovin, of Caton: ibid.
1628. Geoffrey Stovyne, of Caton: ibid.
1720. Richard Stoving, of Heysham: ibid. ii. 241.
MDB. (co. Lincoln), 3.

Stow, Stowe. — Local, 'of Stow.' A.S. and M.E. stów, a place; cf. Chepstow, i. e. the market - place, and Plaistow, the play-place, the open space for games, &c. There are six parishes of Stow and five of Stowe in England (v. Crockford). The parishes in cos. Lincoln and Cambridge seem to have been the chief parents.

Baldwin de Stow, co. Camb., 1273. A.
Warin de Stowe, co. Camb., ibid.
Fulk de Stow, co. Linc., ibid.
Oda de Stow, co. Linc., ibid.
Ricardus de Stowe, 1379: P. T. Yorks. p. 250.
1765. Married — Samuel Stow and Hannah Needham: St. Geo. Han. Sq. i. 141.
London, 5, 2; Philadelphia, 12, 2.

Stowell.—Local, ' of Stowell,' parishes in cos. Gloucester and Somerset; also a tithing in the parish of Overton, co. Wilts.

Richard de Stawell, co. Wilts, 1273. A.
Lecia Stowelle, co. Camb., ibid.
Geoffrey de Stawelle, co. Soms., 1 Edw. III: Kirby's Quest, p. 118.
Adam de Stawell, co. Somerset, Hen. III–Edw. I. K.
Urmfrey de Stoville, co. Wilts, ibid.
1591. John Stowell, co. Somerset: Reg. Univ. Oxf. vol. ii. pt. ii. p. 183.

3 A

1754. Married—John Stowell and Margaret Traley: St. Geo. Han. Sq. i. 54. London, 3; Philadelphia, 1.

Strafford, Stratford.—Local: (1) ' of Strafforth,' in the W. Rid. Yorks; v. Ford and Forth. (2) ' of Stratford,' parishes in cos. Bucks, Warwick, Wilts, Suffolk, &c.

Roger de Stratforthe, co. Bucks, 1273. A.
William de Stratford, co. Oxf., ibid.
Hugh de Stratford, co. Bucks, ibid.
Walter de Stratforde, co. Soms., 1 Edw. III: Kirby's Quest, p. 112.
Thomas Strafforth, 1379: P. T. Yorks. p. 160.
Anthony Stratford, co. Glouc., 1589: Reg. Univ. Oxf. vol. ii. pt. ii. p. 174.
George Stratford, co. Glouc., 1589: ibid.
1620. Bapt.—Roger, s. Edmond Stratforde: St. Jas. Clerkenwell, i. 87.
1803. Married—Edmond Norton and Mary Strafford: St. Geo. Han. Sq. ii. 273.
Leeds, 1, 11; Sheffield, 3, 0; Philadelphia, 3, 1.

Strainbow.—Nick. Cf. Stiffbow, Benbow, &c. Sobriquets from archery taking off moral qualities were of likely occurrence.

John Straynbowe, Pardons Roll, 6 Ric. II.

Strang.—Nick. ' the strang,' i.e. the strong, vigorous. A.S. *strang*; cf. Lang and Long. The surname is Scottish and North English, but generally the former.

Adam Strang, 1379: P. T. Yorks. p. 159.
1767. Married—William Strang and Eliz. Connell: St. Geo. Han. Sq. i. 169. London, 1; Philadelphia, 17.

Strange.—Nick. ' the strange,' i.e. the new-comer, the stranger; cf. Newman.

Stephen le Straunge, co. York, 1273. A.
John le Straunge, co. Camb., ibid.
Hamond le Straunge, co. Berks, ibid.
John le Strange, co. Soms., 1 Edw. III: Kirby's Quest, p. 172.
Willelmus Straunge, 1379: P. T. Yorks. p. 104.
1578. Bapt.—John, s. William Straunge: St. Michael, Cornhill, i. 89.
1780. Married—Thomas Strange and Eliz. Woods: St. Geo. Han. Sq. i. 318. London, 27; Philadelphia, 7.

Strangeman. — Nick. ' the strange man '; v. Strange.

John Strangeman, C. R., 1 Hen. IV. pt. i.

Strangeways. — Local, ' of Strangeways,' an estate now occupied by the Assize Court on the Bury New Road, Manchester. The Strangeways family occupied the hall for centuries (v. Baines' Lancashire, i. 400-1).

1546. John Strangwayes and Gertrude Cutson: Marriage Lic. (London), i. 9.
Giles Strangyuyshe, C. R., 1 Eliz. pt. i.
1589. Giles Strangwaies, co. Dorset: Reg. Univ. Oxf. vol. ii. pt. ii. p. 173.
1601. John Strangewayes, co. Dorset: ibid. p. 253.
MDB. (N. Rid. Yorks), 4; London, 3.

Strangman, Strongman. — Nick. ' the strong man '; cf. Strang and Strong.

Idone Strangman, co. Soms., 1 Edw. III: Kirby's Quest, p. 159.
William Strangman, co. Soms., 1 Edw. III: ibid.
Nicholas Strangman, C. R., 7 Edw. IV.
Harrie, son of John Strongman, 1551: Reg. St. Columb Major, p. 6.
Michell, son of Martin Strangman, 1603: ibid. p. 21.
Katherine, d. of William Strangman, 1604: ibid. p. 22.
London, 1, 0; Boston (U.S.), 4, 2.

Stratford; v. Strafford.

Stratton, Stratten, Strattan. —Local, ' of Stratton,' parishes in cos. Cornwall, Dorset, Gloucester, Norfolk, Wilts, Buckingham, Hants, and Somerset, besides several hamlets, &c.

William de Straton, co. Oxf., 1273. A.
John de Stratton, co. Suff., ibid.
Nicholas de Stratton, co. Norf., ibid.
Ralph de Strattone, co. Bucks, ibid.
1564-5. Robert Stratton and Joanna Harryson, *widow*: Marriage Lic. (London), i. 30.
1795. Married—William Stratton and Martha Dean: St. Geo. Han. Sq. ii. 128. London, 12, 1, 0; Philadelphia, 63, 0, 1.

Stream.—Local, ' at the stream,' from residence thereby. This as a surname seems never to have caught the popular fancy like Beck and Brook.

William atte Streme, co. Soms., 1 Edw. III: Kirby's Quest, p. 270.
1582. Edward Marsh and Ann Streame: Marriage Lic. (London), i. 109.
1613. Married—Thomas Streame and Frances Savidge: St. Antholin (London), p. 49.
New York, 1; Boston (U.S.), 1.

Streat; v. Street.

Streater; v. Streeter.

Streatfeild.—Local, ' of Streatfeild.' Mr. Lower says, ' There may be several places of this name. I only know of one, which is a "borough" of the manor of Robertsbridge, in East Sussex, called in a document before me, of temp. Eliz., Stretfelde; and this locality is within a few miles of that which has been, for three centuries and a half, the chief habitat of the name ' (Patr. Brit. p. 332). The Streatfeilds of Chiddingstone, co. Kent, still maintain this old-fashioned spelling of *field*.

1591. Robert Streatfeild and Eliz. Harris: Marriage Lic. (London), i. 194.
1678. James Adams and Hannah Kellett, at her own disposal: alleged by John Streatfeild, cabinet-maker: Marriage Lic. (Faculty Office), p. 143.
MDB. (co. Kent), 4.

Street, Streat.—Local, ' at the street,' i.e. the paved road, from residence therein.

Alice de la Strete, co. Oxf., 1273. A.
Alexander de la Strete, co. Kent, ibid.
Adam of the Strete, Fines Roll, 11 Edw. I.
William atte Strete, c. 1300. M.
John atte Strete, co. Soms., 1 Edw. III: Kirby's Quest, p. 259.
Thomas del Strete, C. R., 28 Edw. III.
Elyas del Strete, 1379: P. T. Yorks. p. 93.
Alicia del Strete, 1379: ibid. p. 55.
1572. Bapt.—Thomas, s. Robert Streete: St. Jas. Clerkenwell, i. 7.
1803. Married—John Streat and Rose Preedy: St. Geo. Han. Sq. ii. 280. London, 27, 1; Boston (U.S.), 8, 1.

Streetend, Streeten(?), Streeton (?).—Local, ' at the street end '; cf. Woodend and Townsend. Although Streeten and Streeton would seem to be variants of Stretton, q.v., it seems likely that they are but popular variants of Streetend. This was a common mediaeval surname, and yet it has no modern representatives, unless my view be accepted.

Adam de Stretende, co. Kent, 1273. A.
Ralph de Strethende, co. Kent, ibid.
John atte Stretesend, co. Norf. FF.
William Stretende, C. R., 26 Hen. VI.

Of course I may be wrong; if so, Streeten and Streeton are

unquestionable variants of Stretton, q.v.

London, 0, 2, 6; Philadelphia, 0, 0, 10.

Streeter, Streater. — Local, 'the streeter,' he who dwelt in the street; cf. Bridger, Brooker, &c. With Streater, cf. Streat for Street.

1593-4. William Streeter, co. Sussex: Reg. Univ. Oxf. vol. ii. pt. ii. p. 199.
1659. Buried—Jone Streeter: St. Jas. Clerkenwell, iv. 332.
1729. Married — David Streeter and Eliz. Reed, both of Waltham Abbey: St. Geo. Chap. Mayfair, p. 297.
1746. — Robert Streater and Ann Duke: ibid. p. 70.
London, 4, 1; Philadelphia, 8, 0.

Strelley, Striley.—Local, 'of Strelly,' a parish in co. Notts, four miles from Nottingham. Lower, quoting Burke's Landed Gentry, says, 'Strelly, anciently Strellegh, co. Notts, gave name and residence to the knightly family of the Strelleys, one of the oldest and most famous in the county.'

1578. Francis Strellye, co. Notts : Reg. Univ. Oxf. vol. ii. pt. ii. p. 83.
— George Strellye, co. Notts : ibid.
1634. George Strelley and Eliz. Reading: Marriage Lic. (London), ii. 217.
1676. Bapt.—Eliz., d. George Strilley: St. Jas. Clerkenwell, i. 274.
MDB. (co. Leic.), 1, 0; Boston (U.S.), 0, 1.

Stretch. — ? Local. I cannot suggest any satisfactory origin of this surname, except the foreign Stretz. The Philadelphia Directory has three Stretzes and twenty-two Stretches. Nevertheless, seeing that Stretch was a familiar name in co. Ches. so early as the 16th century, it is almost certain that it is of English local origin.

1596. William Stretch, of Gorstich: Wills at Chester, i. 184.
1606. John Stretch, of Chester, *inn-holder*: ibid.
1763. Married—John Potter and Hannah Stretch : St. Geo. Han. Sq. i. 125.
MDB. (co. Ches.), 5; London, 3; Philadelphia, 22.

Strettell, Strettle.—Local, 'of Strettell.' The suffix is doubtless *-hill*; cf. Windle for Windhill, &c. The spot that has originated the surname will probably have to be sought for in co. Chester.

1572. James Strettell and Margaret Braythwa : Marriage Lic. (London), i. 52.
1593. Thomas Strettell, of Marthall : Wills at Chester, i. 184.
1603. Ellen Strettell, of Mobberley, co. Ches.: ibid.
1672. Robert Strethill, of Snelson, in the parish of Rostherne, co. Ches. : East Ches. ii. 643.
Liverpool, 3, 0; Crockford, 1, 0; London, 1, 0; New York, 0, 1.

Stretton.—Local, 'of Stretton,' parishes and places in cos. Chester, Derby, Rutland, Stafford, Warwick, Salop, Hereford, and Leicester. It is quite possible that Streeten and Streeton are variants. But v. Streetend. Of course the derivation lies between one or the other.

Meyler de Stretton, co. Salop, 1273. A.
William de Stretton, co. Notts, ibid.
Roger de Strettun, co. Linc., ibid.
1610. Henry Stretton, of Grappenhall : Wills at Chester, i. 184.
1640. John Stretton, of Marton, Prestbury, co. Ches.: ibid. ii. 210.
1768. Married—Thomas Stretton and Eliz. King : St. Geo. Han. Sq. i. 175.
MDB. (co. Derby), 5; London, 6; Philadelphia, 2.

Strickland.—Local, 'of Strickland,' originally Stirkland, four townships in co. Westmoreland, viz. Great and Little Strickland in the parish of Morland, and Strickland Kettle and Strickland Roger in the parish of Kendal. The surname is now familiar over the English-speaking world.

William de Stirkland, 20 Edw. I: Nicolson and Burn, Hist. Westm. and Cumb. i. 90.
Walter de Stirkeland, 35 Edw. I : ibid. i. 91.
William de Stirkelaunde, co. Westm., 20 Edw. I. R.
1588. Roger Strickland, of Cartmellfell : Lancashire Wills at Richmond, i. 264.
1618. John Strickland, co. Westm.: Reg. Univ. Oxf. vol. ii. pt. ii. p. 368.
1662. James Strickland, of Satterthwaite : Lancashire Wills at Richmond, i. 264.
London, 16; MDB. (co. Lanc.), 9; Philadelphia, 18.

Stringer.—Occup. 'the stringer,' a manufacturer of cord or twine ; cf. Stringfellow, Corder, Roper, or Raper. No doubt the Stringer made the special cord for bows. It is a common Yorkshire entry in the 14th century.

Godwyn̄ Strenger, co. Soms., 1 Edw. III : Kirby's Quest, p. 100.
Willelmus Strynger, 1379: P. T. Yorks. p. 101.
Johannes Strenger, 1379: ibid. p. 172.
Ricardus Stryngar, 1379: ibid. p. 66.
1574. Married — Richard Collie and Bettres Stringer : St. Mary Aldermary (London), p. 5.
1575. George Stringar, co. Staff. : Reg. Univ. Oxf. vol. ii. pt. ii. p. 66.
1646. John Stringer, of Nantwich, *victualler*: Wills at Chester, ii. 210.
West Rid. Court Dir., 2; London, 13; Philadelphia, 21.

Stringfellow. — Occup. 'the stringer,' a maker of bow-strings. All surnames with suffix *-fellow* seem to have sprung from the North of England, especially from co. York; v. Longfellow.

Laurencius Stryngfelagh, 1379: P. T. Yorks. p. 11.
John Strengfellow, of Openshaw, 1616: Wills at Chester, i. 184.
Richard Strengfellow, of Rochdale, 1617: ibid.
1713. Buried — Rebeckah, d. John Stringfellow: St. Mary Aldermary (London), p. 213.
London, 2; Manchester, 4; West Rid. Court Dir., 2; Philadelphia, 6.

Stringlayer. — Occup. 'the stringlayer,' a roper, one who worked on a rope-walk (!).

William le Strenglayer, C. R., 13 Edw. II.

Strode, Strude.—Local, (1) 'of Stroud,' a parish in co. Glouc. ; (2) 'of Strood,' a parish in co. Kent (v. Stroud). Both seem to have been anciently styled Strode. Mr. Lower, quoting Shirley's Noble and Gentle Men, says that 'the name is derived from Strode, in the parish of Ermington, co. Devon, which was in the possession of Adam de Strode in the reign of Henry III' (Patr. Brit. p. 333). However true this may be, it is obvious that the towns of Stroud and Strood have also their representatives in our directories in the form of Strode.

William de Strode, co. Oxf., 1273. A.
William de la Strode, co. Surrey, Hen. III—Edw. I. K.
John de Strode, co. Wilts, ibid.
1571. Swithin Strowde, co. Soms. : Reg. Univ. Oxf. vol. ii. pt. ii. p. 52.
1607. Francis Strode, co. Devon : ibid. p. 297.
1617. William Strodd or Strowde, co. Devon : ibid. p. 361.

1767. Married—William Strode and Ann Fozard : St. Geo. Han. Sq. i. 163. London, 1, 1 ; Philadelphia, 9, 0.

Strong.—Nick. 'the strong'; cf. Strongfellow and Strongman, and also Long, Longman, and Longfellow. Naturally this has taken a firm hold upon our directories, the sobriquet being a popular one. There is no need for many instances.

Simon Strong, co. Camb., 1273. A.
Joscelin le Strong. H.
William le Strong. T.
1539. Bapt.—Peter, s. Martyn Strong, a strannger : St. Dionis Backchurch, p. 71.
London, 29 ; Philadelphia, 31.

Strongbow.—Nick. ; cf. Hotspur, Sharparrow, Stiffbow, or Benbow, a decidedly complimentary sobriquet.

Ranulf Strongbowe, co. Essex, 1273. A.
Simon Strongebowe. H.
Izabell Strongboo, d. of Richard Earl of Pembroke : Visitation of Yorks, Harl. Sdc., p. 282.

Strongfellow. — Nick. 'the strong fellow'; cf. Longfellow. But possibly an imitative corruption of Stringfellow (q.v.) after the origin of this occupative name had become obscured through the variant Strengfellow.

Robert Strongfellowe, temp. Eliz. Z.
Frances Strongfellowe, ibid.

Strongitharm.—Nick. 'strong-in-the-arm'; cf. Armstrong, Brasdefer, &c. This name is still found in co. Cheshire, but is always rare.

1570. Married—Thomas Davenporte and Ellen Strongethearme : Reg. Prestbury, co. Ches., p. 30.
1581. Roger Strongeitharme and Ales Hollynshed : ibid. p. 69.
1597. Richard Stronge in Arme and Margaret Wyatt : Marriage Lic. (London), i. 243.
1621. — William Burghill and Marie Strongitharme : ibid. p. 232.
William Strongitharm, of Swettenham, 1598 : Wills at Chester (1545-1620), p. 184.
George Strongitharm, of Allostock, 1617 : ibid. p. 185.
Barrow-in-Furness, 1.

Strongman. — Nick. ' the strong man '; v. Strangman.

John Strongman, rector of Brunstead, co. Norf., 1389 : FF. ix. 289.
Boston (U.S.), 2.

Strother. — Local, ' of the strother,' i.e. marsh, from residence there beside. 'Strother, a marsh. North Engl.' (Halliwell). This surname has its home in Northumberland. In Newcastle and the district it is commonly met with. It is interesting to note that Chaucer places his Strother in the far North, where Allen, too, was the favourite name. v. Langstroth.

'John highte that on, and Alein highte that other,
Of o toun were they born, that highte Strother,
Fer in the North, I can not tellen where.'
        Chaucer, C. T. 4010-11.

Edward Elliot, of The Strother, 1763 : Brand's Hist. of Newcastle, i. 560.
Alan del Strother, bailiff of Tindall, 1358 : Hodgson, Hist. Northumberland, ii. 542.
William Strother, mayor of Newcastle, 1360 : Hist. Newcastle, Gateshead, i. 160.
Henry del Strother, temp. Henry III : Hodgson, Hist. Northumberland, v. 327.
1706. Bapt. — George, s. William Strother : St. Jas. Clerkenwell, p. 29.
MDB. (co. Northumberland), 2 ; London, 3 ; Philadelphia, 1.

Stroud.—Local: (1) 'of Stroud,' a parish in co. Glouc. ; v. Strode. (2) 'of Strood,' a parish in co. Kent. For further instances, v. Strode.

Edytha atte Stroude, co. Soms., 1 Edw. III : Kirby's Quest, p. 95.
Matilda atte Strode, co. Soms., 1 Edw. III : ibid. p. 202.
Thomas atte Strode, co. Soms., 1 Edw. III : ibid. p. 268.
1641. Buried—Ann, d. Nicholas Stroude: St. Jas. Clerkenwell, iv. 249.
1652. Married—Thomas Harlackenden and Eliz. Stroude: St. Dionis Backchurch, p. 28.
London, 18 ; Philadelphia, 29.

Strude ; v. Strode.

Strutt.—? Nick. 'one who strutted' (?). Sobriquets from gait or peculiarities of walking are endless. The reason is obvious ; they gave individuality, readily seized upon when it became manifest that surnames were necessary to eke out identity.

Simon Strut, C. R., 48 Hen. III.
John le Strut (also John Strutt), co. Wilts, 1273. A.
Robert Strut, co. Camb., ibid.
William Strut, co. Hunts, ibid.
1762. Married—John McDonald and Esther Strutt : St. Geo. Han. Sq. i. 113.
London, 3 ; Philadelphia, 1.

Stuard ; v. Steward.

Stuart ; v. Stewart.

Stubbing, Stubbings, Stubbins, Stubbin.—Local, ' of the stubbings,' from residence beside a number of stumps or stocks of trees ; v. Stubbs (2).

Nicholas de Stubbings, co. Salop, 1273. A.
Henricus de Stubbyng, 1379 : P. T. Yorks. p. 211.
1632. Edmond Stubbing and Jone Wolley : Marriage Lic. (Faculty Office), p. 22.
1674. Bapt. — William, s. William Stubbines : St. Jas. Clerkenwell, i. 264.
London, 1, 4, 2, 0 ; MDB. (co. Camb.), 0, 3, 0, 0 ; Philadelphia (Stubbins), 4 ; (co. Essex), 2, 1, 0, 1.

Stubbs, Stobbs.—Local (1), ' of Stubbs,' a township in the parish of Adwick-le-Street, W. Rid. Yorks, near Doncaster ; (2) ' at the stubs,' one who lived by some stump of a tree or stumps of trees. Cf. Styles, Briggs, Stocks, &c.

George Stobbis, le pownder, per annum 6s. 8d. : Liber Bursarii, Eccles. Dunelmensis, Surtees Soc.
'Old stocks, and stubs of trees.'
        Spenser, F. Q. i. 9. 34.
'Item, una acra et una roda terroe jacent aput Stob-tres,' 1367 : Ext. from grant of John de Clynt, chaplain to David de Wolloure, at Ripon, GGG. i. 194.
Henry de Stubbes, co. York, 1273. A.
Richard de Stubbes, co. York, ibid.
Henricus de Stubbys, 1379 : P. T. Yorks. p. 210.
Alicia de Stubbes, 1379 : ibid. p. 125.
Johannes Stubbe, 1379 : ibid. p. 41.
Johannes de Stubbes, 1379 : ibid. p. 123.
John Stubbe, co. Soms., 1 Edw. III : Kirby's Quest, p. 80.

It is probable that most of our many North-English Stubbs hail from (1), but (2) must have many representatives in our directories. The actual derivation of both (1) and (2) will be the same.

Elizabeth Stobbs, coffee rooms, Pateley Bridge, West Riding Dir.
London, 20, 0 ; Sheffield, 5, 0 ; MDB. (co. Durham), 2, 5 ; New York, 7, 0.

Studdard, Stuttard, Studdert, Stutard. — Occup. ' the stud-herd,' one who kept a stud of horses ; v. Stodart, and cf. Stotherd. One of a large class of North-English surnames with suffix -herd, as in Shepherd ; cf. Calvert,

Coward, Geldard, or Oxnard. The variant Stuttard is, of course, a mere sharpening of the more correct form, as in the case of Calvert for Calve-herd. Studdard evidently represented the old stud-herd, a breeder of horses or mares (v. Skeat on *stud*).

Robertus Studhyrd, 1379 : P. T. Yorks. p. 279.
Johannes Studhyrd, 1379 : ibid. p. 277.
Petrus Studehird, 1379 : ibid. p. 211.
Thomas Studhird, 1379 : ibid. p. 292.
1745. John Studdart, of Hawkshead : Lancashire Wills at Richmond, ii. 242.
1783. Married—Joseph Levermore and Helen Stuttard : St. Geo. Han. Sq. i. 351.
London, 1, 1, 0, 0 ; Crockford, 0, 0, 2, 0 ; Manchester, 0, 3, 0, 1.

Studley, Stoodley. — Local, (1) 'of Studley,' parishes and places in cos. Bucks, Warwick, and W. Rid. Yorks (2) ; (2) 'of Stood-leigh,' a parish in co. Devon, five miles from Bampton. There can be no doubt that the Dorset and Devon Studleys in general represent the last-named place.

William de Stodley, co. Leic., 1273. A.
Thomas de Studle, co. Bedf., 20 Edw. I. R.
Walter de Stodleghe, co. Soms., 1 Edw. III : Kirby's Quest, p. 252.
1584. Nathaniel Studley, co. Dorset : Reg. Univ. Oxf. vol. ii. pt. ii. p. 134.
1586. Thomas Stoodlie, co. Dorset : ibid. p. 153.
1610. Peter Studley, co. Salop : ibid. p. 321.
1644. Bapt. — Ellenor, d. Thomas Studley : St. Dionis Backchurch, p. 108.
London, 1, 0 ; MDB. (co. Devon), 4, 0 ; (co. Dorset), 3, 2 ; New York, 12, 0.

Sturdee, Sturdy.—Nick. 'the sturdy,' the strongly rash or inconsiderate (v. Skeat on *sturdy*, showing how the meaning of the word has changed). M.E. *sturdi*.

Hamond Sturdi, co. Hunts, 1273. A.
Walter Sturdi, co. Oxf., ibid.
Robertus Sturdy, 1379 : P. T. Yorks. p. 227.
1618. Buried — Dyana, wife of James Sturdy : St. Peter, Cornhill, i. 174.
1787. Married — Thomas Atkinson Sturdy and Ann Wood : St. Geo. Han. Sq. i. 410.
London, 2, 3 ; New York, 0, 2.

Sturdevant ; v. Sturtevant.

Sturge, Sturges, Sturgess, Sturgis. — Bapt. 'the son of Thurgis or Turgis,' with prefixed *s*. The surname, like the early

fontal name, is common to all parts of England.

Turgis (without surname), co. Linc., 10 Hen. II : Pipe Roll, p. 22.
Thurgis le Caldecote, co. Norf., temp. King John : FF. vi. 57.
Thurgis (without surname), co. Linc., 1273. A.
Turgis (without surname), co. Linc., ibid.
Turgeus de Corton, co. Suff., ibid.
Turgisius de Heredefeld, co. Kent, ibid.
William Thurgys, co. Wilts, ibid.
Adam Thurgis, co. Bedf., ibid.
Richard Turgis, co. Wilts, ibid.

A century later *s* had stolen to the front :

Johannes Sturgys, 1379 : P. T. Yorks. p. 248.
Johannes Sturgys, junior, 1379 : ibid.
1626. Bapt. — John, son of Sturges Sturgis : St. Dionis Backchurch, p. 100.

The earlier and more correct form lingered on for several centuries.

1629. Buried — John Turges, son of Thomas Turges : St. Dionis Backchurch, p. 220.
1646. Married—Thomas Langham and Sarah Turgis : ibid. p. 25.
1666. Paul Bowes and Bridgett Sturges : Marriage Lic. (Faculty Office), p. 94.
1785. Married—Thomas Sturgis and Sarah Whitmee : St. Geo. Han. Sq. i. 374.
London, 2, 8, 1, 3 ; Oxford, 0, 3, 2, 0 ; Philadelphia, 0, 14, 0, 13.

Sturgeon.—? Nick. 'the sturgeon,' but perhaps a personal name ; cf. Dolphin and Herring, undoubted personal names.

Willelmus Sturgeon, 1379 : P. T. Yorks. p. 299.
John Sturgeon, C. R., 22 Hen. VI.
John Sturgeon, Rot. Pat., 2 Ric. III. pt. i.
1559. Buried—Margery Sturgion : St. Peter, Cornhill, i. 114.
1647. Married — John Scudder and Eliz. Sturgeon : St. Dionis Backchurch, p. 25.
London, 6 ; MDB. (co. Suffolk), 5 ; Philadelphia, 5.

Sturgess, -gis ; v. Sturge.

Sturm ; v. Storm.

Sturman.—(1) ? Occup. 'the steerman' (?) ; cf. Cowman, Bullman, &c., and v. Steer. (2) Occup. 'the steerman,' navigator.

Robert le Steresman, co. Camb., 1273. A.
Roger le Steresman, co. Camb., ibid.

Two early ''Varsity coxes'! Mr. Lower says, ' Stirman or Stirmannus occurs in Domesday as the

designation of an official. Edric Stirman was, t. Edward Confessor, commander of the land and sea forces of the bishop of Worcester for the King's service (Stermannus navis episcopi, et ductor exercitus ejusdem episcopi, ad servicium regis)' : Heming Chartul., quoted in Ellis's Introd. ii. 89.

1548. William Sturman and Eliz. Norryce : Marriage Lic. (London), i. 12.
1553. Bapt.—Mary Sturmanne : St. Peter, Cornhill, i. 6.
1619. Buried—John Styrman : ibid. p. 175.
London, 6 ; Oxford, 2 ; New York, 5.

Sturmy.—Local, 'of Sturmy.' I cannot find the place.

John de Sturmi, co. Heref., Hen. III-Edw. I. K.
Richard de Sturmy, co. York, 1273. A.
William de Sturmy, co. Norf., ibid.
1671. Thomas Sturmy and Eliz. Maddison : Marriage Alleg. (Canterbury), p. 192.
1677. Married — John Sturmey and Elizabeth Clarke : St. Mary Aldermary (London), p. 32.
London, 1.

Sturt. — Local, 'of Stert,' a parish in co. Wilts, near Devizes. As suggested by Mr. Lower, this seems the probable origin. The evidence I furnish below confirms this view :

William de la Sturte, co. Devon, 1273. A.
Thomas atte Sturt, co. Soms., 1 Edw. III : Kirby's Quest, p. 178.
1600. Bapt.—William, s. John Sturte : St. Jas. Clerkenwell, i. 36.
1615. Waymond Stert or Sturt, co. Devon : Reg. Univ. Oxf. vol. ii. pt. ii. p. 343 (see Index).
London, 7 ; MDB. (co. Devon), 3.

Sturtevant, Sturtivant, Sturdevant, Sturdivant. — Nick. At first sight this sobriquet would seem to be a compound of *sturdy*, rash, inconsiderate ; and *avaunt*, a boast, a vaunt, and also an old French sobriquet for some reckless boaster. But I have no doubt it is one of the early nicknames given to pursuivants, harbingers, or heralds, of which this dictionary has so many instances. Thus it means ' go-before,' from *start* (M.E. *stirt* and *stert*), and *avaunt*, forward, to the front. We are still familiar with the *avant-courier*. An exact parallel will be found in the case of Prickadvance (spur-forward) ; v. Pickavance, Purchas, Golightly, Lightfoot, &c.

Willelmus Styrtauant, 1379: P. T. Yorks. p. 273.

Cf. also

Willelmus Stirciuant, 1379: ibid. p. 60.
Robertus Stircyuant, 1379: ibid.
John Sturdyvaunte, 1570: Reg. St. Dionis Backchurch, p. 6.
1604. Buried — Mathew Sturdyvant, Old Buckenham, co. Norf.: FF. i. 392.

A well-known firm of solicitors existed in Preston about 1830 styled Buck and Startifant.

1685. Buried — Elizabeth, wife of Thomas Stertevant: St. Mary Aldermary (London), p. 196.
London, 1, 1, 0, 0; Philadelphia, 2, 0, 3, 0; New York, 8, 0, 0, 0; Boston (U.S.), 34, 0, 0, 6.

Sturton.—Local, 'of Sturton.' Several parishes and townships bear this name in cos. Lincoln, Notts, and W. Rid. Yorks.

Nicholas de Sturton, co. Wilts: Hen. III–Edw. I. K.
1594. David Barnard, *embroiderer*, and Margery Sturton: Marriage Lic. (London), i. 215.
1779. Married — John Rood and Susannah Sturton: St. Geo. Han. Sq. i. 297.
MDB. (co. Lincoln), 4.

Stuttard.—Occup. 'the stud-herd'; v. Studdard.

Stydolph.— ? Bapt. 'the son of Stydulf' (?), one of the endless compounds of Ulf or Wolf, as in Randolph. But Lower says a corruption of St. Edolph, which would make it local, from some chapelry of that name; cf. Sinclair.

Adam Stydulff and Katherine Kingsleye: Dioc. of Chichester.
John Stydulff and Constance Kingsleye: ibid.

I have lost the reference to the above.

1610. Thomas Stydolfe, co. Surrey: Reg. Univ. Oxf. vol. ii. pt. ii. p. 314.
1624-5. William Stydolffe and Mary Lupie: Marriage Lic. (London), ii. 150.

Still existing, I am told, but I cannot find it.

Style, Styles, Stiles, ? Stile.— Local, 'at the stile,' from residence thereby. The seeming plural form Stiles or Styles is really the genitive ; cf. Williams for William (=William's son). So Styles = Style's son ; cf. Holmes, Briggs, Brooks. The genitive form in local surnames is almost entirely confined to monosyllabic surnames.

'For som tyme I served
Symme atte-Style.'
Piers P. 2874.

See also the suggestions with regard to Still.

Alina de la Stigela, C. R., 54 Hen. III.
Richard de la Style, co. Bedf., 1273. A.
John Atte Stile, co. Oxf., ibid.
Robert ate Stiele, co. Oxf., ibid.
Roger atte Styhill, 1379: P. T. Yorks. p. 120.
1575. Nicholas Style and Gertrude Bright : Marriage Lic. (London), i. 67.
1761. Married—Henry Styles and Eliz. Reader : St. Geo. Han. Sq. i. 107.
London, 1, 13, 10, 0; Philadelphia, 0, 7, 68, 1.

Styleman, Stileman, Stillman.—Local, 'the stileman,' i.e. the man who lived at the stile ; v. Style, and cf. Bridgman, Stockman, Steadman, &c.

1586. John Stileman and Alice Hill: Marriage Lic. (London), i. 152.
1661. Bapt. — Elizabeth, d. Nicholas Stillman : St. Jas. Clerkenwell, i. 212.
1701. Married—Andrew Cooper and Sarah Stileman : Reg. St. Dionis Backchurch, p. 50.
London, 0, 2, 2 ; Philadelphia, 0, 0, 14.

Suart.—(1) Occup. 'the sow-herd,' i.e. a keeper of sows ; cf. Swinnart, Hoggard, Calvert, Oxnard, Coward. With the sharpened form, cf. Stuttard. (2) Perhaps sometimes personal for Seward (2), q.v.

Cecilia Sueherd, 1379 : P. T. Yorks. p. 158.
William Suart, 1379 : ibid. p. 298.
1777. Married — James Shuttelworth and Mary Suart: St. Geo. Han. Sq. i. 273.
London, 2 ; Crockford, 1.

Such, Suche, Sutch.—Local, an old form of 'de la Zouch.' I cannot give any satisfactory derivation of this local term. Lower says, 'The baronial family who gave the suffix to Ashby-de-la-Zouch, co. Leic., were a branch of the Earls of Brittany. . . . The founder of the race in England was William le Zusche, who died in the first year of King John. In a charter he calls Roger la Zusche his father, and Alan, Earl of Brittany, his grandfather.' . . . Lower adds that Camden asserts that 'Zouch signifieth the stocke of a tree in the French tongue.' If this be true, Zouch and its variants, such as Souch, Such, Sutch, are but equivalent to the English Stubbs, Stock, Stubbings, &c.

Alan de la Souche, co. Devon, 1273. A.
Roger de la Soche, ibid.
William de la Soche, co. Devon., ibid.
Walter Such, co. Soms., 1 Edw. III : Kirby's Quest, p. 118.
1584-5. Henry Sutche, *yeoman*, and Anne Prentice : Marriage Lic. (London), i. 137.
1602. Francis Souch, London : Reg. Univ. Oxf. vol. ii. pt. ii. p. 260.
1610. Silvester Such, of Ormskirk : Wills at Chester, i. 185.
1615. Thomas Sutch, of Burscough : ibid.
1637. Bapt.—Ann, d. Samuel Sutch : St. Jas. Clerkenwell, i. 137.
London, 6, 1, 3 ; Philadelphia, 0, 0, 9.

Suckbitch. — Local, 'of Soghespich.' Mr. Lower writes: 'This name, borne by more than one respectable family in the West of England, might be supposed to be derived from some legend analogous to that of Romulus and Remus. The earliest form of it, Sokespic, however, excludes such an origin. See Notes and Queries, 1st S. v. 425.' The name is local, and has been turned into an imitative form.

Jordan de Soghespich, co. Devon, 1273. A.

Close beside this entry is the mention of a place Spichwick, no doubt closely connected.

Suckling. — Nick. 'the suck-ling.' This, at least, seems to be the origin. Mr. Lower thinks it is a local surname, but furnishes no evidence ; cf. Child, Ayre, Eyre.

Adam Sucklin, co. Oxf., 1273. A.
Robert Sucling, co. Oxf., ibid.
Walter Sucling, co. Suff., ibid.
1432. John Sokelyng : Cal. of Wills in Court of Husting (2).
1551. Buried—Richard Sucklyne: St. Peter, Cornhill, i. 110.
1801. Married—Charles Suckling and Eliz. Bartlett : St. Geo. Han. Sq. ii. 246.
London, 2 ; Crockford, 3.

Sucksmith.—Occup.; v. Shoe-smith. I may, however, suggest that Sucksmith and Sixsmith may be corruptions of *scythe-smith* or *sickle-smith*, one who manufactured scythes. In Tobacco Tortured (London: Richard Field, 1616) several characters appear whose names are 'Cocke-on-hoope the Cobbler,' 'Martin the Mariner,' 'Thin-gut the Thatcher,' and 'Simkin the Sithe-smith' (v. Notes and Queries, 1885, p. 126).

1754. Married —Charles Dowley and Ann Sucksmith: St. Geo. Chap. Mayfair, p. 276.

Sudbury.—Local,'of Sudbury,' a parish in co. Suffolk.

Robert de Sudbyr, co. Norf., 1273. A.
Ralph de Sudebyre, co. Essex, ibid.
John de Sudbury, co. Bedf., 20 Edw. I. R.
1551. Richard Sudbury, Christ Church: Reg. Univ. Oxf. i. 97.
1580. Benjamin Gilbert, or Bury, of Alta Rothinge, co. Essex, and Eliz. Sudbury: Marriage Lic. (London), i. 97.
MDB. (co. Essex), 2; London, 1; Boston (U.S.), 1.

Sudlow.—Local, ' of Sudlow,' evidently some small spot in the parish of Over Tabley, co. Ches., or the neighbouring parish of Rostherne.

Thomas Stubbs, of Sudloe, parish of Rawsthorne, 1638: Wills at Chester, ii. 210.
William Sudlow, of Witton, 1593: ibid. i. 185.
Richard Newall, of Sudlow, in Over Tabley, *carpenter*, 1663: ibid. iii. 194.
William Sudlow, of Great Budworth, *husbandman*, 1638: ibid. ii. 211.
1763. Married — Robert Sudlow and Catherine Worsdall: St. Geo. Han. Sq. i. 127.
Manchester, 4; London, 2; New York, 4.

Suffolk.—Local, ' of Suffolk'; cf. Kent, Cheshire, Cornwall, &c. These surnames easily arose from migration from one county to another.

Thomas Suffauk, London, 1273. A.
Thomas de Suffolk, London, 20 Edw. I. R.
1733. Married — Manvel Oliver and Mary Suffolk: St. Geo. Han. Sq. i. 11.
1750. — Francis Hughes and Deborah Suffolk: St. Geo. Chap. Mayfair, p. 170. London, 1.

Sugar, Sugars.—Bapt.'the son of Sigher'; v. Sayer and Seager.

Robert Sulgar, 1379: P. T. Yorks. p. 160.
Johannes Sulgar, 1379: ibid.
Jone wyf to Sugero, filio Hemoney Copledale: Visitation of Yorks, p. 40.
Hugh Sugar, Patent Roll, 1 Hen. VII.
1609-10. Gregory Sugar, or Suger, co. Dorset: Reg. Univ. Oxf. vol. ii. pt. ii. p. 309. (v. Index.)
1650. Married—John Sugar and Mary Holten: St. Dionis Backchurch, p. 27.
London, 3, 0; Manchester, 0, 1; New York, 2, 0.

Sugden.—Local, ' of Sugden,' some small spot in W. Rid. Yorks, which I have failed to identify.

Robertus de Sugden, 1379: P. T. Yorks. p. 183.
Willelmus Sugden, 1379: ibid. p. 211.
Robertus de Sugdeyn, 1379: ibid. p. 263.
1555. William Sugden and Catherine Lenyall: Marriage Lic. (London), i. 16.
London, 3; West Riding Court Dir., 30; Philadelphia, 10.

Sully. — Local, ' of Sudeley,' now Sudeley Manor, a parish in co. Gloucester, often written Sully in old records. A family of Sudeleys resided here for centuries.

Bartholomew de Sulley, or Sudeley, co. Glouc., 1273. A.
Henry de Sully, co. Devon, ibid.
Walter de Sully, co. Devon, ibid.
Reymond de Suleye, co. Devon, Hen. III-Edw. I. K.
Mabillia de Suly, co. Glouc., 20 Edw. I. R.
Ralph de Sudlegh, or Sule, or Suley, co. Glouc., Hen. III-Edw. I. K.
Adam Sulleygh, co. Soms., 1 Edw. III: Kirby's Quest, p. 265.
1762. Married —Thomas Leigh and Joan Suly: St. Geo. Han. Sq. i. 109.
London, 8; Philadelphia, 1.

Summer, Summers, Somers, Sommers, Sommer.—Bapt. 'the son of Summer.' Just as ecclesiastical seasons gave us such personal names as Noel, Pentecost, Pask, Christmas, &c., so several centuries earlier popular names for children were descriptive of the natural season in which the child was born, or even the state of the weather. Hence such personal names as Snow, Storm, Winter, Summer, Spring, &c. Several years ago a child was baptized Sou'-wester because born on shipboard in a south-westerly gale. This case I can vouch for.

M.E. *somer*, summer. Cf. such local names as Somerby, Somercoates, Somerford, Somersby, Somersham, Somerton, all implying that the first settler bore the name of Somer (now Summer); v. Winter for further information. Summers, Somers, &c., are the genitive form; cf. Williams and William.

John Somer, co. Soms., 1 Edw. III: Kirby's Quest, p. 133.
1600. Bapt.—Joan, d. Peter Somers: St. Jas. Clerkenwell, i. 37.
1687. — John, s. John Sumer: ibid. p. 322.
1755. Married—Charles Summers and Sarah Mason: St. Geo. Han. Sq. i. 58.
London, 1, 25, 8, 5, 0; Philadelphia, 4, 69, 32, 31, 35.

Summersby.—Local, ' of Somersby,' a parish in co. Lincoln, seven miles from Spilsby.

? Robert de Somerdeby, co. Linc., 1273. A.
London, 1.

Summerscales, Summersgill. — Local, ' of Somerscales.' Summersgill may be of independent origin, but is more probably a corruption of Somerscale; cf. Wintersale and Wintersgill. For prefix v. Summer; for suffix v. Scales.

Johannes de Somerscales, 1379: P. T. Yorks. p. 287.
Johannes de Somerscale, junior, 1379: ibid. p. 288.
Thomas Prockter, of Somerscall, in Botton, 1606: Lancashire Wills at Richmond, p. 222.
1803. Married—John Summersgill and Mary Phillips: St. Geo. Han. Sq. ii. 292. West Rid. Court Dir., 3, 1.

Summerset; v. Somerset.

New York, 1.

Summersford, Summerford. —Local, ' of Somerford,' three parishes in co. Wilts.

William de Sumeford, co. Bucks, 1273. A.
Alexander de Somerford, co. Wilts, ibid.
Richard de Somerford, co. Wilts, ibid.
Nicholas de Somerford, co. Hunts, ibid.
1591. Robert Glover and Anne Somerford: Marriage Lic. (London), i. 193.
1603. Edward Somerford, co. Middlesex: Reg. Univ. Oxf. vol. ii. pt. ii. p. 265.
Crockford, 1, 0; London, 0, 1; Oxford, 3, 1.

Summershall; v. Somersall.

Summerson.—Nick. 'the son of the Sumner' (q. v.), one of several

Yorkshire surnames of a particular class; cf. Taylorson, Herdson, Clarkson, Wrightson, &c.

1752. Married — Thomas Summerson and Ann Hall: St. Geo. Chap. Mayfair, p. 212.

MDB. (co. Durham), 1; New York, 1; Market Weighton (East Rid. Yorks), 1.

Sumner, Sumpner. — Offic. 'the summoner,' a legal officer, the sheriff's messenger. In the Coventry Mysteries it is said:

Sim Somnor, in haste wend thou thi way,
Byd Joseph, and his wyff by name,
At the coorte to apper this day,
Him to purge of her defame.'

The *p* in Sumpner is intrusive, as in Thompson, or Simpson, or Hampton.

Hugh le Sumenor, co. Camb., 1273. A.
Sarra le Sumenur, co. Oxf., ibid.
John le Sumenur, C. R., 20 Edw. I.
Henry le Sumenour. B.
Ralph le Somenur. T.
Adam Somendour, 1379: P. T. Yorks. p. 62.
Henry le Somnor, 1397: Preston Guild Roll, p. 1 (Lanc. and Ches. Rec. Soc.).
1573. Reginald Sumner and Ellinor Sagell: Marriage Lic. (London), i. 57.
1627. Married—Nicholas Sumpner and Dorothy Banes: St. Dionis Backchurch, p. 22.
London, 17, 1; Philadelphia, 3, 0.

Sumpter, Sumter, Sumterman, Sunter. — Offic. 'the sumpter.' O.F. *sommetier*, a pack-horseman, one who carried baggage on horseback; in modern English applied to the horse, not the driver, a sumpter-horse being really a sumpter's horse (v. Skeat, *sumpter*); cf. Palfreyman, q.v.

'Willelmo Mone Sometario ad unum somerum pro armis Regis': Wardrobe of Edward I. p. 77.
Gilbert del Bed prays a reward for long services as 'King's Sumeter': H. i. 156 b.
William le Sumeter, 1273. A.
William le Somter, c. 1300. M.
John le Somyter, co. Soms., 1 Edw. III.: Kirby's Quest, p. 114.
Simon le Someter, varlet of the king's stable: Wardrobe Roll, 19 Edw. II.
Geoffrey le Someter, C. R., 54 Hen. III.
Richard Somterman. RR. 2.
Willelmus Sumpter, 1379: P. T. Yorks. p. 235.

Sunter is, no doubt, a corruption; cf. Sinkinson for Simkinson, &c.

1782. Married—Henry Sumpter and Catherine Davies: St. Geo. Han. Sq. i. 336.
1794. — Henry Sunter and Ann Mills: ibid. ii. 110.
London, 2, 0, 0, 3; Philadelphia, 1, 0, 0, 0.

Sumption, Sumpton.—?—.
Mr. Lower writes, 'This very remarkable name (Sumption) appears to be a contraction of "Assumption" (i.e. of the Virgin Mary), the church festival, and to be cognate with Pentecost, Christmas, Easter, &c.' (Patr. Brit. p. 334). This is quite possible, as nearly all the church festivals are recorded in our directories; but it is more probable, for want of evidence, that both Sumption and Sumpton are variants of Somerton, the *p* being intrusive, as in Thompson or Simpson.

MDB. (co. Glouc.), 2, 0; London, 1, 1.

Sunderland.—Local, 'of Sunderland,' a seaport parish in co. Durham; a great Yorkshire surname that seems early to have passed the borders of the more northern county.

Adam de Sunderland, co. Lanc., 20 Edw. I. R.
Thomas de Sundirland, 1379: P. T. Yorks. p. 184.
1779. Married—John Sunderland and Dina Dickson: St. Geo. Han. Sq. i. 295.
MDB. (West Rid. Yorks), 31; Philadelphia, 11.

Sunman.—Bapt. 'the son of Soneman.' This name occurs as a personal name without surname in the Hundred Rolls (co. Camb.), i. 545.

Soneman ad Cap' Ville, co. Camb., 1273. A.
Sunemanne del Fen, co. Suffolk, ibid.
Soneman de Pote, co. Camb., ibid.
Charles Soneman, co. Camb., ibid.
Roger Soneman, co. Camb., ibid.
William Soneman, co. Suff., ibid.
1887. Married — Henry Sunman, L.R.A.M., of Oxford, to Margaret Elizabeth Noddings: Standard, July 6.
London, 4; Oxford, 1.

Sunnett.—Bapt.; v. Sennett.

Sunter.—Occup.; v. Sumpter. This corruption still occurs in the district where it has existed at least three centuries. Several entries concerning the family of

Sumpter are thus found in the Prestbury registers, East Cheshire:

1560. Buried—Jees Sunter. xxx. Sept., p. 3.
— — Richard Sunter. xviii. Nov., ibid.
I have accidentally omitted to name the register.
Manchester, 3; Boston (U.S.), 1.

Surfleet.—Local, 'of Surfleet,' a parish in co. Lincoln, four miles from Spalding.

(Persona) de Surflet, co. Linc., 1273. A.
1673-4. William Surflett and Mary Gibbs: Marriage Alleg. (Canterbury), p. 108.
MDB. (co. Lincoln), 7.

Surgeon. — Occup. 'the surgeon,' i.e. a chirurgeon. The following entries represent the transition period:

William le Suriegien, co. Northampton, 1273. A.
Robert le Surgien, co. Camb., ibid.
1678. William Holding and Eliz. Surgion: Marriage Alleg. (Canterbury), p. 229.
1719. Bapt.—Abigal, d. Hugh Surgen: St. Jas. Clerkenwell, ii. 115.
MDB. (co. Cumb.), 1; Philadelphia, 2.

Surman, Surmon, Sermon. — Occup. 'the shearman.' A.S. *sciran*, to clip (Skeat); v. Shearman.

Bartholomew Scireman, co. Camb., 1273. A.
Hugh Scireman, co. Camb., ibid.
Mabil Scireman, co. Camb., ibid.
1661. Married—Thomas Knowlls and Elizabeth Surman: St. Dionis Backchurch, p. 37.
1756. — Daniel Sirman and Ann Ross: St. Geo. Han. Sq. i. 62.
London, 3, 2, 0; MDB. (co. Glouc.), 7, 0, 0; New York, 2, 0, 0.

Surr, Surre.—Bapt. 'the son of Sayer,' one of the endless forms of this once popular font-name; v. Sayer.

Ser Manneisin, co. Salop, 1273. A.
Walter fil. Sere, co. Notts, ibid.
1730. John Surr and Eliz. Booth: St. Geo. Chap. Mayfair, p. 161.
1785. — George Surr and Margaret Wilkinson: St. Geo. Han. Sq. i. 376.
London, 3, 0; New York, 0, 2.

Surrage; v. Surridge.

Surrey.—Local, 'of Surrey'; cf. Wiltshire, Darbyshire, Lancaster, Devonish, Cornwall, Kent, &c.

John de Surreye, co. Oxf., 1273. A.
1746. Married—Peter Walker and Eliz. Surry: St. Geo. Chap. Mayfair, p. 66.

1798. Married — Joseph (or John) Metcalf and Tamar Surrey: St. Geo. Han. Sq. ii. 183.
London, 1 ; Philadelphia, 1.

Surreys.—Local, 'the Surreys,' a Surrey man, a man who hailed from that county ; cf. Cornish, Cornwallis, Kentish, &c.
Roger le Surreys, co. Suff., 1273. A.
Seman le Sureys, co. Salop, ibid.
Robert Surreys, co. York, ibid.

Surridge, Surrage. — (1) Local, ' of Surridge,' seemingly some spot in co. Somerset.
Adam de Schirrugge, co. Soms., 1 Edw. III: Kirby's Quest, p. 137.
Edith de Schirugge, co. Soms., 1 Edw. III: ibid.
Thomas de Shirigge, co. Soms., 1 Edw. III: ibid. p. 146.

(2) Bapt. 'the son of Sirich.' This seems the more probable origin ; cf. Aldridge for Aldrich. But as Surrage and Surridge are familiar to co. Somerset, (1) must be looked upon as having a large share in the parentage.
John Soriche, co. Soms., 1 Edw. III: Kirby's Quest, p. 199.
Eylmer fil. Sirich, co. Suff., 1273. A.
Aubert Syrik, co. Linc., ibid.
Robert Syrik, co. Linc., ibid.
1753. Married—John Surridge and Ann Price: St. Geo. Chap. Mayfair, p. 255.
1754. — Thomas Surridge and Sarah Clayton : St. Geo. Han. Sq. i. 55.
London, 7, 0 ; MDB. (co. Essex), 9, 0 ; (co. Soms.), 1, 4 ; New York, 1, 0.

Surtees. — Local, ' Super Teisam' or ' Sur Tees,' from residence upon the bank of the Tees ; an ancient family, co. Durham. Practically of the same class as Tindal, Tweddle, and Teasdale.
Richard super Teisam, 1198. KKK. vi. 63.
John de Surties, bailiff of Newcastle, 1295. PPP.
1787. Married — John Horford and Margaret Surtees: St. Geo. Han. Sq. i. 403.
1802. — Aubone Surtees and Frances Eliz. Honeywood : ibid. ii. 272.
London, 1 ; Newcastle, 2 ; MDB. (co. Durham) 12 ; Philadelphia, 1.

Sutch; v. Such.

Sutcliff, Sutcliffe, Sutliff, Sutlieff. — Local, ' of Sutcliffe,' i.e. the South Cliff, a surname that has made a deep impression upon Yorkshire nomenclature. With Sutliff, cf. Topliff for Topcliff.
Willelmus Sothclyff, of Stanley, 1379: P. T. Yorks. p. 163.

Willelmus de Southclif', of South Owram, 1379: ibid. p. 187.
Adam Southclif', of Wadsworth, 1379: ibid. p. 188.
1588. John Sutcliffe, of Dyneley: Wills at Chester, i. 185.
1746. Married— John Currer and Mary Suttliff: St. Geo. Chap. Mayfair, p. 86.
1794. — Joseph Sutliffe and Mary Richardson : St. Geo. Han. Sq. ii. 106.
MDB. (West Rid. Yorks), 0, 67, 1, 0; Manchester, 2, 31, 0, 0; London, 1, 8, 0, 1; West Rid. Court Dir., 1, 46, 1, 0; Philadelphia, 1, 21, 1, 0.

Suter, Sutter, Sutor.—Occup. ' the souter,' i.e. the shoemaker ; v. Soutar.
Cf. Adam Wild, *sutter*, 1379: P. T. Yorks. p. 17.
Jordan Sutor, co. Hunts, 1273. A.
Adam Sutor, co. Camb., ibid.
Matilda Sutor, co. Hunts, ibid.
Isabel la Sutare, co. Camb., ibid.
1803. Married — William Suter and Ann Williams : St. Geo. Han. Sq. ii. 288.
London, 12, 0, 1 ; Philadelphia, 10, 23, 0.

Suthery, Sutthery. — Local, ' of Southery,' a parish in co. Norfolk.
William de Souther', co. Camb.,1273. A.
Robert de Suthereye, co. Wilts, ibid.
MDB. (co. Bucks), 4, 3 ; Philadelphia, 1, 0.

Sutliff; v. Sutcliff.

Sutterle, Sutterley, Suttley. —Local, possibly sometimes a variant 'of Southery' (v. Suthery), of which the following seems to be an intermediate form :
Roger de Soterle,co.Suff., 20 Edw. I. R.
This closely resembles the American form Sutterle; but more probably Sutterley is a distinct name from Suthery, the one being the Souther-ley, the other the Souther-hey (v. Lee and Hey).
London (Suttley), 1 ; Philadelphia, 3, 3, 0.

Suttle, Suttill. — (1) Local, ' of Soothill,' a township in the parish of Dewsbury, W. Rid. Yorks, in the neighbourhood of which the surname is chiefly found.
Ricardus de Sutill', 1379: P. T. Yorks. p. 182.

(2) Nick. ' the subtle,' the artful. O.F. *sutil*. No doubt this is also represented in our modern directories.

Adam le Sutel, London, 1273. A.
Robert le Sotele, co. Bedf. ibid.
1606. Buried—Thomas Sutle: St. Peter, Cornhill, i. 162.
London, 2, 0; Philadelphia, 2, 1; Otley (West Rid. Yorks), 3, 0.

Sutton. — Local, ' of Sutton,' i. e. the south town, the south enclosure. The places so called are too numerous to mention. Lower says there are over sixty ecclesiastically marked districts, chapelries, and parishes in England of this name. Of course this does not include small manors and farms ; cf. Norton, Weston, Eaton, or Easton.
Johannes de Soutton, 1379 : P. T. Yorks. p. 173.
Johannes de Sutton, 1379 : ibid. p. 100.
Symon de Sutton, 1379 : ibid. p. 98.
Geoffrey de Suttone, co. Hunts, 1273. A.
Saer de Sutton, co. York, ibid.
Albinus de Sutton, co. Notts, 20 Edw. I. R.
1593. Married—Jeames Sutton and Margaret Bonnor: St. Dionis Backchurch, p. 12.
London, 72 ; Philadelphia, 75.

Swabey, Swaby.—Local, ' of Swaby,' a parish in co. Lincoln, near Louth.
Roger de Swaby, co. Linc., 1273. A.
1767. Married—John Sadler and Eliz. Swaby: St. Geo. Han. Sq. i. 164.
1791. — John Miller and Mary Swaby : ibid. ii. 68.
London, 4, 0 ; Crockford, 3, 2 ; MDB. (co. Bucks), 1, 0 ; Philadelphia, 0, 1.

Swaffield. — Local, ' of Swafield,' a parish in co. Norfolk.
William de Swafeld, co. Bedf., 20 Edw. I. R.
1750. Married—George Swaffield and Kezia Overly : St. Geo. Chap. Mayfair, p. 174.
London, 3 ; MDB. (co. Derby), 2.

Swain, Swaine, Swainson. —(1) Bapt. 'the son of Swain,' literally a young lad ; cf. Brown-swain, Boatswain. Swainson is a well-known surname in cos. Lancaster and York.
Alicia Swayneson, 1379: P. T. Yorks. p. 171.
Robertus Swaynne, 1379: ibid. p. 135.
Thomas Swaynesson, 1379: ibid. p. 193.
Sweyn de Canewyk, co. Linc., Hen. III-Edw. I. K.
Adam fil. Suani, co. Linc. 1273. A.
William Svein, co. Suff., ibid.

(2) Occup. 'the swain,' i.e. the peasant, the servant.

John le Swein, co. Oxf., 1273. A.
Robert le Swein, co. Oxf., ibid.
Geoffrey le Sueyn, co. Norf., ibid.
1583. James Swaneson, of Ulverston : Lancashire Wills at Richmond, i. 266.
London, 21, 4, 4 ; Philadelphia, 39, 0, 0.

Swainston, Swanston. — Bapt. 'the son of Swain.' A corruption of Swainson and Swanson ; cf. Johnston and Johnstone, strongly represented in the London Directory, and not always local. Also cf. Snelston and Snelson.

1754. Married—Thomas Swanston and Anne Butler : St. Geo. Chap. Mayfair, p. 274.
1787. — John Brown and Eliz. Swanston : St. Geo. Han. Sq. i. 408.
London, 3, 2.

Swale, Swales. — Local : (1) 'of Swallow Hill,' a hamlet near Barnsley, co. Yorks. At least there is evidence in favour of this view. (2) 'At the Swale,' from residence beside the river of that name, whence Swaledale. Doubtless this will be deemed the more satisfactory solution. Swales is the genitive form ; cf. Williams, Jones, Brooks, Styles, &c. The first reference is in Darton, the parish in which Swallow Hill lies.

Isabella de Swahill, 1379 : P. T. Yorks. p. 88.
Robertus de Swaloughill, 1379 : ibid. p. 51.
Ricardus Swale, 1379 : ibid. p. 70.
Thomas de Swale, 1379 : ibid. p. 252.
1754. Married — Matthew Swales and Dorothy Johnson : St. Geo. Chap. Mayfair, p. 273.
MDB. (West Rid. Yorks), 15, 7 ; West Riding Court Dir., 6, 2.

Swallow. — (1) Nick. 'the swallow' ; cf. Nightingale, Sparrow, Goldfinch, &c. Fr. *hirondelle*. (2) Local, 'of Swallow,' a parish in co. Lincoln, four miles from Caistor.

Helevisa Swalwe, co. Hunts, 1273. A.
Ralph de Swallwe, co. Linc., Hen. III-Edw. I. K.
John Swalewe, co. Soms., 1 Edw. III : Kirby's Quest, p. 127.
Thomas Swalowe, 1379 : P. T. Yorks. p. 219.
Ricardus Swalough, 1379 : ibid. p. 30.
John Swalowe. H.
1624. Married—Samuell Swallow and Francis Denyson : St. Jas. Clerkenwell, iii. 54.
London, 7 ; Philadelphia, 7.

Swalwell. — Local, 'of Swalwell,' a township in the parish of Whickham, near Gateshead, co. Durham.

MDB. (co. Durham), 2.

Swan, Swann, Swanne, Swanson. — (1) Bapt. 'the son of Swan,' i.e. Swain, q.v.

Hamo fil. Swafi, C. R., 30 Hen. III.
Swan le Riche, co. Linc., 1273. A.
Alexander Swan, co. Camb., ibid.
Agnes Swanson, temp. Eliz. ZZ.
Magota Swan, 1379 : P. T. Yorks. p. 24.
Matilda Swanson, 1379 : ibid. p. 171.

(2) Nick. 'the swan'; cf. our modern 'swanlike.'

Geoffrey Svan, co. Camb., 1273. A.
Simon le Swon, 1307. M.
Henry le Swan. H.
Nicholas le Swon, C. R., 2 Hen. V.

(3) Local, 'at the Swan,' an early sign-name.

Thomas atte Swan, C. R., 2 Hen. IV. pt. ii.
London, 16, 19, 1, 5 ; West Rid. Court Dir. (Swann), 5 ; Philadelphia, 19, 9, 0, 8.

Swancock, Swanncott. — (1) Bapt. 'the son of Swan' (?), q.v., with suffix -*cock* ; v. Cocks, and cf. Willcock, Simcock, &c. (2) Local, 'at the swan-cote' (?), from residence beside the cote wherein the swans were kept. Cf.Glasscock and Glasscott for a similar confusion of suffix.

1548. Buried—Thomas Swancock : St. Michael, Cornhill, p. 178.
1759. Married—John Bye and Mary Swancoat : St. Geo. Han. Sq. i. 85.
London, 0, 1.

Swanherd. — Occup. 'the swanherd,' a keeper of swans, an important calling when this bird was a favourite roast ; cf. Rookherd and Gozzard.

William le Swonherde, c. 1300. M.

Swanson. — A variant of Swainson ; v. Swain and Swan.

London, 5 ; Philadelphia, 8.

Swanston. — Bapt. ; v. Swainston.

Swanton. — Local, 'of Swanton,' three parishes in co. Norfolk, viz. Swanton Abbott, Swanton Morley, and Swanton Novers.

Nicholas de Swanton, co. Kent, 1273. A.
Thomas de Swanton or Swantun, co. Norf., ibid.
William de Swanton, co. Wilts, 20 Edw. I. R.
1685. Married—Thomas Swanton and Christian Roll : St. Dionis Backchurch, p. 40.
1782. — James Simpson and Ann Swanton : St. Geo. Han. Sq. i. 336.
MDB. (co. Hereford), 1 ; Boston (U.S.), 6 ; Philadelphia, 2.

Swanwick. — Local, 'of Swanwick,' a hamlet in the parish of Alfreton, co. Derby. The meaning is 'the *wick* or dwelling of Swan,' the original settler ; v. Swan and Wick.

1604. Margaret Swanwick, of Worswall : Wills at Chester, i. 186.
1619. Hugh Swanwick, of Swanwick Green : ibid.
1668. John Swanwick and Mary Winspeare : Marriage Alleg. (Canterbury), p. 247.
1711. Married—Thomas Parish and Hannah Swanwick : St. Mary Aldermary, p. 41.
MDB. (co. Ches.), 3 ; (co. Derby), 2 ; Manchester, 1.

Swarbrick, Swarbrigg. — Local, 'of Swarbrick' or Swartbrick, some small spot in the neighbourhood of Winmarleigh, co. Lanc. Probably the suffix is -*brigg* =bridge ; cf. Philbrick.

1581. John Swartbrecke, of Rossaker : Lancashire Wills at Richmond, i. 267.
1622. Edward Swarthbrecke, of Much Singleton : ibid.
1669. Margaret Swartbreck, of Winmerleigh : ibid.
1680. Joanna Swarbrick, of Winmerley : ibid.
MDB. (co. Lanc.), 4, 0 ; Manchester, 6, 0 ; Philadelphia, 0, 2.

Swatman ; v. Sweetman.

Swayne. — Bapt. ; v. Swain, of which it is a variant.

1600-1. Ellis Swayne or Swaine, co. Dorset : Reg. Univ. Oxf. vol. ii. pt. ii. p. 246.
1738. Married — Joseph Swayne and Mary Jason : St. Geo. Han. Sq. i. 21.
Crockford, 5 ; Philadelphia, 22.

Sweatinbed. — Nick.

Alan Swet in bedde, Close Roll, 3 Edw. I.

Sweatman. — (1) Bapt. 'the son of Swetman' ; v. Sweetman. (2) Local, 'of Swetenham' ; v. Swetnam.

Crockford (1891), 1.

Sweepstake. — Local. The suffix is -*stake*, as in Copestake, &c.

I simply record it because it so nearly approaches in appearance our modern ' sweepstake.'

Robertus Swepstak, 1379 : P. T. Yorks. p. 208.

Sweet.—(1) Bapt. 'the son of Sweet,' analogous to the early introduced French ' Douce '; v. Dowse. (2) Nick. 'the sweet'; cf. Good.

Swet' le Bone, co. Norf., 1273. A.
Adam Swet, co. Oxf., ibid.
Roger Swet, co. Camb., ibid.
Roger Swet, Fines Roll, 11 Edw. I.
Walter Swete, co. Soms., 1 Edw. III : Kirby's Quest, p. 130.
Johannes Suete, 1379 : P. T. Yorks. p. 89.
Johannes Swete, 1379 : ibid. p. 295.
1578. Robert Sweete and Johanna Sweete : Marriage Lic. (London), i. 80.
1700. Bapt. — Ann, d. James Sweet : St. Jas. Clerkenwell, i. 389.
London, 14 ; Philadelphia, 10.

Sweetapple. — (1) Nick. (?), ' sweet apple '; v. Sweet. (2) Local, 'at the sweet-apple,' from residence beside a particular sweet apple - tree. This is the more probable origin ; cf. Crabb, Crabtree, Appletree, Plumptre, Ash, Nash, Birch, &c. It is evidently a West-country surname.

Edward Swetapple. RR. I.
Roger Sweetappull, C. R., 4 Hen. V.
1585–6. Henry Gatcombe and Alice Sweethable (co. Middlesex) : Marriage Lic. (London), i. 147.
1613. Married — Edmund Sweetaple and Sibille Bennet : Reg. Broad Chalke, co. Wilts, p. 4.
1614. — Thomas Bennet and Margrett Sweetaple : ibid.
1687. Married — John Sweetaple and Elizabeth Brett : St. Michael, Cornhill, p. 45.
MDB. (co. Soms.), 1.

Sweetcock.—Bapt. 'the son of Sweetcock.' The name occurs as a single personal name in the Hundred Rolls. Of course the term is one of endearment originally. ' Nice young fellow ' is our modern equivalent (v. Cocks). The feminine form given below is ' confusion worse confounded.' v. Sweet, and cf. Lovecock, frequently found as a baptismal name at the same period.

Adam Swetcoc, co. Camb., 1273. A.
Swetecoka de Hornden, C. R., 16 Edw. I.

Sweetgood.—Bapt. 'the son of Sweetgood.' One of the many surnames with prefix -sweet or suffix -good ; cf. Scattergood and Sweetlove.

Alicia Swytegode, 1379 : P. T. Yorks. p. 71.
Agnes Swythgode, 1379 : ibid.

Sweeting, Sweeten. — (1) Bapt. 'the son of Sweeting'; v. Sweet. Lower says, ' Sweeting, an old A.S. personal name. In Domesday, Sueting, Suetingus.' The Testa de Neville gives one instance betokening a local origin. But all the East-coast Sweetings are of fontal origin ; v. Browning or Harding.

Richard Swetyne, co. Norf., 1273. A.
Thomas Swetyene, co. Norf., ibid.
Willelmus Swyting, 1379 : P. T. Yorks. p. 221.
Isabella Swyting, 1379 : ibid.
Robert Swyting, 1379 : ibid.

(2) Local, ' of Sweeting.'

John de Sweting, co. Wilts, Hen. III– Edw. I. K.
Robert Swetynge, co. Soms., 1 Edw. III : Kirby's Quest, p. 265.
London, 7, 0 ; Philadelphia, 5, 9.

Sweetlove.—Nick. 'Sweetlove,' a term of endearment. Probably a translation of Douceamour.

Cf. Robert Douceamour, Close Roll, 8 Hen. IV.

It may be a baptismal name, judging by the first reference below ; v. Sweet.

Swetelove (without surname), co. Camb., 1273. A.
Margery Swetelove, co. Camb., ibid.
Peter Swetlove, co. Camb., ibid.
1572. Alexander Sweetlove, of Sharples : Wills at Chester, i. 186.
1614. Jane Sweetlove, of Great Lever : ibid.
1633. Margaret Sweetlove, of Sharples : ibid. ii. 212.
MDB. (co. Kent), 1.

Sweetman, Swetman, Swatman.—(1) Bapt. 'the son of Sweetman,' the same as Sweet, with the augmentative -man appended ; cf. Bateman and Tiddiman ; v. Sweet.

Osmund fil. Swetman, co. Berks, Hen. III–Edw. I. K.
Swetman (without surname), co. Oxf., 1273. A.
Swetman fil. Edith, co. Oxf., ibid.
Swetman de Heligham, co. Norf., ibid.
Sweteman Textor, co. Bucks, ibid.

Adam Swetman, co. Oxf., 1273. A.
John Swetemon, C. R., 51 Edw. III.
1757. Married—William Sweetman and Penelope Dunn : St. Geo. Han. Sq. i. 74.

(2) Local ; v. Swetenham and Swetnam.

London, 3, 0, 2 ; Philadelphia, 5, 0, 0.

Sweetmouth. — Nick. ' with the sweet mouth '; v. Sweet.

Robert Swetemouth. D.
William Swetmouth. Q.
John Swetemouthe, C. R., 35 Hen. VI.

Sweetpintle.—Nick.

John Swetpintel, co. Norf., 1273. A.

Sweetser, Sweitzer, Sweetzer, Sweetsir, Switzer.—? Local. Lower suggests ' Switzer,' a Swiss, a native of Switzerland. The surname is no doubt foreign, but was early settled in England, and has acquired an English appearance. At the time of writing there is being advertised ' Schweitzer's Cocoatina.' Cotgrave quotes :

' A Switzer's bellie and a drunkard's face
Are no true signes of penetentiall grace.'

' Leading three thousand must'red men
in pay,
Of French, Scots, Alman, Swisser, and
the Dutch.'
Drayton's Poems, p. 84.

Richard Swetesire, C. R., 29 Edw. III.
1584. Richard Sweetser and Cecily Harrys : Marriage Lic. (London), i. 131.
1778. Married—John Godfrey Sweetser and Jane Mottea : St. Geo. Han. Sq. i. 283.
London, 2, 0, 0, 0, 0 ; Philadelphia, 1, 13, 0, 0, 11 ; Boston (U.S.) (Sweetsir), 1 ; New York, 7, 5, 2, 0, 14.

Swetenham, Swettenham, Sweetenham, Swetnam.—Local, ' of Swettenham,' a parish in co. Chester, five miles from Congleton ; v. Swetnam for modifications.

Richard Swetinam, co. Bucks, 1273. A.
William de Swetenham, co. Ches., 1297 : East Cheshire, ii. 644.
Roger de Swetenham, co. Ches., 1366 : ibid.
1561. Married — William Swettenam and Agnes Plante : Reg. Prestbury Ch., co. Chester, p. 5.
1584. William Swettnam, co. Ches. : Reg. Univ. Oxf. vol. ii. pt. ii. p. 135.
1597. Laurence Swettenham, of Somerford : Wills at Chester, i. 186.
1611. Thomas Swettenham, of Swettenham : ibid.
MDB. (co. Ches.), 2, 1, 0, 0 ; Manchester, 0, 0, 1, 1.

Swetnam, Swetman. — (1) Local, 'of Swetenham,' q.v. ; cf. Debnam and Deadman for Debenham, Putnam and Putman for Puttenham, &c.

1649. Bapt.—Edmund, s. of Edmund and Jone Swetnam : Reg. Stourton, co. Wilts, p. 11.
1650. — Manuell, s. of Edmund and Jone Swetnam : ibid.
1652. — John, s. of Edmund and Jone Swetman : ibid.
1655. — Abraham, s. of Edmund and Jone Swetman : ibid. p. 12.
1664. — John, s. of John and Deborah Swetnam : St. Jas. Clerkenwell, i. 124.
1666. — Dorothy, d. John and Deborah Swetman : ibid. p. 129.

Afterwards invariably Swetman, the real local origin thus becoming lost. (2) For baptismal origin of Swetman, v. Sweetman.

Swift.—Nick. 'the swift.' One of a class of names implying speed, comprehending Purchas, Shearwind, Lightfoot, Golightly, Bullet, &c., given to pursuivants and couriers. Purchas was the favourite.

Matilda Swyft, co. Camb., 1273. A.
Roger Swyft, co. Bucks, ibid.
Arnulph Swyft, co. Norf., ibid.
Ralph Swyft, courier to Edward III : Issues of the Exchequer, edited by Frederick Devon.
Henricus Swyft, 1379 : P. T. Yorks. p. 16.
1754. Married — Godfrey Swift and Christiana Williams : St. Geo. Han. Sq. i. 55.
London, 24 ; Philadelphia, 51.

Swinbank.—Local, 'of Swinbank,' probably the bank where the swine fed. The spot is somewhere in or near the parish of Ravenstonedale, co. Westm.

Reynold Sywnebank, 1541 : Hist. and Traditions of Ravenstonedale, co. Westm., W. Nicholls, p. 113.
Cuthbert Swynebank, 1541 : ibid.
Liverpool, 1 ; MDB. (co. Durham), 2.

Swinburn, Swinburne, Swinborn, Swinborne, Swinburne. — Local, 'of Swinburn,' a township in the parish of Chollerton, co. Northumberland.

William de Swinburne, 1278, co. Northumb.: Lower's Patr. Brit. p. 336.
John de Swynburne, co. Northumb., 20 Edw. I. R.
Nicholas de Swynburne, co. Northumb.: ibid.
William de Swyneburne, co. Northumb.: ibid.

1576. Henry Swynburn, co. Yorks : Reg. Univ. Oxf. vol. ii. pt. ii. p. 71.
1793. Married—Paul Binfield and Mary Frances Swinburne : St. Geo. Han. Sq. ii. 101.
London, 1, 2, 1, 1, 0 ; MDB. (co. Northumberland), 1, 1, 0, 0, 0 ; (co. Hereford), 0, 0, 0, 0, 1.

Swindell, Swindle. — Local, 'of Swindale,' a chapelry in the parish of Shap, co. Westmoreland.

1540. Buried — Alys Swyndelle : St. Dionis Backchurch, p. 178.
1608. Richard Westrawe and Agnes Swindell : Marriage Lic. (London), i. 308.
1790. Married — John Swindell and Lydia Mullins : St. Geo. Han. Sq. ii. 36.
London, 4, 0 ; Boston (U.S.), 1, 1.

Swindells, Swindles.—Local, 'of Swindells,' most probably the spot referred to in the following :

'A branch of the family of Howford held a small estate here (Bosden) in the 14th century, called "Swyndelves"': East Cheshire, i. 264.

This was in the parish of Cheadle, in which immediate district all our Swindells have sprung (for the suffix, v. Delf).

Roger Swyndels, of Marple, 1522 : East Cheshire, ii. 52 n.
1561. Married—Humfry Swyndells and Isabell Woorthe : Prestbury Ch. (co. Ches.), p. 5.
William Swindells, of Stockport : Wills at Chester (1545-1620), p. 186.
John Swindells, of Northenden, 1620 : ibid.
1656. Bapt. — Ursula, d. John Swendalls : St. Jas. Clerkenwell, i. 195.
London, 2, 0 ; Manchester, 10, 0 ; MDB. (co. Ches.), 7, 0 ; Boston (U.S.), 1, 0 ; Philadelphia, 1, 1.

Swinden, Swindin. — Local, 'of Swinden,' a township in the parish of Gisburne, W. Rid. Yorks ; also a township in the parish of Kirkby Overblow, W. Rid. Yorks. Only two entries separate the following :

Johannes de Swyndeyn, 1379 : P. T. Yorks. p. 285.
Thomas Swynhyrd, 1379 : ibid.
Adam de Swynden', 1379 : ibid. p. 93.
Johannes de Swyndene, 1379 : ibid.
1790. Married—George Bateman and Martha Swinden: St. Geo. Han. Sq. ii. 46.
Sheffield, 1, 2 ; West Rid. Court Dir., 2, 1 ; Philadelphia, 1, 0.

Swindlehurst, Swinglehurst.—Local, 'of Swindlehurst.' This is a North-English surname, but I cannot find the precise locality. It is quite clear that

Swinglehurst is a corruption of Swindlehurst ; v. Swindell and Hurst. The meaning would seem to be 'the wood in the swine-dale.'

1576. John Swinlehurst, of Chepin Lancashire Wills at Richmond, i. 267.
1594. William Swindlehurst, of Clitheroe : Wills at Chester, i. 186.
1623. Bapt. — Richard, s. Roger Swinglehurst : St. Jas. Clerkenwell, i. 96.
1635. William Swinglehurst, of Chepin : Lancashire Wills at Richmond, i. 267.
Manchester, 0, 1 ; MDB. (West Rid. Yorks), 4, 0 ; Boston (U.S.), Philadelphia, 0, 1.

Swinfen.—Local, 'of Swinfen,' a hamlet in the parish of Wreford, co. Stafford. An old family bearing this name resided here.

1659. Married—Stephen Casingale and Eliza Swinffon : St. Jas. Clerkenwell, i. 103.
1672. Ralph Swynfen and Eliz. Moreton : Marriage Alleg. (Canterbury), p. 203.
1795. Married—Samuel Swinfen and Susanna Durrant : St. Geo. Han. Sq. ii. 130.
London, 2.

Swinford.—Local, 'of Swinford,' parishes in cos. Leicester and Stafford ; also a tithing in the parish of Cumnor, co. Berks.

William de Swyneford, co. Suff., 1273. A.
William de Swynneford, co. Hunts, ibid.
1626. Bapt.—Marye, d. Peeter Swinford : Reg. Canterbury Cath., p. 6.
1633. — Eliz., d. Peter Swinforde : ibid. p. 7.
MDB. (co. Kent), 5.

Swingler.—Occup. 'the swingler,' i.e. a flax-beater, possibly a wool-beater, hence 'swingling-stick, a stick used for beating or opening wool or flax. Lanc.' (Halliwell). 'Fleyhe, swyngyl, tribulum': Prompt. Parv. 'Swingle, a staff for beating flax' (Skeat, and see his article).

Nicholas Swingler, 1682 : St. Peter, Cornhill, p. 9.
London, 3 ; Derby, 5.

Swinhoe.—Local, 'of Swinhoe,' a township in Northumberland.

Newcastle, 1 ; Oxford, 2.

Swinnart, Swinyard, Swinehart.—Occup. 'the swine-herd' ; cf. Calvert, Coward, Stoddart, &c. Swinyard is almost certainly a corruption of swine-herd. No traces of the local term ; cf. *y* in Sawyer, Bowyer, &c. 'Swinyard, a keeper of swine. "Chandlers, herdsmen, or swinyards, coopers, blacksmiths," &c. (Bishop's Marrow of Astrology, p. 36)': Halliwell.

Walter le Swynhurde, co. Soms., 1 Edw. III: Kirby's Quest, p. 200.
Thomas le Swenhurde, co. Soms., 1 Edw. III: ibid. p. 207.
Robert Swynherd, C. R., 7 Edw. III. pt. ii.
John Swynhird, co. York. W. 2.
Clement Swynhird, 1379: P. T. Howdenshire, p. 9.
Nicholas Swynard, 1379: P. T. Yorks. p. 150.
Johannes Swyndherd, 1379: ibid. p. 59.
Wylymot Swynhirde, 1379: ibid. p. 256.
1668. Nicholas Swinnarde and Susanne Andrews: Marriage Alleg. (Canterbury), p. 233.
London, 0, 3, 0; Philadelphia, 0, 0, 1; New York, 0, 2, 0.

Swinnerton, Swinerton. — Local, 'of Swinnerton,' a parish in co. Stafford, three miles from Stone.

Robert de Swinnerton, co. Staff.: Hen. III-Edw. I. K.
John de Swynnerton, co. Derby, 20 Edw. I. R.
1563. John Swynerton and May Fawnte: Marriage Lic. (London), i. 27.
1609. Henry Swinarton, London: Reg. Univ. Oxf. vol. ii. pt. ii. p. 305.
1617. Randle Swinnerton, of Church Lawton: Wills at Chester, i. 186.
1802. Married—William Utterston and Henrietta Swinerton: St. Geo. Han. Sq. ii. 258.
MDB. (co. Stafford), 1, 0; London, 1, 0; New York, 1, 0; Boston (U.S.), 0, 2.

Swinstead.—Local, 'of Swinstead,' a parish in co. Lincoln.

Gocelin de Swynested, co. Linc., 1273. A.
1583. Richard Swinsted, *farrier*, of Chesthunt, co. Herts, and Judith Hammond: Marriage Lic. (London), i. 119.
MDB. (co. Bedford), 3; London, 2; Oxford, 1.

Swinyard; v. Swinnart.

Swire, Swyer. — Offic. 'the squire,' early corrupted to Swyer or Swire.

Ricardus Sqwyer, 1379: P. T. Yorks. p. 268.
Thomas Swyer, 1379: ibid. p. 266.
Willelmus Swyer, 1379: ibid.
1618. Bapt.—Anna, d. of John Squire, *vulgaritur*, John Swyer, of Skipton: Reg. Skipton Ch.

In the same church is a mural tablet to John Swire, 1760.

1807. Married—William Coates and Mary Swyer: St. Geo. Han. Sq. ii. 362.
London, 3, 3; West Rid. Court Dir., 2, 0; Philadelphia, 4, 0.

Swithenbank, Swithinbank. —Local, 'of Swithenbank,' i. e. the bank on which Swithen, the first proprietor, had settled; v. Swithin. I cannot find the spot. It is a North-English surname; cf. Gillbanks, Windebank, &c.

Manchester, 1, 0; MDB. (West Rid. Yorks), 2, 0; London, 0, 1; New York, 1, 0.

Swithin.—Bapt. 'the son of Swithin'; cf. local Swithinbank.

Thomas Swethyne, co. Norf., 1273. A.
1609. Bapt. — Anne, d. William Swythen: St. Jas. Clerkenwell, i. 57.
1751. Married — John Tuckman and Margaret Swithin: St. Geo. Chap. Mayfair, p. 203.
Tynemouth, 1.

Switzer; v. Sweetser.

Sworder.—Occup. 'the sworder,' a bladesmith, a maker of swords. M.E. *swerd*.

John le Serdere, c. 1300. M.
John Swerder. Z.
Henry Swerder. H.
William Serdier, Close Roll, 16 Edw. III. pt. ii.
London, 1.

Swordslipper. — Occup. 'a sheather,' one who made swordslips; v. Sheather.

Johannes Swerdslyper, 1379: P. T. Yorks. p. 251.
Johanna Swerdsliper, 1379: ibid. p. 25.

This name as a specific occupation occurs in the registers of St. Nicholas, Newcastle, till the close of the 16th century.

William Browne, *sword-slipper*, 1576: Brand's Newcastle, ii. 360.
Robert Heslop, *sword-slipper*, 1586: ibid.

Swyer; v. Swire.

Sybry; v. Sibary.

Syddall; v. Siddall.

Sydenham.—Local, 'of Sydenham,' a parish in co. Kent, near Blackheath.

John de Sydenham, co. Soms., 1 Edw. III: Kirby's Quest, p. 182.
Simon de Sidenham, co. Soms., 1 Edw. III: ibid. p. 192.
1586-7. Roger Raston and Rachael Sydnam: Marriage Lic. (London), i. 159.
1674. Humphey Sydenham and Eliz. St. Johns, *widow*: Marriage Alleg. (Canterbury), p. 231.
1803. Married—Thomas Sydenham and Frances Bunbury: St. Geo. Han. Sq. ii. 295.
London, 4.

Sydney; v. Sidney.

Syer, Syers.—Bapt. 'the son of Saier,' one of the many forms of Sayer, q.v. The fuller form was Sigher or Sighar.

Saier Perkesgate, C. R., 17 Ric. II.
1637. Married—Roberte Syers and Ann Washington: St. Jas. Clerkenwell, i. 69.
1768. — Robert Syer and Ann Brown: St. Geo. Han. Sq. i. 173.
1796. — John Syer and Catherine Greene: ibid. ii. 157.
London, 3, 2; Philadelphia, 0, 5.

Sykes, Sikes.—Local, 'at the syke,' from residence beside a *sike*, i.e. a stream One of the greatest of Yorkshire surnames. It has ramified in a marvellous manner. '*Sike*, a gutter, a stream. North England' (Halliwell). Sykes is almost the invariable dress; cf. Dykes for Dikes. The suffix -s is the genitive form, as in Jones, Brooks, Holmes, Williams, &c., meaning Sykes' son. Sometimes it may mean residence beside two streams, as in one of my references below; then Sykes is plural. Cf. Beck, Brook, Brooks, Gott, &c.

Robertus del Syke, 1379: P. T. Yorks. p. 190.
Rogerus del Syke, 1379: ibid.
Johannes del Syke, 1379: ibid. p. 211.
Agnes del Syke, 1379: ibid. p. 212.
Henricus del Syke, 1379: ibid. p. 178.
1794. Married—Samuel Weeden Sykes and Jemima Jones: St. Geo. Han. Sq. ii. 115.
1804. — James Sikes and Eleanor Adie: ibid. p. 300.
West Rid. Court Dir., 87, 3; Philadelphia, 58, 3.

Sylvester; v. Silvester.

Symcox; v. Simcock.

Symes, Syms, Symmes. — Bapt. 'the son of Simon,' from the nick. Sim or Sime; v. Sim.

Margret Symes, died in Virginia, 1624: Hotten's Lists of Emigrants, p. 243.
Alexander Symes, bound for Virginia, 1635: ibid. p. 138.
1788. Married — William Syms and Mary Griffiths: St. Geo. Han. Sq. ii. 2.
1794. — Joseph Symes and Amelia Lock: ibid. p. 108.
1802. — John Greenwood and Mary Ann Symmes: ibid. p. 256.
London, 13, 3, 0; Philadelphia, 0, 0, 3.

Symmonds, Symmons, Symonds, Symonds, Symons. —Bapt. 'the son of Simon.' The *d* is excrescent, as fully shown under Simon, q.v. I cannot find any traces of Sigismund, otherwise it might easily be the parent of some of our Symmonds, &c.

Thomas Symond, co. Suff., 1273. A.
Alice fil. Symon, co. Oxf., ibid.
Maurice fil. Symon, co. Oxf., ibid.
1587. Married—Thomas Holland and Christabell Symondes: St. Dionis Backchurch, p. 11.
1664. Buried—Goodwife Symmons, of this parish: ibid. p. 235.
1722. Bapt. — Symmonds Symmonds, the mother a lodger at Mr. Kempton's, *porter*: ibid. p. 158.

London, 1, 8, 20, 2, 29; Philadelphia, 0, 3, 3, 0, 0.

Sympson.—Bapt. 'the son of Simon,' q.v. The *p* is intrusive, as in Thompson, Hampson, &c.

Willelmus Symmeson', 1397 : P. T. Yorks. p. 7.
Johannes Symmeson', 1379 : ibid. p. 10.
1554-5. Married — Dominick Croope and Jone Symson: St. Dionis Backchurch, p. 3.
1763. — John Sympson and Ann Blower : St. Geo. Han. Sq. i. 118.
London, 5; Philadelphia, 1.

Syms.—Bapt.'the son of Simon'; v. Symes and Sim.

Synnett, Synnot, Synnott.—Bapt. ; v. Sennett.

Syratt, Syrett ; v. Sired.

Syre ; v. Sire.

Syson. — Bapt. 'the son of Sybil' ; v. Sisson.

1759. Married—Peter Syson and Mary Dawson : St. Geo. Han. Sq. i. 89.
1772. — Jasper. Syson and Jane Watkin : ibid. p. 223.
West Rid. (Yorks) Court Dir., 1.

T

Tabberer, Taberer, Tabor, Tabrar, Taber. — Occup. ' the taborer,' a player on the tabor or tabour (cf. tambourine), a small drum. There are many entries of this vocation. With the shortened Taber or Tabor, cf. Pepper for Pepperer.

John le Taburer, co. Northants, 1273. A.
Peter le Taburer, Close Roll, 17 Edw. I.
William le Tabourer. B.
Edmund Tabour. V.
Robert Tabur, co. Soms., 1 Edw. III : Kirby's Quest, p. 188.
1616. Humphrey Tabor, co. Somerset : Reg. Univ. Oxf. vol. ii. pt. ii. p. 357.
1775. Married — David Yetman and Eliz. Tabor : St. Geo. Han. Sq. i. 258.
1780. Robert Taber and Ann Atterbury : ibid. p. 314.
London, 1, 2, 4, 1, 0 ; Boston (U.S.), 1, 0, 4, 0, 18.

Taberner.—Occup. ' the taberner,' i.e. innkeeper ; v. Taverner. ' *Tabern*, a cellar (North); see Ray's EnglishWords, 1674, p. 48. *Taberna*, a tabyrn, a tavern, or inn, Nominale MS. Hence Taberner, a tavernkeeper ' (Halliwell). Probably this form still exists as a surname, although I have not met with it in registers of the present century.

William Tabernator, co. Berks, 1273. A.
Benedict Taberner, co. Devon, ibid.
Eustace Tabnar', co. Oxf., ibid.
Willelmus Taburner, 1379 : P. T. Yorks. p. 12.
1764. Married — Henry Taberner and Ann Perry : St. Geo. Han. Sq. i. 135.

Tabler, Tableter. — Occup. ' the tabler ' or ' the tableter,' a maker of tables or tablets for putting down daily expenses, &c., of slate, wax, &c.

' A pair of tables all of ivory,
And a pointel, ypolished fetisly,
And wrote alway the names as he stood.'
    Chaucer, C. T. 7323-5.

Also tables for backgammon or chess.

1530. ' Item, the same daye paied to John the hardewarman for . . . 2 coffers, a payer (pair) of tabulles and chesses, . . . etc.': Privy Purse Expenses, Henry VIII, p. 51.
Roger Tablour, c. 1300. M.
Bartholomew le Tabler, ibid.
Richard le Tableter, ibid.
Geoffrey le Tableter, C. R., 19 Edw. II. pt. ii.
Bartholomew le Tableter, London. X.

Tabor, Tabrar ; v. Tabberer.

Tackley.—Local (1), ' of Tackley,' a parish in co. Oxford ; (2) ' of Takeley,' a parish in co. Essex. These two surnames, Tackley and Takeley, are no doubt inextricably mixed.

William de Takeleye, co. Essex, 1273. A.
Agnes de Takele, co. Oxf., ibid.
Robert de Takkele, co. Oxf., ibid.
(Villani) de Tackeleg', co. Essex, 20 Edw. I. R.
1800. Married — Robert Starling and Ann Tackley : St. Geo. Han. Sq. ii. 225.
London, 4.

Tacon. — Bapt. ' the son of Tacoln.' This is a Norfolk and Suffolk surname. Hence the name of Tacolneston, a parish in co. Norfolk, i.e. the town of Tacoln.

Eustace de Tacolnestun, co. Norf., 1273. A.
MDB. (co. Suffolk), 6.

Tadhunter, Tadman (?). — Occup. ' a fox-hunter ' ; v. Todhunter.

1798. Married—Francis Tadman and Mary Young : St. Geo. Han. Sq. ii. 184.
London, 1, 5.

Tadley. — Local, ' of Tadley,' a parish in co. Hants. Possibly, however, this surname is a modification of Tadlow ; v. Tadloo.

Philadelphia, 3.

Tadloo.—Local, ' of Tadlow,' a parish in co. Camb.

Roysia de Tadelowe, co. Camb., 1273. A.
London, 1.

Tadman ; v. Tadhunter.

Tagg, Tag.—Bapt. ' the son of Agnes,' a great favourite in the 13th and 14th centuries. Nick. Tagg and Taggy. The latter continues to be used in Furness, where Agnes is still almost first favourite. I had a Taggy in my kitchen at Ulverston. We find the French dim. as a suffix in Taggon ; cf. Marion from Mary, Alison from Alice, Gibbon from Gib = Gilbert. v. Agate (2).

Richard Tagg, co. Oxf., 1273. A.
Thomas Tagge, et Sissota uxor ejus, 1379: P. T. Howdenshire, p. 8.
Thomas Tagon, 1379 : P. T. Yorks. p. 82.

Johannes Tagge, 1379 : P.T.Yorks. p. 67.
Robertus Tag, 1379 : ibid. p. 8.
1637. Buried — Tagi Witt, co. Wilts :
Reg. Broad Chalke, p. 45.
1771. Married—James Tagg and Bett
Miles : St. Geo. Han. Sq. i. 209.
London, 6, o ; Sheffield, 1, o ; Oxford,
2, o ; Philadelphia, 4, 7.

Tagget, Taggett, Taggitt.—
Bapt. ' the son of Agnes,' from
nick. Tagg, q.v., with dim. Taggett.
New York, 1, 1, 1.

Tailer, Tailor ; v. Taylor.

Taillefer.—Bapt. ; v. Telfer.
New York, 1.

Taintor, Tainturer, Tainter.
—Occup. ' the teinturer,' or ' teyn-
tour,' a dyer. 'Lystare, or Lytaster
of cloth dyynge, *Tinctor* ' : Prompt.
Parv. Cf. *taint, tint, tinge, tincture.*
For a longer statement, v. my
English Surnames, pp. 322-3 (5th
edit.).

Fulk le Taynturor, C. R., 36 Hen. III.
Robert le Teynturer, co. Linc., 1273. A.
Stephen le Teynterer, co. Kent, ibid.
Alexander Wauteresman, le teynturer
(i. e. Alex. the servant of Walter the
teynturer) : C. R., 25 Edw. I.
Warin le Teyntour. T.
John le Teyntour. T.
Philip le Tentier. H.
1702. Married—William Tainter and
Mary Cleiney : St. Jas. Clerkenwell, i.
224.
New York, 7, o, o ; Boston (U.S.), o,
o, 8.

Tait, Taite, Taitt.—A Scottish
surname, concerning which I have
not gathered any information.
Mr. Lower says, ' Teit was a personal name in Norway in the 11th
century. See the Heimskringla '
(Patr. Brit. p. 338).
London, 9, 2, o ; Philadelphia, 35, 6, 7.

Talbot, Talbott, Talbut.—
Bapt. ' the son of Talbot.'
Richard Talebot, Domesday.
Ricardus Talebot, Pipe Roll, 5 Hen. II.
Talebot de Hadfeld, ibid.
Talebotus Talebot, Fines Roll, 12
Edw. I.
Talebotus de Hintlesham, 34 Edw. I :
BBB. p. 727.
The vexed question of the origin
of this name is absolutely settled
by my last references. It is a per-
sonal name. It was not local, for
it is never found in conjunction
with ' de.' Many surnames may
be seen in Domesday, and Talebot

would simply be Richard's patronymic. This explains to a certain
extent the early use of Talbot as
a dog's name, personal names being
freely used in this manner. Gilbert
as Gib became the recognized name
for a cat, Cuddy (Cuthbert) for a
donkey.
' Ran Colie our dogge, and Talbot, and
    Gerlond.'   Chaucer, C. T. 15386.
Willelmus Talbot, 1379 : P. T. Yorks.
p. 146.
Willelmus Talbot-man, 1379 : ibid.
1580-1. John Hedlea and Susanna Talbott : Marriage Lic. (Westminster), p. 7.
London, 27, 2, 1 ; Philadelphia, 31, o, o.

Talboys.—Local, ' of the underwood.' Two great Anglican Church
musicians, Tallis and Boyce (q.v.),
represent the separate constituents
of Talboys. Tallboy (q.v.) is an imitative corruption.
Isabella Taylbous, co. York, 1477 : W.
11, p. 101.
William Taylbus, co. York, 1512 : ibid.
p. 178.
Walter Talebois. B.
William Tallboys. H.
Thomas Taylebushe, *merchant-taylor*,
1570 : Reg. St. Mary Aldermary, p. 57.
1768. Married — James Nelson and
Hannah Talboys : St. Geo. Han. Sq. i. 173.
Oxford, 9.

Talintyre.—Local, ' of Tallen-
tire,' a township in the parish of
Bridekirk, co. Cumb.
Alexander de Talentir, 1212 : RRR.
p. 144.
Alexander de Tarentir, 1214 : ibid.
p. 154.
Richard Talentire, 1559 ; Reg. Univ.
Oxf. i. 239.
' To Thomas Tallentire, ultra x shill-
ings,' 1619 : VVV. p. 129.
London, 1.

Tallboy.—Local. An imitative
corruption of Talboys, q.v.
1610. Bapt.—William, son of William
Talboy : St. Jas. Clerkenwell, i. 61.
London, 2.

Tallemach ; v. Talmadge and
Tollemache.
London, 2.

Tallis.—Local, ' de la taillis,'
from residence beside a small
copse. O. F. *taillis,* ' a copse,
grove, underwood, such wood as
is felled or lopped every seven or
eight years ' (Cotgrave).
Richard Tailles, co. Cornwall, 1273. A.
Aaron Tallis, 1698 : Reg. St. Mary
Aldermary, p. 36.

1887. Buried—Mary Jane Tallis : Manchester Courier, June 18, 1887.
Manchester, 1 ; Boston (U.S.), 2.

Tallman, Talman.—Nick.' the
tall man ' ; cf. Smallman, Bigg,
Little, &c.
Walter Talman, co. Soms., 1 Edw. III :
Kirby's Quest, p. 186.
1658. Married—Richard Tallman and
Ann Meller : St.Mary Aldermary, p. 28.
1693-4. Married—James Tallman and
Eliz. Millington : St. Dionis Backchurch
(London), p. 43.
Boston (U.S.), 4, o ; Philadelphia, 15, 3.

Talmadge, Talmage, Tall-
madge. — ? Local. Variants of
Tollemache, q.v.
Willelmus Talemasche, 7 Hen. II, Pipe
Roll, iv. 4.
John Talmach, 1677 : Reg. St. Mary
Aldermary, p. 104.
London, 2, 1, o ; Philadelphia, o, 7, 2.

Tamblyn, Tamlin, Tamlyn.
—Bapt. ' the son of Thomas,' from
the nick. Tom (commonly Tam)
and dim. Tomlin (commonly Tamlin). The *b* in Tamblyn is the
usual excrescence; cf. Hamblin for
Hamlin, and v. Tomblin, Tamplin,
and Tomlin. It is interesting to
notice how determinately the *o* in
Tom became *a*. Even Tomlinson
is found as Taminson.
1689. Bapt.—Thomas, son of Thomas
Taminson : St. Jas. Clerkenwell, i. 332.
London, 1, 1, 1.

Tame, Thame.—Local, ' of
Tame,' from residence beside the
river Thame ; an early Oxfordshire
surname.
Claricia de Tame, co. Oxf., 1273. A.
John de Tame, co. Oxf., ibid.
Robert de Tame, co. Bucks, ibid.
Edmund Tame, C. R., 27 Hen. VIII.
pt. ii.
1653. Married—Anthonye Robins and
Sarah Tame : St. Michael, Cornhill, p. 31.
London, 3, o ; MDB. (co. Oxford), 1, 1.

Tamlin, -lyn ; v. Tamblyn.

Tammadge ; a corruption of
Talmadge, q.v.
London, 2.

Tamplin.—Bapt. ' the son of
Thomas.' The order is Thomas,
nick. Tom, dim. Thomelin or Tomlin, North or South-West English
Tamlin, then with intrusive but
inevitable *p*, Tamplin ; cf. Thompson
and Thomson from same root. v.
Tomlin, Tamblyn, and Taplin.

William Tamlen, 1572: Reg. St. Columb Major, p. 8.
Constance Tamblyn, 1743: ibid. p. 272.

The fem. Thomasine is invariably Tamson in the same register.

Tamson, d. of Joane Jenken, 1573: ibid. p. 8.
Tamson, d. of John Adam, 1574: ibid. p. 9.
1785. Married — James Mitchell and Sarah Tamplin: St. Geo. Han. Sq. i. 379. London, 3; Philadelphia, 1.

Tamson, Tams.—Bapt. 'the son of Thomas,' from the nick. Tom (commonly Tam) and patronymic Tams or Tamson; v. Tamblyn, Tamplin, &c.

1753. Married — Moses Waddop and Ann Tams: St. Geo. Chap. Mayfair, p. 263. Philadelphia, 1, 5; Oxford, 0, 1.

Tancock.—Bapt. 'the son of Daniel,' from nick. Dan, pet Dancock, sharpened to Tancock (cf. Tennyson, Dennison, &c.). For suffix, v. *cock*, Introd. p. 25.
London, 1; Penzance, 1.

Tancred; v. Tankard.

Tandy. — Bapt. 'the son of Andrew,' from nick. (Scottish) Dandy, then Tandy; cf. Dennison and Tennyson, Dannett and Tannett, &c.

1582. John, s. of Homfrey Dandy: Reg. St. Dionis Backchurch (London), p. 85.
1584. Joane, d. of Homfrie Tandy: ibid.
1638. Married — Elias Clark and Sarah Tandy: St. Peter, Cornhill, i. 256. London, 2; Oxford, 1; Boston (U.S.), 2.

Tanett; v. Tannett.

Taney; v. Tawney.

Tanfield.—Local,' of Tanfield': (1) a chapelry in the parish of Chester-le-Street, co. Durham; (2) a parish in the N. Rid. Yorks, six miles from Ripon.

Ricardus de Tanfeld, 1379: P. T. Yorks. p. 240.
1544. Robert Tanfyld and Wilgeforda Fitzherbert: Marriage Lic. (Faculty Office), p. 2.
1551. Married—Thomas Tanfelde and Margaret Colman: St. Michael, Cornhill, p. 6.
1610. — Thomas Drayton and Marie Tanfeild: ibid. p. 19.
Sheffield, 2; London, 1; New York, 1.

Tangye. — Bapt. 'the son of Tengy,' a common name in the Hundred Rolls.

Tengy ad Fontem, co. Camb., 1273. A.

Allan Tengy, co. Camb., 1273. A.
Nel Tengy, co. Camb., ibid.
London, 1.

Tankard, Tancred. — Bapt. 'the son of Tancred,' very early written Tankard. It is interesting to note that there are no Tankards in the London Directory, and that they are found chiefly in Yorkshire, where the family of Tancred was originally settled.

Robert Tankard, co. Soms., 1 Edw. III: Kirby's Quest, p. 280.
Emma Tankard, 1379: P. T. Yorks. p. 220.
Johannes Tankerd, 1379: ibid.
Edmund Tankard, Patent Roll, 14 Edw. IV. pt. i.
Ricardus Tankart, 1427, Ripon: GGG. p. 329.
William Tankerd, 1571, Ripon: ibid. p. 308.
1678. Richard Wood and Ursula Tanckred (co. York): Marriage Alleg. (Canterbury), p. 285.
Liverpool (Tancred), 1; West Riding Court Dir., 4, 0; Bradford, 5, 0; Boston (U.S.), 0, 4.

Tann.—(1) Bapt. (?), 'the son of Daniel,' from the nick. Dan, sharpened to Tan; cf. Tancock for Dancock, and Tannett for Dannett. (2) Local, ' of Tan.' I cannot find the spot.

Geoffrey de Tan, co. Camb., 1273. A.
William de Tan, co. Camb., ibid.
Adam Tan, et Ydonia uxor ejus, 1379: P. T. Yorks. p. 114.
London, 4; Oxford, 1.

Tanner.— Occup. 'the tanner,' one who tanned leather. Fr. *tan*, ' the bark of a young oak, wherewith leather is tanned': Cotgrave (v. *tan*, Skeat). Hence Barker, q.v.

Ansketill le Tanur, 1189: RRR. p. 52.
Elfer Tannator, co. Sussex, 1273. A.
John Tannarius, co. Oxf., ibid.
Philip le Tannour, co. Hunts, ibid.
Henry le Tanur, co. Notts, ibid.
Henry le Tanner, co. Soms., 1 Edw. III: Kirby's Quest, p. 177.
1613. Bapt.—Mary, d. James Tanner: St. Jas. Clerkenwell, i. 69.
1699. Married — Stephen Tanner and Alice Adams: St. Peter, Cornhill, ii. 62. London, 30; Philadelphia, 8.

Tannett, Tanett.—Bapt. 'the son of Daniel,' from the nick. Dan, and dim. Danet, sharpened to Tanet (v. Dannett); cf. Tennyson for Dennison, or Tancock for Dancock. The Cheshire Wills contain many references to the

family of Danat, or Dannat, or Dannett. In two instances the initial letter is T, not D.

1670. Thomas Tanat, of Broxton: Wills at Chester, iii. 262.
1674. Ann Tannat, of Broxton: ibid.
1768. Married—Thomas Tannatt and Sarah Jones: St. Geo. Han. Sq. i. 176.
West Rid. Court Dir., 2, 1; Philadelphia, 1, 0.

Tanshelf.—Local, 'of Tanshelf,' a township in the parish of Pontefract, W. Rid. Yorks.

MDB. (East Rid. Yorks.), 1.

Tansley.—Local, 'of Tansley,' a hamlet in the parish of Crich, co. Derby, near Matlock.

1788. Married — Thomas Pooley and Catherine Tansley: St. Geo. Han. Sq. ii. 15.
1806. — James Tansley and Charlotte Ablett: ibid. p. 352.
London, 2; Philadelphia, 2.

Tanton, Taunton.—Local, ' of Taunton'; also ' of Taynton,' parishes in diocs. Oxford, Glouc., and Bristol; v. Taunton.

Guido de Tanton,co. Somerset, 1273. A.
William de Tantun, co. Norf., ibid.
Archid de Tanton, co. Soms., 1 Edw. III: Kirby's Quest, p. 362.
London, 1, 3; Philadelphia, 0, 2; New York, 1, 1.

Tantum.—Local, 'of Taunton'; v. Tanton. This corruption is a very natural one; cf. Ransom for Ranson, or Sansom for Sanson. Also cf. the dictionary word *random* for *randon*.

1753. Married — William Tantum and Mary Ward: St. Geo. Chap. Mayfair, p. 265.
Philadelphia, 1.

Tapiser, Tapner, Tapster(?). — Occup. 'the tapecer' or tapener, a worker of tapestry for decorating walls, &c. ' Tappet, a clothe, *tappis'*: Palsgrave. 'Tapecer, *tapetarius*': Prompt. Parv. The Ordinances for the Guild of St. Katharine, Lynn, are signed by 'Peter Tapeser' (English Gilds, p. 68, E. E. Text Soc.). Simon Tapser (H.). The Couchers and Tapisers went together in the York Corpus Christi Pageant (York Mystery Plays, p. xxiii, Toulmin Smith). Spelt also Tapiters. In the old usages of Winchester, the trade is called Tapener (English

Gilds, Toulmin Smith, p. 350). As Tapner it is in the London Directory.

1783. Married — Thomas Hall and Eliz. Tapner : St. Geo. Han. Sq. i. 354.
Marmaduk Myddylton, *tapitour* : Freemen of York, i. 265 (Surt. Soc.).
Robertus Vessy, *tapitour* : ibid.
London, 0, 1, 1.

Taplay, Tapley.—Local, (1) 'of Tapley,' some small place in co. Devon which I have not succeeded in finding ; (2) 'of Taplow,' a parish in co. Bucks, one mile from Maidenhead, a natural modification of the name.

Adam de Tapplegh, co. Devon, Hen. III–Edw. I. K.
Robert de Tapplegh, co. Devon, ibid.
'Robertus and Adam de Tapplegh, tenent in Tappelegh unum feodum,' etc.: K. p. 175.
1744-5. Married—Thomas Tapley and Mary Keet : Canterbury Cath. p. 87.
London, 2, 1 ; Boston (U.S.), 0, 7.

Taplin, Tapling.—Bapt. 'the son of Thomas,' from 'nick. Tam, and dim. Tamlin, which became Tamplin (q.v.), corrupted to Taplin. Thus the *p* is intrusive as in Tompson, and the *g* excrescent as in Robling or Hewlings ; cf. Tapson for Tampson.

1754. Married — William Powell and Mary Taplin : St. Geo. Chap. Mayfair, p. 276.
1801. — Press Bell and Hannah Taplin : St. Geo. Han. Sq. ii. 244.
London, 9, 2 ; Boston (U.S.), 3, 0.

Tapner.—Occup. ; v. Tapiser.

Toluredus le Tapmer. C.
It is almost a certainty that this is a misprint for Tapiner (v. York Plays, p. lxxvii).

London, 1.

Tappenden.—Local, ' of Tappenden,' an ancient Kentish family, long resident at Sittingbourne, but originally of Tappenden, otherwise Toppenden, in the parish of Smarden (v. Hasted's Kent, vii. 479), quoted by Lower.

1748. Married—John Clare and Mary Tappenden, of Feversham, co. Kent : St. Dionis Backchurch, p. 69.
1799. — James Scartchin and Mary Tappenden : St. Geo. Han. Sq. ii. 210.
MDB. (co. Kent), 1 ; London, 3.

Tapper.—Occup. ' the tapper,' one who tapped the barrel, i.e. the tapster ; the feminine suffix gained ground, as females gradually monopolized the place.

'And every hosteler and gay tapstere.'
Chaucer, C. T. 241.

' Tapper, an inn-keeper. North England ' (Halliwell).

John le Tapper, co. Camb., 1273. A.
Robert le Tappere, c. 1300. M.
1614. Richard Tapper : Reg. Univ. Oxf. vol. ii. pt. ii. p. 333.
1635. Thomas Tapper, aged 18 years, embarked to St. Christopher : Hotten's Lists of Emigrants, p. 128.
1750. Married — William Tapper and Phebe Davies : St. Geo. Chap. Mayfair, p. 177.
Crockford, 1 ; Philadelphia, 8.

Tappin, Tapping.—Bapt. 'the son of Thomas,' a corruption of Tamplin, q.v.

1646. Bapt. — Thomas, s. Walter Tappin, *vintner* : St. Peter, Cornhill, i. 90.
1647. — John, sonn of Richard Tapping : *vintner* : ibid. p. 91.
1651. — Martha, d. William Tapping, *vintner* : ibid. p. 93.
London, 4, 4 ; New York, 9, 1.

Tapson.— Bapt. ' the son of Thomas,' a corruption of Tampson (v. Tamplin and Tamblyn), just as Taplin is a corruption of Tamplin (i.e. Tamlin, or Tomlin).

London, 4 ; Devon Court Dir., 2.

Tapster.—Occup. ' the tapster ' ; v. Tapper. Cf. Tapiser.

1548. Bapt. — William Tapster : St. Peter, Cornhill, i. 4.
1749. Married — Robert Tapster and Mary Adams : St. Geo. Chap. Mayfair, p. 143.
London, 1.

Tarbuck.—Local, ' of Tarbuck,' a township in the parish of Huyton, co. Lanc. (Torboc, Domesday). An early family of Tarbocks was settled here.

Henry Tarbock, of Tarbok, 20 Hen. VII : Baines' Lanc. ii. 271.
Bryan Soothworth, of Tarbocke, 1646 : Baines' Lanc. (Croston), p. 308.
Adam Tarbocke, 1622 : Preston Guild Roll, p. 79.
1580. Edward Torbock, co. Lanc. : Reg. Univ. Oxf. vol. ii. pt. ii. p. 95.
— Thomas Torbock, co. Lanc. : ibid.
Manchester, 1 ; Liverpool, 5 ; London, 1.

Targett.—Local, ' at the target,' from residence thereby, a dim. of *targe*, a shield, something to aim at. The archer practised at the targe or target, hence the local surname for one who lived by the spot.

Richard Targe, co. Linc., 1273. A.
1695. Bapt. — Samuel, s. Christopher Targett : Reg. Stourton, Wilts, p. 19.
1759. Married — Richard Collins and Lucy Targett : St. Geo. Han. Sq. i. 87.
London, 4 ; Philadelphia, 2.

Tarleton.—Local, ' of Tarleton,' a parish in West Lancashire, eight miles from Ormskirk.

Adam de Tarleton, 10 Ric. II : Baines' Lanc. ii. 131.
Magota de Tarlton, 1379 : P. T. Yorks. p. 184.
1580. James Tarleton, of West Derby : Wills at Chester, i. 187.
1588. Katherine Tarleton, of Halewood : ibid.
1618. Thomas Tarleton of Liverpool : ibid.
1779. Married — Richard Myers and Eliz. Tarlton : St. Geo. Han. Sq. i. 305.
Liverpool, 4 ; Philadelphia, 2.

Tarrant, Tarratt, Tarrett.—Local, ' of Tarrant,' the name of several parishes in the county of Dorset. Tarratt and Tarrett are doubtless corruptions.

(Abbatissa) de Tarento, co. Dorset, 1273. A.
(Abbatissa) de Tarente, co. Dorset, Hen. III–Edw. I. A.
1621. George Tarrant, co. Hants : Reg. Univ. Oxf. vol. ii. pt. ii. p. 394.
1784. Married — William Tarrant, of Redbridge, co. Southampton, and Mary Sharp : St. Geo. Han. Sq. i. 361.
London, 12, 1, 1 ; Philadelphia, 1, 0, 0.

Tarry, Tarrie. — Bapt. ; v. Terry ; cf. Darby and Derby, Clark and Clerk, Parkin and Perkin.

1786. Married — James Tarry and Sarah Killick : St. Geo. Han. Sq. i. 394.
London, 7, 0 ; Philadelphia, 0, 1.

Tasker.—Occup. ' the tasker,' one with some fixed work to do, possibly one paid by the job. ' *Triturator*, a tasker, Nominale MS., 15th century ' (Halliwell). Hence a thresher or reaper in some places is called a tasker. I met the word in Burton's Anatomy of Melancholy (Introduction): ' Many poor country vicars, for want of other means, are driven to their shifts . . . as Paul did, at last turn taskers, maltsters, costermongers, graziers.'

Benedict le Taskur, co. Hunts, 1273. A.
Gilbert Tasker, co. Bucks, ibid.
Roger le Tasker, C. R., 7 Edw. I.
Alexander Tasker, 1307. M.
Radulphus Tasker, 1329 : P. T. Yorks.
p. 196.
Willelmus Tasker, 1379 : ibid. p. 205.
1677. Bapt.—Elis., d. William Tasker:
St. Dionis Backchurch, p. 122.
1773. Married — Peter Tasker and
Mary Bowers : St. Geo. Han. Sq. i. 229.
London, 10 ; West Rid. Court Dir., 6 ;
Sheffield, 6 ; Philadelphia, 18.

Tasseler. — Occup. ' the tasseler,' one who scratched cloth,
to make a nap, with teasels, a
prickly plant known as the Fuller's
Thistle.

'Cloth that cometh fro' the wevyng
Is nought comely to wear
Til it be fulled under foot,

And with taseles cracched.'
Piers Plowman.

' Item, that every fuller, from the
said feast of St. Peter, in his craft
and occupation of fuller, rower, or
tayseler of cloth, shall exercise and
use taysels, and no cards, deceit-
fully impairing the same cloth '
(4 Edw. IV, c. 1),—' en sa arte et
occupacion de fuller et scalpier ou
tezeiler de drap, exercise et use
teizels, &c.' ' Tasyl, carduus, cardo
fullonis' : Prompt. Parv. ' Tazills,
5s. 8d. more in tazills, 2s.' (Richmondshire Wills, Surt. Soc. p. 274.
Inventory of property of Edward
Kyrkelands, of Kendall, 1578).

Gilbert le Tasselere. H.
Matilda la Tasselere. H.
Edward Taylzer. W. 9.

This last name occurs (1568) in
the will of Walter Strykland (Richmondshire Wills, p. 224). It is
manifestly connected with tasill,
instanced above. Thus Taylor in
the Kendal district may have absorbed Taziller.

1610. Edward Tesler, or Teasler: Reg.
Univ. Oxf. vol. ii. pt. i. 402.

Tatchell.—Bapt. ' the son of
Tachel,' one of the numerous personal names ending in -el. The
surname is still found in co. Somerset.

Gilbert Tachel, co. Oxf., 1273. A.
William Tachel, co. Soms., 1 Edw. III :
Kirby's Quest, p. 198.
London, 1 ; MDB. (co. Soms.), 2.

Tate.—Bapt. ' the son of Tate'
(Yonge, ii. 498). Probably in some
cases a modern variant of the Scotch
Tait.

Nicholas Tate, co. Camb., 1273. A.
1635. Married — William Tate and
Joane Lewis : St. Dionis Backchurch,
p. 23.
London, 11 ; Philadelphia, 27.

**Tatham, Tattam, Tatum,
Tateham, Tatem.**—Local, ' of
Tatham,' a parish in North Lancashire, which early gave rise to
a surname.

'King John, when Earl of Moreton,
gave the services of William of Tatham,
in Tatham . . . to Robert de Monte
Begon': Baines' Lanc. ii. 625.
Thomas de Tatham, 1379 : P. T. Yorks.
p. 289.
Johannes de Tatam, 1379 : ibid.
John Tatam, 1564 : Reg. Univ. Oxf.
i. 253.
1576. Nicholas Colpotts and Katherine
Tatham : Marriage Lic. (London), p. 74.
1604. Robert Tatum and Dorothy
Bisley : ibid. p. 290.
1606. Buried—Boniface Tatam, vintner : St. Peter, Cornhill, i. 162.
Edwarde Tathame, of Overlocke,
parish of Turnstill, 1597 : Lancashire
Wills at Richmond, pp. 269-270.
James Tatam, of Warton, 1620 : ibid.
Edmund Tatham, of Tunstall, 1627 :
ibid.
1744. Married — Nathaniell Still and
Sarah Tatum : Reg. Stourton, Wilts, p. 56.
1765. Married — Richard Tattam and
Caroline Smart : St. Geo. Han. Sq. i.
141.
London, 27, 2, 6, 0, 0 ; West Rid.
Court Dir. (Tateham), 2 ; Philadelphia,
12, 0, 12, 0, 21.

Tatler. — Nick. ' the tattler,'
one who prated much, a prattler ;
v. Totiller.

Christopher Tatler, de Mapelthorne,
yoman, 7 Hen. VII : HHH. p. 149.
1766. Married — John Tattler and
Anna Maria Norgrave : St. Geo. Han.
Sq. i. 150.
London, 2.

Tatlock.—Local, ' of Tatlock,'
some spot in South Lancashire or
co. Chester.

1593. Richard Tatlock, of Simonswood :
Wills at Chester, i. 188.
1607. Catherine Tatlock, of Cuns-
cough : ibid.
London, 3 ; Manchester, 3 ; Boston
(U.S.), 1.

Tatlow. — Local. Probably
a sharpened form of Tadlow ; v.
Tadloo.

1807. Married — Joseph Tatlow and
Sarah Farmer : St. Geo. Han. Sq. ii. 361.
London, 1 ; Philadelphia, 5.

Tatnall, Tatnell.—Local, ' of
Tattenhall,' a parish in co. Chester.

Thomas Tatnall, co. Chester, 1459 :
Earwaker's East Cheshire, i. 174 n.
Robert Tatnall, of Salghton, 1612 :
Wills at Chester, i. 188.
1748. Married — John Tattnall and
Abigail Kent : St. Geo. Chap. Mayfair,
p. 105.
London, 1, 2 ; Philadelphia, 1, 0.

Tattam ; v. Tatham.

**Tattersall, Tattershall, Tat-
tersill.**—Local, ' of Tattershall,' a
parish in co. Lincoln, nine miles
from Horncastle, corrupted by
imitation into Tortoiseshell (q.v.).

Robert de Tateshale, or Tatteshall,
or Tatersale, 26 Edw. I : BBB. p. 557.
Robert Tatersall, C. R., 9 Hen. IV.
1585. Bapt. — Edwarde, s. James
Tattersall : St. Michael, Cornhill, p. 93.
1803. Married — Thomas Ridgway
and Sarah Tattershall : St. Geo. Han. Sq.
ii. 277.
London, 6, 3, 1 ; Philadelphia, 1, 0, 0.

Tatton.—Local, ' of Tatton,' a
township in the parish of Rostherne,
co. Chester.

Andrewe de Tattone, co. Southampton,
1273. A.
Robert de Tatton, co. Chester, 1290 :
East Cheshire, ii. 308.
Robert de Tatton, of Wythenshawe,
1396 : ibid.
Nicholas de Tatton, co. Chester, 1451 :
ibid.
1579. Robert Tatton, of Wythenshawe:
Wills at Chester, i. 188.
1600. Dorothy Tatton, of the Peele, co.
Chester : ibid.
1601. William Tatton, co. Chester :
Reg. Univ. Oxf. vol. ii. pt. ii. p. 247.
1776. Married — James Tatton and
Sarah Strange : St. Geo. Han. Sq. i. 261.
London, 4 ; Manchester, 2 ; Phila-
delphia, 2.

Tatum ; v. Tatham.

Taunton.—Local, ' of Taunton.'
a well-known market-town in co.
Somerset.

Gilbert de Taunton, co. Somerset,
1273. A.
Gwyde de Tauntone, co. Somerset,
ibid.
John Taunton, abbot of Cirencester,
1440 : Atkyn's Hist. Glouc. p. 178.
1761. Married — Samuel Taunton and
Martha Pidgley : St. Geo. Han. Sq. i. 105.
1780. — John Taunton and Sarah
Thompson : ibid. p. 317.
MDB. (Wilts) 5 ; (Somerset), 4 ; London, 3 ; Philadelphia, 2.

Taverner, Tavner, Tavener, Tavernor, Taviner, Tavinor, Tavnor.—Occup. 'the taverner,' a keeper of a tavern. 'Tavernere, tabernarius': Prompt. Parv. v. Taberner.

'Of which the taverner had spoke beforn.'
Chaucer, C. T. 12619.

Richard le Taverner, co. Camb., 1273. A.
Armvin le Taverner, London, ibid.
Falco le Taverner, London, ibid.
Robert le Taverner, co. Soms., 1 Edw. III : Kirby's Quest, p. 104.
Walter le Taverner. B.
John le Tevernour. C.
1553-4. Robert Taverner and Joanna Blakemor : Marriage Lic. (London), i. 15.
1615. Bapt. — Wyborrowe, d. John Taverner : St. Jas. Clerkenwell, i. 73.
London, 5, 2, 2, 0, 0, 0, 0; MDB. (co. Somerset), 0, 0, 0, 1, 1, 1, 0 ; Boston (U.S.) (Tavener), 6 ; New York (Tavnor), 1.

Tawer, Tawyer.—Occup. 'the tawyer' (lit. tawer, the *y* is intrusive as in Sawyer), one who dressed skins. 'Tewynge of lethyr': Prompt. Parv. Professor Skeat (s.v. *taw, tew*) quotes Wyclif's use of *tawer* for a leather-dresser, where a later version has 'curiour,' i.e. currier. A.S. *tawian*, to prepare. v. Tower (2) and Whittear.

'Item, to John Massy, tawyer, for tawing of a tymbre of hole sables, iiiis.': Wardrobe Accounts of Edw. IV, p. 121.
John le Tawrare, co. Wilts, 1273. A.
Ralph le Tawyere, co. Wilts, ibid.
William le Tawyare, Close Roll, 2 Edw. I.
John le Tawyere, co. Wilts, 20 Edw. I. R.
Cf. 1585. Thomas Castle, *white-tawer*, and Ellen Broke : Marriage Lic. (London), i. 141.
Hugh Tawyer, aged 18 years, 'imbarqued in the Ann and Elizabeth' for Barbadoes, 1635 : Hotten's Lists of Emigrants, p. 121.

Tawny, Tawney, Taney.—Nick. 'the tawny,' i.e. of a tanned complexion ; cf. Black, White, Blount, Russell, &c.

Ida le Tauny, co. Norf., 1273. A.
1645. Married — Adam Buddell and Margret Tauny : St. Mary Aldermary, p. 19.
1742. — William Tawney and Frances Jacobs : St. Geo. Chap. Mayfair, p. 26.
— — Thomas Tawney and Sarah Dobney : ibid. p. 28.
MDB. (co. Norf.), 0, 0, 1 ; Philadelphia, 0, 2, 0.

Taylor, Tayler, Tailer, Tailor.—Occup. 'the taylor,' a cutter-out of cloth, a maker of clothes. M.E.

tailor, taylor; O.F. *tailleur*, a cutter. It is now understood that *tailor* shall be the trade-name, and Taylor and Tayler the surname. The early rolls are full of instances, and as a result Taylor is the fourth commonest patronymic in England, giving precedence only to Smith, Jones, and Williams. The Hundred Rolls (1273) have the following variations: Taillar, Taillour, Taillur, Tailur, Taliur, Tallur, Tallyur, Talur, Talyur, Tayler, Tayllour, Tayllur, Taylour, and Taylur.

Henry le Taliur, co. Norf., 1273. A.
Cecil le Tayllour, co. Camb., ibid.
Roger le Taylur, co. Linc., ibid.
Richard le Taylor, co. Northampt., ibid.
1593. Bapt. — Abel, s. John Tailor : St. Peter, Cornhill, i. 39.
1790. Witnesses to marriage, Eliz. Taylar, Richard Tayler : St. Geo. Han. Sq. ii. 38.
1802. Married — Robert Julian and Mary Taylar : ibid. p. 260.
London, 531, 21, 0, 0 ; Philadelphia, 597, 0, 1, 1.

Tayloress.—Occup. 'the tailoress,' a female cutter-out ; v. Taylor.

Alicia la Tayluresse, co. Hunts, 1273. A.

Taylorson, Taylerson.—Nick. 'the taylor's son'; v. Taylor. Still found in the county of York, where the earliest instances are to be met with ; cf. Smithson, Wrightson, Cooperson. Nevertheless, *-son* as a suffix to a trade-name is rare.

Willelmus Talliorson, 1379 : P. T. Yorks. p. 265.
Robertus Taylourson, 1379 : ibid. p. 33.
Agnes Taylour-doghter, 1379 : ibid.
1776. Married — Richard Taylorson and Sarah Brotherton : St. Geo. Han. Sq. ii. 266.
Ripon, 0, 1 ; MDB. (co. Durham), 1, 1.

Taynton.—Local, 'of Taynton,' parishes in cos. Oxford and Gloucester.

Henry de Teynton, co. Oxf., 1273. A.
John de Teynton, co. Oxf., ibid.
1605. Richard Taynton, co. Worc. : Reg. Univ. Oxf. vol. ii. pt. ii. p. 287.
London, 2.

Teal, Teall, Teel.—Nick. 'the teal,' a small duck ; M.E. *tele*; cf. Duck, Drake. The names of John and Thomas Telcock, co. Oxford, occur in the Hundred Rolls (1273); probably a masculine form, equivalent to Drake.

Matilda Tele, co. Camb., 1273. A.
Martin Tele, co. Camb., ibid.
John Teel, co. Soms., 1 Edw. III : Kirby's Quest, p. 169.
1749. Married — Richard Teale and Mary Haselwood : St. Geo. Chap. Mayfair, p. 157.
1790. — William Teal and Eliz. Wardman : St. Geo. Han. Sq. ii. 38.
London, 1, 1, 0 ; Philadelphia, 16, 0, 1.

Teape.—? Bapt. I can furnish no information about this surname.

Johannes Tepe, co. Devon, 1273. A.
1579. Buried — Richarde Teape, servant to Mathew Joyner : St. Dionis Backchurch, p. 196.
London, 3.

Teas, Teaz ; v. Tees.

Teasdale, Teesdale.—Local, 'of Teesdale,' i.e. the valley of the river Tees ; cf. Tweedale, Tyndale, &c.

William de Tesedal, co. York, 1273. A.
Alan de Teysedale, co. Northumb., 20 Edw. I. R.
Henry de Tesdale, Prior of Finchale, 1295 : The Priory of Finchale, Surt. Soc., p. xxvi.
Hugh de Tesedale, 1350 : DDD. i. 63.
Johannes de Tesedale, 1379 : P. T. Yorks. p. 245.
1613. Thomas Tisdale and Barbara Draper : Marriage Lic. (London), ii. 26.
1646. Buried — A young child of Mr. William Teusdall (sic) and Rose his wife' : St. Peter, Cornhill, i. 241.
Manchester, 5, 1 ; London, 3, 0 ; Philadelphia, 3, 1.

Tebay, Teebay, Tibby, Tebby. — Local, 'of Tebay,' a township in the parish of Orton, co. Westmoreland.

Thomas de Tybay, co. Camb., 20 Edw. I. R.
Walter de Tybay, co. Westm.: ibid.
Johannes Tybey, of Sedburgh, near Tebay, 1379 : P. T. Yorks. p. 289.
1784. Married — John Tebay and Catherine Patience Pritchard : St. Geo. Han. Sq. i. 361.
1801. — John Tibbey and Susanna Woollerton : ibid. ii. 233.
Ulverston, 1, 0, 0, 0 ; Liverpool, 0, 2, 0, 0 ; London, 0, 0, 1, 0 ; Oxford (Tebby), 1.

Tebb, Tebbs, Tibbs. — (1) Bapt. 'the son of Theobald,' from the nick. Tebb or Tibb. (2) Bapt. 'the son of Isabella,' from the nick. Tib ; cf. the Yorkshire Till for Matilda and Tagg for Agnes. This solution is important as helping to the origination of Tib, the once familiar name for a female cat, Gib (Gilbert) standing for the male ; v. Gibb. Tibby is still the pet-name of Isabella in the North of England; and a *tib-cat* still means a female cat in Yorkshire, where Isabella was once so popular as a girl's name. But while all this is true, there can be no doubt that Tib, for a cat's name, was originally masculine and ran side by side with Gib, without particular reference to sex. In Reynard the Fox, Tibald is pussy's name (cf. Tibert, a cat: Halliwell); and the nick. of Tibald (i.e. Theobald) was in England Tib. This is clear from Gower's lines on Tyler's insurrection:

'*Hudde* ferit, quem *Judd* terit, dum *Tibbe* juvatur,
Jacke domosque viros vellit, en ense necat,'

where only masculine names are introduced. Originally, then, Tib for a cat was the nick. of Theobald. By degrees, however, Tib for Isabella ousted the popularity of Tib for Theobald. Besides, Theobald itself was becoming forgotten as a font-name. Hence the idea slowly crept in that Tib stood for the female cat, and had always done so. Of course the convenience of having a female name to correspond with Gib was obvious. In the Elizabethan and Stuart period Isabella was universally Tib (Tib for Theobald having disappeared), and Tib was still the lady cat. In Gammer Gurton's Needle Hodge says:

'And while her staff she took
At Tyb her cat to fling.'

Burton in his Anatomy of Melancholy, in a list of names, includes 'tall Tib, slender Sib'; while the 'Psalm of Mercie,' a Commonwealth squib, says:

'"So, so," quoth my sister Bab;
And "kill 'um," quoth Margerie:
"Spare none," cries old Tib; "no quarter," says Sib,
"And hey for our monarchie."'

No doubt there is an occult connexion between Tib and *tabby*.

Tebbe Molend', i.e. the miller, co. Camb., 1273. A.
John Tybbesone, co. Soms., 1 Edw. III: Kirby's Quest, p. 251.
Walter Tybbe, co. Soms., 1 Edw. III: ibid. p. 116.
Richard Tybbe, co. Soms., 1 Edw. III: ibid. p. 193.
Tebb fil. William. J.

Margery Tebbe, co. York. W. 11.
Thomas Tebbe, co. York. W. 12.
John Tibbs, temp. Eliz. Z.
1606. Thomas Tibbes: Reg. Univ. Oxf. vol. ii. pt. ii. p. 290.
1665. Buried — John, son of John Tebbe: St. Michael, Cornhill, p. 255.
1707. John Cranidge and Eliz. Tibbis: Marriage Lic. (London), ii. 336.
London, 3, 7, 4; Philadelphia, 1, 2, 0.

Tebbitt, Tebboth, Tebbott, Tebbut, Tebbutt, Tebbets, Tebbetts.—(1) Bapt. 'the son of Theobald.' These are not diminutives formed from the nick. Tebb, q.v., though practically they became so. They are corrupted forms of the shorter Tebald. (2) Bapt. 'the son of Isabella,' nick. Tib, dim. Tibot; v. Tebb. Tibet Talkapace is one of the heroines in Udall's Ralph Roister Doister (circa 1550).
'Work, Tibet; work, Annot; work, Margery;
Sew, Tibet; knit, Annot; spin, Margery; Let us see who will win the victory.'

The surnames descended from the above two names are now inextricably mixed.

Tibota Foliot, co. Oxf., 1273. A.
Robert Tebaud, co. Norf., ibid.
Margery Tebbolt, co. Camb., ibid.
Thomas Tedbald, co. Camb., ibid.
Ralph Tebaud, or Tebald, or Tebawd, co. Hunts, ibid.
Robert Tebaud-man, i.e. the servant of Teboud, 1379: P. T. Yorks. p. 148.
Adam Thebaud, *hostiler*, occurs above.
Tibaud de Russell. PP.
Tibot Fitz-Piers. Y.
Tybota Hendre, C. R., 14 Hen. VI.
Roger Tebbott, temp. Elizabeth. Z.
Tybott Creffe, 1592: Cal. State Papers (Domestic), iii. 170.
Lease to Stephen Tebold, alias Theobold, 1591: ibid. p. 17.
London, 1, 1, 2, 2, 1, 0, 0; Boston (U.S.), 0, 0, 0, 0, 0, 3, 7.

Tebby ; v. Tebay.

Tedd. — Bapt. 'the son of Edward,' from the nick. Ted.
London, 3 ; Oxford, 1.

Tedman.—? Local, 'of St. Edmund's' (?) ; cf. Toomer (2). The suffix *-mond* or *-mund* always corrupts to *-man*; cf. Osman, Wayman, &c.
John de St. Edmund, London, 1273. A.
Godfrey de St. Edmund, co. Norf., ibid.
These refer, of course, to Bury St. Edmund.
1632. Buried — Edmond Tedmond, a nurse-child at Goodwife Toppen's, came

out of St. Edmund's parish : St. Michael, Cornhill, p. 232.
London, 1.

Tees, Teese, Teas, Teaz.—Local, 'of the Tees,' from residence beside the river of that name. With Tees and Teesdale, cf. Tweed and Tweedale. With the form Teas, cf. Teasdale. This surname with its variants has spread extensively in the United States. Teaz is very American. v. Surtees.
1608. Valentine Penson and Anne Tees, *widow*: Marriage Lic. (London), ii. 62.
London, 1, 0, 0, 0; Philadelphia, 36, 10, 2, 2.

Teesdale ; v. Teasdale.

Tegg, Tigg, Tegge. — Nick. 'the teg,' a sheep in the second year; still in common use in Oxfordshire and the West country. 'A teg or sheep with a little head, and wooll under its belly': Florio, p. 32 (Halliwell); cf. Lamb, and v. Twentyman.
Thomas Tege, co. Soms., 1 Edw. III: Kirby's Quest, p. 95.
William Tegge, co. Soms., 1 Edw. III : ibid. p. 139.
Thomas Tigge, co. Soms., 1 Edw. III ibid. p. 149.
William Tyg, co. Soms., 1 Edw. III: ibid. p. 189.
London, 1, 1, 0 ; Philadelphia, 0, 0, 1.

Teleress.—Occup. ; v. Teller.
Ida le Teleresse. T.

Telfer, Telford, Telfour.—Bapt. 'the son of Taillefer,' i.e. cut-iron. This surname seems to have originally flourished in the Lowlands, and to have worked its way across the border into Northumberland. The corruption into Telford must not lead us astray, although it looks distinctly local. 'Thomas Telford, the great engineer, used to say, "When I was ignorant of Latin, I did not suspect that Telfor, my true name, might be translated, 'I bear arms' (*tela fero*), and, thinking of unmeaning, adopted Telford"' (Lower). In the neighbourhood of Newcastle the two forms are common, and in recent generations either form was used by people of the same stock. John Taylfar, in 1558, obtained a grant from the Bishop of Durham of the reversion of the office of seneschal in the cities and boroughs of Gateshead, Durham, &c., expectant on the death of Christopher Browne (PPP. ii. 334). This is the earliest instance I can find in the district.

On Nov. 1, 1696, twenty-eight people were drowned at Canoubie, after attending church. Reference is made to one in an inscription in the churchyard :

'Here lyes George Tealfer, who died in the water, Nov. the 1, 1696, being the Lord's day, as they were going home from the Kirk': Trans. Cumb. and Westm.Ant.and Arch. Soc.,vol. viii. p.287.

The famous Taillefer of the battle of Hastings will be familiar to the reader. Lower says that Tailzefer was the Scotch form in the 16th century. Cf. Gulliver and Gulliford.

William Tailefer, co. Kent, 1273. A.
Taylfre de Wyncestre, co. Hertf., 20 Edw. I. R.
London, 8, 3, 0 ; Newcastle, 3, 7, 1 ; Philadelphia, 0, 4, 0.

Teller.—Occup. ' the teller,' i.e. the weaver. O.F. *telier*, a linen-weaver.

Lithulph le Teler, 1257 : KKK. vi. 236.
Henry le Telere, temp. 1310. M.
Johannes Teller, 1379 : P. T. Yorks. p. 235.
Symon Telar', 1379 : ibid. p. 121.
John le Teler. E.
Robert le Teler. J.
1610. William Teler and Mary Holborne : Marriage Lic.(Westminster), p.18.
London, 1, 1 ; Philadelphia, 14, 0.

Telwright, Tellwright, Tilewright.—Occup. 'the tilewright,' a maker of tiles ; later, and more generally, a potter, one who bakes and moulds clay. Tilewright seems to be the true form, *tigel-wyrhta* (Matt. xxvii. 7) occurring in an Anglo-Saxon Gospel (v. Skeat, s.v. *tile*). In the York Mystery Plays (Toulmin Smith : Clarendon Press) they are styled Tielmakers or Tillethekkers (i.e. tile-thatchers). In a statute of 1563 they are Tilemakers (5 Eliz. c. 4–23). In the Potteries the term *tilewright* is still used, and it is there the surname Tellwright or Telwright has existed for centuries.

MDB.(co. Stafford),0, 2, 0 ; Manchester, 0, 1, 0.

Temberli, Temperley ; v. Timperley. The first is an American corruption.

Tempany, Temperly.—Local. Obvious corruptions of Timperley, q.v., the second marking the ' first step from the right path.'

1800. Married — Edmund Tempany and Susanna Tomlin : St. Geo. Han. Sq. ii. 224.
London, 3, 4 ; New York, 0, 1.

Tempest.—?——. I dare not hazard a conjecture as to the class to which this surname belongs. Mr. Lower says, ' This family, who are doubtless of Norman origin, are traced to Roger Tempest (temp. Henry I), who held three carucates and two oxgangs of land in the Shipton Fee, co. York' (Patr. Brit. p. 340).

Isabella Tempest, 1379 : P. T. Yorks. p. 257.
1579. John Tempest, co. York: Reg. Univ. Oxf. vol. ii. pt. ii. p. 89.
1758. Married — Henry Tempest, of Broughton, co. York, and Eleanor Jones: St. Geo. Han. Sq. i. 76.
MDB. (West Rid. Yorks), 9 ; Philadelphia, 4.

Templar, Templer. — Offic. (1) One of the great religious body vowed to protect the Temple and Holy Sepulchre, a Crusader ; (2) the custodian of a temple or church in England ; cf. Churcher, and v. Temple.

William le Templyr et Alicia uxor : C. R., 43 Hen. III.
William Templer, co. Linc., 1273. A.
Agnes le Templer, co. Oxf., ibid.
Adam le Templer, 1307. M.
John Templer, co. Soms., 1 Edw. III : Kirby's Quest, p. 118.
William le Templer. J.
1641. Thomas Hutchinson and Lettice Templar : Marriage Lic. (London), ii. 257.
1766. Married — William Templer and Eliz. Dunn : St. Geo. Han. Sq. i. 155.
London, 1, 2 ; MDB. (co. Devon), 0, 4 ; Philadelphia, 2, 0.

Temple.—Local,' of the temple,' any sacred enclosure. A.S. *tempel*; M.E.*temple*, from residence thereby.

Matilda du Temple, co. Oxf., 1273. A.
Petrus del Tempil, 1379 : P. T. Yorks. p. 294.
Matilda de Tempell, 1379 : ibid.
1576. Leonard Temple, co. Oxon: Reg. Univ. Oxf. vol. ii. pt. ii. p. 69.
1634. William Chapman and Joane Temple : Marriage Lic. (London), ii. 220.
London, 31 ; Philadelphia, 29.

Templeman.—Local or occup. ' the temple-man,' one who lived

at or had charge of a temple ; v. Temple, and cf. Churchman and Kirkman.

Ambrose le Templeman, co. Camb., 1273. A.
Robert Templeman, co. Camb., ibid.
Willelmus Tempulman, 1379 : P. T. Yorks. p. 109.
1696. Married—Mark Warkman and Anne Templeman: St. DionisBackchurch, p. 45.
1780. Married — Thomas Templeman and Eliz.Coulton : St.Geo. Han.Sq.i. 316.
London, 9 ; Boston (U.S.), 5.

Templeton.—Local, ' of Templeton,' a parish in co. Devon, five miles from Tiverton.

1764. Married—James Templeton and Eliz. Lobb : St. Geo. Han. Sq. i. 134.
London, 3 ; Philadelphia, 15.

Tench.—? Nick. ' the tench,' the fish of that name. There are so few fish-names that I hesitate much in suggesting this solution. Salman, Chubb, Spratt, Gudgeon, &c., have no connexion with the finny tribe.

John Tenche, co. Linc., 1273. A.
1599–1600. Married—Willyam Tenche and Joane Eaton : St. Dionis Backchurch, p. 14.
1618. James Tench and Mary Eyres : Marriage Lic. (London), ii. 67.
1640. Married — John Gouldwell and Mabell Tench : St.Mary,Aldermary, p. 18.

Tenison, &c. ; v. Tennyson.

Tennant, Tennent.—Occup. ' the tenant,' one who holds land under another.

Willelmus Tenaunt, 1379 : P. T. Yorks. p. 279.
Johannes Tenant, 1379 : ibid.
Ricardus Tenaunt, 1379 : ibid.
1563-4. Married—Philip Swalowe and Eliz. Tennante : St. Dionis Backchurch, p. 5.
1564-5. Silvester Tenante, Ch. Ch. : Reg. Univ. Oxf. vol. ii. pt. ii. p. 13.
1748. Bapt.—Ann, d. William Tenant: St. Michael, Cornhill, p. 175.
London, 15, 3 ; Philadelphia, 2, 5.

Tenniswood, Tinniswood.— Local, ' of Tenniswood,' some small spot in co. York. There can be no doubt that this is a sharpened form of Denniswood, i.e. the wood that belonged to Denis ; v. Tennyson.

MDB. (North Rid. Yorks), 2, 0 ; Manchester, 0, 1 ; York, 1, 0.

Tenny, Tenney.—Bapt. ' the son of Dennis,' from the pet Denny sharpened into Tenny ; v. Tennyson.

Boston (U.S.), i, 46.

Tennyson, Tenison, Tenni-son, Tenneson.—Bapt. 'the son of Dennis.' O.E. Dionys, Denis, whence Denison, sharpened to Tenison ; cf. Haseltine for Hazeldean, Tancock for Dancock, Tanett and Tannett for Danett and Dannett ; cf. Tenniswood (i.e. Denniswood), York Dir. i. Also note that the surname Toket is referred to as Doket in Index of Visitation of Yorkshire (Harl. Soc.). Yorkshire and the Lincolnshire border strongly affected Denis in the surname period. We also find Dandridge for Tandridge, and Tandy for Dandy. Dogood in the old registers is manifestly Toogood.

Arthur Doegood, 1680 : Reg. St. Mary Aldermary (London), p. 105.
1711. Bapt. — Dorothy, d. Edward Tennison : Canterbury Cath., p. 23.
London, o, o, 1, 1 ; MDB. (East Rid. Yorks), o, o, 4, o ; Boston (U.S.), o, o, 1, o.

Tenter, Teinter, Teinturer.—(1) Occup. 'the tenterer' or tenter, one who looked after the tenter-hooks and the cloth he stretched on the frame thereby. The *tenter* was the frame. 'Tenture, tentowre, for cloth ; *extensorium*': Prompt. Parv. By Statute 1 Ric. III, c. 8, *tentors* must be set in open places, not in houses.

'Item, tenture posts and woodde, 6d., 2 tentures, 20s.,' 1562, Kendal : Richmondshire Wills, p. 156.

(2) Occup. 'the teinturer,' i.e. dyer. 'Lystare, or lytaster, of cloth dyynge ; *tinctor*': Prompt. Parv.

Warin le Teyntour. T.
John le Teynter. H.
William le Teinturer. E.
Richard le Tenter. H.
Philip le Tentier. H.
Thomas le Teynturer, co. Oxf., 1273. A.
Sarra le Teynturere, co. Oxf., ibid.
William le Teynturer, co. Hunts, ibid.
Berenger Tinctor, co. Hunts, ibid.
Sarle Tinctor, co. Hunts, ibid.

Tepper.—Occup. ; v. Tipper.

Termday.—? Nick. With probably some reference to the University Terms.

Margaret Termeday, co. Oxf., 1273. A.
William Termeday, co. Oxf., ibid.

Terrell, Tyrrell, Tirrell, Terrill, Turrell, Turrill.—Bapt. 'the son of Turold,' popularly Tirrell. There can be no doubt as to the personal or baptismal origin of the surname. And it will account for the name of Walter Tyrrel, as a reference to the Index of Freeman's Hist. Norman Conquest will conclusively prove the popularity of Turold in the 11th century.

Henry Tyrel, co. Devon, 1273. A.
Walter Tyrel, co. Norf., ibid.
Roger Tirel, co. Hereford, Hen. III–Edw. I. K.
William Torel, co. Soms., 20 Edw. I. R.
John Tyrell, co. Kent, ibid.
Hugh Tyrel, co. Southampton, ibid.
Thomas Torel, co. Soms., 1 Edw. III : Kirby's Quest, p. 116.
Katerina Terell, 1379 : P. T. Yorks. p. 28.
1623. John Tirell and Jane Stokes: Marriage Lic. (London), ii. 123.
1624. Peter Drapier and Barbara Tirrill : ibid. p. 141.
1641. George Tyrell and Anne Thurlow: ibid. p. 258.
London, 3, 15, 1, 0, 3, 1 ; Boston (U.S.), 46, 5, 2, 1, 1, 3.

Terry, Terrey.—Bapt. 'the son of Theodoric' (Tedric, Domesday), from the nick. Terry, probably from the French nick. Thierry.

David fil. Tirry, E. and F., co. Cumb., p. 140.
Terry (without surname), co. York, 1273. A.
Richard Terry, co. Hunts, ibid.
Terricus le Alemaunde, co. Bucks, ibid.
Geoffrey Terri, co. Oxf., ibid.
Terricus Baril, co. Soms., Hen. III–Edw. I. K.
Johannes Tyrry, 1379 : P. T. Yorks. p. 275.
Petrus Terre, 1379 : ibid. p. 241.
1613. James Browne and Bridget Terry : Marriage Lic. (London), ii. 23.
Terye Robsort, 1629 : Reg. St. Mary Aldermary, p. 166.
Thomas Terrick, 1694, co. Ches. : Earwaker's East Ches. i. 407.
London, 49, 7 ; Boston (U.S.), 16, 0.

Tesseyman, Tyzemon, Tissiman.—Bapt. 'the son of Trasemond.' No doubt the Trasemundus and Trasmundus of Domesday, found in cos. Wilts and Dorset. As a surname, I can only discover instances in Norfolk and the North of England. It has existed four centuries at least in York. The terminative -*mund* or -*mond* becomes -*man* ; v. Osman, Wyman, &c.

Richard Tacyman, 1340, Alnwick. KKK. vi. 40.
John Theysman, 1487. W. 11.
Briand Tossemund, 1523 : W. 11, p. 200.
Bryan Tesymon, 1537 : ibid.
Jac. Tesymond, 1545 : ibid. p. 234.
Richard Thesymon, 1546 : ibid. p. 236.

The last four names above occur among members of the Corpus Christi Guild, York.

Thomas Tesmond, sheriff of Norwich, 1559 : FF. iii. 358.
John Tesmond, mayor of Norwich, 1601 : ibid. p. 359.
1614. William Tessamond and Rebecca Gushe : Marriage Lic. (London), ii. 28.
Mr. Burleigh Tesseman sung at the concert at St. Paul's School, London, July 20, 1887 : Standard, July 21.
York, 3, 0, 0 ; Moor Monkton, near York, 2, 0, 0 ; Sunderland, 1, 0, 0 ; Leeds, 2, 0, 0 ; Scarborough, 0, 0, 2 ; South Shields (Tyzemon), 1.

Tester, Testard.—Bapt. 'the son of Testard,' an early baptismal name ; cf. Fr. Tetard.

Henry Testard, co. Hunts, 1273. A.
Robert Testard, co. Suff., ibid.
Ralph Testard, co. York, ibid.
Richard Testard, co. Surrey, Hen. III–Edw. I. K.
Willelmus Testard, 1379 : P. T. Yorks. p. 145.
Johannes Testard, 1379 : ibid.
1606. Married—Anthony Testard and Martha Cominglby (sic) : St. Dionis Backchurch, p. 45.
London, 4, 0 ; Manchester, 2, 0 ; Philadelphia, 1, 0.

Testimony.—? Nick.

Adam Testimonie, co. Oxf., 1273. A.
Ralph Testimonie, co. Oxf., ibid.

Tetley, Tetlow, Titley, Titlow.—Local, 'of Tetlow' or Tetley, some spot in East Cheshire or South-east Lancashire. The name ramified strongly. Also 'of Titley,' a parish in co. Hereford.

Thomas Tyttelegh, 1539 : Earwaker's East Cheshire, p. 160.
Edmund Tetlowe, 1554 : ibid. p. 127 *n*.
Reginald Tetlawe, of Godley, *husbandman*, 1649 : ibid.
Reginald Tetlaw, 1663 : ibid.
Laurence Hulme, of Tetlow, 1599 : Wills at Chester (1545–1620), p. 103.
Henry Tetlow, of Oldham, 1611 : ibid. p. 191.
John Tetlow, of Coldhurst, Oldham, 1597 : ibid.
London, 5, 0, 2, 2 ; Manchester, 3, 8, 1, 0 ; Philadelphia, 1, 6, 0, 9 ; MDB. (co Hereford), 0, 0, 1, 0.

Teversham.—Local, 'of Teversham,' a parish in co. Cambridge, near Cambridge.

William de Teweresham, co. Camb., 1273. A.
London Court Dir., 2.

Tew.—Local, 'of Tew,' two parishes in co. Oxf., Great and Little Tew.
MDB. (co. Oxf.), 1 ; Crockford, 1 ; Boston (U.S.), 3.

Tewer, Tuer.—Occup. 'the 'tewer,' i.e. the tawyer, one who prepared or dressed skins. To tew, to toil hard (Furness dialect, North Lanc.). 'Tew, or tewynge oflethyr': Prompt. Parv. 'A Tewer of skynnes': Cath. Angl. v. Tawer and Tuer.
1394. 'Item, pro tewyng 14 pellium laporum, 1s. 9d.' : FFF. p. 623.
Richard de Bulmer, *tewer*, 1310-2 : Freemen of York, Surt. Soc., i. 14.
Elyas Tewar, *souter*, 1379 : P. T. Yorks. p. 99.
Robertus Tewer, 1379 : ibid. p. 161.
1584. John Tuer, London : Reg. Univ. Oxf. vol. ii. pt. ii. p. 135.
1594. Daniel Tuer, co. Middlesex : ibid. p. 203.
London, 0, 1.

Tewksbury, Tuxbury.—Local, 'of Tewkesbury,' a parish and market-town in co. Gloucester, ten miles from Gloucester. Oddly enough, I am altogether without English instances.
Mabel de Teuksbury,co.Glouc.,1273. A. Boston (U.S.), 29, 1.

Thacher ; v. Thatcher.

Thacker.—Occup.'the thacker,' a thatcher ; cf. Kirk and Church. Among the craftsmen who went in procession in the performance of the York Mystery were the 'Tille-thekers,' i.e. Tile-thatchers' (The York Mystery Plays, p. 112).
William le Thekere, co. Norf., 1273. A.
William Thecker, 1301. M.
Johannes Theker, *tector*, 1379 : P. T. Yorks. p. 296.
Ricardus Theker, 1379 : ibid.
Stephanus Theker, 1379 : ibid. p. 293.
1565. Married—Robert Thacker and Agnes Blage : St. Jas. Clerkenwell, i. 3.
1748. Married—Edward Thacker and Eliz. Peartree : St. Geo. Chap. Mayfair, p. 116.
London, 6.

Thackeray, Thackery, Thackrah, Thackray, Thack-wray, Thackara, Thackaray. —Local, 'at the thack-wray,' i.e. the corner or place set apart for storing thack, or thatch ; v. Wray.

Not Thackery for Thacker, as Vicary for Vicar. Wray is found in many compounds in Yorkshire place-words.
William de la Thekere, co. Norf., 1273. A.
Johannes de Thakwra, 1379 : P. T. Yorks. p. 238.
Robertus de Thakwra, 1379 : ibid.
Thomas Thackwray, co. York. W. 16.
1748. Married—Joseph Thackeray and Martha Houldroide : St. Geo. Chap. Mayfair, p. 122.
1806. — William Thackray and Hannah Blake : St. Geo. Han. Sq. ii. 352.
West Rid. Court Dir., 1, 2, 5, 10, 1, 0, 0 ; London, 1, 3, 1, 1, 1, 0, 0 ; Philadelphia, 2, 0, 0, 4, 0, 13, 5.

Thackster, Thaxter.—Occup. 'the thacker' (fem. suffix -*ster*) ; v. Thacker, and cf. Baxter and Baker.
Thakstare, *sartitector* : Prompt. Parv.
'The Reders, Thaxters, Rede-sellers,' &c., Norwich Pageant : FF. ii. 148.
Thomas Thackstere. H.
John Thackster, co. Norf. FF.
Johannes Thekester, 1379 : P. T. Yorks. p. 244.
Robert Thakster, rector of Carlton, co. Norf., 1541 : FF. v. 98.
John Thaxter, 1567, Coll. Reg. : Hist. C.C.C., Cambridge.
Edmund Thaxter, bailiff of Yarmouth, 1675 : FF. xi. 330.
I am afraid this surname is obsolete in England, but I dare not speak positively. It is well represented across the Atlantic.
Boston (U.S.), 0, 31.

Thain, Thaine, Thane.—Offic. 'the thane,' equivalent to Earl (q.v.), a man who occupied the high position of a thane.
John le Theyn, co. Wilts, 1273. A.
Adam Theyn, co. Norf., ibid.
Roger le Theyn. T.
Nicholas le Then. T.
Cecilia la Theyn, co. Soms., 1 Edw. III : Kirby's Quest, p. 233.(
1640. Married—Alex. Thayne and Ann Fisher : St. Antholin (London), p. 19.
1770. — David Brodie Thain and Sarah Luntley : St. Geo. Han. Sq. i. 295.
London, 1, 1, 2 ; Boston (U.S.), 4, 0, 0.

Thame.—Local ; v. Tame.

Tharp.—Local, 'at the thorp,' from residence therein. A manifest corruption of Thorp, q.v.
1743. Married — Thomas Tharp and Frances Wheelock : St. Geo. Han. Sq. i. 31.
1760. — Alexander Tharp and Mary Moss : ibid. p. 96.
London, 4 ; Philadelphia, 4.

Thatcher, Thacher.—Occup. 'the thatcher.' For other variants, v. Thacker, Thackster, and Thaxter.
Reginald le Thechare, co. Oxf., 1273. A.
Reginald le Theccher. L.
John le Thacher, c. 1300. M.
1591-2. Robert Thatcher, co. Oxf. : Reg. Univ. Oxf. vol. ii. pt. ii. p. 189.
1593-4. William Thatcher, co. Sussex : ibid. p. 199.
London, 11, 0 ; Philadelphia, 25, 9.

Thaxter ; v. Thackster.

Thayer.— ? Bapt. 'the son of Theodoric' (?), from the O.F. popular nick. Thierry or Thierre (v. Terry). Thayer is, I presume, a modern English modification of the surname. But while it barely exists in England, it is a familiar entry in American directories. I have no actual proof for my conjecture, but I strongly believe I shall be found correct.
1605. Anthony Thayer and Martha Bourman : Marriage Lic. (London), i. 297.
1753. Married — Bartholomew Penny and Ann Thayer : St. Geo. Chap. Mayfair, p. 236.
1756. — John Huggins and Hannah There : St. Geo. Han. Sq. i. 66.
London Court Dir., 1 ; Philadelphia, 27.

Theakston, Theakstone, Thexton. — Local, ' of Theak-stone,' a township in the parish of Burneston, N. Rid. Yorks.
1610. William Thekeston, co. Northts.: Reg. Univ. Oxf. vol. ii. pt. ii. p. 377.
1773. Married—John Willis and Mary Theakstion (sic): St. Geo. Han. Sq. i. 230.
London, 1, 1, 1 ; MDB. (North Rid. Yorks), 2, 2, 0 ; (West Rid. Yorks), 1, 2, 2.

Theed. — Bapt. 'the son of Theodoric' (?), spelt Thedric in the Hundred Rolls. It is almost certain that Theed is a nick. of Thedric. The name was very popular. v. Terry.
Nicholas Thede, co. Camb., 1273. A.
William Thede, co. Camb., ibid.
1611. Richard Theede, co. Bucks: Reg. Univ. Oxf. vol. ii. pt. ii. p. 325.
1748. Married—Christopher Theed and Eliz. Carterledge : St. Geo. Chap. Mayfair, p. 111.
London, 2 ; Crockford, 4.

Thelen.—Bapt. 'the son of Llewelyn,' through the difficulty of pronunciation ; cf. Floyd for Lloyd. This derivation is, of course, beyond dispute.

Richard Thwellin, of Holt, 1618 : Wills at Chester (1545-1620), p. 192.
1607. Married— Edwarde Thwellinge and Jane Cotterill : Reg. Prestbury Ch. (Cheshire), p. 175.
— Bapt. — Margarett Thelline : ibid. p. 173.
1633. Buried — Anne Thewllen : ibid. p. 289.
Edward Twallen, co. Chester, 1695: Farwaker's East Cheshire, ii. 226.
Manchester, 1 ; London, 1 ; Philadelphia, 1.

Thelwall.—Local, ' of Thelwall,' formerly a chapelry in the parish of Runcorn, near Warrington, co. Chester.

1617. Buried—Edward Thelwall, servant to Mr. Craven, *upholster* : St. Michael, Cornhill, p. 221.
1622. John Thelwall, of Bold : Wills at Chester, ii. 216.
1630. Marian Thelwall, of Acton Grange : ibid.
Manchester, 1.

Theobald, Theobalds.—Bapt. ' the son of Theobald.'

Theobald Laver, co. Camb., 1273. A.
Walter Theobald, co. Camb., ibid.
1620. Married—John Castell and Grisogond Theobalde : St. Jas. Clerkenwell, i. 69.
1746. — Richard Theobalds and Sarah Penson : St. Geo. Chapel, Mayfair, p. 73.
1791. Married—Daniel Theobald and Ann Bishop : St. Geo. Han. Sq. ii. 69.
1792. — Jesse Theobald and Sarah Young : ibid. p. 70.
London, 9, 0 ; Liverpool, 0, 1 ; Philadelphia, 12, 0.

Thetford.—Local, ' of Thetford,' a market-town in co. Suffolk, thirty miles from Norwich.

1721. Bapt.—Susanna, d. Arthur Thetford : St. Jas. Clerkenwell, ii. 129.
New York, 2.

Thewlis.—? Local, ' of Thewleys.' This Yorkshire surname, I doubt not, is local, the suffix being the plural of *ley*, a meadow. But I cannot find the spot in question.

Thomas Thewelesse, 1379 : P. T. Yorks. p. 177.
West Rid. Court Dir., 2 ; Philadelphia, 2.

Thexton.—Local, a variant of Theakston, q.v.

Thick, Thicke.—Nick. ' the thick,' plump, fat, compact.

' The grete tour that was so thikke and strong.'
Chaucer, C. T. 1058.

Goscelin Thikke, Pardons Roll, 2 Ric. II.
William le Thikke, co. Soms., 1 Edw. III : Kirby's Quest, p. 101.
John le Thikke, co. Soms., 1 Edw. III : ibid. p. 126.
London, 3, 3 ; Oxford, 3, 1.

Thickbroom.—Local, ' at the thick broom,' from residence thereby.

William de Tikebrom, co. Suff., 1273. A.
Cf. William Thikthorn, co. Soms., 1 Edw. III : Kirby's Quest, p. 109.
London, 1.

Thickness, Thicknesse. — Local, ' of Thickness,' some headland on the English coast that I have not been able to identify ; cf. Holderness, Furness, &c. The suffix is -*ness*, a nose of land. Mr. Lower cruelly writes, ' Thicknesse, *nese* or *nesse*, is O.E. for nose, from A.S. *nese*, and this surname therefore probably refers to the thick nose of the original bearer ' (Patr. Brit. p. 341).

William Thyknes, C. R., 14 Ric. II.
1643. Buried — Mary Thikneys : St. Peter, Cornhill, i. 200.
1675. Ralph Thicknes, of Maldon, Essex, and Mary Pulley : Marriage Alleg. (Canterbury), p. 243.
Crockford, 0, 2.

Thickpenny.— ? ——. I can offer no satisfactory solution of this surname.

1590. Buried — Leonard Thickpenny, minister of Enfeld, brought from the Kinges Bench in a coffen with a flap to open, with a writing one it in verse, laid at Ledenhall gate by night : St. Peter, Cornhill, i. 137.
1748. Married—Christopher Wass and Margaret Thickpenny : St. Geo. Chap. Mayfair, p. 326.
London, 1 ; Philadelphia, 1.

Thimbleby.—Local, ' of Thimbleby,' a parish in co. Lincoln, near Horncastle ; also a township in the parish of Osmotherley, N. Rid. Yorks.

Alice de Thumbleby, co. Linc., Hen. III-Edw. I. K.
1586. George Thymblebie, co. Linc. : Reg. Univ. Oxf. vol. ii. pt. ii. p. 152.
London, 1 ; MDB. (North Rid. Yorks), 1 ; (co. Lincoln), 2.

Thin.—Nick. ' the thin ' ; v. Thynne.
London, 1.

Thirgood ; v. Thurgood.

Thirkell, Thirkettle.—Bapt. ; v. Thurkettle.

Thirlwall, Thirlwell.—Local, ' of Thirlwall,' a chapelry in the parish of Haltwhistle, co. Northumberland ; the Roman wall is in the neighbourhood of Gilsland and Thirlwall Castle. v. Thirlway.

Richard de Thurlewall, temp. Hen. III : KKK. v. 311.
Brice de Thirlwall (no date, but early), John de Thirlwall, 1386 : KKK. iii. 145.
Rouland de Thirwall, 1460 : KKK. iv. 27.
1744. Married — John Thirlwall and Hannah Ringrose : St. Geo. Han. Sq. i. 33.
Liverpool, 1, 0 ; West Rid. Court Dir., 1, 1 ; Crockford, 1, 0.

Thirlway, Thirlaway.—Local, ' at the thirlway,' i.e. the road leading through the breach or gateway in the Roman wall. With Thirlaway, cf. Greenaway or Ottaway for Greenway and Ottway ; v. Thirlwall.

MDB. (co. Durham), 0, 2 ; (West Rid. Yorks), 1, 0 ; Newcastle, 0, 1.

Thirst. — Local. Probably a corruption of Thirsk, co. Yorks.

John de Tresk, *sutor*, 28 Edw. I : Freemen of York, i. 8.
Johannes de Thresk, 1379 : P. T. Yorks. p. 241.
1575. Married—John Lambe and Eliz. Thurske : St. Peter, Cornhill, i. 230.
London, 1.

Thirston.—A variant of Thurston (v. Thurstan).
Boston (U.S.), 1.

Thirticle.—Bapt. ' the son of Thurkettle,' q.v., a curious variant. I have not found any 19th century instances. v. Thirtle.

1675. Bapt. — William, s. Thomas Thirticle : St. Mary Aldermary (London), p. 103.
1677. — Eliz., d. Thomas Thirticle : ibid. p. 104.

Thirtle.—Bapt. ' the son of Thurkettle,' a variant of Thirkell or Thurkle (v. Thurkettle) ; cf. Thurtle. This corruption was seemingly an early one, for a township in the parish of Swine, E. Rid. Yorks, bears the name of Thirtleby, i.e. the dwelling of

Thurkell, the first settler. No doubt it was originally Thurkellby. MDB. (Norfolk), 2.

Thiselton, Thistleton.—Local, ' of Thistleton,' a parish in co. Rutland, eight miles from Oakham. Other places probably existed of this name. It is interesting to notice that my first entry is from a Lincolnshire document. The name still exists in that county.

Adam de Thistelton, co. Linc., 1273. A.
1622. John Thistleton, of Woodplumpton, *husbandman* : Lancashire Wills at Richmond, i. 274.
1662. Thomas Thistleton, of Kellamargh : ibid. p. 275.
Crockford, 2, 0 ; MDB. (co. Lincoln), 2, 1.

Thistlethwaite. — Local, ' of Thistlethwaite,' one of the many local names with suffix *-thwaite*, so common to the North of England (v. Thwaite). I cannot find the exact spot.

1577. Alexander Thistlethwaighte and Mary Lisley : Marriage Lic. (London), i. 78.
1682. Thomas Thistlethwaite and Mary Sturmy : Marriage Lic. (Faculty Office), p. 162.
1784. Married—Arthur Stanhope and Eliz. Thistlethwayte : St. Geo. Han. Sq. i. 355.
MDB. (West Rid. Yorks), 2 ; London, 1.

Thistlewood. — Local, ' of Thistlewood.' Probably some spot in co. Lincoln.

MDB. (co. Lincoln), 5 ; Philadelphia, 1.

Thom, Thoms, Thomes.— Bapt. ' the son of Thomas,' from the nick. Thome or Tom, Thome being the earlier form ; v. Thomson.

Robert fil. Thome, co. Linc., 1273. A.
William Thome, co. York, 20 Edw. I. R.
Richard fil. Thome, co. York, ibid.
Alicia relicta Thome, 1379 : P. T. Yorks. p. 138.
Alicia uxor Thome, 1379 : ibid. p. 119.
Petrus Thome-son, 1379 : ibid. p. 115.
1698. Buried—John Tom, of Gaverigan : Reg. St. Columb Major, p. 245.

The earliest instances of Tom (without the *h*) I can find are :

Johanna Tom-douter, the daughter of Tom, 1379 : P. T. Yorks. p. 88.
Johannes Tom-son, 1379 : ibid.
1791. Married—Samuel Ford and Mary Thoms : St. Geo. Han. Sq. ii. 69.
London, 5, 6, 0 ; Boston (U.S.), 2, 4, 1.

Thomas, Thomason, Thomasson, Thomassin, Thomeson. —(1) Bapt. ' the son of Thomas.' Thomas or Thome (whence Tom) was a universal favourite. The 13th and 14th century registers teem with it ; v. Tomlin, Tomlinson, Thomson, Thompson, Tomkins, Tomkinson, Tombs, &c. (2) Bapt. ' the son of Thomasin ' (q.v.). The two have become mixed.

Roger fil. Thomas, co. Camb., 1273. A.
Richard Thomas, co. Suff., ibid.
Walter Thomas, co. Wilts, ibid.
William Thomas, co. Soms., 1 Edw. III : Kirby's Quest, p. 101.
Adam Thomasson, 1379 : P. T. Yorks. p. 174.
Johannes Thomasson, 1379 : ibid. p.138.
1582. Married — Thomas Bryse and Alyce Thomas : St. Michael, Cornhill, p. 12.
— John Thorne and Anne Thomasyne, *widow* : Marriage Lic. (London), i. 111.
1801. Married — Thomas Wyatt and Nancy Thomason : St. Geo. Han. Sq. ii. 239.
1806. — John Baptiste Thomesin and Jane Prin : ibid. p. 355.
London, 219, 5, 1, 0, 0 ; Boston (U.S.), 220, 0, 0, 1, 0 ; Philadelphia, 693, 12, 3, 0, 1.

Thomasin.—Bapt. ' the son of Thomas,' from the dim. Thomasin. A feminine Thomasina or Thomasine arose about the year 1350, and was popular as a font-name over the whole country till the 18th century. It is found in every register in every conceivable form, including Tamzen and Tomson. No doubt Thomasin, as a surname, has long been lost in Thomason or Thomson.

' Thomasinus, varlet of Nicholas le Herier, C. R., 4 Edw. I.
1538. Married — Edward Bashe and Thomeson Agar : St. Dionis Backchurch (London), p. 1.
1622. Buried—Tomson, d. John Moyer : St. Columb Major, p. 210.
1623. — Tomson Simon, *widow* : ibid.
1640. Buried—Thomasing, filia William Sympson : Wadsworth, co. Derby.
1657. Married — John Galley and Thomison Harte : St. Dionis Backchurch (London), p. 33.

For other instances, v. Thomas.

Thomasset, Tompsett, Thomsett, Tomsett. — Bapt. ' the son of Thomas,' from the dim. Thomas-et. The *p* in Tompsett is intrusive, as in Thompson. Although there cannot be the shadow of a doubt about the origin of this surname, I have not come upon any early instances.

1792. Married—Nicholas Peter Thomasset and Sarah Morgan : St. Geo. Han. Sq. ii. 72.
1801. Bapt.—Frederic John, s. Charlotte Thomsett : Canterbury Cath., p. 41.
1809. Married—Charles Norley and Ann Tomsett : ibid. p. 102.
London, 1, 4, 1, 0 ; MDB. (co. Sussex), 0, 6, 0, 1.

Thomerson. — Bapt. A corruption of Thomasson (v. Thomas).

London, 4.

Thomlinson, Thomlin.—Bapt. ' the son of Thomas,' from the nick. Thom, Thom, and the dim. Thom-lin ; v. Tomlin for early instances.

1528-9. John Thomplynson and Parnell Saunder : Marriage Lic. (London), i. 6.
1572. Bapt.—Alice, d. Thomas Thomlinson : St. Peter, Cornhill, i. 15.
1730. Married—John Thomlin and Jane Golde : St. Geo. Chap. Mayfair, p. 320.
1742. — Richard Thomlinson and Catherine Ferrer : ibid. p. 17.
London, 2, 0 ; Liverpool, 1, 0.

Thoms. — Bapt. ' the son of Thomas,' from the nick. Thom (later on Tom), and genitive Thoms. Hence Thomson. v. Thom.

John Thoms, co. Soms., 1 Edw. III : Kirby's Quest, p. 233.
London, 7 ; Philadelphia, 4 ; Boston (U.S.), 4.

Thomson, Thompson.—Bapt. ' the son of Thome,' i.e. Thomas (v. Thom). The *p* in Thompson is, of course, intrusive ; cf. Simpson for Simson.

Eborard fil. Thome, co. Camb., 1273. A.
Abraham fil. Thome, co. Bedf., 20 Edw. I. R.
1602. Married—Thomas Thomson and Mawdelen Langson : St. Jas. Clerkenwell, iii. 26.
1630. — Robert Thompson and Elline Lettice : ibid. p. 62.
London, 78, 245 ; Philadelphia, 91, 781.

Thor, Thore.—(1) Bapt. ' the son of Thor.'

Orm fil. Thore, 1179 : RRR. p. 167.

(2) Local, ' of Thore,' i.e. Kirkby Thure or Thore, a parish in co. Westmoreland. Nevertheless

(1) seems to be the true derivation.

London, 1, 0; Boston (U.S.), 0, 4.

Thorald; v. Thorold.

Thorburn, Thurburn.—Bapt. 'the son of Thurbern' (Thorbjorn occurs fifty-one times in Iceland Roll, Yonge, ii. 205). Torbern and Thurbern, Domesday; cf. Osbern.

William Thorebern, co. Oxf., 1273. A.
Richard Thorbarn, co. Oxf., ibid.
Dominus Thurbern, co. Suff., ibid.
Nicholas Thurbern, co. Wilts, ibid.
Philip Thorbarn, co. Soms., 1 Edw. III: Kirby's Quest, p. 113.
1574. Miles Case and Agnes Thurbarne: Marriage Lic. (London), i. 61.
1808. Married—John Thorburn and Ann Atkins, or Atkinson: St. Geo. Han. Sq. ii. 380.
London, 4, 2; Boston (U.S.), 2, 0.

Thoreby; v. Thurlby.

Thorley.—Local, 'of Thorley,' a parish in co. Hertford; cf. Thurley.

Robert de Torly, co. Sussex, 1273. A.
Thomas de Torlaye, or Thorlay, or Thorley, co. Linc., ibid.
William de Torleye, co. Hertf., 20 Edw. I. R.
Adam de Thorle, co. Norf., 1337: FF. ix. 476.
Theobald de Thorlee, co. Norf., temp. Hen. V: ibid. ii. 276.
1654. Buried—Anthony Thorley, small-pox: St. Michael, Cornhill, p. 247.
London, 2; Manchester, 6; MDB. (Norfolk), 1; Boston (U.S.), 1.

Thorman, Thurman, Thormund, Thurmond.—Bapt. 'the son of Thormond'; cf. Wyman from Wimond, Osman from Osmund, &c.

Henry Thurmond, co. Oxf., 1273. A.
Walter Thurmond, co. Oxf., ibid.
Alan Thurmod, co. Norf., ibid.
Henry Thurmund, co. Hants, 20 Edw. I. R.
1653. Buried—Edward Thurman: St. Peter, Cornhill, p. 207.
'Messrs. Thurmond and Wilson, woollen manufacturers': West Riding Dir., Batley.
London, 3, 1, 0, 0; Soothill, near Dewsbury, 0, 0, 1, 0; Philadelphia, 3, 9, 0, 0.

Thorn, Thorne, Thornes, Thorns.—Local, 'at the thorn' or thorns, i.e. thorn-bush, or clump of thorns. There is a parish of Thorne in dioc. York, and Thornes in dioc. Ripon.

William ad Spinam, co. Camb., 1273. A.
Hugh Thorne, co. Camb., ibid.
John de Thorn, co. Devon, ibid.

Walter de la Thorne, Fines Roll, 11 Edw. I.
Adam atte Thorne, co. Soms., 1 Edw. III: Kirby's Quest, p. 177.
William de Thorn, co. Soms., 1 Edw. III: ibid. p. 105.
Roger atte Thorn, C. R., 3 Hen. VI.
Robert atte Thornes, ibid., 25 Edw. III.
1579. Philip Thorne and Eliz. Hammond, widow: Marriage Lic. (London), i. 87.
1746. Married—Thomas Thornes and Sarah Truelove: St. Geo. Chap. Mayfair, p. 71.
London, 33, 28, 1, 2; Philadelphia, 46, 26, 0, 0.

Thornbarrow, Thornbery, Thornbury, Thornberry, Thornber.—Local, 'of Thornborough,' co. Oxford, or Thornbury, cos. Exeter, Hereford, &c.; also Thonborough in Allerton Mauleverer, near Knaresborough, co. York. With the Yorkshire variant Thornber, cf. the pronunciation Sedber for Sedbergh, in the same county.

Ricardus de Thornbargh, 1379: P. T. Yorks. p. 273.
Robert Thornbrughe, 1541: Hist. and Traditions of Ravenstonedale, co. West., W. Nicholls, p. 114.
Robert Thorneboroughe, 1541: ibid.
1575. Edward Thorneboroughe, co. Hants: Reg. Univ. Oxf. vol. ii. pt. ii. p. 62.
MDB. (West Rid. York), 0, 0, 0, 0, 3; London, 0, 1, 1, 0, 0; Philadelphia, 0, 0, 0, 1, 0.

Thorncroft; v. Thornycroft.

Thorndyke, Thorndike.—Local, 'at the thorn-dike,' from residence thereby. I cannot find the spot; v. Thorn and Dyke.

1620. Edward Thorndicke: Reg. Univ. Oxf. vol. ii. pt. i. p. 361.
1696. Bapt.—William, s. Herbert Thorndicke: St. Jas. Clerkenwell, i. 369.
1806. Married—John Thorndyke and Eliz. Nunn: St. Geo. Han. Sq. ii. 355.
London, 3, 0; Philadelphia, 0, 1; Boston (U.S.), 0, 28.

Thorne(s; v. Thorn.

Thornhill, Thornell, Thornill.—Local, 'of Thornhill,' an extensive parish six miles from Wakefield, co. York. Thornell is a manifest variant. There is also Thornhill, a tithing in the parish of Stalbridge, co. Dorset.

Walter de Thornhulle, co. Soms., 1 Edw. III: Kirby's Quest, p. 254.
Willelmus Thornyll, 1379: P. T. Yorks. p. 120.
Leticia de Thornhyll, 1379: ibid. p. 126.

1580. Robert Curtys and Katherine Thornell: Marriage Lic. (London), i. 99.
1661. Married—William Thornhill and Jane Terrill: St. Jas. Clerkenwell, i. 108.
London, 7, 1, 0; Boston (U.S.), 1, 1, 0; MDB. (co. Lincoln), 2, 1, 1.

Thornley, Thorneley, Thorniley, Thornalley, Thornally, Thornlay.—Local, 'of Thornley,' a township in the parish of Kelloe, co. Durham; also a township in the parish of Chipping, co. Lancaster. Probably many small spots bore this name.

1581. John Thornelie, co. Ches.: Reg. Univ. Oxf. vol. ii. pt. ii. p. 97.
1588-9. Thomas Thorneley and Johanna Longe: Marriage Lic. (London), i. 176.
1662. Richard Thornley, of Chipping: Lancashire Wills at Richmond, i. 276.
1675. Thomas Thornley, of Chipping: ibid.
London, 1, 1, 1, 0, 0, 0; Philadelphia, 13, 0, 0, 0, 0, 0; MDB. (co. Lincoln), 0, 0, 0, 1, 1, 1.

Thorns; v. Thorn.

Thornthwaite.—Local, 'of Thornthwaite,' a chapelry in the parish of Hampsthwaite, W. Rid. Yorks.

1724. Peter Thornthwaite, of Stock-in-Furness Fells: Lancashire Wills at Richmond, ii. 253.
London, 1.

Thornton.—Local, 'of Thornton,' near Bradford, co. York; also parishes in diocs. Lincoln, Oxford, Chester, Peterborough, Canterbury, &c. The explanation of so many Thorntons in the Yorkshire directories lies in the fact that there are at least three Thorntons in that county—the Thornton above mentioned, Thornton-in-Craven, and Thornton-in-Lonsdale.

Roger de Thorntone, co. Camb., 1273. A.
Hugh de Thorneton, co. York, ibid.
Richard de Thorneton, co. York, ibid.
1549. Buried—John Thornetone: St. Michael, Cornhill, p. 179.
1570. George Thorneton and Johanna Alondon: Marriage Lic. (London), i. 46.
London, 35; West Rid. Court Dir. 41; Philadelphia, 98.

Thornycroft, Thorneycroft, Thornicroft, Thorncroft, Thornecroft.—Local, 'of Thornycroft,' in the township of Siddington, in the parish of Prestbury, East Cheshire. The family that rose here has spread its roots all over England.

'Richard, lord of Siddington, confirms and quit claims to Richard, the son of Hamo de Thornicroft, all his right, &c., in certain lands and tenements in a certain place called Thornicroft, in Sydyngton, &c.': Harl. MSS. 2131.

Richard de Thornicroft, 1361: Earwaker's East Ches. ii. 400.

Hugh Thornicroft, of Thornicroft, 1436: ibid. p. 401.

1631. Edward Thonicroft, of Thornicroft: Wills at Chester, ii. 218.

1692-3. Bapt.—Thomas, s. John Thornycroft: St. Dionis Backchurch, p. 132.

London, 1, 2, 1, 2, 0; Manchester, 0, 1, 0, 0, 1.

Thorogood; v. Thurgood.

Thorold, Thorald.—Bapt. 'the son of Thorald,' a favourite early and even Middle-English personal name. The surname still clings to co. Lincoln, where it was evidently popular as a personal name six centuries ago. v. Terrell and Turrell.

Turold, Domesday.

Thorold the Sheriff: Freeman, Norm. Conq. iii. 778.

Ralph fil. Thorald, co. Linc., 1273. A.

Torold Camerarius, co. Essex, ibid.

Symon Thorald, co. Norf., ibid.

Martin Torald, co. Oxf., ibid.

William Torel or Thorel, London, ibid.

Richard Torel, co. Oxf., ibid.

Ralph Turold, co. Suff., ibid.

Turald de Papileon: Hist. Dunelmensis, Surtees Soc., vii. temp. 1400.

1638. Married—Robert Chesham and Phebe Thorold: St. Michael, Cornhill, p. 28.

1649. — Richard Thorold and Mabella Gay: St. Jas. Clerkenwell, i. 84.

MDB. (co. Lincoln), 16, 1.

Thoroughgood; v. Thurgood.

Thorp, Thorpe, Thripp, Thrupp, Throop, Throup.—(1) Local, 'at the thorp,' i.e. the village. (2) Local, 'of Thorpe.' Many parishes, hamlets, &c., are so named in England.

Adam de la Throppe, co. Wilts, 1272. A.

Augustinus de Thorpe, co. Suff., ibid.

Warin de Thorpe, co. Camb., ibid.

1728. Married — Henry Chamner and Barbara Thorp: St. Geo. Han. Sq. i. 5.

1729. — William Thorpe and Frances Fox: ibid. p. 6.

1745. — John Throp and Mary Lunt: ibid. p. 34.

1770. — John Throop and Mary Burgin: ibid. p. 196.

1778. — Joseph Thrupp and Mary Burgon: ibid. p. 290.

London, 16, 30, 1, 4, 0, 0; Boston (U.S.), 4, 22, 0, 0, 1, 1.

Thorrington.—Local, 'of Thorrington,' a parish in co. Essex, seven miles from Colchester.

Roger de Thorington, co. Camb., 1273. A.

William de Thorinton, co. Devon, Hen. III-Edw. I. K.

Robert de Thorinton, co. Lanc., ibid.

1740. Married — Joseph Thorrington and Eleanor Thorp: St. Geo. Chap. Mayfair, p. 155.

London, 1.

Thousandpound. — Nick. 'Thousand-pound'; cf. Hundred-pound, Centlivre, Ninepence, Twentymark, Twelvepence, Fourpence, &c. Thus in the present day a rich colonial is often nicknamed 'the Nugget.'

'Thomas Thousandpound' appears in the Wardrobe Accounts of Edward I. v. Index.

Thrasher; v. Thresher.

Threadgold, Thridgould, Tredgold.—? Nick. 'Threadgold,' a sobriquet of an embroiderer, or tapiser, or coucher. But far more probably a personal name, one of the many names ending in *good*, *gaud*, *got*, or *gold*; v. Scattergood, which is probably a personal and not a nickname.

Walterus Tredegold, co. Kent, 1273. A.

William Tredegold, co. Warw., ibid.

Robert Dredegold, co. Soms., 1 Edw. III: Kirby's Quest, p. 148.

1746. Married—John Thridgould and Ann Hilder: St. Geo. Chap. Mayfair, p. 68.

1765. Married — Benjamin Growcock and Frances Thridgould: St. Geo. Han. Sq. i. 140.

Adlingfleet, co. Yorks, 1, 0, 0; Sykehouse, co. Yorks, 1, 0, 0; London, 2, 1, 0.

Thredder. — Occup. 'the threader,' a maker of thread.

Willelmus Treder, 1379: P. T. Yorks. p. 15.

Christopher Threder, 1555, rector of Wissingset: FF. x. 86.

1574. Ezekiel Threader and Ellen Cummings: Marriage Lic. (London), i. 60.

1741. Married—William Pening and Ann Threader: St. Geo. Han. Sq. i. 27.

1797. — John Dobbs and Sarah Thredder: ibid. ii. 167.

London, 2.

Threlfall.—Local, 'of Threlfall,' an estate ,in the parish of Kirkham, co. Lancaster. This surname has ramified very strongly, and is extremely familiar in the Palatinate. The family was 'ori-

ginally seated at Threlfall in the Fylde, of which were John and Henry Threlfall in the time of Edward VI, and Edmund Threlfall in 19 Jas. I, who died seised of lands in Threlfall, Goosnargh, and Hothersall': Baines' Lancashire, ii. 605.

Edmund Threlfall, of Threlfall, *yeoman*, 1591: Lancashire Wills at Richmond, p. 278.

William Threlfall, of Goosnargh, 1662: ibid. p. 279.

George Threlfall, of Goosnargh, *husbandman*, 1630: ibid. p. 278.

1747. Married—James Threlfa (sic) and Mary Pryor: St. Geo. Chap. Mayfair, p. 100.

Manchester, 8; Goosnargh, 2; MDB. (Lancashire), 13; Philadelphia, 3.

Threlkeld.—Local, 'of Threlkeld,' a chapelry in the parish of Greystock, co. Cumb., four miles from Keswick.

Henry de Threlkeld, co. Cumb., 14 Edw. II: Nicolson and Burn's Hist. of Cumb. ii. 373.

William de Threlkeld, co. Cumb., 13 Ric. II: ibid.

Richard Thrilkelde, Queen's College, 1565: Reg. Univ. Oxf. vol. ii. pt. ii. p. 23.

1567. Edward Threlkeld, rector of Great Salkeld: Jefferson's History of Leath Ward (co. Cumb.), p. 265.

1793. Thomas Threlkeld left £20 to his executors, the interest of which was to be paid to the poor of the parish of Croglin: ibid. p. 103.

MDB. (co. Cumb.), 2; Boston (U.S.), 1.

Thresher, Thrasher.—Occup. 'the thresher,' a grain thresher.

Robert le Thressher, co. Soms., 1 Edw. III: Kirby's Quest, p. 244.

Ricardus Trescher, 1379: P. T. Yorks. p. 111.

Thomas Thresshere, C. R., 7 Hen. IV.

1696. Married—Samuel Taylor and Hannah Thresher: St. Dionis Backchurch, p. 45.

1752. Married—Edward Bennett and Eliz. Thrasher: St. Geo. Chap. Mayfair, p. 215.

London, 5, 0; MDB. (co. Worcester), 0, 1; Philadelphia, 1, 3.

Thring, Tring. — Local, 'of Tring,' a parish and market-town in co. Hertford.

Robert de Thring, co. Kent, 1273. A.

Edgar Thring, 1606: Reg. Broad Chalke, co. Wilts, p. 42.

Annis Thring, 1606: ibid.

1743. Married—Daniel Thring and Eliz. Stork: St. Geo. Han. Sq. i. 31.

1766. — William Tring and Susanna Norris: ibid. p. 154.

London, 3, 1.

Thripp ; v. Fripp and Thorp.

Throckmorton. — Local, ' of Throckmorton,' a chapelry in the parish of Fladbury, co. Worc. Mr. Lower (quoting Shirley's Noble and Gentle Men) says, 'John de Trockemerton was dwelling there about the year 1200' (Patr. Brit. p. 344).

1571. Arthur Throckmorton, London : Reg. Univ. Oxf. vol. ii. pt. ii. p. 52.
1572. Francis Throckmorton, co. Worc.: ibid. p. 53.
1584. Clement Throckmorton, co. Warwick : ibid. p. 84.
1623. John Throgmorton settled in Virginia : Hotten's Lists of Emigrants, p. 189.
London Court Dir., 1 ; Philadelphia, 1.

Throop, Throup ; v. Thorp.

Thrower. — Occup. ' the thrower,' a thread or silk winder, one who throws thread. It is almost certain that Trower is a corrupted form of Thrower ; cf. Thring and Tring (v. Thunder for a reverse corruption).

John Thrower, rector of Flordon, co. Norf., 1418 : FF. v. 73.
Clemens Thrower, C. R., 28 Henry VII. pt. ii.
1774. Married—Thomas Thrower and Eliz. Philby : St. Geo. Han. Sq. i. 237.
London, 4 ; MDB. (Norfolk), 7.

Thrupp ; v. Thorp.

Thunder.—Occup.'the tunder,' an American imitative corruption ; cf. Thring with Tring and Thrower with Trower. Nevertheless, this same corruption is found in English registers ; v. Tunder and Tunneler.

1669. Bapt.—Honour, d. Pattnoe (sic) Thunder : St. Jas. Clerkenwell, i. 239.
1800. Married—Valentine Riviere and Henrietta Thunder (co. Bucks) : St. Geo. Han. Sq. ii. 230.
1801. — Gregory Staples and Mary Thunder : ibid. p. 248.
Philadelphia, 3.

Thurburn ; v. Thorburn.

Thurgaland.—Local, 'ofThurgoland,' a township in the parish of Silkstone, W. Rid. Yorks.

1620. John Hill and Eliz. Thurguland : Marriage Lic. (Westminster), p. 27.
1621. Avery Thurgoland, co. Yorks : Reg. Univ. Oxf. vol. ii. pt. ii. p. 389.
Philadelphia, 4.

Thurgall.—Bapt. 'the son of Thorkettle'; v. Thurkettle. This Norfolk surname is easily proved to be thus descended. It is only a variant of Thurkle ; cf. Thurkleby, a local surname (i.e. the by or dwelling of Thorkettle).

'In the priory church (Langley, co. Norf.) was buried Sir Robert Thurgelby': FF. x. 149.
'Sir Roger de Thurkelby had a grant of free warrant in the 29th of Hen. III': ibid. viii. 22.

In the same way Thurkle or Thurkell became Thurgall, and is so found to this day in co. Norfolk, where Thirkettle, or Thurkettle, or Thurkell are still familiar. It is simply a variant. In compounds the suffix -kettle almost invariably became -kell or -kle ; v. Arkettle, Oskettle, Thurkettle, &c.

MDB. (Norfolk), 1.

Thurgar, Thurgur. — Bapt. 'the son of Turgar' or Thurgar (Yonge, ii. 206).

Thurger del Childhus, co. Suff., 1273. A.
Pagan Thurgar, co. Bedf., ibid.
John Thurgar, co. Camb., ibid.
Hugh Thurgar, co. Camb., ibid.
1801. Married — Christopher Thurgar and Charlotte King : St. Geo. Han. Sq. ii. 240.
London, 0, 1.

Thurgood, Thirgood, Thorogood, Thoroughgood, Thorowgood, Toogood, Towgood.—Bapt. 'the son of Thurgod' (Turgod, Domesday; cf. Tur-ulf for Thur-ulf, and Tor-ald for Thor-ald). 'William Togod, alias Thogod' (L.). This is an important entry, proving, if proof were wanting, that our Toogoods and Towgoods are the same. That Thurgood should be euphemized to Thoroughgood was as natural as inevitable.

Alicia Thurgod, co. Bedf., 1273. A.
Geoffrey Togod, co. Hunts, ibid.
Isolda Togod, co. Hunts, ibid.
William Togod, co. Soms., 1 Edw. III: Kirby's Quest, p. 174.
Hugo Togod, 1379 : P. T. Yorks. p. 74.
'Edward Togoode, sup. for B.A.,' Jan. 1525-6 ': Reg. Univ. Oxf. i. 141.
1557. Bapt.—Dority Throgood : St. Antholin (London), p. 12.
1650. Bapt. — William, s. Richard Thoroughgood, *fishmonger* : St. Peter, Cornhill, i. 93.

1651. Bapt.—Joseph, s. Richard Thorogood, *fishmonger*: ibid.
London, 4, 2, 8, 1, 1, 10, 2 ; Oxford, 1, 0, 1, 0, 0, 1, 0; Philadelphia, 0, 0, 1, 1, 0, 0, 0.

Thurkettle, Thurkell, Thurkle, Thurkill, Thirkettle, Thirkell.—Bapt. 'the son of Thurkettle,' a compound of Kettle, q.v. *Kettle* as a suffix became -*kell*, -*kill*, or -*kle*. v. Thirticle, Thirtle, Thurtle, Thurtell, all variants.

Turketyl, abbot of Croyland, 946-55.
Thurkill the Sacrist : Freeman, Norm. Conq. iii.432.
Thurcytel Marehead : ibid. i. 344.
Walter fil. Turchilli, temp. 1250 : FFF. p. 221.
Thurkeld le Seneschal, co. Linc., 20 Edw. I. R.
William Thurkel, temp. 1300. M.
Nicholas Thirkle, vicar of Wiggenhall, co. Norf., 1541 : FF. ix. 182.
Robert Thirkettle, vicar of Aldeburgh, co. Norf., 1554 : ibid. v. 353.
Margaret Thurketel, co. Norf., temp. 1580 : ibid. v. 401.
Francis Thyrkill, co. Norf., 24 Hen. VIII : ibid. x. 159.

Just as Thurgood (q.v.) became Thoroughgood, so Thurkettle became Thoroughkettle.

1700. Bapt. — Mary Thoroughkettle : St. James, Piccadilly.
London, 0, 0, 2, 0, 2, 2 ; MDB. (Suffolk), Thurkettle, 3 ; (Norfolk), Thirkettle, 3.

Thurlby, Thoreby. — Local, ' of Thurlby.' Two parishes and a hamlet bear this name in co. Lincoln. Also a township named Thoralby, in the parish of Aysgarth, N. Rid. Yorks. This readily suggests the derivation, viz. the by or dwelling of Thorald.

Nicholas de Thurleby, co. Linc., 1273. A.
Roger de Thurleby, co. Linc., ibid.
1576. Henry Thyrlibe, co. Norf. : Reg. Univ. Oxf. vol. ii. pt. ii. p. 71.
London, 1, 0 ; MDB. (Lincoln), 7, 2.

Thurley.—Local, ' of Thurleigh,' a parish in co. Bedford ; cf. Thorley.

1569-70. Robert Thurley and Eliz. Smithe : Marriage Lic. (London), i. 45.
1794. Married—William Jackson and Eliz. Thurley : St. Geo. Han. Sq. ii. 117.
London, 5.

Thurlow.—Local,'ofThurlow.' Great and Little Thurlow are parishes in co. Suffolk.

Matilda de Threlowe, co. Camb., 1273. A.
John de Thrillowe, co. Camb., ibid.

1795. Married — Samuel Thurlow and Eliz. Lowe : St. Geo. Han. Sq. ii. 125. London, 6 ; Philadelphia, 3.

Thurman.—Bapt. ; v. Thorman.

Thurnam.—Local, ' of Thurnham,' a township in the parish of Lancaster.

Carlisle, 2.

Thursby.—Local, ' of Thoresby.' North and South Thoresby are parishes in co. Lincoln.

Gilbert de Thoresby, co. Linc., 1273. A. John de Thoresby, co. Linc., 20 Edw. I. R.
Robertus de Thoresby, 1379 : P. T. Yorks. p. 278.
1628. Married — Samuel Robins and Katherine Thursby : St. Jas. Clerkenwell, i. 58.
1800. — George Augustus Thursby and Frances Pelham : St. Geo. Han. Sq. ii. 220.
Crockford, 3 ; MDB. (co. Lanc.), 2.

Thursfield.—Local, ' of Thursfield,' a chapelry in the parish of Wolstanton, co. Stafford.

1804. Married—Joseph Thursfield and Eliza Quelch : St. Geo. Han. Sq. ii. 307. London, 2.

Thurstan, Thurston, Tustin, Tustian.—(1) Bapt. ' the son of Thurstan.' Danish Thorstein, i.e. Thorstone.

Turstanus Machinator : Domesday.
Thurstan, abbot of Ely : Freeman, Norm. Conq. iii. 68.
Thurstan Goz : ibid. ii. 203.
Thurstan, housecarl of Eadward : ibid. i. 737.
Robert fil. Thurstani, co. Kent, 1273. A.
Thurstan de Torp, co. Hunts, ibid.
Thurstan de Holland, 1313. M.
Thurstayn de Cruce, co. Soms., 1 Edw. III : Kirby's Quest, p. 144.
Johannes Thurstan, 1379 : P. T. Yorks. p. 15.
Thryston Hodgkin, 1544 : Reg. St. Dionis Backchurch.

The omission of *h* was an early one.
Turstan de Brictewell, co. Oxf., 1273. A.

(2) Local, ' of Thurston,' a parish in co. Suffolk.

Hervey de Thurstan, co. Norf., 1273. A.
William de Thurston, co. Norf., ibid.
London, 0, 16, 1, 2 ; New York, 0, 19, 0, 0.

Thurtle, Thurtell. — Bapt. ' the son of Thurkettle,' variants of Thurkle and Thurkell (v. Thurkettle) ; cf. Thirtle. These surnames are found in Norfolk and Suffolk, where, of course, we

expect to see them, as Thurkettle has been established as a surname there for six centuries.

1802. Married — Samuel Thurtle and Susanna Lucas : St. Geo. Han. Sq. ii. 256.
MDB. (co. Norfolk), 1, 1 ; London, 1, 0.

Thurwood.—Bapt. ' the son of Thurgard,' i.e. Thor's guard.

Agnes Thoreward, co. Oxf., 1273. A.
Richard Thoreward, co. Oxf., ibid.
William Thoreward, co. Oxf., ibid.
London, 1.

Thwaite, Thwaites, Thwaits.—Local, ' of the thwaites' or thwaite, i.e. the meadows, the clearings or clearing, frequently found in such compounds as Thistlethwaite, Cooperthwaite, Thornthwaite, Haverthwaite, or Postlethwaite, which are all North English in origin. Probably connected with *whittle*, a knife. M.E. *thwitel*, a knife. Hence *thwaite*, a woodland clearing.

John del Thwaites, c. 1300. M.
Thomas de Thwaytes. B.
Robertus del Twaytes, 1379 : P. T. Yorks. p. 273.
1607. Samuel Thwaytes, of London : Reg. Univ. Oxf. vol. ii. pt. ii. p. 299.
1718. Buried—John Thwaits, in the new vault : St. Michael, Cornhill, p. 285.
London, 0, 17, 3 ; MDB. (West Rid. Yorks), 4, 3, 0.

Thynne.—Nick. ' the thin,' i.e. lean, slender. M.E. *thinne* and *thynne*.

' My tale is don, for my wit is but thinne.' Chaucer, C. T. 9556.

Cf. Thick, Large, Small, Bigg, Little, Fatt, &c. The old orthography has been maintained in this name. For a strange but unconfirmed story of a local origin, viz. ' John of th' Inne,' one of the Inns of Court, v. Lower's Patr. Brit. p. 345. Until better proof is shown we may be content with the satisfactory derivation given above.

Thomas Thynne, co. Northampton, 1273. A.
1577. Francis Thynne, co. Wilts : Reg. Univ. Oxf. vol. ii. pt. ii. p. 76.
1583. Henry Thynne, co. Wilts : ibid. p. 126.
1758. Married—John Thinn and Sarah Gee : St. Geo. Han. Sq. i. 82.
London, 4.

Tibbalds, Tibbard, Tibbles, Tibbals.—Bapt. ' the son of Theobald '; v. Tebbitt.

' For thus sings the divine Mr. Tibbalds, or Theobalds, in one of his birthday poems :
" I am no scollard, but I am polite ;
Therefore be sure I'm no Jacobite."
Polite Conversation, p. 339, Dean Swift's Works (Chatto and Windus, 1876).

1533-4. John Bastall and Tiballe Schryvener : Marriage Lic. (London), i. 9.
1574. Bapt.—Jesper, s. William Tibbold : St. Peter, Cornhill, i. 16.
1598. John Tibbolls and Eliz. Claye : Marriage Lic. (London), i. 253.
London, 1, 1, 1, 0 ; Boston (U.S.), 0, 0, 0, 1 ; Philadelphia, 0, 0, 0, 4.

Tibbatts, Tibbitts, Tibbutt, Tibbits, Tibbetts, Tibbet, Tibbett, Tibbitt, Tibbott.—Bapt. (1) ' the son of Theobald ' ; (2) ' the son of Isabel ' (v. Tebbitt). The variations are almost innumerable. They have run riot through the vowels.

1568. Richard Tybbott and Alice Haselam : Marriage Lic. (London), i. 39.
1729. Married—Roger Persons and Sarah Tibbets : St. Geo. Han. Sq. i. 6.
1744. — William Tibbitt and Eliz. Cammack : ibid. p. 33.
1802. — John Tibbatts and Martha May : ibid. ii. 257.
1805. — John Cock and Catherine Tibbatt : ibid. p. 333.
London, 1, 5, 1, 0, 0, 0, 0, 0, 0 ; Boston (U.S.), 0, 0, 0, 1, 5, 1, 0, 0, 0 ; Philadelphia, 0, 0, 0, 0, 2, 1, 2, 2, 1.

Tibbenham, Tibenham. — Local, ' of Tibbenham,' a parish in co. Norfolk.

MDB. (co. Suffolk), 2, 1.

Tibbetts, &c. ; v. Tibbatts.

Tibbles ; v. Tibbalds.

Tibbs.—Bapt. ; v. Tebb.

Tibby.—Local ; v. Tebay.

Tibbyson.—Bapt. ' the son of Tib '; v. Tebb.

Johannes Tibbeson, 1379 : P. T. Yorks. p. 219.
1788. Married — George Breffitt and Caroline Tibson : St. Geo. Han. Sq. ii. 10.

Ticehurst.—Local, ' of Ticehurst,' a parish in co. Sussex, ten miles from Tonbridge Wells.

MDB. (co. Kent), 1.

Tichborne.—Local, ' of Tichbourne,' in co. Hants.

Richard de Ticheborn, co. Bucks, 1273. A.
Walter de Tycheburn, co. Wilts, Hen. III–Edw. I. K.
1581. Roger Tutcheborne, co. Hants : Reg. Univ. Oxf. vol. ii. pt. ii. p. 98.
1602. Henry Ticheborne, co. Hants : ibid. p. 256.

1617. John Tychborne, co. Hants : Reg. Univ. Oxf. vol. ii. pt. ii. p. 365.
1783. Married — William Tichborne and Sarah Worthington : St. Geo. Han. Sq. i. 345.
London Court Dir., 1 ; New York, 1.

Tickell, Tickle, Tickel. — Local, 'of Tickhill,' a parish in the Union of Doncaster, co. York. By removal of a branch of this family into Lancashire, the surname is now more familiar in that county than in the county of its parentage.

Jordan de Tykehull, co. Notts, 20 Edw. I. R.
Richard de Tikhill, 28 Edw. I : Freemen of York, i. 8.
Henricus de Tikhill, 1379 : P. T. Yorks. p. 114.
Arthur Tickle, of Ormskirk, 1590 : Wills at Chester (1545-1620), p. 192.
Edward Tickle, of Manchester, *apothecary*, 1616 : ibid.
Alice Tickhill, of Manchester, 1618 : ibid.
1795. Married—Ebenezer Roebuck and Zipporah Tickell : St. Geo. Han. Sq. ii. 138.
London, 2, 2, 0 ; Manchester, 1, 3, 0 ; Liverpool, 0, 3, 0 ; Philadelphia, 0, 0, 1.

Ticklepenny, Tickelpenny. —Local, 'of Ticklepenny,' a place near Grimsby, co. Lincoln ; v. Lower's Patr. Brit. p. 346.

1786. Married—William Marriss and Jane Ticklepenny : St. Geo. Han. Sq. i. 386.
MDB. (co. Lincoln), 1, 0 ; Hull, 0, 1.

Tickner.—?Occup. Mr. Lower, quoting Mr. Ferguson, says, 'Dutch *teekenaar*, a drawer or designer' (Patr. Brit. p. 346). This seems the more probable as the surname is modern in England, and may be the result of immigration.

1575. Henry Tycknor and Agnes Anderson, *widow* : Marriage Lic. (London), i. 67.
1630. Bapt.—Michaell, s. Lawrence Ticknor : St. Peter, Cornhill, i. 81.
1649. — Thomas, s. Thomas Tickner, *grocer* : ibid. p. 92.
1771. Married—Benjamin Tickner and Ann Coles : St. Geo. Han. Sq. i. 212.
London, 6 ; Philadelphia, 9.

Tidball.—Bapt. 'the son of Theobald' ; v. Tudball.

London, 1 ; MDB. (co. Somerset), 5 ; New York, 1.

Tidd.—(1) Bapt. 'the son of Tiddeman,' from the nick. Tidd ; v. Tiddeman. But possibly a nick. of Tiffany, q.v., the old name for Epiphany (i.e. Theophania).

'Tid, Mid, and Miseray,
Carlin, Pome, and Pace-egg Day,'
is a North-English rhyme by which children still learn the chief Sundays from Epiphany to Easter. (2) Local, 'of Tydd,' parishes in cos. Cambridge and Lincoln. Probably these are the chief parents.

Thomas de Tid, co. Camb., 1273 : A.
Johannes Tydde, 1379 : P. T. Yorks. p. 134.
John de Tydd, co. Norf., 27 Edw. III : FF. viii. 133.
1705. Married — Samuel Martin and Eliz. Tidd : St. Geo. Han. Sq. ii. 136.
London, 4 ; Philadelphia, 1 ; Boston (U.S.), 8.

Tiddeman, Tiddiman, Tidyman, Tidman, Titman, Tideman.—Bapt. 'the son of Tiddeman.' I cannot explain its origin, but it seems to have come from the Low Countries.

Tethingman le Auste, co. Glouc., 1273. A.
Tiddeman Boker. H.
Tydyman le Swarte. N.
Robert Tethingman, co. Soms., 1 Edw. III : Kirby's Quest, p. 189.
Tideman de Winchcomb, 1394, bishop of Llandaff : Crockford, p. xl.

Cf. Bateman, Coleman, Sweetman, all baptismal names.

1772. Married — Richard Tiddeman and Sarah Frost : St. Geo. Han. Sq. i. 226.
1788. — William Tidman and Margaret Davison : ibid. ii. 11.
London, 0, 1, 1, 10, 1, 0 ; Philadelphia, 0, 0, 0, 1, 1, 1.

Tidmarsh. — Local, 'of Tidmarsh,' a parish in co. Berks.

1602. John Tidmershe, co. Worc. : Reg. Univ. Oxf. vol. ii. pt. ii. p. 258.
1749. Married — Richard Tidmarsh and Sarah Moythen : St. Geo. Chap. Mayfair, p. 142.
London, 4 ; MDB. (co. Wilts), 2 ; Oxford, 3 ; Philadelphia, 1.

Tidswell, Tidgewell.—Local, 'of Tideswell,' a parish in co. Derby.

Henry de Tideswell, co. Derby, 1273.
Ricardus de Tyddeswelle, 1379 : P. T. Yorks. p. 54.
1545. William Coplande and Joanne Tyddeswell : Marriage Lic. (London), i. 10.

1770. Richard Tidswell and Mary Thorley : St. Geo. Han. Sq. i. 203.
London, 2, 0 ; Boston (U.S.), 1, 1.

Tidy, Tidey. — (1) ? Bapt. 'the son of Tiffany' (?), from the nick. Tidd, and the pet form Tiddy or Tidy ; v. Tiffany. (2) Nick. 'the tidy,' the neat in personal appearance and habit.

Stephen Tydy, C. R., 26 Edw. III.
1788. Married—Joseph Piggon and Henrietta Tidy : St. Geo. Han. Sq. ii. 4.
London, 6, 0 ; Boston (U.S.), 0, 1.

Tidyman.—Bapt. ; v. Tiddeman. Nothing to do with tidiness or orderliness. Not a nickname.

London, 1.

Tierney, Tiernay.—Bapt. 'the son of Tierney.' St. Tigernath or Tierney was an Irish saint of the 6th century, and third bishop of Clogher. In the Philadelphia Directory are six Patricks Tierney, two Michaels, and one Terence. This will sufficiently demonstrate the Irish parentage of the surname.

London, 1, 0 ; Philadelphia, 53, 4.

Tiffany, Tiffen, Tiffin.—Bapt. 'the son of Theophania' (i. e. Epiphany), popularly Tiffany, the pet form being Tiffen and Tiffin. Of course the thin gauzy fabric known as *tiffany* has the same origination. One of our old mysteries include :

'Megge Merrywedyr, and Sabyn Sprynge,
Tiffany Twynkeler fàyle for no thynge.'

The font-name is found in Cornwall in the 17th century :

1600. Bapt. — Tiffeny, d. of Harry Hake : St. Columb Major.
1695. — Epipheney, d. of Humfry Oxnam : ibid.

A curious entry meets us in the Testa de Neville (Hen. III-Edw. I), p. 317 :

'Thephanya Hugo de Harington, prior de Giseburn.'

It reads strangely like a double font-name, a custom supposed to be unknown then. It is a man's name, too. All my instances are feminine. Possibly it was his spiritual name.

Tiffonia de Karduil, Hen. III-Edw.
I : K. p. 289.
Theofania de Bolebek, C. R., 46
Hen. III.
Thifania Simme, co. Camb., 1273. A.
Cristina Typhayn, co. Soms., 1 Edw.
III : Kirby's Quest, p. 102.
Johannes Holand et Tiffan uxor ejus,
1379 : P. T. Yorks. p. 134.
Teffan Danyll, 1379 : ibid. p. 148.
Nicholas fil. Tiffaniae. T.
Tyffanie Seamor, temp. Eliz. Z.
Teffania de Wildeker. E.
John Tyffyn,1536: Reg.Univ. Oxf. i.185.
1540. Married—Robert Yerson and
Isabell Tyffenne: St.Peter, Cornhill,i. 221.
1632. — Edward Somes and Mary
Tiffin : St. Antholin (London), p. 66.
1750. —, Whitelock More and Ann
Tiphaine : St. Geo. Han. Sq. i. 45.
London, 0, 3, 6; West Rid. Court
Dir., 2, 0, 0; Boston (U.S.), 9, 0, 1.

Tigg.—Nick. ; v. Tegg.

Tigh, Tighe.—Local ; v. Tye.

Tilbrook.—Local, 'ofTilbrook,'
a parish in co. Bedford.
William de Tilbroc, co. Linc., 1273. A.
MDB. (co. Suffolk), 2 ; (co. Camb.), 3 ;
Philadelphia, 1.

Tilbury.—Local, 'of Tilbury,'
three parishes in co. Essex.
Richard de Tillebyr', co. Essex,1273. A.
1746. Bapt. — Elizabeth, d. Edward
Tilbury : St. Dionis Backchurch, p. 172.
1753. Married—Thomas Tilbury and
Eliz. Head : St.Geo. Chap.Mayfair, p.240.
London, 8 ; Oxford, 1.

Tilden. — Local, ' of Tilden,'
seemingly some spot in co. Kent.
Perhaps a variant of Tilton, q.v.
But this is improbable. I doubt
not that the place must be sought
in the above-named county.
Henry de Tildenne, co. Kent, 20 Edw.
I. R.
1573. Richard Tylden and Mabell
Lamb : Marriage Lic. (London), i. 56.
1610. Theophilus Tylden, co. Kent :
Reg. Univ. Oxf. vol. ii. pt. ii. p. 313.
Philadelphia, 11.

Tildesley,Tildsley,Tyldsley.
—Local, ' of Tyldesley,' a parish in
South Lancashire. The surname
passed on at some period to London,
and is commoner there than in
Lancashire.
Hugo de Tyldesley, co. Linc., 20 Edw.
I. R.
Henry de Tyldesley, co. Linc., ibid.
Thurstan Tyldslay, co. Lanc., 1563:
Wills at Chester (1545-1620), p. 279.
Richard Tildesley, of Preston, co.
Lanc. : ibid. p. 290.

1593. Thurstan Tyldslay : Lancashire
Wills at Richmond, i. 290.
1624. Married — Philip Tillsley and
Ann Daniell : St. Mary Aldermary, p. 15.
London, 5, 0, 0 ; Manchester, 2, 2, 0 ;
Philadelphia, 0, 0, 1.

Tileston ; v. Tilston.

Tilewright ; v. Telwright.

Tilford, Tillford.—Local, ' of
Tilford,' a tithing in the parish of
Farnham, co. Surrey.
1808. Married — William Gurr May-
mott and Ann Tilford : St. Geo. Han.
Sq. ii. 394.
Philadelphia, 2, 0 ; New York, 7, 1.

Till, Tillson.—Bapt. 'the son
of Matilda,' from the nick. Till ; v.
Tilson.

Tillcock.—? Nick. 'the teal-
cock' (?), the male teal. M.E. tele ;
cf. Peacock, Moorcock, &c. If not
a nickname, then baptismal from
some nick. Till, with suffix -cock ;
cf. Wilcock, Jeffcock, Simcock.
This surname was settled in Oxfordshire for centuries.
John Telcok, co. Oxf., 1273. A.
Thomas Telcok, co. Oxf., ibid.
1548. William Tylcokks, bailiff of
Oxford : Reg. Univ. Oxf. vol. ii. pt. i. p.
296.
1556. William Tilkoke, mayor of
Oxford : ibid. p. 7.
1789. Married—Thomas Coggin and
Eliz. Tillcock : St. Geo. Han. Sq. ii. 24.
London, 1.

Tilleard.—? Bapt. 'the son of
Teyllard.'
John Teyllard, co. Soms., 1 Edw. III :
Kirby's Quest, p. 162.
London, 3.

Tiller ; v. Tillyer.

Tillett. — Bapt. ' the son of
Matilda,' from the nick. Till, and
dim. Till-ett (v. Tillotson).
1593. Married—Richard Tyllett and
Johan Tene : St. Dionis Backchurch,
p. 12.
1798. — William Tillet and Martha
Martin : St. Geo. Han. Sq. ii. 190.
London, 13 ; Philadelphia, 1.

Tilley, Tillie, Tilly. — (1)
Local, ' from Tilly,' a village in
' the department of Calvados in
Normandy,' as described by Lower.
He adds, 'There is a second place
so called in the department of
Eure.'

Phillipa de Tylly, or Tilli, 33 Hen. III :
BBB. p. 21.
Ralph de Tilly, 14 Edw. I : ibid. p. 373.
The latter had property in Nor-
mandy.
John Tylye, co. Soms., 1 Edw. III :
Kirby's Quest, p. 103.
Philip de Tylly, co. Dorset, Hen. III-
Edw. I. K.
Henry de Tilli, co. Devon, ibid.
Johannes Tilly, 1379 : P. T. Yorks.
p. 173.

(2) Bapt. (?). A pet form of Matilda ; v. Till, Tilson, and Tillotson.
This second probable origin will
help to explain the large number
of Tilleys and Tillys in our directories.
1756. Married — John Shipman and
Mary Tillie : St. Geo. Han. Sq. i. 65.
1761. — Thomas Tilley and Susanna
Turnedge : ibid. p. 102.
1774. — Henry Tilly and Susanna
Whittington : ibid. p. 246.
London, 21, 1, 10; Boston (U.S.),
6, 0, 1.

Tilling. — Bapt. 'the son of
Matilda,' from nick. Till, dim.
Till-in, more generally dim. Tillot
(v. Tillotson). The g in Tilling is
excrescent, as in Jenning (v. Jennings). Cornwall, the last home of
many a decayed font-name and pet
form, retained Tillin till modern
times.
Stephanus Tyllyng, 1379 : P. T. Yorks.
p. 79.
1691. Married — John Tilling and
Margaret Joy : St. Jas. Clerkenwell,
i. 209.
1779. Bapt. — Tillane, daughter of
William Hewett : Reg. St. Columb
Major (Cornwall), p. 135.
Colin is spelt Colane in the
same register.
London, 9.

Tillison.—A corruption of Tillotson, q.v. In the same way
Ibbison is often a corruption of
Ibbotson, and Sissison of Sissotson,
all being Yorkshire surnames derived from feminine personal
names, viz. Matilda, Isabel, and
Cecilia.
1677. Married — George Smith and
Hannah Taylor, by Dr. Tillison (i. e.
Tillotson): St. Michael, Cornhill, p. 41.
1748. — Richard Tillison and Margaret Stone : St. Geo. Chap. Mayfair,
p. 121.
Boston (U.S.), 2.

Tillman, Tillmon.—(1)Occup. 'the tileman,' i.e. the tiler, one who covered roofs with tiles; v. Tyler. The tendency would be to the modern spelling and pronunciation. (2) Occup. 'the tillman,' i.e. a husbandman. 'Because there were so fewe tylmen, the erde (earth) lay untilled': Capgrave's Chron., sub. A. D. 1349. (Lower's Patr. Brit. p. 346.)

Geoffrey Tileman, co. Hunts, 1273. A. Walter Tileman. N.
1572. Isaac Tylman, Magdalen Hall: Reg. Univ. Oxf. vol. ii. pt. ii. p. 38.
1661. Buried A child of Mr. Tilman's, the chirurgion: St. Dionis Backchurch, p. 233.
London, 6, 0; Boston (U.S.), 8, 2.

Tillotson, Tillott, Tillottson. —Bapt. 'the son of Matilda,' from the nick. Till, and dim. Till-ot. This was and is a familiar Yorkshire surname. The archbishop sprang from a Yorkshire family.

Cecilia Tillote, co. Oxf., 1273. A.
Tyllot Thompson, co. York. W. 9.
Magota Tillosson (sic), 1379 : P. T. Howdenshire, p. 16.
Tillot Punte, 1379: P. T. Yorks. p. 269.
Tillot Hobwyfe, 1379: ibid. p. 271.
Tillot Clynch, 1379: ibid. p. 273.
Tillot de Carr, 1379: ibid. p. 272.
Tillot de Northwod, 1379: ibid. p. 284.
Willelmus Tillotson, 1379: ibid.
Johannes Tillotson, 1379: ibid.
1777. Married — Thomas Rice and Sarah Tillott : St. Geo. Han. Sq. i. 272.
1800. — George Richardson and Caroline Catherine Tillotson: ibid. ii. 346.
London, 1, 0, 0; West Rid. Court Dir., 5, 0, 0; Philadelphia, 2, 0, 1.

Tilly; v. Tilley.

Tillyer, Tiller.—Occup. 'the tiller,' a tiller of the soil. With Tillyer, cf. Sawyer for Sawer, or *lawyer* for *lawer*.

1769. Married—John Tillier and Ann Pickernell : St. Geo. Han. Sq. i. 183.
1780. — Thomas Roberts and Eleanor Tiller: ibid. p. 317.
London, 0, 1; Philadelphia, 6, 1.

Tilney. — Local, 'of Tilney,' two parishes in co. Norfolk.

Robert de Tilney, co. Norf., 1273. A.
Nicholas de Tilneye, co. Norf., ibid.
1564. Edward Chafforne and Ursula Tylney : Marriage Lic. (London), i. 28.
1583. Married—Edmund Tylney, Esq., and the Lady Bray: St. Jas. Clerkenwell, i. 9.
London, 7; Philadelphia, 1.

Tilson, Till, Tillson, Tills, Tilles.—Bapt. 'the son of Matilda,' from nick. Till. Chiefly found in Yorkshire, where Matilda was extremely popular (v. Tillotson).

Alexander fil. Tylle. DD.
John Tilson, co. York. W. 2.
Robert Tilleson, 1397: Preston Guild Rolls, p. 1.
Agnes Tylleson, 1379: P. T. Howdenshire, p. 16.
Robertus Tilleson, 1379: P. T. Yorks. p. 244.
Willelmus Tyllson, 1379: ibid. p. 273.
John Tills, or Tillis, sheriff of Norwich, 1485: FF. iii. 173.
1690. Bapt. — Benjamin, s. Nathan Tillson : St. Jas. Clerkenwell, i. 339.
1742. Married—James Tilson and Jane Tilson : St. Geo. Han. Sq. i. 28.
1748. — John Bell and Eliz. Till: ibid. p. 40.
London, 0, 16, 1, 1, 0; Boston (U.S.), 2, 3, 8, 0, 1.

Tilston, Tileston.—Local, 'of Tilston,' a parish in co. Chester. Not to be confounded with Tilson or Tillotson, q.v.

1586. Thomas Tylston, co. Salop: Reg. Univ. Oxf. vol. ii. pt. ii. p. 153.
1663. Mary Tilston, of Huxley, *widow*: Wills at Chester, ii. 269.
1672. Peter Tilston, of Tattenhall : ibid. Liverpool, 2, 0; Boston (U.S.), 0, 18.

Tilton, ? Tilden. — Local, 'of Tilton,' a parish in the dioc. of Peterborough. Tilden may possibly be a corruption of Tilton; but v. Tilden.

John de Tylton, co. Linc., 1273. A.
London, 1, 0; Boston, 47, 34.

Tim.—Bapt. ; v. Timm.

Philadelphia, 1.

Timbrell.— ?——.

Robert Tymbrel, co. Soms., 1 Edw. III : Kirby's Quest, p. 174.
London, 2,

Timbs. — Bapt. 'the son of Timothy,' from the nick. Tim, patr. Timbs, with excrescent *b*; cf. Tombs for Toms. Similarly the *b* is excrescent in *timber*.

1752. Married—Edward Tymbs and Heneretta Maria Smith: St. Antholin (London), p. 156.
London, 1; Oxford, 2.

Timbury. — Local, 'of Timsbury': (1) a parish in co. Somerset;

(2) a parish in co. Hants. Possibly a corruption of Timperley, q.v.

1771. Married — John Timbury and Ennis Francis: St. Geo. Han. Sq. i. 209.
1782. — William Jones and Mary Timbery : ibid. p. 333.
London, 1.

Timcock.—Bapt. 'the son of Timothy,' from nick. Tim, and suffix *-cock* (v. Introd. p. 25); cf. Wilcock, Simcock, Jeffcock, &c.

John Tymcock. HH.
John Timcock. V. 5.

Timm, Timms, Tims, Times, Timson, Timmis.—Bapt. 'the son of Timothy,' from the nick. Tim; v. Timbs.

1564-5. Richard Tyms, New Coll.: Reg. Univ. Oxf. vol. ii. pt. ii. p. 22.
1752. Married—Dennis Tims and Mary Edwards: St. Geo. Han. Sq. i. 52.
1764. — Jeremiah Ogbourn and Mary Timson : ibid. p. 133.
1771. — Richard Timms and Mary Hughes: ibid. p. 206.
1785. — Matthew Times and Mary Hall: ibid. p. 376.
London, 0, 1, 3, 2, 3, 0; Manchester (Times), 1; Philadelphia, 4, 1, 1, 0, 1, 0.

Timmins, Timmons, Timins. —Bapt. 'the son of Timothy,' from the nick. Tim, and dim. Tim-in; cf. *viol* and *viol-in*, Rob and Rob-in, Col and Col-in, &c. Hence Robins, Collins, &c.

Gilbert Timin, co. Camb., 1273. A.
Agnes Tymandson, co. York, 1477. W. 11.
1603. Buried—John Timmens, servant to George Timmens: St. Michael, Cornhill, p. 212.
1756. Married—Samuel Timings and Mary Overton: St. Geo. Han. Sq. i. 61.
1784. — Robert Smith and Ann Timmins : ibid. p. 361.
London, 1, 0, 0; Philadelphia, 17, 9, 0; MDB. (co. Kent), 0, 0, 2.

Timothy.—Bapt. 'the son of Timothy.' I find few traces of this name in early records.

'John Timothy was, with a hundred other men, transported from Taunton, co. Somerset, to the West Indies, in 1685': Hotten's Lists of Emigrants, p. 316.
London, 3; Philadelphia, 4.

Timperley, Temberli, Temperley.—Local, 'of Timperley,' a parish in co. Chester.

1611. Thomas Timperley, of Hale: Wills at Chester, i. 192.
1623. Married — Thomas Tymperley and Anne Haygh: Reg. Prestbury Ch., co. Ches., p. 241.

1761. Married—William Timperley and Mary Hone : St. Geo. Han. Sq. i. 105.
London, o, o, 4 ; Manchester, 4, 0, 2 ; Philadelphia, 2, 1, 0.

Timpson, Timson. — Bapt. 'the son of Timothy,' from the nick. Tim. The *p* is intrusive, as in Thompson, Simpson, &c. ; v. Timmins.

1742. Bapt.—Maria, d. Robert Timson : St. Geo. Chap. Mayfair, p. 6.
1764. Married — Jeremiah Ogbourn and Mary Timson : St. Geo. Han. Sq. i. 133.
London, o, 3 ; Boston (U.S.), o, 6 ; Philadelphia, 1, 1.

Tims, Timson ; v. Timm.

Tinckler ; v. Tinkler, of which it is a variant.

Tindal, Tindall, Tindale, Tindell, Tindle, Tindill, Tindel. —Local, 'of Tynedale,' from residence by the first bearer on the banks of the river Tyne ; cf. Coverdale, Tweedale, Lonsdale, Teasdale, &c. v. Tyndale.

William de Tyndale, co. Northumb., 20 Edw. I. R.
Thomas deo Tyndale, 1317 : DDD. i. 34.
William de Tyndale, 1357: ibid. p. 35.
Robertus de Tyndale, 1379 : P. T. Yorks. p. 213.
1575. John Tindall, co. York : Reg. Univ. Oxf. vol. ii. pt. ii. p. 64.
1580. Bapt.—Robert, s. Robert Tyndall : St. Jas Clerkenwell, i. 12.
1720. Married—John Tindle and Anne Powell : St. Geo. Chap. Mayfair, p. 291.
1788. — William Bishop and Mary Tindell : St. Geo. Han. Sq. ii. 6.
London, 2, 3, 8, 2, 0, 0, 0; MDB. (East Rid. Yorks), o, 9, 1, 0, 3, 2, 0 ; Philadelphia, o, 13, 0, 1, 0, 0, 2.

Tingay, Tingey.—Local, ' of Tingay (?). I do not know of such a place, but as it belongs to the fen district it may be ' of Tingrith,' a village parish in co. Bedford, four miles from Woburn. This place is styled Tyngri in the Hundred Rolls (i. 546), and the surname is similarly spelt :

Petrus de Tyngrye, co. Bedf., 1273. A.

The change from Tyngrye to Tingay or Tingey is not at all a surprising one in English nomenclature.

1619 Married—Richard Tingey and Isabell Flyng : St. Jas Clerkenwell, i. 46.
1774. — Edward Tingey and Mary Murrow : St. Geo. Han. Sq. i. 240.

London, o, 5 ; MDB. (Bedford), 2, 2 ; (Cambridge), o, 2.

Tingle.—(1) Local, ' of Tinghill ' (?). Apparently some small spot in co. Yorks.

Ricardus Tynghill, 1379 : P. T. Yorks. p. 199.
Elene Tyngyl, 1424, co. York : W. 11, p. 25.

(2) Local, 'of Tynedale,' a variant of Tindal, q.v. The following entries seem to prove this :

1779. Married—Laurence Tingdall and Margaret Carr : St. Geo. Han. Sq. i. 302.
1784. — John Tingle and Ann Chamberlain : ibid. p. 361.

In spite of (2) it must be manifest that (1) is the chief parent.
London, 2 ; Sheffield, 2 ; West Rid. Court Dir., 1 ; Philadelphia, 6.

Tining.—Local, ' at the tining,' from residence thereby. ' *Tining*, a newly enclosed piece of ground. Co. Wilts' (Halliwell).

Thomas atte Tynyng, co. Soms., 1 Edw. III : Kirby's Quest, p. 116.
William atte Tunyng, co. Soms., 1 Edw. III : ibid.

Tinker.—Occup. ' the tinker.' All the early instances are South English ; v. Tinkler for North-English form. Travelling pedlars were so called because they made their approach known by tinking, i.e. ringing, or making a tinkling noise. The mending of pots and pans does not seem to have been the particular pursuit of the mediaeval tinker. He was a general pedlar.

' No person, or persons commonly called Pedler, Tynker, or Pety Chapman, shall wander or go from one towne to another ...and sell pynnes, poyntes laces, gloves, knyves, glasses, tapes, or any suche kynde of wares whatsoever, or gather connye skynnes ' : 5 & 6 Edw. VI, c. 21.

Thomas le Tyneker, co. Bucks, 1273. A.
Angin' Tineker, co. Hunts, ibid.
Peter le Teneker, co. Soms., ibid.
Richard le Tinekere. T.
William le Tynekar, co. Soms., 1 Edw. III : Kirby's Quest, p. 142.
1574. Buried—John Tynker, of Adlyngton : Reg. Prestbury Ch., co. Ches., p. 47.
1777. Married—John Tinker and Eliz. Durrant : St. Geo. Han. Sq. i. 279.
London, 1 ; Philadelphia, 4.

Tinkerson.—Nick. ' the tinker's son ' ; cf. Taylorson, Smithson, Wrightson, &c.

1588. Married—John Tinkerson and Sibell Lee : St. Antholin (London), p. 33.

Tinkler, Tinckler. — Occup. 'the tinkler,' i.e. Tinker, q.v. The term being North English, so is the surname. ' A tincker or tinkeler ' : Baret's Alvearie, 1580 (Halliwell).

'Hey ! sirs ! what cairds and tinklers, And ne'er-do-weel horse-coupers.'
v. Jamieson on *Caird.*

Tinkle is merely the frequentative of *tink.* Hence both Tinker and Tinkler.

William de Westerdale, *tynkler*, 12 Edw. III : Freemen of York, i. 32.
Roger Tynkeler, C. R., 20 Edw. III. pt. i.
Rogerus Tynkler, 1379 : P. T. Yorks. p. 204.
Ricardus Tyncler, 1379 : ibid. p. 35.
Alice Tynkeller, co. York. W. 9.
Richard Tynkler, co. York. W. 8.
1726. Married—George Fawcett and Ann Tenkler : St. Geo. Han. Sq. i. 2.
1746. — Joseph Tinkler and Elinor Smallwood : St. Geo. Chap. Mayfair, p. 77.
London, 2, 1 ; Newcastle, 2, 0 ; New York, 2, 0.

Tinniswood ; v. Tenniswood.

Tinsley, Tinslay.—Local, ' of Tinsley,' a chapelry in the parish of Rotherham, W. Rid. Yorks.

Lecia de Tyneslawe, 1372 : P. T. Yorks. p. 40.
1648. Married—William Scriven and Amye Tinsly : St. Jas. Clerkenwell, i. 83.
1675. — Edward Burton and Mary Tinsley : ibid. p. 180.
London, 4, 2 ; Philadelphia, 2, 0.

Tipkins.—Bapt. ' the son of Theobald,' from nick. Tib, and pet *kin* ; v. Tebb.

1537. ' Item, payed to Typkyn for cherys, xxd.' : Privy Purse Expenses, Princess Mary.

Tiplady.—Local ; v. Toplady.

Tipler ; v. Tippler.

Tipper, Tepper.—Occup. ' the tipper,' one who mounted mazers, drinking horns, or cups with metals. ' To tip, to put on tips at the ends of horns, brims of drinking vessels, &c.' (Bailey). Possibly he was an arrow-header also, a clumsy term for an important occupation, and sure to have a shorter equivalent.

3 C

'Arowe-heders, maltemen, and corne-mongers.'
   Cocke Lorelle's Bote (1510).
'Arowe-hede, *barbellum*': Cath. Ang. (1483).

Tipper is still strongly represented in the directory.

William le Tipper, co. Suff., 1273. A.
Henry le Tipper, co. Bedf., ibid.
Alice Tippere, co. Camb., ibid.
John le Tipper, 1313. M.
1563. Married — Thomas Beane and Jone Typper: St. Peter, Cornhill, i. 226.
London, 11, 5; Philadelphia, 1, 0.

Tippett, Tippetts, Tippitt, Tippets.—Bapt. (1) 'the son of Theobald,' (2) 'the son of Isabella, sharpened forms of Tibbett, Tibbetts, and Tibbitt (v. Tibbatts). The change from *b* to *p* is exceedingly common; cf. Hobbs and Hopps, Hobson and Hopson. In the registers of St. Columb Major, co. Cornwall, the well-known family of Tippett are also occasionally entered as Tibbett:

1599. Bapt. — Nicholas, son of John Tibbett: Reg. St. Columb Major, p. 19.
1603. — Hughe, son of William Tippett, p. 21.
John Typpet, 1568: Reg. Univ. Oxf. i. 272.
1788. Married — John Burgess and Priscilla Tippett: St. Geo. Han. Sq. ii. 2.
London, 6, 1, 2, 0; Devon Court Dir., 1, 1, 1, 0; Philadelphia, 0, 0, 0, 1.

Tipping, Tippin.—Bapt. 'the son of Thorphin'; a variant of Topping. Turpin (q.v.) was the Yorkshire form; Toppin, later Topping, with excrescent *g*, the Lancashire form. Tipping seems to have arisen in the neighbourhood of Preston, and is unquestionably a variant of Topping, as the Preston Guild Rolls fully demonstrate.

John fil. William Toppyng, 1397: Preston Guild Rolls, p. 3.
John Toppynge, 1415: ibid. p. 7.
Ewan Typpynge, 1542: ibid. p. 15.
John Typynge, 1622: ibid. p. 69.
Thomas Typpyng, of Ribchester, 1563: Wills at Chester (1545-1620), p. 290.
Jenet Typpynge, of Preston, 1572: ibid.
William Tipping, of Shaw, *husbandman*, 1634: ibid. p. 279.
1566. Buried — Margaret Typynge, of Pointon: Reg. Prestbury Ch., co. Ches., p. 20.
London, 2, 0; Preston, 4, 0; Liverpool, 9, 0; Manchester, 3, 0; Philadelphia, 3, 1.

Tipple. — Bapt. 'the son of Theobald,' popularly Tibble sharpened to Tipple; v. Tebbitt (1) and the entries there recorded. For change from *b* to *p*, v. Tippett.

Tipel (without surname), co. Norf., 1273. A.
Alicia Typpell, 1379: P. T. Yorks. p. 21.
1762. Married — James Price and Mary Tibball: St. Geo. Han. Sq. i. 113.
'Bedford Chapel, Bloomsbury. Rev. S. A. Tipple will preach to-morrow at 11 a.m. and 7 p.m.': Standard, Feb. 19, 1887.
London, 2.

Tippler, Tipler.—Occup. 'the tippler'; not one who habitually goes in for small potations, as now understood by the term, but a seller of drink, an alehouse keeper. Mr. Lower quotes two 'communes tipulatores' in the records of the Corporation of Seaford, co. Sussex, 36th Elizabeth, who had broken the assize of bread and beer, and were fined 2s. 6d. The same year one Symon Collingham, of Seaford, is licensed as a tipler, and is to abstain from the use of unlawful games 'duringe the time of his tiplinge' (v. Lower's Patr. Brit. p. 347).

William Tipeler, co. Linc., 1273. A.
1806. Married — Francis Tipler and Sarah Bayley: St. Geo. Han. Sq. ii. 354.
MDB. (co. Linc.), 0, 1; (co. Essex), 1, 1.

Tipton. — Local, 'of Tipton,' a parish in co. Stafford, near Dudley. The family bearing this name seems to have settled somewhat early in the neighbouring county of Salop.

1585-6. John Typton, or Tipton, co. Salop: Reg. Univ. Oxf. vol. ii. pt. ii. p. 149.
1616. Edmund Tipton, co. Salop: ibid. p. 350.
1808. Married — Thomas Copland and Margaret Tipton: St. Geo. Han. Sq. ii. 389.
MDB. (co. Salop), 2; Philadelphia, 7.

Tirebuck.—Local, 'of Tarbock,' a township in the parish of Huyton, seven miles from Liverpool; v. Tarbuck, of which it is a variant.

Liverpool, 1; London, 1.

Tirrell; v. Terrell.

Tisbury.—Local, 'of Tisbury,' a parish in co. Wilts, three miles and a half from Hindon.

London, 1.

Tisdall Tisdale. Local, 'of Teesdale,' from res'dence in the valley of the river Tees; v. Teasdale for early instances.

1585. Edward Tayler and Johanna Tysdalle, *widow*: Marriage Lic. (London), i. 141.
1632. Roger Tisdale and Eliz. Gyles: Marriage Lic. (Faculty Office), p. 18.
London, 5, 0; Boston (U.S.), 0, 11; Philadelphia, 5, 2.

Tissiman; v. Tesseyman.

Tissington.—Local, 'of Tissington,' a parish in co. Derby, four miles from Ashbourn.

1768. Married — George Tissington and Margaret Barker: St. Geo. Han. Sq. i. 179.
London, 1; Crockford, 1; New York, 1.

Titchmarsh.—Local, 'of Titchmarsh,' a parish in the dioc. of Peterborough, co. Northants. To be distinguished from Tidmarsh, q.v.

John de Tichemershe, co. Northampt., 20 Edw. I. R.
Henry de Tichemersh, co. Northampt., ibid.
1756. Married — Philip Foley, *clerk*, M.A., and Ann Titchmarsh: St. Geo. Han. Sq. i. 65.
London, 1.

Titford.—Local, 'of Tetford,' a parish in co. Lincoln, six miles from Horncastle.

London, 4.

Titherington, Titterington, Titrington. — Local, 'of Titherington,' a township in the parish of Prestbury, co. Ches.

Jordan de Tyderinton, 19 Edw. I: East Cheshire, i. 264.
William de Tyveryngton, *furbour*, 11 Edw. II: Freemen of York, i. 17.
John de Tyderynton, vicar of Sandback, 1356: ibid. fi. 334 *n*.
1561. Married — John Burey and Ales Tyderinton (of Tytherington): Reg. Prestbury, co. Ches., p. 5.
1614. Buried — Thomas Tydderingeton (of Tydderinton): ibid. p. 204.
1723. Married — Hewitt Tittrington and Rachel Britton: St. Jas. Clerkenwell, i. 248.
MDB. (West Rid. Yorks), 0, 5, 0; Manchester, 1, 1, 0; Philadelphia, 1, 0, 0; New York, 0, 2, 1.

Tithinglamb.—Nick.

William Tythinglomb, Close Roll, 15 Edw. III. pt. ii.

Titley, Titlow. — Local, 'of Titley,' a parish in co. Hereford. Also v. Tetley and Tetlow, of which in some instances probably these are variants.

1750. Married—Thomas Tittley and Martha Maria Ballord: St. Geo. Chap. Mayfair, p. 183.
1790. — John Titley and Eliz. Newell: St. Geo. Han. Sq. ii. 46.
1798. — Isaac Titlow and Eleanor Cornforth: ibid. p. 181.
Philadelphia, 0, 9.

Titman; v. Tiddeman.

Titmas, Titmus, Titmuss.— Nick. ' the titmouse.' Not to be confounded with Titchmarsh, q.v. ' Tytemose, bryd, *frondator* ': Prompt. Parv. ' The mouse a titti-mouse-was no doubt' (Halliwell).

1651. Married—William Titimouse and Anne Pertus, of Ingerston, co. Essex: Reg. St. Peter, Cornhill, i. 258.
In a list of recusants, 1580, presented by the Vicar of Kirkham, co. Lanc., appears:
' Also Diev. Tytmouse, conversant in the company of two widows, viz. mistress Alice Clyfton and mistress Jane Clyfton': Croston's edit. of Baines' Lanc. p. 240.
London, 1, 4, 1.

Titsworth.—Local, ' of Tittisworth,' a township in the parish of Leek, co. Stafford.
Philadelphia, 1.

Titterington; v. Titherington.

Tobias. — Bapt. ' the son of Tobias.'
1774. Married—Joseph Beal and Ann Tobias: St. Geo. Han. Sq. i. 239.
1788. — John Tobias and Eliz. Jacks: ibid. ii. 2.
London, 3; Philadelphia, 9.

Tobin, Tobyn.—Bapt. ' the son of Tobias,' from the dim. Tob-in; cf. Col-in, Rob-in, &c. I suspect that Tobin is a French importation of somewhat recent date.
1737. Buried — John Tobin: St. Antholin (London), p. 209.
1794. Married—John Harriman and Eliz. Tobin: St. Geo. Han. Sq. ii. 118.
London, 4, 0; Philadelphia, 80, 2.

Tobitt, Tobbutt.—Bapt. ' the son of Theobald '; v. Tebbitt.
London, 1, 3; New York, 1, 0.

Toby, Tobey.—Bapt. · the son of Tobias,' from the nick. Toby.
' And kan telle of Tobye,
And of twelve Apostles.'
         Piers P. 5667-8.
William Toby, co. Linc., 1273. A.
Thomas Toby, co. Soms., 1 Edw. III: Kirby's Quest, p. 221.

1584. Bapt.—Elizabeth Tobye: Reg. Stourton, Wilts, p. 2.
1801. Married — Thomas Jinks and Lovey Tobey: St. Geo. Han. Sq. ii. 240.
London, 7, 0; Philadelphia, 1, 7.

Tod, Todd.—Nick. ' the tod,' i.e. the fox, q.v.; cf. Todhunter, a North-English surname. Halliwell says, 'Tod, a fox, still in use '; v. also Jamieson's Dict. Cf. Lowrie.

John le Tod, c. 1300. M.
1575. Abraham Todde, of Newcastle: Reg. Univ. Oxf. vol. ii. pt. ii. p. 66.
1597. Robert Baker and Jane Todd, *widow*: Marriage Lic. (London), i. 240.
London, 7, 42; Boston (U.S.), 0, 53.

Todhunter.—Occup. ' the tod-hunter,' from North-English *tod*, a fox. The surname is still found in Cumberland and the Lake District, and the local nomenclature (cf. Todbusk, Todbank, &c.) still proves a past familiarity with the word. The tod-hunter would obtain a livelihood by keeping down the number of these farmyard burglars. Afterwards, under a statute of Henry VIII, he got twelvepence per fox-head from the parish warden. Todhunter is a great name within the old limits of the parish of Greystock, co. Cumb.

1585. Thomas Todhunter, co. Cumb.: Reg. Univ. Oxf. vol. ii. pt. ii. p. 147.
1591. Married—Fraunces Hocken and Margret Todhunter: St. Mary Aldermary, p. 8.
MDB. (co. Cumb.), 10; London, 3; Ulverston, 1; New York, 1.

Todman.—Local, ' of Toddenham,' a parish in co. Glouc., near Moreton-in-the-Marsh. The modifications are quite regular, first Toddenham, then Todnam, finally Todman. This is one of a fairly large class; cf. Tottman for Tottenham, Swetman for Swetenham, Deadman for Debenham. All local surnames ending in *-enham* seem by some natural law to become modified into *-man*.

Muriel de Todenham, co. Soms., 1 Edw. III: Kirby's Quest, p. 202.
London, 1.

Tofield, Tuffield, Tuffill.— Local, ' at the to-fall' (?), probably from residence beside or inside a pent-house, once called a 'to-fall.' The *d* in Tofield would thus be

excrescent, and imitative of the word *field*. 'To-falle, schudde, *appendicium*' : Prompt. Parv. p. 495. 'Teefall, a mode of building in the pent-house form, common in Northumberland' (Halliwell); and v. Brockett's North Country Glossary and Jamieson's Dict.

1632. Married—Edward Sneller and Audry Tofeild: St. Jas. Clerkenwell, i. 64.
1729. — William Murril and Abigal Tofell: St. Geo. Chap. Mayfair, p. 296.
1802. — James Tofield and Emily Wiltshire: St. Geo. Han. Sq. ii. 271.
London, 3, 1, 1; West Rid. Court Dir., 4, 0, 0.

Tofts, Toft.—Local, (1) ' of Tofts,' a parish in co. Norf.; (2) ' at the tofts ' or toft. A homestead seemingly amid trees, as it is frequently compounded with tree-names; cf. the old proverb, ' He hath neither toft nor croft,' i.e. without house or land. Tofts implies an aggregation of such dwellings.

Johannes Atte toftes et uxor, 1379: P. T. Yorks. p. 185.

(3) Toft, a township in the parish of Knutsford, co. Chester, is the parent of the Cheshire Tofts.

Gundreda de Toftes, co. Norf., 1273. A.
Eborard de Toft, co. Norf., ibid.
Alan de Toft, co. Camb., ibid.
Robert de Toft, co. Bedf., ibid.
1394. Hugh de Toft, co. Ches.: East Cheshire, ii. 355.
1580. Married—John Hatton and Ales Toft: Reg. Prestbury Ch., co. Ches., p. 66.
1585. William Toft, of Buglawton, *yeoman*: Wills at Chester, i. 193.
Manchester, 0, 5; London, 1, 0; Philadelphia, 0, 1; New York, 1, 1.

Toke; v. Tuck.

Tokelin.— Bapt. ' the son of Toke,' from dim. Tokelin. This is interesting as showing the popularity of Toke; v. Tuck.

Richard Tokelyn, co. Soms., 1 Edw. III: Kirby's Quest, p. 96.
Margery Toklyne, co. Soms., 1 Edw. III: ibid. p. 107.
John Tuckling, co. Soms., 1 Edw. III: ibid. p. 159.

Toleman, Tollman, Tolman.— (1) Occup. ' the tollman,' one who took tolls and taxes; v. Toller.

Thomas Tolman. B.
1752. Married—John Dyer and Susanna Tollman: St. Geo. Chap. Mayfair, p. 229.

1791. Married — Thomas Young and Patty Tollman : St. Geo. Han. Sq. ii. 56. London, 5, 1, 5 ; Boston (U.S.), 1, 0, 6 ; Philadelphia, 0, 0, 46.

Tolfree, Tolfrey.—Bapt. 'the son of Thorfrey' (?) ; v. Fray. I strongly suspect that Tolfree and Tolfrey are modifications of this name.

John Torfray, co. Oxf., 1273. A.
1599. Married—Augustin Clarke and Katherine Tolefree : St. Jas. Clerkenwell, i. 22.
London, 1, 1.

Tollemache, Talmadge, Talmage, Tammadge, Tallemach, Tallmadge.—? Local. I can offer no satisfactory solution of this surname. The county of Suffolk seems to have been its original home.

William Talemasche, 7 Hen. II : Pipe Roll, iv. 4.
Hugo Talemasch, alias Talmach, co. Saff., 1273. A.
Alice Talemache, co. Camb., ibid.
Peter Talemache, co. Oxf., ibid.
Hugo Talemache, co. Norf., Hen. III–Edw. I. K.
William Talemache, co. Hants, ibid.
1568. Buried—Fraunces Talmach : St. Peter, Cornhill, i. 119.
London, 0, 2, 1, 2, 2, 0 ; (Tallmadge), Boston, 1 ; (Tollemache), Crockford, 5 ; Philadelphia, 0, 0, 8, 0, 0, 2.

Toller, Toler. — Offic. 'the toller,' a toll-taker by road or in market ; v. Toleman.

'Taillours and tynkers
And tollers in markettes.'
    Piers Plowman, Prologue, 438–9.
'Tollers' office it is ill,
For they take toll oft against skill,'
i.e. often contrary to reason (v. Halliwell).

Ralph le Toller. B.
Bartholomew le Toller, c. 1300. M.
John le Toller, 28 Edw. I : Freemen of York, i. 8.
Willelmus Toller, 1379 : P. T. Yorks. p. 273.
Robertus Toller, 1379 : ibid. p. 272.
1602. Married — Francis Toler and Bridgitt Rafton : St. Jas. Clerkenwell, i. 26.
1761. — Samuel Toller and Eliz. Haggett : St. Geo. Han. Sq. i. 107.
London, 2, 1 ; Philadelphia, 2, 0.

Tolley, Tolly.—Bapt. 'the son of Bartholomew,' from the nick. Tholy. The following seems to prove a diminutive existed :

'Godus Tholyn-wyf,' i.e. Godus, the wife of Tholyn, 1379 : P T. Yorks. p. 21.

Toly Museye, co. Linc., 1273. A.
Douce Toly, co. Camb., ibid.
Tholy Oldcorn, co. Camb., ibid.
Stephen Toli, co. Camb., ibid.
Johanna fil. Tholy, 39 Hen. III : BBB, p. 65.
William fil. Tholy. E.
William, the son of Tole : English Gilds, p. 150.
1795. Married — William Jude and Mary Tolley : St. Geo. Han. Sq. ii. 127.
London, 10, 1 ; Oxford, 8, 0 ; Philadelphia, 7, 0.

Tollman, Tolman. — Occup. 'the toll-man' ; v. Toleman.

Tolmin, Tolming, Toulmin.—Bapt. 'the son of Thomas,' a curious inversion of Tomlin. I have no absolute proof of this, but I cannot doubt it. If I am wrong, then these names are variants of Toleman, q.v. In Furness and the neighbouring districts, where Tomlin and Tomlinson (now often Townson, q.v.) were very familiar, we find Tolming settled for generations.

John Tolmin, of Bolton juxta Arenas, 1641 : Lancashire Wills at Richmond, i. 280.
Richard Towlmyn, of Bolton-by-the-Sands, 1607 : ibid.
Ellen Tolman, of Bolton-le-Sands, 1699 : ibid. ii. 285.
Thomas Tolming, of Bolton Holms, parish of Bolton, 1728 : ibid.
London, 0, 0, 5 ; Liverpool, 0, 0, 3 ; Boston (U.S.), 0, 0, 1.

Tolson, Toulson, Towlson, Towlsion.—(1) Bapt. 'the son of Thomas.' Odd as it may seem, these are but corruptions of Tomlinson, and in the Lake District and other parts of North England they have gone through the stages of Towlinson and Townson to Towlson. Townson (q.v.) is the popular modern form.

1551. John Towlyngson, of the parish of Mellynge : Lancashire Wills at Richmond, i. 285.
1587. Richard Towlson, or Tounsoun, of Dalton : ibid.
1672. George Toulson, of Poulton : ibid. p. 283.
1673. George Towlnson, of Pilling : ibid.

That this is the true derivation there cannot be the shadow of a doubt.

1650. Married — Christopher Oxnard and Faith Toulson : St. Dionis Backchurch, p. 26.
1713. — John Tolson and Barbara Wanley : St. Michael, Cornhill, p. 57.

Manchester, 0, 3, 0, 0 ; West Rid. Court Dir., 8, 0, 0, 0 ; London, 2, 1, 0, 0 ; Sheffield, 0, 0, 2, 0 ; Leeds, 1, 2, 0, 0 ; Boston (U.S.), 0, 0, 0, 1.

Tom.—Bapt. 'the son of Thomas,' from the nick. Tom ; v. Toms.

MDB. (co. Cornwall), 8 ; Philadelphia, 1 ; Boston (U.S.), 1.

Tomalin.—Bapt. ; v. Tomlin, of which it is a corruption ; cf. Ottaway for Ottway, Greenaway for Greenway, Hathaway for Hathway.

London, 4.

Tombleson.—Bapt. 'the son of Thomas,' a corruption of Tomblinson ; v. Tomblin.

MDB. (co. Camb.), 1 ; (co. Norfolk), 1 ; London, 1.

Tomblin, Tomblinson. — Bapt. 'the son of Thomas,' from the nick. Tom, dim. Tom-lin, with usual excrescent b after m ; cf. Timbs and Tombs, and v. Tomlin. The two following names are contained in the list of high sheriffs of Rutland :

1756. Robert Tomblin, of Edithweston, Esq. : Notes and Queries, 1886, Sept. 18, p. 224.
1796. Robert Tomlin, of Edithweston, Esq. : ibid.
1666. Bapt. — Robert, son of John Tomberlin : St. Jas. Clerkenwell, i. 230.
Cf. Thomas Tomblinson, of Kirkham, 1708 : Lancashire Wills at Richmond, p. 256.
1664. Buried — John Tomblans (Tomlins), servant to one Bateman, taylor : St. Michael, Cornhill, p. 253.
1706. Married — Peter Tombling and Frances Godden : Canterbury Cath., p. 68.
Crockford, 1, 0 ; Philadelphia, 0, 1.

Tombs, Toombs.—Bapt. 'the son of Thomas,' from the nick. Tom, patr. Toms, with intrusive b after m ; cf. Tomblin.

1632. Roger Newcourt and Alice Tomes : Marriage Lic. (Faculty Office), p. 19.
1683. Married — Edward Tomes and Dorothy Collier : St. Jas. Clerkenwell, i. 194.
1701. — Thomas Tombes and Mary Broffe : ibid. p. 223.
1702. — Abraham Russell and Rebeccah Tombs : St. Michael, Cornhill, p. 52.
London, 4, 1 ; MDB. (co. Hereford), 4, 0 ; Oxford, 6, 1 ; Boston (U.S.), 6, 2.

Tomes ; v. Toms, of which it is a variant. Cf. Times, a variant of Tims or Timms ; v. Timm.

Tomkin, Tomkins, Tomkinson, Tomkies.—Bapt. 'the son of Thomas,' from the nick. Thom, by-and-by reduced to Tom, dim. Tom-kin (v. *kin*, Introd. p. 25). Tomkies, of course, is a corruption of Tomkins, as Perkiss or Purkiss is of Perkins.

Robertus Thomkyn, 1379: P. T. Yorks. p. 221.
1586. Married — John Tomkyns and Joane Freeman: St. Jas. Clerkenwell, i. 12.
1621. — John Tomkins and Margery Hill: ibid. p. 49.
1632. — William Tomkin and Mary Trapps: ibid. p. 63.
1738. — William Bacon and Martha Tomkinson: ibid. p. 266.
London, 1, 26, 3, 2; Boston (U.S.), 0, 1, 3, 0.

Tomlin, Tomlins, Tomlinson, Tomlyn.—Bapt. 'the son of Thomas,' from the nick. Tom, and dim. Tom-lin; v. Thomlinson.

John Tomelyn: co. Soms., 1 Edw. III: Kirby's Quest, p. 129.
John Thomelyn, co. Soms., 1 Edw. III: ibid. p. 191.
Robert Thomelynsone: Pardons Roll, 16 Ric. II.
Henricus Thomlynson, 1379: P. T. Yorks. p. 172.
Alicia Tomlyn-wyff, 1379: P. T. Howdenshire, p. 30.
Recardus Tomlynson, 1379: ibid.
Matilda Tomelyn-doghter, 1379: P. T. Yorks. p. 12.
1752. Married — Alex. Tomlyn and Ann Knight: St. Geo. Chap. Mayfair, p. 219.
1763. — Thomas Tomlins and Eliz. Blake: St. Geo. Han. Sq. i. 121.
London, 13, 3, 25, 1; Philadelphia, 30, 0, 84, 0.

Tompkin, Tompkins.—Bapt. 'the son of Thomas,' from the nick. Tom, and dim. Tom-kin. The *p* is intrusive, as in Thompson; cf. Wilkin, Watkin, Simpkin, &c. v. Tomkin.

1566. Richard Tompkyn and Margaret Stevens: Marriage Lic. (London), i. 33.
1580. John Tompkyns and Ellen Stanner: ibid. p. 98.
London, 2, 12; Philadelphia, 0, 35.

Tompsett; v. Thomasset.

Tompson.—Bapt. 'the son of Thomas,' from the nick. Tom. The *p* is intrusive, as in Tompkins, Simpkins, &c.; v. Thomson.

1552. Married — Rycharde Glascock and Hellen Tompson: St. Michael, Cornhill, p. 6.
1574. John Tompson and Emma Frenche, *widow*: Marriage Lic. (London), i. 61.
1744. Married — John Tompson and Laetitia Bliss: St. Geo. Chap. Mayfair, p. 40.
London, 6; Boston (U.S.), 4.

Toms, Tomes, Tomson. — Bapt. 'the son of Thomas,' from the nick. Tom; v. Thom and Tombs.

1736. Buried — Rachiel Toms: St. Antholin (London), p. 209.
1746. Married — Robert Peverel and Mary Toms: St. Geo. Chap. Mayfair, p. 73.
1749. — Clifton Tomson and Anne Hoggor: ibid. p. 139.
1768. — Richard Tomes and Mary Bingham: St. Geo. Han. Sq. i. 176.
London, 2, 19, 1; Philadelphia, 11, 4, 9.

Tomsett; v. Thomasset.

Tong, Tonge, Tongue. — Local, 'of Tonge' or Tong, parishes in cos. Salop, Kent, Lancaster (2), and W. Rid. York. Tongue, of course, is merely imitative. Probably all these places are so termed from the shape of the land (like a tongue). M.E. *tonge* or *tunge*, a tongue. Of Tong in co. Salop it is said, 'The river Werf commences from the union of two brooks at the western extremity of the parish' (Lewis's Topographical Dictionary of England, iv. 357). The tongue of land in this case might lie between the two streams.

John de Tonghe, co. Salop, 1273. A.
Nicholas Tonge, co. Bucks, ibid.
Simon de Tonge, co. Kent, ibid.
Roger Tunge, co. York, ibid.
Willelmus de Tonge, 1379: P. T. Yorks. p. 186.

The township of Tongue is mentioned on the same page.

Peter Tonge, of Chester, *shoemaker*, 1572: Wills at Chester (1543–1620), p. 193.
William Tonge, of Farnworth, co. Lanc., 1583: ibid.
1659–60. Married—Charles Tonge and Mary Hancocke: St. Dionis Backchurch, p. 35.
1770. — John Tongue and Eliz. Griffiths: St. Geo. Han. Sq. i. 204.
London, 1, 1, 2; West Rid. Court Dir., 1, 2, 2; Manchester, 1, 6, 1; Philadelphia, 6, 1, 6.

Tonkinson, Tonkins, Tonks, Tunks, Tonkin, Tonkyn. — (1) Bapt. 'the son of Antony,' from the nick. Tony, and with dim. suffix Ton-kin. *Kins* becomes *ks*; cf. Perks from Perkins, Dawks from Dawkins, &c. (The order of corruption is Perkins, Perkiss, Perkes, Perks.) (2) Bapt. A corruption of Tomkinson and Tomkins; cf. Sinkinson and Sinkins for Simkinson and Simkins.

1569. Bapt. — The daughter of James Tonkinson: St. Antholin (London), p. 20.
1603. Buried—Thomas Tunckes: ibid. p. 151.
1789. Married—John Tonks and Mary Bardwell: St. Geo. Han. Sq. ii. 18.
London, 2, 0, 0, 2, 0, 0; MDB. (co. Cornwall), 0, 0, 0, 0, 8, 2; Philadelphia, 0, 0, 0, 0, 2, 0.

Tonson.—Bapt. (1) 'the son of Anthony,' from the nick. Tony; (2) a corruption of Tomson, v. Toms.

London, 1; New York, 1.

Toogood; v. Thurgood.

Took, Tooke; v. Tuck.

Tooker.—Occup. 'the tucker,' q.v. The Somersetshire form was almost invariably Touker.

Alex. le Toukere, co. Soms., 1 Edw. III: Kirby's Quest, p. 218.
Matilda Toukere, co. Soms., 1 Edw. III: ibid. p. 252.
MDB. (co. Soms.), 1; New York, 24.

Tookey.—Bapt.; v. Tuckey.

Tooley. — Bapt. 'the son of Toly,' probably a nick. of the immense favourite Bartholomew. Lower writes, ' Tooley, a crasis of St. Olave. Tooley Street in Southwark is so called from its proximity to the church of St. Olave.' This is true enough so far as the street is concerned, but it is no help to the elucidation of the surname, which probably existed before Tooley Street was dreamt of. The absence of all prefixes in early registers seems to prove a baptismal origin; v. Tolley. In some instances Tooley may be local; cf.

Richard Tulegh, co. Soms., 1 Edw. III: Kirby's Quest, p. 133.

Tooley is a hamlet in the parish of Peckleton, co. Leic.

Robert Toly, co. Camb., 1273. A.
William Toly, co. Essex, ibid.
William Toll, co. Oxf., ibid.
John Toly, co. Soms., 1 Edw. III:
Kirby's Quest, p. 92.
1631. Married — David Toolye and
Jane Bayle : St. Michael, Cornhill, p. 26.
1649-50. — Edmund Tooley and
Martha Harford : St. Dionis Backchurch,
p. 26.
London, 7 ; Philadelphia, 1.

Toombs ; v. Tombs.

Toomer. — (1) ? Occup. 'the
toomer' (?). 'Toom, to take wool
off the cards' (Halliwell). (2)
? Local, 'of St. Omer' (?).
William de St. Omero, co. Wilts, 1273.
A.
Petronilla de St. Omero, co. Camb.,
ibid.
A common entry in the Hun-
dred Rolls ; probably this is the
origin :
Richard de Tomere, co. Soms., 1 Edw.
III : Kirby's Quest, p. 218.
Thomas de Thomere, co. Soms., 1 Edw.
III : ibid.
These are strongly in favour of
the St. Omer theory.
1608. Married — Tobias Humber and
Sarah Toomer : St. Jas. Clerkenwell,
i. 219.
London, 6.

Toon, Toone ; v. Town.

Toop, Topp, Toope.—? Local.
I dare not hazard a guess at
the derivation of this name. Probably Mr. Lower is right in supposing it to be 'at the top,' from
residence on some summit of a
small hill, corresponding with
Bottom, from residence in some
hollow.
Robert Top, co. Soms., 1 Edw. III :
Kirby's Quest, p. 123.
William Toppe, co. Soms., 1 Edw. III :
ibid. p. 281.
1606-7. Henry Topp, co. Dorset :
Reg. Univ. Oxf. vol. ii. pt. ii. p. 294.
1612. John Toppe, co. Wilts: ibid. p.328.
1580. Bapt.—John Tooppe : Reg. Stourton, Wilts, p. 2.
1639. — David, s. Robert Toope : ibid.
p. 9.
Found also as Top in the same
register.
1669. Married — Edward Top and
Ann Lavington : St. Jas. Clerkenwell, iii.
167.
London, 5, 2, 0 ; New York, 0, 3, 2.

Tootal, Tootle. — Local ; v.
Toothill. It is related of a Mr.

Tootle, who went rather late to
an evening party with wife and
daughters, that much tittering was
caused by the flunkey's loud an-
nouncement of 'Mr. Tootle, Mrs.
Tootle, and the Misses Tootle, too!'
London, 1, 2 ; New York, 0, 2.

Tooth. — ?——. Lower says,
'This name probably has reference
to some peculiarity in the teeth of
the original bearer' (Patr. Brit.
p. 350). Certainly there is some
foundation for this. M.E. toth,
a tooth.
Thomas Toth, co. Northampton, 1273.
A.
William Tothe, rector of Outwell, co.
Norf., 1334 : FF. vii. 474.
Richard Tooth, co. Norf., 40 Edw. III:
ibid. p. 504.
1765. Married—Seth Tooth and Mary
Beck : St. Geo. Han. Sq. i. 142.
London, 1 ; Crockford, 4 ; New York, 1.

Toothacher, Toothaker. —
Local, 'German Todtenacker, field
of the dead, a burying ground ;
analogous to our indigenous name
Churchyard' (Lower, Patr. Brit.
p. 350).
Richard Toothaker, 1641 : St. Jas.
Clerkenwell, p. 150.
Nicholas Toothaker, 1642 : ibid. p. 154.
1675. Married — Thomas Goldington
and Margarett Toothacre : St. Michael,
Cornhill, p. 41.
1774. — William Salter and Isabella
Toothaker : St. Geo. Han. Sq. i. 242.
Philadelphia, 0, 2 ; Boston (U.S.), 0, 3.

**Toothill, Tootle, Tothill,
Toatal, Tottle, Tootell, Tootill,
Tuthill, Tuttle, Toutill.**—Local,
'of Totehill,' i.e. the look-out hill.
Many spots are so called in all
parts of England. A hill with
a good outlook against an enemy's
approach. There are two Tottle
Banks in the old parish of Ulverston,
each with a good outlook. 'Tote-
hyll, montaignette' : Palsgrave.
'A tote-hill is an eminence from
whence there is a good outlook':
Ches. Archaeol. xix. 37.
'Item, the same daye paied for a great
bote ... to wayte upon the Kinges grace
fro Yorke place to Brydewell, and fro
thence to Totehill,' 1531 : Privy Purse
Expenses, Hen. VIII, p. 118.

'Totehylle, specula' : Prompt.
Parv. 'Totehylle, or hey place of
lokynge' : ibid. In Way's notes

thereon he quotes Wyclif's
translation of 2 Kings v. 7 : 'For-
sothe David toke the tote hil Syon,
that is, the citee of David.' For
various instances of the word, v.
Way's note. We still use the
verb to 'tout' or 'toot,' spy about,
and the substantive 'touter' ; v.
Skeat on tout.
'On Tootle Height, in the township of
Dilworth (Ribchester), there is a valuable
stone quarry' : Baines' Lanc. ii. 111.
'Near the Forest Chapel is a small
quadrangular Roman camp, situate on
a hill called Toot-hill' : Earwaker's
East Ches. ii. 437, Macclesfield Forest
Township.
The Romans had used the hill
for the same purpose seemingly.
Custance Totel, co. Camb., 1273. A.
Roger Tothull, co. Oxf., ibid.
Johannes de Totehill, 1379 : P. T. Yorks.
p. 66.
Willelmus de Totehill, 1379 : ibid.
p. 64.
Johannes de Tutill, 1379 : ibid. p. 189.
Agnes fil. Thome de Totehil, 1379 : ibid.
p. 61.
John de Totehill, 1379 : ibid. p. xiv.
Alice Tootell, of Bardsea, 1693 : Lan-
cashire Wills at Richmond, p. 257.
William Tootle, of Atherton, 1587 :
Wills at Chester, p. 193.
Manchester, 1, 0, 0, 1, 0, 6, 1, 0, 0, 0 ;
West Rid. Court Dir., 3, 0, 0, 4, 0, 0, 0,
0, 0, 2 ; London, 0, 2, 3, 1, 1, 0, 0, 0, 2,
0 ; MDB. (co. Norfolk), (Tuthill), 2 ;
(Tuttle), 2 ; New York, 1, 2, 0, 0, 0, 0, 0,
18, 39, 0.

Toovey, Tovey. — (1) Bapt.
'the son of Tofig' or Tovi.
Tofig the Proud was Harold's fore-
runner in the foundation of
Waltham. He appears in Florence
as 'Danicus et praepotens vir
Tovius, Pruda cognomento.' He
signs himself in 1033 as 'Tovi
Pruda.' His surname was needed
to distinguish him from two name-
sakes : 'Tovi hwita' and 'Tovi
reada' (Freeman, Hist. Norm.
Conq. i. 769). The name is found
in Domesday as Tovi or Tovius.
The personal name lingered on
long enough to become hereditary
as a surname. (2) Local (?).
Evidently a Norman surname.
Berenger de Tovi, co. Linc., Hen. III-
Edw. I. K.
1583. William Tovye, co. Wilts : Reg.
Univ. Oxf. vol. ii. pt. ii. p. 131.
1771. Married — Samuel Toovey and
Mary Torr : St. Geo. Han. Sq. i. 213.
London, 6, 5 ; Crockford, 2, 6.

Toplady, Tiplady.—? Local. Tiplady seems the original form. It is almost certain that the parentage of this surname must be sought for in co. Yorks.

John Typlady, co. York, 1477. W. ii. 1664. Bapt.—Sarah, d. of Robert Toplady, *gent* : St. Jas. Clerkenwell.
Benjamin Tiplady, 1691 : St. Peter, Cornhill, ii. 59.
Hull, o, 2 ; West Rid. Court Dir., o, 1; London, o, 2 ; Philadelphia, o, 2.

Topliff.—Local, 'of Topcliffe,' a parish in N. Rid. Yorks, near Thirsk ; cf. Cunliffe for Cuncliff.

Alan de Topclyf, co. Linc., 1273. A.
Richard de Toppeclyve, vicar of Greatham, 1308 : DDJ. iii. 140.
Alicia Topcliffe, 1379 : P. T. Howdenshire, p. 27.
Boston (U.S.), 3.

Topp ; v. Toop.

Toppin, Topping. — Bapt. ; variants of Turpin, q.v.

Topple.—(1 Bapt. 'the son of Theobald' ; v Tebbitt (1). The corruptions of Theobald are almost astounding. (2) Local. The instance below, however, seems to point to a local derivation.

1763. Married — Philip Tophill and Ann Smith : St. Geo. Han. Sq. i. 126. London, 3.

Tordoff. — Bapt. 'the son of Thjodulf' (v. Yonge. ii. 338). This name has ramified somewhat strongly in Yorkshire.

Simon Thudolf, co. Oxf., 1273. A.
Geoffrey Thedolf, co. Bucks, ibid.
London, 1 ; Allerton, Yorks, 1; Liversedge, Yorks, 2 ; North Bierley, Yorks, 6.

Torkington, Talkington, Turkington —Local, 'of Torkington,' a township in the parish of Stockport, a surname familiar to South Lanc. and the Cheshire border.

Simon de Torkinton, 1225 : East Ches. ii. 105.
Robert de Torkinton, 1225 : ibid.
Thomas de Torkinton, 1357 : ibid. 106.
1605. Buried — Alexander Torkinton, of Stockport : Reg. Parish Church, Stockport.
1617. — Ales Torkinton : Reg. Prestbury, Ches., p. 218.
1774. Married — Peter Lefargue and Eliz. Torkington : St. Geo. Han. Sq. i. 244.
Manchester, 3, 1, o ; London, 1, o, o ; Philadelphia, 3, o, 9.

Torpin. — Bapt. ; v. Turpin, a variant.

Philadelphia, 1.

Torr, Torre.—Local, (1) 'of the tower.' O.F. *tur*, later *tour*, 'a tower' (Skeat). (2) 'Of the Torr.' Gaelic *torr*, a hill or mound, specially one of conical form.

Hugh de la Tour. B.
Henry atte Torre. T.
John de la Torre, 31 Edw. I : BBB. p. 645.
Hugh atte Torre, co. Soms., 1 Edw. III : Kirby's Quest, p. 152.
Edith atte Torre, co. Soms., 1 Edw. III : ibid. p. 155.
1804. Married — James Torre and Rosellen Eliza Whitwell : St. Geo. Han. Sq. ii. 316.
London, 6, 2 ; Philadelphia, 9, o.

Torrance, Torrence, Torrens. — ?——. I can supply no satisfactory information in regard to this well-established surname.

1750. Married — John Torrence and Mary Cheldrey : St. Geo. Chap. Mayfair, p. 184.
1769. — George Torrans and Fanny Wilkinson : St. Geo. Han. Sq. i. 191.
1804. — William Manners and Ann Torrance : ibid. ii. 303.
London, 2, o, o ; Philadelphia, 2, 9, 11.

Tortoiseshell. — Local. An imitative corruption of Tattersall, found in Manchester Directory in 1861 and onwards (v. Tattersall).

Tosland ; v. Tozeland.

Tothill.—Local ; v. Toothill.

Totiller.—Nick. 'the totiller,' the whisperer ; *tittle*, *tattle*, and *tottle* seem all to have been in use. A totiller was a whisperer of secrets, an idle and rather mischievous chatterbox. v. Tatler.

'For in your court is many a losengeour,
And many a queinte totoler accusour.'
  Chaucer, Legend of Good Women, l. 353.

'Totelare, *susurro*. Totelynge, susurrium. Totelon Talys, totylyn tale in onys ere, *susurro*' (Prompt. Parv. p. 498). The form *tittler* (*titelere*) was also in use. Has the child's game, 'Tom Tiddler's ground,' any connexion ?

Richard le Titteler, co. Suff., 1273. A.
Simon le Tuteler, co. Suff., ibid.
John Totiller. H.
1766. Married—John Tattler and Anna Maria Norgrave : St. Geo. Han. Sq. i. 150.

Totman, Tottenham.—Local; v. Tottman.

Crockford, o, 4.

Tottie, Totty.—Bapt. 'the son of Otto.' But possibly the Danish Thjod (v. Yonge, ii. 338). But far more probably the nick. of Otty or Oddy (q.v.), one of the most popular names of the time. Several Yorkshire font-names took an initial T as their nick. before a vowel; cf. Tagg and Taggy for Agg and Aggy. Nevertheless, the instance recorded below, Robertus Thotte, looks very like the Danish Thjod.

Beatrix Totty, 1379 : P. T. Yorks. p. 200.
Willelmus Totty, 1379 : ibid.

The following pair are registered together :

Johannes Totty, 1379 : P. T. Yorks. p. 215.
Robertus Thotte, 1379 : ibid.
Robert Totty, co. York, 1519. W. ii, p. 194.
1577. George Tottie and Eliz. Periman, *widow* : Marriage Lic. (London), i. 77.
1789. Married—John Byrne and Mary Tottey : St. Geo. Han. Sq. ii. 25.
West Rid. Court Dir., 1, o ; London, 1, o ; Barnsley, o, 1 ; Boston (U.S.), o, 2.

Tottman, Totman. — Local. 'of Tottenham,' a parish in Middlesex, a corruption ; cf. Deadman, Buckman, Putman, Swetman, &c. This corruption is one of a large class.

In 1632 John Totman was shipped to New England : v. Hotten's Lists of Emigrants, p. 150.

Probably he was the ancestor of the Boston Totmans.

1568. William Moulde and Susanna Totnam : Marriage Lic. (London), i. 39.
1753. Married—Thomas Tattnem and Ann Fat : St. Geo. Chap. Mayfair, p. 243.
1796. — John Tottenham and Mary Eaton : St. Geo. Han. Sq. ii. 155.
London, 1, o ; Boston (U.S.), o, 12.

Touchprick. — Nick. 'a hot rider,' one who spurred his horse.

Robertus Touchepryk, et Alicia uxor ejus, 1379 : P. T. Howdenshire, p. 4.

Toulmin. — Bapt. 'the son of Thomas,' a corruption of Tomlin (q.v.). No connexion, as I take it, with Tollman, a tax-gatherer (v. Toleman). The fact is that Toulmin is a North Lancashire surname, where Tomlinson and Tomlin were almost a clan (v. Townson, Towerson, &c.). Toulmin simply reverses the two letters *m* and *l* (cf. Grundy for Gundry, and v. Broderick).

1607. Richard Towlmyn, of Bolton-le-Sands : Lancashire Wills at Richmond, i. 285.
1623. Richard Towlmyne, of Boulton-by-the-Sands : ibid.
1650. Robert Toulmin, of Bolton-le-Sands : ibid. p. 283.
1664. Edmund Touleming, of Harlocks, Bolton-le-Sands : ibid.
1804. Married — Joseph Toulmin and Maria Sampson : St. Geo. Han. Sq. ii. 301.

Whether I be right or wrong in my solution, one thing is certain, the derivation must be sought for in North Lancashire.

London, 5 ; Preston, 7 ; Boston (U.S.), 1.

Toulson ; v. Tolson.

Tournay.—Local ; v. Turney.

Tout. — ? Nick. ' the stout,' a modification of *tort*. ' *Tort*, large, fat. Co. Glouc.' (Halliwell). It will be observed that my first instance is from Sómerset, and that Tout is unquestionably a Western counties surname.

Robert le Tort, co. Soms., 1 Edw. III : Kirby's Quest, p. 156.
Laurence le Tort, co. Soms., 1 Edw. III : ibid. p. 245.
London, 5 ; MDB. (co. Soms.), 5 ; Philadelphia, 3.

Tovey ; v. Toovey.

Tower. — (1) Local, ' of the tower ' ; v. Torr.

John de la Tour de Shrowesbury, C. R., 21 Edw. III. pt. i.

(2) Occup. ' the tower,' i. e. tawyer, a dresser of skins. To tew, to taw, and to tow seem all to be forms of one verb, and to signify the same thing, viz. to work or operate upon an article ; v. Tewer, Tawer, and Whittear. Also v. *tow* (2) in Skeat's Dictionary.

Gilbert le Tower, 1273. A.
Thomas le Toure, ibid.
Juliana la Touestre, ibid.
London, 2 ; Boston (U.S.), 62.

Towerson.—Bapt. ' the son of Thomas,' one of endless corruptions

of Tomlinson (v. Tolson and Townson). The stages of corruption were first Towlnson, then Towenson, then Towerson ; cf. Catterson for Cattinson, or Patterson for Pattinson.

1559. Married—William Towreson and Margery Hawes : St. Michael, Cornhill, p. 7.
1590. Agnes Towenson, of Kirkby Ireleth ; Lancashire Wills at Richmond, i. 283.
1591. John Toweson, of Channon-house, in Pennington : ibid. p. 285.
1635. Thomas Towenson, or Tomlinson, of Channon-house, Pennington : ibid. p. 283.
1616. William Towerson, co. Hunts : Reg. Univ. Oxf. vol. ii. pt. ii. p. 352.
1681. Married—John Poole and Mary Towerson : St. Jas. Clerkenwell, i. 193.
MDB. (co. Cumb.), 3.

Towgood. — Bapt. ; v. Thurgood.

Towler.—Occup. ; v. Toller, of which it is a variant ; cf. Coulson for Colson or Coulthurst for Colthurst.

Thomas Towler, co. York. W. 16.
1595. Edward Towler (co. Herts) and Mary Howe : Marriage Lic. (London), i. 221.
1788. Married—Thomas Quinney and Ann Towler : St. Geo. Han. Sq. ii. 10.
— — Thomas Drewett and Mary Towlear : ibid. p. 12.
London, 3 ; Rathmell, near Settle, Yorks, 2 ; Boston (U.S.), 3.

Towlson ; v. Tolson.

Town, Towne, Toon, Toone.—Local, ' of the town,' from residence therein ; originally an enclosure, a farmstead, a farm with all its outbuildings. Lowland Scotch *toon* ; v. Skeat's Dict.

Geoffrey de la Tune, co. Sussex, 1273. A.
Robert de Tune, co. Norf., ibid.
Ralph de la Tune. B.
Thomas atte Toune, co. Soms., 1 Edw. III : Kirby's Quest, p. 105.
1602. Thurstan Toone, co. Leic. : Reg. Univ. Oxf. vol. ii. pt. ii. p. 260.
1793. Married — William Green and Ann Towne : St. Geo. Han. Sq. ii. 102.
1801. — Thomas Mockett and Anna Town : ibid. p. 232.
London, 4, 5, 3, 1 ; Philadelphia, 20, 3, 4, 1.

Towndrow, Townroe, Townrow.—Local, ' at the town-row,' the one continuous line of town or farm buildings. Many places would bear this name ; cf. Town-

end and Townsend. The *d* is, of course, intrusive ; cf. *riband, gownd,* &c. ' Town-raw is used to denote the privileges of a township. To "thraw one's self out o' a town-raw," to forfeit the privileges enjoyed in a small community. Roxb. ; *q.* a row of houses ' (Jamieson's Dict.). For the suffix, v. Row (2).

Richard Mercer, of Townrowe, in West Derby (Liverpool), 1628 : Wills at Chester (1621–50), p. 152.
Henry Townerow, or Townroe, 1557 : Reg. Univ. Oxf. i. 234.
1562. Thomas Townraye : ibid. vol. ii. pt. ii. p. 7.
1615. Bapt.—John, s. William Townerawe : St. Michael, Cornhill, p. 111.
London, 3, 0, 0 ; Sheffield, 4, 4, 0 ; Manchester, 0, 0, 1.

Townend ; v. Townsend.

Towner.—Occup. ' the towner,' probably equivalent to Farmer, one who kept or laboured on a town or farm ; v. Townman and Town. A well-known auctioneer in Eastbourne bears this name.

1786. Married — Robert Towner and Eliz. Wordsworth : St. Geo. Han. Sq. i. 390.
1806. — Thomas Towner and Ann Pinock : ibid. ii. 356.
Eastbourne (Sussex), 1 ; Boston (U.S.), 2.

Townherd, Tunnard. — Occup. ' the town-herd,' i. e. the man who guarded the town cattle ; v. Town and Herd, and cf. Coward (Cowherd), Calvert (Calveherd), &c. Lower says, ' Tunnard, an ancient Lincolnshire family. In 1333 the name occurs as Tonnehyrd, and in 1381 as Tunherd. . . . The name may signify the "town-herd," one to whom was entrusted the care of the common herd of a town or village, a well-known office in the Middle Ages ' (Patr. Brit. p. 358).

Augustin Tunherd, co. Camb., 1273. A.
Adam Tonhurde, co. Soms., 1 Edw. III : Kirby's Quest, p. 96.

Townley.—Local, ' of Townley,' an ancient manor in Habergham Eaves, Burnley, co. Lanc. The place gave rise to a family of distinction in very early times. Richard de Townley was sheriff of Lancashire, 1376–1379. The surname is now scattered over the county, either through younger branches of the representative family or humbler stocks. Townley is simply a reversal of the syllables in Layton, or Leyton, or Leighton. Townley emphasizes the relation of the meadow to the farm, the others the relation of the farm to the meadow. Townley means the farm - meadow, the others the meadow-farm. v. Town and Ley.

Cecilia de Tonley, 1330: v. Baines' Hist. Lanc. ii. 36.
Johannes de Townlay, 1379: P. T. Yorks. p. 284.
1588. Bernard Townley, co. Lanc.: Reg. Univ. Oxf. vol. ii. pt. ii. p. 166.
1618. Zouch Townley, co. Lanc.: ibid. p. 373.
London, 6; Manchester, 12; Philadelphia, 5.

Townman. — Occup. 'the townman,' a labourer in or occupier of a town; v. Town.

John Tuneman, co. Bedf., 1273. A.
Ralph Tuneman, co. Bedf., ibid.
John Tounman, co. Soms., 1 Edw. III: Kirby's Quest, p. 96.
1598. Richard Tunman, of Dalton-in-Furness: Lancashire Wills at Richmond, i. 288.
1672. Robert Tunman, of Ireleth-in-Furness: ibid.

I fear the name is extinct, but, of course, cannot be positive.

Townroe, -row; v. Towndrow.

Townsend,   Townshend, Townend.—Local, 'at the town-end' or town's-end, from residence thereby. The *h* in Townshend was an early intrusion. Bridge-end, Pounds-end, Greaves-end, Woods-end, Streets-end, and Wick-end are all found with the same intrusive *h* in mediaeval registers (v. my English Surnames, 3rd edit., p. 114, for a long list). 'At the town-end' is still a familiar phrase in the North of England.

Geoffrey de le Tuneshende, co. Norf., 1273. A.
Henry atte Tunesende, co. Oxf., ibid.
Alice atte Tunishende, co. Bucks, ibid.
Richard de la Tuneshend, Close Roll, 2 Edw. I.
Ricardus atte ye Thounhende, 1379: P. T. Yorks. p. 171.
Johannes atte Tonehende, 1379: ibid. p. 134.
1628. Married — Thomas Townesend

and Anne Bradeshawe: St. Dionis Back-church, p. 22.
1760. Married — Thomas Townshend, Esq., and Elizabeth Powys: St. Geo. Han. Sq. i. 94.
London, 46, 3, 11; West Rid. Court Dir., 13, 0, 14; Philadelphia, 145, 1, 0.

Townson.—Bapt. 'the son of Thomas.' However odd this may seem to be, it is unmistakably true. Townson is a North Lancashire corruption of the great Furness surname Tomlinson through the stage Towenson. Of this there cannot be the shadow of a doubt. Even now Townson is pronounced Tone-son in the district.

1571. Edmund Tollenson, or Townson, of Catton: Lancashire Wills at Richmond, i. 280.
1587. Richard Towlson, or Tounsonn, of Dalton: ibid. p. 283.
1588. Jenet Towenson, or Tomlinson, of Ulverston: ibid.
1594. Thomas Toulnson, or Townson, of Gressingham: ibid.
1620. Thomas Tolnson, or Townson, of Catton: ibid. p. 280.
1635. Thomas Towenson, or Tomlinson, of Pennington: ibid. p. 283.
1683. Eliz. Toulnson, of Pilling: ibid. ii. 257.

The present form in Furness, where Tomlinson has predominated for centuries, is Townson; cf. Rawnson for Rawlinson in the same record, viz. Lanc. Wills at Richmond, i. 227.

1730. Married—William Townson and Mary Blackwell: St. Geo. Chap. Mayfair, p. 320.
London, 2; Crockford, 4; Ulverston, 2; Philadelphia, 1.

Towson. — Bapt. 'the son of Thomas,' an abbreviated form of Townson, q.v. This corruption is early found in North Lancashire, where Townson and Towson, &c., arose. Towson is thus but a modification of Towenson as that is of Tomlinson.

Cf. 1591. John Toweson, of Channonhouse, Pennington: Lancashire Wills at Richmond, i. 280.
1669. John Tomlinson, of Channonhouse, Pennington: ibid. p. 285.
1695. Richard Towson, of Priest Hutton: ibid. ii. 260.
1570. Roger Wildynge and Christian Towson: Marriage Lic. (London), i. 46.
1595. Bapt. — Alice, d. John Towson, or Tyson: St. Jas. Clerkenwell, i. 30.
Philadelphia, 2.

Towster.—Occup., a feminine form of Tower (2), q.v.

Juliana la Touestre, co. Oxf., 1273. A.

Toy, Toye.—? Bapt. 'the son of Toy' (?). This seems to be the only reasonable derivation. Further than that it is an old personal name I cannot go.

Warin Toy, co. Camb., 1273. A.
Wydo Toye, co. Suff., ibid.
Johannes Toye, 1379: P. T. Howdenshire, p. 6.
Willelmus Toye, 1379: ibid.
1600. Griffith Toy, co. Pembroke: Reg. Univ. Oxf. vol. ii. pt. ii. p. 244.
1748. Married — Thomas Toy and Anne Bird: St. Geo. Chap. Mayfair, p. 121.
London, 1, 6; Boston (U.S.), 10, 1.

Tozeland, Tosland. — Local, 'of Toseland,' a parish in co. Hunts, four miles from St. Neots.

1750. Married — Simon Tosland and Margaret Hill: St. Geo. Han. Sq. i. 44.
1780. — Samuel Towesland and Mary Toseland (sic): St. Geo. Han. Sq. p. 308.
London, 1, 1.

Tozer, Towzer, Tozar. — Occup. 'the tozer' or teaser (v. Tasseler), one who tosed or teased cloth, one who carded wool, or raised the nap on cloth.

'What schepe that is full of wulle
Upon his backe they tose and pulle.'
Gower's Confessio Amantis.

A recipe from an old Harleian MS. thus begins, 'Recipe brawne of capons, or of hennys, and dry them well, and towse them small.' 'Toze, the same as touse' (Halliwell). 'Touse, to tug or pull about' (ibid.). Hence 'dog Towzer.' 'Tosynge of wulle' (Prompt. Parv.). 'Tosare of wulle, *carptrix*' (ibid.).

Johannes Tesur, 1379: P. T. Yorks. p. 157.
John Toser, co. Norf. F.
1665-6. Thomas Sowersby and Mary Tozer: Marriage Alleg. (Canterbury), p. 113.
1748. Married — Samuel Touzer and Jane Town: St. Geo. Chap. Mayfair, p. 109.
London, 20, 0, 0; MDB. (co. Devon), 21, 0, 0.

Tracy, Tracey. — Local, 'of Traci-Boccage,' in the arrondissement of Caen. Settled in Barnstaple, co. Devon, the parishes, manors, &c., of Woolcombe-Tracy, Bovey-Tracy, Minet-Tracy, and

Bradford-Tracy bear witness to their local ascendency; v. Fuller's Worthies, i. 558.

Henry de Tracy, co. Devon, 1273. A.
Richard de Tracy, co. Devon, ibid.
William de Tracy, co. Sussex, ibid.
Henry Tracy, co. Soms., 1 Edw. III: Kirby's Quest, p. 145.
1597. Richard Tracy, co. Glouc.: Reg. Univ. Oxf. vol. ii. pt. ii. p. 223.
1601. Samuel Tracy, co. Glouc. : ibid. p. 253.
London, 10, 3; Boston (U.S.), 70, 0.

Trader.—Occup. 'the trader' (?). I find no early references to such a name, and am inclined to think it a corruption of Thredder, q.v.

London, 2; Philadelphia, 4.

Trafford, Traford. — Local, 'of Trafford,' a property in the suburbs of Manchester, whence the baronetage of 'de Trafford' gets its title.

Stephen de Trafford, co. Lanc., 20 Edw. I. R.
Henry de Trafford, co. Lanc., ibid.
1572. George Trafford, of Manchester, *gentleman*: Wills at Chester, i. 194.
1591. Henry Trafford, rector of Wilmslow: ibid.
1589. William Trafforde, co. Ches.: Reg. Univ. Oxf. vol. ii. pt. ii. p. 171.
1610. John Trafforde, co. Ches.: ibid. p. 317.
London, 3, 1; Oxford, 7, 0; Manchester, 2, 0; Philadelphia, 2, 0.

Tragetour.—Occupative, 'the tragetour,' a master of legerdemain, a juggler.

'Swiche as thise subtil tregetoures play.'
Chaucer, C. T. 11451.

My first instance seems to imply a misreading of the latter:

Richard le Tregheler: Kirby's Quest, p. 136.
Symon le Tregetor, co. Camb., 1273. A.
William le Tregetur, co. Camb., ibid.
Simon Tregetour, *webster*, 1379: P. T. Howdenshire, p. 4.

The last instance proves that the merely occupative title had settled down into an ordinary surname, but I fear it has not survived.

Trainer, Tranner; v. Trayner.

Tranter, Traunter.—Occup. 'the tranter,' i.e. a pedlar, a hawker. D. *tranten*, to walk slowly (Annandale). 'Tranter, a carrier. Various dialects' (Halliwell).

'And had some traunting chapman for his sire.' Bishop Hall, Satires.

Agnes Traunter: Churchwardens' Accounts, Ludlow, 1547 : Camden Soc.
Annes Tranter : ibid.
1622. Married—William Tranton and Martha Laine: St. Jas. Clerkenwell, i. 51.
1739. — John Pegg and Eliz. Traunter: St. Geo. Han. Sq. i. 22.
London, 4, 0; Derby, 4, 0; MDB. (co. Lanc.), 0, 1; Boston (U.S.), 1, 0; Philadelphia, 0, 1.

Trantom, Trantum; v. Trentham.

Trapnell.—Bapt. 'the son of Tropinel,' a West-country name, one of the many personal names ending in *-el*.

Walter Tropinel, co. Wilts, 1273. A.
Walter Tropinel, co. Norf., ibid.
John Tropenel, co. Soms., 1 Edw. III: Kirby's Quest, p. 99.
MDB. (co. Soms.), 1.

Trapp.—Local, 'de Trap.' I cannot discover the spot.

John Trappe, co. Hunts, 1273. A.
Richard Trappe, co. Hunts, ibid.
Hanelyn de Trap. H.
Elena Trap, co. Soms., 1 Edw. III: Kirby's Quest, p. 128.
1619. John Trappe, co. Worc.: Reg. Univ. Oxf. vol. ii. pt. ii. p. 376.
1702. Married—Benjamin Trapp and Ann Hale : St. Jas. Clerkenwell, i. 225.
London, 4; Philadelphia, 5.

Traverse, Travers, Travis, Traviss. — Local, Fr. 'de la traverse,' from residence beside a crossway, a point where roads met. Oddly enough, I have no early instance to show, but the origin is unmistakable. The full form Traverse is found at Rainhill, Liverpool. The intermediate stage between Traverse and Travis is seen in such an entry as this:

1640. Bapt. — Cordwell Traverse, son of Phillip Travesse : St. Dionis Backchurch (London).
Walter de Travers, 1219: KKK. vi. 117.
Hugh Travers, co. Linc., 1273. A.
Nigel Travers, co. Bucks, ibid.
Robertus Trauers, 1379: P. T. Yorks. p. 152.
1578. Ann Travis, or Travers, of Burtonwood: Wills at Chester, i. 194.
1614. James Travis, of Burtonwood: ibid.
1609. Elizabeth Travers, of Bold : ibid.
1614. Elizabeth Travis, of Bold, *widow*: ibid.

This is proof beyond question that Travis or Traviss is a corruption of Travers or Traverse.

London, 1, 9, 3, 0; Rainhill, 2, 0, 0, 0; Liverpool (Traviss), 1 ; Boston (U.S.), 0, 31, 13, 0.

Travis(s.—Local ; v. Traverse.

Trawin; v. Trown.

Trayner, Traynor, Trainor, Tranner, Trainer.—Occup. ' the trainer,' probably of horses ; v. Ambler. It seems very natural that this surname should be first found in Yorkshire.

Robertus Trainer, 1379: P. T. Yorks. p. 132.
1746. Married—Edward Trayner (co. Linc.) and Jane Webb: St. Geo. Han. Sq. i. 36.
1807. — Owen Traynor and Sarah Harvey: ibid. ii. 364.
London, 2, 1, 0, 0, 0; Hull, 0, 2, 1, 1, 0; Philadelphia, 0, 7, 53, 0, 34; Boston (U.S.), 0, 0, 5, 0, 33.

Treadhard.—Nick. 'a heavy-footed man' ; cf. Golightly and Lightfoot, q.v.

Symon Tredhard, 1379: P. T. Yorks. p. 141.

Treasure.—?——. O.E. *tresor*, treasure, a hoard. It is manifest that the Somersetshire Treasures are descended from Nicholas Tresor mentioned below. The only difficulty is to account for the sobriquet. Possibly it is a local surname meaning 'at the Treasure,' a treasurer, one in care of his lord's money-bags; v. Treasurer, Countinghouse, Chamberlain, &c.

Nicholas Tresor, co. Wilts, 1273. A.
1596. Edmund Tressur and Margaret Eastfield: Marriage Lic. (London), i. 232.
1803. Married — David Treasur and Janet Forfar : St. Geo. Han. Sq. ii. 274.
MDB. (Somerset), 4 ; London, 1.

Treasurer.—Offic. 'the treasurer.'

Gillam Treasorer, C. R., 1-2 Philip and Mary, pt. iv.
1643. Buried—Gilbert Treasurer, servant to Mr. Stile : St. Dionis Backchurch, p. 224.

Treble.—Bapt. (?). Probably a form of Theobald, q.v. In the Philadelphia Directory is found Treebold, which is eminently suggestive.

Relicta Tyreball, co. Bucks, 1273. A. Robert Trepel, co. Soms., 1 Edw. III : Kirby's Quest, p. 158.

1687. Married — Joseph Trebell and Grace Winstanly : St. Dionis Backchurch, p. 41.

1797. — John Treble and Emma Silvester : St. Geo. Han. Sq. ii. 158. London, 3.

Treblecock, Trebilcock. — Local. A Cornish surname, one of the many local surnames beginning with *Tre* and ending with *-cott*, corrupted to *cock*; cf. Glasscock for Glascott.

1742. Married — John Trebilcock, of St. Colomb Major, co. Cornwall, and Frances Sargent : St. Geo. Han. Sq. i. 29.

1777. — Samuel Freake and Jane Treblecook : ibid. p. 278.

MDB. (co. Cornwall), 0, 5 ; Cornish Court Dir., 0, 1 ; Truro, 0, 1.

Tree, Trees.—Local, 'at the tree' or trees, from residence thereby ; cf. Oak, Birch, Box, &c.

Johannes del Trees, 1379 : P. T. Yorks. p. 258.

1583. William Leevers and Eliz. Tree : Marriage Lic. (London), i. 119.

1665. Married — John Tree and Jane Baily : St. Jas. Clerkenwell, i. 117.

1756. — John Barnaby and Eliz. Tree : St. Geo. Han. Sq. i. 66.

London, 5, 0 ; Darley (co. York), Trees, 1 ; Philadelphia, 1, 0.

Treffry, Trefry.—Local, ' of Treffry.' Mr. Lower says, ' This name is derived from the manor of Treffry, in the parish of Lanhydrock, where it is traced to a very early period' (v. for fuller account his Patr. Brit. p. 353).

MDB. (co. Cornwall), 7, 0 ; Boston (U.S.), 0, 7.

Trefusis, Trefuses. — Local, ' of Trefusis,' an estate in the parish of Milor, co. Cornwall, where the family bearing the name have resided for many centuries.

1578. John Trefusis, co. Cornwall : Reg. Univ. Oxf. vol. ii. pt. ii. p. 82.

1589. Nicholas Trefusis, co. Cornwall : ibid. p. 176.

1605. John Trefusis, co. Cornwall : ibid. p. 282.

Crockford, 1, 0 ; London, 0, 1.

Tregarthen, Tregarthin.— Local, ' of Tregarthian.' ' A place in the parish of Gorran, co. Cornwall, where the family were seated temp. Edw. I, or earlier': Lower, quoting Gilbert's Cornwall.

London, 1, 0 ; Oxford, 0, 1.

Tregear.— Local, 'of Tregeare.' ' A place in the parish of Crowan, co. Cornwall. The family were resident there so lately as 1732. Richard Tregeare, of Tregeare, was sheriff of the county in 1704': Lower, quoting Gilbert's Cornwall.

London, 2.

Treherne, Trehearne, Treharne.—Bapt.' the son of Trahern.' ' An ancient Welsh personal name, as Trahern ap Caradoc, Prince of North Wales, 1073': Lower's Patr. Brit. p. 354.

1578. Bapt. — Marie, d. William Treherne, *cloth-worker* : St. Mary Aldermary, p. 59.

1802. Married — William Laker and Susanna Treherne : St. Geo. Han. Sq. ii. 264.

London, 3, 1, 0 ; Boston (U.S.), 0, 0, 1.

Trelawny. — Local, ' of Trelawny.' Two manors of this name exist in co. Cornwall, one in the parish of Alternon, the other in that of Pelynt. The former was the original seat of the Trelawnys, afterwards the latter, which is still the seat of the family': Shirley's Noble and Gentle Men (Lower).

Tremain, Tremayne, Tremaine. — Local, ' of Tremayne.' ' An estate in the parish of St. Martin, co. Cornwall. The pedigree is traced to Perys de Tremayne of Tremayne, in the reign of Edward III': Lower, quoting Shirley's Noble and Gentle Men (Patr. Brit. p. 354).

1704-5. Married — John Forster and Jane Tremaine : St. Dionis Backchurch, p. 53.

London, 3, 0, 0 ; Crockford, 0, 1, 0 ; Boston (U.S.), 0, 0, 1.

Tremble, Trimble.—Variants of the border name of Turnbull (q.v.), found in co. Cumberland.

MDB. (co. Cumberland), 5, 3 ; Philadelphia, 0, 43.

Tremellen.— ? ——.

William Tremillin, co. Staff., 1273. A. London, 1.

Tremenheere. — Local, ' of Tremenheere.' ' The family name of Tremenheere is derived from lands so named in the parish of Ludgvan, of which Nicholas de Tremenheere was seised before

the reign of Edward I': Gilbert's Cornwall, quoted by Lower, Patr. Brit. p. 354.

Crockford, 2.

Tremeer, -mer; v. Trimmer.

Trenchard. — Nick. ' the trenchant.' Fr. *trenchant*, cutting ; doubtless a sobriquet conferred on some skilled swordsman; cf. Sharparrow, Bruselance, &c.

William Trenchaunt, co. Oxf., 1273. A. London, 1 ; Philadelphia, 1 ; New York, 2.

Trendell.—Local, 'of Trendle'; v. Trundle.

Trent.—Local, ' of Trent,' a parish in co. Somerset, near Sherborne.

Gibert de Trent, co. Soms., 1 Edw. III : Kirby's Quest, p. 216.

London, 1 ; MDB. (co. Soms.), 2 ; Boston (U.S.), 1.

Trentham, Trantum, Trantom.—Local, ' of Trentham,' a parish in co. Stafford, four miles from Newcastle.

John, Prior de Trentham, co. Staff., 20 Edw. I. R.

The American form is almost identical with that of an early emigrant's name.

1635. ' Imbarqued in the Blessing ' for New England, Thomas Trentum, aged 14 years : Hotten's Lists of Emigrants, p. 108.

1747. Married — James Trentam (co. Notts) and Patience Damnall : St. Geo. Chap. Mayfair, p. 100.

London, 1, 0, 0 ; Liverpool, 0, 0, 1 ; Philadelphia, 0, 2, 0.

Tresillian.—Local, ' of Tresillian.' ' Two places in Cornwall are so designated, one in the parish of Newlyn, and the other in Merther. The distinguished Sir Robert Tresillian . . . who fell a victim to the resentment of the barons at Tyburn in 1388, was of this family': Lower, quoting Gilbert's Cornwall.

Trespass.—Nick.

Thomas Trespas, co. Hunts, 1273. A. John Trepas, London, ibid.

Trevarthen.—Local, ' of Trevarthian.' ' The manor of Trevarthian, in the parish of Newlyn, near Truro, is undoubtedly the spot that gave origin to this family, who in former times ranked among the most distinguished names that have been known in the county of Cornwall': Lower, quoting Gilbert's Cornwall (Patr. Brit. p. 355).

London, 1.

Trevelion, Trevelyan, Trevilian, Trevillion.—Local, 'of Trevelyan,' an estate in the parish of St. Veep, near Fowey, co. Cornwall, where dwelt in the reign of Edw. I Nicholas de Trevelyan, whose ancestors had possessed the property from a still earlier period (Shirley's Noble and Gentle Men, quoted by Lower, Patr. Brit. p. 355).

1734. Married—George Trevillion and Mary Allen: St. Michael, Cornhill, p. 66.
London, 1, 1, 1, 2.

Trevitt, Trevett.—Bapt. 'the son of Trivet,' possibly a variant of Troite'; v. Trott.

John Trivet, co. Soms., 1 Edw. III: Kirby's Quest, p. 253.
Edmund Trivet, co. Soms., 1 Edw. III: ibid.
Nicholas Trivet, co. Soms., 1 Edw. III: ibid.

There are a fair number of Trivets in this Exchequer Roll.

Philadelphia, 1, 0; Boston (U.S.), 0, 1.

Trew; v. True.

Trewhitt.—Bapt. 'the son of Troite'; v. Trott. But it must not be forgotten that there is High and Low Trewhitt, a township in the parish of Rothbury, co. Northumberland.

Nicholas Tryut, co. Soms., 1 Edw. III: Kirby's Quest, p. 272.
London, 1.

Trewinnard. — Local, ' of Trewinnard.' 'An estate in the parish of St. Erth, co. Cornwall. The earliest recorded ancestor seems to be William de Trewinnard, a knight of the shire, 28 Edw. III': Lower, quoting Gilbert's Cornwall.

London, 2.

Tricker.—Bapt. 'the son of Troggar,' whence Trigger (q.v.), and the sharpened Tricker; cf. Trickett for Triggett, and cf. also Slagg and Slack.

London, 2; Philadelphia, 6.

Trickett, Triggett. — Bapt. 'the son of Trigot,' possibly a dim. of Trig; but v. Traugott (Yonge, ii. 491). It had an unquestioned footing for a time in North, if not South England. Cf. German Traugott, still in use as a font-name.

'But Traugott Waldteufel, for so he was called, profited by his crime hardly at all': Westall's Two Pinches of Snuff, iii. 230.

Baldewin Triket, co. Bedf., 1273. A.
Thomas Triket, co. Norf., ibid.
Ida Triket, co. Middlesex, Hen. III-Edw. I. K.
Simon Triket, cos. Essex and Herts: ibid.
Emma Trigot, 1379: P. T. Yorks. p. 123.
Sibilla Trigot, 1379: ibid. p. 103.
1706. Married—Jonathan Trickett and Mary Williamson: St. Michael, Cornhill, p. 53.
London, 6, 0; Philadelphia, 7, 0.

Trigg, Triggs. — Bapt. 'the son of Trig,' a favourite old Northern name (Yonge, ii. 414), genitive Triggs; v. Trickett.

'No clown would be considered worth his salt if he could not vault over six horses like King Teutobach, or play with three missiles at the same time like Olaf Trygesson': Standard, March 31, 1887.

Robert Trig, co. Camb., 1273. A.
William Triggs, co. Camb., ibid.
Alan Trig, co. Linc., ibid.
William Tryg, co. Soms., 1 Edw. III: Kirby's Quest, p. 271.
Johannes Tryg, 1379: P. T. Yorks. p. 78.
1549. Henry Nelson and Agnes Triggs: Marriage Lic. (London), i. 12.
1597. Buried — Edward Trygge: St. Michael, Cornhill, p. 208.
1657. Married—Hugh Coles, confecksonor, and Ann Trigg: St. Mary Aldermary, p. 27.
London, 8, 7; Boston (U.S.), 0, 3.

Trigger.—Bapt. 'the son of Troggar'; v. Tricker.

Hugh Troggar, co. Soms., 1 Edw. III: Kirby's Quest, p. 264.
London, 1.

Trimbell, Trimble; v. Tremble.

Philadelphia, 1, 43.

Trimbey, Trimby, Trymby.—Local, 'of Thrimby,' a chapelry in the parish of Morland, co. Westmoreland. Probably some other spot was so called in co. Wilts. As a surname Trimby was certain

to become the popular lazy variant for Thrimby; cf. Trower for Thrower.

1615. Bapt. — Mary, d. Cuthbert Tremby: Reg. Stourton, co. Wilts, p. 6.
1624. — Andrew, s. Cutbert Trimbey: ibid. p. 7.
1713. — John, s. John Trimby: ibid. p. 22.

Found also in the same register as Thrimboy (v. Index).

London, 2, 1, 0; Philadelphia, 0, 0, 3.

Trimmer, Tremeer, Tremer.
—(1) Occup. (?) 'the trimmer,' probably some kind of embroiderer. But I have no proof. (2) Local, ' of Tremere.' Lower suggests 'Tremere,' an estate in Lanivet parish, co. Cornwall. The elder line failed in the 14th century; v. Gilbert's Cornwall.

1658. Bapt. — Robert, s. Edmund Trimmer: St. Jas. Clerkenwell, i. 202.
1792. Married—Edward Trimmer and Mary Hewitt: St. Geo. Han. Sq. ii. 87.
London, 4, 0, 0; MDB. (co. Surrey), 1, 0, 0; (co. Cornwall), 0, 1, 0; Philadelphia, 4, 0, 2.

Trinder.—Occup. 'the trinder.' Probably a wheeler, a maker of trindles. ' Trindles, the felloes of a wheel' (Halliwell); cf. 'Trendelyn, as with a rownd thynge; volvo, trocleo.' 'Trendyl, troclea': Prompt. Parv. p. 502. The instance below is from co. Norf., agreeing with the locale of the two last quotations.

Hugh le Trinder, co. Norf., 1273. A.
1615. Martin Trender, co. Wilts: Reg. Univ. Oxf. vol. ii. pt. ii. p. 342.
— Thomas Trender, co. Wilts: ibid.
1791. Married—Benjamin Trinder and Catharine Barnwell: St. Geo. Han. Sq. ii. 55.
London, 4; Oxford, 9; Philadelphia, 1.

Tring; v. Thring.

Trinity.— ? ——.

1700. Married — Robert Butler and Sarah Trinity: St. Michael, Cornhill, p. 55.

Tripcony.—Local, 'of Tripcony,' a Cornish name.

'Presentment of James Trypconye, deputy for the haven of Hayleford or Helford, touching piracies' on coast of Cornwall, April 30, 1579: Cal. State Papers (Domestic), i. 473.
John Dyer, of Tripcony, 1619: Reg. St. Columb Major, p. 208.
London, 1.

Tripp, Trippet.—Bapt. 'the son of Tripp,' an early personal name.

William Trip, co. Camb., 1273. A.
Robert Trippe, co. Bedf., ibid.
Gilbert Trip, co. Wilts, ibid.
John Tryp, co. Soms., 1 Edw. III: Kirby's Quest, p. 107.
Johannes Trypet, 1379: P.T.Yorks.p.44.
Simon Trippe, 1564: Reg. Univ. Oxf. i. 253.
1580. Married — Reinald Trip, *goldsmith*, and Christian Feelding: St. Mary Aldermary, p. 6.
1629. Buried—Prudence Trippit, a *servant*: ibid. p. 166.
London, 13, 0; West Rid. Court Dir., 2, 0; Sheffield, 1, 0; Boston (U.S.), 37, 0.

Tripper, Trippier.—Occup. 'a tripherd,' a goatherd, cos. York and Lanc. '*Trip*, a flock of sheep, a herd of swine or goats' (Halliwell).

'Item, in pane pro triphyrdes sarculant metent,' 1305: Whitaker's Craven, p. 460, compotus de Bolton.
'Item pro geldherds, pro tripherds,' 1317: ibid. p. 465.

The editor adds, 'Trip is a herd of goats, and has given origin to the surname yet remaining in Lancashire, Tripyer'; cf. Tupper for Tupherd.

Walter Tripper,1379: P.T.Yorks. p. 49.
Willelmus Tripper, 1379: ibid.

A Mrs. Trippier let lodgings at Seascale, co. Cumberland (1887).

Penrith, 0, 1; Liverpool, 0, 1; Treales (near Kirkham, co. Lanc.), 0, 1; Wharles (ibid.), 0, 1.

Trist.—Local, 'at the tryst,' the place of meeting. M.E. *trist*, 'a tryst, meeting-place; station in hunting' (Mayhew and Skeat). Lower says, ' Fr. *triste*, sad, pensive.' It may be so, but I find no evidence.

Peter atte Treste, co. Bucks, 1273. A.
1589. Richard Tryst or Trist, co. Northants: Reg. Univ. Oxf. vol. ii. pt. ii. p. 172.
1679. Buried – Mrs. Sarah Tryst : St. Antholin (London), p. 98.
London, 2; Philadelphia, 3.

Triston.—Bapt. 'the son of Tristram,' familiarly known as Tristam. Once popular in Cornwall.

1622. Buried—Grace Tresteene, *widow*: Reg. St. Columb Major, p. 210.
Adam Trestean, 1629: ibid. p. 212.
1784. Married—Thomas Heseltine and Katherine Triston : St.Geo.Han. Sq. i. 358.
London, 2.

Tristram.—Bapt. 'the son of Tristram.'

Tristram de Haule, co. Suff., 1273. A.
John Tristian, co. Soms., 1 Edw. III: Kirby's Quest, p. 130.
Cecilia uxor Trystrem, 1379: P. T. Yorks. p. 265.
Isolda Trestrem, 1379 : ibid.
1585. John Tristrum and Eliz. Emley: Marriage Lic. (London), i. 139.
Tristram Blaby, 1590: Reg. St. Mary Aldermary (London), p. 8.
London, 1; Crockford, 2; New York, 1.

Troate.—Bapt. ; v. Trott.

Trodd.—Bapt. ; v. Trott.

Trollope.—Local, 'of Trollop.' Probably 'hope' is the suffix (v. Hope). Northumberland seems to be the home of the family, but the spot I have failed to identify. They are also early found in co. Lincoln.

William de Trollop, 1383: Prior of Holy Island : QQQ. p. 61.
John Trolop, 1401: DDD. vol. i. p. 85.
1612. Married, w. Roger Trowlupp (Reg. Crossgate): DDD. i. 91.
1744. Married — John Trollop and Sarah Munvell: St. Geo. Han. Sq. i. 32. London, 7.

Trood.—Bapt. ; v. Trott.

Trotman, Trottman.—Occup. 'Trotisman,' i. e. the servant of Trot or Trote (v. Trott); cf. Matthewman, Addiman, Harriman, &c. One of a somewhat large class of names. No relationship with Trotter.

Bartholomew Troteman, 34 Edw. I: BBB. p. 728.
Samuel Trotman. HH.
1628. Married—Richard Archer and Eliz. Trotman: St. Jas. Clerkenwell, i. 59.
Throgmorton Trotman, a native of Cam, co. Glouc., a London merchant, 1663 : Rudder's Hist. Glouc. p. 318.
1783. Married — Richard White and Mary Trotman : St. Geo. Han. Sq. p. 342.
London, 15, 0; MDB. (co. Glouc.), 7, 0; Philadelphia, 2, 1; Boston (U.S.), 3, 0.

Trott, Troate, Trood, Trout, Trodd.—Bapt. 'the son of Troit' or Trote or Troyt. One of the forms of Trude, found in such compounds as Ger-trude, Hil-trude; formerly a name of itself. Hence 'Dame Trott' in the nursery rhyme (v. Yonge, ii. 235-6). The name is frequently found in the Exchequer Lay Subsidies, co. Soms.,

1 Edw. III, and in various forms is still familiar to that county. Speaking generally, the surname has steadily settled down into Trott.

Robertus fil. Troite, 7 Hen. II, Pipe Roll, iv. 40.
Robert fil. Trote, 1165: RRR. p. 7.
Richard fil. Truite, 1179 : ibid. p. 20.

The first two probably represent the same individual. I furnish both instances because of the twofold spelling. It will be well to furnish some early variants:

Nicholas Truhyt, co. Soms., 1 Edw. III : Kirby's Quest, p. 151.
Thomas Troht, co. Soms., 1 Edw. III : ibid. p. 153.
Robert Trote, co. Soms., 1 Edw. III : ibid. p. 156.
Thomas Trut, co. Soms., 1 Edw. III : ibid. p. 159.
Robert Tryut, co. Soms., 1 Edw. III : ibid. p. 146.
John Trout, co. Soms., 1 Edw. III : ibid. p. 224.
Simon Trot, co. Hunts, 1273. A.
Godwin Trote, co. Norf., ibid.
Philip Troyt, co. Norf., ibid.
Jeffry Trote, bailiff of Yarmouth, 1340 : FF. xi. 323.
1661. Married — William Fitter and Jane Trott : St. Michael, Cornhill, p. 38.
London, 8, 0, 1, 0, 1; MDB. (co. Soms.), 8, 1, 4, 1, 0; Boston (U.S.), 10, 0, 0, 7, 0.

Trotter, Trottier. — Official, 'the trotter,' a messenger, one who trotted. Skeat says (v. *trot*): ' Fr. *trotter*, "to trot" : Cotg. O.F. *troter*, 13th century : Littré. We also find O.F. *trotier*, a trotter, a messenger, Low Lat. *trotarius*, = Lat. *tolutarius*, going at a trot.' It is possible that in some cases it is a nickname from the gait of the progenitor, as 'trotter' for a horse was in use. 'Trottare, horse, *succursarius*': Prompt. Parv. The first, of course, is the natural origin. 'LeonTrottier,French confectioner,' in the London Directory, reminds us of the French equivalent.

Johannes Trotter, 1379: P. T. Yorks. p. 300.
Thomas Trotter. W. 13.
Richard Trotter.
1596-7. Married—Walter Trotter and Eliz. Golding: St. Dionis Backchurch, p. 13.
1581. Edward Mott and Isabel Trotter : Marriage Lic. (London), i. 101.
London, 6, 1; Philadelphia, 27, 0.

Troughton. — Local, ' of Troughton,' a small estate, now Troughton Hall, in Woodlands, near Ulverston, North Lancashire. The surname is very familiar in the district.

1547. Bapt.—William Troghton : St. Mary, Ulverston, p. 4.
— Buried—Anne Troghton : ibid. p. 5.
1549. Bapt.—Elizabeth Troghton : ibid. p. 8.
1584. Ann Troughton, of Ulverston : Lancashire Wills at Richmond, i. 287.
1599. Barnard Troughton, of Riddinge, parish of Ulverston : ibid.
1660. Miles Troughton, of Ulverston : ibid.
1747. Married — James Throughton and Miss Middleton : St. Geo. Chap. Mayfair, p. 98.
London, 4 ; Liverpool, 5 ; Philadelphia, 3.

Trounce ; v. Trown.

Trousdale, Trowsdale, Truesdale, Trowsdall.—Local, ' of Troutsdale,' a township in the parish of Brompton, near Scarborough, N. Rid. Yorks.

1635. Phines Trusedell (aged 18 years) embarked for the Barbadoes : Hotten's Lists of Emigrants, p. 142.
1679. Buried — Ann Trowsdale, St. Michael's, Barbadoes : ibid. p. 433.

Probably Phineas was the parent of the American Trowsdales, Trousdales, or Truesdales. The different forms are still chiefly found, so far as England is concerned, in the N. Rid. Yorks, in the neighbourhood of Troutsdale.

MDB. (N. Rid. Yorks), 1, 1, 0, 1 ; Scarborough, 0, 1, 0, 0 ; Boston (U.S.), 1, 1, 3, 0 ; Philadelphia, 0, 0, 2, 0.

Trout.—(1) Nick. (?) 'the trout,' the fish so named. The earliest instance I can find is in co. York. It is there we find the surname Bucktrout, q.v. (2) Bapt. 'the son of Trote.' This must undoubtedly be considered the parent. For an account of the name, v. Trott. Scarcely a single seeming fish-name like Salmon, Turbot, Chubb, &c., represents the finny tribe.

Thomas Trout, 1379 : P.T.Yorks. p. 121.
1601-2. John Rae and Susan Trowte, widow : Marriage Lic. (London), i. 267.
1602-3. John Trout, co. Somerset : Reg. Univ. Oxf. vol. ii. pt. ii. p. 263.
1776. Married—Jacob Trout and Eliz. Evans : St. Geo. Han. Sq. i. 266.
Philadelphia, 61.

Troutbeck.—Local, ' of Troutbeck,' a parish in co. Westmoreland, five miles from Ambleside.

1568. Edward Troutebecke, or Trutbecke : Reg Univ. Oxf. i. 270.
1591. Robert Trowtebecke, co. Cumb.: Reg. Univ. Oxf. vol. ii. pt. ii. p. 186.
1593. Robert Troutbeck, vicar of Newton-Regny : Jefferson's Hist. of Leath Ward, co. Cumb., p. 151.
1621. Anthony Troutbecke, co. Cumb.: Reg. Univ. Oxf. vol. ii. pt. ii. p. 398.
Crockford, 1 ; MDB. (co. Cumb.), 5.

Trover.—Occup. Probably a shortened form of Troubadour (v. *troubadour*, Skeat's Etym. Dict.).

Simon le Trovur, temp. Hen. III.
William le Trovur, temp. Hen. III.

I have lost my reference to these entries.

London, 1.

Trow.—Local, ' at the trow,' i.e. trough. ' *Trow*, a trough ': Halliwell. Mr. Lower quotes Mr. Ferguson as saying, ' Trow, Troy, and Try are different forms of True, as Old Frieslandic *trowe*, *troiwe*, German *treu*.' It may be so. The evidence is altogether against it as regards Trow. Residence by an artifical trough, or a natural trough in a stream, seems the inevitable solution, judging by my first and earliest instances.

William atte Trowe, co. Wilts, 1273. A.
Thomas atte Trowe, co. Soms., 1 Edw. III : Kirby's Quest, p. 243.
Roger atte Trowe : co. Soms., 1 Edw. III : ibid.
1624-5. Philip Gardner and Anne Trow : Marriage Lic. (London), ii. 148.
1694. Bapt. — Gilbert, s. Thomas Trowe : St. Jas. Clerkenwell, i. 358.
1774. Married — Richard Trow and Jane Harper : St. Geo. Han. Sq. i. 242.
London, 1 ; Boston (U.S.), 4.

Trowbridge.—Local, 'of Trowbridge,' a market-town and parish in co. Wilts.

Richard Trowbrigge, co. Soms., 1 Edw. III : Kirby's Quest, p. 104.
John de Trowbrugge, co. Soms., 1 Edw. III : ibid. p. 179.
William de Trowbrugge, co. Soms., 1 Edw. III : ibid.
1583. George Trobrydge, co. Devon : Reg. Univ. Oxf. vol. ii. pt. ii. p. 125.
1731. Bapt.—John, s. John Trowbridge : Reg. Stourton, co. Wilts.
1809. Married — Charles Bulkeley Egerton and Charlotte Troubridge, co. Sussex : St. Geo. Han. Sq. ii. 419.
London, 3 ; Philadelphia, 4.

Trowell.—Local, (1) 'of Trowell,' a parish in co. Notts, near Nottingham ; (2) ' of Trowle,' a tithing in the parish of Great Bradford, co. Wilts. Both seem to be parents.

Richard de Truwell, co. Linc., 1273. A.
Batin de Trowell, co. Wilts, 1 Edw. III : Kirby's Quest, p. 168.
London, 3 ; Philadelphia, 1.

Trower.—Probably a corruption of Thrower, q.v.

London, 9 ; Boston (U.S.), 2.

Trown, Trawin, Trounce, Trounson.—Bapt. 'the son of Trogne.' Peculiar to co. York, so far as I can discover. Trounce, more correctly Trowns (the *s* as in Jones, Jennings, Williams, &c.), may be compared with Ellice for Ellis, or Pierce for Piers.—Since writing the above I find Trounson in co. Devon. I have still more recently met with it in Southport, co. Lanc.

Magota Trogune, 1379, Kimberworth : P. T. Yorks. p. 67.
Willelmus Trogñe, 1379, Kimberworth : ibid.
Johannes Trogñe, 1379, Kimberworth : ibid.
Rogerus Tron, 1379, Hooton Pagnell : ibid. p. 29.
Stephanus Troune, 1379, Hooton Pagnell : ibid.
Johannes Troune, 1379, Hooton Pagnell : ibid. p. 15.
1582. William Trawnson, *myller*, and Eliz. Johnson : Marriage Lic. (London), i. 112.
1791. Married — Charles Cutter and Mary Eliz. Trounce : St. Geo. Han. Sq. ii. 56.
London, 0, 2, 2, 0 ; West Rid. Court Dir., 1, 0, 0, 0 ; Sheffield, 2, 0, 0, 0 ; Leeds, 0, 1, 0, 0 ; (Trounson) North Lew, co. Devon, 1 ; Plymouth, 1 ; New York, 4, 0, 0, 0.

Trowsdale, &c. ; v. Trousdale.

Trowse.—Local, ' of Trowse,' co. Norfolk. This surname still exists in co. Norfolk, where it existed at least five centuries ago. The parish of Trowse-Newton is in co. Norfolk, one mile from Norwich, and it seems to have been the home of the family. Originally the village must have been called Trowse, and the Newton has been added later.

John de Trowse, bailiff of Norwich, 1387 : FF. iii. 116.
Nicholas de Trowes, co. Norf., 20 Edw. I : ibid. x. 66.
1371. Buried—Thomas de Trows, of Norwich : ibid iv. 137.
Thomas Troys, co. Norf., 1517 : ibid. v. 248.
London, 1 ; MDB. (Norfolk), 1.

Troy.—Local, 'de Troyes,' the French town of that name. It is almost certain that this is the origin. In fact, the following entries concerning one and the same individual may be said to prove it. Copin, let it be noticed. was the pet name for Jacob ; v. Coppin.

Copin' de Troye (London citizen), 1273. A.
Jacobus de Troye (London citizen), ibid.
Jacobus de Troys (London citizen), ibid.
James de Troys (London citizen), ibid.
1793. Married — William Troy and Eleanor Fitzgerald : St. Geo. Han. Sq. ii. 95.
1809. — John Troy and Maria Moore : ibid. p. 416.
London, 1 ; Boston (U.S.), 24.

Trubridge.—Local, a variant of Trowbridge, q.v. A similar form is found in an English register.

1761. Married — Samuel Sitchell and Jane Truebridge : St. Geo. Han. Sq. i. 100.
New York, 1.

True, Trew.—Nick. 'the true,' a faithful and trustworthy man. M.E. *trewe.*

Henry Trewe, co. Bedford, 1273. A.
1595. Bapt.—Eliz., d. John True : St. Dionis Backchurch, p. 89.
1596. Buried—Eliz. Trew : ibid. p. 204.
1807. Married—Charles Walker and Ruth Trew : St. Geo. Han. Sq. ii. 372.
London, 0, 5 ; Philadelphia, 2, 0 ; Boston (U.S.), 17, 0.

Truebody.—Nick. 'truebody,' faithful, loyal (cf. Trueman and Truefellow). In the Countess of Leicester's service (18 Edw. I) were several messengers, all bearing names allusive to their office, viz. Slingaway, Bolett (=Bullet), and Treubodie (v. Household Expenses of Ric. de Swinfield, A.D. 1289-90, Camden Soc., p. 143 *n*).

Stephen Trewbody. H.
1630. Buried—Annes Truboddy : Reg. St. Columb Major, p. 213.

Truecock. — Nick. 'faithful fellow' ; v. Cocks.
John Truccok, co. Derby, 1273. A.

Truefellow. -- Nick. 'truefellow,' an honest companion, a loyal partner ; cf. Goodfellow and Trueman.
Johannes Trewfelagh, 1379 : P. T. Yorks. p. 147.

Truelove.— Nick. 'betrothed' or 'bound,' from the Scandinavian *troe lof*, bound in law, a bondsman (Lower, quoting Ulst. Jour. Arch. No. 2). The late Dr. Littledale suggested to me 'betrothed, from Norse *at trulofa*, to pledge one's faith, to betroth.' Hence the meaning of the paradoxical line in the old song :

'So my true love was false to me.'

The Hundred Rolls form of the surname is Trewelove.

Richard Trewlove. G.
Stephen Truelove. H.
John Trewlove, co. Soms., 1 Edw. III : Kirby's Quest, p. 120.
Willelmus Trewluf, 1379 : P. T. Yorks. p. 146.
Ricardus Trewluff, 1379 : ibid. p. 292.
1597. Rowland Trewlove and Winifred Paynter : Marriage Lic. (London), i. 243.
1802. Married — Robert Ireland and Mary Truelove : St. Geo. Han. Sq. ii. 258.
London, 3.

Trueman, Truman. — Nick. 'the true man,' a true, trustworthy, or faithful man. M.E. *trewe.* Probably the sobriquet of some herald or messenger ; v. Truebody.

Agnes Treueman, co. Camb., 1273. A.
Thomas Treweman, co. Worc., ibid.
Richard Treweman, Rot. Claus., 22 Ric. II. pt. ii.
1621. Married — Rychard Trewman and Eliz. Somner : St. Dionis Backchurch, p. 4.
1792. — William Stukeley Burns and Ann Truman : St. Geo. Han. Sq. ii. 82.
London, 3, 11 ; Philadelphia, 4, 14.

Trumper.—Occup. 'the trumper,' a blower on the trump.

'The trompoures with the loud minstralcie.' Chaucer, C. T. 2673.
William le Trompour, c. 1300. M.
John le Trompour, c. 1300. M.
John Skot, *trumper*, 19 Edw. II : Freemen of York, i. 23.
John Trompour, co. Soms., 1 Edw. III : Kirby's Quest, p. 210.

Walterus Tromper, 1379 : P. T. Yorks. p. 133.
1644. Clare Trumper : Cal. of Wills in Court of Husting (2).
1789. Married — George Elliott and Diana Trumper : St. Geo. Han. Sq. ii. 25.
London, 2 ; MDB. (co. Hereford), 6 ; New York, 2.

Trundle, Trendell.—Local, 'of Trendle,' a tithing in the parish of Pitminster, co. Somerset. The Norfolk Trundles are clearly descended from the Trendle family in that county, found there so early as 1360 (v. infra). Whether they hailed from Trendle in Somersetshire, or from some spot so called in Norfolk, I cannot say. Undoubtedly the Trendells of Abingdon, near Oxford, came from the Somersetshire tithing.

1360. Thomas Trendyl, vicar of Witton, co. Norf. : FF. xi. 84.
1569. John Tryndell, rector of Wimbotsham, co. Norf. : ibid. vii. 519.

The last-named is probably referred to in the following :

1565. John Trundell, rector of Bexwell, co. Norf.: FF. vii. 310.
1631. Thomas Trendle, vicar of Mendham, co. Norf. : ibid. v. 385.
1630. William Trundel, of Hetherset, co. Norf. : ibid. p. 28.
1733. Married—Laurence Allison and Judith Trundle : St. Geo. Han. Sq. i. 12.
London, 0, 1 ; MDB. (Norfolk), 5, 0 ; Crockford, 1, 1 ; Abingdon, 0, 1.

Trussharness.—Nick. for an ostler or stableman.
Agnes Trusseharneys, C. R., 8 Edw. III.

Trustram, Trustrum.—Bapt. 'the son of Tristram,' q.v.

1601. John Tristram or Trustram, co. Devon : Reg. Univ.Oxf. vol. ii. pt. ii. p. 250.
1656-7. Married — John Heath and Bridgett Trustram : St. Dionis Backchurch, p. 32.
London, 1, 1.

Tubb, Tubbs, Tubby.—Bapt. 'the son of Theobald.' There can be no reasonable doubt that this is the case. Theobald and its forms have run riot among the vowels ; v. Tebb. Tubby is the pet form ; cf. Charley and Sibley. Tubbs is, of course, the genitive or patronymic form ; cf. Jones or Williams.

Thomas Tubb', *souter*, 1379 : P. T. Yorks. p. 26.

Matilda Tubb', 1379 : P.T.Yorks. p. 26.
1745. Married—Antony Paul Tubb and Eliz. Bushell: St. Geo. Chap. Mayfair, p. 59.
1748. — John Tubbs and Maria Evers: ibid. p. 119.
London, 8, 7, 2 ; Boston (U.S.), 0, 4, 0.

Tubman. — (1) Occup. 'the tubman,' i.e. the cooper. (2) Occup. 'the man of Tub,' i.e. the servant of Tub ; cf. Addyman, Matthewman, Harriman, &c.; v. Tubb. The first derivation is the most probable. The name is found in Furness, North Lancashire, always noted for cooperage.

Henry Tubman, co. York. W. 16.
John Tubman, co. Norf. F.
1549. Married—Robert Tubman and Jelian Schales: St. Mary, Ulverston, p. 9.
1661. Nicholas Tubman, of Barrowhead, Furness : Lancashire Wills at Richmond, i. 288.
1737. Buried—Thomas, son of Thomas Tubman : St. Mary, Ulverston, p. 260.
1745. William Tubman, of Barrow Head: Lancashire Wills at Richmond, ii. 261.
Philadelphia, 2.

Tuck, Took, Tooke, Tuke, Toke, Tuckson.—Bapt. 'the son of Toke.' The Domesday form was Toke, 'liber homo Stigandi Toka Francigine' (? Toka the Frenchman) ; v. Freeman, Norm. Conq. v. 768. Mr. Lower enumerates among the Domesday forms of this familiar personal name Toc, Tocho, Tochi, and Toka, also the patronymic Godric Tokeson (Godric fil. Toke). Tycho Brahe represented the Danish form (v. Yonge, ii. 410). Friar Tuck, whether an historic or legendary personage, bears unmistakably the same name. For a diminutive v. Tokelin. Of many instances I furnish a few.

Toke Dando, co. Somerset, 1273. A.
Toke Lanarius (i.e. the woolmonger), co. Linc., ibid.
Tokus Bobyning, C. R., 3 Edw. I.
Peter Tuck, C. R., 6 Edw. I.
Thomas Tuke, 1379 : P. T. Yorks. p. 295.
Johannes Tokson, 1379 : ibid. p. 150.
1526. Nicholas Toke, or Tocke, or Tuke : Reg. Univ. Oxf. i. 142.
1571. John Tuke and Margaret Willyams : Marriage Lic. (London), i. 48.
1675. Bapt.—James, s. Henry Tucke: St. Jas. Clerkenwell, i. 269.
1676-7. Thomas Tooke (co. Herts) and Eliz. Atkins: Marriage Lic. (London), ii. 300.

1708. William Toke (co. Kent) and Eliz. Hilton : ibid. p. 337.
1753. Married—Roger Took (co. Norfolk) and Eliz. Grandee : St. Geo. Chap. Mayfair, p. 263.
London, 23, 1, 2, 2, 0, 0 ; Crockford (Toke), 1 ; West Rid. Court Dir., 1, 0, 0, 4, 0, 0 ; Boston (U.S.), 13, 0, 0, 0, 0, 0 ; Philadelphia (Tuckson), 1.

Tucker.—Occup. 'the tucker,' a fuller, or walker of cloth. 'Wollen-weaver, weaving housewiefes, or householde clothe . . . clothe-fuller, otherwise called tucker or walker' (5 Eliz. c. 4, 23). Tucker is still a great Westcountry surname, being very strongly represented in cos. Devon, Wilts, and Dorset. As is Lister or Walker (q.v.) to Yorkshire, so is Tucker to these said parts. v.Tooker.

Roger le Tukere, co. Dorset, 1273. A.
Percival le Toukere, 1301. M.
Robert le Tuckere, C. R., 13 Edw. II.
William le Touker. G.
1582-3. Charles Tooker or Tucker, co. Wilts : Reg.Univ.Oxf. vol. ii. pt. ii. p. 124.
1583. Edmund Gylman and Florence Tucker (of Exeter): Marriage Lic. (London), i. 126.
London, 92 ; MDB. (co. Devon), 75 ; Philadelphia, 73.

Tuckerman. — Occup. 'the tuckerman,' a tucker, a walker, a dyer; cf. Merchantman, Husbandman, &c. v. Tucker.

Barbara Tuckerman, 1660 : Reg. Canterbury Cath. p. 121.
1689. John Tuckerman and Mary Bartlett : Marriage Alleg. (Canterbury), p. 101.
MDB. (co. Devon), 1 ; Philadelphia, 2 ; Boston (U.S.), 13.

Tuckett.—? Bapt. 'the son of Tuket' or Touchet, probably a dim. of Tuke or Tuck, q.v.

Nicholas Tochet, co. Linc., 1273. A.
Simon Tochet, co. Linc., ibid.
Thomas Touchet, co. Derby, ibid.
Nicholas Tuchet, co. Linc., 20 Edw. I. R.
Thomas Tuchet, co. Rutl., ibid.
Robert Touschet, co. Derby, ibid.
Willelmus Tuket, 1379 : P. T. Yorks. p. 127.
Tochet Beston, 7 Hen. VIII : East Cheshire, ii. 86.
1809. Married—Nicholas Tuckett and Martha Hole : St. Geo. Han. Sq. ii. 416.
London, 4 ; Boston (U.S.), 4.

Tuckey, Tuckie, Tookey.—Bapt. 'the son of Tochi,' a variant of Tuck, q.v., where Domesday instances will be found. This

derivation is absolutely certain, as proved by the Hundred Roll references below.

Richard Toky, co. Wilts, 1273. A.
John Toky, co. Oxf., ibid.
Thomas Toky, co. Oxf., ibid.
William Toky, co. Oxf., ibid.
1599. Thomas Tookye, co. Leic.: Reg. Univ. Oxf. vol. ii. pt. ii. p. 236.
1604. Job Tookye, co. Leic. : ibid. p. 273.
William Toky, co. Soms., 1 Edw. III : Kirby's Quest, p. 151.
Adam Toky, co. Soms., 1 Edw. III : ibid. p. 205.
1624. William Elliott and Joane Tuckey : Marriage Lic. (London), ii. 142.
1779. Married — Henry Tookey and Ann Beardshaw: St. Geo. Han. Sq. i. 300.
1782. — Francis Tookie and Eliz. Elborn : ibid. p. 340.
London, 8, 1, 2.

Tuckson.—Bapt. 'the son of Tuck.' It is curious that I should have to go to America for the only modern instance I can find of this very early English surname. Instances of Tuckson will be found under Tuck, q.v.

Philadelphia, 1.

Tudball.—Bapt. 'the son of Theobald,' one more of the many variants of Theobald.

Thomas Tedball, co. Camb., 1273. A.
1578. William Kimloughe and Cicely Tudball: Marriage Lic. (London), i. 80.
MDB. (co. Somerset), 5.

Tudor, Tuder.—Bapt. 'the son of Tudor.' Miss Yonge has an interesting paragraph showing the probability that Tudor was a Welsh form of Theodore (Hist. Christian Names, i. 232).

Tuder fil. Griffini ab Mereduk, 12 Edw. I : BBB. p. 348.
Margaret Holl ap Rees ap Tewdor : Visit. Glouc., Harl. Soc., p. 114.
Rys ap Madoc ap Tudir : Visit. London, 1633, i. 220.
1707. Buried — Albinia, wife of Mr. John Tudor, *scrivener* : St. Mary Aldermary, p. 210.
1751. Married — Francis Tudor and Eliz. Higgs: St. Geo. Chap. Mayfair, p. 187.
London, 7, 0 ; Philadelphia, 6, 3.

Tuer.—Occup. 'the tewer,' a dresser of leather, a currier (v. Tewer). 'Teware, *corridiator*' : Prompt. Parv. p. 490. 'Tewyn lethyr, *corrodio*,' ibid. Possibly Twyer is the same.

Willelmus Twyer, 1379: P. T. Yorks. p. 72.
Robertus Twyer, 1379: ibid.
London, 1.

Tuffield, Tuffill; v. Tofield.

Tuke; v. Tuck.

Tulloch.—Local, 'at the tulloch,' from residence there beside. A Scotch name. Lower writes, 'Tulloch, Gael. *tulach*, a hillock. There are places specifically so called in the shires of Perth, Ross, and Aberdeen': Patr. Brit. p. 358.

London, 3; Philadelphia, 4.

Tumber.—Occup. 'the tumber,' i.e. the tumbler. 'Saltator, *tumbere*': Wright's Voc. i. 39, col. 2 (v. Skeat on *tumble*). Cf. fem. 'tombesteres Fetis and smale' (Chaucer, The Pardoner's Tale).

William le Tumber, c. 1300. M.

Tummon, Tummond, Tummons.—Occup. 'tom-man,' i.e. the servant of Tom. A curious but natural corruption. Tummon is one more instance of the many Yorkshire surnames of this class; cf. Matthewman, Addyman, Jackman, Ladyman, Bartleman, Sandeman, &c. The *d* in Tummond is excrescent, as in Simmonds or Hammond for Simon or Hamon.

Robert Thomasman, Fines Roll, 11 Edw I.
William Thomasman. V. 13.
Willelmus Thomasman, 1379: P. T. Yorks. p. 210.
Hugo serviens Thome, 1379: ibid. p. 157.
Alicia serviens Thome, 1379: ibid. p. 207.

The following two entries placed side by side settle the matter:

Johannes Tomman Cisson (i.e. John, the servant of Tom Cisson), 1379: P. T. Yorks. p. 269.
Thomas serviens Thome Cisson, 1379: ibid.

Also notice:

Willelmus Thomeman, 1379: P. T. Yorks. p. 213.
Thomas Tonman, 1379: ibid.
Sheffield, 4, 0, 0; West Rid. Court Dir., 0, 1, 1.

Tunbridge.—Local, 'of Tunbridge' or Tonbridge, a parish in co. Kent, fourteen miles from Maidstone.

Salomon de Tonebregg, co. Essex, 1273. A.
Robert de Tonebrugge, London, ibid.
London, 2; MDB. (co. Essex), 2.

Tunder, Thunder. — Occup. 'the tunder,' i.e. a vintner, a wine-tunner, one who poured wine into barrels or tuns. Hence such terms as 'tunnel' or 'tun-dish,' the vessel used for transferring the wine from cask to bottle (v. my English Surnames, p. 381). For further information, v. Tunneler and Aletunner.

Edmund le Tunder, bailiff of Norwich, 1237: FF. iii. 58.
Hugh le Tundur, 1273. A.
Richard le Tundur. T.
John de Northfolk, *tounder*, 8 Edw. III: Freemen of York, i. 28.

It was inevitable that an imitative variant in the shape of Thunder should arise after the meaning of the surname Tunder had become forgotten. Indeed, it is only in this form that the name has survived. For modern instances, v. Thunder. Lower's and Ferguson's suggestion that Thunder is a personal name and that it is an alias of Thor, the Jupiter-tonans of Northern mythology, cannot be upheld.

Philadelphia, 0, 3.

Tunks.—Bapt.; v. Tonkinson.

Tunnard; v. Townherd.

Tunneler. — Occup. 'the tunneler,' one who fills casks with wine, &c., from *tunne*, a barrel (v. Skeat on *ton*). The tunneler used the tunnel, or funnel, or tunner to expedite his work. 'Fonel, or tonowre, *fusorium, infusorium*': Prompt. Parv. 'Tonnell, to fylle wyne with': Palsgrave. v. Tunder.

William le Toneleur. H.
Ralph le Toneler (I have lost my reference to this).
John de Tikhill, *toundour*, 4 Edw. II: Freemen of York, i. 19.
Geoffrey le Thuneler, 9 Edw. III: ibid. p. 29.

Tunnicliffe, Tunnacliffe.—Local, 'of Tunnicliff,' in the parish of Rochdale, co. Lanc. For an American variant, v. Dunnicliff.

James Scholfield, of Tunnicliffe, par Rochdale, *husbandman*, 1663: Wills at Chester (1545-1620), p. 237.

1724-5. Married—John Tunnecliff and Eliz. Capp: St. Dionis Backchurch, p. 61.
1753. — Thomas Gould and Eliz. Tunnecliff: St. Geo. Chap. Mayfair, p. 236.
Joseph Tunnicliff, mayor of Macclesfield, 1818: Earwaker's East Cheshire, ii. 467.
Manchester, 2, 1; Rochdale, 1, 0; New York, 1, 0.

Tunnock.—Bapt. 'the son of Tunnoc,' an interesting name, found in co. Northumberland so early as the 12th century, and remains as Tunnock in that district still. I strongly suspect that some of the many Tullochs in the Newcastle Directory are not so Scotch as they look, but are an assimilation. Besides, there is a tendency to this interchange; cf. Bannister for Balister, or *banister* for *baluster*.

John fil. Tunnoc, 1196: KKK. vi. 59.
William fil. Tunnok, 1250: ibid. vi. 220.
Roger Tunnok, 1313: PPP. i. 29.
Robert Tunnokman and Richard Tunnokson were witnesses to the will of Henry of Wallsend, *clerk*, 1319: ibid. p. 149.
William Tunnok, *mariner*, 1335: ibid. p. 92.

In Mr. Welford's Hist. of Newcastle and Gateshead is recorded a benefaction to the Virgin Mary Hospital by

'Robert Tunnikysiman and Matilda his wife in 1305': PPP. i. 9.

This, of course, is Robert Tunnockman, literally Robert Tunnock's servant; cf. Matthewman, Bartleman, Jackman, &c.

Sunderland, 1.

Tunstall, Tunstill. — Local, 'of Tunstall,' parishes in diocs. Canterbury, Lichfield, York, Manchester, and Norwich; also as Townstall in dioc. Exeter. Tunstall, thirteen miles from Lancaster, is the parent of the Lancashire Tunstalls.

Hugh de Tonstalle, co. Kent, 1273. A.
Henry de Tunstal, co. Lanc., 17 Edw. II: Baines' Lanc. ii. 621.
William Tunstal, co. Lanc., 47 Edw. III: ibid.
1547. Married—Thomas Hurthelstone and Alyce Tonstale: St. Michael, Cornhill, p. 5.

Brian Tunstall, of Tunstall, Lancashire, 1609: Lancashire Wills at Richmond, p. 288.
Edmund Tunstall, of Netherburrow, parish of Tunstall, 1636: ibid.
London, 6, 1; Manchester, 1, 2; Lancaster, 1, 0; Philadelphia, 1, 0.

Tunwright. — Occup. 'the tun-wright,' a maker of tuns or casks, a cooper; cf. Arkwright, Sivewright, Cartwright, &c.; v. Tunder and Tunneler.
Johannes Tunwryght, 1379: P. T. Yorks. p. 217.

Tup.—Nick. 'the tup,' i.e. the ram; cf. Buck, Roebuck, Ram, &c.
John Tupp, *carnifex*, 10 Edw. II: Freemen of York, i. 17.
Margareta Tup, 1379: P. T. Yorks. p. 91.
Robertus Tup, 1379: ibid.
1756. Married — George Wilson and Ann Tupp: St. Geo. Han. Sq. i. 61. London, 1.

Tuphead.—Nick. Not a complimentary one.
Robert Tuppeheued, Pardons Roll, 6 Ric. II.

Tupman. — Occup. 'the tup-man,' a tup-herd (v. Tupper); cf. Cowman, Steerman, Bullman. 'Tupman, a breeder of tups or rams': Halliwell. For other Pickwickian names, v. Pickwick and Snodgrass.
1756. Married—William Tupman and Sarah Abbott: St. Geo. Han. Sq. i. 64. London, 1; Philadelphia, 2.

Tupper, Tupherd. — Occup. 'the tup-herd'; cf. Coward, Gelderd, Calvert, Stoddard, &c. The final *d* is also lost in Tripherd (v. Tripper) and sometimes in Gelderd (v. Geldard).
Willelmus Tuphird, 1379: P. T. Yorks. p. 217.
1746. Married — George Tupper and Eliz. Drury: St. Geo. Chap. Mayfair, p. 79.
1792. — Richard Davis and Maria Tupper: St. Geo. Han. Sq. ii. 84. London, 6, 0; Boston (U.S.), 11, 0.

Turbefield, Turbyfield, Turburville.—Local, 'of Turberville.' The locality in Normandy (?) cannot be found. The suffix *-ville* frequently becomes *-field* by corruption.
John de Turbervile, co. Berks, 1273. A.
Robert de Turbervill, co. Glouc., ibid.
Galiena de Turbevile, co. Wilts, ibid.

1566. Bapt.—Basil, s. William Trublefelde: Kensington Parish, i. 5.
1635. Married — Philip Colby and Rebecca Trubellvile: ibid. p. 71.
1639. — Thomas Wilkenson and Mary Turbervile: St. Dionis Backchurch, p. 24. London, 1, 1, 1.

Turbot, Turbat, Turbit, Turbett. — Bapt. 'the son of Turbert,' inevitably corrupted, almost as soon as it arose, into Turbot. In Domesday found as Turbert, a personal name. Not to be confounded with Tebbutt (v. Tebbitt), though it may have become absorbed in it.
Emonus Turberd, co. Yorks, 1273. A.
Eymes Turbert, co. Notts, ibid.
Andreas Turbut, co. Oxf., ibid.
Turbert de Wescot, Pipe Roll, 11 Hen. II, p. 74.
Henry Turbot, C. R., 32 Hen. III.
Adam Turbut, 1379: P. T. Yorks. p. 81.
Daniel Turbot, co. York. W. 20.

Few of the supposed fish-names are what they seem; v. Salman.
1748. Married—John Turbot and Mary Clark: St. Michael, Cornhill, p. 71.
1753. — William Turbitt and Mary Kennedy: St. Geo. Chap. Mayfair, p. 241.
— — William Millington and Margaret Turbutt: ibid. p. 243.
1791. — William Turbett and Eliz. King: St. Geo. Han. Sq. ii. 65.
Liverpool, 0, 1, 0, 0; Boston (U.S.), 0, 0, 1, 0; Philadelphia, 0, 0, 0, 1.

Turk.—Local, 'the Turk,' a Mohammedan; 'all Jews, Turks, Infidels, and Heretics': The Book of Common Prayer. Cf. Sarson.
William le Turc, co. Essex, 1273. A.
John Turk, co. Kent, ibid.
Philip Turk, co. Soms., 1 Edw. III: Kirby's Quest, p. 83.
Jacob le Turk. DD.
1552-3. Richard Petytte and Phillipa Turke: Marriage Lic. (London), i. 14.
1613. Bapt.—Jone, d. Robert Turke: St. Michael, Cornhill, p 111.
1751. Married—Thomas Turk and Eliz. Jones: St. Geo Chap. Mayfair, p. 202. London, 3; Philadelphia, 4.

Turkington.—Local, 'of Torkington,' q.v., an American variant.

Turle.—An abbreviated form of Turrell, q.v.
1641. George Tyrell and Anne Thurlow: Marriage Lic. (London), ii. 258.
1760. Married — Thomas Berry and Mary Tyrrl: St. Geo. Han. Sq. i. 96. London, 2; New York, 1.

Turnbuck.—Nick. This is a name that helps to elucidate the origin of Turnbull, q.v.
Alicia Turnebuk, 1379: P. T. Yorks. p. 66.

Turnbull, Trumble, Trumbull. – ?Nick.'turn-bull'(?). There can be little doubt about the origin of this name. Two great clan nicknames grew up in Liddesdale and the 'Debateable Land,' the Armstrongs and Turnbulls, both significant of that prowess which was so necessary in the times of Scotch and English raids across the border. To turn the bull at the baiting would be an exploit worthy a sobriquet in those rude times, and the possessor would be proud to bear it. The idea that this name is local must be given up. Trumble is a corruption of Turnbull, not Turnbull of Trumble. The earliest form is Turnebull.
Johannes Turnebull, 1379: P. T. Yorks. p. 268.

In the same record we find a similar nickname, that of Turnbuck.
Alicia Turnebuk, 1379: P. T. Yorks. p. 66.

The New York form Trumbull is met with in the 15th century:
David Trumbull or Turnbull, 1494-5: TTT. p. 187.
George Trumbull or Turnbull, 1494-5: ibid. p 188.
Jock Trumble, 1544: ibid. p. lii.
Wat Trombull, 1562: ibid. p. ciii.
1707 Bapt.— James, son of William Trumbal: St. Thomas the Apostle (London), p. 71.
For other variants, v. Tremble and Trimble.
London, 26, 1, 0; West Rid. Court Dir., 5, 1, 0; New York, 20, 2, 5.

Turnell.—?Local. Probably a corruption of the Yorkshire name of Thornhill, which is early found in the form of Thornell (v. Thornhill).
Hugo Turnell', et uxor, 1379: P. T. Yorks. p. 151.
West Rid. Court Dir., 5; London, 3; Philadelphia, 1.

Turner, Turnour. — Occup. 'the turner,' one who worked with a lathe. Lower quotes Mr. Fer-

guson as saying, ' Out of all proportion to the number of persons
engaged in the trade'; also as
suggesting that the name was in
many cases baptismal and of
Norman introduction. In a day
that knew little of ornamental
fictile vessels the turner would be
busy enough, and the only wonder
is that it is not, as a surname, as
common as Smith. A glance at
early registers will show how
familiar the occupation was.
Chaucer's Miller of Trumpington
could ' turn cuppes.'

' There dwelled also turners of beads':
Stow, iii. 174.
'Sponers, torners, and hatters.'
Cocke Lorelle's Bote.

To assert that Turnour is local
from ' de Tour Noire,' the Black
Castle (in Normandy, of course), is
childish ; and little better is Tour-
neour, a tilter. There is no evidence.

Aylbricht le Turnur, London, 1273. A.
Geoffrey le Turner, co. Camb., ibid.
William le Turnor, co. Oxf., ibid.
Johannes Turnour, turnour, 1379:
P. T. Yorks. p. 218.
William le Tournour. G.
Henry le Tornour, co. Soms., 1 Edw.
III: Kirby's Quest, p. 91.
1791. Married — George Turnor and
Ann Eleanor Hanmer: St. Geo. Han. Sq.
ii. 63.
London, 338, 0; Crockford, 62, 1;
Philadelphia, 329, 0.

Turney, Tournay.—Local, ' of
Tournay,' in Artois. Gosfrid
Tornai occurs in the Domesday of
Lincolnshire.

Geoffrey de Turnai, co. Linc., 1273. A.
Richard de Turney, co. Bucks, ibid.
William Turney, co. Notts, ibid.
1692. Married — Nathaniell Peacock
and Mary Turney: St. Michael, Cornhill,
p. 47.
London, 8, 0; MDB. (co. Kent), 0, 3;
Philadelphia, 8, 0.

Turnham.—Local, ' of Turn-
ham.' Turnham Green, formerly
a hamlet, now a parish, in co.
Middlesex. five miles from London.
Perhaps some other spot in North
England bore the same name.

Johannes de Turneham, 1379: P. T.
Yorks. p. 117.
1790. Married—Thomas Turnham and
Martha Emerton: St. Geo. Han. Sq. ii. 44.
London, 7.

Turnour.—Occup.; v. Turner.

Turnpenny. — ? Local, ' of
Turnepeny ' (?). I cannot find the
spot. I suspect, after all, that Twopeny or Twopenny may be one of
the modern forms of this name (v.
Twopenny). From Turnpenny to
Turpeny was inevitable, and the
step from this to the imitative
Twopeny is easy. The assertion
that it hails from Tupigny in
Flanders is only a guess. I have
' Abbas de Turpenay (C.)' in my
notebook. A London firm, Gamble
and Turnpenny, were known for
many years familiarly as ' Pitch and
Toss.'

Matilda Tornepeni. co. Oxf., 1273. A.
Nicholas Turnepeny, co. Oxf., ibid.
William Turnepenny, C. R., 9 Edw. I.
John Tournepeny, co. Soms., 1 Edw.
III: Kirby's Quest, p. 207.
Robert Turnepeny. G.
John Turnpeny. D.
1727. Married—Arthur Tawke and
Eliz. Turnpenny : St. Michael, Cornhill,
p. 64.
London, 3; Stanningley, co. York, 1;
Philadelphia, 2.

Turpin, Toppin, Topping.
—Bapt. ' the son of Thorfin,' a
popular name among the Danes,
which originated some of our
place-names ; e.g. Thorpanstye,
otherwise Thorfinstye Hall, in
the parish of Cartmel, co. Lanc.,
was so named from the owner
Thorfin or Torpin, a great landowner (of twelve manors) at the
time of the Doomsday Survey ; v.
Annals of Cartmel (Stockdale,
pp. 510, 592). Sty, A.S. stig, stigo ;
M.E. stie, stye. Meaning (1) a path,
as in ' Sty Head Pass'; (2) an
enclosure for swine.

'He groneth as our bore, lith in our stie.'
Chaucer, C. T. 7411.

(3) part of a house, probably what
we call ' a dais ' (v. sty, Skeat).
v. Tipping.

John Turpin, co. Oxf., 1273. A.
William Turpyn, 1379: P. T. Yorks.
London, 12, 1, 3; Oldham (Lanc.), 0,
1, 0; Boston (U.S.), 3, 0, 1.

Turrell, Turrill.—Bapt. ' the
son of Turold ' (v. Thorold). The
final d seems to have been dropped
through laziness ; v. Terrell.

Ralph Turold, co. Suff., 1273. A.
Thomas Torel, co. Soms., 1 Edw. III:
Kirby's Quest, p. 116.

Willelmus Turyell, 1379: P. T. Yorks.
p. 301.
1596-7. John Pluckwell and Audrey
Turrall: Marriage Lic. (London), i. 236.
1673. Married — George Martur and
Mary Turrell: St. Jas. Clerkenwell, i. 177.
London, 3, 3 ; Boston (U.S.), 1, 3.

Turtle, Turtill, Turtille.—
Bapt. ' the son of Thurkle'; v.
Thurkettle. This is Mr. Lower's
explanation, and I doubt not it is
the correct one.

Reginald Turtel, co. Camb., 1273. A.
John Turkyl, co. Camb., ibid.
Roger Turtle. D.
1627. Married — Henry Turtle and
Hanna Greene: St. Dionis Backchurch,
p. 22.
1750. — Richard Turtle and Lydia
Thorn: St. Geo. Chap. Mayfair, p. 177.
London, 5, 1, 0 ; West Rid. Court Dir.,
2, 0, 0 ; Sheffield, 4, 0, 0 ; New York, 0,
0, 1.

Turton. — Local, ' of Turton,'
a township in the parish of Bolton,
co. Lancaster. The surname has
crossed the borders into Yorkshire
and ramified strongly there.

1523. Sir Henry Turton, priest, fellow
of Christ's College, Manchester: Wills
at Chester, i. 198.
1563. Married — Rodger Turton and
Eliz. Shrigleye: Prestbury Church (co.
Chester), p. 11.
1601-2. Constantine Turton, co. Hants:
Reg. Univ. Oxf. vol. ii. pt. ii. p. 254.
Manchester, 5 ; London, 4 ; Sheffield,
17 ; Philadelphia, 2.

Turvey, Turvy.—Local, ' of
Turvey,' a parish in co. Bedford,
four miles from Olney.

1621. Richard Turvy, co. Worc.: Reg.
Univ. Oxf. vol. ii. pt. ii. p. 393.
1799. Married — William Turvey and
Sarah Dean : St. Geo. Han. Sq. ii. 200.
London, 4, 1 ; Philadelphia, 3, 0.

Tusler.—Occup. ' the touseler';
v. Tasseler, of which it is but a
variant. Also v. Tozer.

1793. Married—James Tusler and Mary
Denyer : St. Geo. Han. Sq. ii. 96.
London, 1.

Tustian, Tustin. — Bapt.
Thurstan, q.v.

Tuthill, Tuttle. — Local ; v.
Toothill.

Tuxbury.—Local, ' of Tewkesbury,' q.v.

Tuxford.—Local, ' of Tuxford,'
a parish in co. Notts, thirty miles
from Nottingham.

1753. Married—James Entwesle and Eliz. Tuxford: St. Geo. Chap. Mayfair, p. 259.
London, 4.

Twaddle, Tweddell, Tweddle, Twaddell. — Local, 'of Tweddale,' from residence in the valley of the Tweed. Cf. Teasdale, Tindal, Lonsdale, &c.

John Tweddel, 1587, accused of raiding over the Border: Nicolson and Burn, Hist. Westm. and Cumb. i. p. xxxi.
Willie Tweddel, 1587: ibid.
John Twedall, of Strines, 1670: Wills at Chester (1660-80), p. 273.
Edmund Twaddell, of Mierscough, 1666: Lancashire Wills at Richmond, p. 290.
1787. Married—Richard Badham and Grace Tweeddale: St. Geo. Han. Sq. i. 397.

Mr. H. J. Twaddle announced the change of his name to Tweeddale in the Times, Jan. 4, 1890.

London, 1, 1, 1, 0; Philadelphia, 0, 0, 4, 24.

Twamley; v. Twemlow.

Tweed. — Local, 'from the Tweed,' i.e. from the valley of the Tweed. v. Twaddle.

Adam Twede, 1379: P. T. Yorks. p. 196.
London, 2; Philadelphia, 9.

Tweedale, Tweedle.—Local, 'of Tweeddale'; v. Twaddle.

Philadelphia, 10, 3.

Tweedie, Tweedy. — Local, 'of Tweeddale.' Probably a corruption of Tweedale (v. Twaddle).

1624. Married — William Lake and Eliz. Twedy: St. Peter, Cornhill, i. 252.
1745. — Francisco Sisco and Mary Tweedy: St. Geo. Chap. Mayfair, p. 54.
London, 5, 3; Philadelphia, 3, 2.

Twelfthman. — ? Official, 'the twelfthman' (?); cf. Hundred. Twentyman (q.v.) is not of this class; it is occupative.

Johannes Twelfemen, 1379: P. T. Yorks. p. 276.

Twell, Twells, Twelves. — Local, 'at the well,' from residence thereby. In this case Atte-well (v. Attwell) has become Twell; cf. Nash for 'Atten-ash.' Twell, Twells, and Twelves are all found in co. Lincoln, the last being an imitative corruption. The final s in Twells and Twelves is the genitive form; cf. Jennings, Jones, Williams, &c.

1661. Married—George Twell and Ann Bateman: St. Jas. Clerkenwell, i. 107.
1703-4. Walter Wells and Dorothy Twells: Marriage Lic. (London), ii. 331.
1747. Married—John Astrie and Eliz. Twelves: St. Geo. Chap. Mayfair, p. 81.
MDB. (Lincoln), 7, 1, 3; Philadelphia, 0, 4, 3.

Twelvepence.—Nick. 'Twelve-pence'; cf. Fourpence and Nine-pence. The latter, as will be seen by reference, survived several generations; v. Thousandpound.

Fulco Twelpenes, co. Camb., 1273. A.

Twemlow, Twombley, Twomeley, Twamley.—Local, 'of Twemlow,' co. Chester.

Lyulph de Twemlowe, 1208: East Ches. ii. 42.
William de Twemlowe, 1376: ibid. p. 50 n.
1578. Married—Rauffe Brodehurst and Margery Twamlowe: Reg. Prestbury, Ches., p. 59.
1587. Thomas Beeche and Jone Twamlowe: ibid. p. 93.
William Kenedy, of Twemlow, 1591: Wills at Chester (1545-1620), p. 113.
John Twemlow, of Mere, co. Chester, husbandman, 1649: ibid. (1621-50), p. 222.
Manchester, 3, 0, 0, 0; Philadelphia, 0, 1, 1, 0; Crockford (Twamley), 4.

Twentyman. — Occup. 'the twinterman,' North English, one who tended twinters, i.e. two-year-old beasts. A.S. twy-winter. Mr. Lower says, 'The officer who commanded twenty armed men was called a vintenarius; and of this word I take Twentyman to be a translation' (Patr. Brit. p. 359). There is no evidence in support of this. The corruption to Twenty-man is imitative.

'At Fenham, 20 stirks and twynters, 1428: QQQ. p. 118, Accounts of Monastery on Holy Island.
'20 oxen, 26 stotts, 12 wedders and twints, 9 tupps,' Stock at Bolton Abbey, 1526: Whitaker's Craven, p. 403.
'6 oxen, 18 steres, 11 heifers, 21 twenters, 23 stirks,' 1556: Richmondshire Wills, Surt. Soc., p. 93.
Cf. Cowman, Steerman or Stierman, Bullman. The surname is still familiar in co. Cumberland.

Henry Twentyman. TT.
1618. Buried — Joseph XXman, of Woodhouses: Reg. Great Orton Church, Carlisle.
1748. Married — Henry Twentyman and Ann Martin: St. Geo. Han. Sq. i. 41.

1787. — John Spinks and Mary Twenty-man: ibid. p. 401.
London, 5; Crockford, 2.

Twentymark. — Nick.; cf. Twentypence. The old English mark was a coin valued at 13s. 4d. Possibly a sobriquet affixed on one whose salary was set down at that sum.

Geoffrey Tventimarc, co. Camb., 1273. A.
1342. June 21. Ralph changed with John Twentimark for Warsop in Yorkshire': The Rectory of Brisingham, co. Norf.: FF. i. 64.

Twentypence.—Nick.

Roger Twentipens, Close Roll, 39 Hen. III.

Cf. Fivepence, Sevenpence, Nine-pence, Twelvepence. Probably a translation; cf.

Roger Vint-deners, co. Berks, 1273. A.

Twiceaday, Twisaday. — ? ——. This curious name has existed for centuries in the district of Furness, North Lancashire. Probably it is a form of Tuesday, as other day-names exist, or existed (v. Saturday, Friday, Monday). Perhaps, like Christmas, Pentecost, &c., it was a personal name given to the child because born or baptized on that day.

Thomas Twysday. H.
Thomas Twisaday, Patent Roll, 1 Hen. VII. pt. iii.
1548. Married—Harry Twisedaie and Katherine Naila: St. Mary, Ulverston, i. 7.
1551. Buried—Harry Twisedaie: ibid. i. 15.
1618. Henry Twisaday, of Ulverston: Lancashire Wills at Richmond, i. 290.
1661. Edward Twiceaday, of Ulverston: ibid.
1664. George Twiseaday, of Ulverston: ibid.
'The account of Henry Twiceaday, collector of the window tax for the year ended March 25, 1725': Annals of Cartmel, p. 262.

The name still exists in Furness in both the above forms.

MDB. (co. Lanc.), 1, 2.

Twichell; v. Twitchell.

Twidale.—Local, 'of Tweed-dale'; v. Twaddle.

Manchester, 1.

Twiddy, Twidy.—Local. A variant of Tweedie, q.v.; cf. Twidale for Tweedale.

London, 3, 0 ; New York, 0, 1.

Twin, Twinn, Twine. — Nick. ' the twin,' one of twin brothers or sisters, a natural sobriquet.

Edmund Twyn, C. R., 8 Hen. IV.
Thomas Twyne, 1564 : Reg. Univ. Oxf. i. 254.
Laurence Twine, 1564 : ibid. p. 255.
1612-3. Stephen Newson and Avice Twine : Marriage Lic. (London), i. 19.
1624. William Clarke and Anne Twynn : ibid. p. 145.
1698. Married — Francis Palmer and Catharine Twine : St. Dionis Backchurch, p. 47.
1750. — Henry Twin and Mary Johns : St. Geo. Chap. Mayfair, p. 185.
London, 1, 1, 1 ; New York, 0, 1, 2.

Twineham, Twyman, Twynam, Twynham, Twinem. — Local, ' of Twineham,' a parish in the dioc. of Chichester, co. Sussex ; cf. Deadman and Putman for Debenham and Puttenham ; also Swetman for Swettenham.

1565. Edward Preston and Anne Twynam : Marriage Lic. (London), i. 30.
1671-2. Married — Thomas Fidge and Hester Twyman : Canterbury Cath., p. 61.

Mr. G. Twyman played for Kent v. Essex in a cricket match, Aug. 15, 1887 ; v. Standard.

London, 1, 3, 1, 0, 0 ; Manchester, 0, 0, 0, 1, 0 ; Liverpool, 0, 0, 0, 0, 1 ; Philadelphia (Twyman), 1 ; Boston (U.S.) (Twynam), 1.

Twining.—Local, ' of Twining,' a parish in co. Gloucester, two miles from Tewkesbury.

1804. Married — Martin Kelly and Hester Twining : St. Geo. Han. Sq. ii. 298.
London, 5 ; Philadelphia, 21.

Twisaday ; v. Twiceaday.

Twisden.—Local,' of Twysden.' Mr. Lower, quoting Shirley's Noble and Gentle Men, writes, ' This surname is derived from Twysden, or Twysenden-Brough, an estate in the parish of Goudhurst, co. Kent . . . where Adam de Twysden resided in the reign of Edw. I. His descendants sold it in the reign of Henry VI.' Mr. Lower adds that ' at Sandhurst in the same county there is another Twysden,

also said to have been a seat of the family, temp. Edw. I ' (Patr. Brit. p. 359).

1591. Charles Tuisden, co. Kent : Reg. Univ. Oxf. vol. ii. pt. ii. p. 186.
— Roger Tuisden, co. Kent : ibid.
1609. Thomas Dalyson and Eliz. Twisden, of East Malling, co. Kent : Marriage Alleg. (Canterbury), p. 175.
London, 1 ; MDB. (co. Kent), 2.

Twiss, Twisse, Twist. — Local, ' of Twiss.' The spot is undoubtedly either the hamlet styled Twiss Green, in the parish of Newchurch-Kenyon, co. Lanc., or a place so called in the immediate vicinity. All the earlier instances hail from that district. With Twist, cf. Gorst for Gorse in the same neighbourhood.

Richard Twiss, of Kenion, 1619 : Wills at Chester (1545-1620), p. 196.
Randle Twisse, of Coppenhall, 1585 : ibid.
Thomas Twist, of Kenyon, 1593 : ibid.
1787. Married — Thomas Twist and Ann Gray : St. Geo. Han. Sq. i. 402.
1805. Married—Rev. Robert Twiss and Fanny Walker : ibid. ii. 320.
Manchester, 3, 1, 3 ; Liverpool, 3, 0, 3 ; London, 3, 0, 1 ; Philadelphia, 4, 0, 4.

Twitchell, Twichell.—Local, ' at the twitchel,' a passage, an alley, from residence thereby. For further information, v. Twitchin.

1655. Married — Edward Nethercoate and Eliz. Twichell : St. Michael, Cornhill, p. 35.
1665. Andrew Atkins and Eliz. Twitchell : Marriage Alleg. (Canterbury), p. 129.
1806. Married—Josiah Spencer Twitchell and Eliz. Watson : St. Geo. Han. Sq. ii. 341.
Crockford, 1, 0 ; New York, 1, 0 ; Philadelphia, 3, 0 ; Boston (U.S.), 22, 4.

Twitchin, Twitching, Twitchings,Twitchen.—Local, ' at the twitchen,' an alley that led from one parish to another, or between two main thoroughfares. ' Twitchel, a narrow passage, an alley. North ' (Halliwell). In the South it was Twitchen. The g in Twitching and Twitchings is an excrescence, the final s being genitive (cf. Jennings from Jenin). In Wood's City of Oxford, edited by Mr. Clark, I find, ' A messuage in " Kibald's twychen," that is, I sup-

pose, " Kibaldi bivium," a double way, or a way having two parts, and common to tow parishes, as that was without doubt to St. Maries and St. Johns ' (i. 187). Further on I find mention of ' Kepeharme's Twychen ' (p. 199) ; and again, ' Sewey's Twychen ' (p. 223). That the word was familiar in the hereditary surname period is clear from the following entries :

Richard Twychenweye, co. Soms., 1 Edw. III : Kirby's Quest, p. 238.
Henry Twychenweye, co. Soms., 1 Edw. III : ibid. p. 234.
Nicholas Twycheenweye, co. Soms., 1 Edw. III : ibid.

i.e. ' at the Twychen way,' the way that led to the twitchen, or more probably the passage or alley itself. The surname still lingers in the neighbourhood of Oxford.

Richard de la Twichena, co. Devon, 1273. A.
1604. Andrew Twitchin, co. Hants : Reg. Univ. Oxf. vol. ii. pt. ii. p. 278.
1744. Married—James Twickten (sic) and Mary Benson : St. Geo. Han. Sq. i. 33.
London, 1, 1, 1, 0 ; MDB. (co. Berks),0, 0, 0, 1 ; New York, 2, 0, 1, 0.

Twombley, Twomeley ; v. Twemlow.

Twopenny, Twopeny.—Said to be from Tupigny in Flanders (Edin. Review, April, 1855), presumably because there happens to be a place so called. The twopenny piece was an early coin in England; v. topens (Halliwell). Both Fourpence and Fourpenny (q.v.) were English surnames. I suspect Twopenny is a nickname, if it be not a corruption of Turnpenny, q.v.

Twoyearold.—Nickname ; cf. Twentyman.

Thomas Twoyearolde, co. Lanc. AA. 1.
William Twoyearold, of Wich Malbank, Nantwich, 1660 : Wills at Chester (1660-80), p. 273.

Twycross.—Local, ' of Twycross,' a parish in co. Leicester, six miles from Atherstone. The place probably took its name from some spot on which was fixed a double cross ; v. Twyford.

1586. William Twycross, or Tuicrosse : Reg. Univ. Oxf. iii. 134.

1689. John Blisse, of Oxford, *grocer*, and Dorothye Twycrosse, of the same: Marriage Alleg. (Canterbury), p. 114. London, 1; Boston (U.S.), 1.

Twydell.—Local, ' of Tweeddale'; v. Twaddle.

London, 1.

Twyford, Twiford. — Local, ' of Twyford,' parishes in cos. Bucks, Leicester, Norfolk, and Hants. Also chapelries in cos. Wilts and Derby. Probably the place-name arose from the fact that there was a double ford there. Hence the commonness of the place-name; cf. Twycross. Of Tiverton, in Devonshire, Lewis writes, 'This place, formerly called Twyford, Twyfordton, or Twofordton, derives its name from its situation between two rivers, the Exe and the Lowman': Top. Dict. iv. 349.

(Dominus) de Twyford, co. Bucks, 20 Edw. I. R.
1642. Thomas Twyford and Mary Henwood: Marriage Lic. (Westminster), p. 40.
1770. Married — Henry Twiford and Martha Wheeler: St. Geo. Han. Sq. i. 202.
London, 3, 0; Philadelphia, 0, 1; New York, 1, 0.

Twyman, Twynam, Twynham.—Local; v. Twineham.

Tyas, Tyers, Tyars.— ?——. I can furnish no satisfactory solution of this surname.

Walerand le Tyeis, co. Soms., 1273. A.
Henry le Tyeys, co. Oxf., ibid.
Franco le Tyeys, co. York, ibid.
Terric le Tyes, cos. Essex and Hereford, Hen. III–Edw. I. K.
1770. Married — Richard Tyas and Eliz. White: St. Geo. Han. Sq. i. 109.
1783. — Jonathan Thompson and Mary Tyers: ibid. p. 350.
London, 2, 2, 2; Philadelphia, 0, 2, 0.

Tydd.—Bapt.; v. Tidd.

Oxford, 1.

Tye, Tighe, Tygh, Tyghe, Tigh.—Local, 'at the Tye.' ' *Tye*, an extensive common pasture': Halliwell. ' *Tye*: it generally means a small piece of common land close to a village, as Telscombe Tye, a few miles from Brighton': Lower, Patr. Brit. p. 359.

Hugh de la Tye, co. Sussex, 1273. A.
Peter atte-Tye, co. Norf., 10 Edw. III: FF. vi. 114.

Peter de Ty, co. Norf., 1342: ibid. vii. 395.
John Tye, co. Norf., 3 Hen. IV: FF. x. 67.
1574. Married—Bartholomew Milborn and Parnell Tye: St. Thomas the Apostle (London), p. 5.
1608. — Thomas Tye and Marie Collins: St. Michael, Cornhill, p. 19.
1703. — Richard Bridgman and Eliz. Tigh: St. Mary Aldermary (London), p. 37.
1784. — James Tye and Sarah Lord: St. Geo. Han. Sq. i. 357.
London, 4, 3, 0, 0, 0; MDB. (Norfolk), 4, 0, 0, 0, 0; Philadelphia, 0, 0, 3, 2, 0; Boston (U.S.), 2, 40, 0, 0, 2.

Tyerman.—Occup. ' the tireman,' ' a dealer in dresses and all other kinds of ornamental clothing' (Halliwell).

John Tyerman, temp. Eliz. Z.
John Tireman, co. Norf. FF.
1638. Buried — John Tyreman: Kensington Parish Church, p. 114.
1663. Married — John Tyreman and Eliz. Wood: St. Jas. Clerkenwell, i. 111. London, 3.

Tyers; v. Tyas.

Tygh, Tyghe.—Local; v. Tye.

Tyldsley.—Local, ' of Tyldesley'; v. Tildesley.

Tyler, Tylor.— Occup. ' the tiler,' one who bakes clay into tiles, a tiler. A.S. *tigele*, Latin *tegula*, a tile, from *tegere*, to cover.

Geoffrey le Tylere, co. Hunts, 1273. A.
Ralph le Tilere, co. Hunts, ibid.
Hugh le Tygheler. H.
Adam le Tyghelere, c. 1300. M.
Robert le Tiegheler, co. Soms., 1 Edw. III: Kirby's Quest, p. 187.
1611. Robert Tyler and Alice Callis: Marriage Lic., ii. 7.
1658. Married — Thomas Nash and Mary Tiler: St. Jas. Clerkenwell, i. 99.
London, 58, 3; Philadelphia, 40, 0.

Tyndale, Tyndall. — Local, ' of Tynedale,' from residence in the valley of the Tyne; cf. Tweedale and Tweedall; for early references v. Tindal.

1643-4. Francis Butler and Amphillis Tyndall: Marriage Lic. (London), ii. 273.
1798. Married — Samuel Phelps and Anne Catherine Tyndale: St. Geo. Han. Sq. ii. 177.
London, 2, 2; Philadelphia, 12, 1.

Tyrrell; v. Terrell.

Tyson. — Bapt. ' the son of Dionise,' from the nick. Dy, whence

Dyson, sharpened to Tyson. In spite of adverse criticism I still cleave to this as the true solution; cf. Tennyson (q.v.) for Dennison from the same once popular North-English personal name. The name Tyson has almost assumed the dimensions of a Scottish clan in Furness and South Cumberland. Of the truth of this derivation I have not a doubt; v. Denny, Dennis, Dyson, &c.

1553. Married — William Tyson and Esabell Cowhird: St. Mary, Ulverston, p. 20.
1557. Buried — Esabell Tyson: ibid. p. 28.
1567. Bapt. — Mathewe Tyson: ibid. p. 49.
1577. Leonard Tyson, of Broughton-in-Furness: Lancashire Wills at Richmond, i. 291.
1593. William Tyson, of Dalton-in-Furness: ibid.
1598. John Tyson, of parish of Aldingham: ibid.
London, 5; MDB. (co. Cumb.), 22; Philadelphia, 82.

Tytherleigh. — Local, ' of Tytherley.' East and West Tytherley are two parishes in co. Hants, near Stockbridge.

1790. Married—Jacob Bown and Mary Tytherleigh: St. Geo. Han. Sq. ii. 39.
London, 3; MDB. (co. Devon), 1.

Tyzack.—? Local. This curious-looking name perplexed me for years, being well established in Yorkshire, yet without representatives in the Yorkshire Poll Tax, 1379. Several allusions in Brand's History of Newcastle, published in 1789, explain its history. In 1619 Sir Robert Mansell built some glass-works at Newcastle, bringing several skilled artisans, with their families, from France. Of these there were two brothers, married, called Teswicke.

1619. Bapt.—John Teswicke, sonne of Tymothie Teswicke, *glasse-maker*, a Frenchman (Reg. St. Nicholas): Brand, Hist. Newcastle, ii. 43.
1620. Samuel Tizick, *glasmaker* (ibid.): ibid. p. 43.
1647. Robert Tizzick, *broadglasmaker* (ibid.): ibid.
1679. William Tizacke obtained a lease of the 'Western glass-houses': ibid. p. 45.
1684. Peregrine Tizack obtained a lease of the 'Eastern glass-houses': ibid. p. 46.

1679. Buried — Abigail, d. of John Tizacke: Brand, Hist. Newcastle, i. 340.

The surname spread with surprising rapidity, all the branches being prolific. Henzell and Tittery were two other French families introduced into Newcastle with the glass-works. The three names monopolized glassmaking in the district for generations. I feel deeply indebted to the clerk of St. Nicholas for adding that one magic word 'Frenchman' to the first entry, occurring as it does in the very year that glass-works were set up.

West Rid. Court Dir., 7; Sheffield, 9; Leeds, 1.

Tyzemon; v. Tesseyman.

U

Ubank.—Local, 'of the yew-bank,' from residence on the bank or slope where the yew-trees grew. For further instances of U for Yew, v. Udall (= Yewdale).

1541. Thomas Ubanke: Reg. St. Peter, Cornhill, i. 105.
1573. Henry Ewbanke, London: Reg. Univ. Oxf. vol. ii. pt. ii. p. 56.
1600. Bapt.—Marie, d. Henry Vbancke: St. Jas. Clerkenwell, i. 37.
1604-5. Toby Ewbanke, co. Durham: Reg. Univ. Oxf. vol. ii. pt. ii. p. 280.
1754. Married—William Ubank and Eliz. Fox: St. Geo. Chapel, Mayfair, p. 270.
Crockford, 1.

Udall, Udell, Udale.—Local, 'of or from Yewdale,' a valley at the north end of Coniston Lake; cf. Ubank for Yewbank.

1586. Thomas Arneway and Margaret Udall: Marriage Lic. (Westminster), p.9.
Agnes Udall, widow of Yewdale, Furness, 1613: Lancashire Wills at Richmond, i. 291.
1747. Married—Benjamin Capon and Mary Vdall: St. Geo. Chap. Mayfair, p. 98.
London, 3, 0, 0; Manchester, 3, 1, 0; MDB. (co. Derby), 0, 0, 1; (co. Stafford), 0, 0, 2; Oxford, 0, 1, 0; Philadelphia, 1, 2, 0.

Udy.—Bapt. 'the son of Udie,' seemingly peculiar to Cornwall and parts of Devon.

1544. Married — Richard Udie and Alse Nanskevell: Reg. St. Columb Major, p. 137.
1545. Bapt. — Richard, son of Udie Myli: ibid. p. 3.
1546. — John, son of Udie Geyne: ibid. p. 4.
1548. — Dorothie, son of Udie Typpett: ibid. p. 5.
1550. — Robert, son of Udie Hodge: ibid. p. 6.
1553. — Thomas, son of Robert Udie: ibid. p. 7.
Cornwall Dir. (Farmers' List), 5; MDB. (Cornwall), 3.

Uff.—Local, 'of Ulph,' q.v.; a corruption.

MDB. (co. Hertford), 1; (co. Bucks), 1.

Ufford. — Local, 'of Ufford,' parishes in cos. Suffolk and Northants.

Robert de Ufford, co. Suffolk, 1273. A.
1635. Bapt.—Diana, d. Joseph Vfforde: St. Jas. Clerkenwell, i. 129.

Uglow.—? Local. The derivation of this name must be sought for in co. Cornwall.

1750. Married — James Dudding and Sarah Uglow: St. Geo. Chap. Mayfair, p. 184.
MDB. (co. Cornwall), 12.

Ulfkettle. — Bapt. 'Ulf-ketel' or 'Wulf-ketel,' i.e. 'Ulf's cauldron.' The Domesday form is 'Ulchetel,' one more of many compounds of *kettle*; v. Chettle and Kettle. This form is again reduced to Ulkell and Ulchel (v. Kell and Chell) in Hist. Dunelm., Surtees Soc., pp. 19, 20.

Ulfcytel of East Anglia marries a daughter of Æthelred: Freeman, Norm. Conq. i. 412.

Ulger.—Bapt. 'the son of Ulger,' no doubt a form of Algar, q.v.

William Ulgar, co. Oxf., 1273. A.
Cristina Ulger, co. Oxf., ibid.
1667. Thomas Atkins and Susanne Ulgar: Marriage Alleg. (Canterbury), p. 134.

Ullathorne.—Local. Probably a variant of the North-English Ellithorne, q.v.

1596. Roger Ullathorne, of Netherburrow, parish of Tunstall: Lancashire Wills at Richmond, i. 291.
1633. Richard Vllathornes, of Dalton: ibid. p. 292.

1729. Married—Gilbert Remphrey and Eliz. Ullithorn: St. Geo. Han. Sq. i. 7.
London, 3.

Ullmer, Ulmer, Ulmar. — Bapt. 'the son of Ulmar' or Wulmar; v. Woolmer for early English instances of this personal name.

1578. Johann Rodolph Ulmerus (Zurich): Reg. Univ. Oxf. vol. ii. pt. ii. p. 82.
1768. Married — Matthew Frederick Ullmer and Susanna Collins: St. Geo. Han. Sq. i. 175.
London, 6, 0, 0; Boston (U.S.), 0, 3, 3.

Ullock, Hullock.—Local, 'of Ullock,' a part-township in the parish of Dean, near Cockermouth, co. Cumb.

1611. Jenet Vllocke: Lancashire Wills at Richmond, i. 292.
1667. Married — Henry Ullock and Margaret Johnson: Parish Church, Kensington, p. 78.
1680. William Vllock: Lancashire Will at Richmond, i. 292.
1800. Bapt. — Eleanor, d. George Ullock: Parish Church, Ulverston, p. 539.
MDB. (co. Cumb.), 1, 2; (co. Westmoreland), 1, 1.

Ulph.—(1) Bapt. 'the son of Ulf,' a favourite personal name at the time of the Conquest and for a century onward; v. Wolff (v. Yonge, ii. 267). (2) Local, 'of Ulph,' a parish in the dioc. of Norwich.

London, 2; MDB. (Norfolk), 3.

Ulyat, Ulyatt, Ulyeat.— Local. The suffix is doubtless -yate (i.e. gate); v. Yate. I cannot discover any spot of this name. (2) Bapt. Possibly a corruption of Elliot, q.v.; cf. Ulgar for Elgar and Algar.

1742. Married—John Ulyat and Ann Clasan: St. Geo. Chap. Mayfair, p. 24. MDB. (co. Cambridge), Ulyatt, 6; London, 0, 1, 1; Crockford, 2, 0, 0; West Rid. Court Dir., 0, 1, 0.

Umfreville, Umfrewill, Umphreville.
—Local, 'de Umframville,' evidently of Norman descent.

Gilbert de Umfraunville, co. Northumberland, 1273. A.
John de Umfravile, co. Devon, ibid.
Ingram de Umframville, co. Northumberland, 20 Edw. I. R.
Gilbert de Umframville, co. Northumberland, ibid.

I find only one representative of this great old name in the London Directory.

Samuel Umfrewill, boot and shoe maker.
London, 0, 1, 0; MDB. (Essex), 0, 0, 1; (co. Kent), 1, 0, 0.

Umpleby, Umphelby.
—Local, 'of Umpleby.' This is another local surname of whose history I can find no trace. It evidently represents some locality in co. York.

MDB. (West Rid. Yorks), 11, 0; London, 0, 1.

Unchaste.
—Nick. 'the unchaste.'

Symon Incaste, co. Wilts, 1273. A.

Uncle, Uncles, Unkles.
—Nick. 'the uncle'; cf. Cousin and Neave. Uncles doubtless represents the patronymic or genitive s, as in Williams, Jones, Neaves, &c.

John le Uncle, co. Essex, 1273. A.
Walter Unkle, co. Linc., ibid.
Robert Unkle. H.
'Lease to Thomas Unkle of a wood within the Manor of Bolynbroke, Nov. 30, 1485': Materials for Hist. Henry VII, p. 593.
1551. Married—John Lucas and Jone Unkulles: St. Dionis Backchurch, p. 3.
1557. — John Clyffe and Jone Unckell: ibid.
1607. John Uncle, co. Sussex: Reg. Univ. Oxf. vol. ii. pt. ii. p. 205.
1670. John Uncle, d. John Uncle: St. Jas. Clerkenwell, i. 247.
1792. Married — Thomas Uncle and Louisa Maria Noble: St. Geo. Han. Sq. ii. 79.
London, 0, 2, 0; New York, 0, 0, 4.

Uncleson.
— Nick. (?). Eliza Uncleson occurs in the Philadelphia Directory. Probably it is a corruption of some other surname.

Underdown.
—Local, 'of the under-down,' i.e. below the down or hill. Synonymous with Underhill; v. Downe.

Richard Underdoune, co. Devon, Hen. III-Edw. I. K.
1580. Married—Raphaell Hearne and Allice Underdowne: St. Dionis Backchurch, p. 9.
London, 3; Philadelphia, 6.

Underhay.
— Local, 'under the hay,' i.e. hedge; v. Hay, one who lived below the hedge.

Cf. William Underwalle, co. Oxf., 1273. A.
1752. Married—Edward Underhay and Eleanor Asher: St. Geo. Chap. Mayfair, p. 230.
London, 5.

Underhill.
—Local, 'under the hill,' one who resided below the hill.

William Underhill, co. Bedf., 1273. A.
John Underhelde, C. R., 33 Edw. I.
1751. Married —John Carruthers and Betty Underhill: St. Dionis Backchurch, p. 70.
1752. — George Manley and Catherine Underhill: St. Geo. Chap. Mayfair, p. 219.
London, 11; Oxford, 8; Philadelphia, 5.

Underwood.
—Local, 'of the under-wood,' living at the foot of the wood.

Robert Underwode, C. R., 33 Hen. III.
John Underwode, co. Oxf., 1273. A.
Hugh Underwod, co. Camb., ibid.
Alexander de Sub-bosco, co. Camb., ibid.
Robertus Vndrewode, 1379: P. T. Howdenshire, p. 27.
1650. Married—Benjamin Underwood and Margrett Buxton: St. Dionis Backchurch, p. 27.
London, 38; Philadelphia, 14.

Undrell.
— Local, 'under the hill,' one who resided below the hill; a corruption of Underhill, q.v. This solution is easily proved.

1625. Francis Lee and Sarah Underell: Marriage Lic. (Westminster), p. 31.
1646. Bapt.—Elissabeath, d. Humphrey and Elissabeathe Undrill: Parish Church, Kensington, p. 36.
1656. — Rebeckea, d. Humphray Undrell: ibid. p. 42.
1659. Buried—Thomas Underell: ibid. p. 129.
London, 1.

Unett.
—? ——. I cannot suggest any derivation of this surname at all satisfactory to myself.

1598-9. Richard Unet, co. Hereford: Reg. Univ. Oxf. vol. ii. pt. ii. p. 233.

1612. John Unett, son of Walter Unett: St. Dionis Backchurch (London), p. 95.
1753. Married — Robert Miller and Frances Unett: St. Geo. Chap. Mayfair, p. 248.
London, 3; MDB. (co. Hereford), 2.

Unsworth, Hunsworth.
— (1) Local, 'of Unsworth,' a parish, once a chapelry in the ancient parish of Oldham, three miles from Bury, co. Lancaster. (2) Local, 'of Hunsworth,' a township in the parish of Birstall, three miles from Bradford, W. Rid. Yorks. No doubt these two surnames have become inextricably mixed.

David de Honneswrth, co. Staff., 1273. A.
Robertus Hunsworth, 1379: P. T. Yorks. p. 73.
John Unsworth, of Golborne (co. Lanc.), 1590: Wills at Chester (1545-1620), p. 196.
Richard Unsworth, of Bury (co. Lanc.), 1590: ibid.
James Unsworth, of Bolton (co. Lanc.), 1608: ibid.
Henry Unsworth, 1682: Preston Guild Rolls, p. 196.
London, 4, 0; Manchester, 13, 0; Philadelphia, 0, 8.

Unthank, Onthank.
—Local, 'of Unthank.' There are two townships of this name, one in Cumberland, the other in Northumberland.

'To George Clementson for xvi. bushells of wheat to sow at Unthanke, £vi. ivs.' 1623: VVV. p. 217.
William de Unthanc, 1233: KKK. vi. 163.
John de Unthanc, 18 Edw. I: KKK. iv. 218.
Richard de Unthank, co. Cumb., 20 Edw. I. R.
Edmond Unthank, 1539: PPP. pp. 174-194.
John Unthanke, 1561: QQQ. p. xxxii.
1577. Henry Unthancke and Margery Maye: Marriage Lic. (London), i. 76.
'James Unthank, in 1732, gave by will £20 to the poor of the township of Culgarth': Jefferson's Hist. and Ant. of Leath Ward, co. Cumberland, p 452.
MDB. (co. Cumb.), 1, 0; (co. Durham), 1, 0; Worcester (U.S.), 0, 2.

Unwin.
—Bapt. 'the son of Unwin.' This surname has ramified in a most extraordinary manner. Lower records an Onwen, a manumitted slave (Cod. Dipl. 971). One of the many personal names with -win as suffix; cf. Baldwin, Aylwin, Goodwin.

Unwona, bishop of Dorchester: Parker, Early Hist. of Oxford, p. 138.
Philip Unwyne, co. Hunts, 1273. A.
William Unwine, co. Camb., ibid.
William Onwinne, co. Oxf., ibid.
Reginald Hunwyn, co. Camb., ibid.
Simon Unnewyn, co. Linc., ibid.
1617. Bapt. — Katharine, d. George Unwen : St. Jas. Clerkenwell, i. 80.
1794. Married — Samuel Unwin and Hannah Hawkridge : St. Geo. Han. Sq. ii. 123.
London, 16 ; West Rid. Court Dir., 12.

Upcher, Upsher.—(1) Local, 'of Upshire,' a hamlet in the parish of Waltham Abbey, co. Essex. (2) Local, 'of Upchurch,' a parish in co. Kent. Possibly occasionally a corruption. But (1) must be considered the true parent.

1620-1. Thomas Upcher (of Colchester, co. Essex) and Anne Ayre : Marriage Lic. (London), i. 96.
1639. Buried—Roger, s. William Upchurch : St. Thomas the Apostle (London), p. 122.
Crockford, 7, 0 ; London, 0, 1 ; MDB. (Huntingdon), 0, 1.

Upcott.—Local, ' of Upcott.' There are four hamlets of this name in co. Devon, in the parishes of Culmstock, Dowland, North Molton, and Rockbeare.

Robert de Uppecote, co. Soms., 1273. A.
Joel de Uppecote, co. Devon, ibid.
John de Uppecot, co. Devon, ibid.
Reginald de Uppecot, co. Devon, Hen. III-Edw. I. K.
1600. John Upcott, co. Devon : Reg. Univ. Oxf. vol. ii. pt. ii. p. 243.
1789. Married—John Tucker and Ann Upcott : St. Geo. Han. Sq. ii. 18.
London, 1 ; Crockford, 1 ; MDB. (Devon), 4.

Upcraft.—Local, 'at the upcroft,' i. e. the upper enclosure (v. Craft), from residence therein or thereby.

1643. Married — John Upcraft and Eustace Warren : St. Jas. Clerkenwell, iii. 75.
1774. — James Upcroft and Mary Pearson : St. Geo. Han. Sq. i. 246.
London, 1 ; New York, 1.

Upfold, Upfill.—Local, 'at the up-fold,' i.e. the upper pen or enclosure, from residence thereby. Upfill represents a common corruption of *-fold* or *-field* as a suffix.

1713. William Upfold and Anna Maria Cockayne : Marriage Lic. (London), ii. 339.
London, 1, 1 ; MDB. (Sussex), 1, 0 ; (co. Hereford), 0, 2.

Upham.—Local, ' of Upham,' a parish in Hampshire. This surname has ramified in an extraordinary manner in the United States.

Nicholas de Upham, co. Wilts, 1273. A.
1749. Married — Joseph Upham and Anne Holt: St. Geo. Chap. Mayfair, p. 130.
1753. — Edward Upham and Mary Empson : ibid. p. 249.
London, 1 ; MDB. (Soms.), 3 ; Boston (U.S.), 51.

Uphill.—Local, ' of Uphill,' a parish in co. Somerset.

Henry Uppenhull, co. Wilts, 1273. A.
Robert Uppehull, co. Oxf., ibid.
Geldanus Uppehill, co. Devon, Hen. III-Edw. I. K.
John Uppehulle, co. Soms., 1 Edw. III : Kirby's Quest, p. 89.
1629. Bapt.—Ann, d. Robert Uphill : St. Jas. Clerkenwell, i. 112.
1675. Richard Uphill and Ellinor Leigh : Marriage Alleg. (Canterbury), p. 239.
Boston (U.S.), 1.

Upholster.—Occup. ' the upholsterer,' obsolete as a surname.

1397. Alice Upholdesterr : Cal. of Wills in Court of Husting (2).

Upjohn.—Bapt. ' the son of John,' a corrupted form of the Welsh patr. Ap-john (= English Johnson). Such corruptions seem to have been common, as the following entries will testify :

Nycholas up-Thomas, 1557: St. Dionis Backchurch (London), p. 77.
1563. Buried—John Upharrye, prentice with John Cooke : ibid. p. 187.
1571. — Hughe Uprice, servant with William Poole: St. Michael, Cornhill, p. 192.
1585. Married — John Peycocke and Margarete Updavi: St. Dionis Backchurch, p. 10.
Robert Upprichard, 1637 : St. Mary Aldermary (London), p. 18.
Roger ap-John, of Worthenbury, 1638 : Wills at Chester (1621-50), p. 124.
Ellis ap-John, of Allington, 1641 : ibid.
1750. Bapt.—Francis, — of James and Mary Upjohn: St. Jas.Clerkenwell, ii. 293.
Of all the above specimens I have only found two, Upjohn and Uprichard, in modern directories.
London, 4.

Upperton.—Local, ' of Uppington.' Probably a corruption ; cf. Catterson for Cattinson, or Patterson for Pattinson. Uppington is a parish in co. Salop.

(Dominus) de Uppiton, co. Salop, 1273. A.

1578. Thomas Upperton, co. Berks : Reg. Univ. Oxf. vol. ii. pt. ii. p. 82.
1619. John Uppington, co. Soms. : ibid. p. 377.
1780. Married—Joseph York and Eliz. Upperton : St. Geo. Han. Sq. ii. 23.
London, 2 ; Boston (U.S.), 1.

Uprichard.—Bapt. ' the son of Richard'; v. Upjohn.

Philadelphia, 1 ; New York, 1.

Upright.—Nick. ' the upright.'

Symon Upriht, co. Camb., 1273. A.
Five centuries later this surname turns up in co. Sussex :
1787. Married—John Upright, of Heatfield, Sussex, and Ann Holgate : St. Geo. Han. Sq. i. 397.
Philadelphia, 1 ; New York, 2.

Upsall.—Local, ' of Upsall,' two townships in the parishes of South Kilvington and Ormsby, N. Rid. Yorks.

Geoffrey de Upsal, co. York, 1273. A.
Richard de Upsale, co. York, ibid.
Robertus de Vpsale, 1379 : P. T. Yorks. p. 67.
Cecilia de Vpsale, 1379 : ibid. p. 62.
1727. Married — Joseph Upstale (sic) and Mary Poulton : St. Geo. Han. Sq. i. 3.
London, 2.

Upshire, Upsher.—Local, 'of Upshire,' a hamlet in co. Essex.

London, 0, 1 ; New York, 1, 0.

Upton.—Local, ' of Upton,' parishes in cos. Bucks, Glouc., Chester, Lincoln, Norfolk, Somerset, &c., besides many townships scattered over the whole country.

John de Upton, co. Berks, Hen. III-Edw. I. K.
Henry de Upton, co. Hunts, 1273. A.
Richard de Upton, co. Wilts. ibid.
Thomas de Upton, co. Salop, ibid.
Walter de Upton, co. Soms., 20 Edw. I. R.
1662. Buried — Ralfe, son of Allice Upton, *widow*: St. Dionis Backchurch, p. 233.
London, 23 ; Philadelphia, 10.

Upwood, Upward. — Local, ' of Upwood,' a parish in the dioc. of Ely. Upward is an imitative corruption.

Thomas de Upwode, co. Hunts, 1273. A.
Alice de Upwode, co. Hunts, ibid.
1697. Thorowgood Upwood (co. Norfolk) and Eliz. Cockayne : Marriage Lic. (Faculty-Office), p. 227.
1776. Married—William Upward and Maria Gretton : St. Geo. Han. Sq. i. 264.

1789. Bapt.—Eliz., d. Henry Upward: Reg. Stourton, co. Wilts, p. 43. London, 4, 1.

Urban.—Bapt. 'the son of Urban,' i.e. polished, city-mannered, a name common to Western Europe, the opposite of Pagan, rustic, simple (v. Pain). Pope Urbanus gave it an impetus. Lat. *urbs*, a city. Cf. Italian Urbani in London Directory.

Urbanus de Lecheworth, Hen. III–Edw. I. K.
William Urban, co. Hereford, 1273. A.
William Urbane, 1519: Reg. Univ. Oxf. i. 3.
London, 1 ; Philadelphia, 12.

Urcy, Hearsey, Hersee, Hersey.—Bapt. 'the son of Ursey,' the popular form of Urse or Ursel, i.e. Ursula. The aspirate is found invariably in names beginning with a vowel; cf. German Herschell for Urschel = Ursula. Fitz-Urse was one of the assassins of Thomas à Becket.

Ralph fil. Urcy, co. Wilts, Hen. III–Edw. I. R.
Henry Urs', co. Berks, 1273. A.
Walter Urs', co. Essex, ibid.
Cok' fil. Ursell', co. Worc., ibid.
Ursellus (without surname), co. Linc., ibid.
Hursel (without surname),co. Linc.,ibid.
Henry Hurs, co. Norf., ibid.
London,0,2,3,3; Boston (U.S.),0,3,2,10.

Urian, Urion, Uren, Urin, Uran.—Bapt. 'the son of Urian.' Both the masculine Uranius and feminine Urania were in use as personal names. On a Welsh variant Urien, v. Yonge, i. 172. A surname founded on this name seems to have crept into Staffordshire and Cheshire, and thence into Lancashire.

John fil. Urian, co. Hunts, 1273. A.
Uryene (without surname), co. Camb., ibid.
1633. Bapt.—Henry, s. Finsby Vrin: St. Jas. Clerkenwell, i. 123.
1635. —Joan, d.Finlye Eurin: ibid.p.131.
1671. John Urran, of Everton: Wills at Chester, iii. 275.
1680. Alice Urian, of Christleton: ibid. iii. 274.
Manchester, 1, 0, 0, 0, 0; Liverpool, 0, 0, 0, 0, 1; London, 0, 0, 1, 0, 0; MDB. (co. Stafford), 0, 2, 0, 0, 0; Philadelphia, 17, 0, 0, 0, 0.

Uridge. — Local, 'de Eweregge'; cf. Udall for Yewdale. Lower says, 'An East Sussex name.

It is found in that district, temp. Edw. II, in the form of de Eweregge (Sussex Arch. Coll. xii. 25).'
London, 1 ; MDB. (co. Sussex), 3.

Urlwin, Urling.—Bapt. 'the son of Urlwin,' one of the endless compounds in *-win*; cf. Baldwin and Unwin. *-win* invariably becomes *-ing* as the surname descends to modern times. Hence the form Urling; cf. Golden, and v. Herlwin.

Richard Urlewyn, co. Oxf., 1273. A.
1581. Roger Urlen, co. Middlesex: Reg. Univ. Oxf. vol. ii. pt. ii. p. 102.
1665. Thomas Urlin and Rebecca Mills: Marriage Alleg. (Canterbury), p. 110.
1666. Bapt. — Margaret, d. Richard Urlwin : Kensington Parish Ch. p. 49.
1671. Simon Urlin, of Ampthill, co. Bedf., and Anne Robinson: Marriage Alleg. (Canterbury), p. 197.
1764. Married — Richard Payne and Mary Urlwin : St. Geo. Han. Sq. i. 131.
London, 1, 1.

Urmson.—Local, 'of Urmston,' a township in the parish of Flixton, on the Cheshire border ; an early corruption, *not* a form of Ormson (v. Orme). The family of Urmston have many entries in the Prestbury Church registers. Two early ones are given below :

1570. Married—Raffe Urmeson and Isabell Manyfold : Reg. Prestbury, co. Ches., p. 31.
1572. Bapt. — Ellen Urmeston : ibid. p. 37.
Richard Urmston, of Horwich, 1598 : Wills at Chester (1545-1620), p. 197.
John Urmson, of Wheelton, 1677 : ibid. (1660-80), p. 274.
Liverpool, 4 ; MDB. (co. Chester), 1.

Urquhart.—Local, ' of Urquhart.' There are places called Urquhart in the shires of Moray, Inverness, and Ross. The family are traced to Galleroch de Urchart, who lived temp. Alex. II. His descendants were hereditary sheriffs of Cromarty (Lower's Patr. Brit. p. 362). Not being an English surname I proceed no further.
London, 7 ; Boston (U.S.), 6.

Urry, Urie, Hurry.—? Bapt. 'the son of Urry' (?). Possibly it is the popular form of Urian, q.v. More probably it is local, but I have no proof.

John Hurri, co. Oxf., 1273. A.
Simon Urri, co. Oxf., ibid.

Ricardus Urry, co. Norf., 20 Edw. I. R.
1677. Roger Barton and Anne Drew, with consent of her mother, Dulsabella Urry : Marriage Alleg. (Canterbury), p. 271.
1748. Bapt.—Betty, d. James Hurry : Reg. Stourton, co. Wilts, p. 31.
1777. Married—John Lewis and Elizabeth Urry : ibid. p. 60.
London, 4, 1, 6.

Urwen.—Local ; v. Irving.

Urwick.—Local, ' of Urwick.' Mr. Lower suggests that it is a variant of Urswick, a parish in Furness, North Lancashire. This is very improbable, as Urswick does not appear to have become the parent of an hereditary surname. Besides, Urwick as a surname is almost entirely confined to South, and especially Southwest, England. I suspect it will be found to represent some small spot in the neighbourhood of co. Somerset.

MDB. (co. Soms.), 5 ; London, 5.

Urwin.—Local ; v. Irving.

Usborn, Usborne.—Bapt. 'the son of Osbern,' a variant. We find Osebern in the Hundred Rolls, and this would readily become Usbern ; v. Osborn.

Gerard fil. Osebern, co. Hunts, 1273. A.
1521. Christopher Usborne and Katharine Grene : Marriage Lic. (London), i. 2.
1700. Married—William Usbourne and Eliz. Edwards : St. Peter, Cornhill, ii. 63.
MDB. (co. Kent), 1, 4 ; (co. Hereford), 0, 1.

Usher.—Offic. 'the usher,' 'a door-keeper,' one who introduced strangers. M.E. *vschere* (Skeat).

Peter le Usser, co. Berks, 1273. A.
London, 13 ; Boston (U.S.), 8.

Usherwood. — Local, ' of Usherwood.' I cannot find the spot, but I doubt not it is in co. Lancaster, where in the modern form of Isherwood it is a familiar surname ; v. Isherwood.

1668. Married—Cornelius Thorogood and Jane Usserwood : St. Jas. Clerkenwell, i. 141.
1682. Bapt.—Thomas, s. Thomas Userwood : ibid. p. 296.
1683. — Thomas, s. Thomas Usherwood : ibid. p. 305.
MDB. (co. Kent), 2.

Utley.—Local ; v. Uttley.

Uttermare, Uttermere. — Local. Mr. Lower says from the French 'D'outre mer, from beyond the sea; a foreigner—foreign, that is, in regard to France, from which country the name seems to have been imported. It appears to be almost entirely limited to the county of Somerset.' I must still believe that it is a native of Somerset till further evidence is produced, and that it is sprung from some small locality in that county. No doubt it is of local origin.

MDB. (co. Soms.), 5, 1.

Utterson.—Bapt. 'the son of Oughtred' or Utred. Found early in Northumberland as a patronymic in the form of Utrickson. From Utrickson to Utterson was an inevitable descent. Naturally we find this name in the county where Oughtred was once so popular. v. Outred.

Thomas Utrickson, 1349 : PPP. p. 134. 1797. Married—John Outherson and Eliz. Fountain : St. Geo. Han. Sq. ii. 165.

Utrick as a font-name survived till the 18th century.

'Here lieth interred the body of Utrick Reay, son and heir of Henry Reay, Esq., alderman of Newcastle-upon-Tyne': Brand's Newcastle, ii. 120. Newcastle, 5.

Utting, Outing.—Bapt. 'the son of Utting,' a long-forgotten personal name. As a surname Utting has strongly ramified in co. Norfolk. 'Utting de Cresswell was witness to a deed temp. King John. Gent. Mag., Oct. 1832': Lower.

Hutting de Schipdon, co. York, 1273. A. Richard Uttying, co. Hunts, ibid. Adam fil. Utting, 1379 : FFF. p. 270. Amicia Vttyng-wyf (i. e. the wife of Utting), 1379 : P. T. Yorks. p. 191. Petrus Vttyng', 1379 : ibid. p. 116. Johannes Vttyng', 1379 : ibid. p. 234. Nicholaus Vttyng', 1379 : ibid. John Uttyng, rector of Bridgham St. Mary, co. Norfolk, 1448 : FF. i. 439. 1794. Married—James Utting and Ann Callingham : St. Geo. Han. Sq. ii. 113. London, 5, 1 ; MDB. (Norfolk), 13, 0.

Uttley, Utley.—Local. Probably 'of Otley,' two parishes, one in co. Suffolk, the other in W. Rid. York ; v. Otley.

London, 0, 2 ; MDB. (co. Lanc.), 3, 2 ; Philadelphia, 4, 0.

V

Vacher.—Occup. 'the vacher,' a cow-keeper, a dairyman. Hence in old records the 'vacherie,' a cow-house. 'Vaccary, a cow-pasture. Lanc. "Vachery, a dairy": Prompt. Parv.' (Halliwell).

Alice la Vacher (probably a dairymaid), co. Camb., 1273. A. Robert le Vacher (probably a dairymaid), co. Oxf., ibid. Simon le Vacher, co. Bedf., ibid. Cf. also Richard de la Vache (probably the cow-shed or dairy), co. Derby, ibid.

The Daily Telegraph (March 22, 1898) records the death of Fred. S. Vacher.

London, 3.

Vaizey.—Local ; v. Vesey.

Vale, Vail, Vaile.—Local, 'of the vale' (M. E. val, F. val), from residence therein ; cf. French Duval.

Eustace del Val, co. Northumberland, 1273. A. Hugh de la Val, co. Northumb., ibid. John del Vale, armorer, 18 Edw. I : Freemen of York, i. 22. Robert de la Vale, co. Northumb., 20 Edw. I. R. Hugh de la Vale, Northumb., ibid. Ralph du Val, Guernsey, ibid.

1655. Bapt.—George, son of Godfrey Vale : St. Jas. Clerkenwell, i. 192. 1792. Married— John Vale and Mary Fielder : St. Geo. Han. Sq. ii. 79. London, 8, 3, 3 ; Philadelphia, 0, 9, 0.

Valentine, Vallentine, Valentin, Vallentin.—(1) Nick. 'a valentine, a sweetheart' ; v. Skeat's Dict.

Hugh le Valentyne, Close Roll, 8 Edw. III.

(2) Bapt. 'the son of Valentine.' St. Valentine's day is February 14, the season when birds begin to pair. In either case the saint has originated the name.

Valentine Fairwether, Close Roll, 1–2 Philip and Mary, pt. viii. 1578. Matthew Nicholson and Alice Valentine : Marriage Lic. (London), i. 82. 1803. Married — James Valentin and Ann Halfacer : St. Geo. Han. Sq. ii. 275.

The Italian Valentini is englished into Valentiny in the London Directory.

London, 8, 2, 3, 2 ; New York, 101, 1, 3, 0.

Vallet. — Occup. 'the valet,' a young groom, a young attendant (v. Skeat's Dict.), now valet.

Adam le Vallet, C. R., 5 Edw. II. Walter Vallet, co. Soms., 1 Edw. III : Kirby's Quest, p. 185.

Vallis.—Local, 'of Valois.'

John, son of James Valloyes, 1601 : Reg. St. Columb Major, p. 198. Elizabeth, d. of John Vallyes, 1573 : ibid. p. 8. Olly, d. of Nicholas Vallis, 1591 : ibid. p. 15. Elizabeth, d. of James Valleys, 1602 : ibid. p. 21. 1765. Married—John Wise and Joanna Valless : St. Geo. Han. Sq. i. 142. London, 3.

Vann, Van.—Local, 'at the van,' i.e. the threshing-floor, from residence thereby. Fr. van, a fan, a threshing instrument ; v. Vanner.

Robert atte Vanne, co. Westm., 20 Edw. I. R. Richard atte Vanne, co. Wilts, ibid. 1677. Bapt.—Susan, d. Leonard Van : St. Jas. Clerkenwell, i. 279. 1746. Married — Samuel Vann and Hannah Jenkins : St. Geo. Chap. Mayfair, i. 77. London, 1, 0 ; New York, 0, 2.

Vanner.—Occup. 'the fanner.' Fr. vanneur, a winnower ; v. Fanner and Vann.

Walter le Vanner, co. Oxf., 1273. A.
John le Vannere, co. Oxf., ibid.
Ralph le Vannere, co. Bucks, ibid.
Henry Vannere, City of London. X.
London, 4.

Varley. — Local, 'of Verley,' a parish in Essex; cf. Derby and Darby, Clerk and Clark.

Hugo de Verli, 1184. RRR. p. 168.
William Vyrly, co. Soms., 1 Edw. III : Kirby's Quest, p. 259.
Roger de Virlie, or Verly, bailiff of Norwich, 1335 : FF. iii. 99.

This Roger was bailiff several times. He is entered Verley in 1343, and Verli in 1344 (FF. iii. 99).

1596. William Varleigh, or Varly : Reg. Univ. Oxf. vol. ii. pt. iii. p. 194.
1801. Married—John Varley and Ann Silvester : St. Geo. Han. Sq. ii. 246.
London, 6 ; Philadelphia, 4.

Varney.—Local, a variant of Verney, q.v. ; cf. Clerk and Clark, Parkin and Perkin, &c.

Varnham, Varnum, Varnam.—Local, 'of Vernham Dean,' a parish in co. Southampton. As usual, the American form is Varnum ; cf. Barnum for Barnham. An early instance occurs in the Hundred Rolls, so our friends across the Atlantic have a long precedent in their favour.

Ralph de Vernum, co. Glouc., 1273. A.
1585. James Varnam, or Vernam, London: Reg. Univ. Oxf. vol. ii. pt. ii. p. 148.
1600. Bapt.—Ralph, s. Ralph Varnam, *merchaunt tailor* : St. Peter, Cornhill, i. 50.
1624. John Varnham and Eliz. Holcrofte : Marriage Lic. (London), i. 143.
1802. Married—Charles Varnham and Maria Harris : St. Geo. Han. Sq. ii. 267.
London, 1, 0, 1 ; Philadelphia, 0, 1, 0 ; Boston (U.S.), 0, 5, 1.

Vass.—Bapt. 'the son of Vass.' Of this early personal name I can supply no history.

Vasse le Poynur, co. Camb., 1273. A.
1601. Buried — Jone Vasse : Reg. Prestbury, Ches., p. 152.
1784. Married — Henry Martin and Susan Vass : St. Geo. Han. Sq. i. 356.
1800. — Thomas Vass and Mary Plain : ibid. ii. 213.
London, 3 ; Philadelphia, 1.

Vassar, Vasser.—Offic. 'the Vavasseur' (q.v.), seemingly an early modification.

Nicholas Vausour, 1379 : P. T. Yorks. p. 150.

1743. Married — Henry Vawser and Ann Bullen : St. Geo. Chap. Mayfair, p. 32.
1749. — James Vassar and Ann Johnson : St. Geo. Han. Sq. i. 41.
London, 1, 1 ; Boston (U.S.), 1, 0.

Vaughan, Vaughn. — Nick. Welsh, 'the little' ; cf. English Little, Bigg, &c. Lower says, 'Vaughan, Welsh *vychan*, little in stature, a personal name of great antiquity' : Patr. Brit. p. 364. Vaughn seems to be a modern Americanism.

William Vachan, co. Salop, 1273. A.
Adam ap-Thewely Vachan, co. Cardigan, 20 Edw. I. R.
Owen Vaghan, co. Salop, ibid.
Davey Watkynge Vaghan : Visit. Gloucester, 1623, p. 104.
1601. Evan Vaughan, co. Salop : Reg. Univ. Oxf. vol. ii. pt. ii. p. 254.
Jenkin Vaughan, prebendary of St. David's, 1621 : Hist. and Ant. St. David's, p. 361.
Jerworth Vachan : Visit. London, 1633, i. 220.
London, 40, 0 ; Philadelphia, 47, 14.

Vavasseur, Vavazor, Vavasour. — Offic. 'the vavasour,' a principal vassal, holding of a great lord, a man of second rank, one of the inferior nobility. '*Vavasour*, antiently a Nobleman, next in dignity to a Baron' : Bailey's Dict. (1742).

'Bothe Knightes and vavasour,
   This damisels love paramour.'
Arthour and Merlin, p. 320 (Halliwell).
Reginald le Vavassur, co. Berks, Hen. III-Edw. I. K.
Adam le Vavasour, co. Bucks, 1273. A.
Mauger le Vavasur, co. York, 20 Edw. I. K.

This latter personal name was evidently handed down in the family, as the following entry, four hundred years later, fully demonstrates :

1696. Maugre Vavasour, of St. Ann's, Holborn, *gent.*, and Mary Moor : Marriage Lic. (London), ii. 318.
London, 3, 1, 0 ; Crockford, 0, 0, 1.

Veal, Veale, Veall. — Nick. 'the veal,' i.e. the calf. M.E. *veel*, O.F. *veel*, 'a calfe or veale,' Cotgrave (v. Skeat) ; cf. Bacon.

Thomas le Veyle, co. Norf., 1273. A.
Roger le Vel, co. Hunts, ibid.
John le Vele, co. Soms., 1 Edw. III : Kirby's Quest, p. 205.
Robert le Veel, C. R., 25 Edw. I.
Hubert le Veyll. B.

1576. Edward Veele, co. Glouc. : Reg. Univ. Oxf. vol. ii. pt. ii. p. 71.
1576. Thomas Veale, co Linc. : ibid. p. 72.
1673. Bapt. — Margaret, d. Thomas Veale : St. Jas. Clerkenwell, i. 260.
1790. Married — James Hall and Martha Veall : St. Geo. Han. Sq. ii. 37.
London, 6, 3, 1 ; Philadelphia, 2, 3, 0.

Vear, Veare.—Local ; v. Vere.

Veasey.—Local ; v. Vesey.

Venables, Venable, Vennable. — Local, 'from Venables, a parish in the arrondissement of Louviers, in Normandy' (Lower). One of this family was tenant under Hugh Lupus, temp. William I, so we may say he 'came over with the Conqueror.'

William de Venables, co. Salop, 1273. A.
1616. Venables, co. Bucks : Reg. Univ. Oxf. vol. ii. pt. ii. p. 356.
1621. Richard Venables, co. Southampton : ibid. p. 389.
1690. Married — Ann Venables : St. Antholin, Budge Row, London, p. 106.
1754. — John Venable : ibid. p. 157.
1791. Married — John Venables and Eliz. Norman : St. Geo. Han. Sq. ii. 61.
London, 12, 1, 0 ; Philadelphia, 2, 5, 2.

Vender.—Occup. 'the vender,' a seller, a dealer.

William le Vendour. D.
Agnes Vendir, co. York. W. 11.
Thomas le Vyndre, C. R., 7 Ric. II.

I fear this surname is obsolete.

Veness, Venes, Venis, Venus. — Local, 'of Venice' ; an early importation ; cf. Jannaway and Lombard. Lower quotes, 'Stephen de Venuse, *miles*,' but gives no reference.

John de Venuz, co. Essex, 1273. A.
Leonard de Venetia. E.

It is interesting to note that all the above forms exist in co. Sussex, where the surname has long been established.

1623. Married—Henry Venus and Anne Starte : St. Jas. Clerkenwell, p. 53.
1787. — Thomas Venes and Eliz. Grocal : St. Geo. Han. Sq. i. 404.
John Venus, 1745 : Blair's Hist. of Alnwick, p. 457.

It may be added that Venus, representing the goddess of love, became a baptismal name ; but far too late to have any influence upon surnames.

1631. Married — John Cotton and Venus Levat : St. Peter, Cornhill, i. 253.

1756. Buried—Love Venus Rivers : St. Peter, Cornhill, ii. 142.

By Archbishop Peckham's law the minister could have refused to baptize, either of the above. ' The minister shall take care not to permit wanton names, which being pronounced do sound to lascivious-ness, to be given to children baptized, especially of the female sex ; and if otherwise it be done, the same shall be changed by the bishop at confirmation.'

London, 1, 0, 0, 0 ; Crockford, 1, 0, 0, 0 ; MDB. (Sussex), 3, 1, 1, 1 ; New York (Venus), 1.

Venimore.—Nick. ' fin-amour ' (v. Finnemore) : cf. Venn and Fenn, Vidler and Fidler, Vanner and Fanner.

London, 1.

Venn. — Local, ' at the fen,' from residence beside a bog or fen (v. Fenn) ; cf. Vanner and Fanner, &c.

John atte Venne, co. Soms., 1 Edw.III : Kirby's Quest, p. 94.
Simon Ven, alias Fen, temp. 1580 : Visit. London, 1634, ii. 308.
John Ven, alias Fen, 1634 : ibid.
1594. John Ven, draper (London), and Ellinor Clerke : Marriage Lic. (London), i. 217.
1610. Richard Venne, co. Devon : Reg. Univ. Oxf. vol ii. pt. ii. p. 374.
1657. Married—Ambrose Venn and Ellinor Nottingham : St Jas. Clerkenwell, i. 99.
London, 10 ; New York, 1.

Vennell, Vennall, Venel, Fennell.—Local, ' at the vennel,' i.e. a small street or passage ; cf. ' vennel, a gutter, a sink. North ' (Halliwell). Cf. Fr. ' Enfiler la venelle,' to run away. Still in use in Scotland for a small lane or passage. From a large number of entries in the Hundred Rolls a few instances may be given.

Geoffrey de la Venele, Fines Roll, 11 Edw. I.
Alexander in Venella, co. Hunts, 1273. A.
Thomas in Venello, co. Hunts, ibid.
Isabel de la Venele, co. Hunts, ibid.
Richard en le Venel. co. Bedf., ibid.
Matilda de Venella, co. Oxf., ibid.

Also in cos. Rutland and Cambridge.

' Simon Venell, alias Fennell, priest,' 1592 : Cal. State Papers (Domestic), iii. 176, 452, &c.
London, 2, 1, 0, 10 ; Philadelphia, 0, 0, 1, 10.

Venner, Fenner.—Occup. ' le veneur,' a huntsman. Lower's explanation is unsatisfactory (Patr. Brit. p. 111). Besides, there is no difficulty in the solution of the name. The early instances are conclusive. Venner must be carefully distinguished from Vanner, q.v. As regards the initial F in Fenner, cf. Fanner, Venn, Vowell, Fennell, &c.

Robert le Venur, co. Linc., 1273. A.
William Venator, co. York, ibid.
Geoffrey le Venour, co. Salop, ibid.
Robert le Veneur, co. Linc., 20 Edw. I. R.
John le Venour. B.
Thomas le Veneur. T.
Robert Hunter, alias Venour : London Visit. 1633, i. 405.
1691-2. Buried—Alce (Alice) Venner, widow : St. Dionis Backchurch, p. 259.
1707. Married — Nathaniel Walker and Margaret Fenner : St. Michael, Cornhill, p. 54.
London, 3, 16 ; Boston (U.S.), 5, 3.

Ventris, Ventriss, Venters. —Local (?). I find no trace of this surname in the early rolls. Probably it is of later and foreign importation. Lower suggests La Ventrouse in the arrondissement of Montagne, Normandy, as the home of the family.

1586-7. Married — Thomas Ventris and Annes Lynge : St. Dionis Backchurch, p. 11.
1614. Bapt. — George, son of Robert Ventresse : St. Michael, Cornhill, p. 111.
1650. Married — John Ventris and Eliz. Gillett : St. Thomas the Apostle (London), p. 19.
London, 1, 1, 2.

Venus.—Local ; v. Veness.

Verdin, Verdon.—Local, ' of Verdun,' a town in the department of Meuse, N.E. France.

Rosa de Verdon, co. Linc., 1273. A.
Wydo de Verdum, co. Norf., ibid.
Bertram de Verdum, 7 Hen. II : Pipe Roll, iv. 41.
1796. Married — Robert Whitton and Sarah Verdon : St. Geo. Han. Sq. ii. 151.
1802. — George Verdin and Ann Aikman : ibid. p. 255.
London, 2, 3 ; New York, 0, 4.

Vere, Vear, Veare. — Local, ' of Ver,' ' a parish and château in the canton of Guvray, in La Manche, Normandy ' (Lower). Clutterbuck, in his Hist. of Hertfordshire, says, ' de Veer,' from a town so called

in the island of Walcheren in Holland. All the early entries by their spelling confirm the former view, save the instance with Baldwin for a Christian name. One single Vere in the London Directory saves the name from complete extinction, save in the variant Vear or Veare.

Albric' de Ver, co. Camb., 1273. A.
Baldewin de Ver, co. Oxf., ibid.
Henry de Ver, co. Suff., ibid.
1581. Robert Vere, co. Essex : Reg. Univ. Oxf. vol. ii. pt. ii. p. 113.
1605. Henry de Vere : ibid. i. 236.
1780. Married—William Sercome and Jane Vear : St. Geo. Han. Sq. ii. 23.
London, 1, 2, 1 ; Boston (U.S.), 1, 0, 0.

Verey, Veary. — ? Bapt. ; v. Verry. Oxford, 1, 1.

Verge.—Local, ' at the verge,' from residence therein. Probably for verger (Chaucer), a garden ; F. vergier. Chaucer has the form verge:
' Ne had Idlenesse thee convaid
In the verge where Mirth him pleid.'
Rom. of Rose.
Richard de la Verge, C. R., 3 Edw. I.

Oddly enough, I cannot light on any instances in modern church registers. But the one quotation above is worth a hundred such entries, as it at once settles the origin of the surname.

London, 2 ; Boston (U.S.), 4.

Verity. — ? ——. I cannot classify this surname. The earliest form found in Yorkshire is Verty.

Agnes Verty, vidua, 1379 : P. T. Yorks. p. 252.
1745. Married—Christopher Verity and Ann Clarke : St. Geo. Chap. Mayfair, p. 56.
1751. — Timothy Cahill and Eleanor Verty : ibid. p. 204.
London, 5 ; Pudsey (Yorks), 4.

Verney, Varney.—Local, ' of Vernai,' ' a parish in the arrondissement of Bayeux' (Lower). The variant Varney seems to be the most popular modern form ; cf. Parkin and Perkin, Clark and Clerk, Darby and Derby, &c.

Lucya de Vernai, co. Oxf., 1273. A.
Simon de Vernay, co. Northampton, ibid.
Ralph de Verney, co. Oxf., ibid.
1600. Francis Verney, London : Reg. Univ. Oxf. vol. ii. pt. ii. p. 241.
1563. Buried — Jeames Verney : St. Peter, Cornhill, i. 117.
1637. Bapt.—Francis, s. John Varney : St. Jas. Clerkenwell, i. 137.

London, 0, 6 ; Oxford, 1, 4 ; Crockford, 1, 0 ; Boston (U.S.), 3, 27.

Verrall, Verrill. — ? Local. Mr. Lower says, 'This name, abundant in East Sussex and seldom found out of it, may be a corruption of Firle, a parish near Lewis—sometimes in old documents written Ferle, and usually pronounced as a dissyllable' (Patr. Brit. p. 367).

1575. Edmund Wyllson and Johanna Ferrall : Marriage Lic. (London), i. 67. MDB. (Sussex), 7, 0 ; Philadelphia, 1, 3.

Verrer, Verrier.—Occup. 'the verrour' or verrer, a glazier.

'In alle the erthe y-halowed and y-holde, In a closet more clere than verre or glas.'
Lydgate (v. *verre*, Halliwell).

The Verrours walked in the York Pageant (York Mystery Plays, p. xxvi, ed. Toulmin Smith).

Edward le Verrer, Close Roll, 39 Hen. III. pt. i.
John le Verrer, Close Roll, 54 Hen. III.
Thomas le Verer, co. Oxf., 1273. A.
Simon le Verrour, co. Northampton, ibid.
Walter le Verrour : Freemen of York, i. 15.
Laurence de Stok, *verrour* : 7 Edw. II ibid.
1750. Married – William Willis and Ann Verrier : St. Michael, Cornhill, p. 72.
London, 0, 1 ; MDB. (co. Kent), 0, 2 ; (Somerset), 0, 1.

Verry, Very. — ? Bapt. 'the son of Everard' (?), from a supposed nick. Very. This is Mr. Lower's suggestion, and there is much to be said in its favour. Everard, being so popular a personal name in the surname period, was bound to have a nick., and Very seems the natural one ; v. Everson.

1600. Married — William Very and Margerie Knight : St. Jas. Clerkenwell, i. 24.
1613. Robert Verey : Reg. Univ. Oxf. vol. ii. pt. ii. p. 331.
1795. Married — Samuel Verry and Susanna Edgley : St. Geo. Han. Sq. ii. 135.
London, 2, 0 ; Boston (U.S.), 5, 7.

Vertue ; v. Virtue.

Vesey, Vezey, Pheysey, Voisey, Vaizey, Veasey. — Local, 'de Veci' or Vesci. Lower says, ' Robert de Veci assisted William I to conquer England, and was rewarded with great estates in the counties of Northampton, Leicester, Warwick, and Lincoln. Ivo or John de Veschi

was his near kinsman, and from him in the female line descended Lord Vesey' (Kelham's Domesday) ; v. Patr. Brit. p. 366.

Willelmus de Vesci, 7 Hen. II : Pipe Roll, iv. 23.
Eustace de Vescy, co. Linc., 1273. A. Richard de Vescy, co. York, ibid.
1512. John Veys-y, or Vesey, or Voysye, or Pheysy : Reg. Univ. Oxf. i. 81.
1603. Walter Veysey, co. Devon : ibid. vol. ii. pt. ii. p. 266.
1603-4. James Voyzey, co. Devon : ibid. p. 269.

Other spellings of the names of the two students last mentioned are Voysey, Vesey, and Veisey (v. Index). For other instances, v. Pheysey.

London, 1, 1, 1, 1, 1, 0 ; Philadelphia, 2, 2, 0, 0, 0, 1.

Vestmentmaker. — Occup. 'the vestment maker,' a maker of robes, especially embroidered ones.

'To Thomas Cheiner, of London, in discharge of £140 lately due to him, for a vest of velvet embroidered with divers work,' July 15, 24 Edw. III : Issues of the Exchequer.

Vestment-makers (York Pageant); v. York Mystery Plays, ed. Toulmin Smith, p. xxiii. In a note the editor says, ' Old-fashioned people in Yorkshire still remember the vests made of well-dressed skins, often handsomely embroidered.' It is in Yorkshire I find the surname.

Robert Vestmentmaker : Testimente Ebor., Surt. Soc., v. Index.

Coke Lorelle's Bote has it ' vestyment-swoers' (sewers).

Viall(s ; v. Viel.

Vicary, Vickery, Vicarey, Vittery.—Offic. 'the vicar.' The absence of ' Vicar' or ' Vicker,' and the great frequency of Vicary and Vickery, prove these to be official and not local.

'Sire preest, quod he, art thou a Vicary ? Or art thou a Person ? say soth by thy fay.
Chaucer, The Persones Prologue.
Richard Vicary. B.
1574-5. Stephen Vyccarye and Margaret Johnson : Marriage Lic. (London), i. 63.
1585. John Vicary, co. Devon : Reg. Univ. Oxf. vol. ii. pt. ii. p. 144.
1749. Married -- Thomas Platt and Anne Vickery : St. Geo. Han. Sq. i. 133.
1749. Married—James Brown and Jane Vickery : ibid.

Vittery seems to be a West-country corruption.

London, 5, 10, 1, 0 ; MDB. (co. Devon), 10, 4, 0, 2 ; Philadelphia, 1, 16, 0, 0.

Vickerage, -idge ; v. Vickridge.

Vickerman. — Occup. ' the vicar's man,' the servant of the vicar ; cf. Priestman, Matthewman, Bartleman, Addiman, &c. Found early in co. York, where the surname is still common.

Willelmus Vikarman, 1379 : P. T. Yorks. p. 100.
Willelmus serviens Vicarii, 1379 : ibid. p. 201.
Beatrix serviens Vicarii, 1379 : ibid. Cf. Adam Parsonman : ibid. p. 241.
Emma Parsonwoman, 1379 : ibid.
Isabella Vikerwoman, 1379 : ibid. p. 50.

In South England it is found as Vicars-man.

Richard le Wycarisman, co. Camb., 1273. A.
London, 3 ; West Rid. Court Dir., 6 ; New York, 1 ; Philadelphia, 1.

Vickers.—(1 Nick. ' the vicar's son ' (v. Vickerson) ; cf. Williams, the genitive of William. (a) Local, ' at the vicar's,' i.e. at the vicar's house, from residence therein. The first is the chief parent.

Peter atte Vicars, 1379 : P. T. Howdenshire (co. York), p. 19.
1581. John Vicars, London : Reg. Univ. Oxf. vol. ii. pt. ii. p. 106.
1618. Edward Wilkinson and Sarah Vicars, *widow* : Marriage Lic. (London), ii. 60.
1655. Bapt. — Parnell, d. Rowland Vickars : St. Jas. Clerkenwell, i. 191.
1689. Married — Francis Vickers and Eliz. Lamden : St. Peter, Cornhill, ii. 59.
London, 22 ; Philadelphia, 16.

Vickerson.—Nick. ' the son of the vicar' ; v. Vickers and Vickress. I can find but one modern instance, and it is in the United States.

William Vikeresson, C. R., 14 Ric. II. Boston (U.S.), 1.

Vickery ; v. Vicary.

Vickress.—Nick. 'the son of the vicar,' from the old popular Vicary, a vicar, genitive Vicarys, corrupted to Vickress (v. Vicary). Thus Vickress is equivalent to Vicars or Vickers, q.v. (cf. Williams, the genitive of William = William's son).

1614-5. William Collins and Margaret Vicares : Marriage Lic. London), ii. 30.
1617-8. John Wells and Joan Viccaries : ibid. p. 57.

1765. Married—William Vickress and Sarah Oliver: St. Geo. Han. Sq. i. 149.
1795. — Edward Godsall and Rebecca Vickress: ibid. ii. 130.
London, 3.

Vickridge, Vickerage, Vickeridge —Local, 'of the vicarage,' from residence thereat (cf. Parsonage); probably the housekeeper for the vicar. I can produce no early instance, but the origin needs no explanation.

1547. John Vicarish and Margery Gerard: Marriage Lic. (Faculty Office), p. 11.
1665. John Hatton and Alice Vicaridge: Marriage Alleg. (Canterbury), p. 111.
Thomas Vicaridge, 1703: Reg. St. Mary Aldermary (London), p. 37.
1710. Married — Richard Eycott and Eliz. Vicaridge: St. Jas. Clerkenwell, iii. 232.
1770. — William Harwich and Kezia Vickredge: St. Geo. Han. Sq. i. 195.
London, 1, 0, 0; MDB. (co. Somerset), 0, 1, 0; (co. Glouc.), 0, 0, 1.

Vidler.—Occup. 'the fiddler,' a player on the fiddle (v. Fidler). The *V* here is a connecting link between *viol* and *fiddle*; cf. Vowler for Fowler, Venn for Fenn, Vanner for Fanner, and probably the Devonshire Vivash for Fiveash. For further instances, v. Vowler.

Reginald le Vielur, co. Oxf., 1273. A.
Robert Vidulator, co. Oxf., ibid.
1786. Married — Matthew Vidler and Frances Barnes: St. Geo. Han. Sq. i. 393.
1808. Edmund Vidler and Ann Meager: ibid. ii. 370.
London, 5; MDB. (co. Sussex), 2; Boston (U.S.), 1.

Viel, Vial, Vialls, Vialle, Viall.—Bapt. 'the son of Viel.' Probably a French form of Vitalis. I have furnished but few of the Hundred Roll entries, which prove Viel to have been a fairly familiar font-name. Vialls is the genitive; cf. Williams, Jones, &c.

Vitalis de Engayne, co. Essex, Hen. III-Edw. I. K.
Viel Engayne, co. Northampton, ibid.
William fil. Viel, co. Hunts, 1273. A.
Juliana Vyel, co. Essex, ibid.
Agnes Viel, co. Oxf., ibid.
1731. Married—Daniel Vial and Sarah Larching: St. Geo. Han. Sq. i. 12.
1775. — John Viall and Sarah Colquhoun: ibid. p. 251.
1780. — Walter Mason and Eliz. Vialls: ibid. 316.
London, 0, 1, 2, 0, 0; Boston (U.S.), 1, 0, 0, 10, 5.

Vigers, Vigurs, Viguers.— ? Official. Probably a modern corruption of Vicars or Vickers (q.v.) through defective and lazy pronunciation; cf. Hicks and Higgs, Hickson and Higson, and endless instances throughout this dictionary. This view is confirmed by the fact that these forms are found in co. Devon and the surrounding districts, where Vowler for Fowler. and Vivash for Fiveash, &c., are, or were, familiar.

1598. Lewis Vigures, co. Devon: Reg. Univ. Oxf. vol. ii. pt. ii. p. 227.
1609. Christopher Vigures, co. Devon: ibid. p. 304.
1642. Married — Walter Vigures and Eliz. Raminge: St. Jas. Clerkenwell, i. 75.
1746. — Samuel Vigars and Grace Bridam: St. Geo. Han. Chap. Mayfair, p. 66.
1801. — William Vigers and Anne Hitchen: St. Geo. Han. Sq. ii. 238.
London, 4, 1, 0; Philadelphia, 0, 0, 7.

Vigourous.—Nick. 'the vigorous,' i.e. the strong. O.F. *vigoureux*; cf. Strong, Strongitharm, &c.

William Vigerus, co. Oxf., 1273. A.
Nicholas Vigorous, co. Northumb., 20 Edw. I. R.
John Viggorus, 1396: FFF. p. 584.
Richard Vigerous, rector of Downham, co. Norf., 1449: FF. vii. 343.
1585. Robert Vigerous and Mary Roberts: Marriage Lic. (London), i. 142.
London, 1.

Villain, Vilain.—Occup. 'the villain,' i.e. the small farmer, the bondman, servant. The surname, though common, gradually got dropped as the term became de graded to its later sense.

William le Vileyn, co. Hunts, 1273. A.
Hugh le Vilein, co. Salop, ibid.
Richard le Vilein, co. Oxf., ibid.
John Vyleyn, C. R., 20 Edw. I.
New York, 0, 1.

Vinall, Vinal. — Local, ' of Vine-hall,' an estate in the parish of Watlington, co. Sussex, which was possessed by the family in the 14th century. The estate gave name to the Vynehalls, afterwards of Kingston, near Lewes, who, as Vinalls, in 1657, obtained a grant of arms (Sussex Arch. Coll. ix. 75, and v. Lower's Patr. Brit. p. 367. The variant Vinal has ramified strongly in the United States of America.

1579. Buried — Ales Fletewood, servant to George Vynoll: St. Mary Aldermary, p. 141.
1752. Married—John Mierr and Mary Vinall: St. Geo. Chap. Mayfair, p. 225.
1780. — William Taylor and Hannah Vinall: St. Geo. Han. Sq. i. 314.
London, 7, 0; Boston (U.S.), 2, 37.

Vince. — Bapt. ' the son of Vincent,' from the nick. Vince (v. Vincent).

1794. Married — William Vince and Grace Salter: St. Geo. Han. Sq. ii. 116.
1809. — John Vince and Sarah Larkin: ibid. p. 413.
London, 11.

Vincent, Vincett.—Bapt. 'the son of Vincent.' Vincett must be looked on not as a dim., but a corruption. It might naturally be deemed a dim. of Vince, the nick. of Vincent, just as Emmett is of Emma, or Hewett of Hugh, but there is no evidence of such a dim. being in use, and no doubt it is a modern corruption of the full name Vincent.

Roger Vincent, co. Berks, 1273. A.
Richard fil. Vincent, co. Hunts, ibid.
Vincent atte More, co. Soms., 1 Edw. III: Kirby's Quest, p. 220.
Johannes Vynsand, 1379: P. T. Yorks. p. 102.
1581. Married — Richard Hart and Judith Vincent: St. Thomas the Apostle (London), p. 6.
1582. Francis Vincent, co. Surrey: Reg. Univ. Oxf. vol. ii. pt ii. p. 121.
1583. James Vincente and Lucy Batchellor: Marriage Lic. (London), i. 121.
London, 42, 1; New York, 37, 0.

Vine.—Local, 'at the vine,' i.e. the vine-tree, from residence there beside; cf. Box, Birch, Plumptre, Crabb, Crabtree, Oak, &c.

Matilda la (? de la) Vine, co. Oxf., 1273. A.
Richard Vygn, co. Soms., 1 Edw. III: Kirby's Quest, p. 271.
1554. Henry Vyne and Jane Dowdyng: Marriage Lic. (London), p. 15.
1689. Buried — Ann Vyne: St. Mary Aldermary, p. 199.
1740. Married — Edward Fidler and Hannah Vine: St. Geo. Han. Sq. i. 24.
London, 14.

Viner, Vyner.—Occup. 'the viner,' probably a vine-grower—not a taverner, but one who superintended a vineyard.

Adam de Viner, C. R., 2 Edw. I.
William le Vinyour, co. Hunts, 1273. A.
Reginald le Vinour, co. Bedf., ibid.
John le Vynor, co. Oxf., ibid.

1577. Henry Vyner, co. Salop: Reg. Univ. Oxf. vol. ii. pt. ii. p. 75.

1655. Married — William Joyner and Mary Chillingsworth, by Alderman Thomas Vyner: St. Michael, Cornhill, p. 34.

1756. Married — Benjamin Viner and Susanna Spearing: St. Geo. Han. Sq. i. 63.

London, 1, 1; Boston (U.S.), 1, 0.

Vinson, Vinsun.—(1) Bapt. 'the son of Vincent' (q.v.), manifest corruptions. (2) Bapt. 'the son of Vincent,' from the nick. Vince (q.v.) and patr. Vince-son. The first is probably the true parent.

1582. Bapt. — Lucrece, d. Humfrey Vincent or Vinson: St. Jas. Clerkenwell, i. 15.

1611. Married — Francis Vinson and Frances Ewers: ibid. p. 38.

1776. — Thomas Vincen and Ann Lee: St. Geo. Han. Sq. i. 271.

London, 1, 1; Boston (U.S.), 8, 0.

Vinter.—Occup. 'the vinter.' Fr. *vinetier*, a tavern keeper, a wine-seller.

Juliana la Vynetar, C. R., 45 Hen. III.
Abellus Vinetar, co. Bedf., 1273. A.
Richard le Viniter, co. Oxf., ibid.
William le Vineter, co. Northampton, ibid.
Robert Vyneter, co. Soms., 1 Edw. III: Kirby's Quest, p. 250.
William le Vyneter, co. Soms., 1 Edw. III: ibid.

1582-3. John Farrante, *husbandman*, and Mary Vinter: Marriage Lic. (London), i. 115.

1772. Married — William Vinter and Harriott Row: St. Geo. Han. Sq. i. 225. London, 3.

Vintner.—Occup. 'the vintner,' a taverner, a wine-seller. The second *n* is intrusive; v. Vinter, which is the older and more correct form. 'Vyntenere, *vinarius*': Prompt. Parv.

Thomas Vyntener, 1379: P. T. Yorks. p. 150.

1560. Married—Thomas Sherson and Ellen Vintener: St. Peter, Cornhill, i. 225.

1605. John Vintener: Reg. Univ. Oxf. vol. ii. pt. ii. p. 356.

1631. John Gerard and Mary Vintner: Marriage Lic. (London), ii. 203.

I find no instances in the modern directories, but probably the surname still exists.

Violett.—(1) Nick.; from the light purple attire of the wearer; cf. Borrell, Burnell, &c. In Some

---

Extracts from Somerset Wills, by A. J. Monday, occurs a bequest (1565) of a 'violett coate,' p. 157, Somerset. Arch. Soc. (2) Bapt. 'the son of Violet,' probably in use early enough to become a surname.

Nicholas Vyolet, Close Roll, 9 Edw. IV.

1526. Robert Fabyan and Marion Violett: Marriage Lic. (London), i. 5.

1581. Nicholas Violett, London: Reg. Univ. Oxf. vol. ii. pt. ii. p. 104.

Violat Mumford, 1637: Reg. St. Mary Aldermary (London), p. 85.

Francis Violet, 1698: Reg. St. Peter, Cornhill, i. 61.

London, 2.

Vipan, Vipon, Vipond. — ? Local, 'of Vipont.' Lower says: 'v. pont, v. pon, latinized "de Veteri Ponte," of the Old Bridge. There are several places in Normandy called Vieupont, and the great Anglo-Norman family so designated (i. e. Vipont) came from Vipont, near Lisieux'; v. Sussex Arch. Coll. ii. 77.

Robert de Veteri Ponte, co. Oxf., 1273. A.

Richard de Veteri Ponte, co. Devon, Hen. III–Edw. I. K.

John de Veteri Ponte, co. Notts and Derby, ibid.

Ivo de Veteri Ponte, co. York, 20 Edw. I. R.

1662. Bapt. — Catherine, d. Thomas and Rosamond Vipin: St. Jas. Clerkenwell, i. 216.

1761. Married — Thomas Lasey and Mary Vipoint: St. Geo. Han. Sq. i. 107.

1772. — Thomas Vipond and Mary Eagle: ibid. p. 222.

London, 1, 0, 0; MDB. (co. Camb.), 13, 0, 0; (co. Norfolk), 5, 0, 2; Crockford, 2, 0, 0; Boston (U.S.), 0, 0, 1; Philadelphia, 0, 1, 0.

Virgin.—Nick. (?) 'the virgin,' probably given to some one who had taken the part of the Virgin Mary in one of the Miracle Plays; cf. King and Virtue.

1581. William Virgyn (co. Essex) and Lettice Sheppie: Marriage Lic. (London), i. 105.

1587. John Virgin, co. Somerset: Reg. Univ. Oxf. vol. ii. pt. ii. p. 158.

1610. Married — John Vergine and Margaret Barrowes: St. Jas. Clerkenwell, i. 36.

1637. — John Virgin and Lenia Harrington: ibid. p. 68.

1800. — George Wellen and Mary Virgin: St. Geo. Han. Sq. ii. 217.

Oxford (1895), 1; Boston (U.S.), 5.

Virtue, Vertue. — Nick. (?). Probably a sobriquet affixed to one who had represented Virtue in one of the early Miracle Plays; cf. King, and v. Virgin. M.E. *vertu*, F. *vertu*, virtue.

1510. Simeon Vertu, Benedictine: Reg. Univ. Oxf. i. 69.

1579. Nathaniel Vertwe, or Virtu, co. Berks: ibid. vol. ii. pt. ii. p. 89.

1617-8. Married—Christopher Vertue and Ann Saull: St. Dionis Backchurch, p. 19.

1682. — Nicolas White and Mary Vertue: St. Jas. Clerkenwell, i. 195.

1792. — Samuel Vertue and Elenor Rowles: St. Geo. Han. Sq. ii. 88.

London, 2, 2; Philadelphia, 10, 0.

Viscount. — Offic. 'a vice-count,' one who supplied the place of a count; cf. vice-gerent, vice-chancellor, &c. This surname, unlike many others of the same official class, does not seem to have lasted long. I find no modern instances.

John le Viscont, C. R., 29 Hen. III.
Eustace le Vehounte, 1273. A.
John le Viscounte. B.

Visick.—Local, a corruption of Fishwick, q.v. A more imitative corruption is found in Physick, q.v.

'Visick and Norman, ladies' boarding school, 82, Carlton Hill, London, N.W.': London Dir. 1870.

London, 1; Devon Court Dir., 1.

Vittery; v. Vicary, of which it is a corruption.

Vivash.—? Local, 'at the Five-ash-trees.' 'A name still of some distinction in the neighbourhood of Devizes, betraying the Western pronunciation of Five-Ashes'; so says a correspondent of Mr. Lower, who adds, 'I should prefer deducing it from the Fr. *vivace*, which Cotgrave defines as "livelie, lustie . . . full of life, mettall, spirit"'; v. Fiveash, and cf. Vowler for Fowler or Venn for Fenn.

1771. Married — Joshua Jackson and Betty Vivesh: St. Geo. Han. Sq. i. 215.

1774. — Thomas Mills and Mary Vivish: ibid. p. 243.

1784. — Thomas Vivaish and Betty Croom: ibid. p. 356.

The Daily Telegraph, May 16, 1894, records the marriage of Simeon Viveash.

Vivian, Vyvyan.—Bapt. 'the son of Vyvyan' or Viviana, the name of the enchantress of King Arthur's Court (v. Yonge, i. 407-8); cf. Phythian.

Vivianus Gernet, co. Lanc., 30 Hen. III : BBB. p. 11.
Isabel fil. Viviani, co. Camb., 1273. A.
John Vivian, or Vivien, or Vivyan, London, 20 Edw. I. R.
Viviana fil. Clementi le Bonde, Close Roll, 10 Edw. II.
Vivian, son of John Browne, 1544 : Reg. St. Columb Major, Cornwall, p. 3.
Vivian, son of Luke Pollard, 1544 : ibid.
Vivian, son of Edward Merifield, 1544 : ibid.
Emblen, d. of Thomas Vivian, 1544 : ibid. p. 10.
1586. Humphrey Vivian, co. Merioneth : Reg. Univ. Oxf. vol. ii. pt. ii. p. 153.
1593-4. Michael Vivian, co. Cornwall : ibid. p. 200.
London, 11, 1 ; MDB. (co. Cornwall), 17, 4 ; Boston (U.S.), 3, 0.

Vizard.—Bapt. ; v. Whiskard. An early use of v for w, the name gradually assuming an imitative form.

Warin Vischard, co. Bucks, 1273. A. London, 3.

Vizer. — Occup. ? Perhaps a maker of vizors or vizards. The more correct form, however, would be Vizerer, and this does not correspond with the first instance below.

John le Visur, co. Worc., 1273. A.
1616. Robert Vizer, co. Somerset : Reg. Univ. Oxf. vol. ii. pt. ii. p. 354.

1805. Married — William Vizer and Mary Henrahan : St. Geo. Han. Sq. ii. 331. London, 2 ; New York, 2.

Voisey ; v. Vesey, of which it is an undoubted variant.

Voller ; a variant of Vowler, q. v.

Oxford, 1.

Voss, Vos.—Nick. Vos, a Dutch and Low German form of Fox, q.v. (Lower's Patr. Brit. p. 367). Its importation into England is comparatively modern.

1692. Bapt. — John, s. David Voss : St. Jas. Clerkenwell, i. 346.
1694. — Eliz., d. David Voss : ibid. p. 356.
London, 8, 2 ; New York, 37, 1.

Vowell, Vowle, Vowles, Voules.—(1) Nick. 'the fowl.' A West-country form of Fowell and Fowle, a fowl, a bird ; cf. Vivash and Visick for Fiveash and Fishwick. Especially cf. Vowler for Fowler. The genitive of Vowle is Vowles ; cf. Brooks for Brook, or Williams for William. (2) Bapt. 'the son of Voel,' an ancient Welsh personal name. Just as Hoel became Howell, so Voel has become Vowell. It is probable that, so far as Vowell is concerned, (2) is the chief parent.

Walter le Fowel, co. Oxf., 1273. A.
Matthew le Fowel, co. Oxf., ibid.
John le Fouel, co. Oxf., ibid.
Nicholas le Foghele, c. 1300. M.
1578. William Vouell, co. Pembroke : Reg. Univ. Oxf. vol. ii. pt. ii. p. 83.

1586. George Voyell, co. Pembroke : ibid. p. 153.
1609. William Voile, co. Hereford : ibid. p. 308.
1608. Buried — Thomas Vowell, the father of John Vowell, *poulter*, dwelling in Gratious (Gracechurch) streete : St. Peter, Cornhill, i. 163.
1620. Frauncis, the sonne of Allexander Brounescome and Effym his wife, brought a bead at Mr. Vowelles howse : ibid. p. 68.
London, 0, 0, 2, 0 ; MDB. (co. Somerset), 0, 0, 29, 2.

Vowler, Voller.—Occup. 'the fowler.' A West-country surname, just where we should expect to find it ; cf. Vidler for Fidler. v. Vidler for other instances of v for f ; but some from a Somersetshire Roll may be quoted :

John Vox (Fox), co. Soms., 1 Edw. III : Kirby's Quest, p. 93.
Stephen le Vrye (Fry), co. Soms., 1 Edw. III : ibid. p. 171.
John le Vreynch (French), co. Soms., 1 Edw. III : ibid. p. 230.
Raph Voulcr, co. Bucks, 1273. A.
John le Voulere, C. R., 20 Edw. II. pt. ii.
Edward le Vowelar, co. Soms., 1 Edw. III : Kirby's Quest, p. 256.

The variant Voller occurs in the Oxford Directory (1896). It is found in church registers.

1761. Married — John Voller and Dorothy Hanson : St. Geo. Han. Sq. i. 104.
MDB. (co. Devon), 4, 0 ; Oxford, 0, 1.

Vyner.—Occup. ; v. Viner.

Vyvyan ; v. Vivian.

W

Wace. — Bapt. 'the son of Wace,' a long-forgotten personal name, found at first in the Eastern counties, on the sea border.

Wacius fil. Robert, co. Linc., 1273. A.
Geoffrey Wace, co. Norf., ibid.
Philip Wase, co. Norf., ibid.
Wacius fil. Huberti, co. Linc., ibid.
John Wason, co. Soms., 1 Edw. III : Kirby's Quest, p. 239.
Johannes Wase, 1379 : P.T. Yorks. p. 145.
1568. Leonard Waice, or Wace : Reg. Univ. Oxf. vol. ii. pt. ii. p. 29.
London, 2 ; Crockford, 4.

Wackett, Waggett, Weggett. —? Bapt. 'the son of Waket' (?). Whatever be the origin, Waggett and Weggett must be considered as simple variants ; cf. Slagg and Slack.

Henry Waket, co. Linc., 1273. A.
Hugh Waket, co. Berks, ibid.
Ralph Waket, co. Linc., ibid.
1581. John Waggatt, or Waggotte (co. Surrey) : Reg. Univ. Oxf. vol. ii. pt. ii. p. 110.
In 1635 Thomas Waggitt, aged 17, sailed in the Thomas and John, for Virginia : Hotten's Lists ot Emigrants, p. 85.
1731. Married — Thomas Pepper and Mary Wackkett : St. Geo. Han. Chap. Mayfair, p. 322.
1742. Bapt.—William Thomas Wagget : ibid. p. 4.
London, 3, 6, 0 ; Boston (U.S.), 0, 1, 1.

Waddecar, Waddacor, Waddicar.—Local, 'of Wedacre,' in the parish of Garstang, co. Lanc.

'Wedicer Hall, commonly called Woodacre, belonged to the family of Rigmaden, and in a charter concerning Cockersand Abbey, in 37 Edw. III. (1363), Thomas de Rigmayden is styled lord of the manor of Wedacre': Baines' Hist. of Lanc. ii. 534.

Willelmus ffyfe de Waddicar, 1642: Preston Guild Rolls, p. 122.

Willelmus ffyfe de Waddaker, 1662: ibid. p. 144.

Ralph Wediker, of Goosnargh, 1672: Lancashire Wills at Richmond, ii. 304.

Ann Wadiker, of Longton, 1675: Wills at Chester (1660–80), p. 276.

Manchester, 0, 1, 0; Preston, 1, 0, 0; Ramsbotham, 0, 0, 1.

Waddell, Waddle. — Local, 'of Odell,' a parish in co. Bedford. For proof, v. Odell. Waddle is a natural variant, but seems confined to America.

Robert de Wadhulle, co. Bedf., 1273. A.

1658. Married — John Waddell and Mary Saint: Reg. Canterbury Cathedral, p. 59.

1706. Married—William Waddell and Alice Ball: St. Jas. Clerkenwell, iii. 28.

1764. — Adam Waddell and Helen Elliot: St. Geo. Han. Sq. i. 131.

London, 4, 0; Philadelphia, 9, 2; Boston (U.S.), 4, 0.

Waddilove,   Waddilow, Wadlow. — Personal or bapt. 'the son of Wadelief,' one of several personal names ending in -lief, dear; cf. Spendlove, Leifchild, &c.

John Wadeinlove, co. Hunts, 1273. A.

Henry Wadeinlove, co. Hunts, ibid.

Agnes Wadylove, 1379: P. T. Yorks. p. 30.

Henricus Wadyloef, 1379: ibid. p. 241.

Robertus Wadyloef, 1379: ibid.

Adam Wadinlof, 1379: ibid. p. 120.

1564. Thomas Wadloffe admitted to be a parchment-seller: Reg. Univ. Oxf. vol. ii. pt. ii. p. 322.

1683–4. Francis Land and Susanna Wadlow: Marriage Alleg. (Canterbury), p. 157.

1686. Thomas Halton and Eliz. Wadloe: ibid. p. 252.

London, 2, 0, 0; MDB. (West Rid. Yorks.), 2, 0, 0; Philadelphia, 0, 0, 3.

Waddington. — Local, 'of Waddington,' a village and parish near Clitheroe, co. York. It is natural to find the name crossing the border into Lancashire. This surname has ramified very strongly in the Northern counties.

Laurencius de Wadyngton, 1379: P. T. Yorks. p. 284.

Johannes de Wadyngton, 1379: ibid. p. 273.

1588. George Waddington, of Leyland: Wills at Chester, i. 198.

1610. Matthew Waddington, co. York: Reg. Univ. Oxf. vol. ii, pt. ii. p. 315.

— Nicholas Waddington, co. York: ibid.

1616. Margaret Waddington, of Over Darwen: Wills at Chester, i. 198.

London, 3; Manchester, 9; Sheffield, 4; West Rid. Court Dir., 11; Boston (U.S.), 1; New York, 2.

Waddle; v. Waddell.

Waddster.—Occup. 'a wadster,' one who used woad (A.S. wád) in dyeing cloth (v. woad, Skeat). As a Yorkshire entry it may be the parent of Walster and Waltster (q.v.), found in the Sheffield Directory. The corruption would easily arise.

Thomas Waddester, 1379: P. T. Yorks. p. 285.

Waddup.—Offic. 'of the Wardrobe,' q.v. In Heyford, co. Oxf., and the surrounding districts the variants are Waddrupp, Wadrup, Wadrop, Wardrup, and Waddup. Like wardrober, one who looked after the wardrobe, a somewhat high official position.

Wade.—(1) Local, 'at the wade.' 'Wath, a ford. N.E.' (Halliwell). This surname has made such a deep impression upon our registers that there is no need to furnish modern instances. With Wade and Waythe, cf. Ford and Forth.

Henry de la Wade, co. Oxf., 1273. A.

Johannes atte Waythe, 1379: P. T. Yorks. p. 71.

Alicia de Wath', 1379: ibid.

Hekyn of Wath', 1379: ibid. p. 70.

(2) Bapt. 'the son of Wade'; v. Wadeson. But (1) is probably the source of most of our Wades.

Andrew Wade, co. Camb., 1273. A.

Rosa Wade, co. Camb., ibid.

Roger Wade. H.

Johannes Wade, 1379: P. T. Yorks. p. 162.

London, 54; Philadelphia, 40; Boston (U.S.), 67.

Wader.—Occup. 'the wader,' one who waded in the Ouse, and probably netted fish.

William de Adle, wayder, 25 Edw. I: Freemen of York, i. 6.

John le Walder, 21 Edw. I: ibid. p. 5.

Robert de Walcheford, wayder: ibid. p. 2.

This occupative term occurs frequently in the above-quoted work. Possibly the following entry may refer to the surname:

1545. William Lyghtfot and Agnes Wadder: Marriage Lic. (Faculty Office), p. 5.

Wadeson.—Bapt. 'the son of Wade'; v. Wade (2). In Domesday found as a personal name in the form of Wada (co. Dorset), Wade (co. Dorset), Wado (co. Wilts).

Nicholas Wodeson. H.

1614. Married—Tobias Waideson and Alice Graye: St. Peter, Cornhill, i. 248.

Thomas Wadeson, of Dalton, 1697: Lancashire Wills at Richmond, ii. 264.

Jenetta Waideson, of Burton, 1718: ibid.

London, 4.

Wadham.—Local, 'of Woodham,' q.v., a natural corruption.

William de Wodham, co. Norf., 1273. A.

1522. John Waddeham, or Waddam: Reg. Univ. Oxf. i. 126.

1764. Married—John Bull and Mary Wadham: St. Geo. Han. Sq. i. 130.

London, 4; Boston (U.S.), 1.

Wadley, Wadleigh.—Local, 'of Wadley,' a tithing in the parish of Great Farringdon, co. Berks. Seemingly meaning 'the ford by the meadow'; v. Wade (1).

Hugh de Wadele, co. Norf., 1273. A.

1652. Bapt. — Ann, d. Thomas Wadly: Reg. Stourton, co. Wilts, p. 11.

1776. Married—Lewis Price and Eliz. Wadeley: St. Geo. Han. Sq. i. 267.

London, 3, 0; Boston (U.S.), 1, 28; Philadelphia, 0, 2; New York, 2, 2.

Wadlow; v. Waddilove.

Wadsworth, Wordsworth. —Local, 'of Wadsworth,' a large township in the parish of Halifax, co. York. In the parish church of Silkstone the name is variously found as Waddysworth (1556), Wardsworth (1656), Wadsworth (1666), and Wordsworth (1668, and forward). Longfellow had for his second name Wadsworth, and was on both father and mother's side of Yorkshire lineage. Query, was the poetic fire of Wordsworth and Wadsworth Longfellow kindled on the same original hearth ? The poet's family must have journeyed by degrees from the Yorkshire border, across Westmoreland, into Cumberland, where, at Cockermouth, John Wordsworth, attorney, was agent for the estates of the first Earl of Lonsdale. His son, the poet, was born there in 1770.

Peter de Waddeworth, *sellarius*, 4 Edw. II : Freemen of York, i. 13.
Alicia de Waddesworth, 1379 : P. T. Yorks. p. 57.
1592. Married — Thomas Hudde and Dorothie Wadsworth : St. Jas. Clerkenwell, iii. 16.
1791. Married — John Hockley and Ann Wordsworth : St. Geo. Han. Sq. ii. 54.
London, 6, 3 ; West Rid. Court Dir., 16, 5 ; Philadelphia, 10, 0 ; Boston (U.S.), 15, 0 ; New York, 0, 1.

Waferer, Wafer. — Occup. 'the waferer,' a wafer-baker, also a wafer-seller. Wafer, a small thin sweet or spiced cake, 'a thin leaf of paste' (Skeat).

'Singers with harpes, baudes, wafereres,
Which ben the veray devils officeres.'
    Chaucer, C. T. 12413.
' Than Haukyns wif the wafrer.'
    Piers Plowman, Vision, 8956.
' Yermongers, pybakers, and waferers.'
    Cocke Lorelle's Bote.
'Pay to Ralph Crast, the waferer, 40s. of our gift' : Issues of Exchequer, 26 Hen. II.
' Cakes of fine flour mingled with oil, or unleavened wafers' : Lev. ii. 4.
Simon le Waffrer, co. Hereford, Hen. III–Edw. I. K.
Robert le Wafre, co. Salop, 1273. A.
William le Wayfre. J.
John the Wafferer, co. Glouc., 1290 : Household Exp., Bishop Swinfield, Cam. Soc., p. 149.
Lambert le Wafrer, Close Roll, 10 Edw. II.
Theobald Wayferer, co. York. W. 2.
1618. Married — William Lovitt and Ann Wafer : St. Jas. Clerkenwell, iii. 46.
1638. Buried—Mr. Edward Wayferrer : St. Michael, Cornhill, p. 235.
1667. Myrth Waferer, of Winchester, D.D., and Mrs. Eliz. Wroth, of Blenden Hall, Bexley, Kent : Marriage Lic. (Canterbury), p. 141.

I do not find any existing examples in England, but I doubt not they exist. Perhaps Weaver has absorbed this surname.

Philadelphia, 0, 5.

Wager.—Occup. 'the wager,'

one who paid or was paid by fixed wages (?) ; cf. Tasker.

Willelmus Wagur et Cecilia, uxor, *smyth*, 1379 : P. T. Yorks. p. 116.
Margareta Wagur, 1379 : ibid.
1603. Buried—John Wager, *a poor man* : St. Jas. Clerkenwell, iv. 76.
1614. Married — Edward Wager to Margret Congrie : St. Peter, Cornhill, i. 248.
London, 3 ; Philadelphia, 6 ; New York, 4.

Wagg. — (1) ? Nick. probably connected with *wag*, to move from side to side, as in wag-tail ; v. Wagstaff, Wagspear, &c. (2) Local, 'at the wagg,' probably a wall (v. *waghe*, Halliwell) ; cf. Wall.

John Wagge, co. York, 1273. A.
Robert Wagge, co. Linc., ibid.
Robert le Wag, co. Oxf., ibid.
William Wag, co. Oxf., ibid.
Robert atte Wagge, co. Soms., 1 Edw. III : Kirby's Quest, p. 195.
Henry atte Wagge, co. Soms., 1 Edw. III : ibid.
1607. Buried — Thomasen, d. David Wagg : St. Jas. Clerkenwell, iv. 99.
1720. Bapt.—Mary, d. Edward Wagg : ibid. ii. 122.
London, 3 ; New York, 1 ; Boston (U.S.), 1.

Waggett ; v. Wackett.

Waghorn, Waghorne.—Nick. ' Waghorn' ; v. Shakespear ; cf. Wagspear and Wagstaff.

John Waghorne, C. R., 17 Ric. II.
John Waghorne, C. R., 9 Hen. IV.
1736. Married — William Lane and Mary Waghorne : St. Michael, Cornhill, p. 67.
1795. Married—Daniel Waghorn and Mercy Wait : St. Geo. Han. Sq. ii. 137.
London, 6, 2.

Wagner, Waggener, Wag-goner, Wagoner, Wagener.— Occup. 'the wagoner,' a wainman, a carter. Wagon, wain (Dutch), a cart for carriage of goods. Probably as 'Wainman' (q.v.) was the common English term, Wagner is generally of German importation. The following entry confirms this :

James Waggoner, son of James Waggoner, christened at the Dutch Church, 1610 : Reg. St. Dionis Backchurch (London), p. 94.
Godemar le Waghener. DD.
John Wiggoner, co. York. W. 16.
1808. Married—Anthony Wagner and Sarah Harby : St. Geo. Han. Sq. ii. 381.

London, 14, 0, 0, 0, 1 ; Philadelphia, 384, 2, 1, 6, 0 ; Boston (U.S.), 34, 1, 0, 0, 0.

Wagspear.—Nick. *Wag* and *shake* were the two invariable verbs that went to the formation of those vigorous sobriquets by which all officious officials were nicknamed by the railing crowd. Hence Wag-spear, Wag-tail, Wag-staff, Wag-horn (for others not in nomenclature, v. Halliwell). Shakespeare having immortalized this class of names, my chief remarks will be found under that name.

Mabill Wagsper, co. York : W. 1 (Index).
' Elias Gile gave all his land in Haverbrec, which William Knipe and William Wagspear held ' : Revenues of the Priory of Conishead, v. West's Ant. of Furness, p. 191.

Wagstaff, Wagstaffe.—Nick. ' Wagstaff,' an official who was officious ; v. Shakespear ; v. also the statement under Wagspear.

Walter Waggestaf, co. Norf., 1273. A.
Robert Waggestaff, co. Oxf., ibid.
Edward Wagstaffe. PP.
1585. Thomas Wagstaffe, co. Warw. : Reg. Univ. Oxf. vol. ii. pt. ii. p. 144.
1696. Bapt.—Ellen, d. Thomas Wagstafe : St. Jas. Clerkenwell, i. 368.
1737. Married—John Wagstaffe and Alice Littler : St. Michael, Cornhill, i. 67.
London, 21, 3 ; Philadelphia, 6, 0 ; Boston (U.S.), 2, 0.

Wagtail.—Nick. ' wagtail' ; v. Shakespear and Wagspear.

Richard Wagetail. Y.

Waight. — Offic. ' the wait' (q.v.), a natural corruption. This variant led on to the imitative Weight, q.v.

1595. Bapt.—Alice, d. Richard Waight, *poulter* : St. Peter, Cornhill, i. 45.
1610. Rondulph Waight, co. Ches. : Reg. Univ. Oxf. vol. ii. pt. ii. p. 311.
1665. Buried — Mary Waight died of the plague : St. Jas. Clerkenwell, iv. 367.
1795. Married — John Waight and Charlotte Griffith : St. Geo. Han. Sq. ii. 135.
London, 6.

Wailes.—Local, 'of Wales' ; v. Wales. That Wailes is a corrupted spelling can easily be proved. The family of Wales, long connected with Furness and North

Lancashire, are found described indiscriminately as Wales and Wailes.

John Wailes, of Kirkby Ireleth, 1587: Lancashire Wills at Richmond, p. 292.
James Wales, of Kirkby Ireleth, 1612: ibid. p. 293.
Edmond Wales, of Boulton-by-the-Sands, 1623: ibid.
Ellen Wailes, of Bolton-juxta-Arenas: 1635: ibid. p. 292.
London, 1; Philadelphia, 3.

Wainman, Wenman. — Occup. 'the wainman,' a wagoner, a carter. Clemens Hall, wayneman (Liber Bursarii, Eccles. Dunelmensis, Sur. Soc.). Wainmen, wagoners (Halliwell).

Henry Wayneman. F.
Hugh Wayneman. W. 3.
Thomas Wenman. Z.

Evidently a common term in its day. Wagon = wain, the earlier form; cf. Charles's Wain, Wainwright.

Johannes Wayneman, 1379: P. T. Yorks. p. 135.
Johannes Wayneman, 1379: ibid. p. 255.
1583. Thomas Wenman, co. Glouc.: Reg. Univ. Oxf. vol. ii. pt. ii. p. 132.
1587. Ferdinand Wainman, or Waynman, co. Bucks: ibid. p. 161.
1604. Bapt.—Elizabeth, d. Syr Ferdinando Wenman: St. Peter, Cornhill, i. 55.
1802. Married—Mark Wainman and Harriott Potts: St. Geo. Han. Sq. ii. 266.
Manchester, 1, 0; London, 0, 4; New York, 3, 4.

Wainwright, Wainewright. — Occup. 'the wainwright,' a wagon-maker, a cartwright. With the instance Wenwright infra, cf. Wenman for Wainman.

1568. Edward Waynwright, Magd. Coll.: Reg. Univ. Oxf. i. 323.
1577. Bapt.—Annes, d. Thomas Wenwright: St. Peter, Cornhill, i. 19.
1678. — Hanna, d. John Waneright: St. Jas. Clerkenwell, i. 283.
London, 14, 2; Philadelphia, 27, 0; New York, 8, 1.

Wait, Waite, Waitt, Wayte, Wayt. — Offic. 'the wait,' i. e. watchman (v. Wayt for a longer notice); also musicians in general.

'The waytis blew lowde.'
'Grete lordys were at the assent, Waytys blewe, to mete they wente.' Halliwell.

Robert le Weyte, co. Oxf., 1273. A.
Sarra le Weyte, co. Oxf., ibid.

Ralph le Weyte, or Wayte, co. Essex, ibid.
Henry le Weyte. D.
Robert le Weyte. H.
Johannes Wayte, 1379: P. T. Yorks. p. 74.
Willelmus Wayte, 1379: ibid. p. 42.
1636. Buried—Barbara, wife of Tho. Waite: St. Jas. Clerkenwell, iv. 227.

Further instances are needless.

London, 5, 20, 1, 2, 1; Philadelphia, 1, 20, 3, 1, 0; Boston (U.S.), 13, 24, 40, 0, 0.

Waithman, Wayman, Weyman. — Occup. 'the waithman,' a hunter, Scotch and North Eng. M.E. waith, to hunt, fish. Jamieson says: 'Waithman, waythman, a hunter.

"Lytil John and Robyne Hude,
Waythmen ware commendyd gude."
Wyntown, vii. 10. 432.
"About this tyme was the waithman Robert Hode with his fallow litil Johne."
Bellend. Cron. B. xiii. c. 19.'

This surname was for several centuries settled in the neighbourhood of Lancaster. From this district it seems now to have disappeared.

Richard Waitheman, of Newtoun, 1566: Lancashire Wills at Richmond, i. 292.
Jean Wayman, or Waithman, of Warton, 1612: ibid. p. 303.
Thomas Wayman, or Waithman, of Warton, 1613: ibid.
Jarvis Waythman, of Carnforth, 1625: ibid.
James Waythman, chantry-priest at Cheadle, co. Ches.: Hist. East Cheshire, i. 202.
1777. Married—Richard Waithman, of Lancaster, and Jane Law: Reg. Ulverston Ch., p. 421.
1778. Bapt.—Mary, d. Capt. Waithman: ibid. p. 494.
London, 0, 2, 0; West Rid. Court Dir., 2, 1, 0; Philadelphia, 0, 4, 10; Boston (U.S.), 0, 0, 1.

Wake.—Nick. 'the wake' (?), i. e. the vigilant, the watchful (?). Hereward the Wake is said to have acquired his surname thus.

Isaac Wake was University orator in 1607. Dr. Sleep was the foremost preacher in Cambridge at the same time. James I, who dearly loved a pun, said 'he always felt inclined to wake when he heard Sleep, and to sleep when he heard Wake': Brooke's Puritans, ii. 180.
John Wake, co. Linc., 1273. A.
Nicholas Wake, co. Derby, ibid.
Thomas le Wake, co. Derby, 20 Edw. I. R.
Baldwin de (le?) Wake, co. Northampton, ibid.

1687. Married—George Wake and Eliz. Sherman: St. Jas. Clerkenwell, p. 204.
London, 16; New York, 4.

Wakefield.—Local, 'of Wakefield,' co. York.

Thomas de Wakefeld, co. Derby, 20 Edw. I. R.
Johannes de Wakfeld', 1379: P. T. Yorks. p. 222.
Willelmus Waykfeld, barker, 1379: ibid. p. 95.
Thomas Wakefeld, lyster, 1379: ibid.
1563. Married—John Cocklowe and Alice Wakefild: St. Thomas the Apostle, (London), p. 3.
1714. Married—George Roberts and Mary Wakefield: St. Mary Aldermary, p. 44.
London, 16; Philadelphia, 9; Boston (U.S.), 25.

Wakeling, Wakelin.—Bapt.; v. Wanklyn. In addition to the earlier instances given under Wanklyn, I add the following:

1763. Married — John Wakeling and Eliz. Harrison: St. Geo. Han. Sq. i. 127.
1775. — John Wakelin and Martha Phillips: ibid. p. 252.
London, 6, 6; Oxford, 0, 12.

Wakeman.—Offic. 'the wakeman,' i. e. watchman. In Ripon Cathedral, if I remember rightly, there is a mural monument commemorating the social and official virtues of the City Wakeman. 'Wakmen, watchmen': Halliwell.

Johannes Wakemen, 1379: P. T. Yorks. p. 203.
Jacob Waykman, co. Norf. F.
Joan Wakemen. H.
John Wakeman, bailiff of Yarmouth, 1586: FF. xi. 328.
1809. Married—James Wakeman and Ann Pirkiss: St. Geo. Han. Sq. ii. 415.
London, 2; Boston (U.S.), 1; Philadelphia, 1.

Walborn; v. Whalebone.

Walcock.—Bapt. 'the son of Walter,' from nick. Wal, and suffix -cock, as in Wilcock, Simcock, &c. (v. Cocks). The probable reason why this surname can scarcely be found now is because it has become absorbed into Walcott (q.v.). For a parallel case, v. Glasscock.

Edith, relict of Walekoc, co. Camb., 1273. A.
Thomas Walkoc, 1379: P. T. Yorks. p. 138.
Willelmus Walcok, 1379: ibid.
1611. Buried — William Walcock, a poor man: St. Jas. Clerkenwell, iv. 117.

Walcot, Walcott.—Local, 'of Walcott': (1) a parish, co. Lincoln; (2) a hamlet in the parish of Misterton, co. Leic.; (3) a chapelry in the parish of Billinghay, co. Linc.; (4) a parish in co. Norfolk, a parish in co. Somerset, a hamlet in the parish of Holy Cross, co. Worc.

Savaric de Walecote, co. Oxf., Hen. III-Edw. I, K.
Symon de Walcote, co. Linc., ibid.
Roger de Walecote, co. Salop, 1273. A.
Thomas de Walecote, co. Norf., ibid.
Nicholas de Walcote, co. Linc., ibid.
Emma de Walecote, co. Linc., 20 Edw. I. R.
Walter de Walecot, co. Norf., ibid.
1625. Buried — Francis Walcott: St. Jas. Clerkenwell, iv. 166.
1639. — Mary Peplow, servant to Richard Walcott: St. Thomas the Apostle (London), p. 121.
London, 2, 0; Crockford, 1, 2; Philadelphia, 1, 4; Boston (U.S.), 0, 19.

Walden.— (1) Local, ' of Walden,' a well-known and ancient town in co. Essex, now Saffron Walden. A monastery at Walden gave impetus to the surname. This I have found to be commonly the case. Two parishes, also in co. Herts, have helped, no doubt, to swell the total.

Alice de Waledene, co. Camb., 1273. A.
Richard de Waledene, co. Camb., ibid.
John de Waledene, co. Bucks, 20 Edw. I. R.

(2) Bapt. 'the son of Waldron.' Naturally and easily corrupted to Waldin and Walding, now Walden.

Walden fil. Gospatrick, co. Cumb., Hen. III-Edw. I. K.
Thomas Waldyng', 1379: P. T. Yorks. p. 143.
Johannes Waldyng', 1379: ibid.
1573. Thomas Walden, Ch. Ch.: Reg. Univ. Oxf. iii. 40.
London, 14; Philadelphia, 8; Boston (U.S.), 15.

Waldie, Waldo; v. Waldy.

Waldron.—Bapt. 'the son of Waleran' (?). The *d* is intrusive. For other forms, v. Walrand. The name seems to have been fairly popular in the hereditary surname period.

Walarinus de Cartone, 1273. A.
1522. John Walronde or Walderon: Reg. Univ. Oxf. i. 25.
1600. John Walrond, co. Devon: ibid. vol. ii. pt. ii. p. 245.
1603. Francis Waldron, co. Soms.: ibid. p. 265.

1730. Bapt.—Sarah, d. William Waldron: St. Mary Aldermary (London), p. 125.
London, 6; Philadelphia, 24; Boston (U.S.), 40.

Waldy, Waldie, Waldo, Wilthew.—Bapt. 'the son of Waldeve.' No doubt an abbreviation, or nick. of Waldeve or Waltheof, an early English personal name. This was early corrupted to Waldew, and the present forms were inevitable. The name was common (I have many more instances) and must have left descendants. As Waltho or Waldie the name crept northwards into co. Roxburgh, and there the surname has flourished for centuries.

Waldief de Haulton, 7 Hen. II: Pipe Roll, iv. 24.
Willelmus fil. Waldief, 7 Hen. II: ibid.
Waldeve fil. Gamel, temp. Hen. II: Hist. Westm. and Cumb. i. 345.
Waldeof, or Waltheof, or Waldew, fil. Gospatric: E. and F., co. Cumb., v. Index.
Waldeof, fil. Dolphin, Hen. II: ibid. p. 42.
Waldeof de Langthwait, Hen. II: ibid.

Almost all the instances are confined to North England.

Waldive Lagoe, 1661, Manchester: Exchequer Depositions, co. Lanc., p. 35.

Wilthew, a surname found in Newcastle and the neighbourhood, must be looked upon as an unquestionable descendant of some Walthew or Waldew.

Adam Walthawe, *spicer*, 1379: P. T. Yorks. p. 281.
London, 0, 1, 1, 0; Crockford, 3, 1, 1, 0; Philadelphia, 0, 3, 0, 0; Boston (U.S.), 0, 0, 4, 0.

Wale.—(1) Nick. 'the whale'; v. Whale. (2)—— ? —— ? Perhaps local, as the ' Prior de Wale ' is mentioned in R. p. 828, in relation to some land in Guernsey.

William Wale, co. Linc., 1273. A.
Adam Wale, co. Oxf., ibid.
Walter Wale, co. Camb., ibid.
Thomas Wale, co. Northampt., Hen. III-Edw. I. K.
Prior de Wale, Guernsey, 20 Edw. I. R.
1655. Buried—Jone, d. William Wale: St. Jas. Clerkenwell, iv. 306.
1808. Married—Richard Wale and Ann Tringham: St. Geo. Han. Sq. ii. 387.
London, 7; Oxford, 2; New York, 1.

Wales.—Local, ' of Wales,' a parish ten miles from Sheffield, W. Rid. York. A family of this name must have settled early on the Yorkshire border of North Lancashire. In the course of time they penetrated into Furness, and spelt their name Wales and Wailes (q.v.).

Cecilia de Wales, 1379: P. T. Yorks. p. 118.
William Wales, of Over Kellett, 1587: Lancashire Wills at Richmond, p. 293.
John Wales, of Cockin (Dalton-in-Furness), 1661: ibid.
London, 3; Philadelphia, 2; Boston (U.S.), 39.

Walesby, Walsby. — Local, ' of Walesby': (1) a parish near Market Rasen, co. Linc.; (2) a parish near Ollerton, co. Notts.

Osbert de Walesby, co. Linc., 1273. A.
William de Walesby, co. Notts, ibid.
1764. Married—Edward Mortimer and Ann Walesby: St. Geo. Han. Sq. i. 132.
1793. — Edward Walsby, D.D., and Henrietta Bisset: ibid. ii. 98.
1815. Buried—Edward Walsby, D.D.: Canterbury Cath., p. 94.
London, 1, 1.

Walford.—Local, 'of Walford': (1) a parish near Ross, co. Hereford; (2) a township in the parish of Leintwardine, co. Hereford.

1572. Clement Walforde, St. Alban Hall: Reg. Univ. Oxf. vol. ii. pt. ii. p. 41.
1663. Thomas Houghton and Hannah Walford: Marriage Alleg. (Canterbury), p. 91.
1672. Thomas Francke and Eliz. Walford: Marriage Lic. (Westminster), p. 201.
1787. Married—Thomas Walford and Mary Coleback: St. Geo. Han. Sq. i. 408.
London, 15; Philadelphia, 3; New York, 2.

Walkden.—Local, ' of Walkden,' now a parish called Walkden Moor, in the ancient parish of Eccles, near Manchester.

John de Walkedene, 1408: East Ches. ii. 335 n.
1610. Robert Walkden, Rochdale: Baines' Lanc. i. 489.
1619-20. Francis Walkeden, co. Lanc.: Reg. Univ. Oxf. vol. ii. pt. ii. p. 381.
1661-2. Simon Harker and Mary Walkadine: Marriage Alleg. (Canterbury), p. 25.
1622. Hugh Walkden, of Bolton: Wills at Chester, ii. 224.
1640. Alexander Walkden, of Sharples: ibid.
Manchester, 6; London, 3.

Walker.—Occup. 'the walker,' i.e. fuller: 'a term applied to a fuller of cloth (from his stamping on or pressing it). A.S. *wealcere*' (Skeat). For a curious fem. suffix, v. Walkster.

> 'Cloth that cometh fro the wevyng
> Is nought comely to wear
> Til it be fulled under foot.'
>   Piers Plowman.

An Elizabethan statute speaks of 'cloth-fuller, otherwise called Tucker, or Walker' (5 Eliz. c. 4. 23).

'Of William Reynolds, *walker*, for half a pewe with Edward Doughtie,3s.4d.: Churchwardens' Expenses, Ludlow,p.154.

In the Chester Play, 1339, the weavers and walkers marched together (Ormerod's Hist. Cheshire, i. 300).

Geoffrey le Walkare, London, 1273. A.
Peter le Walkar, co. Glouc., 20 Edw. I. R.
Ralph le Walkere. T.
Johanna Walkar, 1379: P. T. Yorks. p.159.
Robertus Megson, *walkare*, 1379: P. T. Yorks. p. 159.
Robertus Welos, *walkare*, 1379: ibid.
Willelmus Walkere, *fullo*, 1379: ibid. p. 267.

No modern instances are needed. Their name is legion.

London, 307; Philadelphia, 512; Boston (U.S.), 299.

Walkington. — Local, 'of Walkington,' a parish in the union of Beverley, E. Rid. Yorks.

Thomas de Walkynton, 1379: P. T. Howdenshire, p. 9.
1795. Married—James Crump and Eliz. Walkington : St. Geo. Han. Sq. ii. 125.
London, 1.

Walklate, Walklett.—? Local. Seemingly some small spot on the borders of Cheshire and Derbyshire.

1637. William Walklate, of Charlesworth, co. Derby: Wills at Chester, ii. 226.
1653. Married—Ralph Britall and Elizabeth Walklate, Reg. Mottram, co. Ches.: East Ches. i. 135.
1796. — Richard Gallsworthy and Ann Walklate : St. Geo. Han. Sq. ii. 150.
1803. — George Walklett and Elenor Hodgson : ibid. p. 295.
London, 2, 0; Manchester, 0, 1; Oxford, 0, 5.

Walkling.—Bapt.; v. Wanklyn.

Walkmill.—Local, 'of Walkmill,' a township in the parish of

Warkworth, co. Northumberland, originally the place where the cloth was thickened by the walker (v. Walker).

1394. 'Item, pro 3 bands ad walk-mylne, 20d.': FFF. p. 617.
1609. Richard Wharffe for ye Walk-Mylne . . . one barne, and one little croft, £5 6s. 8d. : Dawson's Hist. of Skipton, p. 275.
Johannes de Walkmylne, 1379: P. T. Yorks. p. 41.

Walkster.—Occup. 'a walker,' a fuller, with fem. *-ster*. Probably the Walster and Waltster (q.v.) of the Sheffield Directory. Yorkshire was famous for its love of the fem. suffix ; v. Slaster, &c.

Johannes Walkester, *fullo*, 1379: P. T. Yorks. p. 186.

Wall, Walle.—Local, 'at the wall,' from residence thereby. One of the walls that defended towns and cities ; cf. Barr and Wagge (2).

Godfrey atte Wall, co. Essex, 1273. A.
Walter de la Walle, co. Devon, ibid.
Lecia Atte-wal, C. R., 18 Edw. I.
John of the Wall (Hereford), Pardons Roll, 6 Ric. II.
Thomas atte Walle, co. Soms., 9 Edw. II : Kirby's Quest, p. 113.
Adam del Wall, 14 Edw. III : Freemen of York, i. 34.
Willelmus atte Wall', 1379: P. T. Yorks. p. 242.
1630. John Wall, of Helsby : Wills at Chester, ii. 226.
1682. Bapt.—Richard, s. George Wall : Reg. Canterbury Cath., p. 17.
London, 34, 0; Philadelphia, 88, 0; Boston (U.S.), 91,0; (Walle), New York, 1.

Wallace, Wallis, Walsh, Welch, Welsh. — Local, 'the Welsh,' from Wales, i. e. the Welshman. Many of the instances in the directories must be looked upon as of Scottish descent ; v. Gales.

> 'And Rose the dyssheres;
> Godefray of Garlekhithe,
> And Gryffyn the Walshe.'
>   Piers Plowman, 3124.

A regulation of Edw. III concerning wool speaks of 'merchandises en Engleterre, Gales (i. e. Wales), ou Irlande' ; also of 'merchantz Engleis, Galeis (i. e. Waleis), ou Irreis' (Stat. of Realm, i. 334). Henry le Galeys (i. e. Welsh) was Lord Mayor in 1298.

Henry le Waleis, co. Wilts, 1273. A.
Roger le Waleis, co. Oxf., ibid.
Adam le Waleys, co. Oxf., ibid.
Iggelram le Waleys, co. Wilts, ibid.
William le Waleys, co. Sussex, ibid.
Howell le Walsshe. J.
John le Waleis. B.
Ingleram le Waleys. B.
Mabil le Walleys. J.
'Richard Walensis, a name afterwards called le Walays and Walsh,' c. Hen. III : Baines' Lanc. ii. 400.
'Richard le Walais, lord of Litherland,' c. Hen. III : ibid.
'Richard le Walays, 15 Edw. II' : ibid.
Roger Walsche, 1379 : P. T. Yorks. p. 74.
Richard Walays, 1379 : ibid. p. 280.
William Wallays, 1379 : ibid.
Alicia Walas, 1379 : ibid. p. 162.
London, 21, 65, 19, 61, 4 ; Philadelphia, 328, 11, 199, 58, 377; Boston (U.S.), 121, 23, 317, 428, 43.

Wallen, Walling, Wallin, Wallon. — Bapt. 'the son of Walter,' from the nick. Wal, dim. Wal-in or Wal-on. The *g* in Walling is excrescent ; cf. Jennings, Wareing, &c. v. Walcock for a similar proof of the use of this nick. But it did not make much headway, as Wat soon became the popular abbreviation of Walter. The same individual is thus described :

Walter Scalpyn, co. Berks, 1273. A.
Walton Scalpyn, co. Berks, ibid.
1615. Married—John Tucker and Jane Wallin : St. Jas. Clerkenwell, iii. 42.
1622. Buried—John Wallen : St. Peter, Cornhill, i. 179.
London, 2, 2, 0, 0 ; Philadelphia, 8, 7, 4, 0 ; Boston (U.S.), 0, 2, 0, 2.

Waller.—Occup. 'the waller,' one who builds walls, a mason. A mason is still a 'waller' in Furness, N. Lanc. I constantly entered the occupation in my church registers at Ulverston. M.E. *wal*. 'Wallare, that werkythe wythe stone and morter, *cementarius*': Prompt. Parv.

William le Waller, bailiff of Norwich, 1232 : FF. iii. 58.
Robert le Walur, co. Norf., 1273. A.
Peter le Walur, co. Oxf., ibid.
Thomas Dyekok, *waller*, 1379 : P. T. Yorks. p. 110.
Willelmus Goderd, *waller*, 1379 : ibid. p. 31.
1608. Edmund Waller, co. Bucks : Reg. Univ. Oxf. vol. ii. pt. ii. p. 301.
1731. Married—William Waller and Honour Spicer : St. Mary Aldermary, p. 49.

London, 53; MDB. (Norfolk), 7; Philadelphia, 7; New York, 23.

Walley.—Local; v. Whalley.

Wallin, Walling; v. Wallen.

Wallingford. — Local, ' of Wallingford,' a borough and market-town in co. Berks. Oddly enough, I find no intervening references, although the surname still exists, and has crossed 'to the other side.'

Wygod de Walingford, co. Berks, Hen. III-Edw. I. K.
Symon de Wallingford, co. Oxf., 1273. A.
Bryan de Walingeford, co. Bucks, ibid.
London, 1; Boston (U.S.), 13.

Wallington. — Local, ' of Wallington.' Parishes in cos. Hertford and Norfolk, also a hamlet near Croydon, Surrey.

Ralph de Walington, co. Devon, 1273. A.
1635. Joseph Wallington sailed for the Barbadoes, in the Ann and Elizabeth, aged 19 : Hotten's Lists of Emigrants, p. 70.
— William Wallington sailed for Virginia in the Transport, aged 32 : ibid. p. 101.
1668. Married—Peeter Grin and Margarett Wallington : St. Jas. Clerkenwell, p. 149.
1743. Buried—T. Wallington: St. Mary Aldermary, p. 226.
1749. Married—John Smith and Mary Wallington : St. Geo. Chap. Mayfair, p. 154.
London, 10; Philadelphia, 8.

Wallis; v. Wallace.

Wallraven, Walraven, Walravin. — Bapt. ' the son of Walraven.' In Domesday, 'Walrauen,' co. Lincoln. It does not seem to have obtained a strong footing in England, and possibly some of our Wallravens are later immigrants from Scandinavia; cf. Raven and Wolfraven.

Walrafnus de Muirteus, co. Camb., 1273. A.
1679. Buried—Prudence Wallraven, related to Mr. Loverow: St. Dionis Backchurch, p. 246.
1687-8. Married—Lancelott Copleston and Hakell Wallraven : ibid. p. 41.
1702. — Matthias Wallraven and Mercy Waymarke : ibid. p. 51.
Philadelphia, 0, 6, 1.

Wallwork, Wallworth, Walworth.—Local, ' of Wallworth.' A well-known Lancashire local surname, although I cannot

identify the spot. No doubt Wallworth is the proper orthography, the suffix -worth (v. Worth) being common in the local nomenclature of South Lancashire ; cf. Whitworth, Butterworth, Wardleworth, all places and surnames in the same district where Wallwork or Wallworth is found. Probably the first two following entries concern relatives, as they hail within a mile from one another :

1605. Margaret Walworth, of Prestwich : Wills at Chester, i. 201.
1618. Lawrence Walwork, of Crumpsall : ibid. p. 201.
1748. Married — Thomas Davis and Hannah Wallwork : St. Geo. Chap. Mayfair, p. 122.
1777. — Stephen Wallworth and Eliz. Scurfield: St. Geo. Han. Sq. i. 279.
Manchester, 11, 3, 0 ; London, 0, 2, 0; Philadelphia, 5, 0, 1 ; Boston (U.S.), 0, 0, 8.

Walmsley, Walmesley, Walmisley. — Local, ' of Walmersley,' a township in the parish of Bury, co. Lanc. This surname is very familiar to the southern portion of the County Palatine.

1600. Married—John Walmsley and Luce Dunster: St. Jas. Clerkenwell, iii. 24.
— Alice Walmesley, widow : Wills at Chester, i. 200.
1608. Henry Walmsley, of Accrington : ibid.
1620. Richard Walmisley, co. Lanc. : Reg. Univ. Oxf. vol. ii. pt. ii. p. 384.
1639. Robert Walmsley, of Walmsley : Wills at Chester, ii. 227.
1746. Married—John Walmesley and Mrs. Warrington : St. Geo. Chap. Mayfair, p. 73.
Manchester, 23, 1, 0 ; London, 7, 1, 3 ; Philadelphia, 24, 0, 0 ; Boston (U.S.), 1, 0, 0.

Walpole.—Local, 'of Walpole.' 'Walpole in Mershland, co. Norfolk, gave name to this historical family, and here Joceline de Walpole was living in the reign of Stephen' : Shirley's Noble and Gentle Men (quoted by Lower).

Alexander de Walepol, 34 Edw. I : BBB. p. 722.
Henry de Walpol, Rot. Fin., 4 Edw. II.
Walter de Walepole, co. Suff., 1273. A.
William de Walepole, co. Suff., ibid.
1579. Married—Roberte Kenigame and Alice Waullpoole : St. Michael, Cornhill, p. 12.
1662. George Bromley and Margaret Walepoole : Marriage Alleg. (Canterbury), p. 32.

1666-7. William Walpool and Luce Draper : ibid. p. 203.
London, 4; MDB. (Norfolk), 9 ; Boston (U.S.), 3 ; New York, 3.

Walrand, Walrond. — Bapt. ' the son of Walrand.' Probably, as suggested by Miss Yonge, founded upon Valerian (v. Christian Names, i. 327). The excrescent d is common after n ; cf. Simond or Simmonds and Hammond, and the provincial gownd for gown. v. Waldron.

Waleran Venator, Domesday. B.
Walrand Clerke, 1273. A.
Walran Oldman, co. Suff., ibid.
Walerand le Tyes, co. Cornwall, ibid.
Robert Wallerond. G.
1621. William Dermer and Ann Walrond : Marriage Lic. (London), ii. 105.
1662. Buried — Eliz., d. Humphry Walrond: St. Jas. Clerkenwell, iv. 347.
Crockford, 0, 3.

Walraven, Walravin ; v. Wallraven.

Walsby.—Local ; v. Walesby.

Walsh; v. Wallace.

Walsham.—Local, ' of Walsham,' parishes in cos. Norfolk and Suffolk.

Roger de Walesham, co. Camb., 1273. A.
Nicholas de Walsham, co. Norf., ibid.
Gilbert de Walsham, co. Norf., Hen. III-Edw. I. K.
Roger de Walsham, co. Camb., 20 Edw. I. R.
1630. Buried—William Wallsham : St. Mary Aldermary, p. 166.
1677-8. Maximilian Walsham and Ann Marryott : Marriage Alleg. (Canterbury), p. 198.
London, 2.

Walsingham. — Local, ' of Walsingham.' Great and Little Walsingham are parishes in co. Norfolk.

Reginald de Walsyngham, co. Norf., 1273. A.
1546. Walter Myldmay and Mary Walsyngham : Marriage Lic. (Faculty Office), p. 7.
1584. Francis Walsingham : Reg. Univ. Oxf. i. 369.
1614. Clement Terry and Catherine Walsingham : Marriage Lic. (Westminster), p. 21.
London, 1 ; MDB. (co. Suff.), 1.

Walster, Waltster.—Occup. (1) ' the waller ' (q.v.), with fem. suffix -ster. Almost all occupative names in Yorkshire took this suffix; cf. Walkster for Walker, Slaster for Slater, Wimplester for Wimpler, and endless others. A waller was a mason, a builder. (2) Probably sometimes a corruption of Waddster, q.v.

Sheffield, 1, 1.

Walter, Walther, Walters. —Bapt. 'the son of Walter.' This once popular font-name has left an indelible mark upon our nomenclature; v. Watt, Watkin, Wallen, Waters, and Waterson.

Baruntinus Walter, C. R., 20 Edw. I.
Edmund fil. Walter, co. Camb., 1273. A.
Walter Walrond, co. Oxf., ibid.
1598. Charles Walter, co. Monm.: Reg. Univ. Oxf. vol. ii. pt. ii. p. 227.
1663. John Walters and Grace Plumer: Marriage Alleg. (Canterbury), p. 101.
London, 43, 3, 29; Philadelphia, 158, 13, 126; Boston (U.S.), 23, 9, 24.

Waltham. — Local, 'of Waltham,' parishes in cos. Kent, Lincoln, Essex, Hants, Berks, Sussex, Hertford, and Leicester. From the instances furnished below it will be seen that several of the localities mentioned above may claim the honour of originating the surname.

Matilda de Waltham, co. Norf., 1273. A.
Maurice de Waltham, London, ibid.
William de Waltham, co. Linc., ibid.
Henry de Waltham, co. Leic., Hen. III-Edw. I. K.
Thomas de Waltham, co. Sussex, 20 Edw. I. R.
Roger de Waltham, co. Bedf., ibid.
1604. David Waltham, co. Devon: Reg. Univ. Oxf. vol. ii. pt. ii. p. 272.
1663. William Waltham and Anne Winch: Marriage Alleg. (Canterbury), p. 97.
London, 6.

Walton.—Local, 'of Walton.' There are twenty-five parishes of Walton in England. It would seem to suggest a stead or dwelling built of stone in place of wood; v. Wall and Town.

Alicia de Walton, 1379: P. T. Yorks. p. 302.
William de Walton, 1415: Preston Guild Rolls, p. 8.
John de Walton, 1415: ibid.'

The last two extracts will represent Walton-le-dale, near Preston.

1578. Married — Hugh Walton and Margaret Woulerrye: St. Thomas the Apostle, p. 4.
London, 50; Philadelphia, 192; Boston (U.S.), 29.

Walworth; v. Wallwork.

Wanklyn, Wakeling, Walkling, Wakelin, Wanklin. — Bapt. 'the son of Walkelin.' A Domesday personal name. The *l* was gradually lost, but in the effort to preserve it, it was resolved into *n*, and Wanklyn became the later English form. Where the *l* was entirely lost, the name took the forms of Wakelin and Wakeling, which now figure more largely in our directories. In Wakeling the *g* is excrescent, as in Wareing or Jennings.

Walchelin the Moneyer, Pipe Roll, 5 Hen. II.
William fil. Wakelin, cos. Notts and Derby, Hen. III-Edw. I. K.
Walkelinus fil. Walkelini, co. Linc., 1273. A.
Andrew Wakelyn, co. Norf., ibid.
Ywud Walklin, co. Oxf., ibid.
Thomas Walkelyn, co. Northampt, 20 Edw. I. R.
Isabella Walklyn, 1379: P. T. Yorks. p. 8.
'Walkelyn Dennis, of Rosington, co. Derby' (living circa 1550): Earwaker's East Cheshire, ii. 647.
Mrs. Walkling, mother of the landlord of the Hop Pole, Swanley Junction, Kent, died Jan. 13, 1887, aged 103 years: Standard, Jan. 14, 1887.
London, 1, 6, 0, 6, 0; Crockford, 0, 2, 0, 0, 0; Manchester, 2, 0, 0, 0, 0; Tiverton, 0, 0, 1, 0, 0; Philadelphia, 0, 3, 0, 0, 0; New York, 0, 4, 0, 0, 0; Boston (U.S.), (Wakeling), 2.

Want.—Nick. 'the want,' i. e. the mole (Halliwell).

John Wante, co. Norf., 1273. A.
Walter le Wante. J.
London (Court Dir.), 1; Philadelphia, 2.

Waple.—Local, 'of Walpole,' q.v. A somewhat curious though natural corruption.

1557. Married—Hillary Wapolle to Joane Garret: St. Peter, Cornhill, i. 223.
London, 3.

Warbleton.—Local, 'of Warbleton,' a parish in co. Sussex. Doubtless lost in Warburton; cf. Hamilton and Hamerton.

Osbert de Warbeltone, co. Sussex, 1273. A.
Amice de Warbilton, co. Camb., ibid.
William de Warbilton, co. Camb., ibid.
1555. Married—James Caterall and Elyne Warbillton: St. Dionis Backchurch, p. 3.

Warboys, Warboise, Worboys, Worboyse. — Local, 'of Warboys,' a parish in the dioc. of Ely, seven miles from Huntingdon. The favourite and natural variant seems to be Worboys.

Alan de Wardeboys, co. Hunts, 1273. A.
Richard de Wardeboys, co. Hunts, ibid.
Persona de Wardeboys, i. e. the Vicar of W., co. Hunts, ibid.
William Wardeboys, C. R., 1 Hen. IV. pt. i.
1519. John Warboys, abbot of Ramsey: Reg. Univ. Oxf. i. 112.
1741. Married — William Nixon and Ann Worbiss: St. Jas. Clerkenwell, iii. 270.
1804. — Thomas Worboyes and Mary Ann Poskett: St. Geo. Han. Sq. ii. 314.
London, 1, 0, 7, 2.

Warbrick.—Local, 'of Warbrick,' a township in the parish of Bispham, co. Lancaster.

1566. John Warbricke, Bras. Coll.: Reg. Univ. Oxf. vol. ii. pt. ii. p. 27.

His college almost claims him as of Lancashire extraction.

Richard Warbreck, of Warbreck, 1671: Lancashire Wills at Richmond, i. 300.
Henry Warbrecke, of Laton, 1580: ibid. p. 301.
Robert Warbrick, of Goosnargh, 1666: ibid.

Layton and Goosnargh are in the immediate neighbourhood of Warbrick.

1628. Richard Warbreck, of Orendall (?): Wills at Chester, ii. 228.
Liverpool, 1; Bolton, 2; Philadelphia, 3; New York, 2.

Warburton, Warburtan.— Local, 'of Warburton,' a village six miles from Warrington, co. Chester. The surname sprung from this place has ramified in a remarkable manner.

1412. Richard de Warberton: East Cheshire, ii. 488.
1593. Hamlet Warburton, of Carrington: Wills at Chester (1545-1620), p. 202.
1594. Edward Warburton, co. Ches., *pleb.*: Reg. Univ. Oxf. vol. ii. pt. ii. p. 205.
1596. Married—Richard Warborton and Joane Blagrove: St. Jas. Clerkenwell, iii. 20.
1597. Thomas Warburton, of Warburton, *clerk*: Wills at Chester (1545-1620), p. 201.
1663. Buried—Thomas Warbaton: St. Antholin (London), p. 191.
MDB. (Cheshire), 24, 0; Manchester, 41, 0; London, 3, 0; Boston (U.S.), 0, 1; Philadelphia, 11, 0; New York, 5, 0.

Warcup.—Local, 'of Warcop,' a parish in co. Westm., three miles from Brough. Query, 'the fortified hill' (v. Cope).

William de Warthecop, 23 Hen. III : Hist. West. and Cumb. i. 89.

1588. Thomas Warcoppe, co. Westm., *pleb.* : Reg. Univ. Oxf. vol. ii. pt. ii. p. 164.

1608. Buried—Awdry, d. Alex. Warcope : St. Jas. Clerkenwell, iv. 105.

1613. — Alex. Warcopp : ibid. p. 123.

1641. Joseph Littlewood and Ann Warcupp : Marriage Lic. (London), ii. 260.

1689. Joseph Leech and Margarett Warcap : Marriage Alleg. (Canterbury), p. 100.

London, 2.

Ward, Warde.—(1) Offic. 'the ward,' a guard, a watchman. This surname has naturally grown to great dimensions in our modern directories, and recent registers need not be quoted.

Robert le Warde, co. Oxf., 1273. A.

Simon le Ward, co. Bucks, ibid.

John le Warde, co. Hunts, ibid.

Warin Warde, co. Camb., ibid.

Willelmus Warde, 1379 : P. T. Yorks. p. 279 (a common entry in this register).

(2) Local, 'of the ward,' at the place of guard.

Walter de la Warde, co. Suff., 1273. A.

1541. Bapt. — Andrew Warde : St. Peter, Cornhill, i. 56.

1606. Buried—Peter, sonne of Thomas Ward, *upholster*, whoe loged att the Blacke Bull in Leadenhall Streete : ibid. p. 106.

London, 237, 0 ; West Rid. Court Dir., 64, 0 ; Philadelphia, 416, 1 ; Boston (U.S.), 227, 1.

Wardale, Wardell. — Local ; variants of Wardle, q.v.

Oxford, 1, 0.

Warden. — (1) Offic. 'the warden'; cf. *churchwarden, way-warden.* (2) Local, 'of Warden,' parishes in cos. Kent, Northumberland, Northants, and Bedford.

William de Wardon, co. Oxf., 1273. A.

Elyas Wardeden, co. Bucks, ibid.

Walter Warden, co. Oxf., ibid.

1595. Buried—Annes, wife of Robert Warden, *poulter* : St. Peter, Cornhill, i. 144.

1684. Buried — Edward, s. Thomas Warden : St. Mary Aldermary, p. 114.

1700. Bapt.—John, s. John Wardin : ibid. p. 195.

London, 8 ; Philadelphia, 14 ; Boston (U.S.), 3.

Warder.—Offic. 'the warder,' the guard. With my first two instances, cf. *ward* and *guard* (v. Ward). A warder was generally a doorkeeper ; cf. Durward.

Robert le Gardur, co. Hunts, 1273. A.

Robert le Garder, co. Oxf., ibid.

1594. Edward Wardoure, co. Middlesex : Reg. Univ. Oxf. vol. ii. pt. ii. p. 202.

1629. Walter Wardour and Margaret Thrower : Marriage Lic.(London), ii. 196.

1685. William Wardour and Anna Sophia Rodd : ibid. p. 307.

London, 1 ; Philadelphia, 4.

Wardle, Wardell, Wardill. —Local, (1) 'of Wardle,' a township in the parish of Bunbury, co. Chester ; (2) a township in the parish of Rochdale, co. Lanc. The suffix is clearly *-hill.*

Richard de Wardle, co. Linc., 1273. A.

Nicholas de Werdhyl, co. Lanc., 20 Edw. I. R.

Johannes de Wardale, 1379 : P. T. Yorks. p. 298.

1602. John Wardell, of Liverpool, *gent.* : Wills at Chester, i. 202.

1649. Humphrey Wardle, of Wardle, *yeoman* : ibid. ii. 228.

1649-50. Timothy Osborne and Arbella Wardell : Marriage Lic. (Faculty Office), p. 44.

1770. Married—Richard Wardle and Susan Porter : St. Geo. Han. Sq. i. 202.

London, 3, 3, 2 ; Manchester, 6, 0, 0 ; Philadelphia,13,11,0 ; Boston (U.S.),0,2,0

Wardman.—Offic. 'the wardman,' a guardian, a warder (v. Ward and Warden). This surname seems to have found its final home in America.

1617. Eliz. Wardman, of Lathom, *widow* : Wills at Chester, i. 202.

1750. Married—Henry Wardman and Eliz. Mulinex : St. Antholin (London), p. 155.

1779. — Jonathan Gaven and Jane Wardman : St. Geo. Han. Sq. i. 302.

New York, 1.

Wardrobe,Wardrop,Wardroper, Wardropper, Wardrupp.—Offic. 'the wardrober,' or in local form 'de la wardrobe'; the keeper of the wardrobe. O.F. *warderobe, garderobe.* The Book of Curtasye says :

'The usshere shalle bydde the wardropere
Make redy for alle, night before they fere.'

'*Wardrope*, a dressing - room. Yorkshire' (Halliwell). It will thus be seen that the *b* was early changed into *p.*

Thomas de la Wardrobe, co. Camb., 1273. A.

John atte Warderobe, C. R., 8 Edw. III.

Adam de la Garderobe. B.

Thomas de la Wardrobe. R.

Elizabeth Wardraper. Z.

Robert Wardropper, co. York. W. 17.

Wardrupp is found in co. Oxf. in the neighbourhood of Lower Heyford.

1570. Buried — Thomas Wardroppe : St. Thomas the Apostle (London), p. 90.

1574-5. Walter Wardroper, co. York : Reg. Univ. Oxf. vol. ii. pt. ii. p. 62.

London, 0, 1, 0, 0. 0 ; Crockford, 0, 0, 3, 0, 0 ; Sheffield, 4, 0, 0, 0, 0 ; New York, 1, 3, 0, 0, 0 ; Philadelphia, 0, 2, 0, 0, 0 ; Boston (U.S.), 0, 2, 0, 0, 0 ; (Wardrope), 1.

Ware, Warr, Warre. — (1) Local, 'at the weir,' from residence thereby, i. e. the weir or wear. '*Ware*, a weir or dam ' (Halliwell).

Ralph de la Ware, co. Essex, 1273. A.

William atte Ware, co. Kent, ibid.

Maurice de la War, co. Devon, Hen. III–Edw. I. K.

Jordan de la Ware, co. Wilts, ibid.

Henry atte Warr, co. Soms., 1 Edw. III : Kirby's Quest, p. 134.

(2) Local, ' of Ware,' a parish in dioc. of St. Albans.

Jordan de Ware, co. Norf., 1273. A.

Henry de Ware, London, ibid.

1585. Humphrey Weare, co. Devon : Reg. Univ. Oxf. vol. ii. pt. ii. p. 147.

1635. William Warr sailed to the Barbadoes in the Expedition : Hotten's Lists of Emigrants, p. 141.

London, 25, 11, 2 ; Philadelphia, 51, 9, 0 ; Boston (U.S.), 64, 3, 0.

Wareham, Warham, Waream.—Local, (1) 'of Wareham,' a town in co. Dorset ; (2) 'of Warham,' a parish in co. Norfolk.

Henry de Warham, co. Norf., 1273. A.

1583. Edward Warum (Waram), co. Dorset : Reg. Univ. Oxf. vol. ii. pt. ii. p. 130.

London, 4, 0, 0 ; Philadelphia, 4, 0, 2.

Wareing, Waring, Warin.—Bapt. 'the son of Warin.' O.F. Guarin. For excrescent *g* in Wareing, cf. Jenning for Jennin. This was one of the most popular of the Norman - introduced names, and though now obsolete, it has left many memorials. The diminutives Guarinot and Warinot remain in Garnett and Warnett, the full patronymic in Garrison and Warison, while simple Waring, Wareing, and Warren (v. Warren, 2) fill columns of the London Directory.

Fulco fil. Warin, co. Salop, 1273. A.

Symon fil. Warin, co. Hunts, ibid.

Warin de la Stane, co. York, ibid.

Guarinus de Chancy. E.

Ivo fil. Guarin. C.

1591-2. Edward Wareinge, co. Staff.: Reg. Univ. Oxf. vol. ii. pt. ii. p. 189.
1615. William Waring, of Chorley: Wills at Chester, i. 202.
1659. Bapt.—John, s. Robert Wareing, *free sadler*: St. Peter, Cornhill, i. 99.
1661. John Waryn and Catherine Twist: Marriage Lic. (London), ii. 41.
London, o, 9, 2 ; Crockford (Wareing), 2 ; Philadelphia, o, 5, o ; Boston (U.S.), o, 1, o.

Warham; v. Wareham.

Warin(g; v. Wareing.

Warinot, Warnett. — Bapt. 'the son of Waren' (O.F. Guarin), from dim. Warin-ot ; cf. Philipot, Mariot, Wilmot (Philip, Mary, William). The present form is Warnett. I had a modern instance, but have lost it.

Robert Warinot, co. Hunts, 1273. A.
William Warinot, co. Kent, 20 Edw.I. R.

Warison.—Bapt. 'the son of Warin' (v. Wareing). This surname is quite enough to prove the early popularity of the Norman font-name of Guarin. The abbreviation of Warinson to Warison presents no difficulty ; cf. Pattison for Pattinson.

Warinus fil. Warin. B.
John Warison. B.
Mabil Warison. G.

Wark.—Local, 'of Wark,' a parish in co. Northumberland.

1349. Richard de Werk : Freemen of York, i. 42.
London, 2 ; Philadelphia, 17.

Warman.—Bapt. 'the son of Warmund' (Yonge, ii. 412) ; -*mond* or -*mund* becomes -*man* by corruption ; cf. Osman, Wayman, &c.

Wormundus de Portu, Hen. III–Edw. I. K.
Wormund de Bremore, co. Devon, 1273. A.
Wormund de Porremore, co. Devon, ibid.
John Waremund, co. Berks, ibid.
1602. Bapt. — Bennet (Benedicta), d. William Warman : St.Peter,Cornhill,p.51.
London, 8 ; Boston (U.S.), 1.

Warmington. — Local, ' of Warmington' : (1) a parish near Oundle, co. Northampton ; (2) a parish in co. Warwick, near Banbury.

Robert de Wermington, co. Hunts, 1273. A.
William de Wermingtone, co. Hunts, ibid.
Henry de Wermyngton, co. Hunts, ibid.

1577. William Warmyngton, co. Dorset : Reg. Univ. Oxf. vol. ii. pt. ii. p. 75.
1779. Married — Thomas James and Mary Warmington : St. Geo. Han. Sq. i. 297.
London, 3.

Warn, Warne. — Local, ' at the warn,' from residence thereby. What this local term means I cannot say ; it belongs to the West country. Possibly 'Warren' (q.v.); cf. Warner for Warrener.

Jervase de Werne, co. Soms., 1273. A.
John de Werne, co. Soms., ibid.
Alex. atte Werne, co. Soms., ibid.
Roger Warne, co. Norf., ibid.
Gervase de Werne, 1 Edw. III : Kirby's Quest, p. 280.
1607. Edward Warne, co. Glouc. : Reg. Univ. Oxf. vol. ii. pt. ii. p. 296.
1661. Robert Browne and Mary Warne : Marriage Alleg. (Canterbury), p. 13.
1702. Bapt. —William, son of Stephen Warne : Reg. St. Columb Major, Cornwall.
1707. — John, son of Stephen Warne : ibid.
London, 4, 22 ; MDB. (co. Cornwall) 4, 14 ; Philadelphia, o, 10 ; Boston (U.S.), o, 1.

Warner.—Two distinct origins, accounting for its large numbers in the present day—one official, one baptismal. (1) Offic. ' the warrener.' '*Warrener*, a keeper of a warren': Bailey's Dict. '*Warnere*, *warinarius*': Prompt. Parv. Warren, preserved ground or water for rabbits, hares, fish, &c. O.F. *warrene* (v. Skeat, *warren*).

Robert le Warner, C. R., 1 Edw. I.
Richard le Warner, co. Camb., 1273. A.
Jacke le Warner, co. Norf., ibid.
Eustace le Warner. T.

Langland speaks familiarly of 'Watte the Warner' as frequenter of a tavern. '*Warren*, a place privileged for the keeping of conies, hares, partridges, and pheasants' (Bailey's Dict.).

> ' The warriner knows
> There are rabbits in breeding.'
>   Cobbe's Prophecies, 1614.

(2) Bapt. Warner. O.F. Garnier. Warnerus and Warnerius (Domesday).

' Warnerus avunculus Radulfi fil. Rogeri ': Pipe Roll, 5 Hen. II.
Warnerus de Lisoriis, ibid.
Warner Buckston, co. Hunts, 1273. A.
Wariner le Botiler, co. Hunts, ibid.
Henricus Warner, 1379 : P. T. Yorks. p. 21.

Modern instances are needless. The directories teem with them. I simply supply one or two quaint spellings.

1572. Bapt.—Richard Warinor : Reg. Stourton, co. Wilts, p. 1.
1621. — John, s. Ann Warrenner : Kensington Parish Church, p. 20.
London, 53 ; Philadelphia, 184 ; Boston (U.S.), 63.

Warnett; v. Warinot.

Warr(e.—Local ; v. Ware.

Warren, Warrin.—(1) Local, ' at the warren,' from residence by or in the privileged inclosure for rabbits, hares, partridges, &c. v. Warner.

Richard de Warenne, co. Norf., 1273. A.
John de Warenne, co. York, ibid.
William de Warren, co. York, ibid.

(2) Bapt. 'the son of Warin' (v. Wareing). O.F. Guarin. Very early Warren became the popularized form.

Warren le Latiner. H.
' Agnes, the widow of Warren de Menyngwarin (Mainwaring, i. e. the manor of Warin), and William Trussell, junior, and Matilda, his wife,' 1307 : Earwaker's East Cheshire, ii. 425.
Sir John Borlase Warren, of Stapleford, co. Notts, is great-great-great grandson of Sir Arnold Waring, knighted March 4, 1632-3, who was son of William Waring : ibid. p. 281.

One and the same individual is thus described :

Warinus de Engayne : Hen. III–Edw. I. K. p. 302.
Warrenus de Engayne, ibid. p. 309.
John Warren, alias Waryng, sup. for B.A., 1512 : Reg. Univ. Oxf. i. 80.
1583. Bapt.—Mary, d. Rafe Warren : Kensington Parish Ch., p. 9.
London, 117, o ; Philadelphia, 110, 3 ; Boston (U.S.), 100, 2.

Warrener, Warrender, Warriner.—Offic. ' the warrener.' His duties were similar to those of the parker, forester, or woodward, all custodians of the forest, chase, park, or warren. The *d* in Warrender is, of course, intrusive.

Robert le Warrener, co. Somerset, 1273. A.
Thomas le Wariner, London, ibid.
William le Warenner, co. Glouc., ibid.
' John Theerles, waryner ' (the Earl's warrener) : C. R., 15 Edw. III. pt. i.

For modern and other instances, v. Warner.

London, o, 1, o ; Philadelphia, o, o, 1 ; Boston (U.S.), 1, o, 2.

Warrick; v. Warwick.

Warring.—Bapt. 'the son of Warin' or Waring. O.F. Guarin (v. Wareing and Warren). The _g_ is excrescent, as in Jennings.

William Waryn or Warryng: Reg. Univ. Oxf. i. 90.
1653. Bapt. — Robert, s. Robert Warrin: St. Peter, Cornhill, i. 94.
London, 1; Philadelphia, 1; Boston (U.S.), 2.

Warrington.—Local, 'of Warrington,' co. Lancaster. It were idle to furnish more than two or three examples of this familiar place and name.

Roger de Warinton, co. Derby, 1273. A.
1587. Hugh Warrington, of Whalley: Wills at Chester (1545-1620), p. 203.
1619. Robert Warrington, of Lawton: ibid.
1743. Married—John Warrington and Eliz. Lightfoot: St. Antholin (London), p. 152.
London, 7; Manchester, 7; Philadelphia, 26; New York, 1.

Warwick, Warwicke, Warrick.—Local, 'of Warwick,' the chief town of the county of that name.

John de Warrewyc, co. York, 1273. A.
Matilda de Warewyck, co. Camb., ibid.
John de Warewyk, co. Oxf., ibid.
1601. Married—Richard Warwick and Hester Thruxton: St. Mary Aldermary, p. 10.
1619. — John Baker and Joane Warricke: St. Jas. Clerkenwell, p. 47.
London, 25, 1, 1; Philadelphia, 26, 0, 7; Boston (U.S.), 6, 0, 0.

Washbourne, Washburn, Washbourne.—Local, 'of Washbourn,' a parish in co. Gloucester; also a chapelry in the parish of Overbury, co. Worcester. According to Lower the latter place gave rise to a patronymic at an early period. As with all surnames ending in the local _-bourn_, the variants are many.

William de Wassebourn, co. Hunts, 1273. A.
Walter de Wasseburne, co. Devon, ibid.
1593. Anthony Washbourne, co. Worc.: Reg. Univ. Oxf. vol. ii. pt. ii. p. 198.
1598. Norman Washeborne and Margaret Midnall: Marriage Lic. (London), i. 254.
1599. Daniel Washbourne, or Washburne, of London: Reg. Univ. Oxf. vol. ii. pt. ii. p. 237.
1616. Bapt. — Sammuell, s. Robert Washborne: St. Antholin (London), p.51.

London, 3, 1, 0; Philadelphia, 0, 4, 2; Boston (U.S.), 0, 54, 4; New York (Washbourne), 1.

Washington. — Local, 'of Washington': (1) a parish in co. Durham, five miles from Gateshead; (2) a parish in co. Sussex, ten miles from Shoreham.

Laurence Wasshington, 1567: Reg. Univ. Oxf. i. 266.
1588. Christopher Washington, co. Northants: ibid. vol. ii. pt. ii. p. 167.
1594. Laurence Washington, co. Herts, _gent_: ibid. p. 203.
1605. Philip Washington, co. York: ibid. pt. iii. p. 288.
1780. Married — Thomas Read and Mary Washington: St. Geo. Han. Sq. p. 312.
London, 5; Philadelphia, 47; Boston (U.S.), 18.

Wass, Wasse. — Local, 'of Wass,' a township in the parish of Kilburn, near Helmsley, N. Rid. Yorks. This is an established Yorkshire name. Probably the two following entries do not concern this name:

Nicholas Waz, co. Wilts, 1273. A.
William Waz, co. Oxf., ibid.
1748. Married—Christopher Wass and Margaret Thickpenny: St. Geo. Chap. Mayfair, p. 326.
1765. — Samuel Lane and Rose Wass: St. Geo. Han. Sq. i. 145.
Manchester, 0, 1; London, 2, 0; MDB. (North Rid. Yorks), 1, 0; (West Rid. Yorks), 2, 0; Philadelphia, 2, 0; Boston (U.S.), 7, 0.

Wasselin.—Bapt. 'the son of Wace,' from dim. Wacelin; cf. Hewlin for Hewelin, little Hew, i.e. Hugh. Wasselin still struggles on for a place in the directory.

Richard Wacelyn, 1273. A.
Andrew Wascelyn, ibid.
Walter Wacelin, ibid.
Nicholas Wascelyn, co. Suff., 1 Edw. II. R.
Andrew Wascelin, co. Norf., ibid.
1662. Samuel Wasling and Eliz. Ayling: Marriage Alleg. (Canterbury), p. 35.
1742. Married — William Hyde and Eliz. Waslyn: St. Geo. Chap. Mayfair, p. 24.
London, 1.

Watcher.—Offic. 'the watcher,' a watchman. M.E. _wacche_, a watch, a keeping guard. With the third instance (Waker), cf. Wakeman.

Ellis le Wacher, co. Camb., 1273. A.
William le Wacher, co. Camb., ibid.

Roger Waker, co. Bedf., ibid.
Peter Waker, co. Dorset, ibid.

Waterbailiff. — Official. 'Water-bailiffs (in port towns) were certain officers formerly appointed for certain ships': Bailey's Dict.

Henry Waterbailiff de Cales: Close Roll, 13 Ric. II. pt. ii.

Waterbearer. — Occup. 'the water-bearer'; v. Waterman (2), Waterleader.

Richard Waterbearer. H.
1648. Buried — Richard Randall, _water-bearer_: St. Michael, Cornhill, p.242.

Waterfall. — Local, 'at the waterfall,' from residence thereby.

Richard de Watterfall, co. Devon, 1273. A.
Johanna Waterfall', 1379: P.T. Yorks. p. 58.
1692. Married—Robert Mathews and Rachell Waterfall: St. Jas. Clerkenwell, iii. 212.
1750. — William Waterfall and Margaret Eglestone: St. Geo. Chap. Mayfair, p. 162.
London, 1.

Waterfield.—Local, 'at the water-field,' from residence thereby. I cannot find a spot so named.

1600-1. John Waterfield: Reg. Univ. Oxf. vol. ii. pt. ii. p. 245.
1636. Buried—Joseph Waterfeild: St. Jas. Clerkenwell, iv. 225.
1798. Married — William Waterfield and Eliz. Weeke Patey: St. Geo. Han. Sq. ii. 185.
London, 2; Philadelphia, 2.

Waterhouse.—Local, 'at the water-house,' from residence thereby. Evidently many small localities were so called in various districts.

1585. Henry Waterhouse, co. Herts: Reg. Univ. Oxf. vol. ii. pt. ii. p. 146.
1591. Edward Waterhowse, co. Sussex: ibid. p. 182.
1567. Married—Thomas Waterhowse and Marie Kirbie: St. Mary Aldermary, p. 4.
1666. Stephen Waterhowse and Eliz. Cod: Marriage Alleg. (Canterbury), p. 194.
London, 10; Philadelphia, 26; Boston (U.S.), 36.

Waterleader. — Occup. 'the water-leader,' a water-carrier. Farmers still _lead_ hay (i.e. carry) in Furness, N. Lanc., and in the North generally. v. Waterbearer.

William Waterleader. D.
Rogerus Devonys Waterleder, 19 Edw. III : Freemen of York, i. 38 (Surt. Soc.).

Waterman.—(1) Occup. 'the servant of Water,' i.e. Walter ; cf. Matthewman, Addiman, &c. ; v. Waters and Waterson.

Geoffrey Walterman, co. Sussex, 1273. A.

The following occur in the roll of a small hamlet, but the nick. Wat is used instead of the fuller Water :

Walterus Nelesthorp, 1379 : P. T. Yorks. p. 210.
Robertus Watman, 1379 : ibid.
Ricardus Watman, 1379 : ibid.
Johannes Watson, 1379 : ibid.
Thomas Watman, 1379 : ibid. p. 145.

(2) Occup. 'the waterman,' i.e. the water-carrier, water-bearer, water-leader.

William le Waterman, co. Oxf., 1273. A.
Adam le Waterman, co. Oxf., ibid.
Robert le Waterman, co. Oxf., ibid.
Julian Waterman, Pat. R., 3 Edw. VI. pt. iii.
1613. Peter Weterman : Reg. Univ. Oxf. vol. ii. pt. ii. p. 330.
1655. Buried — Ann, wife of Hugh Waterman : St. Jas. Clerkenwell, iv. 304.
1729. Married — Joseph Bull to Anne Waterman : St. Mary (London), p. 48.
London, 6 ; West Rid. Court Dir., 2 ; Sheffield, 2 ; Philadelphia, 26 ; New York, 38.

Watermill.—Local, 'at the water-mill,' from residence thereby.

Reginald de Watermill, co. Northampt., 20 Edw. I. R.
1692. Married — John Monke and Sarah Watermill : St. Jas. Clerkenwell, iii. 212.

Waters, Waterson. — Bapt. the son of Walter.' M.E. Water, O.F. Wauter and Watier.

'My name is Walter Whitmore. How now! why start'st thou? what! doth death affright?
Suffolk. Thy name affrights me, in whose sound is death.
A cunning man did calculate my birth, And told me that by *Water* I should die.'
2 Henry VI, Act iv. sc. 1, ll. 31-5.
'The account of Wattare Taylor and Wyllyam Partrynge, benge churchewardens': Churchwardens' Accounts, Ludlow, 1541, Cam. Soc., p. 6.
Wauter de Cornwaille, 1313. M.
Alicia Wartson, 1379 : P. T. Yorks. p. 160.
Johannes Wauterson, 1379 : ibid. p. 226.
William Watterson, 1495, co. York.
W. 11.

John Waterson, co. York. W. 16.
1579. Judith, d. of Water Arksone, *stranger* : St. Dionis Backchurch (London), p. 84.
1563. Bapt. — William, son of Water Lancaster : St. Antholin (London), p. 15.
— Buried — Water Right, servant to Ric. Clarke : ibid.
1588. Margaret Watterson, of Cartmell : Lancashire Wills at Richmond, i. 303.
1607. Married — Edward Waterson and Jane Harrison : St. Michael, Cornhill, p. 18.
London, 39, 0 ; Philadelphia, 93, 3 ; Boston (U.S.), 75, 2.

Watford.—Local, 'of Watford' : (1) a parish in co. Hertford ; (2) a parish in co. Northampton, near Daventry.

Eustace de Watforde, co. Northampt., 1273. A.
Walter de Wateford, London, ibid.
1621. Robert Watford and Ellen Ruddeford : Marriage Lic. (London), ii. 100.
1748. Married — Thomas Hains and Martha Watford : St. Geo. Chap. Mayfair, p. 104.
London, 3 ; Philadelphia, 1.

Watkin, Watkins, Watkinson, Watkiss.—Bapt. 'the son of Walter,' nick. Wat, dim. Watkin. Watkiss is a corruption of Watkins, as Perkiss is of Perkins ; cf. the curious Popkiss for Hopkins. Watkin, which is still familiar in Wales, was a general favourite throughout England in the hereditary surname period.

Watkin, son of Henry Balistarius : Wardrobe Account, 36 Hen. III. 1/5.
Thomas ap-Watkin. B.
Watkynge Llooyde : Visit. Gloucester, 1623, p. 104.
1547. Bapt. — Jane Watkinnes : St. Peter, Cornhill, i. 4.
1580. Edward Watkinson, co. York : Reg. Univ. Oxf. vol. ii. pt. ii. p. 92.
1594. Edward Watkine, co. York : ibid. p. 204.
1662. Thomas Watkys : Preston Guild Rolls, p. 155.
1700. Married — Henry Watkinson and Mary Clarke : St. Peter, Cornhill, ii. 63.
London, 0, 91, 5, 3 ; Philadelphia, 10, 46, 3, 0 ; Boston (U.S.), 1, 30, 0, 0.

Watling.—(1) Bapt. 'the son of Watelin,' from Walter, nick. Wat, dim. Watelin, and with excrescent *g* Watling ; cf. Hewling for Hew-elin. (2) Local, 'of Wateling,' some locality. probably in co. Suffolk.

Geoffrey Wateling, co. Norf., 1273. A.
John de Wateling, co. Suff., ibid.
1639-40. Abraham Watling and Katherine Clances : Marriage Lic. (London), ii. 249.
1689. Bapt. — Robert Wattlin : St. Mary Aldermary (London), p. 109.
London, 13 ; New York, 1.

Watmough, Watmuff, Whatmore, Whatmough. — Nick. 'Wat's brother-in-law,' i.e. the brother-in-law of Walter, familiarly Wat. A very interesting North-English surname, and one of a small but distinct class (v. Muff and Hitchmough) compounded of the Christian name and *maghe* or *mauf*, probably in general a brother-in-law, though other relationships are included. ' Maug, a brother-in-law. North E.' (Halliwell). ' Mauf, Maugh, or Meaugh, a brother-in-law ' (Brockett). 'Mow, husbondys syster, or wyfys systyr, or syster-in-lawe' (Prompt. Parv.). ' Mauf denotes a brother-in-law. N. of E.' (Grose). 'A.S. *mæg* or *mag*, the guttural sound being changed into that of *f*, as in laugh ' (Jamieson). Only a few of these compounds have come down to us in the form of surnames, Watmough and its variants being the prominent instance. The Yorkshire Poll Tax, however, has several others, which although now obsolete are uncontrovertible evidence of the former familiarity of such titles.

William Barnmawe, the child's brother-in-law, co. York, 1273. A.

With the above we must cf. the Yorkshire Barnfather (the child's father).

Cf. also Robert Susannemagh, Fines Roll, 10 Edw. I.
Johannes Elysmagh (Ellis's brother-in-law) : P. T. Yorks. p. 272.
Willelmus Hudmagh (Richard's brother-in-law) : ibid. p. 251.
Ricardus Gepmouth (Geoffrey's brother-in-law) : ibid. p. 114.
Johannes Tailliourmoghe (the tailor's brother-in-law), ibid. p. 283.

Coming to Watmough we find :
Robertus Watmaghe (Walter's brother-in-law) : ibid. p. 287.

Later we find it as Watmouth (now Watmuff) :

Myles Watmough, vicar of Medomsley, 1582 : DDD. ii. 287.

Hugo Watmouth, rector of Thornton-in-Craven,1599 : Whitaker's Craven,p.120.

The modern variant Whatmough is imitative. With this class of surname cf.

William Gamelstepsone (the stepson of Gamel), 25 Edw. I : BBB. p. 544.

Henricus Parson-cosyn, 1379 : P. T. Yorks. p. 91.

Thomas Viker-cosyn, 1379 : P. T. Yorks. p. 226.

1581. Hugh Watmoughe, co. York : Reg. Univ. Oxf. vol. ii. pt. ii. p. 114.

I am glad to find that this most interesting North-country name has reached America.

West Rid. Court Dir., 2, 2, 1, 0 ; Huddersfield, 4, 0, 0, 0 ; Manchester, 2, 0, 0, 3; Philadelphia, 6, 0, 1, 0.

Watt, Watts, Watson, Wattson.— Bapt. 'the son of Walter,' from nick. Wat. Walter being one of the great fontal names of the 13th and 14th centuries, and Wat being the popular nick., it can scarcely be a matter for surprise that Watts and Watson are two of our most familiar surnames. They are confined to no particular district. There is no need to quote from modern registers. Everybody has a friend or acquaintance bearing one or other of the above forms.

William Wattes, co. Oxf., 1273. A.

John Wattessone, C. R., 12 Edw. III. pt. iii.

Johannes Watson, 1379 : P. T. Yorks. p. 144.

Alicia Wat-wyf, 1379 : ibid. p. 92.

Johannes Wattson', 1379 : ibid. p. 279.

Johannes Watte, 1379 : ibid. p. 159.

1598. Married—Thomas Chamberlaine and Jane Wattes : St. Mary Aldermary, p. 9.

London, 13, 107, 212, 1 ; Philadelphia, 57, 61, 339, 7 ; Boston (U.S.), 15, 59, 207, 0.

Watters.—Bapt. A variant of Waters, q.v. Similarly Watterson was a variant of Waterson.

1791. Married — Joseph Watters and Deborah Perry : St. Geo. Han. Sq. ii. 60.

London, 3 ; Philadelphia, 6 ; Boston (U.S.), 5.

Waud.—Local, 'of the wood.'

Thomas de la Waude, co. Bucks, 1273. A.

1793. Married — John Sievier and Francis Waud : St. Geo. Han. Sq. ii. 102.

London, 8.

Waugh.—?———. This name is occasionally found in co. Cumb., especially in the neighbourhood of

Wigton. Probably it is of Scotch descent, having crossed the Border. Mr. Lower says (Patr. Brit. p. 374), 'The Waughs of Help, co. Roxburgh,held these lands from the 13th to the 17th century.' In this case the name does not come within the scope of this dictionary.

Willelmus Wahh, 1379 : P. T. Yorks. p. 26.

1696-7. Adam Runciman and Jane Waugh : Marriage Lic. (London), ii. 320.

1699. Dr. John Waugh and Eliz. Fiddes: ibid. p. 325.

London, 11 ; Philadelphia, 13 ; Boston (U.S.), 18.

Way, Waye.—Local, 'at the way' (M.E. wey), from residence by the wayside ; cf. Lane, and v. Ridgway.

John ate Wey, co. Camb., 1273. A.

Robert de le Weye, co. Devon, ibid.

Thomas de la Weye, co. Kent, ibid.

1584. John Weaye, co. Somerset : Reg. Univ. Oxf. vol. ii. pt. ii. p. 134.

1605. Henry Waie, or Waye, co. Dorset : ibid. p. 280.

1637. Married — William Way and Eliz. Harris : St. Jas. Clerkenwell, iii. 68.

London, 16, 1 ; Philadelphia, 32, 0 ; Boston (U.S.), 13, 0.

Waygood.—Bapt. 'the son of Wigod' ; v. Wiggett, and cf. Wayman for Wyman, and Waymark for Wymark.

1623. Buried—Thomas Waygood, free of the Cookes (buried by night): St. Peter, Cornhill, i. 181.

London, 1.

Wayland, Waylen, Weyland.—Local, 'of Wayland,' a hundred in the county of Norfolk. There is no evidence in favour of a personal origin, although Wayland was familiar to legendary history. But v. Welland.

(Ballivus Hundred) de Wayland, co. Norf., 1273. A. i. 439.

Thomas de Weyland, or Waylaunde, co. Suff., 1273. A.

Richard de Weylaund, co. Suff., ibid.

Nicholas Weylond, co. Norf., ibid.

Rither de Wayland, co. York, 20 Edw. I. R.

Hubert de Weylaund, co. Suff., ibid.

1622. William Flookes and Eliz. Wayland : Marriage Lic. (London), ii. 112.

1669. Married — Mark Weyland and Mary Underwood : St. Jas. Clerkenwell, iii. 158.

1741. Bapt. — John, s. Frederic and Susanna Weiland: ibid. ii. 257.

1770. Married — Swithin Waylen and Maria Jeanetta Alt : St. Geo. Han. Sq. i. 203.

London, 3, 2, 0 ; MDB. (co. Suff.), 2, 0, 0 ; (co. Norfolk) 1, 0, 0 ; Philadelphia, 2, 1, 3 ; Boston (U.S.), 5, 0, 0.

Wayman.—(1) Bapt. ; v. Wyman. (2) Occup. ; v. Waithman.

Waymark ; v. Wymark.

Wayt, Wayte.—Official, 'the wait,' i.e. the watchman. O.F. waite, a sentinel, a guard. 'Wayte, a spye. Wayte, waker' : Prompt. Parv. Still survives in the Christmas waits. For further instances than recorded below, v. Wait.

Adam le Wayte, co. Camb., 1273. A.

Robert le Wayte, co. Hunts, ibid.

Ralph le Wayte. B.

Stephen le Wayte. T.

Johannes Wayt, 1379 : P. T. Yorks. p. 242.

Willelmus Wayt, 1379 : ibid.

1643. Buried—John Wayt, Esq., in the Chauncel : St. Jas. Clerkenwell, iv. 257.

London, 1, 2 ; Philadelphia, 0, 0.

Weakley, Weekley, Weakly.—Local, 'of Weekley,' a village near Kettering, co. Northampton.

1647. Timothy Reyner and Anne Weekely (co. Bedf.): Marriage Lic. (London), ii. 279.

1676. Thomas Weekely and Anne Bishop : Marriage Alleg. (Cant.), p. 252.

1792. Married—Thomas Weakly and Jane Brown : St. Geo. Han. Sq. ii. 73.

London, 1, 0, 0 ; Philadelphia, 7, 2, 4 ; New York, 2, 0, 0.

Weakling, Weaklin.—Bapt.; v. Wakeling and Wanklyn.

London, 0, 1.

Weakspear.—Nick. for a poor spearman ; cf. Shakespear, Wagspear, Breakspear, &c.

William Hudde, alias Weykspere : Pat. R., 14 Hen. VII.

Weald ; v. Weld.

Weale, Weall.—Local, 'of the wele' or weld ; v. Weald.

Simon del Wele, 17 Edw. II : Freemen of York, i. 22.

1609. John Boomer and Mary Weale : Marriage Lic. (London), i. 316.

1749. Married — Lancelot Weale and Tabitha Lucas: St. Geo. Chap. Mayfair, p. 136.

London, 2, 1 ; Philadelphia, 2, 0 ; Boston (U.S.), 2, 0.

Wear, Weare, Weir.—Local, 'at the wear.' A.S. wer, a dam, a fence, a wear or weir; v. Ware.

John de la Were, co. Oxf., 1273. A.

Robert de la Were, co. Glouc., ibid.

1665. Married — Thomas Weare and Isabella Wilkinson: St. Jas. Clerkenwell, p. 120.
1805. — Charles Weir and Mary Harding: St. Geo. Han. Sq. ii. 333.
London, 2, 2, 13; Philadelphia, 8, 2, 60; Boston (U.S.), 2, 4, 27.

Wearing.—Bapt.; v. Wareing.
Ulverston, 1; New York, 1.

Weatherby, Wetherby, Weatherbee, Wetherbee. — Local, 'of Wetherby,' a market-town in the parish of Spofforth, W. Rid. Yorks. This surname has thriven better in the United States than in England. Wetherbee is an Americanism, but not entirely unknown in this country; cf. Applebee.

Robertus de Wethirby, 1379: P. T. Yorks. p. 249.
London, 1, 0, 0, 0; Philadelphia, 5, 4, 0, 2; Boston (U.S.), 0, 0, 6, 48.

Weatherhead, Wetherherd, Weathered, Wethered. — Occup. 'the wether-herd'; v. Herd, and cf. Coward, Stoddart, Oxnard, Calvert, &c. The wether-herd was a tender of rams. The change of the suffix -herd into -head was a natural one, and is now all but universal.

John le Wetherhurde, co. Soms., 1 Edw. III: Kirby's Quest, p. 218.
John Wetherhird. O.
Johannes Wetherhyrd, faber, 1379: P. T. Yorks. p. 290.
Thomas Jonson Wetherhird (i.e. Thomas, the son of John Wetherherd), 1379: ibid.
Agnes Wederhead, of Hornby, 1580: Lancashire Wills at Richmond, i. 304.
1583–4. William Smithe, yeoman, and Joan Wetherhedd: Marriage Lic. (London), i. 128.
1618. Edward Wethered, co. Oxf.: Reg. Univ. Oxf. vol. ii. pt. ii. p. 372.
1633. Bapt. — Mary, d. Nicholas Wetherhead: St. Michael, Cornhill, p. 123.
London, 3, 0, 0, 0; Philadelphia, 0, 1, 0, 0; New York, 0, 0, 1, 1.

Weatherhog, Weatherhogg. —Nick. 'the wether-hog.' 'A male, or heder-hog. Also a surname in the county. Linc.' (Halliwell); cf. Hoglamb, an early Lincolnshire surname.

MDB. (co. Lincoln), 1, 6; London, 0, 1.

Weaver.—Occup. 'the weaver.' Webster, with the fem. suffix

-ster as in spinster, was so much more popular that Weaver has not pushed its way into the directories so successfully as might have been expected. But in America it has prospered wonderfully. The simple Webb (q.v.) also took from the success of this name.

1522. George Wever: Reg. Univ. Oxf. i. 129.
1585. Thomas Weaver, of Wetten-hall, gent.: Wills at Chester, i. 204.
1610. Married — Henrie Planncon, Dutchman, and Margrett Weaver: St. Peter, Cornhill, i. 247.
1646. Cecilia Weever, of Warrington, widow: Wills at Chester, ii. 230.
Nicholas Weever, of Goosnargh, 1670: Lancashire Wills at Richmond, ii. 305.
London, 21; Philadelphia, 112; Boston (U.S.), 22.

Webb, Webbe.—Occup. 'the webbe,' i.e. a weaver. M.E. webbe; A.S. webba.

'My wife was a webbe,
And woolen cloth made.'
Piers Plowman.
'An haberdasher, and a carpenter,
A webbe, a deyer, and a tapiser.'
Chaucer, C. T. 363-4.

This surname does not require any modern instances. The directories teem with representatives. v. Weaver and Webster.

Adam le Webbe, co. Essex, 1273. A.
Elyas le Webbe, co. Bucks, ibid.
Roger le Webbe. B.
Simon le Webbe. N.
Robert le Webbe, co. Soms., 1327: Tax Roll.
Johannes Wybbe, 1379: P. T. Yorks. p. 67.
1603. Nicholas Webbe, of Chester: Wills at Chester, i. 204.
1623. William Webb, of Chester: ibid. ii. 230.
London, 210, 3; Oxford, 33, 0; Philadelphia, 125, 0; Boston (U.S.), 61, 0.

Webber.—Occup. 'the webster,' a webb, a webster, a weaver.
'Coryers, cordwayners, and cobelers, Gyrdelers, forborers, and webbers.'
Cocke Lorelle's Bote.

The popular form webster ousted webber to a certain extent at an early date.

Robert le Webber. B.
Clarice le Webbere. B.
1524. John Webber and Eliz. Letyll: Marriage Lic. (London), i. 4.
1577. Matthew Webber, co. Cornwall: Reg. Univ. Oxf. vol. ii. pt. ii. p. 75.
1603. Buried — Freze Webber, a poor woman: St. Jas. Clerkenwell, iv. 69.

1658. Buried — Thomas Webber: St. Michael, Cornhill, p. 250.
London, 45; Philadelphia, 10; Boston (U.S.), 91.

Webster.—Occup. 'the webster,' a cloth weaver, lit. feminine of Webb or Webber, a weaver.

John le Webestere, co. Norf., 1273. A.
Alicia Wryght, huswyfe, webster, 1379: P. T. Yorks. p. 66.
Robertus Webester, webster, 1379: ibid. p. 99.
Willelmus Webester, webster, 1379: ibid.
John le Webstere. G.
1575. Buried — Eliz. Webster: Kensington Parish, p. 88.
London, 68; MDB. (West Rid. Yorks), 26; Philadelphia, 86; Boston (U.S.), 124.

Weddell, Weddle, Wedell. —Local, 'of Wedhill.' I cannot find the spot. Weddle is the usual variant in these cases; cf. Windle for Windhill, or Pickles for Pick-hills.

Walter de Wedhulle, co. Wilts, 1273. A.
1680. John Weddell and Jane Jones: Marriage Lic. (London), ii. 302.
1745. Married — George Weddel and Mary Gibson: St. Geo. Chap. Mayfair, p. 48.
1778. Married—William Weddle and Betty Windmill: St. Geo. Han. Sq. i. 286.
London, 1, 1, 0; Philadelphia, 2, 0, 3; New York, 0, 3, 0.

Weddicombe; v. Widdicombe.

Wedge; v. Wegg.

Wedgwood, Wedgewood.— Local, 'of Wedgewood,' a township in the parish of Wolstanton, three miles from Burslem, co. Staff. The surname is still familiar to the county, and has become historic.

1592. William Wedgwood, co. Warw.: Reg. Univ. Oxf. vol. ii. pt. ii. p. 191.
1621. John Wegewood, co. Staff.: ibid. p. 395.
1658. Buried — Leonard Wedgwood: St. Jas. Clerkenwell, iv. 323.
1753. Married — Robert Goodall and Mary Wedgewood: St. Geo. Chap. Mayfair, p. 263.
1795. — Richard Wedgewood and Jane Evans: St. Geo. Han. Sq. ii. 127.
London, 2, 0; MDB. (co. Stafford), 4, 0; Boston (U.S.), 0, 5.

Wedlake, Wedlock.—? Local. Lower, quoting Ferguson, says, 'from an old German personal name Widolaic'(Patr. Brit. p. 375). I find no trace of this name on

English soil. Wedlock is evidently imitative.

1593. John Widlocke, vicar of Acton, co. Glouc. : Atkyns' Hist. Glouc., p. 105.
1690. Married—Richard Bedford and Alice Wedlock : St. Jas. Clerkenwell, iii. 207.
1740. Buried — Joseph Wedlock, a German : St. Dionis Backchurch, p. 308.
1744. Married — Richard Warburton and Eliz. Wedlock : St. Geo. Chap. Mayfair, p. 34.
London, 4, 0 ; MDB. (co. Devon), 0, 1 ; Philadelphia, 0, 1 ; New York, 0, 2.

Wedmore.—Local, ' of Wedmore,' a parish six miles from Axbridge, co. Somerset.

Egidius de Wedmor, co. Soms., 1 Edw. II : Kirby's Quest, p. 173.
MDB. (co. Somerset), 5.

Weeden, Weedon. — Local, ' of Weedon ' : (1) a hamlet in the parish of Hardwicke, co. Bucks ; (2) a parish near Daventry, co. Northampton.

John de Wedon', co. Bucks, 1273. A.
Ralph de Wedone, co. Bedf., ibid.
Nicholas de Wedon, co. Notts, Hen. III-Edw. I. K.
Henry de Wedon, co. Bucks, 20 Edw. I. R.
1582. Robert Weedon, or Weeden, co. Bucks : Reg. Univ. Oxf. vol. ii. pt. ii. p. 121.
— William Weedon, co. Bucks : ibid. p. 122.

The three following entries evidently relate to the same individual :

1606. Buried — Mary, wife of Robert Weedon : St. Jas. Clerkenwell, iv. 94.
1608. — Sisley, wife of Robert Weedone : ibid. p. 102.
1611-2. — Fayth, d. of Robert Weeden : ibid. p. 118.
London, 12, 17 ; Philadelphia, 2, 2 ; Boston (U.S.), 3, 0.

Weekley, Weekly ; v. Weakley.

Weeks, Weekes.—Local, ' at the wyke,' a corruption of Wykes, q.v.

1571. Married — John Weekes and Isabell Parkin : St. Thomas the Apostle, London, p. 5.
1581-2. Anthony Weekes, or Wikes, co. Wilts : Reg. Univ. Oxf. vol. ii. pt. ii. p. 115.
1618. Thomas Weekes, co. Sussex : ibid. p. 373.
1603. Bapt.—Jane, d. Thomas Weekes : St. Jas. Clerkenwell, i. 41.
1747. Married — Richard Weeks and Ann Additer : St. Geo. Chap. Mayfair, p. 99.

London, 22, 11 ; Philadelphia, 51, 0 ; Boston (U.S.), 88, 1.

Weeper.—Nick. ' the weeper,' an emotional fellow. I am afraid the surname has not survived.

John le Wepere, co. Oxf., 1273. A.
Henry le Wepere, co. Oxf., ibid.
Robert le Weper, C. R., 25 Edw. I.

Wegg, Wegge, Wege, Wedge.—Bapt. ' the son of Wig ' ; v. full statement under Wigg. There can be little doubt that Wedge is a softened form of Wegg.

John Wegge, co. Soms., 1 Edw. III : Kirby's Quest, p. 92.
Willelmus Wege, 1379 : P. T. Yorks. p. 75.
1625. George Peirse and Joyce Wedge : Marriage Lic. (London), ii. 152.
1646. Buried — Grace, d. Robert Wedge : St. Jas. Clerkenwell, iv. 267.
1719. Bapt.—John, s. George Wegge : St. Peter, Cornhill, ii. 31.
1785. Married — Edmund Rush Wegg and Ann Manwaring : St. Geo. Han. Sq. i. 371.
London, 2, 0, 0, 2 ; MDB. (co. Soms.), Wedge, 1 ; New York, 0, 1, 1, 0 ; Boston (U.S.), 0, 0, 0, 3.

Weggett ; v. Wackett.

Weigall, Weigel, Weigell.—Local, ' of Wighall.' I cannot find the spot, but the derivation is clear, ' the hall of Wiga,' a Domesday personal name. v. Wigg.

Katerina de Wyghehale, 1379 : P. T. Yorks. p. 269.
London, 1, 1, 0 ; New York, 0, 8, 2.

Weight.—Official, ' the wait,' i.e. the watchman (v. Wayt and Wait). This, of course, is an imitative form. Weight conveyed a meaning when the original sense of Wait was forgotten.

1610. Buried — Richard Weight, free of the Poulterer : St. Peter, Cornhill, i. 165.
1805. Married — Samuel Weight and Joyce Smith : St. Geo. Han. Sq. ii. 326.
London, 3 ; Philadelphia, 1 ; New York, 2.

Weightman. — Nick. ' the wightman,' i.e. the brave strong man. Although *weightman*, ' a weigher,' seems the natural derivation, we are on much safer ground in referring it to Wightman (q.v.), as being a variant of that name.

1613. Bapt. — Eliz., d. Peter Weightman : St. Peter, Cornhill, i. 62.

1796. Married—John Weightman and Matilda Hardum : St. Geo. Han. Sq. ii. 146.
London, 6 ; West Rid. Court Dir., 1 ; Philadelphia, 20 ; Boston (U.S.), 1.

Weir ; v. Wear.

Welbourn, Welbourne, Wellborne, Welburn, Wellburn.—(1) Local, ' of Welborne ' : a parish in co. Norf. ; (2) ' of Welbourn,' a parish in co. Lincoln ; (3) ' of Welburn,' a township in the parish of Bulmer, N. Rid. Yorks.

Hugh de Welleburn, co. Linc., 1273. A.
1680. John Glyn and Robert Welbourne : Marriage Lic. (Faculty Office), p. 151.
1706. Married — Rowland Welborne and Eliz. Douthwaite : St. Dionis Backchurch (London), p. 53.
1749. — Francoise Polus le Caan and Mary Wellborn : St. Geo. Han. Sq. i. 42.
London, 1, 0, 3, 0, 0 ; MDB. (co. Linc.), 8, 1, 0, 0, 0 ; (North Rid. Yorks), 1, 0, 0, 2, 6.

Welby.—Local, ' of Welby ' : (1) a parish five miles from Grantham, co. Lincoln ; (2) a chapelry in the parish of Melton Mowbray, co. Leicester.

Richard de Wellebie, co. Linc., 1273. A.
Richard de Welbe, co. Middlesex, temp. Edw. I. R.
1544-5. John Welby and Eliz. Mannyng : Marriage Lic. (Faculty Office), p. 3.
1574-5. Thomas Welbie, co. Linc., gent. : Reg. Univ. Oxf. vol. ii. pt. ii. p. 59.
1637. Married—Toby Welbe and Margret Evans : Kensington Parish, p. 71.
1791. — John Wellby and Mary Ashly : St. Geo. Han. Sq. ii. 61.
MDB. (co. Linc.), 4 ; London, 1 ; Boston (U.S.), 1.

Welch.—Local ; v. Wallace.

Welchman.—Nick.'the Welshman ' ; v. Wallace.

Willelmus Walesman, 1379 : P.T. Yorks. p. 272.
1564. John Welsheman and Ann Pallydaye : Marriage Lic. (London), i. 29.
1621. Thomas Welchman, of Samlesbury : Wills at Chester, ii. 231.
1627. William Welshman, of Mollington : ibid.
1638. Thomas Walchman, of Blackburn, *woollen-webster* : ibid. p. 225.
Edward Welchman, Archdeacon of Cardigan, 1727 : Hist. and Ant. St. David's, p. 360.
London, 6.

Welcome, Wellicome, Willicombe.—(1) Nick. ' the welcome.' M.E. *wilkome*. (2) Local, ' of

Wellcombe,' a parish in co. Devon, five miles from Hartland.

Picotus Wilicom, co. Camb., 1273. A.
Robert de Welcombe, co. Somerset, 1 Edw. III : Kirby's Quest, p. 235.
1584. Thomas Welcom, or Welcombe, co. Linc. : Reg. Univ. Oxf. vol. ii. pt. ii. p. 137.
1609. Married—John Willicome and Jone Lemman : St. Michael, Cornhill, p. 19.
1631. Thomas Welcome, of Dalton (Furness): Lancashire Wills at Richmond, i. 305.
London, o, 1, 2 ; Philadelphia, 1, o, o ; Boston (U.S.), 3, o, o.

Weld, Weald, Welde, Wold.—
Local, 'at the weld,' from residence thereby. A woody or stubbly waste, a wold ; cf. Fenn ; v. also Weale.

Walter de la Wolde, Fines Roll, 11 Edw. I.
John atte Welde, Rot. Pat.,4 Edw. III. pt. ii.
Willelmus del Weld, 1379 : P. T. Yorks. p. 33.
1614. James Welde : Reg. Univ. Oxf. vol. ii. pt. ii. p. 334.
1632. Sir John Cutts and Anne Weld : Marriage Lic. (Faculty Office), p. 21.
1656. Married—WilliamKery,*kalinder*, and Roes Weld : St. Mary Aldermary, p. 26.
London, o, 1, o, o ; Crockford, 1, o, o, o ; Philadelphia, 5, o, 5, o ; Boston (U.S.), 48, o, o, 1.

Weldon.—Local, ' of Weldon,' two parishes in dioc. of Peterborough, co. Northants.

Geoffrey de Weldone, co. Hunts, 1273. A.
Lucas de Weldon, co. Linc., ibid.
Hugh de Weledon, co. Linc., ibid.
1545-6. George Duke and Philippa Weldon : Marriage Lic. (Faculty Office), p. 6.
1596. William Weldon, co. Northants: Reg. Univ. Oxf. vol. ii. pt. ii. p. 216.
1600. Francis Weldon, co. Berks : ibid. p. 241.
London, 5 ; MDB. (Northants), 2.

Welfare, Welfear. — ? Nick. ' well fare,' an expression of good will (?). I see no reason to doubt this origin. Nevertheless, Lower writes, ' Probably from Wifare, or rather Wulpher, a personal name, occurring in Domesday' : Patr. Brit. p. 376. This, of course, was the old personal name Ulfr, coming in such local names as Ulverston, Wolverhampton, &c. My instance is so early in its unaltered form

that I prefer my own view ; cf. Welcome.

Simon Welfare, co. Norf., 1273. A.
1654. Buried—Alse Welfare: Kensington Church, p. 124.
London, 1, 1 ; MDB. (co. Sussex), 2, o.

Welford. — Local, ' of Welford,' parishes in cos. Berks, Northants, and Warwick.

Richard de Welleford, London, temp. Edw. II. R.
1606. Andrew Welford, Magd. Coll. : Reg. Univ. Oxf. vol. ii. pt. iii. 265.
1650. Married—Clement Welford and Mary Haines : St. Jas. Clerkenwell, iii. 85.
London, 6 ; Oxford, 3.

Welham.—Local, ' of Welham,' a parish in co. Leic., four miles from Harborough ; also a township in the parish of Norton, E. Rid. York. The variant Wellum looks like an Americanism (cf. Barnum for Barnham). But it is not found now either in England or the States.

Walter de Welham, co. Soms., 1 Edw. III : Kirby's Quest, p. 224.
1612. Thomas Quilche and Mary Wellam (co. Essex): Marriage Lic. (London), ii. 12.
1665. — John Wellum and Ann Warrener : St. Jas. Clerkenwell, iii. 118.
1696. Married—Mark Sayer and Anne Welham : St. Mary Aldermary (London), p. 35.
1790. — Samuel Wellum and Eliz. Butler : St. Geo. Han. Sq. ii. 47.
London, 4.

Welk, Welkshorn. — Nick. ' the whelk.' The *h* is intrusive ; cf. Winkle.

Matilda le Welke, co. Camb., 1273. A.
William Welkeshorn, co. Suff., ibid.
Philadelphia, 2, o ; New York, 1, o.

Well, Wells.—Local, ' at the well.' Of course Wells, saving in particular cases, has nothing to do with the city of Wells in the West country. The final s is added in common with other monosyllabic local surnames ; cf. Styles, Brooks, Bridges, &c. There is also a parish Wells-by-the-Sea, in dioc. Norwich.

Gilbert de Welles, co. Norf., 1273. A.
William de Welles, co. Linc., ibid.
Hervy del Welle, vicar of Mendham, co. Norf., 1320 : FF. v. 385.
Johannes del Well, 1379 : P. T. Yorks. p. 139.
1583. Anthony Welles, co. Sussex : Reg. Univ. Oxf. vol. ii. pt. ii. p. 130.

1617-8. John Wells and Joane Vicaries : Marriage Lic. (London), ii. 57.
London, o, 141 ; Philadelphia, 1, 144 ; Boston (U.S.), o, 137; New York (Well), 3.

Welland.—(1) Bapt. ' the son of Welland.' In Domesday Welland (co. Devon). (2) Local, ' of Welland,' a parish in co. Worc.

William de Welond, co. Glouc., 1273. A.
Thomas Welond, co. Oxf., ibid.
Richard Welond, co. Suff., ibid.
1787. Married—Thomas Welland and Alice Peach : St. Geo. Han. Sq. i. 405.
London, 3.

Wellard ; v. Willard.

Wellbeloved. — Nick. ' the well-beloved.' A common mode of address by prince or ecclesiastic in formal declarations. The Rev. C. Wellbeloved published a translation of the Bible in 1838, printed by Smallfield & Co., London.

Thomas Welebeloved, C. R., 2 Edw. IV.
William Welbilove. O.
1527-8. John Welbelovyd, of Feltham, and Johanna Farr of Ashford : Marriage Lic. (London), i. 6.
1596. Hugh Welbeloved, *yeoman*, and Anne Hyne, of Feltham, co. Middlesex : ibid. p. 232.
1634. Richard Wellbeloved and Helen Galfield : ibid. ii. 217.
1729. Married—Charles Welbeloved, of Thorpe, co. Surrey, and Margaret Chapman: St. Antholin (London), p. 143.
1766. — Joseph Copeland and Jane Wellbeloved: St. Geo. Han. Sq. i. 157.
London, 2 ; Leeds, 2 ; West Rid. Court Dir., 2.

Wellborne, -burn ; v. Welbourn.

Weller.—Occup. ' the weller,' one who resided by a well, and probably plied the occupation of a Wellman, Waterman, or Waterleader, q.v. (cf. Crossweller, Fielder, Crofter, Bridger, &c. Probably the last took toll for crossing the bridge).

1683. Bapt. — Cornelius, s. Thomas Weller : St. Jas. Clerkenwell, i. 303.
1756. Married—Christian Weller and Ann Poll : St. Geo. Han. Sq. i. 90.
London, 10 ; Oxford, 11 ; New York, 12 ; Boston (U.S.), 5.

Wellesley.—Local, ' of Welesley.' Mr. Lower says, ' a locality in Somersetshire.' A standard-bearer of this name served under Hen. II. The name soon became corrupted to Wesley, and only at the beginning of the 18th century a branch of the family resumed the original form. Patr. Brit. p. 376. v. Wesley and Wolsey.

Wellicome; v. Welcome.

Welling, Wellen.—Local, ' of Welling,' a village, partly in the parish of Bexley and partly in that of East Wickham, co. Kent.

William de Wellynge, co. Norf., 1273. A.
1578. Richard Welling, co. Lanc.: Reg. Univ. Oxf. vol. ii. pt. ii. p. 81.
1619. George Horwood and Anne Wellinge: Marriage Lic. (London), ii. 73.
1654-5. Buried — Eliz., wife of Na-thaniell Wellen, a stranger: St. Dionis Backchurch (London), p. 229.
1757. Married — John Welling and Eliz. Wainwright: St. Geo. Han. Sq. i. 71.
MDB. (co. Sussex), 1, 1; (co. Glouc.), 0, 1; Boston (U.S.) 1, 0; Philadelphia, 1, 0.

Wellington.—Local, ' of Wellington,' parishes in cos. Hereford, Salop, and Somerset.

Robert de Welinton, co. Salop, 1273. A.
Johannes de Welington, co. Devon, 20 Edw. I. R.
William de Welynton, co. Somerset, ibid.
Johannes de Welinton, 30 Edw. I: BBB. p. 621.
1581. James Wellington, co. Heref.: Reg. Univ. Oxf. vol. ii. pt. ii. p. 104.
1583. Peter Wellington, co. Devon: ibid. p. 132.
1661. Married — Richard Wellington and Eliz. Marriott: St. Jas. Clerkenwell, iii. 106.
London, 6; Philadelphia, 5; Boston (U.S.), 17.

Well-liking.—Nick. ' the well-liking,' i.e. of comely appearance; cf. Wellbeloved.

' Well-liking lips they have.'
    Love's Labour's Lost, act v. sc. 2.
Alice Welikeing, co. Oxf., 1273. A.

Wellman.—Occup. ' the well-man,' one who resided by a well as water-carrier; v. Weller.

1752. Married — Thomas Rayner and Mary Welman: St. Geo. Chap. Mayfair, p. 223.
1730. — Richard Wellman and Jone Cox: ibid. p. 316.
London, 4; New York, 10.

Wellock; v. Wheelock.

Wells.—Local; v. Well.

Wellspring.—Local, ' at the well - spring,' from residence thereby. This surname has held a precarious existence for six centuries.

Walter Wilspryng, C. R., 14 Edw. III. pt. ii.
1780. Married — Thomas Wellspring and Lucy Nutt: St. Geo. Han. Sq. i. 316.
London, 1.

Wellstead, Wellsted, Well-steed, Welstead, Welsted, Wellstood.—Local, ' at the well-stead,' i.e. the dwelling or home-stead by the well. I cannot find the spot. It is clear, however, that it is a West-country name. The variants are somewhat numer-ous. Wellstod, entered below, shows the way to Wellstood.

1585. Robert Welsted, co. Somerset: Reg. Univ. Oxf. vol. ii. pt. ii. p. 144.
1606. Henry Welsteed, co. Dorset: ibid. 291.
1608. Married — Henrie Welstod and Katharine Clarke: St. Jas. Clerkenwell, iii. 33.
1741. Bapt. — Richard, s. Richard Wellstead: ibid. ii. 255.
London, 1, 1, 1, 0, 0, 0; Oxford (Well-stood), 4; New York, 1, 0, 0, 2, 1, 6.

Welsh.—Local; v. Wallace.

Welshman, Welchman, Welsman.—Local, ' the Welsh-man'; v. Wallace.

Alan Walseman. R.
William Walssheman, London. X.
Lewis Welsheman. XX. 1.
Johannes Walseman, 1379: P. T. Yorks. p. 143.
1544. Buried—Davye Welchman: St. Dionis Backchurch, p. 180.
1564. John Welsheman and Ann Pally-daye: Marriage Lic. (London), i. 29.
1623. John Welshman, of Newton: Wills at Chester, ii. 231.
London, 2, 6, 2.

Welstead; v. Wellstead.

Welton.—Local, ' of Welton,' parishes in cos. Lincoln, Northants, E. Rid. Yorks.

Roger de Weltone, co. Bedf., 1273. A.
Stephen de Weltone, co. Bedf., ibid.
Hugh de Weltone, co. Oxf., ibid.
1574-5. Basil Smithe and Johanna Welton, widow: Marriage Lic. (London), i. 63.
1638. Edmund Welton and Hester Everard: ibid. ii. 235.
1796. Married—William Welton and Eliz. Sleet: St. Geo. Han. Sq. ii. 141.
London, 6; New York, 6; Phila-delphia, 2.

Wend, Wende; v. Went.

Wenden, Wendon. — Local, ' of Wenden,' or Wendon. I cannot find the locality. It will

have to be sought for in the Fen country.

Peter de Wendon, co. Linc., 1273. A.
Alex. de Wenden, co. Camb., ibid.
1626-7. Isaac Downham and Sarah Wendon: Marriage Lic. (London), ii. 186.
1652. Reginald Wendon and Sicely Dennys: ibid. i. 24.
1798. Married—Samuel Sanderson and Ann Wendon: St. Geo. Han. Sq. ii. 180.
London, 6, 0; Philadelphia, 0, 1.

Wendling, Wendlin.—Local, ' of Wendling,' a parish near East Dereham, co. Norf.

William de Wendling, co. Norf., 1273. A.
London, 1, 0; Philadelphia, 3, 0; New York, 6, 1.

Wenham.—Local, ' of Wen-ham.' There are two parishes of this name in co. Suffolk.

Selithe de Wenham, co. Suff., 1273. A.
Hawisa de Wenham, co. Soms., 9 Edw. II: Kirby's Quest, p. 70.
1682-3. Thomas Wenham and Eliz. Upshaw: Marriage Alleg. (Canterbury), p. 110.
1788. Married — Francis Wenham, of Nevis, West Indies, and Anne Williams: St. Geo. Han. Sq. ii. 14.
London, 3.

Wenman.—Occup. ' the wain-man,' a wagoner; v. Wainman.

London, 4; New York, 4.

Wenn.—Local, ' at the wen,' from residence on a fen; a variant of the Somerset Venn (v. Fenn and Venn).

Johannes atte Wenne, co. Soms., 9 Edw. II: Kirby's Quest, p. 71.
1742. Married — James Wenn and Sarah Merris: St. Geo. Chap. Mayfair, p. 29.
1803. — William Day and Mary French (witness R. Wenn): St. Geo. Han. Sq. ii. 286.
London, 1.

Wensley.—Local, ' of Wensley,' a parish in N. Rid. Yorks. Also Wensley-Fold, a township in the parish of Blackburn, co. Lanc.

1609. Bapt.—Jane, d. John Wendesley: St. Mary Aldermary, p. 70.
1625. Buried—Danniell, s. John Wen-desle: ibid. p. 163.
1707. Married — Peter Wensley and Eleanor Parker: St. Antholin (London), p. 121.
London, 1; Crockford, 1; New York, 1; West Rid. Yorks, 1.

Went, Wend, Wende, Wente.—Local, ' at the went.' M.E. went, a passage. There are one or two

3 F

wents, still so called, in my late parish (Ulverston). 'Went, a cross-way, a passage' (Halliwell). Literally, a small passage leading from one main street to another.

Henry de la Wente, co. Suff., 1273. A.
Stephen ad le Wente, co. Camb., ibid.
William atte Wend, rector of Scoulton, co. Norf., 1368: FF. ii. 344.
Hugo de Went, 1379: P. T. Yorks. p. 135.
Ricardus de Went, 1379: ibid. p. 134.
John atte Wend, of Great Ellingham, co. Norf., 1381: FF. i. 485.
1664. Buried — Moses Went, a youth that belonged to my Lord Bishop of London's house: St. Jas. Clerkenwell, iv. 355.
1807. Married — William Went and Sarah Brown: St. Geo. Han. Sq. ii. 371.
London, 1, 0, 0, 0; New York, 0, 1, 1, 1.

Wentworth. — Local, ' of Wentworth,' a chapelry in the parish of Wath-upon-Dearne, W. Rid. Yorks. This surname has ramified strongly both in England and America. There is also a parish of this name in co. Camb., four miles from Ely. There is clear evidence that this place has helped to swell the total.

Willelmus de Wynteworth, 1379: P. T. Yorks. p. 10.
Johannes de Wynteworth, 1379: ibid. p. 25.
Johannes Wyntworth, 1379: ibid. p. 73.
1586. Paul Wentworthe, co. Bucks: Reg. Univ. Oxf. vol. ii. pt. ii. p. 151.
1593-4. George Wentworth, co. York: ibid. p. 199.
1610. Peter Wentworth, co. Northants: ibid. p. 313.
1622. John Welbore and Anne Wenthworth (co. Bedf.): Marriage Lic. (London), ii. 112.
1677. Buried—Mary Wentworth: Reg. St. Antholin (London), p. 97.
London, 6; Philadelphia, 3; Boston (U.S.), 118.

Werry, Gery, Gerry.—Bapt. ' the son of Werry' or Gerry; cf. Warin and Guarin, Warner and Garner, &c. The surname seems to have settled down as Gery at an early period.

Thomas Gery, co. Oxf., 1273. A.
Gerri de Planastre, co. Oxf., ibid.
Warin Gery, co. Camb., ibid.
Werry de Cadamo, co. Camb., ibid.
Henry Werri, co. Camb., ibid.
Peter Werri, co. Camb., ibid.
1598. James Gery, co. Heref.: Reg. Univ. Oxf. vol. ii. pt. ii. p. 230.
1601. John Gery, co. Camb.: ibid. p. 247.

1642-3. George Gery and Elis. Stoner: Marriage Lic. (London), ii. 369.
1808. Married — Edward Gearry and Mary Button: St. Geo. Han. Sq. ii. 389.
London, 0, 1, 0; Philadelphia, 0, 4, 2; Boston (U.S.), 0, 0, 36.

Weaker; v. Whiskard.

Wealake; v. Westlake.

Wesley.—Local, ' of Westley': (1) a parish in co. Suffolk, near Bury St. Edmunds ; (2) a parish in co. Cambridge, near Newmarket. (The *t* was naturally elided ; cf. Weslake for Westlake, q.v.) ; (3) a variant of Wellesley; v. Wolsey. Other small spots would easily acquire the name.

William de Westle, co. Camb., 1273. A.
Walter de Westleghe, co. Soms., 1 Edw. III: Kirby's Quest, p. 232.
1581. Bapt. — Margaret, d. Robert Wesley: St. Michael, Cornhill, p. 91.
1600. Thomas Westley, co. Warw.: Reg. Univ. Oxf. vol. ii. pt. ii. p. 240.
1602-3. John Westley, co. Warw.: ibid. p. 263.
1749. Married — William Williamson and Ann Wesly: St. Geo. Chap. Mayfair, p. 153.
London, 4; Philadelphia, 20.

West.—Local, ' from the West.' One who had settled eastwards ; cf. Western, Westerman, and Westray. This surname is so universal that to furnish modern instances were idle.

Algar West, co. Oxf., 1273. A.
Albricius West, co. Camb., ibid.
Robert del West, 1379: P. T. Yorks. p. 208.
Ricardus del West, 1379: ibid. p. 210.
Magota del West, 1379: ibid. p. 119.
1575. Richard Weste, co. Devon: Reg. Univ. Oxf. vol. ii. pt. ii. p. 65.
1615. Buried — Joane, d. Michaell Weste: St. Jas. Clerkenwell, iv. 132.
London, 142; West Rid. Court Dir., 9; Philadelphia, 211; Boston (U.S.), 136.

Westacott; v. Westcott.

Westall.—Local, ' of the West-hall,' from residence thereby or therein.

Richard atte Westhalle, alias Westalle de Amcotes (co. Linc.), 30 Edw. I: BBB. p. 619.
1564-5. Owen Westall, New Coll.: Reg. Univ. Oxf. vol. ii. pt. ii. p. 21.
1569-70. Jerome Westall and Margaret Lewes : Marriage Lic. (Westminster), p. 2.
1793. Married — James Flintoft and Martha Westall: St. Geo. Han. Sq. ii. 92.
London, 10; New York, 3.

Westbrook.—Local, ' of Westbrook,' a tithing in the parish of Boxford, co. Berks. No doubt other and smaller localities bear the same name ; cf. Easterbrook.

Richard de Westbrek, co. Surrey, temp. Edw. I. R.
1584. Mark Westbrooke, co. Surrey: Reg. Univ. Oxf. vol. ii. pt. ii. p. 139.
1628. Thomas Westbrook, of Hockley, co. Essex, and Joane Aylet: Marriage Lic. (London), ii. 194.
1741. Bapt.—Mary, d. William Westbrook: St. Geo. Chap. Mayfair, p. 3.
1747. Married — William Westbrooke and Ann Rosewell: ibid. p. 94.
London, 8; Philadelphia, 7; New York, 9.

Westbury.—Local, ' of Westbury,' parishes in diocs. Bath and Wells, Hereford, Oxford, Salisbury.

Agnes de Westburi, co. Bucks, 1273. A.
William de Westburi, co. Bucks, ibid.
John de Westbyr, co. Southampt., Hen. III–Edw. I. K.
1649. Buried — William, s. William Westberry: St. Jas. Clerkenwell, iv. 282.
1651. — Eliz., d. Thomas Westbury: ibid. p. 290.
1748. Married—Thomas Croucher and Sarah Westbury: St. Geo. Chap. Mayfair, p. 112.
London, 3; Oxford, 1.

Westby, Westerby, Westoby, Westbay. — Local, ' of Westby,' a parish in co. Lincoln. With Westerby and Westoby, cf. Westaway and Greenaway for Westway and Greenway. The surname still flourishes in co. Lincoln as Westerby.

Johannes de Westeby, 1379: P. T. Yorks. p. 38.
1542. Buried — Robert Westerbe: St. Peter, Cornhill, i. 106.
1595. Married — John Slawter and Margaret Westabie: St. Jas. Clerkenwell, iii. 19.
London, 2, 3, 4, 0; MDB. (co. Linc.), 0, 4, 0, 0; New York, 0, 0, 0, 1.

Westcott, Westcoatt, Wesscott, Westacott. — Local, ' of Westcott,' parishes and hamlets in cos. Gloucester, Bucks, Berks, &c. West, and cot, a hut, a small dwelling, situated westward of some other dwelling or dwellings ; cf. Northcot.

Ricardus de Westkote, co. Bucks, 1273. A.
Nicholas de Westcote, co. Oxf., ibid.
William de Westcote, co. Somerset, ibid.

Richard de Wescote, co. Soms., 1 Edw. III: Kirby's Quest, p. 182.
Dennys Wescott, 1593: Reg. St. Columb Major, p. 16.
1611. Bapt. — Margrett, d. Thomas Westcott, *baker*, of Cornhill: St. Peter, Cornhill, i. 60.
1689. John Seager and Ann Westcote: Marriage Alleg. (Canterbury), ii. 130.
London, 8, 1, 0, 2; Philadelphia, 32, 0, 3, 1; Boston (U.S.), 9, 0, 15, 1.

Westend. — Local, 'at the West-end' of the town, still a familiar phrase with a somewhat altered sense; cf. Townsend, Wood-end, &c.

Matilda atte Westende, co. Oxf., 1273. A.

Westerby; v. Westby.

Westerman, Westman. — Local, 'the western-man,' one from the West. Found in Yorkshire, where surnames from the points of the compass were common (v. Western and Westray). The following entries lie close together:

Johannes Westeman et Peronilla uxor ejus, 1379: P. T. Yorks. p. 115.
Thomas Westman, 1379: ibid. p. 116.
Johanna del West, 1379: ibid.

Among the householders of Wakefield in the same register are:

Willelmus de West, 1379: P. T. Yorks. p. 159.
Willelmus Westrynneman, i.e. Westerman, 1379: ibid. p. 160.

'George Westerman, blacksmith,' may be seen in my Wakefield Directory (1868).

1628. Married—John Smith and Francesse Westerman: St. Dionis Backchurch, p. 22.
London, 1, 0; West Rid. Court Dir., 2, 0; Leeds, 1, 0; Thorpe Audlin, near Pontefract, 1, 0; Philadelphia, 12, 1; Boston (U.S.), 0, 4.

Western, Westren, Westron. — Local, 'the western,' a man from the West; cf. Southern, and v. Westerman.

Henricus Westryn, 1379: P. T. Yorks. p. 124.
Johannes Westryn, 1379: ibid.
1600. Samuel Western and Anna Maria Finch: Marriage Lic. (London), ii. 312.
1735. Married—James Dolliffe and Anne Western: St. Geo. Chap. Mayfair, p. 12.
1749. — Joseph Westron and Martha Palmer: ibid. p. 149.
London, 11, 0, 0; Sheffield, 0, 1, 0; Leeds, 1, 0, 0; Philadelphia, 3, 0, 0; Boston (U.S.), 0, 0, 1.

Westgarth.—Local, 'of the west garth'; v. Garth.
London, 1; Ulverston, 1.

Westgate. — Local, 'at the west gate,' from residence thereby, probably as warder.

'And at the west gate of the toun, quod he, A carteful of donge ther shalt thou see.'
Chaucer, C. T. 15023-4.

Williamde Westgate, co. Norf., 1273. A.
Berthona de Westgate, co. Kent, ibid.
John de Westgate, 20 Edw. I. R.
William atte Westgate, Fines Roll, 16 Edw. II.

I find no Westgates in our English directories, the name having gradually assimilated itself to Westcott, Wesscott, and Westacott, q.v. The true form, however, is preserved in America.
Philadelphia, 1; Boston (U.S.), 6.

Westhead.—Local, 'of West-head,' a hamlet in the parish of Ormskirk, co. Lanc. This local surname is still chiefly confined to the county Palatine.

Gilbert Westhead, of Ormskirk, 1590: Wills at Chester (1545-1620), p. 205.
Hugh Houghton, of Westhead, parish of Ormskirk, 1610: ibid. p. 102.
Peter Westhead, of Westhead, in Lathom, 1613: ibid. p. 205.
Thomas Westhead, of Lathom, 1619: ibid.

Lathom in the above entries means Lathom, a township in the parish of Ormskirk.

1658. Married—William Clayton and Eliza Westead: St. Jas. Clerkenwell, p. 100.
Manchester, 2; Liverpool, 5; MDB. (co. Lanc.), 4.

Westlake, Weslake.—Local, 'at the west lake,' or pool, from residence thereby. I cannot find the spot. It seems to be a West-country name. For the omission of *t* in Weslake, cf. Wesscott or Wesley.

1566. Raymond Westlake, Ex. Coll.: Reg. Univ. Oxf. i. 244.
1729. Married — Richard Perry and Sarah Westlake: St. Geo. Chap. Mayfair, p. 303.
1805. — John Nankivell and Jane Westlake: St. Geo. Han. Sq. ii. 325.
London, 15, 2; MDB. (co. Soms.), 13, 0; New York, 5, 0.

Westley.—Local; v. Wesley.
London, 5.

Westmarland, Westmoreland, Westmorland. — Local, 'of Westmoreland,' a native of that county who has gone to reside outside its borders; cf. Wiltshire, Darbyshire, &c.

Johannes Westmerland, 1379: P. T. Yorks. p. 141.
1600. Married—Mathyas Westmerland and Elyzabeth Pecke: St. Antholin (London), p. 40.
1791. — Robert Westmorland and Mary Keen.
London, 1, 1, 0; West Rid. Court Dir., 0, 0, 2; MDB. (co. Cumb.), 0, 0, 6.

Westoby; v. Westby.

Westover.—Local, 'of West-over' (v. Over and West); cf. Northover. Westover is a tithing in the parish of Wherwell, near Andover, co. Hants.

William Weshovere (sic), co. Soms., 1 Edw. III: Kirby's Quest, p. 236.

The next entry to this is:

Ivone Esthovere, i. e. East-over.

1572. William Westofer and Alice Younge: Marriage Lic. (Faculty Office), p. 16.
1602. James Westover, co. Devon: Reg. Univ. Oxf. vol. ii. pt. ii. p. 256.
1732. William Westover and Amy Ranes: St. Geo. Han. Sq. i. 10.
MDB. (co. Somerset), 3; Boston (U.S.), 2.

Westray.—Local, 'at the west wray,' i.e. at the west corner, from residence therein. Alike singly and in compound local place-names *wray* plays an important part in North England; v. Wray, Thackeray, Dockreay, &c.

1549. Buried — Joane Westra: St. Peter, Cornhill, i. 110.
1552. Married—Richard Westray and Joane Fullor: St. Antholin (London), p. 9.
1582-3. Edward Hill and Ellen Westwraye: Marriage Lic. (London), i. 116.
1604-5. John Westwray, co. Essex, *gent.*: Reg. Univ. Oxf. vol. ii. pt. ii. p. 279.
1666. Married — Ralph Sauidge and Eliz. Westraie: St. Jas. Clerkenwell, iii. 124.
London, 1; MDB. (co. Cumb.), 2; New York, 1; Boston (U.S.), 1.

Westren, -ron; v. Western.

Westrop, Westrup, Westropp. — Local, 'of Westrop,' a tithing in the parish of Highworth, co. Wilts, i. e. West-thorp; cf. Winthrop, Northrup; v. Thorp.

1656-7. Buried — John, s. John Westropp: St. Jas. Clerkenwell, iv. 314.
1687. Francis Westthorpe and Ann Griffin: Marriage Alleg. (Canterbury), p. 14.
— George Westthrop and Amy Norden: bid. p. 36.
1693-4. Samuel Westthropp and Sarah Booth: ibid. p. 280.
1746. Married — John Pettit and Dorothy Westrop: St. Geo. Chap. Mayfair, p. 64.
London, 1, 3, 0 ; New York, 0, 0, 1.

Westwick.—Local, 'of Westwick': (1) a hamlet in the parish of Oakington, co. Camb. ; (2) a township in the parish of Gainford, co. Durham; (3) a parish in the county of Norfolk ; (4) a township in the parish of Ripon, co. York.

John de Westwik, co. Camb., 1273. A.
Katerina de Westwyc, co. Camb., ibid.
Isabella de Westwyk, co. Camb., ibid.
London, 3.

Westwood.—Local, ' of Westwood,' parishes in diocs. Exeter, Worcester, Lincoln, and Salisbury. Many small localities would, no doubt, be similarly called.

Richard de Westwode, co. Kent, 1273. A.
Henry de Westwode, co. Camb., ibid.
Henry de Westewode, co. Devon, Hen. III—Edw. I. K.
Willelmus de Westwod', 1379 : P. T. Yorks. p. 268.
1579. William Westwood, co. Glouc.: Reg. Univ. Oxf. vol. ii. pt. ii. p. 91.
1608. Rowland Westwood, London : ibid. p. 302.
1746. Married — John Westwood and Eliz. Edwards : St. Geo. Chap. Mayfair, p. 78.
London, 9 ; Philadelphia, 6 ; Boston (U.S.), 1.

Wetherall, Wetherell, Wetherill.—Local, 'of Wetheral,' a parish near Carlisle. This North-English surname has made a fair impression upon our directories on both sides of the water.

Adam de Wederhale, *horner*, 3 Edw. II : Freemen of York, i. 12.
Hugh de Wederhale, co. Cumb., 20 Edw. I. R.
Humfrey de Wederhall : E. and F., co. Camb., p. 164.
1617. Thomas Wethereld, co. Cumb. : Reg. Univ. Oxf. vol. ii. pt. ii. p. 362.
1618. Rowland Wetherall and Margaret More : Marriage Lic. (London), fi. 64.
1628. Nicholas Searle and Eliz. Wetherill : ibid. p. 193.
1744. Married—Peter Scott and Eliz.

Weatherell : St. Geo. Chap. Mayfair, p. 37.
London, 1, 4, 0 ; New York, 0, 3, 3 ; Philadelphia, 0, 4, 42 ; Boston (U.S.), 0, 14, 0.

Wetherby, Wetherbee ; v. Weatherby.

Wethered ; v. Weatherhead.

Wetherfield.—Local, 'of Wethersfield,' a parish in co. Essex.

Roger de Wetheresfeld, co. Camb., 1273. A.
Geoffrey de Wethirisfeld, co. Camb., ibid.
London, 2.

Wetherherd ; v. Weatherhead.

Wetherill.—Local; v. Wetherall.

Philadelphia, 42 ; New York, 3.

Wethey.—Local ; v. Withey.

Wetweather. — Nick. One who threw a damper on things in general ; cf. Fairweather.

Thomas Wetwedder : Charters, Davies.

Wewer ; v. Wooer.

Weyland ; v. Wayland.

Weyman ; v. Waithman.

Weymouth.—Local, 'of Weymouth,' a seaport and market-town in co. Dorset.

1572. Hugh Weymouthe, St. Alban's Hall : Reg. Univ. Oxf. vol. ii. pt. ii. p. 40.
1749. Married—Alex. Chatto and Mary Weymouth : St. Geo. Chap. Mayfair, p. 130.
London, 3 ; Boston (U.S.), 19 ; New York, 3.

Whale, Whal. — Nick. 'the whale,' probably affixed like Oliphant, i. e. the elephant, on account of the ponderous and ungainly build of the bearer.

Thomas Wal, co. Oxf., 1273. A.
Ralph le Wal, co. Oxf., ibid.
Thomas le Whal, 31 Edw. I : BBB. p. 651.
Philemon Whale, Pat. Roll, 19 Eliz. pt. iii.
1613. Richard Whale (co. Essex) and Mary Drywood : Marriage Lic. (London), ii. 19.
1642. Bapt.—Marye, d. William Whale : St. Jas. Clerkenwell, i. 151.
— Buried — Alice, wife of William Whale : ibid. iv. 254.
1795. Married — William Whale and Ann Lamb : St. Geo. Han. Sq. ii. 123.
London, 18, 0 ; New York, 0, 1.

Whalebelly. — ? Local. An imitative corruption of some such local surname as Walbury. This name is borne by a respectable family in south-east England.

Robert Whalebelly, Saham Toney, co. Norfolk : MDB. (1875).

Whalebone, Walborn. — ? Local. A manifest corruption, possibly a variation of Wellborne.

George Whalebone, *coach painter* : London Dir., 1870.
Philadelphia, 0, 4.

Whalley, Walley, Whally.—Local, ' of Whalley,' a parish in co. Lanc., famous for its abbey. Walley is a comparatively modern rendering of the surname.

'Robert de Whalley, who died before 1193, was rector of Rochdale': Baines' Lanc. i. 485.
1415. Geoffrey Whalley : Preston Guild Rolls, p. 8.
1590. Thomas Whalley, of Blackburn, *carpenter* : Wills at Chester (1545-1620), p. 200.
1592. Edmund Walley, of Blackburn : ibid. p. 205.
1604. Raffe Walley, Middlewich : Exchequer Depositions (co. Chester), p. 113.
Manchester, 12, 8, 0 ; London, 1, 0, 0 ; Preston, 4, 1, 0 ; Philadelphia, 8, 1, 14 ; Boston (U.S.), 3, 7, 0.

Wharmby.—Local,'of Wharmby,' some small spot, seemingly in East Cheshire, in the vicinity of Stockport.

1578. Thomas Wharmeby : East Cheshire, ii. 61 n.
1580. Henry Wharmby, of Offerton, *husbandman* : Wills at Chester, i. 205.
1592. Robert Wharmby, of Manchester, *butcher* : ibid.
1603. William Wharmby, of Bredbury : ibid.
Manchester, 4 ; MDB. (co. Ches.), 1 ; New York, 1.

Whately, Whatley, Wheatley, Wheatly.—Local, (1) ' of Whatley,' a parish in dioc. of Bath and Wells; (2) 'of Wheatley,' parishes in diocs. Oxford and Southwell ; (3) ' of Wheatley,' three separate hamlets in co. York, one a township in the parish of Doncaster, one a hamlet in the parish of Ilkley, and one a hamlet in the parish of Ovenden.

Peter de Watele, co. Oxf., 1273. A.
Henry de Watele, co. Oxf., ibid.

Alexander de Whately, or Watteleye, London, ibid.
John de Whateleghe, co. Dorset, ibid.
John de Watelegh, co. Wilts, ibid.
Robert de Whateleg, co. Wilts, Hen. III-Edw. I. K.
Mathew de Wateley, co. Oxf., ibid.
John de Weteley, *sauser*, 25 Edw. I : Freemen of York, i. 6.
Johannes de Whetlay, 1379 : P. T. Yorks. p. 99.
Henricus de Wytlay, 1379 : ibid. p. 91.
London, 2, 7, 22, 3 ; West Rid. Court Dir. (Wheatley), 6 ; Philadelphia, 0, 2, 16, 0 ; Boston (U.S.), 0, 0, 1, 0 ; New York, 2, 1, 4, 2.

Whatman.—Occup. 'the servant of Wat,' i.e. Walter. If this be so, the *h* is intrusive ; cf. Addiman, Matthewman, Wilman, &c.

Richard Whatteman, co. Soms., 9 Edw. II : Kirby's Quest, p. 129.
1557. Christning of Richard Whatman : St. Peter, Cornhill, p. 7.
1565. Bapt.—Sara, d. John Whattman : St. Dionis Backchurch, p. 79.
1591. Francis Whatman, co. Sussex, *pleb.* : Reg. Univ. Oxf. vol. ii. pt. ii. p. 186.
1794. Married—Roger Whatman and Jane Webb : St. Geo. Han. Sq. ii. 111.
London, 2.

Whatmore, -mough ; v. Watmough.

Wheatcroft.—Local, 'at the wheat-croft,' from residence thereby ; cf. Rycroft ; v. Croft or Craft.

Seman de Wetecroft, co. Suff., 1273. A.
Matilda de Wetecroft, co. Suff., ibid.
Robert de Wetecroft, co. Linc., Hen. III-Edw. I. K.
Thomas Whitecroft, C. R., 27 Edw. III.
1604. Married — Cutbert Crackplace and Anne Whitcraft : St. Peter, Cornhill, i. 244.
1703. William Legg and Eliz. Whitcroft : Marriage Lic. (Faculty Office), p. 245.
London, 1 ; Manchester, 3 ; Philadelphia, 2 ; New York, 1.

Wheatley, -ly ; v. Whately.

Wheatman.—Bapt. ; v. Wightman.

Wheeler, Wheeller.—Occup. 'the wheeler,' a maker of wheels, a wheelwright. This surname, representing an occupation of so much importance, is naturally found in large numbers. Modern references are needless.

Hugh le Welere, co. Camb., 1273. A.
Richard le Whelere, C. R., 21 Edw. III. pt. i.

Robert le Whelere. G.
William Wheler, co. Soms., 1 Edw. III : Kirby's Quest, p. 186.
1591. Married — Arthure Mayo and Ann Wheler : St. Michael, Cornhill, p. 15.
1593-4. Gilbert Wheeler, or Wheler, co. Worc. : Reg. Univ. Oxf. vol. ii. pt. ii. p. 200.
1691. Married—Thomas Wheeler and Judith Hiliard : St. Mary Aldermary, p. 34.
London, 76, 2 ; Philadelphia, 73, 0 ; Boston (U.S.), 220, 0.

Wheelhouse.—Local, 'of the wheel-house,' from residence thereby, the place where wheels were made or stored ; cf. Wheeler and Wheelwright. This surname is distinctly indigenous to W. Rid. Yorks.

Willelmus de Whelehous, 1379 : P. T. Yorks. p. 253.
Willelmus de Welchous, *carpenter*, 1379 : ibid. p. 221.
1747. Married—Robert Wheelhous and Ann Bethell : St. Geo. Chap. Mayfair, p. 91.
1795. Married — Samuel Wheelhouse and Lucy White : St. Geo. Han. Sq. ii. 133.
London, 3 ; West Riding Court Dir., 4.

Wheelock, Wellock, Whillock, Whellock. — Local, ' of Wheelock,' a parish in co. Chester.

John de Whelok, co. Ches., 2 Hen. IV (1400) : East Cheshire, i. 240.
1657. Married — William Beuer and Jane Wheellocks : St. Mary Aldermary, p. 28.
Randle Wheelock, of Wheelock, 1661 : Wills at Chester (1660-80), p. 287.
Hugh Wheelock, of Wheelock, 1677 : ibid.
1743. — Thomas Tharp and Francis Whellock : St. Geo. Han. Sq. i. 31.
Manchester, 1, 1, 0, 0 ; MDB. (Cheshire), 0, 0, 1, 0 ; London, 1, 0, 0, 2 ; Philadelphia, 3, 1, 0, 0 ; Boston (U.S.), 52, 6, 0, 0.

Wheelspinner.—Occup. ' the wheelspinner ' ; v. Spinner.

Isabella Whelespynner, 1379 : P. T. Yorks. p. 296.

Wheelwright. — Occup. 'the wheelwright' ; v. Wheeler, and cf. Cartwright and Wainwright. This is still a familiar surname in W. Rid. York.

Walter Welwryhte, co. Essex, 1273. A.
Willelmus Whelewryght, 1379 : P. T. Yorks. p. 125.
Robertus Whelewryght, 1379 : ibid. p. 242.
1778. Married—William Wheelwright and Eliz. Gibbs : St. Geo. Han. Sq. ii. 291.

1785. — John Smith and Rachel Wheelwright : ibid. p. 368.
West Rid. Court Dir., 9 ; Philadelphia, 1 ; Boston (U.S.), 22.

Wheen. — Nick. 'the wheen,' i.e. the queen (q.v.) ; cf. *wheencat*, a female cat (Halliwell). Also *wheene*, a queen ; North England (Halliwell). 'That es called the wheene of the Amazonnes,' Hampole MS. Bowes, p. 136, quoted by Halliwell ; cf. *wick* or *whick* for *quick* (Lancashire dialect).

Nicholas le Whene, Close Roll, 23 Edw. III. pt. ii.
New York, 2.

Whelp. — Nick. 'the whelp (cf. Kenn) ; M.E. *whelp*.

Richard le Whelp, C. R., 6 Edw. I.
Thomas Whelp, co. Soms., 1 Edw. III : Kirby's Quest, p. 223.
New York, 1.

Whenman.—Occup. ; a curious corruption of Wenman, q.v. ; cf. Whyman for Wyman, or Whatman for Watman.

London, 4.

Whetstone.—Local, 'of Whetstone,' a parish in co. Leicester, five miles from the capital. Also a hamlet, partly in co. Herts and partly in co. Middlesex.

1615. Edward Whytestone, or Whetstone, co. Bedf. : Reg. Univ. Oxf. vol. ii. pt. ii. p. 337.
1719. Married — John Whetstone and Jane Price : St. Antholin (London), p. 132.
1750. — Nicholas Wetstone and Mary Bowman : St. Geo. Chap. Mayfair, p. 158.
1752. — Edward Whetstone and Margt. Watkins : ibid. p. 229.
London, 2 ; MDB. (co. Leic.), 2 ; Philadelphia, 10.

Whichcord.— Bapt. A corruption of Guichard (?), q.v.

Whillock ; v. Wheelock.

Whimple, Whipple, Whippell.—Local, 'of Whimple,' a parish in co. Devon, four miles from Ottery St. Mary. The surname, however, has apparently been modified into Whipple, &c. Nevertheless, v. Whipple for another origin.

Hugo de Curteney habet . . . apud Wympel : A., co. Devon, i. 92 (1273).
Richard Bysothewympel (i. e. by South Wympel) : ibid. p. 67.
1657. Married—Richard Simons and

Mary Whimple: St. Thomas the Apostle (London), p. 20.
London, 1, 2, 0; MDB. (co. Devon), 0, 1, 2; Philadelphia, 0, 4, 0; Boston (U.S.), 0, 24, 0.

Whineray, Whinnerah, Winrow, Whinery, Whinnery, Winroe.—Local, 'at the whin-wray,' i.e. the corner where the whin was stored for bedding cattle, or the corner of the field where the whin grew. Whin is still used for bedding purposes in Furness and Cumberland; cf. Thackeray (i.e. the thack-wray), and v. Wray.

1584. John Whinwray, of Tatham: Lancashire Wills (Richmond), i. 307.
1595. John Whinrow, of Dalton-in-Furness: ibid. p. 306.
1597. Margaret Whinerawe, of Dalton: ibid.
1631. Robert Whinwrey, of Dalton: Lancashire Wills at Richmond, i. 307.
Barrow-in-Furness, 1, 1, 0, 0, 0, 0; Ulverston, 1, 0, 0, 0, 0, 0; Manchester, 0, 1, 0, 0, 0; London, 1, 0, 0, 0, 0, 0; Philadelphia, 0, 0, 1, 5, 1, 0; New York, 0, 0, 2, 0, 0, 2.

Whipp, Whipps, Whip.— ? Bapt. 'the son of Whip' (?). Although I have put a query to this statement, there can be little doubt of its accuracy. There are no local prefixes to the early entries, and the surname is found in widely separated districts.

Nicholas Wipe, co. Norf., 1273. A.
Allan Wyppe, co. Camb., ibid.
Henry Whippe, Fines Roll, 4 Edw. III.
Johannes Wippe, 1379: P. T. Yorks. p. 6.
Johannes Whyppe, 1379: ibid. p. 91.
James Whippe, of Twiston, 1677: Wills at Chester (1660-80), p. 287.
Richard Whipp, of Castleton, Rochdale, 1678: ibid. p. 275.
1687. Richard Whipp, goldsmith, and Eliz. Morse: Marriage Alleg. (Canterbury), ii. 11.
London, 2, 1, 0; Manchester, 1, 0, 1; Philadelphia, 2, 0, 0; New York, 1, 0, 0.

Whipple.—Local, 'of Whiphill.' I cannot find the spot. The suffix is -hill, as proved below; cf. Tickle or Tickell for Tickhill, &c. But v. Whimple.

Richard Wiphulle, co. Wilts, 1273. A.
William de Whiphulle, co. Soms., 1 Edw. III: Kirby's Quest, p. 192.
Richard de Whyphull, co. Soms., 1 Edw. III: ibid. p. 174.
London, 2; Boston (U.S.), 24.

Whiskard, Whisker, Wiscar, Wesker, Wisker.—Bapt. 'the son of Wisgar,' or Wiscar. In Domesday described thus: 'Wiscar,' co. Suffolk; 'Wisgar,' co. Suffolk; 'Wisgarus,' co. Essex. The long article on 'Whiskers' appended to this name in Lower is quite out of place. The solution has nothing to do with 'facial ornaments.' The modern form Whisker is simply imitative.

Nicholas Wiscard, co. Salop, 1273. A.
Wiscard Litel, co. Hunts, ibid.
Whischard de Charrum, 1269: KKK. vi. 275.
Wiscard, or Wyschardus Ledet, Hen. III–Edw. I. K.
1805. Married—George Redpath and Charlotte Whisker: St. Geo. Han. Sq. ii. 335.
London, 1, 3, 2, 0, 0; Sheffield (Wesker), 1; Manchester (Whisker), 1; New York, 0, 2, 0, 0, 2.

Whistler, Whisler, Wisler, Wissler.— Nick. 'the whistler,' one who was constantly whistling. The sobriquet would readily fasten itself upon the bearer, and as it denoted a cheery spirit would not be unacceptable to the nominee.

Thomas le Whistlar, co. Soms., 9 Edw. II: Kirby's Quest, p. 138.
Johannes Whisteler, 1379: P. T. Yorks. p. 13.
1607-8. Hugh Whistler (co. Oxford), Trinity Coll.: Reg. Univ. Oxf. vol. ii. pt. ii. p. 300.
1626-7. Philip Hinslow and Eleanor Whistler: Marriage Lic. (London), ii. 184.
1678. Bapt.—Ann, d. Thomas Whistler: St. Mary Aldermary, p. 105.
1800. Married—Webster Whistler (co. Sussex) and Jane Mackay: St. Geo. Han. Sq. ii. 228.
London, 5, 0, 0, 0; MDB. (co. Sussex), 1, 0, 0, 0; Philadelphia, 0, 1, 15, 4; New York, 0, 0, 4, 2.

Whiston, Wiston.—(1) Local, 'of Whiston,' parishes, hamlets, &c., in cos. Lancaster, Stafford, Yorkshire, Worcester, and Northampton.

Arnald de Wiston, co. Notts, 1273. A.
William de Whiston, co. Northampt., 20 Edw. I. R.

(2) Bapt. 'the son of Wistan,' an early form of Wulstan.

William Wlefstan, co. Norf., 1273. A.
Wystan, or Wolstan de Paston, co. Norf., temp. Ric. I: FF. vi. 481.
1742. Buried—Elizabeth Whiston: St. Mary Aldermary, p. 226.

London, 1, 0; Crockford, 2, 0; Boston (U.S.), 5, 1.

Whitacre,-aker; v. Whittaker.

Whitbourne. — Local, 'of Whitbourne,' a parish in co. Hereford, six miles from Bromyard.

Thomas de Wytebourne, co. Soms., 1 Edw. III: Kirby's Quest, p. 275.
1794. Married—Francis Whitburn and Sarah Mildred: St. Geo. Han. Sq. ii. 112.
1796. — John Whitburn and Catherine Earl: ibid. p. 143.
London, 1.

Whitbread, Whitebread.— Nick. (?). (1) A direct translation of the earlier Blanchpain (?), (q.v.). (2) But perhaps a corruption of Whitebeard, of which an early instance seems to be found below; cf. Blackbeard, Brownbeard. The first derivation is feasible as translations of the French were common.

William Wytebred, co. Linc., 1273. A.
John Witbred, London, ibid.
Nicholas Wytberd, co. Glouc., ibid.
Henry Whitbread. H.
1589. Married—Nicholas Wiblen and Katherine Whytebread: St. Dionis Backchurch, p. 11.
1661. — Thomas Whitebread and Debora Boden: St. Mary Aldermary, p. 29.
1750. Buried—Benjamin Whitebread, parish clerk: St. Michael, Cornhill, p. 299.
London, 10, 0; New York, 1, 0.

Whitby, Witby.—Local, 'of Whitby,' a seaport, borough, and market-town in N. Rid. Yorks.

Ricardus de Whiteby, 21-2 Edw. I: Freemen of York, i. 5.
Robertus de Whytby, smyth, 1379: P. T. Yorks. p. 99.
1585. Thomas Whitbey, co. Warw.: Reg. Univ. Oxf. vol. ii. pt. ii. p. 145.
1619. Oliver Whitbie, co. Bedf.: ibid. p. 377.
— Married — Mathew Whitby and Prudence Spencer: St. Dionis Backchurch, p. 19.
London, 7, 0; Philadelphia, 13, 1; Boston (U.S.), 2, 0.

Whitchurch; v. Whitechurch.

White, Whyte.—Nick. 'the white,' of fair complexion; cf. Black, Brown, Read, Russell, Blunt, &c. There is no need to furnish modern illustrations.

Geoffrey le Whyte, co. Camb., 1273. A.
Roger le Whyte, co. Sussex, ibid.
William the White, C. R., 13 Edw. III. pt. iii.

Thomas White, *souter*, 1379: P. T. Yorks. p. 98.
Magota Whyt, 1379 : ibid. p. 72.
London, 402, 10; Boston (U.S.), 619, 9; Philadelphia, 724, 6.

Whitebeard.— ? Nick. 'with the white beard' (?). But v. Wiberd; if an offshoot of this, then the surname is baptismal.

Philip Wytberd. T.
William Witberd, co. Glouc., 20 Edw. I. R.
Cf. Johannes Blakberd, 1379: P. T. Yorks. p. 197.
Alicia Wytberd, 1379 : ibid. p. 270.

Whitebelt.—Nick. 'with the white belt'; cf. Broadgirdle.

Johannes Whitebelt, 1379: P. T. Yorks. p. 160.
Cecilia Whytebelt, 1379 : ibid. p. 167.

Whitebreast. — Nick. 'with the white breast'; cf. *robin redbreast.*

John Whitebrest, Pat. Roll, 15 Ric. II. pt. i.

Whitebull.—Nick. 'the white bull.'

Johannes Whytebull, 1379 : P. T. Yorks. p. 98.
Johannes Whyttebull, 1379 : ibid. p. 101.

Whitechild.—Nick. 'the white child.'

John Whitechild, C. R., 17 Hen. VI.

Whitechurch, Whitchurch.—Local, (1) 'at the White Church'; (2) 'of Whitchurch,' parishes in diocs. Lichfield, Exeter, Hereford, Oxford, Winchester, &c.

William de la Wytechirch, C. R., 33 Hen. III.
William de Witchirch, co. Oxf., 1273. A.
Nicholas de Withchurch, co. Bucks, ibid.
John del Whitechirche, C. R., 5 Edw. I.
1706. Bapt. —John, s. James Whitchurch : St. Dionis Backchurch, p. 145.
London, 2, 3 ; Philadelphia, 1, o ; Boston (U.S.), 3, 1.

Whitefield; v. Whitfield.

Whitefoot.—? Local. But v. Whitehand and Barefoot. It is likely enough to be a nickname. As a rule, however, *-foot* is a local suffix; v. Foot (1).

Roger Wytfot, co. Devon, Hen. III-Edw. I. K.
John Whitefot, C. R., 9 Edw. III.
1634. Married — Edmond Whitefoot

and Martha Walker : St. Antholin (London), p. 68.
London, 1.

Whitehalgh.—Local, 'of the white halgh'; cf. Ridehalgh or Greenhalgh. v. Halgh.

Gilbert del Whithalgh, 1397 : Preston Guild, p. 4.
William de Whitehalgh, 1397: ibid. p. 8.

Whitehand.—Nick. 'with the white hand.' Oddly enough, a fairly common sobriquet in the 13th and 14th centuries. Perhaps a translation of Blanchmains; cf. Humbert Blanchmains (Nicholls, Hist. Leicestershire, Index). The surname still lives. Cf. Whitehead.

Robert Whithond, C. R., 13 Edw. I.
Alexander Whitehand, 3 Edw. III : Freemen of York, i. 25.
Adam Whythand, 1379: P. T. Yorks. p. 95.
Gilbert Whithand. T.
Humbert Whitehand. PP.
Bartholomew Whitehande, of London, Oriel Coll., 1578 : Reg. Univ. Oxf. vol. ii. pt. ii. p. 83.
1583. Buried—Alyce Breese, who dyed in bow lane in ye house of John Whitehande : St. Michael, Cornhill, p. 198.
William Whitehand, 1665: Hist. C. C. Coll., Camb.
London, 1.

Whitehead.—Nick. 'with the white head,' a common sobriquet, as our records prove, especially in North England; cf. Hoar. There is no evidence of a local origin, although Redhead and Blackett (Blackhead) are, like Greenhead, local occasionally. Modern instances are needless. The name exists wherever Englishmen settle.

Roger Witheved, co. Hunts, 1273. A.
William Witheved, co. Camb., ibid.
Adam Whitehead, 1379: P. T. Yorks. p. 240.
Johannes Whittehed, 1379 : ibid. p. 149.
Robertus Qwytheued, 1379 : ibid. p. 266.
John Qhwitheved, co. York. W. 9.
Rauf Whytehed, co. York. W. 2.
1745. Married — Owen Whitehead to Mary Russel : St. Michael, Cornhill, p. 70.
London, 60 ; Manchester, 50 ; Philadelphia, 60 ; Boston (U.S.), 12.

Whitehorse.—(1) Local, 'at the White Horse,' a sign-name ; cf. Whitelam, Grayhorse, and Roebuck.

William del Whithors, Fines Roll, 2 Edw. I.
Mary Whithors : Household Book of Queen Isabella, 1358 ; Cott. MS. Galba, E. xiv.
Walter Whitehors. O.

(2) Possibly in some cases a translation of French Blaunchival; cf. Whitbread for Blanchpain.

Henry Blaunchival, co. Somerset, 1273. A.
1651. Buried—Robert Whitehorse : St. Peter, Cornhill, i. 205.
1714. Married — Hugh Rance and Sarah Whitehorse : St. Jas. Clerkenwell, iii. 238.

Whitehouse.—Local, 'at the white house,' from residence therein ; cf. Wodehouse, Parkhouse, Moorhouse, &c. I cannot light upon the precise spot.

Stephen atte Whitehous, co. Soms., 1 Edw. III : Kirby's Quest, p. 138.
1720. Married—Gualtero Bernard and Mary Whitehouse : St. Michael, Cornhill, p. 61.
1788. — John Nottage and Mary Whitehouse : St. Geo. Han. Sq. ii. 4.
London, 22 ; Philadelphia, 12 ; Boston (U.S.), 22.

Whiteknave. — Nick. 'the white knave,' i.e. the white servant; v. Goodknave.

Acelin Wyteknave, co. Hunts, 1273. A.
Thomas Whitteknave, 1379: P. T. Yorks. p. 206.
Johannes Whiteknafe, 1379: ibid.

Whiteknight. — Nick. 'the white knight'; cf. Halfknight, and v. Knight.

Maurice Whiteknyght, Pat. Roll, 2 Hen. IV. pt. ii.

Whitelam, Whitlam.—Nick. 'the white lamb,' possibly a signname, 'at the White Lamb'; cf. Whitehorse.

Isabel Whitlamb, co. York. W. 14.
Alicia Whitlambe, 1379: P. T. Yorks. p. 230.
Richard Whitelomb, Inc. of Long Ichington, 1428: Dugdale's Warwickshire, p. 230.
1769. Married—Cotton Whitelamb and Eliz. Stone: St. Geo. Han. Sq. i. 188.
1804. — Thomas Whitelam and Ann Field : ibid. ii. 302.
London, 1, 0 ; Swinton, near Rotherham, 0, 1 ; Philadelphia, 1, 1.

Whitelegge, Whitelegg. — Local, 'of the white legh' (v. Lee). The same as Whiteley or Whitley; v. Whately for a similar form.

1584. Married—William Hudson and Agnes Whytlegge: St. Jas. Clerkenwell, iii. 11.
Mary Whitlegg, of Gatley, 1672: Wills at Chester (1660–80), p. 288.
James Whitelegg, of Northendon, 1680: ibid.
'Thomas Whitelegg was the next witness.' Inquest at Coroner's Court, Salford, July 22, 1887: Manchester Courier, July 23, 1887.
Crockford, 2, 0; Manchester, 2, 6; New York, 1, 0.

Whiteley, Whitley, Whitely.—Local, 'of Whiteley' (the white meadow); v. preceding article. There are many places naturally bearing this name. Whitley is a tithing in the parish of Cumnor, co. Oxf.; a hamlet in the parish of St. Giles, Reading; a chapelry in the parish of Tynemouth, co. Northumb.; also townships in W. Rid. Yorks, &c.

William de Witeleye, co. York, 1273. A.
Simon de Whitleghe, co. Soms., 1 Edw. III: Kirby's Quest, p. 187.
1582. William Whitleaye, or Whyteley, co. Linc.: Reg. Univ. Oxf. vol. ii. pt. ii. p. 119.
1688. Thomas Whitlee, *lighterman*, and Mary Ambros: Marriage Alleg. (Canterbury), ii. 55.
London, 3, 7, 0; Philadelphia, 31, 6, 6.

Whitelock, Whitlock.—(1) Nick. 'white-lock,' from the complexion of the hair or a particular tress; cf. Blacklock, Silverlock, Lovelock. This is quite satisfactory. But it may be an imitative form of Witlac, a Scandinavian personal name; cf. Goodlake. (2) Local, 'at the white lake,' from residence thereby.

Emma fil. Witlok, co. Hunts, 1273. A.
William Witlohc, co. Oxf., ibid.
William atte Whytelak, co. Soms., 1 Edw. III: Kirby's Quest, p. 178.
Walter Whytelock, co. Soms., 1 Edw. III: ibid. p. 105.
John Wytlock, C. R., 29 Edw. III.
1581. William Whitlock, co. Berks: Reg. Univ. Oxf. vol. ii. pt. ii. p. 103.
1601. Married—John Baber and Jane Whitlocke: St. Michael, Cornhill, p. 17.
1799. — Edward Whitelock and Mary Ann Mullard: St. Geo. Han. Sq. ii. 208.
London, 8, 15; Philadelphia, 7, 11; Boston (U.S.), 0, 2.

Whiteman, Whitman.—(1) Bapt.; v. Wightman. (2) Nick. 'the white man,' from the pallid appearance of the bearer; cf. Blackman and Greenman.

Agnes Wyteman, co. Oxf., 1273. A.
John Wyteman, co. Camb., ibid.
Thomas Wyteman, co. Oxf., ibid.
William Wytman, co. Hunts, ibid.
1607. Buried—John, s. Peter Whitman, *vintner*: St. Peter, Cornhill, i. 163.
1637-8. Christopher Whiteman and Alice Aldrington: Marriage Lic. (Westminster), p. 37.
London, 10, 1; Philadelphia, 64, 33; Boston (U.S.), 0, 51.

Whiteoak, Whittock, Whittick.—Local, 'at the white oak,' from residence thereby. The variants here given were inevitable.

1702. Bapt.—Sarah, d. Samuel Whittock: St. Jas. Clerkenwell, ii. 11.
1726. — Eliz., d. Peter Whittick: ibid. p. 159.
London, 0, 0, 4; Keighley (West Rid. Yorks), 1, 1, 0; New York, 0, 0, 1.

Whiter; v. Whittear.

Whiteside. — Local, 'at the white side,' i.e. from residence at the white side of some wood, orchard, hill, &c.; cf. Garside, i.e. the side of the garth or orchard; or Akenside, i.e. the side of the clump of oak-trees.

Richard Whitside, co. Camb., 1273. A.
Willelmus Whitesyde, 1379: P. T. Yorks. p. 253.
1575. Buried—Agnes Whiteside: St. Jas. Clerkenwell, iv. 7.
1752. Married — James Clough and Frances Whiteside: St. Geo. Chap. Mayfair, p. 212.
London, 2; Manchester, 1; New York, 7.

Whiteskirts.—Nick.

Henry Whiteskyrtes, Close Roll, 12 Edw. I.

Whitesmith. — Occup. 'the whitesmith,' a worker in tin-plate. I think the surname is obsolete; cf. Brownsmith, Blacksmith, Greensmith, and Redsmith. Whitesmith and Blacksmith are still occupative terms.

William le Wyteswyth (sic), co. Camb., 1273. A.
Robert le Withsmyth, co. Camb., ibid.
Richard le Wytesmith, C. R., 45 Hen. III.
William le Wytesmyth, 1313. M.

Whitey, Whitty, Wittey, Witty, Wittie.—Local, 'at the white hay,' i.e. hedge, from residence thereby; v. Hay.

Thomas ate Wythey, co. Oxf., 1273. A.
William ate Wythey', co. Oxf., ibid.
Nicholas de la Wytheg', co. Oxf., ibid.

Walter de la Wythege, co. Southampt., ibid.
1574-5. — Whitty, Ireland, *gent.*: Reg. Univ. Oxf. vol. ii. pt. ii. p. 59.
1632. Walter Williams and Jane Witty: Marriage Lic. (Faculty Office), p. 18.
1676. George Withey and Alice Cotton: Marriage Alleg. (Canterbury), p. 174.
London, 1, 3, 1, 1, 0; Philadelphia, 1, 7, 0, 2, 2; Boston (U.S.), 0, 3, 0, 0, 0.

Whitfield, Whitefield. — Local, 'of Whitfield,' parishes in diocs. Canterbury, Newcastle, Southwell, and Peterborough.

Margery de Wytefeld, co. Oxf., 1273. A.
Peter de Whytefeld, co. Norf., ibid.
Walter de Wytefeld, co. Salop, Hen. III-Edw. I. K.
Elyas de Wytefeld, co. Oxf., ibid.
1610. Henry Whitfeld, co. Kent: Reg. Univ. Oxf. vol. ii. pt. ii. p. 314.
1610. Jevan ap-Hugh and Katherine Whitfield: Marriage Lic. (Westminster), p. 18.
1675. Guy Miege and Mary Whitefeild: Marriage Alleg. (Canterbury), p. 146.
London, 19, 5; Philadelphia, 9, 7; Boston (U.S.), 0, 2.

Whitgift.—Local, 'of Whitgift,' a parish in the W. Rid. Yorks. I fear this name is extinct.

Johannes Thomson de Whidgift, 1379: P. T. Yorks. p. 112.
'John Whitgift, Archbishop of Canterbury, was born 1530, at Great Grimsby, Lincolnshire': Lemprière's Universal Biography.

Witham.—Local; v. Witham.

Whiting, Whitting. — (1) ? Bapt. I think there can be no question of two separate origins, but the first I cannot exactly elucidate; cf. the many hamlets called Whittington and Whittingham, where the A.S. family suffix comes in.

Adelina Wyting, co. Hunts, 1273. A.
John Witting, co. Oxf., ibid.
Felicia Wyting, co. Camb., ibid.
Gerin Wyting, co. Bedf., ibid.

(2) Local.

Thomas de Wytin, co. Notts, 1273. A.
John de Wyten, co. Hereford, Hen. III-Edw. I. K.
Robert de Whyten, co. Notts, 20 Edw. I. R.
1689-90. Samuel Starkey and Eliz. Whiting: Marriage Alleg. (Canterbury), p. 136.
1706. Bapt.—Noell, son of Noell Whiting: St. Dionis Backchurch, p. 145.
London, 25, 4; Philadelphia, 12, 2; Boston (U.S.), 87, 0.

Whitlam; v. Whitelam.

Whitley; v. Whiteley.

Whitlock; v. Whitelock.

Whitman; v. Whiteman.

Whitmore, Witmore.—Local, ' of Whitmore,' a parish in dioc. of Lichfield, co. Stafford, formerly Whittimere.

William de Witimere, co. Salop, 1273. A.
Johannes Whittemore, 1379: P. T. Yorks. p. 157.
1581. Peter Whitmore, co. Staff., *gent.*: Reg. Univ. Oxf. vol. ii. pt. ii. p. 98.
1612. Bapt.—John, s. Humphrey Whitmoore: St. Michael, Cornhill, p. 110.
1616. Thomas Whitmore, co. Salop, *pleb.*: Reg. Univ. Oxf. vol. ii. pt. ii. p. 357.
London, 13, 0; Philadelphia, 8, 1; Boston (U.S.), 18, 0.

Whitnell, Whitnall.—Local, ' of Whitenhull.' I cannot find the exact locality. Evidently it must be sought for in the West country.

Ralph de Whitenhull, co. Soms., 9 Edw. II: Kirby's Quest, p. 140.
Stephen de Whitenhull, co. Soms., 9 Edw. II: ibid. p. 142.
1793. Married — James Whitnell and Ann Stabler: St. Geo. Han. Sq. ii. 92.
MDB. (co. Soms.), 1, 0; London, 0, 1.

Whitney. — Local, 'of Whitey,' a parish in co. Hereford. It is quite clear that co. Hereford is the chief home of this family. Nevertheless Witney, the formerly well-known town in co. Oxford, must have swelled the total.

John de Witteneye, co. Suff., 1273. A.
Thomas de Whytene, co. Notts, ibid.
Robert de Wyttenye, co. Hereford, Hen. III-Edw. I. K.
1604. Henry Whitney, co. Heref.: Reg. Univ. Oxf. vol. ii. pt. ii. p. 275.
1605. Thomas Whitney, co. Heref.: ibid. p. 285.
1676. George Whitney and Sarah Todd: Marriage Alleg. (Canterbury), ii. 169.
London, 8; MDB. (co. Hereford), 1; Philadelphia, 28; Boston (U.S.), 216.

Whitsunday.—†Bapt. Pentecost was once a familiar font-name; cf. Nowell, Pask, and Christmas. As confirmations were general on Whitsunday, and it was a common circumstance to change the baptismal name then, it was natural that Pentecost, or 'Whitsunday,' should sometimes become the new name. The candidates were addressed by name till 1552. For the rule concerning the exchange of names—under exceptional circumstances—laid down by Archbishop Peckham, v. my Curiosities of Puritan Nomenclature, p. 75.

William Wytesoneday, co. Somerset, 1273. A.

Whittaker, Whitacre, Whitaker, Whittiker. — Local, ' of the white acre.' No doubt many small localities scattered over the country bearing this name have helped to swell the large total of Whitakers found in our modern directories. Over and Nether Whitacre are parishes in co. Warwick.

Simon de Withacre, co. Leic., Hen. III-Edw. I. K.
Alan Witacur, co. Oxf., 1273. A.
Richard de Whitacre, co. Northampton, ibid.
Jordan de Whitacre, co. Northampton, 20 Edw. I. R.
Henricus Wyteacre, 1379: P. T. Yorks. p. 194.
Willelmus de Wetaker, 1379: ibid. p. 195.
Rogerus Whitteacres, 1379: ibid. p. 271.
1618. Married — John Whitaker and Mary Storey: St. Dionis Backchurch, p. 19.
London, 10, 0, 41, 0; West Rid. Court Dir., 4, 1, 35, 0; New York, 11, 0, 9, 1; Philadelphia, 32, 0, 72, 0.

Whittam, &c.; v. Witham.

Whittear, Whittier, Whityer, Whiter.—Occup. ' the white tawer' or tower, one who dressed the lighter kid skins for the glover; v. Tawer and Tower (2).

Eustace le Wittowere, co. Hunts, 1273. A.
Thomas le Wytewere, co. Hunts, ibid.
Geoffrey le Whitetawier. N.
1634. William Lilley and Grace Whityer: Marriage Alleg. (Westminster), p. 34.
1674-5. Edward Ap-Price and Mary Whitter: ibid. p. 237.
1782. Married — Thomas Short and Eliz. Whitear: St. Geo. Han. Sq. i. 241.
London, 0, 0, 0, 5; Philadelphia, 0, 2, 0, 0; Boston (U.S.), 0, 47, 0, 0.

Whitteridge, Whittredge.—Local, ' of Whitrigg,' co. Cumb. ; ' a long white rigg upon the banks of the Wathinpool ' (E. and F., co. Cumb. p. 75).

William Wyterik, co. Camb., 1273. A.
Robert de Whyterigg, or Whyterik, or Whyteryk, co. Cumb., 20 Edw. I. R.
Walter de Whyteryk, co. Cumb., ibid.

Thomas de Whitrigg: E. and F., co. Cumb. p. 26.
London, 1, 0; Boston (U.S.), 0, 8.

Whittick; v. Whiteoak.

Whittier; v. Whittear.

Whitting; v. Whiting.

Whittingham. — Local, ' of Whittingham,' a parish in co. Northumberland, eight miles from Alnwick; also a township in the parish of Kirkham, co. Lanc.

1608. William Whittingham, co. Ches.: Reg. Univ. Oxf. vol. ii. pt. ii. p. 301.
1608-9. Thomas Whittingham, co. Ches. : ibid. p. 304.
1669. George Whittingham and Susanne Seagood: Marriage Alleg. (Canterbury), p. 15.
1766. Married—Thomas Whittingham and Sarah Hudson: St. Geo. Han. Sq. i. 152.
London, 11; New York, 5.

Whittington. — Local, ' of Whittington,' parishes in diocs. Glouc. and Bristol, Southwell, Lichfield, Norwich, Manchester, and Worcester.

Johannes de Whityngton, 1379: P. T Yorks. p. 259.
Isabella de Wetyngton, 1379: ibid. p. 61.
1590-1. Thomas Whittington, co. Heref.: Reg. Univ. Oxf. vol. ii. pt. ii. p. 182.
1617. Henry Whittington, co. Glouc.: ibid. p. 358.
1713. Bapt.—Richard, s. John Wittington: St. Peter, Cornhill, ii. 29.
— Buried — Richard Whittington, under the gallery: ibid. p. 121.
London, 4; Philadelphia, 24; Boston (U.S.), 3.

Whittle.—Local, (1) ' of Whittle,' generally called Whittle-in-the-Woods, a township in the parish of Leyland, co. Lanc.; (2) also hamlets and townships in cos. Northumberland and Derby. All the Lancashire Whittles, a numerous progeny, hail from (1). This name is commonly found in the Chorley and Preston district. It reached London in, or earlier than, the 17th century.

1581. John Whittle, of Chorley, co. Lanc. : Wills at Chester (1545-1620), p. 208.
1617. Robert Whittle, of Leyland, co. Lanc. : ibid.
1662. Gulielmus Whittle: Preston Guild Rolls, p. 139.

1667. Sackvill Whittle, *barber-chirur-geon*, and Margaret Fox: Marriage Alleg. (Canterbury), p. 141.
London, 8; Manchester, 8; Chorley, 5; Preston, 8; Philadelphia, 9; Boston (U.S.), 20.

Whittock, Whittuck. — ? Nick. 'the white cock'(?). What may be the origin of this name I dare not say, but one thing is absolutely certain, Wytcok below is the parent. But v. Whiteoak.
Robert Wytcok, co. Wilts, 1273. A.
1690. Bapt.—William, s. Samuel Whittock : St. Jas. Clerkenwell, i. 338.
1696. — Joseph, s. Samuel Whittock : ibid. i. 365.
MDB. (co. Soms.), 2, 2.

Whitty ; v. Whitey.

Whitwell.—Local, 'of Whitwell,' a hamlet in the parish of Tinsley, near Sheffield; also parishes in cos. Derby, Norfolk, and Rutland; also townships in cos. Westm. and York (N. Rid.). It is manifest that several of these places, north and south, have originated the surname.
Eborard de Wytewelle, co. Camb., 1273. A.
Walter de Wytewelle, co. Camb., ibid.
Johannes de Whitwell, 1379: P. T. Yorks. p. 292.
Thomas de Whitewell, 1379: ibid. p. 250.
1608. Miles Whitwell, Kendall : Wills at Chester, i. 208.
1630. Edmund Whitwell, of Burton : Lancashire Wills at Richmond, i. 309.
1701. Bapt. — Richard, s. Anthony Whittwel : St. Jas. Clerkenwell, ii. 2.
1713. — Eleanor, d. Anthony Whitwel : ibid. p. 70.
London, 4; Boston (U.S.), 16.

Whitworth.—Local, 'of Whitworth,' a chapelry in the parish of Rochdale, co. Lanc. This surname has a vigorous existence in the county Palatine.
1615. Susanna Whitworth, of Castleton, parish of Rochdale : Wills at Chester, i. 208.
1619. James Whitworth, of Brandwood, parish of Rochdale : ibid.
1635. Married—Jeremy Whitworth and Mary Pecke : St. Mary Aldermary, p. 18.
1646. Edmund Whitworth, of Prestwich, *husbandman* : Wills at Chester, ii. 235.
Manchester, 19; Philadelphia, 6; Boston (U.S.), 2.

Wholesworth ; v. Holdsworth.

Whyatt ; v. Wyatt.

Whybreu, Whybrow, Wybroo, Wybrow.—(1) Bapt. 'the son of Werburgha.' A nun of this name is said to have been patron saint of the ancient abbey of St. Werbergh, Chester; v. Chambers' Book of Days, i. 215. (2) Local; v. Wybroo.
1560. Buried—Whitburga, d. Robert Soham, Beetley, Norfolk : St. Mary, Beetley.
1564. Married—Rycharde Johnson and Wyboroe Wylson : St. Michael, Cornhill, p. 8.
London, 3, 5, 1, 3; New York (Whybrew), 1.

Whyman.—Bapt. 'the son of Wymond'; v. Wyman.
London, 2; New York, 2.

Whyte.—Nick.; v. White.

Wiberd, Wiber, Wybert.— Bapt. 'the son of Wiberd,' i.e. Wigbert (Yonge, ii. 409). Found in Domesday as Wiber and Wibert (co. York).
Wibert fil. Hacun, 1188 : RRR. p. 50.
Wybert, rector de Gynynton, 1273. A.
Thomas Wyberd, co. Suff., ibid.
Adam Wyberd, co. Kent, ibid.
Robert Wyberd, co. Norf., ibid.
William Wyberd, co. Glouc., Hen. III-Edw. I. K.
William fil. Wiberti, Pipe Roll, 5 Hen. II.
Wybert de Littelton, Pat. R., 4 Edw. III. pt. ii.
Hugo Wyberd, 1379 : P. T. Yorks. p. 30.
1579. Married — Christopher Dodson and Agnes Wyberde : St. Michael, Cornhill, p. 12.
1611-2. Walter Wyberd (co. Essex) and Eliz. Swifte : Marriage Lic. (London), i. 9.
1718. Married—Thomas Johnson and Eliz. Wibard : St. Mary Aldermary, p. 44.
London, 0, 1, 0; New York, 0, 0, 1.

Wick, Wicks, Wickes, Wicke. —(1) Local, 'at the wyke'; v. Wike and Wykes. (2) Bapt. 'the son of William'; v. Wilkerson and Wilkes.
London, 0, 20, 2, 0; Philadelphia, 18, 5, 1, 4; Boston (U.S.), 0, 4, 0, 0,

Wicken(s ; v. Wickin.

Wicker, Wickers, Whicker, Whickers.—Bapt. 'the son of Wyger.' But v. Wilkerson and Wilkes.
Thomas Wyger', co. Camb., 1273. A.
Henry Wyger, co. Devon, ibid.
William Wyger, co. Hunts, ibid.
Johannes Wykir, *shereman*, 1379 : P. T. Yorks. p. 25.

Robertus Wyker, 1379 : ibid. p. 26.
1581. Thomas Whicker, co. Devon : Reg. Univ. Oxf. vol. ii. pt. ii. p. 105.
1798. Married—Thomas Middleton and Ann Wickers : St. Geo. Han. Sq. ii. 179.
1807. — William Wicker and Eliz. Vining : ibid. p. 378.
London, 3, 2, 1, 0; Philadelphia, 3, 0, 0, 0; New York, 3, 1, 0, 0.

Wickerson ; v. Wilkerson.

Wickett.—(1) Local, 'at the wicket,' a small gate, from residence thereby ; cf. Barr.
Robert atte Wychit, Close Roll, 14 Edw. II.
Walter Wyket, Close Roll, 2 Edw. I.

(2) Bapt. A sharpened form of Wiggett, q.v.
1541. Bapt.—Jane Wicket : St. Peter, Cornhill, i. 2.
1717. Married — George Wickett and Ann Cotes : St. Michael, Cornhill, i. 59.
1750. — William Grace and Mary Wickett : St. Geo. Chap. Mayfair, p. 169.
Sheffield, 2; New York, 2.

Wickham.—Local, 'of Wickham.' There are many spots and parishes of this name in cos. Kent, Glouc., Essex, Suffolk, Hants, Berks, Lincoln, Oxford, Camb., &c. Its meaning seems to be exactly equivalent to our 'homestead'; v. Wickstead and Wykes.
William de Wykham, co. Oxf., 1273. A.
1572. Married—John Wyckham and Mary Ovenden : St. Dionis Backchurch (London), 7.
1577. Edward Wickam, co. Oxf. : Reg. Univ. Oxf. vol. ii. pt. ii. p. 74.
1594. Richard Wickham, co. Kent : ibid. p. 205.
1762. Buried—Susanna Wickham : St. Peter, Cornhill, i. 144.
London, 14; Philadelphia, 1; Boston (U.S.), 4.

Wickin, Wicken, Wickins, Wickens, Wicking.—(1) Bapt. 'the son of William,' corruptions of Wilkin and Wilkins (q.v.). (2) Bapt. 'the son of Wiggin,' sharpened to Wickin. This is a more probable derivation. The *g* in Wicking is excrescent, as in Jennings.
'Thomas Wykynsone holds lands, and tenements, 5s. 3d.' : Rental of Halifax, 1439, Cotton MS. Vespasian, F. 15, Brit. Mus.
'John Wykynsone holds lands, and tenements, 8d.' : ibid.
Willelmus Wykyn, 1379 : P. T. Yorks. p. 25.
Johanna Wykyn, 1379 : ibid. p. 35.

For corroborative evidence of (2), v. Wiggin, where the popularity of the personal name is conclusively shown.

1667. Bapt. — Thomas, s. Samuell Wickins: St. Peter, Cornhill, i. 88.
1669. Buried—Eliz., servant to Samuel Wickens: ibid.
1678. Married — John Wicken and Isabel Mellen: St. Jas. Clerkenwell, iii. 185.
1808. Married—Edward Radclyff and Harriot Wicking: St. Geo. Han. Sq. ii. 385.
London, 0, 1, 0, 8, 3; Boston (U.S.), 0, 0, 0, 4, 0.

Wickliffe; v. Wycliffe.

Wicks; v. Wykes.

Wickstead, Wicksted, Wicksteed.—Local, 'at the wick-stead,' from residence therein; v. Wykes, and cf. *homestead.* Lower says the name hails from a manor called Wicksted in co. Ches. That this is true is evident. Any number of references can be quoted from that county.

1602. John Whicksteed, or Weecksteede, London: Reg. Univ. Oxf. vol. ii. pt. ii. p. 257.
1611. Henry Wicksted, of Wick Malbank: Wills at Chester, i. 209.
1648. Thomas Wickstead, of Wickstead, co. Chester: ibid. ii. 235.
1649. Hugh Wickstead, of Chester, *glover*: ibid.
1796. Married — William Boles and Eliz. Wicksted: St. Geo. Han. Sq. ii. 158.
1799. Married — John Wicksteed and Honoria Tichborne: St. Geo. Han. Sq. ii. 203.
London, 0, 1, 4; MDB. (co. Ches.), 1, 0, 1; New York, 0, 0, 4.

Widder(s; v. Widow.

Widdicombe, Widicombe, Weddicombe, Withecomb, Widdicombe.—Local, 'of Widecombe-in-the-Moor,' a parish in co. Devon, six miles from Ashburton; also Widcombe, a parish in co. Somerset. These probably share the parentage.

Robertus Wythecumbe, co. Soms., 9 Edw. II: Kirby's Quest, p. 76.
Walter de Wydecu'be, co. Soms., 9 Edw. II: ibid. p. 95.
Ammyra de Wydecombe, co. Soms., 9 Edw. II: ibid. p. 119.
Elena de Wydecombe, co. Soms., 9 Edw. II: ibid. p. 131.
London, 3, 0, 0, 0; Devon Court Dir., 0, 1, 1, 0, 0; New York, 0, 0, 0, 0, 1; Manchester, 0, 0, 0, 1, 0

Widdows; v. Widow.

Widdowson; v. Widowson.

Widger.—? Bapt. 'the son of Wicher' (?). Widger seems to be quite a modern, even recent, variant; cf. Wickersley (the meadow of Wicker), a parish in W. Rid. Yorks. This represents the harder N.E. pronunciation.

John Wycher, co. Camb., 1273. A.
Juliana Wycher, co. Camb., ibid.
William Wycher, co. Hunts, ibid.
Robert Wiger, co. Suff., ibid.
1753. Married — John Dawkins and Abigail Whitcher: St. Geo. Chap. Mayfair, p. 235.
1754. — Thomas Whitchar and Hannah Snow: ibid. p. 269.
London, 1; Philadelphia, 2; Boston (U.S.), 2.

Widgington; v. Wigginton.

Widmer.—Local, 'of Widmerpool,' a parish in co. Notts, nine miles from the capital.

Durand de Wydmerpol, London, temp. Edw. II. R.
Walter de Wythmer, co. Soms., 1 Edw. III: Kirby's Quest, p. 260.
Stephen Wedmer, co. Soms., 1 Edw. III: ibid. p. 272.
1581. Thomas Widmerpooll, co. Notts: Reg. Univ. Oxf. vol. ii. pt. ii. p. 110.
1586. Nicholas Wydmer, or Widmore, co. Bucks: ibid. p. 151.
1789. Married — Thomas Shotter and Eliz. Widmer: St. Geo. Han. Sq. ii. 22.
1806. — William Bowles and Maria Widmor: ibid. p. 340.
London, 1; Boston (U.S.), 3; New York, 2.

Widow, Widders, Widdows, Widder, Wider, Widdos, Widdoes, Widows.—Bapt. 'the son of Wydo,' English for Guido (Guy) (v. Widowson, 2); cf. Warin for Guarin, &c.

William fil. Wydo, co. Norf., 1273. A. Reg. fil. Wydonis, co. Hunts, ibid.
Thomas Wydowe, C. R., 20 Ric. II. pt. i.
Annabella Wydow, 1379: P. T. Yorks. p. 146.

Widders is a natural corruption of Widows with the patronymic s. 'Beware of widders' does not apply in this case, but points to a similar corruption.

London, 0, 1, 4, 0, 0, 0, 0, 1; Philadelphia, 0, 0, 2, 0, 0, 1, 2, 0; New York, 0, 0, 0, 3, 10, 0, 0, 0.

Widowhood.—Nick.
Reginald Widewohod, Close Roll, 49 Hen. III.

Widowson, Widdowson, Widows, Widdison. — (1) Nick. 'the widow's son.' (2) Bapt. 'the son of Wydo'; v. Widow. Doubtless (1) is the chief parent.

Andrew fil. Vidue, co. Camb. 1273. A. Symon fil. Vidue, co. Oxf., ibid.
Edmund fil. Vidue, co. Soms., 1 Edw. III: Kirby's Quest, p. 101.
Willelmus Wydowson, 1379: P. T. Yorks. p. 215.
Ricardus Widowson, 1379: ibid.
Adam Wydouson, 1379: P. T. Howdenshire, p. 25.
1571. Richard Widoson, co. Notts: Reg. Univ. Oxf. vol. ii. pt. ii. p. 52.
1583. Garrett Florence and Ann Wyddowson, relict of Robert Wyddowson: Marriage Lic. (London), i. 118.
1666. Married—Adam Wydeson and Alice Ranen: St. Jas. Clerkenwell, iii. 124.
London, 0, 1, 4, 0; West Rid. Court Dir. (Widdison), 2; Sheffield (Widdowson), 8; New York, 0, 1, 0, 0.

Wigan.—(1) Local, 'of Wigan,' an important town in South Lanc. (2) Bapt. 'the son of Wigan'; v. Wiggin. Although it is certain that our Cheshire and Lancashire Wigans hail from the town, it is equally certain that the surname, generally speaking, belongs to (2).

Willelmus de Wygan, *ffranklayn*, 1379: P. T. Yorks. p. 127.
1592. William Wigan, of Great Harwood: Wills at Chester, i. 209.
1617. John Wigan, of Heap: ibid.
1638. Benjamin Wigan, of Atherton: ibid. ii. 236.
1801. Married—James Lambley and Grace Wigan: St. Geo. Han. Sq. ii. 243.
London, 3; Liverpool, 1; Philadelphia, 1; Crockford, 3.

Wigand, Wigans; v. Wiggin.

Wigfall, Wigfull.—Local, 'of Wigfall,'some small spot in co. York.
Henricus de Wigfall, *webester*, 1379: P. T. Yorks. p. 82.
Ibota de Wigfall, 1379: ibid.
Johannes Wigfall', 1379: ibid. p. 81.
1654. Buried—Henry Wigfall, servant with Mr. Thomas Chewning: St. Michael, Cornhill, p. 246.
1701. Married — Richard Wigfall and Alice Hull: St. Jas. Clerkenwell, iii. 223.
West Rid. Court Dir., 5, 4; Sheffield, 4, 3; Philadelphia, 3, 0; Boston (U.S.), 1, 0.

Wigg, Wiggs, Wigson. — Bapt. 'the son of Wig' (v. Lower, Patr. Brit. 'Wigg,' and Yonge,

Christian Names, ii. 409). As a personal name the forms in Domesday are Wiga (cos. York and Bucks), Wige (co. York), and Wig (co. Bedford). Another early form of Wig was Vig (Yonge, ii. 409), whence possibly Figg, Figgs, and Figgin (q.v.). Another form, Wigel, was once common in Holland, and is found in Wigglesworth, co. York.

Thomas Wigge, Close Roll, 3 Edw. I.
Robert Wygge, co. Kent, 20 Edw. I. R.
William Wygge, Pardons Roll, 5 Ric.II.
1586. Bapt.—Agnes Wigges, daughter of William Wigs: St. Peter, Cornhill, i. 30.
1715. Married — Charles Trinquand and Mary Wigg: St. Michael, Cornhill, p. 58.
1804. — William Wigson and Sarah St. John: St. Geo. Han. Sq. ii. 314.
London, 6, 4, 0; New York, 1, 0, 0; Boston (U.S.), 1, 0, 0.

Wiggett.—Bapt. 'the son of Wigod' or Wigot. In Domesday Wigod is found in co. Devon, and Wigot in cos. Sussex, Bedford, and Berks. As a font-name Wigot or Wigod lasted till the 14th century.

Tokig, son of Wiggod (Freeman, Hist. Norm. Conq. iv. 47), called Wiggod, of Wallingford (ibid. iv. 45, 728).
'Walter de Ganto, 3 carucates, which Wigotus holds': Lincolnshire Survey, p. 18, temp. 1109.
Adam Wigod, co. Hunts, 1273. A.
Thomas Wigod, co. Camb., ibid.
Margaret fil. Wyggotti, co. Linc., ibid.
John Wygot, co. Oxf., 20 Edw. I. R.
Robertus Wygot, co. Linc., ibid.
Robertus Wygott, 1379: P. T. Howdenshire, p. 32.
Constance Wygood, C. R., 1 Hen. IV. pt. i.
London, 3; Philadelphia, 1.

Wiggin, Wiggins, Wigan, Wigans, Wiggan, Wiggans, Wigand.—Bapt. 'the son of Wigand' (v. Yonge, ii. 409). This personal name has made a deep impression upon English nomenclature, and just as Stigand became Stiggin and Stiggins, so Wigand became Wiggin and Wiggins. As regards Wigan, this has in some cases a local parentage (v. Wigan). The final s in Wiggins, &c., is genitive; cf. Williams, Jones, &c.

Wyganus Marescall, Hen. III–Edw. I: K. p. 88.
Wuganus de Wyleby, ibid. p. 89.
William Wygeyn, co. Norf., 1273. A.
Wygan le Bretun, co. Essex, ibid.

Eva Wigeyn, co. Oxf., 1273. A.
Thomas Wygan, 1379: P. T. Howdenshire, p. 7.
Robert Wyghene, 1379: P. T. Yorks. p. 81.
1705. Married—Daniel Wiggen and Mary Bridge: St. Mary Aldermary (London), p. 38.
1760. — John Wigans and Mary Spong: St. Geo. Han. Sq. i. 98.
1789. — George Neves and Mary Wiggin: ibid. ii. 22.
1790. — Thomas Wiggins and Anna Maria Adcock: ibid. p. 50.
1793. — Thomas Wiggens and Eliz. Beakley: ibid. p. 93.
London, 2, 17, 3, 1, 0, 0, 0; West Rid. Court Dir., 2, 1, 0, 0, 0, 0, 0; Philadelphia, 1, 38, 1, 0, 2, 0, 7; Boston (U.S.), 65, 3, 0, 0, 0, 0, 0.

Wigginton, Wiginton, Widgington.—Local, 'of Wigginton,' parishes in cos. York, Hertford, Oxford, and Stafford. Lit. 'the town of Wiggin'; v. Wiggin, and cf. the local Wiggenhall, Wigginthorpe, Wiggonby, and Wiggonholt. Several of the local Wigginton are represented in the instances below:

Guido de Wygynton, co. Oxf., 1273. A.
Roger de Wygynton, co. Oxf., ibid.
John de Widington, co. Linc., ibid.
Samuel de Wygenton, co. Hertf., Hen. III–Edw. I. K.
1682. Edward Wiggington and Hanna Jackson: Marriage Alleg. (Canterbury), p. 118.
1785. Married—Richard Pim and Eliz. Widginton: St. Geo. Han. Sq. i. 375.
London, 3, 2, 2; New York, 1, 0, 0.

Wigglesworth. — Local, 'of Wigglesworth,' a township of Long Preston, W. Rid. Yorks.

Johannes de Wykelsworth, 1379: P. T. Yorks. p. 255.
Willelmus de Wyglesworth, 1379: ibid. p. 257.
Matthias Wiglesworth, co. Yorks: Reg. Univ. Oxf. vol. ii. pt. ii. p. 114.
1795. Married—Benjamin Wiglesworth and Hanna Johnson: St. Geo. Han. Sq. ii. 125.
London, 2; West Riding Court Dir., 8; Boston (U.S.), 1.

Wight.—Nick. 'the wight,' i.e. the active, strong; v. Wightman.

'Y schalle gyf the two greyhowndys,
As wyghte as any roo.' Halliwell.
William le Wyhte, co. Sussex, 1273. A.
John le Wighte, co. Soms., 1 Edw. III: Kirby's Quest, p. 90.
1729. Married—Joseph Wight and Mary Hart: St. Geo. Chap. Mayfair, p. 289.
1792. — Nicolas Joseph Henrij and Margt. Wight: St. Geo. Han. Sq. ii. 80.
London, 3; New York, 19.

Wightman, Weightman, Whiteman, Wheatman.—(1) Nick. 'the wightman.' A.S. wight, active, brave, strong.
'A wightman of strengthe.'
Piers P. 5195.
(2) Bapt. 'the son of Wigmann' (Yonge, ii. 410). It is clear from the evidence that there was some difficulty in pronouncing this early personal name:

Alexander Wigman, co. Northampton 1273. A.
Geoffrey Wygeman, or Wygman, or Wigeman, co. York, ibid.
Johannes Wygh'man, 1379: P. T. Yorks. p. 63.
Willelmus Wyghman, 1379: ibid.
Johannes Wyghman, 1379: ibid.
Richard Wightman, co. York. W. 15.
William Whytman. B.
Audrey Whiteman, temp. Eliz. Z.

I strongly suspect the baptismal origin (2) is the correct one. I believe also that all the four modern directory forms given above are varieties of one name. If there were evidence enough (1) would be a tempting solution.

Sheffield, 4, 0, 0, 2; London, 7, 6, 10, 0; Philadelphia, 8, 20, 64, 0; Boston, 6, 1, 2, 0.

Wigley.—Local, 'of Wigley,' i.e. the meadow that belonged to Wigg (q.v.). I cannot find the spot, but it is manifest that it must first be looked for in co. Derby.

John de Wyggeley, co. Derby, 20 Edw. I. R.
1601. Edmund Wigley, co. Derby, pleb.: Reg. Univ. Oxf. vol. ii. pt. ii. p. 251.
1793. Married — Joseph Wigley and Mary Heath: St. Geo. Han. Sq. i. 95.
London, 6; Philadelphia, 1; Boston (U.S.), 2.

Wigman; v. Wikman.

Wigmore.—Local, 'of Wigmore,' a parish in co. Hereford, ten miles from Leominster.

Richard de Wigmore gave land to the Church of St. Peter, Gloucester, in 1239: Atkyns' Hist. Gloucestershire, p. 75.
1596. Warnecombe Wigmor, co. Heref.: Reg. Univ. Oxf. vol. ii. pt. ii. p. 216.
1602. Michael Wigmor, co. Soms.: ibid. p. 262.
1688. Henry Wigmore, or Wigmor, and Sarah Croke: Marriage Alleg. (Canterbury), p. 55.
1771. Married—Richard Wigmore and Mary Weston: St. Geo. Han. Sq. i. 208.
London, 5; MDB. (co. Gloucester), 2; Philadelphia, 6; Boston (U.S.), 1.

Wignall.—Local, 'of Wiggenhall.' There are several parishes so named in co. Norfolk.

William de Wigenhale, co. Norf., temp. Hen. III : FF. vii. 352.
Richard de Wigenhale, co. Norf., 1273. A.
1588. Buried — Anne, wife of William Wignell : St. Mary Aldermary, p. 144.
1604. Elizabeth Wignall, of Chester : Wills at Chester (1545-1620), p. 209.
1605. Thomas Wignall, of Tarleton : ibid.
London, 2 ; MDB. (Norfolk), 1 ; Philadelphia, 6 ; Boston (U.S.), 1.

Wigsell.—Local, ' of Wigsell,' 'anciently Wigsale, an estate in the parish of Salehurst, co. Sussex ' (Lower).

London, 1.

Wike.—Local, ' at the wike,' from residence therein. ' *Wike*, a home, a dwelling ' (Halliwell) ; v. Wykes.

William del Wik, or Wike, co. Kent, Hen. III–Edw. I. K.
Walter de la Wike, co. Bucks, 1273. A.
Henry de la Wyke, co. Oxf., ibid.
1777. Married—Robert Betterton and Mary Wike : St. Geo. Han. Sq. i. 273.
London, 1 ; Philadelphia, 1.

Wikman, Wigman, Wichman, Wickman.—Bapt. 'the son of Wigman' (v. Yonge, ii. 410).

' Haec nomina sunt eorum, et hic census per annum, Johannes xii denarios, Osbernus 18*d.*, Gualterus presbyter 8*d.*, ... Wikemanus, 10*d.*'(Norwich) : FF. iv. p. 430 *n.*
William Wygeman, co. Soms., 1 Edw. III : Kirby's Quest, p. 93.
Alex. Wigman, co. Northampton, 1273. A.
Alan Wichman, co. Suff., ibid.
Geoffry Wygeman, co. York, ibid.
1565. John Wickman, Ch. Ch. : Reg. Univ. Oxf. vol. ii. pt. ii. p. 12.
London, 1, 0, 0, 0 ; Philadelphia, 0, 1, 1, 0 ; New York, 0, 0, 2, 1.

Wilberforce.—Local, ' of Wilberfoss,' a parish in E. Rid. Yorks, five miles from Pocklington.

Robert de Wylberfosse, co. York, 1273. A.
Peter de Wilberfoss, *potter*, 4 Edw. II : Freemen of York, i. 13.
John de Wilberfosse, *potter*, 4 Ric. II : ibid. i. 78.
1586. Edward Wilberfosse and Ann Monioye, alias Mountioye : Marriage Lic. (London), i. 152.
London, 1 ; Crockford, 3.

Wilbraham.—Local, ' of Wilbraham,' a manor in co. Ches.

Richard de Wilburgham, of Wilburgham, 43 Hen. III : Shirley's Noble and Gentle Men, quoted by Lower.
William de Wilburgham, 1286 : Cal. of Patent Rolls, i. 239.
Randle de Wylberham, co. Ches. : East Ches. ii. 397.
1508. William Wylbram : Reg. Univ. Oxf. i. 59.
1572. Richard Wilbraham, of Worleston : Wills at Chester, i. 209.
1611. Thomas Wilbraham, of Woodhey : ibid.
1622. Married — Randoll Wilbraham and Martha Markham : St. Michael's, Cornhill, p. 23.
London, 3 ; Philadelphia, 13.

Wilby.—Local, ' of Wilby,' villages in cos. Norfolk, Suffolk, and Northampton.

Robert de Wyleby, co. Northampton, Hen. III–Edw. I. K.
Wigan de Wyleby, co. Leicester, ibid.
Juliana de Wylleby, co. Notts, 1273. A.
1577-8. Richard Wilbie and Emma Tailor : Marriage Lic. (London), i. 79.
1603. Thomas Wilbe, or Wilbee, or Wilbie, co. York : Reg. Univ. Oxf. vol. ii. pt. ii. p. 264.
1687. John Wilby (co. Kent) and Mary Putnume : Marriage Alleg. (Canterbury), ii. 41.
London, 1 ; Philadelphia, 7 ; Boston (U.S.), 2.

Wilcock, Wilcocke, Wilcocks, Wilcockson, Wilcox, Wilcoxon, Wilcoxen. — Bapt. ' the son of William,' from nick. Will, and suffix *-cock* (v. Cocks) ; cf. Jeffcock, Simcock, &c.

Wilecoc Rossel, co. Devon, 1273. A.
Ricardus Wilkokson, 1379 : P. T. Yorks. p. 266.
Adam Wylkokson, 1379 : ibid.
Radulfus Wylcok', 1379 : ibid. p. 145.
Willelmus Wilkocson, 1379 : ibid. p. 174.
1526-7. Lawrence Hillis and Wynefred Wylcoks : Marriage Lic. (London), i. 5.
1576. Bapt.—John, s. Robert Wylecockes : St. Michael, Cornhill, p. 89.
1617. William Wilcock, of Flixton : Wills at Chester, i. 209.
1666. Richard Wilcoxen (co. Ches.) and Eleanor Starkey : Marriage Lic. (Faculty Office), p. 93.
London, 3, 3, 2, 2, 24, 1, 0 ; Philadelphia, 4, 0, 0, 0, 53, 0, 0 ; New York, 1, 0, 0, 0, 39, 1, 1.

Wild, Wilde, Wyld, Wylde. —Nick. ' wild, violent, untamed.' It was a popular sobriquet in Yorkshire, judging by the 1379 Poll Tax and the present county directory.

Emma la Willde, co. Oxf., 1273. A.
Walter le Wilde, co. Suff., ibid.
William le Wilde, co. Hunts, ibid.
William le Wild, 1313. M.

Johannes Wylde, 1379 ; P. T. Yorks. p. 119 (common in this roll).
1660. Married— John Wray and Rachell Wylde : St. Dionis Backchurch, p. 36.
London, 40, 12, 3, 10 ; Sheffield, 28, 4, 0, 0 ; Philadelphia, 36, 38, 2, 0 ; Boston (U.S.), 29, 33, 0, 0.

Wildash, Wildish. — Local, ' at the wild ash,' from residence thereby ; cf. Ash, Nash, Birch, Rowntree, &c. The above seems to be the natural solution, but I have no proof.

1799. Married—Thomas Wildish and Mary Beale : St. Geo. Han. Sq. ii. 202.
1893. — Thomas Wildash and Hannah Beatson : Daily Telegraph, June 28, 1893.
London, 1, 4.

Wildblood.—Nick. 'an untamed spirit.' The earliest instance I can discover is met with in Yorkshire. The surname still remains there.

Richard Wyldeblode, co. Yorks. W. 9.
Leonard Wildblood, 1607 : St. Mary Aldermary, p. 11.
1607. Bapt.—Edward, s. Richard Wildbloud : St. Jas. Clerkenwell, i. 48.
1626. James Carr and Mary Wildbloud : Marriage Lic. (London), ii. 164.
1633. George Johnson and Susanna Sturt, with consent of mother, Susanna Wildblood : ibid. p. 216.
West Rid. Court Dir., 1.

Wildbore.—Nick. ' the wild boar'; cf. Wildgoose, Pigg, Hogg, Weatherhog, &c.

Willelmus Wyldebore, 1379 : P. T. Yorks. p. 193.
Johannes Wildebore, 1379 : ibid. p. 15.
Richard Wildbore, C. R., 35 Hen. VI.
1630. Married—Tobit Wildebore and Prissila Jonsonn : St. Antholin (London), p. 64.
1792. — Geo. Augustus Wildbore and Caroline Matilda Meadows : St. Geo. Han. Sq. ii. 76.
London, 2 ; West Rid. Court Dir., 1 ; Boston (U.S.), 1.

Wildern.—Local, ' at the wildern,' from residence in a wild, desert place, a wilderness ; v. Skeat on *wilderness*.

John atte-Wilderne, Fines Roll, 11 Edw. I.

Wilderspin ; v. Witherspoon.

Wildgoose.—Nick. ' the wildgoose,' from some characteristic resemblance to the habits of the bird.

Alicia Wyldguse, 1379 : P. T. Yorks. p. 172.
Robertus Wyldgose, *souter*, 1379 : ibid.

Simon Wildegose, C. R., 2 Ric. II.
1582-3. John Wylgose, co. Sussex: Reg. Univ. Oxf. vol. ii. pt. ii. p. 126.
1603. Buried — William Wildgoose, servant to William Pickering: St. Dionis Backchurch, p. 207.
1774. Married — John Wildgoose and Catherine Garvie: St. Geo. Han. Sq. i. 240.
Sheffield, 1.

Wildish; v. Wildash.

Wildman.—Nick. 'wild man.' In this case it is merely the familiar nickname Wild, with an augmentative -*man*; cf. Merry and Merriman.

John Wildeman, C. R., 18 Ric. II.
Willelmus Wyldman, 1379 : P. T. Yorks. p. 286.
1748. Married—Thomas Wissett and Ann Wildman: St. Michael, Cornhill, p. 71.
London, 1 ; West Riding Court Dir., 1 ; Leeds, 3 ; Philadelphia, 8 ; New York, 1.

Wildsmith, Wyldsmith. — Occup. I cannot discover an early instance. I do not know the origin. My first example is Woolsmith, but that seems as hard of solution as the rest. Nevertheless, as the surname is almost entirely confined to Yorkshire, the centre of the woollen trade, some connexion may exist.

John Wollesmyth, C. R., 32 Hen. VI.
1659. Married—Afery Welsmith, Canterbury Cath. p. 59.
1787. Married—Joshua Jones and Anne Wilesmith: St. Geo. Han. Sq. i. 398.
London, 1, 0 ; West Rid. Court Dir., 3, 0 ; Sheffield, 1, 1 ; Leeds, 1, 0.

Wileman; v. Willman.

Wiley; v. Wylie.

Wilford.—Local, 'of Wilford,' alias 'Wilfrid's-Ford,' a parish in co. Notts.

Henry de Wylleford, co. Notts, 1273. A.
Gervase de Wyleford, co. Notts, Hen. III–Edw. I. K.
Thomas de Wilford, co. Notts, 20 Edw. I. R.
1555. Christopher Wilford and Frances Jackes: Marriage Lic. (London), i. 16.
1559. Married—Thomas Wylforde and Eliz. Hawes: St. Michael, Cornhill, p. 7.
1584. Robert Wylforde, co. Kent: Reg. Univ. Oxf. vol. ii. pt. ii. p. 134.
London, 1 ; Philadelphia, 2 ; New York, 6.

Wilful.—Nick. 'the wilful,' the obstinate.

William le Wilfulle, co. Wilts, 1273. A.

Wilkerson, Wickerson.— Bapt. 'the son of William,' corruptions of Wilkinson (v. Wilkin); cf. Dickerson for Dickinson, Catterson for Cattinson, &c.

1782. Married — Robert Girling and Ann Wilkerson: St. Geo. Han. Sq. i. 341.
London, 1, 0 ; New York, 1, 0 ; Boston (U.S.), 1, 0.

Wilkes, Wilks.—Bapt. 'the son of William,' from nick. Will, and dim. Wil-kin (v. Wilkin); a corruption of Wilkins through Wilkiss or Wilkess. Cf. Perks and Perkes for Perkins, Dawks and Dawkes for Dawkins, &c. So early as the 14th century we find Wilkson for Wilkinson.

Thomas Wylkson, 1379 : P. T. Yorks. p. 144.
Johannes Wylkson, 1379 : ibid.
1574. Robert Wylkes, co. Northampt.: Reg. Univ. Oxf. vol. ii. pt. ii. p. 58.
1632. Bapt. — Dennys, d. Richard Wilkes : St. Jas. Clerkenwell, p. 121.
1737. Married—Henry Wilks and Mary Crafts: St. Geo. Han. Sq. i. 18.
London, 19, 16 ; Philadelphia, 2, 7 ; New York, 3, 5.

Wilkey, Wilkie.—Bapt. 'the son of William,' a pet form of Wilkin, q.v. We also find Wilkison for Wilkinson.

1663-4. Buried—Susanna, wife of James Wilkey : St. Dionis Backchurch (London), p. 234.
1756. Married—Alex. Wylkie and Mary Francis : St. Geo. Han. Sq. i. 62.
1788. Married — James Forward and Sarah Wilkison : ibid. ii. 15.
London, 1, 12 ; Philadelphia, 3, 9 ; New York, 2, 7.

Wilkin, Wilkins, Wilkinson.—Bapt. 'the son of William,' from nick. Will, and dim. *kin* (v. *kin*, Introd. p. 25) ; cf. Wat-kin, Tomp-kin.

Wilechin fil. Monetarii, 1167: KKK. vi. 11.
Willekin de Laurecost, 1196: RRR. p. 78.
Ralph Wylekin, co. Norf., Hen. III–Edw. I. K.
Amice Wylekun, co. Sussex, ibid.
Wilekin fil. Austen. C.
Wilkin le Furmager. O.
Thomas Wylkynson, 1379 : P. T. Yorks. p. 145.
Adam Wylkynson, 1379 : ibid. p. 89.
Matilda Wylkyn, *doghter*, 1379 : P. T. Yorks. p. 99.
London, 11, 64, 122 ; Philadelphia, 0, 86, 157 ; Boston (U.S.), 1, 64, 55.

Wilks; v. Wilkes.

Wilkshire.—Local, a corruption of Wiltshire, q.v.

Boston (U.S.), 2.

Will.—(1) Local, 'at the well,' from residence thereby. This form occurs with fair frequency in Kirby's Quest. (2) Bapt. 'the son of Will,' gen. Wills ; v. Willis.

William atte Wille, co. Soms., 1 Edw. III : Kirby's Quest. p. 261.
1743. Married—John Will and Patience Gardener : St. Geo. Han. Sq. i. 30.
London, 3 ; Philadelphia, 18 ; Boston (U.S.), 3.

Willan, Willans.—Bapt. 'the son of William,' from nick. Will, and dim. Will-in, corrupted in the North to the familiar Willan (v. Willin); cf. *violin*, a little viol, or Colin, little Cole (Nicholas).

1584. William Willeyne, co. Westm.: Reg. Univ. Oxf. vol. ii. pt. ii. p. 137.
Rychard Willen, 1602, Hackthorp: Hist. Westm. and Cumb. i. 97.
Christopher Wyllen, 1602, Hackthorp: ibid.
1678. Married — Geffrey Willan and Judeth Fawcett : St. Dionis Backchurch, p. 39.
London, 3, 3 ; West Rid. Court Dir., 3, 3 ; Philadelphia, 0, 5 ; New York, 0, 1.

Willard, Wellard.—Bapt. 'the son of Willihard' (Yonge, ii. 227). Although not confined to Kent, that is the district in which the surname is chiefly found.

Wihelardus de Trophil, 1168: KKK. vi. 202.
Wilard de Pikeden, 1227: ibid. vi. 150.
Emayn Wylard, 1379: P. T. Yorks. p. 294.
1602. William Willarde, co. Kent: Reg. Univ. Oxf. vol. ii. pt. ii. p. 258.
1690-1. Nicholas Willard (co. Sussex) and Jane Coumber: Marriage Alleg. (Canterbury), ii. 175.
1750. Married—Sarah Willard : Reg. Canterbury Cath.
London, 2, 2 ; Philadelphia, 42, 0 ; Boston (U.S.), 63, 0.

Willets, Willett, Willetts, Willet. — Bapt. 'the son of William,' from the nick. Will, and dim. Will-et or Will-ot ; v. Gillott.

Richard Wylyot, co. Norf., 1273. A.
John Wylot (co. Soms.), c. 1300. M.
Thomas Wiliot. J.
Thomas Wylott. F.
John Wilot, co. Soms., 1 Edw. III : Kirby's Quest, p. 264.
1586. Buried, the wife of John Willet : St. Thomas the Apostle (London), p. 97.
1764. Married—George Avery and Eliz. Willett : St. Geo. Han. Sq. i. 138.

London, 1, 20, 2, 0; Manchester, 0, 6, 0, 0; Philadelphia, 5, 8, 5, 2; New York, 24, 17, 1, 3.

Willey.—(1) Local; v. Wylie. (2) Bapt.; v. Willy.

Willgoose.—A corruption of Wildgoose, q.v.

'Her bridesmaids, Miss Willgoose, Miss Leatherbarrow, . . . wore pretty costumes of cream colour': The Southport Visitor, Aug. 4, 1888.

Williams, Williamson, Willyams, William.—Bapt. 'the son of William.' For nearly eight centuries William and John have raced for first place in popularity. Legion is the name of their offspring, and to furnish instances would be absurd.

Johannes fil. Willelmi, 1379: P. T. Yorks. p. 144.
Hugo Williamson, 1379: ibid.
London, 464, 58, 1, 0; Philadelphia, 944, 154, 0, 8.

Willicombe; v. Welcome.

Willie; v. Willy.

Willimott; v. Wilmot.

Willin, Willing, Willings, Willinson, Willins, Wyling.—Bapt. 'the son of William,' from nick. Will, dim. Will-in (v. Willan). The *g* in Willing, &c., is excrescent, as in Jennings or Wareing.

Cecilia Wylyn, 1379: P. T. Yorks. p. 266.
Ricardus Wylyn, 1379: ibid.
Johannes Willion, 1379: ibid. p. 268.
1578-9. John Willins, co. Cardigan: Reg. Univ. Oxf. vol. ii. pt. ii. p. 86.
1704. Henry Willinson, of Docker: Lancashire Wills at Richmond, p. 283.
1750. Married—Frederic Willing and Eliz. Franklin: St. Geo. Chap. Mayfair, p. 161.
London, 1, 3, 2, 0, 0, 0; Philadelphia, 0, 8, 2, 0, 0, 1; New York, 0, 0, 5, 1, 0, 1, 0.

Willis, Willison, Wills, Willies, Williss.—Bapt. 'the son of William,' from the nick. Will, Willy, or Willie. The final *s* represents the patronymic, as in the case of Williams, Jones, &c.

Johannes Willeson, 1379: P. T. Yorks. p. 231.
Willelmus Willeson, 1379: ibid. p. 62.
Adam Wylis, 1379: ibid. p. 174.
Robert Wylis. F.
Henry Wyllys, or Wylles, 1508: Reg. Univ. Oxf. i. 65.
1579. Bapt.—William, s. Henrie Willison: St. Mary Aldermary, p. 59.

1795. Married—Henry Willis and Sarah Linden: St. Geo. Han. Sq. ii. 140.
London, 82, 1, 36, 1, 0; West Rid. Court Dir., 11, 0, 1, 0, 2; Philadelphia, 59, 1, 61, 0, 0; New York, 68, 0, 13, 0, 0.

Willmer, Willmore, Wilmer, Wilmore, Willmire.—Bapt.' the son of Wilmar' (Yonge, ii. 227).

Roger fil. Wilmer, co. Notts, 1273. A.
Nicholas Wilmar, co. Hunts, ibid.
Peter Wlmar, co. Camb., ibid.
1689. Bapt. — Edward Wilmore: St. John Bapt. on Wallbrook.
1730. Buried—John Willmore: St. Mary Aldermary (London), p. 221.
1806. Married—Matthew Willmer and Ann Warner: St. Geo. Han. Sq. ii. 357.
London, 3, 3, 0, 0, 0; Philadelphia, 0, 1, 20, 1, 1; New York, 2, 0, 4, 2, 0.

Willoughby.—Local, ' of Willoughby,' parishes in cos. Lincoln, Warwick, Notts, and Leicester.

Robert de Wylugheby, co. Linc., Hen. III-Edw. I. K.
Henry de Wiluby, co. Bucks, 1273. A.
William de Wilughby, co. Northampt., 20 Edw. I. R.
Richard de Willughby, co. Notts, ibid.
Robert de Willughby, co. Derby, ibid.
1582. Edward Willoughbey, co. Linc.: Reg. Univ. Oxf. vol. ii. pt. ii. p. 119.
1591. Henry Willughby, or Willabie, co. Wilts: ibid. p. 187.
1620. Bapt. — Ann, d. John Willobie: St. Michael, Cornhill, p. 115.
London, 15; Philadelphia, 7; Boston (U.S.), 10.

Willows.—Local, ' at the willows,' one who lived by a clump or stretch of willow trees.

Johannes atte Wylowes, 1379: P. T. Howdenshire, p. 16.
1579. William Willowes and Mary Westwoode: Marriage Lic. (London), i. 93.
1803. Married—Charles Willows and Eliz. Alderson: St. Geo. Han. Sq. ii. 281. London, 2.

Wills; v. Willis.

Willsher, Willshire.—Local. From Wiltshire, q.v.

London, 5, 1.

Willson; v. Wilson.

Willy, Willie, Willey.—(1) Bapt. 'the son of William,' from nick. Will, popularly Willy (v. Willis).

Thomas Wyly, 1379: P. T. Yorks. p. 150.

(2) Local; v. Wylie.

1586. Bapt.—Mary Willy, daughter of Richard Willye: St. Peter, Cornhill, i. 30.
1614. Thomas Williams and Eliz.

Willey: Marriage Lic. (Westminster), p. 22.
London, 6, 1, 11; West Rid. Court Dir., 0, 0, 7; Philadelphia, 0, 4, 0; New York, 0, 2, 8.

Wilman, Wileman, Willman.—Occup. 'Will-man,' i.e. the servant of Will; cf. Matthewman, Addiman, Harriman, Ladyman, Vickerman, &c. Nearly all this class of surnames hails from Yorkshire.

Adam Willeman, 1379: P. T. Yorks. p. 171.

The first three following dwelt in the village of Harewood.

Willelmus Thome-man, 1379: P. T. Yorks. p. 213.
Thomas Jon-man, 1379: ibid.
Walterus Wilman, 1379: ibid.
Simon Willeman, co. Camb., 1273. A.
1563. Married—Harry Willman and Alis Worship: St. Antholin (London), p.15.
1753. Married—William Willman and Eliz. Jackson: St. Geo. Chap. Mayfair, p. 266.
London, 0, 2, 1; West Rid. Court Dir., 4, 0, 0; Philadelphia, 2, 0, 1; New York, 0, 2, 0.

Wilmer v. Willmer.

Wilmington.—Local, 'of Wilmington,' parishes in cos. Kent and Sussex.

Stephen de Wilminton, co. Kent, Hen. III-Edw. I. K.
Robert de Wilmiton, co. Kent, ibid.
Jacob de Wylmingtun, co. Kent, 1273. A.
1599. John Willmington, co. Soms.: Reg. Univ. Oxf. vol. ii. pt. ii. p. 234.
London, 1; Philadelphia, 2; Boston (U.S.), 1.

Wilmot, Wilmott, Willimott.— Bapt. 'the son of William,' from dim. William-ot, used for both sexes. It existed in Cornwall as a girl's name till the close of the last century.

Williametta Cantatrix. E.
Gwillimett (without surname). E.
Gilemota Carrecke, co. York. W. 2.
Henry Wilmot, co. Camb., 1273. A.
Wylymot Swynhird, 1379: P. T. Yorks. p. 256.
Matilda Wylymot, 1379: ibid. p. 116.
1579. Hugh Wyllymott, of Knutsford, co. Ches.: East Cheshire, i. 309.
1583. Bapt. — John, son of Wyllmott Scobeld: Reg. St. Columb Major, p. 12.
1592. — Willmott, daughter of Robert Edwardes: St. Jas. Clerkenwell, p. 26.
1613. — Symon, s. Symon Willimott, *vintner*: St. Peter, Cornhill, i. 62.

1631. Bapt. — Wilmote, d. Patient Wilmote : Reg. St. Columb Major, p. 213.
London, 11, 3, 1 ; Philadelphia, 4, 1, 0 ; Boston (U.S.), 7, 0, 0.

Wilsher.—Local. From Wiltshire, q.v.
1653. Married—John Cane and Marye Wilshire : St. Michael, Cornhill, p. 31.
London, 5.

Wilson, Willson.—Bapt. 'the son of William,' from nick. Will. This surname rivals, in the multitude of its representatives, the famous patronymics Johnson, Jackson, Robinson, and Dickson or Dixon ; v. Willis.
Adam Wyllson, 1379 : P. T. Yorks. p. 279.
Thomas Wyllson, 1379 : ibid.
1604. Edw. Willson, or Wilson, co. Lanc. : Reg. Univ. Oxf. vol. ii. pt. ii. p.272.
London, 321, 32 ; Philadelphia, 930, 6.

Wilthew.—Bapt. ; v. Waldy, an undoubted descendant of Walthew or Waldew.
Newcastle-on-Tyne, 2.

Wilton.—Local, 'of Wilton,' a parish and borough in co. Wilts, on the river Wily, whence its name.
Margery de Wiliton, co. Berks, 1273. A.
Ralph de Wylyton, co. Wilts, ibid.
Ralph de Wyliton, co. Glouc., Hen. III-Edw. I. K.
Simon de Wiltone, co. Soms., 1 Edw. III : Kirby's Quest, p. 194.
1591. Bapt.—Mary, d. George Wilton : St. Jas. Clerkenwell, i. 25.
1751. Married—William Wilton and Mary Pearson : St. Geo. Han. Sq. i. 46.
London, 9 ; MDB. (co. Soms.), 10 ; Boston (U.S.), 10.

Wiltshire, Wiltsheare, Wiltsher, Wiltshier, Wiltshear.—Local, 'from Wiltshire.' This surname has now many forms ; v. Willsher, Wilsher, &c.; cf. Darbyshire, Cheshire, Kentish, Cornish, &c.
Hunfridus de Wilechier, 7 Hen. II : Pipe Roll, iv. 13.
Michael de Wyltesire, co. Camb., 1273. A.
William de Wyltesyre, co. Soms., ibid.
Roger de Wilteschire, co. Salop, ibid.
Almaric de Wilteshire, 1313. M.
Richard Wilteshire. B.
John Wiltsheere, 1680 : Reg. St. Mary Aldermary (London), p. 105.
1794. Married—William Wiltshire and Ann Hazell : St. Geo. Han. Sq. ii. 109.
1798. — Isaac Wiltshear and Sarah Dalloway : ibid. p. 184.

London, 19, 1, 1, 1, 0 ; MDB. (co. Oxford), 0, 0, 0, 0, 1 ; Philadelphia, 4, 0, 0, 0, 0 ; New York, 3, 0, 0, 0, 0.

Wimble.—Local, 'of Wymbhull.' I cannot find the spot. The suffix is -hill (v. Hull). It is quite natural to find the surname drop into the form of Wimble. Such modifications are common ; cf. Cockle, Windle, &c.
Roger de Wymbhull, co. Bedf., Hen. III-Edw. I. K.
Probably Wimple is a variant. It is found in the same district as the above.
1690. Thomas Foster and Mary Wimple (co. Essex) : Marriage Alleg. (Canterbury), ii. 163.
1789. Married—James Wimble and Martha Challand : St. Geo. Han. Sq. ii. 34.
London, 4.

Wimbush, Winbush.—Local, 'of Wimbush,' a parish in dioc. of St. Alban's, co. Essex.
Thomas de Winebise, co. Leic., Hen. III-Edw. I. K.
John de Wymbisse, co. Camb., 1273. A.
John Wimbis, co. Essex, ibid.
Simon de Wymbisse, co. Essex, ibid.
The modern corruption was early anticipated in the following entry :
John Wymbusch, Patent Roll, 1 Hen. VI. pt. v.
London, 1, 1 ; Philadelphia, 0, 1.

Wimer; v. Wymer.

Wimpler. — Occupative, ' the wimpler,' a maker of wimples.
'Full seemly her wimple pinched was.'
Chaucer, C. T. 151.
Of Shame :
' Humble of her port, and made it simple, Wearing a vaile, instede of wimple, As nuns done in their abbey.'
id. R. Rose, 3863-5.
Alan le Wympler : Wardrobe Account, 49 Hen. III. 1/31.
Henry le Wimpler, co. Hunts, 1273. A.
William le Wimpler, C. R., 34 Hen. III.
William le Wympler. N.

Wimplester. — Occup. ' the wimplester,' a curious feminine of Wimpler. The only instance I have met with is that below ; cf. Slaster for Slater, or Walkster for Walker in the same county.
Crystiana Wympylster, 1379 : P. T. Howdenshire, p. 3.

Wimpory ; v. Winpenny.

Winbolt.—Bapt. ' the son of Winibald ' (v. Yonge, ii. 224).

Hence such place-names as Wimbledon, anciently written Wymbaldon, i.e. the dune or down of Wimbald, or Wimbald ; or Wimbotsham, a parish in co. Norf., i.e. the ham of Wimbot ; cf.
1618. Ellen Whishall, widow, of Wimbolsley (i. e. the meadow of Wimbald) : Wills at Chester, i. 205.
William Wernbald, co. Camb., 1273. A.
Matilda Weribold, co. Camb., ibid.
Wynebold de Balon gave half a hide to St. Peter of Glouc. in 1126 : Atkyns' Hist. of Glouc. p. 71.
1628. Married—Steeven Winnibote and Alis Eshbeach : St. Antholin (London), p. 62.
1795. — John Marscott and Rebekah Winboult : St. Geo. Han. Sq. ii. 132.
1746. — Edward Stallard and Eliz. Winbolt : St. Dionis Backchurch, p. 69.
Winbolt is now the accepted form. With this variant cf. Newbolt for Newbold.
London, 1.

Winbush ; v. Wimbush.

Winch.—(1) Local, 'of Winch.' There are two parishes in Norfolk of this name, viz. East and West Winch.
Peter de Winch, vicar of Ameringhall, co. Norf., 1382 : FF. v. 419.
(2) Local, ' at the winch,' from residence beside some particular windlass for drawing water from a deep well, &c.
Thomas atte Wynch, 19 Edw. I : BBB. p. 434.
1628. Bapt.—Nathaniell, d. William Winch, grocer : St. Peter, Cornhill, i. 78.
1752. Buried—Ann Winch, in the churchyard : St. Michael, Cornhill, p. 300.
It is probable that (1) has furnished us with most of our Winches.
London, 16 ; MDB. (Norfolk), 2 ; Philadelphia, 6 ; Boston (U.S.), 14.

Winchester.—Local, ' of Winchester,' a city in co. Hants.
Ralph de Wincestre, co. Norf., 1273. A.
Nicholas Winchestre, co. Suff., ibid.
John de Wynchestre, piscarius, 7 Edw. II : Freemen of York, i. 15.
Robertus Wynchester, 1379 : P. T. Yorks. p. 91.
1724. Bapt.—John, son of John Winchester : St. Jas. Clerkenwell, p. 151.
1804. Married—James Winchester and Eliz. Edge : St. Geo. Han. Sq. ii. 312.
London, 5 ; Oxford, 4 ; Philadelphia, 18 ; Boston (U.S.), 21.

Winckle ; v. Winkle.

Wincott, Winnicott.—? Bapt. 'the son of Wingod.' The name looks local, but I find no spot of that shape or form, while Wynegod was early turned into a surname, and its inevitable corruption would be Wincot. Nevertheless, on the face of it the origin would seem to be local.

Robert Wynegod, co. Oxf., 1273. A.
William Wynegod, co. Soms., ibid.
1582-3. Charles Wincote, co. Warw.: Reg. Univ. Oxf. vol. ii. pt. ii. p. 125.
1590. William Wyncott, co. Warw.: ibid. p. 180.
1761. Married—John Dipple and Sarah Wincote: St. Geo. Han. Sq. i. 102.
London, 2, 1.

Windebank. — Local, ' of Windebank,' probably from residence 'at the windy bank.' Many small spots would naturally bear this name; cf. Swithenbank, Brooksbank, &c.

Nan of Windebank, 1422, Ashton-under-Lyne: Custom Roll and Rental, Cheth. Soc.
1599. Francis Windebank, or Wyndebancke, London: Reg. Univ. Oxf. vol. ii. pt. ii. p. 234.
1686. Sir Francis Windebanke, Bart., and Eliz. Parkhurst: Marriage Lic. (Faculty Office), p. 179.
1792. Married—Ottewell Timmess and Sarah Windebank: St.Geo. Han. Sq.ii.85.
London, 1.

Windel(1; v. Windle.

Winder.—Local, (1) 'of Winder,' a township in parish of Lamplugh, co. Cumb.; (2) Low Winder, a township in parish of Barton, co. Westm.; (3) High Winder, near Carnforth, North Lanc. There can be no doubt as to the local origin of the Cumberland and North Lancashire Winders. The home of the latter is High Winder.

Thomas Winder, of Hygh Winder, 1616: Lancashire Wills at Richmond, p. 318.
Christopher Winder, of Hye Winder, 1618: ibid. p. 317.
Elizabeth Winder, of High Winder, 1676: ibid.
1604. Samuel Winder, co. Berks: Reg. Univ. Oxf. vol. ii. pt. ii. p. 278.
1736. Bapt.—Sarah, d. Michael Winder: St. Jas. Clerkenwell, ii. 230.
London, 7; Lancaster, 1; Ulverston, 1; Philadelphia, 5; New York, 3.

Windhouse; v. Windus.

Windle, Windell, Windel.—Local, ' of Windhill,' a hamlet in the township of Idle, co. York. The tendency of the suffix -hill is to become -le; cf. Cockle, Wimble, &c. Also ' of Windle,' a township in the parish of Prescot, co. Lanc.

Willelmus de Wyndhill, 1379: P. T. Yorks. p. 55.
Johannes de Wyndhill, 1379: ibid.
1577. Christopher Windle, co. York: Reg. Univ. Oxf. vol. ii. pt. ii. p. 79.
1607. George Rowley and Margaret Windle: Marriage Lic. (London), i. 301.
1684. William Cooper and Isabel Windell: Marriage Alleg. (Canterbury), p. 166.
1726. Bapt.—Mary, d. George Windall: St. Jas. Clerkenwell, ii. 159.
London, 6, 2, 0; Philadelphia, 12, 2, 0; New York, 0, 0, 1.

Windmill. — Local, 'at the windmill,' from residence thereby, a miller.

1683. Buried—Richard Windmill: St. Mary Aldermary, p. 195.
1779. Married—William Windmill and Mary Elsley: St. Geo. Han. Sq. i. 299.
MDB. (co. Soms.), 4.

Windmiller, Winemiller.—Occup. 'the wind-miller.' I do not think this is English. I find no traces of it. But v. Windmillward.

Philadelphia, 1, 0; Boston (U.S.), 0, 1.

Windmillward.—Offic. 'the custodian of a windmill'; v. Millward.

William Wyndmilward. D.

Windows.—Local; v. Windus.

Oxford, 2.

Windross.—Local, 'of Winderhouse.' The local term winder is common in North Lancashire; v. Winder.

Nicholas Winderhouse, of Tarniker, 1672: Lancashire Wills at Richmond, i. 318.
George Windresse, of Bispham, 1661: ibid.
William Windress, of Lower Wyersdales, 1678: ibid.
Robert Windrass, of Lytham, 1707: ibid. ii. 287.
Manchester, 1.

Windsor.—Local,'of Windsor,' a parish, borough, and market-town, co. Berks, anciently Windleshora, said to have arisen from the winding course of the Thames.

Hugh de Windelsor, London, 1273. A.
John de Wyndesoure, co. Oxf., ibid.
1564-5. Miles Wyndser, Corp. Christi Coll.: Reg. Univ. Oxf. vol. ii. pt. ii. p. 15.

1620. Buried—Dorothy, d. Henry Windsore: St. Jas. Clerkenwell, iv. 149.
1734. Married— — Windsor and Eliz. Perkins: St. Geo. Han. Sq. i. 14.
London, 10; Philadelphia, 2; Boston (U.S.), 3.

Windus, Windhouse.—Local, ' of the wind-house,' probably a place for winding threads; v. Windross. With the suffix -us for house, cf. Loftus, Kirkus, Bacchus.

Willelmus de Wyndhows, 1379: P. T. Yorks. p. 275.
1674. Robert Dowling and Frances Windowes: Marriage Alleg. (Canterbury), p. 120.
1692. Married—Arthur Windus and Mary Soloman: St. Jas. Clerkenwell, iii. 211.
London, 2, 0; New York, 0, 1.

Winfarthing. — Local, ' of Winfarthing,' a parish in Norfolk.

Thomas de Wynneferthyn, co. Camb., 1273. A.
Walter de Wynneferthing, Close Roll, 5 Edw. I.
Robert de Winfarthing, rector of Bergh-Apton, 1342: FF. x. 99.

Winfield. — Local, ' of Winfield,' a township in the parish of Wrotham, co. Kent. Occasionally this surname represents Wingfield, q.v.

Richard de Winfeld, co. Northumb., 1273. A.
1773. Married — Joseph Winfield and Mary Nickolls: St. Geo. Han. Sq. i. 229.
1788. — James Wynfield and Eliz. Adams: ibid. ii. 12.
MDB. (co. Kent), 1; (co. Derby), 3; London, 3; New York, 4; Boston(U.S.),6.

Wing. — Local, ' of Wing,' parishes in cos. Rutland and Bucks. It is found at an early period in the district.

Geoffrey Wenge, co. Hunts, 1273. A.
William Wenge, co. Hunts, ibid.
1599. John Wynge, co. Oxf.: Reg. Univ. Oxf. vol. ii. pt. ii. p. 235.
1621. Matthew Winge, co. Oxf., ibid. p. 402.
1626. Married — Richard Gwynn and Dyonis Winge: St. Jas. Clerkenwell, iii. 56.
London, 11; MDB. (co. Oxf.), 3; (co. Bedford), 3; Philadelphia, 5; New York, 23.

Wingate, Winget.—(1)? Bapt. 'the son of Wingod' (?). This might be easily corrupted to Wingate. Both prefix and suffix are common ingredients in early personal names; cf. Baldwin, Selwin, Oswin, Unwin, and Osgood, Thoroughgood, &c. Wingod is simply Godwin reversed.

John Wynegod, co. Oxf., 1273. A.
Robert Wynegod, co. Oxf., ibid.
William Wynegod, co. Soms., ibid.
1776. Married — Charles Nevill and Mary Wingod: St. Geo. Han. Sq. i. 269.

(2) Local, 'of Wingate,' a township in the parish of Kelloe, co. Durham.

John de Wyngate, co. Kent, Hen. III–Edw. I. K.
1672. Married—Sir Francis Wingate, Kt., and Ann Fish: St. Mary Aldermary, p. 31.

(1) needs more confirmatory evidence before it can be accepted.

London, 2, 1; Philadelphia, 11, 0; Boston (U.S.), 4, 0.

Wingfield.—Local, 'of Wingfield,' parishes in cos. Suffolk and Derby (2). Winfield is the present form in Derbyshire of this local surname; v. Winfield.

1674. Buried — Edward Wingfeild, Esq., under the gallery: Kensington Parish Church, p. 146.
1703. Married—Henry Wingfeild and Mary Bunby: St. Mary Aldermary, p. 37.
London, 14; New York, 1.

Wingham.—Local, 'of Wingham,' a parish nine miles from Canterbury, co. Kent. From the evidence below it would seem that other spots were so called.

Henry de Wyngeham, co. Kent, 1273. A.
Henry de Wingham, co. Linc., ibid.
Walter de Wingham, co. Som., ibid.
William de Wingham, co. Wilts, ibid.
William de Wingham, co. Surrey, 20 Edw. I. K.
Hugh de Wyngeham, co. Soms., Hen. III–Edw. I. K.
1616. Arthur Wingham, London: Reg. Univ. Oxf. vol. ii. pt. ii. p. 356.
1618. Roger Bragg and Mary Wingham: Marriage Lic. (London), ii. 66.
London, 3; New York, 1.

Winkfield.—Local, 'of Winkfield,' parishes in co. Berks and co. Wilts.

1558. Bapt. — Ellen Winckefeeld, daughter: St. Peter, Cornhill, i. 8.
London, 2; Manchester, 2.

Winkle, Winckle, Winkel.—(1) Local, 'of Wincle,' a township near Macclesfield, on the extreme border of Cheshire, only separated from Staffordshire by the river Dane. It is called 'Winchul,'

c. 1200 (East Cheshire, ii. 432), so we may presume that -hill is the suffix; cf. Windle, Cockle, &c.

1565. Richard Winkle: Reg. Univ. Oxf. i. 424.
Jane Winckle of Leyland, husbandman, 1635: Wills at Chester (1621-50), p. 239.
1675. James Clowse and Mary Winckle: Marriage Alleg. (Canterbury), ii. 143.
1779. Married — John Grange and Mary Winkell: St. Mary Aldermary, i. 298.

(2) Nick. 'the winkle,' the periwinkle. I do not suppose this bears any relation to our present Winkles, but it is worth while recording the following entry:

John le Wenchel, co. Bucks, 1273. A.
Manchester, 1, 0, 0; Liverpool, 0, 1, 0; New York, 5, 2, 0; Philadelphia, 2, 3, 0.

Winkley. — Local, (1) 'of Winkley,' or Winckleigh, a parish in co. Devon; (2) 'of Winckley,' a hall and estate in the township of Aighton, and parish of Mitton, co. Lanc. Hence the Lancashire surname. 'In the Coucher Book of the neighbouring abbey of Whalley, the name of Robert de Wynkedelegh occurs in 4 Edw. I' (Lower's Patr. Brit. p. 385).

Michael de Wynklegh, co. Devon, 1273. A.
Richard de Wynklegh, co. Devon, ibid.
Michael de Wynkeleg, co. Devon, Hen. III–Edw. I. K.
1677-8. William Winckley and Magdalen Taylor: Marriage Alleg. (Canterbury), ii. 215.
Francis Winckley, of Preston, 1746: Lancashire Wills at Richmond (1681-1748), p. 286.
Thomas Winckley, of Preston, 1714: ibid.
1807. Married—Thomas Winkley and Eliz. Watson: St. Geo. Han. Sq. ii. 375.
London, 3; Manchester, 1; Boston (U.S.), 12.

Winks, Wink.—? Bapt. 'the son of Wink' (?). This surname is firmly established in co. York; cf. Winkfield and Winkley.

Ricardus Wynk', 1379: P. T. Yorks. p. 4.
Alexander Wynk, 1379: ibid. p. 163.
Robertus Wynk, 1379: ibid.
1587. Richard Wyncke and Johanna Bonner: Marriage Lic. (London), i. 161.
1727. Married—Robert Kyll and Margaret Wincks: St. Jas. Clerkenwell, iii. 254.
West Rid. Court Dir., 3, 0; Sheffield, 3, 0; London, 3, 0.

Winn(e.—Nick.; v. Wynn.

Winnicott; v. Wincott.

Winpenny, Wimpeny, Wimpery, Wimpory.—? Nick. 'Winpenny' (cf. Pennyfather). Perhaps what it looks, 'Win-penny,' a sobriquet for one of 'acquisitive habits.' But the entry

John Vympany: Pat. Roll, 3 Edw. VI. pt. iii.

which manifestly is the same name, seems a somewhat early contradiction of this view. In any case, Wimpory appears to be a corruption.

Henry Winpenny, bailiff of Bristol, 1316: Barrett's Hist. Bristol.
William Wynpeny, co. York, 1468. W. 11.
1794. Married — William Cross and Sarah Winpenny: St. Geo. Han. Sq. ii. 6.
Manchester, 2, 0, 0, 2; Philadelphia, 6, 0, 0, 0; New York, 1, 0, 0, 0.

Winrow.—Local; v. Whineray.

Winscombe.—Local, 'of Winscombe,' a parish in co. Somerset, two miles from Axbridge.

William Wynscombe, co. Soms., 9 Edw. II: Kirby's Quest, p. 134.
MDB. (co. Soms.), 2.

Winser, Winsor.—Local, 'of Windsor,' a natural modification; v. Windsor.

1605. Married — Griffith Evan and Ann Winsor: St. Mary Aldermary (London), p. 11.
Robert Masone, of Winsore, 1626: ibid. p. 16.
1794. — Joseph Winsor and Mary Miller: St. Geo. Han. Sq. ii. 106.
London, 5, 6; Philadelphia, 0, 4; Boston (U.S.), 0, 25.

Winsome. — Nick. 'the winsome,' attractive, lovely. M.E. winsom.

Matilda Wensom, co. Hunts, 1273. A.

Winstanley.—Local, 'of Winstanley,' a township in the parish of Wigan, co. Lanc.

Roger de Winstanleg', temp. John: Baines' Lanc. ii. 189.
1555. James Winstanley, of Winstanley: Wills at Chester (1545-1620), p. 212.
1603. Edward Winstanley, of Woodhouses, Wigan: ibid.
1575. Married — Thomas Porte and Margaret Wynstanley: St. Michael, Cornhill, p. 11.
Manchester, 8; London, 6; Philadelphia, 2.

Winston, Winstone, Winson.—Local, 'of Winston': (1)

a hamlet near Barnard Castle, co. Durham; (2) a hamlet near Debenham, co. Suffolk; (3) a hamlet near Cirencester, co. Gloucester. The variant Winson is fairly familiar. In a similar way Kelson is a modification of Kelston.

John de Wynston, co. Kent, 1273. A.
William de Wynestone, co. Suff., ibid.
Adam de Wynestone, co. Hunts, ibid.
Thomas Wynston, 1379: P. T. Howden-shire, p. 27.
1651. Married — William Smith and Anne Winston: St. Dionis Backchurch, p. 27.
1657. Buried — Francis, wife of Edmond Browne, from Mr. Winstons: St. Mary Aldermary, p. 180.
1790. — John Winson and Maria Allison: St. Geo. Han. Sq. ii. 41.
London, 0, 5, 0; Philadelphia, 7, 0, 3; Boston (U.S.), 10, 0, 0.

Winter, Wynter.—Bapt. 'the son of Winter.' The ecclesiastical seasons all made their mark on the font; cf. Pentecost, Whitsunday, Noel, Nowell, Christmas, Middlemass (Michaelmas). The natural seasons gave personal names in the same way. 'Summer and Winter are both ancient names; in the *Cod. Dip. Alamannioe* there are two brothers called respectively Sumar and Winter, A.D. 858.' Winter was also the name of one of the companions of Hereward the Saxon' (Ferguson, Surnames as a Science, p. 182). Although a pre - Norman personal name, Winter survived the Conquest, and attained hereditary honours as a surname in the 13th cent. We may observe here that Winter is compounded with several local surnames, such as Wintersgill, Winterbotham, Winterburn, or Winterflood. Professor Skeat shows that *winter* means literally the wet season. In these place-words we recognize low-lying hollows or streams liable to be flooded by winter rains, although dry in the summer.

Philip Winter, C. R., 48 Hen. III.
John Winter. H.
Wynter Mariot, co. Norf., 1273. A.
Gelle Winter, co. Camb., ibid.
Emma Wynter, 1379: P. T. Yorks. p. 300.
London, 47, 0; Crockford, 18, 2; Philadelphia, 51, 0; Boston (U.S.), 18, 0.

Winterborn, Winterburn, Winterbourn.—Local, 'of Winterburn,' a township in the parish of Gargrave, near Skipton, co. York. There are also twenty parishes called Winterbourne in England. For suggested origin, v. Winter and Burn.

Walter de Winterburne, co. Oxf., 1273. A.
Thomas de Wynterburn, 1379: P. T. Yorks. p. 258.
1672. Bapt. — Warrdell, s. William Winterborne: St. Jas. Clerkenwell, p. 253.
London, 2, 1, 2; Oxford (Winterborne), 2; Philadelphia, 0, 1, 0; New York, 0, 3, 0.

Winterbottom, Winterbotham. — Local, 'of Winterbottom'; for origin, v. Winter. Like most of the surnames whose suffix is the local -*bottom*, Winterbottom arose in the south-east corner of Lancashire, on the Cheshire and Yorkshire borders. It is believed that Saddleworth is its precise and original habitat; v. Higginbotham, Shufflebottom, and Botham.

1564. Married — John Dowleye and Agnes Wintrebothom: Reg. Prestbury Ch. (Cheshire), p. 14.
1590. Orme Winterbottom, parish of Ashton-under-Lyne: Wills at Chester (1545-1620), p. 213.
1593. Jarvis Winterbottom, of Mosley, Ashton-under-Lyne: ibid.
1618. Richard Winterbotham, of Hartshead, Ashton-under-Lyne: ibid.
1644. Buried—George Winterbothom, stewarde of Stockport: Reg. Stockport Parish Ch. (vide East Cheshire, i. 408).
1653. Robert Winterbothom, mayor of Stockport: ibid. p. 347.
Manchester, 7, 2; London, 3, 3; Philadelphia, 27, 1; New York, 8, 0.

Winterflood. — Local, 'of Winterflood'; v. Winter for origin. I do not find the spot.

Walter Winterflod, co. Essex, 1273. A.
Ralph de Wynterfled, co. Essex, ibid.
1567. Thomas Sedgewyke and Grace Winterfloode, co. Norf.: Marriage Lic. (Faculty Office), p. 14.
1808. Married—John Ellison and Eliz. Winterflood: St. Geo. Han. Sq. ii. 383. London, 4.

Winterscale, Wintersgill.—Local, 'of Winterscale,' i. e. the winter cot or hut; v. Scales. Wintersgill is a corruption, though -*gill* is a local suffix; cf. Summerscales and Summersgill. The spot

whence the surname arose lies in the parish of Ingleton, W. Rid. Yorks.

William Proctor, of Winterscall, parish of Ingleston (sic), 1611: Wills at Chester (1545-1620), p. 156.
Magota de Wynterscale, 1379: P. T. Yorks. p. 290.
Johannes Wynterscalle, 1379: ibid. p. 288.

Of these two, Magota lived in Ingleton, and John in Dent, in the immediate district. No further evidence is needed as regards the precise spot.

1638. Married—William Winterscale and Jane Hurd: St. Jas. Clerkenwell, iii. 20.
1769. — Thomas Loomes and Ann Wintersgill: St. Geo. Han. Sq. i. 189.
West Rid. Court Dir., 0, 1; Leeds, 0, 1; Manchester, 0, 1.

Winterton.—Local, 'of Winterton,' two parishes, one in co. Norf., the other in that of Lincoln.

Richard de Winterton, co. Norf., 1273. A.
Walter de Winterton, co. Warw., ibid.
Henry de Wyntreton, co. Staff., Edw. I. R.
1626. Robert Winterton and Mary Bateman: Marriage Lic. (London), i. 181.
1636. Buried — A still-born child of Thomas Winterton: St. Jas. Clerkenwell, iv. 219.
London, 3; New York, 2; Boston (U.S.), 3.

Winthrop.—Local, 'of Winthorpe,' parishes in cos. Lincoln and Notts. v. Thorp.

1539. Bapt. — Alice, d. Ade Wintrop: St. Peter, Cornhill, i. 1.
1543. — Bridget Wintrope: ibid. p. 3.
1652. — Margrat, the dafter (sic) of Stephen Winthrop: Kensington Parish Church, p. 39.
1714. Married — Peter Wentrup and Jane Archer: St. Jas. Clerkenwell, iii. 237.
Crockford, 1; New York, 13.

Winton.—Local, 'of Winton': (1) a township in parish of Kirkby-Sigston, N. Rid. Yorks; (2) a township in parish of Kirkby-Stephen, co. Westmorland.

Thomas de Wineton, co. Kent, 1273. A.
John de Wintun, co. Kent, ibid.
1576. Roger Robynson and Alice Wynton: Marriage Lic. (London), i. 72.
1645. Scudamor Winton and Faith Scott: ibid. ii. 276.
London, 3; Philadelphia, 2; Boston (U.S.), 1.

Winyard.—Local, 'at the wine-yard,' from residence thereby. A.S. *win-geard*, vineyard.

William atte Wyneard, co. Soms., 1 Edw. III : Kirby's Quest, p. 138.
1506. William Wynnyarde : Reg. Univ. Oxf. i. 49.
1577. Richard Wynyard, Merton Coll.: ibid. vol. ii. pt. ii. p. 456.
1665. Married — Edward Winniyard and Mary Banister : St. Jas. Clerkenwell, iii. 118.
1729. — Thomas Whinyard and Eliz. Larcomb : St. Antholin (London), p. 143. London, 4.

Wiredrawer. — Occup. ' the wire-drawer.'

'Cappers, wyerdrawers, pynners,' Chester Play, 1339 : Ormerod's Hist. Cheshire, i. 300.
'Bedmakers, fedbedmakers, and wyre-drawers ': Cocke Lorelle's Bote.
Robert le Wyrdraere : Wardrobe Account, 49 Hen. III, 1/31.
Will. de Pontefracto, *wyrdragher*, 42 Edw. III : Freemen of York, i. 65.
William de Wirdrawere, London. X.
Rauf le Wyrdrawere, ibid.

This surname I believe to be extinct.

Wisbey, Wisby.—Local, ' of Whisby,' a chapelry in the parish of Doddington, co. Linc.

1758. Married — Thomas Wisbey and Margaret Ryan : St. Geo. Han. Sq. i. 77. London, 1, 2.

Wiscar.—Bapt. ; v. Whiskard.

Wisdom.—Local, 'of Wisdom,' a place or estate in the parish of Cornwood, co. Devon. v. Lower's Patr. Brit. p. 386. All my instances prove the surname to be West Anglian.

Wymund Wysdom, co. Somerset, 1273. A.
Hugh Wysdam, co. Somerset, ibid.
Richard Wysdem, co. Somerset, 20 Edw. I. R.
Robert Wisdom, co. Soms., 1 Edw. III : Kirby's Quest, p. 206.
Thomas Wisdom, M.P. for Wilton, C. R., 51 Edw. III.
Elizabeth Wisedome, 1542 : Reg. Broad Chalke, co. Wilts, p. 6.
Dorothy Wisedom, 1551 : ibid.
1653. Married—Henry Wisdome and Alyce Haward : St. Jas. Clerkenwell, iii. 89.
1756. — John Wisdom and Lydia Beedal : St. Geo. Han. Sq. i. 67. London, 4 ; Philadelphia, 4 ; Boston (U.S.), 1.

Wise, Wyse.—Nick. 'the wise,' the learned ; v. Wiseman. Of the nine instances of Wise in the Hundred Rolls (vol. ii), eight resided either in Oxfordshire or Cambridgeshire. No doubt all were University men !

Elias le Wyse, co. Oxf., 1273. A.
Henry le Wyse, co. Hunts, ibid.
William le Wyse, C. R., 4 Edw. II.
Thomas le Wys, Pat. Roll, 3 Edw. VI. pt. iii.
1668-9. Stephen Dring and Patience Wyse, d. John Wise : Marriage Alleg. (Canterbury), ii. 262.
London, 30, 0 ; Philadelphia, 92, 0 ; New York, 36, 1.

Wisehead.—Nick. ' the wise-head '; cf. Wise and Wiseman.

Johannes Wysehede, 1379 : P. T. Yorks. p. 158.

Wiseman. — Nick. ' the wise man,' the clever, the learned man ; v. Wise. It is curious and interesting to note that the in-stances of Wise and Wiseman in the Hundred Rolls are nearly all from the two University counties.

Roger Wyseman, co. Oxf., 1273. A.
Alan Wysman, co. Camb., ibid.
John Wysman, co. Oxf., ibid.
Johannes Wysman, 1379 : P. T. Yorks. p. 152.
Petrus Wysman, 1379 : ibid. p. 145.
1656. Married — Thomas Duncombe and Margaret Wiseman : St. Michael, Cornhill, p. 37.
London, 17 ; Philadelphia, 15 ; Boston (U.S.), 9.

Wisker ; v. Whiskard.

Wisler, Wissler ; v. Whistler.

Wiston ; v. Whiston.

Witby; v. Whitby.

Witcomb.—Local, 'of Witcomb Magna,' a parish in co. Glouc., near Painswick.

1757. Married — James Rendall and Rachael Witcomb : St. Geo. Han. Sq. i. 68.
London, 1 ; Oxford, 2 ; New York, 1.

Witham, Whitham, Whit-tome, Whittum, Whittam, Whittem.—Local, ' of Witham,' parishes in cos. Essex, Somerset, and Lincoln (3). The variant Whittum is American; cf. Barnum for Barnham.

John de Wytham, ' the king's chaplain,' 1286 : Cal. of Patent Rolls, i. 240.
1583-4. John Cramp and Thomasine Wyttham: Marriage Lic. (London), i. 127.

1625. Buried — A childe of William Wittam's : St. Jas. Clerkenwell, iv. 184.
1752. Bapt. — Thomas, s. John Whit-tam : ibid. ii. 302.
1777. Married—Philip Paine and Mary Witham : St. Geo. Han. Sq. i. 278.
London, 6, 1, 3, 0, 1, 0 ; MDB. (co. Camb.), Whittome, 3 ; Philadelphia, 0, 3, 0, 0, 0, 1 ; Boston (U.S.), 20, 0, 0, 2, 0, 1.

Withecomb ; v. Widdicombe and Withycomb.

Withers.—Bapt. ' the son of Wither.' Lower writes : ' Wither occurs in Domesday as a tenant prior to that census.' The surname constantly appears in the Hundred Rolls, but always without prefix, suggesting that its origin is personal ; cf. Witherslack, Withersfield, Withersdale, Witherley, all parishes set down in Crockford.

Agnes Wyther, co. Camb., 1273. A.
Richard Wyther, co. Oxf., ibid.
Simon Wyther, co. Hunts, ibid.
Walter Wythor, co. Camb., ibid.
1590. Married—Jeames Wythers and Ann Graye : St. Michael, Cornhill, p. 15.
London, 28 ; Oxford, 3 ; Philadelphia, 11 ; Boston (U.S.), 4.

Witherspoon, Wodder-spoon, Wilderspin, Wother-spoon. — ? ——. I can make nothing out of this surname, and leave it to the consideration of more enlightened students. I can furnish them with materials, but that is all. My Yorkshire references clearly represent some of its an-cestors.

Adam Wytherpyn, co. Norf., 1273. A.
Adam Wyerpin, co. Norf., ibid.
Johannes Withspone, 1379 : P. T. Yorks. p. 36.
Willelmus Wythspone, 1379 : ibid.
John Wetherpyn, vicar of Thrickby, co. Norf., 1419 : FF. xi. 254.
Liverpool Court Dir., 1, 0, 0, 0 ; London, 1, 1, 1, 4 ; Philadelphia, 0, 0, 0, 3 ; Boston (U.S.), 4, 0, 0, 0.

Withey, Wethey, Withy, Withye.—Local, 'at the white hay,' i.e. the white hedge (v. Hay), from residence thereby ; cf. Whit-field, Whitworth, &c., and v. Whitey.

William ate Wythege, co. Oxf., 1273. A.
Nicholas de la Wythege, co. Oxf., ibid.
Walter de la Wythege, co. Hants, ibid.
Richard Whitheye, co. Linc., ibid.
Thomas atte Withigh, co. Soms., 9 Edw. II : Kirby's Quest, p. 154.
1564. William Withie, Ch. Ch. : Reg. Univ. Oxf. vol. ii. pt. ii. p. 12.

1799. Married — Thomas Withy and Mary Pratt: St. Geo. Han. Sq. ii. 202. London, 9, 2, 0, 0; MDB. (co. Soms.), 0, 0, 4, 1; New York, 2, 0, 0, 0; Boston (U.S.), 3, 0, 0, 0.

Withipoll.—Local, 'of Withypoole,' a parish in dioc. Bath and Wells. Blomefield seems to speak of another place :

The manor of West Bradenham, co. Norf., came by marriage to Sir William Wythypole, of Whythypole, in Shropshire : FF. vi. 143.
Poule Withipoule, *taillour* : Rutland Papers, Camden Soc.
1599. Buried — Edmund, s. Edmund Withypoole, Esq.: St. Jas. Clerkenwell, iv. 64.

Withthebeard.—Nick. Either to distinguish from another man of the same Christian name, or because the beard was rarely worn at the period.

William Withtheberd, Close Roll, 23 Edw. III. pt. ii.
John Wytheberd. RR. 1.
Peter Wi-the-berd. D.

Cf. Brownbeard and Blackbeard, q.v. ; also cf. Hugh Barbatus (Domesday).

Withy ; v. Withey.

Withycomb, Withecomb.— Local, ' of Withycombe,' a parish in co. Somerset. Cf. Widdicombe.

Walter de Wydecombe, co. Soms., 1327 : Tax Poll.
1665. Buried — William Withecom : St. Jas. Clerkenwell, iv. 368.
1793. Married — John Mortimer and Martha Withycombe : St. Geo. Han. Sq. ii. 105.
MDB. (co. Somerset), 3, 0 ; Manchester, 0, 1.

Witmore ; v. Whitmore.

Witney, Withney. — Local, 'of Witney,' a parish in co. Oxford ; v. Whitney.

John de Witteneye, co. Suff., 1273. A.
1619. Buried — Helline Witney : St. Jas. Clerkenwell, iv. 144.
1806. Married — Wright Witney and Amelia Worrall : St. Geo. Han. Sq. ii. 350.
London, 2, 0 ; New York, 0, 1.

Witton.—Local, ' of Witton'; parishes in cos. Lanc., Yorkshire, and Durham.

Johannes de Wytton, 1379: P. T. Yorks. p. 206.
1681. Married — Mathew Wytton and Eliz. Harden : St. Jas. Clerkenwell, iii. 192.

1740. Buried — Eliz. Witton : St. Dionis Backchurch, p. 308.
London, 4 ; Philadelphia, 1.

Witty, Wittey.—Local, 'at the white hay,' from residence thereby ; v. Withey for early instances.

1697. Married — Griffith Roberts and Eliz. Wittie : St. Dionis Backchurch, p. 46.
1767.— James Wittey and Eliz. French: St. Geo. Han. Sq. ii. 170.
London, 1, 1.

Wix.—Local ; v. Wykes, and cf. Dix for Dicks, Rix for Ricks, or Nix for Nicks. All these variants are more or less modern.

1756. Bapt.—Sarah, d. Edward Wix : St. Peter, Cornhill, ii. 46.
1803. Married—Joseph Wix and Amy Minall : St. Geo. Han. Sq. ii. 273.

The death of Jemima Wix, Peckham, was announced in the Standard, Nov. 10, 1886.

London, 1 ; Philadelphia, 1.

Wodderspoon ; v. Witherspoon.

London, 1.

Wode ; v. Wood.

Wodehouse, Woodhouse.— Local,'at the wood-house,' probably the woodward's residence.

Richard del Wodehus, co. Hunts, 1273. A.
Robert de Wodehous, co. Notts, 20 Edw. I. R.
William de la Wodehouse, Close Roll, 12 Edw. I.
John atte Wodehouse. X.
Petronil de la Wodehouse. B.
Johannes de Wodhous, 1379: P. T. Yorks. p. 99.
1624. Married — William Wodhowse and Mary Ship : St. Peter, Cornhill, i. 252.
London, 0, 22 ; Crockford, 7, 19 ; Philadelphia, 0, 13 ; New York, 0, 7.

Wogan.—? Bapt. ' the son of Wogan' (?).

John Wogan, co. Cumb., 21 Edw. I. R.
John Wogan, 14 Edw. III : Furness Coucher Book, i. 132.
Rogerus Wargan, 1379: P. T. Yorks. p. 32.
Richard Wogan, prebendary of St. David's, 1426 : Hist. and Ant. St. David's, p. 362.
David Wogan, prebendary of St. David's, 1487 : ibid.
1741. Married—William Worgan and Elizabeth Hide : St. Antholin (London), p. 151.
Philadelphia, 3 ; Boston (U.S.), 3.

Wold.—Local, 'at the wold,' from residence thereon ; v. Weald or Weld.

John atte Wold, C. R., 6 Edw. III. pt. ii.
Stephanus del Wold, 21-2 Edw. I : Freemen of York (Surt. Soc.), i. 5.
Boston (U.S.), 1.

Wolf(e ; v. Wolff.

Wolfenden, Woolfenden, Wolfendine, Wolffinden, Woofenden. — Local, ' of Wolfenden,' a district, once a hamlet, in Rossendale, co. Lanc. There are many variants of this surname.

George Hey, of Wolfenden, forest of Rossendale, 1620 : Wills at Chester (1545-1620), p. 91.
James Wolfenden, of Rochdale, 1614 : ibid. p. 214.
1620. Bapt. — Marie, d. Robert Wolfendene : St. Thomas the Apostle (London), p. 44.
1792. Married — Thomas Francis and Eliz. Wolfinden : St. Geo. Han. Sq. ii. 80.
Manchester, 6, 3, 0, 0, 0 ; MDB. (West Rid. Yorks) Wooffenden, 1 ; Philadelphia, 9, 2, 1, 1, 1.

Wolferstan.—Local, 'of Woolverstone,' a village near Ipswich, co. Suff.

Hamo de Wolfreston, co. Suff., 20 Edw. I. R.
1621. Edmund Wolferston and Mary Preston : Marriage Alleg. (Westminster), p. 27.
1791. Married—James Wolferstan and Mary Langford : St. Geo. Han. Sq. ii. 68.
London, 2 ; Plymouth, 1.

Wolff, Wolf, Wolfe, Woolf, Woolfe, Wulff, Wulf, Wulfe. —(1) Nick. 'the wolf'; concerning the extermination of wolves in England, see Wolfhunt.

John le Wlf, co. Sussex, 1273. A.
Agnes le Wolf, co. Hunts, ibid.
Emma le Wolf, co. Bedf., ibid.
Adam le Wolf. H.
Philip le Wolf, 1306. M.

(2) Bapt. 'the son of Wolf,' or Ulf, a personal name, once so familiar that our local nomenclature could not escape its influence, as in Ulverston, Wolverton, Wolvesey, Wolvercote, Wolverley, Wolverhampton, Wolferton, &c. The Index to Freeman's Norm. Conq. will show that Ulf or Wolf was almost as common a personal name in England as in Iceland or Den-

mark. See also Miss Yonge, ii. 267. Ulf, son of Tur-ulf, witnessed the foundation charter of St. Mary's Priory, Lancaster (Baines' Lanc. ii. 654). Another Ulf married Canute's sister; yet a third was Bishop of Dorchester.

Ulf de Appelbi, 1163 : RRR. p. 5.
Ulf Stodhyrda, 1196 : RRR. p. 78.
Roger Ulfe, temp. 1250: FFF. pp. 444–6.
William fil. Ulfe, temp. 1250 : ibid.
Peter Ulfe, temp. 1250: ibid.
Magota Wlfe, 1379 : P. T. Yorks. p. 157.
Thomas Wolphe, or Wulph, co. Wilts, 1586 : Reg. Univ. Oxf. vol. ii. pt. ii. p. 150.
London, 17, 5, 6, 26, 4, 3, 0, 0 ; Philadelphia, 10, 255, 35, 3, 0, 1, 2, 3 ; Boston (U.S.), 18, 24, 13, 7, 0, 0, 1, 0.

Wolfhound.—Nick. 'the wolfhound'; one more incidental proof of the existence of wolves at the period.

Robert Wolfhound, Fines Roll, 12 Edw. I.

Wolfhunt. — Occup. 'the wolf-hunt,' a hunter of wolves, from *wolf*, and Middle English *hunte*, a hunter, the latter being a later form (v. Hunt). Wolves were found in England longer than is supposed. A writ of Edward I (1281) commissions Peter Corbet to kill wolves in Gloucester, Worcester, Hereford, Shropshire, and Stafford (Rymer, i. 591). A family of this name held lands in Derbyshire by service of keeping down the wolves in Peak Forest (Arch. Assoc. Journal, vii. 197). John Engayne held lands (1273) in Huntingdonshire by tenure of maintaining dogs for the king's wolf-hunting (Hundred Rolls, ii. 627, quoted by Lower). An entry still later, relating to the district about Whitby, co. York, is interesting :

' Item, pro tewynge 14 pellium luporum, 1s. 9d.,' 1394 : FFF. p. 623.
Richard le Wulfhunt, co. Kent, 1273. A.
Walter le Wolfhunt. B.
John Wolfehunt. G.
Robert Wolfhunte, co. Notts, Pardons Roll, 6 Ric. II.

Wolfnoth, Woolnough. — Bapt. 'the son of Wolfnoth.' A.S. Ulnoth. 'An ancient baptismal

name, common in Domesday' (Lower).

Wolnotus Hostiarius, 1154 : GGG. p. 259.
Robert Welnoth, co. Norf., 1273. A.

The name occurs two centuries earlier (v. quotation from Freeman on 'Hacon').

1799. Married — Simon Woolnough and Eliz. Tagg : St. Geo. Han. Sq. ii. 196.
London, 0, 8.

Wolford ; v. Woolford.

Wolfraven.—Bapt. 'the son of Wolfraven'; cf. Wallraven and Raven.

Thomas Wlfraven, co. Oxf., 1273. A.
William Wlfraven, co. Oxf., ibid.

Wolfson, Woolfson, Wulfson.—Bapt. 'the son of Wolf,' or Ulf; v. Wolf (2). Wolfsohn is in the London Directory, a German immigrant of the same origin.

William fil. Ulfe, temp. 1200: FFF. p. 444.
Uctred Ulfson, temp. 1200 : ibid. p. 93 n.
London, 0, 1, 1 ; Philadelphia, 2, 0, 0 ; Boston (U.S.), 9, 0, 0.

Wollaston.—Local, 'of Wollaston': (1) a parish in co. Glouc. near Chepstow ; (2) a parish in co. Northampton, near Wellingborough ; (3) a chapelry in co. Salop, nine miles from Shrewsbury; (4) a manor in the parish of Old Swinford, co. Stafford, which early gave rise to a surname (v. Lower's Patr. Brit. p. 388).

Ivo de Wolastone, co. Staff., 1273. A.
William de Wolastone, co. Salop, ibid.
Saer de Wolaveston, co. Northampt., ibid.
John de Wolaston, co. Bedf., 20 Edw. I. R.
William de Wolaston, co. Northampt., ibid.
1661. Buried — Margaret, d. John Woollaston : St. Jas. Clerkenwell, iv. 342.
1611–2. Samuel Wollerston, co. Northants : Reg. Univ. Oxf. vol. ii. pt. ii. p. 325.
London, 3 ; Philadelphia, 2.

Woller ; v. Wooler.

Wollmer ; v. Woolmer.

Wolman, Wollman; v. Woolman.

Wolrige ; v. Woolrich.

Wolsdenholme ; v. Wolstenholme.

Wolseley.—Local, ' of Wolseley,' a hamlet in the parish of Colwich, co. Stafford.

Robert de Wolsley, vicar of Addingham in Craven, 1353 : Whitaker, p. 292.
1674. John Berry and Ann Wolseley, of Wolseley, co. Staff.: Marriage Alleg. (Canterbury), p. 233.
Crockford, 3.

Wolsey, Woolsey. — Bapt. ' the son of Wulsi.' At first sight the name seems local, and an abbreviation of Wolseley, q.v. A parallel is found in the case of the famous founder of Wesleyanism, whose latest biographer shows that his progenitors were Wellesleys. But no doubt can exist on the subject. Wolsey is a modern form of the personal name Wolsi or Wulsi. Lower (Patr. Brit. p. 388), quoting from Fuller's Worthies, reminds me that St. Wulsy was first abbot of Westminster.

William Wulsi, co. Camb., 1273. A.
1605. Bapt.—Israell,'s. Israell Wolsey: St. Dionis Backchurch, p. 92.
1613. Richard Letten and Mary Wolsey : Marriage Lic. (London), ii. 21.
1680. William Greene and Cassandra Wolsey : Marriage Alleg. (Canterbury), p. 30.
Philadelphia, 1, 2.

Wolstencroft, Wolsoncroft, Woolstencroft, Wozencroft, Worsencroft.—Local, ' of Wolstancroft,' i.e. the field or enclosure of Wulstan, the first settler or owner ; cf. Wolstenholme, found in the same district of South Lanc. The corrupted Wozencroft looks queer. It is merely a variant of the already modified Wolsoncroft.

1584. Buried — Joane, d. James Wolsoncroft ; St. Thomas the Apostle (London), p. 96.
1610. Bapt.—Francis, s. Thomas Worsencroft : St. Jas. Clerkenwell, i. 58.
1613. William Woolstencroft, of Manchester: Wills at Chester, i. 217.
1635. John Wossencroft, of Poulton, co. Lanc. : ibid. ii. 244.
1637. Jeremy Wolstencroft, of Middleton, Manchester : ibid. p. 240.
1640. Robert Wolsoncroft, of Failsworth, Manchester : ibid.
1703. Married—Samuel Woosencrafte and Thomasine Blake : ibid. iii. 226.
1732. — Thomas Wosancroft and Eliz. Wilkes : ibid. p. 258.
Manchester, 3, 0, 3, 1, 1 ; Philadelphia, 7, 1, 0, 0, 0.

Wolstenholme, Woolsten-holme, Wolsdenholme, Wol-stenholmes.—Local, 'of Wolsten-holme,' an ancient manor in Spotland, in the parish of Rochdale, co. Lanc.; literally, 'the holm of Wolfstan'; v. Holm, and cf. Wolstencroft.

Andrew de Wolstenholme, 1180: Baines' Lanc. i. 512.
1604. Margaret Wolstenholme, of Wolstenholme: Wills at Chester (1545-1620), p. 214.
1608. Robert Wolstenholme, of Stansfield, parish of Rochdale: ibid.
Manchester, 13, 3, 1, 1; Sheffield, 13, 0, 0, 0; London, 2, 0, 0, 0; Philadelphia, 8, 0, 0, 0; Boston (U.S.), 3, 0, 0, 0.

Wolston; v. Woolston.

Wolton.—Local, 'of Wolton.' I cannot find the place, and probably now the surname is lost in that of Walton, q.v.

Jordan de Wolton, co. Oxf., Hen. III-Edw. I. K.
Odo de Wolton, co. Worc., ibid.
Robert de Woltun, co. Kent, 1273. A.
1809. Married—Matthew Wolton and Jane Ludgater: St. Geo. Han. Sq. ii. 408. London, 2.

Wolverton, Woolverton.—Local, 'of Wolverton,' i.e. the stead or dwelling of Wolf, the first settler (v. Wolff). Parishes in cos. Bucks, Norf., Hants, and Warwick are so named.

London, 1, 2; New York, 2, 0; Philadelphia, 0, 3.

Womack.—?—. Evidently a south-eastern counties' name, probably local.

Henry Womock, vicar of Great Ellingham, co. Norf., 1601: FF. i. 486.
1779. Married — James Womack and Ann Summers: St. Geo. Han. Sq. i. 295.
MDB. (co. Suffolk), 5; London, 5.

Wombwell, Wombell, Wombill. — Local, 'of Womb-well,' a village in the parish of Darfield, co. York. Wombill is a natural modification, but is probably somewhat modern.

Hugo de Wambewell, *zonarius*, 1277: Freemen of York (Surt Soc.), i. 3.
Isabella de Wombewell, 1379: P. T. Yorks. p. 102.
Avicia de Womwell, 1379: ibid. p. 74.
1558. Married — Thomas Wombwell, Knt., and Annie Perye: St. Michael, Cornhill, p. 7.
1632. William Wombwell and Frances Veale: Marriage Lic. (London), ii. 105.

1806. Married—William Wombill and Honor Triptree: St. Geo. Han. Sq. ii. 349.
London, 1, 0, 0; Sheffield, 2, 1, 0; Crockford (Wombill), 1.

Womersley.—Local, 'of Womersley,' a parish near Pontefract, co. York.

1789. Married — Edward Bunn and Hannah Womersley: St. Geo. Han. Sq. ii. 24.
London, 3; Halifax, 2.

Wonter, Wontner. — Occup. 'the wonter,' the mole-catcher. A.S. *want, wont*, a mole.

Henry le Wantur, co. Salop, 1273. A.
London, 0, 2; New York, 1, 0.

Wood, Wode.—Local, 'at the wood,' from residence thereby. Common to every mediaeval register all over the country. With Wode, cf. Wodehouse.

Andrew ate Wode, co. Oxf., 1273. A.
Richard de la Wode, co. Oxf., ibid.
Elias in le Wode, co. Camb., ibid.
Walter de la Wode, co. Heref., Hen. III-Edw. I. K.
Robertus del Wodde, *webster*, 1379: P. T. Yorks. p. 133.
Thomas del Wode, *smythe*, 1379: ibid. p. 91.
Robertus del Wode, 1379: ibid. p. 218.

Modern instances are needless.

London, 317, 0; Philadelphia, 450, 0; New York (Wode), 2.

Woodall.—Local, 'at the wood-hall,' from residence therein or thereby. Doubtless several places would bear this title, and each might originate a surname; cf. Wodehouse.

Adam de Wodhall, 1379: P. T. Yorks. p. 25.
Matilda atte Wodhall, 1379: P. T. Howdenshire, p. 32.
1600. William Woodhall, co. Essex, Reg. Univ. Oxf. vol. ii. pt. ii. p. 242.
1613. Thomas Woodall (co. Herts) and Alice Jeffereys: Marriage Lic. (London), ii. 20.
London, 9; Philadelphia, 3; Boston (U.S.), 1.

Woodard.—(1) Bapt. 'the son of Odard,' or Wodard.

Wadard 'homo episcopi' held lands of Bishop Odo: Freeman, Norm. Conq. iii. 571.
John fil. Wudardi, 1168: KKK. vi. 13.
John fil. Odard, 1161: ibid. p. 6.

The last two entries concern, I believe, the same individual.

Cristiana fil. Odard, temp. Hen. III. T.
Alan Wodard, 1273. A.
Wodard atte Barre, C. R., 3 Edw. I.

I furnish two other possible sources of the name, but the above is the undoubted parent of nine-tenths of the bearers of this patronymic. (2) Official. An abbreviation of Woodward, q.v. (3) Occup. 'the wood-herd,' probably a hog-tender; v. Herd. Cf. Coward for Cowherd.

Richard le Wodeherd, co. Norf., 20 Edw. I. R.
Richard le Wodehirde, co. Norf., 1273. A.
1682. Married — Thomas Woodard and Alice Dobbey: St. Jas. Clerkenwell, iii. 197.
London, 7; Philadelphia, 1; Boston (U.S.), 4.

Woodberry, -borough; v. Woodbury.

Woodbridge. — Local, ' of Woodbridge,' a parish in the county of Suffolk, seven miles from Ipswich.

John de Wudebrege, co. Camb., 1273. A.
Thomas de Wudebrige, co. Wilts, ibid.
1596. John Woodbridge, co. Oxf.: Reg. Univ. Oxf. vol. ii. pt. ii. p. 215.
1668. Married—Thomas Woodbridge and Ellin Davis: St. Jas. Clerkenwell, iii. 145.
London, 10; Philadelphia, 1; Boston (U.S.), 11.

Woodburn, Woodburne.—Local, 'at the wood-burn,' i.e. the woodland stream; v. Burn. Not in London Directory; a well-known surname in Furness, North Lanc. The register of the parish church of Ulverston teems with this patronymic.

1591. Gillian Woodburn, of Kirkbie Ireleth: Lancashire Wills at Richmond, i. 319.
1617. Richard Woodborne, of Kirkbie Ireleth: ibid.
1654. Bapt.—Jane, d. Rodger Woodburne, *tourney*: St. Mary, Ulverston, i. 127.
1656. — John, s. William Woodburne, *marcer*: ibid. p. 128.
1700. Married — Christopher Woodborne and Bridget Dawson: St. Jas. Clerkenwell, iii. 222.
Ulverston, N. Lanc., 5, 2; Philadelphia, 8, 1; Boston (U.S.), 4, 0.

Woodbury, Woodberry, Woodborough. — Local, ' of Woodbury,' or Woodborough: (1) of Woodborough, a parish in co. Notts; (2) of Woodbury, a parish in co. Devon. Both places are parents of the name.

David de Wodebir, co. Devon, 1273. A.
Edmund de Wodeburg', co. Suff., ibid.
Henry de Wodeburg', co. Notts, ibid.
Ralph de Wodeburg', co. Notts, ibid.
London, 3, 0, 1; Philadelphia, 6, 0, 0; Boston (U.S.), 74, 10, 0.

Woodcock.—Nick. 'the wood-cock'; cf. Nightingale, Pidgeon, Jay, Dove, &c.

Adam Wodecok, co. Linc., 1273. A.
Wydo Wodcok, co. Suff., ibid.
Willelmus Wodcok, 1379 : P. T. Yorks. p. 40.
Johannes Wodecok, ibid. p. 233.
1516. Lawrence Wudcocke, or Wode-cocke : Reg. Univ. Oxf. i. 103.
1554. Thomas Cable and Emma Wodde-cokk : Marriage Lic. (London), i. 15.
1611. Married — Thomas Woodcock and Phillip (= Philippa) Phelps : St. Michael, Cornhill, p. 20.
London, 21; Philadelphia, 17; Boston (U.S.), 2.

Woodcroft. — Local, 'at the wood-croft,' i.e. the enclosure by the wood, from residence thereby ; v. Croft or Craft.

1584-5. Geoffrey Woodcrofte, *weaver*, and Margaret Smithe : Marriage Lic. (London), i. 138.
1615. Bapt. — Anthony, s. Nicholas Woodcrofte : St. Dionis Backchurch, p. 22.
1626. Married—John Parey and Eliz. Woodcraft : ibid. p. 96.
London, 1.

Woodend. — Local, 'at the wood-end,' one who lived at the end of the wood; cf. Fieldsend, Townsend, and the place-name Gravesend. This surname still exists in Furness, North Lancashire. My instances prove it to have been there for 300 years at least. No doubt it has existed there for six centuries.

Adam de Wodeshende, co. Dorset, 1273. A.

With this, cf. Townend and Townshend. The *h* is, of course, intrusive.

1601. Bapt. — Richard, s. Nicholas Woodend : St. Mary, Ulverston, i. 91.
Nicholas Woodend, of Ulverston, 1624: Lancashire Wills at Richmond, i. 320.
James Woodend, of Lowick, 1662: ibid.
Blawith-in-Furness, 2; Boston (U.S.), 3.

Wooder ; v. Woodger.

Wooderson, Woodson. — Bapt. 'the son of Wodard' (?) ; v.

Woodard. The only other ety-mology is 'Widowson,' q.v. But this seems somewhat forced. Upon careful consideration I see no reasonable doubt in accepting Woodard as the parent. It must be remembered that that baptismal name was popular in the hereditary surname period.

1565. Alex. Woodson, Ch. Ch.: Reg. Univ. Oxf. vol. ii. pt. ii. p. 13.
1604-5. John Woodsonne, Bristol : ibid. p. 280.

In this register the name is also spelt Wooddeson, Woddeson, and Wodison. It is manifest, therefore, that Wooderson is a member of the family ; cf. Patterson for Pattison.

1634. Buried — Richard Woodison, servant to Mr. Darrell : St. Jas. Clerkenwell, iv. 214.
1674. George Wooddeson and Mary Balston : Marriage Alleg. (Canterbury), p. 230.
1803. Married—John Wooderson and Ann Oliver : St. Geo. Han. Sq. ii. 282.
London, 2, 0; Philadelphia, 0, 5; New York, 0, 1.

Woodford, Woodforde. — Local, 'of Woodford' : (1) a parish in co. Wilts, four miles from Salis-bury ; (2) a parish in co. Essex, eight miles from London. Both places seem to have had a share in the origination of the surname.

Geoffrey de Wodeford, co. Wilts, 1273. A.
Symon Wodeford, co. Bucks, ibid.
Nicholas de Wodeford, co. Glouc., ibid.
Geoffrey de Wodeford, co. Soms., 1 Edw. I : Kirby's Quest, p. 180.
1577. Bapt.—Thomas Wodford, son of Gamaliel Woodford : St. Peter, Cornhill, i. 19.
1581. Robert Wodforde, co. Bucks: Reg. Univ. Oxf. vol. ii. pt. ii. p. 96.
1620. — Adryan, s. Emanuel Wood-ford : St. Jas. Clerkenwell, i. 87.
London, 6, 3 ; New York, 7, 0 ; Boston (U.S.), 3, 0.

Woodgate, Woodgates. — Local, 'at the wood-gate,' from residence beside the entrance into the wood. Such a spot would naturally lend itself to a surname.

Robert atte Wodgate, C. R., 2 Edw. I.
1585-6. Peter Woodgate, or Wodgate, co. Kent : Reg. Univ. Oxf. vol. ii. pt. ii. p. 149.
1618. Francis Quarles and Ursely Woodgate : Marriage Lic. (London), ii. 60.

1651. Buried — Eliz. Woodgate : St. Peter, Cornhill, i. 206.
London, 9, 1 ; New York, 2, 0.

Woodger, Woodyer, Wood-yeare, Wooder. — Occup. (1) 'the wooder,' i.e. the woodman ; (2) 'the wood-hewer,' i.e. a wood-chopper. Both these names have resolved themselves into Woodger and Woodyer ; cf. Sawyer for Sawer, or *lawyer* for *lawer*, or *pavier* for *paver*. With the cor-rupted Woodger for Woodyer, cf. Goodger for Goodier. As re-gards Woodhewer, that would naturally and inevitably become Woodyer.

Matthew le Woder, C. R., 35 Edw. I.
Robert le Wodehyewere. H.
John Wodhewher, 1379 : P. T. Yorks. p. 209.
Robert Wodhewer, 1379 : ibid. p. 267.
William Wodhewer, 1379 : ibid. p. 223.
1605. Richard Woodyere : Reg. Univ. Oxf. i. 356.
1663. John Woodger and Mary Huds-don : Marriage Alleg.(Canterbury), ii. 98.
1790. Married — John Woodrow and Ann Woodyer : St. Geo. Han. Sq. ii. 37.
1799. — William Woodyer and Cathe-rine Wood : ibid. p. 210.

The present form of the name is now all but universally Wood-yer.

London, 9, 0, 0, 1 ; West Rid. Court Dir. (Woodyeare), 1.

Woodhacker.—(1) Occup. 'a woodcutter.'

William le Wodehagger, Close Roll, 10 Edw. II.

Jack is Jagge in Piers Plowman, and Hick is Higg (v. Higg and Hick). (2) Nick. ; the above applied to a bird, woodpecker, &c. 'Wodehake, or reyne fowle, -*picus*' : Prompt. Parv. ; v. *woodwale*, in Skeat.

Woodham.—Local, 'of Wood-ham,' three parishes in co. Essex ; v. Wadham.

Peter de Wodeham, co. Northampton, 1273. A.
Egidius de Wodeham, London, ibid.
Reginald de Wodeham, co. Gloucester, ibid.
Thomas de Wodeham, co. Essex, ibid.
1613. John Woddam : Reg. Univ. Oxf. vol. ii. pt. ii. p. 330.
1625. Thomas Woodham (co. Middle-sex) and Eliz. Mussate : Marriage Lic. (London), ii. 157.

1789. Married—James Woodham and Mary Rodam (or Rodman) : St. Geo. Han. Sq. ii. 31. London, 9.

Woodhay. -- Local, ' at the wood-hay' (v. Hay), from residence thereby.

Richard de la Wodehaye, co. Linc., 20 Edw. I. R.
Thomas de la Wodehaye, co. Linc., ibid.
1654. Married—Charles Woodey and Ann Hayle : St. Jas. Clerkenwell, iii. 92.
1668. — Philip Lancedowne and Mary Wooddey : ibid. p. 143.

Woodhead.—Local, ' of Wood-head,' a great Yorkshire surname. Literally, ' at the wood-head,' at the top of the wood ; cf. Akenhead, Birkenhead, i.e. the head of the oaks or birches. The great tunnel between Lanc. and Yorkshire is called the Woodhead tunnel from the name of the locality ; cf. Wood-end, q.v.

Rogerus de Wodehed, 1379 : P. T. Yorks. p. 199.
1686. William Woodhead and Margarett Birkhead : Marriage Alleg. (Canterbury), p. 245.
1789. Joseph Woodhead and Eliz. Parker : St. Geo. Han. Sq. ii. 28.
London, 8 ; West Rid. Court Dir., 30 ; Philadelphia, 8 ; Boston (U.S.), 3.

Woodhouse ; v. Wodehouse.

Woodhull, Woodill.—Local, ' at the wood-hill,' from residence thereby ; v. Hull. In Woodill the *h* is elided. The surname seems to have been closely confined to co. Northampton. Its present refuge is the United States.

1545. John Leveson and Ann Woodhull : Marriage Lic. (Faculty Office), p. 5.
1581. Anthony Wodhill, co. Warw. : Reg. Univ. Oxf. vol. ii. pt. ii. p. 98.
— Laurence Wodhill, co. Northampt. : ibid.
1598. Fulcke Wodhull, or Woodhull, co. Northampt. : ibid. p. 231.
— Giles Wodhull, co. Northampt. : ibid.
Philadelphia, 6, 2 ; New York, 11, 0.

Woodland, Woodlands.—Local, ' at the wood-laund' (cf. Buckland, Lund), a grassy space or glade in the heart of a wood.

Cicely de la Wodeland, Close Roll, 52 Hen. III.
Peter de Wodelonde, co. Soms., 9 Edw. II : Kirby's Quest, p. 75.

John de Wodelond, co. Soms., 9 Edw. II : ibid. p. 194.
1561. John Woodland and Joanna Darby : Marriage Lic. (London), i. 22.
1793. Married—James Woodland and Hannah Shadbolt : St. Geo. Han. Sq. ii. 105.
London, 5, 1 ; Philadelphia, 14, 0 ; Boston (U.S.), 1, 0.

Woodlark.—Nick. ' the wood-lark ' ; cf. Lark.

Robert Wodlarke, C. R., 29 Hen. VI.

Woodley.—Local, (1) ' of Wood-ley,' a parish in co. Berks ; (2) ' of Woodleigh,' in co. Devon.

London, 9 ; Oxford, 1 ; Philadelphia, 2.

Woodman.—(1) Occup. ' the woodman,' generally one who resided in a wood, a woodcutter. (2) Bapt. ' the son of Wodemund'; cf. Osman for Osmund, or Wyman for Wymund, &c.

Thomas Wodemund, co. Oxf., 1273. A.
Thomas Wodeman, co. Oxf., ibid.
William Wudeman, co. Kent, ibid.
Eudo Wudeman, co. Linc., ibid.
Johannes Wodman, *laborer*, 1379 : P.T. Howdenshire, p. 15.
1621. Bapt.—Mary, d. Robert Woddman : St. Michael, Cornhill, p. 115.
1659. Married—Thomas Woodman and Jane Humphrey : St. Thomas the Apostle (London), p. 20.
London, 29 ; Philadelphia, 7 ; Boston (U.S.), 56.

Woodmansey, Woodmancy, Woodmansee. — Local, ' of Woodmansey,' a township in the parish of St. John, Beverley, E. Rid. Yorks.

MDB. (East Rid. Yorks), 2, 0, 0 ; Philadelphia, 0, 1, 1 ; Boston (U.S.), 0, 2, 0 ; New York, 0, 0, 2.

Woodmason. — Occup. ' the wood-mason.'

1773. Bapt. — James, s. James Woodmason : St. Peter, Cornhill, ii. 54.
1774. — Mary Magdalen, d. James Woodmason : ibid.
1798. Married — James Woodmason and Ann Bursey : St. Geo. Han. Sq. ii. 185.
London, 1 ; Bigbury (Devon), 1 ; MDB. (co. Devon), 1.

Woodmonger.—Occup. ' the woodmonger,' a seller of wood for firing purposes, &c.

Robert Wudemongere, London, 1273. A.

Woodnott, Woodnutt. — Bapt. ' the son of Godinot,' dim. of Godin, i.e. Godwin (v. Godinot); cf. Guyat and Wyatt, Gillott and Willott, Guillaume and William.

Ralph Wodenot, R. Pat., 4 Edw. III. pt. ii.
William Wodenotte. L.
Thomas Woodnotte, *grome* : Privy Purse Exp., Eliz. of York, p. 98.
1510. Richard Wodnet, or Wotnet : Reg. Univ. Oxf. i. 67.
1703. Bapt.—Winifred Woodnot : St. Jas. Piccadilly.
1720. Married—Thomas Williams and Ann Woodnutt : St. Geo. Chap. Mayfair, p. 300.
1745. — Richard Pulford and Rebecca Woodnott : ibid. p. 58.
London, 0, 2 ; Philadelphia, 0, 4.

Woodroffe, Woodroof, Woodrooffe, Woodrough, Woodruff.—Offic. ' the wood-reeve ' or wood-bailiff, but I cannot find the term in official use ; from A.S. *róf*, active (v. *reeve*, Skeat) ; cf. *sheriff*, *port-reeve*, *borough-reeve*. v. Woodward.

John Woderove, co. Oxf., 1273. A.
Robert Woderove, co. Hunts, ibid.
Henry Woderoue, co. Linc., ibid.
Thomas Woderoue, 1379 : P. T. Yorks. p. 88.
1524. William Woddrof, or Woderof : Reg. Univ. Oxf. i. 133.
George Woodruffe, temp. Eliz. Z.
1733. Married—Daniel Woodrooffe to Jemima Archer : St. Mary Aldermary (London), p. 49.
London, 9, 2, 1, 2, 6 ; Philadelphia, 6, 0, 0, 0, 47 ; Boston (U.S.), 2, 0, 0, 3, 12.

Woodside.—Local, ' of Wood-side,' townships in the parishes of Westward, co. Cumb. ; Shiffnall, co. Salop ; and Wigton, co. Cumb. Cf. Woodend and Woodhead.

Philadelphia, 16 ; Boston (U.S.), 18.

Woodson.—Bapt. ; v. Wooder-son.

Woodstock.—Local, ' of Wood-stock,' a borough and market-town, co. Oxford.

Hudde de Wodestok, co. Oxf., 1273. A.
John de Wodestok, co. Oxf., ibid.
1546. John Wodstocke and Eliz. Taylor : Marriage Lic. (Faculty Office), p. 8.
1635. Robert Woodstock, aged 40, sailed for St. Christopher's, in the Matthew, from London : Hotten's Lists of Emigrants, p. 81.
1653. Buried—Agnes, d. Jeremy Woodstocke : St. Jas. Clerkenwell, iv. 298.
1801. Married—William Bridgland and Ann Woodstock : St. Geo. Han. Sq. ii. 245.
London, 2 ; New York, 1.

Woodward, Woodwards.—Offic. ' the woodward,' a forest officer who looked after wood and vert. ' Wodewarde, or walkare in

a wode for kepynge, *lucarius*':
Prompt. Parv. p. 531.

'John Keeper, or Woodward, of Buck-holt-wood,' 31 Hen. VIII: Rudder's Gloucestershire, pp. 140-1.
Roger le Wodeward, Hen. III-Edw.
I. K.
Aylward le Wodeward, co. Essex, 1273. A.
Adam le Wodeward, co. Oxf., ibid.
William le Wodewarde, co. Soms., 1 Edw. III: Kirby's Quest, p. 220.
Richard le Wodeward, co. Sussex, 20 Edw. I. R.
Johannes Woddeword, 1379: P. T. Yorks. p. 86.

Modern instances are needless.

London, 44, 2; Philadelphia, 70, 0; Boston (U.S.), 67, 0.

Wooer, Wewer.—Nick. 'the wooer,' i.e. lover.

Geoffrey le Wowere, co. Suff., 1273. A.
Nicholas le Wowere, co. Suff., ibid.
John le Wower, co. Camb., ibid.
Hugo le Wewer, co. Wilts, 20 Edw. I. R.
Philadelphia, 0, 2.

Wooeress.—Nick. 'a female wooer'; v. Wooer.

Emma le Woweres, co. Oxf., 1273. A.

Woofenden; v. Wolfenden.

Wookey.—Local, 'of Wookey,' a parish in co. Somerset, near Wells.

1620-1. Nicholas Wookey, co. Soms.: Reg. Univ. Oxf. vol. ii. pt. i. p. 386.
1690. Bapt.—John, s. John Wookey: St. Jas. Clerkenwell, i. 338.
1808. Married—William Wookey and Alice Pritchard: St. Geo. Han. Sq. ii. 382. MDB. (co. Soms.), 8.

Woolard.—Bapt.; v. Woollard.

London, 1.

Woolchapman. — Occup. 'a chapman who dealt in wool.'

Robertus Wulchapman, 1379: P. T. Yorks. p. 159.

Wooldridge, Wooldredge.—Bapt. 'the son of Wulfric'; v. Woolrich. The *d* is intrusive.

Wooler, Wooller, Woller.—Local, 'of Wooler,' a parish in co. Northumberland. The surname having settled in Yorkshire has led to the impression that it meant a wool-merchant. There is, I believe, no evidence of this. The above is the natural solution.

Issabel Woller, 1487, co. York. W. 11.
1694. Married—Thomas Wooller and Abigail Dawson: St. Jas. Clerkenwell, iii. 213.
1710. Bapt. — Richard, s. Richard Woller: ibid. ii. 53.
1728. Married — William Wooller and Mary Morgan: ibid. iii. 254.
London, 0, 1, 0; Bierley, 3, 0, 0; Brad-ford, 2, 0, 0; Philadelphia, 2, 0, 1; New York, 0, 0, 1.

Wooley; v. Woolley.

Woolf(e; v. Wolff.

Woolfenden; v. Wolfenden.

Woolford, Woollford, Wol-ford.—Local, 'of Wolford,' a parish in co. Warwick, near Shipston.

1669. Married — Samson Hisscockes and Ane Woolford: St. Jas. Clerkenwell, iii. 162.
1801. — Matthew Woolford and Eliz. Clayton: St. Geo. Han. Sq. ii. 247.
London, 2, 2, 0; Philadelphia, 6, 0, 8; Boston (U.S.), 2, 0, 1.

Woolfson; v. Wolfson.

Woolgar, Woolger. — Bapt. 'the son of Wulgar.' In Domesday the form is Wlgar, co. Warwick, and Vlgar, co. Cheshire.

William fil. Wulgar, 1164: KKK. vi. 7.
1678. Bapt.—Anne, d. William Wolgar: St. Michael, Cornhill, p. 150.
1683. Buried — William, s. William Woolgar: ibid. p. 268.
1685. William Woolger and Eliz. Forth: Marriage Alleg. (Canterbury), ii. 213.
London, 3, 1.

Woolhouse. — Local, 'at the wool-house,' the store-house for wool, from residence thereby. The stock at Bolton Abbey (1526) included: 'Item, Wolle in the Woolhouses, £45 4s. 0d.' (Whit-aker's Craven, p. 403). Naturally we expect this to be a Yorkshire surname.

Sibota del Wolhouse, 1379: P. T. Yorks. p. 198.
Robertus del Wolhouse, 1379: ibid.
William Woolhouse, bailiff of Yar-mouth, 1545: FF. xi. 327.
1687-8. John Woolhouse, B.A., admit-ted fellow of Magd. Coll. Oxf.: Reg. Univ. Oxf. vol. ii. p. 238.
1697. John Bush and Margaret Wool-house: Marriage Lic. (Faculty Office), p. 223.
Sheffield, 8; West Rid. York (Court Dir.), 4.

Woollard, Woollett, Wool-latt.—Bapt. From some long-

forgotten Wolfgard or Wolfhard. With Woollard, cf. Millard for Mill-ward. The following first two entries occur on same page and in close proximity:

Wlward Hutlawe, co. Kent, 1273. A. ii. 544.
Reymund Wlward, co. Kent, ibid.
Wulward(without surname), co. Camb., 1273. A.
Thomas Wulward, co. Camb., ibid.
Geoffrey Wlvard, co. Suff., ibid.
Michael Woleward, co. Camb., ibid.
Walter Woleward, co. Soms., 1 Edw. III: Kirby's Quest, p. 216.
William Woleward, co. Soms., 1. Edw. III: ibid.
1629. Married—Thomas Woollard and Collat Hargrave: St. Peter, Cornhill, i. 253.
1750. — John Woollett and Anne Holmes: St. Geo. Chap. Mayfair, p. 180.
London, 9, 6, 2; Boston (U.S.), 4, 0, 0; New York, 0, 1, 0.

Wooller; v. Wooler.

Woolley, Wooley.—Local, 'of Wooley,' a parish in dioc. Bath and Wells; also 'of Woolley,' parishes in diocs. Ely and York. The North-English Woolleys hail from Yorkshire. The references will show that the origin is Wolf-ley, 'the meadow of Ulf,' or Wolf, a common personal name.

Johannes de Wulley, 1379: P. T. Yorks. p. 159.
Elena de Wolley, 1379: ibid.
Thomas de Wollay, 1379: ibid. p. 92.
Adam de Wolueley, 1379: ibid. p. 90.
Robert de Woluelay, 1379: ibid.
1594. John Wooly, London: Reg. Univ. Oxf. vol. ii. pt. ii. p. 203.
1601. Thomas Woolley, co. Warw.: ibid. p. 248.
1682-3. John Bright and Ann Woolley: Marriage Alleg. (Canterbury), ii. 125.
London, 21, 2; Philadelphia, 16, 2; Boston (U.S.), 8, 0.

Woollford; v. Woolford.

Woollven, Woolven, Wool-vine, Wolven.—Bapt. 'the son of Wulwin.' In Domesday found as Wluuen.

Wulfwine the Reeve: Parker, Early Hist. of Oxford, p. 179.
Wulwinus Monetarius, 10 Hen. II: Pipe Roll, p. 3.
1730. Married—Thomas Woolven and Mary Haycraft: St. Mary Aldermary (London), p. 49.
1747. Married—Henry Whitaker and Ann Woolvan: St. Geo. Chap. Mayfair, p. 99.
London, 1, 1, 1, 0; New York (Wolven), 1.

Woolman, Wolman, Woll-man.—Occup. 'the woolman,' a wool-buyer. This surname crossed the Atlantic, and has 'increased and multiplied' there. The original emigrant must have started early in the 17th century. If he had several boys, who lived, married, and had large families, the large number of Woolmans in America is easily accounted for. For opposite reasons Woolman is in danger of extinction in England.

John Gammwell, *wolman* (Beverley, co. York), 16 Hen. VI: HHH. p. 137.
1523. Richard Wulman: Reg. Univ. Oxf. i. 132.
1584. Bapt.—Griffith, s. John Woollman: St. Jas. Clerkenwell, p. 16.
1635. Richard Wollman, aged 22, sailed to Virginia in the Globe, of London: Hotten's Lists of Emigrants, p. 120.
1761. Married—John Woollman and Susanna Field: St. Geo. Han. Sq. p. 103.
London, 1, 0, 0; Philadelphia, 17, 1, 0; New York, 1, 0, 2.

Woolmer, Wollmer.—Bapt. 'the son of Wulmar,' or Ulmar. Wlmar, co. Linc., Wlmaer, co. Yorks; Wlmarus Presbyter, co. Bucks (Domesday). v. Ullmer.

Wulmar Bradfot, 1171: RRR. p. 14.
Wolmer le Essex (London citizen), 1273. A.
Wlmerus de Neuton, co. Suff., ibid.
Wolmar de Estchep, London, ibid.
Ralph Wolmer, co. Norf., ibid.
John Wolmere, co. Soms., 1 Edw. III: Kirby's Quest, p. 86.
1579-80. Anthony Wollmer and Agnes Vincente: Marriage Lic. (London), i. 93.
1588. Bapt.—Cecily, d. Edwarde Woolmer: St. Jas. Clerkenwell, i. 20.
London, 5, 0; Philadelphia, 0, 1; New York, 0, 2.

Woolmonger. — Occup. 'the woolmonger,' a merchant in wool, often Flemings. Hence Morkin in the first instance. Cf. Woolman.

Morekinus le Wolmongere, London, 1273. A.
Walter le Wollemongere, co. Hunts, ibid.
Henry Wollemongere, co. Hunts, ibid.
Roger le Wolemongere, C. R., 9 Edw. II.

A curious corruption is found in the following entry:

1759. Married — Thomas Whitehead and Mary Willomanger: St. Geo. Han. Sq. i. 88.

Woolnough.—Bapt. ; v. Wolfnoth.

Woolrich, Woolrych, Wolrige, Woollright, Wooldredge, Woolridge, Wooldredge. — Bapt. 'the son of Wulfric' (v. Ulfric, Yonge, ii. 269), one of the many compounds of Ulf or Wolf; cf. Orme and Worm, Ulph and Wolff (2). Adam Wulfric was admitted to the Roll of Guild Merchants of Shrewsbury in 1231. He is the ancestor of the Shropshire Wolryches (Shirley's Noble and Gentle Men, quoted by Lower). With regard to the forms Woolright and Wooldridge, cf. the analogous Allwright and Aldridge from Aldrich.

William Wulurich, co. Wilts, 1273. A.
Robert Wolurich, co. Oxf., ibid.
Adam fil. Wlfric, co. Salop, ibid.
Astill fil. Wlfriche, co. Oxf., ibid.
Thomas Wlfrich, co. Bucks, ibid.
1658. Bapt. — Sarah, d. John Woolldrig: St. Mary Aldermary (London), p. 97.
1659. — Ann, d. Edward Wollrich: ibid.
1763. Married—Thomas Oxford and Olley Woolldridge: St. Geo. Han. Sq. i. 118.
London, 1, 1, 1, 1, 10, 0, 0; MDB. (co. Glouc.), Woolwright, 1; Boston (U.S.), 0, 0, 0, 0, 1, 1, 1.

Woolsey ; v. Wolsey.

Woolstencroft, -holme ; v. Wolstencroft, -holme.

Woolston, Woolson, Wolston, Wolson.—(1) Local, (a) ' of Wolstan,' a parish in co. Warw., near Rugby ; (b) ' of Woolstone,' two parishes near Newport Pagnell, co. Bucks ; (c) ' of Woolston,' a hamlet in the parish of North Cadbury, co. Somerset ; and (d) ' of Woolstone,' a tithing in the parish of Hound, co. Devon. With the corrupted Woolson, cf. Kelson for Kelston (q.v.). There can be little doubt that in some instances Wollaston and Wolston have become mixed up. (2) Bapt. 'the son of Wolfstan' (v. Yonge, ii. 269). The probability is that (1) is the correct derivation.

William de Wolstone, co. Bucks, 1273. A.

1567. Christopher Gyll and Emma Woolson: Marriage Lic.(Faculty Office) p. 14.
1573. Buried — Richard Wolston: St. Thomas the Apostle, p. 91.
1581. Edward Woolson and Mary Tirrey: Marriage Lic. (London), i. 101.
1601. James Woolston, or Wolston, co. Devon: Reg. Univ. Oxf. vol. ii. pt. ii. p. 249.
1787. Married — William Woolstone and Eliz. White: St. Geo. Han. Sq. i. 377.
London, 1, 0, 0, 0 ; New York, 0, 2, 0, 0; Boston (U.S.), 0, 3, 1, 1 ; Philadelphia, 12, 3, 0, 0.

Woolven, -vine ; v. Woollven.

Woolverton ; v. Wolverton.

Woolvet, Woolvett. — Bapt. 'the son of Wulvard.' For strong corroborative evidence, v. instances under Woollard.

1590. Buried—William Wollfett: St. Jas. Clerkenwell, iv. 41.
1799. William Woolfett and Mary Sutton: St. Geo. Han. Sq. ii. 195.
London, 1, 1.

Wooster.—Local, ' of Worcester,' a corruption ; v. Worcester.

1567. Buried—Abraham, son of Reynold Woster: St. Antholin (London), p. 19.
1625. — Henry, s. John Woster: St. Jas. Clerkenwell, iv. 170.
1658. Married—John Watson and Alice Wooster: ibid. iii. 100.
1726. Bapt.—John, s. Robert Wooster: ibid. ii. 164.
London, 3 ; Philadelphia, 5 ; Boston (U.S.), 3.

Wootton, Wootten, Wooton, Wotton, Wooten.—Local, ' of Wootton': (1) a parish in co. Bedford ; (2) a parish in co. Berks, near Abingdon ; also parishes in cos. Kent, Lincoln, Northampton, Oxford, Southampton, Stafford, &c., besides many hamlets and manors scattered over the country; also Wotton, a parish in co. Surrey. No doubt the origin is Wood-town, ' the enclosure in the wood.' This would at once explain the frequency of its occurrence as a place-name.

Robert de Wottone, co. Devon, Hen. III-Edw. I. K.
Fredeshet de Wottone, co. Bucks, 1273. A.
John atte Wodeton, London, ibid.
Thomas de Wodeton, co. Devon, ibid.

John de Wodeton or John de Wutton, co. Oxf., 1273. A.
1670. John Hill and Mary Wootton: Marriage Lic. (Westminster), p. 45.
1667. George Wotton and Eliz. Bagshaw: Marriage Alleg. (Canterbury), p. 141.
London, 14, 1, 1, 3, 0; Oxford, 2, 3, 0, 0, 0; Philadelphia, 1, 11, 0, 0, 1; New York, 1, 0, 0, 2, 0.

Worboy(s; v. Warboys.

Worcester, Wurster. — Local, 'of Worcester,' the capital of the county of that name, anciently Wigornaceastre.

Richard de Wygorn', co. Wilts, 1273. A.
Henry de Wygornia, co. Wilts, ibid.
1596. Thomas Worcester, or Worcettor: Reg. Univ. Oxf. vol. ii. pt. ii. p. 216.
1619. Arthur Blunt and Ann Worster: Marriage Lic. (London), ii. 72.
1663. Richard Worcester and Mary Gardner: Marriage Alleg. (Canterbury), p. 80.
1796. Married — Thomas Worcester and Sarah Hammond: St. Geo. Han. Sq. ii. 150.
Philadelphia, 1, 18; Boston (U.S.), 23, 1.

Wordsworth. — Local, 'of Wadsworth,' q.v.

Worger. — Bapt. 'the son of Orgar' (q.v.); cf. Ulf and Wulf, Orme and Worm, Oddard and Woodard, &c.

1674. Bapt. — Eliz., d. John Worgar: St. Jas. Clerkenwell, i. 263.
1677. — John Worgar, s. John Worger: ibid. p. 279.
London, 2.

Work. — Local, 'at the work,' the construction, i.e. the place where the work of defence is being carried on, from A.S. (ge)weorc, a fortification; cf. modern 'works,' a place where manufactures are carried on.

Robertus del Werk, 1379: P.T.Yorks. p. 161.
Philadelphia, 22; Boston (U.S.), 4.

Workman. — Occup. 'the workman,' a labourer, artisan. Cf. preceding article.

Gilbert le Worcman, co. Oxf., 1273. A.
Nicholas Workman, Close Roll, 35 Edw. I.
Johannes Werkman, 1379: P. T. Yorks. p. 243.
Robertus Warkman, 1379: ibid. p. 95.
1665. Giles Workman, vicar of Alderley, co. Glouc.: Atkyns' Hist. Glouc. p. 107.

This surname has ramified strongly in the county of Gloucester.

1696. Married — Mark Warkman and Anne Templeman: St. Dionis Backchurch, p. 45.
London, 3; West Rid. Court Dir., 1; MDB. (co. Glouc.), 12; Philadelphia, 13; Boston (U.S.), 3.

Worm. — Bapt. 'the son of Worm,' i.e. Orme, q.v. W precedes o and u in many names; cf. Ulf and Wolf, Oddard and Woodard, &c.

John Worme, Close Roll, 1 Hen. IV. pt. ii.
Thomas Worme, 1379: P. T. Yorks. p. 81.
William Worme, 1519: GGG. p. 315.
1569. Married — John Worme and Bridgett Vaughan: St. Jas. Clerkenwell, iii. 4.
1612. Cordwell Hamond and Margaret Worme: Marriage Lic. (London), ii. 16.
New York, 2; Philadelphia, 1.

Wormald. — Bapt. 'the son of Wormbald.' Wormald was an inevitable variant. It will be seen that the surname has its chief habitat in W. Rid. Yorks, where I find the personal name at an early period.

Wormboldus Harlam, 1429, co. York: W. ii. 245.
1797. Married — Edward Wolley and Ann Wormald: St. Geo. Han. Sq. ii. 170.
London, 6; West Rid. Court Dir., 11; Leeds, 9.

Wormall, Wormull, Wormell, Wormelle. — Local, (1) 'of Wormhill,' a chapelry in the parish of Tideswell, co. Derby.

Roger de Wormhyll, C. R., 3 Hen. V.

(2) 'Of Wormwall.'

Alex. de Wormwall, 1379: P.T.Yorks. p. 188.

As the Lancashire Aspinwall became Aspinall, so Wormwall would become Wormall, &c.

1730. Married — William Batt and Grace Wormell: St. Geo. Han. Sq. i. 7.
London, 0, 3, 0, 0; Boston (U.S.), 0, 0, 1, 1.

Wormet. — Bapt. 'the son of Worm' (Orme), dim. Wormet. If not this, it must be a corruption of Wormald.

Wormet Orfeour, Close Roll, 6 Hen. IV.

Worrall, Worrell, Worrill. — (1) Local, 'of Wirral.' The district of Wirral, co. Ches., has originated most of the Worralls, &c., of Lancashire and Cheshire. The surname seems to have reached London at a somewhat early period. (2) Local, 'of Worrall,' a hamlet four miles from Sheffield.

John Wirrall, of ——, co. Chester, 1576: Wills at Chester (1545-1620), p. 213.
Thomasin Worrall, of Whiston, widow, 1590: ibid. p. 217.
Margaret Worrall, of Comberbach, 1611: ibid.
Hugh Wirrall, co. Ches., 1630: East Cheshire, ii. 12.
William Wyrhall, co. Ches., 1664: ibid. i. 22.
1586. Married — Robert Worrell and Joane Childe: St. Mary Aldermary (London), p. 7.
1590. Thomas Worrall, co. Ches.: Reg. Univ. Oxf. vol. ii. pt. ii. p. 176.
1797. Married — William Richardson and Susanna Worrell: St. Geo. Han. Sq. ii. 167.
Manchester, 11, 1, 0; London, 9, 2, 1; Sheffield, 4, 1, 0; Philadelphia, 18, 56, 0; Boston (U.S.), 1, 1, 0.

Worsdale, Worsdell. — Local, 'of Wyresdale,' a manor in the parish of Garstang, North Lancashire, situated on the river Wyre; also the valley itself, which is still beautifully wooded.

Johannes de Wyresdale, 1379: P. T. Yorks. p. 78.
William de Wiresdall, 1379: ibid.
1667. Married — John Woodeson and Ane Worsdall: St. Jas. Clerkenwell, iii. 137.
1793. — John Worsdale and Mary Chamberlain: St. Geo. Han. Sq. ii. 92.
London, 2, 0; Ulverston, 0, 1.

Worsencroft; v. Wolstencroft.

Worship. — Nick. a title of respect, short for worth-ship, honour. We say 'your Worship' or 'your Honour.'

Thomas Worthshipp, Close Roll, 16 Edw. III. pt. i.
Thomas Worthship. G.
Hugh Worshipp, temp. Eliz. Z.
1561. Bapt. — Elizabeth, d. William Worship: St. Antholin (London), p. 14.
1615. William Worship, D.D., and Eliz. Beale: Marriage Lic. (London), ii. 34.

Worsley, Worseley. — Local, 'of Worsley,' a parish near Manchester. But the instances below seem to suggest other small localities in South England. The Lancashire and Cheshire Worsleys, however, hail from the above, and have strongly ramified.

John de Wereslle, co. Hunts, 1273. A.
Alan de Weresle, co. Camb., ibid.
Robert de Weresl', co. Suff., ibid.
1571. James Worselye, co. Dorset : Reg. Univ. Oxf. vol. ii. pt. ii. p. 49.
1593. Ottiwell Worsley, of Barton, Manchester : Wills at Chester, i. 217.
1618. Ellen Worsley, of Pendleton, Manchester : ibid.
1622. William Stane and Bridget Worsley : Marriage Lic. (London), ii. 113.
1639. Thomas Worseley and Eliz. Bosvile : ibid. p. 241.
London, 2, 0 ; Manchester, 15, 0 ; Philadelphia, 5, 0 ; Boston (U.S.), 0, 1.

Worsted.—Local, 'of Worsted' or Worstead, a village in co. Norfolk, whence came the thread so called. Flemish weavers, no doubt, settled there early.

Eustace de Wurstede, co. Norf., 1273. A.
Robert de Wurstede, co. Norf., ibid.
Simon Worsted, C. R., 6 Ric. II. pt. ii.
1625-6. Nathaniel Rickard and Grace Wosted : Marriage Lic. (London), ii. 163.

Worswick.—Local, ' of Urswick,' a parish in Furness, North Lanc. This place is popularly called Ursick, but in the past it was evidently Worswick or Worsick (cf. Physic for Fishwick). There is no difficulty about the initial *w* ; cf. Worm and Orme, &c.

1670. Anne Worswick, of Plumpton : Lancashire Wills at Richmond, i. 321.
1673. Thomas Worswick, of Catforth : ibid.
1731. Alex. Worsick, of Great Singleton ; ibid. ii. 289.
1735. Robert Worsick, of Poulton : ibid.

The surname seems to have crossed the Morecambe Sands into the Fylde district of the county.

Manchester, 2 ; Boston (U.S.), 1.

Worth.—Local, 'at the worth,' from A.S. *worth*, an enclosed homestead, a habitation with surrounding land (Bosworth and Toller) ; hence an estate or manor, as in Whitworth, Rickmansworth, &c.

William de la Worthe, co. Soms., 1273. A.
Richard de la Worthe, co. Devon, 20 Edw. I. R.
Reginald de la Wurth. E.

Philip atte Worthe, co. Soms., 1 Edw. III : Kirby's Quest, p. 134.
1581. Anthony Worthe, co. Warw. : Reg. Univ. Oxf. vol. ii. pt. ii. p. 97.
1672. William Worth and Eliz. Dalling : Marriage Lic. (Faculty Office), p. 123.
London, 8 ; Oxford, 5 ; Philadelphia, 16 ; Boston (U.S.), 15.

Worthington. — Local, ' of Worthington,' a township in the parish of Standish, co. Lanc.

'Hugh de Worthyngton and John de Heton hold of the said John half of one knight's fee in Worthyngton,' &c. : Knights' Fees, 23 Edw. III : Baines' Lanc. ii. 695.
Johannes de Worthyngton, *bocher*, 1379 : P. T. Yorks. p. 160.
1598. John Worthington, of Warrington : Wills at Chester, i. 218.
1613. Edward Worthington, of Worthington : ibid.
1616-7. Married—John Hollywell and Joyce Worthington : St. Dionis Backchurch, p. 19.
Manchester, 33 ; London, 7 ; Philadelphia, 57 ; Boston (U.S.), 11.

Worthy. — Local, 'at the worthy,' i.e. the worth, q.v. ; cf. Kenworthy, Langworthy, &c.

1730. Bapt.—John, s. John Worthy : St. Jas. Clerkenwell, p. 187.
1806. Married—William Worthy and Ann Griffiths : St. Geo. Han. Sq. ii. 352.
New York, 1.

Wortley.—Local, 'of Wortley,' two villages, near Leeds and Sheffield.

John de Wortlay, *taillour*, 8 Edw. III : Freemen of York, i. 28.
Johannes de Wortelay, 1379 : P. T. Yorks. p. 89.
1608-9. Francis Wortley, co. York : Reg. Univ. Oxf. vol. ii. pt. ii. p. 304.
1621. Thomas Wortlye, co. York : ibid. p. 395.
1746. Married — Joseph Wortley and Eliz. Ryall : St. Dionis Backchurch, p. 69.
Sheffield, 4 ; West Rid. Court Dir., 5 ; London, 3 ; New York, 2.

Worton.—Local, ' of Worton,' several villages so called in co. Oxford.

Adam de Worton, co. Oxf., 1273. A.
Nicholas de Worton, co. Oxf., ibid.
1669. Married—Richard Worton and Mary Pace : St. Jas. Clerkenwell, p. 167.
London, 2 ; Philadelphia, 2 ; Boston (U.S.), 3.

Wostenholm, Wostinholm, Wostenholme. — Local ; v. Wolstenholm. Variants peculiar to Yorkshire.

Sheffield, 7, 1, 0 ; Philadelphia, 5, 0, 2.

Wotherspoon ; v. Witherspoon.

Wotton ; v. Wootton.

Wozencroft ; v. Wolstencroft.

Wragg, Wragge, Wraggs.—Bapt. 'the son of Ragg,' q.v. The early form is Ragg, clearly allied to Ragn, ' judgement' (Yonge, ii. 374), the chief element of such names as Ragner, Reginald, Raginbald, Raginmund (Raymond), and once a familiar nick. of Ragner, or Ragnar. For *w*, cf. Wray and Ray. Wragg has almost ousted Ragg, but the reason is obvious. The name seems peculiar to Yorkshire.

Peter Ragge, co. York, 1273. A.
William Ragge, co. York, ibid.
Johannes Ragge, 1379 : P. T. Yorks. p. 124.
1620. Thomas Wragg and Jane Smith : Marriage Lic. (London), ii. 91.
1695. Thomas Wragge and Eliz. Houblon : ibid. ii. 316.
West Rid. Court Dir., 12, 0, 0 ; London, 11, 1, 1 ; Philadelphia, 3, 0, 0 ; New York, 0, 1, 0.

Wray, Ray.—Local, 'at the wray,' i.e. in the corner, from residence therein (v. Wroe). Ray in North Lanc. represents Wray as a surname, although surrounded with numberless spots called Wray, or of which Wray is an element. This word means a corner (as of a field or yard) or secluded place. Mr. Atkinson (N. and Q. 1885, p. 252) finds a case of 'in le Wra' or 'del Wra' translated into ' in angulo' and 'in le herne' (v. Hearn and Nangle), and quotes ' Roger in le Wra' in Whorlton, 'Walter del Wra,' in Marske, and 'Robert in le Wra' in Thorgenby (1301). (Taxatio quindecimoe D'no Regi concessor in Com. Ebor: in parte de Northridinge.) Among the compounded place-names are Dockwray, Whin-wray, Capon-wray, and Thack-wray, all self-explanatory ; cf.

Isabel Dockraye, 1560 : Lancashire Wills at Richmond, i. 95.
John Whinwray, of Dalton, 1591 : ibid. i. 307.

Also cf.

Antony Sawraye, of Plumpton, 1623 : ibid. p. 245.
John Blackburne, of Caponwray, 1636 : ibid. p. 36.

In fact, the compounds are many ; cf.

Johannes de Somerscalewra, et uxor, 1379 : P. T. Yorks. p. 286.
Johannes de Somerscale, junior, et uxor, 1379 : ibid.

Amongst many instances I select the following :

Thomas de Ireby, in le Wra, in Villa de Bolton : E. & F., co. Cumb., p. 175.
Thomas del Wra, 1379 : P. T. Yorks. p. 242.
1598. Married—Thomas Johnson and Jane Wraie : St. Jas. Clerkenwell, iii. 21.
1616. — Richard Phelke and Eliz. Raye : ibid. iii. 42.
1640. — Edward Wraye and Eliz. How : ibid. p. 72.
London, 19, 32 ; Philadelphia, 51, 59 ; Boston (U.S.), 5, 58.

Wreaks.—Local, ' of Wreaks.' I cannot find the spot. Wreaks-end (i. e. the end of the Wreak or Wreaks) is the name of an estate near Broughton-in-Furness.
Alicia de Wrekes, 1379 : P. T. Yorks. p. 236.
1730. Bapt. — Leonard, s. Leonard Wreaks : St. Jas. Clerkenwell, ii. 186.
West Rid. Court Dir., 1 ; Sheffield, 2 ; New York, 2.

Wren, Wrenn.—Nick. ' the wren.' M.E. *wrenne*. Cf. Sparrow, Nightingale, Woodcock, &c.

Alice Wrenn, co. Camb., 1273. A.
William Wrenne, co. Camb., ibid.
Wulfy Wrenne, co. Norf., ibid.
Adam Wrenne, 1379 : P. T. Yorks. p. 235.
1630. Married — Thomas Wrenn to Agnis Merceye : St. Mary Aldermary, p. 17.
1661. Buried—Isaac, son of Margarett Wrenn : St. Michael, Cornhill, p. 251.
London, 11, 1 ; Philadelphia, 6, 0 ; New York, 8, 3.

Wrench.—? Bapt. ' the son of Wrench' (?). Found without prefix in the Hundred Rolls. It is a common entry, and scattered over many counties. The conclusion that it is baptismal is almost irresistible. One entry below seems to decide the question.

John Wrenche, co. Wilts, 1273. A.
Robert Wrench, co. Oxf., ibid.
Peter Wrench, co. Suff., ibid.
Warin Wrench, co., Bedf. ibid.

Wrennoc fil. Maurice, co. Salop, Hen. III–Edw. I. K.
1572. Buried — Joan, wife of John Wrenche : St. Peter, Cornhill, i. 121.
1577. Bapt. — Fraunces, s. Simon Wrenche : St. Mary Aldermary(London), p. 59.
London, 6 ; Philadelphia, 4 ; New York, 3.

Wright, Wrightson.—Occup. ' the wright,' often latinized in mediaeval rolls into *faber*, a skilled workman in various materials.

' He was a well good wright, a carpenter.'   Chaucer, C. T. 616.

v. Cheesewright, Glasswright, Cartwright, Wheelwright, Arkwright, &c.

Robert le Wricte, co. Camb., 1273. A.
Roger le Wricte, co. Camb., ibid.
Margery le Wrytte, co. Camb., ibid.
Adam Wrygson, 1379 : P. T. Yorks. p. 84.
Johannes Redebarn, *wryght*, 1379 : ibid. p. 80.
Robert Wreghtston, 1379 : P. T. Yorks. p. 281.
Ann Wrighteson, co. York. W. 9.
1741. Bapt.—James, s. James Wrightson : St. Geo. Chap. Mayfair, p. 2.
1742. Married—Alex. Wright and Mary Harwood : ibid. p. 22.

Wrightson belongs to an extremely small but interesting class ; cf. Smithson, Hinson, Taylorson, and Herdson.

London, 380, 3 ; Philadelphia, 586, 4.

Wrigley.—Local, ' of Wrigley.' This name seems to have passed over the borders from the W. Rid. Yorks. into South-East Lanc. *via* Saddleworth, in which district it still possesses a strong foothold.

Willelmus Wryglegh, 1379 : P. T. Yorks. p. 173.
John Wrigley, of Millington, 1576 : Wills at Chester, i. 219.
John Wrigley, of Saddleworth, 1620 : ibid.
1635. Margaret Wrigley, of Saddleworth : ibid. ii. 246.
1747. Married—John Spatcher and Eliz. Wrigley : St. Geo. Chap. Mayfair, p. 100.
London, 1 ; Manchester, 18 ; Oldham, 13 ; Philadelphia, 36 ; Boston (U.S.), 2.

Wringrose ; v. Ringrose.

Wringrose : Church Defence Report, 1890-91.
Rugby, 1.

Wroe.—Local, ' at the wroe,' i.e. in the corner, a shelter for cattle, &c. ; v. Wray, Nangle, and Hearn.

' Nere Sendyforth ther is a wroo,
And nere that wro is a welle.'
True Thomas, Jamieson's Pop. Ball. ii. 39.

Thomas del Wro, co. Suff., 1273. A.
Adam del Wroo, 6 Edw. III : Old Homesteads, Crompton (Oldham Guardian).
John del Wroo, 6 Edw. III : ibid.
Johannes del Wroo, 1379 : P. T. Yorks. p. 78.
Matilda in ye Wro, 1379 : ibid. p. 200.
Eva in ye Wro, 1379 : ibid.
Thomas del Wro, 1379 : ibid. p. 138.
1742. John Ellis and Mary Wroe : St. Geo. Chap. Mayfair, p. 28.
1759. Married — John Wroe and Eliz. West : St. Geo. Han. Sq. i. 84.
London, 1 ; Manchester, 9 ; Oldham, 2 ; Philadelphia, 2.

Wulf(e, Wulff ; v. Wolff.

Wulfkettle, Wulfkill.—Bapt. ' the son of Wolf-kettle ' (v. Ulf-kettle). The abbot of Croyland, 1062-86, was Ulfcytel or Wulfketyl. His predecessors were Osketyl in 992, and Turketyl in 941. All compounds of Kettle (q.v.).

Wulfkill of Lincoln : Freeman's Norman Conq. iv. 217.

Wulfson ; v. Wolfson.

Wurster ; v. Worcester.

Wyard, Wyart.—Bapt. ' the son of Wygard ' (Yonge, ii. 410). Now almost entirely lost in Wyatt, q.v.

Lena Wyard, co. Suff., 1273. A.
Adam Wyard, co. Camb., ibid.
Robert Wyard. D.
John Wyard. D.
John Wyhard, co. Worc., Hen. III–Edw. I. K.
Wiard le Corner, Wardrobe Accounts, 3 Edw. III.

The following may be placed here, but probably is a variant of Wyatt, q.v. :

1788. Married—Samuel Jesse and Mary Wyett : St. Geo. Han. Sq. ii. 10.
London, 1, 0 ; New York, 0, 1.

Wyatt, Whyatt, Wiatt.—Bapt. ' the son of Guy,' from dim. Guy-ot, in England Wyot (cf. Warin for Guarin, Warner for Garnier, Wilmot for Guillemot) ; v. Guion.

' Adam, son of Wyot, held an oxgang of land ' : De Lacy Inquisition.
Ayote uxor Wyot, co. Salop, 1273. A.
Henry Wyot, co. Camb., ibid.
Wyott le Carpenter, co. Bucks, ibid.
Wyot de Dudelebury, co. Salop, ibid.

Wyot fil. Helias. DD.
Wyot Balistarius. E.
Wiotus de Colebrok, C. R., 8
Edw. II.
Margaret Wyotte, 1379: P. T. Yorks.
p. 66.
Mergeria Wyot, 1379: ibid. p. 134.
1575. John Wyot, co. Devon: Reg.
Univ. Oxf. vol. ii. pt. ii. p. 65.
1576. William Wyatt, co. Devon: ibid.
p. 73.
1581. John Wyatt, or Wiat, co. Worc.:
ibid. p. 103.
1603. Francis Wiat, co. Kent: ibid.
p. 267.

It is clear from the above that
the present form Wyatt is of fairly
recent growth, and will now remain
the recognized orthography for the
coming ages.

London, 55, 0, 0; Philadelphia, 12, 1,
1; Boston (U.S.), 9, 0, 0.

Wybert; v. Wiberd.

Wybroo, Wybrow.—(1) Local,
'of Wigborough.' Great and Little
Wigborough, parishes about seven
miles from Colchester, in co. Essex.
As will be seen from this dictionary,
the suffix -bury or -borough frequently becomes modified into
-brow; cf. Hembrow for Hem-
bury. (2) Bapt.; v. Whybreu.

Richard de Wygebere, co. Soms., 1
Edw. III : Kirby's Quest, p. 242.
Richard de Wigebergh, co. Soms.,
Hen. III–Edw. I. K.
1760. Married—Frederick Wybrow and
Mary Munden : St. Geo. Han. Sq. i. 98.
1802. — George Wybrow and Hannah
Hockley : ibid. ii. 269.
London, 1, 3.

Wyburn.—Bapt. 'the son of
Wyborn.' This surname looks
wonderfully local, but, as suggested
by Mr. Lower (Patr. Brit. p. 391),
the probability is that it is an early
personal name. There is no local
prefix to it in the Hundred Roll
records; cf. Osborne.

Robert Wyborn, co. Oxf., 1273. A.
1575. — Wyburne, co. Kent: Reg.
Univ. Oxf. vol. ii. pt. ii. p. 69.
1805. Married—William Fred Parkes
and Maria Wyborn : St. Geo. Han. Sq.
ii. 338.
London, 2.

Wycliffe, Wickliffe.—Local,
'of Wycliffe,' the parish so called
in North Yorks, 'the white cliff.'
Any one who has seen it will readily

see the origin of the name in the
dull, whitey-grey cliff by which it
stands.

John Whitclive, co. Soms., 1 Edw. III:
Kirby's Quest, p. 138.
Johanna de Wyclayf, 1379: P. T.
Yorks. p. 122.
Willelmus Whyttloffe, 1379: ibid. p. 42.
Johannes Wytloffe, 1379: ibid.

These will probably be immediate
relatives of the Reformer.

Geoffrey Whiteclef, M.P. for Suth-
werk, Close Roll, 4 Ric. II.
1578. Bapt.—Bridget, d. John Wicklif:
St. Mary Aldermary, p. 59.
New York, 0, 1.

**Wykes, Wicks, Wickes,
Wix.**—Local, 'at the wyke,' i.e.
the home, the dwelling; v. Wike.
The suffix s is common to all local
surnames of one syllable; cf. Sykes,
Dykes, Brooks, Styles, &c. 'Wick,
Anglo-Saxon wic, an abode, related
to the Latin vicus' (Isaac Taylor,
Words and Places, p. 484). v.
Wix.

William atte Wyk, co. Oxf., 1273. A.
Henry de la Wyke, co. Oxf., ibid.
Roger de la Wyke, co. Sussex, ibid.
William de la Wyk, co. Soms., ibid.

Cf. John de la Wykhend, co.
Bedf., in the same record (A.).
This is analogous to Townend or
Townshend, i.e. 'at the wyke-
end.' The h is intrusive.

Agneta atte Wykes, co. Soms., 1 Edw.
III : Kirby's Quest, p. 82.
1675. Richard Wykes and Mary West :
Marriage Alleg. (Canterbury), p. 242.
1691. Married—Benjamin Tiplady and
Ann Wicks : St. Peter, Cornhill, ii. 59.
London, 7, 20, 2, 1; Oxford (Wicks), 5;
Boston (U.S.), (Wyke), 2; Philadelphia,
1, 5, 1, 1.

Wyld; v. Wild.

Wyldsmith; v. Wildsmith.

**Wylie, Wyllie, Willey,
Wiley.**—(1) Local, 'of Willey,'
parishes in the diocs. of Hereford
and Worc. (2) 'of Wylye' or
Wyly, a parish in the dioc. of
Salisbury, co. Wilts.

Nicholas de Wyly, co. Wilts, Hen. III–
Edw. I. K.
Richard de Wileye, co. Camb., 1273. A.
Roger de Wylye, co. Bedf., ibid.
Hugh de Wyly, co. Wilts, 20 Edw.
I. R.
1595. Edmund Willie, co. Soms.: Reg.
Univ. Oxf. vol. ii. pt. ii. p. 209.

1614. Thomas Williams and Eliz.
Wylley : Marriage Lic. (Westminster),
p. 22.
1621. Francis Willy, co. Herts : Reg.
Univ. Oxf. vol. ii. pt. ii. p. 402.
1746. Married — William Rogers and
Eliz. Wily : St. Geo. Chap. Mayfair, p.63.
London, 7, 5, 11, 4; Boston (U.S.), 6,
2, 40, 49; Philadelphia, 29, 0, 2, 116.

**Wyman, Wayman, Way-
men.**—Bapt. 'the son of Wimond.'
The baptismal name lasted till the
Reformation :

Wimond Cary, Patent Roll, 2 Eliz.
pt. xiv.

The London Directory proves its
common use in the past. With
Wyman cf. Osman for Osmund, and
with Wayman cf. Waymark (v.
Wymark).

Reginald fil. Wymundi, Hen. III–Edw.
I. K.
Wymundus de Ralegh, ibid.
Wymund le Lyngedraper, 1273. A.
Wymond Brother, Close Roll, 13
Edw. II.
John Wyman, sup. for B.A., Jan. 27,
1527–8 : Reg. Univ. Oxf. i. 150.

Wymond is the name of the
third soldier in the Shearmen's
Play :

'We, howe! Sir Wymond, howe?'
     York Mystery Plays, p. 339.

'Goffridus, 1 carucate, which Widmun-
dus holds': Lincolnshire Survey, temp.
1109, p. 14.
Johannes Wymond, 1379: P. T. Yorks.
p. 134.
1582. Married — Peter Wayman and
Ann Bondde : St. Mary Aldermary
(London), p. 7.
1753. — James Wyman and Jane
McAulay: St. Geo. Chap. Mayfair, p. 225.
London, 8, 2, 1; Philadelphia, 14, 4, 0;
Boston (U.S.), 82, 0, 0.

Wymark, Waymark.—Bapt.
'the son of Wymarc.' 'On either
side of his bed stood the two great
chiefs of his realm, Harold the
Earl, and Stigand the Archbishop.
At the bed's head stood the Staller,
Robert the son of Wymarc, a man
of Norman birth' (Death of Eadward,
Freeman, iii. 9). Several Wymarcs
occur in Domesday. 'Wymarck
Piggesteyl, inhabitant of Win-
chelsea, 20 Edw. I' (Lower, Patr.
Brit.).

Wymarc Mercatrix, co. Hunts, 1273. A.
Wymarc Brown, co. Bedf., ibid.
Wymarca fil. Roberti, Henry III. T.

Wymarca Fraunceys, Henry III. T. Johannes Wymarkson, 1379: P. T. Yorks. p. 271.
Wymerk de Bland, 1379: ibid. p. 246.
John Wymerk, fellow of Merton, 1451: Reg. Univ. Oxf. i. 16.
1551. Buried — Ellis Wimarke: St. Antholin (London), p. 8.
1702. Married—Matthias Wallraven and Mercy Waymarke: St. Dionis Back-church, p. 51.

With the variant Waymark, cf. Wayman for Wyman, q.v.

London, 2, 1.

Wymer, Wimer.—Bapt. 'the son of Wigmar' (Yonge, ii. 410). In England popularly Wymer or Wimer. Once decidedly a favour-ite, and incorporated with many local terms. Lord Winmarleigh takes his title from Winmarleigh in co. Lanc., formerly Winnerlie or Wimerlegh; cf. Wymersley in

the same county (v. Baines' Lanc. ii. 535).
Wimer de Eppeworth, Hen. III–Edw. I. K.
Wymer atte Grene, 1273. A.
John Wymer, co. Camb., ibid.
Peter Wymere, co. Camb., ibid.
Wimerus Dapifer, temp. Edw. I: Blomefield's Norfolk (edit. 1805), vol. x. p. 52.
Wymer de Alesham, 1364: ibid. p. 121.
Wyhomarus de Aske: Visitation of Yorkshire, p. 365.
London, 3, 0; Philadelphia, 0, 18.

Wynn, Wynne, Winn, Winne.—Nick.'Gwynn'(Welsh), white, fair (v. Gwinn); cf. Gwalter and Gwilliam for Walter and William, both Welsh forms.

Oto Gwyn, or Hwyn, 1513: Reg. Univ. Oxf. i. 84.
Robert Wynne, or Gwinne, 1568: ibid. p. 271.
1593-4. Ellis Wynn, or Win, co. Carnarvon: ibid. vol. ii. pt. ii. p. 200.
1605. John Wynn, co. Carnarvon: ibid. p. 286.

1605. Morgan Wynne, or Winn, co. Denbigh: ibid. p. 285.
1719. Buried — Hugh Winn, in the middle isle: St. Peter, Cornhill, ii. 125.
London, 5, 9, 15, 0; Philadelphia, 19, 12, 20, 2; Boston (U.S.), 1, 4, 36, 2.

Wynter; v. Winter.

Wyon.—Bapt. 'the son of Guy,' from the dim. Guion. Just as another dim. Guiot became Wyot and Wyatt, so Guion became Wyon. No connexion with Wynn, q.v.

William Wyonn, co. Soms., 9 Edw. II: Kirby's Quest, p. 174.
1629. Married — Simon Wyan and Joane Charnocke: St. Thomas the Apostle (London), p. 14.
1632. — Robert Wyan and Mary Went-worth: St. Jas. Clerkenwell, iii. 64.
1670. — Oliver Beecher and Sarah Wyan: St. Michael, Cornhill, i. 39.
London, 3.

Wyse; v. Wise.

Y

Yalden.—Local, 'of Yalding,' a parish in co. Kent, near Maid-stone. This seems to be the most satisfactory solution.

London, 2.

Yalland; v. Yelland.

Yapp.—? Local, 'at the gap'; v. Gapp; cf. Yates for Gates.

1620. Christopher Baylie and Eliz. Yapp: Marriage Lic. (London), ii. 91.
Richard Yapp, *haberdasher*, 1655: Reg. St. Peter, Cornhill, i. 250.
1792. Married — Francis Yapp and Lydia Shorland: St. Geo. Han. Sq. ii. 71.
London, 3; Philadelphia, 2; Boston (U.S.), 2.

Yarborough, Yarbrough, Yerburgh, Yarboro.—Local, (1) 'of Yarborough' or Yarburgh, a parish in the union of Louth, co. Lincoln; (2) also a hamlet in the parish of Croxton, co. Lincoln.
Gilbert de Yerdeburc, co. Linc., 1273. A.
Robert de Yerdeburch, co. Linc., ibid.

John de Yerbury, co. Soms., 1 Edw. III: Kirby's Quest, p. 227.
1635. Richard Yerbergh and Frances Proctor: Marriage Lic. (London), ii. 223.
1635-6. Rowland Hacker and Eliz. Yerborowe: ibid. p. 225.
1660-1. William Gilbert and Katherine Yarborough: Marriage Alleg. (Canter-bury), p. 54.
Crockford, 1, 0, 2, 0; MDB. (Lincoln), 2, 2, 1, 1.

Yard, Yarde.—Local, 'at the yard' (M.E. *yerd*, an enclosure), from residence therein.

John de la Yhurde, co. Southampton, Hen. III–Edw. I. K.
William de la Yerd, C. R., 2 Edw. I.
William atte Yurd, C. R., 17 Edw. III. pt. i.
Hugh atte Yeurd, co. Soms., 1 Edw. III: Kirby's Quest, p. 167.
Walter atte Yurd, co. Soms., 1 Edw. III: ibid. p. 180.
1676. Buried—Mary, d. Thomas Yard: St. Thomas the Apostle (London), p. 141.
1807. Married—William Shergold and Mary Yard: St. Geo. Han. Sq. ii. 366.
London, 0, 2; Crockford, 1, 2; Phila-delphia, 16, 0.

Yardley.—Local, 'of Yardley': (1) a parish in co. Hertford; (2) a parish near Birmingham, co. Worcester; (3) two parishes, Yardley - Gobion and Yardley - Hastings, in co. Northampton.

Richard de Yardele, co. Linc., 1273. A.
1592. Bapt.—Eliz., d. William Yardley: St. Jas. Clerkenwell, i. 26.
1612. Married — Richard Hinde and Anne Yardlye: St. Michael, Cornhill, p. 20.
London, 6; Philadelphia, 13.

Yarker.—? Offic. 'a whipper-in' (?); v. *yark* in Halliwell.

Johannes Yarkar, 1379: P. T. Yorks. p. 211.
Johannes Yarker, 1379: ibid. p. 199
Manchester, 1; Pennington, near Ulverston, 1.

Yarnold, Yarnall. — Bapt. 'the son of Arnold.' The corruption was an early one. With Yarnall, cf. Arnall for Arnold.

Richard fil. Yarnord, co. Salop, 1273. A. 1783. Married—John Brill and Sarah Yarnould : St. Geo. Han. Sq. i. 351. London, 2, 0 ; Philadelphia, 0, 44.

Yarnton, Yarranton, Yarrington.—Local, ' of Yarington ' or Yarnton, a parish in co. Oxford. The London Directory form is manifestly a corruption of Yarrington as found below :

1626. John Ward and Eliz. Yarrington : Marriage Lic. (London), ii. 168.
— Arthur Croome and Dorothy Yarrington : ibid. p. 178.
London, 0, 1, 0 ; MDB. (co. Worc.), 0, 2, 0 ; Oxford, 1, 0, 0 ; Philadelphia, 0, 0, 1 ; Boston (U.S.), 0, 0, 7.

Yarrow.—Local, ' of Yarrow,' a parish in co. Selkirk.

1573. Buried — Sare Yarrowe, d. of Marques Yarrow, *a stranger* : St. Dionis Backchurch, p. 193.
1766. Married — John Yarrow and Susanna Merredith : St. Geo. Han. Sq. i. 151.
London, 10 ; Philadelphia, 7.

Yate, Yates.—Local, ' at the gate.' M.E. *gate, yate.* Monosyllabic local surnames frequently take a final *s*, perhaps the patronymic, as in Williams, Jennings, &c.; cf. Stubbs, Styles, Stones, Bridges, Brooks. Hence Yates for Yate. ' Gate (or yate), *porta, foris* ': Prompt. Parv. Other forms of this surname are Yeatts, Yeates, and Yeats. q.v. Evidently the two following names were closely related :

1606. Laurence Yate, of Nether Darwen : Wills at Chester, i. 221.
1608. Laurence Yates, of Blackburn : ibid.

No doubt the family were known indifferently as Yate or Yates.

William atte Yete, co. Soms., 1 Edw. III : Kirby's Quest, p. 91.
Batin atte Yete, co. Soms., 1 Edw. III : ibid. p. 92.
Richard atte Yate, co. Soms., 1 Edw. III : ibid. p. 94.
Johannes atte Yate, 1379 : P. T. Yorks. p. 134.
Adam atte Yate, 1379 : ibid. p. 184.
1725. Married—Thomas Yate and Eliz. Collyer : St. Dionis Backchurch, p. 61.
London, 0, 37 ; Crockford, 2, 8 ; Philadelphia, 0, 47 ; Boston (U.S.), 0, 13.

Yate-, Yatman ; v. Yeatman.

Yaxley.—Local, ' of Yaxley,' parishes in cos. Hunts and Suffolk.
London, 3.

Yea ; v. Yeo.

Yeadon.—Local, ' of Yeadon,' a township in the parish of Guisley, near Leeds, W. Rid. Yorks.
John de Yedon, co. York, 1273. A.
Robert de Yedona, co. York, ibid.
MDB. (West Rid. Yorks), 2.

Yeaman ; v. Yeman.

Yeamans ; v. Yeoman.

Yearling. — Nick. ' the yearling ' ; cf. Tegg and Weatherhog.
John Yerling, co. Soms. 1 Edw. III : Kirby's Quest, p. 238.

Yeates ; v. Yeats.

Yeatman, Yatman.—Occup. ' the gate-man,' one who had care of a road or gate, or more simply one who lived on the road by the gate. *Yate* for gate is still in common use in the North. A farm in Ulverston is called Bowstead Yeats. v. Yates and Yeats.

1603. Bapt.—John, s. John Yateman : St. Jas. Clerkenwell, i. 41.
1758. Married — Thomas Wight and Ann Yeatman : St. Geo. Han. Sq. i. 77.
1775. — David Yetman and Eliz. Tabor : ibid. p. 258.
London, 6, 0 ; Crockford, 3, 1 ; Oxford (Yateman), 1 ; Philadelphia, 6, 0 ; Boston (U.S.), 0, 1.

Yeats, Yeates, Yeatts ; v. Yate and Yeatman.

1753. Married—John Yeats and Ann Davis : St. Geo. Han. Sq. i. 50.
1760. — John Baynom and Ann Yeates : ibid. p. 94.
London, 6, 6, 0 ; Philadelphia, 0, 0, 4.

Yeilding, Yelden.—Local, ' of Yielding,' otherwise ' Yelden,' a parish in co. Bedford, near Higham Ferrers.
1615. James Yeldinge, co. Hants : Reg. Univ. Oxf. vol. ii. pt. ii. p. 344.
London, 1, 1.

Yeldham. — Local, ' of Yeldham,' two parishes (Great and Little Yeldham) near Halsted, co. Essex.
1796. Married—John Smith and Lucy Yeldham : St. Geo. Han. Sq. ii. 148.
1801. — Joseph Yeldom and Letitia Lawrence : ibid. p. 242.
London, 2.

Yelland, Yeolond, Yolland, Yalland.—Local, ' of Yealand.' Yealand Conyers and Yealand

Redmayne are two townships in the parish of Warton, co. Lanc. Yealand Hall still remains ; v. Baines' Hist. Lanc. ii. 604.
John de la Yaldelonde, co. Devon, 1273. A.
William de Yelaund, co. Northumberland : ibid.
Adam de Yelland, warden of the Honor of Lancaster, 13 Hen. III : Baines' Hist. Lanc. ii. 604.
Willelmus de Yeland, 1379 : P. T. Howdenshire, p. 4.
MDB. (co. Devon), 7, 0, 3, 2 ; London, 1, 0, 0, 0 ; Sheffield, 0, 1, 0, 0 ; Philadelphia, 3, 0, 0, 0 ; Boston (U.S.), 1, 0, 0, 0.

Yellowley, Yellowly, Yellowlee.—Local, ' of Yellowley.' I cannot find the spot. It seems to be a North-English surname. Its meaning is simple, viz. ' the golden meadow,' whether from its yellow flowers or yellow clayey soil, I cannot say.
Northumberland Court Dir., 3, 1, 0 ; Crockford, 0, 1, 0 ; New York, 0, 0, 1.

Yelverton. — Local, ' of Yelverton,' a parish in co. Norfolk, about six miles from Norwich.
MDB. (co. Devon), 4 ; London Court Dir., 2 ; New York, 1.

Yeman, Yeaman. — Occup. ' the yeoman ' ; v. Yeoman.
William Yeaman, temp. Eliz. Z.
1805. Married — Thomas Shields and Frances Yeaman : St. Geo. Han. Sq. ii. 319.
London, 2, 0 ; New York, 0, 2.

Yeo, Yea, Yoe, Yohe.—Local, ' at the yew,' from residence thereby, a West-country name ; cf. Box, Ash, Birch, Plumptre, &c. Lower says, ' An ancient Devonshire family. The Yeo is a small river of that county, a tributary of the Cready, into which it falls near the town of Crediton. C. S. Gilbert derives the name from Tre-yeo, in the parish of Lancells, near Stratton, co. Cornwall.—Hist. Cornw. ii. 335.' In some cases this is probably true.
Geoffrey de la Ya, co. Devon, Hen. III–Edw. I. K.
Nicholas de la Ya, co. Devon, ibid.
William atte Yoo, co. Soms., 1 Edw. III : Kirby's Quest, p. 89.
John atte Yo, co. Soms., 1 Edw. III : ibid. p. 182.

3 H

John atte Yoo, co. Soms., 1 Edw. III : Kirby's Quest, p. 251.
1547. William Yeo and Anne Turton : Marriage Lic. (London), i. 10.
1683. Bapt.—William, son of Richard Yeo : St. Jas. Clerkenwell, i. 302.
1722. Married—Arthur Yeo and Mary Dowling : St. Antholin (London), p. 137.
1739. — George Sikes and Mary Yoe : St. Dionis Backchurch, p. 67.
MDB. (Somerset), 2, 4, 0, 0 ; (Devon), 10, 0, 0, 0 ; London, 6, 0, 0, 0 ; New York, 0, 0, 1, 0 ; Philadelphia, 2, 0, 0, 5 ; Boston (U.S.), 4, 0, 0, 0.

Yeoland; v. Yelland.

Yeoman, Yeomans, Yeomanson, Yeamans. — Occup. 'the yeoman,' one of some small position or estate. The s in Yeomans is the patronymic ; cf. Jones for Johnson, Roberts for Robertson, &c.

Henricus Yhoman, 1379 : P. T. Yorks. p. 106.
Johannes Yomanne, 1379 : ibid. p. 250.
Robert Yomanson. F.
1539-40. Married—John Trevisam and Agnes Yemerson : St. Dionis Backchurch, p. 1.
1582. — Nycholas Speringe and Ellyn Yeomans : St. Michael, Cornhill, p. 13.
Fraunce Yeoman, 1596 : Reg. St. Columb Major, p. 17.
1781. Married—Thomas Yeoman and Hannah Neale : St. Geo. Han. Sq. i. 319.
London, 4, 10, 1, 0 ; Philadelphia, 0, 3, 3, 3 ; New York, 4, 0, 0, 1.

Yeowart; v. Youard.

Yerburgh.—Local ; v. Yarborough.

Yetts.—Local ; v. Yate.
London, 3.

Yew, Yews; v. Ewes.

Yewdall, Yeudall, Youdale.—Local, 'of Yewdale.' Probably the Yorkshire Yewdalls are sprung from some small dale of that name in the West or North Riding. There is a Yewdale at the northern end of Coniston Lake, which seems to have originated a surname. As the first instance below is found in the immediate neighbourhood of Skipton, it may be that the Coniston vale is the true parent of all the Yewdalls.

Alicia de Yowdall', 1379 : P. T. Yorks. p. 266.
1600. Geoffrey Yeodell, of Dalton in Furness : Lancashire Wills at Richmond, i. 324.

1616. William Yeodall, or Yewdell, of Cartmel, Furness : ibid.
1727. Bapt.—Timothy, s. of Eliz. Youdall : Reg. St. Mary, Ulverston, p. 315.
1788. Married—Joseph Ambrose and Mary Yewdall : St. Geo. Han. Sq. ii. 1.
West Rid. Court Dir., 7, 0, 0 ; Boston (U.S.), 1, 0, 0 ; Philadelphia, 0, 0, 3 ; New York, 0, 0, 1.

Yewen.— Bapt. 'the son of Jevan'; v. Jevon.
Yevan de Yhtefelt, co. Salop, 1273. A.
Heine fil. Yevan, co. Salop, ibid.
London, 2.

Yoe, Yohe; v. Yeo.

Yohman; v. Yeoman.
New York, 1.

Yolland.—Local ; v. Yelland.

Yonge, Yung. — Nick. 'the Young,' q. v. M.E. yong and yung.
John le Yonge, co. Wilts, 1273. A.
London, 2, 0 ; Philadelphia, 1, 3 ; Boston (U.S.), 1, 0.

Yool, Youle, Youll, Youell.—Bapt. 'the son of Yule,' a name given to children born on Christmas Day ; cf. Noel, Nowell, Christmas, Midwinter, Pentecost, Pace, Pascal, &c. From Yorkshire the surname seems to have gone northwards, as Youll is fairly familiar to the present directories of Durham and Northumberland.
William Yole, pelter, 8 Edw. III : Freemen of York, i. 29.
Isabella Yoll', 1379 : P. T. Yorks. p. 123.
Johannes Yoll', 1379 : ibid.
Robertus Youle, 1379 : ibid. p. 6.
Willelmus Youle, 1379 : ibid.
1620. Thomas Youll and Eliz. Moseley : Marriage Lic. (London), ii. 97.
1778. Married—James Youell and Jane Franks : St. Geo. Han. Sq. i. 288.
London, 2, 3, 0, 0 ; Northumberland Court Dir., 0, 0, 2, 0 ; Philadelphia, 0, 0, 0, 3 ; New York, 0, 2, 0, 0.

Yorath. — Bapt. 'the son of Yerworth,' a Welsh personal name found at an early period.
Iorwerth, alias Gervase, bishop of St. David's, 1215 : Hist. and Ant. St. David's, p. 357.
John Yerworthe, co. Ches., 1581 : Reg. Univ. Oxf. vol. ii. pt. ii. p. 97.
Edward Yerworth, or Yearewarth, co. Ches., 1602 : ibid. p. 256.
1610. Samuel Yaroth, co. Dorset : ibid. p. 319.
1626. John Coles and Catherine Yarath, widow : Marriage Lic. (London), ii. 181.
'W. L. Yorath, who followed, was dis-

missed without scoring'; Glamorganshire v. M.C.C. and ground : South Wales Daily News, Aug. 23, 1889.
Swansea, 2 ; Cardiff, 3.

York, Yorke. — Local, ' of York.' Naturally, a name likely to become familiar to our directories.
Gilbert de Ebor', co. York, 1273. A.
William de Ebor', co. York, ibid.
Agnes de York, 1379 : P. T. Yorks. p. 155.
1557. Married—Guylberte Yorke and Amye Bonde : St. Michael, Cornhill, p. 7.
1659. Buried — Rebecca, d. Richard Yorke, hosier : St. Dionis Backchurch, p. 231.
London, 8, 2 ; West Rid. Court Dir., 3, 5 ; Philadelphia, 15, 2 ; Boston (U.S.), 44, 0.

Youard, Youart, Yeowart, Youatt.—Occup. ' the ewe-herd,' recorded as 'yowhird' (v. Ewart) ; cf. Calvert for Calveherd, Swinnart for Swineherd, &c.

'A ring for my cozen, Mrs. Ellen Yoward' . . . Will of Ric. Tempest, of Bracewell, 1657 : Whitaker's Craven, p. 97.
The live stock at Bolton Abbey (1526) included 'xx oxen, xxvi stotts, ix tuppers, x yowes': ibid. p. 403.
Matilda Yowhyrd, 1379 : P. T. Yorks. p. 266.
Thomas Yowhyrd, 1379 : ibid. p. 264.
Willelmus Euerhyrd, 1379 : ibid. p. 271.
Johannes Euerhyrd, 1379 : ibid.
1611. Married—Richard Yeowart and Penelope Parker : Marriage Lic. (London), ii. 6.
1787. — William Jones and Martha Yourd, or Youd : St. Geo. Han. Sq. i. 401.
London, 0, 0, 0, 2 ; MDB. (North Rid. Yorks), 1, 0, 0, 0 ; Liverpool, 0, 0, 1, 0.

Youdale; v. Yewdall.

Youell, Youll; v. Yool.

Youmans; v. Yeomans.
New York, 8.

Young, Younge.—Nick. 'the Young.' M.E. yong and yung. Probably in many cases the nickname was applied in the sense of junior, to distinguish father and son when both bore the same personal name (v. Senior) ; cf. Younger. Over a thousand people bear this name in London alone.

Hugh le Yunge, co. Oxf., 1273. A.
Ralph le Younge, co. Staff., ibid.
William le Yunge, co. Northumb., 20 Edw. I. R.

1561. Bapt. — John, son of Gregory Yong, *grocer*: St. Peter, Cornhill, i. 10. London, 240, 1; Philadelphia, 762, 0; Boston (U.S.), 396, 0; New York (Younge), 1.

Youngcock. — Nick. 'young cock,' a familiar term of address; cf. the modern 'Well, old cock, how are you?' v. Cocks and Cox.

Willelmus Yongcok, 1379: P. T. Yorks. p. 29.

Younger, Yunger. — Nick. 'the younger,' i.e. the younger of two bearing the same name; cf. Elder and Senior.

Edmundus Yonger, 1379: P. T. Yorks. p. 279.
Walter Yonger, C. R., 1 Hen. V.
1788. Married — John Younger and Eliz. Russell: St. Geo. Han. Sq. ii. 3.
London, 4, 0; Philadelphia, 8, 6; Boston (U.S.), 1, 0.

Youngerman, Yungerman. —Nick. 'the younger man,' to distinguish the original bearer of the name from the elder man; v. Elder and Younger.

Boston (U.S.), 2, 0; Philadelphia, 0, 1,

Younghusband.—Nick. 'the young husband,' the young householder; v. Husband; cf. Youngsmith.

Roger le Yonghusband. G.
Thomas le Yonghusband, temp. 1300. M.

Radulphus Yong' Hosband et Agnes uxor ejus, 1379: P. T. Yorks. p. 164.
Bertram Younghusband: PPP. p. 19.

The following is a natural and yet curious corruption :

Richard Youngsband, vicar of Thorpmarket, co. Norf., 1608: FF. viii. 174.
1806. Married—William Younghusband and Anne Younghusband: St. Geo. Han. Sq. ii. 341.
London, 4; Boston (U.S.), 1.

Youngling, Yungling. — Nick. 'the youngling,' a young man (v. Wyclif, Mark xvi. 5). I cannot find any instances in modern English directories. It seems to be one of many names which have died out in the old country and survived in the United States.

John Yonglyng, C. R., 9 Hen. IV.
Richard Yonglyng, C. R., 1 Hen. V.
New York, 1, 1; Philadelphia, 0, 1.

Youngman, Yungman. — Nick. 'the young man'; cf. Younghusband. An East Anglian surname, common in Norfolk and Suffolk.

William Yungman, co. Linc., 20 Edw. I. R.
Nicholas Youngman, 1365, co. Norf.: FF. i. 298.
1787. Married—John Youngman and Sarah Vanryne: St. Geo. Han. Sq. i. 401.

London, 8, 0; MDB. (Norfolk), 8, 0; (Suffolk), 13, 0; Philadelphia, 0, 1; New York, 0, 1; Boston (U.S.), 1, 0.

Youngmay.—Nickname, 'the young may,' i.e. the growing boy; v. May (1).

Martin le Yungemey, co. Sussex, 1273. A.

Youngsmith. — Nick. 'the young smith,' as distinguished from the old. The surname ought to be extant, judging by the number of early entries, but I have not discovered it. It is found in the sixteenth century.

Johannes Yong', *smyth*, 1379: P. T. Yorks. p. 165.
Johannes Yongsmyth, 1379: ibid. p. 24.
John Yongsmith, temp. Eliz. F.
Bartholomew Youngsmithe, co. York. W. 16.
Bertram Youngsmith, 1502: PPP. p. 10.

Youngson.—Nick. 'the son of Young' (q.v.), or probably the younger as distinguished from the elder son; v. Younger.

MDB. (East Rid. Yorks), 1.

Yung; v. Yonge.

Yunger; v. Younger.

Yungerman; v. Youngerman.

Yungling; v. Youngling.

Yungman; Youngman.

Z

Zachary.—Bapt. 'the son of Zachary,' the English form of Zachariah (v. Yonge, i. 124).

1586. Bapt.—Isabell, d. Thomas Zachary: St. Jas. Clerkenwell, i. 18.
London, 1; Crockford, 1.

Zeal, Zeall. — Local. Mr. Lower says, 'of Zeal, a parish in Devonshire, usually called Zeal-Monachorum.' There is also South Zeal in the same county, and Zeals is a tithing in co. Wilts. I find no

early instance of this surname, and think it is more probably a variant of Seal, q.v.; and cf. Zouch and Such.

London, 0, 1.

Zealey.—? Nick. I find no traces of this name in early records, so conclude that it is a corruption of Seeley, q.v.

1749. Married — Simon Zealey and Abigail Churchill: St. Geo. Chap. Mayfair, p. 129.
London, 1.

Zouch.—Local, 'de la Zouch.' 'Zuches = stumps of trees': Halliwell. v. Such.

Ivo de la Zusch, co. Devon, 1273. A.
Ivo de la Zoche, ibid.
Alan de la Zouche, co. Wilts, Hen. III–Edw. I. K.
Guy de la Zouch, co. Sutherland, 20 Edw. I. R.
Olive de la Zouche, co. Hants, ibid.
1580. Married — Robert Arras and Elizabeth Zouche: St. Jas. Clerkenwell, iii. 8.
1641. William Zouch and Anne Bowling: Marriage Lic. (London), ii. 261.

ADDENDA ET CORRIGENDA

Abbey, Abbee, Abbe. — v. p. 37. The two local instances from Freemen of York were added after the publication of that work in 1897. The article remains as originally written, when the Author had only found the local instance in the Lay Subsidy (Rylands).

Bannerman.—Offic. 'the bannerman,' the ensign bearer. Though this name, being Scotch, has no place of right in this dictionary, it is interesting as being the equivalent of Penniger, q.v.; also v. Mr. Lower's article in Patr. Brit. p. 17.

Manchester, 1; Philadelphia, 1.

Bramble.—Local, 'of Bramble.' I cannot find the place. It is probably some small spot in co. Kent.

Thomas de Bremble, co. Kent, 1273. A.
Helena Bramble, co. Kent, 13 Edw. IV, pt. ii.
1606-7. Richard Bramble (Dorset): Reg. Univ. Oxf. vol. ii. pt. ii. p. 293.
1623. John Bramble, 'Maior of Poole,' co. Dorset: Visitation of Dorsetshire, p. 1.
London, 3; Penzance, 1; Philadelphia, 10.

Brearley, Brierley, Brierly. —Local, 'of Brierley,' a township in the parish of Felkirk, West Riding, co. York; v. Brear.

John de Brerelay, 13 Ric. II: Freemen of York, i. 89.
1782. Married—John Croker and Mary Brearley: St. Geo. Chap. Mayfair, p. 234.
London, 0, 4, 2; West Rid. Court Dir., 4, 8, 1.

Brooker, Brucker. — Local, 'the brooker,' one who lived by the brook (M.E. *brok* and *broke*, Mayhew and Skeat). Cf. Bridger, and v. next article. For instances, v. Broker, to which this should be added as an additional meaning.

Oxford, 3, 2.

Brookman.—Local, 'the brookman,' one who lived by the brook; cf. Bridgman, Pullman, &c.

John Brokeman. C.
1592. Francis Mason and Anne Brokeman: Marriage Lic. (London), i. 205.
1601. Edward Cooke and Katherine Brookeman: ibid. p. 264.
London, 2; Philadelphia, 1.

Butts.—Local, 'at the butts,' from residence thereby. Mr. Lower says, 'Butts, the marks for archery. In old times all corporate towns, and most parishes, had a provision for this sport, and numerous fields and closes where the long bow was exercised are still called 'The Butts' (Patr. Brit. p. 48). v. Sowerbutts.

1563. Edmund Buttes and Thomasine Bedell: Marriage Lic. (London), i. 26.
1619. Richard Butts, co. Hereford: Reg. Univ. Oxf. vol. ii. pt. ii. p. 379.
London, 3; Boston (U.S.), 13.

Cambden, Camden.—Local, 'of Campden': (1) Chipping Campden; (2) Broad Campden, a parish and a hamlet in co. Glouc.

Hugh de Campeden, co. Glouc., 1273. A.
John de Campeden, co. Northampt., ibid.
1570. William Camden: Reg. Univ. Oxf. i. 270.
1573. William Campden: ibid. vol. ii. pt. iii. p. 40.
London, 4, 1; Philadelphia, 0, 10.

Crawley.—Local, 'of Crawley.' Parishes and townships bear this name in cos. Northumb., Hants, and Sussex. There is also Crawley, a hamlet in co. Oxf., and North Crawley in co. Bedford.

Hugh de Craule, co. Bedford, 1273. A.
Margaret de Craule, co. Oxf., ibid.
Alan de Craule, co. Oxf., 20 Edw. I. R.
1659. Married—Thomas Crawley and Amye powell (sic): St. Peter, Cornhill, p. 261.
London, 24; Boston (U.S.), 11.

Glanfield, Glanvill, Glanville.—Local, 'de Glanville.' Mr. Lower says, 'A place in the arrondissement of Pont l'Evéque in Normandy.' The change to Glanfield was natural; cf. Merrifield for

Merivale. Mr. Lower, quoting Shirley's Noble and Gentle Men, says, 'Ranulf de Glanville entered England with the Conqueror' (Patr. Brit. p. 130).

Ranulf de Glanvile, co. Camb., 1273. A.
Reginald de Glanvil, co. Oxf., ibid.
1724. Bapt. — Mary, d. Samuel and Mary Glanvil: Reg. St. Columb Major, p. 97.
1727. — Eliz., d. Samuell and Mary Glanfield: ibid.

Evidently the parents were the same in the last two entries.

London, 4, 4, 8; Oxford, 1, 0, 3; Philadelphia, 0, 0, 1.

Lovegrove. — Local, 'of the grove,' or collection of trees, belonging to Love. v. Love and Grove.

1616. Buried — John, s. John Lovegrove: St. Jas. Clerkenwell, iv. 136.
1621. John Lovegroave and Agnes Whitmill: Marriage Lic. London, ii. 102.
London, 10; Oxford, 4; Philadelphia, 4.

Lyman, Lynam.—Local, (1) 'of Lyneham,' a chapelry near Burford, co. Oxf.; (2) 'of Lineham,' a parish in co. Wilts. The interchange of letters is common; cf. Adnam and Adman for Addingham; Swetnam and Swetman for Swetenham; Debnam and Deadman for Debenham, &c.

William de Linham, co. Oxf., 1273. A.
William de Linham, co. Notts, ibid.

The following entries refer to the same individual:

1613. Richard Lynam (Queen's): Reg. Univ. Oxf. vol. ii. pt. ii. p. 331.
1616-7. Richard Lyman (Liman, Lynam) (Queen's): ibid. pt. iii. p. 353.
London, 1, 0; Oxford, 0, 3; Philadelphia, 13, 8.

Lyndhurst.—Local, 'of Lyndhurst,' a parish in the New Forest, co. Hants.

Henry de Lindherste, co. Hants, 1273. A.

Maydwell.—Local, 'of Maidwell,' a parish in co. Northampton. v. Maidwell.

Simon de Maydewell, co. Northampt., 1273. A.
Henry de Maydewelle, co. Oxf., ibid. London, 2.

Ovenell, Overnell. — Local, 'of Ovenell.' I cannot find the spot, but the following entry seems to refer to this name :

Hugh de Ovonill, co. Salop, 20 Edw. I. R.
London, 0, 1 ; Oxford, 3, 0.

Penington, Pennington. — Local, 'of Pennington,' (1) a parish in the union of Ulverston, in the North Division of co. Lanc. ; (2) a township in the parish of Leigh, in the South Division of the same county ; (3) a hamlet in co. Hants. v. Pinnington. The name seems to have arisen in the northern county.

Alan de Penyngton, co. Lanc., 20 Edw. I. R.
Mabel Penington, of Ulverston, 1588 : Lancashire Wills at Richmond, i. 213.
John Pennington, of Ulverston : ibid. p. 214.
Myles Penyngton, of Hauxhead, 1611 : ibid.
1548. Bapt.—John Pennington : Reg. St. Mary, Ulverston, i. 6.
—— elin pennington (sic), ibid.
1803. Bapt. — William, s. George Pennington : ibid. ii. 628.

London, 0, 7 ; Ulverston, 0, 5 ; Philadelphia, 2, 47.

Salvage.—Nick. ; v. Savage, of which it is a variant.

London, 1.

Twelvetrees.—Local, 'at the twelve trees,' from residence by a clump of trees ; cf. Fiveash and Snook.

London, 1.

Watmough. — I have come across an interesting entry corroborative of the article on Watmough, q.v. ; also v. Barnmaw and *cock*, p. 25.

Cok ffenwick, the Maugh of Willy Charleton : Patent Roll, 14 Hen. VII.

www.ingramcontent.com/pod-product-compliance
Lightning Source LLC
Chambersburg PA
CBHW050600270326
41926CB00012B/2123